Lecture Notes in Computer Science 12731

More information about this subseries at http://www.springer.com/series/7409

Ruben Verborgh · Katja Hose ·
Heiko Paulheim · Pierre-Antoine Champin ·
Maria Maleshkova · Oscar Corcho ·
Petar Ristoski · Mehwish Alam (Eds.)

The Semantic Web

18th International Conference, ESWC 2021
Virtual Event, June 6–10, 2021
Proceedings

Springer

Editors
Ruben Verborgh
Ghent University
Ghent, Belgium

Katja Hose
Aalborg University
Aalborg, Denmark

Heiko Paulheim
University of Mannheim
Mannheim, Germany

Pierre-Antoine Champin
ERCIM
Sophia Antipolis, France

Maria Maleshkova
University of Siegen
Siegen, Germany

Oscar Corcho
Universidad Politécnica de Madrid
Boadilla del Monte, Spain

Petar Ristoski
eBay Inc.
San Jose, CA, USA

Mehwish Alam
FIZ Karlsruhe - Leibniz Institute
for Information Infrastructure
Eggenstein-Leopoldshafen, Germany

ISSN 0302-9743   ISSN 1611-3349   (electronic)
Lecture Notes in Computer Science
ISBN 978-3-030-77384-7   ISBN 978-3-030-77385-4   (eBook)
https://doi.org/10.1007/978-3-030-77385-4

LNCS Sublibrary: SL3 – Information Systems and Applications, incl. Internet/Web, and HCI

Preface

What does it mean to have a conference in these strange times? Semantic drift is biting us once again. The word "conference" has its roots in Latin, where it means bringing things together. If there is one thing we cannot do yet, it is bringing people together.

While we have become moderately good at online meetings and virtual gatherings of all kinds, we still have not found an adequate replacement for a coffee break. The power of spontaneous interactions is immense; undoubtedly, some of the best collaborations in our field have started over coffee — or liquids with similar cohesive abilities — in Crete.

However, "to confer" also means to have discussions and exchange opinions. We believe that dialogue is one of the most important aspects of a healthy research community, and we have made it one of our goals to see how we can further drive such conversations. The results of several of those exchanges can be found in these proceedings, and in the echoes of this year's online conference, which surely will have planted new seeds for the exciting times to come once the world opens up again.

Since these times bring great changes, we took the opportunity to introduce a few more novelties for the 18th edition of the European Semantic Web Conference (ESWC 2021). While the world was closing down, we decided to make the reviewing process more open and switch from the well-established, closed Easychair platform to OpenReview. As a result, the submissions, reviews, and discussions for all papers are now available to the public, moving the paper decisions away from back room discussions to provide a transparent process.

Moreover, some new research track topics were proposed. Two of the more experimental ones are "replication studies", which gives a strong case for analyzing whether research efforts stand the test of time, and "problems to solve before you die", which aims to shift the focus from sometimes very specific solutions for particular problems to a wider research agenda. Moreover, for the first time, "negative result" submissions were invited across all tracks, which garnered particularly good feedback.

Overall, the research track attracted 121 submissions of which 30 were ultimately accepted, with a third undergoing a shepherding process, yielding an acceptance rate of 24.8%. It is particularly remarkable that the acceptance rate for negative results papers was comparable to the overall acceptance rate, which shows that reporting negative results is actually appreciated by the research community.

In the research track, most contributions were submitted to the knowledge graph track, while tracks such as (i) NLP and information retrieval, (ii) matching, integration, and fusion, (iii) data dynamics, quality, and trust, and (iv) ontologies and reasoning also attracted significant numbers of contributions. Moreover, we observed some emerging topics: not quite surprisingly, knowledge graph embeddings were a hot topic among the accepted papers, but there were also enough submissions on autonomous driving to fill a dedicated session in the program.

The resources track attracted a total of 36 submissions, 11 of which were accepted. The track demonstrated very well that the community is not only producing theoretical research but also datasets and artifacts that can be reused by researchers and practitioners. Finally, the in-use track attracted 10 submissions, 2 of which were finally accepted for presentation at the conference. Both the resources and the in-use track demonstrated that the field is clearly moving towards adoption of the developed methods on a large scale and in real projects.

With its 18th edition, ESCW 2021 has officially stepped into adulthood, and it clearly shows in the vibrant and active community. An event like ESWC, be it offline or online, is never the outcome of the work of a few people but an effort that takes a lot of hands. Overall, ESWC 2021 had 23 people on the organization team, plus 20 track chairs for the various topical areas of the research track. 240 reviewers produced a total of 545 reviews, many of them signing with their name and thereby making the review process more transparent. We would like to give a big shout-out to everybody in this community who lent a hand to help - ESWC would not be the same without your contribution! Moreover, we would like to thank STI, OpenReview, and Springer for their support. We finally would like to thank our sponsors for supporting ESWC 2021.

Here's to meeting you all in person for a Greek salad and raki, while making new memories.

April 2021

Ruben Verborgh
Katja Hose
Heiko Paulheim
Pierre-Antoine Champin
Maria Maleshkova
Oscar Corcho
Petar Ristoski
Mehwish Alam

Organization

General Chair

Ruben Verborgh   Ghent University, Belgium

Program Chairs

Katja Hose   Aalborg University, Denmark
Heiko Paulheim   University of Mannheim, Germany

In-Use Chairs

Oscar Corcho   Universidad Politécnica de Madrid, Spain
Petar Ristoski   IBM Research, USA

Resources Chairs

Pierre-Antoine Champin   Université Claude Bernard Lyon 1, France
Maria Maleshkova   University of Bonn, Germany

Digital Conference Chairs

Violeta Ilik   Adelphi University Libraries, USA
Christian Hauschke   Leibniz Information Center for Science and
     Technology, University Library (TIB), Germany

Workshop and Tutorial Chairs

Femke Ongenae   Ghent University, Belgium
Riccardo Tommasini   University of Tartu, Estonia

Posters and Demo Chairs

Anastasia Dimou   Ghent University, Belgium
Aidan Hogan   Universidad de Chile and IMFD, Chile

PhD Chairs

Ilaria Tiddi   Vrije Universiteit Amsterdam, the Netherlands
Claudia d'Amato   University of Bari, Italy

viii   Organization

Track Chairs

Simon Mayer	University of St. Gallen, Switzerland
Arne Bröring	Siemens AG, Germany

Sponsors Chair

Daniele Dell'Aglio	Aalborg University, Denmark
Christian Dirschl	Wolters Kluwer Deutschland GmbH, Germany

Project Networking Chair

Alexandra Garatzogianni	Leibniz Information Center for Science and Technology, University Library (TIB), Germany

Web and Publicity Chair

Cogan Shimizu	Kansas State University, USA

Semantic Chair

François Scharffe	Columbia University, USA

Proceedings Chair

Mehwish Alam	FIZ Karlsruhe - Leibniz Institute for Information Infrastructure and Karlsruhe Institute of Technology, Germany

Subtrack Chairs

Ontologies and Reasoning

Cogan Shimizu	Kansas State University, USA
Jacopo Urbani	Vrije Universiteit Amsterdam, the Netherlands

Knowledge Graphs

Marta Sabou	TU Wien, Austria
Axel Polleres	Vienna University of Economics and Business, Austria

Semantic Data Management, Querying and Distributed Data

Maribel Acosta	Ruhr-University Bochum, Germany
Hala Skaf-Moli	LS2N and University of Nantes, France

Data Dynamics, Quality, and Trust

Emanuele Della Valle   Politecnico di Milano, Italy
Anisa Rula   University of Milano-Bicocca, Italy

Matching, Integration, and Fusion

Catia Pesquita   LASIGE and Universidade de Lisboa, Portugal
Ernesto Jimenez-Ruiz   City, University of London, UK, and University
    of Oslo, Norway

NLP and Information Retrieval

Klaus Berberich   Saarland University of Applied Sciences, Germany
Ziqi Zhang   University of Sheffield, UK

Machine Learning

Michael Cochez   Vrije Universiteit Amsterdam, the Netherlands
Daria Stepanova   Bosch Center for AI, Germany

Science Data and Scholarly Communication

Andrea Giovanni Nuzzolese   National Research Council, Italy
Rafael Gonçalves   Stanford University, USA

Problems to Solve Before You Die

Harald Sack   FIZ Kalrsruhe - Leibniz Institute for Information
    Infrastructure and Karlsruhe Institute
    of Technology, Germany
Frank van Harmelen   Vrije Universiteit Amsterdam, the Netherlands

Program Committee

Aaron Eberhart   Kansas State University, USA
Achim Rettinger   Trier University, Germany
Adam Funk   University of Sheffield, UK
Adila Krisnadhi   Universitas Indonesia, Indonesia
Aditya Mogadala   Saarland University, Germany
Adrian Soto Suarez   Universidad Adolfo Ibáñez, Chile
Adrian Brasoveanu   Modul Technology GmbH, Austria
Aidan Hogan   DCC, Universidad de Chile, Chile
Alasdair Gray   Heriot-Watt University, UK
Alessandra Russo   Imperial College London, UK
Alessandro Adamou   Bibliotheca Hertziana - Max Planck Institute
    for Art History, Italy
Alessandro Faraotti   Sapienza University of Rome, Italy
Alsayed Algergawy   University of Jena, Germany
Anastasia Dimou   Ghent University, Belgium

Andrea Pomp	University of Wuppertal, Germany
Andrea G. B. Tettamanzi	University of Nice Sophia Antipolis, France
Andreas Thalhammer	Karlsruhe Institute of Technology, Germany
Andreea Iana	University of Mannheim, Germany
Andriy Nikolov	KMI - Open University, UK
Angelo Salatino	KMI - Open University, UK
Anisa Rula	University of Bonn, Germany
Anna Fensel	University of Innsbruck, Austria
Antoine Isaac	Europeana, the Netherlands
Antoine Zimmermann	Mines Saint-Etienne, France
Arkaitz Zubiaga	Queen Mary University London, UK
Armando Stellato	University of Rome Tor Vergata, Italy
Armin Haller	Australian National University, Australia
Audun Stolpe	Norwegian Computing Center, Norway
Baris Sertkaya	Frankfurt University of Applied Sciences, Germany
Blake Regalia	University of California, USA
Blerina Spahiu	University of Milan-Bicocca, Italy
Carlos Bobed Lisbona	Universidad de Zaragoza, Spain
Carlos Buil-Aranda	Universidad Técnica Federico Santa María, Chile
Carole Goble	University of Manchester, UK
Carolina Scarton	University of Sheffield, UK
Cassia Trojahn	Institut de Recherche en Informatique de Toulouse, France
Catherine Faron	University of Cote d'Azur, France
Catherine Roussey	INRAE, France
Catia Pesquita	Universidade de Lisboa, Lisbon
Cedric Pruski	Paris Sud University, France
Christoph Lange	RWTH Aachen University, Germany
Christopher J. O. Baker	University of New Brunswick, Canada
Claudia d'Amato	University of Bari, Italy
Claudia Marinica	Polytech Nantes, France
Cord Wiljes	Bielefeld University, Germany
Dag Hovland	University of Oslo, Norway
Dagmar Gromann	University of Vienna, Austria
Danh Le Phuoc	TU Berlin, Germany
Daniel Faria	INESC-ID, Portugal
Daniel Garijo	USC/ISI, USA
Daniela Oliveira	University of Lisbon, Portugal
Davide Buscaldi	École Polytechnique, France
Dennis Diefenbach	Jean Monnet University, France
Diego Moussallem	Paderborn University, Germany
Dimitris Plexousakis	FORTH-ICS, Greece
Domagoj Vrgoc	Pontificia Universidad Católica de Chile, Chile
Dominic Seyler	University of Illinois Urbana-Champaign, USA
Edna Ruckhaus Magnus	Universidad Simón Bolívar, Venezuela
Eero Hyvonen	University of Helsinki, Finland

Maria Angela Pellegrino   University of Salerno, Italy
Maria Koutraki   L3S, Germany
Mariano Fernandez-Lopez   Universidad CEU San Pablo, Spain
Marieke van Erp   KNAW Humanities Cluster, the Netherlands
Martin G. Skjæveland   University of Stavanger, Norway
Martin Theobald   University of Luxembourg, Luxembourg
Matteo Palmonari   University of Milan-Bicocca, Italy
Matthias Klusch   German Research Center for AI, Germany
Maulik Kamdar   Stanford University, USA
Maurizio Atzori   University of Cagliari, Italy
Mauro Dragoni   University of Trento, Italy
Maxime Lefrancois   Mines Saint-Etienne, France
Mayank Kejriwal   USC/ISI, USA
Mehwish Alam   FIZ Karlsruhe - Leibniz Institute for Infrastructure,
        Germany
Michael Cochez   VU Amsterdam, the Netherlands
Miguel A. Martinez-Prieto   University of Valladolid, Spain
Milan Dojchinovski   Leipzig University, Germany
Muhammad Saleem   Leipzig University, Germany
Mustafa Jarrar   Birzeit University, Palestine
Nadine Steinmetz   TU Ilmenau, Germany
Nandana   IBM, USA
    Mihindukulasooriya
Naouel Karam   Fraunhofer FOKUS, Germany
Natanael Arndt   Leipzig University, Germany
Nathalie Aussenac-Gilles   CNRS, France
Nathalie Hernandez   IRIT, France
Nathalie Pernelle   University Sorbonne Paris Nord, France
Natthawut Kertkeidkachorn   National Institute of Advanced Industrial Science
        and Technology, Japan
Nicolas Heist   University of Mannheim, Germany
Oana Inel   Delft University of Technology, the Netherlands
Olaf Hartig   Linköping University, Sweden
Oliver Lehmberg   University of Mannheim, Germany
Olivier Corby   University Cote d'Azur, France
Ondej Zamazal   Prague University of Economics and Business,
        Czech Republic
Oscar Corcho   Universidad Politécnica de Madrid
Panos Alexopoulos   Textkernel, the Netherlands
Pascal Hitzler   Kansas State University, USA
Pascal Molli   University of Nantes, France
Paul Groth   University of Amsterdam, the Netherlands
Pavel Shvaiko   University of Trento, Italy
Pavlos Fafalios   ICS-FORTH, Greece
Petar Ristoski   eBay, USA
Peter Bloem   Vrije Universiteit Amsterdam, the Netherlands

Pierre-Antoine Champin	ERCIM, France
Rafael Berlanga	Universitat Jaume I, Spain
Rafael S. Goncalves	Stanford University, USA
Raghava Mutharaju	Indraprastha Institute of Information Technology, India
Ralf Krestel	Hasso Plattner Institute, Germany
Raphael Troncy	Eurecom, France
Ricardo Usbeck	Fraunhofer IAIS, Germany
Riccardo Tommasini	University of Tartu, Estonia
Rigo Wenning	ERCIM, France
Rinke Hoekstra	Elsevier, the Netherlands
Roghaiyeh Gachpaz Hamed	Trinity College Dublin, Ireland
Roman Kontchakov	Birkbeck, University of London, UK
Ruben Taelman	Ghent University, Belgium
Rui Zhu	UC Santa Barbara, USA
Ruijie Wang	University of Illinois Urbana-Champaign, USA
Russa Biswas	Karlsruhe Institute of Technology, Germany
Ryutaro Ichise	National Institute of Informatics, Japan
Sabrina Kirrane	Vienna University of Economics and Business, Austria
Sahar Vahdati	Leipzig University, Germany
Sebastian Neumaier	University of Applied Sciences St. Pölten, Austria
Sebastian Richard Bader	Fraunhofer IAIS, Germany
Sebastian Tramp	eccenca GmbH, Germany
Sebastijan Dumancic	KU Leuven, Belgium
Serena Villata	CNRS, France
Sergio José Rodríguez Méndez	Australian National University, Australia
Simon Gottschalk	Leibniz University of Hannover, Germany
Simon Razniewski	Max Planck Institute for Informatics, Germany
Simon Steyskal	Vienna University of Economics and Business, Austria
Simona Colucci	Politecnico di Bari, Italy
Songmao Zhang	Academy of Mathematics and Systems Science, Chinese Academy of Sciences, China
Stasinos Konstantopoulos	NCSR Demokritos, Greece
Stefan Dietze	GESIS and HHU, Germany
Steffen Staab	University of Stuttgart, Germany
Sven Hertling	University of Mannheim, Germany
Tassilo Pellegrini	University of Applied Sciences St. Pölten, Austria
Tobias Kaefer	Karlsruhe Institute of Technology, Germany
Tobias Weller	University of Mannheim, Germany
Tomi Kauppinen	Aalto University, Finland
Torsten Hahmann	University of Maine, USA
Umberto Straccia	ISTI-CNR, Italy
Vadim Ermolayev	Zaporizhzhia National University, Ukraine
Valentina Anita Carriero	University of Bologna, Italy
Valentina Presutti	University of Bologna, Italy
Varish Mulwad	General Electric, USA

Victor de Boer	Vrije Universiteit Amsterdam, the Netherlands
Vinh Nguyen	U.S. National Library of Medicine, USA
Wei Hu	Nanjing University, China
Wolfgang Faber	Alpen-Adria University of Klagenfurt, Austria
Xander Wilcke	Vrije Universiteit Amsterdam, the Netherlands
Xingyi Song	University of Sheffield, UK
Ying Ding	University of Texas at Austin, USA
Yuan-Fang Li	Monash University, Australia
Ziqi Zhang	University of Sheffield, UK

Sponsors

Platinum

Silver

Bronze

Supporter

Contents

Data Dynamics, Quality, and Trust

Matching, Integration, and Fusion

NLP and Information Retrieval

Machine Learning

Science Data and Scholarly Communication

Problems to Solve Before You Die

Resources

In-Use Track

Ontologies and Reasoning

Streaming Partitioning of RDF Graphs for Datalog Reasoning

Temitope Ajileye$^{(\boxtimes)}$ ⬡, Boris Motik ⬡, and Ian Horrocks ⬡

Department of Computer Science, University of Oxford, Oxford, UK
{temitope.ajileye,Boris.motik,Ian.horrocks}@cs.ox.ac.uk

Abstract. A cluster of servers is often used to reason over RDF graphs whose size exceeds the capacity of a single server. While many distributed approaches to reasoning have been proposed, the problem of data partitioning has received little attention thus far. In practice, data is usually partitioned by a variant of hashing, which is very simple, but it does not pay attention to data locality. Locality-aware partitioning approaches have been considered, but they usually process the entire dataset on a single server. In this paper, we present two new RDF partitioning strategies. Both are inspired by recent *streaming* graph partitioning algorithms, which partition a graph while keeping only a small subset of the graph in memory. We have evaluated our approaches empirically against hash and min-cut partitioning. Our results suggest that our approaches can significantly improve reasoning performance, but without unrealistic demands on the memory of the servers used for partitioning.

1 Introduction

The *Resource Description Framework* (RDF) is a popular data format, where *triples* represent relationships between *resources*. The *Web Ontology Language* (OWL) is layered on top of RDF to structure the data and support *reasoning*: a reasoner can derive fresh triples using domain knowledge. Thus, developing efficient reasoning algorithms for RDF has received considerable attention.

A popular way to realise OWL reasoning is to encode the rules of inference in a prominent rule-based formalism called *datalog*. For example, the OWL 2 RL profile is a fragment of OWL designed to support datalog reasoning. Datalog reasoning is often implemented in practice by *materialisation*: all consequences of the data and the rules are precomputed in a preprocessing step so that queries can later be evaluated without any further processing of the rules.

Modern RDF datasets can be very large; for example, the UniProt[1] dataset contains over 34 billion triples. Complex reasoning over such large datasets is infeasible on a single server, so a common solution is to partition the data in a cluster of shared-nothing servers. Many such approaches for RDF querying have been proposed [4,10–13,16,22,23,28,30]. Reasoning is more involved since

---

[1] https://www.uniprot.org/.

R. Verborgh et al. (Eds.): ESWC 2021, LNCS 12731, pp. 3–22, 2021.
https://doi.org/10.1007/978-3-030-77385-4_1

it requires interleaving queries and updates, but nevertheless several distributed RDF reasoners have been developed [9,17,24,26,27,29].

Rule application during reasoning requires distributed join processing, which can be costly if the triples to be joined are stored in different servers; moreover, derived triples need to be distributed across the cluster. Thus, data should ideally be partitioned in a locality-aware way to minimise overheads. Little attention has been paid thus far to the data partitioning problem. Systems based on Hadoop and Spark store the data in a distributed file system and thus typically cannot influence data placement. Systems that explicitly control data placement usually determine a triple's destination by hashing some or all of the triple's components (usually the subject). Hashing is very simple to implement and requires little resources, but it can incur significant overhead, particularly for subject–object and object–object joins. Other systems use min-cut graph partitioning [15] to obtain locality-aware partitions; however, this usually requires loading all data into a single server, which defeats the main goals of using a cluster.

Streaming methods aim to produce good graph partitions without loading the entire graph into memory at any point in time (but by possibly reading the graph data several times). Such techniques have been developed primarily for general graphs, rather than RDF. Motivated by the desire to improve the performance of distributed RDF reasoners, in this paper we adapt the HDRF [21] and 2PS [19] state-of-the-art streaming graph partitioning algorithms to RDF. Unlike HDRF and 2PS, our $HDRF_3$ and $2PS_3$ algorithms have to take into account certain idiosyncrasies of the RDF data model. For example, it is well known that subject–subject joins are very common in RDF queries, so colocating triples with the same subject is really important in RDF; however, honouring this requires modifications to HDRF and 2PS.

By comparing our approaches empirically with hash and min-cut partitioning, we investigated how different data partitioning strategies affect reasoning times and network communication. We based our evaluation on the DMAT distributed datalog reasoner [3]. The reasoning algorithm of DMAT is unique in that it is independent of any specific data partitioning strategy: as long as a certain index is provided that informs the system of how data is distributed in the cluster, the algorithm can correctly compute the materialisation.

We show empirically that partitioning the data into highly connected subsets can be very effective at reducing communication and thus reducing reasoning times; however, it can also lead to workload imbalances among servers, which can lead to increases in reasoning when the communication overhead is small. Overall, our $2PS_3$ method seems to be very effective: while requiring only modest resources for partitioning, it can more than halve the reasoning times compared to hash partitioning. Thus, we believe our technique provides an important building block of truly scalable distributed RDF reasoners.

The proofs of our results, all datasets and rule sets used for testing, and the DMAT system are available as online supplementary material[2].

---

[2] https://krr-nas.cs.ox.ac.uk/2021/stream-graph-partitioning/.

2 Preliminaries

We next recapitulate some common definitions. An *RDF graph* G is a finite set of triples of the form $\langle s, p, o \rangle$, where s, p, and o are *resources* (i.e., IRIs, blank nodes, or literals) called *subject*, *predicate*, and *object*, respectively. The *vocabulary* of G is the set of all resources occurring in G. Given a resource r, let $G^+(r) = \{\langle s, p, o \rangle \in G \mid s = r\}$ and $G(r) = \{\langle s, p, o \rangle \in G \mid s = r \text{ or } o = r\}$. We call $|G^+(r)|$ and $|G(r)|$ the *out-degree* and the *degree* of r, respectively.

A *partition* $\mathcal{P}$ of an RDF graph G is a list of RDF graphs $\mathcal{P} = G_1, \ldots, G_n$ such that $G_i \cap G_j = \emptyset$ for $1 \leq i < j \leq n$ and $G = \bigcup_{i=1}^{n} G_i$. We call graphs G_i *partition elements*. The *replication set* of a resource r is $A(r) = \{k \mid G_k \cap G(r) \neq \emptyset\}$. For V the vocabulary of G, the *replication factor* of a partition $\mathcal{P}$ is defined as

$$\mathsf{RF}(G, \mathcal{P}) = \frac{1}{|V|} \sum_{r \in V} |A(r)|.$$

Given a fixed tolerance parameter $\alpha \geq 1$, the objective of graph partitioning is to compute a partition $\mathcal{P}$ of G such that $|G_i| \leq \alpha \frac{|G|}{n}$ holds for each $1 \leq i \leq n$, while minimising the replication factor $\mathsf{RF}(G, \mathcal{P})$. Thus, each G_i should hold roughly the same number of triples, while ensuring that resources are replicated as little as possible. Solving this problem exactly is computationally hard, so the objective is usually weakened in practice. The algorithms we present in this paper will honour the restrictions on the sizes of G_i; moreover, they will aim to make the replication factor small, but without minimality guarantees.

A *datalog* rule is an expression of the form $H \leftarrow B_1, \ldots, B_n$, where H and B_i are *atoms* of the form $\langle t_s, t_p, t_o \rangle$, and t_s, t_p, and t_o are variables or resources. Atom H is called the *head*, and $B_1, \ldots, B_n$ are called the rule *body*. A *substitution* σ is a mapping of variable to resources, and $A\sigma$ denotes the result of replacing each variable in atom x with $\sigma(x)$. A rule is applied to an RDF graph G by enumerating each substitution σ such that $\{B_1\sigma, \ldots, B_n\sigma\} \subseteq G$, and then extending G with $H\sigma$. To compute the *materialisation* of G for a set of datalog rules P, this process is iteratively repeated for each rule $r \in P$ as long as possible—that is, until no new triples can be derived. In this work, we study how different partitioning strategies affect the performance of computing the materialisation when the RDF data is partitioned across a cluster of servers.

3 Related Work

In this section, we present an overview of the related approaches to distributed querying, distributed reasoning, and RDF data partitioning.

Distributed Query Processing. To compute a join in a distributed setting, facts participating in the join must be brought to a server in the cluster. Many solutions to this key technical problem have been developed. Numerous systems (e.g., HadoopRDF [13] and S2RDF [23], to name a few) are built on top of big data frameworks such as Hadoop or Spark. Systems such as YARS2 [11] and Trinity.RDF [30] compute joins on a single server after retrieving data from the cluster. Systems such as H-RDF-3X [12], SHAPE [16], and SemStore [28] split a query into parts that can be evaluated without communication, and then combine the partial answers in a final join phase. Finally, systems such as AdPart [4] and TriAd [10] compute distributed joins by exchanging partial answers between servers. Recently, 22 systems were surveyed and 12 of those were compared experimentally [1], and TriAd and AdPart were identified as fastest. The *dynamic data exchange* [22] approach was later shown to be also very competitive.

Distributed Reasoning. Matching rule bodies corresponds to query evaluation, so distributed reasoning includes distributed querying; however, it also involves distributed data updates, which introduces additional complexity. SociaLite [24] handles datalog extended with a variant of monotonic aggregation. Many distributed RDF reasoners can handle only limited datalog subsets [5]. For example, RDFS reasoning can be performed without any communication [27]. WebPIE [26] handles the OWL-Horst fragment using Hadoop, while CiChild [9] and SPOWL [17] handle the OWL-Horst and the OWL 2 RL fragments, respectively, in Spark. PLogSpark [29], also implemented in Spark, is one of the few distributed RDF reasoners that can handle arbitrary datalog rules.

DMAT. Our DMAT system [3] supports distributed seminaïve evaluation of arbitrary datalog rules by extending the distributed query answering technique by Potter et al. [22]; the system uses RDFox [20] for triple storage, indexing, and retrieval. DMAT uses an index to locate the relevant data in the cluster, allowing it to be used with any partitioning strategy. This is different from most existing approaches, where the reasoning algorithms depend on the details of data partitioning. We use DMAT in our evaluation since it allows us to vary the partitioning strategies only and study how this affects the performance of reasoning. While the absolute reasoning times are specific to DMAT, the number of joins that span servers are the same for all implementations, so other systems should exhibit similar relative performance for different partitioning strategies.

Data Partitioning. Although it is intuitive to expect that partitioning the data carefully to minimise communication should improve the performance of distributed systems, the effects of data partitioning remain largely unknown. Existing approaches to data partitioning can be broadly divided into three groups. The first groups consists of systems that use Hadoop or Spark to store their data in a distributed file system. The data is usually allocated randomly to servers, which makes exploiting data locality during querying/reasoning difficult. The second group consists of hash-based variants, where the destination for a triple is determined by hashing one or more triple's components (usually subject). The third group consists of variants based on min-cut graph partitioning [15], which aims to minimise the number of edges between partitions and thus reduce the cost of communication. Such approaches are sometimes combined with data replication (e.g., [10,12]), where a triple is stored on more than one server. All systems in the latter two groups colocate triples with the same subjects to eliminate communication for the most common subject–subject joins [8].

4   Motivation and Our Contribution

Distributed reasoning requires network communication for evaluating rule bodies and for distributing the derived triples, and communication is much slower than RAM access. One can thus intuitively expect that communication will critically determine the performance of reasoning, and that, to reduce communication and thus improve performance, joining triples are colocated whenever possible.

Janke et al. [14] studied this problem for distributed query processing. Interestingly, they concluded that reducing communication can be detrimental if done at the expense of uneven server workload. However, it is unclear to what extent this study applies to reasoning. Reasoning over large datasets involves evaluating millions of queries and distributing derived triples, both of which can incur much more communication than for evaluating a single query. Moreover, imbalances in single queries could even out over all queries.

Another question is how to effectively partition RDF data in a locality-aware way. As we mentioned in Sect. 3, subject hashing is commonly used in practice; while very efficient, it does not take the structure of an RDF graph into account and thus provides no locality guarantees for subject–object or object–object joins. Other commonly used approaches are based on min-cut partitioning. The METIS partitioner requires loading the entire graph into a single server, which is clearly problematical. This problem can be mitigated by using the parallelised version of METIS called ParMETIS; however, graph partitioning is an NP-hard problem, so such a solution is still likely to use considerable resources.

Thus, how to partition RDF data effectively, and how this affects distributed reasoning, is still largely unknown. To answer the former question, we draw inspiration from recent work on *streaming graph partitioning* [2,6,18,19,21,25,31] methods, which process the graph edges a fixed number of times without ever storing the entire graph in memory. The memory used by these algorithms is often proportional to the number of graph vertices, which is usually at least an order of magnitude smaller than the number of edges.

These approaches seem to provide a good basis for RDF partitioning, but they are typically formulated for general (directed or undirected) graphs. Several RDF-specific issues must be taken into account to obtain adequate partitions in the context of RDF. For example, colocating triples with the same subject was shown to be crucial for practical applications (cf. Sect. 3). Thus, in Sects. 5 and 6, we present two new streaming RDF partitioning techniques, which we obtain from the state-of-the-art algorithms HDRF [21] and 2PS [19]. The idea behind the former is to prefer replicating vertices of higher degree so that a smaller number of vertices has to be replicated overall, and the idea behind the latter is to assign to each server communities of highly connected vertices.

In Sect. 7 we empirically investigate the connection between data partitioning and reasoning performance. To this end, we compare the performance of reasoning for different data partitioning strategies: our two new techniques, subject hash partitioning, and a variant of min-cut partitioning [22]. Our results suggest that data partitioning can indeed have a significant impact on reasoning performance, sometimes cutting the reasoning times to less than half.

5   The HDRF₃ Algorithm

We now present our HDRF₃ algorithm for streaming partitioning of RDF data. We follow the 'high degree replicated first' principle from the HDRF algorithm for general graphs [21]. In Sect. 5.1 we briefly discuss the original idea, and in Sect. 5.2 we discuss in detail how we adapted these principles to RDF.

5.1   High Degree Replicated First Streaming Partitioning

The HDRF algorithm [21] targets large undirected graphs whose vertex degree distribution resembles the power-law distribution. The algorithm aims to replicate (i.e., assign to more than one server) vertices with higher degrees, so that a smaller number of vertices is replicated overall. It processes sequentially the edges of the input graph and assigns them to servers. For each server $k \in \{1, \ldots, n\}$, the algorithm maintains the number N_k of eges currently assigned to server k; all N_k are initially zero. For each vertex v, the algorithm maintains the degree $deg(v)$ of v in the subgraph processed thus far, and the replication set $A(v)$ for v. For each v, the degree $deg(v)$ is initialised to zero, and $A(v)$ is initialised to the empty set. To allocate an undirected edge $\{v, w\}$, the algorithm first increments $deg(v)$ and $deg(w)$, and then for each candidate server $k \in \{1, \ldots, n\}$ it computes the score $C(v, w, k)$. The algorithm sends the edge $\{v, w\}$ to the server k with the highest score $C(v, w, k)$, and it increments N_k.

The score $C(v, w, k)$ consists of two parts. The first one estimates the impact that placing $\{v, w\}$ on server k will have on replication, and it is computed as

$$C_{REP}(v, w, k) = g(v, w, k) + g(w, v, k), \qquad \text{where}$$

$$g(v, w, k) = \begin{cases} 1 + \frac{deg(w)}{deg(v) + deg(w)} & \text{if } k \in A(v), \\ 0 & \text{otherwise.} \end{cases}$$

To understand the intuition behind this formula, assume that vertex v occurs only on server k, vertex w occurs only server k', and $deg(v) > deg(w)$. Then, we have $g(v, w, k) < g(w, v, k')$, which ensures that edge $\{v, w\}$ is sent to server k'—that is, vertex v is replicated to server k', in line with our desire to replicate higher-degree vertices. The sum $deg(v) + deg(w)$ in the denominator of the formula for $g(v, w, k)$ is used to normalise the degrees of v and w.

Considering $C_{REP}(v, w, k)$ only would risk producing partitions of unbalanced sizes. Therefore, the second part of the score is used to favour assigning edge $\{v, w\}$ to the currently least loaded server using formula

$$C_{BAL}(k) = \frac{maxsize - N_k}{\epsilon + maxsize - minsize},$$

where *maxsize* and *minsize* are the maximal and minimal possible partition sizes.

Scores $C_{REP}(v, w, k)$ and $C_{BAL}(k)$ are finally combined using a fixed weighting factor λ as

$$C(v, w, k) = C_{REP}(v, w, k) + \lambda \cdot C_{BAL}(k)$$

By tuning λ, we can determine how important is minimising imbalance in partition sizes as opposed to achieving low replication factors.

The version of the algorithm presented above makes just one pass over the graph edges, and $g(v, w, k)$ and $g(w, v, k)$ are computed using the partial vertex degrees (i.e., degrees in the subset of the graph processed thus far). The authors of HDRF also discuss a variant where exact degrees are computed in a preprocessing pass. The authors also show empirically that this does not substantially alter the quality of the partitions that the algorithm produces.

5.2 Adapting the Algorithm to RDF Graphs

Several problems need to be addressed to adapt HDRF to RDF graphs. A minor issue is that RDF triples correspond to labelled directed edges, which we address by simply ignoring the predicate component of triples. A more important problem is to ensure that all triples with the same subject are colocated on a single server, which, as we already mentioned in Sect. 4, is key to ensuring good performance of distributed RDF systems. To address this, we compute the destination for all triples with subject s the first time we see such a triple.

The pseudo-code of HDRF$_3$ is shown in Algorithm 1. It takes as input a parameter α determining the maximal acceptable imbalance in partition element sizes, the balance parameter λ as in HDRF, and another parameter δ that we describe shortly. In a preprocessing pass over G (not shown in the pseudo-code), the algorithm determines the size of the graph $|G|$, and the out-degree $|G^+(r)|$ and the degree $|G(r)|$ of each resource r in G. The algorithm also maintains (i) the replication set $A(r)$ for each resource, which is initially empty, (ii) a mapping T of resources occurring in subject position to servers, which is initially undefined on all resources, and (iii) the numbers $N_1, \ldots, N_n$ and $R_1, \ldots, R_n$ of triples and resources, respectively, assigned to servers thus far, which are initially zero.

The algorithm makes a single pass over the graph and processes each triple $\langle s, p, o \rangle \in G$ using the function PROCESSTRIPLE. Mapping T keeps track of the servers that will receive triples with a particular subject resource. Thus, if $T(s)$ is undefined (line 2), the algorithm sets $T(s)$ to the server with the highest score (line 3) in a way analogous to HDRF. All triples with the same subject encountered later will be assigned to server $T(s)$, so counter $N_{T(s)}$ is updated with the out-degree of s (line 4). Finally, the triple is sent to server $T(s)$ (line 5),

---

Algorithm 1. HDRF_3

Require: tolerance parameter $\alpha > 1$
the balance parameter λ
the degree imbalance parameter δ
the target number of servers n
$|G|$, $|G^+(r)|$, and $|G(r)|$ for each resource r in G are known
$A(r) := \emptyset$ for each resource r in G
Mapping T of resources to servers, initially undefined on all resources
$N_k := R_k := 0$ for each server $k \in \{1, \ldots, n\}$

1: **function** PROCESSTRIPLE(s, p, o)
2:     **if** $T(s)$ is undefined **then**
3:         $T(s) := \arg\max_{k \in \{1,\ldots,n\}} \text{SCORE}(s, o, k)$
4:         $N_{T(s)} := N_{T(s)} + |G^+(s)|$
5:     Add (s, p, o) to $G_{T(s)}$
6:     **if** $T(s) \notin A(s)$ **then** Add $T(s)$ to $A(s)$ and increment $R_{T(s)}$
7:     **if** $T(s) \notin A(o)$ **then** Add $T(s)$ to $A(o)$ and increment $R_{T(s)}$

8: **function** SCORE(s, o, k)
9:     $C_{REP} := 0$
10:    **if** $k \in A(s)$ and $\text{DEG}(k) \leq \min_{\ell \in \{1,\ldots,n\}} \text{DEG}(\ell) + \delta$ **then**
11:        $C_{REP} := C_{REP} + 1 + \frac{|G(o)|}{|G(s)| + |G(o)|}$
12:    **if** $k \in A(o)$ and $\text{DEG}(k) \leq \min_{\ell \in \{1,\ldots,n\}} \text{DEG}(\ell) + \delta$ **then**
13:        $C_{REP} := C_{REP} + 1 + \frac{|G(s)|}{|G(s)| + |G(o)|}$
14:    $C_{BAL} := 1 - n\frac{N_{k'} + |G^+(s)|}{\alpha |G|}$
15:    **return** $C_{REP} + \lambda\frac{\sum_k N_k}{|G|} C_{BAL}$

16: **function** DEG(k)
17:    **return** $(R_k = 0)$? 0 : N_k/R_k

---

and the replication sets of s and o and the number of resources $R_{T(s)}$ on server $T(s)$ are updated if needed (lines 6 and 7).

The score of sending triple $\langle s, p, o \rangle$ to server k is calculated as in HDRF. The replication part C_{REP} of the score is computed in lines 11 and 13. Unlike the original HDRF algorithm, we assign all triples with subject s to a server the first time we encounter resource s, so having complete degree is important to take into account the impact of further triples with the same subject. Moreover, we observed empirically that it is beneficial for the performance of reasoning to have partition elements with roughly similar average resource degrees. Function DEG estimates the current average degree of resources in server k as a quotient of the currently numbers of triples (N_k) and resources (R_k) assigned to server k. Then, in lines 11 and 13, C_{REP} is updated only if the average degree of server k is close (i.e., within δ) to the minimal average degree.

The balance factor is computed in line 14, and it is obtained by taking into account that the maximum size of a partition element is $\alpha|G|/n$.

Finally, C_{REP} and C_{BAL} are combined using λ in line 15. However, unlike the original HDRF algorithm, factor $\frac{\sum_k N_k}{|G|}$ ensures that partition balance grows in importance towards the end of partitioning.

As we mentioned in Sect. 2, producing a balanced partition while minimising the replication factor is computationally hard, so the minimality requirement is typically dropped. The following result shows that Algorithm 1 honours the balance requirements, provided that α and λ are chosen in a particular way.

Proposition 1. *Algorithm 1 produces a partition that satisfies $|G_i| \leq \alpha\frac{|G|}{n}$ for each $1 \leq i \leq n$ whenever α and λ are selected such that*

$$\alpha > 1 + n\frac{\max_r |G^+(r)|}{|G|} \quad and \quad \lambda \geq \frac{4\alpha}{n\left(\frac{\alpha-1}{n} - \frac{\max_r |G^+(r)|}{|G|}\right)^2}.$$

6   The 2PS$_3$ Algorithm

We now present our 2PS$_3$ algorithm for RDF, which adapts the *two-phase streaming* algorithm 2PS [19]. In Sect. 6.1 we discuss the original idea, and in Sect. 6.2 we discuss in detail how to apply these principles to RDF.

6.1   Two-Phase Streaming

The 2PS algorithm processes undirected graphs in two phases. In the first phase, the algorithm clusters resources into communities with the goal of placing highly connected resources into a single community. This is achieved by initially assigning each resource in the graph to a separate community. Then, when processing an edge $\{v, w\}$ in the first phase, the current sizes of the current communities of v and w are compared, and the resource belonging to the smaller community is merged into the larger community. Thus, communities are iteratively coarsened as edges of the input graph are processed in the first phase. The entire first phase can be repeated several times to improve community detection.

After all edges are processed in the first phase, the identified communities are greedily assigned to servers. Then, the graph is processed in the second phase, and edges are assigned to the communities of their vertices.

6.2   The Algorithm

Just like in the case of HDRF, the main challenge in extending 2PS to RDF is to deal with the directed nature of RDF triples, and to ensure that triples with the same subject are assigned to the same server.

The pseudo-code of 2PS$_3$ is shown in Algorithm 2. As in HDRF$_3$, the algorithm uses a preprocessing phase to determine the size of graph $|G|$ and the

---

Algorithm 2. 2PS₃

Require: tolerance parameter $\alpha > 1$
the target number of servers n
$|G|$ and $|G^+(r)|$ for each resource r in G are known
$C(r) := c_r$ and $S(c_r) := |G^+(r)|$ for each resource r in G, where
c_r is a community unique for r

18: **function** PROCESSTRIPLE-PHASE-I(s, p, o)
19:    Let $r_{max} := \arg\max_{r \in \{s,o\}} S(C(r))$, and let r_{min} be the other vertex
20:    **if** $S(C(r_{max})) + |G^+(r_{min})| < (\alpha - 1)\frac{|G|}{n}$ **then**
21:        $S(C(r_{max})) := S(C(r_{max})) + |G^+(r_{min})|$
22:        $S(C(r_{min})) := S(C(r_{min})) - |G^+(r_{min})|$
23:        $C(r_{min}) := C(r_{max})$

24: **function** ASSIGNCOMMUNITIES
25:    $N_k := 0$ for each server $k \in \{1, \ldots, n\}$
26:    **for** each community c occurring in the image of the mapping C **do**
27:        $T(c) := \arg\min_{k \in \{1,\ldots,n\}} |N_k|$
28:        $N_{T(c)} := N_{T(c)} + S(c)$

29: **function** PROCESSTRIPLE-PHASE-II(s, p, o)
30:    Add (s, p, o) to $T(C(s))$

---

out-degree $|G^+(r)|$ of each resource. Thus, 2PS₃ uses three phases; however, to stress the relationship with the 2PS algorithm, we call the algorithm 2PS₃.

The algorithm maintains a global mapping C of resources to communities—that is, $C(r)$ is the community of each resource r. Thus, two resources r_1 and r_2 are in the same community if $C(r_1) = C(r_2)$. Initially, each resource r is placed into its own community c_r. As the algorithm progresses, the image of C will contain fewer and fewer communities. Once communities are assigned to servers, a triple $\langle s, p, o \rangle$ will be assigned to the server of community $C(s)$, thus ensuring that all triples with the same subject are colocated.

The algorithm also maintains a global function that maps each community c to its size $S(c)$. Please note that $S(c)$ does not hold the number of resources currently assigned to community c; rather, $S(c)$ provides us with the number of triples whose subject is assigned to community c. Because of that, $S(c_r)$ is initially set to $|G^+(r)|$ for each resource r, rather than to 1.

After initialisation, the algorithm processes each triple $\langle s, p, o \rangle \in G$ using function PROCESSTRIPLE-PHASE-I. In line 19, the algorithm compares the sizes $S(C(s))$ and $S(C(o))$ of the communities to which s and o, respectively, are currently assigned. It identifies r_{max} as the resource whose current community size is larger, and r_{min} as the resource whose current community size is smaller (ties are broken arbitrarily). The aim of this is to move r_{min} into the community of r_{max}, but this is done only if, after the move, we can satisfy the requirement on the sizes of partition elements: if each community contains no more than $(\alpha - 1)\frac{|G|}{n}$ triples, we can later assign communities to servers greedily and the resulting partition elements will contain fewer than $\alpha\frac{|G|}{n}$ triples. This is reflected in the condition in line 19: if satisfied, the algorithm updates the sizes of the communities of r_{max} and r_{min} (lines 21–22), and it moves r_{min} into the community of r_{max} (line 23). If desired, G can be processed repeatedly several times using function PROCESSTRIPLE-PHASE-I to improve the communities.

Once all triples of G are processed, function ASSIGNCOMMUNITIES assigns communities to servers. To this end, for each server k, the algorithm maintains the number N_k of triples currently assigned to partition element k. Then, the communities from the image of C (i.e., the communities that have 'survived' after shuffling the resources in the first phase) are assigned by greedily preferring the least loaded server. Finally, using function PROCESSTRIPLE-PHASE-II, each triple $\langle s, p, o \rangle \in G$ is assigned to the server of community $C(s)$.

As in HDRF$_3$, our algorithm is not guaranteed to minimise the replication factor. However, the following result shows that the algorithm will honor the restriction on the sizes of partition elements for a suitable choice of α.

Proposition 2. *Algorithm 2 produces a partition that satisfies $|G_i| \leq \alpha\frac{|G|}{n}$ for each $1 \leq i \leq n$ whenever α is selected such that*

$$\alpha > 1 + \frac{\max_r |G^+(r)|}{|G|}.$$

7 Evaluation

To see how partitioning affects distributed reasoning, we computed the materialisation for three large datasets, which we partitioned using subject hash partitioning (Hash), a variant of min-cut partitioning [22] (METIS), and our HDRF$_3$ and 2PS$_3$ algorithms. We introduce our datasets in Sect. 7.1; we present the test protocol in Sect. 7.2; and we discuss our results in Sect. 7.3.

7.1 Datasets

Apart from the well-known LUBM[3] benchmark, we are unaware of publicly available large RDF datasets that come equipped with complex datalog programs. Thus, we manually created programs for two well-known large datasets. All programs and datasets are available from the Web page from the introduction, and some statistical information about the datasets is shown in Table 1.

LUBM-8K. We used the LUBM dataset for 8,000 universities, containing 1.10 billion triples. Moreover, we used the *extended lower bound* datalog program by Motik et al. [20]. The program was constructed to stress-test reasoning systems, and it was obtained by translating the OWL 2 RL portion of the LUBM ontology into datalog and manually adding several hard recursive rules that produce many redundant derivations. To the best of our knowledge, this program has not yet been used in the literature to test distributed RDF reasoners.

---

[3] http://swat.cse.lehigh.edu/projects/lubm/.

WatDiv-1B. The WatDiv[4] benchmark was developed as a test for SPARQL querying. We used the 1.09 billion triples provided by the creators of WatDiv. Since WatDiv does not include an ontology or datalog program, we manually produced a program consisting of 32 chain, cyclical, and recursive rules.

MAKG*. The *Microsoft Academic Knowledge Graph* (MAKG) [7] is an RDF translation of the Microsoft Academic Graph—a heterogeneous dataset of scientific publication records, citations, authors, institutions, journals, conferences, and fields of study. The original MAKG dataset contains 8 billion triples and includes links to datasets in the Linked Open Data Cloud. To obtain a more manageable dataset, we selected a subset, which we call MAKG*, of 3.67 billion core triples. Since MAKG does not have an ontology, we manually created a datalog program consisting of 15 chain, cyclical, and recursive rules.

Table 1. Datasets & programs

Dataset	Dataset stats			Program stats			Mat. stats		λ
	Triples (G)	Res. (M)	Deg.	Rules	Recr.	Avg. body	Triples (G)	Der. (G)	
LUBM-8K	1.10	260	4.21	103	3	1.20	2.66	63.45	819
WatDiv-1B	1.09	100	11.29	32	2	2.10	1.77	2.09	800
MAKG*	3.67	490	7.48	15	2	2.20	5.63	17.47	800

Legend: res. = #resources; deg. = triples/res.; recr. = #recursive rules; avg. body = average #body atoms; der. = #derivations; λ = a HDRF$_3$ parameter

7.2   Test Protocol

As mentioned in Sect. 3, our DMAT system can be used with an arbitrary data partitioning strategy, so it provides us with an ideal testbed for our experiments. We ran our experiments on the Amazon EC2 cloud, with servers connected by 10 Gbps Ethernet. To compute the materialisation, we used ten servers of the r5 family, each equipped with a 2.3 GHz Intel Broadwell processor and 128 GB of RAM; the latter was needed since DMAT stores all data in RAM. We used an additional, smaller coordinator server to store the dictionary (i.e., mapping of resources to integers) and distribute the datalog program and the graphs to the cluster; this server did not participate in reasoning. Finally, we used another server with 784 GB of RAM to partition the data using METIS.

To speed up loading times, we preprocessed all datasets by replacing all resources with integers. The coordinator distributed the triples to the workers for Hash, HDRF$_3$, and 2PS$_3$; for METIS, we loaded the precomputed partitions directly into the workers. To hash the triples' subjects, we simply multiplied the integer subject value by a large prime in order to randomise the distribution of the subjects. In our algorithms, we used $\alpha = 1.25$. With HDRF$_3$, we used

---

[4] https://dsg.uwaterloo.ca/watdiv/.

$\delta = 0.25$ and we set λ to the lowest value satisfying Proposition 1; the values of λ thus vary for each dataset and are shown in Table 1. Finally, with 2PS$_3$, we processed the graphs twice in the first phase. After loading the dataset and the program into all servers, we computed the materialisation while recording the wall-clock time and the total number of messages sent between the servers.

7.3 Test Results and Discussion

For each of the four partitioning strategies, Table 2 shows the minimum, maximum, and median numbers of triples in partition elements, given as percentages of the overall numbers of triples. The table also shows the replication factor (see Sect. 2 for a definition) and the time needed to compute the partitions. Finally, the table shows the reasoning times and the numbers of messages.

Partition Times and Balance. All partitioning schemes produced partition elements with sizes within the tolerance parameters: Hash achieves perfect balance if the hash function is uniform; METIS explicitly aims to equalise partition sizes; and our two algorithms do so by design and the choice of parameters. For all streaming methods, the partitioning times were not much higher than the time required to read the datasets from disk and send triples to their designated servers. In contrast, METIS partitioning took longer than materialisation on LUBM-8K and WatDiv-1B, and on MAKG* it ran out of memory even though we used a very large server equipped with 784 GB of RAM.

Replication, Communication, and Reasoning Times. Generally lowest replication factors were achieved with 2PS$_3$: only METIS achieved a lower value on WatDiv-1B, and HDRF$_3$ achieved a comparable value on MAKG*. The replication factor of Hash was highest in all cases, closely followed by HDRF$_3$. Moreover, lower replication factors seem to corelate closely with decreased communication overhead; for example, the number of messages was significantly smaller on LUBM-8K and MAKG* with 2PS$_3$ than with other schemes. This reduction seems to generally lead to a decrease in reasoning times: 2PS$_3$ was the fastest than the other schemes on LUBM-8K and MAKG*; for the former, the improvement over Hash is by a factor of 2.25. However, the reasoning times do not always corelate with the replication factor: on WatDiv-1B, METIS and 2PS$_3$ were slower than Hash and HDRF$_3$, despite exhibiting smaller replication factors.

Workload Balance. To investigate further, we show in Fig. 1 the numbers of derivations and the total size of partial messages processed by each of the ten servers in the cluster. As one can see, partitioning the data into strongly connected clusters can introduce a workload imbalance: the numbers of derivations and messages per server are quite uniform for Hash and, to an extent, for HDRF$_3$; in contrast, with 2PS$_3$ and METIS, certain servers seem to be doing much more work than others, particularly on WatDiv-1B and MAKG*. Thus, reducing communication seems to be important, but only to a point. For example, 2PS$_3$ reduces communication drastically on LUBM-8K, and this seems to 'pay off' in terms of reasoning times. On MAKG*, the reduction in communication seems to lead to modest improvements in reasoning times, despite a more pronounced workload imbalance. On WatDiv-1B, however, communication overhead does not appear to be significant with any partitioning strategy, so the workload imbalance is the main determining factor of the reasoning times.

Overall Performance. In general, 2PS$_3$ seems to provide a good performance mix: unlike METIS, it can be implemented without placing unrealistic requirements on the servers used for partitioning; it can significantly reduce communication; and, while this can increase reasoning times due to workload imbalances, such increases do not appear to be excessive. Thus, 2PS$_3$ is a good alternative to hash partitioning, which has been the dominant technique used thus far.

Table 2. Partition & reasoning

Method	Partitioning stats [n=10]					Reasoning stats	
	Min (%)	Max (%)	Med (%)	RF	Time (s)	Time (s)	Messages (G)
LUBM-8K[1.10G triples]							
Hash	10.00	10.00	10.00	1.60	**530**	17,400	71.67
METIS	9.24	10.66	9.98	1.19	15,300	12,580	15.44
HDRF$_3$	9.35	10.47	10.00	1.43	590	15,740	46.05
2PS$_3$	9.06	10.35	10.00	**1.08**	700	**7,740**	**9.22**
WatDiv-1B[1.09G triples]							
Hash	10.00	10.00	10.00	2.48	**520**	1,870	8.95
METIS	9.70	10.35	10.00	**2.16**	15,100	2,690	**4.54**
HDRF$_3$	10.00	10.00	10.00	2.48	590	**1,850**	8.95
2PS$_3$	9.92	10.02	10.00	2.40	1,080	2,520	8.81
MAKG*[3.66G triples]							
Hash	10.00	10.00	10.00	1.99	**2,220**	8,000	29.24
METIS	Partitioning exhausted 784 GB of memory						
HDRF$_3$	10.00	10.00	10.00	**1.66**	3,500	7,160	26.15
2PS$_3$	9.91	10.06	10.00	1.67	3,640	**6,870**	**24.70**

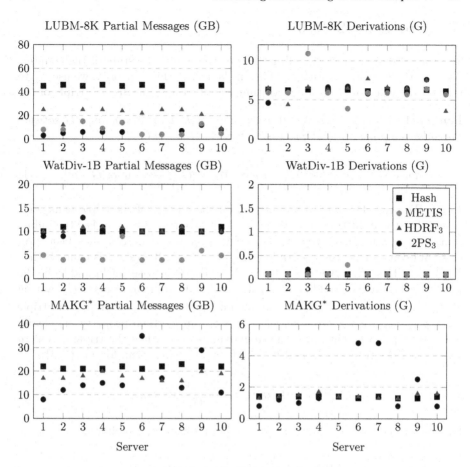

Fig. 1. Reasoning by servers

8   Conclusion and Future Work

We have presented two novel algorithms for streaming partitioning of RDF data in distributed RDF systems. We have compared our methods against hashing and min-cut partitioning, which have been the dominant partitioning methods thus far. Our methods are much less resource-intensive than min-cut partitioning, and they are not significantly more complex than hashing. Particularly the $2PS_3$ method often exhibits better reasoning performance, thus contributing to the scalability of distributed RDF systems. In our future work, we will aim to further improve the performance of reasoning by developing ways to reduce imbalances in the workload among servers. One possibility to achieve this might be to analyse the datalog program before partitioning and thus identify workload hotspots.

Acknowledgments. This work was supported by the SIRIUS Centre for Scalable Access in the Oil and Gas Domain, and the EPSRC project AnaLOG.

A   Proofs for Sect. 5

To prove Proposition 1, we will need to reason about the state of the counters N_k from the $HDRF_3$ algorithm. Thus, in the rest of this appendix, we use N_k^i to refer to the value of N_k from Algorithm 1 after processing the i-th triple of G.

Lemma 1. *For $\alpha > 1$ and $\lambda > 0$, each run of Algorithm 1 on a graph G satisfies the following property after processing the i-th triple of G:*

$$\max_k N_k^i - \min_k N_k^i < M_\lambda, \quad where \ M_\lambda = |G|\sqrt{\frac{4\alpha}{n\lambda}} + \max_r |G^+(r)|. \quad (1)$$

Proof. We prove the claim by induction on the index i of the triple being processed. For the induction base, the claim is clearly true for $i = 0$. For the induction step, assume that property (1) holds after the i-th triple has been process, and consider processing triple $\langle s_{i+1}, p_{i+1}, o_{i+1} \rangle$. If $T(s_{i+1})$ is defined, then $N_k^{i+1} = N_k^i$ for each server k, so (1) clearly holds. Otherwise, let k_1 and k_2 be the servers such that $N_{k_1}^{i+1}$ and $N_{k_2}^{i+1}$ are minimal and maximal, respectively, among all N_k^{i+1} at step $i + 1$. If $N_{k_2}^i$ is also maximal among all N_k^i at step 1 and triple $\langle s_{i+1}, p_{i+1}, o_{i+1} \rangle$ is sent to a server different from k_2, then property (1) clearly holds at step $i + 1$. Thus, the only remaining case is when the triple is sent to server k_2. The scores for k_1 and k_2 are of the following form, for $j \in \{1, 2\}$:

$$\text{SCORE}_j = (C_{REP})_j + \lambda \frac{\sum_k N_k^i}{|G|}(C_{BAL})_j$$

For convenience, let $\sum_k N_k^i = S$. We can bound SCORE_1 as follows:

$$\text{SCORE}_1 = (C_{REP})_1 + \lambda \frac{S}{|G|}(C_{BAL})_1$$

$$\geq \lambda \frac{S}{|G|}(C_{BAL})_1$$

$$= \frac{\lambda S}{|G|}\left(1 - n\frac{N_{k_1}^i + |G^+(s_{i+1})|}{\alpha|G|}\right)$$

Moreover, we can bound SCORE_2 as follows, where we use the fact that the definition of $(C_{REP})_2$ clearly ensures $(C_{REP})_2 < 4$:

$$\text{SCORE}_2 = (C_{REP})_2 + \frac{\lambda S}{|G|}(C_{BAL})_2$$

$$< 4 + \frac{\lambda S}{|G|}\left(1 - n\frac{N_{k_2}^i + |G^+(s_{i+1})|}{\alpha|G|}\right)$$

Triple $\langle s_{i+1}, p_{i+1}, o_{i+1} \rangle$ is sent to k_2, so we have $\text{SCORE}_1 \leq \text{SCORE}_2$. Combined with the above bounds for SCORE_1 and SCORE_2, we observe the following.

$$\frac{\lambda S}{|G|} \left(1 - n \frac{N^i_{k_1} + |G^+(s_{i+1})|}{\alpha |G|} \right) < 4 + \frac{\lambda S}{|G|} \left(1 - n \frac{N^i_{k_2} + |G^+(s_{i+1})|}{\alpha |G|} \right)$$

$$\frac{\lambda S}{|G|} \left(-n \frac{N^i_{k_1}}{\alpha |G|} \right) < 4 + \frac{\lambda S}{|G|} \left(-n \frac{N^i_{k_2}}{\alpha |G|} \right)$$

$$N^i_{k_2} - N^i_{k_1} < 4 \frac{\alpha |G|}{n\lambda} \frac{|G|}{S}$$

Now $N^i_{k_2} - N^i_{k_1} < S$ clearly holds at each step i, which ensures

$$N^i_{k_2} - N^i_{k_1} < 4 \frac{\alpha |G|}{n\lambda} \frac{|G|}{N^i_{k_2} - N^i_{k_1}}.$$

We make the following observations.

$$(N^i_{k_2} - N^i_{k_1})^2 < 4 \frac{\alpha |G|^2}{n\lambda}$$

$$N^i_{k_2} - N^i_{k_1} < |G| \sqrt{\frac{4\alpha}{n\lambda}}$$

$$N^i_{k_2} + |G^+(s_{i+1})| < N^i_{k_1} + |G| \sqrt{\frac{4\alpha}{n\lambda}} + \max_r |G^+(r)|$$

$$N^{i+1}_{k_2} < N^i_{k_1} + M_\lambda$$

Finally, $N^i_{k_1} = N^{i+1}_{k_1}$ since the triple is sent to server k_2, so the last observation proves our claim. $\qquad \square$

Proposition 1. *Algorithm 1 produces a partition that satisfies* $|G_i| \leq \alpha \frac{|G|}{n}$ *for each* $1 \leq i \leq n$ *whenever* α *and* λ *are selected such that*

$$\alpha > 1 + n \frac{\max_r |G^+(r)|}{|G|} \quad and \quad \lambda \geq \frac{4\alpha}{n \left(\frac{\alpha - 1}{n} - \frac{\max_r |G^+(r)|}{|G|} \right)^2}.$$

Proof. Let $\alpha > 1$ and λ be as stated in the proposition. Note that the condition on α ensures

$$\frac{\alpha - 1}{n} - \frac{\max_r |G^+(r)|}{|G|} > 0.$$

We now show that $M_\lambda \leq (\alpha - 1)\frac{|G|}{n}$ holds. Towards this goal, we make the following observations:

$$\lambda \geq \frac{4\alpha}{n\left(\frac{\alpha-1}{n} - \frac{\max_r |G^+(r)|}{|G|}\right)^2}$$

$$\frac{4\alpha}{\lambda n} \leq \left(\frac{\alpha - 1}{n} - \frac{\max_r |G^+(r)|}{|G|}\right)^2$$

$$\sqrt{\frac{4\alpha}{\lambda n}} \leq \frac{\alpha - 1}{n} - \frac{\max_r |G^+(r)|}{|G|}$$

$$|G|\sqrt{\frac{4\alpha}{\lambda n}} \leq |G|\frac{\alpha - 1}{n} - \max_r |G^+(r)|$$

$$|G|\sqrt{\frac{4\alpha}{\lambda n}} + \max_r |G^+(r)| \leq (\alpha - 1)\frac{|G|}{n}$$

Now $\mathcal{P} = G_1, \ldots, G_n$ be the partition produced by Algorithm 1. Clearly, we have $\min_k |G_k| \leq \frac{|G|}{n}$. Now consider an arbitrary server k. Property (1) of Lemma 1 ensures $|G_k| \leq |G|/n + M_\lambda$. Moreover, the condition on M_λ proved above ensures

$$|G_k| \leq \frac{|G|}{n} + (\alpha - 1)\frac{|G|}{n} = \alpha\frac{|G|}{n}.$$

This holds for every server k, which implies our claim.   □

B   Proofs for Sect. 6

Proposition 2. *Algorithm 2 produces a partition that satisfies $|G_i| \leq \alpha\frac{|G|}{n}$ for each $1 \leq i \leq n$ whenever α is selected such that*

$$\alpha > 1 + \frac{\max_r |G^+(r)|}{|G|}.$$

Proof. For each community c, the following property holds at each point during algorithm's execution:

$$S(c) = \sum_{r \text{ with } C(r)=c} |G^+(r)| \tag{2}$$

To see this, note that S is initialised by setting $S(c_r) = |G^+(r)|$ for each resource r. Moreover, lines 21 and 22 clearly ensure that the property is preserved when mapping C is updated in line 23.

We prove by induction that function AssignCommunities ensures the following inequality:

$$\max_k N_k - \min_k N_k \leq (\alpha - 1)\frac{|G|}{n}. \tag{3}$$

For the induction base, all N_k are initialised to zero, so (3) holds after line 25. For the induction step, assume that (3) holds before line 28 is evaluated for some community c. Let $k_1 = \arg\min_k N_k$ and $k_2 = \arg\max_k N_k$, and let N'_k be the updated values of N_k after line 28; we clearly have $N'_k = N_k$ for all $k \neq k_1$, $N'_{k_1} = N_{k_1} + S(c)$, and $\min_k N'_k \geq \min_k N_k$. We have two possibilities.

– $N'_{k_1} \leq N_{k_2}$. Then, $\max_k N'_k = N_{k_2}$ and so the following condition holds, where the induction assumption ensures the second inequality:

$$\max_k N'_k - \min_k N'_k \leq \max_k N_k - \min_k N_k \leq (\alpha - 1)\frac{|G|}{n}.$$

– $N'_{k_1} > N_{k_2}$. Then, $\max_k N'_k = N_{k_1} + S(c)$. Moreover, the requirement on the choice of α in our claim and the condition in line 20 of the algorithm ensure that $S(c) \leq \frac{(\alpha-1)|G|}{n}$ holds for each community c at any point in time during an algorithm's run. This, in turn, ensures the following property:

$$\max_k N'_k - \min_k N'_k = S(c) \leq (\alpha - 1)\frac{|G|}{n}.$$

Thus, (3) holds. In addition, at the end of function ASSIGNCOMMUNITIES, we have $\min_k N_k \leq \frac{|G|}{n}$ because $\sum_k N_k = |G|$. This, in turn, ensures

$$\max_k N_k \leq \min_k N_k + (\alpha - 1)\frac{|G|}{n} \leq \alpha\frac{|G|}{n}.$$

In the second phase, each triple $\langle s, p, o \rangle$ is assigned to $T(C(s))$. But then, (2) clearly ensures $|G_k| = N_k$ for each k, which implies our claim. $\square$

References

1. Abdelaziz, I., Harbi, R., Khayyat, Z., Kalnis, P.: A survey and experimental comparison of distributed SPARQL engines for very large RDF data. PVLDB **10**(13), 2049–2060 (2017)
2. Agathangelos, G., Troullinou, G., Kondylakis, H., Stefanidis, K., Plexousakis, D.: Incremental data partitioning of RDF data in SPARK. In: ESWC, pp. 50–54 (2018)
3. Ajileye, T., Motik, B., Horrocks, I.: Datalog materialisation in distributed RDF stores with dynamic data exchange. In: ISWC, pp. 21–37 (2019)
4. Harbi, R., Abdelaziz, I., Kalnis, P., Mamoulis, N., Ebrahim, Y., Sahli, M.: Accelerating SPARQL queries by exploiting hash-based locality and adaptive partitioning. VLDB J. **25**(3), 355–380 (2016). https://doi.org/10.1007/s00778-016-0420-y
5. Antoniou, G., et al.: A survey of large-scale reasoning on the web of data. Knowl. Eng. Rev. **33**, e21 (2018)
6. Echbarthi, G., Kheddouci, H.: Streaming METIS partitioning. In: ASONAM, pp. 17–24 (2016)
7. Färber, M.: The microsoft academic knowledge graph: a linked data source with 8 billion triples of scholarly data. In: ISWC, pp. 113–129 (2019)
8. Gallego, M.A., Fernández, J.D., Martìnez-Prieto, M.A., de la Fuente, P.: An Empirical Study of Real-World SPARQL Queries. CoRR abs/1103.5043 (2011)

9. Gu, R., Wang, S., Wang, F., Yuan, C., Huang, Y.: Cichlid: efficient large scale RDFS/OWL reasoning with spark. In: IPDPS, pp. 700–709 (2015)
10. Gurajada, S., Seufert, S., Miliaraki, I., Theobald, M.: TriAD: a distributed shared-nothing RDF engine based on asynchronous message passing. In: SIGMOD, pp. 289–300 (2014)
11. Harth, A., Umbrich, J., Hogan, A., Decker, S.: YARS2: a federated repository for querying graph structured data from the web. In: ISWC, pp. 211–224 (2007)
12. Huang, J., Abadi, D.J., Ren, K.: Scalable SPARQL querying of large RDF graphs. PVLDB **4**(11), 1123–1134 (2011)
13. Husain, M.F., McGlothlin, J.P., Masud, M.M., Khan, L.R., Thuraisingham, B.M.: Heuristics-based query processing for large RDF graphs using cloud computing. IEEE TKDE **23**(9), 1312–1327 (2011)
14. Janke, D., Staab, S., Thimm, M.: On data placement strategies in distributed RDF stores. In: SBD, pp. 1:1–1:6 (2017)
15. Karypis, G., Kumar, V., Comput, S.: A fast and high quality multilevel scheme for partitioning irregular graphs. SIAM J. Sci. Comput. **20**, 359–392 (1998)
16. Lee, K., Liu, L.: Scaling queries over big RDF graphs with semantic hash partitioning. PVLDB **6**(14), 1894–1905 (2013)
17. Liu, Y., McBrien, P.: Spowl: spark-based owl 2 reasoning materialisation. In: BeyondMR 2017 (2017)
18. Mayer, C., et al.: ADWISE: adaptive window-based streaming edge partitioning for high-speed graph processing. In: ICDCS, pp. 685–695 (2018)
19. Mayer, R., Orujzade, K., Jacobsen, H.: 2ps: High-quality edge partitioning with two-phase streaming. CoRR abs/2001.07086 (2020)
20. Motik, B., Nenov, Y., Piro, R., Horrocks, I., Olteanu, D.: Parallel materialisation of datalog programs in centralised, main-memory RDF systems. In: AAAI, pp. 129–137 (2014)
21. Petroni, F., Querzoni, L., Daudjee, K., Kamali, S., Iacoboni, G.: HDRF: stream-based partitioning for power-law graphs. In: CIKM, pp. 243–252 (2015)
22. Potter, A., Motik, B., Nenov, Y., Horrocks, I.: Dynamic data exchange in distributed RDF stores. IEEE TKDE **30**(12), 2312–2325 (2018)
23. Schätzle, A., Przyjaciel-Zablocki, M., Skilevic, S., Lausen, G.: S2RDF: RDF querying with SPARQL on spark. PVLDB **9**(10), 804–815 (2016)
24. Seo, J., Park, J., Shin, J., Lam, M.: Distributed socialite: a datalog-based language for large-scale graph analysis. PVLDB **6**, 1906–1917 (2013)
25. Stanton, I., Kliot, G.: Streaming graph partitioning for large distributed graphs. In: KDD, pp. 1222–1230 (2012)
26. Urbani, J., Kotoulas, S., Maassen, J., van Harmelen, F., Bal, H.: WebPIE: a web-scale parallel inference engine using MapReduce. JWS **10**, 59–75 (2012)
27. Weaver, J., Hendler, J.A.: Parallel materialization of the finite RDFS closure for hundreds of millions of triples. In: ISWC, pp. 682–697 (2009)
28. Wu, B., Zhou, Y., Yuan, P., Jin, H., Liu, L.: SemStore: a semantic-preserving distributed RDF triple store. In: CIKM. pp. 509–518 (2014)
29. Wu, H., Liu, J., Wang, T., Ye, D., Wei, J., Zhong, H.: Parallel materialization of datalog programs with spark for scalable reasoning. In: WISE, pp. 363–379 (2016)
30. Zeng, K., Yang, J., Wang, H., Shao, B., Wang, Z.: A distributed graph engine for web scale RDF data. PVLDB **6**(4), 265–276 (2013)
31. Zhang, W., Chen, Y., Dai, D.: AKIN: a streaming graph partitioning algorithm for distributed graph storage systems. In: CCGRID, pp. 183–192 (2018)

Parallelised ABox Reasoning and Query Answering with Expressive Description Logics

Andreas Steigmiller[✉] and Birte Glimm

Ulm University, Ulm, Germany
{andreassteigmiller,birteglimm}@uni-ulm.de

Abstract. Automated reasoning support is an important aspect of logic-based knowledge representation. The development of specialised procedures and sophisticated optimisation techniques significantly improved the performance even for complex reasoning tasks such as conjunctive query answering. Reasoning and query answering over knowledge bases with a large number of facts and expressive schemata remains, however, challenging.

We propose a novel approach where the reasoning over assertional knowledge is split into small, similarly sized work packages to enable a parallelised processing with tableau algorithms, which are dominantly used for reasoning with more expressive Description Logics. To retain completeness in the presence of expressive schemata, we propose a specifically designed cache that allows for controlling and synchronising the interaction between the constructed partial models. We further report on encouraging performance improvements for the implementation of the techniques in the tableau-based reasoning system Konclude.

1 Introduction

Description Logics (DLs) are a family of logic-based representation formalisms that provide the logical underpinning of the well-known Web Ontology Language (OWL). The knowledge expressed with DLs is typically separated into terminological (aka TBox or schema) and assertional knowledge (aka ABox or facts), where the former describes the relationships between concepts (representing sets of individuals with common characteristics) as well as roles (specifying the relationships between pairs of individuals) and the latter asserts these concepts and roles to concrete individuals of the application domain. Automated reasoning systems derive implicit consequences of the explicitly stated information, which, for example, allows for detecting modelling errors and for enriching queries by additional answers that are implied by the knowledge. Expressive DLs, such as $\mathcal{SROIQ}$ [11], allow for describing the application domain in more detail, but require sophisticated reasoning algorithms and are typically more costly in terms of computational resources. Nevertheless state-of-the-art reasoning systems are usually able to handle real-world ontologies, which often also use expressive language features, due to a large range of developed optimisation techniques.

The increasing volume of data in many application domains leads, however, also to larger amounts of assertional knowledge. For less expressive schemata (where

A. Steigmiller—Funded by the German Research Foundation (Deutsche Forschungsgemeinschaft, DFG) in project number 330492673.

R. Verborgh et al. (Eds.): ESWC 2021, LNCS 12731, pp. 23–39, 2021.
https://doi.org/10.1007/978-3-030-77385-4_2

reasoning is usually deterministic), the interest in ontology-based data access (OBDA) led to several advancements, e.g., query rewriting, materialization techniques, or combined approaches. To cope with the reasoning challenges in the presence of an expressive schema several techniques have been developed, which often complement each other. There are, for example, summarisation [3,6] and abstraction techniques [8], which derive consequences for representative individuals and transfer the results to many other individuals with the same or a similar (syntactical) structure. These techniques do not necessarily work well for all ontologies, may be limited to certain queries or (fragments of) DLs, or require expensive computations, e.g., justifications. Several techniques also reduce reasoning to datalog [1,5,21] since datalog engines are targeted towards data intensive applications. This reduction, however, often leads to some additional overhead and, in some cases, it can be necessary to fall back to a fully-fledged DL reasoner, e.g., for handling non-deterministic features. Other approaches partition the ABox or extract modules out of it [20] such that each part can be processed independently [19]. Moreover, approaches based on big data principles such as map and reduce have been proposed [18]. However, they are typically also limited to specific language features and/or queries and do not work for arbitrary ontologies. Particularly challenging is the support of conjunctive queries with complex concept atoms or with existential variables that may bind to anonymous individuals, which are only implied by the knowledge base, since these features typically make it difficult to appropriately split the ABox upfront in such a way that queries can correctly be answered without too much data exchange.

Many state-of-the-art reasoners directly integrate techniques that improve ABox reasoning, e.g., (pseudo) model checking [10] or bulk processing with binary retrieval [9]. Most reasoners for expressive DLs are based on (variants of) tableau algorithms, which construct abstractions of models called completion graphs. By caching (parts of) the completion graph from the initial consistency check, subsequent reasoning tasks and queries can be answered more efficiently [12,16]. However, constructing and caching entire completion graphs for knowledge bases with large ABoxes requires significant amounts of (main) memory, which may be more than what is typically available.

In this paper, we propose to dynamically split the model construction process for tableau algorithms. This allows for (i) handling larger ABoxes since not everything has to be handled at once and for (ii) exploiting parallelisation. The proposed splits lead to similarly sized work packages that can be processed concurrently without direct synchronisation. To ensure that the partial models constructed in parallel are "compatible" with each other, we employ a cache where selected consequences for individuals are stored. For processing new or reprocessing incompatible parts of the knowledge base, we retrieve cached consequences and ensure with appropriate reuse and expansion strategies that the constructed partial models are eventually compatible with the cache, such that it can (asynchronously) be updated. Conjunctive query answering is supported by adapting the expansion criteria and by appropriately splitting the propagation work through the (partial) models for determining query answers.

The paper is organised as follows: Sect. 2 introduces some preliminaries about DLs and tableau algorithms; Sect. 3 describes the cache; Sect. 4 discusses the adaptations for query answering and Sect. 5 presents implementation details and results of experiments before we conclude in Sect. 6. An accompanying technical report [14] provides further details, examples, proofs, and evaluation results.

Table 1. Core features of $\mathcal{SROIQ}$ (#M denotes the cardinality of the set M)

		Syntax	Semantics
Individuals:	Individual	a	$a^{\mathcal{I}} \in \Delta^{\mathcal{I}}$
Roles:	Atomic role	r	$r^{\mathcal{I}} \subseteq \Delta^{\mathcal{I}} \times \Delta^{\mathcal{I}}$
	Inverse role	r^-	$\{\langle \gamma, \delta \rangle \mid \langle \delta, \gamma \rangle \in r^{\mathcal{I}}\}$
Concepts:	Atomic concept	A	$A^{\mathcal{I}} \subseteq \Delta^{\mathcal{I}}$
	Nominal	$\{a\}$	$\{a^{\mathcal{I}}\}$
	Top	$\top$	$\Delta^{\mathcal{I}}$
	Bottom	$\bot$	$\emptyset$
	Negation	$\neg C$	$\Delta^{\mathcal{I}} \setminus C^{\mathcal{I}}$
	Conjunction	$C \sqcap D$	$C^{\mathcal{I}} \cap D^{\mathcal{I}}$
	Disjunction	$C \sqcup D$	$C^{\mathcal{I}} \cup D^{\mathcal{I}}$
	Existential restriction	$\exists r.C$	$\{\delta \mid \exists \gamma \in C^{\mathcal{I}} : \langle \delta, \gamma \rangle \in r^{\mathcal{I}}\}$
	Universal restriction	$\forall r.C$	$\{\delta \mid \langle \delta, \gamma \rangle \in r^{\mathcal{I}} \to \gamma \in C^{\mathcal{I}}\}$
	Number restriction, $\bowtie \in \{\leqslant, \geqslant\}$	$\bowtie n\, r.C$	$\{\delta \mid \#\{\langle \delta, \gamma \rangle \in r^{\mathcal{I}} \text{ and } \gamma \in C^{\mathcal{I}}\} \bowtie n\}$
Axioms:	General concept inclusion	$C \sqsubseteq D$	$C^{\mathcal{I}} \subseteq D^{\mathcal{I}}$
	Role inclusion	$r \sqsubseteq s$	$r^{\mathcal{I}} \subseteq s^{\mathcal{I}}$
	Role chains	$r_1 \circ \dots \circ r_n \sqsubseteq S$	$r_1^{\mathcal{I}} \circ \dots \circ r_n^{\mathcal{I}} \subseteq S^{\mathcal{I}}$
Assertions:	Concept assertion	$C(a)$	$a^{\mathcal{I}} \in C^{\mathcal{I}}$
	Role assertion	$r(a, b)$	$\langle a^{\mathcal{I}}, b^{\mathcal{I}} \rangle \in r^{\mathcal{I}}$
	Equality assertion	$a \approx b$	$a^{\mathcal{I}} = b^{\mathcal{I}}$

2 Description Logics and Reasoning Preliminaries

The syntax of DLs is defined using a vocabulary consisting of countably infinite pairwise disjoint sets N_C of *atomic concepts*, N_R of *atomic roles*, and N_I of *individuals*. A role is either atomic or an *inverse role* r^-, $r \in N_R$. The syntax and semantics of complex *concepts* and *axioms* are defined in Table 1. Note that we omit the presentation of some features (e.g., datatypes) and restrictions (e.g., number restrictions may not use "complex roles", i.e., roles that occur on the right-hand side of role chains or are implied by such roles) for brevity. A knowledge base/ontology $\mathcal{K}$ is a finite set of axioms. One typically distinguishes terminological axioms in the TBox $\mathcal{T}$ (e.g., $C \sqsubseteq D$) and assertions in the ABox $\mathcal{A}$ (e.g., $C(a)$) of $\mathcal{K}$, i.e., $\mathcal{K} = (\mathcal{T}, \mathcal{A})$. We use $\mathsf{inds}(\mathcal{K})$ to refer to the individuals of $\mathcal{K}$. An *interpretation* $\mathcal{I} = (\Delta^{\mathcal{I}}, \cdot^{\mathcal{I}})$ consists of a non-empty *domain* $\Delta^{\mathcal{I}}$ and an *interpretation function* $\cdot^{\mathcal{I}}$. We say that $\mathcal{I}$ *satisfies* a general concept inclusion (GCI) $C \sqsubseteq D$, written $\mathcal{I} \models C \sqsubseteq D$, if $C^{\mathcal{I}} \subseteq D^{\mathcal{I}}$ (analogously for other axioms and assertions as shown in Table 1). If $\mathcal{I}$ satisfies all axioms of $\mathcal{K}$, $\mathcal{I}$ is a *model* of $\mathcal{K}$ and $\mathcal{K}$ is *consistent/satisfiable* if it has a model.

A tableau algorithm decides the consistency of a knowledge base $\mathcal{K}$ by trying to construct an abstraction of a model for $\mathcal{K}$, a so-called *completion graph*. A completion graph G is a tuple $(V, E, \mathcal{L}, \neq)$, where each node $v \in V$ (edge $\langle v, w \rangle \in E$) represents one or more (pairs of) individuals. Each node v (edge $\langle v, w \rangle$) is labelled with a set of concepts (roles), $\mathcal{L}(v)$ ($\mathcal{L}(\langle v, w \rangle)$), which the individuals represented by v ($\langle v, w \rangle$) are instances of. The relation $\dot{\neq}$ records inequalities between nodes. We call $C \in \mathcal{L}(v)$ $(r \in \mathcal{L}(\langle v, w \rangle))$ a *concept (role) fact*, which we write as $C(v)$ $(r(v, w))$. A node v is a *nominal node* if $\{a\} \in \mathcal{L}(v)$ for some individual a and a *blockable node* otherwise. For $r \in \mathcal{L}(\langle v, w \rangle)$ and $r \sqsubseteq^* s$, with $\sqsubseteq^*$ the reflexive, transitive closure over role inclusions of $\mathcal{K}$ (including their inverses), we call w an *s-successor* of v and v an *s-predecessor* of w. A node w is called an *s-neighbour* of v if w is an *s-successor* of v or v an s^--*successor* of w. We use *ancestor* and *descendant* as the transitive closure of the predecessor and successor relation, respectively. We say that v_n is an *implied descendant* of v_0 if there is a path $v_0, v_1, \ldots, v_n$ such that v_{i+1} is a successor of v_i for $0 \leq i < n$ and each v_j with $j > 0$ does not represent an individual of $\mathsf{inds}(\mathcal{K})$.

A completion graph is initialised with one node for each individual in the input knowledge base. Concepts and roles are added to the node and edge labels as specified by concept and role assertions. For simplicity, we assume that, for each individual $a \in \mathsf{inds}(\mathcal{K})$, a nominal $\{a\}$ is added to $\mathcal{L}(v_a)$. This allows for easily handling equality assertions by adding $\{b\}$ to $\mathcal{L}(v_a)$ for $a \approx b \in \mathcal{A}$. As a convention, we write v_a to refer to the node representing $a \in \mathsf{inds}(\mathcal{K})$, i.e., $\{a\} \in \mathcal{L}(v_a)$. Note that v_a and v_b can refer to the same node if $\{a\}$ and $\{b\}$ are in its label. Complex concepts are then decomposed using a set of expansion rules, where each rule application can add new concepts to node labels and/or new nodes and edges, thereby explicating the structure of a model. The rules are applied until either the graph is *fully expanded* (no more rules are applicable), in which case the graph can be used to construct a model that is a *witness* to the consistency of $\mathcal{K}$, or an obvious contradiction (called a *clash*) is discovered (e.g., a node v with $C, \neg C \in \mathcal{L}(v)$), proving that the completion graph does not correspond to a model. $\mathcal{K}$ is consistent if the rules (some of which are non-deterministic) can be applied such that they build a fully expanded, clash-free completion graph. Cycle detection techniques such as *pairwise blocking* [11] prevent the infinite generation of new nodes.

3   Caching Individual Derivations

Since tableau-based reasoning algorithms reduce (most) reasoning tasks to consistency checking, parallelising the completion graph construction has general benefits on the now ubiquitous multi-core processor systems. Partitioning the ABox upfront such that no or little interaction is required between the partitions [19] no longer works for expressive DLs, such as $\mathcal{SROIQ}$, or complex reasoning tasks, such as conjunctive query answering (with complex concepts and/or existential variables). This is, for example, due to implied connections between individuals (e.g., due to nominals) or due to the consideration of new concept expressions at query time. The effect of parallelisation is further hindered by the multitude of optimisations, required to properly deal with real-world ontologies, which often introduce dependencies between rules and (parts of) completion graphs, resulting in the need of data synchronisation. For example, the anywhere blocking optimisation (cycle detection) investigates all previously constructed nodes in the completion graph in order to determine whether a node is blocked. Hence, a parallelisation approach where a completion graph is modified in parallel can be difficult to realise since it could require a lot of synchronisation.

For ontologies with large ABoxes, it seems more suitable to build completion graphs for parts of the ABox separately (by independent threads) and, since independence of the parts cannot be assumed, to align the results afterwards. Such an alignment can, however, be non-trivial on several levels: For example, if different non-deterministic decisions have been made for individuals in overlapping parts or due to technical details of the often complex data structures for completion graphs, e.g., efficient processing queues, caching status of node labels, etc.

Our parallelisation approach focuses on aligning completion graphs for ABox parts and we address the challenges by employing a cache for certain derivations for individuals, which facilitates the alignment process. For this, consistency checking roughly proceeds as follows: We randomly split the ABox into equally sized parts that are distributed to worker threads. When a thread begins to process one of these ABox parts, it retrieves stored derivations from the cache for (possibly) affected individuals in that part. The thread then tries to construct a fully expanded and clash-free *local* completion graph for the ABox part by reusing cached derivations and/or by expanding the processing to individuals until they are "compatible" with the cache. Compatibility requires that the local completion graph is fully expanded as well as clash-free and that it can be expanded such that it matches the derivations for the remaining individuals in the cache. If it is required to extend the processing to some "neighbouring" individuals for achieving compatibility (e.g., if different non-deterministic decisions are required for the already processed individuals), then also the cached derivations for these individuals are retrieved and considered. If this process succeeds, the cache is updated with the new or changed derivations for the processed individuals.

If compatibility cannot be obtained (e.g., due to expansion limitations that ensure similarly sized work packages), then the cache entries of incompletely handled individuals are marked such that they are considered later separately. For this, a thread loads the data for (some) marked individuals and tries to construct a fully expanded and clash-free completion graph for them until full compatibility is obtained. If clashes occur that depend on reused (non-deterministic) derivations from the cache, then the corresponding individuals can be identified such that their expansion can be prioritized and/or the reuse of their derivations can be avoided. As a result, (in)consistency of the knowledge base can eventually be detected, as soon as all problematic individuals are directly expanded and all relevant non-deterministic decisions are investigated together.

Before describing the different aspects of the approach and the work-flow in more detail, we define a basic version of the cache and how derivations are stored and used.

Definition 1 (Individual Derivations Cache). *Let $\mathcal{K}$ be a knowledge base. We use* fclos($\mathcal{K}$), rols($\mathcal{K}$), *and* inds($\mathcal{K}$) *for the sets of concepts, roles, and individuals that can occur in $\mathcal{K}$ or in a completion graph for $\mathcal{K}$. An individual derivations cache C is a (partial) mapping of individuals from* inds($\mathcal{K}$) *to cache entries, where the cache entry for an individual $a \in$* inds($\mathcal{K}$) *consists of:*

- $K^C \subseteq 2^{\text{fclos}(\mathcal{K})}$ *and* $P^C \subseteq 2^{\text{fclos}(\mathcal{K})}$: *the sets of known and possibly instantiated concepts of a, respectively,*
- $I \subseteq 2^{\text{inds}(\mathcal{K})}$: *the individuals that are (indirectly) connected via nominals to a,*
- $\exists$: rols($\mathcal{K}$) $\rightarrow \mathbf{N}_0$: *mapping a role r to the number of existentially derived successors for a and r, and*
- K^R: rols($\mathcal{K}$) $\rightarrow 2^{\text{inds}(\mathcal{K})}$ *and* P^R: rols($\mathcal{K}$) $\rightarrow 2^{\text{inds}(\mathcal{K})}$: *mapping a role r to the sets of known and possible neighbours of a and r, respectively.*

We write $K^C(a, C)$, $P^C(a, C)$, $I(a, C)$, $\exists(a, C)$, $K^R(a, C)$, and $P^R(a, C)$ to refer to the individual parts of the cache entry $C(a)$. We write $a \in C$ if C is defined for a.

Note that we distinguish between known and possible information in the cache, which mostly correspond to the deterministically and non-deterministically derived consequences in completion graphs. Non-deterministically derived facts in completion graphs can usually be identified via branching tags for dependency directed backtracking [2,17]. If the cache is clear from the context, we simply write $K^C(a)$ or $K^R(a)(r)$, where the latter returns the known (deterministically derived) r-neighbours of a.

Let $\mathcal{K} = (\mathcal{T}, \mathcal{A})$ be a knowledge base and $\mathcal{A}_j \subseteq \mathcal{A}$ the processed ABox part. In addition to the usual initialisation of a completion graph $G = (V, E, \mathcal{L}, \neq)$ for $\mathcal{K} = (\mathcal{T}, \mathcal{A}_j)$, we add $K^C(a)$ to $\mathcal{L}(v_a)$ and r to $\mathcal{L}(\langle v_a, v_b \rangle)$ if $b \in K^R(a)(r)$, for each $v_a, v_b \in V$. If a node $v \in V$ exists with $\{c\} \in \mathcal{L}(v)$ or $\neg\{c\} \in \mathcal{L}(v)$, but $v_c \notin V$, then we add v_c with $\{c\} \in \mathcal{L}(v_c)$ to V and initialise v_c analogously. Once G is extended into a fully expanded and clash-free completion graph, we identify the derivations for cache entries for each individual a with $v_a \in V$. Since deterministically derived consequences remain valid for all possible completion graphs, we update the corresponding cache entries by adding the deterministically derived consequences, e.g., for K^C, whereas non-deterministically derived consequences may change and, thus, replace existing cache entries, e.g., for P^C. A completion graph for $(\mathcal{T}, \mathcal{A}_j)$ is *compatible* with the cache if it can be extended to a fully expanded and clash-free completion graph for $(\mathcal{T}, \mathcal{A}_1 \cup \ldots \cup \mathcal{A}_j)$, where $\mathcal{A}_1 \cup \ldots \cup \mathcal{A}_{j-1}$ are the previously processed (and cached) ABox parts. As argued above, this might require the integration and processing of individuals from the cache during the completion graph expansion. Hence, we define when individuals in the cache *potentially influence* or are *influenced by* the completion graph.

Definition 2 (Cache Influence and Compatibility). *Let* $\mathcal{K} = (\mathcal{T}, \mathcal{A})$ *be a knowledge base,* $G = (V, E, \mathcal{L}, \neq)$ *a completion graph for* $(\mathcal{T}, \mathcal{A}_j)$ *with* $\mathcal{A}_j \subseteq \mathcal{A}$*, and* $v_a \in V$*. We use* #exrols$_r(v_a)$ *for the number of* r*-neighbours of* v_a *that do not represent an individual of* inds$(\mathcal{K})$ *and* neighb$_r(v_a)$ *for the* r*-neighbours of* v_a *that represent an individual of* inds$(\mathcal{K})$*. For an individual derivations cache* C *(c.f. Definition 1), an individual* $b \in C$ *with* $v_b \notin V$ is *potentially influenced by* G *if*

D1 $\forall r.C \in \mathcal{L}(v_a)$, $b \in K^R(a)(r) \cup P^R(a)(r)$, and $C \notin K^C(b) \cup P^C(b)$;
D2 $\leqslant n\, r.C \in \mathcal{L}(v_a)$, $b \in K^R(a)(r) \cup P^R(a)(r)$, and $\{C, \neg C\} \cap (K^C(b) \cup P^C(b)) = \emptyset$;
D3 $\leqslant n\, r.C \in \mathcal{L}(v_a)$, $b \in K^R(a)(r) \cup P^R(a)(r)$, and #$[\{d \mid d \in K^R(c)(r) \cup P^R(c)(r)$ with $\{c\} \in \mathcal{L}(v_a)\} \cup$ neighb$_r(v_a)] +$ #exrols$_r(v_a) > n$;
D4 $b \in I(a)$ and $C \in \mathcal{L}(v_a)$, $C \notin K^C(a) \cup P^C(a)$ or $\leqslant n\, r.C \in \mathcal{L}(v_a)$ with $\exists(a)(r) > 0$;
or
D5 $\{c\} \in \mathcal{L}(v_a)$, $\{c\} \notin K^C(a) \cup P^C(a)$, $a \in K^R(b)(r) \cup P^R(b)(r)$ and $c \notin K^R(b)(r) \cup P^R(b)(r)$ or $b \in K^R(a)(s) \cup P^R(a)(s)$ and $b \notin K^R(c)(s) \cup P^R(c)(s)$.

An individual $b \in C$ *with* $v_b \notin V$ *is potentially* influencing *the completion graph* G *if*

G1 $b \in P^R(a)(r)$;   G3 $b \in I(a)$, $C \in P^C(a)$, $C \notin \mathcal{L}(v_a)$; or
G2 $b \in K^R(a)(r)$, $C \in P^C(a)$, $C \notin \mathcal{L}(v_a)$;   G4 $\{a\} \in P^C(b)$ or $\neg\{a\} \in P^C(b)$;

We say that G *is* compatible *with a cache* C *if there is no individual* b *that is potentially influenced by* G *or potentially influencing* G.

Roughly speaking, an individual is potentially influenced by a completion graph if integrating it into the completion graph could lead to new consequences being propagated to it. In contrast, an individual potentially influences a completion graph if the integration of it could result in new consequences for the local completion graph.

The conditions for determining influenced individuals have a strong correspondence with the tableau expansion rules (cf. [11]). In fact, Condition D1, D2, and D3 basically check whether the ∀-, the **choose**-, or the ⩽-rule could potentially be applicable, i.e., whether the handling of $\forall r.C$ or $\leqslant r n.C$ concepts requires the consideration of neighbours from the cache. The first part of Condition D4 further checks whether some individual is indirectly connected to a via a nominal for an implied descendant for an individual b and whether new consequences could be propagated to that descendant. This could be the case if the label for a differs to the concepts for a in the cache. The second part handles potential cases where new nominals may have to be introduced and may influence b or descendants of b. Finally, Condition D5 ensures that neighbours are integrated if individuals are newly merged such that their neighbour relations in the cache can be updated.

Instead of mirroring Conditions D1–D4 for determining influencing individuals, we use the relatively simple Conditions G1–G4 since they allow for simpler data structures and efficient cache updates. Condition G1 and G2 simply check whether some possible instances are missing in the local completion graph, which may stem from a neighbouring individual from the cache. Condition G3 analogously checks for a potentially influencing individual b that is indirectly connected via the nominal $\{a\}$ in the label of an implied descendant of b. Condition G4 checks for merges and inequality information caused by non-deterministically derived nominal expressions for other individuals.

The following example, inspired by the well-known UOBM ontology, illustrates consistency checking with the cache.

Example 1. Suppose an ABox consisting of the two parts:

$$\mathcal{A}_1 = \{ \; \forall enr^-.(\forall takes.GC \sqcup \forall takes.UGC)(uni), \quad likes(stud, soccer), \quad enr(stud, uni),$$
$$\forall likes^-.SoccerFan(soccer), \qquad\qquad takes(stud, course)\},$$

$$\mathcal{A}_2 = \{ \; \exists hc.\exists likes.\{soccer\}(prof), \qquad\qquad teaches(prof, course),$$
$$\forall teaches.\forall takes^-.\neg TennisFan(prof), \quad likes(prof, soccer)\}.$$

We abbreviate *Undergraduate Course* as *UGC*, *Graduate Course* as *GC*, *enrolled in* as *enr*, *has child* as *hc*, and *student* as *stud*. For checking $\mathcal{A}_1$, we initialise a completion graph with nodes and edges that reflect the individuals and assertions in $\mathcal{A}_1$ (cf. upper part of Fig. 1). To satisfy the universal restriction for v_{soccer}, we apply the ∀-rule, which propagates *SoccerFan* to v_{stud}. Analogously, the universal restriction for v_{uni} propagates $\forall takes.GC \sqcup \forall takes.UGC$ to v_{stud}. We assume that the disjunct $\forall takes.GC$ is checked first, i.e., it is non-deterministically added to $\mathcal{L}(v_{stud})$. Then the concept GC is propagated to v_{course}. The completion graph for $\mathcal{A}_1$ is now fully expanded and clash-free. We next extract the data for the cache (as shown in the lower part of Fig. 1).

The completion graph for $\mathcal{A}_2$ is analogously initialised (cf. upper part of Fig. 2). For the concept $\exists hc.\exists likes.\{soccer\} \in \mathcal{L}(v_{prof})$, the ∃-rule of the tableau algorithm builds a blockable hc-successor for v_{prof} with $\exists likes.\{soccer\}$ in its label, for which another successor is created that is merged with v_{soccer} (due to the nominal) lead-

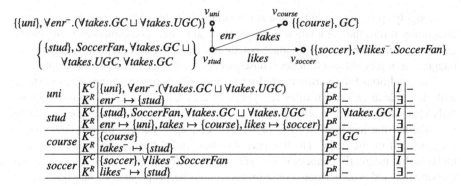

Fig. 1. Local completion graph (upper part) and entries of the individual derivations cache (lower part) for handling ABox $\mathcal{A}_1$ of Example 1

ing to the depicted edge to v_{soccer}. Due to the universal restriction $\forall likes^-.SoccerFan$ in $\mathcal{L}(v_{soccer})$, $SoccerFan$ is propagated to v_1 and to v_{prof}. For the universal restriction $\forall teaches.\forall takes^-.\neg TennisFan \in \mathcal{L}(v_{prof})$, we propagate $\forall takes^-.\neg TennisFan$ to v_{course}. Now, there are no more tableau expansion rules applicable to the constructed completion graph, but it is not yet compatible with the cache and we have to integrate (potentially) influenced or influencing individuals. In fact, *course* causes two incompatibilities: On the one hand, Condition **D1** identifies *stud* as (potentially) influenced due to $\forall takes^-.\neg TennisFan \in \mathcal{L}(v_{course})$ and because *stud* is a $takes^-$-neighbour of *course* according to the cache (cf. Fig. 1). On the other hand, Condition **G2** is satisfied (since $GC \notin \mathcal{L}(v_{course})$ but $GC \in P^C(course)$) and, therefore, the neighbour *stud* listed in $K^R(course)(takes^-)$ is identified as potentially influencing. We integrate *stud* by creating the node v_{stud}, by adding the concepts $\{stud\}$ and $\forall takes.GC \sqcup \forall takes.UGC$ from the cache to $\mathcal{L}(v_{stud})$, and by creating an edge to v_{course} labelled with *takes* as well as an edge to v_{soccer} labelled with *likes*. Now, the rule application for $\forall takes^-.\neg TennisFan \in \mathcal{L}(course)$ propagates $\neg TennisFan$ to v_{stud}. In addition, by reprocessing the disjunction $\forall takes.GC \sqcup \forall takes.UGC$ for v_{stud}, we obtain $GC \in \mathcal{L}(v_{course})$ if the same disjunct is chosen. As a result, the completion graph is fully expanded and clash-free w.r.t. $\mathcal{A}_2$ and it is compatible with the cache. Hence, the cache can be updated resulting in the entries depicted in the lower part of Fig. 2. Note that only v_{uni} has not been integrated in the completion graph for $\mathcal{A}_2$, but there is usually a bigger gain for larger ABoxes.

For parallelising the work-flow with the cache, one has to update and use the entries in a consistent/atomic way such that the state is clear. This can efficiently (and asynchronously) be realised by associating an update id with each cached individual and allow them to have an "inconsistent state" in the cache (see technical report for details). If an update extracted from a constructed completion graph refers to a cache entry of an individual with a changed update id (i.e., the cache entry has been changed by another thread), then the non-deterministically derived consequences are simply added and the state of the individual is set inconsistent (e.g., by adding $\bot$ to $P^C(a)$). If all parts of the ABox are processed, then we repeatedly retrieve individuals with inconsistent states from the cache and reprocess them until compatibility is achieved. Repeatedly deriv-

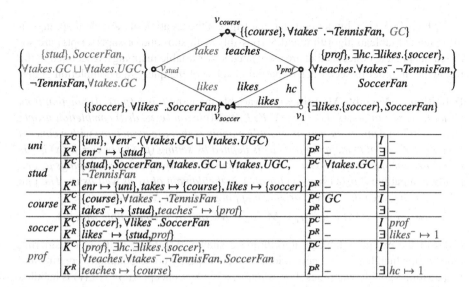

Fig. 2. Local completion graph (upper part, expansions from cache due to incompatibilities in red) and entries of the individual derivations cache (lower part, changes in blue) for handling ABox $\mathcal{A}_2$ of Example 1. (Color figure online)

ing different consequences for individuals and correspondingly updating the cache in parallel can, however, threaten termination of the procedure. To retain termination, we simply increase the number of individuals that are processed by one thread such that, in the worst-case, all individuals with inconsistent states are eventually processed together.

A naive expansion to all influenced individuals can cause a significant work imbalance for knowledge bases that use complex roles or have intensively connected individuals. In fact, if many neighbour individuals are influenced by universal restrictions or by the merging of nodes, then the expansion to all of them could result in an enormous completion graph processed by one thread, which could limit the effectiveness of the parallelisation. This can be addressed by "cutting the propagation" in the completion graph, for which we then notify the cache that the states of the remaining individuals have to be considered inconsistent such that their processing can be continued later. This cannot avoid the (theoretical) worst-case of processing the whole knowledge base in the end, but it seems to work well for many real-world ontologies, as indicated by our evaluation.

4   Query Answering Support

Compared to other more sophisticated reasoning tasks, conjunctive query answering is typically more challenging since an efficient reduction to consistency checking is not easy. However, a new approach for answering (conjunctive) queries has recently been introduced, where the query atoms are "absorbed" into several simple DL-axioms [13]. These "query axioms" are of the form $C \sqsubseteq {\downarrow} x.S^x$, $S^x \sqsubseteq \forall r.S_r^x$, $S^x \sqcap A \sqsubseteq S_A^x$, and $S^x \sqcap S^y \sqsubseteq$

S^{xy}, where $\downarrow x.S^x$ is a binder concept that triggers the creation of variable mappings in the extended tableau algorithm and S (possibly with sub- and/or superscripts) are so-called query state concepts that are associated with variable mappings, as defined in the following, in order to keep track of partial matches of the query in a completion graph.

Definition 3 (Variable Mappings). *A variable mapping μ is a (partial) function from variable names to nodes. Let $G = (V, E, \mathcal{L}, \dot{\neq}, M)$ be an (extended) completion graph, where $M(C, v)$ denotes the sets of variable mappings that are associated with a concept C in $\mathcal{L}(v)$. A variable mapping $\mu_1 \cup \mu_2$ is defined by setting $(\mu_1 \cup \mu_2)(x) = \mu_1(x)$ if x is in the domain of μ_1, and $(\mu_1 \cup \mu_2)(x) = \mu_2(x)$ otherwise. Two variable mappings μ_1 and μ_2 are compatible if $\mu_1(x) = \mu_2(x)$ for all x in the domain of μ_1 as well as μ_2. The join $M_1 \bowtie M_2$ between the sets of variable mappings M_1 and M_2 is defined as:*

$$M_1 \bowtie M_2 = \{\mu_1 \cup \mu_2 \mid \mu_1 \in M_1, \mu_2 \in M_2 \text{ and } \mu_1 \text{ is compatible with } \mu_2\}.$$

Rules of the extended tableau algorithm are shown in Table 2 (without considering blocking), which handle the new axioms and concepts by correspondingly creating and propagating variable mappings. For example, a binder concept $\downarrow x.S^x \in \mathcal{L}(v)$ is handled by adding S^x to $\mathcal{L}(v)$ and by creating a mapping $\{x \mapsto v\}$ that is associated with S^x for v, i.e., $\{x \mapsto v\} \in M(S^x, v)$. Although conjunctive query answering with arbitrary existential variables is still open for $\mathcal{SROIQ}$, the approach works for knowledge bases where only a limited number of new nominal nodes is enforced (by using an extended analogous propagation blocking technique) [13], which is generally the case in practice.

As an example, a simple query with only the atoms $r(x, y)$ and $s(y, x)$ (with x, y both answer variables) can systematically be absorbed into the axioms $\top \sqsubseteq \downarrow x.S^x$, $S^x \sqsubseteq \forall r.S_r^x$, $S_r^x \sqsubseteq \downarrow y.S^y$, $S_r^x \sqcap S^y \sqsubseteq S^{xy}$, $S^{xy} \sqsubseteq \forall s.S_s^{xy}$, and $S_s^{xy} \sqcap S^x \sqsubseteq S^{xyx}$. The query state concept S_r^x, for example, represents the state where bindings for x are propagated to r-successors, i.e., $r(x, y)$ is satisfied. For bindings that are propagated back over s-edges via $\forall s.S_s^{xy}$, the final binary inclusion axiom checks whether the cycle is closed. If it is, the joined variable mappings are associated with S^{xyx} from which answer candidates can be extracted once a fully expanded and clash-free completion graph is found.

Note that with sophisticated absorption techniques, variable mappings can often be derived deterministically, i.e., they directly constitute query answers. Non-deterministically obtained variable mappings do, however, require a separate entailment check to verify that there exist no counter example with the query variables equally bound as in the non-deterministically derived variable mapping. This can be realised by restricting the generated binder concepts of the absorption process to only create corresponding bindings and by triggering a clash with the additional axiom $S^{xyx} \sqsubseteq \bot$.

While query answering by absorption is able to process queries for many (expressive) real-world ontologies [13], especially queries with existential variables can require a substantial amount of computation. A significant bottleneck is often the (variable mappings) *propagation task*, i.e., the creation and propagation of the variable mappings to get all potential answers from a completion graph. Building and using completion graphs for partial ABoxes (possibly in parallel) is difficult since it is unclear which joins of bindings can occur in answers and, hence, how the ABox can suitably be partitioned. The individual derivations cache can, however, also help to split the propagation work for variable mappings such that each thread can completely determine a few

Table 2. Tableau rule extensions

$\downarrow$-rule:	
if	$\downarrow x.C \in \mathcal{L}(v)$, and $C \notin \mathcal{L}(v)$ or $\{x \mapsto v\} \notin \mathcal{M}(C, v)$
then	$\mathcal{L}(v) = \mathcal{L}(v) \cup \{C\}$, $\mathcal{M}(C, v) = \mathcal{M}(C, v) \cup \{\{x \mapsto v\}\}$

$\forall$-rule:	
if	$\forall r.C \in \mathcal{L}(v)$, there is an r-neighbour w of v with $C \notin \mathcal{L}(w)$ or $\mathcal{M}(\forall r.C, v) \not\subseteq \mathcal{M}(C, w)$
then	$\mathcal{L}(w) = \mathcal{L}(w) \cup \{C\}$, $\mathcal{M}(C, w) = \mathcal{M}(C, w) \cup \mathcal{M}(\forall r.C, v)$

$\sqsubseteq_1$-rule:	
if	$S^{x_1 \cdots x_n} \sqsubseteq C \in \mathcal{K}$, $S^{x_1 \cdots x_n} \in \mathcal{L}(v)$, and $C \notin \mathcal{L}(v)$ or $\mathcal{M}(S^{x_1 \cdots x_n}, v) \not\subseteq \mathcal{M}(C, v)$
then	$\mathcal{L}(v) = \mathcal{L}(v) \cup \{C\}$, $\mathcal{M}(C, v) = \mathcal{M}(C, v) \cup \mathcal{M}(S^{x_1 \cdots x_n}, v)$

$\sqsubseteq_2$-rule:	
if	$S^{x_1 \cdots x_n} \sqcap A \sqsubseteq C \in \mathcal{K}$, $\{S^{x_1 \cdots x_n}, A\} \subseteq \mathcal{L}(v)$, and $C \notin \mathcal{L}(v)$ or $\mathcal{M}(S^{x_1 \cdots x_n}, v) \not\subseteq \mathcal{M}(C, v)$
then	$\mathcal{L}(v) = \mathcal{L}(v) \cup \{C\}$, $\mathcal{M}(C, v) = \mathcal{M}(C, v) \cup \mathcal{M}(S^{x_1 \cdots x_n}, v)$

$\sqsubseteq_3$-rule:	
if	$S_1^{x_1 \cdots x_n} \sqcap S_2^{y_1 \cdots y_m} \sqsubseteq C \in \mathcal{K}$, $\{S_1^{x_1 \cdots x_n}, S_2^{y_1 \cdots y_m}\} \subseteq \mathcal{L}(v)$, and $(\mathcal{M}(S_1^{x_1 \cdots x_n}, v) \bowtie \mathcal{M}(S_2^{y_1 \cdots y_m}, v)) \not\subseteq \mathcal{M}(C, v)$
then	$\mathcal{L}(v) = \mathcal{L}(v) \cup \{C\}$, $\mathcal{M}(C, v) = \mathcal{M}(C, v) \cup (\mathcal{M}(S_1^{x_1 \cdots x_n}, v) \bowtie \mathcal{M}(S_2^{y_1 \cdots y_m}, v))$

Algorithm 1. recPropTask(R, i)

Input: Variable binding restrictions R and the index of the next to be handled variable

1: **if** $i \le n$ **then**
2:     $B \leftarrow$ recPropTask$(R, i + 1)$
3:     **for each** x_j with $1 \le j < i$ **do**
4:         $R(x_j) \leftarrow B(x_j)$
5:     **end for**
6:     **while** $|B(x_i)| \ge l$ **do**
7:         $R(x_i) \leftarrow R(x_i) \setminus B(x_i)$
8:         $B_t \leftarrow$ recPropTask$(R, i + 1)$
9:         $B(x_i) \leftarrow B_t(x_i)$
10:     **end while**
11:     $B(x_i) \leftarrow \emptyset$
12: **else**
13:     $G \leftarrow$ buildComplGraph(R, l)
14:     $C \leftarrow C \cup$ answerCands(G)
15:     $B \leftarrow$ extractBoundIndis(G)
16: **end if**
17: **return** B ▷ Returning the bound individuals from the last constructed completion graph

answer candidates over a part of the ABox. This enables (a uniform) parallelisation of the propagation task. Note that a partitioning of individuals for the first variable can be used for a naive parallelisation: We create several propagation tasks and restrict the $\downarrow$-rule to bind the first variable only to the individuals of the handled partition. This can, however, lead to a work imbalance if many answers are based on the same individual for the first variable and we cannot easily impose restrictions for the other variables since we do not know which combinations of individuals can occur in answers.

We can, however, use a dynamic approach, where we limit the number of individuals to which a variable can be bound. Each individual bound to such a "binding-limited" variable is recorded and in the next propagation task we exclude bindings to already tested individuals. This can, for example, be realised with the recursive function recPropTask sketched in Algorithm 1, which takes as input a mapping R from variables to (still) allowed bindings for individuals and the index i of the current variable (assuming that the variables are sorted in the order in which they are absorbed). The function accesses and modifies some variables via side effects, namely l, denoting the limit for the number of allowed bindings for each variable, n, standing for the number of variables in the query, and C, denoting the set of answer candidates. The function is initially called with $R(x) = \text{inds}(\mathcal{K})$ for each variable x in the query and with $i = 1$ such that the restrictions for the first variable are managed first. As long as there are more variables to handle, the function calls itself recursively for the next variable (cf. Line 2) and checks for the returned sets of bound individuals, denoted with B, from the last generated completion graph whether the limit l has been reached for the current variable. If this is the case, then the bindings for previous variables are "frozen", i.e., they are interpreted as the only allowed bindings (cf. Line 3–5), and the used bindings for the current variable are excluded for the next propagation task (cf. Line 7). This ensures that all combinations are tested step-by-step and that each propagation task only creates and propagates a limited amount of variable mappings. In fact, if the restrictions for all variables are set, then they are used for constructing the next completion graph (Line 13), where R and l are checked by an adapted $\downarrow$-rule. Subsequently, we can extract the found answer candidates (Line 14) and the individuals that have been used for bindings (Line 15).

Note that the concepts from the query absorption typically cause an expansion of the local completion graph due to influence criteria, e.g., if $\forall r.S_r^x$ is in the label of some node, then Condition G1 identifies all r-neighbours from the cache as (potentially) influenced and the corresponding nodes need to be integrated into the completion graph to propagate the associated variable mappings to them. This can result in significant propagation work, in particular, for complex roles and individuals with many neighbours. Moreover, exhausted binding restrictions for the next variable might prevent us from actually using the mappings. To address this, one can impose propagation restrictions for universal restrictions of the form $\forall r.S_r^x$ such that the local completion graph is only expanded to nodes for which bindings are possible for the next variable. This can easily be implemented by adapting the query absorption to annotate universal restrictions with the variable of the role atom to which the propagation occurs. For example, a concept of the form $\forall r.S_r^x$ resulting from the query atom $r(x, y)$ is annotated with y, denoted as $\forall r_{\to y}.S_r^x$. Condition D1 is then adapted to only identify individuals as influenced that are allowed as bindings for the labelled variable of the universal restriction.

Definition 4 (Query Propagation Influence). *Let* $G = (V, E, \mathcal{L}, \neq, M)$ *be an (extended) completion graph for a knowledge base* $\mathcal{K}$, *C an individual derivations cache (c.f. Definition 1),* $v_a \in V$ *a node representing the individual a, and y a query variable. A restriction set* $R(y) \subseteq \text{inds}(\mathcal{K})$ *for y restricts the individuals to which y can be bound, i.e., only to a node* v_a *if* $a \in R(y)$. *An individual* $b \in C$ *such that no node in V contains* $\{b\}$ *in its label is* (query propagation) *influenced if*

Q1 $\forall r_{\to y}.S_r^{x_1,\dots,x_n} \in \mathcal{L}(v_a)$, $b \in K^R(a)(r) \cup P^R(a)(r)$, *and* $b \in R(y)$.

As mentioned, if the restrictions for a variable are not known upfront, then one can collect them dynamically by only imposing a limit for the number of individuals for the restriction set. While we check whether an individual b is query propagation influenced w.r.t. a variable y and the amount of individuals in the restriction set $R(y)$ is less than the limit, we simply add b to $R(y)$ such that Condition G1 is satisfied. Analogously, we add b to $R(y)$ when we test whether we can bind y to b for $\downarrow$-concepts and the limit is not yet reached. When the limit is reached, no more individuals are added to the restriction set and, therefore, no other (combinations of) variable mappings are created and the completion graph is not further expanded to other individuals. The collected restrictions are then used in the next propagation task to enforce the exploration of other (combinations of) variable mappings.

Note, however, that steering the expansion with the query propagation influence condition cannot straightforwardly be used for roles with recursive role inclusion axioms (e.g., transitive roles) due to the unfolding process and since it would be too restrictive. One could possibly improve the handling for complex roles with non-trivial adaptations to the tableau algorithm, but it is unclear whether this is worth the effort. In particular, even if the individuals are expanded, the binding restrictions are already adhered to by the $\downarrow$-rule and one can simply prioritise the absorption of other roles first.

5   Implementation and Experiments

We implemented the individual derivations cache with the sketched extensions in the tableau-based reasoning system Konclude with minor adaptations to fit the architecture and the optimisations of Konclude. In particular, we use Konclude's efficient, but incomplete saturation procedure [15] to initialise the cache entries for all individuals. If completeness of the saturation cannot be guaranteed for an individual, we mark the corresponding cache entry as inconsistent such that it is reprocessed with the tableau algorithm. Parallel processing (via small batches) is straightforward for the saturation as individuals with their assertions are handled separately. This automatically leads to a very efficient handling of the "simple parts" of an ABox and it only remains to implement the (repeated) reprocessing of individuals with inconsistent cache entries.

Since tableau algorithms are usually quite memory intensive, scalability of the parallelisation not only depends on the CPUs but also on the memory bandwidth and access. Hence, the memory allocator must scale well and the data must be organised in a way that allows for effectively using the CPU caches (e.g., by writing the data of entries with one thread in cohesive memory areas). We investigated different memory allocators (hoard, tcmalloc, jemalloc) and integrated jemalloc [7] since it seems to work best in our scenario. The worker threads for constructing completion graphs only extract the data for cache updates. A designated thread then integrates the cache updates, based on the update ids introduced on page 8, which reduces blocking, improves memory management, and allows for more sophisticated update mechanisms.

To further improve the utilisation of multi-processor systems and to avoid bottlenecks, we also parallelised some other processing steps, e.g., parsing of large RDF triple files, some preprocessing aspects (i.e., extracting internal representations from RDF triples), and indexing of the cache entries for retrieving candidates for query answering. Also note that some higher-level reasoning tasks of Konclude are already (naively) parallelised by creating and processing several consistency checking problems in parallel.

For evaluating the approach,[1] we used the large ontologies and the appertaining queries from the PAGOdA evaluation [21], which includes the well-known LUBM and UOBM benchmarks as well as the real-world ontologies ChEMBL, Reactome, and

---

[1] Source code, evaluation data, all results, and a Docker image (koncludeeval/parqa) are available at online, e.g., at https://zenodo.org/record/4606566.

Table 3. Evaluated ontologies, number of queries (from the PAGOdA+VLog evaluation), and parsing times with different number of threads in seconds (speedup factor in parentheses)

Ontology	DL	#Axioms	#Assertions	#Q	K-1	K-2	K-4	K-8
ChEMBL	$\mathcal{SRIQ}(\mathcal{D})$	3,171	$255.8 \cdot 10^6$	6 + 3	1830	935 (2.0)	497 (3.7)	268 (6.8)
LUBM$_{800}$	$\mathcal{ALEHI}^+(\mathcal{D})$	93	$110.5 \cdot 10^6$	35 + 3	363	184 (2.0)	102 (3.6)	56 (6.5)
Reactome	$\mathcal{SHIN}(\mathcal{D})$	600	$87.6 \cdot 10^6$	7 + 3	66	34 (1.9)	19 (3.6)	11 (6.2)
Uniprot$_{100}$	$\mathcal{ALCHOIQ}(\mathcal{D})$	608	$109.5 \cdot 10^6$	–(see footnote 2)	409	229 (1.8)	119 (3.5)	63 (6.7)
Uniprot$_{40}$	$\mathcal{ALCHOIQ}(\mathcal{D})$	608	$42.8 \cdot 10^6$	13 + 3	215	113 (1.9)	59 (3.6)	33 (6.5)
UOBM$_{500}$	$\mathcal{SHIN}(\mathcal{D})$	246	$127.4 \cdot 10^6$	20 + 0	431	227 (1.9)	121 (3.5)	66 (6.5)

Uniprot[2] from the European Bioinformatics Institute. To improve the evaluation w.r.t. the computation of large amounts of answers, we further include the queries from tests for the datalog engine VLog [4], but we use them w.r.t. the original TBoxes. We run the evaluations on a Dell PowerEdge R730 server with two Intel Xeon E5-2660V3 CPUs at 2.4 GHz and 512 GB RAM under a 64bit Ubuntu 18.04.3 LTS. For security reasons and due to multi user restrictions, we could, however, only utilise 480 GB RAM and 8 CPU cores of the server in a containerised environment (via LXD).

Metrics of the evaluated ontologies are depicted on the left-hand side of Table 3, whereas the right-hand side shows the (concurrent) parsing times for the ontologies in seconds, where K-1, K-2, K-4, and K-8 stand for the versions of Konclude, where 1, 2, 4, and 8 threads are used, respectively. Since the parallel parsing hardly requires any synchronisation and only accesses the memory in a very restricted way, it can be seen as a baseline for the achievable scalability (there are minor differences based on how often the different types of assertions occur).

The left-hand side of Table 4 shows the (concurrent) pre-computation times, i.e., the time that is required to get ready for query answering after parsing the ontology, which includes the creation of the internal representation, preprocessing the ontology (e.g., absorption), saturating the concepts and individuals, repeatedly reprocessing the individuals with inconsistent cache entries, classifying the ontology, and preparing data structures for an on-demand/lazy realization. Consistency checking clearly dominates the (pre-)computation time such that the other steps can mostly be neglected for the evaluation (e.g., classification takes only a few milliseconds for these ontologies). As shown in Table 4, our parallelisation approach with the individual derivations cache is able to significantly reduce the time required for consistency checking, but the scalability w.r.t. the number of threads depends on the ontology. For LUBM and ChEMBL, the approach scales almost as well as the parsing process, whereas the scalability w.r.t. Reactome seems limited. The Reactome ontology intensively relies on (inverse) functional roles such that many and large clusters of same individuals are derived in the reasoning process. With a naive implementation of the cache, we would store, for each individual in a cluster, all derived neighbour relations, which easily becomes infeasible if large clusters of same individuals are linked. For our implementation of the cache,

---

[2] We evaluated query answering on a sample (denoted with Uniprot$_{40}$) since the full Uniprot ontology (Uniprot$_{100}$) is inconsistent and, hence, not interesting for evaluating query answering.

Table 4. (Pre-)computation and accumulated query answering times for the evaluated ontologies with different numbers of threads in seconds (speedup factor in parentheses)

Ontology	(Pre-)computing				Query answering			
	K-1	K-2	K-4	K-8	K-1	K-2	K-4	K-8
ChEMBL	2421	1244 (1.9)	663 (3.7)	397 (6.1)	12767	8927 (1.4)	4507 (2.8)	3231 (4.0)
LUBM$_{800}$	2793	1658 (1.7)	831 (3.4)	437 (6.4)	2777	1829 (1.5)	1026 (2.7)	569 (4.8)
Reactome	1408	687 (2.0)	427 (3.3)	361 (3.9)	935	524 (1.8)	333 (2.8)	232 (4.0)
Uniprot$_{100}$	1343	742 (1.8)	429 (3.1)	302 (4.4)	N/A(see footnote 2)	N/A(see footnote 2)	N/A(see footnote 2)	N/A(see footnote 2)
Uniprot$_{40}$	1090	532 (2.0)	289 (3.7)	198 (5.5)	28	21 (1.3)	16 (1.8)	14 (2.0)
UOBM$_{500}$	1317	735 (1.8)	394 (3.3)	245 (5.4)	3774	1799 (2.1)	947 (4.0)	554 (6.8)

we identify and utilise representative individuals to store the neighbour relations more effectively, but we require consistent cache entries for this. If the clusters of same individuals are updated in parallel, which often leads to inconsistent cache entries, more neighbour relations must be managed and, thus, the parallelisation of ontologies such as Reactome only works to a limited extent with the current implementation. Also note that the enormous amounts of individuals in these ontologies make it impossible for the previous version of Konclude to build full completion graphs covering the entire ABox, i.e., the version of Konclude without the cache quickly runs out of memory for these ontologies. Also note that the individuals from the cache are mostly picked in the order in which they are indexed, i.e., more or less randomly due to hashing of pointers. Nominals, however, are indexed first and, hence, are prioritised in the (re-)processing. Clearly, the processing order can have a significant influence on how much (re-)processing is required, but the runs for the evaluated real-world ontologies showed hardly any variance since most consequences could be derived locally.

The right-hand side of Table 4 reveals the query answering times (and scalability), accumulated for each ontology. Since not all steps are parallelised and the version of Konclude with only one thread uses specialised and more efficient implementations in some cases (e.g., an optimised join algorithm for results from several sub-queries, whereas the parallelised version is based on several in-memory map-reduce steps), query answering scalability leaves still room for improvement. Nevertheless, without splitting the propagation tasks, several queries cannot be computed, i.e., the version of Konclude without the presented (query answering) splitting techniques cannot answer all of the queries within the given memory and time limits. Moreover, the parallelisation significantly improves the query answering times and the improvements are larger, the more computation is required. As a comparison, PAGOdA requires 19, 666 s for loading and preprocessing all ontologies and more than 101, 817 s for query answering, where it reached the memory limit for one query and for two the time limit of 10 h.

6 Conclusions

We show how the now ubiquitous multi-core processors can be used for parallelising reasoning tasks such as consistency checking and (conjunctive) query answering for expressive Description Logics. For this, we split the assertional knowledge of an ontology to similarly sized work packages for tableau-based reasoning. The technical foundation is a cache that stores chosen consequences derived for individuals and appropriate expansion as well as cache maintenance strategies to ensure correctness and termination. Our experiments with the reasoning system Konclude show promising performance improvements. The approach may even be a suitable basis for distributed reasoning in a compute cluster, where cache entries are distributed over different machines, and for incremental/stream reasoning, where a few assertions are (frequently) added or removed.

References

1. Allocca, C., et al.: Large-scale reasoning on expressive Horn ontologies. In: Proceedings of 3rd International Workshop on the Resurgence of Datalog in Academia and Industry, vol. 2368. CEUR (2019)
2. Baader, F., Calvanese, D., McGuinness, D., Nardi, D., Patel-Schneider, P. (eds.): The Description Logic Handbook: Theory, Implementation, and Applications, 2nd edn. Cambridge University Press, Cambridge (2007)
3. Bajraktari, L., Ortiz, M., Simkus, M.: Compiling model representations for querying large ABoxes in expressive DLs. In: Proceedings of 27nd International Joint Conference on Arti. Intelligence (2018)
4. Carral, D., Dragoste, I., González, L., Jacobs, C.J.H., Krötzsch, M., Urbani, J.: VLog: a rule engine for knowledge graphs. In: Proceedings of 18th International Semantic Web Conference (ISWC 2019) (2019)
5. Carral, D., González, L., Koopmann, P.: From horn-SRIQ to datalog: a data-independent transformation that preserves assertion entailment. In: Proceedings of 33rd AAAI Conference on Artificial Intelligence (AAAI 2019). AAAI Press (2019)
6. Dolby, J., Fokoue, A., Kalyanpur, A., Schonberg, E., Srinivas, K.: Scalable highly expressive reasoner (SHER). J. Web Semant. **7**(4), 357–361 (2009)
7. Evans, J.: A scalable concurrent malloc(3) implementation for FreeBSD. In: Proceedings of 3rd Technical BSD Conference (BSDCan 2006) (2006)
8. Glimm, B., Kazakov, Y., Tran, T.: Ontology materialization by abstraction refinement in Horn $\mathcal{SHOIF}$. In: Proceedings of 31st AAAI Conference on Artifical Intelligence (AAAI 2017), pp. 1114–1120. AAAI Press (2017)
9. Haarslev, V., Möller, R.: On the scalability of description logic instance retrieval. J. Autom. Reason. **41**(2), 99–142 (2008)
10. Haarslev, V., Möller, R., Turhan, A.-Y.: Exploiting pseudo models for TBox and ABox reasoning in expressive description logics. In: Goré, R., Leitsch, A., Nipkow, T. (eds.) IJCAR 2001. LNCS, vol. 2083, pp. 61–75. Springer, Heidelberg (2001). https://doi.org/10.1007/3-540-45744-5_6
11. Horrocks, I., Kutz, O., Sattler, U.: The even more irresistible $\mathcal{SROIQ}$. In: Proceedings of 10th International Conference on Principles of Knowledge Representation and Reasoning. AAAI Press (2006)
12. Sirin, E., Cuenca Grau, B., Parsia, B.: From wine to water: optimizing description logic reasoning for nominals. In: Proceedings of 10th International Conference on Principles of Knowledge Representation and Reasoning (KR 2006). AAAI Press (2006)
13. Steigmiller, A., Glimm, B.: Absorption-based query answering for expressive description logics. In: Ghidini, C., Hartig, O., Maleshkova, M., Svátek, V., Cruz, I., Hogan, A., Song, J., Lefrançois, M., Gandon, F. (eds.) ISWC 2019. LNCS, vol. 11778, pp. 593–611. Springer, Cham (2019). https://doi.org/10.1007/978-3-030-30793-6_34

14. Steigmiller, A., Glimm, B.: Parallelised ABox reasoning and query answering with expressive description logics - technical report. Technical report, Ulm University, Ulm, Germany (2021). https://www.uni-ulm.de/fileadmin/website_uni_ulm/iui.inst.090/Publikationen/2021/StGl2021-PARQA-TR-ESWC.pdf
15. Steigmiller, A., Glimm, B., Liebig, T.: Coupling tableau algorithms for expressive description logics with completion-based saturation procedures. In: Demri, S., Kapur, D., Weidenbach, C. (eds.) IJCAR 2014. LNCS (LNAI), vol. 8562, pp. 449–463. Springer, Cham (2014). https://doi.org/10.1007/978-3-319-08587-6_35
16. Steigmiller, A., Glimm, B., Liebig, T.: Completion graph caching for expressive description logics. In: Proceedings of 28th International Workshop on Description Logics (DL 2015) (2015)
17. Tsarkov, D., Horrocks, I., Patel-Schneider, P.F.: Optimizing terminological reasoning for expressive description logics. J. Autom. Reason. **39**, 277–316 (2007)
18. Urbani, J., Kotoulas, S., Maassen, J., van Harmelen, F., Bal, H.E.: Webpie: a web-scale parallel inference engine using mapreduce. J. Web Semant. **10**, 59–75 (2012)
19. Wandelt, S., Möller, R.: Distributed island-based query answering for expressive ontologies. In: Proceedings of 5th International Conference on Advances in Grid and Pervasive Computing (GPC 2010) (2010)
20. Wandelt, S., Möller, R.: Towards ABox modularization of semi-expressive description logics. J. Appl. Ontol. **7**(2), 133–167 (2012)
21. Zhou, Y., Cuenca Grau, B., Nenov, Y., Kaminski, M., Horrocks, I.: PAGOdA: pay-as-you-go ontology query answering using a datalog reasoner. J. Artif. Intell. Res. **54**, 309–367 (2015)

Analysing Large Inconsistent Knowledge Graphs Using Anti-patterns

Thomas de Groot[(✉)], Joe Raad, and Stefan Schlobach

Department of Computer Science, Vrije Universiteit Amsterdam, Amsterdam,
The Netherlands
{t.j.a.de.groot,j.raad,k.s.schlobach}@vu.nl

Abstract. A number of Knowledge Graphs (KGs) on the Web of Data
contain contradicting statements, and therefore are logically inconsistent.
This makes reasoning limited and the knowledge formally useless. Understanding how these contradictions are formed, how often they occur,
and how they vary between different KGs is essential for fixing such
contradictions, or developing better tools that handle inconsistent KGs.
Methods exist to explain a single contradiction, by finding the minimal
set of axioms sufficient to produce it, a process known as justification
retrieval. In large KGs, these justifications can be frequent and might
redundantly refer to the same type of modelling mistake. Furthermore,
these justifications are –by definition– domain dependent, and hence difficult to interpret or compare. This paper uses the notion of anti-pattern
for generalising these justifications, and presents an approach for detecting almost all anti-patterns from any inconsistent KG. Experiments on
KGs of over 28 billion triples show the scalability of this approach, and
the benefits of anti-patterns for analysing and comparing logical errors
between different KGs.

Keywords: Linked open data · Reasoning · Inconsistency

1 Introduction

Through the combination of web technologies and a judicious choice of formal
expressivity (description logics which are based on decidable 2-variable fragments of first order logic), it has become possible to construct and reason over
Knowledge Graphs (KGs) of sizes that were not imaginable only few years ago.
Nowadays, KGs of billions of statements are routinely deployed by researchers
from various fields and companies. Since most of the large KGs are traditionally built over a longer period of time, by different collaborators, these KGs are
highly prone for containing logically contradicting statements. As a consequence,
reasoning over these KGs becomes limited and the knowledge formally useless.

Typically, once these contradicting statements in a KG are retrieved, they
are either logically explained [22] and repaired [20], or ignored via non-standard
reasoning [13]. This work falls in the first category of approaches where the

© Springer Nature Switzerland AG 2021
R. Verborgh et al. (Eds.): ESWC 2021, LNCS 12731, pp. 40–56, 2021.
https://doi.org/10.1007/978-3-030-77385-4_3

focus is to find and explain what has been stated in the KG that causes the inconsistency. Understanding how these contradictions are formed and how often they might occur is essential for fixing and avoiding such contradictions. At least, it is a necessary step for developing better tools that can handle inconsistent KGs. For explaining contradictions, the notion of *justification*, which is a minimal subset of the KG that is sufficient for the contradiction to hold, plays a key role [12].

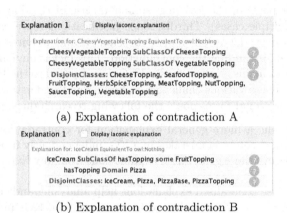

(a) Explanation of contradiction A

(b) Explanation of contradiction B

Fig. 1. Screenshot of the ontology editor Protégé showing the explanations of two contradictions found in the Pizza ontology

Example 1. In the renowned *Pizza ontology*[1] that serves as a tutorial for OWL and the ontology editor Protégé, we can find two contradictions that were asserted by its developers on purpose. The first contradiction (A) demonstrates the unsatisfiable class *CheesyVegetableTopping*, that has two disjoint parents *CheeseTopping* and *VegetableTopping*. The second contradiction (B) demonstrates a common mistake made with setting a property's domain, where the class *Pizza* is asserted as the domain of the property *hasTopping*. This statement means that the reasoner can infer that all individuals using the *hasTopping* property must be of type *Pizza*. On the other hand, we find in the same ontology a property restriction on the class *IceCream*, stating that all members of this class must use the *hasTopping* property. However, since it is also specified that the classes *Pizza* and *IceCream* are disjoint, now enforcing an unsatisfiable class to have a member leads to an inconsistency in the ontology. As presented in Fig. 1, justifications serve to explain such contradictions, by showing the minimal set of axioms from the ontology that causes the contradiction to hold.

Although justifications provide a good basis for debugging data quality and modelling issues in the KG, their specificity in explaining the contradictions

---

[1] https://protege.stanford.edu/ontologies/pizza/pizza.owl.

increases in some cases the complexity for analysing and dealing with these detected contradictions. Particularly in large KGs, these complexities are amplified and encountered in different dimensions. Firstly, existing methods to retrieve entailment justifications do not *scale* to KGs with billions of triples. Secondly, these retrieved contradictions with their justifications can be too *frequent* to manually analyse and understand the modelling mistakes made by the ontology designer. This is especially inconvenient when a significant number of these retrieved justifications actually refer to the same type of mistake, but instantiated in different parts of the KG (e.g. similar misuse of the domain and range properties in multiple cases). Thirdly, since justifications represent a subset of the KG, they are by definition *domain dependent*, and requires some domain knowledge for understanding the contradiction. This fact is obviously more limiting in complex domains, such as medical KGs, as opposed to the Pizza ontology example above. These various challenges in finding and understanding justifications in their traditional form, poses the following research questions:

Q1: Can we define a more general explanation for contradictions, that categorises the most common mistakes in a KG, independently from its domain?

Q2: Can we retrieve these generalised explanations from any KG, independently from its size?

Q3: How can these generalised explanations help analysing and comparing certain characteristics between the most commonly used KGs in the Web?

This paper introduces a method for extracting and generalising justifications from any inconsistent KG. We call these generalised justifications *anti-patterns*, as they can be seen as common mistakes produced either in the modelling or population phases, or possibly stemming from erroneous data linkage. We have developed an open-source tool that can retrieve these anti-patterns from any (inconsistent) KG. We test the scalability and the completeness of the approach on several KGs from the Web, including *LOD-a-lot, DBpedia, YAGO, Linked Open Vocabularies*, and the *Pizza* ontology, with a combined size of around 30 billion triples. Despite deploying a number of heuristics to ensure scalability, our experiments show that our method can still detect a large number of anti-patterns in a KG, in reasonable runtime and computation capacity. Finally, we publish these detected anti-patterns in an online catalogue encoded as SPARQL queries, and show how these anti-patterns can be put to use for analysing and comparing certain characteristics of these inconsistent KGs.

The rest of the paper is structured as follows. Section 2 presents related works. Section 3 presents the preliminaries and notation. Section 4 introduces our notion of anti-patterns and describes our approach for detecting them. Section 5 presents the evaluation of the approach. Section 6 presents inconsistency analyses conducted on several large inconsistent KGs. Section 7 concludes the paper.

2   Related Work

Dealing with inconsistent knowledge bases is an old problem, and solutions have been proposed as early as 1958 by Stephen Toulmin [24], where reasoning over consistent subbases was proposed. Explaining why a knowledge base entails a certain logical error (or entailment in general) has taken up traction in the last decade, leading to the most prevalent form of explanation in OWL knowledge bases called justification: minimal subsets of the graphs preserving entailments [15,22]. A number of approaches, described in [3], aims at supporting users' understanding of *single* justifications for single entailments. Such approaches focus on reducing the axioms in justifications to their relevant parts and remove superfluous information [12,14], providing intermediate proof steps to explain subsets of justifications [11], or attempting to improve understandability of an explanation by abstracting from the logical formalism to natural language [17].

In this work, we focus on a complementary part of the problem, where the goal is to facilitate the understandability of *multiple* justifications, of logically incorrect entailments, that share the same structure. For this, we rely on the notion of *anti-pattern* that represents a generalisation of such justifications. The term 'anti-pattern' appears in the work of [21], where the authors manually classify a set of patterns that are commonly used by domain experts in their DL formalisations, and that normally result in inconsistencies. In addition anti-patterns are also studied in [19], where the authors use a combination of reasoning and clustering methods for extracting common patterns in the detected justifications. However, this approach cannot be applied to any inconsistent KG, as it requires the KG to be mapped to the foundational ontology DOLCE-Zero.

Moreover, the notion of justifications with the same structure has been previously investigated but not formalised by [16], while the more complex notion of justification template has been introduced by [3], where several equivalence relations over justifications has been explored. In comparison with the mentioned works, this is the first work that relies on a simpler notion of justifications' generalisation, for the goal of analysing common logical errors in KGs, at the scale of the Web. Our method for detecting such anti-patterns reuses part of the work of [18], where the authors propose the efficient algorithm for path finding that we use in our subgraph generation. Our work can also be compared to an earlier large scale justification retrieval approach that uses MapReduce [26] but was mainly evaluated over synthetic data sets, and recent analyses [4,7,8], that aim at studying general characteristics of large KGs in the Web.

3   Background

In this section, we give the preliminary background and introduce the notation.

We consider a vocabulary of two disjoint sets of symbols[2]: L for literals and I for IRIs (Internationalised Resource Identifiers). The elements of $T = L \cup I$ are called RDF terms, and those of $I \times I \times T$ are called RDF triples. An RDF knowledge graph $\mathcal{G}$ is a set of RDF triples.

Let V be a set of variable symbols disjoint from T, a triple pattern is a tuple $t \in (I \cup V) \times (I \cup V) \times (T \cup V)$, representing an RDF triple with some positions

---

[2] We do not consider blank nodes in this work.

replaced by variables. Any finite set of triple patterns is a basic graph pattern (BGP) P, and forms the basis of SPARQL for answering queries (matching a BGP to a subgraph of $\mathcal{G}$ by substituting variables with RDF terms).

We use $var(t)$ and $var(P)$ to denote the set of variables occurring in a triple pattern t and a BGP P, respectively[3]. A substitution μ is a total mapping from V to T i.e., $\mu\colon V \to T$. The domain of μ, denoted by $dom(\mu)$, is the subset of V where μ is defined. Given a triple pattern t and a mapping μ such that $dom(\mu) := var(t)$, $\mu(t)$ is the triple obtained by replacing the variables in t according to μ. Similarly, given a BGP P and a substitution μ such that $dom(\mu) := var(P)$, $\mu(P)$ is the set of triples obtained by replacing the variables in the triples of P with respect to μ.

Finally, we use the standard notions of *entailment, satisfiability* and *consistency* for RDF(S) and OWL [2,10]. Most importantly, *an inconsistent KG* is a graph for which no *model* exists, i.e. a formal interpretation that satisfies all the triples in the graph given the semantics of the used vocabularies. Let E be some entailment relation, and e a triple such that $\mathcal{G} \models e$. A subgraph $J(e)$ of $\mathcal{G}$ is called a justification for the inferred triple e, if $J(e) \models e$, and $\nexists J'$ s.t. $J' \subset J(e)$ and $J' \not\models e$ (i.e. a justification is a minimal subset of the knowledge graph that is responsible for the inferred triple). When e is involved in a contradiction, then naturally, its justification $J(e)$ will play a key role in explaining the contradiction.

4 Defining and Detecting Anti-patterns

In this section, we introduce the notion of anti-patterns, and describe our approach for retrieving anti-patterns from any inconsistent KG.

4.1 Anti-patterns

As previously defined, a justification is a minimal description of a single entailment (or contradiction), which can be represented as an instantiated BGP. If $\mathcal{G}$ is consistent w.r.t. some entailment relation E, one could call a BGP P a pattern for $\mathcal{G}$ if there is a substitution $\mu(P)$ such that $\mathcal{G} \models \mu(P)$. In other words, if there is a variable assignment such that all instantiated graph patterns are entailed by the knowledge graph.

Suppose now that the knowledge graph $\mathcal{G}$ is inconsistent w.r.t E. In that case, trivially not every BGP would be a pattern. Therefore we define, the more interesting syntactic notion of a BGP as an anti-pattern for $\mathcal{G}$ w.r.t E, as a minimal set of triple patterns that can be instantiated into an inconsistent subset of $\mathcal{G}$. We define the notion of *anti-patterns* as follows.

Definition 1 (Anti-Pattern). *P is an anti-pattern of a Knowledge Graph $\mathcal{G}$ if there is a substitution $\mu(P)$ s.t. $\mu(P) \subseteq \mathcal{G}$, and $\mu(P)$ is minimally inconsistent w.r.t some entailment relation E, i.e. $\nexists P'$ s.t. $P' \subset P$ and $\mu(P')$ is inconsistent.*

---

[3] Therefore, $var(t) \subseteq var(P)$ whenever $t \in P$.

For an anti-pattern P, we denote by $|P|$ the size of this anti-pattern, defined as the number of triple patterns in P. We define also the notion of *support* $sup(P)$ for an anti-pattern, as the number of substitutions $\mu(P)$. Intuitively, $\mu(P)$ refers to a particular justification in $\mathcal{G}$, and the support refers to the number of justifications occurring in the KG for a certain anti-pattern.

In order to transform a justification into an anti-pattern, we replace the elements in the subject and object position of the BGP with variables. In order to prevent breaking the contradiction, elements appearing in the predicate position of a justification are not replaced in the anti-pattern, with the exception of one case: elements appearing in the predicate position and also appearing in the subject or object position of the same justification.

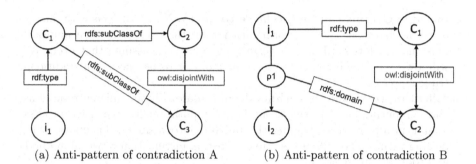

(a) Anti-pattern of contradiction A   (b) Anti-pattern of contradiction B

Fig. 2. Graphical representation of the anti-patterns of the two contradictions found in the Pizza ontology of Example 1, with circles representing the variables V and rectangles representing the RDF terms T.

Going back to Example 1, we presented two explanations of contradictions found in the Pizza ontology. Contradiction A shows an inconsistency in the ontology in which the unsatisfiable class *CheesyVegetableTopping*, that is a subclass of the two disjoint classes *CheeseTopping* and *VegetableTopping*, is instantiated. While this example refers to a specific case of a contradiction entailed from the description of these three classes, it also refers to a common type of modelling or linking mistake that can be present in another (part of the) ontology. For instance, using the same principle, the modeller could have also created the class *FruitVegetableTopping* as subclass of the two disjoint classes *FruitTopping* and *VegetableTopping*. This formalisation of certain types of mistakes is what we refer to as anti-patterns. Figure 2 presents the two anti-patterns generalising the justifications of contradictions A and B. For instance in the anti-pattern of contradiction A, the three classes *CheesyVegetableTopping*, *CheeseTopping* and *VegetableTopping* are replaced with the variables C_1, C_2 and C_3, respectively. In this anti-pattern, replacing the predicate *owl:disjointWith* with a variable p_1 would break the contradiction, since p_1 could potentially be matched in the KG with another predicate such as *rdfs:subClassOf*. On the other hand, we can see in the anti-pattern of contradiction B that the predicate *hasTopping* is replaced with the variable p_1, since it also appears in the subject position of the triple ⟨*hasTopping, rdfs:domain, Pizza*⟩. This allows the same anti-pattern to generalise other justifications in the KG, that follow the same pattern but involve a different property than *hasTopping*.

4.2 Approach

This section describes our approach for finding anti-patterns from any inconsistent KG. Finding anti-patterns from a KG would mainly consist of two steps: retrieving justifications of contradictions, and then generalising these detected justifications into anti-patterns. Such approach is expected to deal with multiple dimensions of complexity, mainly:

Knowledge Graphs can be too large to query. Now that KGs with billions of triples have become the norm rather than the exception, such approach must have a low hardware footprint, and must not assume that every KG will always be small enough to fit in memory or to be queried in traditional triple stores.

Justification retrieval algorithms do not scale. Finding all contradictions, and computing their justifications is a computationally expensive process, as it typically requires loading the full KG into memory. Therefore, when dealing with KGs of billions of triples, existing justification retrieval methods and tools do not scale [5].

Theoretically, guaranteeing the retrieval of *all* anti-patterns given any inconsistent KG requires firstly finding *all* contradictions with their justifications, and then generalising these justifications into anti-patterns. In practice, and as a way to tackle the above listed challenges, our approach introduces a number of heuristics in various steps of the approach. These heuristics emphasises the scalability of the approach, opposed to guaranteeing its completeness regarding the detection of all anti-patterns. Mainly, an initial step is introduced in the pipeline that consists of splitting the original KG into smaller and overlapping subgraphs. Depending on the splitting strategy, this step can impact the number of retrieved justifications, which in its turn can potentially impact the number of the retrieved anti-patterns. In the following, we describe the mains steps of our approach consisting of (1) splitting the KG, (2) retrieving the contradictions' justifications, and (3) generalising these justifications. Figure 3 summarises these three steps.

1. Splitting the KGs. Due to the large size of most recent KGs, running a justification retrieval algorithm over the complete KG to retrieve all contradictions is impractical. To speed up this process or even make it feasible for some larger KGs, we split the KG into smaller subgraphs. Each subgraph is generated by extending a root node as a starting point, that is retrieved by taking a distinct RDF term that appears in the subject position of at least one triple. As a result, the number of generated subgraphs is always equal to the number of distinct

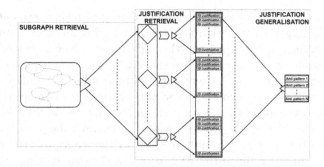

Fig. 3. Diagram that shows the pipeline used to extract subgraphs, find justifications in these subgraphs, and generalise these justifications to anti-patterns.

subjects in a KG. Using a breadth-first search, the graph is expanded by finding all the triples that have the root node as the subject, and these triples are added to the subgraph. Next, all the nodes in the object position are expanded, together with the predicates, and the graph is expanded as long as possible, or until the maximum amount of triples G_{max} set by the user is reached[4]. In Sect. 5, we empirically estimate the optimal G_{max} value for large general domain KGs, based on the trade-off between scalability of the approach and its completeness in terms of the detected anti-patterns.

2. Justification Retrieval. Out of these newly formed subgraphs, we are only interested in the ones that are inconsistent. Therefore, we firstly check for the consistency of each of these subgraphs and discard the consistent ones. Then, for each of the inconsistent subgraphs, we run a justification retrieval algorithm to retrieve the detected inconsistencies with their justifications. For this, we use the justification retrieval algorithm in the Openllet reasoner with the OWL 2 EL profile, that walks through the graph and finds the minimal justification for each contradiction. It continues to search for justifications until no more justification can be found in the graph[5]. This step is executed for each subgraph, and all the justifications are then pushed to the final stage of the pipeline.

3. Justification Generalisation. While most justifications are different, as each one represents a set of instantiated triple patterns, the underlying non-instantiated BGPs do not have to be. The underlying BGP forms the basis of the anti-patterns. To retrieve all anti-patterns from the detected justifications, we first generalise the justification to an anti-pattern by removing the instantiated

---

[4] Alternatively one can use a neighbourhood radius to limit the size of a subgraph instead of G_{max}.

[5] since justification retrieval algorithms can potentially run for a long time in the search for additional justifications in a KG, we set a runtime limit between 10 and 20 s based on the considered subgraph size.

subject and object on the nodes (when applicable, also the instantiated predicate is removed, such as the case described in Sect. 4.1). Justifications with the same underlying pattern are grouped together. Therefore, given a justification and its generalisation into anti-pattern, we check whether an anti-pattern with the same structure already exists. Comparing anti-patterns with different variable names consists in checking whether these anti-patterns are isomorphic. For this, we implement a version of the VF2 algorithm [6], with the addition of matching the instantiated edges of the anti-patterns (i.e. matching the predicates that do not appear in the subject or object position of the same justification). If the anti-pattern P of a certain justification is matched to an existing anti-pattern, we group this justification with the other justifications generalised by this anti-pattern, and increment $sup(P)$ by 1. Otherwise, a new anti-pattern is formed as a generalisation of this justification. This algorithm continues until all justifications have been matched to their corresponding anti-patterns.

Implementation. The source code of our approach is publicly available online[6]. It is implemented in JAVA, and relies on a number of open-source libraries, mainly *jena*[7], *hdt-java*[8], *openllet*[9], and *owlapi*[10]. All experiments in the following sections have been performed on an Ubuntu server, 8 CPU Intel 2.40 GHz, with 256 GB of memory.

5 Experiments

As a way of emphasising scalability over completeness, our approach for finding anti-patterns from any inconsistent KG implements an initial step that consists of splitting the KG into smaller and overlapping subgraphs.

   In the first part of these experiments (Sect. 5.1), we empirically evaluate the impact of the subgraph size limit G_{max} on the efficiency of the approach. Then, based on the G_{max} estimated from the first experiment, we show (in Sect. 5.2) the scalability of our approach on some of the largest KGs publicly available on the Web.

5.1 Completeness Evaluation

In this section, we measure the impact of splitting the KG both on the number of detected anti-patterns, and the runtime of the approach. The goal of this experiment is to ultimately find the optimal subgraph size limit to consider in the first step of the approach. For evaluating completeness, this experiment requires datasets in which *Openllet* can retrieve (almost) all inconsistencies with their justifications. For this, we rely on the three following datasets:

---

[6] https://github.com/thomasdegroot18/kbgenerator.
[7] https://jena.apache.org.
[8] https://github.com/rdfhdt/hdt-java.
[9] https://github.com/Galigator/openllet.
[10] https://owlcs.github.io/owlapi.

- **Pizza ontology:** dataset of 1,944 triples serving as a tutorial for OWL. We choose this dataset based on the fact that its contradictions and anti-patterns are known, and therefore can represent a gold standard for our approach.
- **Linked Open Vocabularies (LOV):** dataset of 888,017 triples representing a high quality catalogue of reusable vocabularies for the description of data on the Web [25]. We choose this dataset since it is small enough to retrieve almost all of its contradictions and their justifications using *Openllet*.
- **YAGO:** dataset of more than 158 million triples covering around 10 million entities derived from Wikipedia, WordNet and GeoNames [23]. We choose this dataset to observe whether the optimal size limit varies significantly between the previous datasets and this relatively larger one.

In the following experiments, we vary the subgraph size limit G_{max}, and observe the number of detected anti-patterns and the corresponding runtime for each of the three steps of our approach. Table 1 presents the first experiment, conducted on the only considered dataset which all of its contradictions are known and can be computed on the whole graph. These results show that splitting the Pizza dataset into smaller, but overlapping, subgraphs does not impact the coverage of the approach, as both available anti-patterns in this dataset are detected even when small subgraph size limits are considered.

Table 1. Impact of the subgraph size limit G_{max} on the number of detected anti-patterns and the runtime of the approach (in seconds) for the Pizza dataset.

G_{max}	Detected anti-patterns	Total runtime	Step 1 runtime	Step 2 runtime	Step 3 runtime	Number of subgraphs
50	2	3	1	2	0.01	335
100	2	4.3	1.3	3	0.01	186
250	2	8	3	5	0.05	77
500	2	13	6	7	0.04	38
750	2	18	8	10	0.08	25
1K	2	23	10	13	0.08	19
No limit	2	3.2	–	3.1	0.1	–

Table 2 presents the results of the same experiment conducted on the LOV and YAGO datasets. We adapt the considered G_{max} to the size of these datasets. These results show that in both datasets, choosing a subgraph size limit of *5,000 triples* provides the optimal trade-off between the runtime of the approach and the number of detected anti-patterns for both these KGs. Moreover, and similarly to the previous experiment, we observe that the justification retrieval step (i.e. Step 2) is the most time consuming step, accounting in some cases up to 94% of the total runtime. Finally, and as it was not possible to run *Openllet* on graphs larger than 100K triples, this experiment does not guarantee for both datasets that all possible contradictions and anti-patterns can be detected when splitting

Table 2. Impact of the subgraph size limit G_{max} on the number of detected anti-patterns and the runtime of the approach (in seconds) for LOV and YAGO.

	G_{max}	Detected anti-patterns	Total run-time	Step 1 run-time	Step 2 run-time	Step 3 run-time	Number of subgraphs
LOV	500	0	1,783	216	1,566	2	101,673
	1K	2	3,505	429	3,073	3	50,960
	5K	39	4,525	668	3,829	28	10,218
	10K	39	5,106	739	4,349	18	5,109
	25K	39	5,347	835	4,493	18	2,041
	50K	39	5,497	858	4,615	24	1,014
	100K	39	5,758	946	4,792	20	507
YAGO	500	0	3,403	649	2,753	1	18,203,648
	1K	0	39,41	1,223	2,717	1	9,123,936
	5K	135	14,342	2,125	12,004	214	1,829,442
	10K	135	18,283	2,265	15,739	279	914,721
	25K	135	19,174	2,938	16,013	223	365,422
	50K	135	34,177	3,289	30,684	204	181,547
	100K	135	68,264	3,976	64,081	206	90,773

the graph. Moreover, it does not guarantee that the optimal subgraph size limit for these two datasets can be generalised to other datasets. Therefore, we only consider the *5,000 triples* limit as an *estimation* for an optimal G_{max} when splitting large general domain KGs, for the goal of detecting anti-patterns in any inconsistent dataset.

5.2   Scalability Evaluation

In the second part of these experiments, we evaluate the scalability of our approach on some of the largest KGs publicly available on the Web. In addition to the YAGO dataset, we choose the two following datasets:

- **LOD-a-lot:** dataset of over 28 billion triples based on the graph merge of 650K datasets from the LOD Laundromat crawl in 2015 [9].
- **DBpedia (English):** dataset of over 1 billion triples covering 4.58 million entities extracted from Wikipedia [1].

Based on the results of the previous experiment, we set the value of G_{max} to 5,000 triples and run our approach for each of these three datasets. Table 3 shows that finding most anti-patterns from some of the largest KGs is feasible, but computationally expensive. Specifically, detecting 135 and 13 different anti-patterns in *YAGO* and *DBpedia* takes approximately 4 and 13 h, respectively. Moreover, detecting 222 different anti-patterns from the *LOD-a-lot* takes almost a full week. This long runtime is mostly due to our naive implementation, as the most costly step of retrieving justifications could be parallelised, instead of sequentially retrieving these justifications for each subgraph.

Table 3. Results of detecting anti-patterns from three of the largest KGs in the Web: LOD-a-lot, DBpedia and YAGO.

	LOD-a-lot	DBpedia	YAGO
Number of triples	28,362,198,927	1,040,358,853	158,991,568
Number of distinct namespaces	9,619	20	11
Number of distinct anti-patterns	222	13	135
Largest anti-pattern size	19	12	16
Runtime (in hours)	*157.56*	*13.01*	*3.98*

6 KG Inconsistency Analysis

In the previous section, we showed that it is feasible to detect anti-patterns from some of the largest KGs in the Web, when the KG is split into overlapping subgraphs with a maximum size of 5,000 triples. In this section, we further analyse these retrieved anti-patterns and compare the detected logical errors between these three KGs.

6.1 What is the Most Common Size of Anti-patterns?

We already saw from Table 3 that the largest anti-patterns in the *LOD-a-lot*, *DBpedia*, and *YAGO* contain respectively 19, 12, and 16 edges. Looking at their size distribution, Fig. 4 shows that the most common size of an anti-pattern $|P|$ ranges between *11* and *14* triple patterns for *LOD-a-lot* and *YAGO*, and between *6* and *11* triple patterns for *DBpedia*. This result, in addition to a manual verification of some of these anti-patterns, shows that most inconsistencies in *DBpedia* stem from direct instantiations of unsatisfiable classes, while the ones in *LOD-a-lot* and *YAGO* require following longer transitive chains, such as *rdfs:subClassOf* chains.

6.2 What are the Most Common Types of Anti-patterns Found in These KGs?

Anti-patterns represent a generalised notion of justifications that describe common mistakes in a KG. In our analysis of the detected anti-patterns in these three KGs, we found that a number of the different anti-patterns refer to an even more general type of mistakes, and can be further grouped together. This general type of anti-patterns consists of anti-patterns with the same structure of nodes

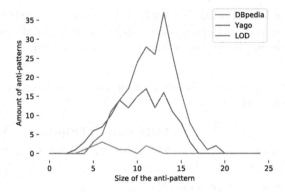

Fig. 4. Size distribution of the anti-patterns in these three KGs.

and edges, but with different size. Based on this principle, we can distinguish between three general types of anti-patterns found in these investigated KGs: *kite graphs*, *cycle graphs*, and *domain or range-based graphs*. Figure 5 presents a sample of detected anti-patterns referring to these three general types, and Table 4 presents their distribution in the three investigated KGs. It shows that kite graphs anti-patterns are the most common in the *LOD-a-lot* and *YAGO*, whilst cycle graph anti-patterns are the most common in *DBpedia*. All detected variants of these three general type of anti-patterns can be explored online[11].

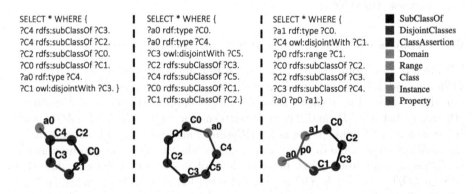

Fig. 5. Sample of three anti-patterns, referring to three general types: kite graph (left), cycle graph (middle), and domain or range-based graph (right).

---

[11] https://thomasdegroot18.github.io/kbgenerator/Webpages/statisticsOverview.html.

Table 4. General types of anti-patterns found in these three KGs.

Type of anti-patterns	LOD-a-lot	DBpedia	YAGO
Kite graphs	156	1	108
Cycle graphs	54	12	11
Domain or Range-based graphs	12	0	16

6.3 What is the Benefit in Practice of Generalising Justifications into Anti-patterns?

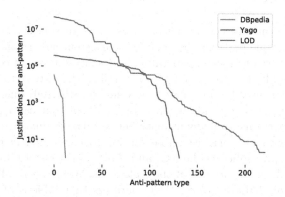

Fig. 6. Distribution of anti-pattern support.

In addition to the fact that justifications are domain-dependent and possibly complex, understanding and analysing justifications of contradictions can also be impractical due to their redundancy and frequency. This is particularly true in the three large investigated KGs, as we can see in Fig. 6. This plot presents the distribution of the anti-pattern support $sup(P)$ in these three KGs. It shows that the detected anti-patterns make the millions of retrieved justifications in the *LOD-a-lot*, *DBpedia*, and *YAGO* more manageable, by generalising them into *222*, *13*, and *135* anti-patterns, respectively. Specifically, Table 5 shows that on average each anti-pattern generalises around 5M, 7.7K, and 133K justifications in the *LOD-a-lot*, *DBpedia*, and *YAGO*, respectively. It also shows that a single anti-pattern in the *LOD-a-lot* generalises more than 45M retrieved justifications. Interestingly, the *LOD-a-lot* –a dataset that represents the largest publicly available crawl of the LOD Cloud to date– contains over a billion justifications, while *DBpedia* and *YAGO* –two of the most popular available RDF datasets–contain around 100K and 18M justifications, respectively. Thus, indicating that the quality of *DBpedia* (0.0009%), estimated by the number of detected justifications per triple in $\mathcal{G}$, is significantly higher in comparison with *LOD-a-lot* (3.9%) and *YAGO* (11.3%).

Table 5. Impact of generalising justifications to anti-patterns

$sup(P)$	LOD-a-lot	DBpedia	YAGO
Minimum	2	1	1
Maximum	45,935,769	32,997	379,546
Average	4,988,176.9	7,796.07	133,998.31
Median	23,126	4,469	106,698
Total	1,107,375,273	101,349	18,089,773
Total per triple	3.9%	0.009%	11.3%

7   Conclusion

In this work, we introduced anti-patterns as minimal sets of (possibly) unin-stantiated basic triple patterns that match inconsistent subgraphs in a KG. We can use anti-patterns to locate, generalise, and analyse types of contradictions. Retrieving contradictions from a KG and finding the extent to which a KG is inconsistent can now be formulated as a simple SPARQL query using anti-patterns as BGPs. Our second contribution is a tool that can extract a large number of anti-patterns from any inconsistent KG. For evaluating our approach, we showed on relatively small KGs that our approach can detect in practice all anti-patterns despite splitting the KG, and showed on KGs of billions of triples that our approach can be applied at the scale of the Web. Specifically, we showed on the *LOD-a-lot*, *DBpedia*, and *YAGO* datasets that billions of justifications can be generalised into hundreds of anti-patterns. While these findings prove the spread of billions of logically contradicting statements in the Web of Data, this work also shows that these contradictions can now be easily located in other KGs (e.g. using a *SELECT* query), and possibly repaired (e.g. using a *CON-STRUCT* query). The source code, as well as the list of detected anti-patterns from these KGs are publicly available as SPARQL queries, with their support in each dataset.

We are aiming to extend this work by (1) including additional datasets such as Wikidata and additional commonly used domain specific datasets, (2) exploiting the previously computed transitive closure of more than half a billion *owl:sameAs* links [4], 3 billion *rdf:type* statements with 4 million *rdfs:subClassOf* in the LOD-a-lot, for the goal of detecting additional types of anti-patterns, and (3) analysing the origins of these anti-patterns which consists of analysing billions of detected justifications, and in the case of the LOD-a-lot dataset also consists of obtaining the provenance of each statement from the LOD Laundromat crawl.

References

1. Auer, S., Bizer, C., Kobilarov, G., Lehmann, J., Cyganiak, R., Ives, Z.: DBpedia: a nucleus for a web of open data. In: Aberer, K., et al. (eds.) ASWC/ISWC -2007. LNCS, vol. 4825, pp. 722–735. Springer, Heidelberg (2007). https://doi.org/10. 1007/978-3-540-76298-0_52
2. Baader, F., Calvanese, D., McGuinness, D., Patel-Schneider, P., Nardi, D., et al.: The Description Logic Handbook: Theory, Implementation and Applications. Cambridge University Press, Cambridge (2003)
3. Bail, S.: The justificatory structure of OWL ontologies. Ph.D. thesis, The University of Manchester (United Kingdom) (2013)
4. Beek, W., Raad, J., Wielemaker, J., van Harmelen, F.: sameAs.cc: the closure of 500M owl: sameAs statements. In: Gangemi, A., et al. (eds.) ESWC 2018. LNCS, vol. 10843, pp. 65–80. Springer, Cham (2018). https://doi.org/10.1007/978-3-319-93417-4_5
5. Bonte, P., et al.: Evaluation and optimized usage of owl 2 reasoners in an event-based ehealth context. In: 4e OWL Reasoner Evaluation (ORE) Workshop, pp. 1–7 (2015)
6. Cordella, L.P., Foggia, P., Sansone, C., Vento, M.: A (sub) graph isomorphism algorithm for matching large graphs. IEEE Trans. Pattern Anal. Mach. Intell. **26**(10), 1367–1372 (2004)
7. Debattista, J., Lange, C., Auer, S., Cortis, D.: Evaluating the quality of the lod cloud: an empirical investigation. Semant. Web (Preprint) **9**, 1–43 (2018)
8. Färber, M., Bartscherer, F., Menne, C., Rettinger, A.: Linked data quality of dbpedia, freebase, opencyc, wikidata, and yago. Semant. Web **9**(1), 77–129 (2018)
9. Fernández, J.D., Beek, W., Martínez-Prieto, M.A., Arias, M.: LOD-a-lot. In: Gangemi, C., et al. (eds.) ISWC 2017. LNCS, vol. 10588, pp. 75–83. Springer, Cham (2017). https://doi.org/10.1007/978-3-319-68204-4_7
10. Hitzler, P., Krotzsch, M., Rudolph, S.: Foundations of Semantic Web Technologies. CRC Press, Boca Raton (2009)
11. Horridge, M., Parsia, B.: From justifications towards proofs for ontology engineering. In: Twelfth International Conference on the Principles of Knowledge Representation and Reasoning (2010)
12. Horridge, M., Parsia, B., Sattler, U.: Laconic and precise justifications in OWL. In: Sheth, A., Staab, S., Dean, M., Paolucci, M., Maynard, D., Finin, T., Thirunarayan, K. (eds.) ISWC 2008. LNCS, vol. 5318, pp. 323–338. Springer, Heidelberg (2008). https://doi.org/10.1007/978-3-540-88564-1_21
13. Huang, Z., Van Harmelen, F., Ten Teije, A.: Reasoning with inconsistent ontologies. IJCAI **5**, 254–259 (2005)
14. Kalyanpur, A., Parsia, B., Grau, B.C.: Beyond asserted axioms: fine-grain justifications for owl-dl entailments. In: International Workshop on Description Logics DL, vol. 6 (2006)
15. Kalyanpur, A., Parsia, B., Sirin, E., Hendler, J.: Debugging unsatisfiable classes in owl ontologies. J. Web Semant. **3**(4), 268–293 (2005)
16. Nguyen, T.A.T., Power, R., Piwek, P., Williams, S.: Justification patterns for owl dl ontologies (2011)
17. Nguyen, T.A.T., Power, R., Piwek, P., Williams, S.: Measuring the understandability of deduction rules for owl. In: International Workshop on Debugging Ontologies and Ontology Mappings-WoDOOM12, Galway, Ireland, 8 Oct 2012, no. 079 pp. 1–12.. Linköping University Electronic Press (2012)

18. Noori, A., Moradi, F.: Simulation and comparison of efficency in pathfinding algorithms in games. Ciência e Natura **37**(6–2), 230–238 (2015)
19. Paulheim, H., Gangemi, A.: Serving DBpedia with DOLCE – more than just adding a cherry on top. In: Arenas, M., et al. (eds.) ISWC 2015. LNCS, vol. 9366, pp. 180–196. Springer, Cham (2015). https://doi.org/10.1007/978-3-319-25007-6_11
20. Plessers, P., De Troyer, O.: Resolving inconsistencies in evolving ontologies. In: Sure, Y., Domingue, J. (eds.) ESWC 2006. LNCS, vol. 4011, pp. 200–214. Springer, Heidelberg (2006). https://doi.org/10.1007/11762256_17
21. Roussey, C., Corcho, O., Vilches-Blázquez, L.M.: A catalogue of owl ontology antipatterns. In: International Conference on Knowledge Capture, pp. 205–206 (2009)
22. Schlobach, S., Cornet, R., et al.: Non-standard reasoning services for the debugging of description logic terminologies. IJCAI **3**, 355–362 (2003)
23. Suchanek, F.M., Kasneci, G., Weikum, G.: Yago: a core of semantic knowledge. In: International conference on World Wide Web, pp. 697–706. ACM (2007)
24. Toulmin, S.E.: The Uses of Argument. Cambridge University Press, Cambridge (2003)
25. Vandenbussche, P.Y., Atemezing, G.A., Poveda-Villalón, M., Vatant, B.: Linked open vocabularies (lov): a gateway to reusable semantic vocabularies on the web. Semant. Web **8**(3), 437–452 (2017)
26. Wu, G., Qi, G., Du, J.: Finding all justifications of owl entailments using tms and mapreduce. In: International Conference on Information and Knowledge Management, pp. 1425–1434 (2011)

Processing SPARQL Property Path Queries Online with Web Preemption

Julien Aimonier-Davat, Hala Skaf-Molli$^{(\boxtimes)}$ ⓘ, and Pascal Molli ⓘ

LS2N – University of Nantes, Nantes, France
{Julien.Aimonier-Davat,Hala.Skaf,Pascal.Molli}@univ-nantes.fr

Abstract. SPARQL property path queries provide a succinct way to write complex navigational queries over RDF knowledge graphs. However, the evaluation of these queries over online knowledge graphs such as DBPedia or Wikidata is often interrupted by quotas, returning no results or partial results. To ensure complete results, property path queries are evaluated client-side. Smart clients decompose property path queries into subqueries for which complete results are ensured. The granularity of the decomposition depends on the expressivity of the server. Whatever the decomposition, it could generate a high number of subqueries, a large data transfer, and finally delivers poor performance. In this paper, we extend a preemptable SPARQL server with a partial transitive closure operator (PTC) based on a depth limited search algorithm. We show that a smart client using the PTC operator is able to process SPARQL property path online and deliver complete results. Experimental results demonstrate that our approach outperforms existing smart client solutions in terms of HTTP calls, data transfer and query execution time.

1 Introduction

Context and Motivation: Property paths were introduced in SPARQL 1.1 [14] to add extensive navigational capabilities to the SPARQL query language. They allow to write sophisticated navigational queries over Knowledge Graphs (KGs). SPARQL queries with property paths are widely used. For instance, they represent a total of 38% of the entire log of wikidata [5]. However, executing these complex queries against online public SPARQL services is challenging, mainly due to quotas enforcement that prevent queries to deliver complete results [9–11]. In this paper, we focus on *how to execute SPARQL property path queries online and get complete results?*

Related Works: The problem of executing property path queries online and get complete results have been already studied in the context of Triple Pattern Fragment (TPF) [8,17] and Web Preemption [1]. Current approaches decompose property path queries into many triple pattern or BGP queries that are guaranteed to terminate. However, such an approach generates a large number of queries which significantly degrades performance.

© Springer Nature Switzerland AG 2021
R. Verborgh et al. (Eds.): ESWC 2021, LNCS 12731, pp. 57–72, 2021.
https://doi.org/10.1007/978-3-030-77385-4_4

```
PREFIX wd: <http://www.wikidata.org/entity/>
PREFIX wdt: <http://www.wikidata.org/prop/direct/>
SELECT ?creativeWork ?fictionalWork  WHERE {
  ?creativeWork wdt:P144 ?fictionalWork .
  ?creativeWork wdt:P31/wdt:P279* wd:Q17537576 .
  ?fictionalWork wdt:P136 wd:Q8253}
```

(a) Q1: Creative works and the list of fiction works that inspired them on Wikidata

```
@prefix owl: <http://www.w3.org/2002/07/owl#>
@prefix foaf: <http://xmlns.com/foaf/0.1/>
select ?x ?o where {
  ?x foaf:name ?n .
  ?x owl:sameAs* ?o .
}
```

(b) Q2: List of similar entities on DB-Pedia

Fig. 1. Property path queries on online knowledge graphs

Approach and Contributions: In this paper, we extend a preemptable SPARQL server with a preemtable Partial Transitive Closure (PTC) operator based on a depth limited search algorithm. We show that a smart client using the PTC operator is able to compute SPARQL 1.1 property path queries online and get complete results without decomposing queries. In this paper: (i) We show how to build a PTC preemptable operator. (ii) We show how to build a smart-client that computes transitive closures from partial transitive closures. (iii) We compare the performances of our PTC approach with existing smart client approaches and SPARQL 1.1 servers. Experimental results demonstrate that our approach outperforms smart client approaches in terms of query execution time, number of HTTP calls and data transfer.

This paper is organized as follows. Section 2 reviews related works. Section 3 introduces web preemption and property paths. Sections 4 presents the PTC approches and algorithms. Section 5 presents our experimental results. Finally, the conclusion is outlined in Sect. 6.

2   Related Works

Property paths closely correspond to regular expressions and are crucial to perform non-trivial navigation in knowledge graphs. Regular expressions involve operators such as ' * ' (transitive closure operator, zero or more occurrences-kleene star), ' | ' (OR operator), ' / ' (sequence operator), ' ∧ ' (inverse operator), ' ! ' (NOT operator) that allow to describe complex paths of arbitrary length. For instance, the query SELECT ?x ?y WHERE { ?x foaf:knows* ?y } requires to compute the transitive closure of the relation foaf:knows over all pairs (x, y) present in a knowledge graph.

SPARQL Endpoints. Many techniques [4,12] allow to evaluate property paths. There is currently two main approaches: graph traversal based approaches and recursive queries. Whatever the approach we consider, path queries with transitive closures are challenging to evaluate for online Knowledge Graphs such as DBPedia or Wikidata. To ensure a fair usage policy of resources, public SPARQL endpoints enforce quotas [6] in time and resources for executing queries. As queries are stopped by quotas, many queries return no results or partial results. For instance, the query $Q1$ in Fig. 1 returns no result on Wikidata because it has been stopped after running more than 60s. The query $Q2^1$ on DBPedia returns partial results because it has been killed after delivering the first 10000 results.

Decomposition and Restricted Interfaces Approaches. The problem of executing property path queries online and get complete results have been already studied with SPARQL restricted interfaces represented by Triple Pattern Fragment (TPF) [8,17] and Web Preemption [1]. As a TPF server [8,17] ensures the termination of any triple pattern query, a TPF smart client [15] decomposes the evaluation of a property path into multiple triple pattern queries that are sent to the server. This requires to compute several joins on the client, especially to compute transitive closure expressions. This generates many calls and a huge data transfer, resulting in poor performances as pointed out in [1]. As preemptable SPARQL server [10] ensures the termination of any BGP query, the SaGe smart client [1] decomposes the query into BGP queries that are sent to the server. As BGP are supported, performances are better than TPF. However, the preemptable server does not support transitive closures. Consequently, to process the query $Q1$ of Fig. 1a the smart client breaks the Basic Graph Pattern (BGP) of $Q1$ into 3 triple patterns. The triple patterns are then processed using nested loop joins where joins are performed on the client. The transitive closure is processed using a simple Breadth First Search (BFS) algorithm implemented on client-side. This process remains clearly data-transfer intensive and generates a very high number of calls to the server. As each call has to pay for the network latency, the execution time of the query is dominated by the network costs.

3   Web Preemption and Property Paths

Web preemption [10] is the capacity of a web server to suspend a running SPARQL query after a fixed quantum of time and resume the next waiting query. When suspending a query Q, a preemptable server saves the internal state of all operators of Q in a saved plan Q_s and sends Q_s to the client. The client can continue the execution of Q by sending Q_s back to the server. When reading Q_s, the server restarts the query Q from where it has been stopped. As a preemptable server can restart queries from where they have been stopped and makes a progress at each quantum, it eventually delivers complete results after a bounded number of quanta.

However, web preemption comes with overheads. The time taken by the suspend and resume operations represents the overhead in time of a preemptable server. The size of Q_s represents the overhead in space of a preemptable server and may be transferred over the network each time a query is suspended by the server. To be tractable, a preemptable server has to minimize these overheads.

---

[1] $Q1$ and $Q2$ are respectively executed at the public SPARQL endpoints of Wikidata and DBPedia, at August 5 2020.

As shown in [10], suspending a simple triple pattern query is in constant time, i.e., just store the last triple scanned in Q_s. Assuming that a dataset D is indexed with traditional B-Trees on SPO, POS and OSP, resuming a triple pattern query given the last triple scanned is in $O(log(|D|))$ where $|D|$ is the size of the dataset D. Many operators such as join, union, projection, bind and most filters can be saved and resumed in constant time as they just need to manage *one-mapping-at-a-time*. These operators are processed by the preemptable SPARQL server.

However, some operators need to materialize intermediate results and cannot be saved in contant time. For example, the "ORDER BY" operator needs to materialize the results before sorting them. Such operators are classified as *full-mappings* and are processed by the smart client. For example, to process an "ORDER BY", all results are first transferred to the smart client that finally sort them. If delegating some operators to the client-side allows effectively to process any SPARQL queries, it has a cost in term of data transfer, number of calls to the server to terminate the query, and execution time. Unfortunately, to compute property path expressions with transitive closures we need a server-side operator that belongs to the *full-mappings* operators. DFS Graph-traversal based approaches require to store at least the current path in the graph that can be in the worst case, of the size of the graph. Recursive-queries approaches require to store a temporary relation that is incrementally saturated, and that also cannot be saved in constant time. Currently, a BGP containing a path expression with a closure is fully processed by the smart-client following the decomposition approach described in the related works (cf Sect. 2).

The only way to reduce the number of calls is to extend a preemptable server with a transitive closure operator such that BGP containing path patterns can be processed on server-side. However, algorithms that implement transitive closure such as DFS and BFS are not preemptable, i.e., cannot be suspended and resumed in constant time.

Problem Statement: Define an α operator able to compute the transitive closure such that the complexity in time and space of suspending and resuming α is in constant time.

4   The Partial Transitive Closure Approach

To compute SPARQL 1.1 property paths online and deliver complete results, our approach relies on two key ideas:

- First, thanks to the ability of the web preemption to save and load iterators, it is possible to implement a Partial Transitive Closure (PTC) operator that can be saved and resumed in $O(k)$. A PTC operator computes the transitive closure of a relation but cuts the exploration of the graph at a depth k. Nodes that are visited at depth k are called frontier nodes. However, such an operator is not able to compute property path expressions as defined in SPARQL 1.1, i.e., transitive closures may be incomplete and return duplicates.

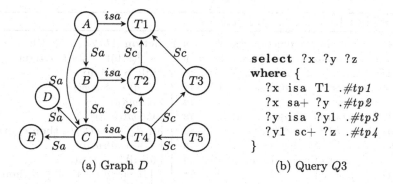

(a) Graph D

```
select ?x ?y ?z
where {
    ?x isa T1 .#tp1
    ?x sa+ ?y .#tp2
    ?y isa ?y1 .#tp3
    ?y1 sc+ ?z .#tp4
}
```

(b) Query $Q3$

Fig. 2. Graph D and query $Q3$

– Second, by sending frontier nodes to the smart client, it is possible to restart the evaluation of a property path query from the frontier nodes. Consequently, a smart client using the PTC operator can fully compute SPARQL 1.1 property paths. Such a strategy to compute property paths outperforms smart client approaches as queries are evaluated on the server without any joins on client-side.

In this paper, we focus on the evaluation of transitive path expressions *without* nested stars. For example, property paths like (ab*)* are not considered and will be the subject of future work. We assume that non-transitive expressions such as alternatives or sequences are decomposed and evaluated following [14].

4.1 The PTC Operator

A *Partial Transitive Closure* $PTC(v, p, k)$ is defined for a starting node v, a non-transitive path expression p and a depth k. $PTC(v, p, k)$ returns all pairs (u, d) with u a node, such that it exists a path from v to u that conforms to the expression $(p)^d$ where $d \leq k$ and d is minimal.

The *frontier nodes* for a $PTC(v, p, k)$ are the nodes reached at depth k, i.e., $\{u \mid (u, d) \in PTC(v, p, k) \wedge d = k\}$.

To illustrate, consider the $PTC(A, Sa, 2)$ that returns all nodes reachable from A through a path that conforms to the expression $(Sa)^d$ with $d \leq 2$. On the graph D of Fig. 2a, $PTC(A, Sa, 2) = \{ (B, 1), (C, 1), (D, 2), (E, 2) \}$ where both D and E are frontier nodes. If $PTC(n, p, k)$ returns no frontier nodes then the transitive closure is complete, i.e., k was large enough to capture the transitive closure for parameters v and p. Otherwise, frontier nodes are used by the smart client to continue the evaluation of the transitive closure until no new frontier nodes are discovered.

In our context, the depth limit k ($maxDepth$) is fixed by the preemptable SPARQL endpoint administrator and can be seen as a global variable of the preemptable server.

Algorithm 1: ALP auxiliary function

---

1 **Let** $eval(v, p)$ be the function that
returns all terms reachable from the
RDF term v, by going through a path
that matches the non-transitive path
expression p.

2 **Let** MaxDepth be the depth limit

3 **Function** *ALP(v:term, p:path)*:

4 $\quad R \leftarrow \emptyset$ // set of terms

5 $\quad V \leftarrow \emptyset$ // set of pairs (Term, Integer)

6 $\quad ALP(v, p, R, V)$

7 $\quad$ **return** R

8 **Function** *ALP(v, p, R, V)*:

9 $\quad S \leftarrow [(v, 0)]$ // stack of terms

10 $\quad$ **while** $S \neq \emptyset$ **do**

11 $\quad\quad (u, d) \leftarrow S.pop()$

12 $\quad\quad R.add(u)$

13 $\quad\quad V.add((u, d))$

14 $\quad\quad$ **if** $d \geq MaxDepth$ **then continue**

15 $\quad\quad X \leftarrow eval(u, p)$

16 $\quad\quad$ **forall** $x \in X$ **do**

17 $\quad\quad\quad$ **if** $\nexists(x, d') \in V$, $d' \leq d$ **then**

18 $\quad\quad\quad\quad S.add((x, d + 1))$

To implement a PTC operator, we rely on a depth-limited search (DLS) algorithm [13] [2]. DLS is fundamentally a depth-first search where the search space is limited to a maximum depth. Algorithm 1 redefines the ALP auxiliary function of the SPARQL 1.1 specification to follow our definition of PTC.

To avoid counting beyond a Yottabyte [2], each node is annotated with the depth at which it has been reached (Line 13). A node is revisited only if it is reached with a shortest path (Line 17). Compared to an existential semantics [2] where nodes can be visited only once, the time complexity is degraded because nodes can be revisited at most k times. However, using an existential semantics does not allow to ensure the PTC semantics, as pointed out in [16]. To illustrate, consider $PTC(A, Sa, 2)$ evaluated previously. Under an existential semantics, starting at node A, node B is first visited at depth 1, then C at depth 2 and both B and C are marked as visited. As C cannot be revisited at depth 1, $PTC(A, Sa, 2)$ returns pairs $\{(B, 1), (C, 2)\}$. In spite of there is a path from A to D and E that match $(Sa)^2$, nodes D and E are not returned. Moreover, C appears as a frontier node and will be explored by the smart client whereas it is not a frontier node.

4.2 pPTC: A Preemptable PTC Iterator

The most important element of an iterative DLS is the stack of nodes to explore. To build a preemptable iterator based on the DLS, its stack must be saved and resumed in constant time. To achieve this goal, we do not pushed nodes on the stack, but iterators that are used to expand nodes and explore the graph.

Algorithm 2 presents our preemptable Partial Transitive Closure iterator, called *pPTC*. To illustrate how a property path query is evaluated using *pPTC*, suppose the server is processing query $Q3$ with the physical query plan of Fig. 3. When the third index loop join iterator is first activated, it pulls the bag of

---

[2] Iterative Deepening Depth-First Search (IDDFS) can also be used, but IDDFS retraverse same nodes many times.

Algorithm 2: A *Preemptable PTC Iterator*, evaluating a kleene star expression without nested stars

---

Require:
p: path expression without stars
v: RDF term
μ: set of mappings
tp_{id}: path pattern identifier
Data:
$MaxDepth$: depth limit
S: empty stack of preemptable iterators
V: set of pairs (RDF term, Integer)
CT: empty set of control tuples

1 **Function** *Open()*:
2   iter ← createIter($v, p, ?o$)
3   S.push(iter.save())
4   μ_c ← nil
5   iter ← nil

6 **Function** *Save()*:
7   **if** $iter \neq nil$ **then**
8   S.push(iter.save())
9   **return** S, path, tp_{id}, μ_c

10 **Function** *Load(S', path', tp$_{id}$', μ_c')*:
11    $S \leftarrow S'$
12   path ← path'
13    $tp_{id} \leftarrow tp_{id}$'
14    $\mu_c \leftarrow \mu_c'$

15 **Function** *GetNext()*:
16   **while** $S \neq \emptyset$ **do**
17   **if** $\mu_c = nil$ **then**
18   **while** $\mu_c = nil$ **and** $S \neq \emptyset$ **do**
19   iter ← S.pop().load()
20   μ_c ← iter.getNext()
21   **if** $\mu_c = nil$ **then return** nil
22   **non interruptible**
23   **if** $iter \neq nil$ **then**
24   S.push(iter.save())
25   iter ← nil
26   n ← $\mu_c[?o]$
27   **if** $\exists(n, d) \in V, d \leq |S|$ **then**
28   **continue**
29   V.add($(n, |S|)$)
30   **if** $|S| < MaxDepth$ **then**
31   child ← createIter($n, p, ?o$)
32   S.push(child.save())
33   CT.add($(tp_{id}, \mu, (n, |S|))$)
34   solution ← $\mu \cup \mu_c$; μ_c ← nil
35   **return** solution
36   **return** nil

---

mappings $\mu = \{ ?x \mapsto A, ?y \mapsto C, ?y1 \mapsto T4 \}$ from its left child. Then, it applies μ to $tp4$ to generate the bounded pattern $b = $ T4 Sc+ ?z, creates a *pPTC* iterator to evaluate b and calls the *GetNext()* operation of the *pPTC* iterator, i.e., its right child.

To expand a node v, *pPTC* creates an iterator $iter = createIter(v, p, ?o)$. Each time $iter.GetNext()$ is called, it returns a solution mapping μ_c where $\mu_c[?o]$ is the next node reachable from v through a path that conforms to p. In Fig. 3 the first time the *GetNext()* operation of the *pPTC* iterator is called, it expands the node $T4$. Expanding $T4$ with $p = Sc$ is equivalent to evaluate the triple pattern T4 Sc ?z. Consequently, *pPTC* calls the function $createIter(T4, Sc, ?z)$ to create a *ScanIterator* on the top of the stack S and calls its *GetNext()* operation to retrieve the first child of $T4$, i.e., $T2$. When *pPTC* want to expand $T2$, the iterator used to expand $T4$ is saved and a new iterator is created at the top of the stack. As depicted in Fig. 3, compared to a traditional DLS like Algorithm 1 (Lines 16-18) the siblings of $T2$ are not stored on the stack before expanding $T2$. Because a preemptable iterator is used to explore $T4$, it can be resumed later to continue the exploration of $T2$ siblings, i.e., only iterators need

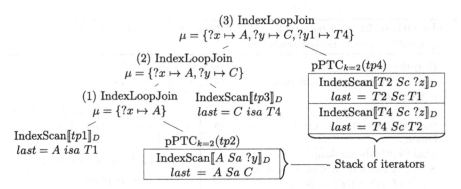

Fig. 3. Physical execution plan of query $Q3$ with the internal state of iterators for $k = 2$

to be saved, one for each node on the current path. As the space complexity of a saved preemptable iterator is bounded by the size of the query plan and not the size of the data [10], by limiting the exploration depth at k, we ensure that the size of S is bounded by k. Consequently, the $pPTC$ iterator can be saved and resumed in $O(k)$.

Quanta and Complexities. During one quantum, the $pPTC$ operator maintains a structure to keep track of visited nodes with their corresponding depth. To be preemptable, this structure has to be flushed at the end of the quantum, keeping only the stack of iterators between two quanta. In the worst case, we can consider visited nodes as always empty. In this case, the $pPTC$ iterator enumerates all simple paths leading to a $\#P$ complexity as described in [2]. In the best case, the $pPTC$ iterator has the same time complexity as PTC.

Controls for the PTC-Client. To allow a smart client to resume a property path query and continue the evaluation beyond the frontier nodes, visited nodes are contextualized and sent to the client. For each visited node, a $pPTC$ iterator generates a *control tuple* $ct = (tp_{id}, \mu, (n, d))$ (Line 33) where tp_{id} is the identifier of the path pattern that produced ct, μ is the current mappings when ct has been produced and (n, d) is a pair representing a visited node with its depth. For example, suppose that the server is processing query $Q3$ using the physical query plan of Fig. 3. When the first index loop join is activated, it pulls the bag of mappings $\{ ?x \mapsto A \}$ from its left child, and next calls the $GetNext()$ operation of the $pPTC$ iterator, i.e., its right child. In this context, the $pPTC$ iterator explores node A at depth 1 by evaluating A Sa $?y$, returns the bag of mappings $\{ ?x \mapsto A, ?y \mapsto C \}$ and generates the control tuple $(TP2_{id}, \{?x \mapsto A\}, (A, 1))$.

All control tuples generated during a quantum are stored in a shared memory which is specific to the query during a quantum. At the end of the quantum, control tuples and solution mappings are sent to the client. The data transfer of the control tuples represents the overhead of our PTC approach. To reduce the data transfer, control tuples $ct_1, ..., ct_n$ that share the same tp_{id} and μ are grouped together into a tuple $(tp_{id}, \mu, [(n_1, d_1), ..., (n_n, d_n)])$.

Algorithm 3: PTC-Client

Data:

$MaxDepth$: depth limit

$FIFO$: empty queue of tuples (query Q, ptc_{id}, frontier node n)

V: maps each ptc_{id} to a set of pairs (node, depth)

R: empty multi-set of solution mappings

1 **Function** $EvalClient(query)$:

2     $FIFO$.enqueue($(query, nil, nil)$)

3   **while** $FIFO \neq \emptyset$ **do**

4        $(Q, ptc_{id}, n) \leftarrow FIFO$.dequeue()

5   **if** $\exists (n', d') \in V[ptc_{id}]$, $n' = n \wedge d' < MaxDepth$ **then continue**

6        $(\omega, ct) \leftarrow$ ServerEval(Q)

7        $R \leftarrow R \cup \omega$

8   **for** $(tp_{id}, \mu, vc) \in ct$ **do**

9           $ptc'_{id} \leftarrow$ hash(μ, tp_{id})

10   **for** $(node, depth) \in vc$ **do**

11   **if** $\exists (n', d') \in V[ptc'_{id}]$, $n' = node$ **then**

12   V$[ptc'_{id}]$.add($node$, min($d', depth$))

13   **else**

14   V$[ptc'_{id}]$.add($node, depth$)

15   **if** $depth = MaxDepth$ **then**

16                   $Q_e \leftarrow$ ExpandQuery($Q, tp_{id}, \mu, node$)

17                   $FIFO$.enqueue($Q_e, ptc'_{id}, node$)

18   **return** R

4.3 The PTC-Client

The general idea of the PTC-Client is to use the control tuples returned by the server-side $pPTC$ iterators to expand frontier nodes until no more frontier nodes can be discovered, i.e., transitive closures are complete.

Algorithm 3 describes the behavior of the PTC-client. It is fundamentally an iterative Breadth-First Search (BFS) algorithm that traverses frontier nodes. The FIFO queue stores the frontier nodes to traverse with their context. R is the multi-set of results. The V variable represents the visited nodes. As a path expression may be instantiated many times, we store a set of visited per instance of path expression, i.e., ptc_{id}.

Figure 4 illustrates the first iteration of Algorithm 3 using query $Q3$ of Fig. 2b. First, the query $Q3$ is evaluated on the server by calling $ServerEval$ (Line 6). $ServerEval$ accepts any SPARQL property path query and returns a set ω of solution mappings and a set ct of control tuples. The sets ω and ct for query $Q3$ are depicted in Fig. 4 by the two tables. As we can, all visited nodes are discovered with a depth $= 1$, as MaxDeph $= 1$, they are all frontier nodes. Consequently, the Algorithm 3 will expand $Q3$ with all these frontiers nodes.

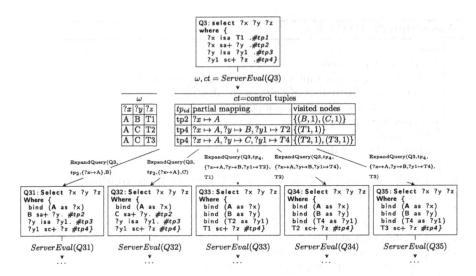

Fig. 4. First iteration of ClientEval($Q3$) as defined in Algorithm 3 with graph D and $MaxDepth = 1$

ExpandQuery takes a query Q, a set of partial mappings and a frontier node n as input (Line 16) and produces a new query as output. *ExpandQuery* processes in three steps. (1) The subject of the path pattern identified by tp_{id} in Q is replaced by n. (2) Triple patterns tp in Q such as $\mu(tp)$ is fully bounded are removed. (3) To preserve the mappings μ from Q to Q_e, a BIND clause is created for each variable in $dom(\mu)$.

Figure 4 illustrates the query returned by *ExpandQuery* for each frontier node returned by *ServerEval*($Q3$). Queries $Q31$, $Q32$, $Q33$, $Q34$ and $Q35$ are finally pushed in the FIFO queue (Line 17) to be evaluated at the next iteration. It could happen that the evaluation of an expanded query reached an enqueued frontier node with a shortest path (Line 12). In this case, the expanded query is not evaluated (Line 5).

5 Experimental Study

In this experimental study, we want to empirically answer the following questions: What is the impact of the $maxDepth$ and the time quantum parameters on the evaluation of SPARQL property path queries, both in terms of data transfer, number of HTTP calls and query execution time? How does the PTC approach perform compared to smart client approaches and SPARQL endpoints?

In our experiments *Jena-Fuseki* and *Virtuoso* are used as the baselines to compare our approach with SPARQL endpoints, while the multi-predicate automaton approach [1] is used as the baseline for the smart client approaches. We implemented the PTC operator in Python as an extension of the SAGE

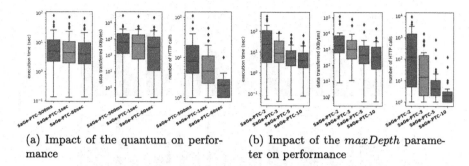

(a) Impact of the quantum on performance

(b) Impact of the *maxDepth* parameter on performance

Fig. 5. Impact of the different parameters on performance for the gMark queries

server, while the PTC client is implemented in JavaScript. The resulting system, i.e., the SAGE server with our PTC operator and the JavaScript client, is called *SaGe-PTC*. The code and the experimental setup are available on the companion website[3].

5.1 Experimental Setup

Dataset and Queries: The dataset and queries are generated by gMark [3], a framework designed to generate synthetic graph instances coupled with complex property path query workloads. We use the "Shop" use-case configuration file[4] to generate a graph instance of 7,533,145 triples and a workload of 30 queries. All our queries contain from 1 to 4 transitive closure expressions, for which numerical occurrences indicators have been replaced by Kleene plus "+" operators.

Compared Approaches: We compare the following approaches:

– *SaGe-PTC* is our implementation of the PTC approach. The dataset generated by gMark is stored using the SAGE HDT backend. The SAGE server is configured with a page size limit of 10000 solution mappings and 10000 control tuples. Different configurations of *SaGe-PTC* are used. (i) *SaGe-PTC-2*, *SaGe-PTC-3*, *SaGe-PTC-5*, *SaGe-PTC-10* and *SaGe-PTC-20* are configured with a time quantum of 60 s and a *maxDepth* of 2, 3, 5, 10 and 20, respectively. (ii) *SaGe-PTC-500ms*, *SaGe-PTC-1sec* and *SaGe-PTC-60sec* are configured with a *maxDepth* of 20 and a time quantum of 500 ms, 1 s and 60 s, respectively.
– *SaGe-Multi* is our baseline for the smart client approaches. Property path queries are evaluated on a SAGE smart client using the decomposition approach defined in [1]. For a fair evaluation, *SaGe-Multi* runs against the *SaGe-PTC* server with a time quantum of 60 s. We did not include Comunica [15] in the setup as it has already been compared with *SaGe-Multi* in [1] and *SaGe-Multi* dominates Comunica for all evaluation metrics.

---

[3] https://github.com/JulienDavat/property-paths-experiments.
[4] https://github.com/gbagan/gmark/blob/master/use-cases/shop.xml.

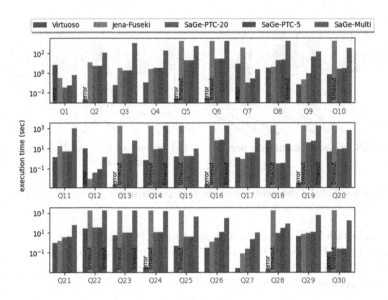

Fig. 6. Execution time per query for SPARQL endpoint and smart client approaches compared to our PTC approach

- *Virtuoso* is the Virtuoso SPARQL endpoint (v7.2.5) as of December 2020. *Virtuoso* is configured **without quotas** in order to deliver complete results. We also configured *Virtuoso* with a single thread to fairly compare with other engines.
- *Jena-Fuseki* is the Apache Jena Fuseki endpoint (v3.17.0) with the same configuration as *Virtuoso*, i.e., without quotas and a single thread.

Evaluation Metrics: Presented results correspond to the average obtained of three successive executions of the queries workload. Each query is evaluated with a time-out of 30 min. (1) *Execution time* is the total time between starting the query execution and the production of the final results by the client. (ii) *Data transfer* is the total number of bytes transferred to the client during the query execution. (iii) *Number of HTTP calls* is the total number of HTTP calls issued by the client during the query execution.

Hardware Setup: We run our experimentations on a google cloud virtual machine (VM) instance. The VM is a c2-standard-4 machine with 4 virtual CPU, 16 GB of RAM and a 256 GB SSD. Both clients and servers run on the same machine. Each client is instrumented to count the number of HTTP requests sent to the server and the size of the data transferred to the client.

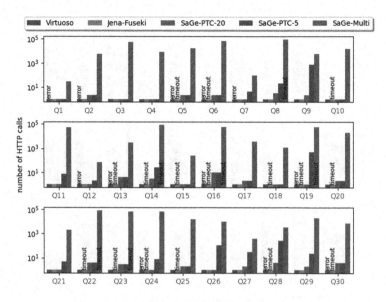

Fig. 7. Number of HTTP calls per query for SPARQL endpoint and smart client approaches compared to our PTC approach

5.2 Experimental Results

What is the Impact of the Quantum on Performance ? To measure the impact of the quantum on performance, we run our workload with different quanta; 500 ms, 1 s and 60 s. The *maxDepth* is set to 20 for each quantum, such as all queries terminate without frontier nodes. Figure 5a presents *SaGe-PTC* performance for *SaGe-PTC-500 ms*, *SaGe-PTC-1 s* and *SaGe-PTC-60 s*.

As expected, increasing the quantum improves performance. With large quantum, a query needs less calls to complete, which in turn improves the execution time. Concerning the data transfer, the visited nodes of *pPTC* iterators are flushed at the end of each quantum, which leads to revisit already visited nodes. Consequently, the less a query needs quanta to complete, the less it transfers duplicates.

What is the Impact of maxDepth on Performance? To measure the impact of *maxDepth* on performance, we run our 30 queries with different values of *maxDepth*; 2, 3, 5 and 10. To reduce the impact of the quantum, we choose a large quantum of 60 s. Figure 5b presents *SaGe-PTC* performance for *SaGe-PTC-2*, *SaGe-PTC-3*, *SaGe-PTC-5* and *SaGe-PTC-10*.

As we can see, the *maxDepth* impacts significantly the performance in terms of execution time, data transfer and number of calls. Increasing the *maxDepth* drastically improves performance because it allows to capture larger transitive closures. This means less control tuples are transferred to the client and less expanded queries are executed on the server.

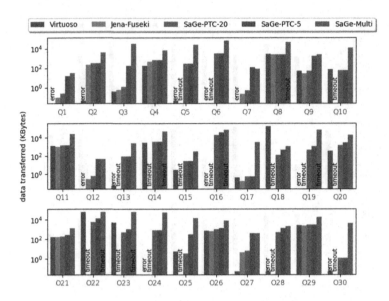

Fig. 8. Data transfer per query for SPARQL endpoint and smart client approaches compared to our PTC approach

How does the PTC Approach Perform Compared to the Smart Client Approaches and SPARQL Endpoints? The PTC approach computes SPARQL property path queries without joins on the client. When $maxDepth$ is high enough, no expanded queries are sent to the server. We just have to pay the web preemption overheads and the duplicates transferred by the PTC approach. Consequently, we expect our approach to be somewhere between SPARQL endpoints and smart clients in terms of performance. Close to SPARQL endpoints when $maxDepth$ is high and better than smart clients in the general case. We compare *SaGe-PTC* with *SaGe-Multi*, *Jena-Fuseki* and *Virtuoso*. We run *SaGe-PTC* with both $maxDepth = 5$ (*SaGe-PTC-5*) and $maxDepth = 20$ (*SaGe-PTC-20*). Figures 6, 8 and 7 respectively present the execution time, the data transfer and the number of HTTP calls for each approach.

As expected, *SaGe-PTC* outperforms *SaGe-Multi* regardless the query. Because *SaGe-PTC* does not decompose BGPs, the number of calls is drastically reduced, as shown in Fig. 7. Concerning the data transfer, both *SaGe-PTC* and *SaGe-Multi* transfer the visited nodes. However *SaGe-PTC* does not transfer any intermediate results, saving a lot of data transfer.

Compared to *Jena-Fuseki* both approaches use a similar graph traversal algorithm. However *Jena-Fuseki* has no overheads, i.e., is optimal in terms of data transfer and number of calls. Only one call is sent per query and only the final results are transferred to the client. Consequently, we expect *Jena-Fuseki* to perform better than *SaGe-PTC*. Surprisingly *Jena-Fuseki* does not dominate the PTC approach. *SaGe-PTC-20* is very close to *Jena-Fuseki* for queries where *Jena-Fuseki* does not time-out. As queries return no frontier nodes, overheads compared to *Jena-Fuseki* are small. The differences between the two approaches are mainly due to a join ordering issue. Compared to *SaGe-PTC-20*, with *SaGe-PTC-5* queries need to send expanded queries to terminate. As expected, *SaGe-PTC-5* offers performance between that of SPARQL endpoints and that of smart clients. For most queries, its performance are very close to *SaGe-PTC-20*. We conjecture that most transitive closures for our queries can be computed with small *maxDepth*. When there is a large number of frontier nodes to explore, performance degrades but remains better than those of smart client approaches.

We expect *Virtuoso* to be optimal as it implements the state of art query optimization techniques. Surprisingly, *Virtuoso* does not dominate *SaGe-PTC*. *Virtuoso* generates errors for 12 queries out of 30. It cannot execute the 12 queries either because of the missing of a starting point or because it has not enough space resources to materialize the transitive closure. *Virtuoso* issues are mainly due to the simple path semantics when dealing with dense graphs. Of course, the number of calls for *Virtuoso* is optimal. However, using a simple path semantics leads to high data transfer when path queries are executed against dense graphs.

6   Conclusion

In this paper, we proposed an original approach to process SPARQL property path queries online and get complete results. Thanks to a preemptable Partial Transitive Closure operator, a smart client is ensured to grab all mappings that are reachable at a depth fixed by the server. Thanks to control information delivered during SPARQL property path queries processing, a smart client generates queries to find missing mappings. Unlike current smart clients, the PTC smart client does not break BGPs containing path patterns. Even in presence of path patterns, all joins are performed on server-side without the need to transfer intermediate results to the client. As demonstrated in the experimentations, the PTC approach outperforms existing smart clients and reduces significantly the gap of performance with SPARQL endpoints. This approach raises several interesting perspectives. First, there is a large room for optimisation: better join ordering in presence of path patterns, pruning some calls when path patterns are "reachability" oriented, and better evaluation of resuming queries according to their shapes. Second, it may be interesting to explore if partial transitive closure is compatible with partial aggregates [7]. If the aggregation functions are computed on client-side, then there is no issue for computing aggregation in presence of path patterns. However, partial aggregates computed with partial transitive closures on server-side may return incorrect results.

Acknowledgments. This work is supported by the ANR DeKaloG (Decentralized Knowledge Graphs) project, ANR-19-CE23-0014, CE23 - Intelligence artificielle.

References

1. Aimonier-Davat, J., Skaf-Molli, H., Molli, P.: How to execute sparql property path queries online and get complete results? In: 4rth Workshop on Storing, Querying and Benchmarking the Web of Data (QuWeDa 2020) Workshop at ISWC2020 (2020)
2. Arenas, M., Conca, S., Pérez, J.: Counting beyond a yottabyte, or how sparql 1.1 property paths will prevent adoption of the standard. In: Proceedings of the 21st International Conference on World Wide Web, pp. 629–638 (2012)
3. Bagan, G., Bonifati, A., Ciucanu, R., Fletcher, G.H., Lemay, A., Advokaat, N.: gmark: schema-driven generation of graphs and queries. IEEE Trans. Knowl. Data Eng. **29**(4), 856–869 (2016)
4. Bonifati, A., Fletcher, G., Voigt, H., Yakovets, N.: Querying graphs. Synth. Lect. Data Manag. **10**(3), 1–184 (2018)
5. Bonifati, A., Martens, W., Timm, T.: Navigating the maze of wikidata query logs. In: The World Wide Web Conference, pp. 127–138 (2019)
6. Buil-Aranda, C., Hogan, A., Umbrich, J., Vandenbussche, P.Y.: Sparql web-querying infrastructure: ready for action? In: International Semantic Web Conference, pp. 277–293 (2013)
7. Grall, A., Minier, T., Skaf-Molli, H., Molli, P.: Processing sparql aggregate queries with web preemption. In: European Semantic Web Conference, pp. 235–251 (2020)
8. Hartig, O., Letter, I., Pérez, J.: A formal framework for comparing linked data fragments. In: International Semantic Web Conference, pp. 364–382 (2017)
9. Hasnain, A., Mehmood, Q., Zainab, S.S., Hogan, A.: Sportal: profiling the content of public sparql endpoints. Int. J. Semant. Web Inf. Syst. (IJSWIS) **12**(3), 134–163 (2016)
10. Minier, T., Skaf-Molli, H., Molli, P.: Sage: Web preemption for public sparql query services. In: The World Wide Web Conference, pp. 1268–1278 (2019)
11. Polleres, A., Kamdar, M.R., Fernández, J.D., Tudorache, T., Musen, M.A.: A more decentralized vision for linked data. In: 2nd Workshop on Decentralizing the Semantic Web (DeSemWeb 2018) co-located with ISWC 2018 (2018)
12. Reutter, J.L., Soto, A., Vrgoč, D.: Recursion in sparql. In: International Semantic Web Conference, pp. 19–35 (2015)
13. Russell, S.J., Norvig, P.: Artificial Intelligence - A Modern Approach. Prentice Hall series in artificial intelligence, 2nd edn. Prentice Hall, Upper Saddle River (2003)
14. Steve, H., Andy, S.: SPARQL 1.1 query language. In: Recommendation W3C (2013). https://www.w3.org/TR/sparql11-query
15. Taelman, R., Van Herwegen, J., Vander Sande, M., Verborgh, R.: Comunica: a modular sparql query engine for the web. In: International Semantic Web Conference, pp. 239–255 (2018)
16. Udupa, A., Desai, A., Rajamani, S.: Depth bounded explicit-state model checking. In: International SPIN Workshop on Model Checking of Software, pp. 57–74 (2011)
17. Verborgh, R., et al.: Triple pattern fragments: a low-cost knowledge graph interface for the web. J. Web Semant. **37**, 184–206 (2016)

Ontology-Based Map Data Quality Assurance

Haonan Qiu[1,2(✉)], Adel Ayara[1], and Birte Glimm[2]

[1] BMW Car IT GmbH, Ulm, Germany
{haonan.qiu,adel.ayara}@bmw.de
[2] Institute of Artificial Intelligence, University of Ulm, Ulm, Germany
birte.glimm@uni-ulm.de

Abstract. A lane-level, high-definition (HD) digital map is needed for autonomous cars to provide safety and security to the passengers. However, it continues to prove very difficult to produce error-free maps. To avoid the deactivation of autonomous driving (AD) mode caused by map errors, ensuring map data quality is a crucial task. We propose an ontology-based workflow for HD map data quality assurance, including semantic enrichment, violation detection, and violation handling. Evaluations show that our approach can successfully check the quality of map data and suggests that violation handling is even feasible on-the-fly in the car (on-board), avoiding the autonomous driving mode's deactivation.

Keywords: Autonomous driving · Digital maps · Ontologies · Rules

1 Introduction

Autonomous cars act in a highly dynamic environment and consistently have to provide safety and security to passengers. A detailed, high-definition (HD) map is needed for a car to understand its surroundings, which provides *lane-level* information to support vehicle perception and highly precise localisation [3]. The creation of a road map involves a series of decisions on how features of the road are to be represented concerning the map scale, level of generalization, projection, datum, and coordinate system. Every step of map creation may introduce an error in one of the map features and Fig. 1 shows a road gap that has been found in a commercially available HD map, which caused a degradation of the autonomous driving (AD) mode and a driver take-over request.

Usually, a take-over request is conducted for safety reasons when the AD system is approaching its limits due to, for example, weather conditions. In general, a take-over request is a complex and risky process and should be avoided as much as possible and, in case of map errors, the request is not even related to system limits. Therefore, the goal of our work is to use ontologies and reasoning to find and fix map errors to extend the AD function's availability. Ensuring (general) data quality with an ontology-based approach has been well-studied recently [6,7,12]. Yilmaz et al. [27,28] have even demonstrated the feasibility

© Springer Nature Switzerland AG 2021
R. Verborgh et al. (Eds.): ESWC 2021, LNCS 12731, pp. 73–89, 2021.
https://doi.org/10.1007/978-3-030-77385-4_5

Fig. 1. Snap shots of a normal driving scenario without map errors and active AD mode (left-hand side) and an error scenario (right-hand side) with deactivated AD mode and a driver take-over request due to a gap in the road model

of using ontological methods for spatial data quality evaluation. The latter work does, however, not consider map-specific concepts, e.g., lanes and the resulting challenges, and neither are the challenges and possibilities of *handling* violations considered. We address these challenges and present an ontology-based approach for ensuring map data quality. The main contributions are:

- We present a workflow for ensuring map data quality based on OWL 2 RL ontologies [13] and Datalog rules [1].
- We present the develop Map Quality Violation Ontology (MQVO) and a set of constraint rules for violation detection.
- We demonstrate violation handling strategies using violation tolerance and resolution.
- We evaluate the performance of violation detection and the correctness of violation resolution using RDFox [21] and realistic map data.

The rest of this paper is structured as follows: Sect. 2 introduces related work, followed by some preliminaries in Sect. 3. Section 4 describes the workflow consisting of semantic enrichment, violation detection, and violation handling. In Sect. 5, we describe the experimental setup and results, and we conclude in Sect. 6. Additional explanations, rules, available resources and evaluation discussion can be found in an accompanying technical report [22].

2   Related Work

Spatial data quality can be assessed with ontology-based approaches. Mostafavi et al. [18] propose an ontology-based approach for quality assessment of spatial databases. The ontology is encoded in Prolog, and queries are used to determine the existence of inconsistencies. Wang et al. [25] investigate the feasibility of applying rule-based spatial data quality checks over mobile data using the Semantic Web Rule Language (SWRL). The authors show that the system has the capability to warn the data collector if there is any inconsistent data gathered in the field. Yilmaz et al. [28] created an ontology associated with spatial concepts from the Open Geospatial Consortium and rules implemented as GeoSPARQL queries for detecting inconsistencies. Yilmaz et al. also developed the Spatial Data Quality Ontology together with SWRL rules for performing quality assessment [27]. Huang et al. [14] investigate the feasibility of combining ontologies and semantic constraints modelled in the Shapes Constraint Language (SHACL) for ensuring the semantic correctness of geospatial data from different levels of detail. A number of RDF stores also support geospatial queries and integrity constraints, e.g., Stardog,[1] Virtuoso,[2] and GraphDB.[3]

The existing ontology-based approaches, however, focus on general spatial data. Map-related concepts and relationships, such as the relationships among coordinate points, lanes, and roads, are not studied. While SHACL is designed for RDF validation, by checking nodes w.r.t. class axioms or paths w.r.t. property axioms, it cannot describe complex (spatial) relationship constraints, which is crucial for map data. Although SHACL provides validation reports, it does not provide a mechanism (e.g., vocabulary) for fixing errors, while we aim at supporting violation detection and handling in a closed loop.

3   Preliminaries

In this section, we present relevant background for map data, the Resource Description Framework, and rules.

3.1   Map Data

Our work is focused on the Navigation Data Standard (NDS) [20]. Map data is partitioned in to adjacent *tiles*. They form approximately rectangular territorial sections. The magnification *level* determines the edge length of a tile. *Nodes* within a map tile represent a point location on the surface of the Earth by a pair of longitude (y-coordinate) and latitude (x-coordinate) coordinates. *Links* represent a stretch of road between two nodes and are represented by a line segment (corresponding to a straight section of the road) or a curve having a shape that is generally described by intermediate points called *shape points* along the link. Shape points are represented by x-y coordinates as nodes, but shape points do not serve the purpose of connecting links, as do nodes. Link and road are synonyms and road has the same meaning as in everyday language use. Links have attributes such as travel direction and types, such as highway. The ordering of the shape points is with respect to the travel direction. The geometry of *Lanes* is described by shape points too. Lanes are connected via *lane connectors*. Each lane is described by two *lane boundaries* with lane marking types (solid/dashed, single/double, etc.). Finally, lanes are organized into *lane groups* with link references. We refer the interested reader to the literature for further details about HD maps [11,15].

---

[1] https://www.stardog.com/.
[2] https://virtuoso.openlinksw.com/.
[3] https://graphdb.ontotext.com/.

3.2 RDF Graphs

Resource Description Framework (RDF) is a W3C standardised model for data interchange in applications on the Web, where a subject (s) and a object (o) are related with an explicit predicate (p). These simple *s-p-o* statements can be seen as a directed, labelled (knowledge) graph. We formally introduce RDF graphs as follows:

Definition 1 (RDF Graph [5]). *Let I, L, and B be pairwise disjoint infinite sets of IRIs, literals, and blank nodes, respectively. A tuple $(s, p, o) \in I \cup B \times I \times (I \cup L \cup B)$ is called an RDF triple, where s is the* subject*, p is the* predicate*, and o is the* object*. An RDF graph G is finite set of RDF triples and induces a set of* vertices $V = \{s \mid (s, p, o) \in G\} \cup \{o \mid (s, p, o) \in G\}$.

On top of RDF, we use the RL (rule language) profile of the Web Ontology Language (OWL) [13] and custom Datalog rules [1] (RDFox syntactic variant) to model complex knowledge and to infer, in particular, spatial relationships.

3.3 Rules

For defining such *Datalog rules*, we fix countable, disjoint sets of *constants* and *variables*. A *term* is a constant or a variable. An *atom* has the form $P(t_1, \ldots, t_k)$, where P is a k-ary predicate and each t_i, $1 \leq i \leq k$, is a term. We focus on unary and binary atoms only (i.e., $1 \leq k \leq 2$), which correspond to classes and properties of the ontology, respectively. An atom is *ground* if it does not contain variables. A *fact* is a ground atom and a *dataset* is a finite set of facts, e.g., as defined in an ontology. A Datalog *rule* is a logical implication of the form $H_1, \ldots, H_j \leftarrow B_1, \ldots, B_k$, where each H_i, $1 \leq i \leq j$, is a *head* atom, and each B_ℓ, $1 \leq \ell \leq k$, is a *body* atom. A Datalog *program* is a finite set of rules.

A *negative* body atom has the form, NOT EXISTS $v_1, \ldots, v_j$ IN B, where each v_i, $1 \leq i \leq j$, is a variable and B is an atom. A rule r is *safe* if variables that appear in the head or in a negative body atom also appear in a positive body atom. A safe Datalog rule can be extended with *stratified negation* by extending the rule to have negative body atoms, where there is no cyclic dependency between any predicate and a negated predicate.

An *aggregate* is a function that takes a multiset of values as input and returns a single value as output. An aggregate atom has the form Aggregate($B_1, \ldots, B_k$ ON $x_1, \ldots, x_j$ BIND $f_1(e_1)$ AS $r_1 \ldots$ BIND $f_n(e_n)$ AS r_n), where each B_i, $1 \leq i \leq k$, is an atom, each x_u, $1 \leq u \leq j$, is a variable that appears in B_i, each f_v, $1 \leq v \leq n$, is an aggregate function, each e_w, $1 \leq w \leq n$, is an expression containing variables from B_i, and each r_z, $1 \leq z \leq n$, is a constant for a variable that does not appear in B_i.

4 Ensuring Map Data Quality

In this section, we present the workflow of ensuring map data quality consisting of: (i) semantic enrichment, (ii) violation detection, and (iii) violation handling (see Fig. 2). We next describe these steps in more detail.

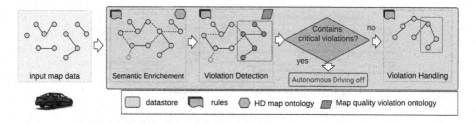

Fig. 2. Workflow diagram of ensuring map data quality

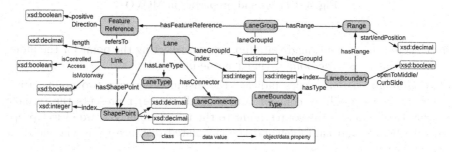

Fig. 3. An HD map ontology based on NDS (partial rendering)

4.1 Semantic Enrichment

We adopt the concept of semantic enrichment [10] and use a set of rules for inferring spatial semantics, e.g., start/end points and direct lane successors. This allows us to express complex spatial relationships, which are the basis for the subsequent violation detection and handling process. We modelled an HD map ontology based on the NDS specification for describing the map entities as shown in Fig. 3. The rules can be categorised into: (1) primitive rules, (2) bounding rules, (3) coordinate distance rules, and (4) topological rules:

(1) Primitive rules enrich instances with one-step inferences regarding relationships and attributes and their results serve as input for all other rules. For a concrete example consider:

$$\text{hasLane}(x,y) \leftarrow \text{LaneGroup}(x), \text{laneGroupId}(x,i), \text{Lane}(y), \text{laneGroupId}(y,i).$$

(2) Bounding rules infer the boundaries of an area or the range of a lane or road, such as a start/end shape point of a lane or the left or right-most lane. As a concrete example, consider:

$$\text{StartShapePoint}(z) \leftarrow \text{Lane}(l), \text{AGGREGATE}(\text{hasShapePoint}(l, p), \text{index}(p, idx) \text{ ON } l$$
$$\text{BIND MIN}(idx) \text{ AS } m), \text{hasShapePoint}(l, z), \text{index}(z, m).$$

AGGREGATE takes the matches for hasShapePoint(l, p) and index(p, idx) as input and groups them based on the lane l. The aggregation function MIN then selects the minimal index per group and assigns this value to m using BIND.

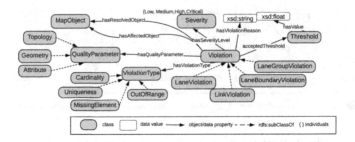

Fig. 4. Classes and properties in MQVO

Since there is no suitable aggregate function for selecting the point for the index m, it remains to get the point z that has the index m.

(3) Coordinate distance rules indicate the distance between two points using coordinates. An auxiliary concept (CoordinateDistance) represents the ternary relation that connects the source point to the target point via two object properties hasSource and hasTarget and the calculated distance value via the data property distance:

$$CoordinateDistance(d), hasSource(d, s), hasTarget(d, t), distance(d, z) \leftarrow$$
$$ShapePoint(s), x(s, x_s), y(s, y_s), ShapePoint(t), x(t, x_t), y(t, y_t),$$
$$BIND(\texttt{sqrt}((x_s - x_t)^2 + (y_s - y_t)^2) \texttt{ AS } z), BIND(\texttt{SKOLEM}(\texttt{"}d\texttt{"}, s, t) \texttt{ AS } d).$$

The SKOLEM function allows for dynamically generating "fresh" IRIs [5] based on the string "d" and the variable bindings for s and t.

(4) Topology rules refer to topological relations, more specifically, lateral (left/right) and longitudinal (predecessor/successor) relations. Connectivity can naturally be expressed using recursive rules. The base case (one-step connectivity) is usually inferred based on a pre-defined connectivity reference. For example, the hasDirectNext relation over lanes is defined based on source and destination connectors, while for links, it is defined by comparing the coordinates of start and end points of links.

4.2 Violation Detection

We developed the Map Quality Violation Ontology (MQVO) and a set of spatial constraint rules to detect violations after the enrichment process. The MQVO describes the type of violation, the affected objects, the severity level, etc. and provides information to guide the subsequent violation handling process. The spatial constraint rules are classified into (1) topology, (2) geometry and (3) attribute checking rules. We first describe MQVO, then we introduce the three types of constraint checking rules.

Map Quality Violation Ontology. We developed MQVO to describe map data errors since, to the best of our knowledge, there are no ontologies for the

Table 1. Constraint axioms as Datalog Constraint Atoms (DCA). We use C for classes, op for object, dp for data, and p for object or data properties.

OWL Axiom	Datalog Constraint Atom (DCA)
Existential quantification	$C(x)$, NOT EXISTS y IN ($C(y)$, p(x, y))
Individual value restriction	$C(x)$, NOT op$(x, individual)$
Literal value restriction	$C(x)$, NOT dp$(x, literal)$
HasKey	$C(x)$, dp(x, z), $C(y)$, dp(y, z), FILTER$(x \neq y)$
Min ($<$)/Max ($>$)	$C(x)$, AGGREGATE(p(x, v) ON x BIND count(v) AS n),
Cardinality restriction	FILTER$(n \bowtie max), \bowtie \in \{>, <\}$

specific purpose of describing map data violations. MQVO supports error detection by defining properties that can identify map objects (e.g., links/lanes) in which a violation is detected. It also provides context information for a violation to guide the repair process. Figure 4 shows the main concept Violation and the related properties and classes. Each violation is associated with a ViolationType, QualityParameter, Severity, affected MapObject, and the reason. Severity is described by one of the individuals Low, Medium, High and Critical. If a violation is repaired, then the involved map objects are linked to it via the hasResolvedObject object property. A violation can have an accepted Threshold, such as the threshold of the distance between two points.

Constraint Rules are classified into (1) topology, (2) geometry, and (3) attribute checking rules based on the map error types. Before describing the details of each rule type, we first introduce *Violation Recording Rule Templates* (VRRTs), which provide patterns for modelling constraint violation detection rules. Table 1 shows OWL axioms used to capture the map data quality requirements together with their corresponding *Datalog Constraint Atoms* (DCA). Constraint violations are recorded using freshly generated instances of Violation as shown in the following rule template:

$$\text{Violation}(v), \text{hasAffectedObject}(v, x), \text{hasReason}(v, "r") \leftarrow$$
$$<\text{DCA}>, \text{BIND}(\text{SKOLEM}("d", x) \text{ AS } v).$$

A concrete example of minimum cardinality constraint of lane shape points using the above template is as follows:

$$\text{Violation}(v), \text{hasAffectedObject}(v, l), \text{hasReason}(v, "MinCardinalityError") \leftarrow$$
$$\text{Lane}(l), \text{AGGREGATE}(\text{hasPoint}(l, p) \text{ ON } l \text{ BIND count}(p) \text{ AS } n),$$
$$\text{FILTER}(n < 2), \text{BIND}(\text{SKOLEM}("d", l) \text{ AS } v).$$

(1) Topology Checking Rules are designed for checking the spatial relationships of map objects. A comprehensive formal categorisation of binary topological relations between regions, lines, and points has been developed by Egenhofer

---

Algorithm 1: Check full coverage

---

    input : $\overline{pq}$: a base line, $L = \{\overline{u_1 v_1}, \ldots, \overline{u_n v_n}\}$: a set of line segments
    output: L_g, L_o: sets of line segments causing gaps and overlappings, resp.

1   $L_g = L_o = \emptyset$;
2   $\overline{u_s v_s} = \text{GETSTARTSEGMENT}(L)$;   `// apply bounding rules`
3   $\overline{u_e v_e} = \text{GETENDSEGMENT}(L)$;   `// apply bounding rules`
4   **if** $u_s > p$ **then**
5      $L_g = L_g \cup \{\overline{u_s v_e}\}$;   `// gap at the start`
6   **if** $v_e < q$ **then**
7      $L_g = L_g \cup \{\overline{u_e v_e}\}$;   `// gap at the end`
8   **for** $i = 1 \ldots n - 1$ **do**
9      $\overline{uv} = \text{GETDIRECTNEXT}(\overline{u_i v_i})$;   `// apply topology rules`
10   **if** $v_i < u$ **then**
11        $L_g = L_g \cup \{\overline{u_i v_i}, \overline{uv}\}$;   `// gap in the middle`
12   **else if** $v_i > u$ **then**
13        $L_o = L_o \cup \{\overline{u_i v_i}, \overline{uv}\}$;   `// overlapping`

---

and Herring [9]. In this paper, we model *full coverage* constraints, checking if a set of other map objects fully covers a given map object. For example, a link should be fully covered by a set of lane groups. To describe such constraints, we first introduce some basic notations.

Definition 2. *A line (segment)* $\overline{pq}$ *is defined by its* start point p *and its* end point q, *where* $p \neq q$. *A (base) line* $\overline{pq}$ *is fully covered by a sequence of lines* $\overline{u_1 v_1} \ldots \overline{u_n v_n}$ *if* $p = u_1$, $q = v_n$, *and* $v_i = u_{i+1}$ *for each* $1 \leq i < n$, *where* $u_i \neq v_i$. *We say that there is a* gap at the start *if* $p < u_1$, *a* gap at the end *if* $v_n < q$, *a* gap in the middle *if* $v_i < u_{i+1}$ *for some* $1 \leq i < n$, *and there is an* overlapping *if* $v_i > u_{i+1}$ *for some* $1 \leq i < n$.

Algorithm 1 presents the pseudo-code of full coverage checking. Given a base line $\overline{pq}$ and a sequence of line segments L without self-loops, the algorithm first identifies the start and end segment in L (lines 2–3) using bounding rules. The algorithm checks if there is a gap at the start or end w.r.t. the base line (lines 4–7). At last, it iterates through the given line segments and, for each segment, it gets the direct next line segment (line 9) through topology rules, checks if there is any gap in the middle (lines 8–10) or any overlapping (lines 11–12).

(2) Geometry Checking Rules are designed to check the geometric representation of links (lanes). The link (lane) model uses an ordered sequence of shape points describing the geometry of a polyline that represents a link (lane). We further subdivide geometry checking rules into *cardinality* and *geometric accuracy* checking rules. Cardinality checking rules use minimum or maximum cardinality restrictions in VRRTs. Geometric accuracy is checked via coordinate proximity using distance thresholds [8] to account for different levels of accuracy and

precision [29] in the collected map data. The following rule, where we abbreviate hasAffectedObject as hao, illustrates the case of checking a radius distance threshold of geometric points in two connected lanes.

$\mathsf{Violation}(v),\ \mathsf{hao}(v, u_p),\ \mathsf{hao}(v, v_q),\ \mathsf{hasReason}(v, \text{"GeometryError"}) \leftarrow$
$\qquad \mathsf{Lane}(p),\ \mathsf{Lane}(q),\ \mathsf{hasDirectNext}(p, q),\ \mathsf{endPoint}(p, u_p),\ \mathsf{startPoint}(q, v_q),$
$\qquad \mathsf{CoordinateDistance}(c),\ \mathsf{hasSource}(c, q),\ \mathsf{hasTarget}(c, p),\ \mathsf{distance}(c, d),$
$\qquad \mathsf{Threshold}(t),\ \mathsf{hasValue}(t, v_t),\ \mathtt{FILTER}(d > v_t),$
$\qquad \mathtt{BIND}(\mathtt{SKOLEM}(\text{"}d\text{"},\ u_p,\ v_q)\ \mathtt{AS}\ v).$

(3) Attribute Accuracy Checking Rules are used to check if the recorded attributes of map data representing real-world entities are correct and consistent. The attributes could be feature classifications, text information for feature names, or descriptions, and they ought to be consistent with each other. For example, if a road is classified as a motorway, it should also have a controlled-access designed for high-speed vehicular traffic. Controlled-access is modelled as a data property with a Boolean value. Hence, the corresponding violation detection rule can be modelled using a literal value restriction in the VRRT.

4.3   Violation Handling

Violations are handled based on the severity level. If a critical violation is detected during the map pre-loading phase, the autonomous driving mode is switched off, and control is handed over to the driver in the corresponding region. For non-critical violations, we rely on *violation tolerance* and *violation resolution* strategies considering the spatial relations. Violation tolerance is feasible because errors in the low-level (raw) data do not necessarily affect the decision taken at the knowledge (human-perceivable) level in intelligent systems [26]. In cases where the violations cannot be tolerated, spatial knowledge, e.g., topological relations, can be used to resolve violations [2,17]. These strategies allow us to support autonomous driving applications, even in the presence of low-level data errors.

We apply graph aggregation [16] for violation tolerance and decomposition [4] for violation resolution to achieve knowledge level consistency. Essentially, these strategies take advantage of graph structure similarity, which is captured by the notion of *isomorphisms* :

Definition 3 (RDF Graph Isomorphism [5]**).** *Let G_1 and G_2 be RDF graphs with V_1, V_2 the induced vertices of G_1 and G_2, respectively. We say that G_1 and G_2 are isomorphic, if there is a bijection $\mu\colon V_1 \to V_2$ such that $\mu(b) \in B$ for each $b \in V_1 \cap B$, $\mu(\ell) \in L$ for each $\ell \in V_1 \cap L$, $\mu(v) \in I$ for each $v \in V_1 \cap I$, and, for each triple $(s, p, o) \in G_1$, $(\mu(s), p, \mu(o)) \in G_2$. We call such μ an isomorphism between G_1 and G_2.*

Based on isomorphism, we introduce graph aggregation and its use for *violation tolerance*. Apart from its use in violation tolerance, graph aggregation is

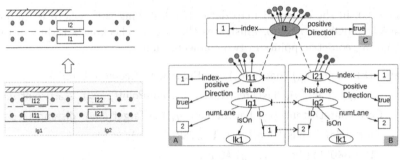

(a) lanes aggregation visual representation.   (b) lanes aggregation graph representation

Fig. 5. A violation-free example of RDF graph aggregation over lanes

helpful in itself to obtain a higher-level view of the map data, with a focus on the details that are important for autonomous driving.

Definition 4 (RDF Graph Aggregation). *Let G_1, G_2, and G be RDF graphs with vertices V_1, V_2, and V, respectively, such that G_1 is isomorphic to G_2 witness by the isomorphism μ. A (partial) function $\alpha\colon V_1 \cup V_2 \to V$ is an* abstraction function *w.r.t. G_1, G_2, and G if, for each $v \in V$, there are nodes $v_1 \in V_1$ and $v_2 \in V_2$ such that $\mu(v_1) = v_2$ and $\alpha(v_1) = \alpha(v_2) = v$. If an abstraction function w.r.t. G_1, G_2, and G exists, we call G an* aggregation graph *of G_1 and G_2.*

We generalise the notion of an abstraction graph to a set of pairwise isomorphic graphs $G_1, \ldots, G_n$ in a natural way.

Figure 5 shows an example where we apply graph aggregation over lanes of two lane groups with ID 1 and 2. We abbreviate lane as l, laneGroup as lg, and link as lk, e.g., l11 stands for lane11. Subfigure (a) shows a map visualisation, while (b) shows the corresponding graph representation, and the aggregation is shown in the upper part. Note that the mapping with a dotted line shows the isomorphism between graph A and graph B (we omit the mapping for identical values such as a mapping from true in graph A to true in graph B). The dashed lines show the abstraction function, where we again omit identical value mappings. The abstraction function only maps the lanes (l11 in graph A and l21 in graph B) as well as the lane index and direction attribute. The lane aggregation aligns with the human perception of l11 and l21 as one continuous lane.

(1) Violation Tolerance. Figure 6 shows an example with a violation, which consists of a duplicate lane group ID. More precisely, lg1 and lg2 both have ID 1 in the map data. As a result of this, the map data is parsed as containing just one lane group (with ID 1), which also causes l11 and l21 to be considered equal as they both have ID 1 and belong to the lane group with ID 1. Hence, we get identical RDF graphs for l11 (graph A) and l21 (graph B), which is a special case of RDF graph isomorphism. Applying the abstraction function (as in Fig. 6, dashed line) results, however, in the same (correct) aggregation graph (graph C) as for the violation-free scenario shown in Fig. 5. Hence, the RDF graph aggregation can tolerate some data errors.

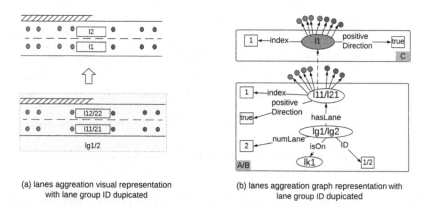

(a) lanes aggreation visual representation
with lane group ID dupicated

(b) lanes aggreation graph representation with
lane group ID dupicated

Fig. 6. An example of lane aggregation with lane group ID uniqueness violation

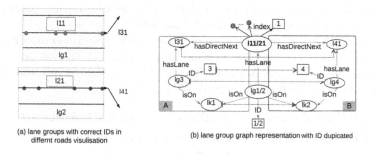

(a) lane groups with correct IDs in
differnt roads visulisation

(b) lane group graph representation with ID dupicated

Fig. 7. A example of lane ambiguity caused by lane group ID duplication.

(2) Violation Resolution. We illustrate how violations can be resolved (in particular, lane ambiguity) using graph decomposition.

Definition 5 (RDF Graph Decomposition). *An RDF decomposition of an RDF graph G is a collection of edge-disjoint, isomorphic subgraphs $G_1, \ldots, G_n$ of G such that every edge of G belongs to exactly one G_i, $1 \leq i \leq n$. We denote such a decomposition of G as $\hat{G} = \{G_1, G_2, \ldots, G_n\}$.*

Figure 7 shows an example of lane ambiguity also caused by a lane group ID duplication. Subfigure (a) shows a normal map visualisation of lg1 and lg2 located in separate roads. Subfigure (b) shows the graph representation resulting from a duplicate ID of lg1 and lg2 which causes l11 and l21 to merge into one lane instance having both lanes' spatial relationships, such as associated points, links and successor lanes. Based on the graph structure of the ambiguous graph, there exists a mapping between subgraph A and B, which indicates the application of RDF decomposition. Hence, we apply RDF graph decomposition to fix the topology and distance measurements to restore geometry. Figure 8 shows the concrete steps: (1) violation detection, (2) topology correction, and (3) assignment of geometric points.

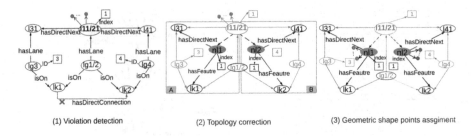

Fig. 8. Lane ambiguity violation resolution steps

In Step 1, a topology violation is detected if a lane group is associated with two disconnected links. This is modelled by checking the existence of a connection between links associated to a lane group using an existential qualification in a VRRT, and an instance of LaneViolation is generated having topology (an instance of class Topology) as its QualityParameter.

In Step 2, the topology correction is achieved via graph decomposition and relationship establishment. The original graph of l11/21 can be decomposed into isomorphic subgraphs A and B. Two new lane instances (nl1 and nl2) are generated with the correct topological relationships.

NewLane(l), hasFeature(n, f), hasDirectNext(l, n), hasOriginalLane(l, m) ←
LaneViolation(v), hasQualityParameter(v, topology), hao(v, m),
hasLane(lg_1, m), isOn(lg_1, f), LaneGrp(lg_2), hasLane(lg_2, n),
isOn(lg_2, f), hasDirectNext(m, n), index(m, i),
BIND(SKOLEM("d", f, i) AS l)

In Step 3, geometric shape point assignment is achieved via a point grouping strategy which compares the distance from each shape point of the lane to the first and last shape point of the lane associated links. The shape points are then grouped if the difference between the calculated distance and the links' length is within a threshold, e.g., 10 m.

hasPossibleLanePoint(f, p) ←
    LaneViolation(v), hasQualityParameter(v, $topology$), hao(v, l), hasShapePoint(l, p),
    hasFeature(l, f), length(f, n), hasFirstShapePoint(f, u), hasLastShapePoint(f, v),
    CoordinateDistance(d_1), hasSource(d_1, p), hasTarget(d_1, u), distance(d_1, t_1),
    CoordinateDistance(d_2), hasSource(d_2, p), hasTarget(d_2, v), distance(d_2, t_2),
    FILTER(ABS(($t_1 + t_2$) − n) < 10).

While assigning the point groups to correct new lanes, geometric point grouping is verified by comparing the number of points in each group to the total number of points of the original lane to prevent wrong point group assignments.

hasShapePoint(n, p) ←

    NewLane(n), hasOriginalLane(n, l), numPoints(l, u), hasFeature(n, f),

    hasPossibleLanePoint(f, p), numPossibleLanePoints(f, m), FILTER$(m < u)$.

5   Evaluation

Tile-based map data is stored as Binary Large Object (BLOB) in an NDS map database. We use SQLite Python APIs to extract map data and construct RDF triples based on the HD map ontology (see Fig. 3). We have implemented the proposed workflow of ensuring map data quality into an application called *SmartMapApp* using RDFox 4.0.0 as reasoner. The evaluation was performed on a 64-bit Ubuntu virtual machine with 8 Intel(R) Core(TM) i7-8550U CPU @ 1.80 GHz running at 33 MHz with 15 GB memory. We first show the performance of semantic enrichment and violation detection and then we evaluate the correctness of violation handling.

5.1   Violation Detection

We used 10 adjacent real map tiles along Federal Motorway 92 (Bundesautobahn 92) in Germany for violation detection evaluation, and record the computation time after doing a warm-up run by executing the tasks 3 times sequentially . Semantic enrichment is performed via 42 rules and violation detection consists of 37 rules (see Table 2). The result of the two phases is summarised in Fig. 9. The computation time for both phases increases with respect to the data size. The average number of input triples is 146, 182, the average execution time of semantic enrichment is 1, 584 ms, and the average execution time of violation detection is 197 ms.

5.2   Violation Handling

We consider the use case of lane group ID uniqueness violations to evaluate violation handling strategies. We show the result of violation tolerance over the error on a high way described in Fig. 1 (see Sect. 1), and violation resolution over an error on separated roads. At last, we discuss the evaluation results.

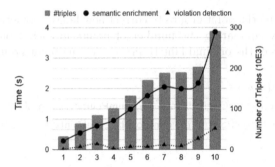

Fig. 9. Performance of semantic enrichment and violation detection over real map data; the left-hand side scale shows the execution time for semantic enrichment (dots on a solid line) and violation detection (diamonds on a dotted line) in seconds; the number of input triples is shown in form of bars using the scale on the right-hand side

Table 2. Number of rules used for semantic enrichment and violation detection

Semantic enrichment rules		Violation detection rules	
Primitive rules	15	Topology checking rules	10
Bounding rules	14	Geometry checking rules	14
Coordinate distance rules	3	Attribute accuracy checking rules	13
Topology rules	10	Total	37
Total	42		

Violation Tolerance. The error in Fig. 1 occurred in the map data containing a highway in Germany. Part of this highway is represented as five continuous lane groups with the same number of lanes. Two of the lane groups have the same ID, which caused the degradation of the autonomous driving mode. We applied graph aggregation over both the ground truth and dirty data. The lane aggregation results agree on both inputs, which shows that the lane group ID issue can be solved (see Table 3).

Violation Resolution. We evaluated the resolution strategy over two lane groups containing only one lane allocated to different links. The ID duplication caused the lanes in these two lane groups to be merged into one lane. Table 4 shows the result of applying graph decomposition over the dirty data. Row 2 (dirty data) shows that the lane is ambiguous as it has the length, number of shape points, successors, and related links of both lanes. Row 3 shows that the graph decomposition can resolve the error and all lane properties are correctly recovered.

Overall, the results demonstrate that our approach can improve map data quality, resulting in a better error-tolerance of AD systems. On the one hand, the performance of the violation detection allows the deployment of the proposed solution in the back-end (cloud side) to check the map data before sending it to the car or on-board (embedded side, in the car) in case of loss of connectivity

Table 3. The violation tolerance over a lane using graph aggregation, both ground truth and dirty data are aggregated results

	Lane	Length (m)	#Points	Successor	Link
Ground truth	BE9D6	2034	54	563E	02
Dirty data	BE9D6	2034	54	563E	02

Table 4. The violation resolution of a lane using graph decomposition

	Lane	Length (m)	#Points	Successor	Link
Ground truth	1116_0	358	14	1117_0	199
Dirty data	1116_0	214, 358	5, 14	1117_0, 1188_0	199, 197
Resolved violation	1116_0	358	14	1117_0	199

with the back-end. On the other hand, the evaluation of the violation handling strategies has shown that we could avoid the deactivation of the AD mode by detecting the error and correcting the map data in both cases of the lane group error. The cost of reasoning generally depends not only on the number of rules but also on the complexity of the combination of certain rules and the input data. For details of how RDFox performs reasoning, we refer interested readers to the description of the materialization algorithm in RDFox [19].

6 Conclusion and Future Work

In this paper, we present an ontology-based approach for ensuring map data quality. We propose a workflow considering semantic enrichment, violation detection and violation handling. Semantic enrichment is achieved via a set of rules combined with an HD map ontology and the results provide the needed spatial knowledge for violation detection and handling. Violation detection is modelled via the novel Map Quality Violation Ontology and suitable constraint violation rules. At last, we show novel violation handling strategies over non-critical violations using graph aggregation and graph decomposition. We evaluate the performance of violation detection and the correctness of violation handling. The results show that our approach can successfully check the quality of map data and suggests that violation handling is even feasible on-the-fly in the car (on-board), avoiding the autonomous driving mode's deactivation. We plan to integrate this approach into the developed knowledge-spatial architecture [23], and test the approach in ROS (Robot Operating System) [24], which requires a re-implementation of the Java-based SmartMapApp in C++.

References

1. Abiteboul, S., Hull, R., Vianu, V.: Foundations of Databases, vol. 8. Addison-Wesley, Reading (1995)

2. Ai, T., Yang, M., Zhang, X., Tian, J.: Detection and correction of inconsistencies between river networks and contour data by spatial constraint knowledge. Cartogr. Geogr. Inf. Sci. **42**(1), 79–93 (2015)
3. Armand, A., Ibanez-Guzman, J., Zinoune, C.: Digital maps for driving assistance systems and autonomous driving. In: Watzenig, D., Horn, M. (eds.) Automated Driving, pp. 201–244. Springer, Cham (2017). https://doi.org/10.1007/978-3-319-31895-0_9
4. Arumugam, S., Hamid, I., Abraham, V.: Decomposition of graphs into paths and cycles. J. Discrete Math. **2013**, 721051 (2013)
5. Cyganiak, R., Wood, D., Lanthaler, M.: RDF 1.1 Concepts and abstract syntax-3. RDF graphs. https://www.w3.org/TR/rdf11-concepts/ (2014). Accessed 14 Sep 2020
6. De Meester, B., Heyvaert, P., Arndt, D., Dimou, A., Verborgh, R.: RDF graph validation using rule-based reasoning. Semant. Web J. **12**, 117–142 (2020)
7. Debattista, J., Lange, C., Auer, S.: daQ, an ontology for dataset quality information. In: Linked Data on the Web (LDOW) (2014)
8. Devillers, R., Jeansoulin, R., Goodchild, M.F.: Fundamentals of Spatial Data Quality. ISTE, London (2006)
9. Egenhofer, M.J., Herring, J.: TheCategorizing binary topological relations between regions, lines, and points in geographic databases. The **9**(94–1), 76 (1990)
10. Eiter, T., Füreder, H., Kasslatter, F., Parreira, J.X., Schneider, P.: Towards a semantically enriched local dynamic map. Int. J. Intell Transp. Syst. Res. **17**(1), 32–48 (2019)
11. Gran, C.W.: HD-Maps in autonomous driving. Master's thesis, NTNU (2019)
12. Heyvaert, P., Dimou, A., De Meester, B., Verborgh, R.: Rule-driven inconsistency resolution for knowledge graph generation. Semant. Web J. **10**, 1071–1086 (2019)
13. Hitzler, P., Krötzsch, M., Parsia, B., Patel-Schneider, P.F., Rudolph, S.: OWL 2 Web Ontology Language: Prime, 2nd edn. http://www.w3.org/TR/owl2-primer/ (27 October 2009)
14. Huang, W.: Knowledge-based geospatial data integration and visualization with semantic web technologies. In: 2019 Doctoral Consortium at the 18th International Semantic Web Conference (ISWC-DC 2019), vol. 2548, pp. 37–45. CEUR-WS (2019)
15. Liu, R., Wang, J., Zhang, B.: High definition map for automated driving: overview and analysis. J. Navigat. **73**(2), 324–341 (2020)
16. Maali, F., Campinas, S., Decker, S.: Gagg: A Graph Aggregation Operator. In: Gandon, F., Sabou, M., Sack, H., d'Amato, C., Cudré-Mauroux, P., Zimmermann, A. (eds.) ESWC 2015. LNCS, vol. 9088, pp. 491–504. Springer, Cham (2015). https://doi.org/10.1007/978-3-319-18818-8_30
17. Majic, I., Naghizade, E., Winter, S., Tomko, M.: Discovery of topological constraints on spatial object classes using a refined topological model. J. Spatial Inf. Sci. **2019**(18), 1–30 (2019)
18. Mostafavi, M.A., Edwards, G., Jeansoulin, R.: An ontology-based method for quality assessment of spatial data bases. In: Third International Symposium on Spatial Data Quality. Geoinfo Series, vol. 1/28a, pp. 49–66 (April 2004)
19. Motik, B., Nenov, Y., Piro, R., Horrocks, I., Olteanu, D.: Parallel materialisation of datalog programs in centralised, main-memory rdf systems. In: Proceedings of the Twenty-Eighth AAAI Conference on Artificial Intelligence (AAAI'2014), pp. 129–137. AAAI Press (2014)
20. NDS Association: The standard for map data. https://nds-association.org/. Accessed 27 May 2020

21. Nenov, Y., Piro, R., Motik, B., Horrocks, I., Wu, Z., Banerjee, J.: RDFox: A Highly-scalable RDF store. In: The Semantic Web - ISWC 2015. pp. 3–20 (2015)
22. Qiu, H., Ayara, A., Glimm, B.: Ontology-Based Map Data Quality assurance-Technical Report. https://cloudstore.uni-ulm.de/s/ftSSDmdnbfx35R7 (2020)
23. Qiu, H., Ayara, A., Glimm, B.: Ontology-based processing of dynamic maps in automated driving. In: 12th International Joint 2020 Conference on Knowledge Discovery, Knowledge Engineering and Knowledge Management, vol. 2. SCITEPRESS (in press)
24. Quigley, M., et al.: ROS: an open-source Robot Operating System. In: ICRA Workshop on Open Source Software, vol. 3, p. 5 (2009)
25. Wang, F., Mäs, S., Reinhardt, W., Kandawasvika, A.: Ontology based quality assuranc e for mobile data acquisition. In: EnviroInfo. pp. 334–341 (2005)
26. Xu, X., Huang, H.H.: Exploring data-level error tolerance in high-performance solid-state drives. IEEE Trans. Reliabil 64(1), 15–30 (2014)
27. Yilmaz, C., Comert, C., Yildirim, D.: SDQO and sfQ, ontologies for spatial data quality. IN: ISPRS - International Archives of the Photogrammetry, Remote Sensing and Spatial Information Sciences XLII-2/W13, pp. 1275–1280 (2019)
28. Yilmaz, C., Cömert, Ç.: Ontology based quality evaluation for spatial data. Int. Arch. Photogram. Remote Sens. Spatial Inf. Sci. 40, 95–99 (2015)
29. Zheng, L., Li, B., Yang, B., Song, H., Lu, Z.: Lane-level road network generation techniques for lane-level maps of autonomous vehicles: a survey. Sustainability 11(16), 4511 (2019)

Knowledge Graphs (Understanding, Creating, and Exploiting)

Applying Grammar-Based Compression to RDF

Michael Röder[1,2](✉) ⓘ, Philip Frerk[1], Felix Conrads[1],
and Axel-Cyrille Ngonga Ngomo[1,2] ⓘ

[1] DICE Group, Department of Computer Science, Paderborn University,
Paderborn, Germany
{michael.roeder,axel.ngonga}@upb.de
[2] Institute for Applied Informatics, Leipzig, Germany

Abstract. Data compression for RDF knowledge graphs is used in an increasing number of settings. In parallel to this, several grammar-based graph compression algorithms have been developed to reduce the size of graphs. We port gRePair—a state-of-the-art grammar-based graph compression algorithm—to RDF (named RDFRePair). We compare this promising technique with respect to the compression ratio to the state-of-the-art approaches for RDF compression dubbed HDT, HDT++ and OFR as well as a k^2-trees-based RDF compression. We run an extensive evaluation on 40 datasets. Our results suggest that RDFRePair achieves significantly better compression ratios and runtimes than gRePair. However, it is outperformed by k^2 trees, which achieve the overall best compression ratio on real-world datasets. This better performance comes at the cost of time, as k^2 trees are clearly outperformed by OFR w.r.t. compression and decompression time. A pairwise Wilcoxon Signed Rank Test suggests that while OFR is significantly more time-efficient than HDT and k^2 trees, there is no significant difference between the compression ratios achieved by k^2 trees and OFR. In addition, we point out future directions for research. All code and datasets are available at https://github.com/dice-group/GraphCompression and https://hobbitdata. informatik.uni-leipzig.de/rdfrepair/evaluation_datasets/, respectively.

Keywords: RDF compression · Graph compression · Benchmarking

1 Introduction

The first prominent use of data compression can be traced back to the 19th century with works such as the Morse code, which uses a precursor of entropy-based compression by assigning shorter codes to high-frequency letters [16]. Data compression is now used in an ever growing number of settings, especially due to the steadily increasing size of application-relevant datasets [7,8,10,12,15,17]. This holds in particular for RDF knowledge graphs, which grow continuously in both number and sheer size [10]. The need for compressing RDF data has hence fueled a considerable body of research.

RDF compression algorithms achieve better compression ratios than human-readable compact RDF representations (e.g., Turtle [3], Notation-3 [4]) by serializing RDF data in a manner which still allows for querying. The wide range of available

© Springer Nature Switzerland AG 2021
R. Verborgh et al. (Eds.): ESWC 2021, LNCS 12731, pp. 93–108, 2021.
https://doi.org/10.1007/978-3-030-77385-4_6

approaches spans algorithms implemented directly in storage solutions [2] over algorithms able to exploit the semantics of RDF knowledge graphs [12, 15] to syntax-based compression techniques [8, 10]. Most of these approaches abide by the general concept of separating an RDF graph into three different parts [8]: a header, a dictionary and a representation of the triples. The *header* contains general statistical information. Since it is not necessary for the decompression of the RDF graph, we will not further take it into consideration throughout the rest of this paper. The *dictionary* maps the URIs and literal values of the graph to ids. These ids are used within the triples file for a space-efficient *representation*. This general concept is wide spread when it comes to the compression of RDF graphs [8, 10].

The graph processing community has also been aware of the need for compression and has developed a range of approaches ranging from tree-based strategies [5] to techniques based on automatically generated graph context-free grammars [13]. Especially the latter work of Maneth et al. attracted our interest since the authors implemented a prototypical compressor and evaluated it on different types of graphs (including some RDF graphs). Based on a comparison with a k^2-trees-based compression they conclude that "[o]ver RDF graphs [...] our compressor gives the best results, sometimes factors of several magnitudes smaller than other compressors" [13]. However, no previous work has addressed the concrete task of porting and comparing the current state of the art in grammar-based graph compression with the current reigning RDF compression algorithms. We address exactly this research gap.

In this paper, we port one of the currently best performing graph compression approaches, i.e., gRePair [13] and adapt it to RDF knowledge graphs. In addition, we develop an efficient implementation of k^2 trees [1, 5] for RDF. The resulting approaches are compared with HDT, HDT++ and OFR in a large-scale evaluation over 40 datasets w.r.t. their runtime and compression ratio. Our results suggest that OFR and k^2 trees achieve comparable results and outperform other RDF compression approaches significantly with respect to compression ratio—including gRePair. Our result analysis unveils more efficient dictionary compression approaches yield the potential for better RDF compression ratios. A comparison with respect to query execution performance is not part of this paper.

In the following section, we present related work. Section 3 comprises preliminaries before our approach is described in Sect. 4. We describe our evaluation and report results in Sect. 5 before we conclude in Sect. 6.

2   Related Work

The existing compression algorithms for RDF data can be separated into two groups—syntactic compression algorithms and semantic compression algorithms. A syntactic compression takes the given RDF graph and uses an economical syntax to encode its information. For example, Fernández et al. [8] present the HDT compression.[1] It is an implementation of a dictionary and several triple representations. The dictionary reduces the space needed to store the URIs by using a prefix tree. The most efficient

---

[1] https://www.w3.org/Submission/HDT/.

triple representation groups triples by their subject and after that by their predicate. The grouped triples are represented by using id arrays and bitsets. Álvarez-García et al. [1,2] the k^2-triples approach that uses k^2 trees to store triples to ensure that even large RDF graphs can be handled by in-memory data stores. However, the authors do not compare the approach with other RDF graph compression approaches. Similar to k^2-triples, Wang et al. [18] proposes the usage of octrees to compress the representation of triples. Their evaluation shows that this approach achieves better compression ratios than HDT for 4 example datasets. However, to the best of our knowledge the implementations of k^2-triples and octrees are not publicly available. Hernández-Illera et al. [10] extend HDT to HDT++ by using predicate families, i.e., combinations of predicates that co-occur very often. Instead of storing the predicate ids for each of these triples, HDT++ stores the id of the predicate family together with the object ids. The evaluation shows that especially for highly structured datasets, HDT++ achieves better compression ratios than HDT. For 3 out of the 4 datasets used for the evaluation, HDT++ outperforms a k^2-tree-based compression. The Objects-First Representation (OFR) presented by Swacha et al. [17] uses a two-staged algorithm. In the first stage, the dictionary and the triples are compressed. Instead of a single dictionary, the algorithm uses several indexes that handle different parts like subject, predicate or object URIs, subject or object names, or literals. The triples are represented as `object, subject, predicate` tuples and subsequently sorted in ascending order, thus allowing the usage of a delta encoding for the objects. This means that only one bit is necessary to encode whether the object of a triple remains the same as the object of the previous triple or whether its ID is increased by 1. The encoding of the subject follows a similar idea with a special handling of large deltas between the IDs. The predicate IDs are encoded as usual numbers. In the second stage of the algorithm, a general compression algorithm is applied. Depending on the data, the first step uses different output streams to write the data. The authors argue that this allows the second-stage algorithm to find more patterns within streams that contain similar data. In their evaluation, the authors show that using either the Deflate or the LZMA algorithm in the second stage outperforms the HDT algorithm using the same algorithms as a post processing. However, the usage of general compression algorithms prevents the execution of queries on the compressed dataset.

The group of semantic compression algorithms aims at the reduction of the number of triples that need to be stored by replacing repetitive parts of the graph. A general approach to the reduction of graphs are grammar-based compressions. Maneth et al. [13] propose the gRePair algorithm. The approach searches for edge pairs—named digrams—that occur often within a graph. The occurrences of the digrams are replaced by hyper edges. In an additional grammar, the rules for replacing the hyper edges with their digrams is stored. The remaining graph is stored using a k^2 tree. Although the authors suggest that this compression can potentially be ported to RDF and used for querying, we are the first to port gRePair to RDF knowledge graphs. Pan et al. [15] propose to search for redundant graph patterns and replace them by triples with newly created predicates and a grammar comprising rules for the decompression. However, a comparison with existing RDF compression approaches like HDT with respect to their compression ratio is missing and the source code is not available. Gayathri et al. [9] propose the mining of logical Horn-rules. Based on these rules, triples that can be inferred are removed from the graph. In the evaluation, the authors show that depending on the dataset 27–40% of the triples can be removed. In a similar way, Joshi et al. [12] propose a compression technique which is based on frequent item set mining. Frequent patterns that can be recovered by applying rules are removed from the graph. Their evaluation shows that for several datasets, more than 50% of the triples can be removed and that the removal can lead to an improvement of the performance of the HDT compression algorithm.

3   Preliminaries

Definition 1 (Sets). *Let U, B and L be the mutually disjoint sets of URI references, blank nodes and literals, respectively [11]. Let $P \subseteq U$ be the set of all properties.*

Definition 2 (RDF triple). *An RDF triple $t = (s, p, o) \in (U \cup B) \times P \times (U \cup B \cup L)$ displays the statement that the subject s is related to the object o via the predicate p [11].*

Definition 3 (RDF graph). *An RDF graph can be defined as directed labeled multi-graph, i.e., as a tuple $G = (V, E, \lambda)$ where $V = \{v_1, ..., v_n\}$ is the set of nodes; E is a multiset of edges $e_i = (v_i^{(t)}, v_i^{(h)}) \in V^2$ and $\lambda : E \to P$ is the edge label mapping.*

Definition 4 (Digram). *A digram $d = (p_i, p_j)$ is defined as two edges that share at least one node and are labeled with two edge labels p_i and p_j. It follows, that each digram can link up to three nodes. Each node is either an external or an internal node, where a node is called external if it has at least one edge that does not belong to the digram.*

Note that in contrast to Maneth et al. [13], we do not define digrams as hyperedges, i.e., we limit ourselves to digrams with one or two external nodes for two reasons: First, this allows the usage of digrams as normal edges in a directed labeled graph as defined above. Second, preliminary implementations showed that digrams with more than two external nodes might not lead to better compression ratios. Our definition leads to 33 different shapes of digrams. 8 examples thereof are depicted in Fig. 1. A digram occurrence is defined as the occurrence of such a digram in a given graph.

Definition 5 (Digram-compressed RDF graph). *Let D be the set of all digrams. A digram-compressed RDF graph is an RDF graph which has an extended label mapping function $\lambda' : E \to P \cup D$.*

Definition 6 (Non-terminal edge). *A non-terminal edge is an edge in a digram-compressed RDF graph that is not mapped to a predicate but to a digram.*

Definition 7 (Grammar). *A grammar $\mathfrak{G}$ is defined as $\mathfrak{G} = (S, D)$, where S is a digram-compressed RDF graph named* start graph *and D is the set of digrams used to compress the graph.*

Definition 8 (Quadrant). *A matrix of dimension $2^n \times 2^n$ can be divided into four sub-matrices of equal size $2^{n-1} \times 2^{n-1}$. These submatrices are called quadrants. The quadrants will represent the following rows and columns of the original matrix:*

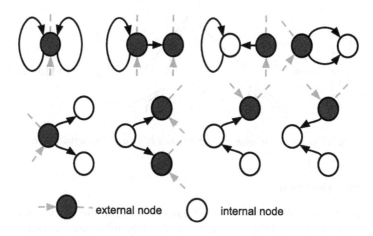

Fig. 1. Examples of digram shapes. The external nodes have additional edges that are not part of the digram (depicted in light gray).

- *First quadrant: $(0, 0)$ to $(2^{n-1} - 1, 2^{n-1} - 1)$;*
- *Second quadrant: $(0, 2^{n-1})$ to $(2^{n-1} - 1, 2^n)$;*
- *Third quadrant: $(2^{n-1}, 0)$ to $(2^n, 2^{n-1} - 1)$;*
- *Fourth quadrant: $(2^{n-1}, 2^{n-1})$ to $(2^n, 2^n)$.*

Definition 9 (Compression Ratio). *Let s_o and s_c be the file size in bytes of the original RDF file and the compressed file, respectively. The compression ratio r is defined as $r = \frac{s_c}{s_o}$. The smaller the compression ratio, the better is the performance of a compression algorithm.*

4   Approaches

We implemented two approaches for RDF compression: RDFRePair and k^2. We begin by presenting RDFRePair, an RDF compression approach based on the gRePair algorithm proposed by Maneth et al. [13]. It adapts the gRePair approach to RDF and combines it with the dictionary of [8]. The workflow of RDFRePair comprises 4 main steps: 1) Indexing the nodes and edge labels of the input graph, 2) running the gRePair algorithm, 3) creating k^2 trees for the remaining, compressed graph and 4) serializing the graph. The second approach skips the second step and solely relies on an efficient implementation of k^2 trees as proposed by Álvarez-García et al. [1]. These steps are explained in the following before we explain the decompression of the graph in Sect. 4.5. The execution of queries on the compressed graph is out of the scope of this paper.

4.1   Indexing

The first step is to load the input RDF graph into memory and index all nodes and edge labels within the graph. Maneth et al. [13] state that "[a]ny method for dictionary compression can be used to additionally compress the dictionary (e.g. [14])". Hence, we use the dictionary implementation of HDT [8].

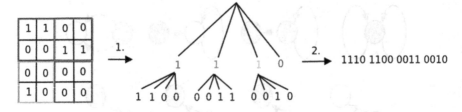

Fig. 2. Example of an adjacency matrix to a k^2 tree and its serialization.

4.2 gRePair Algorithm

In this step, the algorithm will create a Grammar $\mathfrak{G}$ from the indexed graph G as described by Maneth et al. [13]. This step consists of the following sub steps.

1. *Initial digram scan:* The algorithm iterates over all vertices. For each vertex, all pairs of edges connected to that vertex are counted as potential digrams.
2. *Sort digrams:* All digrams with at least two occurrences are sorted descending by their frequency using a priority queue.
3. *Get most frequent digram d:* The most frequent digram is removed from the priority queue.
4. *Replace all occurences of d:* All occurrences of d within the graph are replaced with non-terminal edges and the edges receive the label d. All replaced occurrences are added to a list which is necessary for the later serialization of the digram d.
5. *Find new digrams:* Since new edges have been introduced, new digrams could have been created. All vertices connected to at least one of these newly created non-terminal edges are given to the digram search algorithm to search for new digrams. If new digrams are found, they are added to the queue.
6. *Repeat:* if the queue is not empty, go back to step 2.

4.3 k^2 Trees

The grammar $\mathfrak{G}$ created by the gRePair algorithm is split up in a start graph S and the set of digrams D. As proposed by Maneth et al. [13], an adjacency matrix is created for each edge label in S. The matrix is of dimension $|V| \times |V|$ and its cells represent the edges between the subject (row index) and the object (column index). If an edge with the edge label of the matrix exists between a subject and an object the representing cell is set to 1. Hence, the matrix is typically sparse.

Thereafter, the k^2 trees are built from these matrices. To this end, each path from the root of the k^2 tree to its leaves is built individually before it is merged with all other paths of the matrix. The path creation algorithm is shown in Algorithm 1. First, the matrix is resized to $2^h \times 2^h$ where $h \in \mathbb{N}$ is the lowest integer that fulfills $2^h \geq |V|$. The added rows and columns are filled with zeros. After that, the matrix is transformed into a tree using a recursion. Starting with the root node, the matrix is divided into 4 quadrants as defined in Definition 8 and four child nodes are added to the root node.

Algorithm 1: k^2 tree path creation algorithm.

Input: Matrix M, Integer h
Output: k^2-Tree
1 x1 = 0, y1 = 0, x2 = 2^h, y2 = 2^h
2 root = new TreeNode()
3 currentNode = root
4 **for** *Point p : M.getPoints( )* **do**
5 | quadrant = getQuadrant(p, x1, y1, x2, y2)
6 | child = new TreeNode()
7 | currentNode.set(quadrant, child)
8 | currentNode = child
9 |_   shrinkBoundaries(x1, y1, x2, y2, quadrant)
10 **return** *root*

Algorithm 2: k^2 tree path merge algorithm.

Input: TreeNode node, Map<Integer, TreeNode> map, Integer k, Integer h
Output: List of individual paths in k^2-tree
1 **if** *k==h OR node == null* **then**
2 |_   return
3 **for** *child C : node.getChildren( )* **do**
4 |_   map.get(k).add(C)
5 **for** *child C : node.getChildren( )* **do**
6 |_   merge(C, map, k+1, h)
7 **return** *map*

The value of a child node is either 1 if the quadrant contains at least one cell with a 1 value. Otherwise, the child node gets the value 0. This is done recursively for each child having a 1 until the quadrants are of size 2×2. In that case, the 4 numbers of the quadrant are used for the 4 child nodes.

Instead of implementing the recursion directly, we implemented a more efficient algorithm, which comprises two steps. First, the algorithm iterates over all cells of the matrix having a 1 value. For each of these cells, the path within a k^2 tree is determined as shown in Algorithm 1. Beginning with the complete matrix, the algorithm determines the quadrant in which the cell is located and adds a child node to the path before shrinking the quadrant. Thereafter, all generated paths are merged as shown in Algorithm 2. Afterwards the map represents the k^2 Tree optimized for later serialization.

4.4 Serialization

The serializiation of the created grammar 𝕲 comprises the serialization of the start graph and the serialization of the digrams.

Start Graph. The start graph is serialized as a sequence of its k^2-trees. Each tree is preceded by the ID of its edge label (4 bytes). Each tree node is represented by a single

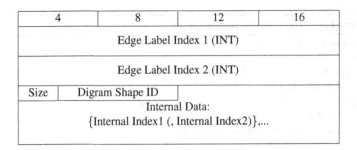

4	8	12	16
Edge Label Index 1 (INT)			
Edge Label Index 2 (INT)			
Size	Digram Shape ID		
Internal Data: {Internal Index1 (, Internal Index2)},...			

Fig. 3. Digram serialization. One line represents 2 bytes.

bit. Hence, the tree is serialized as a sequence of bits representing its nodes from top to bottom. If the tree has an uneven number of nodes, the last byte will be padded with zeros. An example is shown in Fig. 2. In this example the whole tree can be stored using only 2 bytes.

Digrams. The digrams used to reduce the graph are serialized as depicted in Fig. 3. A serialized digram comprises the two edge labels, a size flag, a shape ID and the IDs of all internal nodes of all occurrences of this digram. The edge label IDs are two integers that represent the IDs of the properties or digrams the two edges of the digram have.[2] The size flag uses two bits to decode the number of bytes that are used for the single internal node IDs. This allows the usage of 1, 2, 3 or 4 byte IDs. The shape ID comprises 6 bits that are used to store the ID of the digram shape (i.e., one of the different 33 shapes). The last part of the digram lists the IDs of the internal nodes of all occurrences of the digram. To this end, the occurrences of the digram are sorted based on the ID(s) of its external nodes. Hence, the mapping of internal nodes to the single occurrences of the digram are stored implicitly without taking any additional space. Maneth et al. [13] propose an optimization that reassigns the IDs of vertices in the graph to implicitly store the IDs of internal nodes as well. However, this would raise a new requirement for the dictionary or consume additional space to store the mapping of IDs.

4.5 Decompression

In this section, we briefly describe the process of decompressing a compressed graph. First, the dictionary is loaded. After that all k^2 trees for all terminal edges are loaded and directly transformed into the RDF triples they represent. The digrams are then read and iterated upon in reverse order. The non-terminal edges of each digram's k^2-tree are sorted by the IDs of vertices they connect. Based on this order, the single non-terminals can be replaced by the two edges and the internal nodes. Since the non-terminal edges are handled in the same order as during the serialisation, the internal nodes are read in the correct order. Depending on the two edge labels a digram contains, the generated

---

[2] In the current implementation, we use 32 Bit integers. They can be extended to 64 Bits for very large graphs.

terminal edges are directly written into the result RDF graph. If non-terminals are created, they are added to the list of their digram. The order of digrams ensures that only non-terminal edges of yet unprocessed digrams can be found.

5 Evaluation

Our evaluation aims to answer the following research questions:

- **RQ1**: How do RDFRePair and k^2 perform compared to state-of-the-art RDF graph compression algorithms w.r.t. compression ratio and (de)compression times?
- **RQ2**: To which extent does the dictionary affect the compressed size?
- **RQ3**: Which RDF dataset features influence the compression ratio?

5.1 Experimental Setup

To answer the research questions above, we execute several experiments using different RDF datasets and compression algorithms.[3] For each dataset-algorithm combination, we use the algorithm to compress and decompress the dataset. During that, we gather four measures: 1) the compression ratio, 2) the runtime of the compression, 3) the runtime of the complete decompression and 4) the amount of space of the compressed dataset that is used to store the dictionary. In addition, we analyze the datasets using the following metrics to answer the third question: number of triples, classes and resources, URI resources, properties, as well as star pattern similarity and structuredness. We elaborate upon the last two measures in the following.

In [13], the authors mention that a graph similar to the star pattern is beneficial for gRePair, because gRePair can make use of this structure to find many digram occurrences around those high-degree nodes. A directed graph is described as a star pattern if one node $v \in V$ is connected to all other nodes, whereas no other nodes are connected to each other. Hence, the following necessary (but not sufficient) condition must apply: $\exists v \in V, \forall e \in E : v \in e$. As graphs tend to be more complex than such simple patterns, we define a metric describing how similar a given graph is to a star pattern. Let $deg(v)$ be the degree of a node v. Let N be a list of all nodes sorted by their deg-values in descending order and N_x be the first x nodes of N. We define the star pattern similarity (SPS) metric as follows.

$$SPS = \frac{\sum_{n \in N_x} deg(n)}{\sum_{n \in N} deg(n)} \in [0 : 1] \tag{1}$$

In our experiments we choose $x = 0.001 \cdot |N|$.

Duan et al. [6] compare synthetic and real-world RDF datasets and conclude that synthetic datasets tend to be more structured. To measure this structuredness, they count how regularly properties occur for instances of classes. If all instances of a class have

---

[3] All experiments were executed on a 64-bit Ubuntu 16.04 machine, an Intel(R) Xeon(R) CPU E5-2698 v3 @ 2.30 GHz with 64 CPUs and 128 GB RAM. Only the experiments for WatDiv were executed on a 64-bit Debian machine with 128 CPUs and 1TB RAM.

Table 1. Datasets used for the evaluation.

Name	Abbreviation	#Triples	#Resources	#Classes
dc-2010-complete-alignments	SD0	5 919	821	36
ekaw-2012-complete-alignments	SD1	13 114	1 604	36
eswc-2006-complete-alignments	SD2	6 654	1 259	25
eswc-2009-complete-alignments	SD3	9 456	1 247	34
eswc-2010-complete-alignments	SD4	18 122	2 226	36
eswc-2011-complete-alignments	SD5	25 865	3 071	36
iswc-2002-complete-alignments	SD6	13 450	1 953	36
iswc-2003-complete-alignments	SD7	18 039	2 565	36
iswc-2005-complete-alignments	SD8	28 149	3 877	36
iswc-2010-complete-alignments	SD9	32 022	3 842	36
external_links_en	DB0	49 999	7 070	0
geo_coordinates_en	DB1	49 999	54 870	1
homepages_en	DB2	49 999	12 505	0
instance_types_transitive_en	DB3	49 999	98 666	273
instance_types_en	DB4	49 999	48 913	306
mappingbased_objects_en	DB5	49 998	37 159	0
persondata_en	DB6	49 999	9 516	2
transitive_redirects_en	DB7	49 999	82 386	0
wikidata-20200308-lexemes-BETA	WD0	49 828	9 965	15
wikidata-20200404-lexemes-BETA	WD1	49 827	9 931	15
wikidata-20200412-lexemes-BETA	WD2	49 828	9 932	15
wikidata-20200418-lexemes-BETA	WD3	49 828	9 902	15
lubm-1	LUBM-1	100 545	17 209	15
lubm-10	LUBM-10	1 272 577	207 461	15
lubm-100	LUBM-100	13 405 383	2 179 801	15
lubm-1000	LUBM-1000	133 573 856	21 715 143	15
watdiv	WAT	1 098 871 666	52 120 471	12 500 145
external_links_en	EL	7 772 283	9 128 582	0
geo_coordinates_en	GC	2 323 568	580 897	1
homepages_en	HO	688 563	1 300 927	0
instance_types_en	IT	5 150 432	5 044 646	422
instance_types_transitive_en	ITT	31 254 270	4 737 461	388
mappingbased_objects_en	MO	18 746 173	5 901 219	0
persondata_en	PD	10 310 094	1 522 938	18
transitive_redirects_en	TR	7 632 358	10 404 804	0
archives-hub	AH	1 361 815	135 643	46
jamendo	JA	1 047 950	410 929	11
scholarydata_dump	SDD	859 840	95 016	46
wikidata-20200308-lexemes-BETA	WD	42 914 845	6 061 049	22
dblp-20170124	DBLP	88 150 324	28 058 722	14

triples with the same properties, the class is highly structured. If some of the instances have triples with properties that other instances of the same class do not have, the class is less structured. The structuredness of a dataset is the weighted average of the class structuredness values with a higher weight for classes with many instances and many properties.

5.2 Datasets

Table 1 shows the summary of the datasets.[4] We use 40 datasets in total. Note that gRe-Pair and in part RDFRePair were not able to handle large datasets in our experiments. To still be able to compare them with other approaches, we introduce 4 Wikidata and 8 DBpedia subsets cut at 50 k lines.

5.3 Compression Algorithms

For the evaluation of RDFRePair, we select a subset of the algorithms listed as related work. We choose HDT because of its wide adoption and its usage as reference algorithm in several publications.[5] In addition, we compare our evaluation with HDT++ and OFR since both algorithms are reported to perform at state-of-the-art level and better than HDT.[6] We also use our k^2 implementation since the implementations used in the related work (e.g., [1]) do not seem to be available as open source. In addition, we received a prototypical implementation of the gRePair algorithm from the authors of [13]. Given that the original gRePair implementation is a proof of concept, it is rather far from stable regarding decompression. Apart from that, the implementation does not create a dictionary. To alleviate this problem, the HDT dictionary size was added for a fair comparison. The OFR compression provides several files representing the compressed graph. To combine these files and further compress them the authors suggested to use either Deflate (zip) or LZMA (7z). However, since our goal is to compare comparisons that would be able to answer SPARQL queries, we do not use additional, binary compression algorithms. Instead, we sum up the sizes of the individual files. The addition of other algorithms (see Sect. 2) was prevented by the non-availability of their implementation or their reported poor compression ratio.

5.4 Results

Figure 4 shows the compression ratios achieved by the different algorithms. To compare the compression ratios across the different datasets, we use a one-tailed Wilcoxon signed-rank test for a pairwise comparison of the compression algorithms. Table 2 lists

---

[4] The datasets can be found at https://w3id.org/dice-research/data/rdfrepair/evaluation_datasets/. For scholarly data (DF0–DF9), we use the rich datasets (see http://www.scholarlydata.org/dumps/).

[5] https://github.com/rdfhdt/hdt-java.

[6] HDT++ is available at https://github.com/antonioillera/iHDTpp-src. OFR is not publicly available. However, the authors were so kind to provide us the binaries.

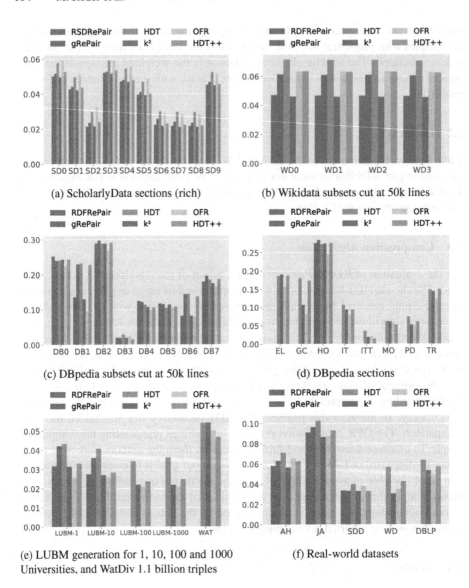

(a) ScholarlyData sections (rich)

(b) Wikidata subsets cut at 50k lines

(c) DBpedia subsets cut at 50k lines

(d) DBpedia sections

(e) LUBM generation for 1, 10, 100 and 1000
Universities, and WatDiv 1.1 billion triples

(f) Real-world datasets

Fig. 4. Compression ratio for the compression algorithms on the single datasets. Smaller values are better.

the p-values of the tests. These results suggest that RDFRePair leads to significantly better compression ratios than the original prototypical gRePair implementation. However, RDFRePair is significantly outperformed by k^2 and OFR. The prototypical implementation of gRePair is outperformed by all other approaches. Overall, OFR and our implementation of the k^2 algorithm lead to the best compression ratios with k^2 performing better on non-synthetic datasets. None of these two algorithms is able to significantly

Table 2. p-value of a one-tailed Wilcoxon signed rank test with respect to compression ratio. A bold value indicates that the algorithm in the row leads to a significantly better compression ratio than the algorithm in the column ($p < \alpha = 0.05$).

$r_1 \setminus r_2$	RDFRePair	gRePair	HDT	k^2	OFR	HDT++
RDFRePair	—	**≈0.0**	0.79	≈1.0	0.99	0.89
gRePair	≈1.0	—	0.95	≈1.0	≈1.0	≈1.0
HDT	0.21	0.05	—	≈1.0	≈1.0	≈1.0
k^2	**≈0.0**	**≈0.0**	**≈0.0**	—	0.51	**≈0.0**
OFR	**0.01**	**≈0.0**	**≈0.0**	0.49	—	0.07
HDT++	0.11	**≈0.0**	**≈0.0**	≈1.0	0.93	—

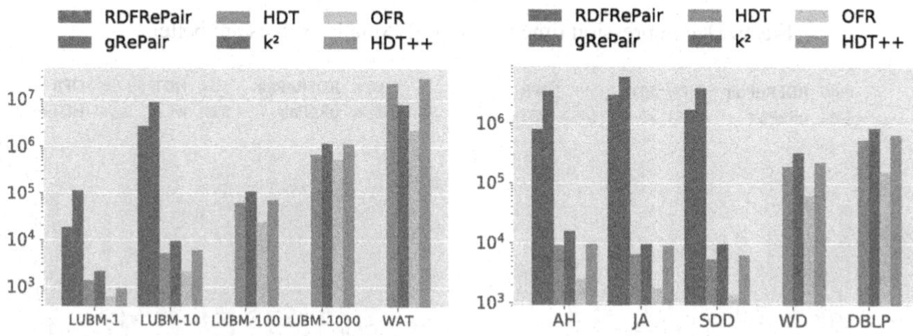

(a) LUBM generation for 1, 10, 100 and 1000 Universities, and WatDiv 1.1 billion triples

(b) Real-world datasets

Fig. 5. Compression time in ms (log). Smaller values are better.

outperform the other one with respect to the compression ratio. Our findings contradict the results of Maneth et al. [13] that gRePair performs better than k^2.

OFR has the shortest runtime w.r.t. compression and decompression time (depicted in Figs. 5 and 6). It is followed by HDT and HDT++. k^2 shows a longer runtime than these three algorithms. The prototypical implementation of gRePair is the slowest algorithm. In addition, gRePair and RDFRePair were not able to compress 12 of the 40 datasets within 2 h, respectively.

Figure 7 depicts the amount of space used to store the compressed dictionary in comparison to the overall size of the compressed dataset. 5 of the 6 approaches share a similar dictionary implementation based on [8]. For all these approaches, the dictionary consumes the majority of the space. Especially for the k^2 compression, the average size of the dictionary over all datasets is 80%. In comparison, the OFR dictionary achieves smaller dictionary sizes on some of the datasets. This suggests that improvements to the dictionary can lead to much better compression ratios for HDT, HDT++ and k^2.

The correlation analysis reveals that all algorithms have a correlation between their performance and the number of classes. However, this seems to be an indirect relation that is caused by the datasets that contain solely one-to-one mappings like

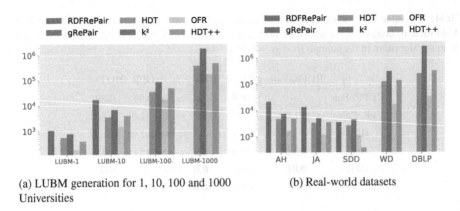

(a) LUBM generation for 1, 10, 100 and 1000 Universities

(b) Real-world datasets

Fig. 6. Decompression time in ms (log). Smaller values are better.

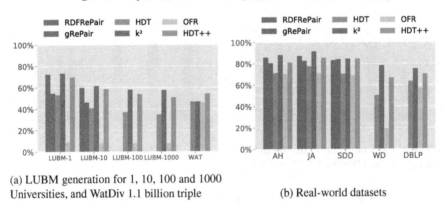

(a) LUBM generation for 1, 10, 100 and 1000 Universities, and WatDiv 1.1 billion triple

(b) Real-world datasets

Fig. 7. Size of the dictionary in comparison to the compressed dataset size in %.

DB0 or EL. These datasets have no classes and are hard to compress because of their one-to-one structure. Neither the SPS nor the structuredness metric show any significant correlations.

The results show that RDFRePair underachieves. A further analysis reveals that the optimization described in Sect. 4.4, i.e., to store the IDs of internal nodes implicitly by renumbering all nodes in the graph, is one of the major features of gRePair.[7] This leads to very good results in the evaluation done by Maneth et al. [13]. This optimization seems to contradict the statement that a dictionary compression as proposed by Martínez-Prieto et al. [14] can be used (see Sect. 4.1) since the dictionary compression needs to allow the gRePair algorithm to freely redefine the IDs of all nodes. However, Martínez-Prieto et al. separate the space of node IDs into several ranges. Based on the role of a node in the graph, it has to receive an ID of a certain range. This allows different indexing and compression strategies for the different ranges. However, such a

---

[7] For a fair comparison, we turned this feature of gRePair in our evaluation off. Otherwise, it couldn't be used with the HDT dictionary.

Table 3. Values of Kendall's Tau rank correlation between compression ratio and dataset metrics. A bold value indicates a significant correlation ($\alpha = 0.02$). * only experiments that terminated in time were taken into account.

	RDFRePair*	gRePair*	HDT	k^2	OFR	HDT++
#Triples	0.27	0.32	0.17	0.13	0.03	0.11
#Classes	**−0.47**	**−0.57**	**−0.51**	**−0.50**	**−0.43**	**−0.52**
#UriResources	0.23	0.27	0.17	0.13	0.04	0.10
#Resources	**0.37**	**0.40**	0.24	0.20	0.12	0.17
#Properties	−0.17	−0.13	−0.22	−0.24	−0.15	−0.19
SPS	0.09	0.14	0.06	0.00	−0.01	0.04
Structuredness	−0.20	−0.24	−0.21	−0.18	−0.30	−0.21

node can not get an ID assigned by gRePair. We measured the amount of space the internal nodes consume. Especially for type graphs with a simple structure (e.g., DB4) the internal nodes consume up to 98% of the memory of the compressed triples (i.e., the memory of the compressed dataset without the dictionary). We call this the *internal node size ratio*. The datasets used by Maneth et al. [13] seem to favor the usage of digrams. Two out of the six datasets have an internal node size ratio of 99% while three other datasets have ratios of more than 50%. In our evaluation, the majority of datasets has an internal node size ratio below 50%. More diverse datasets like SD0–SD9 have ratios between 9% and 16%. Even without storing internal nodes, RDFRePair and gRePair would still show a lower performance than k^2 trees for such datasets but with the cost of a dictionary that may less optimized for querying and compression.

6 Conclusion

This paper presented several contributions. First, we presented RDFRePair—an improved implementation of the gRePair algorithm ported to the compression of RDF graphs. Second, we present an efficient implementation of the k^2 trees for the same goal. Third, we ran a large-scale evaluation comparing RDFRePair and k^2 with HDT, HDT++, OFR and a prototypical implementation of gRePair. Our results could not support the assumption that grammar-based compressions like gRePair are able to outperform existing RDF graph compressions. Instead, our results suggest that in most cases the best compression ratio of RDF datasets can be achieved by using either k^2 trees or OFR with k^2 trees performing best on average when faced with real data. On the other hand, OFR clearly shows a better runtime performance. There are existing implementations for executing SPARQL queries on k^2 trees while an implementation for the query execution for OFR is missing. During the analysis of our results, we couldn't identify significant correlations between the compressor's performance and the features of the datasets. However, our results suggest that future work may focus on further improving the dictionary since it consumes the majority of the space.

Acknowledgements. This work has been supported by the German Federal Ministry for Economic Affairs and Energy (BMWi) within the project SPEAKER under the grant no

01MK20011U and by the EU H2020 Marie Skłodowska-Curie project KnowGraphs under the grant agreement no 860801.

References

1. Álvarez-García, S., Brisaboa, N., Fernández, J.D., Martínez-Prieto, M.A., Navarro, G.: Compressed vertical partitioning for efficient RDF management. Knowl. Inf. Syst. **44**(2), 439–474 (2014). https://doi.org/10.1007/s10115-014-0770-y
2. Álvarez-García, S., Brisaboa, N.R., Fernández, J.D., MartíÂnez-Prieto, M.A.: Compressed k^2-Triples for Full-In-Memory RDF Engines. In: AMCIS 2011 Proceedings. IEEE (2011)
3. Beckett, D., Berners-Lee, T., Prud'hommeaux, E., Carothers, G.: RDF 1.1 Turtle. W3C Recommendation, W3C (February 2014)
4. Berners-Lee, T.: Primer: Getting into RDF & Semantic Web Using N3. Technical Report **W3C**, (October 2010)
5. Brisaboa, N.R., Ladra, S., Navarro, G.: k 2-trees for compact web graph representation. In: International Symposium on String Processing and Information Retrieval (2009)
6. Duan, S., Kementsietsidis, A., Srinivas, K., Udrea, O.: Apples and oranges: a comparison of RDF benchmarks and real RDF datasets. In: Proceedings of the 2011 ACM SIGMOD International Conference on Management of Data (SIGMOD 2011), pp. 145–156. ACM (2011)
7. Fernández, J.D., Gutierrez, C., Martínez-Prieto, M.A.: RDF compression: basic approaches. In: Proceedings of the 19th International Conference on World Wide Web (2010)
8. Fernández, J.D., Gutierrez, C., Martínez-Prieto, M.A, Polleres, A., Arias, M.: Binary RDF Representation for Publication and Exchange (HDT). Web Semant. Sci. Serv. Agents World Wide Web **19**, 22–41 (2013)
9. Gayathri, V., Kumar, P.S.: Horn-rule based compression technique for RDF data. In: Proceedings of the 30th Annual ACM Symposium on Applied Computing (SAC 2015), pp. 396–401. Association for Computing Machinery, New York (2015)
10. Hernández-Illera, A., Martínez-Prieto, M.A., Fernández, J.D.: Serializing RDF in compressed space. In: 2015 Data Compression Conference, pp. 363–372. IEEE (2015)
11. Hitzler, P., Krötzsch, M., Rudolph, S., Sure, Y.: Semantic Web: Grundlagen. Springer (2007). 10.1007/978-3-319-93417-4
12. Joshi, A.K., Hitzler, P., Dong, G.: Logical linked data compression. In: Cimiano, P., Corcho, O., Presutti, V., Hollink, L., Rudolph, S. (eds.) ESWC 2013. LNCS, vol. 7882, pp. 170–184. Springer, Heidelberg (2013). https://doi.org/10.1007/978-3-642-38288-8_12
13. Maneth, S., Peternek, F.: Grammar-based graph compression. Inf. Syst. **76**, 19–45 (2018)
14. Martínez-Prieto, M.A., Fernández, J.D., Cánovas, R.: Compression of RDF dictionaries. In: Proceedings of the 27th Annual ACM Symposium on Applied Computing (SAC 2012), pp. 340–347. Association for Computing Machinery, New York (2012). https://doi.org/10.1145/2245276.2245343
15. Pan, J.Z., Pérez, J.M.G., Ren, Y., Wu, H., Wang, H., Zhu, M.: Graph pattern based RDF data compression. In: Supnithi, T., Yamaguchi, T., Pan, J.Z., Wuwongse, V., Buranarach, M. (eds.) JIST 2014. LNCS, vol. 8943, pp. 239–256. Springer, Cham (2015). https://doi.org/10.1007/978-3-319-15615-6_18
16. Salomon, D.: Data Compression: The Complete Reference. Springer, New York (2004). 10.1007/b97635
17. Swacha, J., Grabowski, S.: OFR: an efficient representation of RDF datasets. In: Languages, Applications and Technologies. pp. 224–235. Springer International Publishing (2015)
18. Wang, K., Fu, H., Peng, S., Gong, Y., Gu, J.: A RDF data compress model based on octree structure. In: 2017 12th IEEE Conference on Industrial Electronics and Applications (ICIEA). pp. 990–994 (2017)

HDT Bitmap Triple Indices for Efficient RDF Data Exploration

Maximilian Wenzel[1(✉)], Thorsten Liebig[2(✉)], and Birte Glimm[1(✉)]

[1] Institute of Artificial Intelligence, University of Ulm, Ulm, Germany
{maximilian.wenzel,birte.glimm}@uni-ulm.de
[2] derivo GmbH, Ulm, Germany
liebig@derivo.de

Abstract. The exploration of large, unknown RDF data sets is difficult even for users who are familiar with Semantic Web technologies as, e.g., the SPARQL query language. The concept of faceted navigation offers a user-friendly exploration method through filters that are chosen such that no empty result sets occur. Computing such filters is resource intensive, especially for large data sets, and may cause considerable delays in the user interaction. One possibility for improving the performance is the generation of indices for partial solutions. In this paper, we propose and evaluate indices in form of the Bitmap Triple (BT) data structure, generated over the Header-Dictionary-Triples (HDT) RDF compression format. We show that the resulting indices can be utilized to efficiently compute the required exploratory operations for data sets with up to 150 million triples. In the experiments, the BT indices exhibit a stable performance and outperform other deployed approaches in four out of five compared operations.

1 Introduction

Exploring large data sets is increasingly important in many scenarios. In the context of Semantic Web technologies, however, the exploration of a large, unfamiliar RDF data set can be very challenging, in particular, for novice users of Semantic Web technologies. Faceted navigation is an approach to ease the exploration process by providing users with filters for a given set of resources such that it is guaranteed that applying the filters yields a non-empty result.

Several approaches and systems support faceted navigation: *Ontogator* [9], */facet* [8], and *BrowseRDF* [15] are among the first text-based, faceted browsers, where the latter provides metrics for an automatic ranking for the available filters. *GraFa* [13] targets large-scale, heterogeneous RDF graphs and employs a materialisation strategy and a full-text index for queries to improve the response time. The browsers *SemFacet* [2,10] and *Broccoli* [3] support faceted search, i.e., they combine faceted navigation with full-text search. Apart from text-based faceted browsers, there are also graph-based visualisation systems such as *gFacet* [7] and *SemSpect* [11].

The operations needed for faceted navigation are, however, very costly, especially for large data sets. To improve the performance of the required operations,

© Springer Nature Switzerland AG 2021
R. Verborgh et al. (Eds.): ESWC 2021, LNCS 12731, pp. 109–125, 2021.
https://doi.org/10.1007/978-3-030-77385-4_7

most (if not all) of the above systems use indices. Sometimes, such indices require, however, even more space than the original data set. Therefore, the development of techniques for keeping such indices as small as possible is of great importance. An established compression format for RDF data is *Header-Dictionary-Triples* (HDT) [5,12], where each resource of the data set is assigned a unique integer ID in a dictionary component. These IDs are then used to generate a compressed representation of all RDF triples in a binary data structure called *Bitmap Triples* (BT). HDT further has the advantage that triple patterns can efficiently be resolved over the BT data structure.

In this work, we propose two BT indices on top of an HDT file for efficiently executing the operations required in faceted navigation. For this, we extend the original BT definition to allow for representing BT indices over subsets of the original RDF graph. An exploration over a given HDT file is especially useful since the HDT format is intended to be an exchange format for RDF data sets. Therefore, using an exchanged HDT file as a basis for a faceted navigation back end might be practical in order to get an overview of an initially unknown data set. In an empirical evaluation, we demonstrate that the generation of these indices is feasible for data sets with up to 150 million triples and that the time and space needed for generating the indices is less than what is required for generating the original HDT file. Based on the indices, a stable and consistently improved performance can be observed compared to executing the operations over the HDT file itself and other in-memory triple stores.

Section 2 introduces the concept of and operations needed for faceted navigation as well as the fundamentals of the HDT format. Section 3 then introduces the novel BT indices and their use in the required exploratory operations. In Sect. 4, we empirically evaluate our approach and other existing approaches over various real-world data sets. Section 5 concludes the paper.

2   Preliminaries

Before going into the details of our proposed indices, we introduce the operations needed for faceted navigation, the basics of Header Dictionary Triples and the Bitmap Triples compression format.

2.1   Faceted Navigation

Faceted navigation is an approach to retrieve data which is organised in facets and facet values. In this paper, we consider faceted navigation over RDF graphs:

Definition 1 (RDF). *Let I, L, and B be pairwise disjoint infinite sets of IRIs, literals, and blank nodes, respectively. A tuple $(s, p, o) \in (I \cup B) \times I \times (I \cup L \cup B)$ is called an RDF triple, where s is the subject, p is the predicate, and o is the object. An RDF graph G is a finite set of RDF triples. We set $S_G = \{s \mid (s, p, o) \in G\}$, $P_G = \{p \mid (s, p, o) \in G\}$, $O_G = \{o \mid (s, p, o) \in G\}$.*

Fig. 1. Screenshot of the GraFa [13] application. Proceeding from an initial class, the user refines the set of instances by the step-wise selection of available filters.

Given an RDF graph G, we define the set C_G of classes as containing all resources C such that G RDFS-entails the triple $(C, rdf: type, rdfs: Class)$. We say that a resource s has type C if G RDFS-entails the triple $(s, rdf: type, C)$ and the instances of a class C are all resources that have the type C in G.

In the context of faceted search, for a triple $(s, p, o) \in G$, we also call p a facet, and we call s and o facet values.

We normally omit "RDF" in our terminology if no confusion is likely and we abbreviate IRIs using the prefixes *rdf*, *rdfs*, and *owl* to refer to the RDF, RDFS, and OWL namespaces, respectively.

The initial step in the faceted exploration of a graph is to filter resources according to classes. Once a user has chosen a class, the instances of the class constitute the *centre* of the exploration. This centre is then step-by-step refined by applying filters.

Definition 2 (Filters). *Let G be an RDF graph, a centre $M \subseteq S_G \cup O_G$ w.r.t. G is a subset of the resources in G.*

Let V be a countably infinite set of variables *disjoint from $I \cup L \cup B$. In order to distinguish variables from resources, we prefix variables with a ?. A* triple pattern *is a member of the set $(I \cup B \cup V) \times (I \cup V) \times (I \cup L \cup B \cup V)$.*

An incoming property-value filter *is a triple pattern of the form $(s, p, ?o)$, while an* outgoing property-value filter *is of the form $(?s, p, o)$. Given a centre M w.r.t. G, applying the property-value filters $(s, p, ?o)$ and $(?s, p, o)$ to M yields $\{o \mid o \in M, (s, p, o) \in G\}$ and $\{s \mid s \in M, (s, p, o) \in G\}$, respectively.*

A property filter *is a triple pattern of the form $(?s, p, ?o)$. Applying $(?s, p, ?o)$ to a centre M yields a set of* incoming resources $M_p^{\rightarrow} = \{s \mid o \in M, (s, p, o) \in G\}$ *and a set of* outgoing resources $M_p^{\leftarrow} = \{o \mid s \in M, (s, p, o) \in G\}$.

Given a centre M w.r.t. G, a filter f is available, *if applying f over M yields a non-empty result.*

In faceted navigation, only available filters must be presented to the user. The above defined notions and operations are used, for example, in the application GraFa [13] as shown in Fig. 1.

Fig. 2. Excerpt from the SemSpect [1] application exploring the Panama Papers data set. (1) A user selects an initial class (in SemSpect denoted as "category"), which then represents the *centre*. (2) Proceeding from the *centre*, all reachable classes are computed. (3) The user chooses one of the reachable classes which subsequently constitutes the new *centre*.

Since the exploration is also often based on classes and their instances, which are then filtered, another important concept is that of *reachable classes*:

Definition 3 (Reachable Classes). *Let G be an RDF graph and M a centre. A class C induces a set of* incoming (outgoing) *facets $\{p \mid (s,p,o) \in G, s \in M, o \text{ has type } C\}$ ($\{p \mid (s,p,o) \in G, o \in M, s \text{ has type } C\}$) w.r.t. M. We say that C is an* incoming (outgoing) reachable class *w.r.t. M, if the induced set of incoming (outgoing) facets is non-empty.*

If the direction (incoming/outgoing) is clear from the context, we simply speak about reachable classes.

From a centre M, a user may choose a reachable class C and an appropriate facet p to continue the exploration. As a result, an *incremental join operation* is performed to join the incoming (outgoing) resources with the instances of the class C. Subsequently, this set becomes the new centre. From there, the available filters and the reachable classes are computed again.

As an example for the reachable classes and incremental join operation, an excerpt from the application SemSpect [1] is shown in Fig. 2.

2.2 RDF Compression

Traditional RDF serialisation formats (e.g., RDF/XML, Turtle, or N3) have a high level of redundancy and a simple lookup requires a sequential scan of the document. The binary Header Dictionary Triples (HDT) [5,12] format addresses these shortcomings by providing a compressed triple structure that can be queried without the need of decompression. An HDT file is composed of three parts: (i) the *Header* provides metadata about the data set in plain RDF format, (ii) the *Dictionary* provides a mapping between strings and unique IDs, and (iii) the *Triples* encode the RDF graph using IDs. We next consider the concrete implementation of the dictionary and the triples component in more detail as they constitute the basis of the proposed indices.

Definition 4 (HDT). *Let $SO_G = S_G \cap O_G$ denote the set of shared resources, $S_{pure} = S_G \setminus SO_G$ the set of pure subjects, and $O_{pure} = O_G \setminus SO_G$ the set of pure objects. For a set S, we use $\overline{S}$ to denote the lexicographic order of elements in S.*

The HDT dictionary *provides a mapping μ such that μ maps a resource r_i at position i (starting with position 1) of a list L to i if $L = \overline{SO_G}$, to $|SO_G| + i$ if $L = \overline{S_{pure}}$, to $|SO_G| + i$ if $L = \overline{O_{pure}}$, and to i if $L = \overline{P_G}$.*

Note that a given ID can belong to different sets, but the disambiguation of the correct set is trivial when we know the position (subject, predicate, or object) of the ID in a triple. Furthermore, the distinction into four sets helps to assign shorter IDs since the entries are stored in a binary sequence, where the length of the sequence depends on the maximal used ID. The ID 0 is reserved as a wildcard character in triple ID queries. The dictionary is eventually stored using *plain front-coding* [4] – a compression format for lexicographically sorted dictionaries based on the fact that consecutive entries are likely to share a common prefix.

The *Triples component* uses the assigned IDs to form a compressed representation of a graph G using the Plain Triples, Compact Triples or Bitmap Triples [5] format.

Definition 5 (Plain Triples). *Given an RDF graph G, the* Plain Triples *representation* $\mathsf{PT}(G)$ *of G is obtained by replacing each triple $(s, p, o) \in G$ with $(\mu(s), \mu(p), \mu(o))$, where μ is the HDT dictionary mapping.*

The *Compact Triples* representation of G is obtained from $\mathsf{PT}(G)$ based on adjacency lists of predicates and objects for the subjects:

Definition 6 (Compact Triples). *For a subject ID s in the plain triples format $\mathsf{PT}(G)$ of an RDF graph G, $\mathsf{pred}(s)$ denotes the ordered sequence of predicate IDs in $\{p \mid (s, p, o) \in \mathsf{PT}(G)\}$; for a subject ID s and a predicate ID p in $\mathsf{PT}(G)$, $\mathsf{obj}(s, p)$ denotes the ordered sequence of object IDs in $\{o \mid (s, p, o) \in \mathsf{PT}(G)\}$.*

Let $s_1, \ldots, s_n$ be the ordered sequence of distinct subject IDs in $\mathsf{PT}(G)$. The Compact Triples *encoding $\mathsf{CT}(G)$ of G consists of two ID sequences: The predicate sequence $S_p = \mathsf{pred}(s_1)0 \ldots 0\mathsf{pred}(s_n)$ and the objects sequence $S_o = S_o^1 \ldots S_o^n$, where each partial object sequence S_o^i, $1 \le i \le n$, is the concatenation $\mathsf{obj}(s_i, p_1)0 \ldots 0\mathsf{obj}(s_i, p_m)0$ and $p_1, \ldots, p_m = \mathsf{pred}(s_i)$.*

Note that the unused ID 0 is used to terminate predicate and object sequences. The *Bitmap Triples* representation of G is obtained from $\mathsf{CT}(G)$ by further compressing the lists with the help of additional bitmap sequences:

Definition 7 (Bitmap Triples). *Let G be an RDF graph and $\mathsf{CT}(G)$ its compact triples representation such that $S_p = S_p^1 0 \ldots 0 S_p^n$ and $S_o = S_o^1 0 \ldots 0 S_o^m$ are the predicate and object sequence of $\mathsf{CT}(G)$, respectively. Let ℓ_p^i and ℓ_o^j denote the length of S_p^i and S_o^j, $1 \le i \le n$, $1 \le j \le m$, respectively.*

The Bitmap Triples *encoding $\mathsf{BT}(G)$ of G consists of two ID sequences $\hat{S}_p = S_p^1 \ldots S_p^n$ and $\hat{S}_o = S_o^1 \ldots S_o^m$, obtained from S_p and S_o by dropping the 0s, and two bit sequences B_p and B_o such that the length of B_p and B_o is the same as the length of $\hat{S}_p$ and $\hat{S}_o$, respectively, and the value at position pos in B_p (B_o) is 1 if $pos = \ell_p^1 + \ldots + \ell_p^i$ for some i, $1 \le i \le n$, ($pos = \ell_o^1 + \ldots + \ell_o^j$, for some j, $1 \le j \le m$) and it is 0 otherwise.*

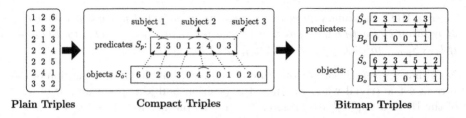

Fig. 3. Example for the compressed triple formats from Fernandez et al. [5]

Figure 3, from an example introduced by Fernandez et al. [5], illustrates the different formats. While we omit the dictionary component, the Plain Triples show that the IDs $1 \ldots 3$ are subject IDs and that the ID 1 denotes a shared resource as it also occurs in the object position. The further (pure) objects have the IDs $2 \ldots 6$. The IDs $1 \ldots 4$ also represent predicates. The subject 1 is used with the (distinct) predicates 2 and 3, hence, pred(1) is 23. Analogously, pred(2) = 124 and pred(3) = 3. In S_p these sequences are separated by a 0 and S_o analogously encodes the objects for each subject–predicate pair. In the Bitmap Triples encoding, the sequences $\hat{S}_p$ and $\hat{S}_o$ simply drop any 0 from S_p and S_o. The bit sequence B_p tells us with a value of 1, when a sequence in $\hat{S}_p$ ends, i.e., the first sequence 23 (of length 2) ends at (and including) position 2. The following sequence 124 (of length 3) starts at position 3 and the next 1 at position 5 $(2 + 3)$ of B_p indicates the end of the sequence. The bit sequence B_o analogously terminates the sequences in $\hat{S}_o$.

HDT is not merely a compression format but also provides the efficient resolution of triple patterns on the compressed representation of an RDF graph by deploying succinct data structures for the BT implementation [5]. SP-O index queries can be efficiently accomplished in $O(log(n))$, i.e., the triple patterns (s, p, o), $(s, p, 0)$, $(s, 0, o)$ and $(s, 0, 0)$ can be resolved, where 0 denotes a wildcard match and s, p, o represent resource IDs at the corresponding triple position. For other triple patterns, the so far discussed solutions do not suffice and Martínez-Prieto et al. [12], therefore, introduced a compact full-index called *HDT Focused on Querying (FoQ)*, which is created over the original HDT file and which consists of a further PS-O and OP-S index.

3   Faceted Navigation Indices Based on HDT BT

In order to efficiently compute the available filters, reachable classes, filter operations and the corresponding incremental joins as described in Sect. 2, we propose the use of additional (in-memory) BT indices over *subsets* of the original RDF data set. Therefore, in order to represent only a sub-graph, an adaptation of the original Bitmap Triples format (Definition 7) is needed. We illustrate this for the standard SP-O triple component order, but the approach can analogously be transferred to the PO-S and PS-O BT indices. We decided against self-indexing individual triples in the Bitmap Triples component of the HDT file because we need to perform efficient triple pattern queries on the subgraphs

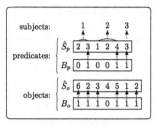
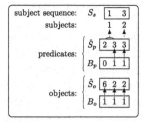

Bitmap Triples   **Partial BT SP-O Index**

Fig. 4. Bitmap triples from the example in Fig. 3 (left-hand side) and for the sub-graph containing triples with subject IDs 1 and 3 (right-hand side) with the additional subject sequence S_s to obtain the original subject IDs

in the triple component order PO-S and PS-O. For instance, in case of triple pattern queries $(?s, p, o)$, the self-indexing approach does not require less space since these patterns can only be efficiently resolved by indexing all subjects for the appropriate predicate-object pairs.

Definition 8 (Partial BT SP-O Index). *Let G be an RDF graph and $G' \subseteq G$ a sub-graph of G. A partial BT index for G' consists of $\mathsf{BT}(G')$ and the ID sequence $S_s = s_1 \cdots s_n$, where $s_1, \ldots, s_n$ is the ordered sequence of distinct subject IDs in $\mathsf{PT}(G')$.*

For an SP-O index over a sub-graph G' of an RDF graph G, the implicit subject ID, which is stored by the bit sequence B_p, does not correspond to the actual subject dictionary ID of the original HDT file. Therefore, the additional ID sequence S_s indicates the actual subject ID from the dictionary to each implicit subject ID.

Figure 4 shows again the Bitmap triples from Fig. 3 (left-hand side) and the Bitmap Triples for the sub-graph containing only triples with subject IDs 1 and 3. The additional subject sequence S_s is used to obtain the original subject IDs for the HDT mapping.

In order to resolve triple patterns of the form $(s, 0, 0)$ (with 0 as wildcard) on a partial SP-O BT index, the subject ID s is first converted into the implicit subject ID of the corresponding partial BT index. For this purpose a binary search operation is executed on the sequence S_s to obtain the position of s in S_s, which corresponds to the implicit subject ID in the bit sequence B_p of $\mathsf{BT}(G')$. Afterwards, the resolution of triple patterns involves the same steps as for the standard Bitmap Triples [12]. However, when iterating over the results from a search over a partial BT index, each subject ID s_r from the search results has to be converted into the appropriate subject ID s_e over the full graph, which can be accomplished by the simple *access* operation $s_e := S_s[s_r]$.

Based on our definition of partial BT indices, we propose the use of two additional (in-memory) BT indices: *Property-Value* and *Class-to-Class* indices.

Definition 9 (Property-Value Index). *Let G be an RDF graph with $C \in C_G$ a class. An* incoming property value (PV) index w.r.t. C *is a partial PS-O BT index over $\{(s, p, o) \in G \mid o$ has type $C\}$. An* outgoing PV index w.r.t. C *is a PO-S BT index over $\{(s, p, o) \in G \mid s$ has type $C\}$.*

Table 1. Data sets utilised in the experiments

Data Set	RDF Dump File (.ttl)	#Triples	#Classes
LinkedMDB[a]	282 MB	3,579,532	41
Lobbying filings[b]	306 MB	5,344,200	7
Panama papers[c]	1,140 MB	19,903,231	18
Reactome[d]	1,350 MB	48,556,891	82
SciGraph[e]	8,500 MB	39,692,376	20
YAGO 2[f]	9,920 MB	158,991,568	373,442
OpenPermID[g]	11,470 MB	152,527,813	21

[a] http://www.cs.toronto.edu/~oktie/linkedmdb/linkedmdb-18-05-2009-dump.nt.
[b] We are not authorized to publish the data set in RDF format. REST API for XML download: https://lda.senate.gov/api/. Accessed 15 Oct 2019.
[c] https://doi.org/10.5281/zenodo.4319930.
[d] https://doi.org/10.5281/zenodo.4415888.
[e] https://www.springernature.com/gp/researchers/scigraph.
[f] http://yago.r2.enst.fr/.
[g] https://permid.org/.

In order to efficiently calculate all available filters and the filter operations, we generate incoming and outgoing PV indices for all classes in an RDF graph. In case of the incoming and outgoing PV indices, the PS-O and the PO-S triple component order has been chosen, respectively, to fetch all relevant triples for a given incoming property-value filter $(s, p, ?o)$ and outgoing property-value filter $(?s, p, o)$, respectively.

In order to efficiently compute reachable classes, we further propose Class-to-Class indices:

Definition 10 (Class-to-Class Index). *Let G be an RDF graph with $C, D \in C_G$ classes. A Class-to-Class (CtC) index w.r.t. C and D is a partial PS-O BT index over $\{(s, p, o) \in G \mid s$ has type C, o has type $D\}$.*

We generate CtC indices for each pair of classes $C, D \in C_G$. The PS-O triple component order facilitates the computation of incremental join operations between instances of the classes C and D since all existing triples in the corresponding index can efficiently be retrieved for a given facet p.

4   Implementation and Evaluation

We next present the empirical evaluation of the proposed additional BT indices. We start by describing used data sets as well as the time and space required to create and store the proposed BT indices for these data sets. We then introduce the different benchmarked approaches and the queries and tasks used in the evaluation before we present the actual results.

All presented experiments were conducted on an Intel(R) Core(TM) i7-3930K CPU @ 3.20 GHz, 6 cores, 64 GB DDR3 @ 1334 MHz.

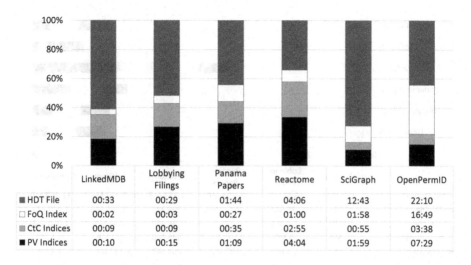

	LinkedMDB	Lobbying Filings	Panama Papers	Reactome	SciGraph	OpenPermID
■ HDT File	00:33	00:29	01:44	04:06	12:43	22:10
□ FoQ Index	00:02	00:03	00:27	01:00	01:58	16:49
▨ CtC Indices	00:09	00:09	00:35	02:55	00:55	03:38
■ PV Indices	00:10	00:15	01:09	04:04	01:59	07:29

Fig. 5. Time required for generating the representations (format mm:ss)

4.1   Data Sets and Index Generation

The (partial) BT indices were implemented in Java with the HDT Java library[1] as foundation and the code is available on GitHub as open-source project.[2] Since our implementation does not support RDFS-entailment, the required inferences (for types of the resources) are materialised upfront using RDFox [14]. For each RDF file, we generate an HDT file, which serves as the basis for the CtC and PV indices. Note that RDF classes, which do not contribute to the semantic domain of the RDF model such as *rdfs:Resource*, are not considered in the indices.

In order to get an impression of the required generation time and resulting file size, the proposed BT indices have been generated for various data sets (see Table 1). For the YAGO 2 data set, the CtC and PV indices could not be generated because of insufficient main memory capacity for the high number of distinct RDF classes.

In Fig. 5, the time required to generate all CtC and PV indices is compared to the time needed to create the HDT file and the compact HDT Focused on Querying (FoQ) full-index [12]. Figure 6 shows the size of the BT indices compared to the size of the original RDF dump file, the HDT file and the HDT FoQ index. Neither the time for generating the CtC nor the PV index exceeds the time for generating the HDT file on any data set. The files that are utilised in an actual faceted exploration, i.e., the PV, CtC, and FoQ indices and the HDT file,

---

[1] https://github.com/rdfhdt/hdt-java.
[2] https://github.com/MaximilianWenzel/hdt-bt-indices-java-lib.

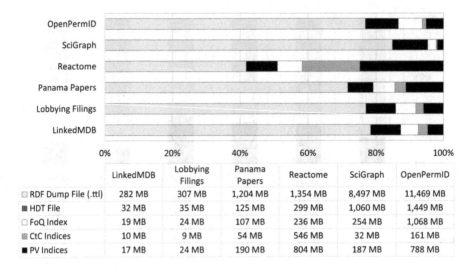

	LinkedMDB	Lobbying Filings	Panama Papers	Reactome	SciGraph	OpenPermID
☐ RDF Dump File (.ttl)	282 MB	307 MB	1,204 MB	1,354 MB	8,497 MB	11,469 MB
■ HDT File	32 MB	35 MB	125 MB	299 MB	1,060 MB	1,449 MB
☐ FoQ Index	19 MB	24 MB	107 MB	236 MB	254 MB	1,068 MB
■ CtC Indices	10 MB	9 MB	54 MB	546 MB	32 MB	161 MB
■ PV Indices	17 MB	24 MB	190 MB	804 MB	187 MB	788 MB

Fig. 6. File size comparison of the various representations

require between 18–30% of the Turtle file size in five out of six data sets. Only for the Reactome data set, 139% of the Turtle file size is needed which is due to the high interconnectivity, i.e., the high number of triples $t = (s, p, o)$ where s and o have an RDF class assigned. The consumed storage space subsequently corresponds to the required main memory capacity during an exploration.

4.2   Performance Benchmark Setup

We consider the following approaches in the experimental evaluation:

1. *HDT Jena:* The Jena ARQ query engine[3] used over an HDT file.
2. *RDFox:* The commercial, in-memory triple store RDFox [14].
3. *Plain HDT:* Our implementation using only the original HDT file and the FoQ index.
4. *PV indices:* Our implementation used with PV indices, the HDT file and the FoQ index. The FoQ index is utilized to perform efficient triple pattern queries that enhance the property-value filter and available filter operations if a given centre M has less resources than a threshold θ, which was experimentally determined [16]. For instance, in case of property-value filter operations, $\theta = 5,000$.
5. *CtC indices:* Our implementation used with CtC indices and the HDT file.
6. *Hybrid:* Our implementation used with PV indices, the CtC indices, the HDT file and the FoQ index.

Our evaluation initially also included other triple stores. However, we limit our result presentation to a comparison with RDFox and HDT Jena as these were

---

[3] https://jena.apache.org/documentation/query/index.html.

the best performing systems for the kinds of queries needed in faceted exploration. When interpreting the results, it should be noted that RDFox and HDT
Jena offer full SPARQL 1.1 support and RDFox further supports incremental
reasoning. This is in contrast to our HDT BT indices which are particularly
optimized but also limited to faceted query answering. Our approach also comes
with a single upfront HDT BT indices creation time. For instance, the largest
considered data set, OpenPermID, can be loaded query ready in 93 s into an
RDFox data store, whereas the generation of our CtC and PV indices alone
requires about 11 m.

The used queries and tasks in the experiments are designed to fulfill the
following two requirements: (i) The queries should be representative for the data
set. We use the principle of stratified randomisation to design queries, which
correspond to a specific level of difficulty. Since it was not always possible to
generate sufficient queries for all difficulty levels, the actual number of queries
in an experiment may vary depending on the data set. We comment on this in
the evaluation results. (ii) The queries should be representative for a faceted
navigation scenario. To address this, we use the following query types and tasks
in our benchmark:

1. *Filter queries* apply a sequence of property-value filters to a given centre M.
   Since incoming and outgoing filters require the same computational effort
   using the PV indices, only outgoing filters are considered. As result, all IRIs
   of the resources from the filtered centre are returned. Overall, we consider 1
   to 3 filters over 3 levels of difficulty with 10 queries per difficulty level, where
   the relevant parameters for the difficulty level comprise the size of M and size
   of the result set obtained by applying the filter. Thus, the maximal number
   of evaluated filter queries per data set is $n_{max} = 3 \cdot 3 \cdot 10 = 90$.
2. The task of *computing all available filters* is based on a filter query, which is
   used to initialise a centre M. Relative to this centre, all available incoming
   and outgoing property-value filters are computed. As result, the number of
   distinct facet values for each facet is subsequently returned. Overall, we use
   1 filter over 3 levels of difficulty with 10 queries per difficulty level, i.e., we
   evaluate at most $n_{max} = 30$ task executions per data set.
3. *Class queries* start with a given initial centre M_0 and perform n incremental
   join operations to an incoming or outgoing reachable class. All IRIs of the
   resources from the final centre M_n are subsequently returned. The number
   of joins n corresponds to the number of used facets. The parameters, which
   were considered in the query generation process for the corresponding level
   of difficulty, are again the size of M_0 and, on the other hand, the number
   of triples that participate in the join operations. We evaluate class queries
   that use 1 to 4 joins over 3 levels of difficulty with 10 queries per difficulty
   level, i.e., we evaluate at most $n_{max} = 120$ task executions per data set. The
   incremental join operations are explicitly indicated in the resulting SPARQL
   queries by using nested subqueries with single result variables to lower the
   number of intermediate results and eventually increase the efficiency, i.e., each
   SPARQL query begins with the resulting centre M_n and the preceding class

M_{n-1} is defined in an appropriate subquery which in turn uses a subquery for its respective predecessor M_{n-2} if present.

4. The task of *computing all reachable classes* starts from a centre of resources, obtained using a class query, and computes the reachable classes relative to this centre. The returned result is the number of reachable classes, i.e., the number of incoming and outgoing facets w.r.t a reachable class as described in Definition 3. We use class queries with 1 join over 3 levels of difficulty and 10 queries per difficulty level. Overall, we evaluate at most $n_{max} = 30$ task executions per data set.

5. *Hybrid queries* combine class and filter queries. We obtain a centre M by executing a class query (which requires a series of joins) and then apply a filter query to the obtained centre. All IRIs of the resulting resources are returned. Again, we consider 3 levels of difficulty which coincide with the number of applied filters and the difficulty level of the underlying class query. We evaluate hybrid queries that use 1 to 4 joins over 3 levels of difficulty with 10 queries per difficulty level, i.e., we evaluate at most $n_{max} = 120$ task executions per data set.

Note that all operations in our experiments compute exact results which is of course more expensive than the calculation of partial results. Partial results, however, often increase the scalability of the eventual application, which is observed, for instance, in the SPARQL query builder *SPARKLIS* [6].

The complete execution of an experiment comprises the following steps: First, the query engine is initialised and the queries are loaded from a file into main memory. Second, a warm-up round begins where all queries are executed before the actual experiment. Afterwards, the execution time of all queries is measured in two consecutive rounds and the minimum required time is documented. If a query requires more than ten seconds for the execution, a timeout occurs and is documented correspondingly. A timeout of ten seconds has been chosen because an execution time beyond ten seconds is unreasonable concerning the user-experience in an exploratory setting.

4.3 Experimental Results

In the following sections all results from the experiments are presented. The collected time measurements were evaluated using the programming language R and are summarized by box plots. The value n represents the actual number of queries from each experiment. Recall that not for all difficulty levels sufficiently many queries could be generated and, hence, $n \leq n_{max}$. We present the experimental results of the four largest data sets from Table 1 for which the PV and CtC indices could be generated. The full experimental results and queries are available online [16].

Figure 7 shows the results of the *filter queries*. The PV indices and the Plain HDT approach perform equally well on all data sets – no considerable benefits are obtained using additional PV indices on top of the original HDT file. Apart from a few outliers, e.g., on the Reactome data set, RDFox is the leading approach for the resolution of filter queries with reference to the median since it is the lowest

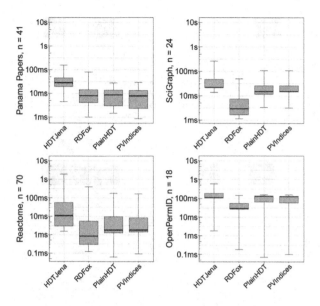

Fig. 7. Results of the filter query experiment

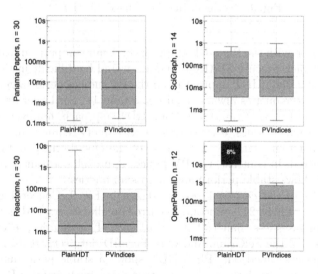

Fig. 8. Results of the available filters experiment

observed on all data sets. RDFox and the Jena ARQ query engine both utilise query planning in contrast to Plain HDT and the PV indices. The performance of our implementation could certainly be improved with additional query planning, which is a topic for future research.

Figure 8 shows the results of the *available filters* experiment. Since the available filters are computed relative to the current *centre*, we only compare the PV

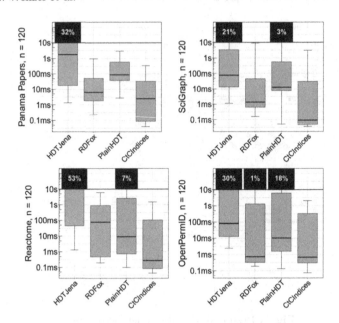

Fig. 9. Results of the class query experiment

indices approach with the Plain HDT approach. A fair comparison with the other approaches, which execute SPARQL queries, would be difficult in this scenario. Apparently, the Plain HDT approach and the PV indices perform generally well in that 50% of the queries always require less than 1 s. For larger data sets such as Reactome and OpenPermID, the Plain HDT approach, however, reveals significant performance issues, where occasionally a query requires more than 5 s in case of the Reactome data set and in case of the OpenPermID data set even a timeout occurred. In contrast, the PV indices approach constantly requires less than 2 s and shows stable performance across all queries.

The results of the *class queries* are shown in Fig. 9. Concerning the HDT Jena approach, at least 21% timeouts occurred on all data sets. Although RDFox requires in all cases less than 1 s for at least 75% of the queries, several outliers appear in case of the SciGraph and OpenPermID data set, where furthermore 1% of the queries timed out. Plain HDT shows a stable performance in case of the Panama Papers data set, but in other cases, such as OpenPermID, 18% timeouts occur and, in sum, about 25% of the queries require more than 5 s for the completion. The CtC indices show an overall stable performance with a maximum required execution time on the SciGraph data set at around 3 s.

In Fig. 10, the results from the *reachable classes* task are presented. Since the reachable classes are computed relative to the current *centre*, we only compare the CtC indices approach with the Plain HDT approach. A fair comparison with the other approaches would be difficult in this scenario. As can be seen, the CtC indices outperform the Plain HDT approach for all data sets. Especially

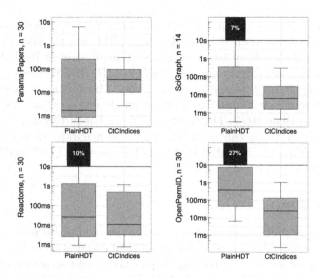

Fig. 10. Results of the reachable classes experiment

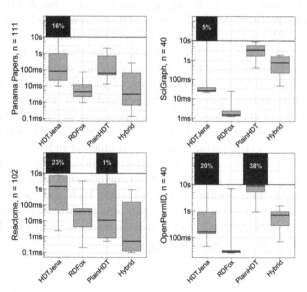

Fig. 11. Results of the hybrid query experiment

concerning the data sets SciGraph, Reactome and OpenPermID, Plain HDT requires in some cases even more than $10\,s$ whereas the CtC indices need at most about $1\,s$ for the execution.

The results of the *hybrid queries* are presented in Fig. 11. Those approaches, which utilise query planing, i.e., the Jena ARQ query engine and RDFox, have evident benefits concerning the resolution of hybrid queries. For instance, in case of RDFox, 75% of the measured times from SciGraph and OpenPermID are considerably lower than those of the Plain HDT and the Hybrid approach. Nevertheless, at least 5% of the queries timed out in case of HDT Jena on all data sets and, in case of Reactome and OpenPermID, RDFox shows a worst case evaluation time of about 3 s and 7 s, respectively. The maximum execution time of the Hybrid approach is considerably lower on all data sets than the maximum time required by Plain HDT. The Hybrid approach has furthermore a worst case evaluation time of 2 s, as can be observed for the SciGraph data set, whereas, e.g., 38% of the queries executed by Plain HDT on the OpenPermID data set led to a time out.

5   Conclusion

In this paper, we propose an approach to generate additional indices on top of the RDF compression format HDT for the efficient exploration of RDF data sets. To achieve this objective, the Bitmap Triples (BT) data structure of the HDT file was extended to a BT index which is able to store subsets of the original RDF graph. In order to cover all required exploratory operations of a faceted navigation scenario, two kinds of BT indices have been introduced, namely the Property-Value (PV) and the Class-to-Class (CtC) indices.

Our evaluation over real-world data sets shows that the generation of the CtC and PV indices is feasible for data sets with up to 150 million triples and 82 RDF classes. Neither the generation time of the PV nor of the CtC indices exceeded the duration for generating the original HDT file. Likewise, the file sizes of the PV and CtC indices do not surpass the original HDT file size.

In the performance benchmark, the CtC indices, the PV indices and the Hybrid approach, i.e., the combination of both kinds of indices, show an overall stable performance for all considered exploratory operations across all data sets with a maximum execution time of 3 s. We conclude that such BT indices represent a significant contribution for the Semantic Web and faceted navigation in particular and that further improvements are possible, when the approach is combined with other optimisations such as query planning and a memory efficient BT indices generation method.

References

1. Semspect by derivo. http://semspect.de/. Accessed 14 Jan 2020
2. Arenas, M., Cuenca Grau, B., Kharlamov, E., Marciuška, Š., Zheleznyakov, D.: Faceted search over RDF-based knowledge graphs. J. Web Semant. **37**, 55–74 (2016)
3. Bast, H., Bäurle, F., Buchhold, B., Haußmann, E.: Easy access to the freebase dataset. In: Proceedings of 23rd International Conference on World Wide Web, pp. 95–98 (2014)
4. Brisaboa, N.R., Cánovas, R., Claude, F., Martínez-Prieto, M.A., Navarro, G.: Compressed string dictionaries. In: Pardalos, P.M., Rebennack, S. (eds.) SEA 2011. LNCS, vol. 6630, pp. 136–147. Springer, Heidelberg (2011). https://doi.org/10.1007/978-3-642-20662-7_12

5. Fernández, J.D., Martínez-Prieto, M.A., Gutiérrez, C., Polleres, A., Arias, M.: Binary RDF representation for publication and exchange (HDT). J. Web Semant. **19**, 22–41 (2013)
6. Ferré, S.: Sparklis: an expressive query builder for SPARQL endpoints with guidance in natural language. Semant. Web **8**(3), 405–418 (2017)
7. Heim, P., Ziegler, J., Lohmann, S.: gFacet: a browser for the web of data. In: Proceedings of International Workshop on Interacting with Multimedia Content in the Social Semantic Web, vol. 417, pp. 49–58. CEUR-WS.org (2008)
8. Hildebrand, M., van Ossenbruggen, J., Hardman, L.: /facet: a browser for heterogeneous semantic web repositories. In: Cruz, I., et al. (eds.) ISWC 2006. LNCS, vol. 4273, pp. 272–285. Springer, Heidelberg (2006). https://doi.org/10.1007/11926078_20
9. Hyvönen, E., Saarela, S., Viljanen, K.: Ontogator: combining view- and ontology-based search with semantic browsing. J. Inf. Retrieval **16**, 17 (2003)
10. Kharlamov, E., Giacomelli, L., Sherkhonov, E., Cuenca Grau, B., Kostylev, E.V., Horrocks, I.: SemFacet: making hard faceted search easier. In: Proceedings of ACM on Conference on Information and Knowledge Management, pp. 2475–2478 (2017)
11. Liebig, T., Vialard, V., Opitz, M.: Connecting the dots in million-nodes knowledge graphs with SemSpect. In: Proceedings of International Semantic Web Conference (Posters, Demos & Industry Tracks) (2017)
12. Martínez-Prieto, M.A., Arias Gallego, M., Fernández, J.D.: Exchange and consumption of huge RDF data. In: Simperl, E., Cimiano, P., Polleres, A., Corcho, O., Presutti, V. (eds.) ESWC 2012. LNCS, vol. 7295, pp. 437–452. Springer, Heidelberg (2012). https://doi.org/10.1007/978-3-642-30284-8_36
13. Moreno-Vega, J., Hogan, A.: GraFa: scalable faceted browsing for RDF graphs. In: Vrandečić, D., et al. (eds.) ISWC 2018. LNCS, vol. 11136, pp. 301–317. Springer, Cham (2018). https://doi.org/10.1007/978-3-030-00671-6_18
14. Nenov, Y., Piro, R., Motik, B., Horrocks, I., Wu, Z., Banerjee, J.: RDFox: a highly-scalable RDF store. In: Arenas, M., et al. (eds.) ISWC 2015. LNCS, vol. 9367, pp. 3–20. Springer, Cham (2015). https://doi.org/10.1007/978-3-319-25010-6_1
15. Oren, E., Delbru, R., Decker, S.: Extending faceted navigation for RDF data. In: Cruz, I., et al. (eds.) ISWC 2006. LNCS, vol. 4273, pp. 559–572. Springer, Heidelberg (2006). https://doi.org/10.1007/11926078_40
16. Wenzel, M.: HDT bitmap triple indices - results of the experiments (Mar 2021). https://doi.org/10.5281/zenodo.4608413

Programming and Debugging
with Semantically Lifted States

Eduard Kamburjan[✉], Vidar Norstein Klungre, Rudolf Schlatte,
Einar Broch Johnsen, and Martin Giese

Department of Informatics, University of Oslo, Oslo, Norway
{eduard,vidarkl,rudi,einarj,martingi}@ifi.uio.no

Abstract. We propose a novel integration of programming languages
with semantic technologies. We create a semantic reflection mechanism
by a direct mapping from program states to RDF knowledge graphs. This
mechanism enables several promising novel applications including the use
of semantic technology, including reasoning, for debugging and validating the sanity of program states, and integration with external knowledge graphs. Additionally, by making the knowledge graph accessible
from the program, method implementations can refer to state semantics
rather than objects, establishing a deep integration between programs
and semantics. This allows the programmer to use domain knowledge
formalized as, e.g., an ontology directly in the program's control flow. We
formalize this integration by defining a core object based programming
language that incorporates these features. A prototypical interpreter is
available for download.

1 Introduction

Knowledge graphs and ontologies are eminently useful representations of formal
knowledge about individuals and universals. They are less suitable for the representation of change, and in particular dynamic behavior. Different approaches
have been proposed that attempt to express program behavior in terms of actions
on a DL interpretation [26] or a DL knowledge base [1]. A recent approach has
combined a guarded command language with DL reasoning [6] to enable probabilistic model checking over the combination. Each of these approaches entails
its own set of technical challenges, and they are also quite different from current
state-of-the-art programming paradigms.

In this work, we present a comparatively simple connection between programs
and knowledge graphs: we give a direct mapping of program states in an object-
based language to an RDF graph, including the running program's objects, fields,
and call stack. An immediate application of this mapping is to use semantic
technology for program debugging, visualisation, querying, validation, reasoning,
etc. In this paper, *semantic debugging* refers to the process of detecting and
correcting conceptual mistakes at the appropriate level of global object access
instead of interacting with only individual objects, as in conventional debuggers.

© Springer Nature Switzerland AG 2021
R. Verborgh et al. (Eds.): ESWC 2021, LNCS 12731, pp. 126–142, 2021.
https://doi.org/10.1007/978-3-030-77385-4_8

The RDF graph can be exposed within the programming language, which adds a semantic reflection layer to the programs. This enables *semantic programming* where the semantic view of the state can be exploited in the program. In particular, it allows one to use the knowledge of the application domain within the program. The programming language can further support a mechanism that extends the RDF graph with triples based on the results of specially designated methods. The approach is implemented and available.

In this work, the RDF graph is close to the object structure, thus representing an *internal domain* of the program. Our long-term goal is to use the same principles for *external domains* that correspond to a program's application domain. This will enable semantic integration between programs as well as linking them to external knowledge graphs and other data sources, thus extending ontology-based data access and integration (see e.g. [9]) to programs and behavioural specifications [13] that allow modeling of complex concurrent systems [16].

Contributions. The contributions of this paper are (1) the concept of interpreting a program state as a knowledge graph to enable semantic state access, (2) the application enabled by this concepts and (3) the SMOL language that implements the concept and exemplifies the applications.

Paper Overview. Section 2 gives a motivating example of mapping program states to an 'internal' knowledge graph. Section 3 gives syntax and semantics of SMOL, the used programming language, and defines the mapping of SMOL program states to RDF graphs. Section 4 extends SMOL with a statement to access its own knowledge graph, thereby adding reflection by semantic state access. Section 5 extends SMOL with a way to add *computed* triples to the knowledge graph. Section 6 describes the implementation, Sect. 7 discusses related work, and Sect. 8 concludes. Further details of this work may be found in an accompanying technical report [17].

2   Motivating Example

We start by giving an example of the use of domain models in programming to demonstrate semantic bugs and motivate semantic programming. Semantic bugs are programming errors that arise from mismatches between the implementation and the domain that is implemented. Such bugs are unlikely to cause immediate runtime errors and are, thus, harder to catch. Instead, they require to examine the program state through a conceptual lens, i.e., in terms of the implemented domain. *Semantic debugging* is the process of detecting and fixing such errors.

The implemented domain can be external or internal. An external domain relates the implementation to some concept outside the program. For example, a class modeling a car that contains a list of its wheels. If the list contains only one element, this is a semantic bug: the object does not represent a car. An internal domain relates the implementation to itself.

Example 1. Consider 2–3 trees [2], a data structure to access key-value pairs. Such trees have three kinds of nodes: leaves have one or two data values and no children, 2-nodes that have one data value and two children and 3-nodes that have two data values and three children. The keys are sorted within the tree; e.g., in a 2-node, all keys below the left child are smaller than the key stored in the node and all below the right child are larger. Listing 1 shows an implementation of such a tree. In the implementation, a node is a 2-node if the fields `dataR` and `childR` are set to `null` and the other fields are non-null. A node is a 3-node if all fields are non-null. A leaf has no children and at least one data value.

```
1 class Node(dataL, dataR, childL, childM, childR, parent)
2   get(k)
3     if(this.dataL = null)    then r := null; return r; end
4     if(k = this.dataL.key)   then r := this.dataL.value; return r; end
5     if(k <= this.dataL.key) then r := this.childL.get(k); return r; end
6     if(this.dataR = null)    then r := this.childM.get(k); return r; end
7     ...
8   end
9 end
```

Listing 1. Part of the implementation of 2-3 trees in SMOL.

The nodes of a 2–3 tree change their "class" during their lifetime from leaf to 2-node to 3-node. It would be highly inefficient to create a new object every time this happens, as the addition of a value to the tree may cause several such changes. This exemplifies how the application "domain" (here: 2–3 trees) and the needs of the implementing language (here: efficiency) can collide.

In this example, the distinction between leaf nodes, 2-nodes and 3-nodes is *semantic* in the sense that these nodes share the same syntactic structure. It is not visible in the code that certain nodes are not supposed to exist; e.g., nodes where only `dataR` is set to `null` are so-called *faulty nodes*. This means that erroneous insertion algorithms may cause *semantic bugs*: they may violate the domain model of 2–3 trees. Note that faulty nodes as discussed above cannot be described by means of an ontology for the syntax—the domain model is a model of runtime states (i.e., the three kinds of nodes), not one of syntax.

An interpretation of the runtime state as a knowledge graph opens for *semantic state access*; i.e., the runtime state can be queried by means of semantic tools via this interpretation. In our example, all three kinds of node can be described as both SHACL shapes and SPARQL queries for debugging.

Semantic bugs may cause *delayed* and *non-local* runtime errors. Semantic debugging requires to perform semantic queries on a program state to access the complete program state, not only the current stack trace. The faulty node described above causes the tree to effectively ignore the values below `childR` by the `get` method. Thus, the error is delayed (observable only after the faulty insertion) and non-local (not observable with a single stack trace). Similarly, the car with a single wheel may not cause *any* runtime error at all.

Semantic programming is the application of this conceptual lens from *within* the program: As we interpret every runtime state as a model for a domain, we can also perform queries automatically during execution, for example, querying for all faulty nodes and calling a repair function that fixes the tree.

Terminology. There are some conflicts of terminology between programming languages and semantic technologies, of which we emphasis the following: In programming languages the word *semantics* describes the runtime behavior of a program, and is unrelated to ontologies and formalized domains.

In programming, a *class* is completely described by (a) its name, (b) its fields and methods and (c) the name of its superclass. We only consider class hierarchies without multiple inheritance, which form a tree. Each *object* has an identifier and belongs explicitly to one class (and its superclasses). The state, i.e., the values in the fields of an object, may change, but the class does *not*. In contrast, an *OWL class* corresponds to a unary predicate in logic and any *resource* belongs to many classes. Classes are identified by their extension and not their name, and resources have no built-in notion of class membership.

3   Core Language SMOL

As our programming model, we consider a semantic minimal object language (SMOL). The language contains the minimal set of features to demonstrate semantic state access: a class system to define objects and a simple while language for statements. To demonstrate the use of reflection, SMOL uses dynamic typing: each value is tagged with its type at runtime.

3.1   Programming Model

A program in SMOL consists of a set of classes and a **main** block. Statements and expressions are standard, including a **null** reference and the self reference **this**. For simplicity all fields are public, fields are always prefixed with the target object and nested object creation and method calls inside expressions are not supported. The syntax of SMOL is given by the following definition.

Definition 1 (Surface Syntax). *Let v range over variables, f over fields, n over $\mathbb{N}$, m over method names and c over class names. The syntax of SMOL is defined below. We assume standard literals and operators in expressions. The notation $\overline{\cdot}$ denotes lists and $[\cdot]$ optional elements.*

Prog ::= $\overline{\text{Class}}$ main s end   Class ::= class C ($\overline{f}$) $\overline{\text{Met}}$ end   Met ::= m($\overline{v}$) s end

s ::= l:=e; | $[$l:=$]$se; | if e then s$[$else s$]$end s | s s | while e do s end s | return e; | skip

se ::= new C($\overline{e}$) | e.m($\overline{e}$)   e ::= null | l | n | e+e | e $\geq$ e | ...   l ::= this.f | e.f | v

The runtime semantics of SMOL is a transition system between runtime configurations. Each such configuration represents the state of the program at a given point of execution. An expression evaluates to a *domain element* (DE), which is either a literal value or an object reference. For method calls, we use runtime statements rs which extend statements s with a special statement l ← stack (explained below). Runtime configurations are defined as follows.

Definition 2 (Configuration). *Let* X, Y *range over object identifiers,* σ, ς *over maps from variables to DEs,* ρ *over maps from fields to DEs and* i *over* $\mathbb{N}$. *Configurations* Conf, *objects* obs *and processes* prcs *are defined by the following:*

$$\text{Conf} ::= \text{CT obs} \langle[\text{prcs}]\rangle \qquad \text{rs} ::= \text{s} \mid 1 \leftarrow \text{stack; s}$$
$$\text{obs} ::= (\text{C}, \rho)_X \mid \text{obs obs} \qquad \text{prcs} ::= (\text{m}, X, \text{rs}, \sigma)_i \mid \text{prcs, prcs}$$

where CT *maps class names to a list of field names and a set of method entries. These are accessed by the auxiliary functions* fields(CT, C) *and* methods(CT, C), *respectively. We use* vars(CT, C, m) *to access the variables and* body(CT, C, m) *the body of a method. Terms* obs *are treated as sets.*

A runtime configuration Conf contains a set of objects and a stack of processes. An object has a unique name X and contains its class name C and memory ρ. A process has an id i and contains the name m of the method is executing, the object identifier X to resolve this, a runtime statement rs and a local store σ.

Observe that in a configuration, $\langle$prcs$\rangle$ realizes a *stack* of processes corresponding to nested method calls. In a process, the statement $1 \leftarrow$ stack denotes that location 1 waits for a return value from the next process on the stack.

Definition 3 (Initial Configuration). *Given a program* Prog, *the initial configuration has the form* CT_{Prog} (Entry, $\emptyset$)$_\text{E}$ $\langle$(entry, E, s, $\emptyset$)$_1\rangle$, *where* CT_{Prog} *is extracted as defined in Definition 2, but with an additional class* Entry *that has a single method* entry *with the statement of the main block as its body.*

The runtime semantics of SMOL is now presented as a structured operational semantics [24], i.e., a set of conditional rewrite rules which describe transitions from a runtime configuration into another. An expression evaluates to a pair X, f or a variable v if applied to a left-hand side and to a domain element if applied to a right-hand side. We denote by $[\![e]\!]_Y^{\sigma,\text{obs}}$ the evaluation function for expressions e, where Y is the value of this, σ the local variables, and obs a set of objects (such that their memories ρ may be accessed). For brevity's sake, we refrain from introducing the full runtime semantics here and refer to our technical report [17].

Definition 4 (Transition System). *The most important rules of the transition system are given in Fig. 1.*

The transition system is defined with two layers. A global layer that performs a step of the whole system and local layer that performs a step of a single statement. To connect the two layers, rule **(lift)** performs a step in the top-most process, using a local transition relation $\xrightarrow{\text{CT}}_X$. The local transition relation considers only (a) the active statement (b) the current local memory and (c) all objects. We give three rules to illustrate this: **(af)** executes an assignment to some field. The left-hand side expression evaluates to the pair of object identifier and field name and the right-land side to a literal or reference to be stored

$$(\text{lift}) \; \frac{s, \sigma, \text{obs} \xrightarrow{\text{CT}}_X s'', \sigma', \text{obs}'}{\text{CT obs} \; \langle \text{prcs}, (\text{m}, \text{X}, s \; s', \sigma)_i \rangle \rightarrow \text{CT obs}' \; \langle \text{prcs}, (\text{m}, \text{X}, s'' \; s', \sigma')_i \rangle}$$

$$(\text{af}) \; \frac{\llbracket e \rrbracket_Y^{\sigma, \text{obs}} (C, \rho)_X = v \qquad \llbracket 1 \rrbracket_Y^{\sigma, \text{obs}} (C, \rho)_X = \text{X}, \text{f}}{1 \; := \; e;, \sigma, \text{obs} \; (C, \rho)_X \xrightarrow{\text{CT}}_X \text{skip};, \sigma, \text{obs} \; (C, \rho[\text{f} \mapsto v])_X} \qquad (\text{av}) \; \frac{\llbracket e \rrbracket_Y^{\sigma, \text{obs}} = v \qquad \llbracket 1 \rrbracket_Y^{\sigma, \text{obs}} = v}{1 \; := \; e;, \sigma, \text{obs} \xrightarrow{\text{CT}}_X \text{skip};, \sigma[v \mapsto v], \text{obs}}$$

$$(\text{new}) \; \frac{|\bar{e}| = |\text{fields}(\text{CT}, C)| \qquad \text{Y fresh} \qquad \bigwedge_{1 \leq i \leq |\text{fields}(\text{CT}, C)|} \rho(\text{f}_i) = \llbracket e_i \rrbracket_Y^{\sigma, \text{obs}}}{1 \; := \; \text{new } C(\bar{e});, \sigma, \text{obs} \xrightarrow{\text{CT}}_X 1 \; := \; \text{Y};, \sigma, \text{obs} \; (C, \rho)_Y}$$

Fig. 1. Selected rules of the transition system for SMOL.

there. The rule updates the heap of the target object and reduces the statement to **skip**. Rule (av) is similar if the left-hand side expression evaluates to a variable name. Rule (new) adds a new object after evaluating all parameter expressions.

Premises in the rules realize *dynamic checking*: mismatching parameters, null access and all other errors are caught at runtime. A runtime configuration for which no rule is applicable is *terminated*. A terminated runtime configuration with a non-empty stack is *stuck*. A program may get stuck if, e.g., a method is called on an object and this method is not defined in the object's class.

3.2 Semantic State Access

The formal definitions given in the previous section describe the global state of a program execution. The established way to examine this state in debuggers is to evaluate expressions in the top-most context and navigation of the process stack. To enable semantic state-access on the overall state without manual navigation, we map a configuration into an knowledge base using our SMOL domain model.

Definition 5 (Knowledge Base). *A knowledge base $\mathcal{K} = (\mathsf{T}, \mathsf{A})$ is a pair of a TBox T and an ABox A. We represent the ABox as a set $E \times P \times E$, where each element is a triple over entities E and predicates P. A triple (e_1, p, e_2) is also written $p(e_1, e_2)$.*

Entities are, e.g., domain elements or method names. We remind the reader that literal values are domain elements. The sets of predicates and entities may overlap: a field is used as both an entity (to express that a class has a field), as well as a property (to connect an object with the value stored within this field).

The TBox consists of axioms. Some axioms are generated as part of the mapping and stem from the SMOL domain. Additionally axioms to reflect the application domain can be provided by the user.

Definition 6 (SMOL Domain and Mapping). *The generic SMOL domain model without the subdomain for statements is the OWL model pictured in Fig. 2.*

The set of axioms defining the above model is denoted T_{SMOL}. Given a configuration Conf, the mapping $\mu(\mathsf{Conf})$ generates a ABox as defined in Fig. 3.

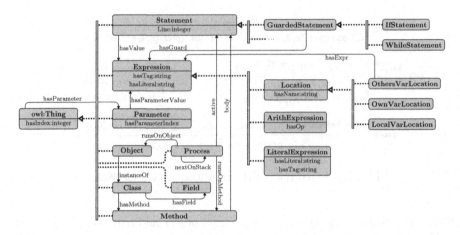

Fig. 2. OWL domain model for `SMOL` configurations. Common prefix `smol:` omitted. Boxes denote classes, arrows object properties and dotted arrows subclassing. Entries within the boxes are data properties.

$$\mu(\text{CT obs } \langle \text{prcs} \rangle) = \mu(\text{CT}) \cup \mu(\text{obs}) \cup \mu(\langle \text{prcs} \rangle)$$

$$\mu(\text{CT}) = \bigcup_{\text{C} \in \mathbf{dom}(\text{CT})} \big\{ \mathtt{smol:hasField}(f_P(\text{C}), f_P(\mathtt{f})), \mathtt{rdfs:subProperty}(f_P(\mathtt{f}), \mathtt{smol:Field}) \mid \mathtt{f} \in \text{CT}(\text{C}) \big\}$$

$$\cup \bigcup_{\text{C} \in \mathbf{dom}(\text{CT})} \big\{ \mathtt{smol:hasMethod}(f_P(\text{C}), f_P(\mathtt{m})), \mathtt{rdf:type}(f_P(\mathtt{m}), \mathtt{smol:Method}) \mid \mathtt{m} \in \text{CT}(\text{C}) \big\}$$

$$\cup \big\{ \mathtt{rdf:type}(f_P(\text{C}), \mathtt{smol:Class}) \mid \text{C} \in \mathbf{dom}(\text{CT}) \big\}$$

$$\mu(\text{obs}_1 \ \text{obs}_2) = \mu(\text{obs}_1) \cup \mu(\text{obs}_2) \qquad \mu((\text{C}, \rho)_\text{X}) = \{ \mathtt{smol:instanceOf}(f_R(\text{X}), f_P(\text{C})) \} \cup \bigcup_{\mathtt{f} \in \mathbf{dom}(\rho)} \{ \mathtt{f}(\text{X}, \rho(\mathtt{f}))$$

$$\mu(\langle \rangle) = \emptyset \qquad \mu(\langle \mathtt{p}_i \rangle) = \mu(\mathtt{p}_i) \qquad \mu(\langle \mathtt{p}_i \ \mathtt{p}_j \rangle) = \{ \mathtt{smol:nextOnStack}(f_R(\mathtt{i}), f_R(\mathtt{j})) \} \cup \mu(\mathtt{p}_i) \cup \mu(\mathtt{p}_j)$$

$$\mu(\langle \text{prcs } \mathtt{p}_i \ \mathtt{p}_j \rangle) = \{ \mathtt{smol:nextOnStack}(\mathtt{i}, \mathtt{j}) \} \cup \mu(\langle \text{prcs } \mathtt{p}_i \rangle) \cup \mu(\mathtt{p}_j)$$

$$\mu((\mathtt{m}, \text{X}, \mathtt{rs}, \sigma)_i) =$$

$$\{ \mathtt{smol:runsMethod}(f_R(\mathtt{i}), f_P(\mathtt{m})), \mathtt{smol:runsOnObject}(f_R(\mathtt{i}), f_R(\text{X})), \mathtt{rdf:type}(f_R(\mathtt{i}), \mathtt{smol:Process}) \}$$

$$\cup \{ \mathtt{smol:active}(f_R(\mathtt{i}), \mu(\mathtt{rs})) \} \cup \bigcup_{\text{V} \in \mathbf{dom}(\sigma)} \{ f_P(\mathtt{v})(f_R(\mathtt{i}), \sigma(\mathtt{v})) \}$$

Fig. 3. Mapping configurations. Statements and expression ommited for space reasons. f_P adds a prefix that identifies the program, f_R adds a prefix that identifies the run.

Fields and locations have two roles: All fields are properties (datatype or object properties, depending on the type), and they are elements of `Field`. Treating them as properties, we can use them to connect an object `O1` with an object `O2` stored in its field `f` using the triple `f(O1, O2)`. Treating them as individuals, we can express that they belong to a class. E.g., if `O1` is of class `C`, by using the triple `hasField(C, f)`. Analogously for variables and `Location`. The domain model also structures the statements, e.g., `IfStatement` and `WhileStatement` are both subclasses of `GuardedStatement`.[1]

---

[1] For space reasons, the complete version of this part of the domain model is given in the repository, and the following figures have been slightly simplified.

In the mapping, every class and object property is prefixed with an IRI unique to this version the program. We stress that each field is a subproperty of **Field** and every variable is a subproperty of **Location**. The **SMOL** domain is not merely a reformulation of the grammars in Definitions 1 and 2—it introduces terms like guarded statements which are not given in the grammar. Exactly one state is mapped to a knowledge base at a time, not a whole trace.

Example 2. Figure 4 shows a program and the main part of the mapping of its configuration. It exemplifies that the knowledge graph contains information about three layers of the program state: A syntactic layer describes the class information (in blue), an object layer describes the object instances (in brown) and a process layer describes the current stack (in yellow). The layers are not strict for fields and variables: **f** is both at the syntactic layer (**f** is a field of class **C**) and at the object layer (object **X** stores **2** in **f**) – the double line denotes equality.

```
1 class C(f) m(v) return this.f + v; end end
2 main o = new C(2); o.m(3); end
```

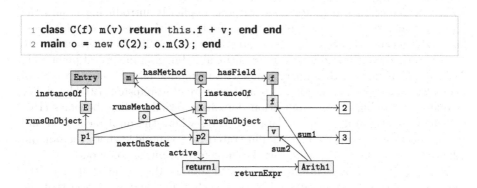

Fig. 4. A SMOL program and its mapping into a knowledge graph after o.m(3) is called.

The representation as a knowledge base allows us to access information beyond the basic notations of runtime semantics by inferring additional information through inference rules. We are generic in the access and inference mechanisms itself and assume some representation of axioms and queries.

Definition 7 (Queries). *An answering engine is a function that maps a knowledge base and a query to a set of answers:*

$$\mathsf{ans}((\mathsf{T},\mathsf{A}),q) = \{\overline{x} \mid (\mathsf{T},\mathsf{A}) \models q(\overline{x})\}$$

The satisfiability relation $\models$ *depends on the concrete nature of the query.*

Query engines can also handle boolean queries, such as description logic assertions, by returning either an empty set for true or a non-empty set for false.

Semantic Debugging. The mapping allows the programmer to debug a program by simple and efficient access to the runtime configuration through queries. This does not require an axiomatisation of the application domain, but if one is available, it can be used to additionally debug in terms of the application domain.

Example 3 (Semantic Debugging). Continuing with Example 1, we can formalize the notion of leaves, 2-nodes, 3-nodes and faulty nodes with the OWL class expressions from Fig. 5. To access a configuration Conf for semantic debugging with a query q, one needs to compute

$$\mathsf{ans}\big((\mathsf{T}_{\mathrm{SMOL}} \cup \mathsf{T}_{\mathbf{user}}), \mu(\mathsf{Conf})\big), q\big)$$

where $\mathsf{T}_{\mathbf{user}}$ are user input axioms that define the domain of the application.

Note that the axioms $\mathsf{T}_{\mathrm{SMOL}}$ and the mapping μ are part of the language and need *not* be provided by the user. The vocabulary is partially given by the language itself and partially by the user-defined classes. The overhead for the programmer is, thus, only to provide additional axioms if needed.

Recall that semantic state access is performed on a single state. For example, if the construction of the 2–3 tree in Example 1 temporarily contains a faulty node, then this node will not be retrieved by a semantic state access *after* the construction has completed (if the construction indeed fixes the node). If one wishes to detect such a faulty node without explicitly introducing it into the domain model, one can either use a query language with negation or a language for validation such as SHACL, whose integration into SMOL we discuss in Sect. 6.

Semantic debugging differs from traditional debugging in several points: (1) Access is performed with a query language to examine larger states, instead of manually investigating the call and heap structure of a snapshot. (2) The ability to query and debug using application domain knowledge. This becomes critical when investigating complex data structures where the implementation and the application domain conflict, as illustrated by Example 1 where the domain differentiates 3 classes of nodes, but the implementation has only one.

Semantic technologies are not a standard tool for debugging, but given the complexity of some current debugging tools, such as profilers, we expect that the overhead for the programmer is acceptable for complex structures, especially if they have an application domain component.

Root	$\equiv$ parent : null
Leaf	$\equiv$ (childL : null) $\sqcap$ (childM : null) $\sqcap$ (childR : null) $\sqcap$ ($\exists$dataL.$\exists$instanceOf.Pair)
TwoNode	$\equiv$ (childR : null) $\sqcap$ (dataR : null) $\sqcap$ ($\exists$childL.$\exists$instanceOf.Node)
	$\sqcap$ ($\exists$childM.$\exists$instanceOf.Node) $\sqcap$ ($\exists$dataL.$\exists$instanceOf.Pair)
ThreeNode	$\equiv$ ($\exists$dataL.$\exists$instanceOf.Pair) $\sqcap$ ($\exists$dataR.$\exists$instanceOf.Pair)
	$\sqcap$ ($\exists$childL.$\exists$instanceOf.Node) $\sqcap$ ($\exists$childM.$\exists$instanceOf.Node) $\sqcap$ ($\exists$childR.$\exists$instanceOf.Node)

Fig. 5. Domain model for 2–3 trees as OWL classes in DL syntax.

Verification. Before we investigate semantic state access further, we note that using established programming language constructs for control flow allows us to directly use results from programming languages. For example, we can carry over verification techniques and verify invariants. For a more detailed treatment of the following statement, we again refer to our technical report. We say that a formula is *state-based* if it contains as predicates only (a) instanceOf and (b) subproperties of Field and Expression. An ontology is *state-based* if its axioms contain only such predicates.

Proposition. *Let* Prgm *be a* SMOL *program, such that type inference succeeds. Let* O *be a state-based domain ontology,* C *a class in* Prgm *and* φ *be a state-based description logic formula. There is a sound and complete (relative to integer arithmetic) proof system that checks whether* φ *is an invariant for* C.

4   Internal Semantic State Access

So far, semantic state access is used to query the program state from the outside to realize semantic debugging. Next, we integrate domain knowledge directly into the runtime semantics of the program: the control flow is expressed not in terms of data structure implementations, but in terms of the implemented domain. To do so, we add a new statement to retrieve information about the state through the conceptual lens of ontologies about the program state from the *inside*.

Definition 8 (Extended Surface Syntax). *Let str range over string literals. The syntax of* SMOL$^+$ *is defined by extending statements from Definition 1 as follows:*

$$s ::= \ldots \mid \text{l:=access}(str, \overline{e});$$

The runtime semantics of the access statement map the current program and use the *inferred* knowledge graph to perform some query. The query is not static: additional parameters are evaluated and mapped to nodes inside the knowledge graph. We use $\%i$ as placeholders in the query string to add the additional parameters. We require the existence of a List class to represent the results of the statement for further computations.

Definition 9. *The runtime semantics* SMOL$^+$ *are defined by all rules from Definition 3 and the following additional rule for the access statement. We remind that* I *and* R *are available as user inputs.*

$$\text{(acc)} \frac{q = str\left[\%i \setminus [\![e_i]\!]_Y^{\sigma,\text{obs}}\right]_{i \leq n} \qquad l = \text{ans}\big(((\mathsf{T}_{\text{SMOL}} \cup \mathsf{T}_{\text{user}}), \mu(\text{Conf})), q\big)}{\underbrace{\text{CT obs } \langle \text{prcs}, (\text{m}, \text{Y}, \text{v} := \text{access}(str, e_1, \ldots, e_n); \text{ s}, \sigma)\rangle}_{=\text{Conf}} \rightarrow_\mathsf{T} \text{CT obs } \langle \text{prcs}, (\text{m}, \text{Y}, \text{s}, \sigma[\text{v} \mapsto l])\rangle}$$

We illustrate internal SSA ith two examples: domain-specific control and reflection. We can apply the *domain* ontology in the queries, inspired by the 'ontology-mediated symbols' introduced by Dubslaff et al. [5], to directly control the program in terms of the domain. An ontology-mediated symbol is a query over the extended knowledge graph and can be expressed in our system.[2]

---

[2] Dubslaff et al. use description logic formulas for queries, not SPARQL, but our approach is general w.r.t. the query language.

Example 4. Consider the upper code in Listing 2. The scheduler uses the domain knowledge to determine which of the platforms is overloaded and accordingly moves servers between platforms. The critical point here is that :Overloaded is defined by the background knowledge and can, thus, be changed according to different scenarios outside the simulation.

```
1 class Platform(serverList) ... end  class Server(taskList) ... end
2 class Scheduler(platformList)
3   reschedule()
4     over := access("SELECT ?x WHERE{?x a :Overloaded }");
5     tasks := this.collectExcessiveTasks(over);
6     this.reschedule(tasks);
7   end
8 end
```

```
1 m(o)
2   callable :=
3   access("SELECT ?y WHERE{%1 :instanceOf ?y. ?y :hasMethod n }",o);
4   if callable <> null then o.n();  else .../*report error*/ end
5 end
```

Listing 2. Upper code: Using ontology-mediated symbols in SMOL. Lower code: Reflection with semantic state access.

Exchanging the background knowledge can be used to change the specification when a platform is overloaded—the language concepts of ontology-mediated programming are thus subsumed by semantic programming.

The class table and stack structure are both available in the knowledge graph. We can, thus, reason about these structures at runtime *in terms of the formal (runtime) semantics and domain.* I.e., this does not merely expose the structure of the implementing runtime environment but adds domain knowledge—in this case, the domain of runtime configurations. The actual implementation in the interpreter, or other runtime, may for efficiency be quite different.

Example 5. The method in the lower part of Listing 4 checks that a passed parameter is from a class that implements n before calling the method.

The above example illustrates a common pattern in languages with dynamic types or reflection and is based on the static information. As the knowledge graph underlying the state also enables access to the processes, one can also use it to make control based on the stack. E.g., one can bound recursion without an additional counter or reflect on the calling method without passing a parameter.

5   Computational Semantic State Access

So far, we can access the data in a configuration and, beyond merely serialising it into another format, use inference to ontologise it. However, we cannot access data that is implicit in the configuration. Consider Listing 3: The Rectangle class has a width w and a height h, but its area is not directly available. Even worse: each rectangle is part of a scene that may scale all its elements (and apply further operations, which we omit here). While the final step of the computation of an area is a multiplication, the overall computation involves a method call.

```
1 class Scene(scaling) getScale() return this.scaling; end end
2 class Rectangle(scene, w, h)
3  rule area() s := scene.getScale(); return s*this.w*this.h; end
4 end
5 main sc := new Scene(2); ... r := new Rectangle(sc, 5, 1); end
```

Listing 3. A rectangle inside a scene.

Our solution is *computational semantic state access* (CSSA): certain methods, here **area** are directly encoded as inference rules to enrich the knowledge graph. This makes data that is a *computational* result available for inference. Furthermore, this allows one to determine based on a query where a computation has to be performed (instead of pre-performing it on all possible targets).

The language allows the programmer to mark methods as available for inference by exposing them with the **rule** keyword.

Definition 10 (Extended Surface Syntax with CSSA). *The syntax of Definition 8 is extended by replacing the method definition (from Definition 1) with*

$$\mathsf{Met}:: = [\mathtt{rule}]\ \mathtt{m}(\overline{\mathtt{v}})\ \mathtt{s}\ \mathbf{end}$$

For wellformedness, we demand that m is guaranteed to terminate if it is modified by **rule**.[3] The semantics of a **rule** method is not a transition rule, but an extension of the translation.

Definition 11. *The semantics of SMOL$^+$ is defined by the original transition system of SMOL$^+$ and by replacing the definition of $\mu((\mathtt{C}, \rho)_\mathtt{x})$ in Fig. 3 by*

$$\mu((\mathtt{C}, \rho)_\mathtt{x}) = \{\mathtt{smol} : \mathtt{instanceOf}(f_{\mathrm{run}}(\mathtt{X}), f_{\mathrm{prog}}(\mathtt{C}))\} \cup$$

$$\bigcup_{\mathtt{f} \in \mathrm{dom}(\rho)} \{f_{\mathrm{prog}}(\mathtt{f})(f_{\mathrm{run}}(\mathtt{X}), \rho(\mathtt{f}))\} \cup \bigcup_{\substack{\mathtt{m}\ is\ a \\ \mathbf{rule}\ of\ \mathtt{C}}} \{f_{\mathrm{prog}}(\mathtt{exec\_C\_m})(f_{\mathrm{run}}(\mathtt{X}), l)\}$$

where l is a literal computed as follows. Let $\mathcal{K}$ be a knowledge graph and $\mu_{obj}^{-1}(\mathcal{G}) = (\mathtt{CT\ obs}\ \epsilon)$ its state without the processes. Let $\mathtt{X}$ be the object id of the object bound to $?o$. The configuration $\mathtt{CT\ obs}\ \langle(\mathtt{m}, \mathtt{X}, \mathtt{s}, \{\})_1\rangle$ finishes in a configuration of the form $\mathtt{CT\ obs'}\ \langle(\mathtt{m}, \mathtt{X}, \mathbf{return}\ \mathtt{e}, \sigma)_1\rangle$. The literal l is defined as the evaluation of $\mathtt{e}$ in this configuration. If the execution does not finish in a configuration of the required form, we set $l = \mathtt{smol:null}$.

The execution is not performed on $\mu(\mathsf{Conf})$ itself. This means that any state change, e.g., object creations or changes of fields, are *not* recorded in $\mu(\mathsf{Conf})$. We stress that the **access** statement is still part of the language.

---

[3] Via a timeout, a syntactic check that no (mutual) recursion and no loops occur during its execution, or a termination proof. We do not commit to a concrete restriction.

Example 6. Consider the final configuration of the program in Listing 3. Let X be the created object. The method `area` is syntactically guaranteed to terminate and application to X results in the following added triple:

$$\texttt{prog:exec\_Rectangle\_area}(\texttt{run}: X, 10)$$

We remind the reader that this is not merely an arithmetic expression, but requires a method call to include the scaling of the overall scene—`rule`-methods allow one to include such computations directly into the knowledge graph.

A method exposed with `rule` takes no parameters to avoid spurious triples. If a call with a particular parameter is required, one may introduce a wrapper class that is created before $\mu(\mathsf{Conf})$ is computed.

Example 7. To lookup 5 in Example 1 in a query, one may introduce the following class and create an instance `new Wrap(tttree, 5)` before a `get` call.

```
1 t.get(key); return v; end end
```

CSSA is not redundant to method calls: it extends the knowledge base at *every* instance and allows to select in the graph depending on these attributes.

6   Implementation

An implementation is available at `github.com/Edkamb/SemanticObjects`. It supports a superset of SMOL⁺ and adds inheritance and some convenience features for the program, such as output. Several examples are provided, including the example from Sect. 2 with complete, and a SMOL⁺ implementation of a subset of the geological assistant [4], a simulator for geological processes.

Interpreter. SMOL⁺ is implemented by an interpreter written in Kotlin that builds on Apache Jena and HermiT [10] for the semantic state access. The interpreter implements an interactive shell to realize a Read-Evaluate-Print-Loop (REPL) that allows the user to step through the execution and semantically access the current state. The user may query the state with SPARQL, validate it against SHACL shapes or retrieve all members of an OWL class defined by a class expression. As a domain ontology, a file containing OWL classes can be loaded. It is possible to run a program without stepping through the execution; the language is extended with a `breakpoint` statement that stops the execution in this case. Additionally, the interpreter uses the prefixes `prog:` (for f_P) and `run:` (for f_R) to simplify referencing elements of the current state. CSSA is implemented by introducing a Jena-functor for each `rule` method and a rule with this functor in its head. The functor copies the complete interpreter state without the stack and executes the corresponding method.

Performance. We have evaluated the performance of internal SSA by adding n elements to a 2–3 tree and the querying OWL class expression using HermiT. For $n = 100$, the system used 150 s. To evaluate CSSA, we have similarly added n elements and then used the `rule` wrapper from Example 7 to retrieve a value. Here, for $n = 3000$, the system used 205 s. 3000 added values correspond to approximately 9000 created `SMOL` objects[4] and 60k triples. This shows that our proof-of-concept can handle non-trivial amounts of data, and complex data structures and queries. We conjecture that the most significant bottleneck concerning the performance is the non-optimised interpreter, and the explicit generation of the knowledge base. To increase efficiency, we plan to make the knowledge base virtual and only access object states as required to answer queries. Backward reasoning can be included e.g. by query rewriting for OWL QL ontologies.

7   Related Work

Ontologies for Java's core concepts by Kouneli et al. [18] and for connecting object-oriented languages by de Aguiar et al. [3] have similarities to `SMOL`'s ontology, but aim at communication between users and not at semantic state access.

Imperative programming languages and transition systems can operate directly on knowledge graphs through atomic actions. Golog [22] uses first-order logic guards to examine and pick elements from its own state. *knowledge-based* programs [8] support an epistemic knowledge modality K. Zarrieß [26] integrates description logic in a concurrent extension of Golog to verify CTL properties with description logic assertions. These assertions are easily realised using `assert` in `SMOL`$^+$, while our object invariants are orthogonal to CTL checking of traces. When operating on a knowledge graph, an ABox may change and violate a TBox. Calvanese et al. [1] propose two operations `ASK` and `TELL` for transition systems defined *explicitly* over knowledge bases. `ASK` corresponds roughly to our `access`, while `TELL` performs an action required by the explicit representation. In contrast, the transition system in `SMOL`$^+$ is *implicit* such that well-established principles from programming languages carry over to avoid reinvestigations of modularity, runtime semantic structure and control flow for knowledge bases. While all changes to the knowledge graph are global in Calvanese et al., global changes in `SMOL`$^+$ only happen in the part of the knowledge graph inferred from user-provided axioms; the part inferred from the mapping only changes locally.

Our work has not investigated programming languages that operate directly on DL interpretations or knowledge graphs, as done by [1,26], but rather how programming languages can be enhanced by semantic technologies. Closest to our work, *ontology-mediated* programming [5,6] defines an interface to integrate additional knowledge into a stochastic model checking tool, using external knowledge graphs to influence control flow. In contrast, we use internal knowledge graphsfor debugging. Neither the application to debugging nor an integration with rule-based inference as in CSSA has been studied in any of these approaches. Additionally, these approaches all use unconventional operators or highly specialised paradigms, while `SMOL`$^+$ allows external semantic state access for a standard object-oriented language; the `access` and `rule` extensions are optional

---

[4] Partly because the implementation still lacks a garbage collector for rewritten nodes.

and based on a clear interface and established query language, instead of low-level logic-based operations. For these reasons, SMOL$^+$ appears as conceptually simpler.

Ontologies can be used to type programs. Leinberger et al. [19] study DL concept expressions as static types in a λ-calculus, and type check using SHACL constraints [21]. Existing programming languages can be integrated with RDF data using the type systems of Paar and Vrandecic [23] and Leinberger et al. [20]. The difference between ontologies and regular types is not merely one of taste: (a) concepts allow more expressive structure than type hierarchies and (b) classes in programming languages are designed by the user to fit the needs of its application, while the concepts of the domain are designed to accomodate the needs of a general domain. While this work attempts to unify two tools made for different tasks, our approach is to give a sensible interface. SMOL is dynamically typed and the concepts of the domain and mapping in SMOL are disjoint and need to be connected using additional axioms. The connection to types has also been investigated through mappings [15] and code generation [25].

Eiter et al. [7] explore answer set programming to embed rules over DL knowledge graphs in the declarative setting of logic programs. Their rules are more expressive than our CSSA rules and aim to be a general programming approach. Käfer and Harth [14] perform actions on RDF files in the semantic web using linked data, operating on a set of user-input rules for an abstract state machine. Horne et al. define an operational semantics for SPARQL updates [12] and a system that internalizes queries into a process algebra [11].

8   Conclusion

This paper presents a novel approach to combine semantic technologies and programming languages. By regarding runtime configurations as knowledge graphs, we can use semantic state access to query such configurations for semantic debugging. By adding a semantic reflection layer to the programming language, computations can be driven by the result of queries from within a program. Finally, a deep integration of inference and computation allows inference to trigger method executions through computational semantic state access.

Future Work. As discussed, we plan to make the knowledge base virtual for performance reasons. We are also considering to develop an extension with special statements to manipulate the TBox and investigate how further programming languages concepts, such as garbage collection and encapsulation, carry over.

Acknowledgements. We thank Clemens Dubslaff and Patrick Koopmann for inspiring discussions on ontology-mediated verification. We are grateful to the anonymous reviewers for very constructive comments. This work was supported by the Research Council of Norway via *SIRIUS* (237898) and *PeTWIN* (294600).

References

1. Calvanese, D., Giacomo, G.D., et al.: Actions and programs over description logic knowledge bases: a functional approach. In: Knowing, Reasoning, and Acting: Essays in Honour of Hector J. Levesque. College Press (2011)
2. Cormen, T.H., Leiserson, C.E., Rivest, R.L., Stein, C.: Introduction to Algorithms, 2nd edn. The MIT Press (2001)
3. de Aguiar, C.Z., de Almeida Falbo, R., Souza, V.E.S.: OOC-O: a reference ontology on object-oriented code. In: Laender, A.H.F., Pernici, B., Lim, E.-P., de Oliveira, J.P.M. (eds.) ER 2019. LNCS, vol. 11788, pp. 13–27. Springer, Cham (2019). https://doi.org/10.1007/978-3-030-33223-5_3
4. Din, C.C., Karlsen, L.H., Pene, I., Stahl, O., Yu, I.C., Østerlie, T.: Geological multi-scenario reasoning. In: Proceedings of Norsk Informatikkonferanse (NIK) (2019)
5. Dubslaff, C., Koopmann, P., Turhan, A.-Y.: Ontology-mediated probabilistic model checking. In: Ahrendt, W., Tapia Tarifa, S.L. (eds.) IFM 2019. LNCS, vol. 11918, pp. 194–211. Springer, Cham (2019). https://doi.org/10.1007/978-3-030-34968-4_11
6. Dubslaff, C., Koopmann, P., Turhan, A.: Give inconsistency a chance: semantics for ontology-mediated verification. In: Description Logics, Volume 2663 of CEUR Workshop Proceedings. CEUR-WS.org (2020)
7. Eiter, T., et al.: Combining answer set programming with description logics for the semantic web. Artif. Intell. **172**(12–13), 1495–1539 (2008)
8. Fagin, R., Halpern, J.Y., Moses, Y., Vardi, M.Y.: Knowledge-based programs. Distrib. Comput. **10**, 4 (1997)
9. Giese, M., et al.: Optique: zooming in on big data. IEEE Comput. **48**(3), 60–67 (2015)
10. Glimm, B., Horrocks, I., Motik, B., Stoilos, G., Wang, Z.: HermiT: an OWL 2 reasoner. J. Autom. Reason. **53**(3), 245–269 (2014). https://doi.org/10.1007/s10817-014-9305-1
11. Horne, R., Sassone, V.: A verified algebra for linked data. In: FOCLASA, Volume 58 of EPTCS (2011)
12. Horne, R., Sassone, V., Gibbins, N.: Operational semantics for SPARQL update. In: Pan, J.Z., et al. (eds.) JIST 2011. LNCS, vol. 7185, pp. 242–257. Springer, Heidelberg (2012). https://doi.org/10.1007/978-3-642-29923-0_16
13. Johnsen, E.B., Hähnle, R., Schäfer, J., Schlatte, R., Steffen, M.: ABS: a core language for abstract behavioral specification. In: Aichernig, B.K., de Boer, F.S., Bonsangue, M.M. (eds.) FMCO 2010. LNCS, vol. 6957, pp. 142–164. Springer, Heidelberg (2011). https://doi.org/10.1007/978-3-642-25271-6_8
14. Käfer, T., Harth, A.: Rule-based programming of user agents for linked data. In: LDOW@WWW, Volume 2073 of CEUR. CEUR-WS.org (2018)
15. Kalyanpur, A., Pastor, D.J., Battle, S., Padget, J.A.: Automatic mapping of OWL ontologies into Java. In: SEKE (2004)
16. Kamburjan, E., Hähnle, R., Schön, S.: Formal modeling and analysis of railway operations with active objects. Sci. Comput. Program. **166**, 167–193 (2018)
17. Kamburjan, E., Klungre, V.N., Schlatte, R., Johnsen, E.B., Giese, M.: Programming and debugging with semantically lifted states (full paper). Research report 499, Department of Informatics, University of Oslo, March 2021. https://ebjohnsen.org/publication/rr499.pdf

18. Kouneli, A., Solomou, G., Pierrakeas, C., Kameas, A.: Modeling the knowledge domain of the Java programming language as an ontology. In: Popescu, E., Li, Q., Klamma, R., Leung, H., Specht, M. (eds.) ICWL 2012. LNCS, vol. 7558, pp. 152–159. Springer, Heidelberg (2012). https://doi.org/10.1007/978-3-642-33642-3_16

19. Leinberger, M., Lämmel, R., Staab, S.: The essence of functional programming on semantic data. In: Yang, H. (ed.) ESOP 2017. LNCS, vol. 10201, pp. 750–776. Springer, Heidelberg (2017). https://doi.org/10.1007/978-3-662-54434-1_28

20. Leinberger, M., Scheglmann, S., Lämmel, R., Staab, S., Thimm, M., Viegas, E.: Semantic web application development with LITEQ. In: Mika, P., et al. (eds.) ISWC 2014. LNCS, vol. 8797, pp. 212–227. Springer, Cham (2014). https://doi.org/10.1007/978-3-319-11915-1_14

21. Leinberger, M., Seifer, P., Schon, C., Lämmel, R., Staab, S.: Type checking program code using SHACL. In: Ghidini, C., et al. (eds.) ISWC 2019. LNCS, vol. 11778, pp. 399–417. Springer, Cham (2019). https://doi.org/10.1007/978-3-030-30793-6_23

22. Levesque, H.J., Reiter, R., Lespérance, Y., Lin, F., Scherl, R.B.: GOLOG: a logic programming language for dynamic domains. J. Log. Program. 31(1–3), 59–83 (1997)

23. Paar, A., Vrandečić, D.: Zhi# – OWL aware compilation. ESWC 2011. LNCS, vol. 6644, pp. 315–329. Springer, Heidelberg (2011). https://doi.org/10.1007/978-3-642-21064-8_22

24. Plotkin, G.: A structural approach to operational semantics. J. Log. Algebr. Program. 60, 17–139 (2004)

25. Stevenson, G., Dobson, S.: Sapphire: generating Java runtime artefacts from OWL ontologies. In: Salinesi, C., Pastor, O. (eds.) CAiSE 2011. LNBIP, vol. 83, pp. 425–436. Springer, Heidelberg (2011). https://doi.org/10.1007/978-3-642-22056-2_46

26. Zarrieß, B., Claßen, J.: Verification of knowledge-based programs over description logic actions. In: IJCAI. AAAI Press (2015)

Do Embeddings Actually Capture Knowledge Graph Semantics?

Nitisha Jain[1]([✉]), Jan-Christoph Kalo[2], Wolf-Tilo Balke[2], and Ralf Krestel[1]

[1] Hasso-Plattner-Institut, University of Potsdam, Potsdam, Germany
{nitisha.jain,ralf.krestel}@hpi.de
[2] Technische Universität Braunschweig, Braunschweig, Germany
{kalo,balke}@ifis.cs.tu-bs.de

Abstract. Knowledge graph embeddings that generate vector space representations of knowledge graph triples, have gained considerable popularity in past years. Several embedding models have been proposed that achieve state-of-the-art performance for the task of triple completion in knowledge graphs. Relying on the presumed semantic capabilities of the learned embeddings, they have been leveraged for various other tasks such as entity typing, rule mining and conceptual clustering. However, a critical analysis of the utility as well as limitations of these embeddings for semantic representation of the underlying entities and relations has not been performed by previous work.

In this paper, we performed a systematic evaluation of popular knowledge graph embedding models to obtain a better understanding of their semantic capabilities as compared to a non-embedding based approach. Our analysis brings attention to the fact that semantic representation in the knowledge graph embeddings is not universal, but restricted to a small subset of the entities based on dataset characteristics. We provide further insights into the reasons for this behaviour. The results of our experiments indicate that careful analysis of benefits of the embeddings needs to be performed when employing them for semantic tasks.

Keywords: Knowledge graph embeddings · Semantic representation · Entity similarity

1 Introduction

Knowledge graphs (KGs) serve as structured repositories of real-world facts in the form of triples comprising of entities and relations e.g. *(head entity, relation, tail entity)*. Popular KGs such as Yago [17], Freebase [4] and DBpedia [2] have been applied to a number of applications including question answering, rule mining and web search. Despite being composed of millions of facts, KGs still suffer from the issue of incompleteness, where entities or facts about entities are missing. A number of solutions have been suggested to cope with KG incompleteness, from statistical methods [22,27] to the more recent latent embedding

© Springer Nature Switzerland AG 2021
R. Verborgh et al. (Eds.): ESWC 2021, LNCS 12731, pp. 143–159, 2021.
https://doi.org/10.1007/978-3-030-77385-4_9

based techniques. Following the introduction of the *TransE* embeddings by Bordes et al. in 2013 [5], a flurry of different models have been proposed in the recent years, as summarized by Wang et al. [30].

The fundamental idea behind latent embedding models or knowledge graph embedding models (used interchangeably throughout this paper) is the representation of entities and relations by low-dimensional dense vectors that can capture the interactions within the knowledge graph. Due to their success on the link prediction task towards knowledge graph completion, these models have garnered considerable attention. The intense popularity and frequency of novel ideas towards better KG embedding models has also encouraged the research community to exploit these embeddings for other tasks as well. Since the basic premise of KG embeddings is centered around the semantic relationships between various entities, there is a widespread notion that embeddings must be able to capture the semantics and features of KG entities and relations very well. As such, embeddings have been used for many similarity-based tasks including entity similarity [26] and relation similarity [16], as well as conceptual clustering [9,10,29]. Moreover, several previous works have attempted to leverage KG embeddings for performing reasoning with rules [12,31,32].

While the results look promising, none of these previous works have performed a detailed analysis of the benefits of the embeddings across different datasets as well as across different entities within a single dataset. In some cases, a measurement of the consistency and scalability of the proposed embedding-based approach for different real-world datasets is largely lacking. The oversight of the limitations of KG embeddings and emphasis on the success for the simpler cases might prove misleading to research community. Our work aims to address this issue by studying the characteristics of the latent vectors obtained from several KG embedding models and quantitatively measuring their ability for semantic representation. With the aid of a systematic evaluation, we report that while embeddings can learn certain semantic features of KG entities on which they are trained, this learning is non-uniform and the quality of semantic representation varies largely across different entities within the dataset.

Our analysis shows that though it seems intuitive to leverage KG embeddings for semantic interpretability (just like word embeddings successfully have been), this is not always the case. The performance of embeddings is, in fact, limited in reality and heavily dependent on the dataset characteristics. We show that even straightforward tasks, such as finding semantically similar entities, do not yield uniformly good results for all entities in the data when relying on the vector representations of these entities. These observations raise doubts about the applicability of KG embeddings not only for semantic reasoning, but also for triple completion and link prediction. Other recent works have also put the efficacy of KG embeddings techniques under scrutiny [1,24,25]. These papers evaluate and criticize the KG embedding models primarily in terms of their performance on the link prediction task. In this work, we focus instead on the utility of the KG embeddings for providing semantic interpretations (or rather, the lack thereof). Furthermore, we provide a detailed discussion of the insights from our experimental analysis and identify the factors that determine a good semantic representation of the entities and relations for any given KG as well as the reasons for the shortcomings of current embedding models. We hope our efforts towards a first comprehensive analysis on semantics in KG embeddings will encourage further investigation into this problem space and assist researchers with a proper inspection of the popular KG embedding models for different semantic tasks. Our datasets and code are publicly available[1].

2   Related Work

KG embeddings have been used for a variety of applications over the years. We provide an overview of the related works that follow embeddings-based approach and discuss them in the context of semantics in the embeddings.

Entity Typing. Finding missing type information for entities in KGs has been a long standing problem. Early techniques usually relied on probabilistic methods for predicting the class membership of entities based on their properties [22]. More recently, KG embeddings have been used together with classification algorithms. As an example, Nickel et al. use RESCAL to predict new type information in a small Yago dataset and show good results on high-level classes such as *persons, locations* and *movies* [21]. Moon et al. propose a new embedding technique for performing entity typing [19]. In the example illustration for clustering shown in this paper, it can already be observed that the embedding technique seems to be problematic at distinguishing fine-granular classes such as *author* and *actor*. To a certain degree, their results show that entity typing with KG embeddings is far from being an ideal solution. More recently, an improved embedding technique for entity typing has been proposed [33]. Similar to us, the authors perform an evaluation of embeddings on Freebase and Yago for the entity typing task. While the results already reveal some problems when using entity embeddings for typing, a larger analysis is not performed. In contrast, our work undertakes a detailed analysis of the limits of entity typing when using KG embeddings and shows how classical techniques (e.g. *SDType* [22]) are often superior.

Entity Clustering. Besides link prediction, entity clustering is another popular application of KG embeddings. In [9], Gad-elrab et al. perform a limited analysis of several clustering algorithms on fine-grained classes. In a related work, the authors leverage rules and embeddings in conjunction to derive explainable clusters from the dataset [10]. However, the results have been shown to work well only for relatively easy relational datasets having well-defined relations between the entities and for small, targeted subsets of Yago. A scalability analysis of these techniques for actual knowledge graphs where their applicability would be most useful is missing. Another related work is presented by Jain et al. [15] where

---

[1] https://github.com/nitishajain/KGESemanticAnalysis.

the authors incorporate type information of entities to design better embedding models and demonstrate their results on entity clustering. However, clustering results are illustrated only for limited classes such as persons, organizations and locations without any details on the performance across all classes in the dataset.

Another branch of research concerns with using path-based graph embeddings to perform node classification and clustering tasks [13]. Generally, these techniques aim at creating node (or entity) embeddings using longer paths, instead of relying only on triples like common KG embeddings. However, these techniques are usually evaluated on datasets that do not share the characteristics of knowledge graphs in terms of having fine-grained entity types. Still, as a representative for path-based embeddings, we also evaluate RDF2Vec [23] in this work.

Other Applications. Besides knowledge graph completion, KG embeddings have been employed in a number of other settings. Similar to previous tasks, it is crucial that KG semantics are captured properly for embeddings to scale well for arbitrary real-world datasets. Embedding approaches have been explored in the context of rule mining on KGs by many previous works with seemingly good results. Existing techniques have either attempted to mine rules directly from the embeddings [31], or use embeddings to support rule mining for confidence computation [12,32] such that rules of higher quality can be mined. The latter works have not studied or quantified the benefits of embeddings on their work or explored which entities are positively impacted by them.

Furthermore, embeddings are often used to measure the semantic similarity of the entities and relations to perform data integration via entity or relation alignments [7,16]. An overview of several entity alignment techniques which are based on embeddings is presented in [26]. In our work, embeddings based approaches are compared to classical non-embedding approaches showing no real advantages. This result may already imply that entity semantics is not represented properly in embeddings.

Criticism of KG Embedding Models. For several years, a large variety of knowledge graph embeddings has been developed to perform link prediction to cope with incomplete information in KG. A recent re-evaluation of knowledge graph embedding methods shows several quality problems in the evaluation of KG embedding models as well as the carefully curated benchmark datasets that have been universally used for performance comparison [1]. Akrami et al. demonstrate that existing datasets show several redundancies and cross-product relations. Redundancies in the datasets lead to heavy data leakage thereby making them unrealistically simple in contrast to real-world KG. Furthermore, cross-product relations, connecting all entities to all other entities are frequently used. The authors point out that predictions for these relations is trivial and leads to overestimating the performance of embedding techniques. They show that cleaning the datasets from these defects significantly reduces the link prediction quality of KG embeddings. In another study, the performance gains claimed by newer and more complex models in comparison with the first KG embedding models has also been questioned [25]. Our work extensively analyzes the problems of current embedding models in terms of their semantic utility, casting doubt on their overall usability in complex real-world KG settings.

3 Analysis of the Semantics of Embeddings

In this section, we explain our approach to perform a systematic evaluation of the embeddings for checking their semantic soundness. We also elaborate on the design of our experiments based on popular benchmark datasets.

3.1 Categorization of Entities

KG embeddings are trained to capture the structural information of the underlying dataset. Ideally, if latent embeddings were able to embody all the latent features of entities, then entities with similar features would be similar in the vector space as well. That is, entities belonging to a particular *type*, and therefore having similar features would result in similar vectors [29]. Inversely, the embeddings that are close to each other in the vector space would correspond to entities having similar types or features [19]. This implies that it should be possible to identify the entities belonging to a particular type from the KG embeddings. Therefore, in this work we focus on verifying whether the entities can be categorized or assigned to their respective types from their corresponding latent vector representations.

While this is similar to the task of *entity typing* as discussed in Sect. 2, in this work we chose to follow a comparatively straightforward approach to analyse whether the embeddings in high dimensional space can indeed express the similarities between entities belonging to the same class or concept. We perform a systematic investigation with two distinct sets of *classification* and *clustering* experiments for the entity embeddings in the vector space.

Both these methods are suitable for semantic analysis as they can identify salient features of the embeddings, if any. These can be used to assign the correct class label to the entities in the case of classification, and segregate the entities into separate clusters as per their classes in the case of clustering. If latent embeddings are able to capture the connotations of entities, then this should be reflected in the performance of classification and clustering results obtained by using the embedding vectors as representation. The intentional choice of these techniques is also, in part, to their simplicity, which will enable us to lay the focus on the quality of the embeddings instead of the quality of the evaluation technique itself.

Classification. With the aid of the supervised approach of classification, we hope to discover the salient semantic features that the latent embeddings are assumed to have learned and use these features to identify the correct class labels for entities. Since an entity can belong to multiple classes in a KG, this entity typing task is a multi-label classification problem where one or many class/type labels can be assigned to an entity. For our experiments, we employed three different types of classification algorithms which work well for multi-label data. The *Multi Layer Perceptron* (MLP) classifier is a neural-network-based classifier using a simple feed-forward network. We chose the most basic architecture with a single hidden layer with 100 units. As a second classification technique, we chose a *K-Nearest-Neighbour* (KNN) classifier. Lastly, *Random Forest* (RF) classification is used as a decision-tree-based algorithm.

Clustering. Being an unsupervised task, clustering is used for identifying the class membership of entities by assigning them to separate clusters, each cluster ideally representing a class. For our experiments, since the ground truth for class labels of entities is known, we are able to measure the quality of clustering by comparing the actual labels with the predicted class labels. Previous works have attempted to identify conceptual clusters in a vector space by applying simple techniques such as *K-Means* to entity embeddings obtained from KG embedding models [10]. We expand our analysis to multiple clustering techniques to weigh the merits and flaws of the techniques and draw conclusions about the characteristics of the underlying embeddings on which clustering is performed. In our experiments, we leverage *Spectral* clustering, *Optics* clustering as well as *Hierarchical Agglomerative* clustering techniques in addition to the simple *K-Means* technique. While hierarchical clustering is particularly suitable for representing the class hierarchy present in most KG ontologies, *Spectral* clustering has shown promising performance for graph based data. *Optics* is a density-based technique that is suited for identifying clusters in spatial data and fits well to our use case.

It is to be noted that our intention for performing clustering in this work is not to discover new concepts but rather to re-discover the existing concepts that the entities are already associated with. Therefore, we provide the required parameter of the number of expected clusters and calculate cluster quality based on ground truth class labels of the entities under consideration.

3.2   Datasets

For the experiments, we have chosen the popular benchmark datasets Yago3-10 and FB15K-237. This allows for our results to be put in the correct context with regard to the numerous other related works that have shown good performance on these datasets [6]. Here, we discuss the main characteristics of these datasets and describe the selection of a suitable subset for the clustering and classification experiments.

Yago3-10. This dataset was created from the Yago3 knowledge graph [17] by filtering out the entities having less than 10 relations. It consists of a total of 1,079,040 triples with 123,181 entities and 37 relations. Yago is a semantic knowledge base associated with a hierarchical ontology that was derived from *Wordnet* taxonomy [18] combined with Wikipedia categories that are often fine-grained and noisy.

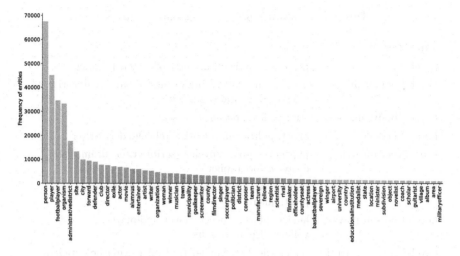

Fig. 1. Yago3-10 class frequency analysis.

In order to explore the differences in semantic representation for entities with varying type granularity, we proceeded to extract entities belonging to classes at different levels of the Yago ontology that resembles a tree-like structure. We limited our analysis to the concepts in Yago that are directly mapped to the *Wordnet* taxonomy to obtain a clean sub-tree of classes that are related to each other. Starting with the main branches of Yago class hierarchy, we chose the classes *person, organization, body_of_water* and *product*, then progressively explored their sub-trees to design experiments at different levels of the class hierarchy. For this, we manually performed a systematic analysis of the sub-classes of the above four classes and chose the most frequent classes for our experiments. This was a non-trivial task for the Yago3-10 dataset due to the presence of a highly skewed class frequency distribution. As reported previously [11], a large proportion of the entities in this dataset belongs to very few classes, while a long list of classes have very few representative entities. Almost 62% of all the entities belong to the 1% most frequent classes in this dataset. The frequency distribution of the classes (having at least 1000 entities) is graphically represented by Fig. 1 which shows that the class frequency distribution follows Zipf's law.

Due to the constraint of sparse entities in many cases, for each class, a list of sub-classes having entities above a minimum threshold were explored and used for designing the experiments (sub-classes leading to a high skew were omitted to ensure data balance). This was done for three levels starting with the main Yago classes as stated above. Each experiment contains a set of classes that belong to the same level in the ontology. This is important for a fair comparison of the semantic representation of the classes at different granularity levels of the class hierarchy. Table 1 lists all the experiments at different levels along with their classes. For each experiment all the entities belonging to the set of classes in the experiment was compiled from the Yago dataset, then the corresponding

Table 1. Yago3-10 experiments for different levels.

Experiment	Classes
Level-1	person, organization, body_of_water, product
Level-2-organization	institution, musical_organization, party, enterprise, nongovernmental_organization
Level-2-body_of_water	stream, lake, ocean, bay, sea
Level-2-person	artist, politician, scientist, officeholder, writer
Level-3-person-writer	journalist, poet, novelist, scriptwriter, dramatist, essayist, biographer
Level-3-person-artist	painter, sculptor, photographer, illustrator, printmaker
Level-3-person-player	hockey_player, soccer_player, ballplayer, volleyball_player, golfer
Level-3-person-scientist	social_scientist, biologist, physicist, mathematician, chemist, linguist, psychologist, geologist, computer_scientist, research_worker

Table 2. FB15K-237 experiments for different levels.

Experiment	Classes
Level-1	person, organization, body_of_water, product
Level-2-organization	institution, musical_organization, party, enterprise, nongovernmental_organization
Level-2-person	artist, politician, scientist, officeholder, writer
Level-3-person-writer	journalist, poet, novelist, scriptwriter, dramatist, essayist, biographer

embeddings for these entities was extracted from pre-trained KG embeddings models to serve as data for the clustering and classification experiments.

FB15K-237. This second dataset is a subset of the Freebase knowledge graph, frequently used by knowledge graph embedding models. FB15K-237 [27] comprises 272,115 triples with 14,541 entities and 237 relations. It was derived from the FB15k [5] dataset by filtering out redundant and inverse relations. With regard to the domains, it mainly pertains to *persons*, *organizations* and *products* and we aimed to design our experiments with a similar structure. We performed the mapping of Freebase entities to Yago through existing *sameAs* links and chose classes and sub-classes by following the Wordnet taxonomy. The experiments were designed in the same way as described above for the Yago dataset for allowing direct comparisons. The Freebase dataset is significantly smaller than the Yago dataset, such that the number of entities reduces dramatically when considering the classes at level-3. Therefore, we had to limit ourselves to fewer experiments as listed in Table 2.

3.3   Knowledge Graph Embeddings

For all the experiments, we obtain the pre-trained embeddings models for the benchmark datasets from the LibKGE library [6] since extensive hyper parameter tuning has already been performed. We used five different embedding techniques that are widely popular: TransE [5], RESCAL [20], Complex [28], DistMult [31] and ConvE [8]. Since for Yago3-10 only the Complex embeddings were available, we trained the remaining embeddings ourselves by adapting the parameters that were used for the Freebase dataset[2]. Another popular branch of embedding approaches is based on paths in a knowledge graph, usually showing good results in entity typing tasks as discussed in Sect. 2 [23]. RDF2Vec was trained using paths created by a random walker algorithm which created paths of length 4. Then the model was trained for 50 iterations using pyRDF2Vec library[3].

4   Experiments

In this section we present the results of our experiments for clustering and classification on Yago3-10 and FB15k-237 datasets. Additionally, we draw comparisons with a traditional statistical approach.

4.1   Non-Embedding Baseline

To ensure that the results are not driven solely by the performance of clustering and classification algorithms, we found it important to include a baseline that is unrelated to the embeddings. For this, we leveraged the *SDType* approach as introduced by Paulheim et al. in 2013 [22]. This is a heuristics based technique that simply uses the links between the entities to infer their type. Based on the incoming and outgoing relations associated with a particular entity, the average probability of each type for an entity is calculated. Purely relying on the statistical distributions of the entity links, this method is robust to noisy facts in the dataset and agnostic to existing type information. We rely on this approach to stipulate whether any semantic features are present in the underlying data that can help with the deduction of type information for the entities. If the statistical approach can already leverage the semantic features in data to identify the types for entities, this indicates that unsatisfactory scores for classification or clustering on embeddings must be due to the failure of embedding models to capture these semantic features during training. We report the performance of *SDtype* for our experiments along with the classification results in terms of the best F1 measure obtained (P-R curves are available on github link).

---

[2] The training parameters and performance scores are available on github link.
[3] https://github.com/IBCNServices/pyRDF2Vec.

4.2   Evaluation Metrics

Similar to previous works [10], we measured the Adjusted Rand Index (ARI), Normalized Mutual Information (NMI) and the V-measure to estimate the quality of the clusters. With the true and predicted labels as input, ARI measures the similarity of the assignments with values between -1 and 1 (0 stands for random assignment, 1 is the perfect score). NMI measures the agreement of the assignments and V-measure is the harmonic mean of homogeneity and completeness of the clusters. For both, the values lie between 0 and 1, with 1 being a prefect score. For the evaluation of classification experiments, an 80–20 ratio was used to split the dataset (consisting of entity embeddings and class labels) into train and test set. Since the task is a multi-label classification, the weighted average of F1 measures per class (in %) in the test set was used as an evaluation measure.

4.3   Classification Results

Figure 2 shows the weighted F1 measures for Yago3-10 dataset across all the embedding models (color coded) as well the different classifiers (pattern coded). It can be seen from this figure that all the classifiers perform very well for level-1 experiment (refer to Table 1), where the considered classes are coarse-grained and distinct from one another. However, the performance starts degrading once experiments at level-2 are considered and becomes worse for level-3, where the F1 measure drops below 20 for sub-classes of the *scientist* class. This is due to the fact that classes are finer-grained for these experiments, where they all have a common parent class and share certain common features. For instance, different types of *persons*, and further, different types of *artists*, *scientists* etc. would all share common properties of the *person* class (discussed in detail in Sect. 5). Even though the considered classes are conceptually distinct from one another, the classification algorithms find it hard to perform label matching correctly based on embeddings. This behaviour is uniform across all clustering algorithms and all embedding models, with no setting performing particularly better or worse. Though fine-grained entity typing is indeed a hard problem, our experiments are designed only for the top three levels of classes. It is indicated by these results that embeddings simply do not possess the necessary semantic features such that classification could identify correct entity types beyond the highly coarse-grained classes.

Similar trends are also seen for the FB15k-237 dataset (Fig. 3) where classification performs very well for the level-1 experiment, but gets worse progressively for level-2 and level-3. A few exceptions in this trend are noticed when the dataset is highly skewed towards entities of a particular class, such as *players* in case of Yago and *artists* in case of Freebase. In this case, the performance is improved to some degree as compared to other experiments at the same level. The performance of Freebase is generally better than Yago due to the presence of more relations in the dataset. Overall, the drop in classifier performance with increasing levels indicates a lack of sufficient semantic representation in embeddings for fine-grained entities for both the datasets.

To compare and contrast the performance of the *SDType* baseline approach, the F1 measures for *SDType* are also shown in Figs. 2 and 3 (coded with a different color and symbol). Significantly, it can be seen that *SDType* is able to achieve quite competitive results as compared to the embeddings, notably for the level-3 classes. This provides strong evidence for the shortcomings of embeddings for representing fine-grained classes for which even simple statistical approach can already give comparable results.

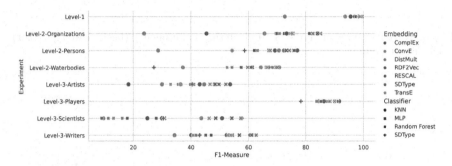

Fig. 2. F1 measure for Yago3-10 classification experiments (best viewed in color). (Color figure online)

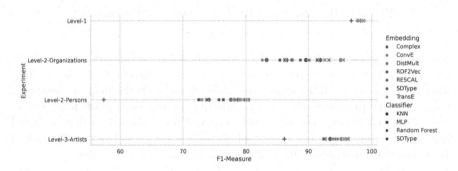

Fig. 3. F1 measure for FB15K-237 classification experiments.

4.4 Clustering Results

The results for the clustering experiments are reported in terms of the NMI scores and shown in Fig. 4 for the Yago3-10 dataset and Fig. 5 for the FB15k-237 dataset. Overall, clustering performs worse than classification, which raises doubts over the expected spatial closeness of similar entities in the vector space. Further, the clustering results also demonstrate a similar pattern to the classification results. The NMI scores are relatively better for level-1 classes but get

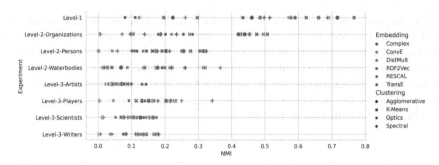

Fig. 4. NMI measure for YAGO3-10 clustering experiments (best viewed in color). (Color figure online)

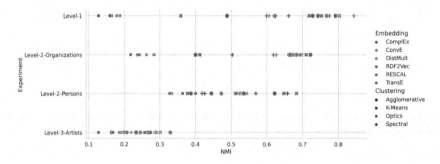

Fig. 5. NMI measure for FB15K-237 clustering experiments.

progressively worse for lower levels[4]. All embedding techniques fair similarly, thus conveying that it is difficult to identify or re-discover even the existing entity types or classes from any of the embeddings with the help of clustering, except for very high-level classes. Considering the different algorithms, *Optics* shows worse clustering scores in many cases. Since *Optics* is a density-based clustering technique, the low quality of clusters again point towards the lack of proper conceptual representation in the embeddings in vector space.

5   Discussion

From the experimental results on both supervised and unsupervised tasks, it is clear that KG embeddings are unable to capture the latent features that would be sufficient for a good semantic representation for all entities of a KG. While entities belonging to a small set of high-level *easy* classes are relatively well-represented, the same does not hold true for most of the entities corresponding to other important classes in the dataset. We investigated further to understand the plausible reasons for this shortcoming and discuss our findings here.

---

[4] ARI and V-measure show similar trend, full results are available on github link.

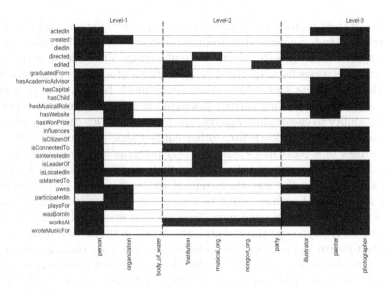

Fig. 6. Representation of outgoing relations at different levels in Yago.

Looking beyond the flaws in the training and evaluation process of the KG embedding models (that has been the focus of previous works as discussed in Sect. 2), we studied the characteristics of the underlying KG datasets on which the various embeddings are trained. Knowledge graphs such as Yago and Freebase are comprised of real world entities that frequently belong to more than one semantic type or class e.g. an artist can also be a politician in real life. Since such entities would reflect the characteristics of multiple classes, they are associated with a number of different relations that are neither unique nor indicative of any single class in particular.

To explore this further, we performed an analysis of the relations associated with the different classes that were used in our experiments for the Yago3-10 dataset. For each class, the incoming and outgoing relations associated with all the entities of the class were separately identified. Thereafter, the classes were compared to each other in terms of their relations within the same experiment as well as across experiments at different levels (as listed in Table 1). Figure 6 shows a comparison for classes at different levels based on their outgoing relations for a few representative experiments. Here, a slot is shaded depending on the premise that the relation was found for a minimum number of entities of the class. The figure demonstrates that the classes at level-1 have different sets of relations associated with them, i.e. there are few overlapping relations. This is less so for level-2 classes where several relations are found to be common. Finally, at level-3 there are hardly any unique relations that could distinguish one class from another and the relations overlap is quite substantial.

These results stem directly from the characteristics of real-world data where, for instance, all persons have similar properties (e.g. *wasBornIn, isCitizenOf*) regardless of their profession. In Yago3-10, any specific relations that could have uniquely identified, e.g. an *artist* from a *politician* seem to be either missing or very sparse. This directly affects the embeddings since they are trained to learn the associations between the different entities of a KG (a heuristics based approach like *SDType* can exploit sparse links much better). The presence of overlapping relations among entities belonging to different semantic types hinders their ability to encapsulate *type-specific* features. In this case, an embedding model can only hope to learn from other entities that are found in the triples of the entities of a particular class, and find patterns and features from those entities. However, recent work has shown that relations in knowledge graphs can be ambiguous in the way they connect different entities [14]. This means that various types of entities might be connected to a particular entity by the same relation. Such generic and noisy links make it even harder for embedding models to derive type-specific features about the entities, thus limiting their capability to learn similar entities or identify any common traits for all entities belonging to the same class. It is worthwhile to note that some classes such as *musical_instrument* and *tv_program* in Freebase have been shown to cluster well in the vector space [19]. A closer inspection reveals that these classes have very few and unique incoming relations such that the embeddings would be able to learn their features well. However, classes with unique representative properties are not very common in real-world datasets.

The key insight from our detailed analysis in this work is that while KG embeddings are assumed to be representing the semantics for entities and relations, in reality their semantic soundness is severely restricted and highly dependent on the datasets on which they are trained. Experimental results have clearly shown that several prominent embedding models often record worse semantic capability for a majority of the entities in real-world datasets as compared to a simple heuristics based approach that can derive the semantics directly from KG triples without any additional information. These findings indicate that a thorough inspection of the advantages and weaknesses of KG embeddings is necessary when employing them for semantic tasks. While the semantic web community is focused on novel architectures for training the KG embeddings models, a careful eye on the generalizability of these models in terms of their semantic representation also deserves more attention. We hope this work will guide further research in this direction. Recent efforts towards the explainability in KG embedding models [3,10] could be the first steps towards understanding these models that could benefit all semantic tasks that leverage them.

6   Conclusion

In this paper, we performed a comprehensive analysis of the popular knowledge graph embedding models in terms of their semantic utility. The results from our classification and clustering experiments on top of these embeddings brings attention to the weaknesses in semantic representation of embeddings. We have shown that embeddings fare poorly in terms of identifying the concepts or classes for a majority of the entities in the underlying knowledge graph and simple statistical approaches can compete very well with them. We also presented a detailed analysis of the reasons for limited semantic understanding of the embeddings relating to sparse and noisy links in real-world datasets. We hope the results from this work would serve as a precautionary tale and help the research community become cognizant of the realistic semantic benefits of knowledge graph embeddings, such that they can make prudent decisions when applying these embeddings to new problem statements and semantic tasks. We plan to extend this analysis to include further and more recent embedding techniques.

References

1. Akrami, F., Saeef, M.S., Zhang, Q., Hu, W., Li, C.: Realistic re-evaluation of knowledge graph completion methods: an experimental study, pp. 1995–2010 (2020)
2. Auer, S., Bizer, C., Kobilarov, G., Lehmann, J., Cyganiak, R., Ives, Z.: Dbpedia: a nucleus for a web of open data. In: International Semantic Web Conference, pp. 722–735 (2007)
3. Bhowmik, R., de Melo, G.: Explainable link prediction for emerging entities in knowledge graphs. In: Pan, J.Z., Tamma, V., d'Amato, C., Janowicz, K., Fu, B., Polleres, A., Seneviratne, O., Kagal, L. (eds.) ISWC 2020. LNCS, vol. 12506, pp. 39–55. Springer, Cham (2020). https://doi.org/10.1007/978-3-030-62419-4_3
4. Bollacker, K., Evans, C., Paritosh, P., Sturge, T., Taylor, J.: Freebase: a collaboratively created graph database for structuring human knowledge. In: Proceedings of the 2008 ACM SIGMOD International Conference on Management of Data, pp. 1247–1250 (2008)
5. Bordes, A., Usunier, N., Garcia-Duran, A., Weston, J., Yakhnenko, O.: Translating embeddings for modeling multi-relational data. In: Advances in Neural Information Processing Systems, pp. 2787–2795 (2013)
6. Broscheit, S., Ruffinelli, D., Kochsiek, A., Betz, P., Gemulla, R.: LibKGE - A knowledge graph embedding library for reproducible research. In: Proceedings of the 2020 Conference on Empirical Methods in Natural Language Processing: System Demonstrations, pp. 165–174 (2020)
7. Chen, W., Zhu, H., Han, X., Liu, Z., Sun, M.: Quantifying similarity between relations with fact distribution. In: Proceedings of the 57th Conference of the Association for Computational Linguistics pp. 2882–2894 (2019)
8. Dettmers, T., Minervini, P., Stenetorp, P., Riedel, S.: Convolutional 2D knowledge graph embeddings. In: 32nd AAAI Conference on Artificial Intelligence, AAAI 2018, vol. 32, pp. 1811–1818 (2018)
9. Gad-Elrab, M.H., Ho, V.T., Levinkov, E., Tran, T., Stepanova, D.: Towards utilizing knowledge graph embedding models for conceptual clustering. In: Proceedings of the ISWC 2020 Demos and Industry Tracks, vol. 2721, pp. 281–286 (2020)
10. Gad-Elrab, M.H., Stepanova, D., Tran, T.K., Adel, H., Weikum, G.: ExCut: explainable embedding-based clustering over knowledge graphs. In: International Semantic Web Conference, pp. 218–237 (2020)
11. Hao, J., Chen, M., Yu, W., Sun, Y., Wang, W.: Universal representation learning of knowledge bases by jointly embedding instances and ontological concepts. In: Proceedings of the 25th ACM SIGKDD International Conference on Knowledge Discovery & Data Mining, pp. 1709–1719 (2019)

12. Ho, V.T., Stepanova, D., Gad-Elrab, M.H., Kharlamov, E., Weikum, G.: Rule learning from knowledge graphs guided by embedding models. In: International Semantic Web Conference, pp. 72–90 (2018)
13. Hussein, R., Yang, D., Cudré-Mauroux, P.: Are meta-paths necessary? revisiting heterogeneous graph embeddings. In: Proceedings of the 27th ACM International Conference on Information and Knowledge Management, pp. 437–446 (2018)
14. Jain, N., Krestel, R.: Learning fine-grained semantics for multi-relational data. In: International Semantic Web Conference, 2020 Posters and Demos (2020)
15. Jain, P., Kumar, P., Chakrabarti, S., et al.: Type-sensitive knowledge base inference without explicit type supervision. In: Proceedings of the 56th Annual Meeting of the Association for Computational Linguistics (Volume 2: Short Papers), pp. 75–80 (2018)
16. Kalo, J.C., Ehler, P., Balke, W.T.: Knowledge graph consolidation by unifying synonymous relationships. In: International Semantic Web Conference, pp. 276–292 (2019)
17. Mahdisoltani, F., Biega, J., Suchanek, F.: YAGO3: a knowledge base from multilingual Wikipedias. In: 7th Biennial Conference on Innovative Data Systems Research (2014)
18. Miller, G.A.: WordNet: a lexical database for english. Commun. ACM **38**(11), 39–41 (1995)
19. Moon, C., Jones, P., Samatova, N.F.: Learning entity type embeddings for knowledge graph completion. In: Proceedings of the 2017 ACM on Conference on Information and Knowledge Management, pp. 2215–2218 (2017)
20. Nickel, M., Tresp, V., Kriegel, H.P.: A three-way model for collective learning on multi-relational data. In: Proceedings of the 28th International Conference on Machine Learning, ICML 2011, pp. 809–816 (2011)
21. Nickel, M., Tresp, V., Kriegel, H.P.: Factorizing yago: scalable machine learning for linked data. In: Proceedings of the 21st International Conferen on World Wide Web, pp. 271–280 (2012)
22. Paulheim, H., Bizer, C.: Type inference on noisy RDF data. In: International Semantic Web Conference, pp. 510–525 (2013)
23. Ristoski, P., Paulheim, H.: Rdf2vec: Rdf graph embeddings for data mining. In: International Semantic Web Conference, pp. 498–514 (2016)
24. Rossi, A., Matinata, A.: Knowledge graph embeddings: are relation-learning models learning relations? In: EDBT/ICDT Workshops (2020)
25. Ruffinelli, D., Broscheit, S., Gemulla, R.: You {can} teach an old dog new tricks! on training knowledge graph embeddings. In: International Conference on Learning Representations (2020)
26. Sun, Z., Zhang, Q., Hu, W., Wang, C., Chen, M., Akrami, F., Li, C.: A benchmarking study of embedding-based entity alignment for knowledge graphs. Proc. VLDB Endow. **13**(12), 2326–2340 (2020)
27. Toutanova, K., Chen, D.: Observed versus latent features for knowledge base and text inference. In: Proceedings of the 3rd Workshop on Continuous Vector Space Models and their Compositionality, pp. 57–66 (2015)
28. Trouillon, T., Welbl, J., Riedel, S., Gaussier, E., Bouchard, G.: Complex embeddings for simple link prediction. In: Proceedings of the 33rd International Conference on Machine Learning - Volume 48, ICML 2016, pp. 2071–2080 (2016)
29. Wang, C., Pan, S., Hu, R., Long, G., Jiang, J., Zhang, C.: Attributed graph clustering: a deep attentional embedding approach (2019)

30. Wang, Q., Mao, Z., Wang, B., Guo, L.: Knowledge graph embedding: a survey of approaches and applications. IEEE Trans. Knowl. Data Eng. **29**(12), 2724–2743 (2017)
31. Yang, B., Yih, S.W.t., He, X., Gao, J., Deng, L.: Embedding entities and relations for learning and inference in knowledge bases. In: Proceedings of the International Conference on Learning Representations (ICLR) 2015, May 2015
32. Zhang, W., et al.: Iteratively learning embeddings and rules for knowledge graph reasoning. In: Proceedings of the 2019 World Wide Web Conference, WWW 2019, pp. 2366–2377 (2019)
33. Zhao, Y., Xie, R., Liu, K., Xiaojie, W., et al.: Connecting embeddings for knowledge graph entity typing. In: Proceedings of the 58th Annual Meeting of the Association for Computational Linguistics, pp. 6419–6428 (2020)

A Semantic Framework to Support AI System Accountability and Audit

Iman Naja[1]([envelope]), Milan Markovic[1], Peter Edwards[1], and Caitlin Cottrill[2]

[1] Computing Science, University of Aberdeen, Aberdeen AB24 3UE, UK
{iman.naja,milan.markovic,p.edwards}@abdn.ac.uk
[2] Centre for Transport Research, University of Aberdeen, Aberdeen AB24 3UE, UK
c.cottrill@abdn.ac.uk

Abstract. To realise accountable AI systems, different types of information from a range of sources need to be recorded throughout the system life cycle. We argue that knowledge graphs can support capture and audit of such information; however, the creation of such accountability records must be planned and embedded within different life cycle stages, e.g. during the design of a system, during implementation, etc. We propose a provenance based approach to support not only the capture of accountability information, but also abstract descriptions of accountability plans that guide the data collection process, all as part of a single knowledge graph. In this paper we introduce the SAO ontology, a lightweight generic ontology for describing accountability plans and corresponding provenance traces of computational systems; the RAInS ontology, which extends SAO to model accountability information relevant to the design stage of AI systems; and a proof-of-concept implementation utilising the proposed ontologies to provide a visual interface for designing accountability plans, and managing accountability records.

Keywords: AI · Provenance · Accountability · Ontology

1 Introduction

Artificial Intelligence (AI) solutions are increasingly being deployed in diverse domains such as finance, law and healthcare. However, this widespread adoption does not come without risks and AI systems are increasingly linked to grievously erroneous, unintended or even undesirable behaviours (e.g. perpetuating racism and sexism) [25]. Naturally, then, there is a desire to introduce accountability measures for such systems; and over the past decade this has attracted considerable attention from developers and researchers [6,14], professional bodies [1,25], as well as regulators and policy makers [12,24].

Supported by the award made by the UKRI Digital Economy programme to the RAInS project (ref: EP/R033846). The authors acknowledge Jatinder Singh and Richard Cloete for their involvement in the early stages of the Accountability Fabric's design.

The original version of this chapter was revised: Figure 3 has been corrected. The correction to this chapter is available at https://doi.org/10.1007/978-3-030-77385-4_44

R. Verborgh et al. (Eds.): ESWC 2021, LNCS 12731, pp. 160–176, 2021.
https://doi.org/10.1007/978-3-030-77385-4_10

For the purpose of this paper, the term AI system refers to software comprising 'core AI' components (e.g. a machine learning model) and other supporting functions (e.g. API wrappers) [19] allowing it to function either as a standalone solution, or as a part of a larger system. We consider the development and use of an AI system in terms of four high-level life cycle stages: *Design, Implementation, Deployment*, and *Operation*; this conforms to the recommendation by Amershi *et al.* [2] that standard software engineering practices should apply to such systems. *Design* involves all aspects associated with designing an AI system; *implementation* encompasses all activities associated with building and testing the system; *deployment* includes installing and configuring the system and, if applicable, integrating it with other systems, producing documentation, and training users. Finally, *operation* consists of the actual use of the system and (routine) monitoring. Moreover, by accountability, we mean the ability to inspect, review or otherwise interrogate an AI system with the goal of (*i*) making processes associated with each of its life cycle stages transparent [1,6,7,14,24,25]; (*ii*) demonstrating compliance with hard laws (i.e. laws and regulations), and soft laws (i.e. standards and guidelines) [14,24]; and (*iii*) aiding investigations into the cause(s) of failure or erroneous decisions and supporting the identification of responsible parties [1,6,7,14,24].

To realize accountable AI systems, different types of information from a range of sources need to be recorded throughout the system life cycle. We argue that knowledge graphs can support accountability of such systems by capturing and linking critical transparency information across the different life cycle stages. However, such transparency information must be meaningful and its collection must be proactive (i.e. planned) so it can be enforced through the means of hard and soft laws. We introduce the concept of *accountability plans*, which represent the information that should be captured at different stages of an AI system's life cycle. Accountability plans are linked to *accountability traces*, which are records representing the actual manifestation of those plans. These traces capture structured information describing crucial outcomes of activities influencing the accountability of the AI system. Such activities may represent, for example, the creation of tangible artefacts (e.g. design specifications, implemented system components) or decisions made by key staff members (e.g. approving a design specification) during the system life cycle. Similar to the idea of model cards presented by Mitchell *et al.* [20] which is gaining popularity in the machine learning community, the instances of "accountable outputs" produced by activities recorded in the accountability traces may be understood as reports or cards detailing the key accountability information. To model *accountability plans* and *accountability traces*, we rely on a provenance-based approach by reusing the W3C recommendation PROV-O [16] and its extension EP-Plan [17]. We extend PROV-O's concepts *entity, activity*, and *agent* to represent the *accountability traces* as causal provenance graphs and EP-Plan's concepts *step* and *variable* to describe abstract plans corresponding to such provenance records.

In this paper, we focus on exploring the feasibility of our proposed approach through exploring the core mechanisms for capturing accountability plans and their corresponding traces. We then evaluate this idea by implementing a proof of concept software tool for documenting the design stage of AI systems which incorporate machine learning systems. Specifically, our three main contributions are:

1. The System Accountability Ontology (SAO), a generic, reusable, lightweight core ontology which introduces a set of concepts to model accountability plans and their corresponding traces to support accountability of computational systems.
2. The Realising Accountable Intelligent Systems (RAInS) ontology, an extension of SAO, for supporting accountability during the design stage of AI systems, specifically those which employ machine learning.
3. The *Accountability Fabric*, a proof-of-concept implementation utilising SAO and RAInS to provide a visual interface for designing accountability plans, and managing accountability records.

The remainder of this paper is organised as follows: Sect. 2 discusses related work; Sect. 3 describes the methodology used when creating the SAO and RAInS ontologies; Sect. 4 discusses the knowledge representation requirements influencing the design of SAO and RAInS; Sect. 5 describes SAO and RAInS; Sect. 6 discusses the implementation of the *Accountability Fabric* and an evaluation of SAO and RAInS; and finally, Sect. 7 concludes the paper with discussion of future work.

2   Related Work

The challenge of how to realise accountable AI systems has attracted considerable attention over the past decade. Professional bodies such as ACM and IEEE have published statements and reports listing principles for accountable algorithms and trustworthy AI systems [1,25]. National and international regulatory bodies have been working to understand and address the implications of AI systems use; and legislation is being developed across a number of jurisdictions, including the UK and the European Union, with a focus on accountability and maintaining ethical principles [8,12,24]. Developers and researchers have also been involved in underscoring the need for accountable AI and have proposed a range of methods to address related issues [28]. Many of these involve documenting how AI systems are designed and developed and how they operate [6,11,14,20]. Typically, such approaches include questions or prompts which designers and developers of AI systems need to consider and for which they should document outcomes. This process is largely manual; however, semi-automated approaches such as the Model Card toolkit[1] are also emerging. Ontologies which describe AI systems and processes that lead to their creation have also been proposed (e.g. MEX [9], ML Schema [22], and KBCE [27]). However, tools to support community uptake (e.g. to automatically produce metadata from running the code of a machine learning model) are still largely missing and possibly hinder widespread adoption[2]. In the same context, PROV-O has

---

[1] https://github.com/tensorflow/model-card-toolkit.
[2] https://github.com/ML-Schema/core/issues/23.

been proposed as a means to record the provenance of decisions made by AI systems [4,13]; while this has some similarities with the approach we describe here - it has a much narrower scope. In our work, we utilise PROV-O's concept of a plan, which represents intended steps or actions so that an objective may be realised; however, PROV-O provides no detailed vocabulary for representing such plans. Extensions to PROV-O to document plans were originally proposed for the scientific workflow domain, for example, by the ProvOne [3] and P-Plan [10] ontologies. More recently, P-Plan, and its extension EP-Plan [18], has been applied in other domains. For example, Pandit and Lewis [21] proposed an extension of P-Plan for use in the GDPR context, while Markovic *et al.* [17] discussed the role of EP-Plan in increasing transparency of Internet of Things deployments. Both demonstrated the cross-domain re-usability of P-Plan's simple approach to modelling abstract plans as a series of *steps* interlinked through their input and output *variables* into an acyclic graph.

In summary, while ontologies have been proposed to describe AI systems (and may be used to enhance their transparency), and extensions to PROV-O have been proposed to enable richer descriptions of plans associated with provenance traces, to date we are not aware of any approaches that combine these two to address the challenge of accountable AI.

3   Ontology Development Methodology

The NeOn methodology [23] was adopted to guide the process of ontological modelling of *accountability plans* and their corresponding *accountability traces*. Knowledge representation requirements for accountable design of AI systems were gathered from the academic literature, statements and guidelines released by professional bodies, and publications from regulatory bodies. An application use-case from the healthcare domain was also analysed to identify information elements that should be captured as part of *accountability traces*. The use case is based on plans by the Scottish Breast Screening Programme to address a shortage of trained radiologists [26] by examining how a deep-learning image classifier[3] can be used to replace one of the two human radiologists currently required to analyse mammography images. A number of indicative competency questions were collected, which were then grouped via further analysis under six broad themes discussed in Sect. 4.

A modular approach to ontology development was adopted which commenced with formalising the core reusable concepts for modelling *accountability plans* and corresponding *accountability traces* applicable to computational systems - resulting in SAO. This was followed by formalising RAInS, which extends SAO, for the specific domain of AI system design. The ontologies were implemented using Protégé and further evaluated via a proof-of-concept application for generating and managing accountability knowledge graphs described using SAO and RAInS (details in Sect. 6).

---

[3] https://www.abdn.ac.uk/news/12398/.

4 Knowledge Capture Requirements

Competency questions (CQs) were extracted from existing literature [4–8,11,13, 14,20,24]. These covered a range of topics relating to AI systems and their development, including documentation requirements for specific components (e.g. machine learning models) and explanation of automated decision-making. While the literature did not always explicitly link the identified CQs to a specific life cycle stage (e.g. design), we used our experience from the aforementioned medical use case scenario and our own judgement to identify CQs applicable to the design stage of an AI system utilising machine learning. The CQs were then transformed into knowledge capture requirements organised under the following themes to identify what should be recorded by *accountability traces*:

1. **System-level information:** the intended purpose of the system [4,20,24]; the intended users of the system [5,7,20]; and the compliance specifications which apply to the system, i.e. the hard laws that must be followed and soft laws that should be followed [5,24].
2. **Dataset information:** characteristics of the dataset (e.g. size, composition of instances, number of features) [4,5,7,11,20,24]; collection method [8,11]; any associated pre-processing (e.g. sampling, aggregation) [5,11,20,24]; and tasks for which it should be used [5,11] and those for which it should not [11].
3. **Model information:** characteristics of the model (e.g. decision threshold, excluded dataset features) [6,13,20]; details related to implementation (e.g. algorithm used) [6,20,24]; associated evaluation procedures [6,20,24]; and tasks for which it should [8,20,24] and should not be used [20].
4. **Supporting infrastructure information:** the specification of system components which are not 'core AI' but may still be the source of erroneous behaviour of an AI system (e.g. user interface, API wrappers); the characteristics of supporting infrastructure relevant to the accountability of systems such as specification of human agency and oversight mechanisms (e.g. human-in-the-loop or human-in-command [24]); specification of audit mechanisms [8,24]; and specification of the level of explanations to be provided by the system [5,8,24].
5. **Limitations and risks:** the known or expected limitations of the datasets used to train the decision-making models [5,8,24] and the resulting models [5,20,24]; and the known or expected risks, including biases, associated with datasets [5–8,11,14,24] and models [5–8,20,24].
6. **Human decision making and approvals:** who is accountable for the creation of various specifications including the dataset [11,13], model [20] and supporting infrastructure specifications; who assessed the fitness of the dataset [8,24], model, and supporting infrastructure specifications against the system's purpose (and how was this done); which hard and soft laws requirements were included in dataset [5,8,24], model [5,24], and supporting infrastructure [5,24] specifications and who assessed the compliance of such specifications against those laws (and how was this done); and finally who approved the various specifications that influence the later life cycle stages (e.g. implementation stage).

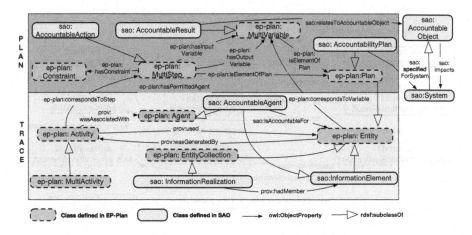

Fig. 1. An overview of core concepts defined in the SAO ontology.

5   Modelling System Accountability

5.1   The SAO Ontology

SAO[4] (Fig. 1) is a generic model for describing plans and corresponding traces to support accountability of computer systems. SAO introduces *sao:Accountable-Object* to model an abstract representation of any meaningful grouping (software component, dataset, model, evaluation process, etc.) that may be used to organise system-related accountability information. The definition is deliberately generic so it can be adapted to the needs of any organisation thus allowing flexibility in how a system description should be decomposed into different reference categories that may be used by an audit mechanism. In this context, the system itself (*sao:System*) is an accountable object. A larger system may thus be described as a group of sub-systems or a single system may be broken down into a number of layers/components (e.g. a decision logic layer).

Each instance of *sao:System* may be linked to one or more accountability plans (*sao:AccountabilityPlan*) which specify the information that should be collected to support future accountability. The mechanism for capturing plans and their corresponding execution traces is reused from the EP-Plan ontology [17]. Plans consist of steps which take variables as their inputs or outputs; these are then linked to corresponding accountability traces represented as core PROV-O concepts which are sub-classed in EP-Plan (Fig. 1). SAO extends EP-Plan with two concepts for describing accountability plans: *sao:AccountableAction* and *sao:AccountableResult*, and three concepts to describe the corresponding elements of the accountability trace: *sao:InformationRealization, sao:Information-Element* and *sao:AccountableAgent*. An accountable action is any process that produces an output (*sao:AccountableResult*) which should be documented for

---

[4] https://w3id.org/sao.

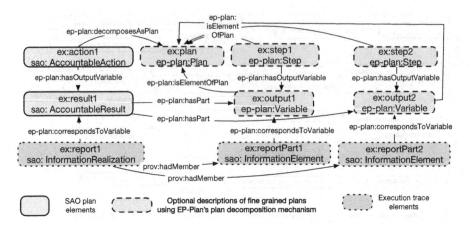

Fig. 2. An example decomposition of *sao:AccountableAction* into a sub-plan containing two steps producing variables describing in more detail the composite *sao:AccountableResult* multivariable and matching execution traces.

accountability purposes. A description of such an output in the accountability trace then represents the information available at a specific point in its production. For example, a specification of a machine learning model may include characteristics that were believed to be achievable at the design stage (and for which members of the design team were accountable); however, this may differ from the characteristics of the implemented model recorded as an accountable output later in the system life cycle (and for which developers, not designers were accountable). At the accountability trace level, the information corresponding to *sao:AccountableResult* is modelled as a collection (*sao:InformationRealization*). This is because, at the plan level, *sao:AccountableResult* is expected to provide only a high level reference to the expected information. For example, consider a model specification that takes the form of a written report. Here, the plan does not define all the individual steps corresponding to the separate report sections containing the different types of information as output variables (e.g. algorithm details, associated limitations, etc.). Instead, the plan records a high level reference to an *sao:AccountableResult* denoting the expected report. The corresponding execution trace instance is recorded as a collection (*sao:InformationRealization*), which can be linked to any number of *sao: InformationElement*(s) describing the individual records (e.g. algorithm details). The decision to only represent high-level descriptions of plans was made to support reusability of template plan specifications - thus avoiding detailed plans which could be more difficult to match to the existing internal development processes of organisations. However, if required, detailed plan descriptions are supported by EP-Plan through descriptions of sub-plans [18] (Fig. 2). This mechanism could be utilised, for example, within large organisations where different agents contribute different information elements and a detailed provenance trace of their individual contributions is required.

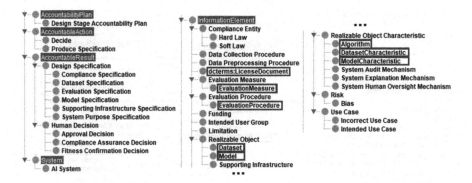

Fig. 3. RAInS classes as subclasses of SAO classes (in blue-filled rectangles). Third party classes reused from ML Schema and Dublin Core vocabulary have green borders. (Color figure online)

SAO also defines *sao:AccountableAgent* to indicate agents that can be held to account for their actions. These are also subtypes of *sao:InformationElement* and may therefore be mentioned as part of an *sao:InformationRealization*. For example, a model specification may specify certain agents that are assumed to be accountable for the realised model. The relationship *sao:isAccountableFor* explicitly denotes the direct link between accountable agents and the entities for which they are accountable. It is also possible to indicate expected responsibilities of agents within an organisation for specific accountable actions and results, by linking *sao:AccountableAgent* to *sao:AccountableAction* using *ep-plan:hasPermittedAgent*.

Finally, the concept *ep-plan:Constraint* can be used to record details about any constraints that were associated with the planned *sao:AccountableAction*, thus providing mechanisms to further customise generic plans to the requirements of individual organisations, allowing further context to be provided on how accountable results were produced (e.g. explaining why certain information elements were included as part of the information realization).

5.2   The RAInS Ontology

The RAInS[5] ontology extends SAO for the AI systems domain by defining a set of concepts required to document the *design* stage of such systems. Figure 3 depicts the classes defined in RAInS.

Subclasses of *sao:AccountableAction* and *sao:AccountableResult* are defined to provide a minimal set of high-level constructs for describing *accountability plans* consisting of actions producing *design specifications* (e.g. a machine learning model design specification) and *human decisions* (e.g. approval of a specification by an accountable person). By design specifications we mean a collection of requirements or expected characteristics associated with

---

[5] https://w3id.org/rains.

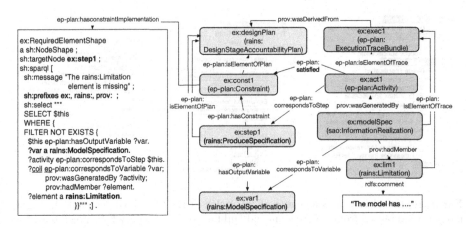

Fig. 4. An illustration of linking a SHACL constraint to a plan step using *ep-plan:Constraint*. The constraint states that an instance of type rains:Limitation must be present as part of the *sao:InformationRealization*

aspects of an AI system. Such specifications are produced by the system designers and should be complied with when the system is realised later in the life cycle. These specifications are not intended to describe specific steps and the order in which they should be performed - i.e. plans. Subclasses of *rains:DesignSpecification* are defined to cover descriptions of dataset, model, evaluation, and supporting infrastructure specifications (see Sect. 4). Further subclasses of *rains:DesignSpecification* are also defined to describe additional metadata through *rains:SystemPurposeSpecification* and *rains:ComplianceSpecification* to indicate the intended qualities of the expected system, which influence the other individual specifications (e.g. a step producing a dataset specification using inputs defining the system purpose and desired compliance specification). Subclasses of *rains:HumanDecision* are used at the plan level to describe the various decisions (e.g. specification approvals) expected to be made by the accountable decision-makers within an organisation.

At the *accountability trace* level, RAInS extends *sao:InformationElement* with a number of subclasses for capturing metadata relating to risks, compliance, intended and incorrect use cases, intended user groups, data collection methods, and data pre-processing methods. Furthermore, information elements may describe a *rains:RealizableObject* which represents a tangible system asset that will be realised during the *implementation* stage, e.g. training dataset, machine learning model, component of supporting infrastructure, etc. Here, the data property *rains:isReusedObject* indicates with a Boolean value whether the resource already exists and is being reused. However, at this stage this system asset is still referred to in abstract terms using *rains:RealizableObject* as it is not yet an implemented AI component. Each *rains:RealizableObject* may be linked using the *rains:hasRealizableObjectCharacteristic* object property to *rains:RealizableObjectCharacteristic*, which may be used to structure the description of *rains:RealizableObject* into separate information elements (e.g. discussing model performance) within *sao:InformationRealization*.

To allow for a range of potential applications, the RAInS ontology does not dictate what information elements (if any) should be part of an information realization. Users can associate constraints with plan steps that may be used to validate the quality of generated knowledge graphs. Figure 4 illustrates a SHACL [15] constraint specifying that the *rains:Limitation* element must be present in a collection corresponding to the *rains:ModelSpecification*. Ensuring the completeness of information captured in the knowledge graph would be an important factor, for example, if the collection of *accountability traces* was used to demonstrate compliance with hard or soft laws. If required, constraints may be defined at an abstract level (i.e. they cannot be automatically validated by rules) and their compliance or violation may be determined manually by the information provided by a human agent contributing the relevant *accountability trace* information. This may be implemented via, for example, a question such as "has this activity been performed without any conflicts of interest?", where the user is expected to provide a direct answer to this question.

5.3   Design Rationale and Alignment to Other Ontologies

EP-Plan (an extension of PROV-O) defines core concepts used for modelling the execution traces corresponding to plan specifications. SAO extends EP-Plan to define concepts for recording accountability plans and corresponding accountability traces for computational systems. RAInS then extends SAO further with domain specific concepts relating to the design stage of AI systems. Accountability plans represent simple and generalisable workflows which document record keeping protocols, whereas much of the *actionable information* is recorded in the accountability traces. This approach is similar to the pattern implemented by the Information Object ontology[6]. Its concept *information object* describes an abstract conceptualisation of an object (e.g. a written text) while the corresponding *information realization* describes a realisation of that object (e.g. a specific report). In our approach, the abstract conceptualisation is the description of *sao:AccountableResult* at a plan level; its subsequent realisation is captured by *sao:InformationRealization*. The latter describes a specific information instance (e.g. a specification report) as part of the accountability trace.

RAInS includes subclasses of *sao:InformationElement* to provide descriptions of information captured in the execution traces. Here, concepts from ML Schema (MLS) and the Dublin Core Vocabulary (DC)[7] such as *mls:Dataset*, *mls:Model*, and *dc:LicenseDocument* are reused as subclasses of *sao:InformationElement*. Classes defined in SAO and RAInS may be extended for more detailed domain specific descriptions. For example, concepts from the Decision Provenance ontology[8] such as *dp:Question*, *dp:Answer*, and *dp:Option* may be used as subclasses of *rains:InformationElement* to further describe documented human decisions.

---

[6] http://www.ontologydesignpatterns.org/ont/dul/IOLite.owl.

[7] https://www.dublincore.org/specifications/dublin-core/dcmi-terms/.

[8] https://promsns.org/def/decprov/decprov.html.

6 Evaluation

We performed a two stage evaluation[9] process where we first verified the design of SAO and RAInS and then validated their intended application within the accountability context (see Sect. 1) through prototype implementation and an example knowledge graph.

To enhance the clarity of both ontologies we produced standard documentation using Widoco[10]. The automated OOPS! Pitfall Scanner[11] was used throughout the ontology development process to prevent common pitfalls and bad modelling practices. The scanner did not highlight any issues directly related to SAO or RAINS[12]. We then implemented the *Accountability Fabric* prototype, a web-based tool for managing accountability plans and accountability traces. The tool (available on GitHub[13]) is a *Spring Boot*[14] app with HTML/JavaScript/CSS front end. It comprises three modules: *Accountability Plan Design Module, Provenance Capture Module*, and *Audit Module*. The *Accountability Plan Design Module* provides a web interface to design *accountability plans*, using steps and variables defined by SAO and RAInS. The *Provenance Capture Module* is responsible for recording the execution traces and associating them with the accountability plans. This module currently only generates web forms for manual human input, which was sufficient to evaluate SAO and RAInS against our knowledge capture requirements identified in Sect. 4. However, in future we plan to extend it to enable programmatic access for automated logging (see Sect. 7). The *Audit Module* provides a simple visual interface which allows the inspection of an AI system's accountability traces. Accountable agents are displayed along with their accountable actions and corresponding accountable results. Lastly, the storage and querying of the knowledge graphs is supported by the GraphDB[15] graph store, SPARQL and RDF4J library[16]. Information is described using PROV-O, EP-Plan, SAO, RAInS, DC and MLS (see Sect. 5).

The *Accountability Fabric* was used to create an accountability plan[17] for the design stage of an example machine learning-based medical image classification

---

[9] Evaluation results and instructions on how to reproduce them are available in the GitHub repository: https://github.com/RAINS-UOA/ESWC_2021_Evaluation.

[10] https://w3id.org/widoco.

[11] http://oops.linkeddata.es/.

[12] The tool produced one incorrect suggestion about potential class equivalence between *sao:System* and *prov:Organisation*. For completeness, we note that the reused ontologies PROV-O, DC, P-PLAN (which EP-Plan extends) and MLS - which we have no control over - produce a number of warnings related to missing domains and ranges, missing inverse properties, etc.

[13] https://github.com/RAINS-UOA/rains-workflow-builder/tree/ESWC-2021.

[14] https://spring.io/projects/spring-boot.

[15] https://www.ontotext.com/products/graphdb/.

[16] https://rdf4j.org/.

[17] The example plan was created with 19 steps, each producing one output variable.

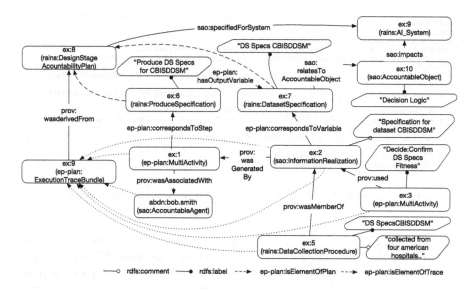

Fig. 5. A section of the knowledge graph from the medical image classification example.

system. It was then used to create an accountability trace[18] associated with the plan. Figure 5 depicts a portion of the generated knowledge graph[19] modelling the accountability plan and its corresponding trace. It illustrates an example where a dataset specification (*ex:2*) is described as an information realization containing an information element (*ex:5*); the latter describes its data collection procedure.

The knowledge graph was imported into Protégé[20] and the built-in Hermit reasoner was used to evaluate the consistency of the populated ontology and to infer additional relationships. The inferences were then inspected manually to validate their correctness. While all the inferences were correct, the Hermit reasoner identified an inconsistency originating from the MLS ontology which was initially imported in RAInS for the evaluation (*owl: Nothing EquivalentTo mls: Experiment*). However, this inconsistency does not affect the concepts reused by RAInS and MLS ontology is not imported by default. To validate whether our ontologies satisfy the three goals of accountability as outlined in Sect. 1 and the knowledge capture requirements described in Sect. 4, we used the *Audit Module* user interface to retrieve relevant information associated with the design stage of an AI system. The *Audit Module* presents an agent-centric interface focused on

---

[18] The trace contained: 19 activities (corresponding to the 19 steps); 19 information realizations (corresponding to the 19 variables); 16 accountable agents; and 48 information elements, including the 16 accountable agents.

[19] https://github.com/RAINS-UOA/ESWC_2021_Evaluation/tree/main/ exampleKnowledgeGraph.

[20] https://protege.stanford.edu.

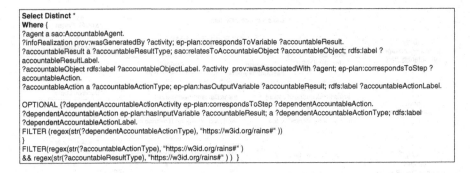

```
Select Distinct *
Where {
?agent a sao:AccountableAgent.
?infoRealization prov:wasGeneratedBy ?activity; ep-plan:correspondsToVariable ?accountableResult.
?accountableResult a ?accountableResultType; sao:relatesToAccountableObject ?accountableObject; rdfs:label ?
accountableResultLabel.
?accountableObject rdfs:label ?accountableObjectLabel. ?activity  prov:wasAssociatedWith ?agent; ep-plan:correspondsToStep ?
accountableAction.
?accountableAction a ?accountableActionType; ep-plan:hasOutputVariable ?accountableResult; rdfs:label ?accountableActionLabel.

OPTIONAL {?dependentAccountableActionActivity ep-plan:correspondsToStep ?dependentAccountableAction.
?dependentAccountableAction ep-plan:hasInputVariable ?accountableResult; a ?dependentAccountableActionType; rdfs:label
?dependentAccountableActionLabel.
FILTER (regex(str(?dependentAccountableActionType), "https://w3id.org/rains#" ))
}
FILTER(regex(str(?accountableActionType), "https://w3id.org/rains#" )
&& regex(str(?accountableResultType), "https://w3id.org/rains#" ) ) }
```

Fig. 6. An example SPARQL query for auditing accountability traces.

identifying how agents were involved in different aspects of the system design, the decisions they made and the outputs they produced. The *Audit Module* executes SPARQL queries[21] to populate the interface. Figure 6 illustrates a query used by the tool to retrieve details about the accountable agents who performed accountable actions along with the corresponding results. Figure 7 depicts a screenshot of the interface driven by the data in Fig. 5; the accountable actions of a selected agent (abdn:caitlin.d.c) are listed in the *Results* table. By clicking on the individual values within the table, more information about the corresponding instance is presented in the *Object Details* window.

Using this interface we were able to demonstrate that a system life-cycle stage can be made transparent by retrieving information about accountable agents, their activities, and accountable results described using SAO and RAINS to provide answers satisfying our knowledge requirements (see Sect. 4). This directly relates to the first of the three accountability goals discussed in Sect. 1. However, we also note that both SAO and RAInS are incomplete as they require extensions to cover specific domain applications and other life-cycle stages respectively. To satisfy the second accountability goal we inspected the information about human agent decisions (e.g. to assure system compliance with relevant hard and soft laws). Coverage provided by RAInS in this context is greater than the MLS ontology, and positions SAO and RAInS in a wider context encompassing social, technical and legal perspectives[22].

To demonstrate the ability of our approach to support identification of errors and responsible parties, consider Fig. 8. Here, it is evident that agents responsible for producing the design specification of the dataset and those responsible for its approval could be potentially held to account for the incorrect choice of the

---

[21] Relevant Java file https://github.com/RAINS-UOA/rains-workflow-builder/blob/master/rains-workflow-builder/src/main/java/uoa/web/handlers/SystemRecord Manager.java.

[22] The mapping of the CQs from Sect. 4 to the SAO and RAInS concepts that were created to address them, is summarised here: https://github.com/RAINS-UOA/ESWC_2021_Evaluation/blob/main/exampleKnowledgeGraph/DesignCQs.xlsx.

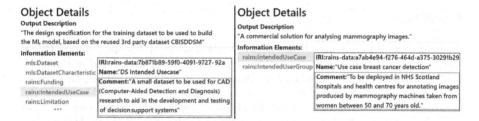

Fig. 7. The user interface of the *Accountability Fabric* audit module.

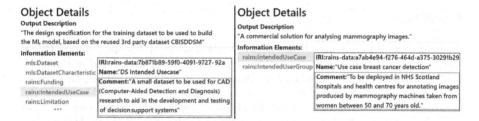

Fig. 8. Comparison between the *intended use cases* associated with the reused third party training *dataset* and the overall *system*. A discrepancy exists - as the dataset is not suitable for production ready solutions.

training dataset because of the mismatch between its intended use case and the intended use case of the AI system.

7 Conclusions and Future Work

In this paper, we have presented an ontology-based approach for supporting accountability of AI systems by increasing the transparency of their design stage using knowledge graphs. We demonstrated, via a proof of concept implementation, the application of SAO and RAInS ontologies to record *accountability traces* by following *accountability plans*.

In our future work, we aim to extend the RAInS ontology with further concepts applicable to other AI system life cycle stages such as implementation, deployment and operation. At the same time, we will expand the functionality of the *Accountability Fabric* framework to evaluate the practical application of the ontology. We also intend to enable data exchange pipelines between the *Accountability Fabric* and external frameworks through API access. For example, by integrating with the Model Card Toolkit used by developers to generate model cards [20], the *Fabric* would be able to extract information related to the implementation of AI systems. Another strand of activity will investigate whether the information contained in accountability plans can be passed to a development environment such as Jupyter Notebook[23] to prevent further model development if accountability information is not provided. Future versions of the *Accountability Fabric* are also set to be evaluated with real users (such as developers of AI systems) to identify real life implications of using such a tool. This may include, for example, issues related to commercial sensitivity of AI development if too much information is required by the accountability plan.

Finally, because the *Accountability Fabric* is designed to support collection of information from different sources, we also propose to investigate the challenges relating to the veracity of such information, considering questions such as who created the accountability trace, when was it created, etc. and how emerging standards such as RDF*[24] may help to address them.

References

1. ACM U.S. Public Policy Council (USACM) and ACM Europe Council Policy Committee (EUACM): Statement on algorithmic transparency and accountability, May 2017. https://www.acm.org/binaries/content/assets/public-policy/2017_joint_statement_algorithms.pdf. Accessed 24 Jan 2019
2. Amershi, S., et al.: Software engineering for machine learning: a case study. In: 2019 IEEE/ACM 41st Int'l Conference on Software Engineering: Software Engineering in Practice (ICSE-SEIP), pp. 291–300. IEEE (2019)
3. Cuevas-Vicenttín, V., et al.: Provone: a prov extension data model for scientific workflow provenance (2015). https://purl.dataone.org/provone-v1-dev
4. Curcin, V., Fairweather, E., Danger, R., Corrigan, D.: Templates as a method for implementing data provenance in decision support systems. J. Biomed. Inform. **65**, 1–21 (2017)
5. Department of Health & Social Care (UK): Code of conduct for data-driven health and care technology, July 2019. https://www.gov.uk/government/publications/code-of-conduct-for-data-driven-health-and-care-technology/initial-code-of-conduct-for-data-driven-health-and-care-technology
6. Diakopoulos, N.: Algorithmic accountability reporting: On the investigation of black boxes (2014), Tow Center for Digital Journalism, Columbia University
7. Diakopoulos, N., et al.: Principles for accountable algorithms and a social impact statement for algorithms. http://www.fatml.org/resources/principles-for-accountable-algorithms. Accessed 10 Jan 2019

---

[23] https://jupyter.org/.

[24] https://w3c.github.io/rdf-star/.

8. Digital Catapult Machine Intelligence Garage Ethics Committee: Ethics framework, April 2020. https://www.migarage.ai/wp-content/uploads/2020/05/MIG_Ethics-Report_2020_v6.pdf. Accessed 09 Jan 2020

9. Esteves, D., et al.: Mex vocabulary: a lightweight interchange format for machine learning experiments. In: Proceedings of the 11th International Conference on Semantic Systems, SEMANTICS 2015, pp. 169–176. ACM, September 2015

10. Garijo, D., Gil, Y.: Augmenting prov with plans in p-plan: scientific processes as linked data. In: Proceedings of the 2nd International Workshop on Linked Science (2012)

11. Gebru, T., et al.: Datasheets for datasets. In: Proceedings of the 5th Workshop on Fairness, Accountability, and Transparency in Machine Learning, PMLR 80 (2018)

12. House Of Lords Select Committee on Artificial Intelligence: AI in the UK: Ready, Willing and Able, April 2018, HL Paper 100

13. Huynh, T.D., Stalla-Bourdillon, S., Moreau, L.: Provenance-based Explanations for Automated Decisions: Final IAA Project Report. Technical report (2019)

14. IBM: Everyday ethics for artificial intelligence (2019). https://www.ibm.com/watson/assets/duo/pdf/everydayethics.pdf

15. Knublauch, H., Kontokostas, D.: Shapes constraint language (SHACL). W3C recommendation, W3C, July 2017. https://www.w3.org/TR/2017/REC-shacl-20170720/

16. Lebo, T., Sahoo, S., McGuinness, D.: PROV-O: The PROV ontology. W3C recommendation, W3C, April 2013. http://www.w3.org/TR/2013/REC-prov-o-20130430/

17. Markovic, M., et al.: Semantic modelling of plans and execution traces for enhancing transparency of IoT systems. In: 6th International Conference on Internet of Things: Systems, Management and Security (IOTSMS), pp. 110–115. IEEE (2019)

18. Markovic, M., Garijo, D., Edwards, P.: Linking abstract plans of scientific experiments to their corresponding execution traces. In: Proceedings of the 3rd International Workshop on Capturing Scientific Knowledge (Sciknow 2019). CEUR-WS (2019)

19. Menzies, T.: The five laws of SE for AI. IEEE Softw. **37**(1), 81–85 (2020)

20. Mitchell, M., et al.: Model cards for model reporting. In: Proceedings of the Conference on Fairness, Accountability, and Transparency, pp. 220–229. ACM (2019)

21. Pandit, H.J., Lewis, D.: Modelling provenance for GDPR compliance using linked open data vocabularies. In: Privacy and the Semantic Web - Policy and Technology workshop (PrivOn 2017), co-located with ISWC (2017)

22. Publio, G.C., et al.: ML Schema: exposing the semantics of machine learning with schemas and ontologies. In: 2nd Reproducibility in Machine Learning Workshop at ICML 2018, July 2018. poster

23. Suárez-Figueroa, M.C., Gómez-Pérez, A.: Neon methodology for building ontology networks: a scenario-based methodology. In: Proceedings of the International Conference on Software, Services & Semantic Technologies (2009)

24. The European Commission Independent High-Level Expert Group on Artificial Intelligence: Ethics Guidelines for Trustworthy AI, April 2019. https://ec.europa.eu/newsroom/dae/document.cfm?doc_id=60419

25. The IEEE Global Initiative on Ethics of Autonomous and Intelligent Systems: Ethically aligned design: A vision for prioritizing human well-being with autonomous and intelligent systems. Technical report, IEEE (2019). https://standards.ieee.org/content/ieee-standards/en/industry-connections/ec/autonomous-systems.html

26. The Royal College of Radiologists: Clinical radiology Scotland workforce 2019 summary report, August 2020. https://www.rcr.ac.uk/sites/default/files/clinical-radiology-scotland-workforce-census-2019-summary-report.pdf
27. Tianxing, M., Zhukova, N., Meltsov, V., Shichkina, Y.: A knowledge-based computational environment for real-world data processing. In: MisraMisra, S., et al. (eds.) ICCSA 2019. LNCS, vol. 11619, pp. 257–269. Springer, Cham (2019). https://doi.org/10.1007/978-3-030-24289-3_20
28. Wieringa, M.: What to account for when accounting for algorithms: a systematic literature review on algorithmic accountability. In: Proceedings of the 2020 Conference on Fairness, Accountability, and Transparency, FAT* 2020, pp. 1–18. ACM (2020)

Semantic Data Management, Querying
and Distributed Data

Comparison Table Generation from Knowledge Bases

Arnaud Giacometti, Béatrice Markhoff, and Arnaud Soulet[✉]

Université de Tours, LIFAT, Blois, France
{arnaud.giacometti,beatrice.markhoff,arnaud.soulet}@univ-tours.fr

Abstract. Comparison table is an efficient tool for comparing a small number of entities for decision making to analyze the main similarities and differences. The manual choice of their comparison features remains a complex and tedious task. This paper presents VERSUS, which is the first automatic method for generating comparison tables from knowledge bases of the Semantic Web. For this purpose, we introduce the contextual reference level to evaluate whether a feature is relevant to compare a set of entities. This measure relies on contexts that are sets of entities similar to the compared entities. Its principle is to favor the features whose values for the compared entities are reference (or frequent) in these contexts. We show how to select these contexts and how to efficiently evaluate the contextual reference level from a public SPARQL endpoint limited by a fair-use policy. Using our publicly available benchmark based on Wikidata, the experiments show the interest of the contextual reference level for identifying the features deemed relevant by users with high precision and recall. In addition, the proposed optimizations significantly reduce the execution time and the number of required queries.

1 Introduction

A comparison table is a double-entry table with entities that you want to compare in columns and comparison features in rows. The comparison table is a particularly useful tool for decision making by isolating the common points and major differences between compared entities. Therefore, this analytical technique is popular in science to compare works, in culture to compare art works or in commerce to compare products or services. This paper aims to fully automate the process of generating a comparison table of a set of entities by querying a knowledge base available on the Semantic Web such as DBpedia [2], YAGO [13] or Wikidata [16]. For instance, starting from Ada Lovelace and Alan Turing, we want to obtain a comparison table like the one presented by Table 1 built from Wikidata (the last column related to our method will be explained later). Beyond people, we aim to compare any entities such as places (countries, cities), objects (tapestries, statues), institutions (universities, political parties), events (tournaments, festivals) and so on. Unfortunately, there is no theoretical framework for the design of comparison tables to determine if a feature is interesting for comparing entities. This task is non-trivial since in 17% of the cases a human

© Springer Nature Switzerland AG 2021
R. Verborgh et al. (Eds.): ESWC 2021, LNCS 12731, pp. 179–194, 2021.
https://doi.org/10.1007/978-3-030-77385-4_11

evaluator does not know whether a feature is interesting or not (see Sect. 6.1 for details). In Table 1, it seems natural to use gender to compare two people. Besides, specifying that Turing was a member of the Royal Society is only interesting because two scientists are compared. Thus, the main challenge is to formalize the notion of *interesting* comparison feature. In addition, we want to benefit from the huge knowledge bases available on the Semantic Web, which raise a problem of robustness and efficiency. Indeed, these knowledge bases are relatively reliable but they most often suffer from incompleteness [10,18]. For this reason, it would be desirable that a feature considered interesting at a given moment remains so despite the subsequent addition of facts. For instance, in Table 1, completing Ada Lovelace's religion should not prevent the selection of "religion" as a comparison feature. Furthermore, rather than centralizing the data, we would like to directly query public SPARQL endpoints to build the comparison tables. This has the advantage of guaranteeing an optimal level of freshness. Nevertheless, the fair-use policy of these public endpoints, which cut off queries that are too expensive, raises optimization needs [12].

Table 1. A comparison table of Ada Lovelace and Alan Turing as running example

Features	Ada lovelace	Alan turing	*crl*
sex or gender	female	male	0.908
spoken language	English	English	0.472
member of		Royal Society	0.205
field of work	mathematics, computing	mathematics, logic, cryptanalysis, cryptography, computer science	0.110
manner of death	natural causes	suicide	0.100
religion	?	atheism	0.015

Along these lines, we investigate the first fully-automatic method for generating comparison tables for a particular set of entities without any information other than the knowledge base (meaning no manually-specified comparison features). Our entity-centric approach leads to the following contributions:

- We define a new interestingness measure, called *contextual reference level*, in order to judge if a feature is relevant for comparing a given set of entities. Its principle is to favor the reference features whose values are often used by other sets of similar entities, called *contexts*.
- We show with VERSUS how to select the contexts and how to efficiently evaluate the contextual reference level of a feature while minimizing the number of knowledge base queries. The idea is to estimate bounds and to interrupt the computation as soon as its interest is guaranteed or not.
- We evaluate VERSUS on a publicly available benchmark, named *Comparison Feature Benchmark* (CFB), that we developed to assess the quality of comparison features. It relies on comparison tables built from Wikidata and manually evaluated. On this benchmark, the contextual reference level leads,

with equal precision, to better recall and better accuracy than the state-of-the-art baselines including automatic facet generation. In addition, our optimized evaluation is significantly faster as it requires fewer queries.

The rest of the paper is organized as follows. Section 2 presents related work. Section 3 formalizes our problem. We introduce the contextual reference level and the VERSUS algorithm in Sects. 4 and 5. The experiments in Sect. 6 evaluate the approach qualitatively and quantitatively.

2   Related Work

To the best of our knowledge, there is no work to build a comparison table of a set of entities. We could resort to machine learning methods that learn to rank RDF properties [4]. Unfortunately, it would be difficult to gather feedback specific to our problem to build a training dataset. Besides, as the ranking of the properties depends on the compared entities (for example, `located in` is relevant for only 84.3% of comparison tables in our benchmark), this would require the construction of a training dataset of considerable size to cover all cases.

Most techniques that compare two entities in a knowledge base rely on a similarity measure [1,3]. Such measures are relevant for estimating the resemblance between two entities, but they do not explicitly give the comparison features [14]. In this direction, [9] builds relation paths in knowledge bases between two entities to identify all similarities and differences. Unfortunately, no interestingness measure filters out irrelevant paths leading to too many attributes (including irrelevant ones like identifiers). The tasks closest to ours are the infobox template generation [11,17] and the facet extraction [5,6,8,15]. First, an infobox is a set of attribute-value pairs describing an entity. The choice of attributes is based on a template defined for each class (grouping a set of entities). For instance, persons[1] are described by their name, birth date, nationality, highlights and so on. Many templates have been produced collaboratively by Wikipedia contributors, but methods have also been proposed to automatically refine these templates for more specific classes [11,17]. More recently, [11] proposed an unsupervised metric-based method that favors frequent attributes with popular values with respect to the PageRank. Unfortunately, as for [9], most of the attributes of the infoboxes describe *one* entity in a singular way and therefore cannot be used to compare *several* entities. For instance, image or notable works are not features that can be shared by two persons.

Second, faceted search consists of restricting a collection of entities by selecting only those with a certain value for a given attribute, called facet [15]. A relevant facet has frequently shared values among the observed entities. Typically, facets are temporal (publication date, birth date), spatial (conference location, birth place), personal (author, friend), material (subject, color) or energetic (activity, action) attributes [15]. There are a few automatic facet extraction methods. For a given class, [6] extracts from the infobox templates the attributes

---
[1] https://en.wikipedia.org/wiki/Template:Infobox_person.

whose values are frequently observed. Similarly, [8] measures the quality of an attribute by favoring frequently used attributes whose values are few and uniformly distributed. Recently, [5] proposes very similar measures to extract facets but a preprocessing method groups the quantitative values (which we do not consider in this paper) and a postprocessing method filters out the redundant facets. These methods mainly derive attributes for a limited number of classes containing a lot of entities. Evaluating very similar entities (like Ada Lovelace and Alan Turing) requires considering smaller groups of much more specific entities (e.g., persons employed by the University of Cambridge). Therefore, the main limitation of automatic facet extraction methods is to miss some very specific but very relevant features. Finally, unlike the facets used for navigation, it does not matter if a comparison feature has a lot of values in the knowledge base with an unbalanced distribution.

3   Problem Statement

A knowledge base on a set of relations $\mathcal{R}$ and a set of constants $\mathcal{E}$ (representing entities and values) is a set of facts $\mathcal{K} \subseteq \mathcal{R} \times \mathcal{E} \times \mathcal{E}$. We write the facts in the form $r(s, o) \in \mathcal{K}$, where r is the relation, s is the subject and o is the object. For instance, `religion(Turing, atheism)` indicates that Alan Turing was an atheist[2]. Given a relation r, $r^{-1}(s, o) \in \mathcal{K}$ means that $r(o, s) \in \mathcal{K}$ where r^{-1} is the inverse relation of r. Besides, $r_{\mathcal{K}}(s)$ (or more simply, $r(s)$ when the knowledge base $\mathcal{K}$ is clear) is the set of objects associated to the subject s for the relation r in $\mathcal{K}$. For instance, `field of work(Turing)` returns the set {`mathematics`, `logic`, `computer science`, `cryptanalysis`, `cryptography`}.

The notion of comparison table is formalized as follows:

Definition 1 (Comparison table). *Given a knowledge base $\mathcal{K}$, the comparison table of a set of entities $E \subseteq \mathcal{E}$ by a set of features $F \subseteq \mathcal{R}$ is a table with $|F|$ rows and $|E|$ columns where each cell intersecting a feature f and an entity e contains the values $f(e) = \{o \in \mathcal{E} : f(e, o) \in \mathcal{K}\}$.*

Definition 1 limits the comparison features to the relations of the compared entities. With this definition, to use relation paths [5,9] of greater length (such as "the country of the birth place"), it would be necessary to enrich the knowledge base (which we do not consider in this paper). Table 1 illustrates Definition 1 with the comparison table of the set of entities $E = \{$`Lovelace, Turing`$\}$ by the set of features $F = \{$`sex or gender, spoken language,` $\dots \}$. The cell at the intersection of `field of work` and `Turing` contains the values `field of work(Turing)`.

An interestingness measure $m : \mathcal{R} \times 2^{\mathcal{E}} \times 2^{(\mathcal{R} \times \mathcal{E} \times \mathcal{E})} \rightarrow [0, 1]$ evaluates the interest $m(f, E, \mathcal{K})$ of using the relation f as a feature for comparing the entities of E in the knowledge base $\mathcal{K}$.

Definition 2 (Interesting feature). *Given a KB $\mathcal{K}$, a set of entities $E \subseteq \mathcal{E}$, an interestingness measure $m : \mathcal{R} \times 2^{\mathcal{E}} \times 2^{(\mathcal{R} \times \mathcal{E} \times \mathcal{E})} \rightarrow [0, 1]$ and a threshold $\gamma \in [0, 1]$, an interesting feature $f \in \mathcal{R}$ (for m and γ) satisfies $m(f, E, \mathcal{K}) \geq \gamma$.*

---

[2] The `Typewriter` font denotes the literals from Wikidata that are used as illustrations.

Given a KB $\mathcal{K}$, a set of entities E, an interestingness measure m and a threshold γ, we aim at extracting all the interesting features $F = \{f \in \mathcal{R} : m(f, E, \mathcal{K}) \geq \gamma\}$ to build a comparison table of E by F.

For this purpose, we have to address two challenges. The first challenge consists in defining an interestingness measure that estimates the relevance of a feature from a knowledge base (see Sect. 4). The second challenge is to efficiently evaluate this measure by minimizing the number of SPARQL queries (see Sect. 5).

4 Contextual Reference Level of a Feature

4.1 Definition

Intuitively, to understand and to be able to interpret a comparison table, a feature is interesting if the values describing the compared entities are known by the user. In psychology, it is well known that the user needs at least one *reference* value to compare two values [14]. In particular, if these values are too rare (or even only characterize one compared entity), the user of the table is unlikely to know them because he has never been confronted with them. Sometimes such values are informative, but they do not help to compare the entities with each other. For instance, the place of burial of Ada Lovelace is Hucknall Church St Mary Magdalene while that of Alan Turing is Working Crematorium. There is no particular conclusion to draw from this difference (except perhaps that Alan Turing was atheist unlike Ada Lovelace, but the feature `religion` is much better suited to underline this point). Of course, this notion of scarcity is dependent on the compared entities. Even if there are only few people who are members of the Royal Society, this feature makes sense to compare two persons employed by the University of Cambridge. The key idea of our interestingness measure is to evaluate the relevance of a feature according to entities that are similar to the compared entities (for instance, those "being employed by Cambridge" or those "speaking English" for Ada Lovelace and Alan Turing). We formalize this intuition by introducing the notion of context:

Definition 3 (Context). *Given a set of entities $E \subseteq \mathcal{E}$ and a relation-object couple $(r, o) \in \mathcal{R} \times \mathcal{E}$ such that $E \subseteq r^{-1}(o)$, the context C for E stemming from (r, o) is the set of entities $r^{-1}(o) \backslash E$. $\mathbb{C}_E$ denotes the set of all contexts for E.*

Intuitively, a context C is a set of entities that are similar but different from the entities of E with respect to a relation-object couple (r, o) shared by all the entities of E. For the comparison table provided by Table 1, an example of context is the set of entities having English as spoken language (here, the relation-object couple is (`spoken language`, `English`)). Naturally, the classes are conducive to contexts. For example, all persons (i.e., entities with couple (`instance of`, `human`)) could constitute a context for Lovelace and Turing.

Given a set of entities $E \subseteq \mathcal{E}$, a feature $f \in \mathcal{R}$ and a context $C \in \mathbb{C}_E$, the more the set of values $f(e)$ with an entity $e \in E$ describes the entities of C, the more this feature f has a chance to be a referent for the user of the table. From this intuition, given an entity $e \in E$, we deduce that the interest of a feature f should increase with the probability of observing the values in $f(e)$ in the set of values $f(s)$ of similar entities $s \in C$: $Pr[f(s) \cap f(e) \neq \emptyset \mid s \in C]$. Then, given a set of entities $E = \{e_1, \ldots, e_P\}$ and a context $C \in \mathbb{C}_E$, we define the *contextual reference level* of a feature f, denoted by $crl_C(f, E, \mathcal{K})$, as the probability of observing the values $f(e_i)$ of at least one entity $e_i \in E$ in the set of values $f(s_i)$ of similar entities $s_i \in C$:

$$crl_C(f, E, \mathcal{K}) = Pr\big[(f(s_1) \cap f(e_1) \neq \emptyset) \vee \ldots \vee (f(s_P) \cap f(e_P) \neq \emptyset) \mid s_1 \in C, \ldots, s_P \in C\big]$$
$$= Pr\big[(\exists e_i \in E)(f(s_i) \cap f(e_i) \neq \emptyset) \mid s_i \in C\big]$$

It is indeed a probability because if a similar entity s_i shares features with several entities in E, it is counted only once. In practice, entities belong to several relevant contexts. For example, for Ada Lovelace and Alan Turing, we will consider the contexts stemming from four couples (see Sect. 5.2 for details): (field of work, mathematics), (employer, Univ. of Cambridge), (occupation, computer scientist) and (spoken language, English). For this reason, we extend the definition of $crl_C(f, E, \mathcal{K})$ to a set of contexts $\mathcal{C} = \{C_1, \ldots, C_K\}$ as follows:

Definition 4 (Contextual reference level). *Given a set of entities $E = \{e_1, \ldots, e_P\} \subseteq \mathcal{E}$ and a set of contexts $\mathcal{C} = \{C_1, \ldots, C_K\} \subseteq \mathbb{C}_E$, the contextual reference level of a feature f is defined as :*

$$crl_{\mathcal{C}}(f, E, \mathcal{K}) = Pr\big[(\exists e_i \in E)(\exists k \in [1..K])(f(s_i^k) \cap f(e_i) \neq \emptyset) \mid s_i^k \in C_k\big]$$

It is important to note that the compared entities E play a very strong role in this definition because they limit the choice of $\mathcal{C}$ in the set of potential contexts $\mathbb{C}_E$. The fourth column of Table 1 indicates the contextual reference level of each feature computed from Wikidata in the four contexts mentioned above. For instance, 0.908 corresponds to the probability of observing the value female or male (respectively stemming from Ada Lovelace or Alan Turing for e_i) as sex or gender of an entity s_i that is a mathematician or an employee of Cambridge or a computer scientist or an English speaker. With Definition 4, it would be possible to directly calculate the contextual reference level of a feature with a SPARQL query (not reported here due to the space limit). However, this statistical query would often be too costly not to be interrupted by the fair-use policy of public SPARQL endpoints [12]. Nevertheless, this definition implicitly assumes that the entities s_i^k are identically and independently drawn in the different contexts C_k. With this i.i.d. assumption, the following property rewrites the contextual reference level:

Property 1. Given a set of entities $E \subseteq \mathcal{E}$, a set of contexts $\mathcal{C} \subseteq \mathbb{C}_E$ and a feature $f \in \mathcal{R}$, we have:

$$crl_{\mathcal{C}}(f, E, \mathcal{K}) = 1 - \prod_{C \in \mathcal{C}} \prod_{e \in E} (1 - Pr[f(s) \cap f(e) \neq \emptyset] \mid s \in C]) = 1 - \prod_{C \in \mathcal{C}} (1 - crl_C(f, E, \mathcal{K}))$$

Due to lack of space, we omit the proofs, but this follows from Morgan's law. Interestingly, each probability $Pr\big[f(s) \cap f(e) \neq \emptyset \mid s \in C\big]$ can easily be calculated independently by a low-cost SPARQL query. We will see in Sect. 6.3 that in practice, the error rate of this kind of query is under 0.5%. In addition, considering Property 1, it is easy to see that the contextual reference level increases with the probability $Pr\big[f(s) \cap f(e) \neq \emptyset \mid s \in C\big]$ and that its range is $[0,1]$. The contextual reference level of the feature f is zero when no entity among those of the contexts $\mathcal{C}$ has a common value with the entities of E. Conversely, $crl_{\mathcal{C}}(f, E, \mathcal{K})$ is equal to 1 as soon as a value in $f(e)$ is shared by all the entities of at least one context C.

4.2   Quality Criteria Analysis

Properties 2–4 present three quality criteria that a well-behaved interestingness measure for evaluating features should satisfy. First, the following property proves that contextual reference level is monotone with respect to contexts:

Property 2. Given a KB $\mathcal{K}$, a feature f and a set of entities E, we have $crl_{\mathcal{C}}(f, E, \mathcal{K}) \leq crl_{\mathcal{C}'}(f, E, \mathcal{K})$ if the two sets of contexts satisfy $\mathcal{C} \subseteq \mathcal{C}' \subseteq \mathbb{C}_E$.

This result is explained by the addition of factors less than 1 in the double product of Property 1 when a context is added to $\mathcal{C}$. Interestingly, the addition of a new context favors the emergence of new interesting features (e.g., if a new relation is added to the knowledge base). However, we will see in Sect. 5.2 that this also raises problems of redundancy between contexts. The following property goes further by showing that contextual reference level is also robust against incompleteness for the feature f:

Property 3. Given two KBs $\mathcal{K}$ and $\mathcal{K}'$, a set of contexts $\mathcal{C} \subseteq \mathbb{C}_E$ and a feature f such that $f_{\mathcal{K}}(e) \subseteq f_{\mathcal{K}'}(e)$ for each $e \in E$, we have $crl_{\mathcal{C}}(f, E, \mathcal{K}) \leq crl_{\mathcal{C}}(f, E, \mathcal{K}')$.

This property underlines that the value of contextual reference level is always underestimated when some facts are missing. If new facts are added in the knowledge base, then the contextual reference level of a feature can only increase (if the context $\mathcal{C}$ remains unchanged). For this reason, the extracted features will remain interesting for crl if the knowledge base is completed. In Table 1, the feature `religion` was selected despite the lack of value for Ada Lovelace. Whatever the value could be stated, this feature would remain interesting for crl.

Finally, the next property proves that contextual reference level of a feature f is zero when it is an identifier (i.e., an injective function $f(x) = f(y) \Rightarrow x = y$):

Property 4. Given a set of entities E and a set of contexts $\mathcal{C}$, we have $crl_{\mathcal{C}}(f, E, \mathcal{K}) = 0$ for any feature f that is an identifier.

This result is explained by observing that for an injective function f, we have $f(e) \cap f(s) = \emptyset$ for any entity $e \in E$ and subject $s \in C$ because the set of entities E and any context C in $\mathcal{C}$ are disjoint (see Definition 3). Interestingly, an identifier f is not relevant for a comparison table because all values of f uniquely identifies an entity. For instance, for a set of countries, the property `GeoNames ID` is not an interesting feature w.r.t. crl.

Algorithm 1. VERSUS: extracting the set of interesting features w.r.t. *crl*

Input: A knowledge base $\mathcal{K}$, a set of entities $E \subseteq \mathcal{E}$ and a threshold γ
Output: The set of interesting features $F \subseteq \mathcal{R}$
 1: $F := \emptyset$
 2: $\mathcal{R}_E := \{r \in \mathcal{R} : e \in E \wedge r(e,s) \in \mathcal{K}\}$
 3: **for all** $f \in \mathcal{R}_E$ **do**
 4:    Select the set of contexts $\mathcal{C}$ for the entities E and the feature f with Algorithm 2
 5:    **if** $crl_{\mathcal{C}}(f, E, \mathcal{K}) \geq \gamma$ (using Algorithm 3) **then** $F := F \cup \{f\}$
 6: **end for**
 7: **return** F

---

5   VERSUS: A Method for Extracting Interesting Features

5.1   Overview

The overall idea is to analyze each relation f that describes at least one entity in E to determine whether it is an interesting feature in $\mathcal{K}$: $crl_{\mathcal{C}}(f, E, \mathcal{K}) \geq \gamma$. Algorithm 1 sketches this process. First, the set F that will contain all the interesting features is initialized with the empty set (Line 1) and the set of all the candidate relations $\mathcal{R}_E$ gathers the relations that describe at least one entity in E (Line 2). After, each relation in $\mathcal{R}_E$ is separately processed (Lines 3–6). Line 4 selects the set of contexts $\mathcal{C} \subseteq \mathbb{C}_E$ without considering the relation f (see Algorithm 2). This set of contexts is immediately used by Algorithm 3 in order to decide whether the relation f is an interesting feature for the entities in E. If f is really interesting for *crl*, it is added to the set of interesting features F. Finally, this set is returned at Line 7.

The rest of this section details Lines 4 and 5 based respectively on Algorithms 2 and 3. Section 5.2 gives the method for selecting the set of contexts. Of course, this choice is decisive in the calculation of the contextual reference level. Section 5.3 presents an efficient algorithm for evaluating the contextual reference level. Indeed, the naive evaluation of the contextual reference level is expensive, as for each feature, it requires to calculate $|\mathcal{C} \times E|$ queries for the numerators and $|\mathcal{C}|$ queries for the denominators (see Definition 4).

5.2   Context Selection

This step aims to select a small number of relevant contexts among all the contexts of $\mathbb{C}_E$ that may be redundant. Indeed, in the case where a large number of contexts in $\mathcal{C}$ are correlated, the contextual reference level might be abnormally overestimated (see Property 2). For example, since all employees of the University of Cambridge are necessarily humans, the context stemming from (instance of, human) does not provide additional information, but it increases the contextual reference level. It is however important to keep a set of contexts that cover all the specificities of the entities similar to E: $\bigcap \mathbb{C}_E$. For example, the context stemming from (occupation, computer scientist) is important because

---

Algorithm 2. Selecting a set of contexts

Input: A knowledge base $\mathcal{K}$, a set of entities $E \subseteq \mathcal{E}$ and a feature $f \in \mathcal{R}$
Output: A set of contexts $\mathcal{C} \subseteq \mathbb{C}_E$
1: $\mathcal{C} := \{r^{-1}(o) \backslash E : r \in (\mathcal{R} \backslash \{f\}) \land (\forall e \in E)(r(e, o) \in \mathcal{K})\}$
2: Sort the contexts of $\mathcal{C}$ by ascending cardinality
3: **for all** context $C_i \in \langle C_1, \ldots, C_n \rangle$ **do**
4:     **if** $\bigcap(\mathcal{C} \backslash C_i) = \bigcap \mathcal{C}$ **then** $\mathcal{C} := \mathcal{C} \backslash C_i$
5: **end for**
6: **return** $\mathcal{C}$

Table 2. Relation-object couples common to Ada Lovelace and Alan Turing

Relation r	Object o	$|r^{-1}(o) \backslash E|$
`field of work`	`mathematics`	2,018
`employer`	`Univ. of Cambridge`	3,129
`occupation`	`computer scientist`	7,943
~~`described by source`~~	~~`Obalky knih.cz`~~	47,563
`spoken language`	`English`	165,714
~~`instance of`~~	~~`human`~~	6,389,426

it distinguishes Ada Lovelace and Alan Turing from mathematicians at the University of Cambridge who have not contributed in computer science. In this way, we choose one of the smallest sets of contexts $\mathcal{C}^* \subseteq \mathbb{C}_E$ that characterizes the same set of entities as $\mathbb{C}_E$ by intersecting: $\mathcal{C}^* \in \arg \min_{\mathcal{C} \subseteq \mathbb{C}_E} \{|\mathcal{C}| : \bigcap \mathcal{C} = \bigcap \mathbb{C}_E\}$. The exact resolution of this problem is NP-hard and it would require a large number of knowledge base queries. We therefore propose a heuristic algorithm, which eliminates superfluous contexts from the smallest one to the largest one.

Given a knowledge base $\mathcal{K}$, a set of entities E and a feature f, Algorithm 2 returns a set of contexts $\mathcal{C}$. Line 1 builds the set of contexts $\mathbb{C}_E$ except it excludes the context stemming from the feature f (i.e., $r \neq f$). The contexts are then sorted from the smallest to the largest (Line 2) to favor the removal of overly general contexts. The loop (Lines 3–5) iterates over each context C_i starting with the smallest one. Line 4 tests whether the intersection of contexts without C_i gives the same set of entities as with C_i. If this is the case, it means that this context does not provide any specificity and it is discarded from $\mathcal{C}$. Once the loop is completed, Line 6 returns the set of non-redundant contexts.

Table 2 presents the relation-object couples (r, o) from which contexts are computed considering Ada Lovelace and Alan Turing. After having been sorted by ascending cardinality in Wikidata (i.e., $|r^{-1}(o) \backslash E|$), the two redundant contexts were eliminated by Lines 3–7 of Algorithm 2. For example, the restriction "instance of human" does not delete any entity among those belonging to all other contexts. It is important to note that the interest of an approach centered on entities is to consider contexts that do not depend only on classes (i.e., there are other relations than `instance of`). However, the number of contexts in $\mathcal{C}$ remains reasonable in practice (7 at most in our experiments). Most often, the iteration of Lines 3–5 removes few contexts, but in some cases, many redundant contexts are eliminated (for example, 167 in the most extreme case).

5.3 Efficient Evaluation of the Contextual Reference Level

Rather than calculating the exact contextual reference level of a feature, the idea is to do a partial calculation of this value in order to only determine whether $crl_C(f, E, \mathcal{K})$ is greater than γ. It is easy to see that the complement to 1 of the contextual reference level (i.e., $1 - crl_C(f, E, \mathcal{K})$) decreases with each multiplication by a factor of the form $\left(1 - Pr\big[f(s) \cap f(e) \neq \emptyset \mid s \in C\big]\right)$. With this observation, it is possible to derive a lower bound for the contextual reference level. In the process of calculation, when this lower bound exceeds the threshold γ, we have the guarantee that $crl_C(f, E, \mathcal{K}) \geq \gamma$. Conversely, it is possible to derive an upper bound of the contextual reference level by using $Pr[f(s) \cap f(e) \neq \emptyset, s \in \mathcal{E}]$ as an upper bound of the joint probability $Pr[f(s) \cap f(e) \neq \emptyset, s \in C]$. The following property formalizes these two bounds:

Property 5. Given a knowledge base $\mathcal{K}$, the contextual reference level of a feature f for the entities E is bounded for any $\mathcal{S} \subseteq \mathcal{C} \times E$:

$$crl_C(f, E, \mathcal{K}) \geq 1 - \prod_{(C,e) \in \mathcal{S}} \left(1 - Pr\big[f(s) \cap f(e) \neq \emptyset \mid s \in C\big]\right)$$

$$\leq 1 - \left[\prod_{(C,e) \in \mathcal{S}} \left(1 - Pr\big[f(s) \cap f(e) \neq \emptyset \mid s \in C\big]\right) \right.$$

$$\left. \times \underbrace{\prod_{(C,e) \in (\mathcal{C} \times E) \backslash \mathcal{S}} \left(1 - \frac{\min\{|\{s \in \mathcal{E} : f(s) \cap f(e) \neq \emptyset\}|, |C|\}}{|C|}\right)}_{\text{optimistic factor}} \right]$$

Algorithm 3 benefits from these bounds for efficiently evaluating if $crl_C(f, E, \mathcal{K}) \geq \gamma$. More precisely, Lines 1 and 2 respectively initialize the product p and the optimistic factor o discussed above by considering all the couples in $\mathcal{C} \times E$. The loops of Lines 3 and 4 enumerate the different entities $e \in E$ and the different contexts $C \in \mathcal{C}$. At each iteration, Line 5 refines the calculation of p taking into account the probability $Pr\big[f(s) \cap f(e) \neq \emptyset \mid s \in C\big]$ while Line 7 updates o. If the current contextual reference level is higher than the threshold γ, Line 6 returns *true* because $1 - p$ is a pessimistic approximation of the final contextual reference level. Conversely, Line 8 returns *false* when the upper bound $1 - p \times o$ is lower than γ.

Let us illustrate Algorithm 3 with the computation of the contextual reference level of two features for Ada Lovelace and Alan Turing with a threshold $\gamma = 0.01$ illustrated by Table 3. The probability of having an entity with a natural death (like Ada Lovelace) among those who studied mathematics is 0.025. From this evaluation, it is certain that `manner of death` is an interesting feature because its exact contextual reference level exceeds the lower bound $1 - (1 - 0.025)$ which is higher than the threshold γ. In this case, this avoids the evaluation of 7

Algorithm 3. Computing the contextual reference level of a relation

Input: A knowledge base $\mathcal{K}$, a set of entities $E \subseteq \mathcal{E}$, a threshold γ, a set of contexts $\mathcal{C}$ and a relation f

Output: Return true if the relation f is interesting i.e., $crl_\mathcal{C}(f, E, \mathcal{K}) \geq \gamma$

1: $p := 1$
2: $o := \prod_{(C,e)\in\mathcal{C}\times E} \left(1 - \frac{\min\{|\{s\in\mathcal{E}: f(s)\cap f(e)\neq\emptyset\}|,|C|\}}{|C|}\right)$
3: **for all** $e \in E$ **do**
4:     **for all** $C \in \mathcal{C}$ **do**
5:         $p := p \times (1 - (|\{s \in C : f(s) \cap f(e) \neq \emptyset\}|)/(|C|))$
6:         **if** $1 - p \geq \gamma$ **then** *true*
7:         $o := o/\left(1 - \frac{\min\{|\{s\in\mathcal{E}: f(s)\cap f(e)\neq\emptyset\}|,|C|\}}{|C|}\right)$
8:         **if** $1 - p \times o < \gamma$ **then** *false*
9:     **end for**
10: **end for**
11: **return** *false*

Table 3. Computation of crl of two features for Ada Lovelace and Alan Turing

Contexts $\mathcal{C}$	Entities E	field of work	employer	occupation	spoken language
manner of death	Lovelace	**0.025**	0.018	0.017	0.038
	Turing	0.002	0.001	0.002	0.003
student of	Lovelace	**0,000**	0,000	0,000	0,001
	Turing	0,001	0,000	0,000	0,001

queries that would have been necessary for the exact calculation of the contextual reference level. For the feature `student of`, the optimistic factor after the first evaluation is equal to 0.998. It is therefore sure that the contextual reference level of this feature is at most equal to $1 - (1 - 0) \times 0.998 = 0.002$ which is lower than the threshold γ. Again, the contextual reference level computation can be interrupted (Line 8) avoiding the evaluation of 7 queries.

6 Experiments

After presenting the evaluation benchmark in Sect. 6.1, our experiments aim to answer the following two questions: Does the contextual reference level really isolate the best features? (Q1) and What is the gain of the optimized evaluation? (Q2). These questions are respectively answered in Sects. 6.2 and 6.3. VERSUS is implemented in Java using the Jena library to query the public Wikidata SPARQL endpoint. VERSUS was run on Windows 10 with an Intel core i7 processor and 32 GB of RAM. Due to the few operations performed on the client side, the execution times correspond essentially to the processing time of SPARQL queries on the server side[3]. Although execution times vary with server

---

[3] https://query.wikidata.org/.

load and available data, they shape the behavior of the approaches. Note that the source code of VERSUS, the evaluation tool and the results are available on the website https://lovelace-vs-turing.com and github.com/asoulet/versus.

6.1   Comparison Feature Benchmark (CFB)

As comparison table generation is a new problem, we had to develop a benchmark, named *Comparison Feature Benchmark* (CFB). Its twofold objective is to constitute a reference dataset to compare the speed of different approaches and a gold standard to assess the quality of the discovered comparison features. This section starts by describing the method to select from Wikidata the sets of entities to be compared with their candidate comparison features. For simplicity, we consider only pairs of entities to be compared. Then, we explain how the quality of the candidate comparison features have been manually evaluated.

First, we randomly draw from Wikidata 1,000 types T_i ($i \in [1..1000]$) that have between 10k and 1k instances. This random sample guarantees to cover a wide variety of entities (person, place, objects, events and so on) in order to best reflect Wikidata diversity. Second, for each type T_i, we select the two entities e_i^1 and e_i^2 that have the highest degree of incoming facts (i.e., maximizing $\deg(e) = |\{s \in \mathcal{E} : r(s, e) \in \mathcal{K} \wedge e \in T_i\}|$). This in-degree ranking favors popular entities of the type T_i. For instance, the entities Paris (Q90) and London (Q84) are selected for the type city (Q515). Then, for each pair of entities $E_i = \{e_i^1, e_i^2\}$, we define the set F_i of relations r_j where $r_j \in \mathcal{R}$ has URI as objects, r_j is a direct property of Wikidata (by using the prefix http://www.wikidata.org/prop/direct/) and $r_j(e_i^1)$ or $r_j(e_i^2)$ is not empty (note that we do not consider the inverse relations less likely to be features). Thus, F_i is the set of candidate comparison features to compare entities in E_i. Finally, for each pair of entities $E_i = \{e_i^1, e_i^2\}$, we store in our benchmark CFB all the facts $r_j(e_i^k, o_i^k)$ ($k \in \{1, 2\}$) where $r_j \in F_i$ and o_i^k is an object randomly drawn from the values in $r_j(e_i^k)$ (if $r_j(e_i^k)$ is the empty set, then o_i^k is null). For each type T_i ($i \in [1..1000]$), this process builds a comparison table with $|F_i|$ rows and two columns to compare e_i^1 and e_i^2.

Second, 1,195 candidate features (out of the 11,852, or about 10%) were drawn at random and evaluated manually by one of the 6 evaluators. Each time, we asked if the candidate feature $r_j \in F_i$ was relevant to compare the pair of entities $E_i = \{e_i^1, e_i^2\}$ (by selecting in CFB the facts $r_j(e_i^1, o_i^1)$ and $r_j(e_i^2, o_i^2)$). The evaluator can answer "No", meaning that the feature r_j is not relevant (44.9% of the evaluations), "Yes" (37.9%) or "I don't know" (17.2%). Only 80 evaluations were common, of which 74 agreed. It leads to a Cohen's kappa coefficient of 0.832 that corresponds to an *almost perfect* agreement [7].

6.2   Q1: Quality of the Extracted Features

Figures 1 and 2 respectively report the precision-recall results (ignoring "I don't know" evaluations) and the number of comparison features. First, we benefit from the CFB benchmark described in the previous section for comparing the

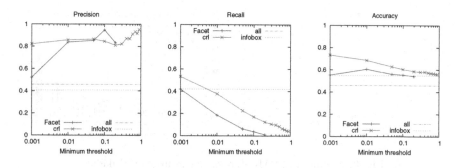

Fig. 1. Precision, recall and accuracy for crl, Facet, infobox and all

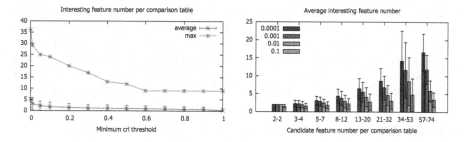

Fig. 2. Number of interesting features per comparison table

contextual reference level used by VERSUS (denoted by crl) with the metric used by automatic facet generation [8] (denoted by Facet). For the facet-oriented metric, the type T_i of the two entities (see above) is used to define the collection on which the metric is computed. We also use two baselines: the all method [9] that selects all the candidate features of the benchmark and the infobox method that selects all the candidate features present in at least one of the Wikipedia infoboxes of the entities E_i. Figure 1 reports the precision, recall and accuracy for these methods by varying the minimum threshold for crl and Facet. For the reasons mentioned in related work, we observe that the precision of all and infobox, less than 50%, is catastrophic. When the precision of Facet is better than that of crl, the recall of Facet is dramatically low (less than 20 features are extracted). Overall, the contextual reference level is much better than facet-oriented metric with comparable precision but higher recall and higher accuracy. This result is not surprising because, unlike Facet, our method brings out features specific to the two compared entities.

The precision of the contextual reference level, always above 76%, is generally high with regard to the baselines whose precision is less than 50%. Interestingly, this precision increases with the minimum contextual reference level threshold (from 76% for $\gamma = 0.0001$ to 86% for $\gamma = 0.05$). This demonstrates the ability of our measure to isolate the most relevant features. However, the recall decreases very quickly with the minimum contextual reference level threshold. This is

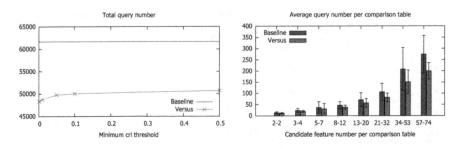

Fig. 3. Number of SPARQL queries executed on Wikidata

explained by the decrease in the number of interesting features with γ as shown in Fig. 2. With $\gamma = 0.1$, the left-hand side graph indicates that a comparison table contains only three features on average. However, the right-hand side graph shows strong disparities depending on the initial number of candidate features describing the entities (note that slices are non-linear). In practice, to have a good compromise, it seems appropriate to set γ with a value less than 0.1.

6.3   Q2: Efficiency of the Method

This section assesses the efficiency gain of the optimized method (VERSUS benefiting from Property 5) with a baseline where the exact value of the contextual reference level is calculated (baseline based on Property 1).

Figure 3 indicates the number of SPARQL queries required to build the 1,000 comparison tables of the benchmark. The left-hand side figure plots the total number of queries required by baseline and by VERSUS with respect to the minimum crl threshold. It is always more advantageous to use the optimized method because fewer queries are executed (around -20% of queries). VERSUS is even more efficient for low thresholds (i.e., $\gamma \leq 0.1$). For $\gamma = 0.01$, we observe on the right-hand side figure that the number of queries increases linearly with the number of candidate features to be tested. This result is expected because the number of contexts (between 1 and 7) is relatively independent of the number of features. Again, VERSUS is always more efficient.

The average execution time for building a comparison table with VERSUS is 58.8 s. In the worst case, it requires 693.1 s to generate that of two authors, namely the botanist Miguel Colmeiro and the poet Manuel Curros Enríquez. More precisely, Fig. 4 (left-hand side) details the average execution time to construct a comparison table according to the number of features. Unlike the number of queries, the execution time of the construction of a comparison table does not increase linearly with the number of features. In addition, the standard deviations are very high. This phenomenon is explained by the fact that not all queries have the same complexity. For instance, it is more expensive to evaluate a query with the person as context than with the country as context because the latter contains fewer entities. In particular, very few queries ($< 0.5\%$) have an execution time that exceeds the limit of the fair-use policy of Wikidata and fail

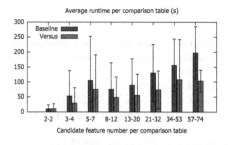 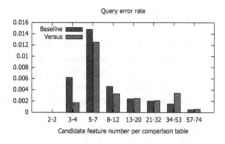

Fig. 4. Average running time and query error rate

as shown by the error rates on Fig. 4 (right-hand side). Interestingly, the gain in execution time of VERSUS is around 30%, better than the gain in number of queries (only 20%).

7 Conclusion

We presented VERSUS that automatically generates a comparison table of a set of entities from a knowledge base by querying its public SPARQL endpoint. To this end, we introduced the contextual reference level that evaluates whether a feature has values for the compared entities which are sufficiently common among other similar entities. We have broken down the computation of the contextual reference level into several low-cost SPARQL queries so that it satisfies the fair-use policy of Wikidata public endpoint. Finally, this computation is also optimized in VERSUS to reduce this number of queries. Experiments on our Comparison Feature Benchmark show the good precision of the contextual reference level for isolating the most relevant features. Interestingly, our entity-centric approach has a higher recall and accuracy than a baseline using facet-oriented metric, which relies on classes. Moreover, thanks to our optimization, VERSUS is about 30% faster than a naive approach. In future work, we would like to investigate other kinds of interestingness measures not based on the contextual reference level, but on the contrary, on exceptionality. If such measures are likely to have a weak recall, they could be used in addition to the contextual reference level for extracting unexpected features. Instead of evaluating each feature one by one, it would also be relevant to extract an interesting *set* of features so as to avoid redundancies. This would be essential to combine several endpoints from the Linked Open Data cloud that necessarily contain repeated information.

Acknowledgments. We thank the evaluators for the time they took to annotate the features. This work was partially supported by the grant ANR-18-CE38-0009 ("SESAME").

References

1. Anyanwu, K., Maduko, A., Sheth, A.: SemRank: ranking complex relationship search results on the semantic web. In: Proceedings of the 14th International Conference on World Wide Web, pp. 117–127 (2005)
2. Auer, S., Bizer, C., Kobilarov, G., Lehmann, J., Cyganiak, R., Ives, Z.: DBpedia: a nucleus for a web of open data. In: Aberer, K., et al. (eds.) ASWC/ISWC -2007. LNCS, vol. 4825, pp. 722–735. Springer, Heidelberg (2007). https://doi.org/10.1007/978-3-540-76298-0_52
3. d'Amato, C., Fanizzi, N., Esposito, F.: A semantic similarity measure for expressive description logics. arXiv preprint arXiv:0911.5043 (2009)
4. Dessi, A., Atzori, M.: A machine-learning approach to ranking RDF properties. Future Gener. Comput. Syst. **54**, 366–377 (2016)
5. Feddoul, L., Schindler, S., Löffler, F.: Automatic facet generation and selection over knowledge graphs. In: Acosta, M., Cudré-Mauroux, P., Maleshkova, M., Pellegrini, T., Sack, H., Sure-Vetter, Y. (eds.) SEMANTiCS 2019. LNCS, vol. 11702, pp. 310–325. Springer, Cham (2019). https://doi.org/10.1007/978-3-030-33220-4_23
6. Hahn, R., et al.: Faceted Wikipedia search. In: Abramowicz, W., Tolksdorf, R. (eds.) BIS 2010. LNBIP, vol. 47, pp. 1–11. Springer, Heidelberg (2010). https://doi.org/10.1007/978-3-642-12814-1_1
7. Landis, J.R., Koch, G.G.: The measurement of observer agreement for categorical data. Biometrics, pp. 159–174 (1977)
8. Oren, E., Delbru, R., Decker, S.: Extending faceted navigation for RDF data. In: Cruz, I., et al. (eds.) ISWC 2006. LNCS, vol. 4273, pp. 559–572. Springer, Heidelberg (2006). https://doi.org/10.1007/11926078_40
9. Petrova, A., Sherkhonov, E., Cuenca Grau, B., Horrocks, I.: Entity comparison in RDF graphs. In: d'Amato, C., et al. (eds.) ISWC 2017. LNCS, vol. 10587, pp. 526–541. Springer, Cham (2017). https://doi.org/10.1007/978-3-319-68288-4_31
10. Razniewski, S., Suchanek, F., Nutt, W.: But what do we actually know? In: Proceedings of the 5th Workshop on Automated Knowledge Base Construction, pp. 40–44 (2016)
11. Sáez, T., Hogan, A.: Automatically generating Wikipedia info-boxes from Wikidata. In: Companion Proceedings of the Web Conference 2018, pp. 1823–1830 (2018)
12. Soulet, A., Suchanek, F.M.: Anytime large-scale analytics of linked open data. In: Ghidini, C., Hartig, O., Maleshkova, M., Svátek, V., Cruz, I., Hogan, A., Song, J., Lefrançois, M., Gandon, F. (eds.) ISWC 2019. LNCS, vol. 11778, pp. 576–592. Springer, Cham (2019). https://doi.org/10.1007/978-3-030-30793-6_33
13. Suchanek, F.M., Kasneci, G., Weikum, G.: Yago: a core of semantic knowledge. In: Proceedings of the 16th International Conference on World Wide Web, pp. 697–706 (2007)
14. Tversky, A.: Features of similarity. Psychol. Revi. **84**(4), 327 (1977)
15. Tzitzikas, Y., Manolis, N., Papadakos, P.: Faceted exploration of RDF/S datasets: a survey. J. Intell. Inf. Syst. **48**(2), 329–364 (2017)
16. Vrandečić, D., Krötzsch, M.: Wikidata: a free collaborative knowledgebase. Commun. ACM **57**(10), 78–85 (2014)
17. Wu, F., Weld, D.S.: Automatically refining the Wikipedia infobox ontology. In: Proceedings of the 17th International Conference on World Wide Web, pp. 635–644 (2008)
18. Zaveri, A., Rula, A., Maurino, A., Pietrobon, R., Lehmann, J., Auer, S.: Quality assessment for linked data: survey. Semantic Web **7**(1), 63–93 (2016)

Incremental Schema Discovery at Scale for RDF Data

Redouane Bouhamoum$^{(\boxtimes)}$, Zoubida Kedad, and Stéphane Lopes

DAVID Lab, University of Versailles Saint-Quentin-en-Yvelines, Versailles, France
{redouane.bouhamoum,zoubida.kedad,stephane.lopes}@uvsq.fr

Abstract. The lack of a descriptive schema for an RDF dataset has motivated several research works addressing the problem of automatic schema discovery. The goal of these approaches is to generate a structural schema of a given RDF dataset from its instances. However, as new instances are added, the generated schema may become inconsistent with the dataset.

In this paper, we propose an incremental schema discovery approach for massive RDF datasets. It is based on a scalable and incremental density-based clustering algorithm which propagates the changes occurring in the dataset into the clusters corresponding to the classes of the schema. Our approach is implemented using big data technology to scale up schema discovery while providing a high quality clustering result. We present some experiments which demonstrate the efficiency of our proposal on both synthetic and real datasets.

Keywords: Incremental schema discovery · RDF data · Big data · Clustering

1 Introduction

The Web of data represents a huge information space consisting of an increasing number of interlinked datasets described using the Resource Description Framework (RDF)[1]. One important feature of such datasets is that they contain both the data and the schema describing the data. However, these schema-related declarations are not mandatory, and are not always provided. As a consequence, the schema may be incomplete or missing.

The lack of schema offers a high flexibility while creating interlinked datasets, but can also limit their use. Indeed, it is not obvious to query or explore a dataset without any knowledge on its resources, classes or properties. The exploitation of an RDF dataset would be easier with a schema describing the data.

We have proposed in previous works a schema discovery approach suitable for very large datasets, which relies on a scalable density-based clustering algorithm [3]. It enables fast density-based clustering on large datasets and provides

---

[1] RDF: https://www.w3.org/RDF/.

© Springer Nature Switzerland AG 2021
R. Verborgh et al. (Eds.): ESWC 2021, LNCS 12731, pp. 195–211, 2021.
https://doi.org/10.1007/978-3-030-77385-4_12

a good quality schema. However, RDF datasets are subject to frequent evolutions over time, and new instances may be inserted. For example, between version 3.5 and version 3.9 of DBpedia[2], the number of triples having the class *Person* as their object has been multiplied by 45 [14]. Due to such evolution, the ability to perform incremental updates on the schema has emerged as a new challenge.

In this work, we introduce an incremental schema discovery approach for large RDF datasets. Our contribution is an incremental density-based clustering algorithm for building and updating the clusters that represent the classes of the schema. Our algorithm incrementally updates the classes describing an RDF dataset in order to keep the schema consistent with the evolution of the data and ensures that the result is the same as if the clustering algorithm has been executed on the whole dataset in one go. In addition, the incremental clustering process is parallelized to be efficient on large datasets. The source code of the implementation of our algorithm, based on the distributed processing framework Apache Spark[18] is available online[3].

The rest of the paper is organized as follows. Section 2 presents the problem addressed in this paper and provides some preliminary notations. The general idea of our approach is introduced in Sect. 3. Section 4 presents our data distribution principle. Section 5 describes the computation of the neighborhood of the newly inserted entities. Section 6 presents the generation of the new schema. Experimental results are presented in Sect. 7, and Sect. 8 discusses the related works. Finally, a conclusion is provided in Sect. 9.

2 Problem Statement

An RDF *dataset* is a set of RDF(S)/OWL triples $\mathcal{D} \subseteq (\mathcal{R} \cup \mathcal{B}) \times \mathcal{P} \times (\mathcal{R} \cup \mathcal{B} \cup \mathcal{L})$, where $\mathcal{R}$, $\mathcal{B}$, $\mathcal{P}$ and $\mathcal{L}$ represent resources, blank nodes (anonymous resources), properties and literals respectively. In such dataset, an *entity* e is either a resource or a blank node, that is, $e \in \mathcal{R} \cup \mathcal{B}$. We denote by D the set of entities of the dataset $\mathcal{D}$. We define a function, denoted $\overline{}$, which returns the set of properties of an entity: $\overline{e} = \{p \in \mathcal{P} \mid \langle e, p, o \rangle \in D\}$. This function can be extended for a set of entities $E \subseteq D$: $\overline{E} = \bigcup_{e \in E} \overline{e}$. The dataset D is described by the schema S, defined as follows.

Definition 1. *A schema S describing a dataset D is composed of a set of classes $\{C_1, \ldots, C_n\}$, where each C_i is described by the set of properties $\overline{C_i} = \{p_1^i, \ldots, p_{m_i}^i\}$.*

Consider that over time, new sets of entities are added incrementally to the dataset D. The addition of a set of entities denoted Δ_D to the dataset D may result in S to become incoherent with the new dataset $D \cup \Delta_D$.

To deal with this problem, we make the following assumptions:

1. The dataset D and the newly inserted set of entities Δ_D can both be massive.

---

[2] https://www.dbpedia.org/.

[3] https://github.com/BOUHAMOUM/incremental_sc_dbscan.git.

2. The schema S describing the dataset D has been generated using a density-based clustering approach. Among the clustering algorithms, our work focuses on density-based clustering (DBSCAN) [7] which has been used for schema discovery on RDF data and has provided good results [3,11]. We assume in the present work that the schema is produced using this algorithm.
3. The entities of the dataset are compared using the *Jaccard index* which is defined as the size of the intersection of the property sets divided by the size of their union [10]: $\forall e_i, e_j \in D, J(e_i, e_j) = \frac{|e_i \cap e_j|}{|e_i \cup e_j|}$

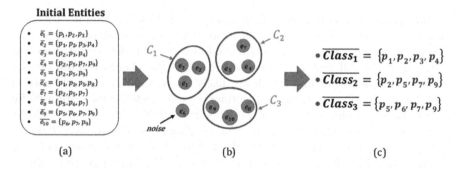

Fig. 1. Example of a set of entities and the corresponding schema

Figure 1 presents a set of entities (Fig. 1a) grouped into three clusters (Fig. 1b) using DBSCAN. The similarity threshold ϵ is set to 0.7 and the density threshold $minPts$ to 2. The resulting clusters represent the classes of the schema (Fig. 1c).

In this work, our aim is to update the schema S considering the entities within Δ_D. In order to update this schema, we have to modify the classes impacted by the insertion of the new entities, or create new classes when necessary. The resulting schema after the propagation of updates in the set of existing classes is a descriptive schema which represents the whole dataset, consisting of both the initial dataset D and the set of newly inserted entities Δ_D.

3   General Approach

We design in this paper an incremental, distributed, density-based clustering algorithm to extract a schema from large RDF datasets that evolve over time. It allows to keep the schema coherent with the dataset when new entities are added. In order to efficiently manage incrementally growing big datasets, the clustering is restricted to new entities and their neighborhood within the old entities. Clustering the new entities and updating the clusters within their neighborhoods ensures providing the same result as executing DBSCAN on the global data [6].

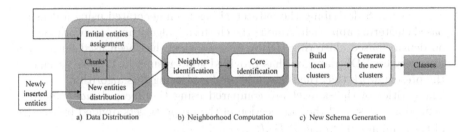

Fig. 2. Overview of the incremental schema discovery approach

Our approach is composed of three main steps parallelized and implemented using big data technology. Figure 2 illustrates these different steps.

First, data are split into subsets, called *chunks*, in order to distribute the entities over the different processes (see Fig. 2a). The chunks contain entities sharing some properties and which are likely to be similar. The new entities from Δ_D are distributed, then the identifiers of the created chunks are used for the assignment of old entities from D. This way, all the entities that could be similar to new ones, whether in D or Δ_D, are grouped in at least one chunk.

Second, in parallel on each node, the neighborhood for each new entity is computed (see Fig. 2b). At the end of this step, entities having dense neighborhoods, called *core entities*, are identified.

Finally, based on the neighborhood of the new entities, the set of clusters is built locally in each chunk. The clusters produced within each chunk are then merged to generate the new clusters that represent the classes of the new schema as illustrated in Fig. 2c.

We have implemented our algorithm using Spark [18], a big data technology offering a fast distributed execution of the approach and allowing to manage massive datasets. The following sections detail our proposal.

4 Data Distribution Principle for Neighborhood Computation

Computing the neighborhood of the new entities may require a very high number of comparisons. We propose to distribute these new entities according to the distribution principle introduced in [3], where the entities of the dataset are split into different subsets according to their properties. The comparison of entities is performed within each chunk in parallel, thus speeding up the clustering process.

The intuition behind our distribution method is to group entities sharing some properties into chunks to ensure that all the pairs of similar entities will be detected. Indeed, according to the similarity index, two entities are similar if they share a number of properties higher than a given threshold. Thus, entities that could be similar are grouped together in at least one chunk, and will be compared during the computation of their neighborhood. If two entities are not grouped in any of the resulting chunks, this means that they are not similar.

This distribution principle allows to skip meaningless comparisons as the similarity between entities in different chunks is not evaluated.

In this section, we first describe how to split the new dataset into chunks, then we show how to assign the initial entities to the created chunks by identifying the ones that could be similar to one of the newly inserted entities.

4.1 Distributing New Entities over Chunks

In our incremental algorithm, we distribute the new entities according to the properties describing them. An entity is distributed according to its properties over several chunks to ensure that it will be compared to all of its neighbors. To optimize the distribution of entities in our approach, we do not consider all the properties of the entities. Thus we limit the duplication of entities in the different chunks and reduce the cost of the comparison process by skipping useless comparisons.

To this aim, the notion of *prefix-filter* is adapted [4]. The intuition behind this notion is that, to be similar, two sets have to share a sufficient number of elements. This number of elements depends on the similarity threshold and on the size of the sets. Moreover, elements must always be chosen in the same order, and thus a total ordering on the elements has to be defined. This result allows to filter candidates considering only their prefix.

From this notion, we define a *dissimilarity threshold* for an entity e as follows:

Definition 2. *Let ϵ be the similarity threshold chosen by the user. The dissimilarity threshold for an entity e is the number $dt_\epsilon(e) = |\overline{e}| - \lceil \epsilon \times |\overline{e}| \rceil + 1$.*

This threshold represents the number of properties to consider in order to decide whether this entity could be similar to any other one. It allows to reduce the number of entities to be considered when searching for the neighborhood of a given entity. Note that the *dissimilarity threshold* as defined in our work is based on the Jaccard similarity index. Using another index would require to propose another definition of this threshold based on this index.

As mentioned above, in order to choose the properties for the prefix, we define a total ordering on the properties.

Definition 3. *Let $<_{\mathcal{P}}$ be a total order on the properties describing a dataset, e an entity with $\overline{e} = \{p_1, p_2, \ldots, p_n\}$ and $p_i <_{\mathcal{P}} p_{i+1}$ for $1 \leq i < n$. The comparison set of e denoted by $cs(e)$ is the set of properties $\{p_1, p_2, \ldots, p_{dt_\epsilon(e)}\}$.*

We will now introduce the definition of a *chunk*.

Definition 4. *A chunk for a property $p \in \mathcal{P}$ denoted by $[p]$ is a subset of entities having the property p in their comparison set: $[p] = \{e \mid p \in cs(e)\}$.*

Previous results about prefix-filter ensure that by comparing only entities inside chunks, all the comparisons required for the clustering will be performed at least once [4]. The proof of the correctness of this proposition is provided in [3]. For example, if $\epsilon = 0.7$, the entity e_1' described by $\overline{e_1'} = \{p_1, p_5, p_8\}$ is assigned to the chunk $[p_1]$ since $dt(e_1') = 1$ and $cs(e_1') = \{p_1\}$, and e_2' described by $\overline{e_2'} = \{p_1, p_3, p_5, p_8\}$ is assigned to $[p_1]$ and $[p_3]$ since $dt(e_2') = 2$ and $cs(e_2') = \{p_1, p_3\}$. These two entities are similar, they are grouped and compared in $[p_1]$.

Algorithm 1 describes the distribution of the new entities over the chunks. It requires as input the list of new entities and the similarity threshold ϵ. The distribution of entities is performed in parallel and defines for each entity the chunks it is assigned to (line 1–3) resulting in partial chunks, which are then merged to build the final chunks.

Algorithm 1. Distributing new entities

Require: the new dataset Δ_D, the similarity threshold ϵ
1: **for all** entity e' in Δ_D **do in parallel**
2:    **for all** property $p \in cs(e')$ **do**
3:        $[p] = [p] \cup \{e'\}$
4: Merge the chunks generated by the parallel execution for the same properties
5: **return** the chunks

Entities of Δ_D are distributed over chunks. As they can be in the neighborhood of entities of D, we need to identify which entities of D have to be added to the generated chunks. This is the focus of the following subsection.

4.2   Assigning Initial Entities to Chunks

As previously stated, the clusters that could be updated due to the insertion of new entities are those within the neighborhood of the new entities. Thus, the entities in D that are in the neighborhood of a newly inserted entity have to be identified. To this end, old entities that share common properties with the new ones are distributed over the generated chunks. By initial entities, we mean the entities in the dataset D prior to the addition of Δ_D, the set of new entities.

To distribute the entities in D, we first determine which properties have to be considered: for each entity $e \in D$, we compute its comparison set $cs(e)$ to select the properties to be considered in order to determine the chunks it will be assigned to. The entities are assigned to the existing chunks according to their comparison set. Note that no new chunk is created: old entities are only assigned to chunks already created during the distribution of the new entities. An old entity e is assigned to a chunk $[p]$ if $p \in cs(e)$ and $\exists e' \in \Delta_D, e' \in [p]$. For example, suppose that the created chunks are $[p_1]$ and $[p_3]$. The old entity e_2 described by $\overline{e_2} = \{p_1, p_2, p_3, p_4\}$ is assigned to the chunk $[p_1]$. Indeed, $cs(e_1) = \{p_1, p_2\}$, however, the chunk $[p_2]$ is not created and e_1 is only assigned to $[p_1]$.

The distribution principle used in this paper ensures that each new entity is grouped with all its candidate neighbors in $D \cup \Delta_D$. New entities are compared with all their candidate similar entities in order to define their neighborhood, and then the clusters that should be updated or created are identified.

5   Computing the Neighborhood of the New Entities

In order to propagate the insertion of new entities into the existing schema, we need to compute the neighborhood of the new entities considering both the newly added entities and the old ones which have been previously assigned to existing clusters. This section first describes neighborhood computation for each new entity, then presents the identification of core entities in order to build the clusters.

As the chunks contain entities which are likely to be similar, the ϵ-neighborhood of a new entity is identified by computing the similarity between this new entity and all the other ones in the same chunk. We evaluate the similarity between two entities e_i and e_j using the *Jaccard index*.

Definition 5. *The ϵ-neighborhood of an entity e' is the set of entities similar to e' with a threshold of ϵ: $neighborhood_\epsilon(e') = \{e \in D \cup \Delta_D \mid J(e',e) \geq \epsilon\}$*

We distinguish between three kinds of entities: *core entities* with at least *minPts* entities in their ϵ-*neighborhood*, *border entities*, that are not core entities but have at least one core entity in their ϵ-*neighborhood*, and *noise entities*, that are not core entities and have no core entity in their ϵ-*neighborhood*. The latters are never assigned to a cluster.

The ϵ-*neighborhood* is computed for each new entity e' in each chunk by comparing e' to all the entities (new or old) within the same chunk. The ϵ-*neighborhood* is calculated in parallel in the different chunks, independently. The computation of the ϵ-*neighborhood* of the old entities is not required since they have already been clustered in previous iterations. However, the neighborhood of an old entity is updated if it is similar to a new entity. Indeed, old entities that were either border or noise entities can become cores or borders, which would result in updating the old clusters.

Since the neighborhood of entities can be distributed over different chunks, the neighbors discovered in each chunk are consolidated, and the list of neighbors for each entity in the whole dataset is built.

This process leads to the identification of the *core entities*, from which the clusters will be initiated; the cores are the entities having a number of neighbors greater or equal to *minPts*. The old border and noise entities that are similar to new ones can become core or border entities; adding new entities to their ϵ-*neighborhood* could make the number of their neighbors higher or equal to *minPts* and they will therefore become core entities, or they can be neighbors of a new core. As a consequence to such change occurring for an old entity, the clusters existing prior to the insertion of the new entities have to be updated.

Old entities that are not similar to a new one within a chunk are removed since they will not induce any change on the existing clusters and they will not be assigned to any new cluster.

6   Generating the New Schema

In order to update the schema, we first modify the clusters locally in the chunks based on the neighborhood of the new entities. This is performed in parallel within each chunk, providing the local clusters, which are then processed in order to determine the ones that have to be merged. Finally, the new schema is generated by propagating the updates on the old clusters.

6.1   Updating Clusters in Each Chunk

After adding the set of entities Δ_D, three situations may occur: (i) existing clusters could be updated by adding new elements, (ii) some clusters could be merged and (iii) new clusters could be created from new core entities.

In a density-based clustering algorithm, the clusters are built according to the density-reachability principle, introduced by the DBSCAN algorithm [7].

Definition 6. *An entity e is* density-reachable *from an entity e' wrt. ϵ and minPts if there is a chain of entities $e_1, \ldots, e_z$, $e_1 = e'$, $e_z = e$ such that e_{i+1} is a core entity and e_i is in its ϵ-neighborhood, $\forall i \in \{1, \ldots, z\text{-}1\}$.*

Based on the core entities, the following change operations can be performed:

- If the ϵ-*neighborhood* of a new core $e' \in \Delta_D$ contains an old core entity $e \in D$ which belongs to an old cluster C, then the entity e' is assigned to C and C is also expanded with entities that are density-reachable from e'.
- If a core entity $e \in D \cup \Delta_D$ has no old core entity in its ϵ-*neighborhood*, then a new cluster is created and the entities that are density-reachable from e are added to this cluster.
- If the ϵ-*neighborhood* of a core entity $e \in D \cup \Delta_D$ contains two of more old core entities, which belong to distinct clusters, then these clusters are merged and the resulting cluster is expanded with the entities that are density-reachable from e.
- If an old core entity has a new entity which is not a core within its neighborhood, then the corresponding new entity is absorbed by the cluster containing this old core entity.

Note that the number of cores is lower than the total number of entities within a chunk. Therefore, iterating over the cores instead of all the entities improves the efficiency of the process.

During this stage, we update the clusters in the neighborhood of the new entities according to the rules defined above. These rules are executed in parallel in the different chunks based on the neighborhood of the entities. Updating the clusters in each chunk is performed considering similar entities within this chunk, providing local clusters.

Algorithm 2 describes the update of the set of clusters within each chunk. It iterates over each core entity within the chunks (line 3); these core entities could be new entities or old ones that have a newly inserted entity in their

---

Algorithm 2. New Local Clusters

Require: CH: the chunks, $Cores$: the new core entities
1: **for all** $[p] \in CH$ **do in parallel**
2:    is-visited $= \emptyset$
3:    **for all** $e \in Cores$ **do**
4:       **if** $e \notin$ is-visited **then**
5:          is-visited $=$ isVisited $\cup \{e\}$
6:          **if** $e.cluster \neq null$ **then**
7:             $C = e.cluster$
8:          **else**
9:             Create a new cluster $C = \{e\}$
10:            $C = C \cup neighborhood_\epsilon(e)$
11:            **for all** $e' \in C \mid e' \in cores$ and $e' \notin$ is-visited **do**
12:               **if** $e'.cluster = null$ **then**
13:                  $C = C \cup \{e'\} \cup neighborhood_\epsilon(e')$
14:               **else**
15:                  $c' = e'.cluster$
16:                  $c = c \cup c'$
17:         local-clusters $=$ local-clusters $\cup C'$
18: **return** local-clusters

---

neighborhood. Then, the algorithm identifies the cluster of the current core in order to expand it (line 6–7) or create a new cluster for this core (line 9), and the cluster is expanded by adding the neighbors of the core (line 10). Next, the algorithm identifies among the added neighbors, those which are cores (line 11), and adds their neighbors to the cluster if they do not belong to any other cluster (line 12–13). If the created cluster C contains a core entity that belongs to another cluster C', then these two clusters are merged (line 15–16).

At the end of this stage, clusters are produced in each chunk. The next section describes the process of building the final clustering result.

6.2 Generating the Final Clusters

Due to data distribution, some clusters may span across multiple chunks. First, the clusters updated independently within the chunks could have elements distributed into different chunks. These clusters share some core entities and will therefore be merged. Second, the clustered entities are either new entities or old entities in the neighborhood of new ones. In order to provide the final result, the updates performed on the clusters have to be propagated in the old entities which have not been distributed in the chunks and have not been considered during the clustering.

In this section, we first describe the identification of the clusters that span across several chunks, and the way the corresponding local clusters are merged. This process is executed on one computing node and is not parallelized. Then, we present the generation of the new schema according to the computed clusters.

According to the density-based clustering algorithm, an entity e is assigned to a cluster C if e is density-reachable from a core entity in C. If this same entity e is also in another local cluster C', e is also density-reachable from a core entity in C'. If e is a core, it represents a bridge between the entities in the clusters C and C', making them density-reachable. The clusters that span across several chunks are therefore identified by finding out the local clusters that share a common core entity within the newly inserted entities. These clusters are merged to produce the final result. For example, the clusters $C_{p_1.1}$ and $C_{p_3.1}$ produced respectively within the chunks $[p_1]$ and $[p_3]$, are merged if they share a common core entity e'_1. The border entities assigned to different clusters are randomly assigned to one of these clusters.

After producing the final clusters representing the new entities and their neighborhood, this result is propagated in the old clusters to construct the new schema. The old clusters to consider at this stage are those which have been merged as a consequence of the insertion of a new core in their neighborhood. The entities previously assigned to these old clusters should therefore be reassigned to the new cluster resulting from the merging.

If two old clusters C_i and C_j are merged to produce a new cluster C', all the elements of these clusters should be assigned to C'. However, not all the old entities are distributed over the chunks. We therefore need to change the assignment of old entities which have not been distributed in the chunks and which belong to clusters that have been merged into a new one.

Finally, all the entities that are not assigned to a cluster, are considered as noise.

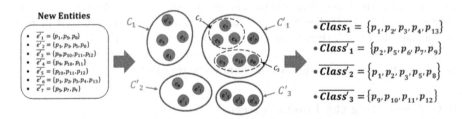

Fig. 3. Updating the schema after the insertion of new entities

Figure 3 presents the updates on the classes introduced in Fig. 1 following the insertion of a set of new entities. For instance, the set of properties describing $class_1$ has been updated in order to represent the new entity e'_6 within the corresponding cluster C_1. The classes $Class_2$ and $Class_3$ are merged into $Class'_2$ since the corresponding clusters C_2 and C_3 have a common core e'_7 that is similar to one of their entities, e_4 and e_9 respectively. Additionally, new classes ($class'_2$ and $class'_3$) are created, representing the newly generated clusters.

This process provides the final clusters, ensuring that they are the same as the ones a sequential DBSCAN algorithm would have generated if executed on the global dataset in one batch.

7   Experimental Evaluations

As previously explained, clustering a dataset using our incremental approach provides the same result as clustering the dataset with the DBSCAN algorithm in one batch. This feature of our approach is important since it ensures the good quality of the extracted schema when using DBSCAN for clustering RDF datasets, which has been shown in previous works [3,11].

In this paper, our experiments are therefore focused on the performances of our approach when applied to large evolving datasets. In our experiments, we evaluate the efficiency of our incremental clustering algorithm compared to the scalable DBSCAN proposed in [3], and derive the speed-up factor when using our incremental approach to reflect the insertion of sets of entities in the clustering result instead of using the scalable DBSCAN algorithm on the dataset composed of the old entities and the newly inserted ones. Both algorithms rely on the Apache Spark 2.0 framework. We have used our implementation of the scalable DBSCAN algorithm, available online[4].

Each time a set of entities Δ_D is added to the initial dataset D, we evaluate the execution time needed by our incremental algorithm to update the clustering result obtained on D so as to reflect the insertion of Δ_D. The execution time of this scenario is compared to the execution time needed by the scalable DBSCAN algorithm in order to cluster the dataset composed of both the initial dataset and the inserted set of entities, i.e. $D \cup \Delta_D$.

First, we have used a synthetic multidimensional dataset of 4 million entities, generated using "IBM Quest Synthetic Data Generator"[5]. In our context, the generator produces the properties of each entity that will be used in our experiments. Second, as the complexity of our incremental approach depends on the number of inserted entities, we have therefore evaluated the incremental algorithm by inserting sets of entities of different sizes. Finally, we illustrate the efficiency of our approach on real datasets. To this end, we apply our approach on 1.2 million entities extracted from DBpedia[6] [1]. All the experiments have been conducted on a cluster running Ubuntu Linux consisting of 5 nodes (1 master and 4 slaves), each one equipped with 30 GB of RAM and a 12-core CPU.

We have first evaluated the scalability of our approach and compared it to the scalable DBSCAN algorithm using several synthetic datasets where we have added datasets of different sizes. Figures 4a, 4b and 4c show both algorithms' runtime as a function of the dataset size. The scalable DBSCAN takes as input the global dataset while the incremental algorithm takes as input the clusters of the previous execution and the newly inserted entities.

The results show that clustering a small dataset is faster using the scalable DBSCAN than using the incremental DBSCAN. This is due to the fact that clustering a small number of entities is very fast and requires a few seconds (22 s to clusters 200k entities). Besides, the incremental algorithm executes extra

---

[4] https://github.com/BOUHAMOUM/SC-DBSCAN.
[5] IBM QSDG: https://sourceforge.net/projects/ibmquestdatagen/.
[6] http://downloads.dbpedia.org/3.9/.

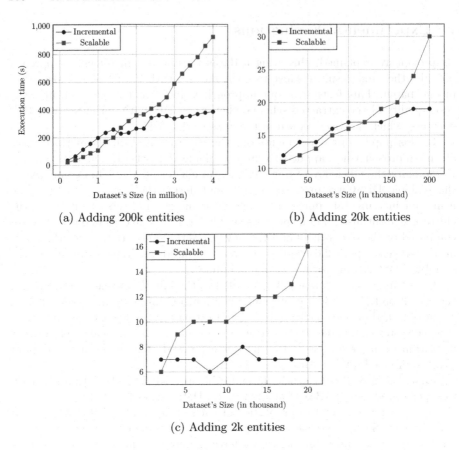

(a) Adding 200k entities

(b) Adding 20k entities

(c) Adding 2k entities

Fig. 4. Incremental vs. sequential scalable algorithm

operations such as the assignment of old entities and the union of the result
produced by this assignment with the chunks created during the distribution
of the new entities, which makes it slower on small datasets compared to the
scalable algorithm.

However, when the number of entities is higher, clustering a dataset using
the incremental DBSCAN algorithm is faster. This is due to the fact that the
clustering is applied on new entities and their neighborhoods, which counterbal-
ances the extra operations, while the scalable DBSCAN algorithm has to build
the clusters by computing the neighborhood of all the entities, which is a more
expensive operation. In addition, the incremental approach produces a lower
number of new clusters compared to the scalable algorithm. Thus, when merging the clusters determined within each chunk, a process which is executed in
one node, the incremental algorithm has to deal with a lower number of clusters
which makes it faster.

We can observe that the bigger the dataset, the larger the gap between the execution time of both algorithms, and the higher the gain achieved by the incremental approach.

Since the complexity of the incremental algorithm is defined by the number of new entities and their neighborhood, we have experimented the insertion of sets of entities Δ_D of different sizes. The results show that the advantage of the incremental algorithm compared to the scalable DBSCAN is noticed at different levels according to the size of the added set of entities. The smaller the sets of added entities, the faster the clustering using the incremental algorithm. In our experiments, when adding 200k entities at each step, the incremental algorithm becomes faster than the scalable algorithm when the whole dataset reaches the size of 1.6M entities, while when adding 20k at each step, it becomes faster when the dataset reaches the size of 140k entities (Fig. 4b). When the size of the inserted datasets is smaller, the gain achieved by the incremental algorithm is more important, as shown in Fig. 4c after the second insertion. These results are explained by the fact that the incremental algorithm generates the clusters only for the new entities and their neighborhood. It does not take into consideration all the dataset. The smaller the inserted set of entities, the fewer the number of entities which have to be managed by the algorithm, which makes its execution faster.

Finally, we have evaluated the efficiency of our approach on real datasets. Figure 5 illustrates the ability of our incremental algorithm to cluster real datasets, such as DBpedia, a large RDF source from which we have extracted more than 1.2 million entities. Similar to the evaluations on the synthetic datasets, we have added in each insertion to the initial dataset D, a set of entities Δ_D containing 100k entities. Then the execution time of the incremental algorithm is compared to the scalable DBSCAN when executed on the entire dataset.

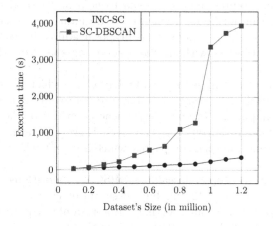

Fig. 5. Clustering a subset of DBpedia

This evaluation shows that the incremental algorithm overcomes the scalable algorithm in terms of performances. In addition, entities in DBpedia have a high number of properties; some entities have more than 600 properties. As a consequence, the scalable algorithm creates big sized chunks; this has a negative impact on its performances because it reaches the calculation's limit of the cluster when computing the ϵ−neighborhood of the entities, as we notice on the dataset having 1 million entities. However, the incremental algorithm is not impacted by entities having a high number of properties since it manages in each clustering only a limited subset of the dataset and computes the ϵ-neighborhood for the new entities only.

8   Related Work

Several approaches have been proposed for schema discovery in RDF datasets. Some of them use clustering algorithms to group similar entities in order to form the classes of the schema [5,11]. Other approaches have used frequent pattern mining algorithms to find the most frequent properties describing the schema [17]. However, these approaches have not dealt with scalability issues, and do not scale to process large datasets.

To manage the incrementality issues, the approach presented in [11] proposes a supervised learning step in order to define the type of a new incoming entity, by introducing the concept of fictive entity representing a class, and by comparing a new entity to each fictive entity to determine its type. However, the goal of this approach is to assign an existing type to an instance, and it does not generate new types.

Some approaches have specifically addressed the scalability of schema discovery, providing algorithms capable of managing large datasets, implemented using big data technology such as Hadoop or Spark. However, unlike our approach, these algorithms rely on type declarations to group entities into classes, and then provide a representative schema to help understand the data [2,15]. Such approaches can not be used when these declarations are not provided. To the best of our knowledge, there is no proposal addressing schema discovery for massive RDF datasets without the assumption that type declarations are provided in the dataset.

Our clustering algorithm is inspired by DBSCAN, which is well suited to the requirements of RDF datasets, mainly because it provides clusters of arbitrary shape, which is important in our context where entities of the same type can be described by heterogeneous property sets. However, the main weakness of DBSCAN is its computational complexity which is $\mathcal{O}(n^2)$, where n is the number of entities.

Many works have proposed scalable DBSCAN algorithms by parallelizing their execution, such as [9,12,16], but these approaches are not incremental. Using these algorithms on an evolving dataset would require repeating their execution on the global dataset after each insertion.

Some approaches have proposed an incremental version of DBSCAN. In [6], the neighborhood of an inserted or deleted entity is computed and some rules are proposed in order to update the corresponding clusters. However, this approach processes one entity at a time. In addition, updating the clusters after the insertion of an entity requires its comparison with the entire dataset, which is a costly operation. [13] proposes to enhance the previous approach by limiting the search space during the neighborhood computation. The dataset is split into partitions based on partition centers, and a new entity is assigned to the partition with the closest center. The neighborhood of the new entity is computed within this partition only. However, defining a center in an RDF dataset is not straightforward. In addition, partitioning data based on centers does not ensure that the result is the same as the one of the DBSCAN algorithm, which could decrease the quality of the clustering. RT-DBSCAN [8] proposes to define the $((minPts\text{-}1) \times \epsilon)$-neighborhood of the new inserted entity and to perform the clustering in this region using DBSCAN. It parallelizes the execution of the approach by dividing the dataset into cells where the incremental algorithm is executed in parallel, then the clusters produced for each cell are merged to build the final clustering result. This algorithm is implemented using Spark streaming. However, this approach is designed for data represented in a 2D space and is not suitable for RDF data.

9   Conclusion

In this work, we have addressed the problem of incremental evolution of the schema of large RDF datasets as new entities are inserted.

We have proposed a novel incremental density-based clustering algorithm which scales up the schema discovery process, making it effective for very large RDF datasets. It builds the clusters which group similar entities by updating the existing clusters or creating new ones according to the neighborhood of the newly inserted entities, and ensures that the resulting set of clusters is the same as the one generated using DBSCAN on the global dataset. The clusters produced by our approach represent the classes of the schema, which capture the structure of the entities contained within an RDF dataset. Our proposal has been implemented using Spark, which has enabled the clustering of large RDF datasets. The performed experiments have shown that incrementally extracting a schema from an RDF dataset using our approach outperforms the existing scalable schema discovery approach using scalable DBSCAN when applied on the global dataset, with both synthetic and real data.

In our future works, we will explore the possible ways of enriching the set of classes provided by our approach, by generating the semantic links between these classes as well as providing some semantic annotations. Besides, as some schema-related declarations could be available in the dataset, another possible way of improving our approach is to extend our algorithms in order to exploit partially available schema-related declarations to guide the discovery process, which could improve significantly the quality of the resulting schema.

References

1. Auer, S., Bizer, C., Kobilarov, G., Lehmann, J., Cyganiak, R., Ives, Z.: DBpedia: a nucleus for a web of open data. In: Aberer, K., et al. (eds.) ASWC/ISWC -2007. LNCS, vol. 4825, pp. 722–735. Springer, Heidelberg (2007). https://doi.org/10.1007/978-3-540-76298-0_52
2. Baazizi, M.A., Lahmar, H.B., Colazzo, D., Ghelli, G., Sartiani, C.: Parametric schema inference for massive JSON datasets. VLDB J. **28**, 497–521 (2019)
3. Bouhamoum, R., Kedad, Z., Lopes, S.: Scalable schema discovery for RDF data. In: Hameurlain, A., Tjoa, A.M. (eds.) Transactions on Large-Scale Data- and Knowledge-Centered Systems XLVI. LNCS, vol. 12410, pp. 91–120. Springer, Heidelberg (2020). https://doi.org/10.1007/978-3-662-62386-2_4
4. Chaudhuri, S., Ganti, V., Kaushik, R.: A primitive operator for similarity joins in data cleaning. In: Proceedings of the 22nd International Conference on Data Engineering, ICDE. IEEE Computer Society, Atlanta (2006)
5. Christodoulou, K., Paton, N.W., Fernandes, A.A.A.: Structure inference for linked data sources using clustering. Trans. Large Scale Data Knowl. Centered Syst. **19**, 1–25 (2015)
6. Ester, M., Kriegel, H., Sander, J., Wimmer, M., Xu, X.: Incremental clustering for mining in a data warehousing environment. In: Gupta, A., Shmueli, O., Widom, J. (eds.) VLDB 1998, Proceedings of 24rd International Conference on Very Large Data Bases, 24–27 August, 1998, New York City, New York, USA, pp. 323–333. Morgan Kaufmann (1998)
7. Ester, M., Kriegel, H.P., Sander, J., Xu, X.: A density-based algorithm for discovering clusters in large spatial databases with noise. In: Proceeding of the Second International Conference on Knowledge Discovery and Data Mining (KDD), pp. 226–231. AAAI Press (1996)
8. Gong, Y., Sinnott, R.O., Rimba, P.: RT-DBSCAN: real-time parallel clustering of spatio-temporal data using spark-streaming. In: Shi, Y., Fu, H., Tian, Y., Krzhizhanovskaya, V.V., Lees, M.H., Dongarra, J., Sloot, P.M.A. (eds.) ICCS 2018. LNCS, vol. 10860, pp. 524–539. Springer, Cham (2018). https://doi.org/10.1007/978-3-319-93698-7_40
9. He, Y., Tan, H., Luo, W., Feng, S., Fan, J.: Mr-dbscan: a scalable mapreduce-based dbscan algorithm for heavily skewed data. In: Proceeding of the 27th International Parallel and Distributed Processing Symposium Workshops (IPDPS), vol. 8, pp. 83–99. Springer, Heidelberg (2013)
10. Jaccard, P.: The distribution of flora in the alpine zone. New Phytol. **11**(2), 37–50 (1912)
11. Kellou-Menouer, K., Kedad, Z.: A self-adaptive and incremental approach for data profiling in the semantic web. Trans. Large Scale Data Knowl. Centered Syst. **29**, 108–133 (2016)
12. Lulli, A., Dell'Amico, M., Michiardi, P., Ricci, L.: Ng-dbscan: scalable density-based clustering for arbitrary data. In: Proceeding of the 42nd International Conference on Very Large Data Bases (VLDB), vol. 10(3), 157–168, November 2016
13. Bakr, A.M., Ghanem, N.M., Ismail, M.A.: Efficient incremental density-based algorithm for clustering large datasets. Alexandria Eng. J. **54**, 1147–1154 (2015). Elsevier B.V
14. Pernelle, N., Saïs, F., Mercier, D., Thuraisamy, S.: RDF data evolution: efficient detection and semantic representation of changes. In: Proceedings of the Posters and Demos Track of the International Conference on Semantic Systems - SEMANTICS, vol. 12 (2016)

15. Sevilla Ruiz, D., Morales, S.F., García Molina, J.: Inferring versioned schemas from NoSQL databases and its applications. In: Johannesson, P., Lee, M.L., Liddle, S.W., Opdahl, A.L., López, Ó.P. (eds.) ER 2015. LNCS, vol. 9381, pp. 467–480. Springer, Cham (2015). https://doi.org/10.1007/978-3-319-25264-3_35
16. Song, H., Lee, J.G.: RP-DBSCAN: a superfast parallel DBSCAN algorithm based on random partitioning. In: Proceedings of the International Conference on Management of Data (SIGMOD), pp. 1173–1187. ACM (2018)
17. Issa, S., Paris, P.-H., Hamdi, F., Si-Said Cherfi, S.: Revealing the conceptual schemas of RDF datasets. In: Giorgini, P., Weber, B. (eds.) CAiSE 2019. LNCS, vol. 11483, pp. 312–327. Springer, Cham (2019). https://doi.org/10.1007/978-3-030-21290-2_20
18. The Apache Software Foundation: Apache Spark (2018). https://spark.apache.org. Accessed 20 Oct 2018

HTTP Extensions for the Management of Highly Dynamic Data Resources

Lars Gleim[1]($\boxtimes$)(iD), Liam Tirpitz[1]($\boxtimes$)(iD), and Stefan Decker[1,2](iD)

[1] Databases and Information Systems, RWTH Aachen University, Aachen, Germany
gleim@dbis.rwth-aachen.de, liam.tirpitz@rwth-aachen.de
[2] Fraunhofer FIT, Sankt Augustin, Germany

Abstract. As Semantic Web Technologies are increasingly employed for the management of highly dynamic data resources, e.g., the Industrial Internet of Things, resource versioning, state synchronization and distributed data management infrastructures are gaining practical relevance. The HTTP Memento protocol has recently been discussed as a promising building block for the implementation of such services for Findable, Accessible, Interoperable and Reusable (FAIR) Data. While this standard already enables the management and discovery of persistent, immutable and versioned resources on the Web and in Knowledge Graphs, it lacks support for the management of data updated at high frequencies and only provides inefficient means for managing resources with many revisions.

To address these shortcomings, we propose three extensions to the HTTP Memento protocol: arbitrary resolution timestamps, resource creation support and range requests for TimeMaps. We provide a reference implementation of our proposals as open source software and quantitatively evaluate the extensions' performance, showcasing superior results in terms of resource capacity, insertion correctness, latency and amount of transferred data. Based on a qualitative analysis, we conclude that in conjunction with our proposed extensions, the HTTP Memento protocol addresses a variety of data management challenges including data *archiving*, *citation*, *retrieval*, *discovery*, *synchronization* and *sustainability* for highly dynamic data on the Web and in Knowledge Graphs, providing a promising foundation for prospective standardized and interoperable data management solutions.

Keywords: HTTP Memento protocol · FAIR data management · Decentralization · Version management · State synchronization · Linked Data · RDF

1 Introduction

Resources on the Web evolve over time and some resources change faster than others. Handling such resources can be problematic because data cannot be referenced and cited reliably if it changes or disappears altogether [8]. To combine

© Springer Nature Switzerland AG 2021
R. Verborgh et al. (Eds.): ESWC 2021, LNCS 12731, pp. 212–229, 2021.
https://doi.org/10.1007/978-3-030-77385-4_13

the opposing requirements for dynamic resources and reliable citations, a suitable versioning and persistent identification mechanism is needed, that allows to reliably capture, identify and retrieve individual, immutable resource revisions. While semantic data management (SDM) and versioning solutions in the Semantic Web community are largely using SPARQL, LDP [22] or plain HTTP as their primary access mechanism, there is no standard for managing highly dynamic resources that would allow the handling of RDF data analogously to any other resource on the Web, as promoted e.g., by the FAIR principles for scientific data management [27]. Especially in the IoT context a joint and standardized mechanism to handle highly dynamic data resources is missing.

The HTTP Memento protocol [20] has been successfully employed for time-based resource access and identification in the context of SDM [9,15,21] and could provide the basis for interoperable solutions, tightly integrated with the HTTP protocol and therefore the core technologies of the Web. However, in its current form, the Memento protocol was created for applications with slowly changing data in mind, such as traditional websites or library resources [20]. As such, Memento does not perform well in scenarios with highly dynamic data resources, because it is limited by design decisions like the use of RFC1123 timestamps [4] with a maximum resolution of one second, limiting the frequency of data changes that can be handled. Nevertheless, the need for standardized identification and retrieval of resource revisions also exists in applications with highly dynamic data resources, for example in the Industrial Internet of Things, where a large variety of different data elements, like sensor and machine data, must be captured at high frequencies [17]. A prominent example is provided by the recently standardized W3C Web of Things API, which promotes, e.g., the direct exposure of current sensor readings through web resources [14]. In such a scenario, a single data resource may describe the state of a machine or sensor, which changes multiple times per second. While stream processing [6], as well as data propagation and notification systems [5], have been actively investigated in recent years, the unified management and identification of individual data points received little attention. Instead, efforts such as the JSON Time Series data format [2] focus primarily on providing a lightweight data-interchange format. At the same time, different approaches for versioning semantic data were developed [16], but those often focus explicitly on RDF data and cannot provide straightforward interoperability with existing Web resources. However, especially in the context of industrial use case scenarios, each individual state of such a resource may need to be persistently identified and retrievable [10,11]. The Memento protocol is a promising candidate to provide these services, however, currently inadequate to handle such highly dynamic resources. Therefore, we propose and evaluate extensions to the existing Memento protocol with the goal to provide a standardized mechanism to create, access and identify revisions for highly dynamic data resources.

Contributions. Based on our discussion of shortcomings of the Memento protocol, we propose three extensions to the HTTP Memento protocol:

- An updated datetime format, allowing arbitrary resolution timestamps, to uniquely identify individual resource revisions, even at high frequencies.
- Support for Memento creation as part of the protocol, to allow clients to reliable cite the resource revisions they created.
- Temporal range requests for TimeMaps, enabling the targeted retrieval of specific temporal ranges of Mementos for a more efficient discovery, especially for resources with large numbers of revisions.

We analyze the practical benefits of our proposals in a both quantitative and qualitative evaluation, concluding them to provide a promising foundation for the standardized management of highly dynamic data resources on the Web.

Paper Organization. The remainder of this paper is structured as follows. Section 2 provides an overview of corresponding related work and fundamental technologies. Section 3 discusses the proposed extensions and their benefits in detail. Section 4 evaluates the proposed extensions using our open source reference implementation. Finally, we conclude our work in Sect. 5.

2   Related Work

In the following, we provide a short overview of prior work towards data versioning and temporal data management on the Web. We then introduce the Memento protocol and discuss its applications in data management on the Web.

WebDAV. As summarized by Whitehead [26], the WebDAV protocol and its extension DeltaV provide capabilities for remote collaborative authoring, metadata management, version control, and configuration management of Web resources. Extending upon HTTP, WebDAV adds operations for overwriting prevention, properties, and namespace management, while DeltaV builds upon WebDAV to offer versioning (checkout and checkin), autoversioning, workspaces, activities, and configuration management. Although both WebDAV and DeltaV are IETF Web standards, their practical adoption remains low to date, in part due to the general complexity of the WebDAV protocol. While Tim Berners-Lee still proposed the usage of the protocol for resource management in his 2009 vision of *Socially Aware Cloud Storage* [3], the later implementation *Solid* [18] instead implements the Linked Data Platform specification [22] standardized by the W3C in 2015.

The Memento Protocol. A more recent and much simpler approach to resource versioning is provided through the HTTP Memento protocol [19], which enables the retrieval of *Mementos* – historic states of resources – via time-based HTTP content-negotiation. As summarized by Gleim and Decker [9], the Memento framework distinguishes four logical components: Original Resource, Memento, TimeGate, and TimeMap. A Memento $\langle u, t \rangle$ captures the state of an Original Resource with URI u at a given point in time t (exposed via the Memento-Datetime HTTP header). Mementos are intended to be *immutable* and may optionally be associated with one or more distinct Memento URI(s) for *referenceability*. Such a URI-M must further identify the URL of its Original Resource in an HTTP Link header. Using the Accept-Datetime HTTP request header, historic states of Original Resources may then be requested from a so-called TimeGate through time-based content-negotiation, and are serviced through either a direct HTTP response or HTTP redirection to external archive locations, providing a simple solution to the archiving problem.

Additionally, the Memento protocol also enables revision discovery and synchronization through TimeMaps, which provide a listing of available Mementos ⟨b, t*⟩ at points in time t* for a given Original Resource b, i.e., a history of available revisions with respective associated distinct Memento URIs. Thus, exposing up-to-date TimeMaps for resources enables trivial change monitoring and the discovery, retrieval, and thus synchronization of resource state. Depending on the application scenario, TimeGate, TimeMap, and/or Mementos may all be provided by the Original Resource provider. It is, however, similarly possible to deploy all components independently of each other, as well as with optional redundancies. Notably, third parties may also provide archiving services by storing Mementos and/or providing lookup services (i.e., an *external* TimeGate) for resources from other domains, such as already provided by archive.org. Thus, adoption does not hinge on the support of any individual group or organization but may be adopted by interested users in backward compatibility with existing resources on the Web. Individual Mementos may further be resolved to multiple URI-Ms, i.e., different storage locations, (e.g. via TimeMaps), supporting explicit redundancy. Gleim and Decker [8] conclude that the Memento protocol provides a promising solution for the *archiving, citation, retrieval, discovery, synchronization* and *sustainability* challenges of data management. Further details, including discovery procedures for TimeGates, Mementos and Original Resources, can be found in RFC7089 [19].

Data Management with the Memento Protocol. In the following, we shortly introduce prior work exploring the application of the Memento protocol in the context of data management solutions. Meinhardt et al. [15] proposed a system for the management of Linked Data enabling access to arbitrary historical data states through the Memento protocol. The authors further implemented a custom REST API to enable incremental updates to the underlying RDF data. Due to its reliance on custom API endpoints, the approach is however not well suited for applications with arbitrary Web services. Verborgh [25] described an approach employing the Memento protocol to query historical datasets using the SPARQL query language. Taelman et al. [23] then adopted the approach for historical access to linked data through the Triple Pattern Fragments API. Extending upon these approaches, Vander Sande [24] proposes an integrated data publishing solution for libraries, providing historical access to Linked Data through various access mechanisms. Anderson [1] proposed the Dydra graph store which implements temporal RDF dataset versioning analogously to the Memento TimeGate pattern. Recently, Gleim et al. [11] employ the Memento protocol for resource versioning in the implementation of the semantic data management system FactStack [11] based on the FactDAG data interoperability model [10]. Nevertheless, the Memento protocol's shortcomings w.r.t. highly dynamic data resources remain unaddressed to date.

3   Optimizing the Memento Protocol

In the following, we propose multiple, independent extensions to the existing Memento protocol, with the goal to enable support for highly dynamic data resources. First, we introduce an exemplary industrial use case scenario to highlight the need for Memento protocol extensions to better support highly dynamic data resources. Motivated by this use case, we propose the adoption of the RFC3339 datetime format [13] which supports arbitrary time resolution, instead of the currently used RFC1123, which is limited to a resolution of one second. Subsequently, we propose to broaden the scope of the Memento protocol beyond pure data retrieval and extend it to support the creation of resources and their revisions via PUT and POST, as well. This especially enables clients to reliably and persistently cite individual resource revisions immediately upon creation. Finally, we propose a ranged request for TimeMaps, which enables clients to retrieve arbitrary sections of a TimeMap with a single request, reducing the communication overhead associated with large TimeMaps commonly associated with highly dynamic resources.

Use Case. To highlight the need to extend the Memento protocol towards highly dynamic resource support, we introduce the example use case illustrated in Fig. 1. We will refer to this use case in the following sections to motivate individual Memento extensions. Our use case considers a production machine in an industrial IoT setting, which can be observed via multiple sensors writing their data to a Web server via HTTP PUT or POST requests with high frequency, possibly following the Linked Data Platform specification [22]. In the following, we refer to this Web server as the *Memento Server*. Each sensor writes to a single resource and each revision of such a resource (stored and subsequently retrievable as a Memento) reflects a specific sensor value, i.e., the state of a sensor at a specific point in time. The use case also consists of multiple reporter processes. These software components consider a certain range of Mementos associated with certain sensor resources to create reports indicating the state of the machine. A reporter process first creates a full report with all relevant information, by updating a resource on the Memento server. The reporter process also creates a short summary of this report directly after the full report is created. To maintain useful provenance information, each summary also references the full report it was generated from. Finally, since the machine produces safety-critical parts, regulated by the government, the summary of the report is also stored externally on a government archive server.

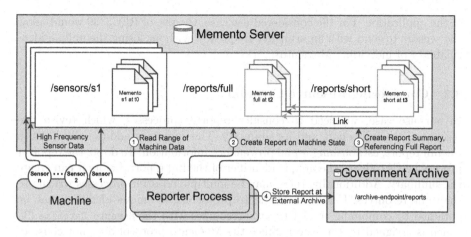

Fig. 1. An example highlighting the need for HTTP extensions to handle highly dynamic resources.

3.1   Changing the Datetime Format

The Memento protocol relies on timestamps to provide access to naturally ordered resource revisions via datetime negotiation or TimeMaps. These timestamps follow the RFC1123 [4] format, which provides a static resolution of one second. However, in industrial applications like the use case illustrated in Fig. 1, we consider sensors updating resources multiple times per second, each change leading to a Memento that needs to be identifiable. The RFC1123 timestamps cannot uniquely identify multiple revisions that occur within the same second and timestamp collisions are unavoidable for high-frequency data. Therefore, we propose a revision to the Memento protocol that changes the format of the timestamps to the more modern and flexible RFC3339 [13]. RFC3339 standardizes the use of datetime formats based on ISO 8601 [12] for use in internet protocols and allows the representation of fractions of seconds with arbitrary precision. The use of RFC3339 in the Memento protocol would allow the natural ordering of resource revisions with an arbitrarily small distance to each other. While computer systems only provide timestamps with a finite resolution, the RFC3339 format would allow the protocol to be used on current systems with the highest possible resolution, as well as with future systems, which may provide an even higher timestamp resolution. Additionally, for most applications, the uniqueness of a timestamp is more important than its actual accuracy. Therefore, even systems with lower resolution timestamps can profit from the additional resolution allowed by the RFC3339 format by simply using the least significant digits as a counter to guarantee the uniqueness of identifiers assigned in the same timestamp interval. While these virtual timestamps are not accurate timestamps up to the least significant digits, they provide uniqueness and natural ordering while still expressing time information with the highest possible precision. Since RFC3339 allows arbitrary fractions, the size of the counter can be chosen to fit the needs of the application. For the considered use case, the use of RFC3339 would allow the sensors to send with an arbitrary frequency, without losing the unique identifiability of individual Mementos.

3.2 Considering Resource Creation

In our use case, we need to consider reporter processes, which revise two resources, the full report and its summary. The summary additionally links to the full report, establishing useful provenance information. To do so, the reporter process needs to learn the unique identifier of the full report, before it can create the summary. Additionally, there may be multiple reporter processes writing to the same resources. Using the Memento protocol, the unique identifier may be obtained by combining the URI of the resources with the Memento-Datetime [9], which is assigned by the server. Since the Memento protocol does not consider the creation of resources via HTTP PUT or POST, there is no standardized way for the client to learn the Memento-Datetime that was assigned to the Memento it created. While the most recent Memento-Datetime may be obtained using an additional GET request to the resource created using PUT or POST, this poses multiple problems. First, following each PUT or POST request with a GET request creates unwanted overhead. Additionally, since multiple clients may write to the same resource, race conditions may occur and it cannot be guaranteed that the returned Memento-Datetime is actually associated with the Memento created by the requesting client, as illustrated in Fig. 2. In our use case, this would lead to a summary that references the wrong full report. Instead, we propose the extension of the Memento protocol to also consider the creation of Mementos through RESTful APIs by reusing the existing Memento-Datetime header as a response header in the context of PUT or POST requests. The server may then further indicate the location that the created resource may be retrieved from through the HTTP Content-Location header. Note, that this approach may be implemented in a backward-compatible manner with arbitrary REST endpoints (as long as they internally guarantee, that individual resource revisions are unique). The Memento protocol considers different scenarios where TimeGates, Original Resources and Mementos may exist distributed across different servers or may be handled by the same entity. We also consider different cases for the creation of Mementos. However, we always assume that an Original Resource acts as its own TimeGate and assigns unique Memento-Datetimes to each resource revision. After a Memento has been created by the Original Resource it may be handed over to another Memento server for storage.

Creating Mementos Through the Original Resource. In the centralized case, the Original Resource (OR) also acts as its own TimeGate. We propose the standardization of PUT and POST requests towards the Original Resource. To create a new revision of the Original Resource, a client may issue a PUT or POST request to the OR. If the request is successful, the current representation is updated to the new revision and a new Memento is created. The

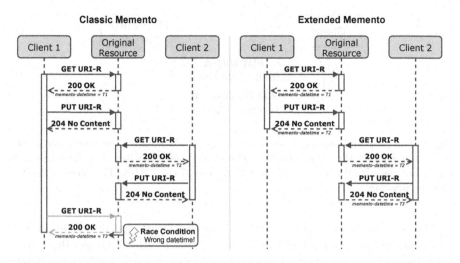

Fig. 2. The necessary requests for Memento creation with and without the proposed extension. The extension avoids additional requests and race conditions, which may lead to wrong datetime associations at the creating client, by returning the assigned Memento-Datetime directly with the response to a request.

server communicates the unique identifier it assigned to the Memento via the Memento-Datetime header. While the classic Memento protocol already specifies the Memento-Datetime response header, its exact meaning is clear from the type of request. Used as a response to a PUT or POST request, the Memento-Datetime header communicates that the content of the request has been persisted with the returned, unique timestamp. This proposed additional response header allows clients to directly and reliably reference the resource revisions they created, as illustrated in Fig. 2.

To achieve the desired immutability for reliable citations, a DELETE request may only create a tombstone object. The current representation of the resource would act like a deleted resource, while the existing Mementos remain available.

Storing Mementos in an External Memento Archive. Our example use case also requires the reporter process to hand over the summary reports to an external archiving service provided by the government. To store already existing Mementos at an external TimeGate, we propose the utilization of an archiving endpoint (URI-A). This archiving endpoint consists of the URI of the Memento server, but also encodes the URI-R of the Original Resource in its path. The archiving endpoint may exist at an arbitrary location on the server, which should be discoverable via a well-known location, e.g., http://archive.tld/.well-known/memento-archive-location/. At this location, clients can learn the actual archive endpoint, e.g. from a JSON representation such as {"archive_location":"http://archive.tld/archive-endpoint"}.

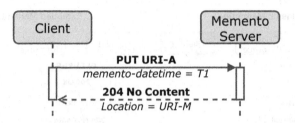

Fig. 3. The proposed process of storing an existing Memento at an archiving server that is not holding the associated OR. The client passes the `Memento-Datetime` as a header and encodes the location of the OR as part of the URI-A. The server responds with the new Memento location.

This way, Memento archiving services provide a clearly specified location that stores and provides access to Mementos belonging to other Original Resources, which may exist in parallel to Original Resources the archiving service maintains itself. Encoding the URI-R as part of the URI-A instead of a separate request header enables a unique endpoint for each OR which acts as a TimeGate for that OR and may even provide resource-specific human-readable information at that location, such as the TimeMap in HTML format. To store a Memento, we reuse the already existing `Memento-Datetime`, as illustrated in Fig. 3. Used as a request header, the `Memento-Datetime` indicates the unique `Memento-Datetime` that the OR assigned to the Memento in the request at its creation. The archiving endpoint responds with the URI-M identifying the storage location of the Memento. Note, that `Memento-Datetime` is used as a request header instead of a response header. Similar to the creation of Mementos at the OR, the semantics of the header is implied by the type of the associated request.

The ability to store Mementos at external archiving services in a standardized way allows for the realization of simple push-based resource state synchronization mechanisms and redundant resource archiving, both of which are relevant challenges for data management solutions on the Web. With regard to our use case, the extension for resource creation allows the reporter processes to reliably reference the full reports from their summaries and to create synchronized copies of the summaries at an external archiving service.

3.3 Range Requests for TimeMaps

In the considered use case, sensors create resource revisions with high frequency. Therefore, a single resource is expected to have a large number of revisions. The reporter processes in this use case are only interested in a specific range of Mementos, i.e., the Mementos that were created since their last execution. The Memento protocol specifies TimeMaps, listing the Mementos for a resource known to the TimeGate that provides the TimeMap. If many Mementos exist, as is the case in our use case, this TimeMap may be long and difficult to handle. However, the clients in our use case are not interested in the full TimeMap, but only in a specific fragment (Fig. 4).

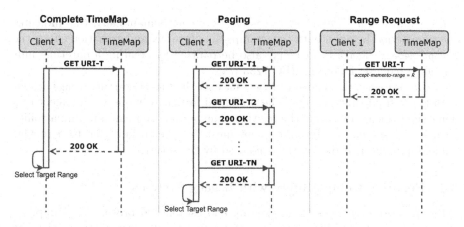

Fig. 4. Comparison of retrieval methods for TimeMap fragments. A complete TimeMap always returns every fragment with a single request, but for large TimeMaps, this is inefficient. Linearly paging through TimeMap fragments transmits fewer data per request, but may require many requests. The proposed range-request returns only the requested range of Mementos with a single request.

The classic Memento protocol provides a paging mechanism, which divides the TimeMap into pieces that can be accessed separately, where each page also points to its predecessor and its successor. Since the URI format identifying the individual pages is not standardized, the TimeMap can only be paged linearly, without skipping ahead or even searching for a certain time range by performing a binary search. Therefore, if a client is looking for a range of Mementos at the end of the TimeMap, the complete TimeMap is downloaded and many requests are necessary to reach the desired part of the TimeMap, which creates a huge overhead for resources with many Mementos. Additionally, the client may need to combine the results from multiple pages locally and remove parts of the first or last page that do not match the target range. The Memento protocol also specifies Index TimeMaps, which only contain links to other TimeMaps and a datetime range that is covered by each linked TimeMap. Index TimeMaps can again point to other Index TimeMaps. However, Index TimeMaps are primarily intended for distributed TimeMaps across multiple archives. While this mechanism can be used to create tree structures of TimeMaps that guide clients to a specific range of Mementos without sending the complete TimeMap, it still requires the client to request multiple TimeMaps and assemble the results from these requests to obtain the intended range of Mementos. Therefore, Index TimeMaps are not considered further. Instead, we propose a new header that clients could use to request a specific range of a TimeMap, the `Accept-Memento-Range` header. Unfortunately, RFC3339 does not cover time periods, but they are specified by ISO 8601, for which RFC3339 is a profile. Therefore, we utilize the time period syntax of ISO 8601, more specifically its *explicit* syntax for periods that connects two timestamps with a forward slash, e.g., *iso-date-time-start / iso-date-time-end*. Semantically, this indicates the time period between both timestamps. In a future standardization effort, the `Accept-Memento-Range` header may also be realized by creating a datetime unit for range requests following RFC 7233 [7].

In our use case, the reporter process may set the `Accept-Memento-Range` header with the desired time period of the presented format to request a fragment of a TimeMap which only covers the relevant time period. To maintain compatibility with legacy servers, a Memento client must be able to fall back to a regular TimeMap request, if the header is ignored by the server.

3.4   Ensuring Compatibility with Legacy Systems

While proposing changes to an existing and established protocol, the implications for the compatibility with the existing protocol revision also need to be considered. Most of the proposed changes can be implemented as an extension, without any impact on existing Memento implementations. The additional request headers for the creation of Mementos or the retrieval of TimeMaps would only be used by a client compatible with the Memento extension. A legacy server would simply ignore the unknown headers and a compatible client must handle a legacy response. Similarly, a modern server may choose not to implement individual extensions to keep its complexity low and a client also needs to handle any combination of enabled extensions. If the server uses extensions, incompatible clients would simply ignore the additional response headers that are returned for HTTP PUT or HTTP POST requests. Therefore, these extensions would not break the existing Memento infrastructure.

However, the datetime format used by the Memento protocol cannot be changed without breaking compatibility with legacy systems. To address this problem, the updated datetime format could be implemented as an extension as well, using an additional header, the `Memento-Version` header. If the client initiates a request with `Memento-Version = 2`, the server has to use RFC3339 timestamps for its responses, if the extended Memento protocol is supported. This holds for TimeMaps as well as `Memento-Datetime` headers. If the client does not set this header, the server acts as a legacy server and uses RFC1123 for the datetime format in its responses. The use of RFC1123 timestamps may lead to ambiguous identification of Mementos, as previously discussed. In that case, the server may use an arbitrary but consistent reduction and ignore additional Mementos in interactions with legacy clients, e.g., the server may only list and return the first Memento that was created within a certain second. If this behavior is undesirable, the server may also reject legacy requests. If a client wants to use the RFC3339 datetime format for its requests, using the `Accept-Datetime` header, it may not know if the server supports that extension. Therefore, the protocol extension must ensure that such an interaction can fall back to classic Memento. This could be achieved by sending two request headers with the initial request. The `Accept-Datetime` header uses the RFC1123 format with reduced resolution and an additional header, `Accept-Datetime-2` for example, specifies the RFC3339 datetime. If the server does not support the extension, it will ignore the second header and the client needs to handle the legacy response, which can be identified by looking at the format of the `Memento-Datetime`. Otherwise, the server supports the extension and the client may send subsequent requests without the legacy headers.

The proposed extensions further maintain HTTP idempotence of all requests. While range request and increased timestamp accuracy clearly have no impact on idempotence, creating Mementos through the Original Resource creates a new Memento with user-provided content and server-assigned `Memento-Datetime` for each `PUT`/`POST` request. It is therefore idempotent w.r.t the latest resource state itself, even though the header is updated. Storing Mementos in a third-party Memento Archive is always idempotent, both w.r.t. the resource state and its Memento header. Therefore, from the viewpoint of the "non-Memento-aware" Web, all described methods are idempotent.

Together, the proposed changes enable the Memento protocol to be used for data management in high-frequency environments, where every revision of a resource has to be captured, while also maintaining compatibility to legacy systems.

4   Evaluation

To evaluate the proposed extensions to the Memento protocol, we implemented a minimal Memento server as a Node.js (v14) application with an in-memory Redis backend (v6), which we released as open source software[1], and evaluate its performance using a single-node deployment of the server application and a client on a workstation with Intel i7-8700K CPU, 64 GB of RAM and NVMe SSD. The goal of the Memento server implementation used for the evaluation was not to provide a highly scalable application but to compare the proposed extensions with the classic Memento protocol. The repository also contains a written description of the implementation details.

We conducted two separate experiments. The first experiment evaluates the use of the RFC3339 datetime format, as well as the benefits of using Memento in the context of resource creation. The second experiment evaluates the proposed range request for the retrieval of Memento TimeMaps. All created resources in both experiments contain random strings of length 20. All plots reflect the averaged result over 10 repetitions of the associated experiment. The error bars indicate the 99% confidence interval.

4.1   Experiment 1 - Inserting Resource Revisions

First, the performance of the `Memento-Datetime` response header for `PUT` and `POST` requests to the OR is evaluated experimentally in combination with the updated timestamps in RFC3339 format. In this experiment, the OR acts as its own TimeGate. We assume an application in which the client needs to reference

---

[1] https://git.rwth-aachen.de/i5/factdag/memento-server.

the exact resource revision it created and therefore needs to learn the unique Memento-Datetime assigned to its revision. Clients create revisions of a single OR using PUT requests to that resource, with different frequencies. The server creates a Memento for each request, assigns unique RFC3339 timestamps and directly returns them via the Memento-Datetime header with the response. An insertion is only considered successful if the server assigns a unique identifier for the inserted resource revision and the client learns the correct identifier so it can reference the associated resource revision.

In the first variation of that experiment, the client ignores the returned MementoDatetime header and issues a subsequent GET request to learn the Memento-Datetime header. This emulates a scenario with the use of high precision RFC3339 timestamps, but without the Memento-Datetime header for PUT or POST requests. In the second variation, the client considers the returned Memento-Datetime header to learn the assigned Memento-Datetime and does not issue a subsequent GET request. The correctness of insertions with the third variation, the classic Memento protocol with RFC1123 timestamps and without the Memento-Datetime response header is not determined experimentally. Instead, the best-case scenario of one correct insertion per second is plotted based on the availability of timestamps and the pigeon-hole principle. Note, that due to effects like jitter or processing delay, requests may collide for a unique timestamp in one second, while the timestamp provided by the following second is not used at all. Therefore, the classic Memento protocol may perform worse in practice, especially for comparably low frequencies of around 1 revision per second.

Correctness of Insertions. Figure 5a plots the percentage of successful insertions for different loads (insertions per second) on the server for the classic Memento protocol, the extended protocol and a hybrid with RFC3339 timestamps but without the resource creation extension and its response headers respectively. In the case of classic Memento, due to the limited timestamp resolution, only a single revision gets a unique identifier per second. That limits the effective load on a single resource to one insertion per second. Otherwise, most of the insertions cannot be uniquely identified. If RFC3339 timestamps are used, but the associated timestamp is not returned with the response to a POST or PUT request, the client must issue a subsequent GET request to learn the exact timestamp. However, between the POST request and the GET request, another insertion may have taken place on the same resource, as illustrated in Fig. 2. In that case, the client learns a timestamp associated with the wrong resource revision. This is increasingly likely for high loads on a single resource. The client checks if the correct timestamp was returned by comparing the inserted resource content with the returned content. If the contents match, the insertion is considered successful otherwise the insertion failed. For the extended Memento protocol, the timestamp associated with an insertion can be learned directly from the response to a POST or PUT request and a subsequent GET request is not necessary.

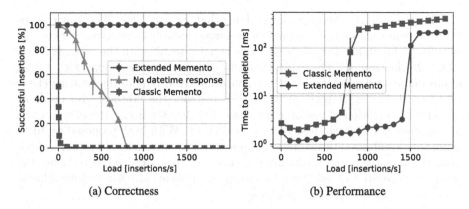

(a) Correctness   (b) Performance

Fig. 5. Results of Experiment 1, comparing the extensions to the classic Memento protocol regarding correctness and performance of citable resource revision insertions.

Performance. The previously presented results show increased correctness for the creation of resource revisions with the extended Memento protocol, but the performance of such creation events is important as well. The experimental results in Fig. 5b show, that the extended Memento protocol is faster for creation events if the client needs to learn the unique identifier of the created resource revision. While the performance of our Memento server implementation could likely be significantly optimized, performance degradation over a certain threshold is to be expected from any implementation. The significant performance drop observed above roughly 1500 requests per second does not hinder the direct comparison of the protocol performance itself. The plot shows that the used implementation can handle twice as many creation events per second if the extended Memento protocol is used, before the time to completion increases notably. These advantages are due to the need for a client to send a subsequent GET request to learn the most recent Memento-Datetime. Therefore, each creation event consists of a PUT or POST request, followed by a GET request. This roughly doubles the load on the server and increases the time to complete the operation for the client, because two sequential requests need to be issued to the server. Since we execute requests against localhost, the impact of network latency on our results is negligible. Increased network latency would impact the traditional Memento protocol (with one or multiple requests) equally or more than our proposal (with only a single request for both Memento creation and TimeMap retrieval). An evaluation with larger resources (compared to the current 20 character strings) would effectively add the same transmission time offset for either protocol version since this affects the initial PUT/POST request time equally for both protocol versions. Subsequently, the relative overhead of the second request diminishes as larger resources are transferred. Nevertheless, the absolute overhead remains effectively unchanged, since an additional round trip is needed in the traditional protocol.

The evaluation of this experiment shows that the use of RFC3339 timestamps with Memento allows the assignment of unique identifiers to resource revisions even for highly dynamic resources, which is not possible with the currently used RFC1123 timestamps. The experiment also shows that timestamps with a high resolution alone are not sufficient in applications that require the creating client to reference the exact revision it created. Instead, the protocol also needs to consider the creation of resource revisions and directly notify the client of the unique identifier that was assigned to the revision. With both proposed protocol extensions combined, the correct assignment and referencing of resource revisions is guaranteed even for highly dynamic data resources, while reducing the overhead generated by additional requests in applications that require reliable references to specific resource revisions.

4.2   Experiment 2 - Accessing TimeMaps

The second experiment considers the proposed extension to the retrieval of TimeMaps, namely the `Accept-Memento-Range` header. To evaluate its performance, and compare it to the already standardized methods of retrieval, we create a resource with 10 000 revisions and set up a client to retrieve a subset of revisions based on a given datetime-range which includes 100 Mementos. The position of the targeted Mementos is varied with each execution so that the first execution needs to isolate the entries on positions 0 to 99 and the last execution targets the entries on positions 9900 to 9999 of the TimeMap. The experiment is executed for the retrieval of a full TimeMap, for the retrieval via a paged TimeMap and for retrieval via the proposed range request, respectively. For each execution, the processing time is measured. In the case of a full TimeMap, that includes the time for the request and the response itself, as well as the time the client spends to identify the targeted elements from the TimeMap. Similarly, in the case of a paged TimeMap, the processing time includes the time for the individual requests, as well as the time the client needs to evaluate if a page lists some or all of the targeted Mementos and the time to create the final list, which may consist of fragments combined from multiple pages. The results plotted in Fig. 6 show that the processing time to retrieve a segment of a TimeMap is constant if the full TimeMap is retrieved and the desired segment is isolated by the client. On the other hand, the processing time for the retrieval of a segment via a paged TimeMap depends on the position of the segment within the TimeMap. If the segment is at the beginning of the TimeMap, the paged approach may be faster than the retrieval of the complete TimeMap. However, since the client needs to page through the TimeMap page by page, the processing time increases linearly if the position of the target range is moved towards the end of the TimeMap. If the target range is at the end of the TimeMap, the processing time for a paged TimeMap is considerably higher than for the retrieval of a full TimeMap, because increasingly many pages need to be requested. Like the retrieval via a complete TimeMap, the processing time for retrieval via a range request is independent of the position of the target range within the Map and can be completed with a single request. Since the transmitted amount of data

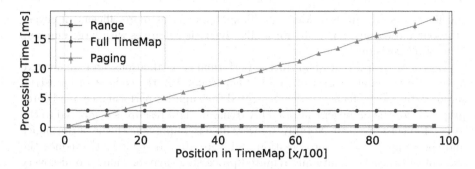

Fig. 6. Processing time for retrieving 100 consecutive entries in a varying position from a TimeMap with 10 000 entries. Retrieving the whole TimeMap always requires the same time, but produces overhead, because the TimeMap is larger than the target range. Linearly paging through the TimeMap with 100 entries per page varies in its duration based on the position of the target range. The proposed datetime-range request results in a consistently low processing time for the client.

may be considerably smaller depending on the relation between map size and range size (1/100 of the user data with the chosen example) the processing time for a range request is lower compared to the retrieval of the full TimeMap. While the retrieval via pages may have similar processing times, this is only possible if the desired range is towards the front of the Map.

Note, that the exact results heavily depend on the size of the TimeMap and the size of the target range in relation to the size of the TimeMap and this experiment only considers a single combination of those parameters. However, the provided data does clearly show how the range request for TimeMaps can have a positive impact on the communication overhead and the processing time for the client. At the same time, depending on the implementation, the range request may increase the computational load on the server, especially compared to statically cached TimeMap pages. Since the extension is optional for the server, it may decide to deactivate this extension if computational resources are limited.

5   Conclusion

In this work, we proposed three independent extensions to the HTTP Memento protocol to address its current shortcomings with respect to the management of highly dynamic data resources, such as increasingly prevalent in the Web through the influence of Industrial Internet of Things technologies. We specifically propose the following modifications: a) An updated datetime format, allowing arbitrary resolution timestamps, to uniquely identify individual resource revisions, even for highly dynamic resources. b) Support for Memento creation as part of the protocol, to allow clients to reliable cite the resource revisions they created. c) Temporal range requests for TimeMaps, enabling the targeted retrieval of specific temporal ranges of Memento TimeMaps for the more efficient discovery of resource revisions, especially for highly dynamic resources with large numbers of resource revisions.

Based on respective quantitative performance evaluations and qualitative analysis in the context of a concrete usage scenario in the context of industrial sensor data management, we demonstrated the superior performance of all three proposals for the management of highly dynamic data resources compared to the plain Memento protocol. Notably, we were able to improve both the performance and correctness of Memento creation and were able to significantly reduce the amount of transferred data and required processing time for Memento discovery through TimeMaps.

Our open source reference implementation of the proposed extension allows for the immediate evaluation of our proposal by the community and may serve as a foundation for future work. We conclude that in conjunction with our proposed extensions, the Memento protocol addresses a variety of data management challenges including data *archiving, citation, retrieval, discovery, synchronization* and *sustainability* for arbitrary and highly dynamic data on the Web and in Knowledge Graphs, providing a promising foundation for prospective standardized and interoperable data management solutions, e.g., in conjunction with the Linked Data Platform specification, which we plan to pursue in future work.

Acknowledgments. Funded by the Deutsche Forschungsgemeinschaft (DFG, German Research Foundation) under Germany's Excellence Strategy – EXC-2023 Internet of Production – 390621612.

References

1. Anderson, J.: RDF graph stores as convergent datatypes. In: MEPDaW@WWW, pp. 940–942 (2019)
2. Argos.io Pty Ltd.: JSON Time Series. https://docs.eagle.io/en/latest/reference/historic/jts.html
3. Berners-Lee, T.: Socially aware cloud storage. Notes on web design, 17 August 2009
4. Braden, R.T.: Requirements for internet hosts - application and support. Technical report 1123, IETF, October 1989 https://rfc-editor.org/rfc/rfc1123.txt
5. Calbimonte, J.P.: Linked data notifications for RDF streams. In: WSP/WOMoCoE@ISWC, pp. 66–73 (2017)
6. Dell'Aglio, D., Calbimonte, J.-P., Della Valle, E., Corcho, O.: Towards a unified language for RDF stream query processing. In: Gandon, F., Guéret, C., Villata, S., Breslin, J., Faron-Zucker, C., Zimmermann, A. (eds.) ESWC 2015. LNCS, vol. 9341, pp. 353–363. Springer, Cham (2015). https://doi.org/10.1007/978-3-319-25639-9_48
7. Fielding, R., Lafon, Y., Reschke, J.: Hypertext transfer protocol (http/1.1): range requests. Technical report 7233, IETF, June 2014. http://www.rfc-editor.org/rfc/rfc7233.txt
8. Gleim, L., Decker, S.: Open challenges for the management and preservation of evolving data on the web. In: MEPDaW@ISWC (2020)

9. Gleim, L., Decker, S.: Timestamped URLs as persistent identifiers. In: MEP-DaW@ISWC (2020)
10. Gleim, L., Pennekamp, J., Liebenberg, M., Buchsbaum, M., et al.: FactDAG: formalizing data interoperability in an internet of production. IEEE IoT J. **7**, 3243–3253 (2020)
11. Gleim, L., Pennekamp, J., Tirpitz, L., Welten, S., Brillowski, F., Decker, S.: FactStack: interoperable data management and preservation for the web and industry 4.0. In: Sattler, K.-U., Herschel, M., Lehner, W. (eds.) BTW 2021, pp. 371–395. Gesellschaft für Informatik, Bonn (2021). https://doi.org/10.18420/btw2021-20
12. International Standardization Organization: ISO 8601: 2004 (E): Data Elements and Interchange Formats, Information Interchange. Representation of Dates and Times, ISO (2004)
13. Klyne, G., Newman, C.: Date and time on the internet: timestamps. Technical report 3339, IETF, July 2002. https://www.ietf.org/rfc/rfc3339.txt
14. Kovatsch, M., Matsukura, R., Lagally, M., Kawaguchi, T., Toumura, K., Kajimoto, K.: Web of Things (WoT) Architecture. W3C Recommendation (2020)
15. Meinhardt, P., Knuth, M., Sack, H.: TailR: a platform for preserving history on the web of data. In: International Conference on Semantic Systems (2015)
16. Pelgrin, O., Galárraga, L.: Towards Fully-fledged Archiving for RDF Datasets (2020)
17. Pennekamp, J., Glebke, R., Henze, M., Meisen, T., Quix, C., et al.: Towards an infrastructure enabling the internet of production. In: IEEE ICPS, pp. 31–37 (2019)
18. Sambra, A.V., Mansour, E., Hawke, S., Zereba, M., et al.: Solid: a platform for decentralized social applications based on linked data. Technical report, MIT CSAIL & QCRI (2016)
19. Van de Sompel, H., Nelson, M., Sanderson, R.: HTTP Framework for Time-Based Access to Resource States – Memento. RFC 7089 (2013)
20. Van de Sompel, H., Nelson, M.L., Sanderson, R., Balakireva, L.L., Ainsworth, S., Shankar, H.: Memento: Time Travel for the Web. arXiv:0911.1112 (2009)
21. Van de Sompel, H., Sanderson, R., et al.: Persistent identifiers for scholarly assets and the web: the need for an unambiguous mapping. Int. J. Digital Curation **9**(1), 331–342 (2014)
22. Speicher, S., Arwe, J., Malhotra, A.: Linked Data Platform 1.0. W3C Recommendation (2015)
23. Taelman, R., Vander Sande, M., Herwegen, J., Mannens, E., Verborgh, R.: Triple storage for random-access versioned querying of RDF archives. J. Web Semant. **54**, 4–28 (2018)
24. Vander Sande, M., Verborgh, R., et al.: Toward sustainable publishing and querying of distributed Linked Data archives. J. Documentation **74**(1), 195–222 (2018)
25. Verborgh, R.: Querying history with Linked Data (2016). https://ruben.verborgh.org/blog/2016/06/22/querying-history-with-linked-data/
26. Whitehead, E.J.: WebDAV and DeltaV: collaborative authoring, versioning, and configuration management for the web. In: HYPERTEXT, pp. 259–260 (2001)
27. Wilkinson, M.D., et al.: The FAIR guiding principles for scientific data management and stewardship. Sci. Data **3**(1) (2016). https://doi.org/10.1038/sdata.2016.18

Expressibility of OWL Axioms
with Patterns

Aaron Eberhart[✉], Cogan Shimizu, Sulogna Chowdhury,
Md. Kamruzzaman Sarker, and Pascal Hitzler

Data Semantics Lab, Kansas State University, Manhattan, USA
aaroneberhart@ksu.edu

Abstract. The high expressivity of the Web Ontology Language (OWL) makes it possible to describe complex relationships between classes, roles, and individuals in an ontology. However, this high expressivity can be an obstacle to correct usage and wide adoption. Past attempts to ameliorate this have included the development of specific, presumably human-friendly syntaxes, such as the Manchester syntax or graphical interfaces for OWL axioms, albeit with limited success. If modelers want to develop suitable OWL axioms it is important to make this as easy as possible.

In this paper, we adopt an idea from the Protégé plug-in, OWLAx, which provides a simple, clickable interface to automatically input axioms of a limited number of types by following simple axiom patterns. In particular, each of these axiom patterns contains at most three classes or roles. We hypothesize that most of the axioms in existing ontologies could be expressed semantically in terms of simple patterns like these, which would mean that more complex patterns can be used very sparingly.

Our findings, based on an analysis of 518 ontologies from six public ontology repositories, confirm this hypothesis: Over 90% of class axioms in the average ontology are indeed expressible with our simple patterns. We provide a detailed analysis of our findings.

1 Introduction

Knowledge graph schema are complex artifacts that can be difficult and expensive to produce and maintain. This is especially true when encoding them in OWL (the Web Ontology Language) as ontologies. The high expressivity of OWL is a boon, in that it makes it possible to describe complex relationships between classes, roles,[1] and individuals in an ontology. At the same time, however, this high expressivity is often an obstacle to its correct usage that can limit adoption. Past attempts to ameliorate this have included the development of specific, presumably human-friendly syntaxes, such as the Manchester syntax [10], or graphical interfaces for OWL axioms, albeit with modest success [16].

---

[1] We refer to properties as **roles**, unless a distinction is relevant, as this is the standard description logic term. These include both object properties and data properties.

© Springer Nature Switzerland AG 2021
R. Verborgh et al. (Eds.): ESWC 2021, LNCS 12731, pp. 230–245, 2021.
https://doi.org/10.1007/978-3-030-77385-4_14

Additionally, certain engineering paradigms and methodologies have been developed, such as eXtreme Design [2] or Modular Ontology Modeling [7,19], that try to simplify the modeling process.

In general, these methodologies aim to guide ontology developers through the complex modeling process by either abstracting the complexity away (for example, through the use of Ontology Design Patterns), or by limiting the scope of the model to something immediately applicable and understandable. In this paper we are particularly interested in the latter, especially during the axiomatization process. We believe that it is important to investigate new avenues for improving the approachability of creating suitable OWL axioms.

One of the core tenets of the Modular Ontology Modeling methodology is to produce schema diagrams and then systematically axiomatize them, with the input of domain experts. This systematic axiomatization is inspired by the OWLAx plugin for Protégé,[2] which provides a simple, clickable interface to automatically input axioms of limited syntactic forms that are all created from simple axiom patterns [17]. In particular, each of these simple axiom patterns contains at most three classes or roles. In [17], it was posited (but not demonstrated) that the 17 axiom patterns provided by the interface were sufficient for *most* modeling purposes. In this paper we test that hypothesis by analyzing 518 ontologies from six public ontology repositories. Concretely, we show the following:

H1. Almost all axioms in OWL ontologies are expressible using a set of simple axiom patterns, like those found in Table 1.

And indeed, as we will see, it holds for over 90% of class axioms in the average ontology using our relatively straightforward analysis. With a more thorough analysis or with different patterns, the percentage may even be higher.

2   Related Work

We are aware of only a very limited amount of research that specifically concerns the semantic, not syntactic, composition and expressibility of ontologies regarding patterns. There are several studies, such as [5,14,23], which investigate the use of OWL syntax and constructs in general. However, a mere syntactic survey of OWL as it is used in practice does not directly address the question we are investigating, namely whether a relatively small set of axiom patterns suffices to express most OWL axioms. Zhang et al. [26] look at ways to measure the design complexity of ontologies. Their work is focused more on ontology quality evaluation than ontology composition. Some have also attempted to measure the effect that axioms like existential quantifiers have on reasoning time, such as Kang et al. [11], although it is only tangentially related to the work that we are presenting.

There are also, as previously mentioned, tools that attempt to simplify OWL ontology development, such as Manchester Syntax [10], WebVOWL [13], CoMo-dIDE [18], Graffoo [3], and ROWLTab [16]. These tools simplify the development

---

[2] See https://protege.stanford.edu/.

process but they do not measure whether OWL axioms are necessarily complex in everyday usage. It could very well be the case that OWL is unavoidably complicated and these tools are needed to deal with this complexity, although we believe our work demonstrates that this is usually not the case.

3 Methodology

Our hypothesis is that most axioms in ontologies could be expressed with simple axiom patterns. In this section, we will define what we mean by simple axioms, then give an example of a set of patterns that generate simple axioms, such as those used in the Protégé plugin OWLAx. Following that, we will describe how to measure the extent to which an ontology is expressible with simple axiom patterns, and then provide some minimal normalizations for ontologies which we will use in our evaluation.

3.1 Simple Axioms

The simple axioms we study in this paper are defined below. We consider description logic syntax for OWL DL, that is, we identify it with the description logic $\mathcal{SROIQ}(D)$ [8].

Definition 1. *A **Simple Axiom** is any OWL axiom that contains at most three class or role names, or a data range, and is not a syntactic shortcut for other OWL axioms as defined in the OWL 2 Specification.[3] Any axiom which is not simple is a **Complex Axiom**.*

Our set of axiom patterns is designed for class axioms, so we restrict our focus to class axioms in the evaluation, although, in principle, the notion of a simple axiom could apply to role (RBox) axioms as well. The limitation of three atoms for simple axioms is an intuitive threshold, in terms of size, because it means that nesting is limited, yet the axiom can still contain expressions and participate in complex inferences in combination with other simple axioms. This would not be the case for axioms limited to size two, where one could only express $A \sqsubseteq B$ for classes, or $R \sqsubseteq S$ for roles, which would radically limit the expressivity of the ontology. Axioms with more than three atomic classes or roles may be more expressive, but are often equivalent through normalization to smaller axioms, so they do not make not good candidates for simple axioms. Note that negation and inverse are not considered complex, since the definition considers only the number of names; of course double negation can be eliminated trivially.

3.2 OWLAx Axiom Patterns

OWLAx [17] is a Protégé plugin that allows users to automatically generate certain simple OWL axioms using a graphical interface. The set of axioms we study in this paper are inspired by the axioms that OWLAx can create, and they are listed in Table 1.

---

[3] See https://www.w3.org/TR/2012/REC-owl2-syntax-20121211/.

Table 1. OWLAx axiom patterns

Subclass	$A \sqsubseteq B$	Functional	$\top \sqsubseteq\, \leqslant 1R.\top$
Disjoint Classes	$A \sqcap B \sqsubseteq \bot$	Qualified Functional	$\top \sqsubseteq\, \leqslant 1R.B$
Domain	$\exists R.\top \sqsubseteq B$	Scoped Functional	$A \sqsubseteq\, \leqslant 1R.\top$
Scoped Domain	$\exists R.A \sqsubseteq B$	Qualified Scoped Functional	$A \sqsubseteq\, \leqslant 1R.B$
Range	$\top \sqsubseteq \forall R.B$	Inverse Functional	$\top \sqsubseteq\, \leqslant 1R^-.\top$
Scoped Range	$A \sqsubseteq \forall R.B$	Inverse Qualified Functional	$\top \sqsubseteq\, \leqslant 1R^-.B$
Existential	$A \sqsubseteq \exists R.B$	Inverse Scoped Functional	$A \sqsubseteq\, \leqslant 1R^-.\top$
Inverse Existential	$A \sqsubseteq \exists R^-.B$	Inverse Qualified Scoped Functional	$A \sqsubseteq\, \leqslant 1R^-.B$
		Structural Tautology	$A \sqsubseteq\, \geqslant 0R.B$

A, B, R are variable terms that contain at most one class or role name, or a data range

The actual implementation details of the OWLAx plugin are not pertinent to our discussion. Rather, we are interested in what it happens to contain: a set of patterns that only make simple axioms. In this sense, the axiom patterns are *simple axiom patterns*, since they can generate only simple axioms. And because it was designed specifically to help create ontologies, we speculate that ontologies will be mostly expressible using these patterns. We now discuss how to assess the extent to which an ontology can be expressed using such *axiom patterns*.

3.3 Axiom Pattern Expressibility

To study whether axioms in an ontology are expressible with simple axiom patterns, we first define the term axiom pattern and then show how a set of axiom patterns can be used to study axioms in an ontology, obtaining multiple metrics to evaluate pattern expressibility.

Definition 2. *An **Axiom Pattern** is a programmatic template for creating new, syntactically correct axioms. An axiom pattern may have variable terms that can be used to obtain specific axioms by substitution. Given an axiom α and a pattern p, we say that p can generate α (or, p is α-generating) if α can be obtained by appropriately substituting variable terms in p.*

For example, the axiom pattern $A \sqsubseteq \exists R.B$ for an existential axiom from Table 1, where A, B, R are variable terms, can be used to generate the axiom Dog $\sqsubseteq$ $\exists$chases.Squirrel by substitution, where "Dog" and "Squirrel" are classes and "chases" is a role. Note that axiom patterns are very different from Ontology Design Patterns (ODPs) [20], because an ODP is a partial ontology representing a generic solution to a recurring ontology modeling problem, while an axiom pattern is a pattern for making single axioms. They are fundamentally different in purpose and nature (although the term *pattern* can be used for either).

Definition 3. *The **axiom pattern expressibility** $ae_{\mathcal{P}}(\alpha)$ of an axiom α w.r.t. a set of axiom patterns $\mathcal{P}$ is the set of patterns $p \in \mathcal{P}$ each of which can generate*

α with the fewest substitutions. Formally, given an axiom α and a pattern p that can generate α, let $s_p(\alpha)$ be the number of substitutions required to generate α from p. Given an axiom α, and a set $\mathcal{P}$ of axiom patterns, let $ae_{\mathcal{P}}(\alpha)$ be the set of α-generating patterns from $\mathcal{P}$ such that, for all $q \in ae_{\mathcal{P}}(\alpha)$ and $p \in \mathcal{P}$, we have $s_q(\alpha) \le s_p(\alpha)$. Note that $ae_{\mathcal{P}}(\alpha)$ may be empty if there are no α-generating patterns in $\mathcal{P}$.

We give an example for these definitions. Let P be the set of axiom patterns from Table 1, and let α be Human $\sqsubseteq \le 1.\mathrm{hasHeart}.\top$. Then $s_{A \sqsubseteq \le 1R.\top}(\alpha) = 2$ and $s_{A \sqsubseteq \le 1R.B}(\alpha) = 3$. It is easy to check that no other patterns in P can generate α. Hence $ae_{\mathcal{P}}(\alpha) = \{A \sqsubseteq \le 1R.\top\}$.

Proposition 1. *For $\mathcal{P}$ the set of axiom patterns from Table 1, and given any axiom α in $\mathcal{SROIQ(D)}$, $ae_{\mathcal{P}}(\alpha)$ is either empty or a singleton set. I.e. if an axiom can be generated from a pattern from P, then there is a unique pattern with the minimal number of required substitutions.*

Proof. It is sufficient to show that no axiom can be created by more than one of our patterns with the fewest substitutions. This can be verified easily by inspecting Table 1 and comparing pairs of patterns. We draft the thought process. Table 1 states that each variable term contains at most one class or role name, therefore subclass, disjoint classes, and structural tautology patterns all have no overlapping patterns which could also produce axioms of those forms. The domain, range, and existential patterns do not mutually overlap except in pairs that vary only in the location of $\top$ or $^-$, so the claim is clearly also true, since $\top$ or $^-$ in the pattern reduces the number of substitutions required to generate an axiom containing it by 1. Functional and inverse functional patterns follow a similar structure, where an axiom is always uniquely obtainable with the fewest substitutions from the pattern containing $\top$ and $^-$ in the same locations.

The following will be used in our evaluations.

Definition 4. *The **Average Axiom Pattern Expressibility** $\overline{ae}_{\mathcal{P}}(\mathcal{A})$ for a set of axioms $\mathcal{A}$ of cardinality $|\mathcal{A}|$ (i.e., $|\mathcal{A}|$ is the number of axioms in $\mathcal{A}$) is defined as*

$$\overline{ae}_{\mathcal{P}}(\mathcal{A}) = \frac{1}{|\mathcal{A}|} \sum_{\alpha \in \mathcal{A}} |ae_{\mathcal{P}}(\alpha)|.$$

*The **Average Ontology Axiom Pattern Expressibility** $\overline{oe}_{\mathcal{P}}(\mathcal{O})$ of a set of ontologies $\mathcal{O}$ having cardinality $|\mathcal{O}|$ and set of axiom patterns $\mathcal{P}$, is given by*

$$\overline{oe}_{\mathcal{P}}(\mathcal{O}) = \frac{1}{|\mathcal{O}|} \sum_{\mathcal{A} \in \mathcal{O}} \overline{ae}_{\mathcal{P}}(\mathcal{A}),$$

where $\mathcal{A}$ represents the set of axioms in each ontology.

It is important to note that average ontology axiom pattern expressibility can be used to evaluate a set of ontologies, and average axiom pattern expressibility can be used to evaluate any number of axioms, e.g. a set of axioms which has been collected from multiple ontologies.

3.4   Normalization

We have discussed our evaluation measures for axiom pattern expressibility of an ontology. However, there remains an issue that ontologies often vary radically in the way they are syntactically expressed, even if semantically they mean similar or even equivalent things. Ontologies are written for completely different purposes and at differing levels of complexity; some ontologies are developed for complex reasoning applications, while others are used for more straightforward data integration. Even within a single ontology, different authors may express equivalent statements in different ways based on personal preference or style. To give an example, class disjointness of two classes A and B can be expressed with any of the (equivalent) axioms $A \sqcap B \sqsubseteq \bot$, $A \sqsubseteq \neg B$, $B \sqsubseteq \neg A$, and others.

Hence, in order to evaluate the pattern expressibility of a large number of ontologies uniformly, we therefore need at least a minimal syntactic normalization strategy taken from community standards that allows us to compare disparate sources without biasing the evaluation in favor of any particular style. For this, we use multiple strategies derived from common OWL practices.

Our normalization begins by filtering out all axioms except class, role, and HasKey axioms. This is necessary because there are many OWL axioms for which our pattern study will not apply. Included in this are assertion (ABox) axioms, since these are primarily axioms about instances rather than classes and roles, but also axioms such as annotations, declarations, and datatype definitions, that are axioms according to the OWL 2 specification but carry no or few formal semantics. HasKey axioms are taken into account because they are logical axioms and not assertions or annotations, although their semantics is different from class and role axioms. Note that none of our axiom patterns matches HasKey axioms. The remaining class and role axioms are then transformed according to the following procedures.

The first transformation that we perform is an equivalence transformation based on the syntactic shortcuts defined in the OWL Structural Specification [15]. Whenever an axiom is found that has one of the forms in Column 1 of Table 2, we perform the designated substitution. These substitutions are equivalent rewritings so they do not alter the semantics of the ontology. It is also possible that other simple transformations of class axioms according to the equivalences defined in the structural specification could improve the evaluation, since these axioms also might be expressible using patterns. Our transformation thus may lead to an undercount in our disfavor; we will come back to this point later. Thus, for EquivalentClasses, DisjointClasses, and DisjointUnion we convert them to sets of SubClass axioms using definitions in the OWL 2 specification.

The second transformation that we perform is obtaining negation normal form (NNF) of all class axioms in an ontology. By using the NNF we can transform all of the class axioms in an ontology into simple syntactic forms that are stripped of unnecessary information that might be due to coincidence rather than semantic equivalence.

The last transformation we apply is splitting SubClass axioms with conjunctions in the consequent, or disjunctions in the antecedent, into separate axioms.

Table 2. Axiom transformations

Ontology axiom	Substituted axiom
ReflexiveObjectProperty(R)	$\top \sqsubseteq \exists R.\mathbf{Self}$
IrreflexiveObjectProperty(R)	$\exists R.\mathbf{Self} \sqsubseteq \bot$
FunctionalObjectProperty(R)	$\top \sqsubseteq \; \leqslant 1R.\top$
FunctionalDataProperty(S)	$\top \sqsubseteq \; \leqslant 1S.\top$
InverseFunctionalObjectProperty(R)	$\top \sqsubseteq \; \leqslant 1R^-.\top$
ObjectPropertyRange(R C)	$\top \sqsubseteq \forall R.C$
DataPropertyRange(S D)	$\top \sqsubseteq \forall S.D$
ObjectPropertyDomain(R C)	$\exists R.\top \sqsubseteq C$
DataPropertyDomain(S C)	$\exists S.\top \sqsubseteq C$

R is an ObjectProperty, S is a DataProperty, C is a
Class, and D is a DataRange

This is a standard procedure in many normalizations, and we simply replace the axiom with a set of axioms formed from the conjuncts or disjuncts whenever an axiom of this type is found. There is a special case that occurs only when the consequent is an ExactCardinality expression whose value is equal to 1. In this case, we do not use a MinCardinality 1 substitution but instead add an existential, since that is equivalent and more compact.

All normalizations are performed sequentially and axioms are output into a separate collection for evaluation. This compartmentalizes the data and ensures that no duplicates are created, even when a single axiom is transformed into a set of axioms. The sets of axioms $\mathcal{A}$ used in our evaluations are these separate normalized sets.

4   Evaluation

We analyze a set of 518 ontologies from various sources, normalizing them, and testing them for axiom pattern expressibility according to the principles described in the previous section. Ontologies were selected from diverse sources with unique design requirements: benchmark ontologies, Ontology Design Patterns (ODPs), ontologies extracted from Linked Open Vocabulary (LOV) [22], as well as medical domain ontologies. It would technically be possible to integrate other types of linked data in this analysis, though semantically it may not be straightforward to interpret the results if the data was mixed, so we use only OWL ontologies. Statistics about the original ontologies gathered before and after normalization can be found in Table 3. The normalization adds a few axioms to the set of axioms from an ontology whenever an axiom is split, so counts increase by a factor of around 7–8 to 10, except for ontologies that contain many assertions that were excluded during the normalization process, like hydrography and anatomy benchmarks. As mentioned previously, the normalized axioms are the axioms used in the evaluation and the equations. We use the set of all normalized axioms from all ontologies for the $\overline{ae}_\mathcal{P}(\mathcal{A})$ numbers and the set of normalized axioms from each ontology for $\overline{oe}_\mathcal{P}(\mathcal{O})$ numbers.

Table 3. Ontology Statistics. Logical axioms are axioms that are neither declarations nor annotations

	LOV	Hydrography	Anatomy	Conference	ODP	Ontobee	Misc
Classes	20075	341	6048	498	577	509925	80796
Roles	10106	121	5	226	600	10453	535
Data properties	8340	77	0	85	71	480	66
Axioms	274991	8873	41407	3037	7378	5071892	816572
Logical axioms	82450	5463	16383	2153	3223	963880	272334
Normalized axioms	94937	1748	9951	2774	3917	1208950	391015
Ontologies	250	4	2	7	80	171	4

In this section, we report the result for all ontologies we tested, then go into details about each source, reporting a separate evaluation for each. Next we break down the results by profile and report the numbers for those as well. In all cases, the expressibility numbers are reported for All Axioms, Class Axioms, and Simple Class Axioms. Our axiom patterns can only express simple class axioms, thus the values for 'All Axioms' represent the evaluation using all class, role, and HasKey axioms, 'Class Axioms' indicates the evaluation using only class axioms, and 'Simple Class Axioms' represents the evaluation for only simple class axioms. In Figures and Tables, the term "miss" is used to indicate a simple axiom that was observed but was inexpressible using our patterns. The last value we report, which is a byproduct of calculations that produce expressibility numbers, is the percent subclass and percent existential, as well as their combination. By this we mean, what percent of all of the axioms in an ontology are expressible with the subclass pattern, the existential pattern, or both. It will turn out in nearly every case that a surprisingly high proportion of most ontologies is expressible with just these two simple axiom patterns. OWL files and source code for the evaluation, except the gene ontology which can't be uploaded due to size restrictions, can be found on the GitHub page https://github.com/aaronEberhart/owlax and the raw data can be inspected in the spreadsheet at https://tinyurl.com/eswc2021.

4.1 Overall Expressibility

The average axiom pattern expressibility and the average ontology axiom pattern expressibility for our simple axiom patterns over all normalized axioms in all ontologies is included in Table 4, as well as the standard deviation for the ontology axiom pattern expressibility.

Figure 1 shows the overall distribution of axioms for the entire collection of ontologies. Complex class axioms, role axioms, miss (inexpressible simple axioms) and HasKey are the axioms that cannot be generated by our patterns; note that only the first two of these play a significant role. Simple subclass is 54.8%, and existential is 23.9%, totaling 78.8%. This is almost the same as the axiom expressibility value for all axioms (82.2%). A more detailed view of axiom type distributions can be found in the next section in Fig. 2.

Table 4. Overall average expressibility

	$\overline{ae}_\mathcal{P}(\mathcal{A})$	$\overline{oe}_\mathcal{P}(\mathcal{O})$	StdDev $\overline{oe}_\mathcal{P}(\mathcal{O})$
All axioms	82.2%	82.9%	0.206
Class axioms	83.8%	92.9%	0.165
Simple class axioms	99.8%	96.5%	0.153

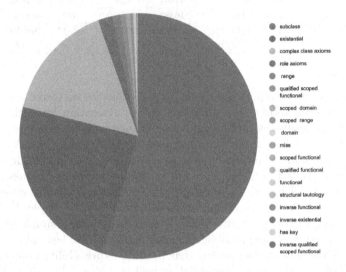

● subclass
● existential
● complex class axioms
● role axioms
● range
● qualified scoped functional
● scoped domain
● scoped range
● domain
● miss
● scoped functional
● qualified functional
● functional
● structural tautology
● inverse functional
● inverse existential
● has key
● inverse qualified scoped functional

Fig. 1. Overall distribution of axioms

4.2 Source Expressibility

As they are all from very different domains, each source was analyzed independently from the whole. Our evaluation includes 250 ontologies that were automatically pulled from LOV using a script that can be found on the project GitHub. We obtained benchmark ontologies that are used for ontology alignment evaluation. There are 4 ontologies from Hydrography, 2 from Anatomy, and 7 from the Conference domains, and each appear in their own column in Tables 5 and 6. We also obtained and evaluated 80 ODPs, as well as a collection of 171 OWL files that are mainly from the medical domain from the ontobee[4] [25] website. Additionally, we gathered 4 ontologies that did not fall neatly into any of these categories but nonetheless seemed interesting to include in the overall result. These ontologies are General Formal Ontology [6], Gene Ontology [4], GeoLink Base Ontology [12], and the Enslaved Ontology [21], and their average is labeled Misc in the tables.

The Gene Ontology tends to dominate the other sources in Misc due to its extremely large size. It also contains a much higher percentage of complex class axioms than any other ontology we tested, which accounts for the difference

---

[4] http://ontobee.org.

Table 5. $\overline{ae}_P(\mathcal{A})$ by source

	LOV	Hydrography	Anatomy	Conference	ODP	Ontobee	Misc
All axioms	78.7%	77.1%	99.9%	89.3%	85.7%	88.7%	62.4%
Class axioms	92.6%	84.5%	100%	96.2%	97.3%	89.9%	62.5%
Simple class axioms	99.2%	96.5%	100%	99.2%	99.1%	99.8%	99.9%

Table 6. $\overline{oe}_P(\mathcal{O})$ by source

	LOV	Hydrography	Anatomy	Conference	ODP	Ontobee	Misc
All axioms	81.3%	77.5%	99.9%	87.3%	76.5%	88.3%	67.2%
Class axioms	92.7%	89.7%	100%	92.8%	96.4%	91.8%	99.4%
Simple class axioms	95.2%	97.6%	100%	95.2%	97.7%	97.9%	99.4%

in Misc between simple class axioms and class axioms. In LOV there are a considerable number of role axioms. This explains why the expressibility is so much higher for class axioms than all axioms.

In Table 7, we see the range of percent subclass and existential among sources. Anatomy, Ontobee, and Misc all contain medical domain ontologies, which may account for the increase in percent existential if they contain more ontologies in the EL profile. LOV and Hydrography, on the other hand, are expressible with very little subclass at all, and both contain many role axioms. Except for the Anatomy Benchmarks, which is actually only two ontologies so a disproportionately small sample size, it does not appear to be the case that any sources are entirely existential and subclass. Neither are any sources completely lacking the two axiom patterns. When we break the results down by profile in the next section, things will look quite a bit different.

Figure 2 shows the actual counts of each axiom pattern used to calculate expressibility in logarithmic scale. In this chart we can see how sources like Ontobee and Misc do contain some of the less common patterns. They are just so large that smaller sources, like ODPs and benchmarks, tend to have higher percentages. The previously mentioned high percentage of complex class axioms for Misc can be seen in the third column. Also, the two ontology sources with the highest percent expressibility of subclass and existential are Anatomy and Ontobee, both medical type ontology sources. If we move farther down the chart to the less common axiom patterns, the larger ontology sources are less prevalent and now the benchmarks and ODPs start to dominate. The last two axiom patterns were never detected by our program and inverse scoped functional occurred once so the log scale in the chart hides this. For the inverse qualified functional axiom pattern it is conceivable that authors rarely had occasion to write axioms like this. Disjoint classes may seem surprising, however we investigated the evaluation and found that, even though our pattern, $A \sqcap B \sqsubseteq \bot$, is expressible in profiles that do not contain negation, authors are likely using Protégé or the OWLAPI [9] to state disjoint classes axioms which the normalization transforms

Table 7. Percent subclass and existential by source

	LOV	Hydrography	Anatomy	Conference	ODP	Ontobee	Misc
Subclass	42.4%	46.2%	66.8%	57.6%	56.4%	60.2%	41.0%
Existential	05.9%	07.4%	33.1%	06.7%	05.7%	26.5%	20.7%
Subclass + Existential	48.3%	53.3%	99.9%	64.3%	62.1%	86.7%	61.7%

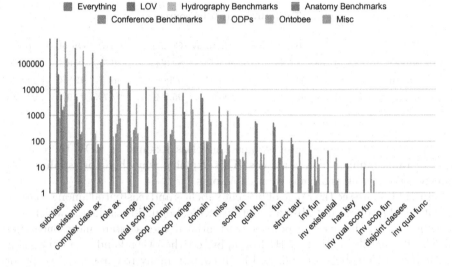

Fig. 2. Axiom expressibility counts, log scale

into subclass axioms containing negation, as defined in the specification. This causes disjoint classes to match the subclass pattern rather than our disjointness pattern, which is not a false negative or a methodological error, but it is technically a misclassification due to conflicting sets of patterns.

4.3 Profile Expressibility

During the analysis we also tested each ontology to see if it was in the OWL profiles EL, QL, RL, or DL, and report the expressibility information for each profile separately. In Tables 8, 9 and 10, the Full column is reproduced from values in Sect. 4.1 and Table 4 for comparison, since every ontology will be in OWL Full. There were 15 ontologies that could be loaded into the evaluation, but the OWLAPI could not test their profile; these ontologies were not included in the profile results but are included in the Full column. Interestingly, for the EL, QL, and RL profiles we see around a ten percent expressibility boost over the overall result. All three also have perfect expressibility for simple class axioms, and nearly perfect expressibility for all class axioms. The expressibility numbers for DL are also slightly higher than the overall numbers, though significantly less so than for the other profiles. The lower values for Full compared to DL are heavily influenced by the Gene Ontology, which was not classified as OWL DL.

Table 8. $\overline{ae}_{\mathcal{P}}(\mathcal{A})$ by profile

	EL	QL	RL	DL	Full
All axioms	98.7%	99.7%	97.8%	91.4%	82.2%
Class axioms	98.8%	100%	100%	92.7%	83.8%
Simple class axioms	100%	100%	100%	99.9%	99.8%

Table 9. $\overline{oe}_{\mathcal{P}}(\mathcal{O})$ by profile

	EL	QL	RL	DL	Full
All axioms	94.6%	87.7%	81.7%	82.8%	82.9%
Class axioms	97.5%	97.1%	95.2%	94.4%	92.9%
Simple class axioms	98.1%	97.1%	95.2%	97.2%	96.5%

Unlike the different sources, where the percent subclass and existential numbers were mostly near the average, we get a much more skewed result when we break the ontologies down by profile in Table 10. EL and DL ontologies seem to be expressible with a similar percentage of subclass axioms as the overall result, though EL has many more existential expressions. QL ontologies, on the other hand, are eighty percent expressible with the simple subclass pattern. And the RL profile ontologies are almost entirely expressible with simple subclass. It is no surprise, then, that EL, QL, and RL ontologies have such high expressibility.

In Table 11, we mark which of our axiom patterns are expressible in each profile with an X symbol, using the OWL 2 Profiles [24] document as a reference. We see that RL expressibility is almost entirely subclass, and the existential pattern is indeed inexpressible in that profile. EL seems to be evenly divided between subclass and existential, which again aligns with the types of statements permitted in the profile. The DL profile allows all the types of expressions and it understandably has a similar result to the overall average.

For the EL profile we also observe a unique result, because our axiom patterns have almost complete overlap with the 4 normal form class axioms defined for $\mathcal{EL}^{++}$ in [1], as shown in Table 12. The only exception is conjunction, which can only match our disjoint classes axiom pattern when the consequent is equal to $\bot$. If we were to define a conjunction axiom pattern, it might be possible to completely express this profile with simple axiom patterns. This could also be done for class axioms in the QL profile, where our axiom patterns could express all simple axioms, and could express any set of QL axioms that was normalized to remove nested quantifiers. Simple class axioms for the RL profile could be expressed in much the same way as EL, missing only conjunction axioms that do not have $\bot$ in the consequent. With the addition of a conjunction pattern and by normalizing to remove nested quantifiers we could also obtain complete class axiom pattern expressibility for RL.

Table 10. Percent subclass and existential by profile

	EL	QL	RL	DL	Full
Subclass	52.5%	78.2%	95.1%	60.9%	54.8%
Existential	46.1%	21.1%	0%	29.2%	23.9%
Subclass + Existential	98.6%	99.3%	95.1%	90.2%	78.8%

Table 11. Profile axiom pattern expressibility

	EL	QL	RL	DL		EL	QL	RL	DL
$A \sqsubseteq B$	X	X	X	X	$\top \sqsubseteq\ \leqslant 1R.\top$				X
$A \sqcap B \sqsubseteq \bot$	X		X	X	$\top \sqsubseteq\ \leqslant 1R.B$				X
$\exists R.\top \sqsubseteq B$	X	X	X	X	$A \sqsubseteq\ \leqslant 1R.\top$			X	X
$\exists R.A \sqsubseteq B$	X		X	X	$A \sqsubseteq\ \leqslant 1R.B$			X	X
$\top \sqsubseteq \forall R.B$				X	$\top \sqsubseteq\ \leqslant 1R^-.\top$				X
$A \sqsubseteq \forall R.B$			X	X	$\top \sqsubseteq\ \leqslant 1R^-.B$				X
$A \sqsubseteq \exists R.B$	X	X		X	$A \sqsubseteq\ \leqslant 1R^-.\top$			X	X
$A \sqsubseteq \exists R^-.B$		X		X	$A \sqsubseteq\ \leqslant 1R^-.B$			X	X
					$A \sqsubseteq\ \geqslant 0R.B$				X

5   Discussion

Our motivation for this study is that we believe *simple axioms*, specifically those that can be created from simple patterns, are easier for non-logicians to understand and utilize for modeling. This is not to say that complex axioms are unnecessary, indeed they may be the most important. However, if most of OWL could be expressed with simple patterns, as we have shown, this seems a good place to focus our attention when we consider ways to facilitate adoption. Alongside improved comprehension, simple axioms made from patterns come with a number of added benefits: attempting to measure the non-local effects of ontological commitments may be easier, they can be easily and automatically created by tools that allow users to specify statements in a graphical interface without a deep technical understanding of the inner-workings of OWL, and simple axioms often do not require normalization before being input to a reasoner. To support this, we determine the current usage characteristics of axioms in existing ontologies to see if they are expressible with simple axiom patterns, as well as how this relates to different sources and OWL profiles.

Our evaluation is limited in a few ways. We have not yet investigated if limiting an ontology engineer to these axiom patterns would pose additional obstacles, such as in writing complex axioms. There is also no way we are aware of to automatically detect if patterns were used to make an ontology, so we are unable to compare ontologies made without patterns to those that were made with patterns. Finally, our evaluation produces a lower bound. So while it shows

Table 12. $\mathcal{EL}^{++}$ axiom pattern expressibility

Axiom pattern	$\mathcal{EL}^{++}$ Normal Class Axiom
A ⊑ B	A ⊑ B
A ⊓ B ⊑ ⊥	A ⊓ B ⊑ C, when C = ⊥
∃R.⊤ ⊑ B	∃R.A ⊑ B, when A = ⊤
∃R.A ⊑ B	∃R.A ⊑ B
A ⊑ ∃R.B	A ⊑ ∃R.B

clearly that axiom patterns can provide sufficient expressibility for most axioms, we do not yet know how much more a more sophisticated evaluation might find.

5.1   Future Work

In the future there are many potential next steps that could build on this study. One approach would be to test different sets of simple axiom patterns and see how the expressibility numbers compare between them. OWLAx was a good basis to create an initial set of simple axiom patterns but there are some obvious common ones that it lacks, for instance conjunction, disjunction, negation, as well as multiple variations on cardinality and role axioms. For the current study we only use simple axioms because there is no clearly defined way to categorize complex axioms, which can be arbitrarily large. It may be interesting to analyze the complex axioms to see if there are any new patterns that can be included.

We also admit that our definition of expressibility is quite simple, intentionally kept this way for clarity. However it may be possible with some more comprehensive statistical tools that a better understanding of axiom pattern expressibility in ontologies is possible. In a future study we may look into different evaluations besides expressibility, perhaps it will be informative to compare.

Additionally, our method normalized many axioms, however it is likely that complex axioms existed in the ontologies we studied that *could* have been normalized but *weren't* because our method only obtained NNF and then split up appropriate conjunction and disjunction axioms. By introducing new terms in the normalization to syntactically split some expressions we might be able to even further increase the expressibility detection capability. Though, as previously mentioned, this would require the addition of new terms, and would be equivalent but also contain more entities, so the comparison would be less obviously appropriate.

6   Conclusion

In this paper we demonstrate that most axioms in OWL ontologies are expressible with a small set of simple axiom patterns. This has implications for how we approach ontology management and development. If ontologies are mostly expressible with simple patterns then focusing on supporting and explaining these types of axiom patterns can lead to easier adoption and maintenance. Complex axioms will of course always be a part of OWL, but we can improve our ontologies most easily by first making sure that the patterns used to create simple axioms are well understood and used correctly.

Acknowledgement. The authors acknowledge partial support from the financial assistance award 70NANB19H094 from U.S. Department of Commerce, National Institute of Standards and Technology and partial support from the National Science Foundation under Grant No. 2033521.

References

1. Baader, F., Brandt, S., Lutz, C.: Pushing the EL envelope. IJCAI **5**, 364–369 (2005)
2. Blomqvist, E., Hammar, K., Presutti, V.: Engineering Ontologies with Patterns - The eXtreme Design Methodology. In: Hitzler, P., Gangemi, A., Janowicz, K., Krisnadhi, A., Presutti, V. (eds.) Ontology Engineering with Ontology Design Patterns: Foundations and Applications, Studies on the Semantic Web, vol. 25, chap. 2, pp. 23–50. IOS Press (2016)
3. Falco, R., Gangemi, A., Peroni, S., Shotton, D., Vitali, F.: Modelling OWL ontologies with graffoo. In: Presutti, V., Blomqvist, E., Troncy, R., Sack, H., Papadakis, I., Tordai, A. (eds.) ESWC 2014. LNCS, vol. 8798, pp. 320–325. Springer, Cham (2014). https://doi.org/10.1007/978-3-319-11955-7_42
4. Gene Ontology Consortium: The Gene Ontology (GO) database and informatics resource. Nucleic Acids Research 32(Database-Issue), 258–261 (01 2004). https://doi.org/10.1093/nar/gkh036
5. Glimm, B., Hogan, A., Krötzsch, M., Polleres, A.: Owl: Yet to arrive on the web of data? arXiv preprint arXiv:1202.0984 (2012)
6. Herre, H.: General Formal Ontology (GFO): a foundational ontology for conceptual modelling. In: Poli, R., Healy, M., Kameas, A. (eds.) Theory and Applications of Ontology: Computer Applications, pp. 297–345. Springer, Dordrecht (2010)
7. Hitzler, P., Krisnadhi, A.: A tutorial on modular ontology modeling with ontology design patterns: The cooking recipes ontology. CoRR abs/1808.08433 (2018). http://arxiv.org/abs/1808.08433
8. Hitzler, P., Krötzsch, M., Rudolph, S.: Foundations of Semantic Web Technologies. Chapman and Hall/CRC Press (2010)
9. Horridge, M., Bechhofer, S.: The OWL API: A Java API for working with OWL 2 ontologies. In: Proceedings of the 6th International Conference on OWL: Experiences and Directions - Volume 529, OWLED 2009, pp. 49–58. CEUR-WS.org, Aachen, DEU (2009)
10. Horridge, M., Patel-Schneider, P.F.: OWL 2 Web Ontology Language Manchester Syntax. W3C Working Group Note (2009)
11. Kang, Y.-B., Li, Y.-F., Krishnaswamy, S.: Predicting reasoning performance using ontology metrics. In: Cudré-Mauroux, P., et al. (eds.) ISWC 2012. LNCS, vol. 7649, pp. 198–214. Springer, Heidelberg (2012). https://doi.org/10.1007/978-3-642-35176-1_13
12. Krisnadhi, A., et al.: The GeoLink modular oceanography ontology. In: Arenas, M., et al. (eds.) ISWC 2015. LNCS, vol. 9367, pp. 301–309. Springer, Cham (2015). https://doi.org/10.1007/978-3-319-25010-6_19

13. Lohmann, S., Link, V., Marbach, E., Negru, S.: WebVOWL: web-based visualization of ontologies. In: Lambrix, P., et al. (eds.) EKAW 2014. LNCS (LNAI), vol. 8982, pp. 154–158. Springer, Cham (2015). https://doi.org/10.1007/978-3-319-17966-7_21

14. Matentzoglu, N., Bail, S., Parsia, B.: A snapshot of the OWL web. In: Alani, H., et al. (eds.) ISWC 2013. LNCS, vol. 8218, pp. 331–346. Springer, Heidelberg (2013). https://doi.org/10.1007/978-3-642-41335-3_21

15. Parsia, B., Patel-Schneider, P., Motik, B.: OWL 2 Web Ontology Language Structural Specification and Functional-Style Syntax (Second Edition). W3C recommendation, W3C, December 2012. http://www.w3.org/TR/2012/REC-owl2-syntax-20121211/

16. Sarker, M.K., Krisnadhi, A., Carral, D., Hitzler, P.: Rule-based OWL modeling with ROWLTab Protégé pugin. In: Blomqvist, E., Maynard, D., Gangemi, A., Hoekstra, R., Hitzler, P., Hartig, O. (eds.) ESWC 2017. LNCS, vol. 10249, pp. 419–433. Springer, Cham (2017). https://doi.org/10.1007/978-3-319-58068-5_26

17. Sarker, M.K., Krisnadhi, A.A., Hitzler, P.: OWLAx: A Protégé plugin to support ontology axiomatization through diagramming. In: Kawamura, T., Paulheim, H. (eds.) Proceedings of the ISWC 2016 Posters & Demonstrations Track co-located with 15th International Semantic Web Conference (ISWC 2016), Kobe, Japan, October 19, 2016. CEUR Workshop Proceedings, vol. 1690 (2016)

18. Shimizu, C.: Towards a comprehensive modular ontology IDE and tool suite. In: Kirrane, S., Kagal, L. (eds.) Proceedings of the Doctoral Consortium at ISWC 2018 co-located with 17th International Semantic Web Conference (ISWC 2018), Monterey, USA, October 8th to12th, 2018. CEUR Workshop Proceedings, vol. 2181, pp. 65–72 (2018)

19. Shimizu, C., Hammar, K., Hitzler, P.: Modular graphical modeling evaluated. In: Proceedings of ESWC (2020, to appear)

20. Shimizu, C., Hirt, Q., Hitzler, P.: MODL: a modular ontology design library. In: Proceedings of the 10th Workshop on Ontology Design and Patterns (WOP 2019) co-located with 18th International Semantic Web Conference (ISWC 2019). CEUR Workshop Proceedings, vol. 2459, pp. 47–58 (2019)

21. Shimizu, C., et al.: The Enslaved Ontology 1.0: People of the historic slave trade. Technical report, Michigan State University, East Lansing, Michigan, April 2019

22. Vandenbussche, P., Atemezing, G., Poveda-Villalón, M., Vatant, B.: Linked open vocabularies (LOV): a gateway to reusable semantic vocabularies on the web. Semantic Web 8(3), 437–452 (2017). https://doi.org/10.3233/SW-160213

23. Wang, T.D., Parsia, B., Hendler, J.: A survey of the web ontology landscape. In: Cruz, I., et al. (eds.) ISWC 2006. LNCS, vol. 4273, pp. 682–694. Springer, Heidelberg (2006). https://doi.org/10.1007/11926078_49

24. Wu, Z., Fokoue, A., Grau, B.C., Horrocks, I., Motik, B.: OWL 2 Web Ontology Language Profiles (Second Edition). W3C recommendation, W3C, December 2012. http://www.w3.org/TR/2012/REC-owl2-profiles-20121211/

25. Xiang, Z., Mungall, C., Ruttenberg, A., He, Y.: Ontobee: a linked data server and browser for ontology terms. In: ICBO (2011)

26. Zhang, H., Li, Y.F., Tan, H.B.K.: Measuring design complexity of semantic web ontologies. J. Syst. Softw. 83(5), 803–814 (2010)

Data Dynamics, Quality, and Trust

Refining Transitive and Pseudo-Transitive Relations at Web Scale

Shuai Wang$^{(\boxtimes)}$ ⓘ, Joe Raad ⓘ, Peter Bloem ⓘ, and Frank van Harmelen ⓘ

Department of Computer Science, Vrije Universiteit Amsterdam,
Amsterdam, The Netherlands
{shuai.wang,j.raad,p.bloem,frank.van.harmelen}@vu.nl
https://krr.cs.vu.nl

Abstract. The publication of knowledge graphs on the Web in the form of RDF datasets, and the subsequent integration of such knowledge graphs are both essential to the idea of Linked Open Data. Combining such knowledge graphs can result in undesirable graph structures and even in logical inconsistencies. Refinement methods that can detect and repair such undesirable graph structures are therefore of crucial importance. Existing refinement methods for knowledge graphs are often domain-specific, are limited to single relations (e.g. owl:sameAs), or are limited in scale. We present a challenge consisting of a number of datasets of transitive and pseudo-transitive relations and hand-labeled gold standards, as well as baselines. We introduce an efficient web-scale knowledge graph refinement algorithm that works for such relations. Our algorithm analyses the graph structure, and allows the use of weighting schemes to heuristically determine which possibly erroneous edges should be removed to make the graph cycle free. When compared against general-purpose graph algorithms that perform the same task, our algorithm removes the least amount of edges to make the graph of transitive relations cycle-free while maintaining a better precision in identifying erroneous edges as measured against a human gold-standard.

1 Introduction

The central tenet of Linked Open Data is the publication and integration of RDF datasets. Such integration can result in logical inconsistencies or undesirable graph structures. For transitive relations, this can result in chains of relation instances forming complex nested cycles involving many entities across datasets in the corresponding graph. In practice, even logically valid cycles may have negative consequences. For example, a cycle of rdfs:subClassOf triples in an intended hierarchy enforces equality of all classes in the cycle, which may prevent algorithms such as query expansion from termination. To ensure data quality, refinement methods have been developed [13]. However, these methods often depend on domain-specific functionalities [7], or limited to a specific relation (e.g. owl:sameAs) [15,18] or suffer from limited scalability [18]. Such limitations call for the development of scalable and domain-independent algorithms.

© Springer Nature Switzerland AG 2021
R. Verborgh et al. (Eds.): ESWC 2021, LNCS 12731, pp. 249–264, 2021.
https://doi.org/10.1007/978-3-030-77385-4_15

This paper presents a new approach for detecting undesirable cycles in transitive relations. It uses graph structural characteristics and a heuristic notion of reliability of triples, without the need for any domain-dependent information such as labels, comments and other textual information in context [7]. Our approach (i) is independent from domain and language, (ii) has a better precision than general-purpose graph-theoretical methods and (iii) maintains good scalability and efficiency.

Graph structure reflects logical properties and vice versa. For example, when a relation is asymmetric, any cycle of size two in its graph violates consistency. Similarly, for irreflexive relations any self-loop is invalid. This suggests the use of graph-theoretic algorithms to detect logical inconsistencies. In OWL, the transitivity of a relation is typically specified directly through *owl:TransitiveProperty*. In this work, we extend to what we call *pseudo-transitive* relations: that of a sub-property or the inverse of a (pseudo-)transitive relation and those whose intended semantics is assumed to be both transitive and anti-symmetric, even if not formally asserted. In this paper, we exclude equivalence relations (e.g. `owl:sameAs`) and those whose (pseudo-)transitivity are mistakenly asserted or implied on the LOD Cloud (e.g. `foaf:knows`).

Besides the graph structure, another feature to be used for the refinement of knowledge graphs that is independent from domain and language is the *reliability* of triples. While there can be different heuristics, we measure reliability of an edge by counting the number of the occurrences of this edge across datasets of the web-scale integrated graph (see more details in Sect. 5.2). For small self-sufficient datasets, this feature is not of great value because the logical foundations of knowledge graphs dictate that repeated statements in datasets are redundant. However, such feature has been shown to be useful for the ranking of documents and entities [6] and the identification of erroneous assertions and improvement of data quality [3] when the sources of data are present. Figure 1 is an example subgraph of `skos:broader` with such weights extracted from the LOD Laundromat 2015 crawl [1]. It is more likely that `dbc:Numbers` is a broader than `dbc:Integers` (weighting 72), while it is unlikely that `dbc:Integers` is a broader concept for `dbc:Numeral_systems` (weighting 1), showing that weights can indicate the reliability of edges. This example also shows that the relation between some entities can be ambiguous, making it difficult to construct a perfect gold standard. For example, some may believe that numbers are parts of numerical systems while others may think the study of numbers includes the study of numerical systems. Finally, it also indicates that the weights of edges in the neighbourhood can have an impact on the reliability of edges.

The hypotheses that we pursue in this paper are as follows:

H1: By taking graph structural properties (how edges are involved in complex nested cycles) into account, we can make knowledge graphs acyclic while removing fewer edges than graph theoretical methods.

H2: Taking the reliability of triples into account improves the accuracy for identifying erroneous edges.

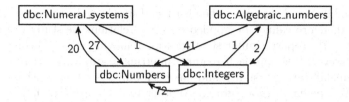

Fig. 1. An example subgraph of `skos:broader` with weights.

This paper presents an algorithm to refine transitive and pseudo-transitive relations for large integrated knowledge graphs at web scale by removing as few edges as possible to obtain acyclic graphs. More specifically, the paper makes the following contributions:

1. a new metric for the hardness of resolving cycles based on strongly connected components.
2. a generic scalable approach for the refinement of (pseudo-)transitive relations using an SMT solver by exploiting Strongly Connected Components.
3. an evaluation that shows how taking into account the reliability of triples can improve the precision of the graph refinement algorithm.
4. a dataset of several widely used (pseudo-)transitive relations with their reliability weights.
5. a new gold standard of thousands of manually annotated triples to be used in the evaluation and comparison of graph refinement algorithms.

This paper is structured as follows: Sect. 2 and 3 discuss related work and present preliminaries. Section 4 describes the dataset and analyses its complexity. Section 5 presents our approach for refining (pseudo-)transitive relations. Section 6 presents the implementation details, our gold standard, and the conducted evaluation. Section 7 discusses the results and concludes the paper.

2   Related Work

2.1   Knowledge Graph Refinement Methods

According to Paulheim's survey [13], there are two main goals for knowledge graph refinement methods: *completing* the knowledge graph with missing knowledge, and *correcting* asserted information. This work falls into the latter category of approaches, as we aim at refining transitive and pseudo-transitive relations by removing edges that lead to unwanted cycles and are potentially erroneous. The closest predecessor of our work is the approach by [18], introduced for refining edges of `rdfs:subClassOf` by exhaustively listing simple cycles[1] and removing minimal edges so that the resulting graph is cycle free. However, this approach

---

[1] A simple cycle is a cycle in which the only repeated vertices are the first and last vertices.

faces a combinatorial explosion when listing all simple cycles of large nested clusters, and therefore cannot be applied on some relations we study in this work. Sun et al. [17] propose similar strategies for removing edges causing cycles in graph. However, this approach requires inferring a graph hierarchy (e.g. using a Bayesian skill rating system), and has been only tested on synthetic datasets and the Wikipedia category graph. Another recent approach that targets the refinement of categorical and list information is introduced by [7]. To our best understanding, this graph-based refinement approach relies on external information of hypernyms, and applies only to English DBpedia categories and lists. Moreover, and similarly to the work presented in [5], these approaches assume the existence of a hierarchy and takes advantage of pre-defined roots. In this work, we show that such hierarchies are frequently violated in the Web, therefore the applicability of such approaches becomes limited in such context. Finally, the graph-based approach presented in this work is similar to other approaches that have also exploited the graph structure for detecting and removing different types erroneous edges at the scale of the Web, such as type [14] and identity links [15].

2.2   General MWFAS Algorithms

In this section we discuss general-purpose graph algorithms for making graphs cycle-free. When restricting to a single relation, the problem of resolving cycles is identical to finding the *Maximum Weighted Directed Acyclic Subgraph* (MWDAS).[2] Historically, the removed edges are also called *arcs* and form a *feedback arc set* (FAS). Therefore, the problem is equivalent to *Minimum Weighted Feedback Arc Set* (MWFAS), and we will use these names for the rest of the paper. The MWFAS problem is APX-hard. Despite the hard limit on its approximability, there are polynomial-time approximation algorithms. The following summarises some algorithms that scale to at least tens of millions of edges according to [16] where more details are presented.

The underlying idea of the **KwikSort(KS)** algorithm is to sort vertices on the number of back arcs induced, and removing the edges with many induced back arcs. The algorithm runs at $\mathcal{O}(n \log n)$ when assuming that arc membership can be tested in constant time. In our experiments we used an optimised implementation that uses $\mathcal{O}(n \log n)$ additional space. Since KS takes a random initial ordering, we take the best result of 200 runs.

The **Greedy(GRD)** algorithm greedily appends all "sink-like" vertices at the end of a sequence s and inserts the "source-like" vertices at the front of s. The implementation in [16] uses bins [12] for the selection of vertices in each iteration. The bins distinguish nodes with only outgoing edges, nodes without outgoing edges, and nodes with both in- and outgoing edges. Each node falls in one of these bins.

---

[2] Note that the resulting graph may not be a spanning tree but a set of directed acyclic graphs (DAGs). Therefore this problem cannot be solved by minimum spanning tree algorithms.

By using s as a linear arrangement and picking all the feedback arcs, it minimize the number of arcs with different orientation. GRD runs in time $\mathcal{O}(m + n)$ and uses $\mathcal{O}(m + n)$ space. It has a guarantee of removing no more than $\frac{1}{2}|E| - \frac{1}{6}|V|$ edges but experiments from [16] observed that the size of FAS is drastically smaller than this worst-case bound.

For a graph G, the **BergerShor(BS)** algorithm begins with a random permutation over the vertices V. It then processes each vertex by comparing its in-degree and out-degree. If a vertex has more incoming arcs than outgoing ones, the incoming ones are removed and added to a set E' while the outgoing arcs are removed and discarded. The collected arcs E' form an acyclic graph G' (its counterpart is the set of arcs removed). The algorithm runs in time $\mathcal{O}(m+n)$ and [16] show that the algorithm far out-performs this worst-case bound.

Finally, we can adopt a **depth-first traversal (DFS)** algorithm and remove all arcs that form a cycle during the search to ensure that the resulting graph is acyclic. Its runtime complexity is $\mathcal{O}(m + n)$. The algorithm does not make any intelligent decision nor minimize the resulting size of FAS.

3   Preliminaries

A knowledge graph is a directed and labelled graph $G = \langle V, E, \Sigma_E, l_E \rangle$, where V is the set of vertices (nodes), $E \subseteq V \times V$ the set of relations (edges), and Σ_E is the set of edge labels. $l_E : E \to 2^{\Sigma_E}$ is a function that assigns to each edge in E a set of labels belonging to Σ_E. For a specific relation $R \in \Sigma_E$, we denote $G_R = \langle V_R, E_R \rangle$ the edge-induced subgraph that only includes those edges whose labels are R, with $V_R \subseteq V$ and $E_R \subseteq E$. In the case of weighted graphs, we introduce an additional weight function $f_w : E \to \mathbb{N}$ that assigns to each edge a weight. In Sect. 5.2, we describe how these weights are calculated.

A walk in a graph G_R is a sequence of vertices $v_0, v_1, \ldots, v_n$, with the edge $(v_i, v_{i+1}) \in E_R$. A walk is a *path* if no edge is repeated. A path between two vertices is *shortest* if the number of vertices on the path is minimal. A path is a *cycle* if it is closed, i.e. $v_0 = v_n$. Apart from reflexive relations, the smallest possible cycle involves two vertices. We denote the set of such size-two cycles by E_{C2} for later convenience. A graph without the corresponding edges of E_{C2} (and vertices if left as singletons) is denoted $G' = G \backslash E_{C2}$.

A Strongly Connected Component (SCC) of G_R is a subgraph where any two of its vertices can be reached by a path (i.e. the subgraph is strongly connected) and is maximal for this property: no additional edges or vertices can be included in the subgraph without breaking strong connectivity.[3] The collection of all SCCs forms a new graph G^{SCC}, and the set of SCCs of G is denoted $\kappa(G)$. In this paper, the process of removing edges in an SCC to make it acyclic is referred to as *resolving cycles*, and graphs with no cycles are referred to as DAGs (directed acyclic graphs). In our datasets, there is often one SCC that is significantly larger (with the most vertices and edges) than others among all the SCCs of a graph. We refer to it as G^B when discussing its properties.

---

[3] All SCCs in this paper are assumed to have more than one node.

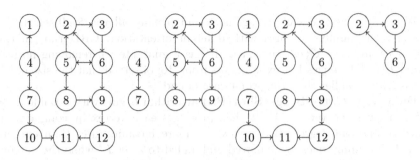

Fig. 2. An example graph and its variants (from left: G, G^{SCC}, G', G'^{SCC}).

Figure 2 presents an example of a graph G with its introduced variants: G^{SCC}, G', and G'^{SCC}. Note that cycles of size two are not necessarily SCCs of size two as they can be nested into other cycles and form a bigger SCC (e.g. size-two cycle between node 5 and 6).

There are efficient algorithms for computing the SCCs of a graph such as Tarjan, which take linear time $\mathcal{O}(|V|+|E|)$ assuming constant time for retrieving edges [9]. It is useful to observe that cycles in a graph G can never span across multiple SCCs (since if there were any such cycle, the SCCs involved would form a bigger SCC, which contradicts its maximality w.r.t. strong connectivity). Therefore, since cycles in G are always contained inside a single SCC, and since the collection of all SCCs of G form a partition of the vertices of G, we can safely divide-and-conquer the process of resolving cycles in G across all SCCs of G. This allow us to focus the cycle resolution locally in comparison with inefficiently and exhaustively listing all simple cycles as in [18].

4   Pseudo-Transitive Relations in the LOD Cloud

4.1   Dataset

In this work, we use the LOD-a-lot dataset [4] as a representative copy of the LOD Cloud. This compressed data file of 28 billion unique triples is the result of the integration of over 650K datasets that are crawled and cleaned by the LOD Laundromat in 2015 [1]. In the LOD-a-lot dataset, there are 2,486 relations explicitly stated as `owl:TransitiveProperty`, used in more than 776 million triples (2.7% of all triples). When the semantics of `rdfs:subPropertyOf` and `owl:inverseOf` is exploited, the number of (pseudo-)transitive relations increases to 8,804 relations, used in around 5.5 billion unique triples (19.5% of the triples). Our manual examination shows that a number of these properties are incorrectly asserted or inferred, such as the widely used `foaf:knows` relation.

For transitive relations, graph characteristics can reflect the logical properties, and vice versa. For instance, irreflexive and antisymmetric relations such as `iwwem:dependsOn` allow for no cycle anywhere in the graph. We consider `skos:broader` a pseudo-transitive relation, as it was not designed to be a transitive property despite being a subproperty of `skos:broaderTransitive`, which is typed `owl:TransitiveProperty` [10]. Unless otherwise specified, we assume that the graph of relations such as `rdfs:subClassOf` and `geo:parentFeature` should be cycle-free despite the logical validity of cycles. Our maual examination also found that many relations are defined together with their inverse (e.g. `skos:broader` and `skos:narrower`). There can also be a relation like that of equivalence (e.g. `owl:sameAs, rdfs:equivalentClassOf`). This paper examines a selection of 10 relations (see e.g. Fig. 3 and Table 1). These are popular relations, all of them directly typed as `owl:TransitiveProperty` with over 100K triples. We exclude the few that actually represent equivalence relations, or whose biggest SCC has less than 10 vertices unless its inverse is to be studied.

4.2 Strongly Connected Components Analysis

To get a sense of how difficult it is to make graphs cycle-free, we introduce in this section a number of metrics. We may turn to standard metrics for the degree of transitivity of a graph, such as the transitivity index T (the number of actual triangles in a graphs as a fraction of the number of all possible triangles), the average clustering index C (the average over the local clustering coefficients of all vertices, where a local clustering coefficient of a vertex is the actual number of edges in the direct neighbourhood of the vertex divided by the possible number of such edges), or the global reaching centrality (GRC) [11]. These measures can be useful for the understanding of graph-theoretical properties. However, our analysis shows that none of T, C or GRC manage to capture the size of SCCs or the hardness of cycle-resolution. Thus they cannot be used as a measure for cycle resolving. We therefore introduce new quantitative measures based on SCCs.

When examining the SCCs of the LOD-a-lot knowledge graph regarding popular relations, we observe two facts: 1) cycles of size two are very common across the graphs. When not nested into other cycles, they are SCCs with two nodes (SCCs of size two), which is the most common type of SCC. This suggests the ambiguity in definition and semantics of the relation; 2) there often exist a very big SCC that covers a majority of nodes involved in the SCCs. This is very different from synthetic models typically used in the evaluation of MWFAS algorithms. The following are measures on how much the SCCs are due to size-two cycles, and other complex nested cycles.

Alpha measure. Let α be the number of edges in cycles of size two divided by the number of all edges in its SCCs $\alpha = f_\alpha(G) = |E_{C2}|/|E^{SCC}|$. By definition, $f_\alpha(G) = f_\alpha(G^{SCC})$. This gives the fraction of edges that can be determined locally if given additional information (e.g. the reliability on each edge).

Beta measure. Remove all the cycles of size two from G and obtain $G' = G \backslash E_{C2}$. The corresponding SCCs of G' form a graph G'^{SCC}. Let β be the number of edges in G'^{SCC} divided by the number of all edges in G^{SCC}: $\beta = |E'^{SCC}|/|E^{SCC}|$. Similarly, we have $f_\beta(G) = f_\beta(G^{SCC})$. This measures the proportion of edges to make decisions on if all edges in size-two cycles are not involved in any SCC. In other words, it gives a measure of the fraction of edges in more complex nested cases.

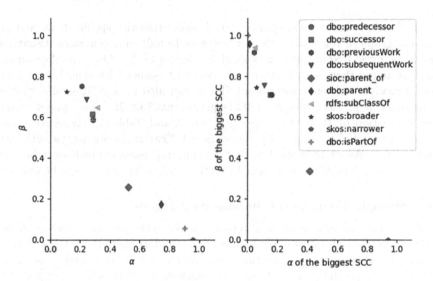

Fig. 3. The Alpha-Beta measures of representative relations

For the graph G in Fig. 2, $\alpha = 0.5$ and $\beta = 0.25$. As for its biggest SCC, $\alpha = 0.4$ and $\beta = 0.3$. Figure 3 reports on the α and β values for the 10 selected relations in Table 1. The figure on the left illustrates the alpha-beta measure. In general, the greater α is, the more size-two cycles there are. The smaller β is, the more likely it is to resolve the cycles by simply making decisions on the edges of cycles of size two (e.g. skos:narrower has $\beta = 0$). On the other hand, skos:broader and dbo:previousWork are examples with more complex cycles nesting into each other. An observation is that the tangent of a line crossing the origin and each point can indicate the hardness. This inspires the following definition.

Gamma measure: For an SCC G, the minimum fraction of decisions to be made to make G cycle-free can be captured by $\alpha + \beta$. Note that an SCC G gets harder when its β is greater, or α is smaller. This can be captured by β/α or $\beta - \alpha$. To avoid cases where $\alpha = 0$ and to make γ a term between 0 and 1, we use the latter and define $\gamma = f_\gamma(G) = (\alpha + \beta)(1 - \alpha + \beta)/2$. This gives a measure of the hardness to make an SCC cycle-free.

Delta measure: Note that using the Gamma measure, we can then estimate the effort required to make each of a graph's SCCs cycle-free. For a graph G in general, $\delta = f_\delta(G) = \sum_{s \in \kappa(G)} f_\gamma(s) * |E|$. It is a sum over the γ value multiplied by the number of edges of each of its SCCs.

Table 1 presents key information of the graphs of the 10 selected relations, together with the values of our metrics. For instance, among the 11.8M skos:broader edges, 356.9K of them are included in a total of 6.7K SCCs. The biggest SCC, G_R^B, captures 227K edges, amounting to 63.6% of the edges in at

Table 1. Popular transitive and pseudo-transitive relations and their measures

Relation (R)	G_R		SCCs of G_R				G_R^B (the biggest SCC)			
	$|E_R|$	$|V_R|$	$|E_R^{SCC}|$	$|V_R^{SCC}|$	$|\kappa(G_R)|$	δ	$|E_R^B|$	$|V_R^B|$	γ	δ
skos:broader	11.8M	5.7M	356.9K	82.0K	6.7K	238.4K	277.0K	43.7K	0.6	188.1K
rdfs:subClassOf	4.4M	3.6M	1.4K	837	196	961.05	780	301	0.9	730.4
dbo:isPartOf	1.0M	408.3K	4.7K	3.8K	1.5K	312.8	60	29	1.0	60.0
skos:narrower	817.1K	737.3K	48	24	7	0.9	16	5	0.0	0.4
dbo:previousWork	551.2K	550.1K	10.6K	8.4K	1.5K	8.0K	710	469	0.9	639.2
dbo:subsequentWork	511.0K	527.5K	15.7K	11.9K	1.8K	10.8K	2.2K	1.5K	0.7	1.6K
dbo:successor	440.7K	417.3K	60.2K	38.0K	5.8K	36.2K	12.5K	5.9K	0.6	8.4K
dbo:predecessor	358.2K	348.1K	40.0K	25.8K	4.2K	22.9K	4.8K	2.4K	0.6	3.2K
dbo:parent	105.8K	97.0K	9.7K	4.3K	921	1.9K	1.5K	979	0.9	1.4K
sioc:parent_of	101.2K	46.6K	6.3K	2.1K	334	1.7K	4.3K	1.1K	0.3	1.5K

least one cycle. Due to its complexity and scale, G_R^B has a big δ. In correspondence, that of G_R is proportionally big. In contrast, the problem of its inverse, skos:narrower, is a much easier problem with only 48 edges involved in cycles with a very small δ value. Thus, it is possible to resolve the cycles by manually annotating each edge in its E_R^{SCC}. Comparing the entries of skos:narrower with dbo:successor, we can see that the δ measures can reflect cases where some big graphs are not necessarily harder to resolve, which is not captured by graph-theoretical measures. These new measures provide a quantitative evaluation on the hardness of cycle resolving, help to study the nature of its complexity, and serve as references for the design of algorithms, choice of parameters as well as the sampling of data.

5 Algorithms

5.1 Algorithms for Cycle Resolving

We aim to design an algorithm that deals with knowledge graphs of (pseudo-) transitive relations that (i) does not rely on a ranking of nodes; (ii) captures the transitivity of relations; (iii) is capable of handling the complex structure resulted from large amount of nested cycles (graphs with high γ values); (iv) is as conservative as possible in removing edges when resolving the cycles; and (v) is extendable to capture other logical and graph properties. The following section presents our algorithm with an evaluation.

We present Algorithm 1 as a general purpose cycle-resolving method for refinement. The algorithm exploits off-the-shelve technology for SMT solvers (Satisfiability Modulo Theories) [2]. The algorithm does not deal with reflexive edges as they can be processed trivially and in linear time. There are three main steps in the algorithm. We first compute the SCCs of the input graph (line 3). Then, we perform partitioning over big SCCs to a given bound b_1 (line 4). This is due to the limit of SMT solvers' capability to handle large amount of clauses. Finally, we sample some cycles and repeatedly call an SMT solver to identify edges to be removed (line 5–17). In the following, we discuss the strategies adopted to deploy it at web scale.

Algorithm 1: General-purpose algorithm for cycle resolving

---

1 **Input:** a graph G with no reflexive edges, its weight function f_w (optional), a bound b_1 for the number of maximum nodes for each SCC, and a bound b_2 for the number of hard clauses.
   Result: a cycle-free graph H and a set of edges removed A.

2 Initiate A as an empty set;

3 Compute the set of SCCs as S;

4 Follow a graph partitioning strategy and reduce the size of S to bound b_1 as S' with removed edges collected and added to A;

5 **while** S' *is not empty* **do**

6   Initiate S'' as an empty set;

7   **foreach** $s \in S'$ **do**

8   Follow a sampling strategy, and obtain cycles C from s with $|C| < b_2$;

9   Initiate an SMT solver o;

10   Introduce to o a set P of propositional variable p_e for each edge e of s;

11   Encode cycles in C as hard constraints in o;

12   Add to o a clause of each variable $p_e \in P$ as a soft constraint with weight $f_w(e)$ if f_w is present, otherwise 1;

13   Run the solver o for optimal solution and decode the output model m;

14   From the model m, collect the edges E to remove and let $A := A \cup E$;

15   Obtain a graph s' from s with E removed;

16   Compute the SCCs N of s' and update $S'' := S'' \cup N$;

17      $S' := S''$;

18 Remove edges A from G and obtain H.

Strategies for Graph Partition. The graph partition problem is well-studied in graph theory. The minimum k-cut problem requires finding a set of edges whose removal partitions the graph to at least k connected components. There exist efficient algorithms and open-source implementations. However, our experiments show that breaking an SCC s into k partitions directly results in a significant amount of edges being removed, whereas our goal is to be as conservative as possible in our repair strategy. For reducing the amount of edges to be removed, our **Strategy P1** partitions the graph into two subgraphs and then computes the SCCs. This process is repeated until each of the resulting SCCs are within the size bound b_1. For weighted graphs (see the next section for how weights are computed), we can adopt a **Strategy P2** by first removing the edges with the lower weights in size-two cycles, and then use Strategy P1.

Strategies for Cycle Sampling. The bottleneck for the earlier work in [18] was the combinatorial explosion when exhaustively listing all cycles of a graph. We therefore focus on sampling an amount of cycles in each iteration that balances the tradeoff between representative capacity and redundancy. **Strategy S1** focuses on the edges: choose a random edge (s, t) in an SCC, then compute the shortest path from (t, s). This forms a cycle. In total we collect b_2 such cycles. As an alternative strategy, we can adopt the **Strategy S2** that selects two nodes randomly and computes the shortest path from one to the other, and back.

Resolving Cycles with an SMT Solver. This section gives details of the interaction with the SMT solver (line 9 and 13 in the algorithm). The SMT solver is used for two purposes: to satisfy all hard constraints and to satisfy the maximal amount of soft constraints.[4] The use of an SMT solver makes it possible to easily extend the current algorithm to weighted cases. In each iteration, for every $s \in S'$, we introduce a propositional variable p_e for each edge e. When there is a cycle $v_1, \ldots . v_k$, we add a hard clause $[\neg p_{(v_1, v_2)} \vee \cdots \vee \neg p_{(v_{k-1}, v_k)} \vee \neg p_{(v_k, v_1)}]$ to the SMT solver (accumulated in conjunction). The clause is satisfied when at least one of the $p_{i,j}$ is assigned False in the returned model of the solver, which indicates the removal of the edge (i, j). To keep the maximal amount of edges, we add a soft clause $[p_e]$ for each edge e. The SMT solver performs a constrained optimisation process within a bounded time. The result of this is a near-optimal solution with the least amount of propositional variables set to False. From the model, we can retrieve edges to be removed to resolve all the encoded cycles. We repeat this process until all the SCCs are resolved and return the DAG and the removed edges. This approach can be easily extended to weighted cases, with the weight for each soft clause as the reliability for each edge.

5.2   Weights

Due to the logical foundation of knowledge graphs, repetition of statements is ignored because of the idempotency of the conjuction operator: $(\phi \wedge \phi) \leftrightarrow \phi$. Nevertheless, we believe that there is an important signal to be gained: the occurrence of the same triple in multiple knowledge graphs is an informal signal that multiple information providers have expressed support for. Thus, the chance that a statement is erroneous decreases with the number of knowledge graphs including this statement. Our algorithm takes the two kinds of weights for soft constraints (Algorithm 1, line 12). **Counted Weights:** the simplest way to obtain the weight of a triple is to count the number of occurrences across the graphs. The LOD-a-lot file consists of 650K datasets (graphs), making it feasible to compute such weights for popular relations; **Inferred Weights:** inspired by the observation and analysis in Sect. 4.1, we take advantage of the logical redundancy between implied properties to compute weights. If a triple (A `rdfs:subClassOf` B) is present in the integrated graph, and there is also an equivalence relation (A `owl:equivalentClass` B) or (B `owl:equivalentClass` A), then we make its weight 2 (i.e. we give more credence to (A `rdfs:subClassOf` B), otherwise 1). For `skos:broader`, we can take advantage of its inverse relation `skos:narrower`. If together with the triple (A `skos:broader` B) the triple (B `skos:narrower` A) exists in the dataset, then we assign weight 2 to the triple (A `skos:broader` B), otherwise 1. While counted weights always exist, inferred weights are more restricted and less common and requires some manual examination. Still, we experiment different weighting scheme for the sake of comparison in evaluation.

---

[4] A sub-optimal result is returned when an SMT solver reaches timeout.

6   Experiments and Evaluation

6.1   Implementation and Parameter Settings

We implemented our algorithm[5] in Python. We adopt the Python binding of METIS[6], a graph partitioning package based on the multilevel partitioning paradigm providing quick and high-quality partitioning. We use Z3[7] as SMT solver [2], and the `networkx` package[8] for the handling of graphs and SCCs.

Based on some trial-and-error experience, in the following experiments we set $b_1 = 15,000$ (i.e. maximum size of an SCC before requiring graph partitioning), and apply Strategy P1 with $k = 2$. To balance the trade-off between efficiency against accuracy, we obtain $b_2 = 3,000$ clauses at most and set the time limit for the SMT solver to 10 s for each SCC.

All experiments were conducted on a 2.2 GHz Quad-Core i7 laptop with a 16 GB memory running Mac OS. All reflexive edges were eliminated in preprocessing.

6.2   Gold Standard

For the evaluation of hypothesis H2, we annotated a number of statements from the two most frequent (pseudo-)transitive relations (`rdfs:subClassOf` and `skos:broader`, according to Table 1). For each relation, we have two gold standards. In the first gold standard **G1**, we randomly pick 500 edges from E_R^{SCC}. The second gold standard separates SCCs of two nodes (**G2-a**, 200 edges) from the rest (**G2-b**, 500 edges). When sampling **G2-b**, we first assign a number on each SCC according to their δ-value and then sample the amount of edges assigned to each SCC randomly, thus providing an evaluation set for edges in complex nested cases. There are 1,199 unique edges in the gold standard of `skos:broader` with a total of 632 (52%) annotated 'remain' in contrast to 401 (33%) 'remove'. This analysis suggests that its under-specified definition caused confusion and subsequently resulted in a complex faulty graph structure. The great proportion of unknown entries for `rdfs:subClassOf` is discussed in Sect. 7.2.

The annotation process was conducted using the platform ANNit[9]. These gold standard datasets are online[10] together with detailed criteria, analysis and limitations. Its consistency was validated manually and by a Python script.

6.3   Efficiency Evaluation

In this section, we compare our refinement algorithm against other MWFAS algorithms. Table 2 presents the results of the number of edges removed for ten

---

[5] https://github.com/shuaiwangvu/Refining-Transitive-Relations.

[6] https://github.com/inducer/pymetis.

[7] https://github.com/Z3Prover/z3.

[8] https://networkx.github.io.

[9] https://github.com/shuaiwangvu/ANNit.

[10] https://zenodo.org/record/4610000.

Table 2. The number of removed edges (with best results highlighted)

Method		skos: broader	rdfs: subClassOf	dbo: isPartOf	skos: narrower	dbo: previousWork	dbo: subsequentWork	dbo: successor	dbo: predecessor	dbo: parent	sioc: parent_of
BS	Overall	1.1M	4.3M	18.8K	57.7K	113.4K	107.1K	85.5K	67.8K	16.9K	6.5K
	SCCs	327.0K	1.1K	3.2K	33	7.5K	11.1K	43.7K	28.9K	7.2K	6.0K
GRD	Overall	493.1K	25.3K	2,175	3.4K	11.9K	12.4K	24.8K	17.2K	5.2K	1.8K
	SCCs	356.9K	430	2,153	**20**	2.5K	3.7K	17.6K	11.8K	3.9K	1.6K
KS	Overall	5.9M	219.2K	459.3K	405.9K	267.6K	253 .5K	218.1K	176.4K	52.4K	46.9K
	SCCs	177.1K	716	2.3K	21	5.3K	7.9K	29.9K	19.9K	4.8K	2.5K
DFS		125.6K	529	2.2K	21	2.3K	3.5K	17.0K	11.4K	**3,943**	1.9K
P1S1-unweighted		**114.8K**	**330**	**2,143**	22	**1.9K**	**2.9K**	**13.3K**	**9.0K**	3,988	**1.2K**
P1S2-unweighted		144.0K	360	2,169	22	2.1K	3.2K	20.1K	10.1K	4.1K	2.6K

subgraphs of LOD-a-lot, both overall and within the SCCs. The highlighted cells show that our approach removes fewer edges during refinement. The result supports our Hypothesis H1. Both approaches are fast: general-purpose MWFAS algorithms take 2–12 s except KS, which may take up to 1 min. Our algorithm takes 8–115 s except for skos:broader, which can take up to 8 min. Details of benchmarks are included in the repository of gold standard. The results in Table 2 are the best records of three runs. Finally, the results are validated to be free from SCCs except singletons.

6.4 Accuracy Evaluation

As for Hypothesis H2, we evaluate our algorithm's unweighted version against the two weighted versions (counted and inferred weights), as well as the MWFAS algorithms. Table 3 presents the precision (p) and recall (r) as well as the number of removed edges ($|A|$) for skos:broader and rdfs:subClassOf. Each entry represents the average of three runs. Taking weights into account (especially counted weights) has a positive impact on precision while maintaining a similar recall. Our approach achieves the best precision among all methods while removing the least amount of edges. As for rdfs:subClassOf, the impact on precision can be positive but unstable due to the limits to be discussed in the next section. When weights are not provided, P1S1 removes the least amount of edges. Otherwise, P2S1 is more optimal for our approach considering the balance between efficiency and accuracy. Overall, this evaluation gives positive support to our Hypothesis H2 and further enhances our conclusion for Hypothesis H1.

7 Discussion and Future Work

7.1 Summary

This paper presented a new algorithm for the refinement of transitive relations and pseudo-transitive relations in very large knowledge graphs. We employed an SMT solver in implementation and evaluated on 10 datasets and validated our Hypothesis H1. As a proof-of-concept, we extended our work to weighted knowledge graphs and evaluated on our gold standard. The results provided positive support for our Hypothesis H2 and we also showed that taking weights into account during refinement has a good potential.

Table 3. Number of removed edges $|A|$, precision p, and recall r for refinement

Method	skos:broader							rdfs:subclass						
	$|A|$	G1		G2-a		G2-b		$|A|$	G1		G2-a		G2-b	
		p	r	p	r	p	r		p	r	p	r	p	r
BS	1.1M	0.32	**0.85**	0.68	**0.72**	0.31	**0.91**	4.3M	0.40	**0.74**	0.40	**0.67**	0.54	**0.79**
GRD	493.1K	0.42	0.22	0.71	0.50	**0.40**	0.26	25.3K	0.42	0.40	0.35	0.45	0.57	0.21
KS	5.9M	0.33	0.52	0.74	0.53	0.28	0.46	2.1M	0.38	0.43	0.43	0.55	0.54	0.53
DFS	125.6K	0.35	0.37	0.68	0.49	0.34	0.34	529	0.43	0.42	**0.49**	0.63	0.55	0.29
P1S1-unweighted	114.8K	0.32	0.26	0.73	0.52	0.30	0.28	**330**	0.50	0.51	0.45	0.57	0.40	0.11
P1S2-unweighted	142.6K	0.32	0.35	0.73	0.52	0.31	0.37	350	0.49	0.44	0.45	0.57	0.58	0.15
P1S1-inferred	115.0K	0.31	0.25	0.73	0.52	0.30	0.28	**330**	0.50	0.51	0.45	0.57	0.40	0.11
P1S2-inferred	143.8K	0.33	0.38	0.73	0.52	0.30	0.36	354	0.49	0.46	0.45	0.57	0.60	0.14
P2S1-inferred	114.8K	0.31	0.25	0.73	0.50	0.30	0.29	**330**	0.50	0.51	0.45	0.57	0.40	0.11
P2S2-inferred	142.7K	0.33	0.35	0.73	0.52	0.31	0.37	356	0.50	0.47	0.45	0.57	0.58	0.15
P1S1-counted	95.4K	0.40	0.33	**0.78**	0.55	0.34	0.26	335	**0.53**	0.49	0.45	0.57	0.67	0.16
P1S2-counted	98.3K	0.42	0.38	**0.78**	0.55	0.34	0.28	354	0.51	0.45	0.45	0.57	**0.70**	0.20
P2S1-counted	**93.4K**	0.43	0.32	**0.78**	0.55	0.34	0.26	335	**0.53**	0.49	0.45	0.57	0.67	0.16
P2S2-counted	94.6K	**0.44**	0.35	**0.78**	0.55	0.32	0.24	357	0.50	0.45	0.45	0.57	0.66	0.17

7.2 Discussion

The graph of rdfs:subClassOf has 4.4 million triples, of which 1.4K are in SCCs. Only 17 triples have inferred weights greater than 1, while 292 triples have such counted weights. The skos:broader graph has 11.8 million triples, of which 265.9K are among SCCs. There are only 39 triples with inferred weights of 2 compared to 284.6K for counted cases. It is clear that far fewer triples are assigned inferred weights than counted weights, making it a less general weighting scheme. Table 3 shows that inferred weights have no significant impact on the results due to their small number. The following focuses on counted weights.

Figure 4 plots the frequency distribution of counted weights for both datasets. It shows a power law distribution for the weights of skos:broader, implying that some relation instances have been stated repeatedly across the web. This justifies the use of frequency of triples as a heuristic for reliability. In comparison, rdfs:subClassOf is less popular and its frequency distribution is less clear and thus less reliable for decision making.

Finally, the unstable result of rdfs:subClassOf is mostly due to the biggest SCC which has 780 edges, amounting to 52% of all the edges in SCCs. All these edges come from a single big faulty dataset, and are all annotated 'unknown'. This explains the big variance for precision and recall as in Table 3.

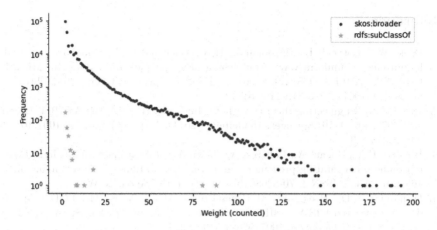

Fig. 4. The frequency distribution of counted weights in SCCs

7.3   Limitations and Future Work

The algorithm essentially grounds relations to propositional logic, thus making it possible to combine it with additional logical constraints with optimisation in the future.

For symmetric relations, we can map the vertices in size-two cycles to one in a new graph while keeping track of the correspondence between the new graph and the original graph. If an edge in the new graph is removed, we remove the corresponding edges of the original graph.

Graph partition is an imprecise step in the algorithm. For example, among the 121.2K edges removed in the case of skos:broader, around 99.6K were identified during the graph partitioning step, amounting to 82.2%. Future work may optimise the parameters to balance the trade-off between accuracy and efficiency.

Figure 4 shows that the frequency distribution of skos:broader follows a power-law distribution. It can mislead the algorithm when an edge with a great weight is actually erroneous. Different weighting scheme can be explored such as that in [8]. Another possible way to improve the accuracy of weights and reduce the number of ties of weights in size-two cycles is by taking the reliability or centrality of sources into account as in [3] for example. General-purpose MWFAS algorithms can be adapted to their weighted cases for future evaluation.

Our recall is limited due to the small amount of edges removed. In Sect. 6.4, we restricted to these two relations due to their popularity and the great effort required for manual annotation. We plan to extend the gold standard to relations with different alpha-beta measures.

References

1. Beek, W., Rietveld, L., Bazoobandi, H.R., Wielemaker, J., Schlobach, S.: LOD laundromat: a uniform way of publishing other people's dirty data. In: Mika, P. (ed.) ISWC 2014. LNCS, vol. 8796, pp. 213–228. Springer, Cham (2014). https://doi.org/10.1007/978-3-319-11964-9_14

2. Bjørner, N.: Engineering theories with Z3. In: Yang, H. (ed.) APLAS 2011. LNCS, vol. 7078, pp. 4–16. Springer, Heidelberg (2011). https://doi.org/10.1007/978-3-642-25318-8_3

3. Bonatti, P.A., Hogan, A., Polleres, A., Sauro, L.: Robust and scalable linked data reasoning incorporating provenance and trust annotations. J. Web Semant. 9(2), 165–201 (2011). ISSN 1570-8268. Provenance in the Semantic Web

4. Fernández, J.D., Beek, W., Martínez-Prieto, M.A., Arias, M.: LOD-a-lot. In: d'Amato, C. (ed.) ISWC 2017. LNCS, vol. 10588, pp. 75–83. Springer, Cham (2017). https://doi.org/10.1007/978-3-319-68204-4_7

5. Fossati, M., Kontokostas, D., Lehmann, J.: Unsupervised learning of an extensive and usable taxonomy for dbpedia. In: International Conference on Semantic Systems, pp. 177–184 (2015)

6. Harth, A., Kinsella, S., Decker, S.: Using naming authority to rank data and ontologies for web search. In: ISWC (2009)

7. Heist, N., Paulheim, H.: Entity extraction from wikipedia list pages. In: ESWC, pp. 327–342 (2020)

8. Hertling, S., Paulheim, H.: WebIsALOD: providing hypernymy relations extracted from the web as linked open data. In: ISWC, pp. 111–119 (2017)

9. Hsu, D., Lan, X., Miller, G., Baird, D.: A comparative study of algorithm for computing strongly connected components. In: 15th IEEE International Conference on Dependable, Autonomic and Secure Computing (DASC), pp. 431–437 (2017)

10. Miles, A., Bechhofer, S.: SKOS simple knowledge organization system reference. W3C recommendation (2009)

11. Mones, E., Vicsek, L., Vicsek, T.: Hierarchy measure for complex networks. PLOS ONE 7(3), (2012)

12. Öncü, H., Agi, M.A.N., Guérin, J.: A fast and effective heuristic for smoothing workloads on assembly lines: algorithm design and experimental analysis. Comput. Oper. Res. 115, 104857 (2020)

13. Paulheim, H.: Knowledge graph refinement: a survey of approaches and evaluation methods. Semant. web 8(3), 489–508 (2017)

14. Paulheim, H., Bizer, C.: Improving the quality of linked data using statistical distributions. Int. J. Semant. Web Inf. Syst. (IJSWIS) 10(2), 63–86 (2014)

15. Raad, J., Beek, W., van Harmelen, F., Wielemaker, J., Pernelle, N., Saïs, F.: Constructing and cleaning identity graphs in the LOD cloud. Data Intell. 2(3), 323–352 (2020)

16. Simpson, M., Srinivasan, V., Thomo, A.: Efficient computation of feedback arc set at web-scale. VLDB 10(3), 133–144 (2016)

17. Sun, J., Ajwani, D., Nicholson, P.K., Sala, A., Parthasarathy, S.: Breaking cycles in noisy hierarchies. In: Proceedings of the 2017 ACM on Web Science Conference, pp. 151–160 (2017)

18. Wang, S., Bloem, P., Raad, J., van Harmelen, F.: SUBMASSIVE: Resolving subclass cycles in very large knowledge graphs. In: Workshop on Large Scale RDF Analytics (2020)

Data Reliability and Trustworthiness Through Digital Transmission Contracts

Simon Mangel[1], Lars Gleim[1]([✉]), Jan Pennekamp[2], Klaus Wehrle[2], and Stefan Decker[1,3]

[1] Databases and Information Systems, RWTH Aachen University, Aachen, Germany
gleim@dbis.rwth-aachen.de
[2] Communication and Distributed Systems, RWTH Aachen University, Aachen, Germany
[3] Fraunhofer FIT, Sankt Augustin, Germany

Abstract. As decision-making is increasingly data-driven, *trustworthiness and reliability* of the underlying data, e.g., maintained in knowledge graphs or on the Web, are essential requirements for their usability in the industry. However, neither traditional solutions, such as paper-based data curation processes, nor state-of-the-art approaches, such as distributed ledger technologies, adequately scale to the complex requirements and high throughput of continuously evolving industrial data. Motivated by a practical use case with high demands towards data trustworthiness and reliability, we identify the need for *digitally-verifiable data immutability* as a still insufficiently addressed dimension of data quality. Based on our discussion of shortcomings in related work, we thus propose *ReShare*, our novel concept of digital transmission contracts with bilateral signatures, to address this open issue for both RDF knowledge graphs and arbitrary data on the Web. Our quantitative evaluation of ReShare's performance and scalability reveals only moderate computation and communication overhead, indicating significant potential for cost-reductions compared to today's approaches. By cleverly integrating digital transmission contracts with existing Web-based information systems, ReShare provides a promising foundation for data sharing and reuse in Industry 4.0 and beyond, enabling digital accountability through easily-adoptable digitally-verifiable data immutability and non-repudiation.

Keywords: Digital transmission contracts · Trust · Data immutability · Non-repudiation · Accountability · Data dynamics · Linked data · Knowledge graphs

1 Introduction

With current trends in the Internet of Things and Industry 4.0, decision-makers nowadays have access to a wide variety of data sources and platforms, thus enabling a data-driven decision-making process. Developments in Open Data

ⓒ Springer Nature Switzerland AG 2021
R. Verborgh et al. (Eds.): ESWC 2021, LNCS 12731, pp. 265–283, 2021.
https://doi.org/10.1007/978-3-030-77385-4_16

underline the trend towards open data sharing paradigms independent of the domain in question. E.g., supply chains already demonstrate these trends in productive use [3,16], where novel approaches enable multi-hop data sharing [30], effectively forming an Internet of Production (IoP) [29] where multiple stakeholders collaborate. Here, benefits include reductions in costs, increased profit margins, and general improvements in production quality [29].

To realize novel use cases in an IoP, data trustworthiness and reliability are crucial properties to enable sound data-driven decisions [25,26,35]. Neglecting these aspects can cause severe damages, such as miscalculations, economic losses, or even harmful to humans [2,10,24,28]. Apart from trust and reliability, *interoperability* is important for any data sharing [13]. In this matter, Linked Data (LD) [1], a paradigm for inter-business data sharing, is a promising candidate. Additionally, LD also facilitates provenance tracing [15] and thus can positively influence trust. Overall, assessing trust and reliability in the context of LD is extremely relevant.

A promising approach to establish objective trustworthiness is to enrich data with digital signatures [40], as automatic signature creation and verification promise scalable solutions. Related work [7,20,36] proposes several existing approaches regarding the signing of Linked Data, which serves as a foundation for any approach using signatures of Resource Description Framework (RDF) resources. However, the rising needs w.r.t. scalability in the face of increasing data dynamics are rarely considered. Hence, existing approaches towards signing LD nowadays have limited applicability. That is, while coarse signatures often force users to retrieve unnecessary data only to verify signatures, fine-granular signatures, which offer more utility by design, impact the scalability due to the communication and storage overhead caused by a large number of signatures, causing a trade-off which impairs the achievable scalability. Moreover, signatures independently generated by the data source cannot provide immutability, as the data source can simply forge signatures for modified data. The reliability guarantees of existing signature-based approaches are significantly weaker than Distributed Ledger-based approaches, where strong immutability is created by committing the state of data to an immutable ledger [16,34]. However, these systems suffer from limited scalability due to limited throughput and infrastructure overhead [38].

To address the required goals of trustworthiness and reliability through scalable immutability, we propose an on-demand signature scheme, where the sender and receiver actively engage in the transmission process and both sign a so-called **D**igital **T**ransmission **C**ontract (DTC). In contrast to common signature approaches, DTCs establish the *immutability* of data reliably, as both peers of a transmission would have to collude to forge a DTC. Together with the non-repudiation provided by the signatures, immutability further implicates *accountability*, which is relevant in the face of liability conflicts [30]. Thus, DTCs enable transmission peers to exchange trustworthy and reliable data by creating immutability based on bilateral signatures with improved scalability w.r.t. data dynamics through their on-demand methodology. Our mechanism is designed to be flexible towards arbitrary data formats, such as conventional, unlinked data, as well as Linked Data resources by employing canonicalization.

Contributions. Our main contributions in this paper are as follows.

- We coin the need for data immutability as an enabler of trustworthiness and reliability, unlocking new data sharing and collaboration use cases based on well-founded data-driven decision making.
- Addressing today's shortcomings, our novel design of digital transmission contracts allows users to verify and prove immutability besides the integrity and authenticity of exchanged data at a low overhead in terms of both computation and communication.
- We further provide the research community with a detailed assessment of the applicability and feasibility of our approach ReShare and thereby create the foundation for the novel paradigm of on-demand bilateral signatures for scalable immutability.

2   Design Goals

To address the lack of suitable approaches in reliable and trustworthy data sharing, we identify a set of concise design goals, which will guide us through the review of related work and presentation and evaluation of our approach.

G1: Integrity, Authenticity and Non-repudiation. The ability to digitally verify the integrity and authenticity of LD resources is essential to establish objective trustworthiness. Thereby, unauthorized modification is prevented, and the users' trust in data correctness is strengthened. Further, non-repudiation is needed for accountability (cf. **G2**), as the possibility to repudiate a given action hinders a party's accountability for said action. As all three requirements can be fulfilled using digital signatures, we group these three desired properties under a single goal.

G2: Immutability. To strengthen data reliability and to establish accountability, we postulate that any used system must be made immutable. Third parties should not be able to easily question this immutability. That is, the system should provide proofs of immutability, which malicious entities cannot easily forge.

G3: Applicability. To be viable in realistic use cases, the solution should be directly applicable and provide both trustworthiness and reliability. Interoperability and usability further affect the applicability of a system, as they facilitate integration in use cases.

G4: Scalability. Given that the increasing data dynamics, especially in the industrial domain, are a significant challenge for data consumers, any proposed signing and verification approach must scale to future needs, i.e., it should be able to timely react to the frequent creation and modification of data without significantly impairing the design.

G5: Performance. To complement **G4**, we emphasize that unreasonable over-head for any involved party must be strictly avoided. Otherwise, the proposed solution limits their ability to participate and leads to undesired constraints following a restricted throughput and consequently a non-acceptance of the system in real-world settings.

G6: Payload Flexibility. As a scalable approach towards trustworthy and reliable data sharing (cf. **G1**, **G2**) unlocks important use cases in industrial environments where the LD paradigm is not yet well-established, we argue that a sole focus on LD significantly limits the applicability. Thus, we demand flexibility concerning the payload of the created signatures. For improved adaptability, any proposed system should support arbitrary data formats, with a specific focus on commonly employed formats on the Web.

Note that the entirety of our design goals exceeds the needs for applications that are exclusive to the Semantic Web. Indeed, any approach that fulfills **G1–G5** can satisfy the requirements of data trustworthiness and reliability in the Semantic Web. However, we intend to propose a more flexible and all-encompassing industry-ready approach.

3   Background and Related Work

Now, we outline related work and fundamental concepts for the challenge of data trustworthiness and reliability. First, we relate the general problem of data quality to our goals of trustworthiness and reliability, before we summarize existing approaches to signing LD resources. With the issue of data mutability in mind, we briefly discuss distributed ledger technology that promises data immutability. Throughout the section, we discuss the shortcomings of approaches based on our design goals described in Sect. 2.

Data Quality and Trust in the Semantic Web. Data quality is commonly conceived as its *fitness for use* w.r.t. a given application [40]. Thus, it consti-tutes a heterogeneous concept with dimensions that partly are of subjective or context-dependent nature. Zaveri et al. [40] were able to extensively identify and categorize sub-dimensions and metrics of data quality in the context of LD.

As one of the six categories of data quality dimensions, *trust* severely suffers from more dynamic associations of stakeholders, such as prevalent in modern supply chains with increasing flexibility [3,27]. Zaveri et al. [40] investigate trust in detail and identify *reputation, believability, verifiability,* and *objectivity* as dimensions of trust. The metrics of reputation, believability, and objectivity are either only able to indicate trustworthiness, e.g., by checking for the existence of meta-information about the data source, or depend on a sophisticated trust model, which may not exist in real-world use cases.

Consequently, we believe that none of these three dimensions allows for objec-tively assessing the trustworthiness of data independent from its context when the fourth dimension – verifiability – is not given, as fraudulent modification and forgery are not prevented. Contrarily, verifiability can be objectively assessed by the use of digital signatures. As long as the signature is bound to the data source, e.g., by employing a Public-Key Infrastructure (PKI) [31], signatures grant authenticity, integrity, and non-repudiation of the data. We argue that data trustworthiness may be sufficiently asserted through signature verification if the data source is trusted.

Approaches towards LD Signatures. After discussing the concept of data quality in the Semantic Web, we now survey existing approaches that sign LD resources. Note that the discussed approaches fulfill **G1**, i.e., the ability to sign LD resources, by design.

To the best of our knowledge, Carroll et al. [7] were the first to propose a sophisticated signature mechanism specifically for usage with Linked Data. The authors especially focus on the canonicalization algorithm and argue that, even if graph canonicalization is GI-complete, practically graphs can be canonicalized in $\mathcal{O}(n \log(n))$. In this regard, Carroll et al. [7] are relevant for any task which needs a canonical RDF representation. However, the authors focus on the signature mechanism itself and do not propose a complete system, as the use of a PKI and the distribution of signatures are not discussed.

Tummarello et al. [36] followed up on Carroll et al. [7] by proposing a more holistic system for LD signatures. The authors argue that graph-level signatures [7] are often too coarse for practical use cases, as users would always have to request the entire RDF graph to verify the signature. To address this issue, the authors proposed to sign the data at a much finer level, i.e., at the level of Minimum Self-contained Graphs (MSGs). Signatures are attached to an arbitrary triple of the signed MSG, thus internalizing them. By directly attaching signatures and certificate metadata to the data itself, the authors explicitly specify how to apply the system to a knowledge graph (**G3**). However, as also criticized by Kasten et al. [20], the certificate is referenced by a URI, which makes the signature unusable if a certificate can no longer be retrieved. Furthermore, a user has to compute at least a partial partitioning into MSGs to know which statements were signed in a given signature, as such information is not explicitly stated. Moreover, the approach has severe issues concerning scalability (**G4**) and performance (**G5**) caused by the fine granularity of signatures. If no blank nodes are present, each statement is signed separately, resulting in a substantial overhead caused by the signatures, which is even exaggerated if data is modified frequently. Due to the focus on LD, the approach does not support signing other data formats, i.e., it does not provide payload flexibility (**G6**).

Kasten et al. [20] improved on Tummarello et al. [36] by proposing a framework that allows for signatures at different levels of granularity, i.e., reaching from MSG signatures up to signing multiple graphs at once. The authors discuss and formalize the entire signature process in a framework and only give exemplary solutions for the identified functions. Therefore, the work does not constitute a directly applicable solution, but rather aims at building a foundation for applicable solutions through formalization. Due to its improved flexibility, the approach provides better scalability (**G4**) and reduced overhead (**G5**) compared to Tummarello et al. [36]. **G6** is not met, as the approach specifically focuses on

RDF data. Most importantly, all approaches listed above have a common crucial deficiency w.r.t. our design goals, i.e., they do not create immutability (**G2**). As the data source only signs data, this entity can easily forge signatures for modified data at any time, thus violating immutability. This aspect is crucial, as we identified immutability as a core requirement for data reliability in Sect. 2.

To the best of our knowledge, none of the existing approaches to signing LD resources can sufficiently fulfill our design goals, especially w.r.t. immutability (**G2**).

Distributed Ledger-based Immutability. In contrast to signatures, Distributed Ledger (DL) technology is designed to provide strong immutability (**G2**) by committing the state of data to an irreversible ledger [41]. This property is highly desirable and thus celebrated in a wide variety of use cases, such as distributed supply chains [3,16]. Such use cases with little pre-existing trust relations and opportunities to employ LD technology motivate the combination of LD and DL technology to establish immutability. Consequently, use cases and barriers w.r.t. the combination of LD and DLs have been identified [6,12,33]. Furthermore, researchers proposed the first concrete solutions employing DL technology to establish immutability in the context of LD [34].

However, the intersection of the two research fields still is in its infancy, and existing approaches rarely cover the need for immutability holistically. Furthermore, the strong immutability provided by Distributed Ledgers comes with practical disadvantages. Even with new consensus mechanisms such as the Swirlds hashgraph consensus algorithm [4] or the tangle [32], which try to mitigate the negative effect of common, costly consensus mechanisms such as proof-of-work, DL systems always bring a substantial overhead (**G5**). This overhead is infeasible in many use cases, as with huge amounts of data, e.g., produced by IoT sensors, the relative cost for conducting the consensus mechanism exceeds the value of the data written to the ledger. Thus, we decided to refrain from involving DL technology in our system. However, we think that the intersection of Distributed Ledgers and LD in scenarios where LD immutability is crucial and the imposed overhead is acceptable makes for a promising research area for future work.

In conclusion, we found that none of the existing approaches towards LD signatures were able to sufficiently fulfill our design goals, especially due to the missing immutability (**G2**). Research regarding combinations of DL and LD technology to provide strong immutability (**G2**) is still in its infancy, resulting in prohibitive scalability (**G4**) and performance (**G5**) overhead for many use cases as detailed in our supplementary material [18]. Therefore, we identify the requirement for an approach that bridges the needs for immutability, scalability, and performance.

4   ReShare: Reliable Data Sharing Through DTCs

To address the previously identified shortcomings of related work w.r.t. our design goals, we propose *ReShare*, a scalable and flexible on-demand resource signature system. ReShare employs the novel concept of **D**igital **T**ransmission

Contracts (DTCs). Whenever the state of data needs to be proven as immutable, the data sender and receiver partake in a *contract generation handshake*, which results in the creation of a DTC. A DTC is a record comprising the state of the subject data (as checksums), the identities of sender and receiver, as well as a timestamp of contract creation, crafted immutably by adding signatures of *both* peers. In the DTC generation mechanism, the receiver requests a DTC for a set of resources. The sender compiles said DTC by creating checksums for the resources, adding metadata, and signing the record. Finally, the receiver signs the retrieved DTC and sends its signature back to the sender.

The validity of a contract can be automatically verified at any time in a corresponding *contract verification mechanism*, where the identities of the parties, the signatures, and the resource checksums are verified. We expect that creating signatures for data exchanges offers improved scalability (**G4**) compared to existing signature mechanisms in use cases where the amount of produced and modified data outweighs the number of data requests. This expectation is strengthened by ReShare's ability to bundle multiple resources into one DTC, thus reducing the per-resource signature overhead (**G5**). Furthermore, we argue that ReShare provides immutability in addition to the existing benefits of digital signatures, i.e., integrity and authenticity, as a colluding of two parties is needed to forge a valid contract that violates the data immutability.

First, we proceed by motivating a use case in the domain of aerospace engineering. Subsequently, we present details about both the contract generation and verification mechanisms. Finally, we discuss realization aspects of ReShare, i.e., the representation and ontology of DTCs and the integration of ReShare with LD technology.

ReShare's Capabilities Illustrated Using Aerospace Engineering. For our system, aerospace engineering constitutes an interesting use case, as reliability is highly desirable when designing and producing safety-critical products. This need even is legally justified, as federal US-American laws require manufacturers to securely store the *type design*, comprising drawings and specifications, information about dimensions, materials, and processes for as long as the respective *type certificate* of the aircraft is valid (cf. 14 CFR §21.31, §21.41, §21.49 [37]). Thus, such data must be kept available reliably, at least as long as an aircraft of the given type is operational. As a result, manufacturers usually apply specialized archiving systems [22]. However, if we consider modern IoT-backed supply chains, massive amounts of data can hardly be processed by common archiving pipelines, which may still involve humans in paper-based signature mechanisms [39]. Therefore, aerospace engineering is a prime candidate to integrate ReShare.

To further look into this use case, we illustrate the benefits of employing an LD-based approach for tracking and tracing through a practical example: Involving the manufacturer Boing, which conducts the final assembly of an aircraft, the independent supplier ACom, which provides the radio unit for Boing's aircraft together with relevant production data, and regulatory agency FÄA that ensures legal compliance. We further consider the following scenarios to visualize the system's functionality:

Assembly. Boing assembles an aircraft using a radio unit supplied by ACom, while ACom further grants Boing access to all relevant production data. Enriched with metdata, such as provenance information, this data is stored in an LD platform. Boing and ACom also generate a DTC, which is bound to the state of said data. In this context, both Boing and ACom verify their certificates and signatures, thus mutually establishing authenticity. Due to the dataflow direction, we refer to ACom as the *sender* and to Boing as the *receiver*.

Proof of Conformance. After an aircraft was involved in an incident, Boing has to prove to FÄA that certain requirements were met during manufacturing. To this end, Boing presents the relevant data, together with the respective DTCs. The contracts include all relevant context to verify the authenticity and state of the data. If an investigation of the incident concludes that, for example, the data regarding the radio is incorrect, Boing is not liable, as it acted to the best of its knowledge. Rather, ACom can be held accountable.

Tracking and Tracing. To deal with the aftermath of a defective radio unit, Boing traces all other aircraft that use the same type of radio using the data's semantic properties. While an improved tracking & tracing efficiency is not a contribution of our system, we argue that ReShare provides the needed reliability through LD.

After outlining three distinct and common real-world scenarios, we now present ReShare's DTC generation and verification mechanisms.

4.1   Generation Mechanism

The contract generation mechanism constitutes a relatively simple 3-way handshake, which we visualize in Fig. 1. We use this opportunity to address the different types of identifiers used in the system. Resources are identified by unique Resource IDs (RIDs). While ReShare supports arbitrary RIDs, the use of Internationalized Resource Identifiers [11] (IRIs) improves interoperability with LD technology. For identification of the contract itself, ReShare mandates the use of unique IRIs [11] in order to integrate DTCs with common LD technology. The mechanism works as following, where **R** denotes the receiver, and **S** the sender:

R1: **R** chooses a set of RIDs and sends the RIDs and his identity, including a public key certificate, to **S**.

S1: **S** can now assemble the contract associating checksums of the canonicalized resources identified by the RIDs. Then, **S** creates a timestamp and a unique contract IRI and adds them to the contract. Finally, **S** creates its signature with the JSON representation of the contract as input. Then, the signature is added to the contract.

S then sends the assembled contract, including its identity with a public key certificate, its signature, the RIDs with associated checksums, the timestamp, and the contract IRI back to **R**.

R2: **S**'s signature (i.e., `senderSig`) is verified, together with **S**'s certificate (included in the `sender` field). The timestamp recency is checked. **R** signs the contract similarly to **S**.

The complete contract, including both peers' signatures, is finally sent to **S**.

Both signatures are created by omitting any existing signatures in the contract as an input to the signature creation. That is, both the sender and receiver sign the DTC, including the identities, resource checksums, and the timestamp. The computation overhead on the sender's side for creating the contract, which mainly consists of generating checksums and creating the signature, can be reduced using pre-generated checksums in use cases where scalability needs are especially high, or Denial of Service by R1 flooding is a valid threat model. In the latter case, the problem could otherwise also be mitigated by the use of rate limiting or access control.

The messages contain complete, incremental versions of the contract, which allows the sender to remain stateless. This design fits our server-client model nicely, where the sender as a server provides an interface for receivers to request contracts. The handshake is always executed on top of TCP, which guarantees reliable communication. Therefore, an error indicates a faulty or incompatible configuration. A mechanism to deal with errors is not part of ReShare, but could be easily implemented for future work.

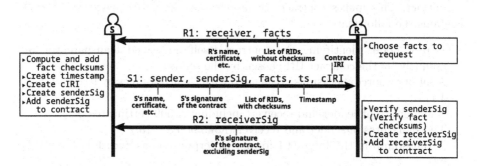

Fig. 1. Visualization of the contract generation handshake. **S** is the *sender*, **R** is the *receiver*. Here, *Fact* is used as a synonym for a persistently identified resource.

4.2   Verification Mechanism

Contract verification relies only on access to the contract and the covered data itself and consists of the following steps (in no particular order):

- Verify the public key certificates using the respective PKI
- Verify the signatures using the JSON-formatted contract and the public keys
- Verify the data checksums

Hence, only access to the contract and the data are needed. As ReShare currently only supports a CA-based PKI with X.509 certificates, the necessary PKI context comprises a set of pre-installed root CA certificates to verify the X.509 certificate chains of both parties. Contracts are explicit about all information needed to verify signatures and checksums, e.g., about the canonicalization and serialization of the data. To verify the checksums, all parties use the same input as during the DTC generation, i.e., the full DTC excluding any existing signatures. Through the simplicity of the verification, only consisting of the three steps described above, the system is applicable (**G3**) in use cases with needs for unambiguous verifiability of the generated DTCs, e.g., in legal conflicts.

4.3 Realization

We implemented ReShare as a Proof-of-Concept Node.js module [18]. We discuss our decisions concerning the implementation and used technologies in the following.

Contract Ontology and Representations. As Tummarello et al. [36] discuss, the ability to internalize signatures into the context of the signed data improves the overall usability, because data and signatures are directly associated. Therefore, contracts are represented as JSON-LD [21] by default. For this, we have defined the ReShare ontology [19], which defines the types and properties in a contract. This makes contracts themselves usable in LD platforms. A DTC contains the following:

- A root node, identifying the contract itself, identified transparently and uniquely by the contract IRI chosen by the sender
- A set of resource checksums, associated with their resources by RIDs (cf. Sect. 4.1)
- The identity of sender and receiver, including X.509 certificates [8]
- The signatures of sender and receiver (RSASSA-PSS [23])
- A timestamp in the ISO 8601 format (interpretable as xsd:dateTimeStamp [9])

An example contract RDF graph with the default structure can be seen in Fig. 2. Note that the notion of *Facts* originates from the FactDAG data interoperability model [13] and its implementation FactStack [14], where a revisioning system is used to create persistence. As this paradigm is not mandatory in ReShare, we use *fact* as a synonym for any persistently identified resource in this paper.

Because we require payload flexibility (**G6**), DTCs should also be compatible with other common technology stacks outside of the Semantic Web. Therefore, in addition to the JSON-LD representation, the context can be omitted, resulting in a pure JSON representation of DTCs, making contracts usable as structured data.

Contract Generation. Given that the contracts are represented as JSON-LD or JSON by default, we decided to rely on a JSON-based protocol for contract

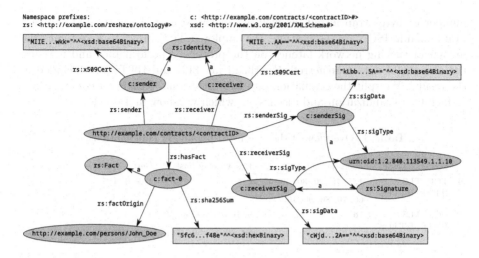

Fig. 2. Structure of an exemplary ReShare contract, visualized as an RDF graph using Turtle notation. http://example.com/contracts/<contractID> here symbolizes the contract IRI chosen by the sender (cf. Sect. 4.1).

generation, where the JSON contracts are wrapped into a minimalistic message structure. The JSON-LD context is automatically added when exporting the contract after generation.

The most basic generation mode corresponds to an execution of the JSON protocol directly on top of TCP, with optional use of TLS. However, this approach requires opening a dedicated port for ReShare. Therefore, we also provide an HTTP(S) mode to integrate ReShare into existing Web servers. Then, the 3-way handshake is wrapped into two HTTP POST requests. Thus, we end up with four modes, which we denote by TCP (i.e., without TLS or HTTP), TLS (i.e., TCP+TLS without HTTP), HTTP, and HTTPS.

5   Evaluation

To assess the benefits, possible limitations, and applicability of ReShare, we first quantitatively evaluate the storage and communication overhead as well as the effects of latency to the generation mechanism, before qualitatively discussing the fulfillment of our design goals as defined in Sect. 2, whilst giving outlooks to promising use cases.

5.1   Quantitative Evaluation

To quantitatively evaluate the performance of the system, we simulated contract generation with varying (i) modes of operation (TCP/TLS/HTTP/HTTPS), (ii) number of facts per contract, and (iii) certificate chain lengths of both peers. We quantitatively evaluate the (a) total duration of the handshake, (b) the number of bytes transferred, as well as (c) the size of the generated contract in its default JSON representation. We employ a TCP proxy to investigate the impact of varying network latency on the protocol's performance and measure the amount of data transferred. Overhead for TLS and HTTP are included in the results. We split the evaluation into two orthogonal parameter combinations to facilitate visualization and discussion, which we show in Table 1.

Table 1. Overview of the evaluated parameter combinations.

	Protocol Mode	Facts/DTC	Proxy delay [ms]	Cert. Chain Len.	Iterations
1	TCP, TLS, HTTP, HTTPS	1, 5, 10, 20, 30, 40, 50, 60, 70, 80, 90, 100	0	1, 2, 3, 4, 5	20
2	TCP, TLS, HTTP, HTTPS	10	0, 10, 20, 30, 40, 50, 60, 70, 80, 90, 100	1	50

Contract Size and Communication Overhead. In Fig. 3, we show how the number of facts in one contract influences contract bytes and communication overhead per fact, split by handshake mode. A per-fact plot brings better comparability to other approaches than per-contract, as contracts are a concept that is specific to our approach. Thus, metrics are plotted on a per-fact (i.e., per-resource) basis.

The total contract size and communication overhead per handshake increase linearly with the number of facts, as fact data is of constant size, consisting of a RID and a checksum. Thus, if m models one of the per-contract metrics, this gives $m(n) = sn + c$, where s is the slope of the curve, i.e., the bytes by which the metric increases if one fact is added per contract, n is the number of facts per contract, and c is the constant overhead which is not influenced by the number of facts. Then, we can model the per-fact metric as $m'(n) = \frac{m(n)}{n} = s + cn^{-1}$. This model is plotted for each metric. The theoretical limit for contract bytes per fact naturally is given by s, which is the slope of the linear per-contract fit. It can be interpreted as the number of bytes that are caused by a fact itself, excluding the static overhead in contracts, which is independent of the number of facts. An analog interpretation of the other metrics slopes is possible. The Figure also shows that the overhead of HTTP is negligible, whereas enabling TLS causes a constant communication overhead of approximately 200 B per contract.

Handshake Duration. To better evaluate the handshake duration in a realistic scenario, we simulate varying degrees of network latency. The results can be seen in Fig. 4. Because the relationship between network latency and total handshake duration expectedly is linear, the slope of a linear fit divided by 2 gives a rough estimate on the number of Round Trip Times (RTTs) a contract generation takes.

As a first observation, our implementation produces a constant overhead of approximately 140 ms in handshake duration. Similar to the previously evaluated communication overhead in bytes, HTTP and TCP add the least latency

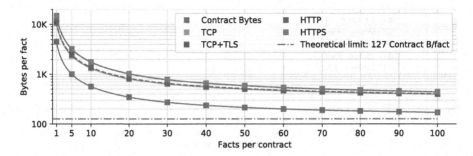

Fig. 3. Contract bytes and communication bytes per fact, by the number of facts in one contract. Dataset 1 from Table 1 was used. Communication bytes are split up by handshake mode, i.e., HTTP enabled/disabled, and TLS enabled/disabled. Compared to a per-contract plot, this representation provides better interpretability when comparing the system to other approaches, as contracts are an unknown concept in other work.

overhead. As the three handshake messages (cf. Sect. 4.1) can directly be sent on top of TCP or HTTP without additional messages, the slope comes close to the baseline of a 3-way handshake. If TLS is enabled, the latency effect is significantly increased by the TLS handshake, i.e., for each TLS handshake, the delay increases by approximately 1 RTT. In TLS mode without HTTP, one socket is used for all messages. Thus, only one TLS handshake is needed, causing a 1 RTT overhead compared to raw TCP. As our implementation currently does not support socket reuse when using HTTP, we need two TLS handshakes in HTTPS mode (one for each POST request), causing a 2 RTT overhead compared to HTTP without TLS, resulting in a maximum handshake duration of approximately 3.5 RTT. Note that reusing cryptographic material from the first request does not reduce latency overhead, as it does not change the number of TLS handshake messages. sages.

For future work, we plan to add socket reuse support for HTTP to our implementation.

5.2 Qualitative Evaluation

After quantitatively evaluating the performance of ReShare, we now classify the quantitative results and discuss the benefits and disadvantages of ReShare w.r.t. the design goals defined in Sect. 2, as well as practical considerations.

Trustworthiness and Reliability. In Sect. 2, we identified signatures as a core enabler of data reliability and trustworthiness (**G1**), which are extremely relevant aspects of data quality (cf. Sect. 1). For the created signatures to create trustworthiness, the entire trust chain, reaching from the PKI as the trust root data checksums, has to be validated as defined in Sect. 4.2. Because the verification algorithms, i.e., X.509 certificate validation, RSA-PSS signature verification, and SHA-2 checksum validation, are generally accepted, our focus is on the availability of the necessary signatures, checksums, and certificates.

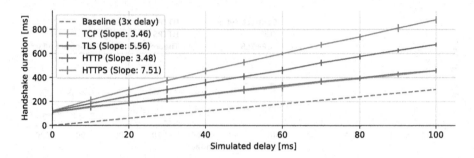

Fig. 4. Visualization of the effect of communication delay in-between sender and receiver simulated with an artificial delay in the TCP proxy. Dataset 2 from Table 1 was used. The data was collected using 10 facts per contract and a certificate chain length of 1. Per mode and artificial delay, 50 contracts were generated. The error bars display the interval of 2σ, thus accounting for approximately 95 % of the measurements. The baseline represents a 3-way handshake without any overhead by computation or additional messages.

First, the material necessary for verifying the signatures themselves is contained within the DTC. Second, for the included certificate to be verifiable, the consumer has to trust the root CA which signed the peer certificates. This assumption is reasonable, as root stores and root programs have long-established extensive CA curation [17]. However, the expiry and revocation of X.509 certificates, as well as the retrievability of the root certificate, which is not included in the contract, hinder verifiability, and thus, reliability (**G1**) in application scenarios with long-term storage requirements. One could counteract this with special approaches for long-term signature preservation, such as Bralić et al. [5], which have detrimental effects on performance (**G5**) or scalability **G4** and require additional infrastructure. We leave this issue to be investigated in future work. Third, the data has to be available in order to verify the included checksum. Here, the structure of DTCs has the advantage that not all included data has to be available in order to keep the signature material verifiable, as individual checksums can be verified. Thus, if certain resources are no longer needed, they can simply be deleted without impacting the verifiability of other resources signed by a contract.

Overall, DTCs are easily verifiable, thus providing good reliability and trustworthiness (**G1**), as long as the certificates are valid and the root certificate is retrievable.

Immutability and Accountability. Usually, data-driven business models with high data reliability needs either depend upon well-trusted business partners or have to resort to both time- and cost-intensive manual data curation [39]. Application of ReShare thus provides promising opportunities to create trustworthiness where trust cannot easily be established otherwise and can further be used as a legal binding of the peers to the underlying transmission, useful in legal conflicts. ReShare provides improved immutability compared to usual signature schemes, as illegally forging a valid DTC requires collusion of both peers of the contract. Because benign behavior of the two peers is a severely limiting assumption, ReShare cannot hold up with DL-based immutability, as successful Distributed Ledgers are considered to be irreversible, unless a large share of the network colludes. Thus, ReShare provides enhanced immutability (**G2**) compared to other signature-based approaches, but cannot keep up with DL technology regarding this aspect. To improve the immutability guarantees of ReShare, one could employ a digital notary, e.g., by adding additional signatures by impartial third parties or committing contracts to a DL. However, to keep scalability, one should incorporate measures to reduce the notary overhead, e.g., by only using the notary for interval-based checksums of all created contracts. We deem this idea an interesting direction for future work.

Performance and Scalability. If a sufficiently large number of resources are signed per-contract, the per-resource storage communication overhead falls below 1 kB relatively quickly. With a handshake latency overhead of less than 200 ms (without delay), less than 5 RTTs, and the simple contract verification mechanism, we argue that the amount of imposed overhead by the use of the system is reasonably low, especially in comparison to traditional proof of transmission approaches, such as paper-based receipts commonly used in industry today [39]. Therefore, the performance goal (**G5**) is met. One could argue that if individual transmissions only consist of a few resources (e.g., only a few RDF statements), the per-resource overhead both for storage of the contracts and the handshake increases relatively fast. This issue also exists in related work w.r.t. LD signatures, as the severity of the overhead imposed to the user when using coarse signatures is exaggerated in this scenario (cf. Sect. 3). However, if, on the one hand, the overall frequency of requests is low, this issue becomes less severe, as the throughput requirements are small. If, on the other hand, higher request frequencies are expected, ReShare provides the opportunity of resource bundling, i.e., requested resources can simply be buffered by the client and bundled into a single DTC, thus mitigating the issue. In environments with high request frequency by many distinct data recipients, DTC bundling may, however, only apply to a lesser degree. However, besides a limitation w.r.t. these specific circumstances, ReShare provides decent scalability (**G4**).

Payload Flexibility. Because DTCs use checksums of canonicalized data, the data format is arbitrary, as long as a canonical representation is specified, which contributes to payload flexibility (**G6**) and allows for applicability to generic Semantic Web data and any other type of resource on the Web. Thus, ReShare constitutes a unified solution for arbitrary data on the Web.

Other Practical Considerations. ReShare has the advantage that it is optionally adaptable both for individual stakeholders and individual transmission, as its use is not mandatory. If one installs ReShare, but opts out to generate contracts for transmissions, made possible through the optionally adaptable design, the system generates little to no overhead. Suppose that it is used in HTTP(S) mode, then, it can be integrated into an already existing web server, and thus does not require additional hardware, infrastructure, or specific software. Such a deployment is useful where manual data curation may be more cost- or time-efficient than generating DTCs, or peers simply do not implement ReShare, making the system fully backward-compatible.

The peer X.509 certificates make up for a majority of the contract data. Thus, removing the certificate data from DTCs and instead of referencing peer certificates with unique identifiers would drastically reduce contract sizes, improving scalability (**G4**) and performance (**G5**). However, as verifiability is the key to the provided trustworthiness and reliability, we argue that making the verifiability of DTCs dependent upon the certificate availability would substantially weaken verifiability, and thus, our core requirement (**G1**). However, to practically reduce the overhead imposed by peer certificates, one could assign unique identifiers to the used certificates in the LD context of DTCs, which allows to only store the certificates once when using an LD platform such as a triple store. This method could be realized with ReShare as part of future work.

ReShare can also be integrated with existing systems and data, i.e., it is backward-compatible. Retrospectively generating DTCs even has an advantage w.r.t. performance (**G5**) and scalability (**G4**), as all resources from a given data source can be bundled into a single DTC, thus reducing the per-resource communication and storage overhead. However, using retrospectively generated contracts, one can not prove possession of the data for the time interval before contract generation due to the contract timestamp.

To conclude, with decent scalability in most use cases and stronger immutability than common signature schemes, we see no significant limitations for ReShare's applicability, making it a promising solution for a variety of use cases with requirements of scalability, trustworthiness, and reliability.

6   Conclusion

In this paper, we expressed the need for immutability as an enabler for data trustworthiness and reliability, paving the way for novel use cases employing LD technology for reliable data sharing and collaboration. After identifying the lack of suitable solutions that bridge the need for scalability and immutability, we present ReShare, our design utilizing digital transmission contracts to establish immutability through signatures by both transmission peers, imposing a reasonably low overhead with good scalability. We provide the research community with a discussion of feasibility and applicability, building a foundation for future work w.r.t. scalable immutability for real-world use.

Trustworthiness and reliability are essential requirements for a more open data sharing paradigm in the industry, as economic outcomes depend on data correctness. Digital signatures can provide integrity, authenticity, and non-repudiation, and therefore, they can be used to create data trustworthiness. However, we argue that simple signatures cannot reliably establish immutability, as the signing authority can forge arbitrary signatures, thus hindering data reliability. Recently, distributed ledgers are frequently proposed to achieve the immutability of information. Unfortunately, their scalability is substantially challenged through limited throughput and infrastructure overhead. To address these issues, we propose ReShare, a system for creating on-demand bilateral signatures contained in digital transmission contracts. Given that both transmission peers would have to collude to forge valid digital transmission contracts, we argue that ReShare provides improved immutability compared to common signature systems, combined with proper scalability through moderate overhead and the ability to sign multiple resources at once.

In our evaluation, we demonstrate that our proposed design shows promising applicability, as its immutability is valuable in use cases with high scalability needs, while being flexible towards the format of signed data and optionally adaptable by concept, imposing little overhead when peers opt-out from usage. Thus, ReShare is a prime candidate to achieve data reliability and trustworthiness for both the Semantic Web and industry. For future work, optionally-adaptable notary systems could further strengthen the immutability of our proposed contracts. However, already in its current state, ReShare allows for novel approaches that profit from and build upon the proposed concept of on-demand bilateral signatures.

Acknowledgments. Funded by the Deutsche Forschungsgemeinschaft (DFG, German Research Foundation) under Germany's Excellence Strategy – EXC-2023 Internet of Production – 390621612.

References

1. Abramowicz, W., Auer, S., Heath, T.: Linked data in business. Bus. Inf. Syst. Eng. **58**(5), 323–326 (2016). https://doi.org/10.1007/s12599-016-0446-0
2. Attaran, M., Attaran, S.: Collaborative supply chain management: the most promising practice for building efficient and sustainable supply chains. Bus. Process Manag. J. **13**(3), (2007)
3. Bader, L., Pennekamp, J., Matzutt, R., Hedderich, D., et al.: Blockchain-based privacy preservation for supply chains supporting lightweight multi-hop information accountability. Inf. Process. Manage. **58**(3), 102529 (2021)
4. Baird, L.: The swirlds hashgraph consensus algorithm: Fair, fast, byzantine fault tolerance. Swirlds-tr-2016, Swirlds, Inc. (2016)
5. Bralić, V., Kuleš, M., Stančić, H.: A model for long-term preservation of digital signature validity: TrustChain. In: INFuture (2017)
6. Cano-Benito, J., Cimmino, A., García-Castro, R.: Towards blockchain and semantic web. In: BIS (2019)
7. Carroll, J.J.: Signing RDF graphs. In: ISWC (2003)
8. Cooper, D., Santesson, S., Farrell, S., Boeyen, S., et al.: Internet X.509 public key infrastructure certificate and certificate revocation list (CRL) profile. RFC **5280**, 1–151 (2008)
9. Cyganiak, R., Wood, D., Lanthaler, M.: RDF 1.1 Concepts and Abstract Syntax. W3C Rec. **25**(02), 1–22 (2014)
10. Dahlmanns, M., Pennekamp, J., Fink, I.B., Schoolmann, B., et al.: Transparent end-to-end security for publish/Subscribe communication in cyber-physical systems. In: ACM SaT-CPS (2021)

11. Duerst, M., Suignard, M.: Internationalized Resource Identifiers (IRIs). RFC 3987 (2005)
12. English, M., Auer, S., Domingue, J.: Block Chain Technologies & The Semantic Web: A Framework for Symbiotic Development. University of Bonn, Technical Report (2016)
13. Gleim, L., Pennekamp, J., Liebenberg, M., Buchsbaum, M., et al.: FactDAG: formalizing data interoperability in an internet of production. IEEE Internet Things J. **7**(4), 3243–3253 (2020)
14. Gleim, L., Pennekamp, J., Tirpitz, L., Welten, S., et al.: FactStack: interoperable data management and preservation for the web and industry 4.0. In: BTW (2021)
15. Gleim, L., Tirpitz, L., Pennekamp, J., Decker, S.: Expressing FactDAG provenance with PROV-O. In: MEPDaW (2020)
16. Gonczol, P., Katsikouli, P., Herskind, L., Dragoni, N.: Blockchain implementations and use cases for supply chains-a survey. IEEE Access **8**, 11856–11871 (2020)
17. Holz, R., Braun, L., Kammenhuber, N., Carle, G.: The SSL landscape - a thorough analysis of the X.509 PKI using active and passive measurements. In: ACM IMC (2011)
18. i5: factcheck.js. https://git.rwth-aachen.de/i5/factdag/factcheck.js
19. i5: ReShare Ontology v0.1. http://i5.pages.rwth-aachen.de/factdag/reshare-ontology/0.1/
20. Kasten, A., Scherp, A., Schauß, P.: A framework for iterative signing of graph data on the web. In: ESWC (2014)
21. Kellogg, G., Champin, P.A., Longley, D.: JSON-LD 1.1. W3C Rec. (2020)
22. LOTAR International: Legal & Business Motivation (2020). https://lotar-international.org/why-lotar/legal-business-motivation/ Accessed 16 Dec 2020
23. Moriarty, K., Kaliski, B., Jonsson, J., Rusch, A.: PKCS #1: RSA Cryptography Specifications Version 2.2. IETF RFC 8017 (2016)
24. Moyaux, T., Chaib-draa, B., D'Amours, S.: Information sharing as a coordination mechanism for reducing the bullwhip effect in a supply Chain. IEEE Trans. Syst. Man Cybern. C **37**(3), 396–409 (2007)
25. Özer, Ö., Zheng, Y.: Establishing trust and trustworthiness for supply chain information sharing. In: Ha, A.Y., Tang, C.S. (eds.) Handbook of Information Exchange in Supply Chain Management. SSSCM, vol. 5, pp. 287–312. Springer, Cham (2017). https://doi.org/10.1007/978-3-319-32441-8_14
26. Özer, Ö., Zheng, Y., Ren, Y.: Trust, trustworthiness, and information sharing in supply chains bridging China and the United States. Manage. Sci. **60**(10), 2435–2460 (2014)
27. Pennekamp, J., Bader, L., Matzutt, R., et al.: Private multi-hop accountability for supply chains. In: BIoTCPS (ICC Workshops) (2020)
28. Pennekamp, J., Dahlmanns, M., Gleim, L., Decker, S., et al.: Security considerations for collaborations in an industrial IoT-based lab of labs. In: IEEE GCIoT (2019)
29. Pennekamp, J., Glebke, R., Henze, M., et al.: Towards an infrastructure enabling the internet of production. In: IEEE ICPS (2019)
30. Pennekamp, J., Henze, M., Schmidt, S., Niemietz, P., et al.: Dataflow challenges in an internet of production: a security & privacy perspective. In: ACM CPS-SPC (2019)
31. Perlman, R.: An overview of PKI trust models. IEEE Netw. **13**(6), 38–43 (1999)
32. Popov, S.: The Tangle. White paper (2016)
33. Third, A., Domingue, J.: LinkChains: exploring the space of decentralised trustworthy linked data. In: DeSemWeb (2017)

34. Third, A., Tiddi, I., Bastianelli, E., Valentine, C., et al.: Towards the temporal streaming of graph data on distributed ledgers. In: LD-DL (2017)

35. Tsai, W.T., Wei, X., Chen, Y., Paul, R., et al.: Data provenance in SOA: security, reliability, and integrity. Serv. Oriented Comput. Appl. **1**(4), 223–247 (2007)

36. Tummarello, G., Morbidoni, C., Puliti, P., Piazza, F.: Signing individual fragments of an RDF graph. In: WWW (2005)

37. U.S. Office of the Federal Register: 14 Code of Federal Regulations, Part 21 (2020). https://www.ecfr.gov/cgi-bin/text-idx?node=pt14.1.21 Accessed 16 Dec 2020

38. Xie, J., Yu, F.R., Huang, T., Xie, R., et al.: A survey on the scalability of blockchain systems. IEEE Netw. **33**(5), 166–173 (2019)

39. Yoon, A.: Data Reuse and Users' Trust Judgments: Toward Trusted Data Curation. Ph.D. thesis, University of North Carolina at Chapel Hill (2015)

40. Zaveri, A., Rula, A., Maurino, A., Pietrobon, R., et al.: Quality assessment for linked data: a survey. Semant. Web **7**(1), 63–93 (2016)

41. Zheng, Z., Xie, S., Dai, H., Chen, X., et al.: An overview of blockchain technology: architecture, consensus, and future trends. In: IEEE BigData Congress (2017)

Matching, Integration, and Fusion

Neural Knowledge Base Repairs

Thomas Pellissier Tanon[✉] and Fabian Suchanek

Télécom Paris, Institut Polytechnique de Paris, Palaiseau, France
thomas@pellissier-tanon.fr

Abstract. The curation of a knowledge base is a crucial but costly task. In this work, we suggest to make use of the advances in neural network research to improve the automated correction of constraint violations. Our method is a deep learning refinement of [23], and similarly uses the edits that solved some violations in the past to infer how to solve similar violations in the present. Our system makes use of the graph content, literal embeddings, and features extracted from Web pages to improve its performance. The experimental evaluation on Wikidata shows significant improvements over baselines.

1 Introduction

The past years have seen the rise of large knowledge bases, completed by a crowd of contributors like Wikidata [28] or Freebase [8], or automatically filled from extraction and conversion pipelines like Yago [27] or DBpedia [4]. Both kind of knowledge bases often contain errors, originating from edge cases in the conversion pipelines, good faith mistakes, or vandalism in the crowd-sourced content. Often, knowledge bases contain a constraint system in order to fight such problems, starting from the OWL distinction between object properties and datatypes properties, and including, e.g., domain and range constraints or more complex expressions such as cardinality constraints and conflict declarations. These constraints are often violated in practice. For example, Wikidata has 1M "domain" constraint violations and 4.4M "single value" constraint violations as of March 20th, 2020. Thus, there is a need for tools to help the knowledge base curators repair these violations in an automated or a semi-automated way.

Recent work [23] shows that, in the case of an actively curated knowledge base like Wikidata, it is possible to use the repairs that have been done in the past in order to learn the repairs for the current constraint violations. The work provides both a formalism and a first algorithm based on rule learning to this end. However, the experiments on Wikidata show that there is still room for improvement: The approach was not able to provide anything meaningful when RDF literals where involved, and the user study presents a low agreement score (less than 50%) for a lot of constraint types.

Hence, we explore in this work a new approach to learn how to repair constraint violations using the edit history, building upon [23]. Our method takes as input a KB with its edit history, a set of constraints, and the statements

R. Verborgh et al. (Eds.): ESWC 2021, LNCS 12731, pp. 287–303, 2021.
https://doi.org/10.1007/978-3-030-77385-4_17

of the KB that constitute violations of the constraints. It produces as output suggestions of statements to add to the KB or to remove from the KB so that the constraint violation disappears. Our new algorithm is based on deep learning, and brings two key advantages over [23]: First, our embeddings take into account the data of the KB in a holistic fashion, as opposed to being limited to the pieces of data captured by logical rules. Second, we are able to make use of data that would be hard to integrate into rule learning approaches, including, e.g., the textual content in the knowledge base. We also keep the ability from [23] to work at the scale of large knowledge bases. Our evaluation on Wikidata shows significant improvements against the state of the art. We also conduct detailed ablation studies to justify our architecture. Finally, we improve the Wikidata evaluation dataset that was introduced by [23], and release it in an easy to use format in the hope that it can be useful to evaluate such systems.

This paper is structured as follows: Sect. 2 discusses related work, and Sect. 3 introduces preliminaries. Section 4 presents a baseline. Section 5 explains our approach and Sect. 6 evaluates it, before Sect. 7 concludes.

2   Related Work

Our work aims at repairing constraint violations in a collaboratively edited knowledge base. It builds on, and improves upon, the approach presented in [23]. Several other approaches are related to this endeavor.

Knowledge Base Cleaning. Several approaches have been developed to repair constraint violations in knowledge bases. Active integrity constraints [11] aim at providing a set of possible repair actions to each constraint. An application to description logic knowledge bases has been presented in [24]. These approaches assume that the user provides a set of possible corrections. In our work, in contrast, we want to learn these corrections automatically from the edit history. Again other works are interactive, and ask the user questions to quickly find a correction [2,3,6,7]. Our work, in contrast, learns the repair directly from the edit history.

Again other approaches use the data in the KB itself in order to improve it. [9] uses knowledge base embeddings, lexical distance, and constraint-based refinements to predict corrections. Our work goes beyond the state of the current KB and learns from the edit history instead.

[22] uses statistics to find errors in the knowledge base and to add new types. [18] exploits the graph structure to find wrong type relations. [21] cleans *sameAs* relations based on the shape of the existing identity and on differences in the graph. [17] uses graph and text distances to look for values for a given subject and predicate. [20] fixes the subject or object of existing relations based on type relations and string matching. [1] uses crowdsourcing to detect quality issues. [26] uses external datasources and statistical data to detect problems in the knowledge base and fix them. Our work differs from all of these works in that we use the past edits as ground truth, and so are able to easily generalize over a

large set of constraint types, instead of focusing on specific cases like *sameAs* or a wrong subject or object. Some works in completely different domains also use the idea of learning repairs from past corrections. For example, [5] learns how to fix errors in source code based on previous error corrections.

Graph Neural Networks. Neural networks are often applied to knowledge base related tasks [30]. However, there does not seem to be any work in the literature that uses neural networks to predict repairs in knowledge bases. Some works use neural networks to reason on top of knowledge bases [15]. Several other works tackle the knowledge graph completion task by mining rules [13] or by link prediction. Our approach takes inspiration from these methods, but ultimately tackles a different problem: We do not want to predict links, but the correction of the violation of a constraint. We refer to [30] for a detailed survey about graph neural networks.

3 Preliminaries

Let us call $\mathcal{T}$ the set of all RDF terms (IRIs, blank nodes and literals). In our work, we see a *knowledge base* (KB) $\mathcal{K}$ as a set of triples of elements of $\mathcal{T}$. These triples are written $\langle s, p, o \rangle$, where s is the subject of the triple (which cannot be a literal), p the predicate (which has to be a IRI), and o the object. We make the unique name assumption in what follows. If this assumption does not hold, and if the KB allows OWL entailment, then $a = b$ can be replaced by $\langle a, \texttt{owl:sameAs}, b \rangle$ in what follows without affecting the validity of our approach.

We define a *conjunctive query* (CQ) as a query of the form $\mathbf{C}(x) = \langle s_1, p_1, o_1 \rangle \wedge \cdots \wedge \langle s_n, p_n, o_n \rangle$, where x is a sequence of variables, the p_i are constants, and the s_i and o_i are variables over x or constants. We write $\mathcal{K} \models \mathbf{C}(x)$ iff there exists a binding for x such that $\langle s_1, p_1, o_1 \rangle \in \mathcal{K}$, ..., $\langle s_n, p_n, o_n \rangle \in \mathcal{K}$. We also define similarly a *disjunctive query* (DQ) as a query of the form $\mathbf{D}(x) = \langle s_1, p_1, o_1 \rangle \vee \cdots \vee \langle s_n, p_n, o_n \rangle$ and we write $\mathcal{K} \models \mathbf{D}(x)$ iff there exists a binding for x and an i such that $\langle s_i, p_i, o_i \rangle \in \mathcal{K}$. We also allow term equalities like $x = y$ and we write $\top$ (true) for the empty CQ and $\bot$ (false) for the empty DQ.

A KB can define *constraints*. Such constraints can enforce, e.g., that some information must be present (e.g. every person should have a birth place), or that some triple combinations may not occur (e.g. a person can have at most one birth place). Following [23], we express these constraints as rules. Such a rule takes the form $\Gamma(x) : \mathbf{B}(x) \rightarrow \exists y \, \mathbf{H}(x, y)$ where x and y are sequences of variables, $\mathbf{B}$ is a CQ and $\mathbf{H}$ a DQ. For example, the rule $\Gamma_1(x) : \langle x, \texttt{rdf:type}, \texttt{schema:Person} \rangle \rightarrow \exists y \, \langle x, \texttt{schema:birthPlace}, y \rangle$ says that all people must have a birth place. The rule $\Gamma_2(x, y_1, y_2) = \langle x, \texttt{schema:birthPlace}, y_1 \rangle \wedge \langle x, \texttt{schema:birthPlace}, y_2 \rangle \rightarrow y_1 = y_2$ says that entities can have at most one birth place. It is clear that any constraint with a combination of $\wedge$, $\vee$ and $\neg$ in the body can be translated into an equivalent conjunction of constraints in this formalism. In particular, the formalism can express constraints such as the following:

- Domain constraints. The rule to enforce that the domain of a property p is d is: $\Gamma(s, o) = \langle s, p, o \rangle \rightarrow \langle s, \texttt{rdf:type}, d \rangle$.
- Range constraints. The rule to enforce that the range of a property p is d is: $\Gamma(s, o) = \langle s, p, o \rangle \rightarrow \langle o, \texttt{rdf:type}, d \rangle$.
- Functional relations. The rule to enforce the functionality of a property p is: $\Gamma(s, o_1, o_2) = \langle s, p, o_1 \rangle \wedge \langle s, p, o_2 \rangle \rightarrow o_1 = o_2$.
- Inverse functional relations. The rule to enforce the inverse functionality of a property p is: $\Gamma(s_1, s_2, o) = \langle s_1, p, o \rangle \wedge \langle s_2, p, o \rangle \rightarrow s_1 = s_2$.
- Symmetric relations. The rule to enforce that p is symmetric is: $\Gamma(s, o) = \langle s, p, o \rangle \rightarrow \langle o, p, s \rangle$.
- Conflicts between properties. The rule to enforce that p_1 and p_2 have disjoint domains is: $\Gamma(s, o_1, o_2) = \langle s, p_1, o_1 \rangle \wedge \langle s, p_2, o_2 \rangle \rightarrow \perp$.

Given a constraint $\Gamma(x) : \mathbf{B}(x) \rightarrow \exists y \mathbf{H}(x, y)$, a *violation* in a KB $\mathcal{K}$ is a binding for x such that (1) $\mathcal{K} \models \mathbf{B}(x)$ and (2) there is no y such that $\mathcal{K} \models \mathbf{H}(x, y)$. For example, if the knowledge base is $\mathcal{K} = \{\langle \texttt{JohnDoe}, \texttt{rdf:type}, \texttt{schema:Person} \rangle\}$ then $x = \texttt{JohnDoe}$ is a violation of Γ_1 in $\mathcal{K}$ because $\mathcal{K} \models \langle \texttt{JohnDoe}, \texttt{rdf:type}, \texttt{schema:Person} \rangle$ and $\nexists y$ $\mathcal{K} \models \langle x, \texttt{schema:birthPlace}, y \rangle$.

The *violation triples* of a violation are the instantiated triples of the body of the constraint. In our previous example, the violation triples would be the single triple $\langle \texttt{JohnDoe}, \texttt{rdf:type}, \texttt{schema:Person} \rangle$.

To repair a violation, we need an *edit action*. Following [23], we define an edit action as a pair $(\mathcal{M}^+, \mathcal{M}^-)$ of one triple to add and one triple to remove. At most one of these triples can be absent, and we write $\emptyset$ for such a triple. The rationale for this representation is that, due to the disjunctive nature of the head of the constraint, the addition of a single triple can remove the violation, and due to the conjunctive nature of the body of the constraint, the removal of a single triple can also fix the constraint. Furthermore, a removal combined with an addition corresponds to a replacement, which is a frequent edit action in KBs. The *result* of an edit action $(\mathcal{M}^+, \mathcal{M}^-)$ on a KB $\mathcal{K}$ is the KB $\mathcal{K}' = (\mathcal{K} \cup \{\mathcal{M}^+\}) \setminus \{\mathcal{M}^-\}$ (omitting either set if the triple is absent in the edit action). An edit action is a *repair* of a violation of a constraint, if the violation no longer exists in the result of the edit action.

For example, the two possible edits to repair a violation of Γ_1 are to remove the triple $\langle x, \texttt{rdf:type}, \texttt{schema:Person} \rangle$ or to add a triple $\langle x, \texttt{schema:birthPlace}, y \rangle$ with a correct instantiation for y.

We aim at learning "good" repair edits that make the KB closer to the real world by adding "true" facts and removing "false" facts. Formally, a "good" edit is an edit $(\mathcal{M}^+, \mathcal{M}^-)$ such that $\mathcal{M}^+$ is absent or in $\mathcal{K}^i$, and $\mathcal{M}^-$ is absent or not in $\mathcal{K}^i$, where $\mathcal{K}^i$ is the "ideal" knowledge base representing the real world [25]. The *edit history* of a KB $\mathcal{K}$ is the sequence of edit actions that have been applied, starting from the empty KB, to yield $\mathcal{K}$. In this paper, we aim at building a predictor that takes as input the edit history of a KB and a set of constraints, and that predicts good repair edits in the sense described above.

4   Baseline Approach

[23] presents a rule learning approach for our problem, called *CorHist*. We introduce this system here briefly, before presenting our new system in the next section. CorHist takes as input the edit history of a KB and constraints. It mines correction rules of the form $\Gamma(\boldsymbol{x}) \wedge \langle s_m, p_m, o_m \rangle \wedge \langle s_c, p_c, o_c \rangle \rightarrow (\mathcal{M}^+(\boldsymbol{x}), \mathcal{M}^-(\boldsymbol{x}))$, where $\Gamma(\boldsymbol{x})$ is a constraint, s_m and s_c are variables in $\boldsymbol{x}$, p_m and p_c are constants, o_m is a constant or a variable in $\boldsymbol{x}$, $(\mathcal{M}^+(\boldsymbol{x}), \mathcal{M}^-(\boldsymbol{x}))$ is the predicted edit action, and o_c is a constant, a variable in $\boldsymbol{x}$ or a new free variable. $\langle s_c, p_c, o_c \rangle$ is optional. This correction rule means that if there exists a violation $\boldsymbol{x}$ of Γ in $\mathcal{K}$, and if $\langle s_m, p_m, o_m \rangle(\boldsymbol{x}) \in \mathcal{K}$ and $\langle s_c, p_c, o_c \rangle(\boldsymbol{x}) \in \mathcal{K}$, then $(\mathcal{M}^+(\boldsymbol{x}), \mathcal{M}^-(\boldsymbol{x}))$ is a good repair. For example, CorHist is able to mine correction rules such as $\Gamma_1(x) \wedge \langle x, \texttt{rdf:type}, \texttt{schema:Person} \rangle \wedge \langle x, \texttt{rdf:type}, \texttt{schema:Place} \rangle \rightarrow (\emptyset, \langle x, \texttt{rdf:type}, \texttt{schema:Person} \rangle)$. This rule repairs violations of the constraint Γ_1 presented in Sect. 3 by stating that "if x violates the constraint Γ_1 and is a $\texttt{schema:Place}$, then the $\texttt{schema:Person}$ type should be removed".

For this purpose, CorHist uses an adaptation of the AMIE algorithm [12]. It takes as input the past corrections dataset and the facts about the entities mentioned in the violation triples. It assumes that there is only one violation triple. It first generates simple rules by taking each past correction from the dataset, and by replacing constants by variables in both the violation triple and the associated correction. This leads to correction rules without context, like $\Gamma_1(x) \rightarrow (\emptyset, \langle x, \texttt{rdf:type}, \texttt{schema:Person} \rangle)$. Then, CorHist refines these correction rules by adding an extra triple to the rule body. For this, it looks for an extra possible pattern in the facts about the entities that are already used in the rule body, and adds this pattern to the rule body.

CorHist ranks the correction rules according to their confidence on the past corrections, i.e. the number of times the rule predicts the correct edit divided by how many times the rule predicts an edit. It also prunes the rules that have too low a confidence, predict less than 10 edits on the training dataset, or have extra triples in the body that do increase the confidence by at least 5%. When CorHist has to predict an edit, it uses the matching correction rule with the highest confidence. The minimal confidence threshold used for pruning is chosen so as to optimize the F1-score on a cross-validation dataset.

CorHist can be improved easily as follows:

- We allow multiple violation triples in the rule by applying exactly the same initialization step, but with multiple triples.
- We allow up to three additional triple patterns $\langle s_c, p_c, o_c \rangle$. These patterns must have a constant predicate and their subject must be a variable in $\boldsymbol{x}$. This allows more specialized rules than CorHist, which supports only one additional triple pattern.
- We allow the system to take into account information from external Web pages about the entities. This information can help the system choose, e.g., between two possible birth places, simply by checking if one of them appears on the Web page.

This last point works as follows: For every URL s that appears in the violation triples, we add two new facts: one is ⟨s, hist:pageStatusCode, XXXX⟩, where XXXX is the HTTP response code of that URL. The other is ⟨s, hist:pageContainsLabel, o⟩, where o is the object of a triple connecting o to s, and one of o's labels (found with the rdfs:label relation) appears in the HTML page of s. For example, if we consider the triple ⟨Douglas_Adams,schema:sameAs,<http://viaf.org/113230702>⟩ from Wikidata, we fetch the external URL from viaf.org, and we add the triples ⟨<http://viaf.org/113230702>, hist:pageStatusCode,200⟩ and ⟨<http://viaf.org/113230702>, hist:pageContainsLabel,Douglas_Adams⟩, because the label "Douglas Adams"@en of the entity Douglas_Adams appears on the page.

We call this improved system *CorHist+*. While we will see in our experiments that CorHist+ improves over CorHist, both systems still suffer from a systematic weakness: They can take into account only triples that explicitly appear in a correction rule – and not shallow signals from the state of the knowledge base. We will now see how to remedy this.

5   Approach

To overcome the limitation of the rule mining approach explored by CorHist, we design a new neural network architecture to implement a correction predictor. Our predictor takes as input the violated constraint, the violation triples, and the facts about the entities that are mentioned in the violation triples. It predicts as output a triple to add and/or a triple to delete. At training time, the input and the outputs come from the edit history of the KB. At prediction time, the input comes from the current state of the KB. In the following, we first present a "conversion" of CorHist+ to a neural network called *Bass-RL*, before adding new components to improve its performance, leading to our final *Bass* architecture[1].

5.1   Bass-RL

The goal of Bass-RL is to build a neural network that mirrors exactly the functioning of CorHist+. Figure 1 shows the basic architecture of our network. It is composed of 3 input components, which all feed into the "edit prediction" component. The dimensions of the internal layers are parametrized by a constant d, which is a hyperparameter of the network. The inputs are:

– **The constraint.** We give to each constraint a unique integer id and then we use a trained embedding matrix to create a d-dimensional vector from the one-hot encoding of the constraint id. This vector is then fed into the edit predictor. This vector gives to the network the information which type of constraint we aim to fix.

---

[1] The "Bass" name derives from "CorHist", because a bass is a singer with a deep voice, and "corhist" is an old English word for "singer".

- **The violation triples.** For each of the k violation triples, we encode the predicate and the object by help of the "term embedding" component. These encodings are concatenated and fed into the edit prediction component. The subject of the violation triple is not used, because it cannot be a constant.
- **The facts about the entities** that appear in the violation triples. We encode only the predicates and the objects, because the subject is already known to the network. For example, if we consider the violation triple $\langle$JohnDoe, schema:birthPlace, Paris$\rangle$, the two entities are JohnDoe and Paris, and we embed their predicates and objects – i.e., {(rdf:type, schema:Person), (schema:gender, schema:Male), ...} for JohnDoe and {(rdf:type, schema:Place), (schema:country, France), ...} for Paris. There are $2k$ mentioned entities, 2 for each of the k violation triples. Each fact is embedded using the "entity fact embedding" component. Then the output vectors are concatenated and fed into the edit prediction component.

Let us now describe each component in detail.

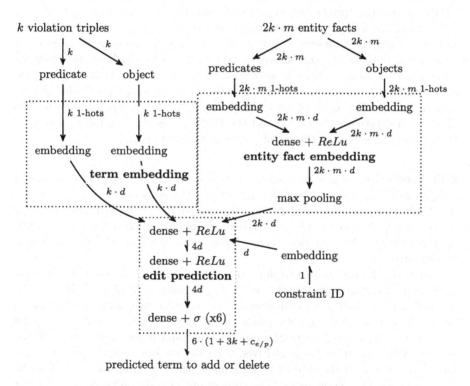

Fig. 1. Network architecture of Bass-RL. d is the vector dimension hyperparameter, k is the max number of violation triples, and m is the max number of facts per entity.

Term Embedding. We embed RDF terms as follows: predicates are one-hot encoded and then embedded into a space of dimension d using an embedding matrix $\mathcal{P}$. We embed similarly the objects using an matrix $\mathcal{E}$. These matrices $\mathcal{E}$ and $\mathcal{P}$ are shared by all object and predicate embedding operations. They are trained at the same time as the neural network. This embedding allows the edit predictor to act on specific predicates and entities in the violation triples.

Entity Fact Embedding. Similarly to CorHist, we give the neural network the facts about the $2k$ entities involved in the constraint violation. A classical approach for this purpose would be to use entity embeddings, i.e., to embed the entity itself. However, entity embeddings have two drawbacks: First, they require expensive pre-training. Second, and more crucially, they do not work with new entities. Therefore, we embed not the entity, but the facts that the entity is involved in. While the objects of these facts will still be encoded using learned embeddings (and thus cannot be entities that are unknown at training time), the subjects can be entities that have never been seen at training time. This allows the network to check constraints on newly added entities.

We encode the (predicate, object) facts of each entity mentioned in the violation triples as follows: we embed the predicates by reusing the same predicate embedding matrix $\mathcal{P}$ described previously. We embed similarly the objects by reusing the same entity embedding matrix $\mathcal{E}$. Then we combine the predicate and the object using a dense layer with a rectified linear unit (ReLU) non linearity[2]. Then we merge the obtained embeddings for each (predicate, object) using a max pooling layer to get a single vector for the entity. If the entity is a URL to an external website, we add the URL triples that we have introduced for CorHist+ (Sect. 4) to the set of (predicate, object) pairs.

Edit Prediction. The edit prediction component takes as input the previous components, i.e. the constraint id embedding, the embeddings of the k violation triple predicates and objects, and the embedding of the facts about the $2k$ entities mentioned in the violation triples. This data is then fed into a multi-layer perceptron. We use two hidden layers of dimensions $4d$ with the ReLU non-linearity.

Our network outputs two triples – one to add and one to delete. Each triple is given by its three components (subject, predicate, and object). Hence, our network has 2×3 output components. Each output component could of course just be the one-hot encoding of a predicate or entity. However, then the network would have to learn each instantiation of a constraint individually (as in "If the subject of the violation triple is Elvis, then the subject of the addition triple should be Elvis", "If the subject is Madonna, then..."). Therefore, we allow the network to output a code, as in "The subject of the addition triple is the object of the first constraint violation triple". To permit nevertheless the output of constants as well, we combine both approaches. With this, each of the 6 outputs

---

[2] This function is defined as $ReLU(x) = max(0, x)$.

(2 × 3 triple components) works in the same way, classifying the output term into one of the following options:

- 1 class to state that the output is not existent (the triple should not be returned), or unknown. We call it the class 0.
- $3k$ classes to state that the output term is the same as the subject/predicate or object of one of the k violation triples. For example, the class 1 corresponds to the subject of the first violation triple, the class 2 to its predicate, the class 3 to its object, the class 4 to the subject of the second violation triple etc.
- c_p or c_e classes to state that the output is one of the c_p predicates (for the predicate to add or delete outputs) or one of the c_e entities (for the other outputs) from a list of predicates/entities found at least t times in the expected outputs from the training data (where t is a hyperparameter).

This leads to $1 + 3k + c_e$ possible classes (and so, output neurons) for each of the four subject/object outputs and $1 + 3k + c_p$ for the two predicate outputs. Each of these outputs are implemented like regular classifiers using a dense layer with a softmax non-linearity[3]. The outputs returns a $1 + 3k + c_{e/p}$ dimensional vector. The ith vector output is the predicted probability of ith class.

To retrieve the final edit, we consider the output for both the "delete" triple and the "add" triple. If the three outputs for the subject, predicate and object of the triple give known values (a known entity or predicate or a known violation triple term given in the input) we build the triple to add or to delete from these outputs. If the three outputs give the "not defined" class, we return no triple. This means that the edit does not contain a triple to add, or a triple to delete, respectively. If there is only one or two components returning "not defined", we assume that the network has not been able to predict a correction.

5.2 Bass

We now present our improved repair predictor, *Bass*. Figure 2 shows the architecture of our network. We designed two improvements over Bass-RL:

RDF Literal Embedding. We want our predictor to be able to act on RDF literals. For example, if every book can have at most one ISBN number, and if a given book has two ISBNs, 2-7654-1005-4 and abc, it is easy to decide that abc should be abandoned, if we allow the network to access the literals.

For this purpose, we first remove the datatype IRI. This leads to strings like "Elvis Presley"@en for a language tagged string or "42" for an integer. Then, we tokenize the string with the BERT tokenizer [10] and apply an embedding matrix on each token. We then apply a max pooling on the embedding sequence to get another d-dimensional vector. We use the BERT tokenizer to provide a better support for out-of-vocabulary words. It also allows to better handle complex values like numbers and dates that a regular tokenizer based on a whitespace

---

[3] $\sigma(x_i) = \frac{e^{x_i}}{\sum_{j=1}^{D} e^{x_j}}$ for all $i \in 1, \ldots, D$ if there are D possible classes.

and/or other characters split. It also allows keeping more significant elements than a simple char based encoding. This input is not used when the objects are IRIs or blank nodes.

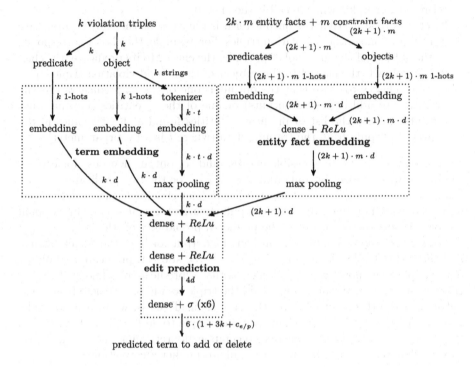

Fig. 2. Bass network architecture when there is just one violation triple. d is the vector dimension hyperparameter, k the max number of violation triples, m the max number of facts per entity, and t the max number of string tokens. Additions compared to Bass-RL are in red.

Constraint Embedding. Bass-RL, like CorHist, encoded a constraint by an ID. This does not allow the network to generalize over the constraints, to treat similar constraints similarly, or to learn new constraints. To remedy this shortcoming, we encode the constraint by a set of (predicate, object) pairs and we encode this set using the entity fact embedding component introduced earlier.

To encode the constraint by a set of (predicate, object) pairs, we rely on *constraint shapes*. The constraint shape of a constraint Γ is a constraint Γ^s where all constants in Γ have been replaced by fresh variables. For example, the shape of the constraint $\Gamma_1(x)$: $\langle x, \texttt{rdf:type}, \texttt{schema:Person} \rangle \rightarrow \exists y\ \langle x, \texttt{schema:birthPlace}, y \rangle$ is $\Gamma_1^s(x)$: $\langle x, p_1, o_1 \rangle \rightarrow \exists y\ \langle x, p_2, y \rangle$. Two constraint shapes are equivalent if they have the same components up to a renaming of variables. With this definition, we encode a constraint $\Gamma(\boldsymbol{x})$: $\varphi(\boldsymbol{x}) \rightarrow \exists \boldsymbol{y}\ \varphi_1(\boldsymbol{x}, \boldsymbol{y}) \vee \cdots \vee \varphi_n(\boldsymbol{x}, \boldsymbol{y})$ by the following set of property value pairs:

- (bass:constraintShape, i) where i is an identifier assigned to the equivalence class of the constraint shape Γ^s.
- (p_i, o_i) for each $\langle s_i, p_i, o_i \rangle$ in φ and φ_i where o_i is a constant.
- $(\hat{p}_i, s_i)$ for each $\langle s_i, p_i, o_i \rangle$ in φ and φ_i where s_i is a constant and $\hat{p}_i$ is the inverse property of p_i.[4]

These components give us our new Bass network.

6   Experiments

6.1   Dataset

We evaluated our algorithm on Wikidata [28]. We considered the same 10 kinds of constraints as in [23]. The dataset provided by [23] contains, for each past correction, the violated constraint and a single violation triple. Thus, running CorHist required access to the Wikidata edit history, so as to extract the other violation triple for "conflict with", "single", and "distinct" constraint types and to retrieve the facts about the entities mentioned in the violation triple. To simplify the re-use of our dataset, we added these items to the data, so that CorHist and Bass can now be trained without having to access the edit history. We also included the content of the external Web pages in the dataset, so that CorHist+ and Bass (and future approaches) do not need to download the pages again.

Different from [23], we limited the number of past corrections to 200k per constraint type (except for "one of" constraints, which have only 23k extracted past corrections in the full dataset). This limitation is made to facilitate the use of the dataset (the previous one had a size of 36GB), and to allow fetching all mentioned Web pages in a week. We split the dataset into 80% training set, 10% cross-validation set, and a 10% test set. This improved dataset is publicly available on FigShare[5].

6.2   Systems

Implementation. We implemented Bass with the Keras API of Tensorflow 2. For the BERT tokenization, we use the HuggingFace "torkenizers" library [29]. Our implementation is publicly available on GitHub[6]. With $\mathcal{E}$ and $\mathcal{P}$, we embed only the entities and predicates with at least 100 occurrences. We do the same for the output by setting $t = 100$. We choose to set all the embedding sizes to $d = 128$. We use the constraint type identifier ("single value", "value type"...) to identify the constraint shape, and we use the Wikidata statement that encodes the constraint to generate the (predicate, object) triples that describe the constraint.

---

[4] Using a new IRI if there is no inverse property of p_i already in the KB.
[5] https://doi.org/10.6084/m9.figshare.13338743.
[6] https://github.com/Tpt/bass-materials.

Table 1. Evaluation of the correction rules mined by Bass, CorHist [23] and CorHist+ and comparison with the baselines. Best F scores in bold.

Constraint type		Micro average			Macro average		
		Prec.	Rec.	F	Prec.	Rec.	F
Type	Add	0.53	0.17	0.26	0.28	0.10	0.14
	Delete	0.04	0.04	0.04	0.08	0.08	0.08
	CorHist	0.88	0.62	0.73	0.96	0.28	0.43
	CorHist+	0.86	0.75	0.80	0.89	0.34	0.49
	Bass	0.92	0.79	**0.85**	0.83	0.36	**0.50**
Value type	Add	0.20	0.07	0.10	0.35	0.11	0.16
	Delete	0.01	0.01	0.01	0.04	0.04	0.04
	CorHist	0.70	0.62	0.66	0.86	0.35	0.50
	CorHist+	0.70	0.63	0.66	0.81	0.43	**0.56**
	Bass	0.78	0.69	**0.73**	0.70	0.28	0.40
One-of	Delete	0.27	0.27	0.27	0.43	0.43	0.43
	CorHist	0.84	0.72	**0.78**	0.84	0.34	**0.48**
	CorHist+	0.84	0.72	**0.78**	0.84	0.34	**0.48**
	Bass	0.86	0.71	**0.78**	0.77	0.26	0.39
Item requires statement	Add	0.99	0.11	0.20	0.92	0.13	0.22
	Delete	0.02	0.02	0.02	0.07	0.07	0.07
	CorHist	0.94	0.30	0.46	0.98	0.17	0.29
	CorHist+	0.85	0.36	**0.51**	0.94	0.19	**0.32**
	Bass	0.89	0.35	0.50	0.76	0.17	0.28
Value requires statement	Add	Nan	0	Nan	Nan	0	Nan
	Delete	0.02	0.02	0.02	0.09	0.09	0.09
	CorHist	0.96	0.64	0.77	0.95	0.33	0.49
	CorHist+	0.90	0.69	0.78	0.89	0.39	**0.55**
	Bass	0.98	0.75	**0.85**	0.72	0.32	0.44
Conflict with	Delete	0.39	0.39	0.39	0.44	0.44	0.44
	CorHist	0.93	0.47	0.63	0.91	0.36	0.51
	CorHist+	0.87	0.84	0.86	0.83	0.46	0.59
	Bass	0.91	0.86	**0.88**	0.77	0.71	**0.74**
Inverse + Symmetric	Add	0.91	0.91	0.91	0.82	0.82	0.82
	Delete	0.07	0.07	0.07	0.11	0.11	0.11
	CorHist	0.95	0.91	0.93	0.91	0.72	0.80
	CorHist+	0.94	0.92	0.93	0.90	0.73	**0.81**
	Bass	0.97	0.94	**0.95**	0.87	0.58	0.69
Single value	Delete	0.45	0.45	0.45	0.42	0.42	0.42
	CorHist	0.85	0.26	0.39	0.90	0.10	0.18
	CorHist+	0.55	0.50	0.53	0.74	0.23	0.36
	Bass	0.74	0.64	**0.69**	0.60	0.52	**0.56**
Distinct values	Delete	0.55	0.55	0.55	0.45	0.45	0.45
	CorHist	0.61	0.53	0.56	0.90	0.16	0.27
	CorHist+	0.58	0.57	**0.57**	0.80	0.26	0.39
	Bass	0.59	0.56	**0.57**	0.48	0.43	**0.46**
Total	Add	0.46	0.14	0.22	0.33	0.11	0.16
	Delete	0.24	0.24	0.24	0.22	0.22	0.22
	CorHist	0.83	0.53	0.65	0.94	0.23	0.37
	CorHist+	0.75	0.64	0.69	0.85	0.30	0.44
	Bass-RL	0.77	0.65	0.70	0.64	0.34	0.44
	Bass	0.80	0.68	**0.73**	0.69	0.39	**0.49**

Training. We trained Bass on the training set for all constraint types at the same time, using the sum of categorical cross-entropy loss[7] for the 6 classification outputs and the Adam [16] optimizer. To ease the training we used the validation set to keep the best epoch according to the loss against the cross-validation dataset. We trained the model for 6 epochs on the full training dataset with a mini-batch size of 256, the best model being found after the 3rd epoch. After loading the dataset into memory, training took 18min using a laptop with an Nvidia Quadro P3000 mobile GPU, an Intel Core i7-7700HQ CPU, and 32 GB of RAM. The rather large batch size was chosen so as to improve the training stability. We experimented with larger batch sizes, but these do not improve the performances.

Baselines. We compare our approach against *CorHist* and *CorHist+* described in Sect. 4, and the two baselines from [23]. For CorHist+, we use a minimal support of 10 and a minimal confidence between 0.1 and 1.

The two baselines *delete* and *add* are basic ones without any learning: *Delete* uses the fact that all Wikidata constraint violations have a "focus" on a single existing triple whose removal would remove the violation. Our baseline just removes this triple. *Add* tries to add a new triple to solve the constraint violation. For "inverse" and "symmetric" constraints, this baseline adds the missing reverse triple and performs very well. For "item requires statement", "value requires statement", "Type" and "Value type", it adds a possibly missing triple only if it is possible to know the expected value(s) from the constraint rule by picking one of the expected values randomly.

6.3   Results

Table 1 compares the performances of *Bass*, *CorHist+*, *CorHist* and the two baselines using our dataset test set. To counter the non-deterministic nature of gradient descent based training, we ran Bass training multiple times. Its performances were stable enough to not change the performance ranking. The other approaches, CorHist(+) and the baselines, are deterministic.

As shown in the evaluations, Bass significantly outperforms CorHist+, which itself significantly improves over CorHist. Indeed, we have conducted a Wilson score test at confidence 95%, and confirm that the confidence interval is of size 0.2% for all approaches – an order of magnitude lower than the score gaps between the different methods. The strongest improvements are seen for the constraint types "Conflict with" and "Single value", which both concern the removal of one value between two choices. CorHist+ significantly improves over CorHist (7% in macro average F-score) by allowing more complex rules, allowing more relevant decisions and integrating metadata from Web pages. The simple move from a rule learning algorithm (CorHist+) to a neural network (Bass-RL) provides a small performance improvement of 1% in micro average F-score.

---

[7] The categorical crossentropy is defined as $CE(x) = \sum_{i=0}^{n} t_i log(p_i)$ where t_i is the expected prediction for the class i, and p_i is the predicted output.

We believe that this improvement stems from the fact that, different from rules, neural networks are able to draw holistic conclusions from the context facts. The addition of textual data and of a structure representation of the constraint, which are hard to take into account with a rule mining approach, allows Bass to outperform Bass-RL by 5% in macro average F-score and by 3% in micro average, suggesting that textual data and a structured representation of the constraints help solving violations of under-represented constraints.

Bass takes around 18 min to train, whereas CorHist took 4 h. Thus, the increase F1 provided by Bass actually comes with a decrease of the training time.

Table 2. Ablation study results.

Approach	Micro average			Macro average		
	Prec.	Rec.	F	Prec.	Rec.	F
Bass	0.80	0.68	**0.73**	0.69	0.39	**0.49**
Bass-RL	0.77	0.65	0.70	0.64	0.34	0.44
Bass minimal	0.65	0.53	0.58	0.50	0.25	0.33
Bass without object literals	0.77	0.65	0.71	0.66	0.36	0.47
Bass without entity facts	0.70	0.59	0.64	0.54	0.31	0.39
Bass without constraint	0.77	0.65	0.71	0.60	0.35	0.44
Bass with one hidden layer edit predictor	0.79	0.67	0.72	0.69	0.38	0.49
Bass with constraint ids	0.80	0.68	0.73	0.66	0.37	0.47
Bass with BiLSTM literals	0.78	0.66	0.71	0.65	0.37	0.47
Bass with entity facts attention	0.76	0.65	0.70	0.63	0.36	0.46
CorHist+	0.75	0.64	0.69	0.85	0.30	0.44
CorHist	0.83	0.53	0.65	0.94	0.23	0.37
Deletion baseline	0.24	0.24	0.24	0.22	0.22	0.22
Addition baseline	0.46	0.14	0.22	0.33	0.11	0.16

6.4   Ablation Study

To understand the contribution of each component of our network, we remove the components one by one, and measure the performance Table 2. We also added Bass-RL and another variant, *Bass minimal*. This variant removes from Bass-RL the constraint embedding and the entity fact embedding. This leads to a network where the edit prediction component receives only the violation triple predicates and objects, embedded with $\mathcal{P}$ and $\mathcal{E}$.

Additionally to the ablation, we investigate some possible variants of our network:

- Replace the constraint description input by the Bass-RL constraint ID encoding. This gives the exact constraint to the model, without the possibility to generalize from the constraint description.

- Replace the max pooling layer in the literal embeddings by a bidirectional long short-term memory network (BiLSTM) [14].
- Replace the max pooling layer that aggregates the embeddings of the (predicate, object) tuples of the involved entities by an attention layer. We define the attention following [19] as $\sigma(q \cdot V^\top) \cdot V$, where σ is the softmax function. This attention layer uses for query q the constraint embedding.

Discussion. Using the description of the constraint instead of the constraint ids does not change the micro average score, but increases the macro average scores. This means that the change helps for constraints with only a few past corrections, which have a weaker weight in the micro average. We thus observe a better generalization with respect to the constraints. Embedding the object literal values brings 2% of improvement on both F-scores, suggesting it brings some value on the 13% of violations where one of the objects is a literal that is not a date or a geographical coordinate. The addition of a bidirectional LSTM and attention would actually be detrimental to the performances of our network.

Overall, our experiments show that our architecture is well-designed, and that it is able to outperform the rule mining approach from [23] by a considerable margin.

7   Conclusion

In this paper, we have presented an approach to automatically repair constraint violations in Wikidata. Our experiments with various sets of constraint types show that our new approach provides significant improvements over the rule-based state of the art, by taking advantage of neural networks. This improvement stems from two factors: First, we find that the neural network can better take into account the shallow context of an entity. Second, the network can take advantage of other input, such as textual values, which is hard to exploit in traditional rule learning approaches.

For future work, we are considering to use the textual information contained in the knowledge base (labels, descriptions) and in the related Web pages. We also plan to update the user study done in [23] using Bass instead of CorHist. It might also be interesting to investigate how well CorHist and Bass perform when less training data is available, and to compare them with other static approaches for KB repairs.

References

1. Acosta, M., Zaveri, A., Simperl, E., Kontokostas, D., Flöck, F., Lehmann, J.: Detecting linked data quality issues via crowdsourcing: a dbpedia study. Semantic Web **9**(3), 303–335 (2018)
2. Arioua, A., Bonifati, A.: User-guided repairing of inconsistent knowledge bases. In: EDBT (2018)
3. Assadi, A., Milo, T., Novgorodov, S.: Cleaning data with constraints and experts. In: WebDB (2018)

4. Auer, S., Bizer, C., Kobilarov, G., Lehmann, J., Cyganiak, R., Ives, Z.G.: Dbpedia: a nucleus for a web of open data. In: ISWC (2007)
5. Bader, J., Scott, A., Pradel, M., Chandra, S.: Getafix: learning to fix bugs automatically. PACMPL **3**, 1–27 (2019)
6. Bergman, M., Milo, T., Novgorodov, S , Tan, W.: QOCO: a query oriented data cleaning system with oracles. PVLDB **8**(12), 1900–1903 (2015)
7. Bienvenu, M., Bourgaux, C., Goasdoué, F.: Query-driven repairing of inconsistent dl-lite knowledge bases. In: IJCAI (2016)
8. Bollacker, K.D., Evans, C., Paritosh, P., Sturge, T., Taylor, J.: Freebase: a collaboratively created graph database for structuring human knowledge. In: SIGMOD (2008)
9. Chen, J., Chen, X., Horrocks, I., Jiménez-Ruiz, E., Myklebust, E.B.: Correcting knowledge base assertions (2020)
10. Devlin, J., Chang, M., Lee, K., Toutanova, K.: BERT: pre-training of deep bidirectional transformers for language understanding. In: NAACL (2019)
11. Flesca, S., Greco, S., Zumpano, E.: Active integrity constraints. In: PPDP (2004)
12. Galarraga, L., Teflioudi, C., Hose, K., Suchanek, F.M.: Fast rule mining in ontological knowledge bases with AMIE+. VLDB J. **24**(6), 707–730 (2015)
13. Ho, V.T., Stepanova, D., Gad-Elrab, M.H., Kharlamov, E., Weikum, G.: Rule learning from knowledge graphs guided by embedding models. In: ISWC (2018)
14. Hochreiter, S., Schmidhuber, J.: Long short-term memory. Neural Computation **9**(8), 1735–1780 (1997)
15. Hohenecker, P., Lukasiewicz, T.: Ontology reasoning with deep neural networks (2018)
16. Kingma, D.P., Ba, J.: Adam: A method for stochastic optimization. In: ICLR (2015)
17. Lertvittayakumjorn, P., Kertkeidkachorn, N., Ichise, R.: Correcting range violation errors in dbpedia. In: ISWC (2017)
18. Liang, J., Xiao, Y., Zhang, Y., Hwang, S., Wang, H.: Graph-based wrong isa relation detection in a large-scale lexical taxonomy. In: AAAI (2017)
19. Luong, T., Pham, H., Manning, C.D.: Effective approaches to attention-based neural machine translation. In: EMNLP (2015)
20. Melo, A., Paulheim, H.: An approach to correction of erroneous links in knowledge graphs. In: K-CAP2017 (2017)
21. de Melo, G.: Not quite the same: Identity constraints for the web of linked data. In: AAAI (2013)
22. Paulheim, H., Bizer, C.: Improving the quality of linked data using statistical distributions. Int. J. Semantic Web Inf. Syst. **10**(2), 63–86 (2014)
23. Pellissier Tanon, T., Bourgaux, C., Suchanek, F.M.: Learning how to correct a knowledge base from the edit history. In: WWW (2019)
24. Rantsoudis, C., Feuillade, G., Herzig, A.: Repairing aboxes through active integrity constraints. In: DL (2017)
25. Razniewski, S., Suchanek, F.M., Nutt, W.: But what do we actually know?. In: AKBC workshop (2016)
26. Rekatsinas, T., Chu, X., Ilyas, I.F., Ré, C.: Holoclean: holistic data repairs with probabilistic inference. VLDB **10**(11), 1190–1201 (2017)
27. Suchanek, F.M., Kasneci, G., Weikum, G.: Yago: a core of semantic knowledge. In: WWW (2007)
28. Vrandečić, D., Krötzsch, M.: Wikidata: a free collaborative knowledgebase. Commun. ACM **57**(10), 78–85 (2014)

29. Wolf, T., et al.: Huggingface's transformers: State-of-the-art natural language processing (2019)
30. Wu, Z., Pan, S., Chen, F., Long, G., Zhang, C., Yu, P.S.: A comprehensive survey on graph neural networks (2019)

Natural Language Inference over Tables: Enabling Explainable Data Exploration on Data Lakes

Mario Ramirez[1(✉)], Alex Bogatu[1], Norman W. Paton[1], and André Freitas[1,2]

[1] Department of Computer Science, University of Manchester, Manchester, UK
mario.ramirezorihuela@postgrad.manchester.ac.uk,
{alex.bogatu,norman.paton,andre.freitas}@manchester.ac.uk
[2] Idiap Research Institute, Martigny, Switzerland

Abstract. Data lakes are repositories of data with potential for analysis. Data lakes aim to liberate data from silos, thereby enabling cross-cutting analyses that were hitherto out of reach. This gives rise to significant challenges for data scientists simply discovering what data sets may be relevant to a task-in-hand. Given a data set of interest, several proposals have been made for indexing schemes that can identify related data sets. However, such schemes tend to build on similarity metrics that stop short of providing a clear explanation as to how an identified data set relates to a provided target. We address this problem by applying Natural Language Inference (NLI) to providing explanations as to how the attributes of discovered data sets relate to those of the target, in terms of a collection of semantic relations. We provide two approaches to inferring semantic relations: (a) by performing unsupervised intensional and extensional analysis of the data sources using Natural Language Processing techniques; and (b) by performing supervised learning of semantic relations by applying BERT over source schema information. The contributions of this paper are: an NLI strategy for providing explicit characterisation of semantic relations between data sets; two approaches to inferring the semantic relations; and an empirical evaluation of the approaches using open government data.

1 Introduction

The growing availability of potentially valuable datasets is leading organisations to develop centralised, scalable repositories, such as data lakes [21]. On-demand infrastructures allow access to such data for analytics and reporting [9]. This creates a data discovery problem, identifying data sources that are relevant to an information requirement.

Commonly, the data discovery problem is formulated as the computation of a similarity function, which aggregates semantic, morphological and distributional features into a similarity score (e.g., [2,4]). More recently, the evolution of neural language models [8] has lowered the barriers for complex language interpretation and inference. Contemporary architectures (e.g. transformer-based models) [22] have consistently delivered accurate language inference capabilities across different tasks. Additionally, variations of these models have been adapted to operate over structured (e.g., [5,10]) and

© Springer Nature Switzerland AG 2021
R. Verborgh et al. (Eds.): ESWC 2021, LNCS 12731, pp. 304–320, 2021.
https://doi.org/10.1007/978-3-030-77385-4_18

Table 1. Semantic relations in NLI.

Semantic relation	Symbol	Abbreviation	Example
Equivalence	$\equiv$	EQ	$couch \equiv sofa$
Forward Entailment	$\sqsubset$	FWD	$crow \sqsubset bird$
Reverse Entailment	$\sqsupset$	REV	$European \sqsupset French$
Negation	$\wedge$	NEG	$human \wedge nonhuman$
Alternation	$\mid$	ALT	$cat \mid dog$
Cover	$\smile$	COV	$animal \smile nonhuman$
Independence	$\#$	IND	$hungry \# hippo$

semi-structured data [24]. However, these models commonly trade interpretability and semantic control for inferential performance, operating by the same principle of a latent space (a black-box) delivering a similarity score.

Approach: In this paper we aim to make explicit the nature of the relationships between tables using Natural Language Inference (NLI). NLI provides a set of atomic natural language inference computations that deliver a step-wise and transparent semantic inference model [13]. For example, NLI can recognise that the text *Kennedy was chosen* can be inferred from *JFK was elected*. Textual Entailment has been seen as a framework for modelling semantic inference that can be generalised into entailment engines for use in many applications [1]. We adapt the formal model of NLI into a variant for structured data, named Relational Natural Language Inference model (RNLI), in which we extend the NLI paradigm to exploit intensional and extensional features of data sets. Given a collection of sources, RNLI outputs a set of entailment relations between pairs of table attributes to qualitatively determine candidate sources for a given query. The specific semantic entailment relations inferred are listed in Table 1.

Motivating Scenario. Consider a data scientist that needs to build a report of the best universities based on their rankings, fees and potential graduate employability. Additionally, it is of interest to know factual information about safety in the cities where universities are based on. The report would be as table H in Fig. 1. To address this task, the data scientist has access to a large collection of data sets related to the domains of the original requirement. Therefore, one key challenge is to find candidate tables in the data lake that contain properties for the expected output. Based on the sources shown in Fig. 1, the aim of the data discovery task is to determine which attributes of candidate sources S_1, S_2 and S_3 are relevant to the target table H. Specifically, it is of interest of the final user to obtain an explainable output to understand in the form of the semantic relations between source and target attributes.

The contributions of this paper can be summarised as:

1. A proposal of an interpretable semantic entailment framework for tabular datasets (RNLI).
2. An implementation of this model using a rule-based linguistic feature model and a transformer-based architecture.
3. An evaluation of the model for the task of explainable table entailment.

S_1: University Rankings

Name	Location	University Rank	Tuition and Fees
Princeton University	Princeton, NJ	1	$45,320
Cornell University	Ithaca, NY	15	$50,953

S_2: Graduate Employability

S_3: City Safety Statistics

University	State	City	Rank
Harvard University	Massachusetts	Cambridge	1
Columbia University	New York	Now York	14

City	Rank	Safety Index
Memphis, TN	1	24,42
New York, NY	34	56,3

H: University Selection Indicators

University	Ranking	Fees	Employability Rank	City	Safety Index
Harvard University	2	$47,074	1	Princeton	30
Columbia University	5	$55,056	14	Now York	60.4

Fig. 1. Running example: source (S_i) and target (H) tables.

This paper is organised as follows. Related work regarding the data discovery problem is described in Sect. 2. Section 3 formalises and describes the proposed RNLI model and the transformer–based alternative as a mechanism to deliver RNLI. Section 4 provides a qualitative and quantitative empirical analysis using large and diverse real-world data collections from open government data. Finally, conclusions are presented in Sect. 5.

2   Related Work

Data discovery approaches can be characterised on the basis of the evidence that informs the discovery process and the nature of its results. For example, Pham *et al.* [19], Das Sarma *et al.* [7] and Ventis *et al.* [23] rely on external databases, such as WebIsA [20] and Freebase [3], to perform entity annotation in tables. These approaches combine string and entity similarities to relate source and target tables. Alternatively, ontology based approaches address the discovery problem by annotating cells and headers in each of the sources [12]. However, these approaches are limited in scope by their dependence on external knowledge bases.

More recent approaches have fewer external dependencies. For example, Aurum [4] adopts a data-driven approach by using data summarization and hashing to capture relationships between sources, to create what are referred to as enterprise knowledge graphs. An extension, SemProp [5], expands the similarity framework to include semantic similarities based on word embeddings. For the most part, these approaches provide quantitative measures of similarity that are used to rank sources.

D^3L [2] provides evidence–based models, where features are extracted from attribute names and values to capture similarity signals. Consequently, a common space of features is generated, from which distance vectors are used for similarity measurements. Like Aurum, D^3L stops short of providing a clear explanation as to how an identified data set relates to other datasets or to a provided target.

There is, therefore, a lack of explanatory information for the identified relationships between tables/attributes in data discovery, a gap that we seek to bridge using *language inference*. In particular, we pioneer the use of NLI [14] to infer explanatory semantic relations between tables and attributes using NLP-based analysis and transformer–based [22] classification. The former builds on a Relational Natural Language Inference Model that exploits intensional and extensional features to compute similarity relationships in an explainable way.

Our second approach builds on a deep-learning transformer architecture [22], specifically BERT [8]. Bidirectional Encoder Representations from Transformers (BERT) [8] is a universal language model pre-trained on large amounts of textual data with the aim of providing a solid base model that can be further fine-tuned to accommodate different downstream tasks (e.g., we use it for NLI-based semantic tagging) in a supervised manner with relatively little additional training. BERT proposes a technique for representing sentences in a similarity-preserving Euclidean space, where semantically similar constructions are close by. We built on this similarity-preserving property to generate representations for schema-level table information (i.e., table and attribute names) and use them to classify the different types of similarity relationships they find themselves in, in accordance to the RNLI model.

3 Relational Natural Language Inference (RNLI)

In this paper, we show that explaining the similarity relationships existing between different tables/attributes of a data lake can be achieved using unsupervised analysis grounded on intentional (i.e., schema–level) and extensional (i.e., instance–level) evidence. Additionally, we also describe a supervised alternative, construed as a classification problem that assumes the existence of training data. The unsupervised proposal, described in this section, builds on Natural Language Inference and aims to support dataset discovery through the generation of semantic alignments between tables in data lakes by relying on various evidence types, as we now describe.

3.1 Semantic Evidence Types

Let $\mathcal{D}$ be a data lake that consists of a set of source tables $\mathcal{D} = \{S_1, ..., S_n\}$. Each $S_i \in \mathcal{D}$ is composed of a set of attributes $\{a_1, ..., a_m\}$. In identifying attribute pairs that are semantically related, we consider four types of semantic evidence:

$\mathbb{N}$: the table descriptors (e.g., table names) of elements in $\mathcal{D}$, with $\mathbb{N} = \{n_1^S, ... n_n^S\}$ the set of table names.

$\mathbb{A}$: the attribute descriptors (e.g., attribute names) of attributes in $\mathcal{D}$, with $\mathbb{A}_i = \{n_i^1 ... n_i^m\}$ the set of attribute names of source S_i.

$\mathbb{T}$: the attribute data types (e.g., numerical, categorical, etc.) of attributes in $\mathcal{D}$, with $\mathbb{T}_i = \{t_i^1 ... t_i^m\}$ the set of attribute types of source S_i.

$\mathbb{D}$: the value domains of attributes in $\mathcal{D}$, with $\mathbb{D}_i = \{d_i^1 ... d_i^m\}$ the set of value domains of attributes of source S_i. Here, a domain d_i^j, is defined as a collection of representative terms, shared by the extents of attributes pertaining to d_i^j, and identified through value extent analysis using specific domain discovery techniques, such as *D4* [18].

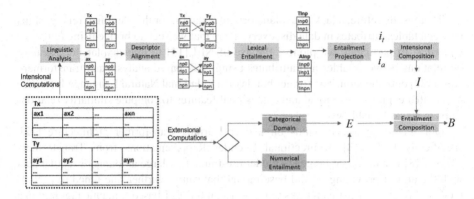

Fig. 2. Relational natural language inference model

As part of our unsupervised NLI–based approach, $\mathbb{N}$ and $\mathbb{A}$ denote *intensional* evidence types, while $\mathbb{T}$ and $\mathbb{D}$ denote *extensional* evidence types. We take a multi–evidence approach and combine both intensional and extensional types of signal to derive similarity features that have the potential of explaining the relationships beyond abstract relatedness.

3.2   Intensional Entailment Computation

This subsection describes how the RNLI model identifies attributes that are semantically related on the basis of intensional information, to determine the conceptual meaning of table and attribute names. We rely on the presence of natural language descriptors as part of table and attribute names and aim to capture these types of signal in the following similarity features:

Full Literal Match: Given a pair of table/attribute names, $(n_i^S, n_j^S)/(n_k^i, n_l^j)$, construed as strings (s_i, s_j), we define $l^f(s_i, s_j)$, the full literal match, as a binary feature (i.e., EQ or IND) between s_i and s_j.

Head Term Literal Match: Given a pair of table/attribute names, $(n_i^S, n_j^S)/(n_k^i, n_l^j)$, construed as strings (s_i, s_j), we define $l^h(s_i, s_j)$, the head term literal match, as a binary feature (i.e., EQ or IND) between s_i's and s_j's head terms. We obtain head terms from noun phrases identified using NLP–specific techniques (e.g., Part of Speech (PoS) tagging).

Head Term Synonymic Match: Given a pair of table/attribute names, $(n_i^S, n_j^S)/(n_k^i, n_l^j)$, construed as strings (s_i, s_j), we define $s^h(s_i, s_j)$, the head term synonymic match, as a binary feature (i.e., EQ or IND) between the Wordnet–specific synsets of s_i's and s_j's head terms.

Head Term Taxonomic Match: Given a pair of table/attribute names, $(n_i^S, n_j^S)/(n_k^i, n_l^j)$, construed as strings (s_i, s_j) in an already determined synonymic equivalence as per s^h, we define $t^h(s_i, s_j)$, the head term taxonomic match, as a multi–valued feature. The value of t^h is determined based on the previously identified head terms and modifiers. Specifically, equality between the two sets of modifiers leads to EQ, containment leads to FWD or REV, partial overlap leads to

COV, and non–overlap leads to ALT because the head terms already match as per s^h.

Given a target table $H \in \mathcal{D}$ (i.e., as in the example from Fig. 1), in order to identify similar attributes to the attributes in H, we perform a pair–wise processing of attributes in H and all the other attributes of tables in $\mathcal{D}$, and extract the above–defined l^f, l^h, s^h, and t^h, for each attribute pair[1]. The process for intensional entailment computation responsible for extracting the above features is depicted in the upper part of Fig. 2 and described next.

Linguistic Analysis. The first step in the process is linguistic analysis of table/attribute names. We parse each table/attribute name to obtain their PoS labels in order to heuristically generate a structured representation. Using PoS tags and Named Entity Recognition (NER) we split each table/attribute name in a sequence of *noun phrases*. We extract the *head terms* of the noun phrases and use them to compute l^h, while l^f is computed using the full table/attribute names. Often, noun phrases contain additional terms called *modifiers* that provide additional information about the concept of the phrase. We use these modifiers next.

Descriptor Alignment. From the collection of noun phrases associated with each table/attribute name we perform phrase alignments to simplify entailment computation. We use the head term of each noun phrase to perform a first conceptual comparison. We use Wordnet to identify synonymic relations between head terms to determine candidate alignments between table/attribute names, i.e., s^h. Additionally, we use the modifiers associated with each head term, when they exist, to discover a taxonomic relation between noun phrases, i.e., t^h. For example when, comparing *Regional University Rank - September* against *University Rank - October* we aim to align the noun phrases (*Regional University Rank, University Rank*) and the modifiers (*September, October*) to determine an entailment relation between noun phrases in terms of their taxonomic representation, as shown in Algorithm 1. In the algorithm, $isSynonymic$ determines the value of s^h based on Wordnet. When $s^h = EQ$, we proceed with a lexical entailment analysis (i.e., GETTAXONOMICREL) described next.

Lexical Entailment. With alignments identified in the previous step we now proceed to determine lexical entailments between noun phrases using GETTAXONOMICREL. First, tokenized table/attribute names are construed as sequences of modifiers plus one head term per name. We perform comparisons between modifier tokens to check for overlapping concepts. We also consider the number of modifier tokens and assume that the more modifiers exist the more specific a concept is being represented. Then, we conclude an entailment relation, i.e., the value of t^h, based on the rules already mentioned in the head term taxonomic match feature definition. For instance, in the previous example, we can see that *Regional University Rank* forward entails *University Rank* and *September* is an alternation of *October*. The composition of these two different relations is described next.

---

[1] In practice, one could drastically reduce the potentially prohibitive space of attribute pairs to process by initially performing general similarity discovery (e.g., using D^3L [2]) and apply RNLI only on the resulted similar pairs.

Algorithm 1. Compute noun phrase entailment

1: *Input:* noun phrases np_x, np_y
2: *Output:* i_{np} entailment relation between noun phrases
3: **function** GETNPRELATION(np_x, np_y)
4:   $h_x \leftarrow x.getHeadToken()$
5:   $h_y \leftarrow y.getHeadToken()$
6: **if** !isSynonymic(h_x, h_y) **then**
7:   $i_{np} \leftarrow independence$
8: **else**
9:
     $i_{np} \leftarrow$ GETTAXONOMICREL(np_x, np_y)
10: **end if**
11: **return** i_{np}
12: **end function**

Algorithm 2. Compute intensional entailment composition

1: *Input:* table, attribute entailments i_t, i_a
2: *Output:* Composite Intensional Entailment I
3: **function**   COMPUTEINTENSIONALVALUE (i_t, i_a)
4: **if** $i_t = IND$ **then**
5:   **if** i_a != IND **then**
6:     $I \leftarrow ALT$
7:   **else**
8:     $I \leftarrow IND$
9:   **end if**
10: **else if** $i_t = FWD$ or $i_t = REV$ **then**
11:   **if** $i_a = EQ$ **then**
12:     $I \leftarrow i_t$
13:   **else**
14:     $I \leftarrow i_a$
15:   **end if**
16: **else**
17:   $I \leftarrow i_a$
18: **end if**
19: **return** I
20: **end function**

Entailment Projection. Given a pair of table/attribute names, the previous steps of our approach can output multiple candidate alignments between associated noun phrases. Consequently, this leads to multiple possible values for t^h. We aggregate such cases according to the rules in Fig. 3. For instance, in the previous example, Algorithm 2 determines that *Regional University Rank - September* is an alternation of *University Rank - October*.

Entailment Composition. The intensional features described at the beginning of this section are extracted separately for each pair of table names and for each pair of attribute names. In considering both table– and attribute–level intensional evidence, we assume that attribute names provide specific information of a concept which requires a contextualisation from the table name. Algorithm 2 is used to compute an intensional entailment by composing table and attribute level entailments. This is a rule-based algorithm in which, based on the table–level and attribute–level intensional entailments, a final intensional entailment is produced.

3.3   Extensional Entailment Computation

We now describe how we extract extensional features from the value extent of each attribute in a given table. We extract three types of extensional similarity features:

Data Type Match: Given a pair of attribute extents, $(\llbracket a_i \rrbracket, \llbracket a_j \rrbracket)$, we define $q^v(\llbracket a_i \rrbracket, \llbracket a_j \rrbracket)$, the data type match, as a binary feature (i.e., EQ or IND) between $(\llbracket a_i \rrbracket$ and $\llbracket a_j \rrbracket)$. We use a simple classification of data types: *categorical* or *numerical*.
Categorical Value Domain Match: Given a pair of attributes (a_i, a_j) with *categorical* value extents, $(\llbracket a_i \rrbracket, \llbracket a_j \rrbracket)$, we define $d^v(\llbracket a_i \rrbracket, \llbracket a_j \rrbracket)$, the categorical value domain

∘	≡	⊏	⊐	^	|	∪	#
≡	≡	⊏	⊐	^	|	∪	#
⊏	⊏	⊏	∪	∪	|	∪	#
⊐	⊐	∪	⊐	∪	|	∪	#
^	^	∪	∪	^	|	∪	#
|	|	|	|	|	|	|	#
∪	∪	∪	∪	∪	|	∪	#
#	#	#	#	#	#	#	#

Fig. 3. Entailment projection rules

match, as a multi–valued feature. The value of d^v is determined based on the value domains of ($[\![a_i]\!]$ and $[\![a_j]\!]$). A domain d_i^j of attribute a_j from a table S_i is a collection of representative tokens shared with $[\![a_j]\!]$). As such, given another domain d_k^i of an attribute a_i from some table S_k, equality between d_i^j and d_k^i leads to EQ, containment leads to FWD or REV, partial overlap leads to COV, and non–overlap (i.e., different domains) leads to IND. In practice however, FWD or REV are not possible because the domain identification process uses $D4$ which aims for a minimal domain identification [18].

Numerical Value Domain Match: Given a pair of attributes (a_i, a_j) with *numerical* value extents, ($[\![a_i]\!]$, $[\![a_j]\!]$), we define $d^k([\![a_i]\!], [\![a_j]\!])$, the numerical value domain match, as a binary feature (i.e., EQ or IND) between ($[\![a_i]\!]$ and $[\![a_j]\!]$). We ground d^k in the Kolmogorov–Smirnov (KS) statistic [6] that allows us to evaluate whether the two corresponding extents, seen as samples, are drawn from the same distribution (i.e., domain).

Given a target table $H \in \mathcal{D}$, similarly to the intensional case, we perform pair-wise processing of attribute extent pairs, as illustrated in the bottom part of Fig. 2 and described next.

Extensional Domain Extraction. In analyzing extensional information, we start from the assumption that in order to produce an entailment relation between two attributes they need to be q^v–equivalent. Once that happens, we use the results of a previous run of $D4$ at data lake–level to obtain the domain of each attribute and to extract d^v for categorical attribute pairs and d^k for numerical attribute pairs. D4 leverages value co-occurrence information across columns in a dataset to output a set of domains discovered by gathering contextual information for terms within columns in a set of tables. Full details of how *D4* achieves domain discovery are available in [18].

Once the extensional features are extracted for a given attribute pair, we employ Algorithm 3 to infer a composite extensional entailment. In the algorithm, we first obtain the domains for each attribute of the input pair (i.e., Lines 4 and 5). Equivalent domains lead to EQ, while attributes with different domains are further processed using GETCONTAINMENTREL, which takes two domains as arguments and applies the rules defined in Table 2 to infer a semantic relation between the given attributes.

Algorithm 3. Compute extensional entailment for categorical attributes

---

1: *Input:* categorical attributes x, y
2: *Output:* e_d entailment relation between categorical attributes
3: **function** GETDOMAINRELATION(x, y)
4:     $d_x \leftarrow x.getDomain()$
5:     $d_y \leftarrow y.getDomain()$
6:     **if** !isSameDomain(d_x, d_y) **then**
7:         $DT_x \leftarrow d_x.getDomainTerms()$
8:         $DT_y \leftarrow d_y.getDomainTerms()$
9:         $e_d \leftarrow$ GETCONTAINMENTREL(DT_x, DT_y)
10: **else**
11:         $e_d \leftarrow equivalence$
12: **end if**
13: **return** e_d
14: **end function**

Table 2. Domain containment relation.

$e_{domain}(a,b)$	Semantic relation
$D_a = D_b$	$\equiv$
$D_a \subset D_b$	$\sqsubset$
$D_a \supset D_b$	$\sqsupset$
$D_a \cap D_b$	$\smile$
$D_a \neq D_b$	$\#$

Finally, for the numerical case, we only consider EQ and IND as the possible values of d^k and heuristically choose between them based on a $d^k_{threshold}$ threshold (i.e., a KS–statistic $> d^k_{threshold}$ results in EQ, and in IND otherwise). $d^k_{threshold}$ is obtained through Eq. 1, a common threshold used with the KS statistic, i.e., the 95% critical value of the KS statistic [6].

$$d^k_{threshold} = 1.36\sqrt{\frac{1}{|[\![a_i]\!]|} + \frac{1}{|[\![a_j]\!]|}} \qquad (1)$$

for a pair of numerical value extents $([\![a_i]\!], [\![a_j]\!])$.

3.4 Entailment Composition

We have described how, given a pair of attributes (a_i, a_j) we extract the NLI–specific value for $[l^f, l^h, s^h, t^h]$ at intensional level, and for $[q^v, d^v, k^v]$ at extensional level. Additionally, we have described how each of the two feature collections is aggregated to a single relation type using Algorithm 2 and Algorithm 3, respectively. We now describe how the two types of relations, *viz.* intensional and extensional, are combined: attributes that are extensionally independent are by default labelled with IND, while extensionally related attributes are labelled by their intensional features. The full set of composition rules is defined in Fig. 4.

Intensional

		≡	⊏	⊐	∧	|	∪	#
Extensional	≡	≡	⊏	⊐	∧	|	∪	#
	⊏	≡	⊏	⊐	∧	|	∪	#
	⊐	≡	⊏	⊐	∧	|	∪	#
	∪	≡	⊏	⊐	∧	|	∪	#
	#	#	#	#	#	#	#	#

Fig. 4. Entailment composition rules

3.5 Transformer-Based RNLI

Given a pair of attributes between which exists a similarity relationship, the RNLI approach described above assigns an explainability dimension to an existing, general–level similarity. Having described how we perform unsupervised NLP–based analysis for similarity explainability, we now discuss a potential alternative for explaining how the attributes of retrieved datasets relate. We construe this explainability task as a fine–tuning BERT step where we rely on a pre–train BERT model to generate similarity-preserving representations for intensional information (i.e., table and attribute names). With these representations in hand, we build a simple downstream classification model that takes as input pairs of attribute intensional representations and labels them with one of the NLI semantic relations from Table 1.

Note that, for this simple alternative approach, we only consider intensional information. This, in turn, requires the assumption that the analyzed data lake presents datasets with semantically–meaningful table and attribute names. We argue that such scenarios are common in practice. For example, most of the datasets available on the public data lake www.data.gov.uk present such table and attribute names. We leave the more complex task of performing transformer–based extensional analysis for future work.

3.6 Intensional Attribute Representations

At its core, BERT is a language representation model capable of generating context–aware embeddings (as opposed to the limited context awareness of Word2Vec [16] models) for words and sentences. Given a name n_i^S of some table S_i (e.g., *University Rankings, Graduate Employability*, etc. from Fig. 1) and an attribute name n_i^j (e.g., *Name, Location*, etc. from Fig. 1), we construe each concatenation $n_i^S || n_i^j$ as a sentence and represent it in an embedding space $\mathbb{R}^d$, offered by the pre–trained BERT model. We, thus, leverage the semantic awareness property of BERT to represent *sentences* and use such representation in a downstream classification task to identify specific semantic similarity types, as we now describe.

3.7 Supervised NLI Labelling

Given a pair of *table name||attribute name* concatenations, for which we already have identified signals of general similarity (e.g., at intensional or extensional levels using

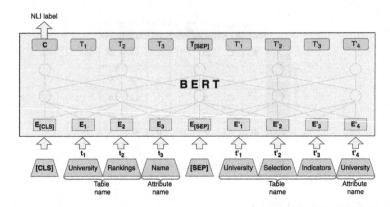

Fig. 5. BERT for NLI labeling. Pre–training is used to generate intensional attribute representations. Fine–tuning is used to label pairs of representations with NLI labels.

approaches such as D^3L [2]), we use the model pictured in Fig. 5 with a fine–tuning BERT task to further explain the type of similarity existing between the two attributes.

Specifically, and with reference to Fig. 1, given the pair (*University Rankings Name, University Selection Indicators University*), corresponding to the first attributes from source S_1 and target H in Fig. 1, respectively, we feed it to a BERT neural network. During training, we also feed the pair's corresponding NLI label (i.e., from Table 1). Using its pre–trained weights, the model firstly generates a semantics–aware attention–based representation for each of the input sentences and optimizes new weights for a classifier whose aim is to label the pair appropriately.

4   Evaluation

We firstly evaluate the quality of our two methods for identifying inter–column entailment. We then compare the results against a similarity discovery technique from the state–of–the–art, $D3L$ [2]. Thirdly, we evaluate the quality of our proposed model when using it to explain the relationship between known similar columns. Finally, we perform an ablation analysis to determine how extensional and intensional features contribute to the explanations.

Evaluation Data: The models are evaluated on ∼600 tables from real–world UK open government data[2], with information from seven domains, such as business, education, salaries, public service, etc. The same dataset in used in [2].

Experimental Setup: To parse and capture linguistic features on dataset elements we used the Stanford Core NLP library [15]. Additionally, we employ Wordnet [17] as an external lexical source to capture semantic features such as synonymic and taxonomic representations of attribute descriptors. For the transformer–based approach, we used a BERT pre–trained model from the Python *transformers* package[3]. During fine–tuning,

---

[2] www.data.gov.uk.

[3] https://pypi.org/project/transformers/.

Table 3. RNLI & BERT results

Class	Precision		Recall		F1-score	
	RNLI	BERT	RNLI	BERT	RNLI	BERT
IND	0.80	1.00	0.99	1.00	0.88	1.00
ALT	0.91	0.81	0.73	1.00	0.81	0.90
EQ	0.83	1.00	0.54	0.63	0.66	0.77
REV	0.56	1.00	0.55	0.88	0.55	0.94
FWD	0.72	1.00	0.87	0.57	0.79	0.73

we trained the model using the Adam optimizer [11] with a linearly–increasing learning rate starting from 10^{-5}, for *10* epochs and with a batch sized of *5*[4]. We trained the model on 70% of the data, validate it (i.e., hyperparameter optimization) on 10% of the data, and tested it on the remaining 20%. All data, source code, baselines and hyperparameter tuning settings are shared[5] for reproducibility purposes.

Baselines and Reported Measures: We evaluate both the composite entailment and the transformer–based models in terms of precision, recall and F1 scores. Using the same measures, we also perform a comparative evaluation between our RNLI proposals and the D^3L similarity framework [2]. For the purpose of computing the evaluation metrics, we use the same ground truth used in [2], where each attribute pair is associated with a binary relatedness representation (i.e., related/unrelated). Out of the approx. *600,000* attribute pairs recorded in the ground truth, we explained *13,000* pairs by labeling each such pair with one of our entailment relationship types from Table 1. Lastly, we use the *600,000* attribute pairs for performing the comparative evaluation against D^3L and the more explicit *13,000* attribute pairs for evaluating the explainability potential of our proposal.

4.1 Inference Performance

Both composite entailment and the transformer–based models are initially evaluated in terms of per–class precision, recall and F1 score. The hypothesis in this experiment is that *our intensional and extensional analysis can indicate not only similar attribute pairs, but also explain the semantic relation type.* Additionally, we hypothesize that, when there is sufficient exemplar data available, *the semantic relation identification can effectively be construed as a BERT fine-tuning task.* We report the per–relationship type results in Table 3.

Overall, the supervised transformer–based approached proves superior to the unsupervised method. However this is conditioned by the existence of labeled training data. In this experiment, approximately 13, 000 attribute pairs had associated NLI labels.

Both RNLI and BERT tend to misclassify related attribute pairs as equivalent. This leads to poorer precision and recall for *EQ*. In the case of *REV* and *FWD* the poor

---

[4] These parameters lead to the best results during validation.

[5] https://bit.ly/3lrb5JD.

Table 4. D3L & RNLI results

Domain	Accuracy		Precision		Recall		F1-score		Δ F1-score
	D3L	RNLI	D3L	RNLI	D3L	RNLI	D3L	RNLI	
Business	0.936	0.952	0.949	0.930	0.855	0.927	0.900	0.929	**0.029**
Schools	0.898	0.933	0.603	0.726	0.660	0.783	0.630	0.753	**0.123**
Elections	0.771	0.779	0.883	0.905	0.216	0.241	0.346	0.380	**0.034**
Flights	0.925	0.937	0.660	0.790	0.224	0.333	0.335	0.469	**0.134**
Food	0.916	0.927	1.000	0.912	0.317	0.454	0.482	0.606	**0.124**
Public Spending	0.764	0.915	0.999	1.000	0.540	0.833	0.701	0.909	**0.208**
Salaries	0.861	0.774	1.000	1.000	0.803	0.678	0.891	0.808	−0.083
Average	0.867	0.888	0.871	0.895	0.516	0.607	0.612	0.694	**0.082**

recall of both RNLI and BERT can be explained by the relatively small number of instances with this label in our test data (i.e., less than 20 in each case). Thus, a single miss can have a significant impact on the recall results.

4.2 Comparative Analysis

In this experiment, we aim to compare the performance of our unsupervised proposal and a similarity–focused baseline, i.e., D^3L [2]. For this purpose we:

1. Transform our multi–class problem to a binary class problem so that the comparison is possible. The mapping that enables this transformation is: $IND \rightarrow dissimilar$; $\{EQ, ALT, REV, FWD\} \rightarrow similar$.
2. Evaluate the two approaches on the entire D^3L ground truth, i.e., *600,000* attribute pairs. Consequently, we do not include the transformer–based approach in this evaluation.
3. Since D^3L is a ranked–retrieval approach, i.e., it retrieves the top–k most similar attributes to a given query attribute, for the purpose of comparison, we randomly pick 20 tables and use their columns as the queries for both the compared approaches. For D^3L, k is set in accordance to the size of each domain existing in the data and present in Table 4. For example, there are approx. 50 tables with *Salary* information and, therefore, for each run of D^3L with a target attribute from the same domain $k = 50$. The purpose of this setting is to avoid penalizing D^3L's recall by setting a fixed, potentially too small, value of k.

Table 4 shows the per–domain (i.e., there are seven different domains in the evaluation dataset) accuracy, precision, recall, and F1–score values, and their average. Overall, it can be concluded that the RNLI approach can be reliably converted to a similarity–focused approach. When this happens, RNLI performs better in most cases. The exception, *Salaries*, is due to a high concentration of numerical attributes that is specially addressed in D^3L.

Table 5. RNLI composite entailment relation performance

Relation	Precision	Recall	F1 score
EQ	0.866	0.742	0.799
REV	0.676	0.556	0.610
FWD	0.545	0.667	0.600
ALT	0.944	0.939	0.942
IND	0.904	1.000	0.950

4.3   Inference Explanations

Previous experiments prove the comparable performance of RNLI to the similarity discovery state–of–the–art. In this experiment, we aim to confirm similar levels of performance, this time with a focus on RNLI's similarity explainability potential. To this end, we consider a scenario in which D^3L is initially employed to efficiently identify similar attributes in a data lake. Then, we employ RNLI as a semantic explainability mechanism to further explain the relationships between the attribute pairs that have been deemed related by D^3L. The results are shown in Table 5.

Overall, RNLI proves reliable in explaining similarity relations grounded on EQ, ALT, and IND. As before, the results are moderate for REV and FWD, mostly due to a relatively small number of instances with these labels in our test data.

4.4   Ablation Study

To have a better understanding of how extensional and intensional features contribute to the final inference, an ablation study is performed in this experiment. To this end, we first isolate intensional features and compute semantic relations. In a second run, we focus exclusively on extensional features to compute the results. Finally we show the results for the combined computation with all feature types considered. Figure 6 shows the obtained results.

Intensional information proves superior to the extensional evidence in identifying NLI relations. In the cases of EQ and IND, this is because, most of the time, the tables and attributes in our test data lake present semantically meaningful names. Reasoning based on these names is more reliable than inferring NLI relations from value domain analysis. In the cases of REV, FWD and ALT, extensional results are close to zero because $D4$ aims for a close to minimal and disjoint domain identification. This means that RNLI will mostly infer EQ or IND when analyzing $D4$ domains. Lastly, in line with our core desideratum in this paper, the combination of intensional and extensional evidence leads to the strongest RNLI results.

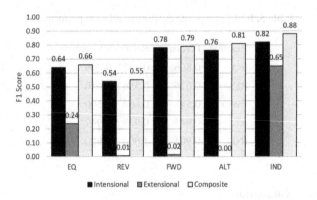

Fig. 6. Ablation study

5 Conclusions

This paper presented the Relational Natural Language Inference Model, a composite entailment framework that models the data lake data discovery problem through natural language inference. We empirically demonstrated an end-to-end process to compute semantic relations at different levels of abstraction by leveraging different sources of signal present in data sources. Additionally, this study was carried out by taking consideration of the explainability of the candidate source relations. Overall, the RNLI model outperforms existing approaches, improving the way inferences are computed and represented in an explainable format. This contributes to a better understanding and semantic control of the inference process. Finally, we see our approach as a mechanism for providing interpretable semantic relations for integration tasks, such as schema matching and entity resolution.

Acknowledgements. Mario Ramirez is supported by the Mexican National Council for Science and Technology (CONACYT). Alex Bogatu is supported by Innovate UK.

References

1. Bar-Haim, R., et al.: The second pascal recognising textual entailment challenge. In: Proceedings of the Second PASCAL Challenges Workshop on Recognising Textual Entailment (2006)
2. Bogatu, A., Fernandes, A.A., Paton, N.W., Konstantinou, N.: Dataset discovery in data lakes. In: 36th IEEE International Conference on Data Engineering (ICDE), pp. 709–720. IEEE (2020)
3. Bollacker, K., Evans, C., Paritosh, P., Sturge, T., Taylor, J.: Freebase: a collaboratively created graph database for structuring human knowledge. In: Proceedings of the 2008 ACM SIGMOD International Conference on Management of Data, pp. 1247–1250 (2008)
4. Castro Fernandez, R., Abedjan, Z., Koko, F., Yuan, G., Madden, S., Stonebraker, M.: Aurum: a data discovery system. In: 34th IEEE International Conference on Data Engineering, ICDE 2018, Paris, France, 16–19 April 2018, pp. 1001–1012 (2018)

5. Castro Fernandez, R., et al.: Seeping semantics: Linking datasets using word embeddings for data discovery. In: 34th IEEE International Conference on Data Engineering, ICDE 2018, Paris, France, 16–19 April 2018, pp. 989–1000 (2018)
6. Conover, W.J.: Practical Nonparametric Statistics. Wiley, New York (1999)
7. Das Sarma, A., et al.: Finding related tables. In: Proceedings of the ACM SIGMOD International Conference on Management of Data, SIGMOD 2012, Scottsdale, AZ, USA, 20–24 May 2012, pp. 817–828 (2012)
8. Devlin, J., Chang, M., Lee, K., Toutanova, K.: BERT: pre-training of deep bidirectional transformers for language understanding. In: Proceedings of the Conference of the North American Chapter of the Association for Computational Linguistics: Human Language Technologies, NAACL-HLT, pp. 4171–4186. ACL (2019). https://doi.org/10.18653/v1/n19-1423
9. Hai, R., Geisler, S., Quix, C.: Constance: an intelligent data lake system. In: Proceedings of the 2016 International Conference on Management of Data, SIGMOD Conference 2016, San Francisco, CA, USA, 26 June– 01 July 2016, pp. 2097–2100 (2016)
10. Hassanzadeh, O., Trewin, S., Gliozzo, A.: Semantic concept discovery over event databases. In: Gangemi, A. (ed.) ESWC 2018. LNCS, vol. 10843, pp. 288–303. Springer, Cham (2018). https://doi.org/10.1007/978-3-319-93417-4_19
11. Kingma, D.P., Ba, J.: Adam: A method for stochastic optimization. In: Bengio, Y., LeCun, Y. (eds.) 3rd International Conference on Learning Representations, ICLR 2015, San Diego, CA, USA, 7–9 May 2015, Conference Track Proceedings (2015)
12. Limaye, G., Sarawagi, S., Chakrabarti, S.: Annotating and searching web tables using entities, types and relationships. PVLDB. **3**, 1338–1347 (2010)
13. MacCartney, B., Galley, M., Manning, C.: A phrase-based alignment model for natural language inference. In: Conference on Empirical Methods in Natural Language Processing, pp. 802–811 (2008)
14. MacCartney, B., Manning, C.: Natural logic for textual inference. In: Workshop on Textual Entailment and Paraphrasing, Association for Computational Linguistics, pp. 193–200 (2007)
15. Manning, C.D., Surdeanu, M., Bauer, J., Finkel, J.R., Bethard, S., McClosky, D.: The stanford corenlp natural language processing toolkit. In: Proceedings of the 52nd Annual Meeting of the Association for Computational Linguistics, ACL 2014, 22–27 June 2014, Baltimore, MD, USA, System Demonstrations, pp. 55–60 (2014)
16. Mikolov, T., Sutskever, I., Chen, K., Corrado, G., Dean, J.: Distributed representations of words and phrases and their compositionality. In: NIPS (2013)
17. Miller, G.A.: WordNet: An Electronic Lexical Database. MIT press, Cambridge (1998)
18. Ota, M., Mueller, H., Freire, J., Srivastava, D.: Data-driven domain discovery for structured datasets. PVLDB **13**(7), 953–965 (2020)
19. Pham, M., Alse, S., Knoblock, C.A., Szekely, P.: Semantic labeling: a domain-independent approach. In: Groth, P. (ed.) ISWC 2016. LNCS, vol. 9981, pp. 446–462. Springer, Cham (2016). https://doi.org/10.1007/978-3-319-46523-4_27
20. Seitner, J., et al.: A large database of hypernymy relations extracted from the web. In: Calzolari, N. (eds.) Proceedings of the Tenth International Conference on Language Resources and Evaluation LREC 2016, Portorož, Slovenia, 23–28 May 2016. European Language Resources Association (ELRA) (2016)
21. Terrizzano, I.G., Schwarz, P.M., Roth, M., Colino, J.E.: Data wrangling: The challenging yourney from the wild to the lake. In: CIDR 2015, Seventh Biennial Conference on Innovative Data Systems Research, Asilomar, CA, USA, 4–7 January 2015, Online Proceedings. www.cidrdb.org (2015)

22. Vaswani, A., et al.: Attention is all you need. In: Advances in Neural Information Processing Systems 30: Annual Conference on Neural Information Processing Systems 2017, 4–9 December 2017, Long Beach, CA, USA, pp. 5998–6008 (2017)
23. Venetis, P., et al.: Recovering semantics of tables on the web. In: PVLDB, pp. 528–538 (2011)
24. Yakout, M., Ganjam, K., Chakrabarti, K., Chaudhuri, S.: Info gather: entity augmentation and attribute discovery by holistic matching with web tables. In: SIGMOD, pp. 97–108 (05 2012)

NLP and Information Retrieval

Grounding Dialogue Systems via Knowledge Graph Aware Decoding with Pre-trained Transformers

Debanjan Chaudhuri[2], Md Rashad Al Hasan Rony[1(✉)], and Jens Lehmann[1,2]

[1] Fraunhofer IAIS, Dresden, Germany
{rashad.rony,jens.lehmann}@iais.fraunhofer.de
[2] Smart Data Analytics Group, University of Bonn, Bonn, Germany
jens.lehmann@cs.uni-bonn.de, s6dechau@uni-bonn.de

Abstract. Generating knowledge grounded responses in both goal and non-goal oriented dialogue systems is an important research challenge. Knowledge Graphs (KG) can be viewed as an abstraction of the real world, which can potentially facilitate a dialogue system to produce knowledge grounded responses. However, integrating KGs into the dialogue generation process in an end-to-end manner is a non-trivial task. This paper proposes a novel architecture for integrating KGs into the response generation process by training a BERT model that learns to answer using the elements of the KG (entities and relations) in a multi-task, end-to-end setting. The k-hop subgraph of the KG is incorporated into the model during training and inference using Graph Laplacian. Empirical evaluation suggests that the model achieves better knowledge groundedness (measured via Entity F1 score) compared to other state-of-the-art models for both goal and non-goal oriented dialogues.

Keywords: Knowledge graph · Dialogue system · Graph encoding · Knowledge integration

1 Introduction

Recently, dialogue systems based on KGs have become increasingly popular because of their wide range of applications from hotel bookings, customer-care to voice assistant services. Such dialogue systems can be realized using both goal and non-goal oriented methods. Whereas the former one is employed for carrying out a particular task, the latter is focused on performing natural ("chit-chat") dialogues. Both types of dialogue system can be implemented using a generative approach. In a generative dialogue system, the response is generated (usually word by word) from the domain vocabulary given a natural language user query, along with the previous dialogue context. Such systems can benefit from the integration of additional world knowledge [12]. In particular, knowledge graphs, which are an abstraction of real world knowledge,

D. Chaudhuri–Equal contribution.

© Springer Nature Switzerland AG 2021
R. Verborgh et al. (Eds.): ESWC 2021, LNCS 12731, pp. 323–339, 2021.
https://doi.org/10.1007/978-3-030-77385-4_19

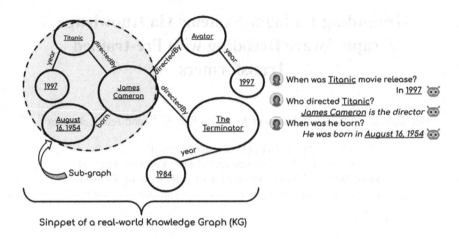

Sinppet of a real-world Knowledge Graph (KG)

Fig. 1. Example of a knowledge grounded conversation.

have been shown to be useful for this purpose. Information of the real world can be stored in a KG in a structured (Resource Description Framework (RDF) triple, e.g., $< subject, relation, object >$) and abstract way (Paris is the capital city of France and be presented in $< Paris, capital city, France >$). KG based question answering (KGQA) is already a well-researched topic [6]. However, generative dialogue systems with integrated KGs have only been explored more recently [7, 12, 20]. To model the response using the KG, all current methods assume that the entity in the input query or a sub-graph of the whole KG, which can be used to generate the answer, is already known [20, 36]. This assumption makes it difficult to scale such systems to real-world scenarios, because the task of extracting sub-graphs or, alternatively, performing entity linking in large knowledge graphs is non-trivial [27]. An example of a knowledge graph based dialogue system is shown in Fig. 1. In order to generate the response *James Cameron is the director*, the system has to link the entity mentioned in the question in the first turn i.e. *Titanic*, and identify the relation in the KG connecting the entities *Titanic* with *James Cameron*, namely *directed by*. Additionally, to obtain a natural dialogue system, it should also reply with coherent responses (e.g. "James Cameron is the director") and should be able to handle small-talk such as greetings, humour etc. Furthermore, in order to perform multi-turn dialogues, the system should also be able to perform co-reference resolution and connect the pronoun (*he*) in the second question with *James Cameron*.

In order to tackle these research challenges, we model the dialogue generation process by jointly learning the entity and relation information during the dialogue generation process using a pre-trained BERT model in an end-to-end manner. The model's response generation is designed to learn to predict relation(s) from the input KG instead of the actual object(s) (intermediate representation). Additionally, a graph Laplacian based method is used to encode the input sub-graph and use it for the final decoding process.

Experimental results suggest that the proposed method improves upon previous state-of-the-art approaches for both goal and non-goal oriented dialogues. Our code is publicly available on Github[1]. Overall, the contributions of this paper are as follows:

- A novel approach, leveraging the knowledge graph elements (entities and relations) in the questions along with pre-trained transformers, which helps in generating suitable knowledge grounded responses.
- We have also additionally encoded the sub-graph structure of the entity of the input query with a Graph Laplacian, which is traditionally used in graph neural networks. This novel decoding method further improves performance.
- An extensive evaluation and ablation study of the proposed model on two datasets requiring grounded KG knowledge: an in-car dialogue dataset and soccer dialogues for goal and non-goal oriented setting, respectively. Evaluation results show that the proposed model produces improved knowledge grounded responses compared to other state-of-the-art dialogue systems w.r.t. automated metrics, and human-evaluation for both goal and non-goal oriented dialogues.

2 Model Description

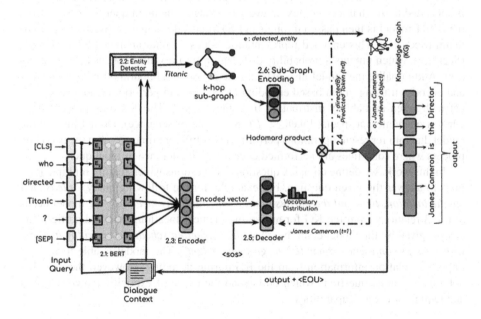

Fig. 2. KGIRNet model diagram.

We aim to solve the problem of answer generation in a dialogue using a KG as defined below.

---

[1] https://github.com/SmartDataAnalytics/kgirnet/.

Definition 1 (Knowledge Graph). *Within the scope of this paper, we define a* knowledge graph *KG as a labelled, undirected multi-graph consisting of a set V of nodes and a set E of edges between them. There exists a function, f_l that maps the nodes and vertices of a graph to a string. The neighborhood of a node of radius k (or k-hop) is the set of nodes at a distance equal to or less than k.*

This definition is sufficiently generic to be applicable to knowledge graphs based on RDF[2] (Resource Description Framework) as well as property graphs [13]. The vertices V of the KG represent entities $e \in V$, while the edges represent the relationships between those entities. A fact is an ordered triple consisting of an entity e (or subject s), an object o and the relation r (a.k.a. predicate p) between them, denoted by (s, p, o).

The proposed model for dialogue generation, which we call KGIRNet, is quintessentially a sequence-to-sequence based model with a pre-trained transformer serving as its input as illustrated in Fig. 2. In contrast to previous works, we introduce an intermediate query representation using the relation information, for training. We also employ a Graph Laplacian based method for encoding the input sub-graph of the KG that aids in predicting the correct relation(s) as well as filter out irrelevant KG elements. Our approach consists of the following steps for which more details are provided below: Firstly, we encode the input query q with a pre-trained BERT model (Sect. 2.1). Next we detect a core entity e occurring in q (Sect. 2.2). Input query q and generated output is appended to the dialogue context in every utterance. The input query, encoded using the BERT model is then passed through an LSTM encoder to get an encoded representation (Sect. 2.3). This encoded representation is passed onto another LSTM decoder (Sect. 2.5), which outputs a probability distribution for the output tokens at every time-step. Additionally, the model also extracts the k-hop neighbourhood of e in the KG and encodes it using graph based encoding (Sect. 2.6) and perform a Hadamard product with token probability distribution from the decoder. The decoding process stops when it encounters a special token, $< EOS >$ (end of sentence). Dotted lines in the model diagram represent operations performed at a different time-step t in the decoding process where solid lines are performed once for each utterance or input query.

In this work, we define complex questions as questions which require multiple relations to answer the given question. For example, for the following query: *"please tell me the location, time and the parties that are attending my meeting"*, the model needs to use 3 relations from the KG for answering, namely location, time and parties. The answer given by the model could be : *"you have meeting scheduled on friday at 10am with boss in conference_room_102 to go_over_budget"*. The model is able to retrieve important relation information from the KG during decoding. However, the model is not able to handle questions which go beyond the usage of explicitly stored relations and require inference capabilities .

2.1 Query Encoding

BERT is a pre-trained multi-layer, bi-directional transformer [32] model proposed in [8]. It is trained on unlabelled data for two-phased objective: masked language model

---

[2] https://www.w3.org/RDF/.

and next sentence prediction. For encoding any text, special tokens [CLS] and [SEP] are inserted at the beginning and the end of the text, respectively. In the case of KGIR-Net, the input query $q = (q_1, q_2, ...q_n)$ at turn t_d in the dialogue, along with the context up to turn $t_d - 1$ is first encoded using this pre-trained BERT model which produces hidden states $(T_1, T_2....T_n)$ for each token and an aggregated hidden state representation C for the [CLS] (first) token. We encode the whole query q along with the context, concatenated with a special token, $< EOU >$ (end of utterance).

2.2   Entity Detection

The aggregated hidden representation from the BERT model C is passed to a fully connected hidden layer to predict the entity $e_{inp} \in V$ in the input question as given by

$$e_{inp} = softmax(w_{ent}C + b_{ent}) \tag{1}$$

where, w_{ent} and b_{ent} are the parameters of the fully connected hidden layer.

2.3   Input Query Encoder

The hidden state representations $(T_1, T_2....T_n)$ of the input query q (and dialogue context) using BERT is further encoded using an LSTM [14] encoder which produces a final hidden state at the n-th time-step given by

$$h_n^e = f_{enc}(T_n, h_{n-1}^e) \tag{2}$$

f_{enc} is a recurrent function and T_n is the hidden state for the input token q_n from BERT. The final representation of the encoder response is a representation at every n denoted by

$$H_e = (h_0^e, h_1^e....h_N^e) \tag{3}$$

2.4   Intermediate Representation

As an intermediate response, we let the model learn the relation or edge label(s) required to answer the question, instead of the actual object label(s). In order to do this, we additionally incorporated the relation labels obtained by applying the label function f_l to all edges in the KG into the output vocabulary set. If the output vocabulary size for a vanilla sequence-to-sequence model is v_o, the total output vocabulary size becomes v_{od} which is the sum of v_o and v_{kg}. The latter being the labels from applying the f_l to all edges (or relations) in the KG.

For example, if in a certain response, a token corresponds to an object label o_l (obtained by applying f_l to o) in the fact (e, r, o), the token is replaced with a KG token v_{kg} corresponding to the edge or relation label r_l of $r \in E$ in the KG. During training, the decoder would see the string obtained by applying f_l to the edge between the entities *Titanic* and *James Cameron*, denoted here as *r:directedBy*. Hence, it will try to learn the relation instead of the actual object. This makes the system more generic and KG aware, and easily scalable to new facts and domains.

During evaluation, when the decoder generates a token from v_{kg}, a KG lookup is done to decode the label o_l of the node $o \in V$ in the KG (V being the set of nodes or vertices in the KG). This is generally done using a SPARQL query.

2.5 Decoding Process

The decoding process generates an output token at every time-step t in the response generation process. It gets as input the encoded response H_e and also the KG distribution from the graph encoding process as explained later. The decoder is also a LSTM, which is initialized with the encoder last hidden states and the first token used as input to it is a special token, $< SOS >$ (start of sentence). The decoder hidden states are similar to that of the encoder as given by the recurrent function f_{dec}

$$h_n^d = f_{dec}(w_{dec}, h_{n-1}^d) \tag{4}$$

This hidden state is used to compute an attention over all the hidden states of the encoder following [19], as given by

$$\alpha_t = softmax(W_s(tanh(W_c[H_e; h_t^d]))) \tag{5}$$

where, W_c and W_s are the weights of the attention model. The final weighted context representation is given by

$$\tilde{h}_t = \sum_t \alpha_t h_t \tag{6}$$

This representation is concatenated (represented by ;) with the hidden states of the decoder to generate an output from the vocabulary with size v_{od}.

The output vocab distribution from the decoder is given by

$$O_{dec} = W_o([h_t; \tilde{h}_t^d]) \tag{7}$$

In the above equation, W_o are the output weights with dimension $\mathbf{R}^{h_{dim} X v_{od}}$. h_{dim} being the dimension of the hidden layer of the decoder LSTM. The total loss is the sum of the vocabulary loss and the entity detection loss. Finally, we use beam-search [31] during the decoding method.

2.6 Sub-Graph Encoding

In order to limit the KGIRNet model to predict only from those relations which are connected to the input entity predicted from step 2.2, we encode the sub-graph along with its labels and use it in the final decoding process while evaluating.

The k-hop sub-graph of the input entity is encoded using Graph Laplacian [16] given by

$$G_{enc} = D^{-1}\tilde{A}f_{in} \tag{8}$$

Where, $\tilde{A} = A + I$. A being the adjacency matrix, I is the identity matrix and D is the degree matrix. f_{in} is a feature representation of the vertices and edges in the input graph. G_{enc} is a vector with dimensions $\mathbf{R}^{ik}$ corresponding to the total number of nodes and edges in the k-hop sub-graph of e. An example of the sub-graph encoding mechanism is shown in Fig. 3.

The final vocabulary distribution $O_f \in R^{v_{od}}$ is a Hadamard product of this graph vector and the vocabulary distribution output from the decoder.

$$O_f = O_{dec} \odot G_{enc} \tag{9}$$

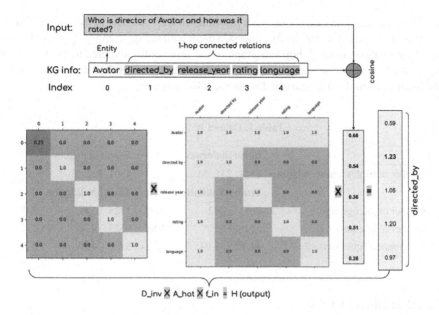

Fig. 3. Sub-graph encoding using graph laplacian.

This step essentially helps the model to give additional importance to the relations connected at k-hop based on its similarity with the query also to filter(mask) out relations from the response which are not connected to it. For the query in 3 *who is the director of Avatar and how was it rated* ? The graph laplacian based encoding method using only relation labels already gives higher scores for the relations directed_by and rating, which are required by the question. This vector when multiplied with the final output vocabulary helps in better relation learning.

3 Experimental Setup

3.1 Datasets

Available datasets for knowledge grounded conversations are the *in-car dialogue* data as proposed by [12] and *soccer dialogues* over football club and national teams using a knowledge graph [7]. The former contains dialogues for assisting the driver of a car with data related to weather, schedules and navigation, in a goal-oriented setting. The soccer dataset contains non-goal oriented dialogues about questions on different soccer teams along with a knowledge graph consisting of facts extracted from Wikipedia about the respective clubs and national soccer teams. Both the datasets were collected using Amazon Mechanical Turk (AMT) by the respective authors [7,12]. The statistics of the datasets are provided in Table 1. As observed, the number of dialogues for both the dataset is low.

To perform a KG grounded dialogue as in KG based question-answering [10], it is important to annotate the dialogues with KG information such as the entities and relations, the dialogues are about. Such information were missing in the soccer dataset, hence we have semi-automatically annotated them with the input entity e_{inp} in the query q and the relations in the k-hop sub-graph of the input entity required to answer q. For the domain of in-car it was possible to automatically extract the entity and relation information from the dialogues and input local KG snippets.

Table 1. Dataset statistics.

	In-car dialogues			Soccer dialogues		
Number of triples, entity, relations	8561, 271, 36			4301, 932, 30		
	Train	**Validation**	**Test**	**Train**	**Validation**	**Test**
Number of dialogues	2011	242	256	1328	149	348
Number of utterances	5528	657	709	6523	737	1727
KG-grounded questions (%)	44.95	33.94	43.84	6.53	4.61	3.88

3.2 Evaluation Metrics

We evaluate the models using the standard evaluation metrics BLEU [25] and Entity F1 scores as used in the discussed state-of-the-art models. However, unlike [20] we use Entity F1 scores based on the nodes V of the KG, as inspired by previous works on KG based question answering [3]. Additionally, we use METEOR [1] because it correlates the most with human judgement scores [30].

3.3 Model Settings

Table 2. Evaluation on goal and non-goal oriented dialogues.

Models	In-car dialogues			Soccer dialogues			Inference time
	BLEU	*Entity F1*	*METEOR*	*BLEU*	*Entity F1*	*METEOR*	*Utterances/sec*
Seq2Seq	4.96	10.70	21.20	1.37	0.0	7.8	133
Mem2Seq [20]	9.43	24.60	28.80	0.82	04.95	7.8	88
GLMP [36]	9.15	21.28	29.10	0.43	22.40	7.7	136
Transformer [32]	8.27	24.79	29.06	0.45	0.0	6.7	7
DialoGPT [39]	7.35	21.36	20.50	0.76	0.0	5.5	2
KG-Copy [7]	–	–	–	1.93	03.17	**10.89**	262
KGIRNet	**11.76**	**32.67**	**30.02**	1.51	**34.33**	8.24	37

For entity detection we used a fully connected layer on top of CNN-based architecture. Size of the hidden layer in the fully connected part is 500 and a dropout value of 0.1 is used and ReLU as the activation function. In the CNN part we have used 300 filters with kernel size 3, 4 and 5. We use BERT-base-uncased model for encoding the input query. The encoder and decoder is modelled using an LSTM (long short term memory) with a hidden size of 256 and the KGIRNet model is trained with a batch size of 20. The learning rate of the used encoder is 1e−4. For the decoder we select a learning rate of 1e−3. We use the Adam optimizer to optimize the weights of the neural networks. For all of our experiments we use a sub-graph size of k = 2. For calculating f_{in} as in Eq. 8, we use averaged word embedding similarity values between the query and the labels of the sub-graph elements. The similarity function used in this case is cosine similarity. We save the model with best validation Entity f1 score.

Table 3. Relation linking accuracy on SQB [37] dataset.

Method	Model	Accuracy
Supervised	Bi-LSTM [21]	38.5
	HR-LSTM [38]	64.3
Unsupervised	Embedding Similarity	60.1
	Graph Laplacian (this work)	**69.7**

4 Results

In this section, we summarize the results from our experiments. We evaluate our proposed model KGIRNet against the current state-of-the-art systems for KG based dialogues; namely Mem2Seq [20], GLMP [36], and KG-Copy [7][3]. To include a baseline method, the results from a vanilla Seq2Seq model using an LSTM encoder-decoder are also reported in Table 2, along with a vanilla transformer [32] and a pre-trained GPT-2 model, DialoGPT [39] fine-tuned individually on both the datasets.

We observe that KGIRNet outperforms other approaches for both goal (in-car) and non-goal oriented (soccer) dialogues except for BLEU and METEOR scores on the soccer dataset. The effect of knowledge groundedness is particularly visible in the case of soccer dialogues, where most models (except GLMP) produces feeble knowledge grounded responses. The Entity F1 score used here is adapted from [3] and is defined as the average of F1-scores of the set of predicted objects, for all the questions in the test set.

In addition to evaluating dialogues, we also evaluate the proposed graph laplacian based relation learning module for the task of knowldge-graph based relation linking. Although, it is a well-researched topic and some systems claim to have solved the problem [26], but such systems are not able to handle relations which are not present in the training data [37]. The latter also proposed a new, balanced dataset (SQB) for simple question answering which has same proportions of seen and unseen relations in the test or evaluation set. We have evaluated our unsupervised graph laplacian based method for relation linking on the SQB dataset against supervised methods namely Bi-LSTM [21], hr-bilstm [38] and unsupervised method such as text embedding based similarity between the query and the relations connected to the subject entity with 1-hop.

---

[3] KG-Copy reports on a subset of the in-car testset hence it is not reported here.

The results are reported in Table 3. As observed, Graph Laplacian performs better wrt. supervised methods on unseen relations and also better than shallow embedding based similarity. This is one of the motivation for using this simple method during KGIRNet's decoding process. We run all the inference on a setup with 32 GB of RAM and 8 GB of VGA and a Bandwidth of 256.3 GB/s.

5   Discussion

For in-car dialogues, we train and evaluate on queries which require knowledge from the KG, hence we omit the scheduling conversations where the driver asks the car to schedule a meeting/conference. In order to get the knowledge graph candidate triples for all the other models (Mem2Seq and GLMP), we provide them with the 2-hop sub-graph of the correct input entity instead of the local knowledge as used in the respective models; this, represents a scenario closer to a real-world KG grounded conversation. For the in-car dataset, the human baseline BLEU score as reported in [12] is 13.5 (the KGIRNet score is 11.76). The BLEU scores for soccer are low because non-goal oriented dialogues are more complicated to model due to large vocabulary sizes (more than 3 times the vocabulary size of the of in-car dataset). Also in the case of soccer dialogues, number of factual conversation is low (4%) compared to the total number of utterances and also the conversations are more generic and repetitive in nature.

Table 4. Analyzing sample predictions.

Input query	True response	Predicted responses		
		GLMP	Mem2Seq	KGIRNet
(S) who is currently coaching bvb dortmund	lucien favre	*the is the coach*	*yes , they have a good*	*lucien favre is the coach of bvb dortmund*
(S) when did italy last win the world cup	2006	*italy won the world cup in 2006*	*i think they have a good team*	*italy won the world cup in 2006*
(C) what time is my doctorappointment?	your doctorappointment is scheduled for friday at 11am	*your next is at 1pm at 7pm*	*your doctorappointment is at 1pm*	*your doctorappointment is on friday at 11am*
(C) i need gas	Valero is 4_miles away	*there is a valero away*	*chevron is gas_station away chevron is at away*	*there is a valero nearby*

5.1   Human Evaluation

We perform a human-based evaluation on the whole test dataset of the generated responses from the KGIRNet model and its closest competitors, i.e. Mem2Seq, GLMP and DialoGPT models. We asked 3 internal independent annotators who are not the authors of this paper (1 from CS and 2 from non-CS background) to rate the quality of the generated responses between 1–5 with respect to the dialogue context (higher is better). Note that for each dataset, we provide the annotators with 4 output files in CSV format (containing the predictions of each model) and the knowledge graph in RDF format. Each of the CSV files contains data in 5 columns: question, original response, predicted response, grammatical correctness, similarity between original and predicted response. In the provided files, the 4th (grammatically correctness) and 5th (similarity between original and predicted response) columns are empty and we ask the annotators to fill them with values (within a range of 1–5) according to their judgement. The measures requested to evaluate upon are correctness (Corr.) and human-like (human) answer generation capabilities. Correctness is measured by comparing the response to the correct answer object. Reference responses are provided besides the system generated response in order to check the factual questions. The results are reported in Table 5a. Cohen's Kappa of the annotations is 0.55.

5.2 Ablation Study

As an ablation study we train a sequence-to-sequence model with pre-trained fasttext embeddings as input (S2S), and the same model with pre-trained BERT as input embedding (S2S_BERT). Both these models do not have any information about the structure of the underlying knowledge graph. Secondly, we try to understand how much the intermediate representation aids to the model, so we train a model (KGIRNet_NB) with fasttext embeddings as input instead of BERT along with intermediate relation representation. Thirdly, we train a model with pre-trained BERT but without the haddamard product of the encoded sub-graph and the final output vocabulary distribution from Step 2.6. This model is denoted as KGIRNet_NS. As observed, models that are devoid of any KG structure has very low Entity F1 scores, which is more observable in the case of soccer dialogues since the knowledge grounded queries are very low, so the model is not able to learn any fact(s) from the dataset. The proposed intermediate relation learning along with Graph Laplacian based sub-graph encoding technique observably assists in producing better knowledge grounded responses in both the domains; although, the latter aids in more knowledge groundedness in the domain of soccer dialogues (higher Entity F1 scores). We also did an ablation study on the entity detection accuracy of the end-to-end KGIRNet model in the domain of in-car and compared it with a standalone

Table 5. In-depth evaluation of KGIRNet model.

Models	In-Car		Soccer	
	Corr.	Human	Corr.	Human
Mem2Seq	3.09	3.70	1.14	3.48
GLMP	3.01	3.88	1.10	2.17
DialoGPT	2.32	3.43	1.32	3.88
KGIRNet	3.60	4.42	1.59	3.78

(a) Human evaluation.

Models	In-Car Dialogues		Soccer Dialogues	
	BLEU	EntityF1	BLEU	EntityF1
S2S	4.96	10.70	1.49	0.0
S2S_BERT	7.53	09.10	1.44	0.0
KGIRNet_NB	9.52	29.03	0.91	29.85
KGIRNet_NS	11.40	33.03	1.05	28.35
KGIRNet	11.76	32.67	1.51	34.32

(b) Ablation study.

Convolutional neural network (CNN) model which predicts the entity from the input query, the accuracies are 79.69% and 77.29% respectively.

5.3   Qualitative Analysis

The responses generated by KGIRNet are analyzed in this section. Responses from some of the discussed models along with the input query are provided in Table 4[4]. We compare the results with two other state-of-the-art models with the closest evaluation scores, namely Mem2Seq and GLMP. The first two responses are for soccer dialogues, while the latter two are for in-car setting. We inspect that qualitatively the proposed KGIRNet model produces better knowledge grounded and coherent responses in both the settings. In the case of soccer dialogues, predicting single relation in the response is sufficient, while for the case of in-car dialogues, responses can require multiple relation identification. KGIRNet model is able to handle such multiple relations as well (e.g., r:date friday and r:time 11 am for the third utterance).

Table 6. Analyzing fact-fullness of KGIRNet.

Input query	True response	Predicted response	Intermediate response
Who is senegal captain?	Cheikhou kouyate	*Sadio mane is the captain of senegal*	*r:captain is the captain of @entity*
Who is the goalie for iceland	Hannes halldorsson	*Runar alex runarsson*	*r :goalkeeper*

To understand more about the advantages of KG grounded generation process, consider the examples from the soccer dataset below in Table 6, in which the model has failed. We have also included the intermediate responses that are generated from the decoder before the KG lookup phase for the reference. In the first case, while constructing the KG, the captain was *Sadio Mane*, whereas the during the dialogue collection phase the probable captain was *Checikhou Kouyate* (as per the annotator). These errors on temporal information can easily be tackled using Knowledge Grounded dialogue systems, where the system can potentially reflect current information with updated real world knowledge. For the second case, the current main goalkeeper for the Iceland national football team is *Hannes Halldórsson*; however, *Rúnar Alex Rúnarsson* is also among the 3 goalkeepers for the team and the model has no additional information to disambiguate between them to produce the same response as the human annotator. KGIRNet is also able to infer conversational context implicitly in dialogues with the system (Table 7).

---

[4] In the table **(S)** and **(C)** refers to example from Soccer and In-car dataset respectively.

Table 7. A conversation with KGIRNet.

User:	what s the weather forecast for today and tomorrow ?
KGIRNet:	what city do you want the weather for
User:	los angeles
KGIRNet:	it will be 40f - 60f on monday warm on tuesday windy on wednesday hot on thursday
User:	thanks
KGIRNet:	you are welcome

5.4   Error Analysis

To analyze more on the shortcomings of our proposed KGIRNet, we stated some sample erroneous responses from the model in Table 8. The first three are from soccer and the rest in-car dialogues. The model often produces generic responses for soccer as in the first example. Our model is only able to handle simple factoid queries and not able to answer queries requiring comparative reasoning such as *best player, youngest player* etc., as observable from the second and third cases. In the second case, the model answers with the coach's name and when asked for the best player for Argentina and it replies with the name of an Uruguayan player in the third case. The model also produces generic relations like coach name, number of world cup championship as response when any such keyword is present in the input. For the in-car dataset, the replies are less generic and more coherent; however, in cases like the fourth example, the model is not able to perform logical reasoning (negation). Moreover, the model fails in cases where the input entity is not recognized correctly as in case of the last example. Although, the name of the friend is fetched from the vocabulary, but the predicted entity is wrong hence the model is not able to decode the relation r:address from the KG during decoding.

Table 8. Error analysis of KGIRNet.

Input query	True response	Predicted response
Portugal win the last eurocup?	Yes they won the last europcup	*Portugal has won the world cup*
Who is switzerlandś best player?	Xherdan shaqiri	*Petkovic is the coach of switzerland*
Who is considered their best player?	Traditionally their top scorers	*Luis suarez is the best player in argentina*
will it be warm in grand_rapids on saturday	It will not be warm in grand_rapids on saturday	*It is not predicted to fall on tuesday in grand_rapids*
Where does my friend live?	Tom lives at 580_van_ness_ave	*Tom s house is located at r:address*

In general, the model's entity detection fails in case of conversations with long dialogue contexts. Incorporating KG information into the entity detection process, where we consider the sub-graph of the entity in the first interaction can potentially help in further performance improvements.

6   Related Work

Leveraging background information for dialogue system improvement is a well-researched topic, especially in goal-oriented setting [2,9,35]. [12] proposed the in-car dataset which uses a knowledge base for in-car conversation about weather, location etc. Recently, [20] proposed memory-network based encoder-decoder architecture for integrating knowledge into the dialogue generation process on this dataset. Improved models in this task are proposed by [15,36]. [7] proposed a soccer dialogue dataset along with a KG-Copy mechanism for non-goal oriented dialogues which are KG-integrated. In a slightly similar research line, in past years, we also notice the use of variational autoencoders (VAE) [17,40] and generative adversarial networks (GANs) [18,23] in dialogue generation. However, knowledge graph based dialogue generation is not well-explored in these approaches.

More recently, transformer-based [32] pre-trained models have achieved success in solving various downstream tasks in the field of NLP such as question answering [29] [8], machine translation [34], summarization [11]. Following the trend, a hierarchical transformer is proposed by [28] for task-specific dialogues. The authors experimented on MultiWOZ dataset [5], where the belief states are not available. However, they found the use of hierarchy based transformer models effective in capturing the context and dependencies in task-specific dialogue settings. In a different work, [24] experimented transformer-based model on both the task-specific and non-task specific dialogues in multi-turn setting. In a recent work, [39] investigated on transformer-based model for non-goal oriented dialogue generation in single-turn dialogue setting. Observing the success of transformer-based models over the recurrent models in this paper we also employ BERT in the dialogue generation process which improves the quality of generated dialogues (discussed in Sect. 4 and 5).

In past years, there is a lot of focus on encoding graph structure using neural networks, a.k.a. Graph Neural Networks (GNNs) [4,33]. In the field of computer vision, Convolutional Neural Networks (CNNs) are used to extract the most meaningful information from grid-like data structures such as images. A generalization of CNN to graph domain, Graph Convolutional Networks (GCNs) [16] has become popular in the past years. Such architectures are also adapted for encoding and extracting information from knowledge graphs [22]. Following a similar research line, in this paper, we leverage the concept of Graph Laplacian [16] for encoding sub-graph information into the learning mechanism.

7   Conclusion and Future Work

In this paper, we have studied the task of generating knowledge grounded dialogues. We bridged the gap between two well-researched topics, namely knowledge grounded question answering and end-to-end dialogue generation. We propose a novel decoding method which leverages pre-trained transformers, KG structure and Graph Laplacian based encoding during the response generation process. Our evaluation shows that out proposed model produces better knowledge grounded response compared to other state-of-the-art approaches, for both the task and non-task oriented dialogues.

As future work, we would like to focus on models with better understanding of text in order to perform better KG based reasoning. We also aim to incorporate additional KG structure information in the entity detection method. Further, a better handling of infrequent relations seen during training may be beneficial.

Acknowledgement. We acknowledge the support of the excellence clusters ScaDS.AI (BmBF IS18026A-F), ML2R (BmBF FKZ 01 15 18038 A/B/C), TAILOR (EU GA 952215) and the projects SPEAKER (BMWi FKZ 01MK20011A) and JOSEPH (Fraunhofer Zukunftsstiftung).

References

1. Banerjee, S., Lavie, A.: Meteor: An automatic metric for MT evaluation with improved correlation with human judgments. In: Proceedings of the acl Workshop on Intrinsic and Extrinsic Evaluation Measures for Machine Translation and/or Summarization, pp. 65–72 (2005)
2. Bordes, A., Boureau, Y.L., Weston, J.: Learning end-to-end goal-oriented dialog. arXiv preprint arXiv:1605.07683 (2016)
3. Bordes, A., Usunier, N., Chopra, S., Weston, J.: Large-scale simple question answering with memory networks. ArXiv abs/1506.02075 (2015)
4. Bronstein, M.M., Bruna, J., LeCun, Y., Szlam, A., Vandergheynst, P.: Geometric deep learning: going beyond euclidean data. IEEE Signal Process. Mag. **34**(4), 18–42 (2017)
5. Budzianowski, P., et al.: Multiwoz-a large-scale multi-domain wizard-of-oz dataset for task-oriented dialogue modelling. arXiv preprint arXiv:1810.00278 (2018)
6. Chakraborty, N., Lukovnikov, D., Maheshwari, G., Trivedi, P., Lehmann, J., Fischer, A.: Introduction to neural network based approaches for question answering over knowledge graphs (2019)
7. Chaudhuri, D., Rony, M.R.A.H., Jordan, S., Lehmann, J.: Using a KG-copy network for non-goal oriented dialogues. In: Ghidini, C. (ed.) ISWC 2019. LNCS, vol. 11778, pp. 93–109. Springer, Cham (2019). https://doi.org/10.1007/978-3-030-30793-6_6
8. Devlin, J., Chang, M.W., Lee, K., Toutanova, K.: Bert: Pre-training of deep bidirectional transformers for language understanding. In: NAACL-HLT, (1) (2019)
9. Dhingra, B., et al.: Towards end-to-end reinforcement learning of dialogue agents for information access (2016)
10. Diefenbach, D., Lopez, V., Singh, K., Maret, P.: Core techniques of question answering systems over knowledge bases: a survey. Knowl. Inf. Syst. **55**(3), 529–569 (2018)
11. Egonmwan, E., Chali, Y.: Transformer-based model for single documents neural summarization. In: Proceedings of the 3rd Workshop on Neural Generation and Translation, pp. 70–79 (2019)
12. Eric, M., Krishnan, L., Charette, F., Manning, C.D.: Key-value retrieval networks for task-oriented dialogue. In: Proceedings of the 18th Annual SIGdial Meeting on Discourse and Dialogue (August 2017)
13. Gubichev, A., Then, M.: Graph pattern matching: Do we have to reinvent the wheel? In: Proceedings of Workshop on Graph Data, ACM (2014)
14. Hochreiter, S., Schmidhuber, J.: Long short-term memory. Neural Comput. **9**(8), 1735–1780 (1997)

15. Kassawat, F., Chaudhuri, D., Lehmann, J.: Incorporating joint embeddings into goal-oriented dialogues with multi-task learning. In: Hitzler, P. (ed.) ESWC 2019. LNCS, vol. 11503, pp. 225–239. Springer, Cham (2019). https://doi.org/10.1007/978-3-030-21348-0_15

16. Kipf, T.N., Welling, M.: Semi-supervised classification with graph convolutional networks. arXiv preprint arXiv:1609.02907 (2016)

17. Li, R., Li, X., Chen, G., Lin, C.: Improving variational autoencoder for text modelling with timestep-wise regularisation. In: Proceedings of the 28th International Conference on Computational Linguistics (December 2020)

18. López Zorrilla, A., De Velasco Vázquez, M., Torres Barañano, M.I.: A differentiable generative adversarial network for open domain dialogue (2019)

19. Luong, M.T., Pham, H., Manning, C.D.: Effective approaches to attention-based neural machine translation. arXiv preprint arXiv:1508.04025 (2015)

20. Madotto, A., Wu, C.S., Fung, P.: Mem2Seq: Effectively incorporating knowledge bases into end-to-end task-oriented dialog systems. In: Proceedings of the 56th Annual Meeting of the Association for Computational Linguistics, vol. 1, Long Papers (July 2018)

21. Mohammed, S., Shi, P., Lin, J.: Strong baselines for simple question answering over knowledge graphs with and without neural networks. In: Proceedings of the 2018 Conference of the North American Chapter of the Association for Computational Linguistics: Human Language Technologies, vol. 2, Short Papers (June 2018)

22. Neil, D., Briody, J., Lacoste, A., Sim, A., Creed, P., Saffari, A.: Interpretable graph convolutional neural networks for inference on noisy knowledge graphs (2018)

23. Olabiyi, O., Salimov, A.O., Khazane, A., Mueller, E.: Multi-turn dialogue response generation in an adversarial learning framework. In: Proceedings of the First Workshop on NLP for Conversational AI (August 2019)

24. Oluwatobi, O., Mueller, E.: Dlgnet: a transformer-based model for dialogue response generation. In: Proceedings of the 2nd Workshop on Natural Language Processing for Conversational AI, pp. 54–62 (2020)

25. Papineni, K., Roukos, S., Ward, T., Zhu, W.J.: Bleu: a method for automatic evaluation of machine translation. In: Proceedings of the 40th Annual Meeting on Association for Computational Linguistics, pp. 311–318. Association for Computational Linguistics (2002)

26. Petrochuk, M., Zettlemoyer, L.: SimpleQuestions nearly solved: a new upper bound and baseline approach. In: Proceedings of the 2018 Conference on Empirical Methods in Natural Language Processing (October–November 2018)

27. Rosales-Méndez, H., Poblete, B., Hogan, A.: What should entity linking link? In: AMW (2018)

28. Santra, B., Anusha, P., Goyal, P.: Hierarchical transformer for task oriented dialog systems. arXiv preprint arXiv:2011.08067 (2020)

29. Shao, T., Guo, Y., Chen, H., Hao, Z.: Transformer-based neural network for answer selection in question answering. IEEE Access 7, 26146–26156 (2019)

30. Sharma, S., El Asri, L., Schulz, H., Zumer, J.: Relevance of unsupervised metrics in task-oriented dialogue for evaluating natural language generation. arXiv preprint arXiv:1706.09799 (2017)

31. Tillmann, C., Ney, H.: Word reordering and a dynamic programming beam search algorithm for statistical machine translation. Comput. Linguist. 29(1), 97–133 (2003)

32. Vaswani, A., et al.: Attention is all you need. In: Advances in Neural Information Processing Systems, pp. 5998–6008 (2017)

33. Veličković, P., Cucurull, G., Casanova, A., Romero, A., Lio, P., Bengio, Y.: Graph attention networks. arXiv preprint arXiv:1710.10903 (2017)

34. Wang, Q., et al.: Learning deep transformer models for machine translation. arXiv preprint arXiv:1906.01787 (2019)

35. Wen, T.H., et al.: A network-based end-to-end trainable task-oriented dialogue system. arXiv preprint arXiv:1604.04562 (2016)

36. Wu, C.S., Socher, R., Xiong, C.: Global-to-local memory pointer networks for task-oriented dialogue. arXiv preprint arXiv:1901.04713 (2019)

37. Wu, P., et al.: Learning representation mapping for relation detection in knowledge base question answering. In: Proceedings of the 57th Annual Meeting of the Association for Computational Linguistics (July 2019)

38. Yu, M., Yin, W., Hasan, K.S., dos Santos, C., Xiang, B., Zhou, B.: Improved neural relation detection for knowledge base question answering. In: Proceedings of the 55th Annual Meeting of the Association for Computational Linguistics, vol. 1, Long Papers (July 2017)

39. Zhang, Y., et al.: Dialogpt: Large-scale generative pre-training for conversational response generation (2019)

40. Zhao, T., Zhao, R., Eskenazi, M.: Learning discourse-level diversity for neural dialog models using conditional variational autoencoders. In: Proceedings of the 55th Annual Meeting of the Association for Computational Linguistics, vol. 1, Long Papers (July 2017)

WEB-SOBA: Word Embeddings-Based Semi-automatic Ontology Building for Aspect-Based Sentiment Classification

Fenna ten Haaf, Christopher Claassen, Ruben Eschauzier, Joanne Tjan, Daniël Buijs, Flavius Frasincar$^{(\boxtimes)}$ ⓘ, and Kim Schouten

Erasmus University Rotterdam, PO Box 1738, 3000 DR Rotterdam, The Netherlands
{450812fh,456177cc,480900re,413647jt,483065db}@student.eur.nl,
{frasincar,schouten}@ese.eur.nl

Abstract. For aspect-based sentiment analysis (ABSA), hybrid models combining ontology reasoning and machine learning approaches have achieved state-of-the-art results. In this paper, we introduce WEB-SOBA: a methodology to build a domain sentiment ontology in a semi-automatic manner from a domain-specific corpus using word embeddings. We evaluate the performance of a resulting ontology with a state-of-the-art hybrid ABSA framework, HAABSA, on the SemEval-2016 restaurant dataset. The performance is compared to a manually constructed ontology, and two other recent semi-automatically built ontologies. We show that WEB-SOBA is able to produce an ontology that achieves higher accuracy whilst requiring less than half of user time, compared to the previous approaches.

Keywords: Ontology learning · Word embeddings · Sentiment analysis · Aspect-based sentiment analysis

1 Introduction

One of the most valuable pieces of information for any business is the opinion of their customers. One source of data that can be of great help is the growing mass of online reviews posted on the Web and social media. The review forum Yelp, for example, features more than 200 million reviews about restaurants and other businesses [28]. Interpreting this massive amount of text manually would be difficult and time consuming. This is where the field of *sentiment analysis* plays an important role. It is a subfield of natural language processing (NLP), that encompasses the study of people's emotions and attitudes from written language [14]. In particular, this paper focuses on *aspect-based sentiment analysis* (ABSA), which aims to compute sentiments pertaining to specific features, the so-called 'aspects', of a product or service [22]. This results in a more in-depth sentiment analysis, as reviews can contain varying sentiment *polarities* (negative, neutral, or positive) about different aspects. This means that through ABSA, businesses

ⓒ Springer Nature Switzerland AG 2021
R. Verborgh et al. (Eds.): ESWC 2021, LNCS 12731, pp. 340–355, 2021.
https://doi.org/10.1007/978-3-030-77385-4_20

can identify which specific aspects, such as food quality or atmosphere, need to be improved upon, allowing them to make the right adjustments in their business model [19].

ABSA firstly requires that the aspects and their categories in sentences are identified (*aspect detection*) and consequently determines the sentiment with respect to these aspects (*sentiment classification*) [24]. The focus of this paper is on the sentiment classification component of sentence-level ABSA, using benchmark data where the aspects are already given [21].

Various methods have been used for sentiment classification, many of which rely on machine learning methods [8]. [24] proposes a *knowledge-based* method using domain sentiment ontologies, which represent a formal definition of the concepts that are related to a specific domain. [24] shows that using common domain sentiment knowledge encoded into an ontology gives better performance for sentiment classification, whilst requiring less training data to do so. [23] further shows that even better performance is achieved by a *Two-Step Hybrid Model* (TSHM) approach. For this approach, the first step is to use a domain sentiment ontology to predict a sentiment and, if this is inconclusive, use a machine learning algorithm that predicts the sentiment as a backup solution.

The ontologies needed as an input for these hybrid models can be obtained through different methods. One approach is to manually build an ontology [23,24], but this is time consuming and needs to be done for each domain separately. Automatic ontology construction is also an option as [3] proposes, but this process is less accurate because there is no human supervision in creating the ontology. [31] shows that a semi-automatic approach, where human input is required to control for possible mistakes made by the ontology builder, comes close to the human made ontology in accuracy whilst being more time-efficient. While the authors of [31] made use of word co-occurrences to build their ontology, the use of word embeddings has not been investigated until now for constructing a domain sentiment ontology. The advantage of word embeddings is that words are mapped to vectors, which allows for easy computation with words. Moreover, word embeddings also capture semantic features of the words such as similarity to other words. Previous authors have shown that word embeddings outperform word co-occurrence based methods for various NLP tasks [1].

In this paper, we propose a semi-automatic ontology builder called Word Embeddings-Based Semi-Automatic Ontology Builder for Aspect-Based Sentiment Analysis (WEB-SOBA). We aim to build a domain sentiment ontology from a domain corpus based on word embeddings, to exploit semantic relations between words. The source code written in Java of this project can be found at https://github.com/RubenEschauzier/WEB-SOBA.

The rest of the paper has the following structure. In Sect. 2 we discuss related relevant literature that forms the background of our research. In Sect. 3, an overview of the used datasets is given. Further, we describe our methodology in Sect. 4 and present our evaluation criteria and results in Sect. 5. Last, we give our conclusions and make suggestions for future work in Sect. 6.

2   Related Works

In this section, we provide an overview of the relevant literature on hybrid methods, ontology building, and word embeddings.

2.1   Hybrid Methods

The authors of [7] are among the first to suggest that a combination or 'hybrid' of knowledge-based and machine learning methods are promising in sentiment analysis. Following such a hybrid approach, [23] proposes a combination of knowledge and statistics. The used machine learning approach is the *bag-of-words* (BoW) model, where the authors train a multi-class Support Vector Machine (SVM) that is able to classify an aspect into one of three sentiment values: negative, neutral, or positive. The authors show that using a BoW model only as a backup when making predictions using an ontology (Ont+BoW) results in an improvement compared to alternative models.

Similar to the two-stage approach in [23,27] uses a combination of methods in a framework called HAABSA, to predict the sentiment values in sentence-level ABSA. Instead of using the BoW model, the authors use a Left-Center-Right separated neural network with Rotatory attention (*LCR-Rot*) model from [30]. [27] finds that an alteration of the LCR-Rot model (*LCR-Rot-Hop*) as the backup model, where the rotatory attention mechanism is applied multiple times, has the highest performance measure and is even able to outperform the Ont+BoW model of [23]. For this reason we favor using this approach to evaluate the performance of our ontology.

2.2   Ontology Building

As described by [6], there are various subtasks associated with the development of an ontology. The first step is to gather linguistic knowledge in order to be able to recognize domain-specific terms as well as synonyms of those terms. All terms with the same meaning need to be clustered together to form concepts (e.g., 'drinks' and 'beverage' can both be a *lexicalization* of the concept Drinks). In addition, hierarchical relationships need to be established (e.g., given the class Food and the class Fries, Fries should be recognized as a subclass of Food). Next, non-hierarchical relations between concepts are defined, as well as certain rules in order to be able to derive facts that are not explicitly encoded by the ontology.

A manually built ontology is given in [23]. Since this ontology was made manually, it has great performance by design. However, building the ontology requires a lot of time. [31] shows that using a semi-automatically built ontology substantially decreases the human time needed to create an ontology, while having comparable results to benchmark models. The authors of [31] focus on using word frequencies in domain corpora for ontology building. [9] further extends this work by making use of *synsets*, or sets of synonyms, in term extraction, concept formation, and concept subsumption. However, differently than [9] and [31], we focus on using *word embeddings* for the automated part of the ontology building, meaning that words are mapped to vectors that retain certain similarities between words. As discussed in the previous section, [1] shows that word embeddings outperform word co-occurrences for certain NLP tasks. We hypothesize that word embeddings can be effective for ontology building based on this previous work.

2.3   Word Embeddings

A word embedding is a method for mapping various words to a single vector space. It creates vectors in a way that retains information about the word the vector represents, whilst having relatively low dimensionality when compared to the bag-of-words approach.

Some of the most well-known methods for word embedding are proposed by [16], known as *local context window methods*. These methods primarily consider a word within the local context it appears, such that the vector of the word is determined by its sentence-level neighbours. The authors introduce the Continuous Bag-of-Words model (CBOW) and the Skip-gram model. It is shown that these local window context methods outperform previous *global matrix factorization* methods like Latent Semantic Analysis (LSA) and Latent Dirichlet Allocation (LDA) [16]. CBOW and Skip-gram are not only able to represent words, but can also detect syntactic and semantic word similarities. Relations like Athens→Greece are established by training on large text files that contain similar relations, e.g., Rome→Italy. Implementations of CBOW and Skip-gram are publicly available in the 'word2vec' project.

A different method for embedding words was introduced in response to CBOW and Skip-gram. [20] combines global factorization and local context window methods in a bilinear regression model called the Global Vector method, abbreviated as GloVe. GloVe produces word embeddings by primarily considering non-zero word co-occurrences of the entire document.

A last method for word embedding, called FastText, is introduced by [4]. FastText extends the Skip-gram model by including 'subword' information. The advantage of such an approach is that a vector representation of an unknown word can be formed by concatenating words, e.g., the vector for 'lighthouse' is associated with the vector for 'light' + the vector for 'house'.

There is no well-defined 'best' word embedding amongst word2vec, GloVe, and FastText for all NLP tasks. Some authors suggest that the difference in performance is mainly due to differences in hyperparameter settings between methods [13]. Other authors suggest that the word embedding methods are similar in practice, as can be found in the results of [18] and [25], for example. There are some exclusive features for each method, however. As an example, FastText can generate a word embedding for a word that does not exist in the database. On the other hand, word2vec is training time efficient and has a small memory footprint. For these practical considerations, we opt for the word2vec algorithm in our research.

3   Data

In sentiment analysis, there are a number of standard datasets that are widely used. We focus on datasets for the restaurant domain, because this is also the domain based upon which the ontologies from [9, 23], and [31] were built, lending for easier comparison.

To create an ontology, we need a domain-specific corpus and a contrasting corpus, in order to find how frequent certain words appear in a domain, relative to general documents. The domain-specific corpus is created using the Yelp Open Dataset [28]. This dataset consist of consumer reviews of various types of businesses. We filter out the reviews that are not about restaurants, resulting in with 5,508,394 domain-specific reviews of more than 500,000 restaurants. For the contrasting corpus, we use the pre-trained word2vec model google-news-300 [12], containing vectors for 3 million words with a dimensionality of 300.

To evaluate our ontology, we use the SemEval-2016 Task 5 restaurant data for sentence-level analysis [21]. It is a standard dataset that contains restaurant reviews. It is structured per review and each review is structured per sentence, with reviews having varying amounts of sentences. There are 676 sentences in the test set and 2000 sentences in the training set. Each sentence contains opinions relating to specific `targets` in the sentence. The `category` of a target is also annotated, which is made up of an entity E (e.g., restaurant, drinks) and attribute A (e.g., prices, quality) pairing E#A. Furthermore, each identified E#A pair is annotated with a polarity from the set $\mathcal{P} = \{$negative, neutral, positive$\}$.

When an entity is only implicitly present in a sentence, the target is labeled as `NULL`. Since most machine learning methods need a target phrase to be present, the implicit sentences are not used in the analysis. These implicit aspects make up around 25% of the training set, leaving still 1879 explicit aspects. Figure 1 gives an overview of the aspects and polarities labeled in the dataset.

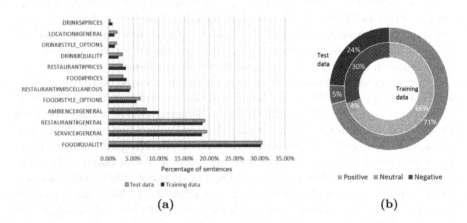

(a)   (b)

Fig. 1. Percentage of occurrence for aspects per sentence (a) and polarities per aspects (b) for the SemEval-2016 Task 5 restaurant dataset.

4   Methodology

In this section, we explain how our ontology builder works, which we refer to as the Word Embedding-Based Semi-Automatic Ontology Builder for Aspect-Based Sentiment Analysis (WEB-SOBA). Additionally, we discuss the user input required at various points in the ontology building process.

4.1   Word Embeddings

The word embedding method we use for our ontology building is word2vec, which uses a two-layer neural network [17]. There are two variations to this. In the Continuous Bag-of-Words (CBOW) model, the embedding is learned by predicting the current word based on its context (the surrounding words). Another approach is to learn by predicting the surrounding words given a current word. This approach is called the Skip-gram model. CBOW is better for frequent words, while Skip-gram does a better job for infrequent words. Moreover, CBOW can be trained faster than Skip-gram. However, in practical applications the performance is fairly similar. For this paper, due to the previously given advantages, we use the CBOW model to make the word embeddings. This model is trained using the following loss function:

$$J = \frac{1}{T} \sum_{t=1}^{T} \log p(w_t | w_{t-c}, \ldots, w_{t-1}, w_{t+1}, \ldots, w_{t+c}), \qquad (1)$$

where $[-c, c]$ is the word context of the word w_t and T represents the number of words in the sequence.

4.2   Ontology Framework

The first step to build our ontology is to decide upon the basic structure that will be used. We use the same structure as the ontology presented by [23]. This ontology contains two main classes: `Mention` and `SentimentValue`. `SentimentValue` consists of the subclasses `Positive` and `Negative`. Please note that our ontology does not model neutral sentiment. This is a deliberate choice, as neutral sentiment has an inherent subjectivity [23]. The skeletal structure already starts with a certain number of `Mention` subclasses based on the entities and attributes that make up categories within the domain, denoted as `ENTITY#ATTRIBUTE` (e.g., `FOOD#QUALITY`). For the considered restaurant domain, the `Mention` subclasses are: *Restaurant, Location, Food, Drinks, Price, Experience, Service, Ambiance, Quality*, and *Style&Options*. In addition we also use the attributes *General* and *Miscellaneous*, but we do not explicitly represent them in sub-classes. Figure 2 illustrates the `Mention` subclasses in our base ontology and how they are related to each other to make `ENTITY#ATTRIBUTE` pairs.

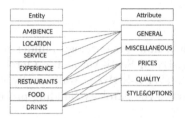

Fig. 2. Entities and Attributes, as E#A pairs.

In this ontology we make a distinction between the part-of-speech of a term, i.e., whether it is a verb (`Action`), noun (`Entity`), or adjective (`Property`). The `Mention` classes are superclasses of classes denoting the aspect and the part-of-speech. For example, `PricesPropertyMention` is a subclass of `PricesMention` and `PropertyMention`. Each of these classes then contains classes which are a subclass of the corresponding `Mention` class and the `SentimentValue` class. For example, a class `LocationPositiveProperty` is a subclass of the classes `LocationPropertyMention` and `Positive`.

There are three types of sentiment-carrying classes: Type-1 (generic sentiment), Type-2 (aspect-specific sentiment), and Type-3 (context-dependent sentiment). The first type always has the same sentiment value regardless in what context the concept is found (e.g., the concept 'good' is always positive). This type of Mention subclasses are also immediately a subclass of the `GenericPositive` or `GenericNegative` classes, which are subclasses of the `SentimentValue` classes `Positive` and `Negative`, respectively. Next, sentiment Type-2 words only apply to a specific category of aspects and with the same sentiment. For example, the word 'delicious' applies to food and drinks but is never used when talking about service. Therefore, when determining the sentiment of an aspect in the service category, this word could be ignored. Finally, Type-3 words indicate different sentiments depending on the aspect category. For example, 'cold' beer is positive whereas 'cold' pizza is negative.

All concepts in the ontology can have two types of properties. The `Mention` classes can first of all have one or multiple aspect properties through which they are linked to all the aspect categories for which they are applicable. For example, `FoodMention` is linked to `FOOD#PRICES`, `FOOD#QUALITY`, and `FOOD#OPTIONS`. Second, differently than the main `Mention` and `SentimentValue` classes, the classes have lexical representations attached.

User Intervention. The user helps initialise the skeletal ontology by providing some lexicalizations for the base classes. In particular, we add some Type-1 sentiment words, such as 'enjoy', 'hate', 'great', and 'bad'. For each of these terms, the 15 most similar words obtained through word embeddings are suggested to the user. The user can then accept or reject adding these words as an extra lexicalization of the corresponding class. The reason to initialise the ontology in this manner is that these generic, context-independent Type-1 words such as 'enjoy' and 'hate' do indicate a sentiment, but are used in a wide range of contexts. Therefore, these words are less likely to be extracted when determining terms specific to the restaurant domain, yet they are still useful if they are added to our ontology.

4.3   Term Selection

To first gather domain-specific words, we use the Yelp dataset [28] containing text about our domain and extract all adjectives, nouns, and, verbs from the text using the *part-of-speech* tagger of the Stanford NLP Processing Group [26]. Adverbs can also be considered for sentiment information, but they sometimes affect the intensity of the sentiment rather than the polarity [11]. Consequently, we only use adjectives, nouns, and verbs for our analysis, as they carry the primary sentiment information of the sentence. Afterwards, we select certain terms from the list of domain-specific words that are to be proposed to the user. We first assign a *TermScore* (TS) to each word, calculated using the *DomainSimilarity* (DS) and the *MentionClassSimilarity* (MCS).

The DS can be computed using the *cosine similarity*. The function for DS of word i is:

$$DS_i = \frac{v_{i,D} \cdot v_{i,G}}{\|v_{i,D}\| \cdot \|v_{i,G}\|}, \tag{2}$$

where $v_{i,D}$ is the vector of word i in the domain-related word embedding model and vector $v_{i,G}$ is generated for word i in the general word embedding model. If a word is domain-specific, the cosine similarity between $v_{i,D}$ and $v_{i,G}$ is low which indicates a low value for DS as well.

The MCS calculates the maximum similarity for word i to one of the *Mention* classes. The function for MCS of word i is:

$$MCS_i = \max_{a \in \mathcal{A}} \left(\frac{v_i \cdot v_a}{\|v_i\| \cdot \|v_a\|} \right), \tag{3}$$

where $\mathcal{A}$ is the set of *Mention* classes, which are *Restaurant, Location, Food, Drinks, Price, Experience, Service, Ambiance, Quality,* and *Style&Options*. The more similar terms are to the lexical representation of the name of one of the mention classes, the higher the value of MCS.

The function TS is defined as the harmonic mean of DS and MCS. Because we want the DS_i value as low as possible, we take its reciprocal value. Both DS and MCS play an important role, because we want words to be both specific to the domain (as represented by DS), and at the same time we want them to be important to the base classes in our domain (as measured by MCS). The function for the TS of each term i is:

$$TS_i = \frac{2}{DS_i + MSC_i^{-1}}, \tag{4}$$

A specific threshold parameter is used, one for each of the three lexical classes (adjectives, nouns, and verbs), to determine whether to suggest terms to the user.

A term will be selected and proposed to the user if its TS exceeds the threshold of the lexical class, which the term belongs to. A critical issue here is deciding the value of the threshold parameter. The value of this parameter determines the amount of terms the user is asked to review. By setting the value of the threshold too low, a lot of terms have to be considered by the user, which is very time consuming. When the value of the threshold parameter is too high, crucial words will be omitted and thus absent from the ontology. The threshold value is defined for lexical class lc (part-of-speech) as follows:

$$TH_{lc}^* = \max_{TH_{lc}} \left(\frac{2}{\frac{n}{accepted} + \frac{1}{accepted}} \right), \tag{5}$$

where TH_{lc} is a threshold score for lexical class lc, n is the number of suggested terms, and *accepted* is the number of accepted terms. TH^* is defined per lexical class so that we maximize the number of accepted terms and the number of accepted terms relative to suggested terms for each lexical class.

User Intervention. After the TermScore of a term exceeds the threshold and the term is suggested to the user, the user can accept or reject whether to add this term to the list of all relevant terms for the ontology. If the term is a verb or a noun, the user decides if the term refers to an aspect, or if it refers to a sentiment. Adjectives are always treated as denoting a sentiment. If the term is added as a *Sentiment Mention*, the user has to decide if the word is a Type-1 *Sentiment Mention* or not, and if so, if the word is positive or negative.

Furthermore, we select all words for each accepted term that are similar to the accepted term using word embeddings. If the cosine similarity is larger than a certain threshold, the word is added to the ontology. We find in preliminary research that a threshold of 0.7 ensures that the vast majority of words added are valuable to the ontology.

4.4   Sentiment Term Clustering

After selecting the important terms for our ontology and letting the user define whether the terms are *Sentiment Mentions* or *Aspect Mentions*, we can create a hierarchy for the words that were deemed to be sentiment words. In this case, we want to determine the `SentimentValue` of each word, as well as determine which `Mention` class(es) the word belongs to if it is not a `GenericPositive` or `GenericNegative` sentiment.

A drawback of using word2vec word embeddings for our application is that the generated vectors do not directly account for sentiment. For example, the vectors for 'good' and 'bad' are very similar to each other because they appear in the same context, even though they convey a different sentiment. This complicates the process of determining the sentiment for our *Sentiment Mention* words. Our proposed solution to this problem is to refine our existing word2vec model, as trained on the Yelp dataset, by making the vectors sentiment-aware.

[29] uses the Extended version of Affective Norms of English Words (E-ANEW) as a sentiment lexicon. This sentiment lexicon is a dataset that attaches emotional ratings to words. Using this sentiment lexicon, the authors find and rank the k (e.g., $k = 10$) most similar words in terms of emotional ratings to the target word that needs to be refined, where the most similar word gets the highest rank. These words are called the neighbours of our target word. The neighbours of our target word are then also ranked in terms of their cosine similarity, where again the word with the highest similarity gets the highest rank. After creating these sentiment and similarity rankings, the vector of the target word is refined so that it is: (1) closer to its neighbours that are sentimentally similar, (2) further away from dissimilar neighbors, and (3) still relatively close to the original vector.

Using these vectors we cluster our *Sentiment Mention* terms. For each term we calculate the cosine similarity between all of our base `Mention` classes and rank them in descending order. Additionally, we calculate the negative and positive score of our *Sentiment Mention* term in the following way:

$$PS_i = \max_{p \in P} \left(\frac{v_i \cdot v_p}{\|v_i\| \cdot \|v_p\|} \right) \qquad NS_i = \max_{n \in N} \left(\frac{v_i \cdot v_n}{\|v_i\| \cdot \|v_n\|} \right) \qquad (6)$$

where PS_i and NS_i are the positive and negative score for $term_i$. $\mathcal{P}$ and $\mathcal{N}$ are a collection of positive and negative words that span different intensities of positivity and negativity, respectively. The set of negative words is as follows: $\mathcal{P}=$ {'good', 'decent', 'great', 'tasty', 'fantastic', 'solid', 'yummy', 'terrific'}. The set of positive words is: $\mathcal{N}=$ {'bad', 'awful', 'horrible', 'terrible', 'poor', 'lousy', 'shitty', 'horrid'}. Finally, we have v_i, v_p, and v_n which are the word embeddings of word i, p, and n, respectively. We predict our $term_i$ to be positive if the PS_i is higher than NS_i. If the PS_i is lower than NS_i, the $term_i$ is considered to be negative.

User Intervention. The user is asked for each *Sentiment Mention* term if it can refer to the base `Mention` class that it has the highest cosine similarity to. If the user accepts the term into the recommended `Mention` class, the user is asked then to confirm if the predicted polarity of the *Sentiment Mention* is correct. Thereafter, the user is asked the same for the `Mention` class that has the second highest cosine similarity to our term. This continues until either all `Mention` classes are accepted or one `Mention` class is rejected. After the process terminates, the *Sentiment Mention* term is added to the ontology in accordance to the decisions made by the user. Each *Sentiment Mention* can be added to multiple `Mention` classes, because a *Sentiment Mention* can convey sentiment for multiple `Mention` classes. An example of this is the word 'idyllic', which can convey sentiment about the restaurant, location, experience, and ambiance.

4.5   Aspect Term Hierarchical Clustering

The next step is clustering and building the ontology's hierarchy for the *Aspect Mention* terms. As previously stated, words can be represented in a vector space using word embeddings, which means it is possible to cluster these terms.

    Building the ontology's hierarchy is done in two steps. First, we implement an adjusted k-means clustering approach to cluster the accepted terms into clusters corresponding to the base `Mention` classes. These clusters are *Restaurant, Location, Food, Drinks, Price, Experience, Service, Ambiance, Quality*, and *Style&Options*. Since the base mention classes are known, we can just add each data point to the base cluster with which it has the highest cosine similarity (using the lexical representations corresponding to the names of these clusters). After clustering the terms into the base subclasses, the next step is building a hierarchy for each subclass using agglomerative hierarchical clustering. Terms start in a single cluster and are slowly merged together per iteration based on a linkage criteria. The method we choose for implementation is called Average Linkage Clustering, abbreviated as ALC, as it is less sensitive to outliers. It is defined as:

$$ALC(A, B) = \frac{1}{|A| \cdot |B|} \sum_{a \in A} \sum_{b \in B} d(a, b) \tag{7}$$

where $d(a, b)$ is the Euclidean distance between vectors a and b, where a is in cluster A and b is in cluster B. At each iteration, terms with the lowest ALC value are clustered, creating the required hierarchy. For our ALC algorithm, we make use of the implementation described by [2]. Based on preliminary experiments of implementing the elbow method, the maximum depth that our dendrogram can possibly have is set to three for each subclass.

User Intervention. For each `Mention` class, each term belonging to that cluster is presented to the user and the user can accept or reject it. If the user rejects it, the user is prompted to specify the right cluster. By doing this, all terms start in the correct cluster before building a hierarchy.

5   Evaluation

In this section, we discuss the procedure by which we evaluate our proposed ontology. We compare the performance of our ontology with benchmark (semi-) manually built ontologies. In Sect. 5.1 we describe the performance measures we use for evaluation. Next, in Sect. 5.2 and Sect. 5.3 we present our results. All results were obtained on an Intel(R) Core(TM) i5-4690k CPU in combination with an NVIDIA GeForce GTX 970 GPU and 16 GB RAM.

5.1   Evaluation Procedure

The output of our proposed methodology is a domain-specific sentiment ontology based on word embeddings. This ontology is used in combination with machine learning methods to classify the sentiment of aspects. We evaluate the quality of our proposed method by looking at the time required to construct the ontology and its performance for sentiment classification. To determine which configuration performs better, we use the Welch t-test to compare the cross-validation outcomes.

As we build the ontology semi-automatically, it is interesting to consider the time required to make a WEB-SOBA ontology. The ontology building time can be divided in human time spent and computer time spent. We try to minimize the total time spent on building the ontology, but value time spent by humans as more expensive than time spent by computers. Ultimately, we expect that our ontology performs better than the ontology of [9] and [31] if the word embeddings truly outperform word co-occurrences. However, we expect the best performance from the ontology of [23] as this ontology was entirely made by hand to perform best.

The experiments are executed on the HAABSA implementation [27]. The experimental setup for testing our ontology is simple, as we can directly plug our ontology into the HAABSA code after it has been semi-automatically constructed. We test the following ontologies: Manual [23], SOBA [31], SASOBUS [9], and WEB-SOBA. These ontologies are evaluated when used by themselves and when used in conjunction with the LRC-Rot-Hop backup model in the HAABSA framework.

5.2   Ontology Building Results

We now evaluate the WEB-SOBA ontology. In the end, 376 classes are added to our ontology, of which there are 15 Type-1 sentiment words, 119 Type-2 sentiment words, and 0 Type-3 sentiment words. These results are not fully unexpected: there are few Type-1 sentiment words, because these words are often not domain-specific and therefore less likely to be selected by the term selection algorithm. There are also no Type-3 sentiment words selected, possibly because there are not many of these in the dataset. To put it into perspective, the manual ontology of [23] has only 15 Type-3 sentiment words. Table 1 presents the distribution of classes, lexicalizations, and synonyms in our ontology, compared to the other benchmark ontologies.

Table 1. Distribution of ontology classes and properties for the manual ontology, SOBA, and WEB-SOBA.

	Manual	SASOBUS	SOBA	WEB-SOBA
Classes	365	558	470	376
Lexicalizations	374	1312	1087	348

It is clear from Table 1 that our ontology is not as extensive compared to the other three ontologies. However, this does not necessarily mean that the ontology should have a worse performance, as it is possible that the most important terms of the domain are captured. Another important factor to consider is the building time duration. Table 2 presents the time that is required for user input and for computing in minutes, compared to benchmark ontologies.

Table 2. Time duration of the building process for the manual ontology, SOBA, and WEB-SOBA.

	Manual	SASOBUS	SOBA	WEB-SOBA
User time (minutes)	420	180	90	40
Computing time (minutes)	0	300	90	30 (+300)

Table 2 shows that with respect to user time required, WEB-SOBA clearly outperforms the other semi-automatic ontology builders, and, obviously, the manual ontology as well. The computing time for running the code between user inputs is only 30 min, which is also lower than the computing time required for the SOBA and SASOBUS ontologies. However, the word embeddings need to be created the first time the program is used and the terms in the Yelp dataset have to be extracted, which requires an additional 300 min of computing time. After the vectors have been made, they can be reused in the same domain. This substantially decreases the time needed to do a different NLP task in the same domain. Additionally, the computation times are higher because the dataset used for this ontology contains millions of reviews compared to the 5001 reviews used to create SOBA and SASOBUS.

5.3 Evaluation Results

We compare the results of WEB-SOBA with the results of the Manual ontology from [23], the SOBA ontology of [31], and the SASOBUS ontology of [9]. Table 3 presents the performance of the ontologies by themselves, while Table 4 presents the results of the Ontology+LCR-Rot-Hop approach [27]. The tables additionally present p-values for the Welch t-test to test for equal means (under unequal variances) for the cross-validation accuracies.

Table 3. Comparison results for different ontologies by themselves on SemEval-2016 Task 5 restaurant data.

	Out-of-sample	In-sample	Cross-validation		Welch t-test			
	Accuracy	Accuracy	Accuracy	St. dev.	Manual	SASOBUS	SOBA	WEB-SOBA
Manual	**78.31%**	**75.31%**	**74.10%**	0.044	–			
SASOBUS	76.62%	73.82%	70.69%	0.049	0.118	–		
SOBA	77.23%	74.56%	71.71%	0.061	0.327	0.685	–	
WEB-SOBA	77.08%	72.11%	70.50%	0.050	0.107	0.636	0.935	–

Table 4. Results for ontologies on SemEval-2016 Task 5 restaurant data, evaluated with LCR-Rot-Hop model as backup.

	Out-of-sample	In-sample	Cross-validation		Welch t-test			
	Accuracy	Accuracy	Accuracy	St. dev.	Manual	SASOBUS	SOBA	WEB-SOBA
Manual	86.65%	87.96%	82.76%	0.022	–			
SASOBUS	84.76%	83.38%	80.20%	0.031	0.052	–		
SOBA	86.23%	85.93%	80.15%	0.039	0.088	0.975	–	
WEB-SOBA	**87.16%**	**88.87%**	**84.72%**	0.017	0.043	0.001	0.005	–

The tables presented above show that WEB-SOBA achieves similar performance to other semi-automatically built ontologies when evaluated by itself, even though it required less than half of the user time to build. When combined with the LCR-Rot-Hop backup method, the WEB-SOBA ontology performs better than all other ontologies including the manual one (at 5% significance level). This shows that our ontology complements the machine learning method well.

Our approach is generalizable to other domains as well. For another domain one only needs to provide the following items: a text corpus, the category classes, and the positive/negative word collections. Even if the overall time is comparable with the one of a manual approach, one major benefit for our approach is that most of the time is spent by system computations instead of user work. As limitations, our solution is not able to deal with polysemous words and our data set was not able to provide for Type-3 sentiment words.

6   Conclusion

For this research paper, we used word embeddings to semi-automatically build an ontology for the restaurant domain to be used in aspect-based sentiment analysis. The ontology builder we propose reduces both computing and user time required to construct the ontology, given that the word embeddings for a specific domain are already made. Furthermore, our method requires less user time compared to recently proposed semi-automatic ontology builders based on word co-occurrences, whilst it achieves similar or better performance. Our proposed ontology even reaches higher accuracy compared to the performance of a manually built one when implemented in a hybrid method with the LCR-Rot-Hop model as backup.

As future work we would like to analyse for which aspects the proposed approach gives the best performance. Also, we suggest that the performance of an ontology used for ABSA can likely be improved by using a contextual word embeddings method, such as BERT [10]. These contextual methods assign a different vector to the same word in a different context. We expect that these contextual word embeddings lead to more accurate sentiment classification, as the various meanings of words are taken into account. However, these methods cannot be directly implemented into the current ontology structure, as the same word gets a different vector in a different linguistic context. As future work we propose to extend the ontology structure by allowing the same word to appear for multiple concepts by conditioning its presence on a certain meaning. In addition, we plan to use domain modelling [5] that complements well our contrastive corpus-based solution by providing domain-specific terms that are more generic than the current ones. Furthermore, the clustering of terms can be improved. Our proposed clustering method works for a relatively moderate amount of domain terms, but is not feasible for a huge number of domain terms. For an efficient hierarchical clustering method for Big Data, one could exploit the BIRCH algorithm as in [15].

References

1. Baroni, M., Dinu, G., Kruszewski, G.: Don't count, predict! A systematic comparison of context-counting vs. context-predicting semantic vectors. In: 52nd Annual Meeting of the Association for Computational Linguistics (ACL 2014), pp. 238–247. ACL (2014)
2. Behnke, L.: https://github.com/lbehnke/hierarchical-clustering-java (2012)
3. Blaschke, C., Valencia, A.: Automatic ontology construction from the literature. Genome Inform. **13**, 201–213 (2002)
4. Bojanowski, P., Grave, E., Joulin, A., Mikolov, T.: Enriching word vectors with subword information. Trans. Assoc. Comput. Linguist. **5**, 135–146 (2017)
5. Bordea, G., Buitelaar, P., Polajnar, T.: Domain-independent term extraction through domain modelling. In: 10th International Conference on Terminology and Artificial Intelligence (TIA 2013) (2013)
6. Buitelaar, P., Cimiano, P., Magnini, B.: Ontology learning from text: an overview. In: Ontology Learning from Text: Methods, Evaluation and Applications, vol. 123, pp. 3–12 (2005)
7. Cambria, E.: Affective computing and sentiment analysis. IEEE Intell. Syst. **31**(2), 102–107 (2016)
8. Cambria, E., Das, D., Bandyopadhyay, S., Feraco, A.: A Practical Guide to Sentiment Analysis. SAC, vol. 5. Springer, Cham (2017). https://doi.org/10.1007/978-3-319-55394-8
9. Dera, E., Frasincar, F., Schouten, K., Zhuang, L.: SASOBUS: semi-automatic sentiment domain ontology building using Synsets. In: Harth, A., et al. (eds.) ESWC 2020. LNCS, vol. 12123, pp. 105–120. Springer, Cham (2020). https://doi.org/10.1007/978-3-030-49461-2_7
10. Devlin, J., Chang, M.W., Lee, K., Toutanova, K.: BERT: pre-training of deep bidirectional transformers for language understanding. In: 2019 Conference of the North American Chapter of the Association for Computational Linguistics: Human Language Technologies (NAACL-HLT 2019) ACL, pp. 4171–4186 (2019)
11. Dragut, E., Fellbaum, C.: The role of adverbs in sentiment analysis. In: Proceedings of Frame Semantics in NLP: A Workshop in Honor of Chuck Fillmore (1929–2014), pp. 38–41 (2014)
12. Google (2013). https://code.google.com/archive/p/word2vec/
13. Levy, O., Goldberg, Y., Dagan, I.: Improving distributional similarity with lessons learned from word embeddings. Trans. Assoc. Comput. Linguist. **3**, 211–225 (2015)
14. Liu, B.: Sentiment analysis and opinion mining. Synth. Lect. Hum. Lang. Technol. **5**(1), 1–167 (2012)

15. Mahmoud, N., Elbeh, H., Abdlkader, H.M.: Ontology learning based on word embeddings for text big data extraction. In: 14th International Computer Engineering Conference (ICENCO 2018), pp. 183–188. IEEE (2018)

16. Mikolov, T., Chen, K., Corrado, G., Dean, J.: Efficient estimation of word representations in vector space. In: 1st International Conference on Learning Representations (ICLR 2013) (2013)

17. Mikolov, T., Sutskever, I., Chen, K., Corrado, G.S., Dean, J.: Distributed representations of words and phrases and their compositionality. In: 27th Annual Conference on Neural Information Processing Systems (NIPS 2013), pp. 3111–3119. Curran Associates (2013)

18. Naili, M., Chaibi, A.H., Ghezala, H.H.B.: Comparative study of word embedding methods in topic segmentation. In: 23rd International Conference on Knowledge-Based and Intelligent Information & Engineering Systems (KES 2019), vol. 112, pp. 340–349 (2017)

19. Pang, B., Lee, L.: Opinion mining and sentiment analysis. Found. Trends Inf. Retrieval $2(1–2)$, 1–135 (2008)

20. Pennington, J., Socher, R., Manning, C.D.: GloVe: global vectors for word representation. In: 2014 Conference on Empirical Methods in Natural Language Processing (EMNLP 2014), pp. 1532–1543. ACL (2014)

21. Pontiki, M., et al.: SemEval-2016 task 5: aspect-based sentiment analysis. In: 10th International Workshop on Semantic Evaluation (SemEval 2016), pp. 19–30. ACL (2016)

22. Schouten, K., Frasincar, F.: Survey on aspect-level sentiment analysis. IEEE Trans. Knowl. Data Eng. $28(3)$, 813–830 (2016)

23. Schouten, K., Frasincar, F.: Ontology-driven sentiment analysis of product and service aspects. In: Gangemi, A., et al. (eds.) ESWC 2018. LNCS, vol. 10843, pp. 608–623. Springer, Cham (2018). https://doi.org/10.1007/978-3-319-93417-4_39

24. Schouten, K., Frasincar, F., de Jong, F.: Ontology-enhanced aspect-based sentiment analysis. In: Cabot, J., De Virgilio, R., Torlone, R. (eds.) ICWE 2017. LNCS, vol. 10360, pp. 302–320. Springer, Cham (2017). https://doi.org/10.1007/978-3-319-60131-1_17

25. Shi, T., Liu, Z.: Linking GloVe with word2vec. arXiv preprint arXiv:1411.5595 (2014)

26. Toutanova, K., Manning, C.D.: Enriching the knowledge sources used in a maximum entropy part-of-speech tagger. In: 2000 Joint SIGDAT Conference on Empirical Methods in Natural Language Processing and Very Large Corpora (EMNLP 2010), pp. 63–70. ACL (2000)

27. Wallaart, O., Frasincar, F.: A hybrid approach for aspect-based sentiment analysis using a lexicalized domain ontology and attentional neural models. In: Hitzler, P., et al. (eds.) ESWC 2019. LNCS, vol. 11503, pp. 363–378. Springer, Cham (2019). https://doi.org/10.1007/978-3-030-21348-0_24

28. Yelp (2019). https://www.yelp.com/dataset

29. Yu, L.C., Wang, J., Lai, K.R., Zhang, X.: Refining word embeddings for sentiment analysis. In: 2017 Conference on Empirical Methods in Natural Language Processing (EMNLP 2017), pp. 534–539. ACL (2017)

30. Zheng, S., Xia, R.: Left-center-right separated neural network for aspect-based sentiment analysis with rotatory attention. arXiv preprint arXiv:1802.00892 (2018)

31. Zhuang, L., Schouten, K., Frasincar, F.: SOBA: semi-automated ontology builder for aspect-based sentiment analysis. J. Web Semant. **60**, 100–544 (2020)

Context Transformer with Stacked Pointer Networks for Conversational Question Answering over Knowledge Graphs

Joan Plepi[1] , Endri Kacupaj[2(✉)] , Kuldeep Singh[3] , Harsh Thakkar[4] ,
and Jens Lehmann[2,5]

[1] Technische Universität Darmstadt, Darmstadt, Germany
joan.plepi@tu-darmstadt.de
[2] Smart Data Analytics Group, University of Bonn, Bonn, Germany
{kacupaj,jens.lehmann}@cs.uni-bonn.de
[3] Zerotha Research and Cerence GmbH, Bonn, Germany
kuldeep.singh1@cerence.com
[4] Zerotha Research and Osthus GmbH, Bonn, Germany
harsh.thakkar@osthus.com
[5] Fraunhofer IAIS, Dresden, Germany
jens.lehmann@iais.fraunhofer.de

Abstract. Neural semantic parsing approaches have been widely used for Question Answering (QA) systems over knowledge graphs. Such methods provide the flexibility to handle QA datasets with complex queries and a large number of entities. In this work, we propose a novel framework named CARTON (Context trAnsformeR sTacked pOinter Networks), which performs multi-task semantic parsing for handling the problem of conversational question answering over a large-scale knowledge graph. Our framework consists of a stack of pointer networks as an extension of a context transformer model for parsing the input question and the dialog history. The framework generates a sequence of actions that can be executed on the knowledge graph. We evaluate CARTON on a standard dataset for complex sequential question answering on which CARTON outperforms all baselines. Specifically, we observe performance improvements in F1-score on eight out of ten question types compared to the previous state of the art. For logical reasoning questions, an improvement of 11 absolute points is reached.

Keywords: Conversational question answering · Knowledge graph · Context transformer · Stacked pointer networks

1 Introduction

Recently, there has been an increased demand for chatbots and voice assistants to communicate and assist humans in different domains such as chitchat, medical, news, enterprise, etc. ([7]). Question answering is a common phenomenon in chatbot conversations to seek specific information. While such questions inherit a conversational

---

J. Plepi and E. Kacupaj–Equal contribution to this research.
Work was done while the author Joan Plepi was a student at University of Bonn.

R. Verborgh et al. (Eds.): ESWC 2021, LNCS 12731, pp. 356–371, 2021.
https://doi.org/10.1007/978-3-030-77385-4_21

Table 1. An example dialog from CSQA dataset [19] describing various states of a conversation.

Turn	State	Utterance
T1	Simple question	**USER**: Can you tell me which cities border Verderio Inferiore ?
	Response	**SYSTEM**: Cornate d'Adda, Bernareggio, Robbiate
T2	Coreference question	**USER**: And which cities flank that one ?
	Clarification	**SYSTEM**: Did you mean Robbiate?
T3	Clarification question	**USER**: No, I meant Cornate d'Adda
	Response	**SYSTEM**: Bottanuco, Busnago, Trezzo sull'Adda
T4	Logical question	**USER**: Which ones share border with Robbiate and are not part of Azerbaijan?
	Response	**SYSTEM**: Trezzo sull'Adda, Busnago, Bottanuco

context, humans also tend to ask questions that require complex reasoning to answer in a real-world scenario. The complexity of questions may differ at various granularity (e.g., simple, logical, quantitative, and comparative). Table 1 presents a few examples from a complex question answering dataset with a conversational context [19]. The example dialogue has several question types and challenges. For example, in the first turn, the user asks a simple direct question, and in the following turn, she asks a question that refers to the context from the previous turn. Furthermore, in the last turn, there is a question that requires logical reasoning to offer a multitude of complexity. Given these questions are from the general knowledge domain, the information required to answer questions can be extracted from publicly available large-scale Knowledge Graphs (KGs) such as DBpedia [11], Freebase [1], and Wikidata [27].

Neural semantic parsing approaches for question answering over KGs have been widely studied in the research community [5,8,9,13]. In a given question, these approaches use a semantic parsing model to produce a logical form which is then executed on the KG to retrieve an answer. While traditional methods tend to work on small KGs [28], more recent approaches also work well on large-scale KGs [8,21]. Often, researchers targeting large scale KGs focus on a stepwise method by first performing entity linking and then train a model to learn the corresponding logical form for each question type [4,8]. Work in [21] argues that the stepwise approaches have two significant issues. First, errors in upstream subtasks (e.g., entity detection and linking, predicate classification) are propagated to downstream ones (e.g., semantic parsing), resulting in accumulated errors. For example, case studies in previous works [4,8,29] show that entity linking error is one of the significant errors leading to the wrong results in the question-answering task. Second, when models for the subtasks are learned independently, the supervision signals cannot be shared among the models for mutual benefits. To mitigate the limitations of the stepwise approach, [21] proposed a multi-task learning framework where a pointer-equipped semantic parsing model is designed to resolve coreference in conversations, and intuitively, empower joint learning with a type-aware entity detection model. The framework combines two objectives: one for semantic parsing and another for entity detection. However, the entity detection model uses supervision signals only from the contextual encoder, and no further signal is provided from the decoder or the semantic parsing task.

In this paper, we target the problem of conversational (complex) question answering over large-scale knowledge graph. We propose CARTON (Context trAnsformeR sTacked pOinter Networks)- a multi-task learning framework consisting of a context transformer model extended with a stack of pointer networks for multi-task neural semantic parsing. Our framework handles semantic parsing using the context transformer model while the remaining tasks such as type prediction, predicate prediction, and entity detection are handled by the stacked pointer networks. Unlike [21] which is current state-of-the-art, CARTON's stacked pointer networks incorporate knowledge graph information for performing any reasoning and does not rely only on the conversational context. Moreover, pointer networks provide the flexibility for handling out-of-vocabulary [26] entities, predicates, and types that are unseen during training. Our ablation study 5.1 further supports our choices. In contrast with the current state of the art, another significant novelty is that the supervision signals in CARTON propagate in sequential order, and all the components use the signal forwarded from the previous components. To this end, we make the following contributions in the paper:

- CARTON - a multi-task learning framework for conversational question answering over large scale knowledge graph.
- For neural semantic parsing, we propose a reusable grammar that defines different logical forms that can be executed on the KG to fetch answers to the questions.

CARTON achieves new state of the art results on eight out of ten question types from a large-scale conversational question answering dataset. We evaluate CARTON on the Complex Sequential Question Answering (CSQA) [19] dataset consisting of conversations over linked QA pairs. The dataset contains 200K dialogues with 1.6M turns, and over 12.8M entities. Our implementation, the annotated dataset with proposed grammar, and results are on a public github[1]. The rest of this article is organized as follows: Sect. 2 summarizes the related work. Section 3 describes the CARTON framework. Section 4 explains the experimental settings and the results are reported in Sect. 5. Section 6 concludes this article.

2   Related Work

Semantic Parsing and Multi-task Learning Approaches. Our work lies in the areas of semantic parsing and neural approaches for question answering over KGs. Works in [6,15,16,31] use neural approaches to solve the task of QA. [15] introduces an approach that splits the question into spans of tokens to match the tokens to their respective entities and predicates in the KG. The authors merge the word and character-level representation to discover better matching in entities and predicates. Candidate subjects are generated based on n-grams matching with words in the question, and then pruned based on predicted predicates. However, their experiments are focused on simple questions. [31] propose a probabilistic framework for QA systems and experiment on a new benchmark dataset. The framework consists of two modules. The first one model the

---

[1] https://github.com/endrikacupaj/CARTON.

probability of the topic entity y, constrained on the question. The second module reasons over the KG to find the answer a, given the topic entity y which is found in the first step and question q. Graph embeddings are used to model the subgraph related to the question and for calculating the distribution of the answer depended from the question q and the topic y. [13] introduce neural symbolic machine (NSM), which contains a neural sequence-to-sequence network referred also as the "programmer", and a symbolic non-differentiable LISP interpreter ("computer"). The model is extended with a key-value memory network, where keys and values are the output of the sequence model in different encoding or decoding steps. The NSM model is trained using the REINFORCE algorithm with weak supervision and evaluated on the WebQuestionsSP dataset [30]. [8] also present an approach that maps utterances to logical forms. Their model consists of a sequence-to-sequence network, where the encoder produces the embedding of the utterance, and the decoder generates the sequence of actions. Authors introduce a dialogue memory management to handle the entities, predicates, and logical forms are referred from a previous interaction. Finally, MaSP [21] present a multi-task model that jointly learns type-aware entity detection and pointer equipped logical form generation using a semantic parsing approach. Our proposed framework is inspired by them; however, we differ considerably on the following points: 1) CARTON's stacked pointer networks incorporate knowledge graph information for performing reasoning and do not rely only on the conversational context as MaSP does. 2) The stacked pointer network architecture is used intentionally to provide the flexibility for handling out-of-vocabulary entities, predicates, and types that are unseen during training. The MaSP model does not cover out-of-vocabulary knowledge since the model was not intended to have this flexibility. 3) CARTON's supervision signals are propagated in sequential order, and all the components use the signal forwarded from the previous component. 4) We employ semantic grammar with new actions for generating logical forms. While [21] employs almost the same grammar as [8].

Other Approaches. There has been extensive research for task-oriented dialog systems such as [10] that induces joint text and knowledge graph embeddings to improve task-oriented dialogues in the domains such as restaurant and flight booking. Work present in [2] proposes another dataset, "ConvQuestions" for conversations over KGs along with an unsupervised model. Some other datasets for conversational QA include CANARD and TREC CAsT [24]. Overall, there are several approaches proposed for conversational QA, and in this paper, we closely stick to multi-task learning approaches for CARTON's comparison and contributions.

3   Carton

Our focus is on conversations containing complex questions that can be answered by reasoning over a large-scale KG. The training data consists of utterances u and the answer label a. We propose a semantic parsing approach, where the goal is to map the utterance u into a logical form z, depending on the conversation context. A stack of three pointer networks is used to fill information extracted from the KG. The final generated logical form aims to fetch the correct answer once executed on the KG. Figure 1 illustrates the overall architecture of CARTON framework.

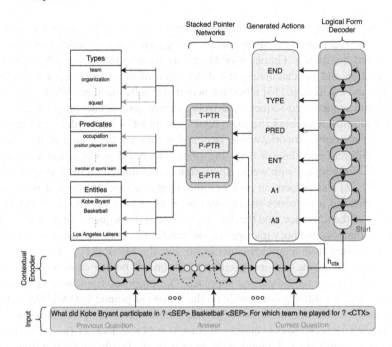

Fig. 1. Context transformer with stacked pointer networks architecture (CARTON). It consists of three modules: 1) A Transformer-based contextual encoder finds the representation of the current context of the dialogue. 2) A logical decoder generates the pattern of the logical forms defined in Table 2. 3) The stacked pointer network initializes the KG items to fetch the correct answer.

3.1 Grammar

We predefined a grammar with various actions as shown in Table 2 which can result in different logical forms that can be executed on the KG. Our grammar definition is inspired by [8] which MaSP [21] also employs. However, we differ in many semantics of the actions and we even defined completely new actions. For example, *find* action is split into *find(e, p)* that corresponds to finding an edge with predicate *p* to the subject *e*; and *find_reverse(e, p)* finds an edge with predicate *p* with object *e*. Moreover, *per_type* is not defined by [8] in their grammar. Table 3 indicates some (complex) examples from CSQA dataset [19] with gold logical form annotations using our predefined grammar. Following [14], each action definition is represented by a function that is executed on the KG, a list of input parameters, and a semantic category that corresponds to the output of the function. For example, *set → find(e, p)*, it has a *set* as a semantic category, a function *find* with input parameters *e, p*. We believe that the defined actions are sufficient for creating sequences that cover complex questions and we provide empirical evidences in Sect. 5. Every action sequence can be parsed into a tree, where the model recursively writes the leftmost non-terminal node until the whole tree is complete. The same approach is followed to execute the action sequence, except that the starting point is the tree leaves.

Table 2. Predefined grammar with respective actions to generate logical forms.

Action	Description
Set $\rightarrow$ find(e, p)	Set of objects (entities) with subject e and predicate p
Set $\rightarrow$ find_reverse(e, p)	Set of subjects (entities) with object e and predicate p
Set $\rightarrow$ filter_by_type(set, tp)	Filter the given set of entities based on the given type
Set $\rightarrow$ filter_mult_types(set_1, set_2)	Filter the given set of entities based on the given set of types
Boolean $\rightarrow$ is_in(set, entity)	Check if the entity is part of the set
Boolean $\rightarrow$ is_subset (set_1, set_2)	Check if set_2 is subset of set_1
Number $\rightarrow$ count(set)	Count the number of elements in the set
Dict $\rightarrow$ per_type(p, tp_1, tp_2)	Extracts a dictionary, where keys are entities of $type_1$ and values are the Number of objects of $type_2$ related with p
Dict $\rightarrow$ per_type_rev(p, tp_1, tp_2)	Extracts a dictionary, where keys are entities of $type_1$ and values are the Number of subjects of $type_2$ related with p
Set $\rightarrow$ greater(num, dict)	Set of entities that have greater count than num
Set $\rightarrow$ lesser(num, dict)	Set of entities that have lesser count than num
Set $\rightarrow$ equal(num, dict)	Set of entities that have equal count with num
Set $\rightarrow$ approx(num, dict)	Set of entities that have approximately same count with num
Set $\rightarrow$ argmin(dict)	Set of entities that have the most count
Set $\rightarrow$ argmax(dict)	Set of entities that have the least count
Set $\rightarrow$ union(set_1, set_2)	Union of set_1 and set_2
Set $\rightarrow$ intersection(set_1, set_2)	Intersection of set_1 and set_2
Set $\rightarrow$ difference(set_1, set_2)	Difference of set_1 and set_2

3.2   Context Transformer

The section describes the semantic parsing part of CARTON, which is a context transformer. The transformer receives input a conversation turn that contains the context of the interaction and generates a sequence of actions. Formally, an interaction I consists of the question q that is a sequence $x = \{x_1, \ldots, x_n\}$, and a label l that is a sequence $y = \{y_1, \ldots, y_m\}$. The network aims to model the conditional probability $p(y|x)$.

Contextual Encoder. In order to cope with coreference and ellipsis phenomena, we require to include the context from the previous interaction in the conversation turn. To accomplish that, the input to the contextual encoder is the concatenation of three utterances from the dialog turn: 1) the previous question, 2) the previous answer, and 3) the current question. Every utterance is separated from one another using a $< SEP >$ token. A special context token $< CTX >$ is appended at the end where the embedding

Table 3. Examples from the CSQA dataset [19], annotated with gold logical forms.

Question Type	Question	Logical Forms
Simple Question (Direct)	Q1: Which administrative territory is the birthplace of Antonio Reguero ?	filter_type(　find(Antonio Reguero, 　　place of birth), 　administrative territorial entity)
Simple Question (Ellipsis)	Q1: Which administrative territories are twin towns of Madrid ? A1: Prague, Moscow, Budapest Q2: And what about Urban Community of Brest?	filter_type(　find(Urban Community of Brest, 　　twinned administrative body), 　administrative territorial entity)
Simple Question (Coreferenced)	Q1: What was the sport that Marie Pyko was a part of ? A1: Association football Q2: Which political territory does that person belong to ?	filter_type(　find(Marie Pyko, 　　country of citizenship), 　political territorial entity)
Quantitative Reasoning (Count) (All)	Q1: How many beauty contests and business enterprises are located at that city ? A1: Did you mean Caracas? Q2: Yes	count(union(　filter_type(　　find_reverse(Caracas, located in), 　　beauty contest), 　filter_type(　　find_reverse(Caracas, located in), 　　business enterprises)))
Quantitative Reasoning (All)	Q1; Which political territories are known to have diplomatic connections with max number of political territories ?	argmax(　per_type(　　diplomatic relation, 　　political territorial entity, 　　political territorial entity))
Comparative Reasoning (Count) (All)	Q1: How many alphabets are used as the scripts for more number of languages than Jawi alphabet ?	count(greater(count(　filter_type(find(Jawi alphabet, 　　writing system), language)), 　per_type(writing system, 　　alphabet, language)))
Comparative Reasoning (All)	Q1: Which occupations were more number of publications and works mainly about than composer ?	greater(filter_type(　find(composer, main subject), 　　occupations), and(　per_type(main subject, publications, 　　occupations), 　per_type(main subject, work, 　　occupations)))
Verification	Q1: Was Geir Rasmussen born at that administrative territory ?	is_in(　find(Geir Rasmussen, 　　place of birth), 　Chicago)

of this utterance is used as the semantic representation for the entire input question. Given an utterance q containing n words $\{w_1, \ldots, w_n\}$, we use GloVe [18] to embed the words into a vector representation space of dimension d_{emb}. More specifically, we get a sequence $x = \{x_1, \ldots, x_n\}$ where x_i is given by,

$$x_i = GloVe(w_i)$$

and $x_i \in \mathbb{R}^{d_{emb}}$. Next, the word embeddings x, are forwarded as input to the contextual encoder, that uses the multi-head attention mechanism from the Transformer network [25]. The encoder outputs the contextual embeddings $h = \{h_1, \ldots, h_n\}$, where $h_i \in \mathbb{R}^{d_{emb}}$, and it can be written as:

$$h = encoder(x; \theta^{(enc)})$$

where $\theta^{(enc)}$ are the trainable parameters of the contextual encoder.

Logical Form Decoder. For the decoder, we likewise utilize the Transformer architecture with a multi-head attention mechanism. The decoder output is dependent on contextual embeddings h originated from the encoder. The decoder detects each action and general semantic object from the KG, i.e., the decoder predicts the correct logical form, without specifying the entity, predicate, or type. Here, the decoder vocabulary consists of $V = \{A_0, A_1, \ldots, A_{18}, entity, predicate, type\}$ where $A_0, A_1, \ldots, A_{18}$ are the short names of actions in Table 2. The goal is to produce a correct logical form sequence. The decoder stack is a transformer model supported by a linear and a softmax layer to estimate the probability scores, i.e., we can define it as:

$$s^{(dec)} = decoder(h; \theta^{(dec)}), \ p_t = softmax(W^{(dec)} s_t^{(dec)}) \qquad (1)$$

where $s_t^{(dec)}$ is the hidden state of the decoder in time step t, $\theta^{(dec)}$ are the model parameters, $W^{(dec)} \in \mathbb{R}^{|V| \times d_{emb}}$ are the weights of the feed-forward linear layer, and $p_t \in \mathbb{R}^{|V|}$ is the probability distribution over the decoder vocabulary for the output token in time step t.

3.3 Stacked Pointer Networks

As we mentioned, the decoder only outputs the actions without specifying any KG items. To complete the logical form with instantiated semantic categories, we extend our model with an architecture of stacked pointer networks [26]. The architecture consists of three-pointer networks and each one of them is responsible for covering one of the major semantic categories (types, predicates, and entities) required for completing the final executable logical form against the KG.

The first two pointer networks of the stack are used for predicates and types semantic category and follow a similar approach. The vocabulary and the inputs are the entire predicates and types of the KG. We define the vocabularies, $V^{(pd)} = \{r_1, \ldots, r_{n_{pd}}\}$ and $V^{(tp)} = \{\tau_1, \ldots, \tau_{n_{tp}}\}$, where n_{pd} and n_{tp} is the total number of predicates and types in the KG, respectively. To compute the pointer scores for each predicate or type candidate, we use the current hidden state of the decoder and the context representation. We model the pointer networks with a feed-forward linear network and a softmax layer. We can define the type and predicate pointers as:

$$p_t^{(pd)} = softmax(\boldsymbol{W}_1^{(pd)} v_t^{(pd)}), \ p_t^{(tp)} = softmax(\boldsymbol{W}_1^{(tp)} v_t^{(tp)}), \qquad (2)$$

where $p_t^{(pd)} \in \mathbb{R}^{|V^{(pd)}|}$ and $p_t^{(tp)} \in \mathbb{R}^{|V^{(tp)}|}$ are the probability distributions over the predicate and type vocabularies respectively. The weight matrices $\boldsymbol{W}_1^{(pd)}, \boldsymbol{W}_1^{(tp)} \in \mathbb{R}^{1 \times d_{kg}}$. Also, v_t is a joint representation that includes the knowledge graph embeddings, the context and the current decoder state, computed as:

$$\begin{aligned} v_t^{(pd)} &= tanh(\boldsymbol{W}_2^{(pd)}[s_t; h_{ctx}] + r), \\ v_t^{(tp)} &= tanh(\boldsymbol{W}_2^{(tp)}[s_t; h_{ctx}] + \tau), \end{aligned} \qquad (3)$$

where the weight matrices $\boldsymbol{W}_2^{(pd)}, \boldsymbol{W}_2^{(tp)} \in \mathbb{R}^{d_{kg} \times 2d_{emb}}$, transform the concatenation of the current decoder state s_t with the context representation h_{ctx}. We denote with d_{kg} the dimension used for knowledge graph embeddings. $r \in \mathbb{R}^{d_{kg} \times |V^{(pd)}|}$ are the predicate embeddings and $\tau \in \mathbb{R}^{d_{kg} \times |V^{(tp)}|}$ are the type embeddings. $tanh$ is the non-linear layer. Please note, that the vocabulary of predicates and types is updated during evaluation, hence the choice of pointer networks.

The third pointer network of the stack is responsible for the entity prediction task. Here we follow a slightly different approach due to the massive number of entities that the KG may have. Predicting a probability distribution over KG with a considerable number of entities is not computationally feasible. For that reason, we decrease the size of entity vocabulary during each logical form prediction. In each conversation, we predict a probability distribution **only** for the entities that are part of the context. Our entity "memory" for each conversation turn involves entities from the previous question, previous answer, and current question. The probability distribution over the entities is then calculated in the same way as for predicates and types where the softmax is:

$$p_t^{(ent)} = softmax(\boldsymbol{W}_1^{(ent)} v_t^{(ent)}), \qquad (4)$$

where $p_t^{(ent)} \in \mathbb{R}^{|V_k^{(ent)}|}$, and $V_k^{(ent)}$ is the set of entities for the kth conversation turn. The weight matrix $\boldsymbol{W}_1^{(ent)} \in \mathbb{R}^{1 \times d_{kg}}$ and the vector v_t is then computed following the same equations as before:

$$v_t^{(ent)} = tanh(\boldsymbol{W}_2^{(ent)}([s_t; h_{ctx}]) + e_k) \qquad (5)$$

where e_k is the sequence of entities for the kth conversation turn. In general, the pointer networks are robust to handle a different vocabulary size for each time step [26]. Moreover, given the knowledge graph embeddings, our stacked pointer networks select the relevant items from the knowledge graph depending on the conversational context. In this way, we incorporate knowledge graph embeddings in order to perform any reasoning and do not rely only on utterance features. Furthermore, the [21] utilizes a single pointer network that only operates on the input utterance to select the already identified entities. Our stacked pointer networks do not use the input utterance but rather directly rely on the knowledge graph semantic categories (types, predicates, and entities).

3.4 Learning

For each time step, we have four different predicted probability distributions. The first is the decoder output over the logical form's vocabulary, and the three others from the stacked pointer networks for each of the semantic categories (entity, predicate, and type). Finally, we define CARTON loss function as:

$$Loss_t = -\frac{1}{m} \sum_{i=1}^{m} \left(log\, p_{i\,[i=y_i^{(t)}]} + \sum_{c \in \{ent,pd,tp\}} I_{[y_i^{(t)}=c]}\, logp_{i\,[i=y_i^{(c_t)}]}^{(c)} \right), \quad (6)$$

where $Loss_t$ is the loss function computed for the sequence in time step t, m is the length of the logical form, $y^{(t)}$ is the gold sequence of logical form, and $y^{(c_t)}$ is the gold label for one of the semantic categories $c \in \{ent, pd, tp\}$.

4 Experimental Setup

Dataset and Experiment Settings. We conduct our experiments on the Complex Sequential Question Answering (CSQA) dataset[2] [19]. CSQA was built on the Wikidata KG. The CSQA dataset consists of around 200K dialogues where each partition train, valid, test contains 153K, 16K, 28K dialogues, respectively. The questions in the CSQA dataset involve complex reasoning on Wikidata to determine the correct answer. The different question types that appear in the dataset are simple questions, logical reasoning, verification, quantitative reasoning, comparative reasoning, and clarification. We can have different subtypes for each one of them, such as direct, indirect, coreference, and ellipsis questions. We stick to one dataset in experiments due to the following reasons 1) all the multi-task learning framework has been trained and tested only on the CSQA dataset. Hence, for a fair evaluation and comparison of our approach inheriting the evaluation settings same as [19,21], we stick to the CSQA dataset. 2) other approaches [2,24] on datasets such as ConvQA, TREC CAsT, etc. are not multi-task learning approaches. Further, we cannot retrain [8,19,21] on these datasets due to their missing logical forms employed by each of these models.

We incorporate a semi-automated preprocessing step to annotate the CSQA dataset with gold logical forms. For each question type and subtype in the dataset, we create a general template with a pattern sequence that the actions should follow. Thereafter, for each question, we follow a set of rules to create the specific gold logical form that extracts the gold sequence of actions based on the type of the question. The actions used for this process are the one in Table 2.

CARTON Configurations. For the transformer network, we use the configurations from [25]. Our model dimension is $d_{model} = 512$, with a total number of $H = 8$ heads and layers $L = 4$. The inner feed-forward linear layers have dimension $d_{ff} = 2048$, (4 * 512). Following the base transformer parameters, we apply residual dropout to the summation of the embeddings and the positional encodings in both encoder and decoder

---

[2] https://amritasaha1812.github.io/CSQA.

stacks with a rate of 0.1. On the other hand, the pointer networks also use a dropout layer for the linear projection of the knowledge graph embeddings. For predicates and types, we randomly initialize the embeddings and are jointly learned during training. The KG embeddings dimension of predicate and types match the transformer model dimension, $d_{kg} = 512$. However, for the entities, we follow a different initialization. Due to a significantly high number of the entities, learning the entity embeddings from scratch was inefficient and resulted in poor performance. Therefore, to address this issue, we initialized the entity embeddings using sentence embeddings that implicitly use underlying hidden states from BERT network [3]. For each entity, we treat the tokens that it contains as a sentence, and we feed that as an input. We receive as output the entity representation with a dimension $d_{ent} = 768$. Next, we feed this into a linear layer that learns, during training, to embed the entity into the same dimension as the predicates and types.

Models for Comparison. To compare the CARTON framework, we use the last three baselines that have been evaluated on the employed dataset. The authors of the CSQA dataset introduce the first baseline: HRED+KVmem [19] model. HRED+KVmem employs a seq2seq [23] model extended with memory networks [12,22]. The model uses HRED model [20] to extract dialog representations and extends it with a Key-Value memory network [17] for extracting information from KG. Next, D2A [8] uses a semantic parsing approach based on a seq2seq model, extended with dialog memory manager to handle different linguistic problems in conversations such as ellipsis and coreference. Finally, MaSP [21] is the current SotA and is also a semantic parsing approach.

Evaluation Metrics. To evaluate CARTON, we use the same metrics as employed by the authors of the CSQA dataset [19] and previous baselines. We use the "F1-score" for questions that have an answer composed by a set of entities. "Accuracy" is used for the question types whose answer is a number or a boolean value (YES/NO).

5   Results

We report our empirical results in Table 4, and conclude that CARTON outperforms baselines average on all question types (row "overall" in the table). We dig deeper into the accuracy per question type to understand the overall performance. Compared to the current state-of-the-art (MaSP), CARTON performs better on eight out of ten question types. CARTON is leading MaSP in question type categories such as *Logical Reasoning (All), Quantitative Reasoning (All), Simple Question (Coreferenced), Simple Question (Direct), Simple Question (Ellipsis), Verification (Boolean), Quantitative Reasoning (Count)*, and *Comparative Reasoning (Count)*. Whereas, MaSP retains the state of the art for the categories of *Clarification* and *Comparative Reasoning (All)*. The main reason for weak results in *Comparative Reasoning (All)* is that our preprocessing step finds limitation in covering this question type and is one of the shortcoming

Table 4. Comparisons among baseline models on the CSQA dataset having 200K dialogues with 1.6M turns, and over 12.8M entities.

Methods	HRED-KV	D2A	MaSP	CARTON (ours)	Δ
Question type (QT)	*F1 score*				
Overall	9.39%	66.70%	79.26%	**81.35%**	**+2.09%**
Clarification	16.35%	35.53%	**80.79%**	47.31%	–33.48%
Comparative reasoning (All)	2.96%	48.85%	**68.90%**	62.00%	–6.90%
Logical reasoning (All)	8.33%	67.31%	69.04%	**80.80%**	+11.76%
Quantitative reasoning (All)	0.96%	56.41%	73.75%	**80.62%**	+6.87%
Simple question (Coreferenced)	7.26%	57.69%	76.47%	**87.09%**	+10.62%
Simple question (Direct)	13.64%	78.42%	85.18%	**85.92%**	+0.74%
Simple question (Ellipsis)	9.95%	81.14%	83.73%	**85.07%**	+1.34%
Question type (QT)	*Accuracy*				
Overall	14.95%	37.33%	45.56%	**61.28%**	**+15.72%**
Verification (Boolean)	21.04%	45.05%	60.63%	**77.82%**	+17.19%
Quantitative reasoning (Count)	12.13%	40.94%	43.39%	**57.04%**	+13.65%
Comparative reasoning (Count)	8.67%	17.78%	22.26%	**38.31%**	+16.05%

of our proposed grammar[3]. We investigated several reasonable ways to cover *Comparative Reasoning (All)* question type. However, it was challenging to produce a final answer set identical to the gold answer set. For instance, consider the question *"Which administrative territories have diplomatic relations with around the same number of administrative territories than Albania?"* that includes logic operators like "around the same number", which is ambiguous because CARTON needs to look for the correct answer in a range of the numbers. Whereas, MaSP uses a BFS method to search the gold logical forms and performance is superior to CARTON. The limitation with *Comparative Reasoning* question type also affects CARTON's performance in the *Clarification* question type where a considerable number of questions correspond to *Comparative Reasoning*. Based on analysis, we outline the following two reasons for CARTON's outperformance over MaSP: First, the MaSP model requires to perform entity recognition and linking to generate the correct entity candidate. Even though MaSP is a multi-task model, errors at entity recognition step will still be propagated to the underlying coreference network. CARTON is agnostic of such a scenario since the candidate entity set considered for each conversation turn is related to the entire relevant context (the previous question, answer, and current question). In CARTON, entity detection is performed only by stacked pointer networks. Hence no error propagation related to entities affects previous steps of the framework. Second, CARTON uses better supervision signals than MaSP. As mentioned earlier, CARTON supervision signals propagate in sequential order, and all components use the signal forwarded from the previous

---

[3] For instance, when we applied the preprocessing step over the test set, we could not annotate the majority of the examples for the *Comparative Reasoning (All)* question type.

Table 5. CARTON ablation study. "W/o St. Pointer" column shows results when stacked pointers in CARTON is replaced by classifiers.

Question type (QT)	CARTON	W/o St. Pointers
Clarification	47.31%	42.47%
Comparative reasoning (All)	62.00%	55.82%
Logical reasoning (All)	80.80%	68.23%
Quantitative reasoning (All)	80.62%	71.59%
Simple question (Coreferenced)	87.09%	85.28%
Simple question (Direct)	85.92%	83.64%
Simple question (Ellipsis)	85.07%	82.11%
Verification (Boolean)	77.82%	70.38%
Quantitative reasoning (Count)	57.04%	51.73%
Comparative reasoning (Count)	38.31%	30.87%

components. In contrast, the MaSP model co-trains entity detection and semantic parsing with different supervision signals.

5.1 Ablation Study

An ablation study is conducted to support our architectural choices of CARTON. To do so, we replace stacked pointer networks module with simple classifiers. In particular, predicates and types are predicted using two linear classifiers using the representations from the contextual encoder. Table 5 illustrates that the modified setting (w/o St. Pointers) significantly under-performs compared to CARTON in all question types. The stacked pointer networks generalize better in the test set due to their ability to learn meaningful representations for the KG items and align learned representations with the conversational context. While classifiers thoroughly learn to identify common patterns between examples without incorporating any information from the KG. Furthermore, our framework's improved results are implied from the ability of stacked pointer networks to handle out-of-vocabulary entities, predicates, and types that are unseen during training.

5.2 Error Analysis

We now present a detailed analysis of CARTON by reporting some additional metrics. Table 6 reports the accuracy of predicting the KG items such as entity, predicate, or type using CARTON. The prediction accuracy of KG items is closely related to the performance of our model, as shown in Table 4. For example, in the *Quantitative (All)* question type (Table 4), predicting the correct type has an accuracy of 73.46% which is lowest compared to other question types. The type prediction is essential in such category of questions, where a typical logical form possibly is: *"argmin, find_tuple_counts, predicate, type1, type2"*. Filtering by the wrong type gets the incorrect result. Please

Table 6. CARTON stacked pointer networks results for each question type. We report CARTON's accuracy in predicting the KG items such as entity, predicate, or type.

Question type (QT)	Entity	Predicate	Type
Clarification	36.71%	94.76%	80.79%
Comparative reasoning (All)	67.63%	97.92%	77.57%
Logical reasoning (All)	64.7%	83.18%	91.56%
Quantitative reasoning (All)	–	98.46%	73.46%
Simple question (Coreferenced)	81.13%	91.09%	80.13%
Simple question (Direct)	86.07%	91%	82.19%
Simple question (Ellipsis)	98.87%	92.49%	80.31%
Verification (Boolean)	43.01%	94.72%	–
Quantitative reasoning (Count)	79.60%	94.46%	79.51%
Comparative reasoning (Count)	70.29%	98.05%	78.38%

note, there is no "entity" involved in the logical forms of *Quantitative (All)* question type. Hence, no entity accuracy is reported.

Another interesting result is the high accuracy of the entities and predicates in *Comparative (Count)* questions. Also, the accuracy of type detection is 78.38%. However, these questions' accuracy was relatively low, only 38.31%, as reported in Table 4. We believe that improved accuracy is mainly affected due to the mapping process of entities, predicates, and types to the logical forms that is followed to reach the correct answer. Another insightful result is on *Simple (Ellipsis)*, where CARTON has a high entity accuracy compared with *Simple Question*. A possible reason is the short length of the question, making it easier for the model to focus on the right entity. Some example of this question type is *"And what about Bonn?"*, where the predicate is extracted from the previous utterance of the question.

We compute the accuracy of the decoder which is used to find the correct patterns of the logical forms. We also calculate the accuracy of the logical forms after the pointer networks initialize the KG items. We report an average accuracy across question types for generating logical form (by decoder) as 97.24%, and after initializing the KG items, the average accuracy drops to 75.61%. Higher accuracy of logical form generation shows the decoder's effectiveness and how the Transformer network can extract the correct patterns given the conversational context. Furthermore, it also justifies that the higher error percentage is generated while initializing the items from the KG. When sampling some of the wrong logical forms, we found out that most of the errors were generated from initializing a similar predicate or incorrect order of the types in the logical actions.

6 Conclusions

In this work, we focus on complex question answering over a large-scale KG containing conversational context. We used a transformer-based model to generate logical forms.

The decoder was extended with a stack of pointer networks in order to include information from the large-scale KG associated with the dataset. The stacked pointer networks, given the conversational context extracted by the transformer, predict the specific KG item required in a particular position of the action sequence. We empirically demonstrate that our model performs the best in several question types and how entity and type detection accuracy affect the performance. The main drawback of the semantic parsing approaches is the error propagated from the preprocessing step, which is not 100% accurate. However, to train the model in a supervised way, we need the gold logical form annotations. The model focuses on learning the correct logical forms, but there is no feedback signal from the resulting answer generated from its logical structure. We believe reinforcement learning can solve these drawbacks and is the most viable next step of our work. Furthermore, how to improve the performance of Clarification and Comparative Reasoning question type is an open question and a direction for future research.

Acknowledgments. The project leading to this publication has received funding from the European Union's Horizon 2020 research and innovation program under the Marie Skłodowska-Curie grant agreement No. 812997 (Cleopatra).

References

1. Bollacker, K.D., Cook, R.P., Tufts, P.: Freebase: a shared database of structured general human knowledge. In: AAAI 2007 (2007)
2. Christmann, P., Saha Roy, R., Abujabal, A., Singh, J., Weikum, G.: Look before you hop: conversational question answering over knowledge graphs using judicious context expansion. In: CIKM (2019)
3. Devlin, J., Chang, M.W., Lee, K., Toutanova, K.: BERT: pre-training of deep bidirectional transformers for language understanding. In: NAACL (2019)
4. Dong, L., Lapata, M.: Language to logical form with neural attention. In: ACL (2016)
5. Dong, L., Lapata, M.: Coarse-to-fine decoding for neural semantic parsing. In: ACL. association for Computational Linguistics (2018)
6. Dong, L., Wei, F., Zhou, M., Xu, K.: Question answering over freebase with multi-column convolutional neural networks. In: ACL (2015)
7. Fensel, D., et al.: Why We Need Knowledge Graphs: Applications. Knowledge Graphs, pp. 95–112. Springer, Cham (2020). https://doi.org/10.1007/978-3-030-37439-6_4
8. Guo, D., Tang, D., Duan, N., Zhou, M., Yin, J.: Dialog-to-action: Conversational question answering over a large-scale knowledge base. In: Advances in Neural Information Processing Systems 31: Annual Conference on Neural Information Processing Systems 2018, NeurIPS 2018 (2018)
9. Jia, R., Liang, P.: Data recombination for neural semantic parsing. In: ACL (Long Papers). Association for Computational Linguistics (2016)
10. Kassawat, F., Chaudhuri, D., Lehmann, J.: Incorporating joint embeddings into goal-oriented dialogues with multi-task learning. In: Hitzler, P. (ed.) ESWC 2019. LNCS, vol. 11503, pp. 225–239. Springer, Cham (2019). https://doi.org/10.1007/978-3-030-21348-0_15
11. Lehmann, J., et al.: Dbpedia - a large-scale, multilingual knowledge base extracted from wikipedia. Seman. Web 6(2), 167–195 (2015)
12. Li, Z., Zhang, Y., Wei, Y., Wu, Y., Yang, Q.: End-to-end adversarial memory network for cross-domain sentiment classification. In: ICAI (2017)

13. Liang, C., Berant, J., Le, Q.V., Forbus, K.D., Lao, N.: Neural symbolic machines: Learning semantic parsers on freebase with weak supervision. In: Proceedings of the 55th Annual Meeting of the Association for Computational Linguistics, ACL Long Papers. Association for Computational Linguistics (2017)
14. Lu, W., Ng, H.T., Lee, W.S., Zettlemoyer, L.S.: A generative model for parsing natural language to meaning representations. In: 2008 Conference on Empirical Methods in Natural Language Processing, EMNLP 2008, ACL (2008)
15. Lukovnikov, D., Fischer, A., Lehmann, J., Auer, S.: Neural network-based question answering over knowledge graphs on word and character level. In: Barrett, R., Cummings, R., Agichtein, E., Gabrilovich, E. (eds.) The Web Conference. ACM (2017)
16. Luo, K., Lin, F., Luo, X., Zhu, K.: Knowledge base question answering via encoding of complex query graphs. In: EMNLP (2018)
17. Miller, A.H., Fisch, A., Dodge, J., Karimi, A., Bordes, A., Weston, J.: Key-value memory networks for directly reading documents. In: Su, J., Carreras, X., Duh, K. (eds.) Proceedings of the 2016 Conference on Empirical Methods in Natural Language Processing, EMNLP (2016)
18. Pennington, J., Socher, R., Manning, C.: Glove: global vectors for word representation. In: Proceedings of the 2014 Conference on Empirical Methods in Natural Language Processing (EMNLP), ACL (2014)
19. Saha, A., Pahuja, V., Khapra, M.M., Sankaranarayanan, K., Chandar, S.: Complex sequential question answering: Towards learning to converse over linked question answer pairs with a knowledge graph. In: Proceedings of the Thirty-Second AAAI Conference on Artificial Intelligence, (AAAI-2018), AAAI Press (2018)
20. Serban, I.V., Sordoni, A., Bengio, Y., Courville, A.C., Pineau, J.: Building end-to-end dialogue systems using generative hierarchical neural network models. In: AAAI (2016)
21. Shen, T., et al.: Multi-task learning for conversational question answering over a large-scale knowledge base. In: Proceedings of the 2019 Conference on Empirical Methods in Natural Language Processing. Association for Computational Linguistics (2019)
22. Sukhbaatar, S., Szlam, A., Weston, J., Fergus, R.: End-to-end memory networks. In: NeurIPS (2015)
23. Sutskever, I., Vinyals, O., Le, Q.V.: Sequence to sequence learning with neural networks. In: Advances in neural information processing systems (2014)
24. Vakulenko, S., Longpre, S., Tu, Z., Anantha, R.: Question rewriting for conversational question answering. arXiv preprint arXiv:2004.14652 (2020)
25. Vaswani, A., et al.: Attention is all you need. In: NeurIPS (2017)
26. Vinyals, O., Fortunato, M., Jaitly, N.: Pointer networks. In: Advances in neural information processing systems (2015)
27. Vrandečić, D., Krötzsch, M.: Wikidata: a free collaborative knowledgebase. Commun. ACM 57(10), 78–85 (2014)
28. Xiao, C., Dymetman, M., Gardent, C.: Sequence-based structured prediction for semantic parsing. In: Proceedings of the 54th Annual Meeting of the Association for Computational Linguistics, vol. 1, Long Papers. Association for Computational Linguistics (2016)
29. Xu, K., Reddy, S., Feng, Y., Huang, S., Zhao, D.: Question answering on Freebase via relation extraction and textual evidence. In: ACL (2016)
30. Yih, W., Richardson, M., Meek, C., Chang, M., Suh, J.: The value of semantic parse labeling for knowledge base question answering. In: Proceedings of the 54th Annual Meeting of the Association for Computational Linguistics, ACL. The Association for Computer Linguistics (2016)
31. Zhang, Y., Dai, H., Kozareva, Z., Smola, A.J., Song, L.: Variational reasoning for question answering with knowledge graph. In: Proceedings of the Thirty-Second AAAI Conference on Artificial Intelligence, (AAAI-2018), AAAI Press (2018)

Machine Learning

Neural Multi-hop Reasoning with Logical Rules on Biomedical Knowledge Graphs

Yushan Liu[1,3](✉), Marcel Hildebrandt[1,3], Mitchell Joblin[1],
Martin Ringsquandl[1], Rime Raissouni[2,3], and Volker Tresp[1,3]

[1] Siemens, Otto-Hahn-Ring 6, 81739 Munich, Germany
{yushan.liu,marcel.hildebrandt,mitchell.joblin,martin.ringsquandl,
volker.tresp}@siemens.com
[2] Siemens Healthineers, Hartmannstraße 16, 91052 Erlangen, Germany
rime.raissouni@siemens-healthineers.com
[3] Ludwig Maximilian University of Munich, Geschwister-Scholl-Platz 1,
80539 Munich, Germany

Abstract. Biomedical knowledge graphs permit an integrative computational approach to reasoning about biological systems. The nature of biological data leads to a graph structure that differs from those typically encountered in benchmarking datasets. To understand the implications this may have on the performance of reasoning algorithms, we conduct an empirical study based on the real-world task of drug repurposing. We formulate this task as a link prediction problem where both compounds and diseases correspond to entities in a knowledge graph. To overcome apparent weaknesses of existing algorithms, we propose a new method, PoLo, that combines policy-guided walks based on reinforcement learning with logical rules. These rules are integrated into the algorithm by using a novel reward function. We apply our method to Hetionet, which integrates biomedical information from 29 prominent bioinformatics databases. Our experiments show that our approach outperforms several state-of-the-art methods for link prediction while providing interpretability.

Keywords: Neural multi-hop reasoning · Reinforcement learning ·
Logical rules · Biomedical knowledge graphs

1 Introduction

Advancements in low-cost high-throughput sequencing, data acquisition technologies, and compute paradigms have given rise to a massive proliferation of data describing biological systems. This new landscape of available data spans a multitude of dimensions, which provide complementary views on the structure of biological systems. Historically, by considering single dimensions (i. e., single types of data), researchers have made progress in understanding many important phenomena. More recently, there has been a movement to develop statistical and

© Springer Nature Switzerland AG 2021
R. Verborgh et al. (Eds.): ESWC 2021, LNCS 12731, pp. 375–391, 2021.
https://doi.org/10.1007/978-3-030-77385-4_22

computational methods that leverage more holistic views by simultaneously considering multiple types of data [40]. To achieve this goal, graph-based knowledge representation has emerged as a promising direction since the inherent flexibility of graphs makes them particularly well-suited for this problem setting.

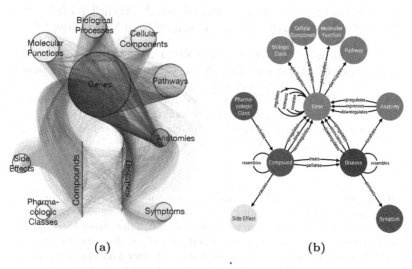

(a)   (b)

Fig. 1. (a) Visualization of the heterogeneous biomedical KG Hetionet [13] (reprint under the use of the CC BY 4.0 license). (b) Schema of Hetionet: Hetionet has 11 different entity types and 24 possible relations between them. Source: https://het.io/about/.

Biomedical knowledge graphs (KGs) are becoming increasingly popular for tasks such as personalized medicine, predictive diagnosis, and drug discovery [9]. Drug discovery, for example, requires a multitude of biomedical data types combined with knowledge across diverse domains (including gene-protein bindings, chemical compounds, and biological pathways). These individual types of data are typically scattered across disparate data sources, published for domain-specific research problems without considering mappings to open standards. To this end, KGs and Semantic Web technologies are being applied to model ontologies that combine knowledge and integrate data contained in biomedical data sources, most notably Bio2RDF [2], for classical query-based question answering.

From a machine learning perspective, reasoning on biomedical KGs presents new challenges for existing approaches due to the unique structural characteristics of the KGs. One challenge arises from the highly coupled nature of entities in biological systems that leads to many high-degree entities that are themselves densely linked. For example, as illustrated in Fig. 1a, genes interact abundantly among themselves. They are involved in a diverse set of biological pathways and molecular functions and have numerous associations with diseases.

A second challenge is that reasoning about the relationship between two entities often requires information beyond second-order neighborhoods [13].

Methods that rely on shallow node embeddings (e. g., TransE [4], DistMult [38]) typically do not perform well in this situation. Approaches that take the entire multi-hop neighborhoods into account (e. g., graph convolutional networks, R-GCN [30]) often have diminishing performance beyond two-hop neighborhoods (i. e., more than two convolutional layers), and the high-degree entities can cause the aggregation operations to smooth out the signal [16]. Symbolic approaches (e. g., AMIE+ [10], RuleN [21]) learn logical rules and employ them during inference. These methods might be able to take long-range dependencies into account, but due to the massive scale and diverse topologies of many real-world KGs, combinatorial complexity often prevents the usage of symbolic approaches [14]. Also, logical inference has difficulties handling noise in the data [24].

Under these structural conditions, path-based methods present a seemingly ideal balance for combining information over multi-hop neighborhoods. The key challenge is to find meaningful paths, which can be computationally difficult if the search is not guided by domain principles. Our goal is to explore how a path-based approach performs in comparison with alternative state-of-the art methods and to identify a way of overcoming weaknesses present in current approaches.

We consider the drug repurposing problem, which is characterized by finding novel treatment targets for existing drugs. Available knowledge about drug-disease-interactions can be exploited to reduce costs and time for developing new drugs significantly. A recent example is the repositioning of the drug remdesivir for the novel disease COVID-19. We formulate this task as a link prediction problem where both compounds and diseases correspond to entities in a KG.

We propose a neuro-symbolic reasoning approach, PoLo (**Po**licy-guided walks with **Lo**gical rules), that leverages both representation learning and logic. Inspired by existing methods [5,12,18], our approach uses reinforcement learning to train an agent to conduct policy-guided random walks on a KG. As a modification to approaches based on policy-guided walks, we introduce a novel reward function that allows the agent to use background knowledge formalized as logical rules, which guide the agent during training. The extracted paths by the agent act as explanations for the predictions. Our results demonstrate that existing methods are inadequately designed to perform ideally in the unique structural characteristics of biomedical data. We can overcome some of the weaknesses of existing methods and show the potential of neuro-symbolic methods for the biomedical domain, where interpretability and transparency of the results are highly relevant to facilitate the accessibility for domain experts. In summary, we make the following contributions:

- We propose the neuro-symbolic KG reasoning method PoLo that combines policy-guided walks based on reinforcement learning with logical rules.
- We conduct an empirical study using a large biomedical KG where we compare our approach with several state-of-the-art algorithms.
- The results show that our proposed approach outperforms state-of-the-art alternatives on a highly relevant biomedical prediction task (drug repurposing) with respect to the metrics hits@k for $k \in \{1, 3, 10\}$ and the mean reciprocal rank.

We briefly introduce the notation and review the related literature in Sect. 2. In Sect. 3, we describe our proposed method[1]. Section 4 details an experimental study, and we conclude in Sect. 5.

2   Background

2.1   Knowledge Graphs

Let $\mathcal{E}$ denote the set of entities in a KG and $\mathcal{R}$ the set of binary relations. Elements in $\mathcal{E}$ correspond to biomedical entities including, e. g., chemical compounds, diseases, and genes. We assume that every entity belongs to a unique type in $\mathcal{T}$, defined by the mapping $\tau : \mathcal{E} \to \mathcal{T}$. For example, $\tau(AURKC) = Gene$ indicates that the entity $AURKC$ has type $Gene$. Relations in $\mathcal{R}$ specify how entities are connected. We define a KG as a collection of triples $\mathcal{KG} \subset \mathcal{E} \times \mathcal{R} \times \mathcal{E}$ in the form (h, r, t), which consists of a head entity, a relation, and a tail entity. Head and tail of a triple are also

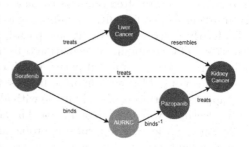

Fig. 2. Subgraph of Hetionet illustrating the drug repurposing use case. The two paths that connect the chemical compound sorafenib and the disease kidney cancer can be used to predict a direct edge between the two entities.

called source and target, respectively. From a graphical point of view, head and tail entities correspond to nodes in the graph while the relation indicates the type of edge between them. For any relation $r \in \mathcal{R}$, we denote the corresponding inverse relation with r^{-1} (i. e., (h, r, t) is equivalent to (t, r^{-1}, h)). Triples in $\mathcal{KG}$ are interpreted as true known facts. For example, the triple $(Sorafenib, treats, Liver\ Cancer) \in \mathcal{KG}$ in Fig. 2 corresponds to the known fact that the kinase inhibitor drug sorafenib is approved for the treatment of primary liver cancer. The *treats* relation is of particular importance for this work since we frame the task of drug repurposing as a link prediction problem with respect to edges of the type *treats*. The domain of *treats* consists of chemical compounds, and the range is given by the set of all diseases.

We further distinguish between two types of paths: instance paths and metapaths. An instance path of length $L \in \mathbb{N}$ on $\mathcal{KG}$ is given by a sequence

$$(e_1 \xrightarrow{r_1} e_2 \xrightarrow{r_2} \dots \xrightarrow{r_L} e_{L+1}) \,,$$

where $(e_i, r_i, e_{i+1}) \in \mathcal{KG}$. We call the corresponding sequence of entity types

$$(\tau(e_1) \xrightarrow{r_1} \tau(e_2) \xrightarrow{r_2} \dots \xrightarrow{r_L} \tau(e_{L+1}))$$

---

[1] The source code is available at https://github.com/liu-yushan/PoLo.

a metapath. For example,

$$(\textit{Sorafenib} \xrightarrow{\textit{treats}} \textit{Liver Cancer} \xrightarrow{\textit{resembles}} \textit{Kidney Cancer})$$

constitutes an instance path of length 2, where

$$(\textit{Compound} \xrightarrow{\textit{treats}} \textit{Disease} \xrightarrow{\textit{resembles}} \textit{Disease})$$

is the corresponding metapath.

2.2 Logical Rules

Logical rules that are typically employed for KG reasoning can be written in the form *head ← body*. We consider cyclic rules of the form

$$(\tau_1, r_{L+1}, \tau_{L+1}) \leftarrow \bigwedge_{i=1}^{L} (\tau_i, r_i, \tau_{i+1}) \,,$$

where $\tau_i \in \mathcal{T}$. The rule is called cyclic since the rule head (not to be confused with the head entity in a triple) connects the source τ_1 and the target τ_{L+1} of the metapath $(\tau_1 \xrightarrow{r_1} \tau_2 \xrightarrow{r_2} \ldots \xrightarrow{r_L} \tau_{L+1})$, which is described by the rule body. The goal is to find instance paths where the corresponding metapaths match the rule body in order to predict a new relation between the source and the target entity of the instance path. For the drug repurposing task, we only consider rules where the rule head is a triple with respect to the *treats* relation.

Define $CtD := (\textit{Compound}, \textit{treats}, \textit{Disease})$. Then, a generic rule has the form

$$CtD \leftarrow \left(\textit{Compound} \xrightarrow{r_1} \tau_2 \xrightarrow{r_2} \tau_3 \xrightarrow{r_3} \ldots \xrightarrow{r_L} \textit{Disease}\right) \,.$$

In particular, the rule body corresponds to a metapath starting at a compound and terminating at a disease. For example (see Fig. 2), consider the rule

$$CtD \leftarrow (\textit{Compound} \xrightarrow{\textit{binds}} \textit{Gene} \xrightarrow{\textit{binds}^{-1}} \textit{Compound} \xrightarrow{\textit{treats}} \textit{Disease}) \,.$$

The metapath of the instance path

$$(\textit{Sorafenib} \xrightarrow{\textit{binds}} AURKC \xrightarrow{\textit{binds}^{-1}} \textit{Pazopanib} \xrightarrow{\textit{treats}} \textit{Kidney Cancer})$$

matches the rule body, suggesting that sorafenib can also treat kidney cancer.

2.3 Related Work

Even though real-world KGs contain a massive number of triples, they are still expected to suffer from incompleteness. Therefore, link prediction (also known as KG completion) is a common reasoning task on KGs. Many classical artificial intelligence tasks such as recommendation problems or question answering can be rephrased in terms of link prediction.

Symbolic approaches have a far-reaching tradition in the context of knowledge acquisition and reasoning. Reasoning with logical rules has been addressed in areas such as Markov logic networks (MLNs) [28] or inductive logic programming [25]. However, such techniques typically do not scale well to modern, large-scale KGs. Recently, novel methods such as RuleN [21] and its successor AnyBURL [19,20] have been proposed that achieve state-of-the-art performance on popular benchmark datasets such as FB15k-237 [31] and WN18RR [7].

Subsymbolic approaches map nodes and edges in KGs to low-dimensional vector representations known as embeddings. Then, the likelihood of missing triples is approximated by a classifier that operates on the embedding space. Popular embedding-based methods include translational methods like TransE [4], more generalized approaches such as DistMult[38] and ComplEx [32], multi-layer models like ConvE [7], and tensor factorization methods like RESCAL [26]. Moreover, R-GCN [30] and CompGCN [34] have been proposed, which extend graph convolutional networks [16] to multi-relational graphs. Despite achieving good results on the link prediction task, a fundamental problem is their non-transparent nature since it remains hidden to the user what contributed to the predictions. Moreover, most embedding-based methods have difficulties in capturing long-range dependencies since they only minimize the reconstruction error in the immediate first-order neighborhoods. Especially the expressiveness of long-tail entities might be low due to the small number of neighbors [11].

Neuro-symbolic methods combine the advantages of robust learning and scalability in subsymbolic approaches with the reasoning properties and interpretability of symbolic representation. For example, Neural LP [39] and Neural Theorem Provers (NTPs) [29] integrate logical rules in a differentiable way into a neural network architecture. The method pLogicNet [27] combines MLNs with embedding-based models and learns a joint distribution over triples, while the Logic Tensor Network [8] inserts background knowledge into neural networks in the form of logical constraints. However, many neuro-symbolic approaches suffer from limited transferability and computational inefficiency. Minervini et al. have presented two more scalable extensions of NTPs, namely the Greedy NTP (GNTP) [22], which considers the top-k rules that are most likely to prove the goal instead of using a fixed set of rules, and the Conditional Theorem Prover (CTP) [23], which learns an adaptive strategy for selecting the rules.

Multi-hop reasoning or path-based approaches infer missing knowledge based on using extracted paths from the KG as features for various inference tasks. Along with a prediction, multi-hop reasoning methods provide the user with an explicit reasoning chain that may serve as a justification for the prediction. For example, the Path Ranking Algorithm (PRA) [17] frames the link prediction task as a maximum likelihood classification based on paths sampled from nearest neighbor random walks on the KG. Xiong et al. extend this idea and formulate the task of path extraction as a reinforcement learning problem (DeepPath [37]). Our proposed method is an extension of the path-based approach MINERVA [5], which trains a reinforcement learning agent to perform a policy-guided random walk until the answer entity to an input query is reached.

One of the drawbacks of existing policy-guided walk methods is that the agent might receive noisy reward signals based on spurious triples that lead to the correct answers during training but lower the generalization capabilities. Moreover, biomedical KGs often exhibit both long-range dependencies and high-degree nodes (see Sect. 4.1). These two properties and the fact that MINERVA's agent only receives a reward if the answer entity is correct make it difficult for the agent to navigate over biomedical KGs and extend a path in the most promising way. As a remedy, we propose the incorporation of known, effective logical rules via a novel reward function. This can help to denoise the reward signal and guide the agent on long paths with high-degree nodes.

3   Our Method

We pose the task of drug repurposing as a link prediction problem based on graph traversal. The general Markov decision process definition that we use has initially been proposed in the algorithm MINERVA [5], with our primary contribution coming from the incorporation of logical rules into the training process. The following notation and definitions are adapted to the use case. Starting at a query entity (a compound to be repurposed), an agent performs a walk on the graph by sequentially transitioning to a neighboring node. The decision of which transition to make is determined by a stochastic policy. Each subsequent transition is added to the current path and extends the reasoning chain. The stochastic walk process iterates until a finite number of transitions has been made. Formally, the learning task is modeled via the fixed-horizon Markov decision process outlined below.

Environment. The state space $\mathcal{S}$ is given by $\mathcal{E}^3$. Intuitively, we want the state to encode the location e_l of the agent for step $l \in \mathbb{N}$, the source entity e_c, and the target entity e_d, corresponding to the compound that we aim to repurpose and the target disease, respectively. Thus, a state $S_l \in \mathcal{S}$ for step $l \in \mathbb{N}$ is represented by $S_l := (e_l, e_c, e_d)$. The agent is given no information about the target disease so that the observed part of the state space is given by $(e_l, e_c) \in \mathcal{E}^2$. The set of available actions from a state S_l is denoted by $\mathcal{A}_{S_l}$. It contains all outgoing edges from the node e_l and the corresponding tail nodes. We also include self-loops for each node so that the agent has the possibility to stay at the current node. More formally, $\mathcal{A}_{S_l} := \{(r, e) \in \mathcal{R} \times \mathcal{E} : (e_l, r, e) \in \mathcal{KG}\} \cup \{(\emptyset, e_l)\}$. Further, we denote with $A_l \in \mathcal{A}_{S_l}$ the action that the agent performed in step l. The environment evolves deterministically by updating the state according to the previous action. The transition function is given by $\delta(S_l, A_l) := (e_{l+1}, e_c, e_d)$ with $S_l = (e_l, e_c, e_d)$ and $A_l = (r_l, e_{l+1})$.

Policy. We denote the history of the agent up to step l with $H_l := (H_{l-1}, A_{l-1})$ for $l \geq 1$, with $H_0 := e_c$ and $A_0 := \emptyset$. The agent encodes the transition history via an LSTM [15] by

$$\boldsymbol{h}_l = \mathrm{LSTM}\left(\boldsymbol{h}_{l-1}, \boldsymbol{a}_{l-1}\right), \tag{1}$$

where $a_{l-1} := [r_{l-1}; e_l] \in \mathbb{R}^{2d}$ corresponds to the vector space embedding of the previous action (or the zero vector for a_0), with r_{l-1} and e_l denoting the embeddings of the relation and the tail entity in $\mathbb{R}^d$, respectively. The history-dependent action distribution is given by

$$d_l = \text{softmax}\left(A_l\left(W_2 \text{ReLU}\left(W_1\left[h_l; e_l\right]\right)\right)\right), \tag{2}$$

where the rows of $A_l \in \mathbb{R}^{|A_{S_l}| \times 2d}$ contain the latent representations of all admissible actions from S_l. The matrices W_1 and W_2 are learnable weight matrices. The action $A_l \in A_{S_l}$ is drawn according to

$$A_l \sim \text{Categorical}\left(d_l\right). \tag{3}$$

The Eqs. (1)–(3) are repeated for each transition step. In total, L transitions are sampled, where L is a hyperparameter that determines the maximum path length, resulting in a path denoted by

$$P := \left(e_c \xrightarrow{r_1} e_2 \xrightarrow{r_2} \ldots \xrightarrow{r_L} e_{L+1}\right).$$

For each step $l \in \{1, 2, \ldots, L\}$, the agent can also choose to remain at the current location and not extend the reasoning path.

Equations (1) and (2) define a mapping from the space of histories to the space of distributions over all admissible actions. Thus, including Eq. (3), a stochastic policy π_θ is induced, where θ denotes the set of all trainable parameters in Eq. (1) and (2).

Metapaths. Consider the set of metapaths $\mathcal{M} = \{M_1, M_2, \ldots, M_m\}$, where each element corresponds to the body of a cyclic rule with CtD as rule head. For every metapath M, we denote with $s(M) \in \mathbb{R}_{>0}$ a score that indicates a quality measure of the corresponding rule, such as the confidence or the support with respect to making a correct prediction. Moreover, for a path P, we denote with $\tilde{P}$ the corresponding metapath.

Rewards and Optimization. During training, after the agent has reached its final location, a terminal reward is assigned according to

$$R(S_{L+1}) = \mathbb{1}_{\{e_{L+1}=e_d\}} + b\lambda \sum_{i=1}^{m} s(M_i)\mathbb{1}_{\tilde{P}=M_i}. \tag{4}$$

The first term indicates whether the agent has reached the correct target disease that can be treated by the compound e_c. It means that the agent receives a reward of 1 for a correct prediction. The second term indicates whether the extracted metapath corresponds to the body of a rule and adds to the reward accordingly. The hyperparameter b can either be 1, i.e., the reward is always increased as long as the metapath corresponds to the body of a rule, or b can be set to $\mathbb{1}_{\{e_{L+1}=e_d\}}$, i.e., an additional reward is only applied if the prediction is also correct. Heuristically speaking, we want to reward the agent for extracting a metapath that corresponds to a rule body with a high score. The hyperparameter $\lambda \geq 0$ balances the two components of the reward. For $\lambda = 0$, we recover the algorithm MINERVA.

We employ REINFORCE [35] to maximize the expected rewards. Thus, the agent's maximization problem is given by

$$\arg\max_{\theta} \mathbb{E}_{(e_c, treats, e_d) \sim \mathcal{D}} \; \mathbb{E}_{A_1, A_2, \ldots, A_L \sim \pi_\theta} \left[R(S_{L+1}) \middle| e_c, e_d \right], \tag{5}$$

where $\mathcal{D}$ denotes the true underlying distribution of $(e_c, treats, e_d)$-triples. During training, we replace the first expectation in Eq. (5) with the empirical average over the training set. The second expectation is approximated by averaging over multiple rollouts for each training sample.

4   Experiments

4.1   Dataset Hetionet

Hetionet [13] is a biomedical KG that integrates information from 29 highly reputable and cited public databases, including the Unified Medical Language System (UMLS) [3], Gene Ontology [1], and DrugBank [36]. It consists of 47,031 entities with 11 different types and 2,250,197 edges with 24 different types. Figure 1b illustrates the schema and shows the different types of entities and possible relations between them.

Hetionet differs in many aspects from the standard benchmark datasets that are typically used in the KG reasoning literature. Table 1 summarizes the basic statistics of Hetionet along with the popular benchmark datasets FB15k-237 [31] and WN18RR [7]. One of the major differences between Hetionet and the two other benchmark datasets is the density of triples, i. e., the average node degree in Hetionet is significantly higher than in the other two KGs. Entities of type *Anatomy* are densely connected hub nodes, and in addition, entities of type *Gene* have an average degree of around 123. This plays a crucial role for our application since many relevant paths that connect *Compound* and *Disease* traverse entities of type *Gene* (see Fig. 1b and Table 2). The total counts and the average node degrees according to each entity type are shown in Appendix A. We will discuss in Sect. 4.5 further how particularities of Hetionet impose challenges on existing KG reasoning methods.

We aim to predict edges with type *treats* between entities that correspond to compounds and diseases in order to perform candidate ranking according to the likelihood of successful drug repurposing in a novel treatment application. There are 1552 compounds and 137 diseases in Hetionet with 775 observed links of type *treats* between compounds and diseases. We randomly split these 755 triples into training, validation, and test set, where the training set contains 483 triples, the validation set 121 triples, and the test set 151 triples.

4.2 Metapaths as Background Information

Himmelstein et al. [13] evaluated 1206 metapaths that connect entities of type *Compound* with entities of type *Disease*, which correspond to various pharmacological efficacy mechanisms. They identified 27 effective metapaths that served as features for a logistic regression model that outputs a treatment probability of a compound for a disease. Out of these metapaths, we select the 10 metapaths as background information that have at most path length 3 and exhibit positive regression coefficients, which indicates their importance for predicting drug efficacy. We use the metapaths as the rule bodies and the confidence of the rules as the quality scores (see Sect. 3). The confidence of a rule is defined as the rule support divided by the body support in the data. We estimate the confidence score for each rule by sampling 5,000 paths whose metapaths correspond to the rule body and then computing how often the rule head holds. An overview of the 10 metapaths and their scores is given in Table 2.

Table 1. Comparison of Hetionet with the two benchmark datasets FB15k-237 and WN18RR.

Dataset	Entities	Relations	Triples	Avg. degree
Hetionet	47,031	24	2,250,197	95.8
FB15k-237	14,541	237	310,116	19.7
WN18RR	40,943	11	93,003	2.2

Table 2. All 10 metapaths used in our model and their corresponding scores.

$s(M)$	Metapath M
0.446	$(Compound \xrightarrow{includes^{-1}} Pharmacologic\ Class \xrightarrow{includes} Compound \xrightarrow{treats} Disease)$
0.265	$(Compound \xrightarrow{resembles} Compound \xrightarrow{resembles} Compound \xrightarrow{treats} Disease)$
0.184	$(Compound \xrightarrow{binds} Gene \xrightarrow{associates^{-1}} Disease)$
0.182	$(Compound \xrightarrow{resembles} Compound \xrightarrow{treats} Disease)$
0.169	$(Compound \xrightarrow{palliates} Disease \xrightarrow{palliates^{-1}} Compound \xrightarrow{treats} Disease)$
0.143	$(Compound \xrightarrow{binds} Gene \xrightarrow{binds^{-1}} Compound \xrightarrow{treats} Disease)$
0.058	$(Compound \xrightarrow{causes} Side\ Effect \xrightarrow{causes^{-1}} Compound \xrightarrow{treats} Disease)$
0.040	$(Compound \xrightarrow{treats} Disease \xrightarrow{resembles} Disease)$
0.017	$(Compound \xrightarrow{resembles} Compound \xrightarrow{binds} Gene \xrightarrow{associates^{-1}} Disease)$
0.004	$(Compound \xrightarrow{binds} Gene \xrightarrow{expresses^{-1}} Anatomy \xrightarrow{localizes^{-1}} Disease)$

4.3 Experimental Setup

We apply our method PoLo to Hetionet and calculate the values for hits@1, hits@3, hits@10, and the mean reciprocal rank (MRR) for the link prediction task. All metrics in the paper are filtered [4] and evaluated for tail-sided predictions. During inference, a beam search is carried out to find the most promising paths, and the target entities are ranked by the probability of their corresponding paths. Moreover, we consider another evaluation scheme (PoLo (pruned)) that retrieves and ranks only those paths from the test rollouts that correspond to one of the metapaths in Table 2. All the other extracted paths are not considered in the ranking.

We compare PoLo with the following baseline methods. The rule-based method AnyBURL [19,20] mines logical rules based on path sampling and uses them for inference. The methods TransE [4], DistMult [38], ComplEx [32], ConvE [6], and RESCAL [26] are popular embedding-based models, and we use the implementation from the LibKGE library[2]. To cover a more recent paradigm in graph-based machine learning, we include the graph convolutional approaches R-GCN [30] and CompGCN [34]. We also compare our method with the neuro-symbolic method pLogicNet [27]. The two neuro-symbolic approaches NTP [29] and Neural LP [39] yield good performance on smaller datasets but are not scalable to large datasets like Hetionet. We have also conducted experiments on the two more scalable extensions of NTP (GNTP [22] and CTP [23]), but both were not able to produce results in a reasonable time. More experimental details can be found in Appendix B.

4.4 Results

Table 3 displays the results for the experiments on Hetionet. The reported values for PoLo and MINERVA correspond to the mean across five independent training runs. The standard errors for the reported metrics are between 0.006 and 0.018.

PoLo outperforms all baseline methods with respect to all evaluation metrics. Applying the modified ranking scheme, our method yields performance gains of 27.7% for hits@1, 14.9% for hits@3, 8.1% for hits@10, and 16.2% for the MRR with respect to best performing baseline.

Figure 3a shows the rule accuracy, i.e., the percentage of correct target entities for extracted paths that follow rule metapaths, for PoLo and MINERVA during training. Both lines behave similarly in the beginning, but the rule accuracy of PoLo increases significantly around epoch 20 compared to MINERVA. It seems that giving the agent an extra reward for extracting rules also improves the probability of arriving at correct target entities when applying the rules. We also compare the metric hits@1 (pruned) for the evaluation of the validation set during training (see Fig. 3b). Around epoch 20, where the rule accuracy of PoLo increases compared to MINERVA, hits@1 (pruned) also increases while it decreases for MINERVA. The additional reward for extracting rule paths could

---

[2] https://github.com/uma-pi1/kge.

Table 3. Comparison with baseline methods on Hetionet.

Method	Hits@1	Hits@3	Hits@10	MRR
AnyBURL	0.229	0.375	0.553	0.322
TransE	0.099	0.199	0.444	0.205
DistMult	0.185	0.305	0.510	0.287
ComplEx	0.152	0.285	0.470	0.250
ConvE	0.100	0.225	0.318	0.180
RESCAL	0.106	0.166	0.377	0.187
R-GCN	0.026	0.245	0.272	0.135
CompGCN	0.172	0.318	0.543	0.292
pLogicNet	0.225	0.364	0.523	0.333
MINERVA	0.264	0.409	0.593	0.370
PoLo	0.314	0.428	0.609	0.402
PoLo (pruned)	**0.337**	**0.470**	**0.641**	**0.430**

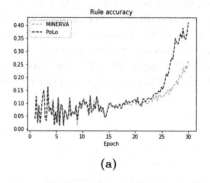 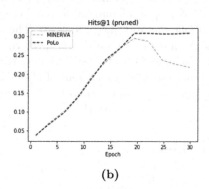

(a)   (b)

Fig. 3. (a) Rule accuracy during training. (b) Hits@1 (pruned) for the evaluation of the validation set during training.

be seen as a regularization that alleviates overfitting and allows for longer training for improved results.

The metapath that was most frequently extracted by PoLo during testing is

$$(Compound \xrightarrow{causes} Side\ Effect \xrightarrow{causes^{-1}} Compound \xrightarrow{treats} Disease)\ .$$

This rule was followed in 37.3% of the paths during testing, of which 16.9% ended at the correct entity.

During testing, PoLo extracted metapaths that correspond to rules in 41.7% of all rollouts while MINERVA only extracted rule paths in 36.9% of the cases. The accuracy of the rules, i.e., the percentage of correct target entities when rule paths are followed, is 19.0% for PoLo and 17.6% for MINERVA.

4.5   Discussion

We have integrated logical rules as background information via a new reward mechanism into the multi-hop reasoning method MINERVA. The stochastic policy incorporates the set of rules that are presented to the agent during training. Our approach is not limited to MINERVA but can act as a generic mechanism to inject domain knowledge into reinforcement learning-based reasoning methods on KGs [18,37]. While we employ rules that are extracted in a data-driven fashion, our method is agnostic towards the source of background information.

The additional reward for extracting a rule path can be considered as a regularization that induces the agent to walk along metapaths that generalize to unseen instances. In particular, for PoLo (pruned), we consider only extracted paths that correspond to the logical rules. However, the resulting ranking of the answer candidates is not based on global quality measures of the rules (e.g., the confidence). Rather, the ranking is given by the policy of the agent (i.e., metapaths that are more likely to be extracted are ranked higher), which creates an adaptive reweighting of the extracted rules that takes the individual instance paths into account.

Multi-hop reasoning methods contain a natural transparency mechanism by providing explicit inference paths. These paths allow domain experts to evaluate and monitor the predictions. Typically, there is an inherent trade-off between explainability and performance, but surprisingly, our experimental findings show that path-based reasoning methods outperform existing black-box methods on the drug repurposing task. Concretely, we compared our approach with the embedding-based methods TransE, DistMult, ComplEx, ConvE, and RESCAL. These methods are trained to minimize the reconstruction error in the immediate first-order neighborhood while discarding higher-order proximities. However, most explanatory metapaths in the drug repurposing setting have length 2 or more [13]. While MINERVA and PoLo can explicitly reason over multiple hops, our results indicate that embedding-based methods that fit low-order proximities seem not to be suitable for the drug repurposing task, and it is plausible that other reasoning tasks on biomedical KGs could result in similar outcomes.

R-CGN and CompGCN learn node embeddings by aggregating incoming · messages from neighboring nodes and combining this information with the node's own embedding. These methods are in principle capable of modeling long-term dependencies. Since the receptive field contains the entire set of nodes in the multi-hop neighborhood, the aggregation and combination step essentially acts as a low-pass filter on the incoming signals. This can be problematic in the presence of many high-degree nodes like in Hetionet where the center node receives an uninformative signal that smooths over the neighborhood embeddings.

The approaches pLogicNet and AnyBURL both involve the learning of rules and yield similar performance on Hetionet, which is worse than PoLo. Most likely, the large amount of high-degree nodes in Hetionet makes the learning and application of logical rules more difficult. Other neuro-symbolic methods such as NTP, its extensions, and Neural LP were not scalable to Hetionet.

To illustrate the applicability of our method, consider the example of the chemical compound sorafenib (see Fig. 2), which is known for treating liver cancer, kidney cancer, and thyroid cancer. The top predictions of our model for new target diseases include pancreatic cancer, breast cancer, and hematologic cancer. This result seems to be sensible since sorafenib already treats three other cancer types. The database ClinicalTrials.gov [33] lists 16 clinical studies for testing the effect of sorafenib on pancreatic cancer, 33 studies on breast cancer, and 6 studies on hematologic cancer, showing that the predicted diseases are meaningful targets for further investigation. Another example of drug repurposing on Hetionet is provided in Appendix C.

4.6   Experiments on Other Datasets

We also conduct experiments on the benchmark datasets FB15k-237 and WN18RR and compare PoLo with the other baseline methods. Since we do not already have logical rules available, we use the rules learned by AnyBURL. We can only apply cyclic rules for PoLo, so we also compare to the setting where we only learn and apply cyclic rules with AnyBURL.

Our method mostly outperforms MINERVA and Neural LP on both datasets. For FB15k-237, PoLo has worse performance than AnyBURL and most embedding-based methods, probably because the number of unique metapaths that occur a large number of times in the graph is lower compared to other datasets [5]. This makes it difficult for PoLo to extract metapaths sufficiently often for good generalization. pLogicNet yields better performance on FB15k-237 than PoLo but worse performance on WN18RR. The results of AnyBURL on FB15k-237 and WN18RR when only using cyclic rules are worse than when also including acyclic rules. It seems that acyclic rules are important for predictions as well, but PoLo cannot make use of these rules. The detailed results for both datasets can be found in Appendix D.

5   Conclusion

Biomedical knowledge graphs present challenges for learning algorithms that are not reflected in the common benchmark datasets. Our experimental findings suggest that existing knowledge graph reasoning methods face difficulties on Hetionet, a biomedical knowledge graph that exhibits both long-range dependencies and a multitude of high-degree nodes. We have proposed the neuro-symbolic approach PoLo that leverages both representation learning and logic. Concretely, we integrate logical rules into a multi-hop reasoning method based on reinforcement learning via a novel reward mechanism. We apply our method to the highly relevant task of drug repurposing and compare our approach with embedding-based, logic-based, and neuro-symbolic methods. The results indicate a better performance of PoLo compared to popular state-of-the-art methods. Further, PoLo also provides interpretability by extracting reasoning paths that serve as explanations for the predictions.

Acknowledgements.. This work has been supported by the German Federal Ministry for Economic Affairs and Energy (BMWi) as part of the project RAKI (01MD19012C).

References

1. Ashburner, M., et al.: Gene Ontology: tool for the unification of biology. Nat. Genet. **25**(1), 25–29 (2000)
2. Belleau, F., Nolin, M.A., Tourigny, N., Rigault, P., Morissette, J.: Bio2RDF: towards a mashup to build bioinformatics knowledge systems. J. Biomed. Inform. **41**(5), 706–716 (2008)
3. Bodenreider, O.: The unified medical language system (UMLS): integrating biomedical terminology. Nucleic Acids Res. **32**(Database), D267–D270 (2004)
4. Bordes, A., Usunier, N., Garcia-Duran, A., Weston, J., Yakhnenko, O.: Translating embeddings for modeling multi-relational data. In: The 27th Conference on Neural Information Processing Systems (2013)
5. Das, R., et al.: Go for a walk and arrive at the answer: reasoning over paths in knowledge bases using reinforcement learning. In: The 6th International Conference on Learning Representations (2018)
6. Defferrard, M., Bresson, X., Vandergheynst, P.: Convolutional neural networks on graphs with fast localized spectral filtering. In: The 13th Conference on Neural Information Processing Systems (2016)
7. Dettmers, T., Minervini, P., Stenetorp, P., Riedel, S.: Convolutional 2D knowledge graph embeddings. In: The 32nd AAAI Conference on Artificial Intelligence (2018)
8. Donadello, I., Serafini, L., Garcez, A.: Logic tensor networks for semantic image interpretation. In: The 26th International Joint Conference on Artificial Intelligence (2017)
9. Dörpinghaus, J., Jacobs, M.: Semantic knowledge graph embeddings for biomedical research: data integration using linked open data. In: SEMANTiCS (2019)
10. Galárraga, L., Teflioudi, C., Hose, K., Suchanek, F.M.: Fast rule mining in ontological knowledge bases with AMIE+. VLDB J. **24**, 707–730 (2015)
11. Guo, L., Sun, Z., Hu, W.: Learning to exploit long-term relational dependencies in knowledge graphs. In: The 36th International Conference on Machine Learning (2019)
12. Hildebrandt, M., Serna, J.A.Q., Ma, Y., Ringsquandl, M., Joblin, M., Tresp, V.: Reasoning on knowledge graphs with debate dynamics. In: The 34th AAAI Conference on Artificial Intelligence (2020)
13. Himmelstein, D.S., et al.: Systematic integration of biomedical knowledge prioritizes drugs for repurposing. Elife **6**, e26726 (2017)
14. Hitzler, P., Krötzsch, M., Rudolph, S.: Foundations of Semantic Web Technologies. Chapman & Hall/CRC Textbooks in Computing (2009)
15. Hochreiter, S., Schmidhuber, J.: Long short-term memory. Neural Comput. **9**(8), 1735–1780 (1997)
16. Kipf, T.N., Welling, M.: Semi-supervised classification with graph convolutional networks. In: The 5th International Conference on Learning Representations (2017)
17. Lao, N., Cohen, W.W.: Relational retrieval using a combination of path-constrained random walks. Mach. Learn. **81**(1), 53–67 (2010)
18. Lin, X.V., Socher, R., Xiong, C.: Multi-hop knowledge graph reasoning with reward shaping. In: The 2018 Conference on Empirical Methods in Natural Language Processing (2018)

19. Meilicke, C., Chekol, M.W., Fink, M., Stuckenschmidt, H.: Reinforced anytime bottom up rule learning for knowledge graph completion. Preprint arXiv:2004.04412 (2020)
20. Meilicke, C., Chekol, M.W., Ruffinelli, D., Stuckenschmidt, H.: Anytime bottom-up rule learning for knowledge graph completion. In: The 28th International Joint Conference on Artificial Intelligence (2019)
21. Meilicke, C., Fink, M., Wang, Y., Ruffinelli, D., Gemulla, R., Stuckenschmidt, H.: Fine-grained evaluation of rule-and embedding-based systems for knowledge graph completion. In: The 17th International Semantic Web Conference (2018)
22. Minervini, P., Bošnjak, M., Rocktäschel, T., Riedel, S., Grefenstette, E.: Differentiable reasoning on large knowledge bases and natural language. In: The 34th AAAI Conference on Artificial Intelligence (2020)
23. Minervini, P., Riedel, S., Stenetorp, P., Grefenstette, E., Rocktäschel, T.: Learning reasoning strategies in end-to-end differentiable proving. In: The 37th International Conference on Machine Learning (2020)
24. Mitchell, T.: Machine Learning. McGraw-Hill Series in Computer Science (1997)
25. Muggleton, S.: Inductive logic programming. N. Gener. Comput. **8**(4), 295–318 (1991)
26. Nickel, M., Tresp, V., Kriegel, H.P.: A three-way model for collective learning on multi-relational data. In: The 28th International Conference on Machine Learning (2011)
27. Qu, M., Tang, J.: Probabilistic logic neural networks for reasoning. In: The 33rd Conference on Neural Information Processing Systems (2019)
28. Richardson, M., Domingos, P.: Markov logic networks. Mach. Learn. **62**(1–2), 107–136 (2006)
29. Rocktäschel, T., Riedel, S.: End-to-end differentiable proving. In: The 31st Conference on Neural Information Processing Systems (2017)
30. Schlichtkrull, M., Kipf, T.N., Bloem, P., Van Den Berg, R., Titov, I., Welling, M.: Modeling relational data with graph convolutional networks. In: The 15th Extended Semantic Web Conference (2018)
31. Toutanova, K., Chen, D., Pantel, P., Poon, H., Choudhury, P., Gamon, M.: Representing text for joint embedding of text and knowledge bases. In: The 2015 Conference on Empirical Methods in Natural Language Processing (2015)
32. Trouillon, T., Welbl, J., Riedel, S., Gaussier, E., Bouchard, G.: Complex embeddings for simple link prediction. In: The 33rd International Conference on Machine Learning (2016)
33. U. S. National Library of Medicine (2000). clinicaltrials.gov
34. Vashishth, S., Sanyal, S., Nitin, V., Talukdar, P.: Composition-based multi-relational graph convolutional networks. In: The 9th International Conference on Learning Representations (2020)
35. Williams, R.J.: Simple statistical gradient-following algorithms for connectionist reinforcement learning. Mach. Learn. **8**(3–4), 229–256 (1992)
36. Wishart, D.S., et al.: DrugBank: a comprehensive resource for in silico drug discovery and exploration. Nucleic Acids Res. **34**(Database), D668–D672 (2006)
37. Xiong, W., Hoang, T., Wang, W.Y.: DeepPath: a reinforcement learning method for knowledge graph reasoning. In: The 2017 Conference on Empirical Methods in Natural Language Processing (2017)
38. Yang, B., Yih, W., He, X., Gao, J., Deng, L.: Embedding entities and relations for learning and inference in knowledge bases. In: The 3rd International Conference on Learning Representations (2015)

39. Yang, F., Yang, Z., Cohen, W.W.: Differentiable learning of logical rules for knowledge base reasoning. In: The 31st Conference on Neural Information Processing Systems (2017)

40. Zitnik, M., Nguyen, F., Wang, B., Leskovec, J., Goldenberg, A., Hoffman, M.M.: Machine learning for integrating data in biology and medicine: principles, practice, and opportunities. Inf. Fusion **50**, 71–91 (2019)

Augmenting Ontology Alignment by Semantic Embedding and Distant Supervision

Jiaoyan Chen[1]($\boxtimes$), Ernesto Jiménez-Ruiz[2,3], Ian Horrocks[1],
Denvar Antonyrajah[4], Ali Hadian[4], and Jaehun Lee[5]

[1] Department of Computer Science, University of Oxford, Oxford, UK
jiaoyan.chen@cs.ox.ac.uk
[2] University of London, London, UK
[3] SIRIUS, University of Oslo, Oslo, Norway
[4] Samsung Research, Staines-upon-Thames, UK
[5] Samsung Research, Seoul, Korea

Abstract. Ontology alignment plays a critical role in knowledge integration and has been widely investigated in the past decades. State of the art systems, however, still have considerable room for performance improvement especially in dealing with new (industrial) alignment tasks. In this paper we present a machine learning based extension to traditional ontology alignment systems, using distant supervision for training, ontology embedding and Siamese Neural Networks for incorporating richer semantics. We have used the extension together with traditional systems such as LogMap and AML to align two food ontologies, HeLiS and FoodOn, and we found that the extension recalls many additional valid mappings and also avoids some false positive mappings. This is also verified by an evaluation on alignment tasks from the OAEI conference track.

Keywords: Ontology alignment · Semantic embedding · Distant supervision · Siamese neural network

1 Introduction

Ontologies are widely used to represent, manage and exchange (domain) knowledge. However, the content of any single ontology is often incomplete even in a single domain and, moreover, many real world applications rely on cross-domain knowledge. Integration of multiple ontologies is therefore a critical task, and is often implemented by identifying cross-ontology mappings between classes that have an equivalent- or sub-class relationship. This process is known as ontology alignment or ontology matching [8,26,29].[1]

---

[1] Ontology alignment also includes mappings between individuals and properties, as well as mappings with more complicated relationships beyond atomic subsumption and equivalence. In this study we focus on mappings between equivalent classes.

© Springer Nature Switzerland AG 2021
R. Verborgh et al. (Eds.): ESWC 2021, LNCS 12731, pp. 392–408, 2021.
https://doi.org/10.1007/978-3-030-77385-4_23

Ontology alignment has been investigated for many years. State of the art (SOTA) systems such as LogMap [17,18] and AgreementMakerLight (AML) [9] often combine multiple strategies such as lexical matching, structural matching and logical reasoning. Such systems typically use lexical matching as their starting point, and while this captures string or token similarity, it fails to capture the contextual meaning of words. Logical reasoning can be used to improve mapping quality, but this often wrongly rejects some valid mappings [27]. In practice, such systems often need (combinations of) hand-craft matching methods to achieve good performance for a new task.

The last decade has seen an extensive investigation of semantic embedding, a branch of machine learning (ML) techniques which can encode symbols such as natural language words, ontology concepts, knowledge graph entities and relations into vectors with their semantics (e.g., correlation with the neighbours) [20,23,31]. This enables us to augment the aforementioned ontology alignment systems with ML algorithms that can exploit richer semantics so as to recall some missed mappings and avoid some false positives.

In this paper we present a ML extension that utilizes distant supervision and semantic embedding, and that can be used to augment classic ontology alignment systems. Briefly, it first uses the original ontology alignment system plus class disjointness constraints (as heuristic rules) to generate high precision seed mappings, and then uses these mappings to train a Siamese Neural Network (SiamNN) for predicting cross-ontology class mappings via semantic embeddings in OWL2Vec*—an ontology tailored language model [3]. We have tested our ML-augmentation with the SOTA systems LogMap and AML in a real world ontology alignment task identified by our industrial partner Samsung Research UK, i.e., the alignment of two food ontologies: HeLiS [7] and FoodOn [6]. The augmentation improved recall by more that 130% while at the same time achieving small improvements in precision. Smaller but still significant improvements in precision and recall were also achieved on an alignment task from the Ontology Alignment Evaluation Initiative (OAEI) [1].

In the remainder of this paper we use LogMap as a concrete example of our ML extension, but the extension can be directly applied to AML and to any other system that is capable of generating high precision mappings to be used in the training phase.

2   Preliminaries and Related Work

2.1   LogMap

LogMap is a scalable logic-based ontology matching system [17,18]. It is often one of the best performing systems for real-world tasks such as those in the biomedical tracks of the OAEI [1].

Figure 1 shows the procedure followed by LogMap to compute an alignment $\mathcal{M}$ given two input ontologies $\mathcal{O}_1$ and $\mathcal{O}_2$. LogMap first builds a lexical index for each ontology based on its entity labels and label variations (e.g., synonyms). These indexes are used to efficiently computing an over-estimation $\mathcal{M}_o$ of the mappings between $\mathcal{O}_1$ and $\mathcal{O}_2$. Mappings in $\mathcal{M}_o$ are not necessarily correct, but they link lexically-related entities and usually have a high recall, while still representing a manageable subset of all possible mappings (i.e., the Cartesian product of the sets of classes in the input ontologies) [16].

From the mapping over-estimation $\mathcal{M}_o$, LogMap identifies a number of high-confidence mappings called *anchor mappings* ($\mathcal{M}_a$). These mappings are used to assess the structural and logical compatibility of the remaining candidate mappings in $\mathcal{M}_o$ via a structural index, which significantly reduces the cost of answering taxonomic and disjointness queries. Mappings in $\mathcal{M}_o$ are also assessed according to the lexical similarity of the involved entities. Finally, LogMap outputs a set of selected mappings $\mathcal{M}$ between $\mathcal{O}_1$ and $\mathcal{O}_2$, and additionally gives as output the anchor mappings $\mathcal{M}_a$ and the mapping over-estimation $\mathcal{M}_o$.

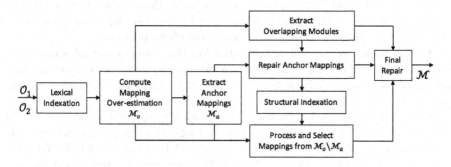

Fig. 1. LogMap system in a nutshell [18]

2.2   Machine Learning for Ontology Alignment

Machine learning (ML) has recently been explored for ontology alignment. ML should facilitate the exploitation of both class information (*e.g.*, names and annotations) and their context in an ontology (*i.e.*, their semantics). However, to develop a robust model, several critical issues have to be addressed. Next we will discuss these issues and current solutions, and compare our method with them.

Features. The symbolic information of a class, such as its textual label and neighbourhood graph structure, should be transformed into real values before they can be utilized by ML algorithms, and informative variables (*i.e.*, features) should be extracted to achieve high performance. One solution, as implemented in, *e.g.*, GLUE [5] and POMap++ [21], is extracting pre-defined features such as edit distance between labels and syntactic similarity. Another solution, as adopted by, *e.g.*, Zhang et al. [33], DOME [13], OntoEmma [30], Bento et al. [2], DeepFCA [22] and VeeAlign [15], is learning relevant features via representation learning models such as neural networks, or/and using pre-trained semantic embeddings (*i.e.*, vectors of characters, words or classes with their semantics kept in the vector space). Some methods such as [25,30] adopt both pre-defined features and semantic embeddings. Meanwhile, instead of word embeddings pre-trained by an external corpus, tailored character embeddings or document embeddings have been explored. ERSOM [32] learns ontology tailored word embeddings via an Auto-Encoder and a similarity propagation method with the classes' meta information and context, while DeepAlignment [19] extends ERSOM by incorporating the synonymy and antonymy word relationships.

Samples. With semantic embeddings, we can identify mappings by calculating the vector distance (or similarity) between classes as in [19,32]. However, such an unsupervised approach depends on how the semantic embeddings are learned. For ontology-tailored embeddings, which usually achieve better performance than pre-trained embeddings, the vector spaces of the two to-be-aligned ontologies are independent and thus two equivalent cross-ontology classes may still have a large vector distance. To address the above issue and further improve the performance, we can utilize (semi-)supervised ML solutions which rely on labeled mappings (*i.e.*, samples) to learn features and train models to predict mappings. Besides costly human annotation for the training samples, one ML solution is transfer learning between tasks, *i.e.*, re-using known mappings from other aligned ontologies. For example, OntoEmma [30] trains the model using 50,523 positive mappings between the ontologies of the Unified Medical Language System, while [25] transfers samples from tasks of one OAEI track to another. However, the effectiveness of such sample transfer significantly depends on the sources to be transferred, and it may be hard to find a suitable source for a new alignment task. In practice, neither [30] nor [25] outperformed the classic systems such as AML and LogMap on the evaluated OAEI tracks.

Scalable Mapping Prediction. Unlike ontology alignment systems based on lexical indexes, an ML-based method usually needs to predict or calculate the scores of all cross-ontology class pairs, which can lead to scalability problems with large ontologies. One solution for this issue is to use blocking techniques such as locality-sensitive hashing [11] and embedding-based lexical index clustering [16]. Another solution, adopted by ERSOM [32] and DeepAlignment [19], is to use optimized search algorithms such as Stable Marriage. The prediction model can also be deployed together with a set of traditional alignment systems, the union of whose outputs can act as a reduced set of candidates with a good recall [25], or with some logic-based constraints or rules which can filter out some candidates and reduce the search space.

In our ML extension, we addressed the feature issue via the combination of an ontology embedding method named OWL2Vec* [3], which is a neural language model tailored to the ontology's text, graph structure and logical axioms; and a SiamNN, which learns features of the input classes and bridges the gap between the two embedding spaces. Unlike current (semi-)supervised learning methods, our ML extension addresses the sample shortage issue via a distant supervision strategy, where some confident mappings derived by the to-be-extended system (such as the anchor mappings of LogMap) are used to generate positive and negative samples, with some high-level class disjointness constraints used to improve sample quality. To reduce the search space when aligning large ontologies, we can optionally use the to-be-extended system (or some other traditional system) to compute a set of candidate mappings with very high recall (similar to [25]); in the case of LogMap we can use its so-called mapping over-estimation.

3   Use Case

Ontologies. In this section we present the use case of aligning HeLiS[2] [7] and FoodOn[3] [6]—two large OWL[4] ontologies. FoodOn captures detailed food knowledge and other knowledge from relevant domains such as agriculture, chemistry and environment, with 359 instances, 28,182 classes and 241,581 axioms within the description logic (DL) $\mathcal{SRIQ}$. HeLiS captures general knowledge on both food and healthy lifestyles with 20,318 instances, 277 classes and 172,213 axioms within the DL $\mathcal{ALCHIQ(D)}$. In order to facilitate alignment, HeLiS instances were transformed into classes, with associated *rdf:type* triples being transformed into *rdfs:subClassOf* triples. This transformation changes the ontology's semantics, but the ontology integration still supports the knowledge graph construction application in industry and does not impact the evaluation of different systems.

A fragment of HeLiS and FoodOn is shown in Fig. 2, where each class is represented by a short name/label for readability.

Motivations. By providing more complete and fine-grained knowledge covering both food and lifestyles, an alignment of HeLiS and FoodOn can be used to improve personalisation and can benefit popular applications in areas such as sport, health and wellbeing. The alignment can also be used for ontology quality assurance (QA) by identifying missing and logically inconsistent relationships through cross checking. One QA example is discovering the missing subsumption relationship between "Soybean Milk" and "Soybean Food Product" in FoodOn (where "Soybean Milk" is only categorized as "Beverage") by mapping them to their HeLiS counterparts "SoyMilk" and "SoyProducts" whose subsumption relationship is defined. We have identified more than 500 such new subsumption relationships between FoodOn classes through aligning FoodOn and HeLiS [14].

Challenges. The technical challenges of aligning HeLiS and FoodOn lie in several aspects. First, as in many ontology matching tasks, we need to address the ambiguity between classes with similar names or with similar neighbourhood structures, the logical inconsistency that can be caused by mappings, the very large search space (with over 580 million candidate mappings), and so on. Second, FoodOn is itself composed of multiple source ontologies, including NCBITaxon and The Environment Ontology, and thus its class hierarchy includes branches covering not only food categorization but also food source categorization (closely related to biological taxonomy), chemical element categorization, etc. Similarly

---

[2] HeLiS project: https://horus-ai.fbk.eu/helis/.
[3] FoodOn project: https://foodon.org/.
[4] Web Ontology Language: https://www.w3.org/TR/owl-features/.

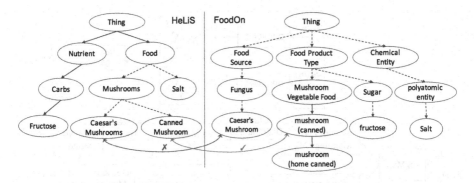

Fig. 2. Fragments of the HeLiS and FoodOn ontologies. The dash arrow means some intermediate classes are hidden. The red (green resp.) arrow denotes false (true resp.) mappings. (Color figure online)

HeLiS has branches of nutrients, food and so on. Similar names and local contexts (*e.g.*, of food products and food sources) can lead to "branch conflicting" mappings whose classes lie in branches with different meanings. One example is the incorrect mapping between "Caesar's Mushrooms" of HeLiS (a food) and "Caesar's Mushroom" of FoodOn (a food source) as illustrated in Fig. 2. Classic systems often fail to identify such errors, even when using logical assessment (as in LogMap) due to missing class disjointness axioms in the source ontologies.

4   Methodology

We will present our ML extension w.r.t. LogMap, as shown in Fig. 3. It comprises three steps: *(i)* compute the seed mappings starting from a set of high precision mappings (such as LogMap's "anchor" mappings) and applying class disjointness constraints (branch conflicts) to further improve precision; *(ii)* construct samples and train a mapping prediction model (a SiamNN whose input is a pair of classes or their associated paths); and *(iii)* compute the output mappings, (optionally) starting from a set of high recall candidate mappings (such as LogMap's overestimation mappings) to reduce the search space. Note this extension can be used with any "traditional" system that is capable of generating high precision mappings for use in the training phase (in our evaluation we use AML as well as LogMap).

4.1   Seed Mappings

To achieve high-confidence seed mappings ($\mathcal{M}_s$) for training, we define a set of disjointness constraints between cross ontology classes to filter out some false-positive mappings from the LogMap anchor mappings ($\mathcal{M}_a$). A disjointness constraint is denoted $\delta = (c_1, c_2)$, where c_1 and c_2 are typically very general classes in $\mathcal{O}_1$ and $\mathcal{O}_2$ respectively, acting as the "root" classes of different knowledge branches. For example, in Fig. 2, "Food" of HeLiS and "Food Source" of

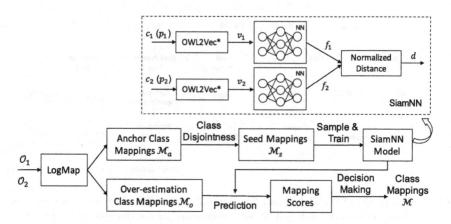

Fig. 3. The ML extension for LogMap

FoodOn comprise one disjointness constraint, while "Food" of HeLiS and "Chemical Entity" of FoodOn comprise another constraint. The set of constraints, which we denote Δ, together with the original alignment system act as heuristic rules in normal distant supervision. In our HeLiS-FoodOn case study, we manually defined four disjointness constraints based on knowledge of the domain and the ontology architectures. Given that disjointness constraints typically involve only very general classes, defining them does not require very detailed knowledge of the domain; moreover, we can use statistical analysis of the mappings computed by LogMap to identify candidate disjointness constraints, or even to fully automate the definition of Δ. For example, given two sibling classes c and c' in $\mathcal{O}_1$ and a class s in $\mathcal{O}_1$, if there are n mappings from subclasses of c to subclasses of s and n' mappings from subclasses of c' to subclasses of s, with $n' \ll n$, then c' is likely to be disjoint with s and (c', s) can be used as a (candidate) disjointness constraint.

When using Δ to filter a mapping $m = (c_1, c_2) \in \mathcal{M}_a$, we consider not just c_1 and c_2, but all subsumers of c_1 and c_2 in the corresponding ontologies $\mathcal{O}_1$ and $\mathcal{O}_2$. For this purpose we use the OWL reasoner HermiT [12] to compute the set of subsumers (both explicitly asserted and entailed) of a given class c, which we denote P_c. Then, given a mapping $m = (c_1, c_2) \in \mathcal{M}_a$, we discard m as a false-positive if there is some $(c_1', c_2') \in \Delta$ such that $c_1' \in P_{c_1}$ and $c_2' \in P_{c_2}$; if this is *not* the case, then we add m to the set of seed mappings $\mathcal{M}_s$.

4.2   Siamese Neural Network

We first generate positive and negative class mappings (samples), then embed these samples as vectors using OWL2Vec*, and finally we train a SiamNN as the mapping prediction model. The seed mappings $\mathcal{M}_s$ are adopted as the positive samples and are randomly divided into a training set $\mathcal{M}_s^t$ and a validation set $\mathcal{M}_s^v$ by a given ratio γ. We then generate the corresponding negative sample sets of $\mathcal{M}_s^t$ and $\mathcal{M}_s^v$, denoted as $\mathcal{M}_s^{t'}$ and $\mathcal{M}_s^{v'}$ respectively, as follows. For each mapping $m = (c_1, c_2)$ in $\mathcal{M}_s^t$ or $\mathcal{M}_s^v$, we generate one negative sample m' by replacing c_1 with a class c_1' randomly selected from $\mathcal{O}_1$, and we generate a second negative sample m'' by replacing c_2 with a class c_2' randomly selected from $\mathcal{O}_2$. Note that the random replacements could produce positive samples from $\mathcal{M}_s$; we discard any such negative samples. We also adopt those anchor mappings that violate the class disjointness constraints, *i.e.*, $\mathcal{M}_a \setminus \mathcal{M}_s$, as negative samples, and randomly partition them into a training set $\mathcal{M}_a^{t'}$ and a validation set $\mathcal{M}_a^{v'}$ with the same ratio of γ. We finally get the training samples as a tuple of $\mathcal{M}_s^t$ and $\mathcal{M}_s^{t'} \cup \mathcal{M}_a^{t'}$ to train the SiamNN, and the validation samples as a tuple of $\mathcal{M}_s^v$ and $\mathcal{M}_s^{v'} \cup \mathcal{M}_a^{v'}$ to adjust the hyper parameters such as the network architecture and the embedding option.

The OWL2Vec* embedding of an ontology is a language model tailored to the given ontology. It can be first pre-trained with a large normal text corpus such as Word2Vec and then fine-tuned with a corpus whose sequences include walks over the ontology's graph structure, the ontology's axioms, the ontology's textual information (*e.g.*, class labels, definitions and comments), etc. It can also be directly trained with the ontology's corpus. In this study, we evaluated both training settings. The OWL2Vec* embedding encodes a class in two ways: directly adopting the vector of the class's URI or calculating the average word vector of the words of the class labels. We prefer the latter as it can utilize both pre-training and fine-tuning, and often performs better for ontologies with rich textual information such as FoodOn. Please refer to [3] for more details on OWL2Vec*. Given a class c, we denote its OWL2Vec* embedding as $v(c)$.

For each mapping sample $m = (c_1, c_2) \in \mathcal{M}_s^t$, we consider two kinds of embeddings to transform it into a tuple composed of two vectors. The first option is directly adopting its OWL2Vec* embeddings $v(c_1)$ and $v(c_2)$, *i.e.*, $v(m) = \{v(c_1), v(c_2)\}$. The second option is to augment the context of c_1 and c_2 by embedding the associated paths of c_1 and c_2, *i.e.*, the sequences of classes obtained by traversing the class hierarchy back to *owl:Thing*. As one class may have multiple such paths, we randomly select at most two paths for each class, and thus one class mapping sample leads to at most four path mapping samples. For two paths associated with c_1 and c_2, denoted as $p_1 = (c_1, ..., c_{n_1}) \in P_1$ and $p_2 = (c_2, ..., c_{n_2}) \in P_2$ respectively, the mapping embedding $v(m)$ is calculated as either $\left\{ \frac{1}{n_1} \sum_{c_i=c_1}^{c_{n_1}} v(c_i), \frac{1}{n_2} \sum_{c_j=c_2}^{c_{n_2}} v(c_j) \right\}$ or $\{[v(c_1), ..., v(c_{n_1})], [v(c_2), ..., v(c_{n_2})]\}$, where $[\cdot, \cdot]$ denotes the vector concatenation. The former embeds a path by averaging the embeddings of its classes, while the latter embeds a path by concatenating the embeddings of its classes. In a given ontology, different paths can have different lengths. To align the vectors of different samples, we fix the path length for the ontology by setting it to the length of the longest path, and pad the shorter paths with placeholders whose embeddings are zero vectors. Note the path lengths of $\mathcal{O}_1$ and $\mathcal{O}_2$ can be different.

The SiamNN is composed of two networks that have the same architecture. The two vectors of an input mapping are fed into the two networks respectively, two features (denoted as f_1 and f_2) are then calculated accordingly, and their normalized distance $d = \frac{\|f_1 - f_2\|}{\|f_1\| + \|f_2\|}$ is further calculated as the output, where $\|\cdot\|$ denotes the Euclidean norm of a vector. A smaller distance indicates that the two classes corresponding to the two input vectors are more likely to constitute a valid mapping, and vice versa. The two networks are learned together by minimizing the following contrastive loss using the Adam optimizer:

$$Loss = \sum_{i=0}^{N} \frac{y_i \times d_i + (1 - y_i) \times max\{\epsilon - d_i, 0\}}{2} \tag{1}$$

where i denotes the ith mapping sample, d_i denotes its output distance, y_i denotes its label ($y_i = 1$ if the mapping is positive, $y_i = 0$ otherwise), N denotes the sample number and ϵ denotes a margin value. Note the insight behind the SiamNN is to map the two input vectors into the same space via two networks (non-linear transformations) which at the same time learn features.

Different network architectures can be adopted for feature learning. We evaluated one simple network (Multi-layer Perception (MLP) with two hidden layers), one classic sequence learning model (Bidirectional Recurrent Neural Networks (BiRNN) with Gate Recurrent Units [4]), and the BiRNN with an additional attention layer (AttBiRNN).

4.3 Prediction, Filtering and Ensemble

We can simply consider all cross-ontology class pairs to be candidate mappings, but this leads to a very large number if the ontologies are large. In our extension to LogMap, we adopt its over-estimation class mappings $\mathcal{M}_o$ as the candidates. This reduces the potential number of candidates from around 580 million to $8,891$ when aligning HeLiS and FoodOn, and at the same time helps to avoid false positive mappings. Each mapping $m = (c_1, c_2) \in \mathcal{M}_o$ is embeded into a tuple of vectors in the same way as in training the SiamNN except that only one path is randomly selected for each class if path embedding is adopted. A distance $d \in [0, 1]$ is then predicted by the SiamNN, and a score y is further calculated as $1 - d$. A higher score indicates a more likely mapping, and vice versa. A score threshold θ is used to filter out unlikely mappings: m is accepted if $y \geq \theta$, and rejected otherwise. To determine θ, we utilized the validation samples: the threshold is increased from 0 to 1 with a small step (*e.g.*, 0.02), and the value leading to the best performance (*e.g.*, the highest F1 score in aligning HeLiS and FoodOn) on $\mathcal{M}_s^v$ and $\mathcal{M}_s^{v'} \cup \mathcal{M}_a^{v'}$ is adopted. The resulting class mappings are denoted as $\mathcal{M}_p$ (predicted mappings).

We filter out any predicted class mappings in $\mathcal{M}_p$ that violate class disjointness constraints Δ as when generating seed mappings (see Sect. 4.1). We further filter the mappings in $\mathcal{M}_p$ using a subsumption-based logical assessment. Specifically, a class in one ontology cannot be equivalent to multiple classes that are in a sub-class relationship in the other ontology. For example, "Canned Mushroom" of HeLiS cannot be equivalent to both "mushroom (canned)" and "mushroom (home canned)" in FoodOn in Fig. 2. If this happens, then the mapping with a lower prediction score should be discarded. More formally, if $\mathcal{M}_p$ includes two mappings (c_1, c_2) and (s_1, s_2) such that either $c_1 = s_1$ and c_2 subsumes s_2 in $\mathcal{O}_2$, or $c_2 = s_2$ and c_1 subsumes s_1 in $\mathcal{O}_1$, then we discard the mapping with the lower prediction score. The remaining mappings are denoted as $\mathcal{M}_p'$.

$\mathcal{M}_p'$ is merged with the seed mappings $\mathcal{M}_s$ to give the final ensemble output: $\mathcal{M} = \mathcal{M}_p' \cup \mathcal{M}_s$. Note that although the seed mappings are used as positive samples for training, it is still possible that some of them will have low prediction scores as embedding, learning and prediction is a probabilistic procedure.

5   Evaluation

5.1   HeLiS and FoodOn

Experiment Setting. We first evaluate the ML extension[5] for aligning HeLiS and FoodOn, where we augment LogMap[6] by using its anchor mappings for the seeds. The augmented system is denoted as LogMap^{anc}-ML. It is compared with the original LogMap and another SOTA system AML v3.1[7] which has been highly ranked in many OAEI tasks [10].

In order to precisely assess an alignment of two ontologies we would need a set of gold standard (GS) mappings against which to measure precision and recall. This is typically not available due to the cost of checking each of a potentially very large number of possible mappings. In the case of HeLiS and FoodOn we have a partial GS consisting of 372 mappings obtained by manually checking a much larger set of candidate mappings computed by LogMap; however, this is still (highly) incomplete, and clearly biased towards mappings that can be found using the techniques employed in LogMap. Therefore, besides the recall of this partial GS (denoted as Recall^{GS}), we have computed approximate precision and recall (denoted Precision$^{\approx}$ and Recall$^{\approx}$, respectively) as follows.

First, given a (possibly empty) set of GS mappings G and a set of computed mappings M, we estimate Precision$^{\approx}$ for G and M (denoted Precision$^{\approx}_{G,M}$) by selecting at random a set $S \subseteq M \setminus G$ and manually checking the mappings in S to identify the set $S_v \subseteq S$ of valid mappings. We then compute:

$$\text{Precision}^{\approx}_{G,M} = \frac{TP_{G,M}}{|M|} = \frac{|M \cap G| + \frac{|S_v|}{|S|} \times |M \setminus G|}{|M|}, \qquad (2)$$

where $|\cdot|$ denotes set cardinality, and $TP_{G,M}$ represents the approximate number of *true positive* mappings. Note that, if $G = \emptyset$ (*i.e.*, no gold standard is available), then this becomes simply $|S_v|/|S|$; if $M \setminus G = \emptyset$ (*i.e.*, all the output mappings are among the GS), then this becomes precision w.r.t. the GS. For the recall, we estimate the total number of valid mappings using the GS as well as the union

---

[5] Codes: https://github.com/KRR-Oxford/OntoAlign/tree/main/LogMap-ML.

[6] https://github.com/ernestojimenezruiz/loap-matcher.

[7] https://github.com/AgreementMakerLight/AML-Project.

of the output mappings of all available systems (*i.e.*, LogMap^{anc}-ML, LogMap and AML), which we denote M'; then, for a given system that computes a set of mappings M, we estimate the recall of the system to be:

$$\text{Recall}^{\approx} = \frac{TP_{G,M}}{|G| + \frac{|S'_v|}{|S'|} \times |M' \setminus G|}, \tag{3}$$

where S' denotes a random set from $M' \setminus G$ and $S'_v \subseteq S'$ are the valid mappings in S' (by manual checking). We further calculate an approximate F1 Score:

$$\text{F1}^{\approx} = \frac{2 \times \text{Precision}^{\approx} \times \text{Recall}^{\approx}}{\text{Precision}^{\approx} + \text{Recall}^{\approx}}. \tag{4}$$

The settings of LogMap^{anc}-ML are adjusted by optimizing the result on the validation mapping set $\mathcal{M}_s^v$, which consists of 10% of all the seed mappings, and the results in Table 1 are based on these optimized settings. For the validation results of different settings, please see the ablation study in Sect. 5.3.

Table 1. The results of aligning HeLiS and FoodOn

Method	Mappings #	Precision$^{\approx}$	Recall$^{\approx}$	F1$^{\approx}$	Recall^{GS}
LogMap (anchor mappings)	311	**0.887**	0.278	0.423	0.602
LogMap	417	0.676	0.284	0.400	0.712
AML	544	0.636	0.349	0.451	0.694
LogMap^{anc}-ML (no ensemble)	1154	0.675	0.785	0.726	0.806
LogMap^{anc}-ML	1207	0.685	**0.833**	**0.752**	**0.839**

Results. In Table 1 we can see that LogMap^{anc}-ML without the ensemble to the seed mappings outputs 1154 mappings—more than twice as many as the original LogMap and AML—while the ensemble (*i.e.*, including the seed mappings) adds 53 more mappings. LogMap^{anc}-ML has much higher recall than AML and LogMap; for example, Recall$^{\approx}$ is increased from 0.284 to 0.833 when the ML extension is added to LogMap. This is consistent with our assumption that SiamNN together with the OWL2Vec* embedding can consider more additional contextual information and word semantics of two to-be-mapped classes. Meanwhile, LogMap^{anc}-ML (no ensemble) has similar precision to LogMap and 6.1% higher precision than AML, while the ensemble with the seed mappings further improves precision from 0.675 to 0.685. As a result, F1$^{\approx}$ of LogMap^{anc}-ML is 88.3% higher than LogMap and 67.0% higher than AML.

5.2   OAEI Conference Track

Experiment Setting. We also evaluated our ML extension on all the 21 class alignments of the 17 ontologies of the OAEI conference track,[8] where the open reference *ra1* with 259 class mappings (*i.e.*, the GS) is adopted to calculate the standard precision, recall and F1 score. Note that we merge the output mappings of the 21 alignments of each system and compare all the mappings to the GS to directly calculate these metrics. The results are shown in Table 2. As the output mappings of AML and LogMap available on the OAEI website of 2020 are slightly different from those generated by our local running of LogMap and AML v3.1 (perhaps this is due to different parameter settings or versions), we report both results, where the former is denoted by the superscript *'oaei'*.

Instead of processing each ontology alignment independently, we merged the seed mappings of all the 21 alignments to train one prediction model and applied this model to predict the candidate mappings of all the alignments. We did not use the LogMap over-estimation mappings but adopted all the cross-ontology class pairs of each alignment, as the total number $(98, 688)$ did not cause scalability issues. As well as LogMap^{anc}-ML, we also report the results of LogMap-ML and LogMap^{oaei}-ML, which adopt the corresponding LogMap output mappings for the seeds. To show the generality, we also applied the ML extension to AML, which we denote AML^{oaei}-ML. Note that the output mappings of LogMap and AML are adopted for training because they have high precision in this case. The reported results of all the ML extensions are based on the class input embedded by the pre-trained OWL2Vec* and the SiamNN with MLP. The baselines include four classic systems (*i.e.*, Wiktionary [28], SANOM [24], LogMap and AML), two SOTA ML-based systems (*i.e.*, VeeAlign [15] and DeepAlignment [19]), and StringEquiv which labels a mapping as true if its class names are the same (case insensitive). Note precision and recall are based on the average of several repetitions of training and prediction, while F1 score is calculated with the averaged precision and recall. The DeepAlignment result is from its paper [19].

Results. From Table 2 we can first confirm the observation from HeLiS and FoodOn, *i.e.*, that the ML extension can improve both the recall and precision of the original alignment system: the F1 score is improved by 9.9%, 4.3%, 3.4% and 2.4% for LogMap^{anc}, LogMap, LogMap^{oaei} and AML^{oaei} respectively. The improvements are not as large as in aligning HeLiS and FoodOn because the to-be-aligned conference ontologies are much smaller and less complex, and the original systems have already been highly optimized for these alignments. Second, our augmented method LogMap^{oaei}-ML is a bit worse than VeeAlign^{oaei}[9] and quite competitive to SANOM^{oaei}, w.r.t. the F1 score. Note these two systems are ranked in the first positions in the 2020 and 2019 rankings, respectively. LogMap^{oaei}-ML also has a slightly higher F1 score than DeepAlignment. Meanwhile, the F1 score of the augmented AML, *i.e.*, AML^{oaei}-ML is very competitive

---

[8] http://oaei.ontologymatching.org/2020/conference/.
[9] VeeAlign has been tailored to the Conference and Multifarm OAEI tracks [15].

Table 2. The results of the OAEI conference track.

Method	Mappings #	Precision	Recall	F1 score
StringEquiv	148	**0.935**	0.498	0.650
AML	223	0.803	0.691	0.743
SANOM^{oaei}	252	0.778	0.757	0.767
Wiktionary^{oaei}	184	0.821	0.583	0.682
VeeAlign^{oaei}	253	0.791	0.772	**0.781**
DeepAlignment	–	0.710	**0.800**	0.750
LogMap^{anc}	139	0.892	0.479	0.629
LogMap^{anc}-ML	157	0.917	0.555	0.691
LogMap	190	0.842	0.618	0.713
LogMap-ML	190	0.881	0.645	0.745
LogMap^{oaei}	198	0.843	0.645	0.731
LogMap^{oaei}-ML	197	0.875	0.665	0.756
AML^{oaei}	220	0.827	0.703	0.760
AML^{oaei}-ML	222	0.842	0.723	0.778

to VeeAlign^{oaei} and is better than the other baselines (*e.g.*, 1.4% higher than SANOM^{oaei}). As the ML extension is trained based on the confident seed mappings from the original systems, the augmented AML and LogMap have much higher precision than VeeAlign^{oaei}, SANOM^{oaei} and DeepAlignment.

5.3 Ablation Study

Experiment Setting. We present the ablation study of the prediction model with different embedding and neural network settings. To this end, standard precision, recall, F1 score and accuracy of the trained model on the validation mapping set are reported. The threshold θ is searched from 0 to 1 with a step of 0.02, and the reported results are based on the threshold that leads to the best F1 score. All the four metrics are calculated by averaging the results of several repetitions of training and validation. Note the model with the best F1 score and its associated optimum θ are adopted in calculating the final output mappings as evaluated in Sect. 5.1. As the validation set, especially its generated negative mappings, are quite simple in comparison with the candidate mappings for prediction, the validation results in Table 3 are much better than the final results in Table 1, but this does not impact our validation of different settings.

We evaluated *(i)* Word2Vec which was trained with a corpus of Wikipedia articles from 2018, OWL2Vec* without pre-training and OWL2Vec* pre-trained with the above Wikipedia corpus; *(ii)* different networks including the SiamNNs, and the original networks (MLP, BiRNN and AttBiRNN) for which the two input vectors are concatenated; and *(iii)* the class vs the path as the input. The dimensions of Word2Vec, OWL2Vec* and the pre-trained OWL2Vec* are set to

200, 100 and 200 respectively. The hidden neural sizes of MLP and BiRNN are both set to 200, while the attention size of AttBiRNN is set to 50. The epoch number and the batch size are set to 14 and 8 in training.

Table 3. The results over the validation mapping set of different embedding and network settings for aligning HeLiS and FoodOn. Class embedding is adopted as the input.

Embedding (class)	Neural network	Precision	Recall	F1 score	Accuracy
Word2Vec	MLP	0.809	0.798	0.803	0.869
	BiRNN	0.741	0.940	0.827	0.869
	AttBiRNN	0.790	0.941	0.859	0.897
	SiamNN (MLP)	0.874	0.941	0.903	0.932
	SiamNN (BiRNN)	0.808	**0.952**	0.874	0.909
	SiamNN (AttBiRNN)	0.828	**0.952**	0.884	0.917
OWL2Vec* (without pre-training)	MLP	0.769	0.869	0.815	0.869
	BiRNN	0.751	0.929	0.830	0.873
	AttBiRNN	0.708	0.976	0.820	0.857
	SiamNN (MLP)	0.854	0.976	0.911	0.936
	SiamNN (BiRNN)	0.924	0.833	0.874	0.921
	SiamNN (AttBiRNN)	0.829	0.905	0.862	0.901
OWL2Vec* (with pre-training)	MLP	0.826	0.845	0.835	0.889
	BiRNN	0.821	0.905	0.859	0.901
	AttBiRNN	0.828	0.860	0.842	0.893
	SiamNN (MLP)	**0.952**	0.905	**0.927**	**0.952**
	SiamNN (BiRNN)	0.914	0.881	0.897	0.933
	SiamNN (AttBiRNN)	0.854	0.893	0.871	0.913

Results. On the one hand we find OWL2Vec* with pre-training has better performance than the original Word2Vec and OWL2Vec* without pre-training; for example, the best F1 scores of these three settings are 0.927, 0.903 and 0.911 respectively. This observation, which is consistent under different settings, is as expected because the pre-trained OWL2Vec* incorporates words' common sense semantics and local context in the ontology. On the other hand we can find the SiamNNs outperform their original networks, and the SiamNN with MLP achieves the best performance. The former validates that the SiamNN architecture, which can align two embedding spaces according to the given training mappings, is more suitable for this task. The latter means further feature learning by RNN over the embedding makes no additional contribution in comparison with MLP. We also validated the above networks using path embedding as input, and the results are worse than their correspondences using the class embedding as input; for example, the best validation F1 score is 0.885 which is worse than 0.927 in Table 3. This may be due to the fact that the relevant predictive information from the class subsumers has already been encoded by OWL2Vec*.

6   Conclusion and Discussion

In this paper we presented a general ML extension to existing ontology alignment systems such as LogMap and AML. Briefly, it first adopts the confident mappings from an original system, such as the anchor mappings of LogMap, as well as some external class disjointness constraints, to generate training samples, then uses an ontology tailored language model OWL2Vec* and a SiamNN to train a model and predict the candidate mappings, and finally filters out invalid mappings according to their predicted scores and a subsumption-based logical assessment. According to the evaluation on an industrial use case and the alignments of the OAEI conference track, the ML extension is shown to be effective in improving both precision and recall. We discuss below some more subjective observations and possible directions for future work.

Running Time. Computation of the ML extension mainly lies in training and validation. With a laptop equipped by 2.3 GHz Intel Core i5 and 16 GB memory, the training of the 6 networks as set out in Sect. 5.3 with the class input using the pre-trained OWL2Vec* and the seeds from LogMap anchors takes 1.3 min for HeLiS and FoodOn, and 1.1 min for the OAEI conference track. It is possible to achieve even better matching performance via an exhaustive exploration of more settings, *e.g.*, the network hidden layer size, but this requires significantly more computation.

Seed Mappings. In distant supervision we assume that the seed mappings used for training are precise. In aligning HeLiS and FoodOn, we also considered extracting the seed mappings from the output mappings of LogMap and AML, both of which have a larger size but lower precision (0.676 and 0.636 respectively) compared to the LogMap anchors. However both lead to lower precision and recall, and the approximate F1 score drops to 0.657 and 0.696 respectively. Class disjointness constraints are also important for filtering out false-positive mappings and generating high precision seeds mappings; in the future work we plan to study semi-automatic neural-symbolic methods for deriving robust class disjointness constraints.

References

1. Algergawy, A., et al.: Results of the ontology alignment evaluation initiative 2019. In: OM@ ISWC, pp. 46–85 (2019). http://oaei.ontologymatching.org/
2. Bento, A., Zouaq, A., Gagnon, M.: Ontology matching using convolutional neural networks. In: Proceedings of LREC, pp. 5648–5653 (2020)

3. Chen, J., Hu, P., Jimenez-Ruiz, E., Holter, O.M., Antonyrajah, D., Horrocks, I.: OWL2Vec*: embedding of OWL ontologies. CoRR (2020)
4. Cho, K., et al.: Learning phrase representations using RNN encoder-decoder for statistical machine translation. In: EMNLP, pp. 1724–1734 (2014)
5. Doan, A., Madhavan, J., Domingos, P., Halevy, A.: Ontology matching: a machine learning approach. In: Staab, S., Studer, R. (eds) Handbook on Ontologies. International Handbooks on Information Systems, pp. 385–403. Springer, Heidelberg (2004). https://doi.org/10.1007/978-3-540-24750-0_19
6. Dooley, D.M., et al.: FoodOn: a harmonized food ontology to increase global food traceability, quality control and data integration. npj Sci. Food **2**(1), 1–10 (2018)
7. Dragoni, M., Bailoni, T., Maimone, R., Eccher, C.: HeLiS: an ontology for supporting healthy lifestyles. In: Vrandečić, D., et al. (eds.) ISWC 2018. LNCS, vol. 11137, pp. 53–69. Springer, Cham (2018). https://doi.org/10.1007/978-3-030-00668-6_4
8. Euzenat, J., Shvaiko, P.: Conclusions. Ontology Matching, pp. 399–405. Springer, Heidelberg (2013). https://doi.org/10.1007/978-3-642-38721-0_13
9. Faria, D., Pesquita, C., Santos, E., Palmonari, M., Cruz, I.F., Couto, F.M.: The agreementmakerlight ontology matching system. In: Meersman, R., et al. (eds.) OTM 2013. LNCS, vol. 8185, pp. 527–541. Springer, Heidelberg (2013). https://doi.org/10.1007/978-3-642-41030-7_38
10. Faria, D., Pesquita, C., Tervo, T., Couto, F.M., Cruz, I.F.: AML and AMLC results for OAEI 2019. In: OM@ISWC, pp. 101–106 (2019)
11. Gionis, A., Indyk, P., Motwani, R., et al.: Similarity search in high dimensions via hashing. VLDB **99**(6), 518–529 (1999)
12. Glimm, B., Horrocks, I., Motik, B., Stoilos, G., Wang, Z.: HermiT: an OWL 2 reasoner. J. Autom. Reason. **53**(3), 245–269 (2014)
13. Hertling, S., Paulheim, H.: DOME results for OAEI 2019. In: OM@ ISWC (2019)
14. Horrocks, I., Chen, J., Jaehun, L.: Tool support for ontology design and quality assurance. In: ICBO 2020 Integrated Food Ontology Workshop (IFOW) (2020)
15. Iyer, V., Agarwal, A., Kumar, H.: VeeAlign: a supervised deep learning approach to ontology alignment. In: OM@ISWC (2020)
16. Jiménez-Ruiz, E., Agibetov, A., Chen, J., Samwald, M., Cross, V.: Dividing the ontology alignment task with semantic embeddings and logic-based modules. In: ECAI (2020)
17. Jiménez-Ruiz, E., Cuenca Grau, B.: LogMap: logic-based and scalable ontology matching. In: Aroyo, L., et al. (eds.) ISWC 2011. LNCS, vol. 7031, pp. 273–288. Springer, Heidelberg (2011). https://doi.org/10.1007/978-3-642-25073-6_18
18. Jiménez-Ruiz, E., Cuenca Grau, B., Zhou, Y., Horrocks, I.: Large-scale interactive ontology matching: algorithms and implementation. In: ECAI (2012)
19. Kolyvakis, P., Kalousis, A., Kiritsis, D.: DeepAlignment: unsupervised ontology matching with refined word vectors. In: Proceedings of NAACL, pp. 787–798 (2018)
20. Kulmanov, M., Smaili, F.Z., Gao, X., Hoehndorf, R.: Semantic similarity and machine learning with ontologies. Brief. Bioinform. (2020)
21. Laadhar, A., Ghozzi, F., Bousarsar, I.M., Ravat, F., Teste, O., Gargouri, F.: POMap++ results for OAEI 2019: fully automated machine learning approach for ontology matching. In: OM@ISWC, pp. 169–174 (2019)
22. Li, G.: DeepFCA: matching biomedical ontologies using formal concept analysis embedding techniques. In: Proceedings of ICMHI, pp. 259–265 (2020)
23. Mikolov, T., Chen, K., Corrado, G., Dean, J.: Efficient estimation of word representations in vector space. CoRR (2013)
24. Mohammadi, M., Hofman, W., Tan, Y.H.: Simulated annealing-based ontology matching. ACM Trans. Manag. Inf. Syst. (TMIS) **10**(1), 1–24 (2019)

25. Nkisi-Orji, I., Wiratunga, N., Massie, S., Hui, K.-Y., Heaven, R.: Ontology alignment based on word embedding and random forest classification. In: Berlingerio, M., Bonchi, F., Gärtner, T., Hurley, N., Ifrim, G. (eds.) ECML PKDD 2018. LNCS (LNAI), vol. 11051, pp. 557–572. Springer, Cham (2019). https://doi.org/10.1007/978-3-030-10925-7_34
26. Otero-Cerdeira, L., Rodríguez-Martínez, F.J., Gómez-Rodríguez, A.: Ontology matching: a literature review. Exp. Syst. Appl. **42**(2), 949–971 (2015)
27. Pesquita, C., Faria, D., Santos, E., Couto, F.M.: To repair or not to repair: reconciling correctness and coherence in ontology reference alignments. In: OM@ISWC, pp. 13–24 (2013)
28. Portisch, J., Hladik, M., Paulheim, H.: Wiktionary matcher. In: OM@ISWC, pp. 181–188 (2019)
29. Shvaiko, P., Euzenat, J.: Ontology matching: state of the art and future challenges. IEEE Trans. Knowl. Data Eng. **25**(1), 158–176 (2013)
30. Wang, L., Bhagavatula, C., Neumann, M., Lo, K., Wilhelm, C., Ammar, W.: Ontology alignment in the biomedical domain using entity definitions and context. In: Proceedings of the BioNLP 2018 Workshop, pp. 47–55 (2018)
31. Wang, Q., Mao, Z., Wang, B., Guo, L.: Knowledge graph embedding: a survey of approaches and applications. IEEE Trans. Knowl. Data Eng. **29**(12), 2724–2743 (2017)
32. Xiang, C., Jiang, T., Chang, B., Sui, Z.: ERSOM: a structural ontology matching approach using automatically learned entity representation. In: EMNLP (2015)
33. Zhang, Y., et al.: Ontology matching with word embeddings. In: Sun, M., Liu, Y., Zhao, J. (eds.) CCL/NLP-NABD-2014. LNCS (LNAI), vol. 8801, pp. 34–45. Springer, Cham (2014). https://doi.org/10.1007/978-3-319-12277-9_4

Convolutional Complex Knowledge Graph Embeddings

Caglar Demir$^{(\boxtimes)}$ and Axel-Cyrille Ngonga Ngomo

Data Science Research Group, Paderborn University, Paderborn, Germany
`caglar.demir@upb.de`

Abstract. We investigate the problem of learning continuous vector representations of knowledge graphs for predicting missing links. Recent results suggest that using a Hermitian inner product on complex-valued embeddings or convolutions on real-valued embeddings can be effective means for predicting missing links. We bring these insights together and propose CONEX—a multiplicative composition of a 2D convolution with a Hermitian inner product on complex-valued embeddings. CONEX utilizes the Hadamard product to compose a 2D convolution followed by an affine transformation with a Hermitian inner product in $\mathbb{C}$. This combination endows CONEX with the capability of (1) controlling the impact of the convolution on the Hermitian inner product of embeddings, and (2) degenerating into ComplEx if such a degeneration is necessary to further minimize the incurred training loss. We evaluated our approach on five of the most commonly used benchmark datasets. Our experimental results suggest that CONEX outperforms state-of-the-art models on four of the five datasets w.r.t. Hits@1 and MRR even without extensive hyperparameter optimization. Our results also indicate that the generalization performance of state-of-the-art models can be further increased by applying ensemble learning. We provide an open-source implementation of our approach, including training and evaluation scripts as well as pretrained models (github.com/dice-group/Convolutional-Complex-Knowledge-Graph-Embeddings).

1 Introduction

Knowledge Graphs (KGs) represent structured collections of facts modelled in the form of typed relationships between entities [13]. These collections of facts have been used in a wide range of applications, including web search [10], cancer research [29], and even entertainment [21]. However, most KGs on the Web are far from being complete [24]. For instance, the birth places of 71% of the people in Freebase and 66% of the people in DBpedia are not found in the respective KGs. In addition, more than 58% of the scientists in DBpedia are not linked to the predicate that describes what they are known for [20]. Link prediction on KGs refers to identifying such missing information [9]. Knowledge Graph Embedding (KGE) models have been particularly successful at tackling the link prediction task [24].

© Springer Nature Switzerland AG 2021
R. Verborgh et al. (Eds.): ESWC 2021, LNCS 12731, pp. 409–424, 2021.
https://doi.org/10.1007/978-3-030-77385-4_24

We investigate the use of a 2D convolution in the complex space $\mathbb{C}$ to tackle the link prediction task. We are especially interested in an effective composition of the non-symmetric property of Hermitian products with the parameter sharing property of a 2D convolution. Previously, Trouillon et al. [35] showed the expressiveness of a Hermitian product on complex-valued embeddings $\mathrm{Re}(\langle \mathbf{e}_h, \mathbf{e}_r, \overline{\mathbf{e}_t}\rangle)$, where $\mathbf{e}_h$, $\mathbf{e}_r$, and $\mathbf{e}_t$ stand for the embeddings of head entity, relation and tail entity, respectively; $\overline{\mathbf{e}_t}$ is the complex conjugate of $\mathbf{e}_t$. The Hermitian product used in [35] is not symmetric and can be used to model antisymmetric relations since $\mathrm{Re}(\langle \mathbf{e}_h, \mathbf{e}_r, \overline{\mathbf{e}_t}\rangle) \neq \mathrm{Re}(\langle \mathbf{e}_t, \mathbf{e}_r, \overline{\mathbf{e}_h}\rangle)$. Dettmers et al. [9] and Nguyen et al. [23] indicated the effectiveness of using a 2D convolution followed by an affine transformation to predict missing links. Additionally, Balažević et al. [3] showed that 1D relation-specific convolution filters can be an effective means to tackle the link prediction task. Chen et al. [6] suggested applying a 2D convolution followed by two capsule layers on quaternion-valued embeddings. In turn, the results of a recent work [28] highlighted the importance of extensive hyperparameter optimization and new training strategies (see Table 1). The paper showed that the link prediction performances of previous state-of-the-art models (e.g., RESCAL, ComplEx and DistMult [26,35,37]) increased by up to 10% absolute on benchmark datasets, provided that new training strategies are applied. Based on these considerations, we propose CONEX—a multiplicative composition of a 2D convolution operation with a Hermitian inner product of complex-valued embedding vectors. By virtue of its novel architecture, CONEX is able to control the impact of a 2D convolution on predicted scores, i.e., by endowing ComplEx with two more degrees of freedom (see Sect. 4). Ergo, CONEX is able to degenerate to ComplEx if such a degeneration is necessary to further reduce the incurred training loss.

We evaluated CONEX on five of the most commonly used benchmark datasets (WN18, WN18RR, FB15K, FB15K-237 and YAGO3-10). We used the findings of [28] on using Bayesian optimization to select a small sample of hyperparameter values for our experiments. Hence, we did not need to perform an extensive hyperparameter optimization throughout our experiments and fixed the seed for the pseudo-random generator to 1. In our experiments, we followed the standard training strategy commonly used in the literature [3,4]. Overall, our results suggest that CONEX outperforms state-of-the-art models on four out of five benchmark datasets w.r.t. Hits@N and Mean Reciprocal Rank (MRR). CONEX outperforms ComplEx and ConvE on all benchmark datasets in all metrics. Results of our statistical hypothesis testing indicates that the superior performance of CONEX is statistically significant. Our ablation study suggests that the dropout technique and the label smoothing have the highest impact on the performance of CONEX. Furthermore, our results on the YAGO3-10 dataset supports the findings of Ruffinelli et al. [28] as training DistMult and ComplEx with new techniques resulted in increasing their MRR performances by absolute 20% and 19%, respectively. Finally, our results suggest that the generalization performance of models can be further improved by applying ensemble learning. In particular, ensembling CONEX leads to a new state-of-the-art performance on WN18RR and FB15K-237.

2   Related Work

A wide range of works have investigated KGE to address various tasks such as type prediction, relation prediction, link prediction, question answering, item recommendation and knowledge graph completion [7,8,14,26]. We refer to [5,16,24,27,36] for recent surveys and give a brief overview of selected KGE techniques. Table 1 shows scoring functions of state-of-the-art KGE models.

RESCAL [26] is a bilinear model that computes a three-way factorization of a third-order adjacency tensor representing the input KG. RESCAL captures various types of relations in the input KG but is limited in its scalability as it has quadratic complexity in the factorization rank [33]. DistMult [37] can be seen as an efficient extension of RESCAL with a diagonal matrix per relation to reduce the complexity of RESCAL [4]. DistMult performs poorly on antisymmetric relations while performing well on symmetric relations [33]. Note that through applying the reciprocal data augmentation technique, this incapability of DistMult is alleviated [28]. TuckER [4] performs a Tucker decomposition on the binary tensor representing the input KG, which enables multi-task learning through parameter sharing between different relations via the core tensor.

Table 1. State-of-the-art KGE models with training strategies. e denotes embeddings, $\overline{e} \in \mathbb{C}$ corresponds to the complex conjugate of e.. $*$ denotes a convolution operation with ω kernel. f denotes rectified linear unit function. $\otimes, \circ, \cdot$ denote the Hamilton, the Hadamard and an inner product, respectively. In ConvE, the reshaping operation is omitted. The tensor product along the n-th mode is denoted by $\times_n$ and the core tensor is represented by $\mathcal{W}$. MSE, MR, BCE and CE denote mean squared error, margin ranking, binary cross entropy and cross entropy loss functions. NegSamp and AdvNegSamp stand for negative sampling and adversarial sampling.

Model	Scoring function	VectorSpace	Loss	Training	Optimizer	Regularizer
RESCAL [26]	$e_h \cdot \mathcal{W}_r \cdot e_t$	$e_h, e_t \in \mathbb{R}$	MSE	Full	ALS	L2
DistMult [37]	$\langle e_h, e_r, e_t \rangle$	$e_h, e_r, e_t \in \mathbb{R}$	MR	NegSamp	Adagrad	Weighted L2
ComplEx [35]	$\mathrm{Re}(\langle e_h, e_r, \overline{e_t} \rangle)$	$e_h, e_r, e_t \in \mathbb{C}$	BCE	NegSamp	Adagrad	Weighted L2
ConvE [9]	$f(\mathrm{vec}(f([e_h; e_r] * \omega))\mathbf{W}) \cdot e_t$	$e_h, e_r, e_t \in \mathbb{R}$	BCE	KvsAll	Adam	Dropout, BatchNorm
TuckER [4]	$\mathcal{W} \times_1 e_h \times_2 e_r \times_3 e_t$	$e_h, e_r, e_t \in \mathbb{R}$	BCE	KvsAll	Adam	Dropout, BatchNorm
RotatE [31]	$- \parallel e_h \circ e_r - e_t \parallel$	$e_h, e_r, e_t \in \mathbb{C}$	CE	AdvNegSamp	Adam	-
QuatE [38]	$e_h \otimes e_r^{\triangleleft} \cdot e_t$	$e_h, e_r, e_t \in \mathbb{H}$	CE	AdvNegSamp	Adagrad	Weighted L2
ConEx	$\mathrm{conv}(e_h, e_r) \circ \mathrm{Re}(\langle e_h, e_r, \overline{e_t} \rangle)$	$e_h, e_r, e_t \in \mathbb{C}$	BCE	KvsAll	Adam	Dropout, BatchNorm

ComplEx [35] extends DistMult by learning representations in a complex vector space. ComplEx is able to infer both symmetric and antisymmetric relations via a Hermitian inner product of embeddings that involves the conjugate-transpose of one of the two input vectors. ComplEx yields state-of-the-art performance on the link prediction task while leveraging linear space and time complexity of the dot products. Trouillon et al. [34] showed that ComplEx is equivalent to HolE [25]. Inspired by Euler's identity, RotatE [31] employs a rotational model taking predicates as rotations from subjects to objects in complex space via the element-wise Hadamard product [16]. RotatE performs well on composition/-transitive relations while ComplEx performs poorly [31]. QuatE [38] extends the complex-valued space into hypercomplex by a quaternion with three imaginary components, where the Hamilton product is used as compositional operator for hypercomplex valued-representations.

ConvE [9] applies a 2D convolution to model the interactions between entities and relations. Through interactions captured by 2D convolution, ConvE yields a state-of-art performance in link prediction. ConvKB extends ConvE by omitting the reshaping operation in the encoding of representations in the convolution operation [23]. Similarly, HypER extends ConvE by applying relation-specific convolution filters as opposed to applying filters from concatenated subject and relation vectors [3].

3   Preliminaries and Notation

3.1   Knowledge Graphs

Let $\mathcal{E}$ and $\mathcal{R}$ represent the set of entities and relations, respectively. Then, a KG $\mathcal{G} = \{(\mathbf{h}, \mathbf{r}, \mathbf{t}) \in \mathcal{E} \times \mathcal{R} \times \mathcal{E}\}$ can be formalised as a set of triples where each triple contains two entities $\mathbf{h}, \mathbf{t} \in \mathcal{E}$ and a relation $\mathbf{r} \in \mathcal{R}$. A relation $\mathbf{r}$ in $\mathcal{G}$ is

- *symmetric* if $(\mathbf{h}, \mathbf{r}, \mathbf{t}) \iff (\mathbf{t}, \mathbf{r}, \mathbf{h})$ for all pairs of entities $\mathbf{h}, \mathbf{t} \in \mathcal{E}$,
- *anti-symmetric* if $(\mathbf{h}, \mathbf{r}, \mathbf{t}) \in \mathcal{G} \Rightarrow (\mathbf{t}, \mathbf{r}, \mathbf{h}) \notin \mathcal{G}$ for all $\mathbf{h} \neq \mathbf{t}$, and
- *transitive/composite* if $(\mathbf{h}, \mathbf{r}, \mathbf{t}) \in \mathcal{G} \wedge (\mathbf{t}, \mathbf{r}, \mathbf{y}) \in \mathcal{G} \Rightarrow (\mathbf{h}, \mathbf{r}, \mathbf{y}) \in \mathcal{G}$ for all $\mathbf{h}, \mathbf{t}, \mathbf{y} \in \mathcal{E}$ [18,31].

The inverse of a relation $\mathbf{r}$, denoted $\mathbf{r}^{-1}$, is a relation such that for any two entities $\mathbf{h}$ and $\mathbf{t}$, $(\mathbf{h}, \mathbf{r}, \mathbf{t}) \in \mathcal{G} \iff (\mathbf{t}, \mathbf{r}^{-1}, \mathbf{h}) \in \mathcal{G}$.

3.2   Link Prediction

The link prediction refers to predicting whether unseen triples (i.e., triples not found in $\mathcal{G}$) are true [16]. The task is often formalised by learning a scoring function $\phi : \mathcal{E} \times \mathcal{R} \times \mathcal{E} \mapsto \mathbb{R}$ [16,24] ideally characterized by $\phi(\mathbf{h}, \mathbf{r}, \mathbf{t}) > \phi(\mathbf{x}, \mathbf{y}, \mathbf{z})$ if $(\mathbf{h}, \mathbf{r}, \mathbf{t})$ is true and $(\mathbf{x}, \mathbf{y}, \mathbf{z})$ is not.

4   Convolutional Complex Knowledge Graph Embeddings

Inspired by the previous works ComplEx [35] and ConvE [9], we dub our approach CONEX (convolutional complex knowledge graph embeddings).

Motivation. Sun et al. [31] suggested that ComplEx is not able to model triples with transitive relations since ComplEx does not perform well on datasets containing many transitive relations (see Table 5 and Sect. 4.6 in [31]). Motivated by this consideration, we propose CONEX, which applies the Hadamard product to compose a 2D convolution followed by an affine transformation with a Hermitian inner product in $\mathbb{C}$. By virtue of the proposed architecture (see Eq. 1), CONEX is endowed with the capability of

1. leveraging a 2D convolution and
2. degenerating to ComplEx if such degeneration is necessary to further minimize the incurred training loss.

CONEX benefits from the *parameter sharing* and *equivariant representation* properties of convolutions [11]. The parameter sharing property of the convolution operation allows CONEX to achieve parameter efficiency, while the equivariant representation allows CONEX to effectively integrate interactions captured in the stacked complex-valued embeddings of entities and relations into computation of scores. This implies that small interactions in the embeddings have small impacts on the predicted scores[1]. The rationale behind this architecture is to increase the expressiveness of our model without increasing the number of its parameters. As previously stated in [35], this nontrivial endeavour is the keystone of embedding models. Ergo, we aim to overcome the shortcomings of ComplEx in modelling triples containing transitive relations through combining it with a 2D convolutions followed by an affine transformation on $\mathbb{C}$.

Approach. Given a triple $(\mathbf{h}, \mathbf{r}, \mathbf{t})$, CONEX $: \mathbb{C}^{3d} \mapsto \mathbb{R}$ computes its score as

$$\text{CONEX}(\mathbf{h}, \mathbf{r}, \mathbf{t}) = \text{conv}(\mathbf{e}_h, \mathbf{e}_r) \circ \text{Re}(\langle \mathbf{e}_h, \mathbf{e}_r, \overline{\mathbf{e}_t} \rangle), \tag{1}$$

where $\text{conv}(\cdot, \cdot) : \mathbb{C}^{2d} \mapsto \mathbb{C}^d$ is defined as

$$\text{conv}(\mathbf{e}_h, \mathbf{e}_r) = f\big(\text{vec}(f([\mathbf{e}_h, \mathbf{e}_r] * \omega)) \cdot \mathbf{W} + \mathbf{b}\big), \tag{2}$$

where $f(\cdot)$ denotes the rectified linear unit function (ReLU), $\text{vec}(\cdot)$ stands for a flattening operation, $*$ is the convolution operation, ω stands for kernels/filters in the convolution, and $(\mathbf{W}, \mathbf{b})$ characterize an affine transformation. By virtue of its novel structure, CONEX is enriched with the capability of controlling the impact of a 2D convolution and Hermitian inner product on the predicted scores. Ergo, the gradients of loss (see Eq. 6) w.r.t. embeddings can be propagated in two ways, namely, via $\text{conv}(\mathbf{e}_h, \mathbf{e}_r)$ or $\text{Re}(\langle \mathbf{e}_h, \mathbf{e}_r, \overline{\mathbf{e}_t} \rangle)$. Equation 1 can be equivalently expressed by expanding its real and imaginary parts:

$$\text{CONEX}(h, r, t) = \sum_{k=1}^{d} \text{Re}(\gamma)_k \text{Re}(\mathbf{e}_h)_k \text{Re}(\mathbf{e}_r)_k \text{Re}(\overline{\mathbf{e}_t})_k \tag{3}$$

$$\begin{aligned}
= \ &\langle \text{Re}(\gamma), \text{Re}(\mathbf{e}_h), \text{Re}(\mathbf{e}_r), \text{Re}(\mathbf{e}_t) \rangle \\
&+ \langle \text{Re}(\gamma), \text{Re}(\mathbf{e}_h), \text{Im}(\mathbf{e}_r), \text{Im}(\mathbf{e}_t) \rangle \\
&+ \langle \text{Im}(\gamma), \text{Im}(\mathbf{e}_h), \text{Re}(\mathbf{e}_r), \text{Im}(\mathbf{e}_t) \rangle \\
&- \langle \text{Im}(\gamma), \text{Im}(\mathbf{e}_h), \text{Im}(\mathbf{e}_r), \text{Re}(\mathbf{e}_t) \rangle
\end{aligned} \tag{4}$$

where $\overline{\mathbf{e}_t}$ is the conjugate of $\mathbf{e}_t$ and γ denotes the output of $\text{conv}(\mathbf{e}_h, \mathbf{e}_r)$ for brevity. Such multiplicative inclusion of $\text{conv}(\cdot, \cdot)$ equips CONEX with two more degrees of freedom due the $\text{Re}(\gamma)$ and $\text{Im}(\gamma)$ parts.

---

[1] We refer to [11] for further details of properties of convolutions.

Connection to ComplEx. During the optimization, $\text{conv}(\cdot, \cdot)$ is allowed to reduce its range into $\gamma \in \mathbb{C}$ such that $\text{Re}(\gamma) = 1 \land \text{Im}(\gamma) = 1$. This allows CONEX to degenerate into ComplEx as shown in Eq. 5:

$$\text{CONEX}(\mathbf{h}, \mathbf{r}, \mathbf{t}) = \gamma \circ \text{ComplEx}(\mathbf{h}, \mathbf{r}, \mathbf{t}). \tag{5}$$

This multiplicative inclusion of $\text{conv}(\cdot, \cdot)$ is motivated by the scaling parameter in the batch normalization (see Sect. 3 in [15]). Consequently, CONEX is allowed use a 2D convolution followed by an affine transformation as a scaling factor in the computation of scores.

Training. We train our approach by following a standard setting [4,9]. Similarly, we applied the standard data augmentation technique, the KvsAll training procedure[2]. After the data augmentation technique for a given pair $(\mathbf{h}, \mathbf{r})$, we compute scores for all $\mathbf{x} \in \mathcal{E}$ with $\phi(\mathbf{h}, \mathbf{r}, \mathbf{x})$. We then apply the logistic sigmoid function $\sigma(\phi((\mathbf{h}, \mathbf{r}, \mathbf{t})))$ to obtain predicted probabilities of entities. CONEX is trained to minimize the binary cross entropy loss function L that determines the incurred loss on a given pair $(\mathbf{h}, \mathbf{r})$ as defined in the following:

$$L = -\frac{1}{|\mathcal{E}|} \sum_{i=1}^{|\mathcal{E}|} (\mathbf{y}^{(i)} \log(\hat{\mathbf{y}}^{(i)}) + (1 - \mathbf{y}^{(i)}) \log(1 - \hat{\mathbf{y}}^{(i)})), \tag{6}$$

where $\hat{\mathbf{y}} \in \mathbb{R}^{|\mathcal{E}|}$ is the vector of predicted probabilities and $\mathbf{y} \in [0, 1]^{|\mathcal{E}|}$ is the binary label vector.

5 Experiments

5.1 Datasets

We used five of the most commonly used benchmark datasets (WN18, WN18RR, FB15K, FB15K-237 and YAGO3-10). An overview of the datasets is provided in Table 2. WN18 and WN18RR are subsets of Wordnet, which describes lexical and semantic hierarchies between concepts and involves **symmetric** and **antisymmetric** relation types, while FB15K, FB15K-237 are subsets of Freebase, which involves mainly **symmetric**, **antisymmetric** and **composite** relation types [31]. We refer to [9] for further details pertaining to the benchmark datasets.

---

[2] Note that the KvsAll strategy is called 1-N scoring in [9]. Here, we follow the terminology of [28].

Table 2. Overview of datasets in terms of number of entities, number of relations, and node degrees in the train split along with the number of triples in each split of the dataset.

Dataset	$|\mathcal{E}|$	$|\mathcal{R}|$	Degr. (M ± SD)	$|\mathcal{G}^{\text{Train}}|$	$|\mathcal{G}^{\text{Validation}}|$	$|\mathcal{G}^{\text{Test}}|$
YAGO3-10	123,182	37	9.6 ± 8.7	1,079,040	5,000	5,000
FB15K	14,951	1,345	32.46 ± 69.46	483,142	50,000	59,071
WN18	40,943	18	3.49 ± 7.74	141,442	5,000	5,000
FB15K-237	14,541	237	19.7 ± 30	272,115	17,535	20,466
WN18RR	40,943	11	2.2 ± 3.6	86,835	3,034	3,134

5.2 Evaluation Metrics

We used the filtered MRR and Hits@N to evaluate link prediction performances, as in previous works [4, 9, 31, 35]. We refer to [28] for details pertaining to metrics.

5.3 Experimental Setup

We selected the hyperparameters of CONEX based on the MRR score obtained on the validation set of WN18RR. Hence, we evaluated the link prediction performance of CONEX on FB15K-237, YAGO3-10, WN18 and FB15K by using the best hyperparameter configuration found on WN18RR. This decision stems from the fact that we aim to reduce the impact of extensive hyperparameter optimization on the reported results and the CO_2 emission caused through relying on the findings of previously works [28]. Strubell et al. [30] highlighted the substantial energy consumption of performing extensive hyperparameter optimization. Moreover, Ruffinelli et al. [28] showed that model configurations can be found by exploring relatively few random samples from a large hyperparameter space. With these considerations, we determined the ranges of hyperparameters for the grid search algorithm optimizer based on their best hyperparameter setting for ConvE (see Table 8 in [28]). Specifically, the ranges of the hyperparameters were defined as follows: d: $\{100, 200\}$; dropout rate:$\{.3, .4\}$ for the input; dropout rate: $\{.4, .5\}$ for the feature map; label smoothing: $\{.1\}$ and the number of output channels in the convolution operation: $\{16, 32\}$; the batch size: $\{1024\}$; the learning rate: $\{.001\}$. After determining the best hyperparameters based on the MRR on the validation dataset; we retrained CONEX with these hyperparameters on the combination of train and valid sets as applied in [17].

Motivated by the experimental setups for ResNet [12] and AlexNet [19], we were interested in quantifying the impact of ensemble learning on the link prediction performances. Ensemble learning refers to learning a weighted combination of learning algorithms. In our case, we generated ensembles of models by averaging the predictions of said models.[3] To this end, we re-evaluated state-of-the-art models, including TucKER, DistMult and ComplEx on the combination

---

[3] Ergo, the weights for models were set to 1 (see the Sect. 16.6 in [22] for more details).

of train and validation sets of benchmark datasets. Therewith, we were also able to quantify the impact of training state-of-the-art models on the combination of train and validation sets. Moreover, we noticed that link prediction performances of DistMult and ComplEx, on the YAGO3-10 dataset were reported without employing new training strategies (KvsAll, the reciprocal data augmentation, the batch normalization, and the ADAM optimizer). Hence, we trained DistMult, ComplEx on YAGO3-10 with these strategies.

5.4 Implementation Details and Reproducibility

We implemented and evaluated our approach in the framework provided by [2,4]. Throughout our experiments, the seed for the pseudo-random generator was fixed to 1. To alleviate the hardware requirements for the reproducibility of our results and to foster further reproducible research, we provide hyperparameter optimization, training and evaluation scripts along with pretrained models at the project page.

6   Results

Tables 3, 4 and 10 report the link prediction performances of CONEX on five benchmark datasets. Overall, CONEX outperforms state-of-the-art models on four out of five datasets. In particular, CONEX outperforms ComplEx and ConvE on all five datasets. This supports our original hypothesis, i.e., that the composition of a 2D convolution with a Hermitian inner product improves the prediction of relations in complex spaces. We used the Wilcoxon signed-rank test to measure the statistical significance of our link prediction results. Moreover, we performed an ablation study (see Table 8) to obtain confidence intervals for prediction performances of CONEX. These results are shown in the Appendix. Bold and underlined entries denote best and second-best results in all tables.

CONEX outperforms all state-of-the-art models on WN18 and FB15K (see Table 10 in the Appendix), whereas such distinct superiority is not observed on WN18RR and FB15K-237. Table 3 shows that CONEX outperforms many state-of-the-art models, including RotatE, ConvE, HypER, ComplEx, NKGE, in all metrics on WN18RR and FB15K-237. This is an important result for two reasons: (1) CONEX requires significantly fewer parameters to yield such superior results (e.g., CONEX only requires 26.63M parameters on WN18RR, while RotatE relies on 40.95M parameters), and (2) we did not tune the hyperparameters of CONEX on FB15K-237. Furthermore, the results reported in Table 3 corroborate the findings of Ruffinelli et al. [28]: training DistMult and ComplEx with KvsAll, the reciprocal data augmentation, the batch normalization, and the ADAM optimizer leads to a significant improvement, particularly on FB15K-237.

During our experiments, we observed that many state-of-the-art models are not evaluated on YAGO3-10. This may stem from the fact that the size of YAGO3-10 prohibits performing extensive hyperparameter optimization

Table 3. Link prediction results on WN18RR and FB15K-237. Results are obtained from corresponding papers. ‡ represents recently reported results of corresponding models.

	WN18RR				FB15K-237			
	MRR	Hits@10	Hits@3	Hits@1	MRR	Hits@10	Hits@3	Hits@1
DistMult [9]	.430	.490	.440	.390	.241	.419	.263	.155
ComplEx [9]	.440	.510	.460	.410	.247	.428	.275	.158
ConvE [9]	.430	.520	.440	.400	.335	.501	.356	.237
RESCAL[†] [28]	.467	.517	.480	.439	.357	.541	.393	.263
DistMult[†] [28]	.452	.530	.466	.413	.343	.531	.378	.250
ComplEx[†] [28]	.475	.547	.490	.438	.348	.536	.384	.253
ConvE[†] [28]	.442	.504	.451	.411	.339	.521	.369	.248
HypER [3]	.465	.522	.477	.436	.341	.520	.376	.252
NKGE [38]	.450	.526	.465	.421	.330	.510	.365	.241
RotatE [31]	.476	.571	.492	.428	.338	.533	.375	.241
TuckER [4]	.470	.526	.482	.443	.358	.544	.394	.266
QuatE [38]	**.482**	**.572**	**.499**	.436	**.366**	**.556**	.401	**.271**
DistMult	.439	.527	.455	.399	.353	.539	.390	.260
ComplEx	.453	.546	.473	.408	.332	.509	.366	.244
TuckER	.466	.515	.476	.441	.363	.553	.400	.268
ConEx	.481	.550	.493	**.448**	**.366**	.555	**.403**	**.271**

even with the current state-of-the-art hardware systems. Note that YAGO3-10 involves 8.23 and 8.47 times more entities than FB15K and FB15K-237, respectively. Table 4 indicates that DistMult and ComplEx perform particularly well on YAGO3-10, provided that KvsAll, the reciprocal data augmentation, the batch normalization, and the ADAM optimizer are employed. These results support findings of Ruffinelli et al. [28]. During training, we observed that the training loss of DistMult and ComplEx seemed to converge within 400 epochs, whereas the training loss of TuckER seemed to continue decreasing. Ergo, we conjecture that TuckER is more likely to benefit from increasing the number of epochs than DistMult and ComplEx. Table 4 shows that the superior performance of ConEx against state-of-the-art models including DistMult, ComplEx, HypER can be maintained on the largest benchmark dataset for the link prediction.

Delving into the link prediction results, we observed an inconsistency in the test splits of WN18RR and FB15K-237. Specifically, the test splits of WN18RR and FB15K-237 contain many out-of-vocabulary entities[4]. For instance, 6% of the test set on WN18RR involves out-of-vocabulary entities. During our experiments, we did not remove such triples to obtain fair comparisons on both

---

[4] github.com/TimDettmers/ConvE/issues/66.

Table 4. Link prediction results on YAGO3-10. Results are obtained from corresponding papers.

	YAGO3-10			
	MRR	Hits@10	Hits@3	Hits@1
DistMult [9]	.340	.540	.380	.240
ComplEx [9]	.360	.550	.400	.260
ConvE [9]	.440	.620	.490	.350
HypER [3]	.533	.678	.580	.455
RotatE [31]	.495	.670	.550	.402
DistMult	.543	.683	.590	.466
ComplEx	.547	.690	.594	.468
TuckER	.427	.609	.476	.331
ConEx	**.553**	**.696**	**.601**	**.474**

datasets. To quantify the impact of unseen entities on link prediction performances, we conducted an additional experiment.

Link Prediction per Relation. Table 5 reports the link prediction per relation performances on WN18RR. Overall, models perform particularly well on triples containing symmetric relations such as also_see and similar_to. Compared to RotatE, DistMult, ComplEx and TuckER, ConEx performs well on triples containing transitive relations such as hypernym and has_part. Allen et al. [1] ranked the complexity of type of relations as R > S > C in the link prediction task. Based on this ranking, superior performance of ConEx becomes more apparent as the complexity of relations increases.

Ensemble Learning. Table 6 reports the link prediction performances of ensembles based on pairs of models. These results suggest that ensemble learning can be applied as an effective means to boost the generalization performance of existing approaches including ConEx. These results may also indicate that models may be further improved through optimizing the impact of each model on the ensembles, e.g., by learning two scalars α and β in $(\alpha \text{ConEx}(s, p, o) + \beta \text{TuckER}(s, p, o))$ instead of averaging predicted scores.

Parameter Analysis. Table 7 indicates the robustness of ConEx against the overfitting problem. Increasing the number of parameters in ConEx does not lead to a significant decrease in the generalization performance. In particular, ConEx achieves similar generalization performance, with $p = 26.63M$ and $p = 70.66M$, as the difference between MRR scores are less than absolute 1%. This cannot be explained with convolutions playing no role as ConEx would then degrade back to ComplEx and achieve the same results (which is clearly not the case in our experiments).

Table 5. MRR link prediction on each relation of WN18RR. Results of RotatE are taken from [38]. The complexity of type of relations in the link prediction task is defined as R > S > C [1].

Relation name	Type	RotatE	DistMult	ComplEx	TuckER	ConEx
hypernym	S	.148	.102	.106	.121	**.149**
instance_hypernym	S	.318	.218	.292	.375	**.393**
member_meronym	C	**.232**	.129	.181	.181	.171
synset_domain_topic_of	C	.341	.226	.266	.344	**.373**
has_part	C	.184	.143	.181	.171	**.192**
member_of_domain_usage	C	**.318**	.225	.280	.213	**.318**
member_of_domain_region	C	.200	.095	.267	.284	**.354**
derivationally_related_form	R	.947	.982	.984	.985	**.986**
also_see	R	.585	.639	.557	**.658**	.647
verb_group	R	.943	**1.00**	**1.00**	**1.00**	**1.00**
similar_to	R	**1.00**	**1.00**	**1.00**	**1.00**	**1.00**

Table 6. Link prediction results of ensembled models on WN18RR and FB15K-237. Second rows denote link prediction results without triples containing out-of-vocabulary entities. CONEX-CONEX stands for ensembling two CONEX trained with the dropout rate 0.4 and 0.5 on the feature map.

	WN18RR				FB15K-237			
	MRR	Hits@10	Hits@3	Hits@1	MRR	Hits@10	Hits@3	Hits@1
DistMult-ComplEx	.446	.545	.467	.398	.359	.546	.397	.265
	.475	.579	.497	.426	.359	.546	.397	.265
DistMult-TuckER	.446	.533	.461	.405	.371	.563	.410	.275
	.476	.569	.492	.433	.371	.563	.411	.275
CONEX-DistMult	.454	.545	.471	.410	.371	.563	.409	.275
	.484	.580	.501	.439	.367	.556	.403	.272
CONEX-ComplEx	.470	.554	.487	.428	.370	.559	.407	.276
	.501	_.589_	_.518_	_.456_	.360	.547	.397	.267
CONEX-TuckER	.483	.549	.494	.449	_.375_	_.568_	_.414_	_.278_
	_.514_	.583	**.526**	**.479**	_.375_	_.568_	_.414_	_.278_
CONEX-CONEX	.485	.559	.495	.450	**.376**	.569	**.415**	**.279**
	.517	**.594**	**.526**	**.479**	**.376**	**.570**	**.415**	**.279**

Table 7. Influence of different hyperparameter configurations for CONEX on WN18RR. d, c and p stand for the dimensions of embeddings in $\mathbb{C}$, number of output channels in 2D convolutions and number of free parameters in millions, respectively.

d	c	p	WN18RR			
			MRR	Hits@10	Hits@3	Hits@1
300	64	70.66M	.475	.540	.490	.442
250	64	52.49M	.475	.541	.488	.441
300	32	47.62M	.480	.548	.491	.447
250	32	36.39M	.479	.545	.490	.446
300	16	36.10M	.479	.550	.494	.445
250	16	28.48M	.477	.544	.489	.443
200	32	26.63M	.481	.550	.493	.447
100	32	10.75M	.474	.533	.480	.440
100	16	9.47M	.476	.536	.486	.441
50	32	4.74M	.448	.530	.477	.401

7   Discussion

The superior performance of CONEX stems from the composition of a 2D convolution with a Hermitian inner product of complex-valued embeddings. Trouillon et al. [35] showed that a Hermitian inner product of complex-valued embeddings can be effectively used to tackle the link prediction problem. Applying the convolution operation on complex-valued embeddings of subjects and predicates permits CONEX to recognize interactions between subjects and predicates in the form of complex-valued feature maps. Through the affine transformation of feature maps and their inclusion into a Hermitian inner product involving the conjugate-transpose of complex-valued embeddings of objects, CONEX can accurately infer various types of relations. Moreover, the number and shapes of the kernels permit to adjust the expressiveness , while CONEX retains the parameter efficiency due to the parameter sharing property of convolutions. By virtue of the design, the expressiveness of CONEX may be further improved by increasing the depth of the $\text{conv}(\cdot, \cdot)$ via the residual learning block [12].

8   Conclusion and Future Work

In this work, we introduced CONEX—a multiplicative composition of a 2D convolution with a Hermitian inner product on complex-valued embeddings. By virtue of its novel structure, CONEX is endowed with the capability of controlling the impact of a 2D convolution and a Hermitian inner product on the predicted scores. Such combination makes CONEX more robust to overfitting, as is affirmed with our parameter analysis. Our results open a plethora of other research avenues. In future work, we plan to investigate the following: (1) combining the convolution operation with Hypercomplex multiplications, (2) increasing the depth in the convolutions via residual learning block and (3) finding more effective combinations of ensembles of models.

Acknowledgments. This work has been supported by the BMWi-funded project RAKI (01MD19012D) as well as the BMBF-funded project DAIKIRI (01IS19085B). We are grateful to Diego Moussallem for valuable comments on earlier drafts and to Pamela Heidi Douglas for editing the manuscript.

Appendix

Statistical Hypothesis Testing. We carried out a Wilcoxon signed-rank test to check whether our results are significant. Our null hypothesis was that the link prediction performances of CONEX, ComplEx and ConvE come from the same distribution. The alternative hypothesis was correspondingly that these results come from different distributions. To perform the Wilcoxon signed-rank test (two-sided), we used the differences of the MRR, Hits@1, Hits@3, and Hits@10 performances on WN18RR, FB15K-237 and YAGO3-10. We performed two hypothesis tests between CONEX and ComplEx as well as between CONEX and ConvE. In both tests, we were able to reject the null hypothesis with a p-value < 1%. Ergo, the superior performance of CONEX is statistically significant.

Ablation Study. We conducted our ablation study in a fashion akin to [9]. Like [9], we evaluated 2 different parameter initialisations to compute confidence intervals that is defined as $\bar{x} \pm 1.96 \cdot \frac{s}{\sqrt{n}}$, where $\bar{x} = \frac{1}{n} \sum_i^n x_i$ and $s = \sqrt{\frac{\sum_i^n (x_i - \bar{x})^2}{n}}$, respectively. Hence, the mean and the standard deviation are computed without Bessel's correction. Our results suggest that the initialization of parameters does not play a significant role in the link performance of CONEX. The dropout technique is the most important component in the generalization performance of CONEX. This is also observed in [9]. Moreover, replacing the Adam optimizer with the RMSprop optimizer [32] leads to slight increases in the variance of the link prediction results. During our ablation experiments, we were also interested in decomposing CONEX through removing conv($\cdot, \cdot$), after CONEX is trained with it on benchmark datasets. By doing so, we aim to observe the impact of a 2D convolution in the computation of scores. Table 9 indicates that the impact of conv($\cdot, \cdot$) differs depending on the input knowledge graph. As the size of the input knowledge graph increases, the impact of conv($\cdot, \cdot$) on the computation of scores of triples increases.

Table 8. Ablation study for CONEX on FB15K-237. *dp* and *ls* denote the dropout technique and the label smoothing technique, respectively.

	FB15K-237			
	MRR	Hits@10	Hits@3	Hits@1
Full	$.366 \pm .000$	$.556 \pm .001$	$.404 \pm .001$	$.270 \pm .001$
No *dp* on inputs	$.282 \pm .000$	$.441 \pm .001$	$.313 \pm .001$	$.203 \pm .000$
No *dp* on feature map	$.351 \pm .000$	$.533 \pm .000$	$.388 \pm .001$	$.259 \pm .001$
No *ls*	$.321 \pm .001$	$.498 \pm .001$	$.354 \pm .001$	$.232 \pm .002$
With RMSprop	$.361 \pm .004$	$.550 \pm .007$	$.400 \pm .005$	$.267 \pm .003$

Table 9. Link prediction results on benchmark datasets. CONEX$^-$ stands for removing conv$(\cdot, \cdot)$ in CONEX during the evaluation.

	ConEx				ConEx$^-$			
	MRR	Hits@10	Hits@3	Hits@1	MRR	Hits@10	Hits@3	Hits@1
WN18RR	.481	.550	.493	.448	.401	.494	.437	.346
FB15K-237	.366	.555	.403	.271	.284	.458	.314	.198
YAGO3-10	.553	.696	.601	.477	.198	.324	.214	.136

Table 10. Link prediction results on WN18 and FB15K obtained from [4,38].

	WN18				FB15K			
	MRR	Hits@10	Hits@3	Hits@1	MRR	Hits@10	Hits@3	Hits@1
DistMult	.822	.936	.914	.728	.654	.824	.733	.546
ComplEx	.941	.947	.936	.936	.692	.840	.759	.599
ANALOGY	.942	.947	.944	.939	.725	.854	.785	.646
R-GCN	.819	.964	.929	.697	.696	.842	.760	.601
TorusE	.947	.954	.950	.943	.733	.832	.771	.674
ConvE	.943	.956	.946	.935	.657	.831	.723	.558
HypER	.951	.958	.955	.947	.790	.885	.829	.734
SimplE	.942	.947	.944	.939	.727	.838	.773	.660
TuckER	.953	.958	.955	.949	.795	.892	.833	.741
QuatE	.950	.962	.954	.944	.833	.900	.859	.800
CONEX	**.976**	**.980**	**.978**	**.973**	**.872**	**.930**	**.896**	**.837**

Link Prediction Results on WN18 and FB15K. Table 10 reports link prediction results on the WN18 and FB15K benchmark datasets.

References

1. Allen, C., Balazevic, I., Hospedales, T.: Interpreting knowledge graph relation representation from word embeddings. In: International Conference on Learning Representations (2021). https://openreview.net/forum?id=gLWj29369lW
2. Balažević, I., Allen, C., Hospedales, T.: Multi-relational poincaré graph embeddings. In: Advances in Neural Information Processing Systems, pp. 4465–4475 (2019)
3. Balažević, I., Allen, C., Hospedales, T.M.: Hypernetwork knowledge graph embeddings. In: Tetko, I.V., Kůrková, V., Karpov, P., Theis, F. (eds.) ICANN 2019. LNCS, vol. 11731, pp. 553–565. Springer, Cham (2019). https://doi.org/10.1007/978-3-030-30493-5_52
4. Balažević, I., Allen, C., Hospedales, T.M.: Tucker: tensor factorization for knowledge graph completion. arXiv preprint arXiv:1901.09590 (2019)
5. Cai, H., Zheng, V.W., Chang, K.C.C.: A comprehensive survey of graph embedding: problems, techniques, and applications. IEEE Trans. Knowl. Data Eng. **30**(9), 1616–1637 (2018)
6. Chen, H., Wang, W., Li, G., Shi, Y.: A quaternion-embedded capsule network model for knowledge graph completion. IEEE Access **8**, 100890–100904 (2020)
7. Demir, C., Moussallem, D., Ngomo, A.-C.N.: A shallow neural model for relation prediction. arXiv preprint arXiv:2101.09090 (2021)
8. Demir, C., Ngomo, A.-C.N.: A physical embedding model for knowledge graphs. In: Wang, X., Lisi, F.A., Xiao, G., Botoeva, E. (eds.) JIST 2019. LNCS, vol. 12032, pp. 192–209. Springer, Cham (2020). https://doi.org/10.1007/978-3-030-41407-8_13
9. Dettmers, T., Minervini, P., Stenetorp, P., Riedel, S.: Convolutional 2d knowledge graph embeddings. In: 32nd AAAI Conference on Artificial Intelligence (2018)
10. Eder, J.S.: Knowledge graph based search system. US Patent App. US13/404,109 (21 June 2012)
11. Goodfellow, I., Bengio, Y., Courville, A.: Deep Learning. MIT Press (2016)
12. He, K., Zhang, X., Ren, S., Sun, J.: Deep residual learning for image recognition. In: Proceedings of the IEEE Conference on Computer Vision and Pattern Recognition, pp. 770–778 (2016)
13. Hogan, A., et al.: Knowledge graphs. arXiv preprint arXiv:2003.02320 (2020)
14. Huang, X., Zhang, J., Li, D., Li, P.: Knowledge graph embedding based question answering. In: Proceedings of the 12th ACM International Conference on Web Search and Data Mining, pp. 105–113 (2019)
15. Ioffe, S., Szegedy, C.: Batch normalization: accelerating deep network training by reducing internal covariate shift. arXiv preprint arXiv:1502.03167 (2015)
16. Ji, S., Pan, S., Cambria, E., Marttinen, P., Yu, P.S.: A survey on knowledge graphs: representation, acquisition and applications. arXiv preprint arXiv:2002.00388 (2020)
17. Joulin, A., Grave, E., Bojanowski, P., Nickel, M., Mikolov, T.: Fast linear model for knowledge graph embeddings. arXiv preprint arXiv:1710.10881 (2017)
18. Kazemi, S.M., Poole, D.: Simple embedding for link prediction in knowledge graphs. In: Advances in Neural Information Processing Systems, pp. 4284–4295 (2018)
19. Krizhevsky, A., Sutskever, I., Hinton, G.E.: ImageNet classification with deep convolutional neural networks. Commun. ACM **60**(6), 84–90 (2017)
20. Krompaß, D., Baier, S., Tresp, V.: Type-constrained representation learning in knowledge graphs. In: Arenas, M., et al. (eds.) ISWC 2015. LNCS, vol. 9366, pp. 640–655. Springer, Cham (2015). https://doi.org/10.1007/978-3-319-25007-6_37

21. Malyshev, S., Krötzsch, M., González, L., Gonsior, J., Bielefeldt, A.: Getting the most out of Wikidata: semantic technology usage in Wikipedia's knowledge graph. In: Vrandečić, D., et al. (eds.) ISWC 2018. LNCS, vol. 11137, pp. 376–394. Springer, Cham (2018). https://doi.org/10.1007/978-3-030-00668-6_23
22. Murphy, K.P.: Machine Learning: A Probabilistic Perspective. MIT Press (2012)
23. Nguyen, D.Q., Nguyen, T.D., Nguyen, D.Q., Phung, D.: A novel embedding model for knowledge base completion based on convolutional neural network. arXiv preprint arXiv:1712.02121 (2017)
24. Nickel, M., Murphy, K., Tresp, V., Gabrilovich, E.: A review of relational machine learning for knowledge graphs. Proc. IEEE **104**(1), 11–33 (2015)
25. Nickel, M., Rosasco, L., Poggio, T.: Holographic embeddings of knowledge graphs. arXiv preprint arXiv:1510.04935 (2015)
26. Nickel, M., Tresp, V., Kriegel, H.P.: A three-way model for collective learning on multi-relational data. In: ICML, vol. 11, pp. 809–816 (2011)
27. Qin, C., et al.: A survey on knowledge graph based recommender systems. Scientia Sinica Informationis **50**, 937 (2020)
28. Ruffinelli, D., Broscheit, S., Gemulla, R.: You can teach an old dog new tricks! on training knowledge graph embeddings. In: International Conference on Learning Representations (2019)
29. Saleem, M., Kamdar, M.R., Iqbal, A., Sampath, S., Deus, H.F., Ngonga Ngomo, A.-C.: Big linked cancer data: integrating linked TCGA and PubMed. J. Web Semant. **27**, 34–41 (2014)
30. Strubell, E., Ganesh, A., McCallum, A.: Energy and policy considerations for deep learning in NLP. arXiv preprint arXiv:1906.02243 (2019)
31. Sun, Z., Deng, Z.H., Nie, J.Y., Tang, J.: RotatE: knowledge graph embedding by relational rotation in complex space. arXiv preprint arXiv:1902.10197 (2019)
32. Tieleman, T., Hinton, G.: Lecture 6.5-rmsprop: divide the gradient by a running average of its recent magnitude. COURSERA: Neural Netw. Mach. Learn. **4**(2), 26–31 (2012)
33. Trouillon, T., Dance, C.R., Gaussier, É., Welbl, J., Riedel, S., Bouchard, G.: Knowledge graph completion via complex tensor factorization. J. Mach. Learn. Res. **18**(1), 4735–4772 (2017)
34. Trouillon, T., Nickel, M.: Complex and holographic embeddings of knowledge graphs: a comparison. arXiv preprint arXiv:1707.01475 (2017)
35. Trouillon, T., Welbl, J., Riedel, S., Gaussier, É., Bouchard, G.: Complex embeddings for simple link prediction. In: International Conference on Machine Learning, pp. 2071–2080 (2016)
36. Wang, Q., Mao, Z., Wang, B., Guo, L.: Knowledge graph embedding: a survey of approaches and applications. IEEE Trans. Knowl. Data Eng. **29**(12), 2724–2743 (2017)
37. Yang, B., Yih, W., He, X., Gao, J., Deng, L.: Embedding entities and relations for learning and inference in knowledge bases. In: ICLR (2015)
38. Zhang, S., Tay, Y., Yao, L., Liu, Q.: Quaternion knowledge graph embeddings. In: Advances in Neural Information Processing Systems, pp. 2731–2741 (2019)

RETRA: Recurrent Transformers for Learning Temporally Contextualized Knowledge Graph Embeddings

Simon Werner[1]([✉]), Achim Rettinger[1], Lavdim Halilaj[2], and Jürgen Lüttin[2]

[1] Trier University, Trier, Germany
{werners,rettinger}@uni-trier.de
[2] Bosch Research, Renningen, Germany
{lavdim.halilaj,juergen.luettin}@de.bosch.com

Abstract. Knowledge graph embeddings (KGE) are vector representations that capture the global distributional semantics of each entity instance and relation type in a static Knowledge Graph (KG). While KGEs have the capability to embed information related to an entity into a single representation, they are not customizable to a specific context.

This is fundamentally limiting for many applications, since the latent state of an entity can change depending on the current situation and the entity's history of related observations. Such context-specific roles an entity might play cannot be captured in global KGEs, since it requires to generate an embedding unique for each situation.

This paper proposes a KG modeling template for temporally contextualized observations and introduces the Recurrent Transformer (RETRA), a neural encoder stack with a feedback loop and constrained multi-headed self-attention layers. RETRA enables to transform global KGEs into custom embeddings, given the situation-specific factors of the relation and the subjective history of the entity.

This way, entity embeddings for down-stream Knowledge Graph Tasks (KGT) can be contextualized, like link prediction for location recommendation, event prediction, or driving-scene classification. Our experimental results demonstrate the performance gains standard KGEs can obtain, if they are customized according to the situational context.

Keywords: Knowledge graph embedding · Contextualized embeddings · Modeling temporal context

1 Motivation

We all play different roles in our lives. In private settings we might act differently than in professional settings. What we represent in a situation depends on contextual factors and there is not a single universally valid representation that captures all roles of a person equally well. In contrast, standard Knowledge Graph Embedding (KGE) methods produce a single vector representation

© Springer Nature Switzerland AG 2021
R. Verborgh et al. (Eds.): ESWC 2021, LNCS 12731, pp. 425–440, 2021.
https://doi.org/10.1007/978-3-030-77385-4_25

for entity instances and relation types in the corresponding Knowledge Graph (KG). Each embedding captures the global distributional semantic of the KG in respect to this entity and is optimized for predicting universally valid facts, a Knowledge Graph Task (KGT) known as link prediction. This assumption of universality rarely holds in real-world inference tasks, since the situational context is crucial for making nuanced predictions. When trying to contextualize global KGEs to a situation, two Research Questions (RQ) come to mind:

RQ1: How can concrete situations, specifically situational context, be modelled appropriately within knowledge graphs?

RQ2: How can static knowledge graph embeddings be transformed into contextualized representations, that capture the specifics of a concrete situations?

In this paper we argue, that a single static KGE per entity and relation is not adequate for many KGTs. Instead, entities and relations need to be put into context by factors specific to the current situation and their subjective history.[1] This requires a different entity embedding for each situation, not just one that attempts to be universally valid. Consequently, there is the need to customize static KGEs to situational and subjective contexts. More precisely, we argue that current models cannot generate relation embeddings that capture the situation-specific relational context (we refer to this limitation as *(Lim1)*) and entity embeddings that contain the subject's history of related observations (we refer to this limitation as *(Lim2)*).

W.r.t. RQ1: We propose *temporally contextualized KG facts* (tcKG facts) as a modelling template for situation-specific information in a KG. This adds a temporal sequence of hyper-edges (time-stamped subject-relation-object triples where the relation is n-ary in order to capture n contextualizing factors) to an existing static KG (see Sect. 3).

W.r.t. RQ2: We contribute the deep learning framework RETRA, which transforms static global entity and relation embeddings into temporally contextualized embeddings, given corresponding tcKG facts. This situation-specific embedding reflects the role an entity plays in a certain context and allows to make situational predictions (see Sect. 4). RETRA uses a novel *recurrent architecture* and a *constrained multi-headed self-attention layer* that imposes the relational structure of temporally contextualized KG facts during training (see Sect. 5).

In order to demonstrate how broadly applicable tcKG and RETRA are we apply and test them in three diverse scenarios, namely location recommendation, event prediction and driving-scene classification. Our empirical results indicates that contextualizing pre-trained KGEs boosts predictive performance in all cases (see Sect. 6).

---

[1] In psychology and neuroscience this distinction might be referred to as semantics vs. episodic memory (see [19]).

2   Related Work

Our work attempts to transfer the success of contextualizing word embeddings in Natural Language Processing to Knowledge Graph Embeddings (KGE).

2.1   Contextualized Word Embeddings

Word embeddings have been the driving force in Natural Language Processing (NLP) in recent years. Soon after the learning of static embeddings of lexical items became popular their drawbacks became apparent since they conflate all meanings of a word into a single point in vector space. More precisely, static semantic representations suffer from two important limitations: *(Lim1)* ignoring the role of situational context in triggering nuanced meanings; *(Lim2)* due to restricting the scope of meaning to individual entities, it is difficult to capture higher order semantic dependencies, such as compositionality and sequential arrangements between entities. Both limitations were recognized early and addressed by approaches that generate contextualized word representations given surrounding words in a sentence. Before the now dominant transformer approach [20], LSTMs where used to contextualize word embeddings [7]. In the area of KGE the need for contextualizing embeddings has not gotten much attention yet, as we will outline next.

2.2   Knowledge Graph Embedding

In recent years KGE has been a very vibrant field in Machine Learning and Semantic Technologies (see [8] for a survey). KGE methods can be roughly characterized by the representation space and the scoring function:

The representation space is traditionally Euclidean $\mathbb{R}^d$, but many different spaces like Complex $\mathbb{C}^d$ (e.g., in [18]) or Hypercomplex $\mathbb{H}^d$ (cmp. [25]) have been used as well. In this work we focus on Euclidean vector spaces only, since they are used for Neural Network embedding models like our RETRA.

The scoring function measures the plausibility of an (unknown) subject-predicate-object triple (referred to as "fact"), given the model parameters. The function produces a scalar score that is obtained by an additive or a multiplicative combination of subject, predicate and object embedding. In this work we focus only on optimizing a given KGE without altering its scoring function.

Standard KGE methods don't take into account temporal information or contextual factors that may influence the plausibility of a fact. In this work we are trying to complement static KGEs without replacing them. To the best of our knowledge there is no existing KGE method that attempts to address both limitations, but they have been addressed individually, as detailed next.

2.3   Knowledge Hypergraph Embedding

Approaches to embed contextualized KG facts is not in the center of current KGE research. However, the use of n-ary relations and the modeling of context as a hypergraph has been proposed before the KGE hype. Such approaches from Statistical Relational Learning were based on graphical models and tensor factorization [16]. A more recent approach extends the current KGE method SimplE [10] to hypergraphs [4] but does not take into account temporal or sequential information. Thus, those approaches address *(Lim1)*, but not *(Lim2)*. In addition, they don't allow to input standard KGE models to transform their embeddings into contextualized KGEs.

2.4   Temporal KGE

Embedding temporal dynamics of a knowledge graph and thus tackling *(Lim2)* has seen some attention recently. Basic approaches to temporal KGE, model facts as temporal quadruples. They are optimized for scoring the plausibility of (unknown) facts at a given point in time [3,11]. A more sophisticated approach is proposed in [14]. It checks the temporal consistency given contextual relations of the subject and object. Besides the inability of those models to model n-ary sequential context, we are also taking a different focus by using the temporal dimension to model the history of experiences of a subject.

A more entity-centric perspective is taken in [17] which attempts to model the temporal evolution of entities. This comes close to what we attempt regarding *(Lim2)*, but again, it does not cover n-ary relations and is not intended to transform given embeddings into contextualized ones, if provided with a history of subjective experiences. [9] take a relation-specific perspective instead, but still suffer from the same limitations as the above mentioned techniques.

2.5   Contextualized KGE

Central to our RETRA-approach is its ability to transform static input embeddings into contextualized KGEs. A similar approach and the same perspective is being adopted in [22]. There, entities and relations are expected to appear in different graph contexts and consequently should change their representation according to the context *(Lim1)*. We agree with this perspective, but argue that temporal evolution is equally important *(Lim2)*. [21] attempt a relation-specific embedding of entities and propose an LSTM-based approach to so. While RETRA is also inspired by Recurrent Neural Networks, we take a more subject-specific perspective. Besides that, temporal and n-ary relations are not considered in [21]. The same limitations apply to [24], but the use of a Transformer is similar to our approach. However, word embeddings are used as inputs to the transformation function instead of pre-trained static KGEs in RETRA.

Summing up, RETRA offers a unique combination that no previous method has attempted: n-ary relations *(Lim1)* and sequential subjective experience *(Lim2)* are exploited to transform static KGE into contextualize ones. RETRA achieves this by two major technical novelties: Modeling KGs with temporally contextualized facts and extending Transformers with a feedback loop and a constrained self-attention layer (Fig. 1).

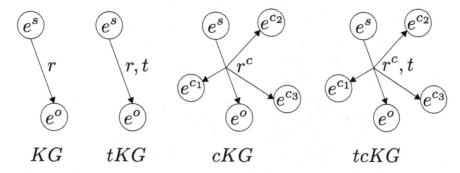

Fig. 1. From subject-predicate-object KG triples, to temporal tKG facts which occur at time t, to contextualized cKG facts which allow to model influencing factors as an n-ary relation, to tcKG facts which contextualize the KG observation at a certain time. This models the observations of a sequence of relations r^c the subject e^o is involved in.

3   Modeling Subjective Temporal Context

To address *RQ1* we start from the assumption that static KG facts act as background knowledge but the inference task depends on the situational context and the subject's memory. Consequently, we need to extend triples as follows:

KG facts are defined as a triple (e^s, r, e^o) where $e^s, e^o \in \{e^1, \dots, e^{n_e}\}$ is from the set of n_e entity instances and $r \in \{r^1, \dots, r^{n_r}\}$ from the set of n_r relation types. KG facts constitute subject-predicate-object statements that are assumed as being static and stable background knowledge.

tKG facts are quadruples (e^s, r, e^o, t) where $t \in \mathbb{N}$ indicates a point in a sequence when the fact occurred. In many scenarios t is obtained from discretizing timestamps and thus creates a globally ordered set of facts, where n_t is the total number of points in time (cmp. [17])[2]. KG facts without a temporal dimension are considered true for any t.

cKG facts are $(n+1)$-tuples $(e^s, r^c, e^o, e^{c_1}, \dots, e^{c_{n_c}})$ that allow to model context as an n_c-ary relation. $e^{c_1}, \dots, e^{c_{n_c}}$ are the n_c context entities influencing the relation r^c between subject e^s and object e^o. As for KG facts, cKG facts are considered non-dynamic background knowledge given the current situation.

tcKG facts are $(n+2)$-tuples $(e^s, r^c, e^o, t, e^{c_1}, \dots, e^{c_{n_c}})$ which represent sequentially contextualized KG facts by combining the features of tKGs and cKGs. Intuitively, they capture a specific situation which subject e^s is experiencing at time t. e^c are influencing factors towards e^s's relation to object e^o.

---

[2] Please note, that temporal KGs have mostly been using t to model the point in time when a fact is being observed. Here, we are taking a slightly different perspective by modeling in which point in time a subject e^s makes an experience in relation to similar experiences it has made at previous points in time.

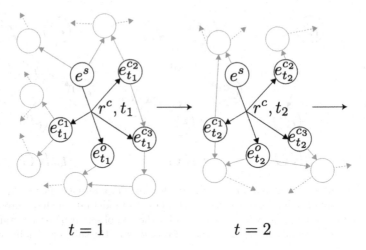

$$t = 1 \qquad\qquad t = 2$$

Fig. 2. tcKG facts (shown in black) and their relation to static background knowledge (KG and cKG facts, shown in gray) as a temporally unrolled KG.

With tcKG facts as additional building blocks, we can now model task-specific temporally contextualized KGs as temporal hypergraphs (i.e., relations are potentially n_c-ary and potentially associated with timestamps t). This subjective temporal context is input to RETRA as follows:

1. Given an n_c-ary relation r^c we first define one entity participating in r^c as the subject e^s whose perspective is represented in respect to an object e^o.[3]
2. The contexts $c_1, \ldots, c_{n_c}$ are given by the remaining entities involved in the n_c-ary relation. They define the influencing factors in a concrete situation.
3. If available, the context can be extended by entities deterministically dependent on e^o. Non-deterministically dependent context of e^o or e^c or facts that are not specific to a certain point in time t only, are not explicitly modelled (see gray edges and gray nodes in Fig. 2).
4. Finally, the temporal context is modeled by n_c relation instances of r^c that involve e^s as the subject. Sorted by time-stamp t, r^c defines the sequential context from the perspective of e^s towards its relation to e^o (see black edges an black nodes in Fig. 2). Note, that the context entities e^c do change in every step, as does e^o, thus $e^o_{t_1} \neq e^o_{t_2}$. Consequently, all the facts associated to e^c and e^o do change in every step (gray edges and gray nodes in Fig. 2). Only e^s and the relation-type of r^c stay fixed as defined above.

With the above selection procedure we obtain a sequence of tcKG facts from the KG by filtering for relations r^c with subject e^s. Consequently, such a model of

---

[3] Note, that this is a deliberate modeling choice that is not due to technical limitations. RETRA can model any sets of subjects and objects since transformers allow variable numbers of inputs and can mask any subset during training. We chose this restriction, since this is pragmatically the most common pattern and avoids a cluttered notation.

dynamic context consists of a sequence of (e^s, r^c)-tuples with varying sequence-length n_t. In each step r^c has an varying object e^o and is characterized by n_c contextual factors e^c.[4]

For illustration purposes, Table 1 shows instantiations of the tcKG modelling pattern according to our three applications domains *location recommendation*, *event prediction* and *driving-scene classification* (see Sect. 6 for details).

Table 1. Illustrating examples of instantiated tcKG patterns for three applications.

Application	Subject e^s	Relation r^c	Object e^o	Contexts $c_1, \ldots, c_{n_c}$
Location recommendation	User	ChecksIn	Location	Time of day, weather, day of week, location type …
Event prediction	Source actor	EventType	Involved target organizations	Target country, source country, sector, …
Driving-scene classification	Ego vehicle	InvolvedIn	Conflict-type	Ego lane, foe road users, foes' lanes, signaling, acceleration, speed, …

4 Embedding Subjective Temporal Context

So far, the tcKG modelling pattern provides an explicit representation of dynamic context of a subject and a relation-type as a sequence of sub-graphs (see Fig. 2). The second contribution of this paper, addressing RQ2, is a machine learning method that captures this information in two embeddings, the subjective context e^s and the relational context r^c.[5] Once we obtain those embeddings we then can use any embeddings-based KGT scoring functions, e.g., for contextualized link prediction.

One way to capture dynamic context in a single embedding is to represent the history of sequential information in a latent state. As common in Hidden Markov Models or Recurrent Neural Nets, all $t - 1$ previous contextualized observation are reduced into one embedding capturing the latent state up to this point. In our model, this memory is captured in the e^s embedding. We thus define the probability P of the contextualized relation representation r^c as being conditioned on $P(r^c | e^s, r, e^o, e^{c_1}, \ldots, e^{c_{n_c}})$. The subjective context representation e^s depends on r^c but also on the previous experience e^s_{t-1} in similar situations: $P(e^s_t | e^s_{t-1}, r^c_t, e^o_t)$. These conditional dependencies are visualized in Fig. 3.

---

[4] Note, that the arity n_c does not need to be fixed in each step and for each e^s. Variable-length context, unknown or missing e^cs can be modelled and handled efficiently with RETRA, since transformers can handle variable input lengths.

[5] We indicate embedding vectors for nodes e and relations r with bold symbols to contrast them to symbolic nodes e and relations r from the KG.

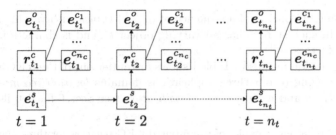

Fig. 3. Sequential context for subject and relation embedding e^s and r. The object e^o and contextual factors e^c refer to a different symbolic KG entity e^o and e^c in every step. They are given by (pre-trained) static KGEs. In contrast e^s and r represent the same symbolic KG node e^s and hyper-edge r, regardless of time and context. However, the embedding is customized with a situation-specific contextualized embedding, depending on the temporal and relational context.

5 RETRA: The Recurrent Transformer

Learning customized embeddings based on subjective sequential context requires a novel Neural Network (NN) architecture.

5.1 The RETRA Architecture

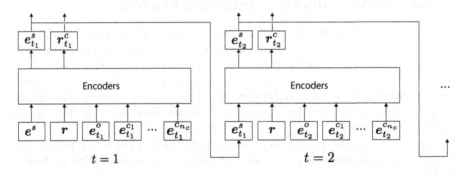

Fig. 4. Recurrency in the RETRA architecture: In the first step, e^s is not temporally contextualized but a static KGE embedding. In $t = 2$ the contextualized $e^s_{t_1}$ is used as input to generate the temporally contextualized $e^s_{t_2}$.

Our model is inspired by the encoder stack of transformers [20] and Recurrent Neural Networks (RNNs) and can thus be called a Recurrent Transformer (RETRA). We can't use common RNN architectures, like LSTMs [7], nor transformer models, since both don't handle multiple variable length inputs per step in a temporal sequence. Regarding input and output, RETRA receives the pretrained static embeddings $e^s, r, e^o, e^{c_1}, \dots, e^{c_{n_c}}$ and outputs the contextualized r^c. In addition, e^s's previous subjective memory e^s_{t-1} is passed on to generate the temporally contextualized embedding e_t^s for the current step. Thus, the only non-pre-trained embedding passed on to the next step is e_{t-1}^s (cmp. Fig. 4).

The final crucial building block to transform $r \longrightarrow r^c$ and $e_{t-1}^s \longrightarrow e_t^s$ is handled inside the encoder stack. Similar to [20] we use a stack of encoder layers, each consisting of a self-attention layer followed by a feed forward network. We adapt each attention head in the self-attention layer to resemble the structure of the relations defined by a tcKG. Thus, we don't need to calculate the pairwise attention for all inputs to the encoder, but can attend r^c only to $\{e^s, r, e^o, e^{c_1}, \ldots, e^{c_{n_c}}\}$. Similarly, we can constrain the attention of e_t^s to $\{e_{t-1}^s, r_t^c, e_t^o\}$ only. This is displayed by the diagonal arrows inside the first encoder layer in Fig. 5.[6]

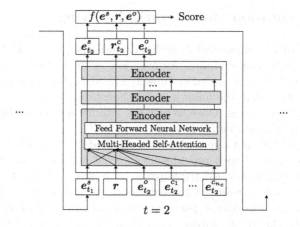

Fig. 5. Inside the Encoders in the RETRA architecture (cmp. Fig. 4): Stacked encoder-layers, each with constrained multi-headed self-attention, followed by the scoring function which returns a scalar score for (e^s, r, e^o)-triple.

5.2   Training RETRA

To optimize the weight matrices in the feed-forward and self-attention layers using backpropagation we need to measure the plausibility of predicted facts (using a scoring function) and its deviation from known facts given in the training data (using a loss function). In principal RETRA is independent of the choice of the scoring function and training objective (see Table 5 in [8] for an overview of state-of-the-art KGE models and their scoring functions). Any scoring functions and training objectives can be plugged into RETRA as long as it allows to calculate a gradient.[7] We settle on the most common KGE training objective,

---

[6] The constraining inside the attention heads is an engineering choice and acts as an inductive bias. Any other constraining is possible including no constraining.

[7] Also, many other self-supervised training objectives are possible. Starting from relation masking to temporal subject masking (mask subject e_t^s and condition the prediction on e_{t-1}^s).

namely link prediction, which we in "transformer terms" refer to as "object masking". The training target is to correctly predict e_{t+1}^o given e_t^s and r_t^c, where e_{t+1}^o is masked out. Thus, the weights need to be adjusted, such that the scoring function $f(e_t^s, r_t^c, e_t^o)$ outputs a high score for the correct e_{t+1}^o from the training data (and a low score for all other entities). Using a soft-max function on the predicted scores for each e^os allows to calculate the cross-entropy loss against the correct triple and backprop the error.

In this paper we are only interested in optimizing the embeddings regardless of the scoring function provided. Thus, we compare the predictive performance of a given KGE model, including its scoring function, to using the same scoring function but transforming the embeddings to temporally contextualized KGEs.

6   Implementation and Empirical Testing

This section provides implementation details and reports empirical results from three diverse application domains. An overview of the features selected in each domain as tcKG facts is provided in Table 1. The SUMO dataset and the parameters used for training in the following experimental section are available in our repository[8] on Github.com. Once we get the internal approval, the code to run the experiments will also be made available there.

The proposed RETRA approach is implemented based on PyTorch's[9] Transformer Encoder layer, which provides an internal self-attention layer. As seen in Fig. 5, we use an embedded triple $(e_{t_1}^s, r, e_{t_2}^o)$ plus its contexts $e^{c_1}, \ldots, e^{c_{n_c}}$ as input and assume the output to contain the contextualized embeddings $e_{t_2}^s$ and $r_{t_2}^c$. Of those embeddings, the contextualized subject embedding replaces or complements the global subject embedding in the next time-step. This is repeated over the whole sequence of experiences of e^s. By doing so, the subject embedding alters based on the history of previous inputs and its current context.

One key feature of RETRA is its complementarity to existing KGE methods. In the use-cases we present here, we use the static KGEs and their respective scoring functions from three established baseline KGE techniques, namely TransE [1], SimplE [10] and HolE [15]. The implementations of the baseline models were acquired using the OpenKE[10] framework, which offers fast implementations of various KGE approaches. The focus of this work is not to obtain the best overall predictive performance but to show how temporal contextualization can improve existing KGEs. For that reason we picked three basic and established baselines.

---

[8] https://github.com/siwer/Retra.
[9] https://pytorch.org/.
[10] https://github.com/thunlp/OpenKE.

6.1   Location Recommendation

For location recommendation, we use the New York City dataset[11] which was created and used for a different recommendation scenario before [23]. The data consists of check-ins from Foursquare[12], which is a location based social network. Every check-in consists of various information, including user, location, location type, country and time. The recommendation target is a *location* or *Point of Interest* (POI) for a particular user, given background knowledge about the locations and the history of *visits* or *checkIns* of users at POIs. The ranking is done by using a scoring function $f(e^s, r, e^o)$ provided by the baseline KGE approaches. The result of a forward step in this scenario is a tensor containing the scores for every potential location in the data. This information plus the information about the known target location given in the training data serves for calculating the cross-entropy loss.

Location Recommendation - Experimental Design: We consider the 'raw' setting provided in the data set, since we are treating every check-in as one distinct time-step. The data set contains 104,991 distinct check-ins, 3,626 distinct locations, 3,754 distinct users and 281 distinct types. For training and testing we were using a random 80–20 split of our data. Users with only one check-in were not considered because a sequence of at least two check-ins is needed for contextualization. In addition to the input of a triple (e^s, r, e^o), we explicitly passed the preceding location and the current location's type as context. The check-ins are not uniformly distributed over users. There are many users with only one or two check-ins, and few users with a lot of check-ins (up to 4,069). The same pattern can be identified with the locations. This extreme imbalance makes this a very challenges task, since we assume that a longer sequence provides more information on a certain user's behaviour than a short sequence would do.

Basic KGE approaches are unable to incorporate the inherent sequential and n-ary relational information provided by such a dataset and are thus fundamentally limited for this task. For both approaches, we have chosen the default number of dimensions (130) as the embedding size.

Location Recommendation - Experimental Results: It can be seen in Table 2, that all baseline approaches have performance issues, which we attribute to the skewed distribution. Still, we use these approaches as our global baseline embeddings to see if it is possible to incorporate more information by modelling the sequence and the context information and thus obtain an increase in performance. When the baseline KGEs are combined with RETRA we indeed obtain a huge relative performance increase. Numbers in bold indicate the best results. While the overall performance is still low, the results show that the usage of sequential and contextual information for enhancing entity embeddings can improve the performance of standard KGE approaches by a factor of up to 15.

---

[11] https://github.com/eXascaleInfolab/LBSN2Vec.
[12] https://foursquare.com.

Table 2. Metrics for the best runs of the baseline and combined approaches. "Imp" refers to the relative percentage of performance change compared to the corresponding baseline metric.

Approach	Hit@10	Hit@3	Hit@1	Imp Hit@10	Imp Hit@3	Imp Hit@1
TransE	0.0100	0.0017	0.0004	-	-	-
SimplE	0.0077	0.0035	0.0013	-	-	-
HolE	0.0038	0.0004	0.0	-	-	-
RETRA+TransE	0.0203	0.0005	0.0001	103%	−70%	−75%
RETRA+SimplE	**0.0592**	**0.0521**	**0.0194**	668%	1388%	1392%
RETRA+HolE	0.0209	0.0005	0.0	450%	25%	0%

When testing different combinations of model parameters, we observed that the learning rate has the strongest influence on the performance. Changing the number of transformer layers does not seem to have a big impact in general. Apparently, the interactions between features is not complex enough to require several attention layers. For all tested scoring functions, the combination with RETRA led to an improvement in performance.

6.2   Driving Situation Classification

Much progress has been made towards automated driving. One challenging task in automated driving is to capture relevant traffic participants and integrated prediction and planning of the next movement by considering the given context and possible interactive scenarios. Here, we define the problem as predicting the driving maneuver (e.g. following, merging, overtaking) of a vehicle given the current state of the driving scene. According to [12] approaches for vehicle motion prediction can be grouped into physics-based, maneuver-based and interaction-based. Interaction-based methods extend maneuver-based methods by modelling the dependencies between pairs of vehicles. Related work based on different deep neural network approaches and feature combinations for trajectory prediction has been described in [13] in which surrounding vehicles and their features are extracted from fixed grid cells. Our approach in comparison uses relational data between the ego and foe vehicles. Our motivation is that explicit representation of triples might lead to improved modelling of interactions between vehicles.

Driving Situation Classification - Experimental Design: We use SUMO[13] (Simulations of Urban Mobility), an open source, highly portable, microscopic and continuous multi-modal traffic simulation package to generate driving data. More than 50,000 driving scenes of a motorway were generated. The vehicle parameters as well as driving styles were varied widely in order to simulate a large variety of vehicles and driving behaviours. This resulted in situations such

---

[13] https://www.eclipse.org/sumo/.

as risky driving situations, abandoned driving maneuvers, unexpected stops and even accidents. We have developed a knowledge graph to represent the simulated data by entities (e.g. scene, situation, vehicle, scenario), relations between entities (e.g. isPartOf, occursIn, type) and their associated features (e.g. speed, acceleration, driving direction, time-to-collision). This resulted in more than 900 Mio. RDF-triples with around 2 million scenes which comprise more than 5 million *Lane Change* and *Conflict* situations, respectively. It represents a valuable benchmark data-set for driving situation analysis. More information on the design and creation process of the data-set is available in [6].

Table 3. Results for the SUMO Driving Situation Classification data set. The task was to predict the correct situation type, given surrounding traffic. All performance metrics (hit@k, mean rank (MR) and mean reciprocal rank (MRR)) indicate that context is crucial and more previous observations information improves the performance more.

Approach	Sequence length	Hit@3	Hit@1	MR	MRR
HolE	0	0.9366	0.5235	1.76	0.72
TransE	0	0.7668	0.2729	2.56	0.53
SimplE	0	-	-	-	-
RETRA+FF	0	**0.9946**	0.8060	1.23	0.89
RETRA+FF	5	0.9731	0.8212	1.23	0.90
RETRA+FF	10	0.9672	0.8382	1.17	0.91
RETRA+FF	15	0.9858	0.8455	1.17	**0.92**
RETRA+FF	20	0.9871	**0.8469**	**1.16**	**0.92**

Driving Situation Classification - Experimental Results: We conducted two sets of experiments on the SUMO data, which both aimed at predicting the type of a conflict. We needed to make this distinction since the baseline KGE methods cannot use context and thus have to make predictions based on the situation-ID. Instead, RETRA learns a dedicated situation embedding based on the context and previous driving scenes. When experimenting with the different baseline KGE scoring functions we noticed that a fully connected feed forward layer (FF) as a trainable scoring function performs better. The results are shown in the first four rows of Table 3. Since various SimplE implementation we tried did not scale to the size of this data set, we can't report any results. Obviously, RETRA+FF considerably outperforms the baselines, even as a non-recurrent version. This is mostly due to its ability to contextualize a situation embedding which avoids the need for explicit situation-IDs.

Since the previous steps in time leading up to the current situation are potentially important in driving scenes, we specifically investigated the influence of previous situations on the predictive performance. The last four rows of Table 3 show how RETRA handles different numbers of recurrence steps, by feeding in the preceding 5–20 driving situations leading up to the current point in time. It can be observed that the longer sequences are the better the results get. This confirms the assumption that the history is important in driving situations and RETRA is able to exploit it.

6.3 Event Prediction

The *Integrated Crisis Early Warning System* [2] contains information on geopolitical events and conflicts and is a widely used benchmark for both static and temporal KGE approaches. We specifically use this dataset to showcase how contextualizing can improve and generalize binary KGE approaches.

Event Prediction - Data Set: For our experiments, we use the 2014 subset[14] of the ICEWS data as described in [5] as a basis, and add contextual information that we take from the original 2014 data[15]. In addition to the triples consisting of *Source, Event Text* and *Target*, we use the entities *Source Sector, Source Country, Target Country* and *Intensity* to contextualize the *Source*.

Event Prediction - Experimental Results: The target is to predict the *target entity*, typically the organization involved in the event, given the *source entity*, aka actor, and the relation. In both setups, we optimize a cross-entropy loss by calculating scores for all possible triples in a query $(s, r, ?)$. The target is to produce the highest score for the original triple given in the ground-truth. In addition to using only the information presented in triples, we also consider contextual information for our training. This is achieved by passing all information through RETRA and using the contextualized subject entity for the query $(s_c, r, ?)$. In this way, the embeddings are learnt in such a manner that they contribute to the contextualizing given a binary scoring function from our baseline

Table 4. Contextualized vs. non-contextualized KGE for different scoring functions on the ICEWS event prediction data set.

Metric	Contextualized			Non-contextualized		
	TransE	SimplE	HolE	TransE	SimplE	HolE
Hits@1	0.519	**0.570**	0.537	0.264	0.264	0.299
Hits@3	0.691	**0.739**	0.703	0.398	0.398	0.463
Hits@10	0.821	**0.843**	0.822	0.532	0.532	0.623
Hits@100	**0.941**	**0.941**	0.940	0.775	0.775	0.840
MR	152.92	91.02	**88.00**	311.85	311.85	193.13
MRR	0.625	**0.669**	0.638	0.358	0.358	0.409

---

[14] https://github.com/nle-ml/mmkb/tree/master/TemporalKGs.

[15] https://dataverse.harvard.edu/dataset.xhtml?persistentId=doi:10.7910/DVN/28075.

KGE methods. As shown in Table 4, using the contextual information results in a huge improvement in performance for all tested baseline scoring functions and evaluation metrics. This, again, indicates that context is crucial and RETRA is able to exploit it, regardless of the KGE scoring function used.

7 Conclusion and Future Work

In this paper we propose the modeling template **tcKG** for temporally contextualized KG facts (addressing *RQ1*) and **RETRA**, a Deep Learning model intended to transform static Knowledge Graph Embeddings into temporally contextualized ones, given a sequence of tcKG facts (addressing *RQ2*). With RETRA we tackle two limitations of current KGE models, namely their lack of taking n-ary relational context into account (*Lim1*) and capturing the evolution of an entity embedding, given its subjective history of similar previous events (*Lim2*). Our experimental results on three data sets from diverse application domains indicate that existing KGE methods for global embeddings can benefit from using RETRA to contextualize their embeddings. We could also demonstrate that both, context and history, does boost performance considerably.

Although there have been a number of recent contributions to the area of contextualized KGEs, we still see large potential for future work beyond additional empirical testing and technical improvements to RETRA. From the perspective of knowledge representation the fundamental question remains how to best capture influencing factors that contextualize the meaning of an entity or relation. We see this as a crucial challenge for making KGs more actionable in concrete real-world situation. Once this is solved efficiently, we expect a similar boost to KGEs as Transformers generated for word embeddings.

References

1. Bordes, A., Usunier, N., Garcia-Durán, A., Weston, J., Yakhnenko, O.: Translating embeddings for modeling multi-relational data. In: Proceedings of the 26th International Conference on Neural Information Processing Systems, NIPS 2013, , Red Hook, NY, USA, vol. 2, pp. 2787–2795. Curran Associates Inc. (2013)
2. Boschee, E., Lautenschlager, J., O'Brien, S., Shellman, S., Starz, J., Ward, M.: ICEWS coded event data (2015). https://doi.org/10.7910/DVN/28075
3. Dasgupta, S.S., Ray, S.N., Talukdar, P.: HyTE: hyperplane-based temporally aware knowledge graph embedding. In: Proceedings of the 2018 Conference on Empirical Methods in Natural Language Processing, pp. 2001–2011 (2018)
4. Fatemi, B., Taslakian, P., Vazquez, D., Poole, D.: Knowledge hypergraphs: prediction beyond binary relations (2020)
5. García-Durán, A., Dumancic, S., Niepert, M.: Learning sequence encoders for temporal knowledge graph completion. CoRR abs/1809.03202 (2018). http://arxiv.org/abs/1809.03202
6. Halilaj, L., Dindorkar, I., Luettin, J., Rothermel, S.: A knowledge graph-based approach for situation comprehension in driving scenarios. In: 18th Extended Semantic Web Conference - In-Use Track (2021). https://openreview.net/forum?id=XBWVwf4lab8

7. Hochreiter, S., Schmidhuber, J.: Long short-term memory. Neural Comput. **9**(8), 1735–1780 (1997)
8. Ji, S., Pan, S., Cambria, E., Marttinen, P., Yu, P.S.: A survey on knowledge graphs: Representation, acquisition and applications. arXiv preprint arXiv:2002.00388 (2020)
9. Jiang, T., et al.: Towards time-aware knowledge graph completion. In: Proceedings of the 26th International Conference on Computational Linguistics: Technical Papers, COLING 2016, pp. 1715–1724 (2016)
10. Kazemi, S.M., Poole, D.: Simple embedding for link prediction in knowledge graphs (2018)
11. Leblay, J., Chekol, M.W.: Deriving validity time in knowledge graph. In: Companion Proceedings of the Web Conference, vol. 2018, pp. 1771–1776 (2018)
12. Lefèvre, S., Vasquez, D., Laugier, C.: A survey on motion prediction and risk assessment for intelligent vehicles. ROBOMECH J. **1**(1), 1–14 (2014). https://doi.org/10.1186/s40648-014-0001-z
13. Lenz, D., Diehl, F., Truong-Le, M., Knoll, A.C.: Deep neural networks for Markovian interactive scene prediction in highway scenarios. In: 2017 IEEE Intelligent Vehicles Symposium IV, Los Angeles, CA, USA, 11–14 June 2017, pp. 685–692. IEEE (2017). https://doi.org/10.1109/IVS.2017.7995797
14. Liu, Yu., Hua, W., Xin, K., Zhou, X.: Context-aware temporal knowledge graph embedding. In: Cheng, R., Mamoulis, N., Sun, Y., Huang, X. (eds.) WISE 2020. LNCS, vol. 11881, pp. 583–598. Springer, Cham (2019). https://doi.org/10.1007/978-3-030-34223-4_37
15. Nickel, M., Rosasco, L., Poggio, T.: Holographic embeddings of knowledge graphs. In: Proceedings of the 13th AAAI Conference on Artificial Intelligence, AAAI 2016, pp. 1955–1961. AAAI Press (2016)
16. Rettinger, A., Wermser, H., Huang, Y., Tresp, V.: Context-aware tensor decomposition for relation prediction in social networks. Soc. Netw. Anal. Min. **2**(4), 373–385 (2012)
17. Trivedi, R., Dai, H., Wang, Y., Song, L.: Know-evolve: deep temporal reasoning for dynamic knowledge graphs. In: Proceedings of the 34th International Conference on Machine Learning, vol. 70, pp. 3462–3471. JMLR.org (2017)
18. Trouillon, T., Welbl, J., Riedel, S., Gaussier, É., Bouchard, G.: Complex embeddings for simple link prediction. In: International Conference on Machine Learning (ICML) (2016)
19. Tulving, E., et al.: Episodic and semantic memory. Organ. Mem. **1**, 381–403 (1972)
20. Vaswani, A., et al.: Attention is all you need. In: Advances in Neural Information Processing Systems, pp. 5998–6008 (2017)
21. Wang, H., Kulkarni, V., Wang, W.Y.: Dolores: deep contextualized knowledge graph embeddings. arXiv preprint arXiv:1811.00147 (2018)
22. Wang, Q., et al.: CoKE: contextualized knowledge graph embedding. arXiv preprint arXiv:1911.02168 (2019)
23. Yang, D., Qu, B., Yang, J., Cudre-Mauroux, P.: Revisiting user mobility and social relationships in LBSNs: a hypergraph embedding approach, pp. 2147–2157 (May 2019)
24. Yao, L., Mao, C., Luo, Y.: KG-BERT: Bert for knowledge graph completion. arXiv preprint arXiv:1909.03193 (2019)
25. Zhang, S., Tay, Y., Yao, L., Liu, Q.: Quaternion knowledge graph embeddings. In: Advances in Neural Information Processing Systems, pp. 2731–2741 (2019)

Injecting Background Knowledge into Embedding Models for Predictive Tasks on Knowledge Graphs

Claudia d'Amato[1,2(✉)], Nicola Flavio Quatraro[1], and Nicola Fanizzi[1,2]

[1] Dipartimento di Informatica, Università degli Studi di Bari Aldo Moro, Bari, Italy
{claudia.damato,nicola.fanizzi}@uniba.it, n.quatraro@studenti.uniba.it
[2] CILA, Università degli Studi di Bari Aldo Moro, Bari, Italy

Abstract. Embedding models have been successfully exploited for Knowledge Graph refinement. In these models, the data graph is projected into a low-dimensional space, in which *graph structural information* are preserved as much as possible, enabling an efficient computation of solutions. We propose a solution for injecting available background knowledge (schema axioms) to further improve the quality of the embeddings. The method has been applied to enhance existing models to produce embeddings that can encode knowledge that is not merely observed but rather derived by reasoning on the available axioms. An experimental evaluation on link prediction and triple classification tasks proves the improvement yielded implementing the proposed method over the original ones.

Keywords: Knowledge graphs · Embeddings · Link prediction · Triple classification · Representation learning

1 Introduction

Knowledge Graphs (KGs) are becoming important for several research fields. Although a standard shared definition for KGs is still not available, there is a general consensus on assuming them as organizations of data and information by means of graph structures [12]. KGs are often the result of a complex (integration) process involving multiple sources, human expert intervention and crowdsourcing. Several examples of large KGs exist, spanning from enterprise products, such as those built by Google and Amazon, to mention a few of them, to other open KGs such as the well known DBpedia, Freebase, Wikidata and YAGO [12]. Despite significant efforts for making KGs as comprehensive and reliable as possible, due to the complex building process they tend to suffer of two major problems: incompleteness and noise [12,20]. As an example, it was found that about 70% of the persons described in DBpedia lack of information regarding their nationality and birth place [8]. Thus, a significant research effort have been devoted to *knowledge graph refinement*, aiming at correcting these issues with KGs [22]. Among the others, two tasks have gained a major attention: *Link Prediction*, aiming at predicting missing links between entities, and *Triple Classification*, that consists in assessing

© Springer Nature Switzerland AG 2021
R. Verborgh et al. (Eds.): ESWC 2021, LNCS 12731, pp. 441–457, 2021.
https://doi.org/10.1007/978-3-030-77385-4_26

the correctness of a statement with respect to a KG. In recent years, numeric approaches to these tasks have gained considerable popularity on account of their effectiveness and scalability when applied to large KGs. Such models typically map entities and relations forming complex graph structures to simpler representations (feature-vectors) and aim at learning prediction functions to be exploited for the mentioned tasks. Particularly, the scalability purpose motivated the interest delved towards *embedding models* [4] which have been shown to ensure good performances on very large KGs. Knowledge graph embedding methods aim at converting the data graph into an optimal low-dimensional space in which *graph structural information* and *graph properties* are preserved as much as possible [4, 15]. The low-dimensional spaces enable computationally efficient solutions that scale better with the KG dimensions. Graph embedding methods differ in their main building blocks: the *representation space* (e.g. point-wise, complex, discrete, Gaussian, manifold), the *encoding model* (e.g. linear, factorization, neural models) and the *scoring function* (that can be based on distance, energy, semantic matching or other criteria) [15]. In general, the objective consists in learning embeddings such that the score of a valid (positive) triple is lower than the score of an invalid triple standing for a sort of negative examples. A major problem with these models is that KGs are mostly encoded exploiting available positive assertions (examples) whilst negative constraints are more rarely found, making negative examples more hardly derivable [2]. As positive-only learning settings may be tricky and prone to over-generalization, negative examples (invalid triples) have to be sought for either by randomly *corrupting* true/observed triples or deriving them having made the *local-closed world assumption* on the data collection. In both cases, wrong negative information may be generated and thus used when training and learning the embedding models; hence alternative solutions are currently investigated [2]. Even more so, existing embedding models do not make use of the additional semantic information encoded within KGs, when more expressive representations are adopted, indeed the need for *semantic embedding methods* has been argued [5, 13, 23].

In this paper we present an approach to graph embeddings that, beyond the graph structural information and properties, is also able to exploit the available knowledge expressed in rich representations like RDFS and OWL. Recent works [19] have proven the effectiveness of combinations of embedding methods and strategies relying on reasoning services for the injection of *Background Knowledge* (BK) to enhance the performance of a specific predictive model. Following this line, we propose TRANSOWL, aiming at injecting BK particularly during the learning process, and its upgraded version TRANSROWL, where a newly defined and more suitable loss function and scoring function are also exploited. Particularly, we focus on the application of this idea to enhance well-known basic scalable models, namely TRANSE [3] and TRANSR [16], the latter tackling some weak points in TRANSE, such as the difficulty of modeling specific types of relationships [2]. We built upon such models to better cope with additional various types of relationships, intervening also on the training process. Indeed, the proposed solutions can take advantage of an informed corruption process that leverages on reasoning capabilities, while limiting the amount of false negatives that a less informed random corruption process may cause.

It is important to note that, in principle, the proposed approach could be applied to more complex (and recent) KG embedding methods. In this work we intended to show the feasibility of the approach, starting with well established models before moving on towards more sophisticated ones, which would need an additional formalization.

The proposed solutions are actually able to improve their effectiveness compared to the original models that focus on structural graph properties with a random corruption process. This is proven through an experimentation focusing on link prediction and triple classification tasks on standard datasets.

The rest of the paper is organized as follows. Basics on KG embedding models that are functional to our method definition are presented in Sect. 2. The formalization of our proposed solutions is illustrated in Sect. 3 while in Sect. 4 the experimental evaluation is provided. Related work is discussed in Sect. 5. Conclusions are delineated in Sect. 6.

2 Basics on Embedding Methods

In the following we assume the reader has familiarity with the standard representation and reasoning frameworks such as RDF, RDFS and OWL, hence we will consider RDF graphs made up of triples $\langle s, p, o \rangle$ of *RDF terms*, respectively the *subject*, the *predicate*, and the *object*, such that $s \in U \cup B$ where U stands for a set of URIs and B as for a set of blank nodes, $p \in U$ and $o \in U \cup B \cup L$ where L stands for a set of *literals*. In the following, given an RDF graph G, we denote as $\mathcal{E}_G$ the set of all entities occurring as subjects or objects in G, and as $\mathcal{R}_G$ the set of all predicates occurring in G.

In this section, basics on *knowledge graph embeddings* methods [4] are recalled, with a special focus on TRANSE [3] and TRANSR [16]. Several models have been actually proposed for embedding KGs in low-dimensional vector spaces, by learning a unique *distributed representation* (or *embedding*) for each entity and predicate in the KG [4] and different representation spaces have been considered (e.g. point-wise, complex, discrete, Gaussian, manifold). Here we focus on vector embedding in the set of real numbers. Regardless of the learning procedure, these models share a fundamental characteristic: given a KG G, they represent each entity $x \in \mathcal{E}_G$ by means of a continuous *embedding vector* $\mathbf{e}_x \in \mathbb{R}^k$, where $k \in \mathbb{N}$ is a user-defined hyperparameter. Similarly, each predicate $p \in \mathcal{R}_G$ is associated to a *scoring function* $f_p : \mathbb{R}^k \times \mathbb{R}^k \to \mathbb{R}$, also referred to as *energy function* [20]. For each pair of entities $s, o \in \mathcal{E}_G$, the score $f_p(\mathbf{e}_s, \mathbf{e}_o)$ measures the *confidence* that the statement encoded by $\langle s, p, o \rangle$ holds true.

TRANSE introduces a very simple but effective and efficient model: each entity $x \in \mathcal{E}_G$ is represented by an embedding vector $\mathbf{e}_x \in \mathbb{R}^k$, and each predicate $p \in \mathcal{R}_G$ is represented by a (vector) *translation operation* $\mathbf{e}_p \in \mathbb{R}^k$. The score of a triple $\langle s, p, o \rangle$ is given by the similarity (negative L_1 or L_2 distance) of the translated subject embedding $(\mathbf{e}_s + \mathbf{e}_p)$ to the object embedding $\mathbf{e}_o$:

$$f_p(\mathbf{e}_s, \mathbf{e}_o) = -\|(\mathbf{e}_s + \mathbf{e}_p) - \mathbf{e}_o\|_{\{1,2\}}. \tag{1}$$

In the case of TRANSR, a different score function f'_p is considered, that preliminarily projects $\mathbf{e}_s$ and $\mathbf{e}_o$ to the different d-dimensional space of the relational embeddings $\mathbf{e}_p$ through a suitable matrix $\mathbf{M} \in \mathbb{R}^{k \times d}$:

$$f'_p(\mathbf{e}_s, \mathbf{e}_o) = -\|(\mathbf{M}\mathbf{e}_s + \mathbf{e}_p) - \mathbf{M}\mathbf{e}_o\|_{\{1,2\}}. \tag{2}$$

The optimal embedding and translation vectors for predicates are learned jointly. The method relies on a *stochastic optimization process*, that iteratively updates the distributed representations by increasing the score of the triples in G, i.e. the observed triples Δ, while lowering the score of unobserved triples standing as negative examples contained in Δ'. Unobserved triples are randomly generated by means of a *corruption process*, which replaces either the subject or the object of each observed triple with another entity in G. Formally, given an observed triple $t \in G$, let $\mathcal{C}_G(t)$ denote the set of all triples derived by corrupting t. Then:

$$\Delta' = \bigcup_{\langle s,p,o \rangle \in \Delta} \mathcal{C}_G(\langle s,p,o \rangle) = \bigcup_{\langle s,p,o \rangle \in \Delta} \{\langle \tilde{s},p,o \rangle \mid \tilde{s} \in \mathcal{E}_G\} \cup \{\langle s,p,\tilde{o} \rangle \mid \tilde{o} \in \mathcal{E}_G\}. \quad (3)$$

The embedding of all entities and predicates in the G is learned by minimizing a *margin-based ranking loss*. Formally, let $\theta \in \Theta$ denote a configuration for all entity and predicate embeddings (i.e. the *model parameters*), where Θ denotes the parameters space. The optimal model parameters $\hat{\theta} \in \Theta$ is learned by solving a constrained optimization problem that amounts to minimizing the following loss functional:

$$\underset{\theta \in \Theta}{\text{minimize}} \sum_{\substack{\langle s,p,o \rangle \in \Delta \\ \langle \tilde{s},p,\tilde{o} \rangle \in \Delta'}} [\gamma + f_p(\mathbf{e}_s, \mathbf{e}_o) - f_p(\mathbf{e}_{\tilde{s}}, \mathbf{e}_{\tilde{o}})]_+ \quad (4)$$

$$\text{subject to } \forall x \in \mathcal{E}_G: \|\mathbf{e}_x\| = 1,$$

where $[x]_+ = \max\{0, x\}$, and $\gamma \geq 0$ is a hyperparameter referred to as *margin*.

The loss functional in the problem enforces the score of observed triples to be higher than the score of unobserved triples. The constraints prevent the training process to trivially solve the problem by increasing the entity embedding norms.

3 Evolving Models Through Background Knowledge Injection

Our approach aims at improving proposed embedding models for KGs, verifying the intuition that the exploitation of expressive schema-level axioms may help increase the model effectiveness. We first present TRANSOWL, injecting BK during the learning process when applied to entity-based models like TRANSE. Then we move on towards a new formalization that is TRANSROWL, which exploits TRANSR, to better handle the various types of relations, besides of adopting a newly defined and more suitable loss function and scoring function.

3.1 TRANSOWL

TRANSOWL aims at enhancing simple but effective and efficient entity-based embedding models like TRANSE with a better use of the available BK. The final goal is showing the feasibility of our approach, that in principle can be applied to more complex models with additional formalization. In TRANSOWL the original TRANSE setting is maintained while resorting to reasoning with schema axioms to derive further triples to be considered for training and that are generated consistently with the semantics of the properties. Specifically, TRANSOWL defines specific constraints on the energy functions for each considered axiom, that guide the way embedding vectors are learned. It extends the approach in [19], generating a model characterized by two main components devoted to inject BK in the embedding-based model during the training phase:

Reasoning: It is used for generating corrupted triples that can certainly represent negative instances, thus avoiding false negatives, for a more effective model training. Specifically, using a reasoner[1] it is possible to generate corrupted triples exploiting the available axioms, specified in RDFS and OWL, namely domain, range, disjointWith, functionalProperty; moreover, false positives can be detected and avoided.

BK Injection: A set of different axioms w.r.t. those mentioned above are employed for the definition of constraints on the energy function considered in the training phase so that the resulting vectors related to such axioms reflect specific properties: equivalentClass, equivalentProperty, inverseOf and subClassOf.

In TRANSOWL the basic loss function minimized in TRANSE (see Eq. 4) is more complex adding a number of terms consistently with the constraints on the energy function based on the underlying axioms. The most interesting one amounts to generating, new triples to be added to the training set on the grounds of the specified axioms. The definition of the loss function along this setting is given as follows:

$$
L = \sum_{\substack{\langle h,r,t \rangle \in \Delta \\ \langle h',r,t' \rangle \in \Delta'}} [\gamma + f_r(h,t) - f_r(h',t')]_+ + \sum_{\substack{\langle t,q,h \rangle \in \Delta_{\mathsf{inverseOf}} \\ \langle t',q,h' \rangle \in \Delta'_{\mathsf{inverseOf}}}} [\gamma + f_q(t,h) - f_q(t',h')]_+
$$

$$
+ \sum_{\substack{\langle h,s,t \rangle \in \Delta_{\mathsf{equivProperty}} \\ \langle h',s,t' \rangle \in \Delta'_{\mathsf{equivProperty}}}} [\gamma + f_s(h,t) - f_s(h',t')]_+ + \sum_{\substack{\langle h,\mathsf{typeOf},l \rangle \in \Delta \cup \Delta_{\mathsf{equivClass}} \\ \langle h',\mathsf{typeOf},l' \rangle \in \Delta' \cup \Delta'_{\mathsf{equivClass}}}} [\gamma + f_{\mathsf{typeOf}}(h,l) - f_{\mathsf{typeOf}}(h',l')]_+
$$

$$
+ \sum_{\substack{\langle h,\mathsf{subClassOf},p \rangle \in \Delta_{\mathsf{subClass}} \\ \langle h',\mathsf{subClassOf},p' \rangle \in \Delta'_{\mathsf{subClass}}}} [(\gamma - \beta) + f(h,p) - f(h',p')]_+ \tag{5}
$$

where $q \equiv r^-$, $s \equiv r$ (properties), $l \equiv t$ and $t \sqsubseteq p$, the sets of triples denoted by Δ_π, where $\pi \in \{\mathsf{inverseOf}, \mathsf{equivProperty}, \mathsf{equivClass}, \mathsf{subClass}\}$, represent the additional triples generated by a reasoner exploiting such properties and $f(h,p) = \|\mathbf{e}_h - \mathbf{e}_p\|$. The different formulation for the case of subClassOf is motivated by the fact that it encodes the additional constraint (expressing major specificity) $f_{\mathsf{typeOf}}(e,p) > f_{\mathsf{typeOf}}(e,h)$ where e is an instance, h subClassOf p and $f_{\mathsf{typeOf}}(e,p) = \|\mathbf{e}_e + \mathbf{e}_{\mathsf{typeOf}} - \mathbf{e}_p\|$ as for the original formulation. This also motivates the adoption of the β factor, that is required to determine the direction of the inequality to be obtained for the energy values associated to subclass entities (one w.r.t. the other). As for the equivalentClass formulation, the rationale is to exploit as much as possible the information that can be made explicit during the training phase. Particularly, we ground on the fact that the typeOf relation is one of the most common predicates in KGs, and as such it is used as a primary target of the training phase. In order to clarify this aspect, let us consider a class A equivalent to a class B. Given the triple $\langle h, \mathsf{typeOf}, A \rangle$ it is possible to derive also $\langle h, \mathsf{typeOf}, B \rangle$. Training the model on those derived triples brings a considerable number of new triples.

---

[1] Facilities available in the Apache Jena framework were used: https://jena.apache.org.

3.2 TRANSROWL

The main motivation for TRANSOWL was to set up a framework that was able to take into account the BK while using a simple model. However, some of the limits of the models grounded on TRANSE originate from an inability to suitably represent the specificity of the various types of properties. Specifically, the main limitations of TRANSE are related to the poor modeling of reflexive and non 1-to-1 relations as well as to their interplay. Such limitations can cause generating spurious embedding vectors with null values or analogous vectors among different entities, thus compromising the ability of making correct predictions. A noteworthy case regards the typeOf property, a common N-to-N relationship. Modeling such property with TRANSE amounts to a simple vector translation; the considered individuals and classes may be quite different in terms of properties and attributes they are involved in, thus determining strong semantic differences (according to [27]) taking place at large reciprocal distances in the underlying vector space, hence revealing the weakness of employing the mere translation.

TRANSR is more suitable to handle such specificity. Thus, further evolving the approach used to derive TRANSOWL from TRANSE, a similar setting is applied to TRANSR, resulting in another model dubbed TRANSROWL, with the variant TRAN-SROWL^R. Particularly, to be more effective on cases involving complex types of relations, a more elaborate vectorial representation is adopted, usually resulting from hyperplane projection [25, 26] or different vector spaces [14, 16]. The underlying model influences the computation of the loss function gradient, that is required to train the model. Hence the main variation introduced by the new model regards the way the entities, within the energy function, are projected in the vector space of the relations, which increases the complexity without compromising the overall scalability. The limitations of TRANSE w.r.t. typeOf can be nearly overcome once the new setting based on TRANSR is adopted. The latter, indeed, associates to typeOf, and to all other properties, a specific vector space where entity vectors are projected to. This leads to training specific projection matrices for typeOf so that the projected entities can be located more suitably to be linked by the vector translation associated to typeOf. Furthermore, methods based on the regularization of the embeddings by exploiting the available axioms [19] prove that resorting to available BK may enhance their effectiveness on account of the addition of more specific constraints to the loss function. As such, the resulting TRANSROWL model maintains the same setting for reasoning adopted by TRANSOWL, but adopt a different utilization of the available axioms in two variants, one analogous to TRANSOWL and the other, dubbed TRANSROWL^R, following the method based on the regularization of the embeddings via equivalence and inverse property axioms [19].

TRANSROWL adapts to the TRANSR by introducing in the loss function (Eq. 5) the TRANSR score function $f'(\cdot)$ (Eq. 2) and additional weighting parameters:

$$L = \sum_{\substack{\langle h,r,t \rangle \in \Delta \\ \langle h',r,t' \rangle \in \Delta'}} [\gamma + f'_r(h,t) - f'_r(h',t')]_+ + \lambda_1 \sum_{\substack{\langle t,q,h \rangle \in \Delta_{\mathrm{inverseOf}} \\ \langle t',q,h' \rangle \in \Delta'_{\mathrm{inverseOf}}}} [\gamma + f'_q(t,h) - f'_q(t',h')]_+$$

$$+\lambda_2 \sum_{\substack{\langle h,s,t \rangle \in \Delta_{\mathrm{equivProperty}} \\ \langle h',s,t' \rangle \in \Delta'_{\mathrm{equivProperty}}}} [\gamma + f'_s(h,t) - f'_s(h',t')]_+ + \lambda_3 \sum_{\substack{\langle h,\mathrm{typeOf},l \rangle \in \Delta \cup \Delta_{\mathrm{equivClass}} \\ \langle h',\mathrm{typeOf},l' \rangle \in \Delta' \cup \Delta'_{\mathrm{equivClass}}}} [\gamma + f'_{\mathrm{typeOf}}(h,l) - f'_{\mathrm{typeOf}}(h',l')]_+$$

$$+\lambda_4 \sum_{\substack{\langle t,\mathrm{subClassOf},p \rangle \in \Delta_{\mathrm{subClass}} \\ \langle t',\mathrm{subClassOf},p' \rangle \in \Delta'_{\mathrm{subClass}}}} [(\gamma - \beta) + f'(t,p) - f'(t',p')]_+ \tag{6}$$

where $q \equiv r^-$, $s \equiv r$ (properties), $l \equiv t$ and $t \sqsubseteq p$ (classes), the different triple sets, denoted by Δ_π with $\pi \in \{\mathrm{inverseOf}, \mathrm{equivProperty}, \mathrm{equivClass}, \mathrm{subClass}\}$, contain additional triples generated by a reasoner exploiting these properties and f' (case of subClass) is defined as for TRANSOWL, considering the embedding vectors coming from TRANSR. The parameters λ_i, $i \in \{1, \ldots, 4\}$, weigh the influence that each function term in Eq. 6 has during the learning phase, analogously to the approach in [19].

In the embedding methods exploiting *axiom-based regularization* [19], the constraints on vectors to be satisfied, representing the related properties of the entities and relations, are explicitly expressed within the loss function. Considering the model TRANSE^R [19], the regularization term based on the equivalence and inverse property axioms is defined as follows:

$$L = \sum_{\substack{\langle h,r,t \rangle \in \Delta \\ \langle h',r',t' \rangle \in \Delta'}} [\gamma + f_r(h,t) - f_r(h',t')]_+ + \lambda \sum_{r \equiv q^- \in \mathcal{T}_{\mathrm{inverseOf}}} \|r + q\| + \lambda \sum_{r \equiv p \in \mathcal{T}_{\mathrm{equivProp}}} \|r - p\| \tag{7}$$

with the hyperparameter λ and where $\mathcal{T}_{\mathrm{inverseOf}} = \{r_1 \equiv q_1^-, r_2 \equiv q_2^-, \ldots, r_n \equiv q_n^-\}$ and $\mathcal{T}_{\mathrm{equivProp}} = \{r_1 \equiv p_1, r_2 \equiv p_2, \ldots, r_n \equiv p_n\}$ stand for the set of inverse properties and equivalent properties following from the axioms in the BK.

To adapt this approach to TRANSROWL, it is required to include constraints on the considered additional properties, such as equivalentClass and subClassOf, and further constraints on the projection matrices associated to each relation. This variant of TRANSROWL, that is dubbed TRANSROWL^R, is formalized as follows:

$$L = \sum_{\substack{\langle h,r,t \rangle \in \Delta \\ \langle h',r',t' \rangle \in \Delta'}} [\gamma + f'_r(h,t) - f'_r(h',t')]_+$$

$$+\lambda_1 \sum_{r \equiv q^- \in \mathcal{T}_{\mathrm{inverseOf}}} \|r + q\| + \lambda_2 \sum_{r \equiv q^- \in \mathcal{T}_{\mathrm{inverseOf}}} \|M_r - M_q\|$$

$$+\lambda_3 \sum_{r \equiv p \in \mathcal{T}_{\mathrm{equivProp}}} \|r - p\| + \lambda_4 \sum_{r \equiv p \in \mathcal{T}_{\mathrm{equivProp}}} \|M_r - M_p\|$$

$$+\lambda_5 \sum_{e' \equiv e'' \in \mathcal{T}_{\mathrm{equivClass}}} \|e' - e''\| + \lambda_6 \sum_{s' \sqsubseteq s'' \in \mathcal{T}_{\mathrm{subClass}}} \|1 - \beta - (s' - s'')\| \tag{8}$$

where $\mathcal{T}_{\mathrm{inverseOf}} = \{r_1 \equiv q_1^-, r_2 \equiv q_2^-, \ldots, r_n \equiv q_n^-\}$, and $\mathcal{T}_{\mathrm{equivProp}} = \{r_1 \equiv p_1, r_2 \equiv p_2, \ldots, r_n \equiv p_n\}$, resp. the sets of inverse and of equivalent properties, $\mathcal{T}_{\mathrm{equivClass}} = \{e'_1 \equiv e''_1, e'_2 \equiv e''_2, \ldots, e'_n \equiv e''_n\}$ and $\mathcal{T}_{\mathrm{subClass}} = \{s'_1 \sqsubseteq s''_1, s'_2 \sqsubseteq s''_2, \ldots, s'_n \sqsubseteq s''_n\}$ resp.

the sets of equivalent classes and subclasses. Parameters λ_i, $i \in \{1, \ldots, 6\}$, determine the weights to be assigned to each constraint and β has the same role mentioned above. The additional term for projection matrices is required for inverseOf and equivProp triples to favor the equality of their projection matrices. This is for having the same energy associated, via score function, to the triples in their respective sets. Considering for instance $\langle h, r, t \rangle$ and $\langle h, p, t \rangle$, if r equivProp p, their energy should be equal.

The idea of taking into account the regularization of the embeddings by means of the axioms, has been experimentally tested (see Sect. 4) in order to assess whether directly imposing such constraints is more advantageous than generating further triples, based on the same constraints, as in the original definition of the TRANSROWL model.

4   Experimental Evaluation

In this evaluation we focused on TRANSOWL, TRANSROWL, TRANSROWL^R compared to the original models TRANSE and TRANSR as a baseline. The evaluation aims at assessing the improvement brought by the choices made for defining new models, grounded on the exploitation of BK injection.

Specifically, we tested the performance of the mentioned models and related systems on the task of *Link Prediction*, together with *Type Prediction* (that, given typeOf-triple for a subject, verifies if the model is able to correctly predict a class the individual belongs to). Then we also tested the models on *Triple Classification* problems, i.e. the ability to classify new triples as true or false. Preliminarily, in the following section, the settings of the experiments are described jointly with the references to the adopted datasets and source code.

4.1   Experiment Setup

Datasets. The models were tested on four datasets drawn from the following KGs, that have been considered in the experimental evaluations of related works [6, 17].

DBpedia. It is a well-known KG with data extracted from Wikipedia. Its vocabulary has 320 classes and 1650 properties. The English version[2] describes 4,58M resources, 4,22M of them classified in an ontology. Its dimensions and the presence of 27M RDF links towards 30+ external sources make it one of the principal reference of the Linked Data cloud. We considered two datasets that were extracted to ensure suitable axioms to test the models under evaluation, namely axioms on domain, range, disjointWith, functionalProperty, equivalentClass, equivalentProperty, inverseOf and subClassOf, in the two variants dubbed[3] *DBpedia100K* [6], containing about 100K entities and 321 relations in 600K triples, and *DBpedia15K*[4] [17], containing about 12.8K entities and 278 relations in 180K triples.

---

[2] https://wiki.dbpedia.org/about.

[3] https://github.com/iieir-km/ComplEx-NNE_AER/tree/master/datasets/DB100K.

[4] https://github.com/nle-ml/mmkb/tree/master/DB15K.

DBPediaYAGO. YAGO [5] is a KG organizing knowledge coming from different sources such as *WordNet, GeoNames* and *Wikipedia*, including 350K+ classes, 10M entities and 120M assertions [22]. It has been exploited to extend and complete *DBpedia15K*, resulting in *DBPediaYAGO* exploiting the many links connecting to DBpedia. *DBPediaYAGO* is characterized by about 290K triples, with 88K entities and 316 relations.

NELL. The dataset[6] comes from a knowledge extraction system for eliciting facts from corpora of Web pages. The resulting KG amounts to 2.810K+ assertions regarding 1.186 different relations and categories. We considered a fragment of NELL2RDF-vanilla[7], that does not contain all of the properties that can be exploited by the proposed model variants. The considered dataset is made up of about 150K triples, with 272 properties and 68K entities. The aim was to test the models on a dataset with a limited set of exploitable properties, namely subClassOf, inverseOf, functionalProperty, disjointWith, range and domain. The abundance of subClassOf-triples, together with a limited number of typeOf-triples for each entity, is meant to test if the models are able to compensate this partial incompleteness and improve the performance of the base models. Considering the inverseOf-axioms allows to compare directly the performance of TRANSROWL and TRANSROWL^R, when generating new triples for training or regularizing the embeddings.

Parameter Settings. All models were set up along the same procedure and parameter values, consistently with the experiments illustrated in [3, 16]: learning rate: 0.001; minibatch dimension: 50; entity/relation vector dimension = 100; epochs: $\{250, 500, 1000\}$. This choice is motivated by the fact that our first aim is to verify the possible improvements of the proposed solutions over the basic models when exactly the same conditions, including the parameter values, apply.

Due to a tendency to *overfitting* that is known to affect TRANSR, it requires an initialization of the embeddings performed via TRANSE (see [16]). Similarly, also TRANSROWL and its variant were initialized with these embeddings. Overfitting has been checked on the models derived from TRANSR along the different numbers of epochs. Moreover, the bern strategy for triple corruption phase was adopted, as this choice led to a better performance compared to the unif strategy in previous experimental evaluations of this class of models [14, 16, 25, 26]. The unif strategy generates negative triples by sampling a pair of entities for subject and object from $\mathcal{E}_G$, assigning uniform probabilities to the possible replacements; bern assigns different chances (along with a Bernoulli distribution) based on the nature (1-to-1,1-to-N, N-to-N) of the relation.

As for the TRANSROWL loss function regularization hyperparameters λ_i, the following values have been found: inverseOf $\lambda_1 = 1$; equivalentProperty $\lambda_2 = 1$; equivalentClass $\lambda_3 = 0.1$; subClassOf $\lambda_4 = 0.01$; whilst as for TRANSROWL^R: $\lambda_1 = \lambda_2 = \lambda_3 = \lambda_4 = \lambda_5 = \lambda_6 = 0.1$;

---

[5] https://yago-knowledge.org/.

[6] http://rtw.ml.cmu.edu/rtw/.

[7] http://nell-ld.telecom-st-etienne.fr/.

Each dataset was partitioned into *training, validation* and *test* sets by randomly selecting 70%, 10%, 20% of the triples per run. Datasets and their partitions, resulting embedding models, together with the source code are available in a public repository[8].

4.2   Link Prediction

Following the standard methodologies for evaluating *Translational Distance Models*, we focus on predicting the missing individuals in given incomplete triples. Specifically the models are used to predict triples $\langle h, r, t \rangle$, with $h, t \in \mathcal{E}_G$ and $r \in \mathcal{R}_G$, corresponding to the patterns $\langle ?, r, t \rangle, \langle h, r, ? \rangle$.

The typical metrics considered for this task are *Mean Rank* and *H@10* (the lower the better, and vice-versa, resp.), that are based on predictions rankings. Two variants are generally taken into account, *Raw* and *Filtered*, where the latter filters off triples that amount to corrupted ones, i.e. negative cases generated for training the model. For a deeper insight, we measured separately the performance considering all properties but typeOf, and then on typeOf only. This allows to verify the improvement brought by the new models considering *Type Prediction* (i.e. classification) problems on the classes of each KG.

As mentioned above, the embeddings were initialized by a first run of TRANSE (1000 epochs), and the training was run for up to further 1000 epochs. To appreciate the performance trends, for TRANSR and its extensions, we also report the test results for models trained in intermediate numbers of epochs, namely 250 and 500. This is in order to check the occurrence of overfitting cases as discussed above.

The complete outcomes of the link prediction experiments are illustrated in Table 1 (best results are bolded, with ties decided by the precise figures).

Preliminarily, comparing the overall performance of TRANSE and TRANSOWL, the latter seems to be able to improve only on classification tasks (those targeting typeOf) and in the experiments on *DBpediaYAGO* and *NELL*, it proves even better, in terms of MR, than TRANSR and derived models. This suggests that TRANSOWL is particularly suitable for classification. However, in most of the cases the best performance on this task was achieved by TRANSROWL especially in terms of *H@10*. Compared to the results achieved by TRANSR, one cannot conclude that the subClassOf axioms have determined the same improvements of TRANSOWL compared to TRANSE, suggesting that more complex models may require more advanced strategies.

Conversely, the results regarding the other properties (no typeOf columns) confirmed that TRANSR and derived models are more suitable for general link prediction problems: TRANSROWL and TRANSROWL^R in most of the cases performed much better than TRANSE and TRANSOWL. Compared to TRANSR, TRANSROWL and TRANSROWL^R showed a better performance, except few cases in which TRANSR resulted slightly better especially in terms of MR, but they were close runner-ups. The improvement w.r.t. TRANSE and TRANSOWL is due to the more suitable representation for the relations. This is more evident from the outcomes on *DBpedia100K* and *DBpediaYAGO*, the latter having been specifically extended to improve the completeness. As argued in [11], a more complete dataset yields a larger number of triples

---

[8] https://github.com/Keehl-Mihael/TransROWL-HRS.

Table 1. Link prediction outcomes (MR = Mean Rank and H@10 = Hits@10)

DBpedia15K

Model	Epochs	no typeOf				typeOf			
		MR (raw)	H@10 (raw)	MR (flt.)	H@10 (flt.)	MR (raw)	H@10 (raw)	MR (flt.)	H@10 (flt.)
TRANSE	1000	587.07	32.46	573.94	35.01	692.29	9.75	67.05	15.68
TRANSOWL	1000	621.06	32.24	607.91	34.85	493.46	13.20	29.14	20.85
TRANSR	250	**583.72**	60.57	**570.54**	63.37	498.58	84.86	26.42	93.09
TRANSR	500	587.37	60.66	574.12	63.42	499.39	85.01	20.15	94.51
TRANSR	1000	600.12	60.67	586.83	63.57	504.13	85.01	13.96	95.50
TRANSROWL	250	584.94	**60.88**	571.74	63.48	493.24	84.91	25.10	93.72
TRANSROWL	500	598.03	60.77	584.79	63.58	487.44	84.97	17.50	95.38
TRANSROWL	1000	606.73	60.59	593.45	63.48	**484.04**	**85.18**	**13.53**	**96.54**
TRANSROWL^R	250	585.84	60.68	572.62	63.40	498.50	84.85	26.60	93.10
TRANSROWL^R	500	592.78	60.66	579.55	63.42	491.98	84.97	19.73	95.52
TRANSROWL^R	1000	607.43	60.71	594.13	**63.65**	497.40	85.12	16.50	96.24

DBpedia100K

Model	Epochs	no typeOf				typeOf			
		MR (raw)	H@10 (raw)	MR (flt.)	H@10 (flt.)	MR (raw)	H@10 (raw)	MR (flt.)	H@10 (flt.)
TRANSE	1000	2233.40	38.56	2204.39	41.11	2224.26	3.62	1615.68	3.86
TRANSOWL	1000	2430.51	38.12	2401.67	40.69	2152.89	5.64	1728.52	6.02
TRANSR	250	2160.79	52.83	2131.51	55.45	1911.06	92.21	1480.79	92.23
TRANSR	500	2152.40	53.02	2122.94	55.67	1927.16	92.17	**1479.44**	92.35
TRANSR	1000	2142.10	53.17	2112.42	55.96	1957.42	92.04	1480.26	92.25
TRANSROWL	250	2165.42	52.67	2136.25	55.26	**1904.80**	92.22	1483.62	92.23
TRANSROWL	500	2147.47	52.92	2118.12	55.59	1933.79	92.22	1498.14	92.37
TRANSROWL	1000	2147.56	**53.24**	2117.87	**56.03**	1961.75	**92.29**	1503.87	**92.43**
TRANSROWL^R	250	2159.51	52.76	2130.29	55.35	1915.67	91.98	1485.03	92.18
TRANSROWL^R	500	2136.73	52.92	2107.29	55.64	1955.90	92.07	1515.07	92.27
TRANSROWL^R	1000	**2121.52**	53.08	**2091.81**	55.95	1971.98	92.24	1511.07	**92.43**

DBpediaYAGO

Model	Epochs	no typeOf				typeOf			
		MR (raw)	H@10 (raw)	MR (flt.)	H@10 (flt.)	MR (raw)	H@10 (raw)	MR (flt.)	H@10 (flt.)
TRANSE	1000	7417.08	19.24	7385.12	20.20	587.19	8.71	**157.14**	19.42
TRANSOWL	1000	7455.49	19.21	7423.56	20.18	**580.29**	8.68	162.03	19.43
TRANSR	250	7279.11	44.04	7247.16	45.13	656.10	83.66	187.91	93.47
TRANSR	500	7256.86	44.03	7224.74	45.18	738.33	81.33	249.10	88.68
TRANSR	1000	7271.50	44.64	7239.09	46.07	844.51	81.98	348.65	88.99
TRANSROWL	250	7279.37	43.76	7247.37	44.92	702.22	84.48	243.45	**94.54**
TRANSROWL	500	7274.77	43.94	7242.67	45.13	796.46	83.44	314.03	92.93
TRANSROWL	1000	7209.02	44.45	7176.64	45.84	868.27	82.81	373.90	91.17
TRANSROWL^R	250	7274.52	43.61	7242.52	44.78	667.70	83.21	208.90	93.22
TRANSROWL^R	500	**7196.12**	44.15	**7164.00**	45.34	752.57	82.08	271.03	90.52
TRANSROWL^R	1000	7226.55	44.13	7194.21	45.52	845.42	81.71	352.16	88.77

NELL

Model	Epochs	no typeOf				typeOf			
		MR (raw)	H@10 (raw)	MR (flt.)	H@10 (flt.)	MR (raw)	H@10 (raw)	MR (flt.)	H@10 (flt.)
TRANSE	1000	7162.08	19.01	6969.07	26.54	2872.45	6.55	2708.90	6.82
TRANSOWL	1000	9622.40	15.54	9423.73	21.72	**2263.09**	6.52	**2092.51**	6.92
TRANSR	250	7118.13	47.13	6921.77	55.10	2796.70	79.28	2628.58	79.70
TRANSR	500	6928.74	47.31	6728.67	55.62	2585.97	79.19	2415.26	79.66
TRANSR	1000	**6891.20**	**47.40**	**6681.76**	**55.93**	2315.08	79.94	2140.16	80.50
TRANSROWL	250	7263.08	46.76	7066.55	54.72	2775.22	79.05	2606.60	79.40
TRANSROWL	500	7005.75	46.86	6804.32	55.07	2545.47	79.44	2374.09	79.86
TRANSROWL	1000	7136.77	46.72	6929.10	55.40	2334.50	**80.00**	2161.67	**80.56**
TRANSROWL^R	250	7530.80	45.89	7334.86	53.51	2714.23	78.40	2547.79	78.75
TRANSROWL^R	500	7300.14	46.04	7098.93	53.89	2527.41	79.81	2357.55	80.20
TRANSROWL^R	1000	7339.53	46.09	7132.22	54.15	2310.11	79.52	2138.99	80.21

describing single entities/relations, as the resulting prediction model, with more parameters to be fitted, can be better trained.

The case of the *NELL* dataset is more peculiar, as it aimed at testing the models in a condition of larger incompleteness and with a smaller number of properties to be exploited for knowledge injection. Specifically, this dataset is characterized by a much lower number of typeOf-triples per entity, thus making classification a much harder task. This lack is (partly) compensated by a wealth of subClassOf axioms that can be exploited during the training of class vectors (an ability, introduced in TRANSOWL, that is shared also by TRANSROWL and TRANSROWL^R). Another type of axioms that abound in the *NELL* dataset is inverseOf. The link prediction results (no typeOf-triples) show a lower performance of both TRANSOWL and TRANSROWL, which suggests that the underlying approach has margins for improvements in its definition and/or calls for a better fitting of the regularization parameters.

Considering the outcomes on intermediate models (after 250 or 500 epochs elapsed) we observe that the methods were not able to improve the resulting models along with the iterations: in a few cases the overall best results were achieved by models trained after fewer epochs had elapsed. This suggests that a more refined regularization would be required.

Lastly, we noticed that TRANSROWL and TRANSROWL^R turned out substantially equivalent in terms of effectiveness, thus indicating efficiency as a criterion for the choice between the alternatives.

4.3 Triple Classification

Triple Classification is another *KG refinement* task that focuses on discerning correct from incorrect triples with respect to the KG. Also for this task, the way for evaluating predictive models has be consistent with the KG embedding methods.

The evaluation procedure introduced in [24] measures the ability to predict whether a triple is positive or negative, i.e. it represents a true or false fact w.r.t. the KG. To make this decision, a threshold s_r is to be determined for each $r \in \mathcal{R}_G$ so to maximize the *False Positive Rate* (FPR), then test triples will be deemed as positive when their energy-based score is greater than s_r, and negative otherwise [18,26]. The value for s_r was estimated considering a random sample of r-triples selected from the training set. They represent the triples that the model has learned to deem as true; for each sampled triple the energy value is computed, measuring the degree of likelihood associated to the triple, setting the threshold s_r to the minimum value. The ability of the model to correctly classify triples is evaluated considering the thresholds obtained for the single relations; this unavoidably increases the chance of predicting as true triples that are actually false, thus it allows to better evaluate the model robustness on the classification of typeOf-triples (especially with simple models such as TRANSE).

Analogously to the previous experiments the performance indices were determined separating the cases of typeOf-triples from those involving the other properties. This allows to better focus on the performance of the proposed models on this relation. The corrupted (negative) triples required for the tests, were generated by reasoning on range and domain axioms for the experiment excluding typeOf, while disjointWith axioms were exploited to get false typeOf-triples.

Table 2. Triple classification outcomes (Accuracy, Precision, Recall and FP Rate)

DBpedia15K

Model	Epochs	no typeOf				typeOf			
		Acc	P	R	FPR	Acc	P	R	FPR
TRANSE	1000	0.663	0.991	0.407	0.006	0.899	0.781	0.958	0.865
TRANSOWL	1000	**0.658**	0.967	**0.407**	0.023	0.975	0.990	0.933	0.127
TRANSR	250	0.655	0.998	0.390	0.002	0.961	0.928	0.954	0.616
TRANSR	500	0.650	0.996	0.380	0.002	0.978	0.979	0.953	0.303
TRANSR	1000	0.641	0.998	0.364	0.001	0.972	0.966	0.946	0.378
TRANSROWL	250	0.646	0.996	0.373	0.003	0.969	0.924	**0.987**	0.857
TRANSROWL	500	0.652	0.997	0.385	0.002	**0.985**	0.993	0.960	0.141
TRANSROWL	1000	0.631	0.997	0.347	0.002	0.962	**0.999**	0.882	**0.006**
TRANSROWL^R	250	0.648	0.997	0.377	0.002	0.937	0.989	0.816	0.049
TRANSROWL^R	500	0.647	0.997	0.376	0.002	0.938	0.994	0.815	0.027
TRANSROWL^R	1000	0.628	**0.998**	0.342	**0.001**	0.981	0.969	0.972	0.523

DBpedia100K

Model	Epochs	no typeOf				typeOf			
		Acc	P	R	FPR	Acc	P	R	FPR
TRANSE	1000	0.742	0.993	0.390	0.004	0.958	0.667	**0.943**	0.891
TRANSOWL	1000	0.714	0.901	0.359	0.058	0.980	0.908	0.835	0.337
TRANSR	250	0.730	0.997	0.359	0.001	0.983	0.890	0.900	0.526
TRANSR	500	0.721	0.998	0.337	0.001	0.980	0.853	0.910	0.635
TRANSR	1000	0.711	0.998	0.313	0.001	0.976	0.884	0.800	0.344
TRANSROWL	250	**0.744**	0.998	**0.392**	0.001	0.983	0.924	0.851	0.321
TRANSROWL	500	0.730	0.995	0.361	0.003	0.979	**0.965**	0.768	0.106
TRANSROWL	1000	0.705	**0.998**	0.300	**0.001**	**0.987**	0.940	0.895	0.353
TRANSROWL^R	250	0.732	0.997	0.364	0.002	0.952	0.635	0.936	0.893
TRANSROWL^R	500	0.717	0.997	0.328	0.002	0.971	0.951	0.668	**0.094**
TRANSROWL^R	1000	0.704	0.998	0.298	0.001	0.981	0.872	0.890	0.543

DBpediaYAGO

Model	Epochs	no typeOf				typeOf			
		Acc	P	R	FPR	Acc	P	R	FPR
TRANSE	1000	0.654	0.914	0.428	0.066	0.962	0.969	0.841	0.144
TRANSOWL	1000	**0.692**	0.887	**0.441**	0.091	0.931	0.961	0.688	0.081
TRANSR	250	0.658	0.953	0.331	0.024	0.885	0.965	0.449	0.029
TRANSR	500	0.656	0.964	0.325	0.017	0.861	0.955	0.335	0.023
TRANSR	1000	0.644	0.964	0.300	0.016	0.844	0.946	0.247	0.018
TRANSROWL	250	0.662	0.965	0.336	0.018	**0.980**	0.982	**0.919**	0.170
TRANSROWL	500	0.658	0.964	0.328	0.018	0.867	**0.988**	0.351	**0.006**
TRANSROWL	1000	0.649	0.968	0.307	0.014	0.905	0.973	0.547	0.032
TRANSROWL^R	250	0.651	0.963	0.315	0.017	0.876	0.965	0.406	0.024
TRANSROWL^R	500	0.648	0.978	0.302	0.010	0.864	0.959	0.349	0.023
TRANSROWL^R	1000	0.636	**0.981**	0.277	**0.007**	0.854	0.953	0.299	0.020

NELL

Model	Epochs	no typeOf				typeOf			
		Acc	P	R	FPR	Acc	P	R	FPR
TRANSE	1000	0.733	0.755	**0.691**	0.420	0.626	0.276	0.900	0.959
TRANSOWL	1000	0.675	0.677	0.671	0.493	**0.819**	**0.430**	0.615	0.680
TRANSR	250	0.751	0.810	0.656	0.311	0.715	0.305	0.672	0.823
TRANSR	500	0.751	0.819	0.644	0.285	0.749	0.311	0.544	0.726
TRANSR	1000	**0.758**	0.843	0.636	0.245	0.803	0.389	0.519	**0.630**
TRANSROWL	250	0.745	0.816	0.632	0.279	0.562	0.246	**0.911**	0.969
TRANSROWL	500	0.744	0.815	0.633	0.282	0.735	0.311	0.610	0.776
TRANSROWL	1000	0.744	0.835	0.608	0.234	0.763	0.334	0.560	0.717
TRANSROWL^R	250	0.737	0.807	0.621	0.281	0.634	0.268	0.804	0.919
TRANSROWL^R	500	0.743	0.830	0.612	0.245	0.723	0.293	0.583	0.771
TRANSROWL^R	1000	0.739	**0.845**	0.587	**0.207**	0.760	0.337	0.598	0.745

The experimental setting is analogous to the first part (see Sect. 4.1). Table 2 reports the complete results for each dataset in terms of accuracy, precision, recall, and false positive rate. Focusing preliminarily on the results of TRANSE and TRANSROWL, we can appreciate a general improvement of the latter especially in terms of FPR (typeOf problems) and in terms of accuracy and recall in (no typeOf) experiments on two datasets in which it outperformed also the other models. The overall results show that TRANSROWL and TRANSROWL^R, achieve the best performance, with a few exceptions, particularly in terms of FPR, also on account of a higher precision and limited decays in terms of recall thus resulting in comparable accuracy measures. These similar performance are likely due to the similar formulation of the respective loss function. In the case of TRANSROWL it determines the generation of further triples, based on the specified axioms, used to train the models: all entities and relations are involved in training. Conversely, in the case of TRANSROWL^R, only entities and relations that comply with the properties in the constraints are considered. This may explain the slightly superior performance of TRANSROWL. Analogously to the experiments in Sect. 4.2, a more incomplete dataset like *NELL* turned out to be more difficult for methods relying on a rich BK, whereas a more complete dataset like *DBpediaYAGO*, yielded a better performance of the newly proposed models with differences between the problems focusing on/excluding typeOf-triples.

Considering the outcomes on intermediate models again there is no clear indication of improvement with the elapsing of the epochs on all performance indexes. This may suggest that involving targeted objectives in the training loop may help.

5 Related Work

The presented knowledge injection approach could be applied to many other embedding models [4] with the aim of exploiting the rich schema-level axioms often available in the context of the Semantic Web. However, various approaches have been proposed that leverage different specific forms of prior knowledge to learn better representations exploited for KG refinement tasks.

In [9] a novel method was proposed jointly embedding KGs and logical rules, where triples and rules are represented in a unified framework. Triples are represented as atomic formulae while rules are represented as more complex formulae modeled by t-norm fuzzy logics admitting antecedents single atoms or conjunctions of atoms with variables as subjects and objects. A common loss over both representation is defined which is minimized to learn the embeddings. The specific form of BK which has to be available for the KG constitutes the main drawback of these approaches.

In [21] a solution based on adversarial training is proposed that exploits Datalog clauses to encode assumptions which are used to regularize neural link predictors. An inconsistency loss is derived that measures the degree of violation of such assumptions on a set of adversarial examples. Training is defined as a minimax problem, in which the models are trained by jointly minimizing the inconsistency loss on the adversarial examples jointly with a supervised loss. A specific form of BK is required and a specific form of *local CWA* is assumed to reason with it. The availability of such clauses and the assumptions on their semantics represent the main limitations of this approach.

Another neural-symbolic approach exploiting prior knowledge through *Logic Tensor Networks* [7] has been applied to similar classification tasks.

A common shortcoming of the related methods is that BK is often not embedded in a principled way. In [10], investigating the compatibility between ontological knowledge and different types of embeddings, they show that popular embedding methods are not capable of modeling even very simple types of rules, hence they are not able to learn the underlying dependencies. A general framework is introduced in which relations are modeled as convex regions which exactly represent ontologies expressed by a specific form of rules, that preserve the semantics of the input ontology.

In [1] the limitations of the current embedding models were identified: theoretical inexpressiveness, lack of support for inference patterns, higher-arity relations, and logical rule incorporation. Thus, they propose the translational embedding model BOXE which embeds entities as points, and relations as a set of hyper-rectangles, which characterize basic logical properties. This model was shown to offer a natural encoding for many logical properties and to be able to inject rules from rich classes of rule languages.

6 Conclusions and Ongoing Work

We have proposed an approach to learn embedding models based on exploiting prior knowledge both during the learning process and the triple corruption process to improve the quality of the low-dimensional representation of knowledge graphs. New models have been defined TRANSOWL, TRANSROWL and TRANSROWL^R, implemented as publicly available systems. An experimental evaluation on knowledge graph refinement tasks has proved the improvements of the derived models compared to the original ones, but also some shortcomings that may suggest valuable research directions to be pursued.

We are currently working on the application of the presented approach to newer embedding models which have been proved more effective than those considered in this work. We intend to extend the approach by exploiting further schema-axioms as well as hierarchical patterns on properties that can be elicited from the embeddings, namely clusters of relations and hierarchies of sub-relations. We are also planning to apply embedding models for solving other predictive problems related to the KGs. Following some previous works, further methods based on embedding spaces induced by specific kernel functions will also be investigated.

Acknowledgment. We would like to thank Giovanni Sansaro who formalized and developed the code for the preliminary version of TransOWL for his bachelor thesis.

References

1. Abboud, R., Ceylan, İ.İ., Lukasiewicz, T., Salvatori, T.: BoxE: a box embedding model for knowledge base completion. In: Proceedings of NeurIPS 2020 (2020)
2. Arnaout, H., Razniewski, S., Weikum, G.: Enriching knowledge bases with interesting negative statements. In: Das, D., et al. (eds.) Proceedings of AKBC 2020 (2020). https://doi.org/10.24432/C5101K

3. Bordes, A., Usunier, N., Garcia-Duran, A., Weston, J., Yakhnenko, O.: Translating embeddings for modeling multi-relational data. In: Burges, C.J.C., et al. (eds.) Proceedings of NIPS 2013, pp. 2787–2795. Curran Associates, Inc. (2013)

4. Cai, H., Zheng, V.W., Chang, K.: A comprehensive survey of graph embedding: problems, techniques, and applications. IEEE Trans. Knowl. Data Eng. **30**(09), 1616–1637 (2018). https://doi.org/10.1109/TKDE.2018.2807452

5. d'Amato, C.: Machine learning for the semantic web: lessons learnt and next research directions. Semant. Web **11**(1), 195–203 (2020). https://doi.org/10.3233/SW-200388

6. Ding, B., Wang, Q., Wang, B., Guo, L.: Improving knowledge graph embedding using simple constraints. In: Proceedings of ACL 2018, vol. 1, pp. 110–121. ACL (2018). https://doi.org/10.18653/v1/P18-1011

7. Donadello, I., Serafini, L.: Compensating supervision incompleteness with prior knowledge in semantic image interpretation. In: Proceedings of IJCNN 2019, pp. 1–8. IEEE (2019). https://doi.org/10.1109/IJCNN.2019.8852413

8. Dong, X.L., et al.: Knowledge vault: a web-scale approach to probabilistic knowledge fusion. In: Proceedings of KDD 2014, pp. 601–610 (2014)

9. Guo, S., Wang, Q., Wang, L., Wang, B., Guo, L.: Jointly embedding knowledge graphs and logical rules. In: Proceedings of EMNLP 2016, pp. 192–202. ACL (2016). https://doi.org/10.18653/v1/D16-1019

10. Gutiérrez-Basulto, V., Schockaert, S.: From knowledge graph embedding to ontology embedding? An analysis of the compatibility between vector space representations and rules. In: Thielscher, M., Toni, F., Wolter, F. (eds.) Proceedings of KR 2018, pp. 379–388. AAAI Press (2018)

11. He, S., Liu, K., Ji, G., Zhao, J.: Learning to represent knowledge graphs with gaussian embedding. In: Proceedings of CIKM 2015, pp. 623–632. ACM (2015). https://doi.org/10.1145/2806416.2806502

12. Hogan, A., et al.: Knowledge graphs. arXiv:2003.02320 (2020)

13. Jayathilaka, M., Mu, T., Sattler, U.: Visual-semantic embedding model informed by structured knowledge. In: Rudolph, S., Marreiros, G. (eds.) Proceedings of STAIRS 2020. CEUR, vol. 2655. CEUR-WS.org (2020). http://ceur-ws.org/Vol-2655/paper23.pdf

14. Ji, G., He, S., Xu, L., Liu, K., Zhao, J.: Knowledge graph embedding via dynamic mapping matrix. In: Proceedings of ACL-IJCNLP 2015, vol. 1, pp. 687–696. ACL (2015). https://doi.org/10.3115/v1/P15-1067

15. Ji, S., Pan, S., Cambria, E., Marttinen, P., Yu, P.S.: A survey on knowledge graphs: representation, acquisition and applications. arXiv:2002.00388 (2020)

16. Lin, Y., Liu, Z., Sun, M., Liu, Y., Zhu, X.: Learning entity and relation embeddings for knowledge graph completion. In: AAAI 2015 Proceedings, pp. 2181–2187. AAAI Press (2015)

17. Liu, Y., Li, H., Garcia-Duran, A., Niepert, M., Onoro-Rubio, D., Rosenblum, D.S.: MMKG: multi-modal knowledge graphs. In: Hitzler, P., et al. (eds.) ESWC 2019. LNCS, vol. 11503, pp. 459–474. Springer, Cham (2019). https://doi.org/10.1007/978-3-030-21348-0_30

18. Lv, X., Hou, L., Li, J., Liu, Z.: Differentiating concepts and instances for knowledge graph embedding. In: Riloff, E., et al. (eds.) Proceedings of EMNLP 2018, pp. 1971–1979. ACL (2018). https://doi.org/10.18653/v1/D18-1222

19. Minervini, P., Costabello, L., Muñoz, E., Nováček, V., Vandenbussche, P.-Y.: Regularizing knowledge graph embeddings via equivalence and inversion axioms. In: Ceci, M., Hollmén, J., Todorovski, L., Vens, C., Džeroski, S. (eds.) ECML PKDD 2017. LNCS (LNAI), vol. 10534, pp. 668–683. Springer, Cham (2017). https://doi.org/10.1007/978-3-319-71249-9_40

20. Minervini, P., d'Amato, C., Fanizzi, N.: Efficient energy-based embedding models for link prediction in knowledge graphs. J. Intell. Inf. Syst. **47**(1), 91–109 (2016). https://doi.org/10.1007/s10844-016-0414-7

21. Minervini, P., Demeester, T., Rocktäschel, T., Riedel, S.: Adversarial sets for regularising neural link predictors. In: Elidan, G., et al. (eds.) UAI 2017 Proceedings. AUAI Press (2017)
22. Paulheim, H.: Knowledge graph refinement: a survey of approaches and evaluation methods. Semant. Web **8**, 489–508 (2016). https://doi.org/10.3233/SW-160218
23. Paulheim, H.: Make embeddings semantic again! In: Proceedings of the ISWC 2018 P&D-Industry-BlueSky Tracks. CEUR Workshop Proceedings (2018)
24. Socher, R., Chen, D., Manning, C.D., Ng, A.Y.: Reasoning with neural tensor networks for knowledge base completion. In: Proceedings of NIPS 2013, pp. 926–934 (2013)
25. Sun, Z., Huang, J., Hu, W., Chen, M., Guo, L., Qu, Y.: TransEdge: translating relation-contextualized embeddings for knowledge graphs. In: Ghidini, C., et al. (eds.) ISWC 2019. LNCS, vol. 11778, pp. 612–629. Springer, Cham (2019). https://doi.org/10.1007/978-3-030-30793-6_35
26. Wang, Z., Zhang, J., Feng, J., Chen, Z.: Knowledge graph embedding by translating on hyperplanes. In: Proceedings of AAAI 2014, pp. 1112–1119. AAAI Press (2014)
27. Yang, B., Yih, W., He, X., Gao, J., Deng, L.: Embedding entities and relations for learning and inference in knowledge bases. In: Proceedings of ICLR 2015 (2015)

Science Data and Scholarly Communication

Structured Semantic Modeling
of Scientific Citation Intents

Roger Ferrod, Luigi Di Caro[✉], and Claudio Schifanella

Department of Computer Science, University of Turin, Turin, Italy
{roger.ferrod,luigi.dicaro,claudio.schifanella}@unito.it

Abstract. The search for relevant information within large scholarly databases is becoming an unaffordable task where deeper semantic representations of citations could give impactful contributions. While some researchers have already proposed models and categories of citations, this often remains at a theoretical level only or it simply reduces the problem to a short-text classification of the context sentence. In this work, we propose *CiTelling*: a radically new model of fine-grained semantic structures lying behind citational sentences able to represent their intent and features. After an extensive and multiple annotation of 1380 citations (https://github.com/rogerferrod/CiTelling), we tested the validity and the reliability of the proposal through both qualitative and quantitative analyses. In particular, we were able to 1) extend the current depth of existing semantic representations when used in computational scenarios, 2) achieve high inter-annotator agreement and 3) obtain state-of-the-art classification results with straightforward neural network models.

Keywords: Citation semantics · Scientific literature exploration · Semantic annotation

1 Introduction

Exploring and understanding the heart of millions of scientific articles is not an easy situation for a young researcher. Actually, only keeping abreast of research progress is becoming an increasingly difficult task even for senior and experienced scientists. Digital technologies are now being adopted since years to lighten such process, by providing advanced *"semantic"* search services based on keywords rather than metadata extraction and filtering procedures.

Numerous techniques have been developed to analyze large amounts of data such as the petabytes produced by the Large Hadron Collider or the hundreds of millions of bases contained in the human genome, but natural language cannot be naturally represented by numbers and easily manipulated by computers. Moreover, the research literature is made of complex textual content which is naturally oriented to be read by humans only.

However, while the actual understanding of the scientific content remains in the researchers' hands, a great support may come from the application of data

© Springer Nature Switzerland AG 2021
R. Verborgh et al. (Eds.): ESWC 2021, LNCS 12731, pp. 461–476, 2021.
https://doi.org/10.1007/978-3-030-77385-4_27

and language technologies to the citational aspect of the articles. Citations, indeed, represent a fundamental mechanism for both making new research and keeping track of what is going on within a scientific field. For example, an article A may cite an article B for different purposes: to extend, to criticize, to compare with, to refer to some used data or technique, and so forth. In other words, citations are crucial for both production and search, but semantic technologies are still far away from being supportive to the daily work of researchers.

Under this light, models such as [22] investigated possible types of citations, together with descriptions and examples. However, categories are sometimes very specific and linked to a few examples, making them difficult to be employed in concrete applications. Alternatively, recent works proposed Machine Learning approaches for the automatic classification of sentences containing citations into few classes such as *extension, use*, etc. The problem with the latter approach is the reduction of the complexity of the single citation semantics into a short-text classification task, where the expected output is simply one label to associate with the sentence containing the citation.

In this contribution, we draw from these experiences to create a fine-grained semantic model of citations which can be instead employed in computational scenarios, manually producing an annotation (available at https://github.com/rogerferrod/CiTelling) of more than one thousand cases for testing its validity through both human agreements and neural network-based classification results. The goal of this work is thus threefold: 1) to propose a computationally-affordable semantic model for citations inheriting and enriching key features of state-of-the-art efforts; 2) to provide an extensive and multiple-user annotation of citational sentences; and 3) to demonstrate the model validity through both human- and machine-based evaluations.

2   Related Work

There exists a large body of literature focusing on the processing of scientific texts for purposes such as data curation (e.g. [17]), search (e.g., [4]), topic modeling (e.g., [3]), summarization (e.g., [25]), and so forth. In this context, our work has similarities with different approaches related to the modeling and use of the citations within large scholar databases, such as *(i)* semantic modeling of citations (e.g., [6,13,16,22]), *(ii)* data analysis and extraction of relevant information (e.g., [9,20,23]), and *(iii)* exploration of the scientific literature by means of faceted search queries and visualization tools (e.g., [1,2,10,11,18]).

In this paper, we focus on the first task of modeling citations, specifically inheriting both the theoretical and top-down approach of *CiTo* [22] and recent state-of-the-art technologies for automatic citation classification [6]. More in details, in [22], the authors identified and formalized different types of possible citation meanings in scientific articles. However, the proposed ontology includes a wide set of complex cases, making it exclusively suitable for manual (and costly) annotations of individual references. In [12], the authors presented an unsupervised technique based instead on a completely automatic clustering process, identifying and describing 11 classes of citations.

More recently, [6] proposed a classifier based on Scaffolds models [24] that was able to identify 6 classes of citations on the ACL-ARC dataset [7] and 3 classes on a larger dataset named *SciCite* [6] with state-of-the-art accuracy levels. In particular, we used these works as baseline for the evaluation, finding that our model allows to achieve comparable performance with extremely simpler neural network-based classifiers on equally-distributed and semantically-deeper citation intents.

3 Motivations and Research Questions

3.1 Semantic Structures in Citations

Our main goal is to build a fine-grained semantic representation of citations to capture and harmonize their *i*) intent type, *ii*) direction, *iii*) objects or concepts involved, and *iv*) context. To better express our idea, let us consider the example below:

> *"We use the Scaffold network classifier (Cohan 2019) to incorporate syntactic structures [...]"*

According to *CiTo* [22], this example should fit the ontological category *use*, as well as for the state-of-the-art classification system proposed in [6]. However, in the latter case the procedure is only limited to the classification of the sentence.

In our work, instead, we face the citation classification problem under a more structured semantic view. In particular, our aim is to model the above citation in the following way:

(a)
```
SUBJECT_PAPER_ID: <this_paper_id>;
INTENT: <uses>;
OBJECT: <scaffold network classifier>;
OF_PAPER_ID: <Cohan_2019_id>;
IN_CONTEXT: <to incorporate syntactic structures>;
```

A part from being more informative than in [22] and [6], our model is able to cope with more complex (but frequent) cases. For instance, consider the citation below:

> *"(Peter et al. 2018) uses the SVD factorization method."*

In this second case, both [22] and [6] approaches would simply associate a label *use* to the whole sentence, as in the previous example. Instead, we model this different case as:

(b)
```
SUBJECT_PAPER_ID: <Peter_2018_ID>;
INTENT: <uses>;
OBJECT: <SVD>;
OF_PAPER_ID: n/a;
CONTEXT: n/a;
```

It is important to note that, in the latter case *(b)*, the *<this_paper_id>* identifier does not enter into the model, since the paper only plays the role of *container*. In other words, *<this_paper_id>* only contains the *<uses>* information that links the cited paper *<Peter_2018_ID>* with the object *<SVD>*. To the best of our knowledge, this is the first attempt to extract source-agnostic knowledge from scholarly databases, as detailed in the next section.

3.2 Active and Passive Roles in Citations

To better understand the advantages of our proposal, one can think at the related work section of a scientific article, which usually expresses definitions, facts and comparative analyses of existing works in the literature. Such section is indeed an extremely rich source of information to model knowledge related to external articles. Usually, semantic analyses of scholarly articles are focused on the modeling of their direct content, whereas they usually contain knowledge about (mentioned) existing works.

A part from the citation class, we further model citational sentences through *active* and *passive* roles. The first case includes a relation of a certain class/intent between a source paper A and a referenced paper B, with a focus on some research objects in B. In the second case, the relationship lies between a referenced paper B (mentioned by the citing paper A) and some research object presented by an unknown third-party paper. In this second situation, it is B that covers the role of subject, proposing, adding or using the object. In other words, the source paper A does not cover any semantic role of interest (while it simply functions as a container for the mentioned citation). Please note that, in the previous Example (b), it would be a mistake to classify the A-B relation with the *"use"* class as currently done by current approaches, since it is not A that uses the mentioned research object. To the best of our knowledge, this represents the first attempt to model structured semantics behind citations, as well as such subject-oriented role. Hereafter we distinguish the two roles by calling them *A-subject* and *B-subject* depending on who holds the role of subject.

In Fig. 1 we illustrate a comparison between current models and our proposal. In particular, *CiTelling* embodies information about roles and relationships that involve fine-grained objects rather than the whole papers. Notice that, while existing state-of-the-art computational models face the problem as a simple short-text classification task, we consider the citation semantics under a semantically richer and structured view. This creates a *knowledge graph* instead of a simpler (labeled) network of articles.

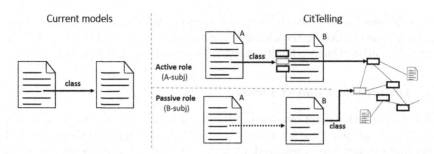

Fig. 1. Comparison of existing models (on the left) with our proposal (right). While the relations of current models involve two papers as a whole (associating an intent with each citation), *CiTelling* is able to highlight particular topics of the cited text (objects marked in red), separating the active from the passive role cases. (Color figure online)

4 Semantic Structuring of Citation Intents

Since the scaffold network model proposed in [6] represents the state of the art on citation classification using the ACL-ARC dataset (developed in [7]), we used its classes as starting point. The original labels were the following: *background, extends, uses, motivation, compare/contrast,* and *future work.* Then, we integrated other two classes from the results of [12]: *propose* and *analyze.* Finally, we added the more formal (and rare) *CiTo* proposals: *critiques* and *data source.* After a careful analysis of their labeling and meaning, we ended up with the five intents (or classes) we thought to be more informative, as shown in Table 1. For example, we decided to exclude the intent *background* as it is often used as a generic "relatedness-based" container.

Table 1. Proposed model of citation intents, integrating features from existing models. **Analyze* is derived from the most specific *Report* label presented in [12].

Intent	Optional subclass	CiTo [22]	SciSite [6]	CitExp [12]
Proposes				x
Uses	[dataset]	x	x	
Extends		x	x	
Analyzes	[critiques]			x*
Compares	[contrasts]		x	

Taking inspiration from the *CiTo* ontology, which contains more specific categories such as *"usesDataFrom"* and *"usesConclusionsFrom"*, we decided to also consider differences within the intents *uses, compares* and *analyzes.* We have therefore added subcategories to highlight the use of *datasets* or *results* in the *use* class and to distinguish dissimilarity (i.e. *contrast*) in *compare.* In the same way, it is useful to capture the negative analyses, which highlight critical issues related to the citation in the *analyze* class; this latter case is extremely rare but very informative, thus we finally opted for its inclusion in our model.

4.1   Object and Context Fields

Another innovative point of our contribution, compared to previous works, is the introduction of two semantic fields *object* and *context* for further modeling the citational semantics, as illustrated in Fig. 2. In this section, we present definitions and examples for these two fields.

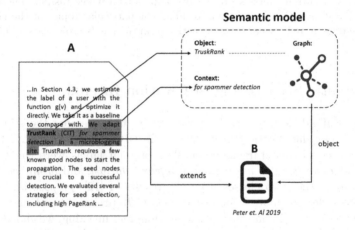

Fig. 2. General overview of the proposed semantic model.

With *object*, we mean a mandatory concept taken into consideration by the citation, whose meaning changes according to the class. For *context*, we mean an optional additional background information, or constraints, which can be useful to disambiguate the *object*. For example, in the sentence:

"*Adaptive modulation techniques over Nakagami-m fading channels were also investigated in [CIT] for mobile wireless channel.*"

the *object* would be "*adaptive modulation techniques*", which is contextualized by "*for mobile wireless channel*".

More in detail, the *object* can be defined as the minimal span of text to which the quotation refers (e.g. the extended or analyzed concept). Consequently, it contains the smallest amount of information able to identify the concept of interest. The *context* is instead represented by a usually larger text surrounding the *object* helping disambiguate or specify it. A direct application of this model could be within a semantic search engine, where the *context* may accompany the object through a tool-tip or other visualization tools, providing additional information on the purpose of the *object* (e.g., "*for matrix factorization*") rather than on the domain of application (e.g., *"in elliptic curve cryptography"*). Additionally, the *context* can be used for integrating additional features into the encoding of *object* meanings (for example, through the employment of recent BERT-like context-dependent embeddings [8]).

Note that we modeled the *object* and the *context* fields in a purely semantic way, avoiding to create lexical-semantic interfaces based on part-of-speech tags, patterns or syntactic structures. While this choice leaves higher margin to subjective evaluations, our aim was twofold: *i*) to deeply evaluate the model through inter-annotation agreements in absence of physical/narrow lexical constraints; and *ii*) to leave room for future automated labeling technologies (e.g. Ontology Learning, Transformer-based Machine Learning, etc.).

4.2   Definition of the Citation Intents

In this section, we provide definitions and examples for the chosen set of intents (or classes) used in our model.

With the exceptions of *propose*[1] and *compare*, all the other classes may be associated with the two roles previously described in Sect. 3.2. For this reason, the formalization that follows will consider both cases. It is possible to generalize the relationships in the following way:

$$[A\text{-}subject]$$
$$A \xrightarrow{\text{class-label}} object \xleftarrow{\text{proposes}} B$$

$$[B\text{-}subject]$$
$$B \xrightarrow{\text{class-label}} object$$

Hereafter we indicate with A the citing paper (i.e. the paper under analysis) and with B the cited paper. Please note that the *propose* relation is implicit in the *A-subject* representation, since the role of B is that of containing *object*.

***Propose* Class.** This class models a particular contribution (i.e. *object*) of a paper. More formally:

$$\exists\ B,\ object\ |\ B \xrightarrow{\text{proposes}} object$$

In words, there exists an article B and one contained concept *object* such that B proposes *object*. Different examples of *propose* citations are shown below:

| (example 1) | *"The relational model was first introduced in the work by* |

Codd [CIT]."

---

[1] *propose* cannot have a relation of type *A-subject* since if the paper A simply proposes *object*, then there is no reason to quote another paper B. Different is the case in which the authors of a paper A propose an *object* referring to a paper B, but in that case the correct relationship is of type *B-subject*.

$\boxed{(example\ 2)}$ "$\underline{\text{Anisotropic diffusion}}$ was   proposed
               $\underset{object}{}$

$\underline{\text{in the context of scale space}}$ [CIT]."
      $\underset{context}{}$

Use Class. This class models the simple use of some object, citing an external article B. More formally:

[A-subject]
∃ A, B, object | A $\xrightarrow{\text{uses}}$ B.object

In words, there exists an article B cited within article A where B.object is used in A.

[B-subject]
∃ B, object | B $\xrightarrow{\text{uses}}$ object

In this case, there exists an article B cited within article A such that B uses some *object* (thus, A plays only the role of article-container). Different examples of *use* citations are shown below:

$\boxed{(A\text{-}subject\ example\ \text{-}\ dataset)}$ "$\underline{\text{For faces,}}$ we used $\underline{\text{FaceScrub dataset}}$
                       $\underset{context}{}$ $\underset{object}{}$

from [CIT]."

$\boxed{(B\text{-}subject\ example)}$ "$\textit{This}$ $\underline{\textit{MMSE representation}}$ was used in [CIT],
                          $\underset{object}{}$

$\underline{\text{to prove the EPI.}}$"
     $\underset{context}{}$

Extend Class. This citation intent models the natural process of scientific evolution, that is the possibility of a paper to modify (adapting or enriching) another work. More formally:

[A-subject]
∃ A, B, object | A $\xrightarrow{\text{extends}}$ B.object

In words, there exists an article B cited within article A where B.object is extended in A.

[B-subject]
∃ B, object | B $\xrightarrow{\text{extends}}$ object

In this case, there exists an article B cited within article A such that B extends some *object*. For example:

$\boxed{(A\text{-}subject)}$ "$\textit{This algorithm is a generalization of the famous}$

$\underline{\textit{min-norm point algorithm}}$ [CIT]."
      $\underset{object}{}$

> (B-subject) "Ernst et al. [CIT] tackle the static ASP by using
> a specialized <u>simplex algorithm</u> for the single runway case and
> object
> <u>extend it to the multiple runway case</u>."
> context

It is important to notice the difference between *extend* and *use*. In particular, extending a work means its use after the application of some changes. This is why cases such as *"Our work is based on CIT"* and *"Following the work of CIT we [...]"* can be also considered instances of the *extend* class.

Analyze Class. This citation type identifies processes of analysis and discussion on specific topics. More formally:

[A-subject]
$\exists$ A, B, object | $A \xrightarrow{\text{analyzes}} B.object$

[B-subject]
$\exists$ B, object | $B \xrightarrow{\text{analyzes}} object$

Examples of *analyze* citations are shown below:

> (A-subject example) "We have conducted a survey to discuss
> <u>Big Data Frameworks</u> [CIT]."
> object

> (B-subject example - critique) "Refer to CIT for a discussion
> <u>on the optical design</u> problem of <u>HMDs</u>."
> context   object

Compare Class. This class identifies similarities or contrasts between articles over a specific research object. More formally:
$$\exists\ A, B, object\ |\ A.object \xleftrightarrow{\text{compares}} B.object$$
This particular relationship is symmetric since the *object* can be either in A or B. Examples of this type of citations are shown below:

> (example 1) "For VGG, our <u>latency</u> is longer than [CIT] due to 45%
> object
> frequency gap."

> (example 2) "This approach is similar to the <u>strategy</u> defined in [CIT]
> object
> <u>as gap recovery</u>."
> context

Notice that, in the first case, *latency* is shared between A and B, meanwhile in the second example there are two different words (*approach* belonging to A, and *strategy* to B) referring to the same concept.

4.3   Data Selection and Annotation

On such modeling basis, we built a balanced dataset with 276 instances for each class, for a total of 1380 instances. As already mentioned, in contrast with the state of the art baselines, we avoided to consider a *background* label since it usually represents a generic class that collects all citations "escaped" from any meaningful classification.

We have randomly sampled 10K papers from the Semantic Scholar corpus[2] obtaining, through ParsCit [15], more than 200K citations. For simplicity, we filtered out the sentences longer than 40 words; however in this way we captured most of the cases. Then, the selection of the candidate citational sentences has been carried out through a first phase of random sampling over such extracted citations, for each class. This process was based on different techniques: for classes such as *use* and *extend* we made use of the classifier provided in [6], while for others (*analyze* and *propose*) we employed a keyword-based random search. The candidate citational sentences were then cleaned out of the noise with a manual validation.

The second phase regarded the annotation of the sentences with the proposed structured semantic model. Three different annotators (the authors of the present paper) separately validated the class label and annotated the *A-Subject* vs *B-Subject* role, the *object* and the *context* fields for each instance. At the same time, the sub-classification operations were carried out, highlighting the sub-types of the classes (e.g. use:data/use:other and analyze:analyze/analyze:critique). The results of the inter-annotation agreement, calculated through the use of the Bleu score [19], are shown in Fig. 4.

In performing this operation we found that there may exist some overlap among the classes and therefore it was useful to set up a disambiguation mechanism. For example, the type *extend* is considered more informative than *propose*. More in detail, we defined an ordered list of the classes to guide the disambiguation of ambiguous cases:

$$extend > analyze > compare > use > propose$$

In this way, it is possible to disambiguate sentences like: "*We use an extension of [CIT]*" (classified as *extend* instead of *use*) and "*We propose a comparative analysis beetween SVC [CIT] and NuSVC*" (labeled with *analyze*).

5   Evaluation

In this section we first report an analysis of the annotation task together with an evaluation of the impact of intent roles (active/passive), intent subclasses (see Table 1), and the obtained inter-annotation agreement. Secondly, we employed the model (through the annotated dataset) in a downstream task, i.e., intent classification, to be able to make comparisons with the current state of the art.

---

[2] https://www.semanticscholar.org/.

5.1   Roles, Subclasses and Inter-annotation Agreement

After the annotation phase, we have identified a clear diversification in the distribution of roles, as shown in Fig. 3. The subclasses are distributed as follows: 10.14% of the instances in the *use* class are further labeled as *"use data/results"*, meanwhile 15.22% of the *compare* class instances were better specified as *"contrast"*. Finally, the rarest, 6.16% of the *analyze* instances are of subtype *"critique/error"*. These statistics suggest the utility of sub-classifying the intents, in order to preserve useful information which can be further processed, analyzed and exploited for automatic classification and reasoning purposes.

Another interesting consideration concerns the nature of the *object* in the various citation intents: classes such as *extend* and *compare* are mostly associated with very generic objects like *method, approach, work* or *study* (respectively 39% and 31% of the total number of objects), meanwhile *use* and *analyze* mention very specific objects (a kind of named entities) such as *LSTM, Vertex-II Pro* or *CPLEX 12.6* (respectively 39% and 15% of the total).

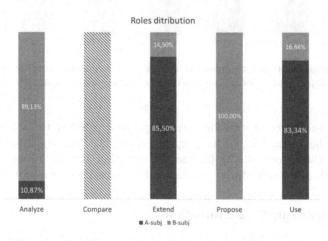

Fig. 3. Predominance of roles types (*A-subject/B-subject*) in the classes distribution. As described in Sect. 4.2, role types are not defined for the *Compare* class.

To calculate the overall agreement on the three annotations of intents {*A1, A2, A3*}, we averaged the scores obtained from the three pairs <*A1,A2*>, <*A1,A3*>, and <*A2,A3*>. More in detail, for each pair we counted a +1 contribution if both annotators labeled the sentence with the same intent. Then, by dividing this value by the number of annotated citations we obtained a global averaged score which was particularly high (0.88).

Then, for the in-text semantic annotations, we computed Bleu scores [19] on *object* and *context*, reaching the scores of 0.78 and 0.55 respectively. These results are in line with our initial expectations: since *context* has a less constrained definition with respect to *object*, it is more susceptible to lexical variations and different textual span interpretations. Moreover, *context* has an average length which is greater than that of *object* (5.77 words vs 2.40 words). The *object* field reached instead high agreement levels. The whole result set broken down by class is reported in Fig. 4. We omitted the results of the agreement on roles as they correspond to an average score of 1.0 (the same considerations hold for the intent subclasses).

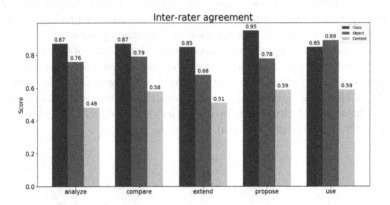

Fig. 4. Averaged inter-rater agreement among the three annotators for each citation intent. The *object* and *context* bars represent averaged inter-annotation Bleu scores.

Among the different citation intents, *propose* resulted to be very easy to classify by the annotators, with an agreement of 0.95. The *object* field goes from an average Bleu score of 0.68 for the *extend* intent to 0.89 for *use*. Then, the *context* field, as already stated, reached values between 0.48 and 0.59.

5.2   Downstream Task Evaluation

We evaluated our model by building a simple classifier on the annotated data, comparing the results with the existing state of the art. In particular, we have focused on the outcomes reported by [6]. Unlike the ACL-ARC (used by [7] and [6]) and SciCite [6] datasets, our dataset is balanced and does not include generic labels such as *background*. The distribution of the classes is shown in Table 2.

Moreover while the *SciCite* dataset contains more than 11k elements, *ACL-ARC* [7] has a number of instances (1941) comparable to our dataset (1380) and a similar number of classes, albeit with a completely different distribution.

In contrast with the state-of-the-art classifiers under comparison in this section, ours is based on an extremely simple architecture. This choice comes from the aim of evaluating the semantic coherence and power of the proposed *CiTelling* model by comparing it with the results of complex neural architectures applied on state-of-the-art citational representation models. In particular, we adopted a single biLSTM layer densely connected to a softmax function,

Table 2. Classes distribution and overlap among datasets.

Intent	ACL-ARC (# 1941)	SciCite (# 11020)	CiTelling (# 1380)
Method	–	29%	–
Result comparison	–	13%	–
Background	51%	58%	–
Future work	4%	–	–
Motivation	5%	–	–
Extend	4%	–	20%
Use	19%	–	20%
Compare	18%	–	20%
Propose	–	–	20%
Analyze	–	–	20%

using the citational sentence as unique input. For the initial word representation layer, we employed pretrained *fastText* word embeddings [14].

Despite the simplicity of the classifier, the results are in line with other more sophisticated existing architectures, in particular with the outcomes reported in [6]. Notice that these methods cannot be directly evaluated on our data since they require further input features and metadata such as section titles and citation markers. Contrariwise, it was possible to apply a simple neural architecture (biLSTM with optimized hyper-parameters[3]) on the existing ACL-ARC data, which reached a significantly low F1 score (38.0%) compared to what obtained by the same neural model on our *CiTelling* data (65.8%). Furthermore, we noticed more balanced values of Precision and Recall with respect to the compared approaches. An overview of the results is reported in Table 3.

Table 3. Intent classification results on *CiTelling* and *ACL-ARC* data.

CiTelling data	F1 score	Precision	Recall
biLSTM	65.8	66.2	66.1
ACL-ARC data	F1 score	Precision	Recall
biLSTM	38.0	44.0	37.0
biLSTM + attention	51.5	53.7	50.6
biLSTM + attention + elmo	54.2	59.2	51.6
[Jurgens et al. 2018]	54.6	64.9	49.9
biLSTM + attention + scaffolds	63.1	71.7	58.2
SciCite classifier	67.9	81.3	62.5

---

[3] 50 input dim, 12 (x2) hidden units, dropout 0.7, L2 penalty 1e-06.

Since our model also integrates directional information (i.e., active and passive roles), we further carried out an additional experimentation by training a neural network performing role classification. By using a *biGRU* architecture [5] with standard settings[4], we obtained a F1-score of 77.6%, with Precision and Recall of 80.6% and 74.8% respectively.

6 Conclusions and Future Work

In this paper, we proposed a new semantic representation for modeling citations within a corpus of scholarly articles. In particular, we took inspiration form both theoretical bases and current computational approaches to both propose a novel semantic model and to create a publicly-available annotated resource. In contrast with the existing approaches aiming at labeling citations with some predefined classes, we put forward a structured model integrating an ontological view of the referenced objects within the literature.

Future developments of this work may include the integration of further articles metadata (e.g., sections, timestamps, etc.) and the management of sentences with multiple types of citations. For example, in the sentence *"CIT used an extension of X but the results are not satisfactory"* the citation plays two roles: it uses an extension of the *object* (therefore categorizable as *extend* with *B-subj* role) while the results of this operation are criticized (*analyze* with *A-subj* role). Furthermore, in the first case the *object* is *X* while in the second case the *object* is *CIT*; thus they are two distinct citation intents that can be extracted separately, enriching in this way the knowledge model.

In order to build a knowledge model capable of integrating and exploiting all the captured concepts, further effort may be spent in the generalization of the objects. This operation could be facilitated by the presence of the *context* field. The objects automatically extracted from the text can then be aligned with existing ontologies such as [21], a large-scale ontology of research mainly in the field of Computer Science.

Our contribution will also enable the construction of a directed citation semantic graph which can be used for advanced analyses (e.g., graph embeddings) rather than semantic web search applications. For example, we can hypothesize the analysis of the knowledge graph with centrality measures, community detection algorithms or temporal analysis, in order to trace the evolution of communities and topics within specific citational paths.

References

1. Akujuobi, U., Zhang, X.: Delve: a dataset-driven scholarly search and analysis system. SIGKDD Explor. Newsl. **19**(2), 36–46 (2017)
2. Alexander, E., Kohlmann, J., Valenza, R., Witmore, M., Gleicher, M.: Serendip: topic model-driven visual exploration of text corpora. In: 2014 IEEE Conference on Visual Analytics Science and Technology (VAST), pp. 173–182. IEEE (2014)

---

[4] 50 input dim, 25 (x2) hidden units, dropout 0.8, L2 penalty 1e-05.

3. Bai, H., Chen, Z., Lyu, M.R., King, I., Xu, Z.: Neural relational topic models for scientific article analysis. In: Proceedings of the 27th ACM International Conference on Information and Knowledge Management, pp. 27–36 (2018)

4. Breitinger, C., Kolcu, B., Meuschke, M., Meuschke, N., Gipp, B.: Supporting the exploration of semantic features in academic literature using graph-based visualizations. In: Proceedings of the ACM/IEEE Joint Conference on Digital Libraries in 2020, pp. 377–380 (2020)

5. Cho, K., et al.: Learning phrase representations using RNN encoder-decoder for statistical machine translation. In: Proceedings of the 2014 Conference on Empirical Methods in Natural Language Processing (EMNLP), Doha, Qatar, pp. 1724–1734. Association for Computational Linguistics, October 2014

6. Cohan, A., Ammar, W., van Zuylen, M., Cady, F.: Structural scaffolds for citation intent classification in scientific publications. In: Proceedings of the 2019 Conference of the North American Chapter of the Association for Computational Linguistics: Human Language Technologies, NAACL-HLT 2019, Minneapolis, MN, USA, 2–7 June 2019, Volume 1 (Long and Short Papers), pp. 3586–3596 (2019)

7. Jurgens, D., Kumar, S., Hoover, R., McFarland, D., Jurafsky, D.: Measuring the evolution of a scientific field through citation frames. Trans. Assoc. Comput. Linguist. **6**, 391–406 (2018)

8. Devlin, J., Chang, M.W., Lee, K., Toutanova, K.: BERT: pre-training of deep bidirectional transformers for language understanding. In: Proceedings of the 2019 Conference of the North American Chapter of the Association for Computational Linguistics: Human Language Technologies, Volume 1 (Long and Short Papers), Minneapolis, Minnesota, pp. 4171–4186. Association for Computational Linguistics, June 2019

9. Šubelj, L., van Eck, N.J., Waltman, L.: Clustering scientific publications based on citation relations: a systematic comparison of different methods. PLoS ONE **11**(4), e0154404 (2016)

10. van Eck, N.J., Waltman, L.: VOS: a new method for visualizing similarities between objects. In: Decker, R., Lenz, H.-J. (eds.) Advances in Data Analysis. SCDAKO, pp. 299–306. Springer, Heidelberg (2007). https://doi.org/10.1007/978-3-540-70981-7_34

11. van Eck, N.J., Waltman, L.: CitNetExplorer: a new software tool for analyzing and visualizing citation networks. J. Informetrics **8**(4), 802–823 (2014)

12. Ferrod, R., Schifanella, C., Di Caro, L., Cataldi, M.: Disclosing citation meanings for augmented research retrieval and exploration. In: Hitzler, P., et al. (eds.) ESWC 2019. LNCS, vol. 11503, pp. 101–115. Springer, Cham (2019). https://doi.org/10.1007/978-3-030-21348-0_7

13. Giosa, D., Di Caro, L.: *What2Cite*: unveiling topics and citations dependencies for scientific literature exploration and recommendation. In: Keet, C.M., Dumontier, M. (eds.) EKAW 2020. LNCS (LNAI), vol. 12387, pp. 147–157. Springer, Cham (2020). https://doi.org/10.1007/978-3-030-61244-3_10

14. Joulin, A., Grave, E., Bojanowski, P., Mikolov, T.: Bag of tricks for efficient text classification. In: Proceedings of the 15th Conference of the European Chapter of the Association for Computational Linguistics: Volume 2, Short Papers, Valencia, Spain, pp. 427–431. Association for Computational Linguistics, April 2017

15. Councill, I.G., Lee Giles, C., Kan, M.-Y.: ParsCit: an open-source CRF reference string parsing package. In: Proceedings of the Language Resources and Evaluation Conference (LREC 2008), Marrakesh, Morrocco, May 2008

16. Kim, J., Kim, D., Oh, A.H.: Joint modeling of topics, citations, and topical authority in academic corpora. Trans. Assoc. Comput. Linguist. **5**, 191–204 (2017)

17. Lo, K., Wang, L.L., Neumann, M., Kinney, R., Weld, D.S.: S2ORC: the semantic scholar open research corpus. In: Proceedings of the 58th Annual Meeting of the Association for Computational Linguistics, pp. 4969–4983 (2020)
18. Nagwani, N.: Summarizing large text collection using topic modeling and clustering based on MapReduce framework. J. Big Data **2**(1), 6 (2015)
19. Papineni, K., Roukos, S., Ward, T., Zhu, W.J.: BLEU: a method for automatic evaluation of machine translation. In: Proceedings of the 40th Annual Meeting on Association for Computational Linguistics, pp. 311–318. Association for Computational Linguistics (2002)
20. Popescul, A., Ungar, L.H., Flake, G.W., Lawrence, S., Giles, C.L.: Clustering and identifying temporal trends in document databases. In: ADL, p. 173. IEEE (2000)
21. Salatino, A.A., Thanapalasingam, T., Mannocci, A., Osborne, F., Motta, E.: (October)
22. Shotton, S.P.D.: FaBiO and CiTO: ontologies for describing bibliographic resources and citations. In: Web Semantics: Science, Services and Agents on the World Wide Web, vol. 17, pp. 33–43 (2012)
23. Mihalcea, R., Corley, C., Strapparava, C.: Corpus-based and knowledge-based measures of text semantic similarity. In: AAAI 2006 Proceedings of the 21st National Conference on Artificial Intelligence, vol. 1, pp. 775–780 (2006)
24. Swayamdipta, S., Thomson, S., Lee, K., Zettlemoyer, L., Dyer, C., Smith, N.A.: Syntactic scaffolds for semantic structures. In: Proceedings of the 2018 Conference on Empirical Methods in Natural Language Processing, Brussels, Belgium, 31 October–4 November 2018, pp. 3772–3782 (2018)
25. Yasunaga, M., et al.: ScisummNet: a large annotated corpus and content-impact models for scientific paper summarization with citation networks. In: Proceedings of the AAAI Conference on Artificial Intelligence, vol. 33, pp. 7386–7393 (2019)

Discovering Research Hypotheses in Social Science Using Knowledge Graph Embeddings

Rosaline de Haan[1], Ilaria Tiddi[2(✉)], and Wouter Beek[1]

[1] Triply, Amsterdam, The Netherlands
{rosaline.de.haan,wouter}@triply.cc
[2] Vrije Universiteit Amsterdam, Amsterdam, The Netherlands
i.tiddi@vu.nl

Abstract. In an era of ever-increasing scientific publications available, scientists struggle to keep pace with the literature, interpret research results and identify new research hypotheses to falsify. This is particularly in fields such as the social sciences, where automated support for scientific discovery is still widely unavailable and unimplemented. In this work, we introduce an automated system that supports social scientists in identifying new research hypotheses. With the idea that knowledge graphs help modeling domain-specific information, and that machine learning can be used to identify the most relevant facts therein, we frame the problem of hypothesis discovery as a link prediction task, where the ComplEx model is used to predict new relationships between entities of a knowledge graph representing scientific papers and their experimental details. The final output consists in fully formulated hypotheses including the newly discovered triples (hypothesis statement), along with supporting statements from the knowledge graph (hypothesis evidence and hypothesis history). A quantitative and qualitative evaluation is carried using experts in the field. Encouraging results show that a simple combination of machine learning and knowledge graph methods can serve as a basis for automated scientific discovery.

Keywords: Scientific discovery · Knowledge graphs · Link prediction · Social science

1 Introduction

Scientific research usually starts with asking a question, followed by doing background research, and then formulating a testable hypothesis. Doing background research to properly substantiate a hypothesis can be a difficult and time-consuming task for scientists. It is estimated that over 3 million scientific articles are published annually, a number that keeps growing of 4% each year [25]. The fast rate at which new publications appear, as well as the inefficient way in which scientific information is communicated (e.g. PDF documents), calls for

© Springer Nature Switzerland AG 2021
R. Verborgh et al. (Eds.): ESWC 2021, LNCS 12731, pp. 477–494, 2021.
https://doi.org/10.1007/978-3-030-77385-4_28

more efficient data analysis and synthesis, in a way that scientists formulating new research hypotheses can be supported rather than overloaded.

The task of significantly speeding up the steps in the scientific process is generally called automated scientific discovery [15]. The latest years have seen Artificial Intelligence approaches for automated scientific discovery in various scientific fields, either relying on symbolic knowledge representation or machine-driven methods. Knowledge graphs such as the Gene Ontology[1] and the ontology collection of the Open Biological and Biomedical Ontology Foundry[2] have been used to encode domain-specific information, such as representing biological systems from the molecular to the organism level. Machine Learning and particularly link prediction methods, that help predicting which missing edges in a graph are most likely to exist, have also been used, e.g. to support medical scientists by showing them new associations between drugs and diseases [15,19].

There is currently not much automated support for social scientists when it comes to getting new insights from scientific information. This is partly due to the more qualitative and uncertain nature of social science data, making it hard to represent, and consequently less machine-interpretable [3]. One effort in this direction is the COoperation DAtabank (CODA), where an international team of social scientists published a structured, open-access repository of research on human cooperation using social dilemmas. The dataset represents about 3,000 research publications with their experimental settings, variables of observation, and quantitative results. Given the large amount of structured information available, and the success of predictive methods seen in other disciplines, it is natural to think that a hybrid method could be designed, to automatically suggest social scientists new hypotheses to be tested.

Here, we study the problem of automatic hypothesis discovery in the field of social sciences. Following approaches in the biomedical field, we propose to frame our problem as a link prediction task, and particularly to exploit the structured representation of the domain to learn research hypotheses in the form of unseen triples over a knowledge graph describing research papers and their experimental settings. Using knowledge graph embeddings, we predict the likelihood of new possible relationships between entities, consisting in the variables studied social science research. These relationships are then used to provide the experts with new research hypotheses structured in a *statement* (the newly predicted associations), *evidence* and *history* (both triples existing in the graph). We quantitatively and qualitatively assess this approach using experts in the field, which helps us evaluating the accuracy and meaningfulness of the discovered hypotheses. Our novelty is not a the prediction algorithm for automated hypothesis discovery, but rather the hybrid method based on link prediction over knowledge graph data. More specifically, we show: (i) how a thorough structured representation of scientific knowledge helps the automatic discovery of research hypotheses, (ii) how our hybrid method can support experts in formulating new research hypotheses and (iii) a practical application in the field of social science.

---

[1] http://geneontology.org/.

[2] http://www.obofoundry.org/.

2   Related Work

Our work relates to three areas, namely (i) existing methods for representing and mining scientific knowledge, (ii) approaches for automated hypothesis discovery in science and (iii) knowledge graph embedding methods and applications.

Representing and Mining Scientific Knowledge. Several methods have been developed to represent scientific knowledge and foster interoperability and reproducibility. Micro- and nanopublications [4,8] have been introduced in the last decade as standardised formats for the publication of minimal scientific claims, i.e. minipublications. Such models allow to describe evidence and nuanced scientific assertions expressing a relationship between two predicates (e.g. a gene relates to a disease), together with provenance information describing both the methods used to derive the assertion and publication metadata. The DISK hypothesis ontology [7] was introduced to capture the evolution of research hypotheses in the neuroscience field, including the provenance and revisions. More precisely, a DISK hypothesis consists of structured assertions (hypothesis statement), some numerical confidence level (hypothesis qualifier), the information of the analysis that were carried out (hypothesis evidence), and prior hypotheses revised to generate the current one (hypothesis history). In the field of medical science, the different elements to be included in a hypothesis can be described with the PICO ontology[3], describing Patients, the Condition or disease of interest and its alternative (Intervention), and the Outcome of the study.

Repositories for storing scientific publications at large scale in the form of knowledge graphs include both domain-specific initiatives (e.g. the AI-KG [5] for Computer Science and the Cooperation Databank [22] for the social sciences), and domain-independent projects such as the Open Research Knowledge Graph (ORKG) project[4]. These initiatives focus on representing research outputs in terms of their content, i.e. describing approach, evaluation methods, results etc., rather than publication context such as year, authors and publication venues. This type of novel representations allows to automatise not only the search for new research, but also to compare it at large scale.

Some work has focused on developing systems that aid with mining claims in the existing literature. The AKminer (Academic Knowledge Miner) system [9] was introduced to automatically mine useful concepts and relationships from scientific literature and visually present them in the form of a knowledge graph. Similarly, [17] uses text-mining to automatically extract claims and contributions from scientific literature and enrich them through entity linking methods. Supervised distant learning was used by [14,24] to extract PICO sentences from clinical trial reports and support evidence-based medicine.

Machine-Supported Hypothesis Discovery. Automated hypothesis discovery using intelligent systems has been interest of study for a long time. Earliest work include the ARROWSMITH discovery support system [21] to help scientists in finding complementary literature for their studies and formulate a

---

[3] https://linkeddata.cochrane.org/pico-ontology.
[4] https://www.orkg.org/orkg/.

testable hypothesis based on the two sets, and the work of [1], which used various machine learning techniques to discover patterns, co-occurrences and correlations in biological data. These approaches inspired the work of [20], which relies on a scientific text collection to discover hypotheses, via Medical Subject Headings (MeSH)-term based text-mining.

Biomedical literature was also used by [10] to develop a link discovery method based on classification, where concepts are learnt and used as a basis for hypothesis generation. An Inductive Matrix Completion method was presented by [12], where the discovered gene-disease associations where supported by different types of evidence learnt as latent factors. The Knowledge Integration Toolkit (KnIT) [11] used methods such matrix factorization and graph diffusion to reason over a network of scientific publications in the biomedical field to generate new and testable hypotheses. The work of [15] shows how scientific insights can be generated using machine support also in the field of astronomy and geosciences. Their model allows to create multiple variants of hypothesised phenomena and their corresponding physical properties; these are matched in the existing empirical data, and scientists can both refine them and use them to justify a stated research hypothesis. The DISK ontology was also used in the field of neuroscience for automated hypothesis assessment [6].

Knowledge Graph Embeddings for Link Prediction. Machine learning methods for knowledge graph completion (or link prediction) use inductive techniques, mostly based on knowledge graph embeddings or rule/axiom mining, to locally and logically predict the likelihood of certain link between two nodes to exist [13]. Currently, the tensor decomposition ComplEx method [23] has proven to be the most stable in terms of performance and scalability [2]. Link prediction methods have been previously used for hypothesis discovery. Authors of [16] first create a knowledge graph from biomedical data and then convert it to a lower dimensional space using graph embeddings. The learnt embeddings are then used to train a recurrent neural network model to predict new drug therapies against diseases. A similar approach is the one of [19] to generate hypotheses on re-purposing drugs for rare diseases; the method relies on graph embeddings learnt over a large knowledge graph including information from the literature of pharmacology, genetics and pathology.

3   Background and Motivating Scenario

The COoperation DAtabank Knowledge Graph. The COoperation DAtabank consists in ~3,000 studies from the social and behavioural sciences published in 3 languages and annotated with more than 300 cooperation-related features, including characteristics of the sample participating in the study (e.g. sample size, average age of sample, percentage of males, country of participants), characteristics of the experimental paradigm (structure of the social dilemma, incentives, repeated trial data), and quantitative results of the experiment (e.g. mean levels of cooperation, variance in cooperation, and effect sizes). The dataset was designed to be fully compliant with the F.A.I.R. principles, and has been published as an openly available knowledge graph[5] to allow domain experts to perform their analyses in minutes, instead of many months of painstaking work [22].

Before continuing with the knowledge graph structure, we need to familiarise the reader with the basic concepts of experimental science. Studies using this methodology may observe a relation between two (one independent, one dependent) variables, which can be quantified as an effect size (representing the quantitative result). The goal of the single experiments carried within in a study is to test whether the dependent variable (DV) changes for when modifying the value of the Independent Variable (IV), which indicates there is a relationship between the two variables. In the case of the Databank, one could imagine an experiment aimed at studying the impact (effect size) of a person's social values (independent variable) over her willingness to cooperate (dependent variable). With this in mind, the CODA knowledge graph includes publications consisting of a `cdo:Paper` class that links to an arbitrary set of `cdo:Study`, i.e. experiments performed in different settings and with different goals. Additional metadata about the paper such as publication date, authors etc. are included as properties of a `cdo:DOI` class. Each `cdo:Study` links to one or more conditions tested, represented by the class `cdo:Observation`, that are in turn modelled as comparisons of one or two different `cdo:Treatment`.

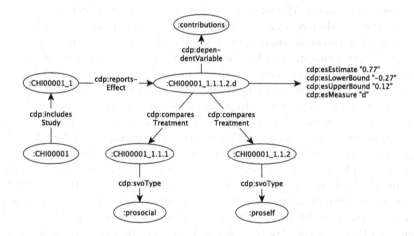

Fig. 1. Example of an observation comparing prosocial vs. proself behaviour.

In a practical example, Fig. 1 shows the paper :`CHI00001` including the study :`CHI00001_1`, which in turns reports the observation :`CHI00001_1.1.1.2.d` comparing treatment :`CHI00001_1.1.1` and :`CHI00001_1.1.2` (we call them T1 and T2 for simplicity). Treatments consist in the experimental settings that the experimenter modifies with the goal of testing how and if the cooperation between

---

[5] http://data.cooperationdatabank.org/.

participants of a game varies significantly. In our example, the experimenter manipulated the property `cdp:svoType` which, recalling what stated above, consists then in the independent variable observed. This is confirmed by the fact that T1 and T2 have a different value for the property (`:prosocial` and `:proself` respectively). Similar to `cdp:svoType`, any RDF property whose domain is the class `cdo:Treatment` is organised in a domain-specific taxonomy of independent variables, representing information relative to cooperation in social dilemmas. Finally, in order to represent how and how much the cooperation varies during an observation/experiment, we use the class `cdo:DependentVariable` for the DV and the datatype property `cdp:esEstimate` for the effect size measurement, e.g. `CHI00001_1.1.1.2.d` measures the DV `:contributions` and its effect size has a value of 0.77[6]. The positive effect size reported by the experimental observation means that T1 scored higher on cooperation than T2, indicating that participants with a pro-social value orientation showed a more cooperative behaviour than participants who had a pro-self value orientation.

Challenge, Solution and Novelty. In the scenario above, it is natural to see how the CODA knowledge graph intrinsically represents research hypotheses that were tested in the human cooperation literature. In other words, one can consider each `cdo:Observation` subgraph as a research hypothesis that aims at testing whether there exists a relation between the `cdo:IndependentVariable` and `cdo:DependentVariable`. The effect size value of each observation then tells us the strength of such relation, identified by the experiment performed to validate the hypothesis. The research question we ask is therefore: is it possible to learn new, plausible observations starting for the representations recorded in CODA? More generally, how to support domain experts in producing new research hypotheses through a more automated method? The solution we propose is to frame the problem of learning research hypotheses as a link prediction task, where we exploit the existing `cdo:Observation` subgraph structures to learn new unseen triples involving a `cdo:IndependentVariable` and `cdo:DependentVariable`. Our hypothesis is that entities and relationships neighbouring the predicted links can help completing the new research hypotheses. Our work main novelty is applying a hybrid method to automatically support social scientists for the first time, following similar approaches in the biomedical field. We train a knowledge graph embedding model to predict the likelihood of a new possible association between an IV and a DV. We then develop a system that suggests new possible research hypotheses including both triples existing in CODA and new predicted triples according to a predefined structure. Accuracy and meaningfulness of the discovered hypotheses are assessed quantitatively and qualitatively in a user-study based on the domain expertise of social scientists from the field.

---

[6] CODA contains two types of effect size measures, i.e. the correlation coefficient ρ and the standardized mean difference d, which can be easily converted to one another. For simplicity, we will only refer to Cohen's d values from now on.

4 Approach

The proposed approach includes three steps: a pre-processing phase for data selection and generation of the model input (Sect. 4.1), a learning phase including parameter tuning, model training, and link prediction (Sect. 4.2), and a last phase for the automated generation of hypotheses (Sect. 4.3).

4.1 Pre-processing

The first step is to choose the right amount of CODA information to retrieve, and create an input for the embedding model to be able to predict new triples.

Observation Selection. First, we define a set of criteria to select the CODA observations, namely:

1. instances of the class `cdo:Observation`;
2. observations reporting using Cohen's d as effect size measure;
3. observations comparing two treatments;
4. observations linking to an instance of a `cdo:DependentVariable`.

The SPARQL query used to get the observations can be found online[7], and results in 4,721 observations, the study, paper and DOI that reported them, the effect size with confidence levels, the experimental design, and sample size and standard deviation per treatment pair.

A further refinement is performed by analysing the independent variables of each observation. We identify the properties-values for which the two treatments compared by an observation differ on, e.g. `cdp:svoType/:prosocial` vs. `cdp:svoType/:proself` in the example of the previous section. To prevent noise and reduce complexity, we dropped observations that had no differing predicates (errors attributed to the large sparsity of the data and to human annotation), or that might differ for more than one property. This left 2,444 observations to train the model, coming from 632 papers and 858 studies, and including 128 unique IVs and 2 unique DVs.

Data Permutation. Since KG embedding methods are generally not capable of learning continuous variables, we learn effect sizes as categorical instead of continuous information. This is also motivated by the fact that Cohen's d is in fact a measure that can be interpreted categorically [18]. To this end, we created a new RDF property `cdp:esType` and a set of 5 instances of the class `cdo:ESType` that a `cdo:Observation` might point to, representing the 5 bins mapping the continuous effect size values to Cohen's categories[8]. Table 1 shows the ranges for each bin/instance, and their respective effect size types.

---

[7] https://data.cooperationdatabank.org/coda/-/queries/link-prediction-selection-query.

[8] Due to the relatively small sets, medium and large effects were grouped together.

Table 1. Effect size ranges, their interpretation and the respective instance created.

Effect size range	Intepretation	Instance
−Infinity, −0.5	Large/medium negative correlation	`:largeMediumNegativeES`
−0.5, −0.2	Small negative correlation	`:smallNegativeES`
−0.2, 0.2	No correlation	`:nullFinding`
0.2, 0.5	Small positive correlation	`:smallPositiveES`
0.5, infinity	Large/medium positive correlation	`:largeMediumPositiveES`

As also explained in Sect. 3, an effect size is an indication of the size of the correlation between an independent and a dependent variable, measured based on the different IV values that two treatments take during an experimentation. This means that, in order to predict a new correlation between IV and DV, one would have to predict multiple triples, i.e. at least one per treatment (and their respective IV values). In order to simplify the task, we summarise the factor that influences the effect size into a single node, by considering IV values pairs as single hypotheses. We therefore combine all possible values for a given IV property into pairs, assigning a hypothesis number to each pair, and create a new node that is linked to the original T1/T2 values through the property `cdp:hypothesis`. The new nodes, shown e.g. in Table 2, are then used for the hypothesis generation. For continuous properties reporting many different values in the object position, four different ranges were automatically created to prevent the generation of an excessive amount of hypotheses. Similarly, pairs with the same IV values in a different order were considered as the same hypothesis (e.g. T1 = proself/T2 = prosocial and T1 = prosocial/T2 = proself were both linked to `:SVOtypeH2`), but the effect size node of the observation was switched (positive to negative, or vice versa) to maintain the direction of the correlation coherent.

Table 2. Hypothesis nodes based on combinations of IV values for T1 and T2.

IV	T1 value	T2 value	Hypothesis node
SVO type	Individualist	Prosocial	`:SVOtype_H1`
SVO type	Prosocial	Proself	`:SVOtype_H2`
SVO type	Individualist	Altruist	`:SVOtype_H3`

We then link the created hypothesis nodes to the dependent variable nodes using three new predicates, related to the type of correlation that is observed: `cdp:hasPositiveEffectOn`, `cdp:hasNoEffectOn`, `cdp:hasNegativeEffectOn`. These properties are based on the statistical significance of the observation, computed using the 95% confidence interval for the effect size. A confidence interval measures the imprecision of the computed effect size in an experiment. When the interval does not include 0, it can be inferred that the association is statistically significant ($p < 0.05$). In other words, the confidence interval tells us how trustworthy is the observation we are analysing, in terms of effect size, population estimate, and direction of the effect. Depending on the confidence interval, we use :hasNoEffectOn if the effect size is not significant, while :hasNegativeEffectOn and :hasPositiveEffectOn are used with observations indicating a significant negative and positive correlation between IV and DV, respectively. When no confidence interval was given in the data, we derive the direction of the correlation using the rule of thumb as reported of [18]: observations with an effect size below -0.2 got a negative effect property, observations that reported effect sizes above 0.2 got a positive effect property, and observations with an effect size between -0.2 and 0.2 got a no effect property. This led us to a total of 751 positive effect triples, 1,017 no effect triples and 676 negative effect triples.

Dataset Creation. The last step of the pre-processing task consists in the conversion into learnable subgraphs, i.e. sets of triples. To do this, we use part of the information already in the data, namely observation ID, the independent and dependent variables, the IV values for the two treatments, and combine them with the computed effect size type, the hypothesis number, and relationship to the dependent variable. A construct query[9] was used to generate subgraphs as depicted in Fig. 2 for 2,444 observations. This led to a dataset of 29,339 triples, that served as input for the link prediction model.

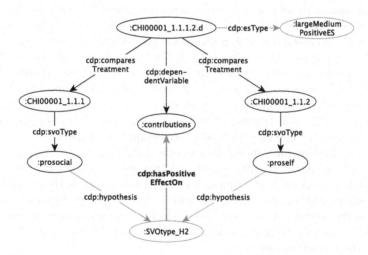

Fig. 2. New graph for the observation CHI00001_1.1.1.2.d used as input for the link prediction task. In red, the nodes and edges created. In bold, the link to be predicted. (Color figure online)

---

[9] https://data.cooperationdatabank.org/coda/-/queries/Rosaline-Construct-Link-Prediction.

Table 3. Final parameter configuration.

Parameter	Value
Batches_count	555
Epochs	100
k (dimensionality)	200
eta (# neg. samples generated per each pos.)	15
Loss	multiclass_nll
Embedding_model_params	{'negative_corruption_entities': 'all'}
LP regulariser params	{'p':1, 'lambda':1e-5}
Xavier initialiser params	{'uniform': False}
Adam optimizer params	{'lr': 0.0005}

4.2 Learning and Predicting Triples

Training and Testing. We use the created dataset to learn a model predicting unseen triples to be used in new hypotheses. Strictly speaking, the prediction consists in identifying triples including a hypothesis number, an effect size predicate and a dependent variable, e.g. ⟨:SVOtype_H2 cdp:hasPositiveEffectOn :contributions⟩. To do this, all triples reporting a negative or a positive effect were gathered. We decided not to make predictions for the no-effect triples, as experts might be less interested in non-interesting relations between variables to frame their hypotheses. Investigating this for future work could be interesting. From the total 1,427 effect triples, the 243 unique hypotheses in subject position, the 2 unique predicates and the 2 unique dependent variables in object position were used to learn how to generate new combinations. This yielded to $243 * 2 * 2 = 972$ total triples, of which 412 were already in the dataset and marked as "seen", while the other 560 were denoted as "unseen".

We used the ComplEx model to learn the likelihood of each triple. We first split the dataset into a training set of 24,539 triples, a test set of 2,400 triples, and a validation set of 2,400 triples. A corruption strategy is then used to generate negative statements. Parameter tuning was finally performed to explore impact on the model performance, see Table 3 for the final configuration. Standard metrics such as mean reciprocal rank, hits@N and mean rank were used to evaluate the trained model.

Link Prediction. The learnt model was used to compute ranks and scores for unseen triples. Ranks indicate the position at which the test set triple was found when performing link prediction, while scores are the returned raw scores generated by the model. Probabilities of unseen triples are also calculated by calibrating the model. We set a positive base rate of 0.5 (50%) to indicate the ratio between positive vs. negative triples. After calibration, a probability for each unseen triple was predicted. We then obtained their ranks, score and probabilities for the 560 unseen triples, to be later used during the hypotheses generation step. A sample of these is in Table 4 below.

Table 4. Prediction example of unseen triples.

Statement	Rank	Score	Prob.
`:iteratedStrategy_H6` `cdp:hasPositiveEffectOn` `:cooperation`	1	7.38	0.98
`:iteratedStrategy_H9` `cdp:hasPositiveEffectOn` `:cooperation`	2	7.32	0.98
			...
`:uncertaintyTarget_H1` `cdp:hasPositiveEffectOn` `:cooperation`	3816	0.10	0.19
`:exitOption_H1` `cdp:hasNegativeEffectOn` `:contributions`	4659	−0.03	0.17

4.3 Hypotheses Generation

The final step is to automatically generate human-interpretable hypotheses, based on the unseen triples predicted by the model. Each statement from Table 4 was converted into a readable text using a prefixed structure following the DISK ontology. A *hypothesis statement* was created by disassembling the triples into respectively the independent variable (the predicted subject), the type of effect (the predicted predicate) and dependent variable (the predicted object). The *hypothesis evidence* was created by querying the CODA knowledge graph for labels of both IVs and DVs, and by converting the effect type property into decapitalised words with spacing. We also retrieve the description of both the IV class and the relevant IV values. The *hypothesis history* was built by retrieving the DOIs of papers that studied that combination of IV values. An example of a generated hypothesis is shown below.

Hypothesis Statement
Partner's group membership has negative effect on contributions

Hypothesis Evidence
Dependent   Variable   (DV):   https://data.cooperationdatabank.org/id/dependentvariable/contributions

Independent   Variable   (IV):   https://data.cooperationdatabank.org/vocab/prop/targetMembership
Whether the participant is interacting with a partner identified as ingroup, outgroup, or stranger.

The IV values to compare in the treatments (T1, T2) are :

Treatment	IV value	Description
T1	ingroup	Partner(s) is a member of the participant's group
T2	ingroup_and _outgroup	When an experimental treatment explicitly provides information that a partner or group belongs to both an ingroup and an outgroup

Hypothesis History
http://dx.doi.org/10.1016/j.joep.2013.06.005
http://dx.doi.org/10.1177/0146167205282149
http://dx.doi.org/10.1016/j.ijintrel.2011.02.017

Implementation. The current approach was implemented using Python 3.7.7. The ComplEx model was implemented using the Ampligraph[10] library. All the code and results can be found on GitHub[11]. The queries were made using the SPARQL API service of the CODA knowledge graph, hosted by TriplyDB[12].

5   Evaluation

We first quantitatively and qualitatively evaluate the model performance through known metrics and inspection of the independent variable embeddings. We then evaluate the generated hypotheses through domain experts.

5.1   Model Performance

We compare our model to the TransE, ComplEx and DistMult models trained with their default parameters. The resulting performance metrics are shown in Table 5. We used three different types of metrics as indication of how well the models were capable of predicting the triples in the test set: mean reciprocal rank (MRR), hits@N, and mean rank (MR). Reciprocal rank measures the correctness of a ranked triple, and mean RR is defined as $MRR = \frac{1}{|Q|} \sum_{i=1}^{|Q|} \frac{1}{rank_i}$, where Q

---

[10] https://github.com/Accenture/AmpliGraph.
[11] https://github.com/roosyay/CoDa_Hypotheses.
[12] https://coda.triply.cc/.

is the number of triples and $rank_i$ the rank of the ith triple predicted by the model. Hits@N indicates how many triples are ranked in the top N positions when ranked against corruptions, i.e.: $Hits@N = \frac{1}{|Q|} \sum_{(s,p,o) \in Q} ind(rank(s,p,o) \leq N)$ where Q is the triples in the test set, (s,p,o) is a triple $\in Q$, and $ind(\cdot)$ is an indicator function returning 1 if the positive triple is in the top N triples, 0 otherwise. We use three values for N, namely 1, 3 and 10. Finally, the MR score is the sum of the true ranks divided by the total amount of ranks, defined as $MR = \frac{1}{|Q|} \sum_{i=1}^{|Q|} rank_{(s,p,o)_i}$. Note that the MR score is not robust to outliers, and is therefore only taken into account together with the other metrics. Overall, these scores indicate a reasonable performance of ComplEx, and confirm our idea that link prediction methods in general can be used for hypothesis discovery. Some room for improvement is left for future work, namely applying our method to other datasets, and fine-tuning additional machine learning techniques.

Table 5. Model comparison.

	MRR	Hits@10	Hits@3	Hits@1	MR
ComplEx	0.60	0.66	0.62	0.56	736.77
DistMult	0.48	0.62	0.57	0.38	683.31
TransE	0.30	0.46	0.35	0.20	330.42
Tuned ComplEx	0.68	0.75	0.69	0.64	279.91

5.2 Qualitative Analysis

To get insight into how the model effectively learnt the data, we created a visualisation of the main independent variables (see Fig. 3). To do this, the 400-dimensional embeddings of 128 unique independent variables were retrieved from the trained model and transformed into an array of (128, 400). We used a UMAP reduction to reduce the 400 dimensions to 2 only, allowing then to display the embeddings in a 2-dimensional space. In order to find the optimal number of clusters in this space, we used an elbow method measuring the Within-Cluster Sums of Squares (WCSS) without finding any significant distinction. We therefore used a silhouette analysis, revealing that 23 clusters was the best balance between the number of clusters and a relatively high silhouette score (silhouette score = 0.49). Clusters were obtained using scikit-learn's KMeans (K = 23) and the visualisation was obtained using the Matplotlib package.

As shown in Fig. 3, most clusters are groups of variables that are rdfs:subClassOf the same class. For example, in clusters 3, 11 and 15, all the variables related to respectively punishment, emotion and leadership are clustered together. Clusters such as 2 and 13 seem to have less cohesion, as no overarching topics can be found that group IVs together. This can be due by a larger variety of the studies that analysed these IV, and potentially a lack of more data. Both clusters also include variables related to reward, showing that studies with reward-related IV are more heterogeneous and were not grouped together.

Fig. 3. Independent variables grouped in 23 clusters. Please cfr. Visualisation.ipynb on Github for better quality.

5.3 Domain Expert Evaluation

In order to qualitatively evaluate the generated hypotheses, 5 domain experts from the CODA team were asked to fill out a user-study. A Google form was created where the experts, after receiving information about the background and the goal of the study, were shown the 10 most likely and 10 most unlikely hypotheses predicted by the model. The 20 hypotheses were shown in a random order using the structure presented in Sect. 4.3. The experts were asked to indicate which 10 hypotheses they considered likely, and which 10 unlikely. A final part for remarks was also included.

Table 6 shows how the experts rated the likelihood of the hypotheses. These can be easily read as "[Hypothesis Statement] *when comparing* [T1 value] vs. [T2 value]", e.g. "SVO type has negative effect on cooperation when comparing a group of individualists vs. a group of competitors". Two hypotheses including miscellaneous IV values did not make sense according to the experts and were omitted. Overall, the majority of the experts rated 12 out of 18 hypotheses as

Table 6. Expert evaluation. #L and #UL refer to the number of experts scoring a hypothesis as likely and unlikely, respectively. *Pred.* indicates the model prediction.

	Hypothesis statement	T1 value	T2 value	#L	#UL	Pred.
1	MPCR has positive effect on contributions	$(-0.401, 0.3)$	$(0.3, 0.5)$	3	2	Likely
2	Partner's group membership has negative effect on contributions	Ingroup	Ingroup and outgroup	0	5	Likely
3	Intergroup competition has positive effect on contributions	Individual group	Intergroup competition	4	1	Likely
4	Anonymity manipulation has positive effect on cooperation	High	Low	3	2	Likely
5	Time pressure has negative effect on contributions	Time-pressure	Time delay	2	3	Likely
6	SVO type has negative effect on cooperation	Individualist	Competitor	3	2	likely
7	Ethnicity (us) has positive effect on cooperation	White	Black or African American	1	4	Likely
8	Iterated strategy has positive effect on cooperation	Predominantly cooperative	Other	4	1	Likely
9	Nationality has negative effect on contributions	JPN	AUS	3	2	Unlikely
10	Exit option has negative effect on contributions	0	1	2	3	Unlikely
11	Exit option has positive effect on contributions	0	1	1	4	Unlikely
12	Emotion has negative effect on cooperation	Neutral	Disappointment	2	3	Unlikely
13	Emotion has positive effect on cooperation	Neutral	Disappointment	2	3	Unlikely
14	Preference for conditional cooperation has negative effect on cooperation	Freeriders	Hump-shaped contributors	4	1	Unlikely
15	Uncertainty target has positive effect on cooperation	Loss	Threshold	4	1	Unlikely
16	Iterated strategy has positive effect on contributions	Tit-for-tat	Tit-for-tat+1	1	4	Unlikely
17	Preference for conditional cooperation has positive effect on cooperation	Freeriders	Hump-shaped-_contributors	1	4	Unlikely
18	Uncertainty target has negative effect on cooperation	Loss	Threshold	0	5	Unlikely

the model did, while only 6 hypotheses were rated opposite of the model. Out of 5 experts, 2 rated more than 9 hypotheses the same as the model, which is higher than chance level, while the other 3 experts scored exactly on chance level. No experts scored below chance level. It should be noted that some experts took more time to fill the evaluation form, as they provided more details in the open-ended questions, and some variety could be seen in how experts rated the hypotheses. We relate this to the complexity of social science data, causing different perspectives to reach different conclusions. Looking at the overall average however, the experts rated 10 hypotheses the same as the model did. This shows that the model output is not random, and that similarities between the expert opinions and the model were found. More in general, we consider our results encouraging enough to confirm the idea that a link prediction-based approach is a valuable method to predict hypotheses over structured data.

6 Conclusions

We have introduced a hybrid approach to automatically support domain experts to identify new research hypotheses. Our novel solution is based on a link prediction task over a knowledge graph in the social science domain, where new edges between nodes are predicted in order to create fully formulated hypotheses in the form of a hypothesis statement, a hypothesis evidence and a hypothesis history. The quantitative and qualitative evaluation carried using experts in the field has shown encouraging results, namely that a simple combination of machine learning and knowledge graphs methods can support designing more complex systems for the automated scientific discovery.

Improvements of our approach could be made as future work, namely by optimising the data modelling and the machine learning approach for social science data. Such type of data has in fact an uncertain nature, and missing information can create an inner bias in the model and have implications for the results. Solutions to cope with such bias should be investigated. As mentioned, the approach should be also tested on datasets of different domains to see how it could perform. Some information from the data was lost due to binning continuous variables (including effect size values), and the learning task could be improved on this aspect. An end-to-end task could be envisioned to learn the subgraphs directly, instead of pre-processing them and reducing the task to predicting one link between two entities. Finally, our model generally predicted only links with the highest probabilities based on statistical frequency learnt from the data structure. An interesting avenue would be to investigate what makes an hypothesis interesting other than popularity, and how to learn them.

References

1. Bahler, D., Stone, B., Wellington, C., Bristol, D.W.: Symbolic, neural, and Bayesian machine learning models for predicting carcinogenicity of chemical compounds. J. Chem. Inf. Comput. Sci. **40**(4), 906–914 (2000). https://doi.org/10.1021/ci990116i
2. Bianchi, F., Rossiello, G., Costabello, L., Palmonari, M., Minervini, P.: Knowledge graph embeddings and explainable AI (April 2020). https://doi.org/10.3233/SSW200011
3. Chen, N.C., Drouhard, M., Kocielnik, R., Suh, J., Aragon, C.R.: Using machine learning to support qualitative coding in social science: shifting the focus to ambiguity. ACM Trans. Interact. Intell. Syst. **8**(2), 1–3 (2018). https://doi.org/10.1145/3185515

4. Clark, T., Ciccarese, P.N., Goble, C.A.: Micropublications: a semantic model for claims, evidence, arguments and annotations in biomedical communications. J. Biomed. Semant. **5**(1), 1–33 (2014). https://doi.org/10.1186/2041-1480-5-28
5. Dessì, D., Osborne, F., Reforgiato Recupero, D., Buscaldi, D., Motta, E., Sack, H.: AI-KG: an automatically generated knowledge graph of artificial intelligence. In: Pan, J.Z., et al. (eds.) ISWC 2020. LNCS, vol. 12507, pp. 127–143. Springer, Cham (2020). https://doi.org/10.1007/978-3-030-62466-8_9
6. Garijo, D., et al.: Towards automated hypothesis testing in neuroscience. In: Gadepally, V., et al. (eds.) DMAH/Poly -2019. LNCS, vol. 11721, pp. 249–257. Springer, Cham (2019). https://doi.org/10.1007/978-3-030-33752-0_18
7. Garijo, D., Gil, Y., Ratnakar, V.: The DISK hypothesis ontology: capturing hypothesis evolution for automated discovery. CEUR Workshop Proc. **2065**, 40–46 (2017)
8. Groth, P., Gibson, A., Velterop, J.: The anatomy of a nanopublication. Inf. Serv. Use **30**(1–2), 51–56 (2010). https://doi.org/10.3233/ISU-2010-0613
9. Huang, S., Wan, X.: AKMiner: domain-specific knowledge graph mining from academic literatures. In: Lin, X., Manolopoulos, Y., Srivastava, D., Huang, G. (eds.) WISE 2013. LNCS, vol. 8181, pp. 241–255. Springer, Heidelberg (2013). https://doi.org/10.1007/978-3-642-41154-0_18
10. Katukuri, J.R., Xie, Y., Raghavan, V.V., Gupta, A.: Hypotheses generation as supervised link discovery with automated class labeling on large-scale biomedical concept networks. BMC Genomics **13**(Suppl 3), 12–15 (2012). https://doi.org/10.1186/1471-2164-13-s3-s5
11. Nagarajan, M., et al.: Predicting future scientific discoveries based on a networked analysis of the past literature. In: Proceedings of the 21th ACM SIGKDD International Conference on Knowledge Discovery and Data Mining, pp. 2019–2028 (2015)
12. Natarajan, N., Dhillon, I.S.: Inductive matrix completion for predicting gene-disease associations. Bioinf. **30**(12), 60–68 (2014). https://doi.org/10.1093/bioinformatics/btu269
13. Nickel, M., Murphy, K., Tresp, V., Gabrilovich, E.: A review of relational machine learning for knowledge graphs (2016). https://doi.org/10.1109/JPROC.2015.2483592
14. Nye, B., et al.: A corpus with multi-level annotations of patients, interventions and outcomes to support language processing for medical literature. In: ACL 2018, vol. 1, pp. 197–207 (2018). https://doi.org/10.18653/v1/p18-1019
15. Pankratius, V., et al.: Computer-aided discovery: toward scientific insight generation with machine support why scientists need machine support for discovery search. IEEE Intell. Syst. **31**(4), 3–10 (2016). https://doi.org/10.1109/MIS.2016.60
16. Sang, S., et al.: GrEDeL: a knowledge graph embedding based method for drug discovery from biomedical literatures. IEEE Access **7**(2016), 8404–8415 (2019). https://doi.org/10.1109/ACCESS.2018.2886311
17. Sateli, B., Witte, R.: Semantic representation of scientific literature: bringing claims, contributions and named entities onto the Linked Open Data cloud. PeerJ Comput. Sci. **2015**(12), 1-e37 (2015). https://doi.org/10.7717/peerj-cs.37
18. Sawilowsky, S.S.: New Effect Size Rules of Thumb. J. Mod. Appl. Stat. Methods **8**(2), 597–599 (2009). https://doi.org/10.22237/jmasm/1257035100

19. Sosa, D.N., Derry, A., Guo, M., Wei, E., Brinton, C., Altman, R.B.: A literature-based knowledge graph embedding method for identifying drug repurposing opportunities in rare diseases. Pacific Symposium on Biocomputing **25**, 463–474 (2020). https://doi.org/10.1142/9789811215636_0041

20. Srinivasan, P.: Text mining: generating hypotheses from MEDLINE. J. Am. Soc. Inf. Sci. Technol. **55**(5), 396–413 (2004). https://doi.org/10.1002/asi.10389

21. Swanson, D.R., Smalheiser, N.R.: An interactive system for finding complementary literatures: a stimulus to scientific discovery. Artif. Intell. **91**(2), 183–203 (1997). https://doi.org/10.1016/S0004-3702(97)00008-8

22. Tiddi, I., Balliet, D., ten Teije, A.: Fostering scientific meta-analyses with knowledge graphs: a case-study. In: Harth, A., et al. (eds.) ESWC 2020. LNCS, vol. 12123, pp. 287–303. Springer, Cham (2020). https://doi.org/10.1007/978-3-030-49461-2_17

23. Trouillon, T., Welbl, J., Riedel, S., Ciaussier, E., Bouchard, G.: Complex embeddings for simple link prediction. In: 33rd International Conference on Machine Learning, ICML 2016, vol. 5, pp. 3021–3032 (2016)

24. Wallace, B.C., Kuiper, J., Sharma, A., Zhu, M., Marshall, I.J.: Extracting PICO sentences from clinical trial reports using supervised distant supervision (2016)

25. Ware, M., Mabe, M.: The STM report: an overview of scientific and scholarly journal publishing (2015)

Problems to Solve Before You Die

Towards a Linked Open Code

Ahmed El Amine Djebri[1]📷, Antonia Ettorre[1]📷, and Johann Mortara[2(✉)]📷

[1] Université Côte d'Azur, Inria, CNRS, I3S, Sophia Antipolis, France
{ahmed-elamine.djebri,antonia.ettorre}@univ-cotedazur.fr
[2] Université Côte d'Azur, CNRS, I3S, Sophia Antipolis, France
johann.mortara@univ-cotedazur.fr

Abstract. In the last two decades, the Linked Open Data paradigm has been experiencing exponential growth. Regularly, new datasets and ontologies are made publicly available, and novel projects are initiated to stimulate their continuous development and reuse, pushing more and more actors to adhere to the Semantic Web principles. The guidelines provided by the Semantic Web community allow to (*i*) homogeneously represent, (*ii*) uniquely identify, and (*iii*) uniformly reference any piece of information. However, the same standards do not allow defining and referencing the methods to exploit it: functions, procedures, algorithms, and code in general, are left out of this interconnected world. In this paper, we present our vision for a Web with *Linked Open Code* in which functionscould be accessed and used as Linked Data, allowing logic harnessing the latter to be semantically described and *FAIR*-ly accessible. Hereafter, we describe the challenges presented by the implementation of our vision. We propose first insights on how to concretize it, and we provide a non-exhaustive list of communities that could benefit from such an ideal.

Keywords: Semantic Web · Ontologies · Feature identification · Linked data · Linked open code

1 Introduction

The Web is growing stronger semantically. More ready-to-consume data, services, and AI-based systems relying on Semantic Web are regularly published. We witness the emergence of the Semantic Web in different unrelated fields such as AI, IoT, networking, medicine, or biology. Within each, papers are being published, wikis are being created, and code is made available. All these different fields share their data through a unique structure, reaching the vision of Tim Berners-Lee who mentioned: *"Semantic Web promotes this synergy: even agents that were not expressly designed to work together can transfer data among themselves when the data come with semantics."* [1].

While Semantic Web offers ways to store metadata to reuse them semantically, code is not used on the Semantic Web to its full potential. Hence, the

© Springer Nature Switzerland AG 2021
R. Verborgh et al. (Eds.): ESWC 2021, LNCS 12731, pp. 497–505, 2021.
https://doi.org/10.1007/978-3-030-77385-4_29

problem we seek to tackle is: *how to take advantage of code as a pre-existing, structured, and functional type of data in Semantic Web?*

Code for data manipulation is actually either (*i*) not needed for simple operations as existing standards offer sufficient functionalities (*e.g.* functions in SPARQL [2]) or (*ii*) used at a higher level in the Semantic Web stack, where users download and build code from open repositories provided to them by the data provider. However, these two approaches exhibit some limitations: in (*i*), the capacities of SPARQL functions are limited and in (*ii*), despite the availability of the code on the Web, the possibility to have a link between the semantics of data and the semantics of code is not fully harnessed. We believe that code should be treated as a special type of data. The use of functions or methods on Semantic Web is usually studied for limited use-cases, such as schema validation (*i.e.* `sh:JSFunction` representing JavaScript functions to be used in *SHACL* engines). We think that the link between code and Semantic Web remains superficial. Functions are not semantically shared as and with data.

We argue that functions, as parts of code, are easily referenceable and can be identified by a defined set of metadata. However, defining their semantics is challenging as functions can be seen from different levels of granularity. Finally, although source code can already be browsed and referenced online at multiple levels of granularity by platforms such as *Software Heritage* [3] or GitHub's permalinks, they do not provide any description of the functionality implemented by the code, thus limiting the code reusability.

2 Code on Semantic Web

Data published on the Semantic Web are often followed by instructions on how to access, read, manipulate, and query them. Ontologies are documented in scientific literature and wikis, offering insights on their semantics, and tools for data manipulation are being provided. An increasing number of developers give open access to public source code repositories hosted on data providers such as GitHub. Academics can publish code directly alongside their paper[1] for frameworks they developed, encouraged by new policies from editors to foster reproduction and reuse of research results[2].

In contrast with Linked Data, code files are often seen as single documents on the Web as the transition between the *document-based* view and the *data-based* one has not affected them on a fine-grained level. Hence, the link between data and the code artifacts directly involved with it remains limited. We believe that since both resources (data and code artifacts related to them) are available on the Web, an effort should be made to provide code in the same format as and alongside data.

---

[1] https://blog.arxiv.org/2020/10/08/new-arxivlabs-feature-provides-instant-access-to-code/.

[2] https://www.acm.org/publications/policies/artifact-review-and-badging-current.

2.1   Adapting Code to Semantic Web

According to the *Web Service Modeling Ontology Primer* (WSMO) [4], a function is not only a syntactical entity but also has defined semantics that allows evaluating the function if concrete input values for the parameters are given. However, the structure of functions defined in most programming languages is more complex than in the definition provided by the WSMO as their computation may rely on data other than the values specified as its parameters such as (*i*) results of other functions defined in the same project or an external library, or (*ii*) attributes of an object for object-oriented methods. These values are provided to the functions by their execution environment, as the *Java Virtual Machine* (JVM) for Java-based systems.

For a function to be compliant with our case, it should (*i*) depend on the standard libraries of a language-version, either directly or transitively through other referenceable functions, and (*ii*) not rely on out-of-scope variables. Property (*i*) applies recursively to any function call inside the function itself. If a code is to be written in an inline mode, any other function call within the same function must be replaced by a set of instructions depending only on the standard libraries of a defined language-version. Achieving (*ii*) requires binding out-of-scope variables to their values.

Many challenges arise from this new definition, starting with the fact that the existing code repositories do not provide a "function-based" view. As a consequence, we should figure out how to turn those into referenceable, reusable resources. The following challenges, presented in Fig. 1, are to be addressed.

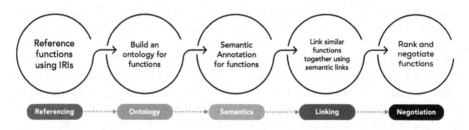

Fig. 1. Challenges to achieve a first working prototype of Linked Open Code

Referencing Functions. Function structure and signature in code make it easily recognizable. The signatures usually contain information such as the function's name and its typed arguments (*cf.* Fig. 2). Such information can be represented as linked data while attributing a unique identifier for function definitions.

The idea is to allow Linked Data providers to publish, following the Semantic Web principles, the code of functions, and their metadata. Furthermore, one may include an additional level of granularity to existing IRIs referencing code entities (repositories, folders, files, fragment), helping to reference functions and keep track of their provenance. For example, a code file archived on *Software*

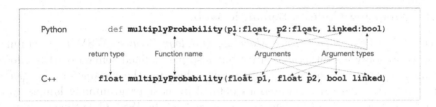

Fig. 2. Comparison of metadata provided function signature in Python and C++

Heritage with the IRI `swh:codeFile` helps addressing the function `fn` using the IRI `swh:codeFile_fn_1` (instead of referencing fragments of code with no defined semantics).

An Ontology for Functions. A crucial step to bring functions to the Semantic Web is the definition of an ontology to represent them. Such ontology must describe four aspects:

1. Versioning: the version of the function, programming language, provenance.
2. Relational: relations between functions (inclusion, dependencies, etc.).
3. Technical: code, arguments, typing, etc.
4. Licensing: although all open source licenses imply free-use and sharing of code[3], some may impose restrictions on the reuse (*e.g.* crediting the original author), hence this information needs to be provided to the user.

Annotating Functions Semantically. During this step, the defined functions are mapped each with their signature and feature metadata. An Abstract Syntax Tree (AST) analysis is applied on each to identify the components constituting the signature of the function (name, parameters, ...) that will then be used as values for the properties defined in the ontology. As a result, the user will be able to query the knowledge base to retrieve the function matching the given constraints. In parallel, a feature identification process is executed to identify the functionalities implemented by each function and annotate them accordingly. The whole process is depicted as in Fig. 3. Multiple techniques for the identification of features have already been proposed [5] and need to be adapted to our context.

Linking Functions. After having identified the features provided by the functions, we can use this information to semantically link functions fulfilling similar goals. Indeed, two functions being annotated with the same feature can be considered as different implementations for the same functionality as perceived by the user. Therefore, we can link them with standard predicates such as `owl:sameAs`, `skos:exactMatch`, `skos:closeMatch` or custom predicates offered by other existing ontologies. Alongside semantics, the dependency

---

[3] https://opensource.org/licenses.

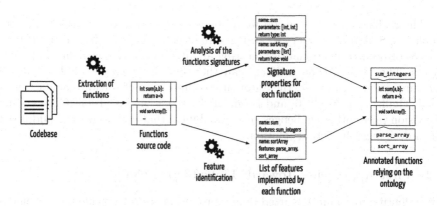

Fig. 3. Overview of the process for semantic annotation of functions

must be taken into account to link related functions together. Based on this criterion, functions relying on the results provided by other functions (including the function itself in the case of recursive calls) will be semantically connected.

Ranking Functions. The same functionality can be implemented in different ways and using different programming languages. To provide the most efficient implementation, there is a need to rank functions according to several parameters. One example can be the feedback of the community, as a repository where usage statistics for functions are being kept for ranking purposes, alongside other information such as the number of times a function was starred, forked, or upvoted by users. It is also possible to signal issues related to security flaws. Performance evaluation can also be used as a ranking criterion. A Semantic Web Engine like *Corese*[4], coded in *Java*, would use functionality implemented in *Java*. However, the same functionality, implemented in *Python*, can deliver better performance for the same tool if used with a *Python* wrapper. This aspect is meant to link code with experience. We can imagine users sharing their execution log, which may contain elements about hardware specification, operating system, language version, etc.

Negotiating Functions. Users may take advantage of the implemented content negotiation to get suitable function definitions for their use-cases. This is done by using HTTP headers, or non-HTTP methods like Query String Arguments (*QSA*). Users negotiate functions that suit their current environment to access and manipulate Linked Data. For instance, a user working with *Corese* may send a request to the function catalog, asking for the *Java* implementation of functions alongside their query for data. Negotiation can rely on the previous step, by proposing the best function to the users according to their specifications.

---

[4] https://github.com/Wimmics/corese.

The realization of this vision would be a framework through which the user would use SPARQL to query a catalog of functions (Sect. 2.1) for the implementations of needed functionalities meeting architectural and user-defined requirements. The fetched code artifacts can then be composed to build a tailored software system. However, the automatic composition of software artifacts is a whole challenge in itself [6] and is out of the scope of this vision. Concretizing the vision raises other challenges (*e.g.* scalability) that will need to be addressed when designing the actual solution.

2.2   First Approaches Towards Linked Open Code

The scientific community started taking promising steps to tackle the aforementioned points and make code semantically and uniformly accessible on the Web.

Initial works such as [7–9] focused on remote execution, through SPARQL queries, of code explicitly written for the Semantic Web. While [7] and [8] deal with SPARQL functions, [9] defines a new scripting language, *LDScript*, but its expressiveness is limited when compared to conventional programming languages. However, none of these approaches enables users to discover, download, and locally execute the best implementation of a given functionality in a required programming language.

More recent works aim to make code written in any language uniformly accessible through semantic queries. Ontologies are defined to describe code either for a specific language, like the *R* ontology [10]; a specific paradigm, such as object-oriented languages with CodeOntology [11]; or independently of the used technology as done by [12]. While [10] does not discuss the link between functions and data and lacks a way to capture the semantics of the functions, [11] and [12] have been extended respectively in [13] and [14–17] to tackle these limitations.

The work presented in [13] relies on CodeOntology for the implementation of a query answering system. The user's queries are translated into SPARQL queries and evaluated against a repository containing the RDF definitions of functions. Those functions are discovered and annotated using CodeOntology to describe their structure and DBpedia for semantics. Though this approach is similar to our vision for what concerns the discovery and semantic annotations of the functions, it differs as it remotely executes functions to answer the user's query while our goal is to find and return the best implementation of the requested functionality. Moreover, we aim to be able to deal with every kind of function despite the paradigm of the language in which they are implemented.

In [14–17], De Meester *et al.* broaden the vision presented in [12] by introducing new concepts, *e.g.* content negotiation. These approaches are very similar to our vision, with the main difference (which is also one of the main challenges of our approach) that we aim to automatically discover, identify and annotate the source code, while these previous works foresee the manual publication of description and implementations by developers. The works discuss briefly ranking the functions, but do not mention what metrics are to be used.

The last very recent initiative is Wikilambda [18] by the Wikimedia foundation. Its aim is to abstract Wikipedia by offering several implementations of functions allowing, firstly, to render the content of Wikidata in natural language using predefined templates and, as a final goal, to make the referenceable functions available on the Web. The main limitation of such an initiative is that the repository needs to be manually populated with functions written by the community, meaning that the success of the approach depends on the expertise and the will of the community, and code already present on the Web cannot be exploited.

3   Long-Term Perspectives

Transitioning from open code to Linked Open Code is challenging, yet it represents tremendous opportunities for diverse communities.

Linking data and code in a standard way would open perspectives to fully open and link libraries of programming languages and tools. This promising step enables to auto-construct, from scratch, small utilities computing data. Initiatives like *DeepCode*[5] for code completion can use this work to improve their models. Later on, frameworks such as GPT-3 can be trained on such data. One can also imagine shareable Deep Learning models in the same way, alongside their data, and in a ready-to-use negotiable format. Another important aspect granted by this transition is datasets of cross-language linked functions, ready to use as a base for code translation projects. We believe that syntactical code translation of code artifacts is not enough to achieve the same performance level obtained by experts of each language. Visual Programming Languages (VPLs) started emerging in the last decades and allow users to create programs and algorithms by assembling visual blocks instead of writing actual code. By providing a consistent organization of the information, they allow better performance in design and problem-solving [19] and bring programming to non-specialists. Visual programming environments are not only developed for teaching purposes[6] but also to support the design of real-world applications [20] and workflows such as the Node-RED[7] language, widely use in the context of the Internet of Things. Providing a structure allowing to reuse code assets as black-boxes would allow the emergence of a global VPL to build software relying on functions available on the Linked Open Code.

We think that the FAIR code vision is not FAIR enough when applied to the Semantic Web. Multiple resources openly available on the Web are not used to their full potential.

---

[5] https://www.deepcode.ai/.
[6] https://scratch.mit.edu/.
[7] https://nodered.org/.

References

1. Berners-Lee, T., Hendler, J., Lassila, O.: The semantic Web. Sci. Am. **284**(5), 34–43 (2001)
2. The W3C SPARQL Working Group. Sparql 1.1 overview. Technical report, World Wide Web Consortium (2013)
3. Di Cosmo, R., Gruenpeter, M., Zacchiroli, S.: Identifiers for digital objects: the case of software source code preservation. In: iPRES 2018–15th International Conference on Digital Preservation, pp. 1–9, Boston, United States, September 2018
4. Arroyo, S., et al.: Web service modeling ontology primer. W3C Member Submission (2005)
5. Dit, B., Meghan, R., Malcom, G., Denys, P.: Feature location in source code: a taxonomy and survey. J. Softw. Evol. Process **25**(1), 53–95 (2013)
6. Benni, B., Mosser, S., Acher, M., Paillart, M.: Characterizing Black-box composition operators via generated tailored benchmarks. J. Object Technol. **19**(2), 1–20 (2020)
7. Atzori, M.: Call: a nucleus for a web of open functions. In: International Semantic Web Conference (Posters & Demos), pp. 17–20 (2014)
8. Atzori, M.: Toward the Web of functions: interoperable higher-order functions in SPARQL. In: Mika, P., et al. (eds.) ISWC 2014. LNCS, vol. 8797, pp. 406–421. Springer, Cham (2014). https://doi.org/10.1007/978-3-319-11915-1_26
9. Corby, O., Faron-Zucker, C., Gandon, F.: LDScript: a linked data script language. In: d'Amato, C., et al. (eds.) ISWC 2017. LNCS, vol. 10587, pp. 208–224. Springer, Cham (2017). https://doi.org/10.1007/978-3-319-68288-4_13
10. Neveu, P., et al.: Using ontologies of software: example of R functions management. In: Lacroix, Z., Vidal, M.E. (eds.) RED 2010. LNCS, vol. 6799, pp. 43–56. Springer, Heidelberg (2012). https://doi.org/10.1007/978-3-642-27392-6_4
11. Atzeni, M., Atzori, M.: CodeOntology: RDF-ization of source code. In: d'Amato, C., et al. (eds.) ISWC 2017. LNCS, vol. 10588, pp. 20–28. Springer, Cham (2017). https://doi.org/10.1007/978-3-319-68204-4_2
12. De Meester, B., Dimou, A., Verborgh, R., Mannens, E.: An Ontology to Semantically Declare and Describe Functions. In: Sack, H., Rizzo, G., Steinmetz, N., Mladenić, D., Auer, S., Lange, C. (eds.) ESWC 2016. LNCS, vol. 9989, pp. 46–49. Springer, Cham (2016). https://doi.org/10.1007/978-3-319-47602-5_10
13. Atzeni, M., Atzori, M.: *What Is the Cube Root of 27?* question answering over CodeOntology. In: Vrandečić, D., et al. (eds.) ISWC 2018. LNCS, vol. 11136, pp. 285–300. Springer, Cham (2018). https://doi.org/10.1007/978-3-030-00671-6_17
14. De Meester, B., Dimou, A., Verborgh, R., Mannens, E., Van de Walle, R.: Discovering and using functions via content negotiation. In: Proceedings of the 15th International Semantic Web Conference: Posters and Demos, pp. 1–4. CEUR-WS (2016)
15. Noterman, L.: Discovering and Using Functions via Semantic Querying. Master's thesis, Ghent University (2018
16. De Meester, B., Noterman, L., Verborgh, R., Dimou, A.: The function hub: an implementation-independent read/write function description repository. In: Hitzler, P., et al. (eds.) ESWC 2019. LNCS, vol. 11762, pp. 33–37. Springer, Cham (2019). https://doi.org/10.1007/978-3-030-32327-1_7
17. Meester, D., B., Seymoens, T., Dimou, A., Verborgh, R.: Implementation-independent function reuse. Futur. Gener. Comput. Syst. **110**, 946–959 (2020)

18. Vrandečić, D.: Architecture for a multilingual Wikipedia. arXiv preprint arXiv:2004.04733 (2020)
19. Whitley, K.N.: Visual programming languages and the empirical evidence for and against. J. Vis. Lang. Comput. **8**(1), 109–142 (1997)
20. Jost, B., Ketterl, M., Budde, R., Leimbach, T.: Graphical programming environments for educational robots: open roberta-yet another one? In: 2014 IEEE International Symposium on Multimedia, pp. 381–386. IEEE (2014)

A Polyvocal and Contextualised Semantic Web

Marieke van Erp[1(✉)] and Victor de Boer[2]

[1] KNAW Humanities Cluster, Amsterdam, The Netherlands
marieke.van.erp@dh.huc.knaw.nl
[2] Vrije Universiteit Amsterdam, Amsterdam, The Netherlands
v.de.boer@vu.nl
https://mariekevanerp.com

Abstract. Current AI technologies and data representations often reflect the popular or majority vote. This is an inherent artefact of the frequency bias of many statistical analysis methods that are used to create for example knowledge graphs, resulting in simplified representations of the world in which diverse perspectives are underrepresented. With the use of AI-infused tools ever increasing, as well as the diverse audiences using these tools, this bias needs to be addressed in both the algorithms analysing data, as well as in the resulting representations. In this *problems to solve before you die* submission, we explain the implications of the lack of polyvocality and contextual knowledge in the semantic web. We identify three challenges for the Semantic Web community on dealing with various voices and perspectives as well as our vision for addressing it.

Keywords: Culturally aware AI · Polyvocality · Contextualisation · Bias

1 Introduction

Biases in data can be both explicit and implicit. Explicitly, 'The Dutch Seventeenth Century' and 'The Dutch Golden Age' are pseudo-synonymous and refer to a particular era of Dutch history. Implicitly, the 'Golden Age' moniker is contested due to the fact that the geopolitical and economic expansion came at a great cost, such as the slave trade. A simple two-word phrase can carry strong contestations, and entire research fields, such as post-colonial studies, are devoted to them. However, these sometimes subtle (and sometimes not so subtle) differences in voice are as yet not often found in knowledge graphs.

One of the reasons is that much of the knowledge found in knowledge graphs is mined automatically and current AI technologies (and their ensuing data representations) often reflect the popular or majority vote. This is an inherent artefact of the frequency bias of many statistical analysis methods that are used to create for example knowledge graphs, resulting in simplified representations

Supported by cultural-ai.nl.

R. Verborgh et al. (Eds.): ESWC 2021, LNCS 12731, pp. 506–512, 2021.
https://doi.org/10.1007/978-3-030-77385-4_30

of the world in which diverse perspectives are underrepresented. With the use of AI-infused tools ever increasing, as well as the diverse audiences using these tools, this bias needs to be addressed in both the algorithms analysing data, as well as in the resulting representations.

Conversations around data bias and polyvocality are taking place in for example the cultural heritage domain (cf. [14,15]) and computational linguistics communities (cf. [8,11]), but do not yet seem mainstream in the Semantic Web discourse. In 2010, Hendler and Berners-Lee already recognised that current knowledge mining mechanisms can bias results and recommend 'Making the different ontological commitments of competing interpretations explicit, and linked together', as this 'can permit different views of data to be simultaneously developed and explored.' [9]. Veltman noted in her 2004 paper that '[Dynamic knowledge will] allow us to trace changes of interpretation over time, have new insights and help us to discover new patterns in knowledge' [20]. Context was also flagged as the next frontier in knowledge representation at the 'Knowledge graphs: New directions for knowledge representation on the semantic web' Dagstuhl seminar in 2018 [5]. While it is known that large knowledge graphs are not always balanced (cf. [12]), that links between linked data resources contain biases (cf. [19]), and that research based on such resources might favour a Western perspective (cf. [6]), the creation of contextualised and polyvocal knowledge graphs has only gained modest traction.

As data-driven applications are permeating everyday life, it is necessary that these applications can serve as many and as diverse audiences as possible. A Dutch visitor to the Rijksmuseum in Amsterdam could recognise the Christian context of a painting depicting Saint Christopher even if s/he does not know that he is the patron saint of travellers. For a Japanese visitor, this might not be immediately apparent, and s/he needs more context to connect this to her/his cultural context, to for example recognise the parallels to Jizō, protector of travellers in some Buddhist traditions. For most other applications (e.g. in the domains of food, health, policy and transportation) a greater awareness of cultural and contextual frameworks of users would be crucial to increase engagement and understanding. Thus far, one of the ways machine learning driven approaches have dealt with this, is to add more data, at the risk of flattening nuances. At times, this has led to painful situations, for example when a Twitter trained chatbot started publishing racist, sexist and anti-semitic Tweets within a day of being released [23]. We argue that addressing this by more intelligently organised datasets to identify bias, and multiple perpectives and contexts is needed. Many of the puzzle pieces for a polyvocal and contextualised Semantic Web are already in place. The different local Wikipedias for example present different perspectives [4,24] with varying levels of in- and between group biases [1] but this is often still expressed implicitly.

In this *problems to solve before you die* submission, we explain the implications of the lack of polyvocality and contextual knowledge in the semantic web, as well as our vision for addressing it. The examples we use come from cultural heritage datasets as we work with those and some of the bias issues are amplified in there due to their longue durée,[1] but these issues and our proposed approach also apply to other domains.

2   What Is a Voice?

Data is not objective, but rather created from a particular perspective or view, representing a *voice*. These perspectives can be informed by cultural, historical or social conventions or a combination of those. Often, these different perspectives are contiguous, rather than disjoint. A cultural view on for example the 'The Dutch Golden Age' is that it was an era in which the Dutch economy and scientific advancements were among the most acclaimed in the world, laying the foundations for the first global multinational corporation and shaping Dutch architecture. A historical view could be that it was an era of unbridled opportunity and wealth for many in the Dutch Republic. A social view could focus on the pride associated with the achievements of this era. However, none of these views tells the entire story. The Dutch Republic maintained several colonies in Africa and Asia and was heavily involved in slave trading; the other side of the coin of wealth and pride.

These different views often come to us through objects in cultural heritage collections which can often be different things throughout their life. For example, many cult figures and other objects were taken and brought back home by missionaries -in some cases to learn about 'the other' from a euro-centric view. Such items were often (dis)qualified as "fetishes" or "idols" and Christian converts were expected to stay away converted from them. Later, these objects were removed from their original ritual settings and became part of ethnographic collections in missionary exhibitions or were sold as works of art. These reframings represent new perspectives on the same object and depend on time, culture and the object provenance. Data models that are perspective-aware should be able to trace the various changes that objects undergo in their trajectory from their original uses in indigenous religious practices into museum collections [13].

A polyvocal Semantic Web provides opportunities, models and tools to identify, represent and show users different perspectives on an event, organisation, opinion or object. Furthermore, identified individual perspectives need to be connected and clustered to be lifted from an individual perspective to a (representative) voice of a group. Identifying, representing and using such groups with fuzzy boundaries that change over time is one of the core challenges.

3   How Can the Semantic Web Deal with Multiple Perspectives and Interpretations?

We identify three main challenges to support polyvocality on the Semantic Web: identification, representation and usage. We describe these challenges below, along with the current state of the art and promising research directions for addressing them.

---

[1] Some collections we work with have been gathered over a span of over 200 years, and the objects they describe go back even longer.

3.1   Identifying Polyvocality in Data Sources

Data sources of various modalities can represent a singular 'voice', and provide a specific perspective on the world. However, within and across data sources, there can also be multiple voices present. Moreover, when aggregating datasets, such voices can become lost in the process. The challenge here is to identify such voices. For natural language data sources, as well as for methods that extract information from structured sources, this requires Information Extraction methods that are 'bias' or 'voice'-aware. In cases where datasets are the result of aggregations, such methods should be able to (re-)identify the separate voices in the combined source.

In cases where human data providers are involved, the voices of the individual users should be maintained. These persons can also represent cultural or societal groups and this information should be available for subsequent representations. As an example, consider a crowdsourcing effort to annotate a Polynesian object in a European museum. Here, annotations provided by the European public on the one hand and annotations provided by members of the source community on the other hand will represent various perspectives. Methods that aggregate such annotations should retain these voices. An example of a method that does this for individual annotators is CrowdTruth [2], which maintains so-called 'disagreement' between annotators. Such methods can be expanded to retain this disagreement to the extent to which it represents a 'voice'.

What holds for these non-professional annotators, also holds for professionals involved in metadating or interpreting information. Different perspectives provided by such professionals should also be maintained in the information processing pipeline. Again, in the cultural heritage domain, with movements towards a diversification of the museum professionals gaining traction [18,22], the different perspectives that such professionals provide should be maintained in the object metadata.

3.2   Representation of Polyvocality: Datamodels and Formalisms

Identifying, extracting and retaining polyvocal information in data sources is one aspect, but this is meaningless if the various voices cannot be represented in the data structures used. Luckily, the Knowledge Graph as a data model and the Semantic Web as an information architecture provide excellent opportunities for maintaining various viewpoints on one subject. Its network structure and distributed nature is well-equipped to deal with such viewpoints. One example is found in Europeana, where the Europeana Data Model [10] allows for multiple publishers to provide information about one cultural heritage object. Building on the OAI-ORE model[2], each data provider provides a "Proxy" resource that represents that object in the context of that provider and all metadata is attached to that Proxy resource, rather than the object representation itself. This allows to have multiple perspectives on a single real-world object. This model has

---

[2] http://www.openarchives.org/ore/1.0/datamodel.

also been applied to represent multiple and potentially disagreeing biographical descriptions of persons [16]. In the NewsReader project,[3] information on events was mined from newspaper articles. Multiple reports on the same event were identified via in- and cross-document coreference resolution and presented using named graphs to group statements about a particular event. Provenance information is then attached to these named graphs to represent the viewpoints of various providers [7,17].

Where a voice corresponds to the view of a data publishers, such models appear adequate. At the other end of the spectrum, we see provenance at the level of the individual annotator or even the individual statement. WikiData for example, represents each statement as a tuple which includes the metainformation about that statement [21]. This allows for the recording of very precise provenance of statements, to the individual level.

The view of a data provider and the view of the individual annotator represent two points on the spectrum that can inform how to represent the more collective and elusive social-cultural voice. Here, we need models and design patterns on how voices can be represented. This means that not only "what is expressed" should be represented, but also "which worldview does this represent". One direction is that of "data lenses" as deployed for example in the OpenPhacts project [3]. Here sets of statements are annotated with provenance information, which in turn represent the scientific worldview of different types of end-users. In our case, we would like such lenses to correspond to various voices regardless of the end-user.

3.3   Usage of Polyvocal Knowledge

Representing and maintaining polyvocal knowledge is meaningless if it cannot be used in end-user facing applications. With the voices being represented in the knowledge graphs, different viewpoints are available for such applications. How to provide access to this more complex information in a meaningful way is a third major research challenge. The Europeana, Wikidata and GRaSP data models are already complex to query, even for Semantic Web experts. Adding another layer, that of the voice or lenses, potentially further complicates this.

Personalisation can be supported by these different views. Developers of end-user applications should take care that such personalisation does not lead to 'filter bubbles'. Effective communication of the various views that exist on specific resources is crucial. One example is objects that are assigned to different categories depending on the cultural context. Many objects in ethnography museums are currently categorised based on older (colonial) classification schemes, that might not represent currently held views, and moreover, such views are likely to differ per culture. If such polyvocal information about the object is maintained, it can be shown to the users in digital interfaces as well as in physical locations.

What is needed are design guidelines and patterns for visualisation of polyvocal Knowledge as well as reusable tools and methods.

---

[3] https://newsreader-project.eu.

4   Discussion

Creating a polyvocal and contextualised Semantic Web will be a community effort driven by interdisciplinary teams. Whilst the Cultural AI consortium is embedded in different cultural heritage institutions in the Netherlands that represent different voices, we have to be aware of the danger that this remains a singular (Western/Northern) voice. To create globally relevant and culturally aware semantic web resources, diversity and inclusivity is key, and for this we can for example take cues from Black in AI[4] and Widening NLP.[5] The Semantic Web community is a diverse one, as our conference attendants, organising and programme committees, editorial boards and mailing lists show. Different voices are present, so let us make our resources, models and projects reflect that.

Acknowledgements. This paper builds upon the core concepts and research agenda of the Cultural AI Lab (https://www.cultural-ai.nl/), the authors would like to thank the co-creators of this research agenda: Antal van den Bosch, Laura Hollink, Martijn Kleppe, Johan Oomen, Jacco van Ossenbruggen, Stephan Raaijmakers, Saskia Scheltjens, Rosemarie van der Veen-Oei, and Lotte Wilms. We also want to thank our colleagues of the "Culturally Aware AI" project funded by the Dutch Research Council's Responsible use of AI programme, from the SABIO project, funded by the Dutch Digital Heritage Network, and from "Pressing Matter: Ownership, Value and the Question of Colonial Heritage in Museums", funded through the National Science Agenda of the Dutch Research Council.

References

1. Álvarez, G., Oeberst, A., Cress, U., Ferrari, L.: Linguistic evidence of in-group bias in English and Spanish Wikipedia articles about international conflicts. Discourse Context Media **35**, 100391 (2020)
2. Aroyo, L., Welty, C.: Truth is a lie: crowd truth and the seven myths of human annotation. AI Mag. **36**(1), 15–24 (2015)
3. Batchelor, C., et al.: Scientific lenses to support multiple views over linked Chemistry data. In: Mika, P., et al. (eds.) ISWC 2014. LNCS, vol. 8796, pp. 98–113. Springer, Cham (2014). https://doi.org/10.1007/978-3-319-11964-9_7
4. Beytía, P.: The positioning matters: estimating geographical bias in the multilingual record of biographies on Wikipedia. In: Companion Proceedings of the Web Conference 2020, pp. 806–810 (2020)
5. Bonatti, P.A., Decker, S., Polleres, A., Presutti, V.: Knowledge graphs: new directions for knowledge representation on the semantic web (dagstuhl seminar 18371). In: Dagstuhl Reports, vol. 8. Schloss Dagstuhl-Leibniz-Zentrum fuer Informatik (2019)
6. Farda-Sarbas, M., Mueller-Birn, C.: Wikidata from a research perspective-a systematic mapping study of wikidata. arXiv preprint arXiv:1908.11153 (2019)

---

[4] https://blackinai2020.vercel.app/.
[5] http://www.winlp.org/.

7. Fokkens, A., Vossen, P., Rospocher, M., Hoekstra, R., van Hage, W.R.: GRaSP: grounded representation and source perspective. In: Proceedings of the Workshop Knowledge Resources for the Socio-Economic Sciences and Humanities associated with RANLP 2017, pp. 19–25. INCOMA Inc., Varna, September 2017. https://doi.org/10.26615/978-954-452-040-3_003

8. Gebru, T., Morgenstern, J., Vecchione, B., Vaughan, J.W., Wallach, H., Daumé III, H., Crawford, K.: Datasheets for datasets. arXiv preprint arXiv:1803.09010 (2018)

9. Hendler, J., Berners-Lee, T.: From the semantic web to social machines: a research challenge for AI on the world wide web. Artif. Intell. **174**(2), 156–161 (2010)

10. Isaac, A.: Europeana data model primer (2013)

11. Jo, E.S., Gebru, T.: Lessons from archives: strategies for collecting sociocultural data in machine learning. In: Proceedings of the 2020 Conference on Fairness, Accountability, and Transparency, pp. 306–316 (2020)

12. Konieczny, P., Klein, M.: Gender gap through time and space: a journey through Wikipedia biographies via the Wikidata human gender indicator. New Media Society **20**(12), 4608–4633 (2018)

13. Meyer, B.: Idolatry Beyond the Second Commandment: Conflicting Figurations and Sensations of the Unseen. Bloomsbury, London (2019)

14. Miles, R.S., Tzialli, A.O.E., Captain, E. (eds.): Inward Outward, Critical Archival Engagements with Sounds and Films of Coloniality - A Publication of the 2020 Inward Outward Symposium (2020). https://doi.org/10.18146/inout2020

15. National Museum for World Cultures: Words matter: An unfinished guide to word choice in the cultural sector. https://www.tropenmuseum.nl/nl/over-het-tropenmuseum/words-matter-publicatie (2018)

16. Ockeloen, N., et al.: BiographyNet: managing provenance at multiple levels and from different perspectives. In: LISC@ ISWC, pp. 59–71. Citeseer (2013)

17. Rospocher, M., et al.: Building event-centric knowledge graphs from news. Journal of Web Semantics **37**, 132–151 (2016)

18. Smith, C.E.: Decolonising the museum: The national museum of the American Indian in Washington, D.C. (2005)

19. Tiddi, I., d'Aquin, M., Motta, E.: Quantifying the bias in data links. In: Janowicz, K., Schlobach, S., Lambrix, P., Hyvönen, E. (eds.) EKAW 2014. LNCS (LNAI), vol. 8876, pp. 531–546. Springer, Cham (2014). https://doi.org/10.1007/978-3-319-13704-9_40

20. Veltman, K.H.: Towards a semantic web for culture. J. Digital Inf. **4**(4) (2004)

21. Vrandečić, D., Krötzsch, M.: Wikidata: a free collaborative knowledgebase. Commun. ACM **57**(10), 78–85 (2014)

22. Wei, L.: Crossing the ethnic boundaries: diversity promotion effort of museum professionals in the United Kingdom. In: Proceedings of the Papers, CAAS 7th Conference at TUFS, October 2016

23. Wolf, M.J., Miller, K.W., Grodzinsky, F.S.: Why we should have seen that coming: comments on Microsoft's Tay "Experiment", and wider implications. ORBIT J. **1**(2), 1–12 (2017)

24. Zhou, Y., Demidova, E., Cristea, A.I.: Who likes me more? Analysing entity-centric language-specific bias in multilingual Wikipedia. In: Proceedings of the 31st Annual ACM Symposium on Applied Computing, pp. 750–757 (2016)

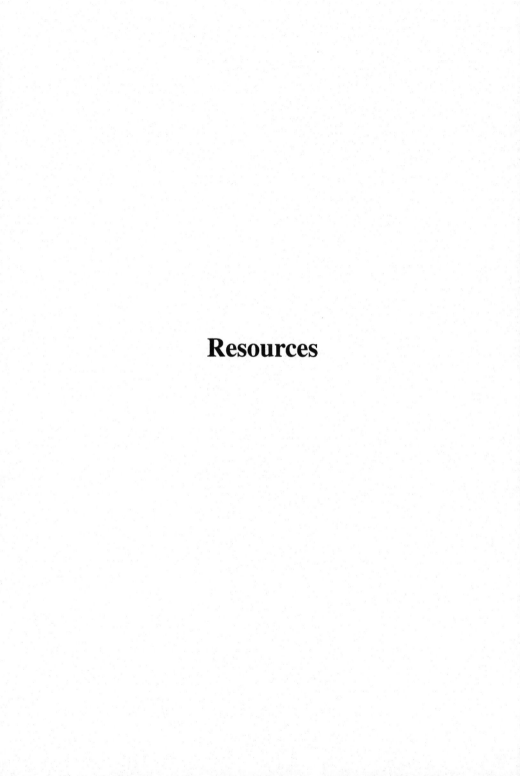

Resources

Resources

The WASABI Dataset: Cultural, Lyrics and Audio Analysis Metadata About 2 Million Popular Commercially Released Songs

Michel Buffa[1]([⊠]), Elena Cabrio[1], Michael Fell[2], Fabien Gandon[1],
Alain Giboin[1], Romain Hennequin[5], Franck Michel[1], Johan Pauwels[3],
Guillaume Pellerin[4], Maroua Tikat[1], and Marco Winckler[1]

[1] University Côte d'Azur, Inria, CNRS, I3S, Nice, France
{michel.buffa,elena.cabrio,maroua.tikat,winckler}@univ-cotedazur.fr,
{fabien.gandon,alain.giboin}@inria.fr, franck.michel@cnrs.fr
[2] Università degli Studi di Torino, Turin, Italy
michaelkurt.fell@unito.it
[3] Queen Mary University of London, London, England
j.pauwels@qmul.ac.uk
[4] IRCAM, Paris, France
guillaume.pellerin@ircam.fr
[5] Deezer Research, Paris, France
rhennequin@deezer.com

Abstract. Since 2017, the goal of the two-million song WASABI database has been to build a knowledge graph linking collected metadata (artists, discography, producers, dates, etc.) with metadata generated by the analysis of both the songs' lyrics (topics, places, emotions, structure, etc.) and audio signal (chords, sound, etc.). It relies on natural language processing and machine learning methods for extraction, and semantic Web frameworks forrepresentation and integration. It describes more than 2 millions commercial songs, 200K albums and 77K artists. It can be exploited by music search engines, music professionals (e.g. journalists, radio presenters, music teachers) or scientists willing to analyze popular music published since 1950. It is available under an open license, in multiple formats and with online and open source services including an interactive navigator, a REST API and a SPARQL endpoint.

Keywords: Music metadata · Lyrics analysis · Named entities · Linked data

1 Introduction

Today, many music streaming services (such as Deezer, Spotify or Apple Music) leverage richmetadata (artist's biography, genre, lyrics, etc.) to enrich listening experience and perform recommendations. Likewise, journalists or archivists

© Springer Nature Switzerland AG 2021
R. Verborgh et al. (Eds.): ESWC 2021, LNCS 12731, pp. 515–531, 2021.
https://doi.org/10.1007/978-3-030-77385-4_31

exploit various data sources to prepare TV/radio shows or music-related articles. Music and sound engineering schools use these same data to illustrate and
explain the audio production techniques and the history or music theory behind
a song. Finally, musicologists may look for hidden relationships between artists
(e.g. influences, indirect collaborations) to support a claim. All these scenarios
have in common that theyshow the need for more accurate, larger and better
linked music knowledge bases, along with tools to explore and exploit them.

Since 2017, the WASABI research project[1] has built a dataset covering more
than 2 M songs (mainly pop/rock and dub) in different languages, 200K albums
and 77K artists. Musicologists, archivists from Radio-France, music schools and
music composers also collaborated. While cultural data were collected from a
large number of data sources, we also processed the song lyrics and performed
audio analyses, enriching the corpus with various computed metadata addressing
questions such as: What do the lyrics talk about? Which emotions do they
convey? What is their structure? What chords are present in the song? What is
the tempo, average volume, etc.? We partnered with the Queen Mary University
of London (QMUL) and the FAST project[2] for extracting chords from the song
audio, and linked to IRCAM's TimeSide[3] audio analysis API which for audio
processings (beat detection, loudness, etc.). We deployed REST and SPARQL
endpoints for requests and a GUI for exploring the dataset [6]. The dataset,
Machine Learning models and processing pipeline are described and available[4]
under an open license.[5]

Section 2 presents the context of the WASABI project and related works.
In Sect. 3, we explain the way we collected and processed data to build the
corpus. Section 4 focuses on the formalization, generation and publication of the
RDF knowledge graph. Section 5 presents several tools and visualizations built
on top of the dataset and services. Finally, Sect. 6 discusses quality assessment
concerns while Sects. 7 and 8 discuss future applications and potential impact of
the dataset and conclude with some perspectives.

2   State of the Art and Related Work

There are large datasets of royalty-free music such as Jamendo (often used [5, 26])
or others found in the DBTunes link directory, but we focus on the ones that
cover commercial popular music (see Table 1) and we will see that few propose
metadata on cultural aspects, lyrics and audio altogether. MusicBrainz offers a
large set of cultural metadata but nothing about lyrics, for example. The Last.fm
dataset contains tags that were used by some researchers for computing moods

---

[1] Web Audio Semantic Aggregated in the Browser for Indexation, (Université Côte
d'Azur, IRCAM, Deezer and Parisson) http://wasabihome.i3s.unice.fr/.

[2] QMUL and the FAST project http://www.semanticaudio.ac.uk/.

[3] TimeSide https://github.com/Parisson/TimeSide.

[4] https://github.com/micbuffa/WasabiDataset.

[5] Creative Commons Attribution-NonCommercial-ShareAlike 4.0 International (CC
BY-NC-SA).

and emotions [7,13]. AcousticBrainz, a public, crowd-sourced dataset, contains metadata about audio and has been used by projects such as MusicWeb [2] and MusicLynx [3] to compute similarity models based on musical tonality, rhythm and timbre features.

The Centre for Digital Music of QMUL collaborated with the BBC on the use of Semantic Web technologies, and proposed music ontologies in several fields including audio effects and organology.

MusicLynx [3] provides an application to browse through music artists by exploiting connections between them, either extra-musical or tangential to music. It integrates open linked semantic metadata from various music recommendation and social media data sources as well as content-derived information. This project shares some ideas with the WASABI project but does not address the same scale of data, nor does it perform analysis on audio and lyrics content.

The Million Song Dataset project (MSD) processed a large set of commercial songs to extract metadata using audio content analysis [4], but did not take advantage of structured data (e.g. from DBpedia) to address uncertainties. Information such as group composition or orchestration can be very relevant to informing Music Information Retrieval (MIR) algorithms, but is only available in certain data sources (BBC, MusicBrainz, ...), and for many little-known artists this information is not available. It is here that the combination of audio and semantics finds its purpose, one reinforcing the other. The WASABI project provides a wider scope than the Million Song Dataset: it started as a challenge to build a datataset that would be twice as big with public domain development of open source tools and a richer cultural and lyric-related set of metadata.

The DOREMUS project [16] overlaps with WASABI but in a rather different context (classical and traditional music). DOREMUS performs the integration of MIDI resources (instead of MIR analysis), recommendation and automatic playlists generation. The WASABI ontology extends the Music Ontology (MO), yet the Performed Music Ontology[6] (part of LD4L) or DOREMUS ontology (based on FRBR) may be considered if future works need to model more accurately the differences between works, performances or expressions.

The Listening Experience Database (LED) collects people's music listening experiences as they are reported in documents like diaries or letters [1]. It mostly relates to legacy music that has little overlap with WASABI.

The MELD framework [21] supports the publication of musicology articles with multi-modal user interfaces that connect different forms of digital resources. Some development could be undertaken to allow musicologists publish articles that would leverage musical data from the WASABI RDF knowledge graph.

The MIDI Linked Data project [17] publishes a large set of MIDI files in RDF. Linked to DBpedia and relying on the Music Ontology, it could complement WASABI to jointly exploit MIDI files and audio and text analyses. Some MIDI content was used in WASABI during the evaluation of the chord extraction.

---

[6] https://wiki.lyrasis.org/display/LD4P/Performed+Music+Ontology.

Table 1. Comparison with other datasets.

	Nb songs	Linked data	Audio analysis	Lyrics analysis	Cultural metadata	Type of music
WASABI	2 M	Yes	Yes	Yes	Yes	Commercial
MSD	1 M	No	Yes	Bag of words	Partial	Commercial
DOREMUS	24k	Yes	No, Midi	Not relevant	Yes	Classical
MusicBrainz	33 M	Yes	No	No	Yes	Commercial
AcousticBrainz	4 M	Yes	Yes	No	MusicBrainz	Commercial
Jamendo	200 k+	No	Chords	No	Yes	Royalty free

3   Building the WASABI Dataset

3.1   Assembling Cultural Data from Multiple Sources

One of the original goals of the WASABI project was to build a dataset comprising metadata produced by natural language processing applied to the lyrics. As shown in Fig. 1, we therefore started from LyricsWikia, a wiki-based, crowd-sourced website gathering a large number of commercial song lyrics, metadata concerning the discography of thousands of artists (name, genre, labels, locations, duration, album release dates etc.). We collected data of 2 M songs, 77K artists and 200K albums, including links and ids to songs, artists and albums on other platforms: Wikipedia, YouTube, MusicBrainz, Last.fm, Discogs, etc.

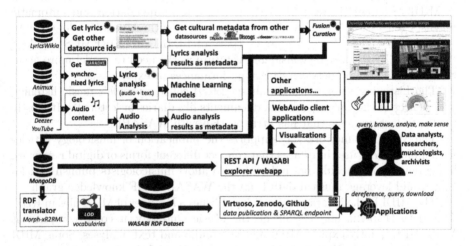

Fig. 1. WASABI pipeline from datasets and corpora to applications and end-users.

Subsequently, we used the links and ids to gather metadata from these multiple platforms. For instance, from several DBpedia language editions we

Table 2. Ratios between external and those in our seed dataset LyricsWikia.

Dataset	Songs	Artists	Albums	Comment
MusicBrainz	57%	78%	45%	
DBpedia	52%	24%	3.8%	
Deezer	57%	64%	63%	87% of the songs if we consider English songs only
Discogs	N/A	69%	41%	Only artists and discographies
Equipboard	N/A	8.4%	N/A	Only famous artists/members had metadata
Final	72%	78%	69%	Entries matched at least once in external sources

retrieved music genres, awards and albums durations; from MusicBrainz: artist type (group, person, etc.), gender, life span, group members, albums' bar code, release date, language; from Discogs: name variations (different ways to call the same song, album or artist) and artist real names that proved to be very relevant for consolidating the dataset; from EquipBoard: content about music gear used by artists (instrument type, brand, model, etc.); from Deezer: songs' popularity rank, flag for explicit song lyrics, tempo, gain, song duration.

Merging was necessary when different properties of the same meaning coming from different data sources provided different, possibly complementary results (e.g. using *owl:sameAs* from DBpedia). The disambiguation properties of Discogs and the availability of multiple URIs from different data sources for the same song/artist/album also made it possible to detect gross errors. Conflict detectors were set up (e.g. for dates) and manual arbitration occasionally took place. We organized "WASABI Marathons" along the project lifetime where participants used the Wasabi Explorer [6] to identify errors. These marathons helped set up scripts to detect and fix errors ranging from spelling errors/variations (e.g. "Omega Man" by The Police is sometimes spelled "Ω Man"), to rules (e.g. several producers for the same song by the same artist generally indicate an anomaly). Table 2 shows the contribution of each data source in the final dataset e.g. we found in MusicBrainz 1,197,540 songs (57% of the 2,099,287 songs retrieved from LyricsWikia, our initial seed). The tools used to collect these metadata are available on the GitHub repository of the WASABI dataset.

3.2 Generating Lyrics Metadata

Lyrics encode an important part of the semantics of a song. We proposed natural language processing methods to extract relevant information, such as:

- *structural segmentation*: we trained a Convolutional Neural Network to predict segment borders in lyrics from self-similarity matrices (SSM) encoding their repetitive structure. Songs are therefore associated to labeled text segments corresponding to verse, chorus, intro, etc. [14]. We showed that combining text and audio modalities improves lyrics segmentation [15].
- *topics*: we built a topic model on the lyrics of our corpus using Latent Dirichlet Allocation (LDA). These topics can be visualized as word clouds of the most characteristic words per topic [10,13];

- *explicitness of the lyrical content*: we compared automated methods ranging from dictionary-based lookup to state-of-the-art deep neural networks to automatically detect explicit content in English lyrics [11];
- *salient passages of a song*: we introduced a method for extractive summarization of lyrics that relies on the intimate relationship between the audio and the lyrics (audio thumbnailing approach) [12];
- *emotions conveyed*: we trained an emotion regression model using BERT to classify emotions in lyrics based on the valence-arousal model [13].

Table 3 gives an overview of the annotations we published relating to the song lyrics. Some of those annotation layers are provided for all the 1.73 M songs with lyrics included in the WASABI corpus, while some others apply to subsets of the corpus, due to various constraints of the applied methods [13].

Table 3. Song-wise annotations - ♣ indicates predictions of our models.

Annotation	Labels	Description	Annotation	Labels	Description
Lyrics	1.73 M	Segments of lines of text	Languages	1.73 M	36 different ones
Genre	1.06 M	528 different ones	Last FM id	326k	UID
Structure	1.73 M	SSM $\in \mathbb{R}^{n \times n}$ (n: length)	Social tags	276k	$\mathbb{S}$ = {rock, joyful, 90s, ...}
Emotion tags	87k	$\mathbb{E} \subset \mathbb{S}$ = {joyful, tragic, ...}	Explicitness ♣	715k	True (52k), False (663k)
Explicitness	455k	True (85k), False (370k)	Summary♣	50k	Four lines of song text
Emotion	16k	(valence, arousal) $\in \mathbb{R}^2$	Emotion♣	1.73 M	(valence, arousal) $\in \mathbb{R}^2$
Topics♣	1.05 M	Prob. distrib. $\in \mathbb{R}^{60}$			
Total tracks	2.10 M	Diverse metadata			

The annotated corpus and the proposed methods are available on the project GitHub repository. As for structure segmentation, for each song text we make available an SSM based on a normalized character-based edit distance on two levels of granularity to enable other researchers to work with these structural representations: line-wise similarity and segment-wise similarity. As for lyrics summarization, the four-line summaries of 50k English lyrics is freely available within the WASABI Song Corpus, as well as the Python code of the applied summarization methods.[7] Concerning the explicitness of the lyrics content, we provide both the predicted labels in the WASABI Song Corpus (715k lyrics, 52k tagged as explicit) and the trained classifier to apply it to unseen text. As for emotion, the dataset integrates Deezer's valence-arousal annotations for 18,000 English tracks[8] [8], as well as the valence-arousal predictions for the 1.73 M tracks with lyrics. We also make available the Last.fm social tags (276k) and emotion tags (87k) to allow researchers to build variants of emotion recognition models. Finally, we provide the topic distribution of our LDA topic model for each song and the trained topic model for future research.

---

[7] https://github.com/TuringTrain/lyrics_thumbnailing.
[8] https://github.com/deezer/deezer_mood_detection_dataset.

3.3   Extracting Chords Through Automatic Audio Content Analysis

We enriched the dataset with automatic chord recognition [23] for reasons of consistency, formatting and coverage. Even though automatic transcriptions are not flawless, at least they are consistent and well-structured. Chord extraction can also be applied to each song for which audio is available, and therefore avoids the popularity bias that would follow from scraping crowd-sourced resources. In order to mitigate algorithmic imperfections, we used a chord recognition algorithm that additionally returns a song-wide measure of confidence in the quality of transcription [22]. Weighing by this measure makes dataset aggregations more reliable, although it obviously is of limited use when an individual song of interest has a particularly low confidence associated with it. A chord vocabulary consisting of sixty chords was imposed: all combinations of twelve possible root notes with five chord types (major, minor, dominant 7th, major 7th, minor 7th).

The Deezer song identifiers provided a link to audio recordings. The actual analysis required access to the raw, unprotected audio and was therefore run by Deezer on their servers. 1.2 million songs in the WASABI dataset have an associated Deezer identifier, so can potentially be enriched with a chord transcription. This process is still ongoing, currently 513K songs have been processed. The chord symbols (without timing due to copyright restrictions) and their confidence measures can be obtained along with the rest of the dataset through the REST API and SPARQL endpoint. Other musical properties based on automatic content analysis can be integrated as future work.

3.4   IRCAM Tools for On-Demand Audio/MIR Analysis

Timeside is an an open, scalable, audio processing framework in Python, enabling low and high level audio analysis, visualization, transcoding, streaming and labelling. Its API supports reproducible and extensible processing on large datasets of any audio or video format. For WASABI, some parts have been created or extended: a secured and documented API with JWT access capabilities, a Provider module to handle automatic extraction of YouTube's and Deezer's tracks or 30 s extracts, an SDK for the development of client applications and a new web front-end prototype. A hosted instance has been connected to the main WASABI API so that every available tracks can be dynamically processed and played back through the multi-track analyzer web player.

4   Formalizing, Generating and Publishing the RDF Knowledge Graph

The WASABI dataset essentially consists of two parts: the initial dataset produced over the last 3 years by integrating and processing multiple data sources, as explained in Sect. 3, and the RDF dataset derived thereof, namely the *WASABI RDF Knowledge Graph* that we describe hereafter. The latter provides an RDF representation of songs, artists and albums, together with the information automatically extracted from lyrics and audio content.

4.1 The WASABI Ontology

The WASABI vocabulary is an OWL ontology to formalize the metadata. It primarily relies on the Music Ontology [24] that defines a rich vocabulary for describing and linking music information, and extends it with terms about some specific entities and properties. It also reuses terms from the Dublin Core, FOAF, Schema.org and the DBpedia ontologies, as well as the Audio Features Ontology[9] and the OMRAS2 Chord Ontology.[10]

The current version of the ontology comprises of 8 classes and 50 properties to describe songs, albums and artists. The number of properties is due to the quite specific features represented in the metadata, for instance multi-track files, audio gain, names and titles without accent, or lyrics-related features such as the detected language or explicitness. Furthermore, no less that 22 properties represent links to the web pages of social networks, either mainstream or specialized in the music domain. Whenever possible, we linked these properties with equivalent or related properties from other vocabularies.

The Music Ontology comes with three terms to represent music performers: *mo:SoloMusicArtist* and *mo:MusicGroup* that are both subsumed by class *mo:MusicArtist*. To distinguish between a music group, an orchestra and a choir, we defined the *wsb:Artist_Person* and *wsb:Artist_Group* classes, respectively equivalent to *mo:SoloMusicArtist* and *mo:MusicGroup*, and two subclasses of *mo:MusicArtist* namely *wsb:Orchestra* and *wsb:Choir*. *wsb:Song* is the class of musical tracks performed by artists. It's a subclass of *mo:Track*, itself a subclass of *mo:MusicalManifestation*. *wsb:Album* is the class of collections of one or more songs released together. It is a subclass of *mo:Record* which itself is a subclass of *mo:MusicalManifestation*.

The ontology namespace[11] (prefix *wsb:*) is also its URI. The ontology can be dereferenced with content negotiation, as well as all the terms of the ontology. It can be downloaded from the repository[12] where graphical visualizations are also available.

4.2 Representing Songs, Artists and Albums in RDF

Beyond the terms of WASABI ontology, the resource descriptions use terms from multiple vocabularies. The namespaces and prefixes are given in Listing 1.1 and the diagram in Fig. 2 is the representation of a song from the WASABI database. This song is linked to its album through the *schema:album* property, and both the album and song are linked to the artist using the *mo:performer* Music Ontology property. Only a small subset of songs' metadata is depicted here: title (*dcterms:title*), audio gain (*wsb:gain*), chords (*chord:chord*)[13] given

---

[9] Audio Features Ontology: http://purl.org/ontology/af/.

[10] OMRAS2 Chord Ontology: http://purl.org/ontology/chord/.

[11] http://ns.inria.fr/wasabi/ontology/.

[12] https://github.com/micbuffa/WasabiDataset/tree/master/ontology.

[13] Due to copyright concerns, the chords ordered sequence and timing were computed but are not provided.

```
@prefix af:       <http://purl.org/ontology/af/>.
@prefix chord:    <http://purl.org/ontology/chord/>.
@prefix dcterms:  <http://purl.org/dc/terms/> .
@prefix foaf:     <http://xmlns.com/foaf/0.1/>.
@prefix mo:       <http://purl.org/ontology/mo/>.
@prefix rdf:      <http://www.w3.org/1999/02/22-rdf-syntax-ns#>.
@prefix rdfs:     <http://www.w3.org/2000/01/rdf-schema#>.
@prefix schema:   <http://schema.org/>.
@prefix wsb:      <http://ns.inria.fr/wasabi/ontology/>.
@prefix xsd:      <http://www.w3.org/2001/XMLSchema#>.
```

Listing 1.1. Namespaces used in the RDF representation of the entities.

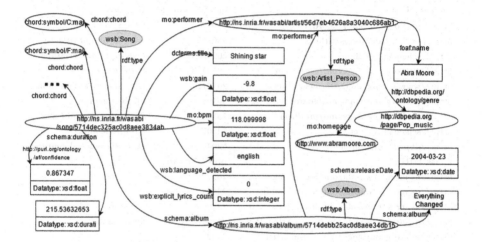

Fig. 2. RDF representation of a song, some properties and its artist and album.

by their URI in the OMRAS2 chord ontology, and number of explicit lyrics (*wsb:explicit_lyrics_count*).

4.3   The RDF Knowledge Graph Generation Pipeline

The dataset described in Sect. 3 consists of a MongoDB database comprising three main collections: songs, artists and albums. The song collection provides not only the metadata, but also a representation of the chords extracted by the audio analysis, and the information extracted from the lyrics.

In a first stage, each JSON document of MongoDB was pre-processed so as to facilitate its translation to RDF, then translated to an RDF representation as described in Sect. 4.2. The translation was carried out by Morph-xR2RML,[14] an implementation of the xR2RML mapping language [19] for MongoDB databases. All files involved in this pipeline are provided under the Apache License 2.0.

---

[14] https://github.com/frmichel/morph-xr2rml/.

Table 4. Statistics of the WASABI dataset.

	No. entities	JSON data	No. RDF triples
Songs	2.08 M	8.8 GB	49.9 M
Artists, groups, choirs and orchestras	77K	378 MB	2.76 M
Albums	208K	424 MB	3.29 M
Total	2.38 M	9.57 GB	55.5 M

Table 5. Selected statistics on typical properties and classes.

Property URI	nb of instances	Comment
http://purl.org/ontology/chord/chord	7595765	Chords of a song
http://purl.org/dc/terms/title	2308022	Song or album title
http://schema.org/album	2099283	Song-to-album relation
http://purl.org/ontology/mo/performer	1953416	Performing artist
http://www.w3.org/2002/07/owl#sameAs	204771	DBpedia/Wikidata links
http://purl.org/ontology/mo/genre	86190	Musical genre
http://purl.org/ontology/mo/producer	75703	Song/album producer
http://schema.org/members	74907	Group members
http://dbpedia.org/ontology/genre	52047	DBpedia musical genre
Class URI	**nb of instances**	
http://ns.inria.fr/wasabi/ontology/Song	2099287	
http://ns.inria.fr/wasabi/ontology/Album	208743	
http://ns.inria.fr/wasabi/ontology/Artist_Group	29806	Group or band
http://ns.inria.fr/wasabi/ontology/Artist_Person	24264	Single artist
http://purl.org/ontology/mo/MusicArtist	23323	
http://ns.inria.fr/wasabi/ontology/Classic_Song	10864	Classic of pop/rock music
http://ns.inria.fr/wasabi/ontology/Choir	44	
http://ns.inria.fr/wasabi/ontology/Orchestra	30	

4.4   Publishing and Querying the WASABI RDF Knowledge Graph

Table 4 synthesizes the amount of data processed to produce the WASABI RDF Knowledge Graph, and reports the number of triples produced. Table 5 reports some statistics about the instances.

Dataset Description and Accessibility. In line with data publication best practices [9], the WASABI RDF Knowledge Graph comes with rich metadata regarding licensing, authorship and provenance information, linksets, vocabularies and access information. These can be visualized by looking up the dataset URI[15]. The dataset is available as a DOI-identified downloadable RDF dump and a public SPARQL endpoint (see Table 6). All URIs can be dereferenced with content negotiation. Further information (modeling, named graphs, third-party vocabularies) are documented in the GitHub repository.

---

[15] WASABI RDF dataset URI: http://ns.inria.fr/wasabi/wasabi-1-0.

Table 6. Dataset accessibility.

RDF dump	https://doi.org/10.5281/zenodo.4312641
Public SPARQL endpoint	http://wasabi.inria.fr/sparql
Documentation	https://github.com/micbuffa/WasabiDataset
Ontology namespace	http://ns.inria.fr/wasabi/ontology/
Data namespace	http://ns.inria.fr/wasabi/
Dataset URI	http://ns.inria.fr/wasabi/wasabi-1-0

Dataset Licensing. Like the rest of the WASABI dataset, the WASABI RDF Knowledge Graph is published under the Creative Commons Attribution-NonCommercial-ShareAlike 4.0 International License. Copyrighted data such as the full text content of the song lyrics and audio are not included but URLs of original source material are given.

Sustainability Plan. We plan several research lines that will exploit and extend the dataset and improve its resilience. We intend to add more audio-related computed metadata from our collaborators at IRCAM and QMUL e.g. links from the song ids to the TimeSide API will ensure that the audio based analyses can be provided or re-triggered even if new songs are added or of the audio data change or vary from the external providers. We also deployed a SPARQL endpoint that benefits from a high-availability infrastructure and 24/7 support.

5   Visualization and Current Usage of the Dataset

The size and the complexity of the dataset require appropriate tools to allow users to explore and navigate through it. This multidimensional dataset contains a large variety of multimedia attributes (lyrics, sounds, chords, musical instruments, etc.) that are interlinked, thus featuring a large and rich knowledge graph. To assist users, we investigate various visualization techniques.

Our goal is to help users explore the dataset by providing answers to common visualization questions such as to get an overview of itemsets fitting some user-defined criteria, exploring details of particular itemsets, identify relationships (such as patterns, trends, and clusters) between itemsets, etc. These common tasks are defined in the information-seeking mantra introduced by Schneidermann [25] which guides the design of all visualization tools. We designed and implemented a large set of visualization techniques using the D3.js library and made these techniques available to the user in a gallery. Figure 3 illustrates some of the visualization techniques currently available and all are interactive so that user can select an itemset and apply zoom and filtering to explore the dataset.

The creation process for the gallery of information visualization techniques is rather opportunistic and incremental. It allows us to explore different alternatives for showing information to the users but also to combine different attributes. The visualization is driven by the type and inner structure of the data that results from the queries embedded into the visualization tools. Whilst visualization tools created this way are not generic, they remove part of the inner complexity of creating (SPARQL) queries, making the tools easier to use and particularly suitable to communicating results to a broad audience.

It is worthy of notice that some of the visualization techniques includes multimedia content, for example the Fig. 4 includes images that refer to cover of albums of an artist. So far, beyond the interactive graphics, only text and images are used in multimedia visualization, we are working to enrich the information visualization gallery with techniques that include audio contents.

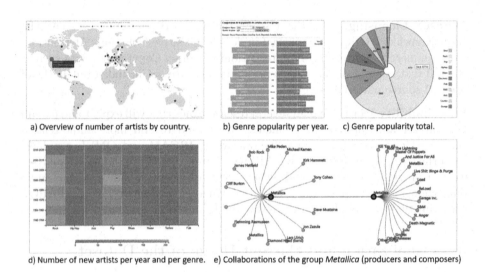

a) Overview of number of artists by country.   b) Genre popularity per year.   c) Genre popularity total.

d) Number of new artists per year and per genre.   e) Collaborations of the group *Metallica* (producers and composers)

Fig. 3. Selected visualization techniques from the WASABI gallery: a) *map view* showing artists per country; b) *barplot* showing a comparison of the popularity of two genres along years; c) *pie chart* showing total genre popularity; d) *heatmap* showing the number of new artists of a genre per year; e) *bifocaltree* showing collaborators of Metallica.

6   Evaluating the Quality of the Dataset, Future Updates

Assessing and ensuring the quality of a large dataset built by aggregating multiple data sources is challenging and continuous process. It is common that metadata coming from various sources be erroneous or conflicting. The multiple hackathons helped in spotting many errors, conflicts and recurring problems, and we wrote a set of scripts (available in the Github repository) to fix some of them. The dataset is meant to be maintained over at least the next three years as we have new ongoing projects that will exploit and extend it. More metadata will be added (in particular from MIR audio analysis of songs, linking songs to existing midi transcriptions or online scores), and we are developing new metadata quality assessment tools (based on visualisations and inferences rules) that

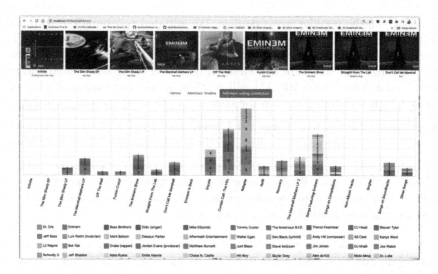

Fig. 4. Example of information visualization including multimedia contents: Eminem collaborations (co-writing of songs) by albums (see cover of albums).

shall allow the community to better detect and report erroneous, conflicting or missing metadata.

On the other hand, the quality of extracted metadata about lyrics have been validated using different methods described in the papers cited in Sect. 3.2.

7   Potential Impact and Reusability

To the best of our knowledge, the WASABI dataset is the first one integrating cultural and MIR data at this scale into a single, coherent knowledge graph that makes it possible to initiate new research. The wide range of metadata resulting from the analysis of song lyrics is one of the remarkable points. Many recommendation systems are based on cultural information and user profiles, sometimes taking into account data from the audio analysis, but few rely on the content of the lyrics or their analysis. Furthermore, mixing the emotions extracted from the textual analysis with results on the analysis of emotions extracted from the audio from other datasets (e.g. AcousticBrainz) provides new prospects for recommendation systems [20]. In addition to being interoperable with central knowledge graphs used within the Semantic Web community, the visualizations show the potential of these technologies in other fields. The availability of this rich resource can also attract researchers from the NLP community.[16]

Interest of Communities in Using the Dataset and Services. The openness of the data and code allow contributors to advance the current state of

---

[16] 1st Workshop on NLP for Music and Audio in 2020 https://sites.google.com/view/nlp4musa.

knowledge on the popular music domain. We initiated collaborations with other groups and, in particular, researchers from the FAST project already used and contributed to the dataset. IRCAM researchers also started cross-domain analyses on songs (i.e. structure and emotion detection using both audio and text [18]). Collaboration with IRCAM will continue as the integration of additional audio data is a priority for us in the coming months and will trigger updates.

Application Scenarios, Targeted Users, and Typical Queries. Following a user-oriented requirement analysis, we designed a set of motivating scenarios:

Scenario 1: research of artists and songs related to current events, set with the help of archivists from Radio-France. E.g. during the "yellow jackets" protest in France, animators of music radio programs repeatedly requested songs about protests, rebellion, anti-government movements, revolution.

Scenario 2: analysis of a particular artist, set with the help of musicologists. To look for an artist's influences, collaborations and themes, and study variations in the compositions (complexity of the songs, recording locations).

Scenario 3: disambiguation of homonyms (artists with the same name) and duplicates (single artist with multiple names or various name spellings), set with the help of Deezer. The goal is to highlight suspicious artist profiles and the sources involved (e.g. homonyms may have different record labels, languages etc.), to display, group and prioritize alerts (e.g. using artists' popularity).

Scenario 4: search for songs of a particular style, in a given key, or containing specific chords, with lyrics with given topics, set with the help of music schools and professional composers. E.g.: look for a blues in E with a tempo of 120 bpm, then get similar songs but with chords outside the key; show artists who wrote a type of songs, sorted by popularity; search for songs with given themes and emotions in the lyrics or with certain types of orchestrations (e.g. guitar and clarinet). Like in scenario 1, these queries involve searches through the dataset, yet they are meant for very different users with different needs that require specific user interfaces: journalists vs. music schools and composers.

Whilst some questions might be answered by showing the correlation between components (e.g., types of collaborations between artists), others might require reasoning (e.g., compute the possible keys from the list of chords), and mix cultural, audio or lyrics related content (e.g., orchestration mixes audio and metadata collected about artists/members' instruments). Answering these complex queries might also require an exploration of the WASABI corpus, and for that we offer a variety of analysis, exploration and visualization tools [6].

8 Conclusion and Future Work

In this paper, we described the data and software resources provided by the WASABI project to make it easier for researchers to access, query and make sense of a large corpus of commercial music information. Applications meant for different types of users (composers, music schools, archivists, streaming services) can be built upon this corpus, such as the WASABI explorer that includes a chord search engine and an augmented audio player [6].

We generated and published an RDF knowledge graph providing a rich set of metadata about popular commercial songs from the last six decades. These metadata cover cultural aspects of songs/albums/artists, lyrics content as well as audio features extracted using Music Information Retrieval techniques. The RDF representation currently uses some free text values coming from the original sources. To be more in line with Linked Data practices, in the future we intend to improve this by reusing, extending or defining thesauruses with respect to musical genres, music instrument types (currently 220 distinct values among which 16 different types of guitar) and equipment types (e.g. microphone, amplifier). We also published the pipeline we set up to generate this knowledge graph, in order to *(1)* continue enriching it and *(2)* spur and facilitate reuse and adaptation of both the dataset and the pipeline.

It is important to note that during the project we had access to copyrighted content (song lyrics, audio files) that we are not allowed to include in the published dataset. Nevertheless, a lot of work has been done on the analysis of song lyrics and the results are available on the GitHub of the project (metadata, ML templates, Python scripts and Jupyter notebooks). It is still possible for researchers to get the lyrics (e.g. via the commercial MusixMatch API[17]) or the audio (via Deezer's public API which offers 30-s clips, or via the YouTube API for example) to reproduce our results. Some computed metadata related to the synchronized chord sequences (used by the augmented audio player in the WASABI online explorer) were published only partially to avoid copyright infringement (as they are too close to music scores). Nevertheless, in collaboration with Deezer and IRCAM, we plan to carry out further audio analyses, mainly for scenarios of interest to music schools, musicologists, archivists and broadcast services.

Results from the lyric processing are provided in the original dataset in different forms (json, csv, etc.). At the time of writing, only the explicitness metadata are included in the RDF knowledge graph, and we are working on a future update that will include other metadata. However, all the components are connected through the WASABI ids, shared by all versions of the dataset.

References

1. Adamou, A., Brown, S., Barlow, H., Allocca, C., d'Aquin, M.: Crowdsourcing linked data on listening experiences through reuse and enhancement of library data. Int. J. Digit. Libr. **20**(1), 61–79 (2019)
2. Allik, A., Mora-Mcginity, M., Fazekas, G., Sandler, M.: MusicWeb: an open linked semantic platform for music metadata. In: Proceedings of the 15th International Semantic Web Conference (2016)

---

[17] https://developer.musixmatch.com/, ex: of lyrics retrieval at https://jsbin.com/janafox/edit.

3. Allik, A., Thalmann, F., Sandler, M.: MusicLynx: exploring music through artist similarity graphs. In: Companion Proceedings of the Web Conference (2018)

4. Bertin-Mahieux, T., Ellis, D.P., Whitman, B., Lamere, P.: The million song dataset. In: Proceedings of the ISMIR Conference (2011)

5. Bogdanov, D., Won, M., Tovstogan, P., Porter, A., Serra, X.: The MTG-Jamendo dataset for automatic music tagging. In: Proceedings of ICML (2019)

6. Buffa, M., Lebrun, J., Pauwels, J., Pellerin, G.: A 2 Million commercial song interactive navigator. In: WAC - 5th WebAudio Conference, December 2019

7. Çano, E., Morisio, M., et al.: Music mood dataset creation based on last. fm tags. In: 2017 International Conference on Artificial Intelligence and Applications (2017)

8. Delbouys, R., Hennequin, R., Piccoli, F., Royo-Letelier, J., Moussallam, M.: Music mood detection based on audio and lyrics with deep neural net. arXiv preprint arXiv:1809.07276 (2018)

9. Farias Lóscio, B., Burle, C., Calegari, N.: Data on the Web Best Practices. W3C Recommandation (2017)

10. Fell, M.: Natural language processing for music information retrieval: deep analysis of lyrics structure and content. Université Côte d'Azur, Theses (2020)

11. Fell, M., Cabrio, E., Corazza, M., Gandon, F.: Comparing automated methods to detect explicit content in song lyrics. In: RANLP - Recent Advances in Natural Language Processing, September 2019

12. Fell, M., Cabrio, E., Gandon, F., Giboin, A.: Song lyrics summarization inspired by audio thumb nailing. In: RANLP - Recent Advances in Natural Language Processing (RANLP), September 2019

13. Fell, M., Cabrio, E., Korfed, E., Buffa, M., Gandon, F.: Love me, love me, say (and write!) that you love me: enriching the WASABI song corpus with lyrics annotations. In: Proceedings of the 12th LREC Conference, pp. 2138–2147, May 2020

14. Fell, M., Nechaev, Y., Cabrio, E., Gandon, F.: Lyrics segmentation: textual macrostructure detection using convolutions. In: Conference on Computational Linguistics (COLING), pp. 2044–2054, August 2018

15. Fell, M., Nechaev, Y., Meseguer-Brocal, G., Cabrio, E., Gandon, F., Peeters, G.: Lyrics segmentation via bimodal text-audio representation. Nat. Lang. Eng. (to appear)

16. Lisena, P., et al.: Improving (re-) usability of musical datasets: an overview of the doremus project. Bibliothek Forschung und Praxis **42**(2), 194–205 (2018)

17. Meroño-Peñuela, A., et al.: The MIDI linked data cloud. In: d'Amato, C., et al. (eds.) ISWC 2017. LNCS, vol. 10588, pp. 156–164. Springer, Cham (2017). https://doi.org/10.1007/978-3-319-68204-4_16

18. Meseguer-Brocal, G., Cohen-Hadria, A., Peeters, G.: Dali: a large dataset of synchronized audio, lyrics and notes, automatically created using teacher-student machine learning paradigm. In: Proceedings of the ISMIR Conference (2018)

19. Michel, F., Djimenou, L., Faron-Zucker, C., Montagnat, J.: Translation of relational and non-relational databases into RDF with xR2RML. In: Proceedings of the 11th WebIST Conference, pp. 443–454 (2015)

20. Monti, D., et al.: An ensemble approach of recurrent neural networks using pre-trained embeddings for playlist completion. In: Proceedings of the ACM Recommender Systems Challenge, RecSys Challenge, pp. 13:1–13:6 (2018)

21. Page, K.R., Lewis, D., Weigl, D.M.: MELD: a linked data framework for multimedia access to music digital libraries. In: 2019 ACM/IEEE Joint Conference on Digital Libraries (JCDL), pp. 434–435. IEEE (2019)

22. Pauwels, J., O'Hanlon, K., Fazekas, G., Sandler, M.B.: Confidence measures and their applications in music labelling systems based on hidden Markov models. In: Proceedings of the 18th ISMIR Conference, pp. 279–285 (2017)
23. Pauwels, J., O'Hanlon, K., Gómez, E., Sandler, M.B.: 20 years of automatic chord recognition from audio. In: Proceedings of the 20th ISMIR Conference (2019)
24. Raimond, Y., Abdallah, S., Sandler, M., Giasson, F.: The music ontology. In: Proceedings of the 8th ISMIR Conference, pp. 417–422 (2007)
25. Shneiderman, B.: The eyes have it: a task by data type taxonomy for information visualizations. In: Proceedings 1996 IEEE Symposium on Visual Languages, pp. 336–343. IEEE (1996)
26. Xambó, A., Pauwels, J., Roma, G., Barthet, M., Fazekas, G.: Jam with Jamendo: querying a large music collection by chords from a learner's perspective. In: Proceedings of Audio Mostly, pp. 1–7 (2018)

RuBQ 2.0: An Innovated Russian Question Answering Dataset

Ivan Rybin[1], Vladislav Korablinov[1], Pavel Efimov[1],
and Pavel Braslavski[2,3(✉)]

[1] ITMO University, Saint Petersburg, Russia
[2] Ural Federal University, Yekaterinburg, Russia
[3] HSE University, Moscow, Russia

Abstract. The paper describes the second version of RuBQ, a Russian dataset for knowledge base question answering (KBQA) over Wikidata. Whereas the first version builds on Q&A pairs harvested online, the extension is based on questions obtained through search engine query suggestion services. The questions underwent crowdsourced and in-house annotation in a quite different fashion compared to the first edition. The dataset doubled in size: RuBQ 2.0 contains 2,910 questions along with the answers and SPARQL queries. The dataset also incorporates answer-bearing paragraphs from Wikipedia for the majority of questions. The dataset is suitable for the evaluation of KBQA, machine reading comprehension (MRC), hybrid questions answering, as well as semantic parsing. We provide the analysis of the dataset and report several KBQA and MRC baseline results. The dataset is freely available under the CC-BY-4.0 license.

Keywords: Knowledge base question answering · Multilingual question answering · Machine reading comprehension · Evaluation resources · Russian language resources

1 Introduction

Question Answering (QA) is an important scientific and applied problem that aims at building a system that can answer questions in a natural language. Two main directions within QA are *Open-Domain Question Answering (ODQA)* and *Knowledge Base Question Answering (KBQA)* (also referred to as *Knowledge Graph Question Answering, KGQA*). ODQA searches for the answer in a large collection of text documents; the process is often divided into two stages: 1) retrieval of documents/paragraphs potentially containing the answer and 2) spotting an answer span within a given document/paragraph (referred to as *machine reading comprehension, MRC*). In contrast, KBQA searches an answer

Ivan Rybin—work done as an intern at JetBrains Research.
Resource location: https://doi.org/10.5281/zenodo.4345696.
Project page: https://github.com/vladislavneon/RuBQ.

in a knowledge base that is commonly structured as a collection of *(subject, predicate, object)* triples, e.g. *(Yuri Gagarin, occupation, astronaut)*. The KBQA task can be formulated as a translation from a natural language question into a formal semantic representation, e.g. a SPARQL query. In many real-life applications, like in *Jeopardy!* winning IBM Watson [12] and major search engines, hybrid QA systems are employed – they rely on both text document collections and structured knowledge bases.

As is typical for all machine learning applications, freely available annotated data for model training and testing is crucial for measurable progress in solving QA tasks. Since the inception of the SQuAD dataset [20], we have seen an avalanche of the available question answering datasets; the most recent trend is non-English and multilingual MRC datasets [5,17,18]. Available KBQA datasets are much scarcer; there are very few non-English datasets among them (see Sect. 2 for details). Russian is among top-10 languages by its L1 and L2 speakers;[1] it has a Cyrillic script and a number of grammar features that make it quite different from English – the language most frequently used in NLP and Semantic Web research.

In this paper, we describe an expansion of **RuBQ** (pronounced ['rubik]) – **Ru**ssian Knowledge **B**ase **Q**uestions, the first Russian KBQA dataset [15]. The first version of the dataset is based on the pairs of questions and answers from online quizzes and contains 1,500 questions along with Wikidata answers, corresponding SPARQL queries, and English machine-translated questions. The dataset is accompanied with a Wikidata snapshot `RuWikidata8M` containing about 212M triples that include 8.1M unique items with Russian labels. The motivation behind RuBQ 2.0 was larger size, higher diversity of questions, as well as the MRC part.

To expand the dataset, we obtained questions from Yandex and Google query suggestion services. A potential advantage of such questions from a search log is that they reflect realistic users' information needs and their wordings. A possible disadvantage of query suggestion services as a source of questions is that we have very little control over the questions' selection criteria, as well as a limited number of returned suggestions for each input. In addition, the services rank the returned queries by their popularity, which may result in shorter, simpler, and less varied questions. As a seed, we used a set of manually crafted question prefixes corresponding to the most popular Wikidata properties, as well as properties with numeric values. To annotate the questions, we employed a pipeline quite different from the version one. We used crowdsourcing to find the answers to the questions and generated SPARQL queries based on automatically extracted question entities and the corresponding properties. We retained those items that produced correct answers. Using this routine, we were able to almost double the dataset: the extended version reached 2,910 questions.

In addition, using automatic methods and subsequent crowdsourced verification, we coupled most of the questions in the dataset with Wikipedia paragraphs containing the answer. Thus, the dataset can be used for testing MRC models, as

---

[1] https://en.wikipedia.org/wiki/List_of_languages_by_total_number_of_speakers.

well as for research on hybrid question answering. We provide several baselines
both for KBQA and MRC that demonstrate that there is an ample room for
improving QA methods. In the reminder of the paper we will refer to the add-on
to the initial dataset as *Query Suggestion Questions* (QSQ), and the merging
of RuBQ 1.0 and QSQ as RuBQ 2.0. Taking into account RuBQ's modest size,
we propose to use the dataset primarily for testing rule-based systems, models based on few/zero-shot and transfer learning, as well as models trained on
automatically generated examples, similarly to recent MRC datasets [1,17]. We
believe that rich and versatile annotation of the dataset will attract researchers
from different communities – Semantic Web, Information Retrieval, and NLP.
RuBQ 2.0 is freely available under the CC-BY-4.0 license in JSON format.[2]

2   Related Work

For a comprehensive survey of KBQA datasets, including the first edition of
RuBQ, see our paper [15]. The majority of KBQA datasets are in English. Few
exceptions are Chinese MSParS [8], multilingual (machine-translated to a large
extent) QALD [25], and the newly introduced Russian RuBQ. A recently published Multilingual Knowledge Questions and Answers (MKQA) dataset [18] contains human translations of 10,000 English questions from the Natural Questions
(NQ) dataset [16] into 25 languages, including Russian. MKQA refrains from
using the existing NQ answers and obtains the answers anew for each language
variant via crowdsourcing. The answers are divided into several types: entity,
long answer, unanswerable, date, number, number with unit, short phrase, as
well as yes/no. Entity answers (4,221 in the English subset, for other languages
the number may slightly differ) are linked to Wikidata. However, the dataset
does not contain annotations of the question entities nor corresponding formal
representations such as SPARQL queries.

Our approach uses search engine query suggestion services to obtain new
questions and is similar to the approach behind the WebQuestions dataset containing 5.8K questions [2]. Later, 81% of WebQuestions were provided with
SPARQL queries and formed the WebQuestionsSP dataset [26]. In contrast to
WebQuestions that started with a single question and iteratively expanded the
pool of questions, we started with a manually crafted list of question prefixes presumably corresponding to the most frequent Wikidata properties and properties
with literal values.

Since the advent of SQuAD [20], a large number of MRC datasets have been
published. In the context of our study, the most relevant datasets are those
built in a semi-automatic manner using existing Q&A pairs. TriviaQA [14]
builds on a collection of 95K trivia and quiz question-answers pairs collected
on the Web. The dataset is enriched with documents from Web search results
and Wikipedia articles for entities identified in the questions, 650K documents
in total. SearchQA dataset [10] exploits a similar approach: it starts from a collection of 140K question-answer pairs from *Jeopardy!* archive and is augmented

---

[2] https://github.com/vladislavneon/RuBQ.

with Google search snippets containing the answer. Each SearchQA Q&A pair is aligned with about 50 such snippets on average. In contrast to these datasets, we conducted an exhaustive crowdsourced annotation of the evidence paragraphs.

Built in 2017 with 50K question-paragraph-answer triples and using SQuAD as a reference, SberQUAD is the largest Russian MRC dataset. A post-hoc analysis revealed that the dataset is quite noisy [11]. Multilingual XQuAD [1] and TyDi QA [5] datasets contain around 1K and 7K Russian items, respectively; summary statistics and comparison of these three resources can be found in our recent paper [11].

Hybrid QA studies start usually with an existing KBQA dataset and complement it with textual evidence using NER and IR techniques [21,22]. A drawback of this approach is that results can be hardly reproduced and compared in absence of a standard dataset. QALD-4 dataset addresses this issues, but is rather small: it contains relevant textual abstracts along with SPARQL queries for 25 questions [24]. Grau and Ligozat [13] built a hybrid QA dataset by recycling questions and answers from TREC and CLEF QA campaigns and augmented them with DBpedia IDs. The resulting dataset contains around 2.2K KB-annotated Q&A pairs, but is not freely available currently. Chen et al. [4] introduced recently the HybridQA dataset that comprises of 13K English Wikipedia tables associated with text passages, as well as 70K questions generated by crowd workers.

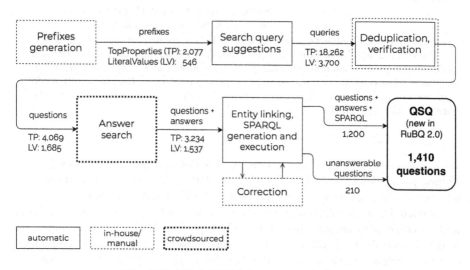

Fig. 1. RuBQ 2.0 KBQA creation pipeline.

3   Data Acquisition and Annotation

The data processing pipeline is presented in Fig. 1. To obtain new questions, we used query suggestion services by Google and Yandex search engines. Firstly,

Table 1. Examples of prefixes for three Wikidata properties and suggested queries; continuations are in **bold**.

Prefix	Returned queries
	height (P2048)
какая высота	какая высота **Эйфелевой башни**
what is the height	*what is the height of the Eiffel tower*
	какая высота **у 9-этажного дома в метрах**[†]
	what is the height of a 9-storey house in meters
какого роста	какого роста **был Наполеон**
how tall	*how tall was Napoleon*
	какого роста **был Илья Муромец**[‡]
	how tall was Ilya Muromets
	educated at (P69)
в каком вузе	в каком вузе **самый низкий проходной балл**[†]
which university	*which university has the lowest passing score*
какой университет окончил	какой университет окончил **Ньютон**[§]
what university did X graduate from	*what university did Newton graduate from*
в каком университете	в каком университете **учился Толстой**
which university	*which university did Tolstoy attend*
в какой школе	в какой школе **учился Гарри Поттер**
what school	*what school did Harry Potter attend*
	noble title (P97)
какой титул у	какой титул у **Кейт Миддлтон**
what title	*what is Kate Middleton's title*
	какой титул у **Хабиба Нурмагомедова**[$]
	what is Khabib Nurmagomedov's title

Notes: [†] questions cannot be answered with Wikidata, we filtered them out manually on the initial stage; [‡] Ilya Muromets (Q1146624) is a legendary hero of the Russian folklore; the question is suitable for KBQA, but the answer is missing in Wikidata; [§] is legitimate, but does not correspond to the expected property; [$] Russian questions do not use auxiliary verbs in contrast to e.g. English, so the subject comes right after the prefix (cf. translated prefix).

we consulted a list of the most popular Wikidata properties,[3] removed cross-linking properties such as *PubMed ID* and *DOI*, and manually crafted question prefixes for the remaining top-200 properties, 2,077 in total. To generate prefixes, we started from the Wikidata property aliases and tried to ensure diversity and coverage, see examples in Table 1. Many prefixes for the same property are almost identical – they differ only in the verb tense/form. Note that the prefixes can be ambiguous and do not uniquely define the property. In addition, we manually compiled 546 question prefixes that imply numerical and date answers, for example: *What is the melting point...*

Search engine suggestion services return up to 10 items for each input. Sometimes the beginnings of returned items do not match the initial prefixes, which is likely due to semantic rather than lexical matching methods. Given a lim-

---

[3] https://www.wikidata.org/wiki/Wikidata:Database_reports/List_of_properties/all.

ited number of returned queries, the simultaneous use of two services allowed to slightly increase the variety of questions. In total, we collected 18,262 queries for prefixes corresponding to popular properties, and 3,700 queries for prefixes with expected numerical answers. These queries have been filtered semi-automatically: we removed duplicates, queries without question words, and questions that cannot be answered using solely a knowledge base, e.g. *What holiday is it today?* After such cleaning, 4,069 unique questions remained, corresponding to 146 properties from the top-200 Wikidata properties, and 1,685 questions with expected numerical answers. We refer to these question samples as *TopProperties* and *LiteralValues*, respectively.

To obtain answers to the questions, we posted a project on the Toloka crowdsourcing platform.[4] The crowd workers' task was to find one or several answers to a question on the Web or indicate that they cannot find any. The interface contained a link to the Google search results for the question, but the workers were instructed that they are free to modify the search query and use other information sources on the Web. Each question was shown to three workers; we kept all the questions where at least two answers matched.[5] In total, we obtained answers for 4,771 questions; Table 2 summarizes the statistics.

In addition, we asked the crowd workers to indicate whether the answer was found as a Google instant answer (also called 'features snippet'). The share of such answers among *TopProperties* questions was 65.3%, i.e. the search engine answers about 2/3 of the questions using question answering capabilities. The share of instant answers for *LiteralValues* group was higher – 87.8%. Note that here we only wanted to get some insight into the search engine answering capabilities and did not use the observed estimates in dataset preparation.

Table 2. Crowdsourced answers' statistics: initial number of questions; questions for which no answers are found; number of questions, where two out of three or all three crowd workers agreed on the answers.

Sample	Q	noA	2/3	3/3	Total
TopProperties	4,069	300	1,278	1,956	3,234
LiteralValues	1,685	148	384	1,153	1,537
				Total:	4,771

To complement questions with SPARQL queries, we firstly applied an IR-based entity linker developed for RuBQ 1.0. For each input string, the linker generates several phrase and free-form queries to a search index of all Russian labels and aliases from Wikidata (about 5.4M items). Returned Wikidata entity candidates are ranked based on a combination of confidence value from

---

[4] https://toloka.ai/.

[5] In case of multiple answers majority voting was applied to individual answers, not the whole list.

the search engine and the popularity of the corresponding Wikipedia pages. The linker proved to be efficient and of high quality, details can be found in the RuBQ 1.0 paper [15]. For the current step, we retained top-5 candidates for each question and answer. Secondly, using the question's anticipated property, we checked whether a triple *(Q_ entity, property, A_ entity)* with any combination of candidate question/answer entities was present in Wikidata.[6] This fully automatic procedure resulted in 746 questions linked to Wikidata (407 in *Top-Properties* and 339 in *LiteralValues*). This approach is quite different from the one of RuBQ 1.0, where entity linking in answers was performed by crowd workers. To increase the number of annotated questions and answers, we manually corrected some questions' properties and entities. This selective in-house annotation allowed us to reach 1,200 annotated questions to double the size of RuBQ compared to the first version.

Since their introduction in SQuAD 2.0 [19], unanswerable questions are featured in many MRC datasets. In the context of an MRC task, such question cannot be answered based on a given paragraph. RuBQ 1.0 and the aforementioned MKQA dataset also contain unanswerable questions. In case of RuBQ, unanswerable questions cannot be answered using the provided Wikidata snapshot. In case of MKQA, this category encompasses ill-formed questions and questions for which no clear answer can be found. We also enriched QSQ with questions, for which the majority of crowd workers agreed on the answer, but the question could not be answered with the current state of Wikidata graph. While many unanswerable quiz questions from the first version of RuBQ can be hardly expressed with Wikidata properties (e.g. *How many noses do snails have?*)[7], unanswerable QSQs are quite common in their form and cannot be answered rather due to KB incompleteness, e.g. *Who is the inventor of streptomycin?*

As can be seen from the Table 3, using the process described above, we were able to almost double the size of the dataset: the number of questions that can be answered using the current version of Wikidata has doubled, while we added slightly fewer unanswerable questions compared to the first version (210 vs. 300). Questions from search engine suggestion services are significantly shorter than quiz questions. Due to the procedure of matching the answers to the Wikidata entities in the first version of the dataset, there were very few questions with numerical and date answers. When working on the extension, we specifically addressed this problem – half of the added answerable questions have a literal answer. Following RuBQ 1.0, we annotated the questions based on the structure of corresponding SPARQL-queries. As in the previous version of the dataset, the majority of questions (911) are *simple*, i.e. they are one-hop questions without aggregation.[8] While the share of simple questions is about the same as in the first

---

[6] Note that prefixes sent to the query suggestion service do not guarantee that the returned question expresses the intended property.

[7] The answer is four; Google returns an instant answer with a supporting piece of text.

[8] Our approach resulted in a slightly lower share of simple questions in QSQ compared to WebQuestions: 76% vs. 85%. It can be attributed to the source of questions and the collection process, as well as to differences in Freebase vs. Wikidata structure.

Table 3. Dataset statistics.

	RuBQ 1.0	QSQ	RuBQ 2.0
Questions	1,500	1,410	2,910
KB-answerable questions	1,200	1,200	2,400
KB-unanswerable questions	300	210	510
Avg. question length (words)	7.9	5.4	6.7
Simple questions (*1-hop* w/o aggregation)	921	911	1,832
Questions with multiple answers	131	244	375
Questions with literals as answers	46	600	646
Unique properties	242	139	294
Unique entities in questions	1,218	1,126	2,114
Unique entities in answers	1,250	1,983	3,166

version, the number of questions with list answers increased significantly. Even though the number of questions doubled, this led to only a moderate increase in unique properties in the dataset – from 242 in the first version to 294 in the second. At the same time, the number of unique entities in questions has almost doubled; the increase in the number of unique answer entities was even more significant. We divided QSQ into dev (280) and test (1,130) subsets maintaining similar ratios of questions types in the subsets. Thus, RuBQ 2.0 contains 580 and 2,330 questions in dev and test sets, respectively. The dataset is available in JSON format; sample entries are shown in Table 4.

Table 4. Sample RuBQ 2.0 entries. Questions are originally in Russian; not all dataset fields are shown.

Question	How many wives did Henry VIII have?
Answer	6
Answer aliases	six

SPARQL query	`SELECT (COUNT(?x) as ?answer)`
	`WHERE {`
	`    wd:Q38370 wdt:P26 ?x.`
	`}`

Tags	count, 1-hop
Paragraphs with answers	51089, 51086
Related paragraphs	51086, 51087, 51088, 51089...
Question	Where is Kutuzov buried?
Answer	Q656 (Saint Petersburg)
Answer aliases	Leningrad, Petersburg, St. Petersburg, Petrograd, Sankt-Peterburg

SPARQL query	`SELECT ?answer`
	`WHERE {`
	`    wd:Q185801 wdt:P119 ?answer`
	`}`

Tags	1-hop
Paragraphs with answers	416
Related paragraphs	416, 417, 418, 419, 420...

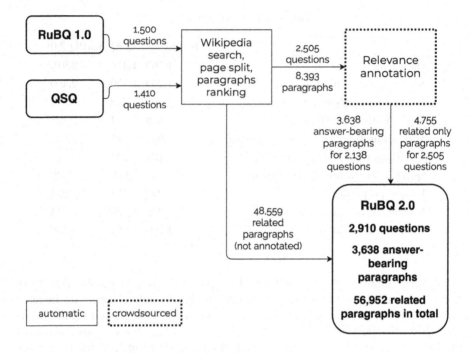

Fig. 2. RuBQ 2.0 MRC creation pipeline.

4   Adding Machine Reading Capabilities

The pipeline of this stage is presented in Fig. 2. To enrich the dataset with machine reading capabilities, we collected all Russian Wikipedia articles corresponding to question and answer entities and split them into paragraphs. For unanswerable questions with no entities linked, we took the top-5 Wikipedia search API results[9] using the question as a query.

Further, we represented questions and answers as bag of words with stopwords removed and entity name synonyms added. The synonyms included Russian and English labels and aliases ("alternate names") from Wikidata, as well as the Wikipedia anchor texts pointing to the entity page. In most cases, the anchor text was an inflectional variant of the entity name (e.g. *Alexandra Pushkina$_{ru}$* – genitive case of *Alexander Pushkin*), a short form (*Pushkin* for *Alexander Pushkin*), or a cross-POS relationship (for example, *Russian$_{adj}$* pointing to *Russia$_{noun}$*). The paragraphs were ranked in descending order of word occurrences from the answer representation; within equal number of occurrences the paragraphs were ranked according to the word occurrences from the question.

Further, the top-4 paragraphs containing at least an answer evidence were annotated on the Toloka crowdsourcing platform. These paragraphs correspond to 2,505 questions out of total 2,910; for 405 questions missing supporting para-

---

[9] https://ru.wikipedia.org/w/api.php.

graphs the answer was often present not in the article body, but in its infobox. The paragraphs were presented to the crowd workers along with the original question, but without the answer. The workers' task was to mark all paragraphs that provide enough information to answer the question. Each question was initially presented to three workers. If the workers disagreed on at least one of the paragraphs, the task was assigned to two more workers. After that, if the difference between positive and negative label counts is three or higher, the corresponding paragraph is considered relevant. Following this procedure, 8,393 paragraphs were annotated in total. Krippendorf's alpha for annotation with three choices (*yes/no/not sure*) is 0.83, which can be considered as a high level of agreement. Crowd workers marked at least one paragraph as providing the answer in case of for 2,138 questions; on average, there are 1.45 supporting paragraphs per question; 367 questions are not provided with an answer-bearing paragraph. Note that 186 (out of 510) KB-unanswerable questions are provided with answer-bearing paragraphs, which can be seen as a potential for hybrid QA.

To be able to use the dataset not only to assess machine reading comprehension, but also paragraph retrieval, we added related paragraphs for each answer. For each question, we added up to 25 paragraphs from top-5 Wikipedia search results using question as a query, ranked by the occurrence of words from the answer and question representations in a similar way to how we ranked paragraphs before crowdsourced annotation. In total, we provide 56,952 unique Wikipedia paragraphs as a part of the dataset; the average length of a paragraph is 62 tokens.

The data preparation process described above has several advantages. Firstly, the annotation process is simpler and faster compared to SQuAD and similar datasets: crowd workers do not need to select a span within a paragraph – only mark a paragraph as sufficient to answer the question. Secondly, the questions are generated independently from the paragraph, which leads to a more natural and realistic task. When questions are generated by crowd workers based on presented paragraphs like in SQuAD or SberQuAD, they tend to be lexically and structurally similar to sentences containing answers and easier to answer as such, see [16]. In contrast to MRC datasets produced fully automatically based on Q&A pairs and search, relevant paragraphs in RuBQ 2.0 are verified manually.

5 Baselines

5.1 KBQA Baselines

Most KBQA research prototypes work with English and Freebase as a target KB. *QAnswer* and *DeepPavlov* are only two available KBQA systems for Russian working with Wikidata. We also employed English version of *QAnswer* along with machine-translated questions, as well implemented a simple rule-based baseline. Thus, the four baseline models reflect a spectrum of approaches to KBQA.

DeepPavlov is an open library featuring models for variety of NLP tasks, including Russian language models [3]. We tested the previous DeepPavlov KBQA system that coped only with simple questions, on RuBQ 1.0 [15]. An improved KBQA model was released by DeepPavlov in summer of 2020.[10] The new release has several components and addresses not only simple questions, but also ranking and counting questions, as well as questions requiring reasoning on numerical values and dates. According to its description, the system sequentially performs query type prediction, entity extraction and linking, relation extraction and path ranking, and finally issues an online SPARQL query to Wikidata.

QAnswer is a rule-based KBQA system that answers questions in several languages using Wikidata [7]. QAnswer returns a (possibly empty) ranked list of Wikidata item IDs along with a corresponding SPARQL query. Since recently, QAnswer accepts Russian questions. We obtained QAnswer's results by sending either original Russian or English machine-translated questions to its API.[11]

We also provide our own rule-based baseline *SimBa* addressing simple questions.[12] The method consists of three components: 1) entity linker based on syntax parsing and a search index, 2) rule-based relation extraction, and 3) SPARQL query generator. The question is parsed with the DeepPavlov parser;[13] interrogative word/phrase is identified using a dictionary, and remaining subtrees from the root are candidate entity mentions. These candidates are mapped to Wikidata entities using a search index. Relation extraction method is quite straightforward: we compiled a list of 100 most frequent Wikidata properties and manually generated regular expressions for them.[14] A question can match regular expressions corresponding to different properties, all of them are added as candidates. Based on the obtained lists of candidate entities and properties, 1-hop SPARQL queries are constructed for all entity–relation pairs. Once the query returns a non-empty answer from Wikidata, the process terminates and the answer is returned.

We calculated the number of correctly answered questions in respective test sets by each of the system. If QAnswer returned a ranked list of answers, only the top answer was considered. In case of multiple correct answers, a system's answer was counted if it matched any of the reference answers. In case of unanswerable questions, an answer was deemed correct if the systems returned either an empty or "no answer/not found" response. DeepPavlov returns an answer as a string rather than a Wikidata item ID, or *not found*, so we compared its answers with the correct answer's label if the correct answer was an entity or with its value if the correct answer was a literal.

---

[10] http://docs.deeppavlov.ai/en/master/features/models/kbqa.html.

[11] https://qanswer-frontend.univ-st-etienne.fr/.

[12] https://github.com/vladislavneon/kbqa-tools/rubq-baseline.

[13] http://docs.deeppavlov.ai/en/master/features/models/syntaxparser.html.

[14] Although these regular expressions and prefixes for collecting QSQs were developed independently and for different sets of properties, this approach can introduce bias in results.

Table 5. Baselines' performance: percent of correct answers on the tests subsets. DP – DeepPavlov; QA-Ru and QA-En – Russian and English versions of QAnswer, respectively; SimBa – our simple baseline. Detailed tag descriptions can be found in RuBQ 1.0 paper [15]. Note that some question types in the lower part of the table are too few to make a reliable comparison.

	DP	QA-Ru	QA-En	SimBa
RuBQ 1.0				
Answerable (960)	**28.9**	23.1	22.0	26.9
Unanswerable (240)	64.2	3.8	8.3	**91.3**
Total (1,200)	35.9	19.3	19.3	**39.8**
QSQ				
Answerable (960)	19.8	30.7	**34.4**	23.6
Unanswerable (170)	36.5	8.8	5.3	**80.6**
Total (1,130)	22.3	27.4	30.0	**32.2**
RuBQ 2.0				
Answerable (1,920)	24.3	26.9	**28.2**	25.3
1-hop (1,460)	30.5	30.8	**32.3**	**32.3**
1-hop + reverse (10)	0.0	0.0	**10.0**	0.0
1-hop + count (3)	0.0	33.3	**66.7**	0.0
1-hop + exclusion (17)	0.0	**5.9**	**5.9**	0.0
Multi-constraint (304)	4.9	19.7	**20.4**	3.6
Multi-hop (55)	3.6	**10.9**	5.5	1.8
Qualifier-constraint (22)	**18.2**	0.0	0.0	4.5
Unanswerable (410)	52.7	5.9	7.1	**86.8**
Total (2,330)	29.3	23.2	24.5	**36.1**

As one can see from the Table 5, the models behave quite differently on answerable questions of the two parts of the dataset. The quality of both versions of QAnswer improves significantly on QSQ compared to RuBQ 1.0, with the improvement of the English version and machine-translated questions being the most striking (from 22.0% to 34.4%). The accuracy of our simple baseline drops from 26.9% to 23.6%; DeepPavlov's drop in quality is more significant – from 28.6% to 19.8%. These results indirectly confirm that expanding the dataset is useful – it allows to get more reliable evaluation results. It is interesting to note that machine translated questions sent to the English version of QAnswer show a better result on QSQ than the original questions on the Russian-language QAnswer (English QAnswer outperforms its Russian counterpart on the whole dataset, but the difference is less pronounced). Perhaps this is due to a more advanced English-language system, or to the fact that shorter and more frequent questions from QSQ get better machine translations.

All systems are expectedly better at handling simple (1-hop) questions that make up the bulk of the dataset. Even the proposed simple baseline copes with simple questions on par with more sophisticated systems. However, the approach explicitly assumes the structure of the query and can only handle questions that correspond to a limited set of popular Wikidata properties. Both versions of QAnswer perform best on complex questions. DeepPavlov's mediocre performance on complex questions can be explained by the fact that the eight patterns that the system operates on are poorly represented among the limited number of RuBQ's complex questions. Few correct answers returned by a simple baseline to complex questions can be considered an artifact. English QAnswer with machine-translated questions achieved the best score on the answerable questions: 28.2% of correct answers. The result suggests that there is an ample room for improvements in multilingual KBQA methods.

The performance of the systems on unanswerable questions sheds some light on their strategies. All the systems in the experiment seem to build a SPARQL query from a question without analyzing the local Wikidata graph or postprocessing the returned results. Due to its cautious strategy, our simple baseline does not return an answer to most of the unanswerable questions. In contrast, QAnswer seems to be a recall-oriented system and returns an answer to almost all questions in both English and Russian versions.

5.2   MRC Baselines

We opted for Multiligual BERT (mBERT) model fine-tuned on MRC task as a baseline. mBERT is a Transformer-based language model pre-trained on the top-100 languages from Wikipedia [6]. Fine-tuned BERT models demonstrated state-of-the-art performance in many downstream NLP tasks, including MRC. Interestingly, BERT-based models show competitive performance in zero-shot cross-lingual setting, when a model is trained on the English data and then applied to the data in another language. Artetxe et al. analyze this phenomenon on multilingual classification and question answering tasks [1]. For our experiments, we fine-tune $BERT_{BASE}$ Multilingual Cased model[15] on three training sets: English SQuAD [20], Russian SberQuAD [11], and a Russian subset of TyDi QA Gold Passage [5]. The number of training question-paragraph-answer triples is 87,599, 45,328, and 6,490, respectively.

MRC model returns a continuous span as an answer for a given paragraph and question. The answer is evaluated against gold answer spans provided by crowd workers. Traditionally, token-based F1 measure of the best match (in case of multiple gold answers) averaged over all questions is used as evaluation metrics. In our case we do not have explicitly marked answer spans within paragraphs, but have a list of correct answer's labels and aliases. Note that considering the way the MRC collection was created, the relevant paragraph must contain an answer in one form or another (see Sect. 4 for details). Since Russian is a highly inflectional language, the surface form of the answer in the paragraph may differ

---

[15] https://huggingface.co/bert-base-multilingual-cased.

from a normalized form in the list. We experimented with three approaches to quantify the match between gold answers and model responses: token-based F1, lemmatized token-based F1, and character-based F1. Token-based metrics treat gold and system answers as bags of words, while the character-based metrics calculate the longest common subsequence (LCS) between the gold and the system answers. In case of the lemmatized version, both gold answers and system responses are processed with *mystem* lemmatizer.[16] We consider the lemmatized token-based F1 as the most reliable metrics; however, its disadvantage is the overhead of lemmatization.

Table 6. MRC baseline results: F1 based either on word overlap (Tokens and Lemmas), or best longest common subsequence (LCS) between gold and system answers. The second column cites the number of training items.

Training set	# items	Tokens	Lemmas	LCS
SQuAD (En, 0-shot)	87,599	0.54	0.70	0.76
SberQuAD (Ru)	45,328	0.48	0.62	0.70
TyDi QA (Ru)	6,490	0.51	0.67	0.73

We applied the models to all 3,638 pairs of questions and relevant paragraphs in the dataset (several relevant paragraphs can be associated with a question). Table 6 reports the performance of the three models. Note that the relative performance of the models is consistent across all metrics. Surprisingly, the model trained on English SQuAD scores the best, while the model trained on a small Russian collection TyDi QA is quite competitive. Although SberQuAD is seven times larger than Russian TyDi QA, it performs worse, probably due to a high level of noise in the annotations as we mentioned in Sect. 2. Although these scores do not account for the paragraph retrieval step and cannot be compared directly with KBQA scores in Table 5, we believe that hybrid KB/text approach to QA can substantially improve the overall results on the dataset.

6   Conclusions

In this work, we described the extension of RuBQ, the Russian dataset for question answering over Wikidata. The first version of the dataset was based on quiz questions and answer pairs harvested on the web. After exhausting this source of questions, we turned to search query suggestion services. This approach proved to be quite efficient: it required manual preparation of question prefixes and a later limited in-house verification; most of the annotation was carried out using crowdsourcing and automated routines. We managed to double the size of the dataset – from 1,500 to 2,910 questions. In addition to questions and Wikidata answers, the dataset contains SPARQL queries, tags indicating query type,

---

[16] https://yandex.ru/dev/mystem/ (in Russian).

English machine translations of the questions, entities in the question, answer aliases, etc. The dataset is accompanied by a Wikidata snapshot containing approximately 8M entities and 212M triples, which ensures the reproducibility of the results. We evaluated three third-party and an own KBQA system on RuBQ. All systems are built on different principles and reflect well the range of approaches to KBQA. Based on the experimental results, we can conclude that the expanded dataset allows for a more reliable evaluation of KBQA systems.

We also expanded the dataset with machine reading comprehension capabilities: most questions are provided with Wikipedia paragraphs containing answers. Thus, the dataset can be used to evaluate machine reading comprehension, paragraph retrieval, and end-to-end open-domain question answering. The dataset can be also used for experiments in hybrid QA, where KBQA and text-based QA can enrich and complement each other. We have implemented three simple MRC baselines that demonstrate the feasibility of this approach.

The main disadvantage of the dataset is a small number of complex questions. In the future, we plan to address this problem and explore different approaches to complex questions generation [9, 23].

The dataset is freely distributed under the CC-BY-4.0 license and will be of interest to a wide range of researchers from various fields – Semantic Web, Information Retrieval, and Natural Language Processing.

Acknowledgments. We thank Yaroslav Golubev, Dmitry Ustalov, and anonymous reviewers for their valuable comments that helped improve the paper. We are grateful to Toloka for their data annotation grant. PB acknowledges support from the Ministry of Science and Higher Education of the Russian Federation (the project of the development of the regional scientific and educational mathematical center "Ural Mathematical Center").

References

1. Artetxe, M., Ruder, S., Yogatama, D.: On the cross-lingual transferability of monolingual representations. In: ACL, pp. 4623–4637 (2020)
2. Berant, J., Chou, A., Frostig, R., Liang, P.: Semantic parsing on Freebase from question-answer pairs. In: EMNLP, pp. 1533–1544 (2013)
3. Burtsev, M., et al.: DeepPavlov: open-source library for dialogue systems. In: ACL (System Demonstrations), pp. 122–127 (2018)
4. Chen, W., et al.: HybridQA: a dataset of multi-hop question answering over tabular and textual data. arXiv preprint arXiv:2004.07347 (2020)
5. Clark, J.H., et al.: TyDi QA: a benchmark for information-seeking question answering in typologically diverse languages. TACL **8**, 454–470 (2020)
6. Devlin, J., Chang, M.W., Lee, K., Toutanova, K.: BERT: pre-training of deep bidirectional transformers for language understanding. In: NAACL-HLT, pp. 4171–4186 (2019)
7. Diefenbach, D., Giménez-García, J., Both, A., Singh, K., Maret, P.: QAnswer KG: designing a portable question answering system over rdf data. In: ESWC, pp. 429–445 (2020)

8. Duan, N.: Overview of the NLPCC 2019 shared task: open domain semantic parsing. In: Tang, J., Kan, M.-Y., Zhao, D., Li, S., Zan, H. (eds.) NLPCC 2019. LNCS (LNAI), vol. 11839, pp. 811–817. Springer, Cham (2019). https://doi.org/10.1007/978-3-030-32236-6_74

9. Dubey, M., Banerjee, D., Abdelkawi, A., Lehmann, J.: LC-QuAD 2.0: a large dataset for complex question answering over Wikidata and DBpedia. In: ISWC, pp. 69–78 (2019)

10. Dunn, M., et al.: SearchQA: a new Q&A dataset augmented with context from a search engine. arXiv preprint arXiv:1704.05179 (2017)

11. Efimov, P., Chertok, A., Boytsov, L., Braslavski, P.: SberQuAD-Russian reading comprehension dataset: description and analysis. In: CLEF, pp. 3–15 (2020)

12. Ferrucci, D., et al.: Building Watson: an overview of the DeepQA project. AI Mag. **31**(3), 59–79 (2010)

13. Grau, B., Ligozat, A.L.: A corpus for hybrid question answering systems. In: Companion Proceedings of the The Web Conference 2018, pp. 1081–1086 (2018)

14. Joshi, M., Choi, E., Weld, D.S., Zettlemoyer, L.: TriviaQA: a large scale distantly supervised challenge dataset for reading comprehension. In: ACL. pp, 1601–1611 (2017)

15. Korablinov, V., Braslavski, P.: RuBQ: a Russian dataset for question answering over Wikidata. In: ISWC, pp. 97–110 (2020)

16. Kwiatkowski, T., et al.: Natural questions: a benchmark for question answering research. TACL **7**, 453–466 (2019)

17. Lewis, P., Oğuz, B., Rinott, R., Riedel, S., Schwenk, H.: MLQA: evaluating cross-lingual extractive question answering. In: ACL, pp. 7315–7330 (2020)

18. Longpre, S., Lu, Y., Daiber, J.: MKQA: a linguistically diverse benchmark for multilingual open domain question answering. arXiv preprint arXiv:2007.15207 (2020)

19. Rajpurkar, P., Jia, R., Liang, P.: Know what you don't know: unanswerable questions for SQuAD. In: ACL, pp. 784–789 (2018)

20. Rajpurkar, P., Zhang, J., Lopyrev, K., Liang, P.: SQuAD: 100,000+ questions for machine comprehension of text. In: EMNLP, pp. 2383–2392 (2016)

21. Savenkov, D., Agichtein, E.: When a knowledge base is not enough: question answering over knowledge bases with external text data. In: SIGIR, pp. 235–244 (2016)

22. Sun, H., Bedrax-Weiss, T., Cohen, W.W.: PullNet: open domain question answering with iterative retrieval on knowledge bases and text. arXiv preprint arXiv:1904.09537 (2019)

23. Talmor, A., Berant, J.: The web as a knowledge base for answering complex questions. In: NAACL, pp. 641–651 (2018)

24. Unger, C., et al.: Question answering over linked data (QALD-4). In: Working Notes for CLEF 2014 Conference, pp. 1172–1180 (2014)

25. Usbeck, R., et al.: 9th challenge on question answering over linked data (QALD-9). In: SemDeep-4, NLIWoD4, and QALD-9 Joint Proceedings, pp. 58–64 (2018)

26. Yih, W., Richardson, M., Meek, C., Chang, M.W., Suh, J.: The value of semantic parse labeling for knowledge base question answering. In: ACL, pp. 201–206 (2016)

A Knowledge Organization System for the United Nations Sustainable Development Goals

Amit Joshi[1(✉)], Luis Gonzalez Morales[1], Szymon Klarman[2],
Armando Stellato[3], Aaron Helton[4], Sean Lovell[1], and Artur Haczek[2]

[1] United Nations, Department of Economic and Social Affairs, New York, NY, USA
{joshi6,gonzalezmorales,lovells}@un.org
[2] Epistemik, Warsaw, Poland
{szymon.klarman,artur.haczek}@epistemik.co
[3] Department of Enterprise Engineering, University of Rome Tor Vergata,
Via del Politecnico 1, 00133 Rome, Italy
stellato@uniroma2.it
[4] United Nations, Dag Hammarskjöld Library, New York, NY, USA
helton@un.org

Abstract. This paper presents a formal knowledge organization system (KOS) to represent the United Nations Sustainable Development Goals (SDGs). The SDGs are a set of objectives adopted by all United Nations member states in 2015 to achieve a better and sustainable future. The developed KOS consists of an ontology that models the core elements of the Global SDG indicator framework, which currently includes 17 Goals, 169 Targets and 231 unique indicators, as well as more than 450 related statistical data series maintained by the global statistical community to monitor progress towards the SDGs, and of a dataset containing these elements. In addition to formalizing and establishing unique identifiers for the components of the SDGs and their indicator framework, the ontology includes mappings of each goal, target, indicator and data series to relevant terms and subjects in the United Nations Bibliographic Information System (UNBIS) and the EuroVoc vocabularies, thus facilitating multilingual semantic search and content linking.

Keywords: United Nations · Sustainable Development Goals · SDGs · Ontology · Linked data · Knowledge organization systems · Metadata

1 Introduction

On 25 September 2015, all members of the United Nations adopted the 2030 Agenda for Sustainable Development [11], centred around a set of 17 Sustainable Development Goals (SDGs) and 169 related Targets, which constitutes a global call for concerted action towards building an inclusive, prosperous world for present and future generations. This ambitious agenda is the world's roadmap

© Springer Nature Switzerland AG 2021
R. Verborgh et al. (Eds.): ESWC 2021, LNCS 12731, pp. 548–564, 2021.
https://doi.org/10.1007/978-3-030-77385-4_33

to address, in an integrated manner, complex global challenges such as poverty, inequality, climate change, environmental degradation, and the achievement of peace and justice for all.

To follow-up and review the implementation of the 2030 Agenda, the United Nations General Assembly also adopted in 2017 a *Global SDG indicator framework* [12], developed by the Inter-Agency and Expert Group on SDG Indicators (IAEG-SDGs), as agreed earlier that year by the United Nations Statistical Commission[1], and entrusted the UN Secretariat with maintaining a Global SDG indicator database of statistical data series reported through various international agencies to track global progress towards the SDGs[2]. After its most recent comprehensive review, approved by the Statistical Commission in March 2020, the current version of the Global SDG indicator framework consists of 231 unique indicators specifically designed for monitoring each of the 169 targets of the 2030 Agenda using data produced by national statistical systems and compiled together for global reporting by various international custodian agencies. While data availability is still a challenge for some of these indicators, there are already more than 450 statistical data series linked to most of these indicators in the Global SDG Indicator database, many of which are further disaggregated by sex, age, and other important dimensions. Data from the Global SDG database is made openly available to the public through various platforms, including an Open SDG Data Hub[3] that provides web services with geo-referenced SDG indicator dataset, as well as an SDG API[4] that can support third-party applications such as dashboards and data visualizations.

In this paper, we describe the formal knowledge organization system (KOS) that has been developed for representing the United Nations Sustainable Development Goals (SDGs). In the following section, we provide the background and related linked data initiatives for the SDGs. Section 3 explains the key SDG terminologies and the ontology depicting the relationship between various SDG elements and concepts, as well as the mapping of terms and concepts in SDGs to external vocabulary and ontology. We evaluate and assess the impact of the SDG KOS in Sect. 4 and provide a brief explanation of LinkedSDG application in Sect. 5 that showcases the importance of such KOS for analysis and visualization of SDG documents. Finally, we provide the concluding remarks in Sect. 6.

---

[1] This global SDG indicator framework is annually refined and subject to periodic comprehensive reviews by the UN Statistical Commission, which is the intergovernmental body where Chief Statisticians from member states oversee international statistical activities and the development and implementation of statistical standards.
[2] https://unstats.un.org/sdgs/indicators/database/.
[3] https://unstats-undesa.opendata.arcgis.com/.
[4] https://unstats.un.org/SDGAPI/swagger/.

2   Towards a Linked Open Data Representation of the SDGs and Their Indicator Framework

The multilingual United Nations Bibliographic Information System (UNBIS) Thesaurus [10], created by the Dag Hammarskjöld Library, contains the terminology used in subject analysis of documents and other materials relevant to United Nations programme and activities. It is used as the subject authority and has been incorporated as the subject lexicon of the United Nations Official Document System. In December 2019, the Dag Hammarskjöld launched a platform for linked data services (http://metadata.un.org) to provide both human and machine access to the UNBIS.

At the second meeting of the Inter-Agency Expert Group on Sustainable Development Goals (IAEG-SDGs) held in Bangkok on October 2015, the UN Environment Programme (UNEP) proposed to develop an SDG Interface Ontology (SDGIO) [3], focused on the formal specification and representation of the various meanings and usages of SDG-related terms and their interrelations[5]. Subsequently, UNEP led a working group to develop the SDGIO, which either created new content or coordinated the re-use of content from existing ontologies, applying best practices in ontology development from mature work of the Open Biological and Biomedical Ontology (OBO) Foundry and Library. Currently, the SDGIO includes more than 100 terms specifying the key entities involved in the SDG process and linking them with the goals, targets, and indicators.

At its thirty-third Session held in Budapest between 30–31 March 2017, the High-level Committee on Management (HLCM) of the United Nations System's Chiefs Executives Board for Coordination adopted the UN Semantic Interoperability Framework (UNSIF) for normative and parliamentary documents, which includes Akoma Ntoso for the United Nations System (AKN4UN)[6]. Akoma Ntoso was originally developed in the context of an initiative by the UN Department of Economic and Social Affairs (UN DESA) to support the interchange and citation of documents among African parliaments and institutions and was subsequently formalized as an official OASIS standard[7].

In 2017, technical experts from across the UN System with backgrounds in library science, information architecture, semantic web, statistics and SDG indicators, agreed to initiate informal working group to develop a proposal for an "SDG Data ontology", based on the global SDG Indicator Framework adopted by the Statistical Commission[8]. The main objective of this effort was to contribute to the implementation of a linked open data approach and allow data users to more easily discover and integrate different sources of SDG-related information

---

[5] This includes terms such as 'access', which occurs 31 times in the SDG Global Indicator Framework.

[6] https://www.w3id.org/un/schema/akn4un/.

[7] https://www.oasis-open.org/.

[8] The group includes representatives from UNSD and other UN offices, including from UN DESA and the UN Library, as well as experts involved in the development of the UN Semantic Interoperability Framework adopted by the High-Level Committee on Management (HLCM) of the CEB.

from across the UN System into end-user applications. The group concluded a first draft of an SDG ontology as part of the SDG Knowledge Organization System (SDG KOS), consisting of a set of permanent Uniform Resource Identifiers (URIs) for the Goals, Targets and Indicators of the 2030 Agenda and their related statistical data series based on the SKOS model.

In order to ensure their fullest possible use, the Identifiers and a formal Statement of Adoption were presented at the second regular session of the UN System Chief Executives Board for Coordination (CEB) in November 2019. At the CEB session, the Secretary-General invited all UN organizations to use them for mapping their SDG-related resources and sign the Statement. Subsequently, at its 51st session held in March 2020, the United Nations Statistical Commission took note of this *common Internationalized Resource Identifiers for Sustainable Development Goals, targets, indicators and related data series*, and encouraged the dissemination of data in linked open data format[9].

3   SDG Knowledge Organization System

3.1   SDG Terminologies

A sustainable development *goal* expresses an ambitious, but specific, commitment, and always starts with a verb/action. Each goal is related to a number of *targets*, which are quantifiable outcomes that contribute in major ways to the achievement of the corresponding goal. An *indicator*, in turn, is a precise metric to assess whether a target is being met. There may be more than one indicator associated with each target. In rare cases, the same *indicator* can belong to multiple *targets*. The global indicator framework lists 247 indicators but has only 231 unique indicators[10].

Finally, a *series* is a set of observations on a quantitative characteristic that provides concrete measurements for an *indicator*. Each *series* contains multiple records of data points organized over time, geographic areas, and/or other dimensions of interest (such as sex, age group, etc.).

To facilitate the implementation of the global indicator framework, all indicators are classified into three *tiers* based on their level of methodological development and the availability of data at the global level, as follows:

- Tier I: Indicator is conceptually clear, has an internationally established methodology and standards are available, and data are regularly produced by countries.
- Tier II: Indicator is conceptually clear, but data are not regularly produced by countries.

---

[9] See https://www.undocs.org/en/E/CN.3/2020/37 - United Nations Statistical Commission, Decision 51/102 (g) on Data and indicators for the 2030 Agenda for Sustainable Development.

[10] See https://unstats.un.org/sdgs/indicators/indicators-list for the updated list of indicators that repeat under two or three targets.

– Tier III: No internationally established methodology or standards are yet available for the indicator.

The updated tier classification contains 130 Tier I indicators, 97 Tier II indicators and 4 indicators that have multiple tiers (different components of the indicator are classified into different tiers)[11].

3.2 Namespaces

The namespace for SDG ontology is http://metadata.un.org/sdg/. The ontology extends and reuses terms from several other vocabularies in addition to UNBIS and EuroVoc. A full set of namespaces and prefixes used in this ontology is shown in Table 1.

Table 1. Namespaces used in SDG ontology

Prefix	Namespace
sdgo:	http://metadata.un.org/sdg/ontology
dc:	http://purl.org/dc/elements/1.1/
owl:	http://www.w3.org/2002/07/owl#
rdf:	http://www.w3.org/1999/02/22-rdf-syntax-ns#
rdfs:	http://www.w3.org/2000/01/rdf-schema#
xsd:	http://www.w3.org/2001/XMLSchema#
skos:	http://www.w3.org/2004/02/skos/core#
wd:	http://www.wikidata.org/entity/
sdgio:	http://purl.unep.org/sdg/
unbis:	http://metadata.un.org/thesaurus/
ev:	http://eurovoc.europa.eu/
dct:	http://purl.org/dc/terms/

3.3 Schema

The SDG ontology formalizes the core schema of SDG goal-target-indicator-series hierarchy, consisting of four main classes namely *sdgo:Goal*, *sdgo:Target*, *sdgo:Indicator* and *sdgo:Series*, which correspond to the four levels of the SDG hierarchy, and three matching pairs of inverse properties – one per each level, as shown in Fig. 1.

The properties are further constrained by standard domain and range restrictions. While logically shallow, such axiomatization avoids unnecessary overcommitment and guarantees good interoperability across different ontology management tools.

---

[11] List is regularly updated and available at https://www.undocs.org/en/E/CN.3/2020/37.

Furthermore, the SDG ontology is aligned with (by extending it) the SKOS Core Vocabulary[12], a lightweight W3C standard RDF for representing tax-onomies, thesauri and other types of controlled vocabulary [8]. This alignment rests upon the set of sub-class and sub-property axioms as shown in Fig. 1, which additionally emphasizes the strictly hierarchical structure of the SDG entities. The top concepts in the resulting SKOS concept scheme are the SDG goals, while the narrower concepts, organized into three subsequent levels, include targets, indicators, and series, respectively.

The choice of SKOS is not restrictive on the nature of SDG items: SKOS and specific OWL constructs can be intertwined into elaborated ontologies that guarantee both strict adherence to a domain (through the definition of domain-oriented properties, such as the aforementioned properties linking the strict 4-layered architecture of the SDGs) and interoperability on a coarser level. For instance, the use of *skos:narrower* and *skos:broader* allows any SKOS-compliant consumer to properly interpret the various levels of the SDG as a hierarchy and to show it accordingly.

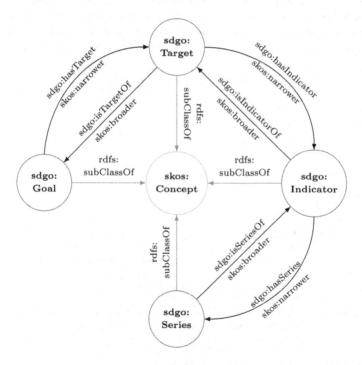

Fig. 1. Core structure of the SDG ontology modelled using SKOS vocabulary

Following from the SKOS specifications, the *skos:broader/narrower* relation is not meant to imply any sort of "subclassification" (e.g. according to the set-

---

oriented semantics of OWL) and indeed it should not for two reasons: a) extensionally, each object in the SDG, be it a goal, target or indicator, is not a class of objects, but rather a specific object itself; b) the SKOS hierarchy does not suggest any sort of specialization, as the relations among the various levels are closer to different nuances of a dependency relation. SKOS properties *skos:broader/narrower* (their name could be misleading) represent a relation meant exclusively for depicting hierarchies, with no assumption on their semantics (see, for instance, the possibility to address a part-of relation as indicated in the SKOS-primer[13]). This is perfectly fitting for the SDG representation, as SDGs are always disseminated as a taxonomy.

Finally, the SDG ontology also covers a three-level Tier classification for Global SDG Indicators, which supports additional qualification of the indicators in terms of their implementation maturity.

3.4   SDG Data

The SDG data, analogously to the schema-level, is represented in terms of two terminologies: the native SDG ontology and the SKOS vocabulary. Every instance is described as a corresponding SDG element and a SKOS concept. As an example, Table 2 presents data pertaining to the SDG Target 1 of Goal 1.

Table 2. RDF Description of SDG Target 1.1

Subject = http://metadata.un.org/sdg/1.1	
Predicate	Object
rdf:type	skos:Concept
rdf:type	sdgo:Target
skos:inScheme	http://metadata.un.org/sdg
skos:broader	:1
sdgo:isTargetOf	:1
skos:narrower	:C010101
sdgo:hasIndicator	:C010101
skos:prefLabel	"By 2030, eradicate extreme poverty for all people everywhere, currently measured as people living on less than \$1.25 a day" @en
skos:prefLabel	"D'ici à 2030, éliminer complètement l'extrême pauvreté dans le monde entier (s'entend actuellement du fait de vivre avec moins de 1,25 dollar des États'Unis par jour)" @fr
skos:prefLabel	"De aquí a 2030, erradicar para todas las personas y en todo el mundo la pobreza extrema (actualmente se considera que sufren pobreza extrema las personas que viven con menos de 1,25 dólares de los Estados Unidos al día)"@es
skos:notation	"1.1" ^^sdgo:SDGCodeCompact
skos:notation	"01.01" ^^sdgo:SDGCode
skos:note	"Target 1.1" @en
skos:note	"Cible 1.1" @fr
skos:note	"Meta 1.1" @es

---

[13] https://www.w3.org/TR/skos-primer/#sechierarchy.

The labels and values of *skos:notation* property reflect the official naming and classification codes of each element.

The codes are represented in two notational variants catering for different presentation and data reconciliation requirements. In several cases the indicators and series have more than one broader concept in the hierarchy, as defined in the Global indicator framework. For instance, the indicator sdg:C200303 appears as narrower concept (*sdgo:isIndicatorOf*) of targets 1.5, 11.5 and 13.1, and is consequently equipped with three different sets of codes: "01.05.01", "1.5.1", "11.05.01", "11.5.1", "13.01.01", "13.1.1". Due to this poly-hierarchy, the indicators are equipped with an additional set of unique identifier codes of the form "*Cxxxxxx*". Table 3 shows the partial RDF description of this indicator C200303.

The unique identifiers of the SDG series, reflected in their URIs and in the values of the *skos:notation* property, follow the official coding system of the UN Statistics Division[14]. As the list of relevant SDG series is subject to recurrent updates, their most recent version captured in the published SDG ontology is represented under the *skos:historyNote* property ("2019.Q2.G.01" at the time of writing).

Table 3. RDF description of SDG indicator C200303 depicting poly-hierarchy

Subject = http://metadata.un.org/sdg/C200303	
Predicate	Object
rdf:type	skos:Concept
	sdgo:Indicator
skos:inScheme	http://metadata.un.org/sdg
skos:broader	:1.5
	:11.5
	:13.1
sdgo:isIndicatorOf	:1.5
	:11.5
	:13.1
skos:narrower	sdg:VC_DSR_AFFCT
	sdg:VC_DSR_DAFF
	sdg:VC_DSR_DDHN
sdgo:hasSeries	sdg:VC_DSR_AFFCT
	sdg:VC_DSR_DAFF
	sdg:VC_DSR_DDHN
sdgo:tier	sdgo#tier_II
skos:prefLabel	"Number of deaths, missing persons and directly affected persons attributed to disasters per 100,000 population" @en
skos:notation	"1.5.1" ^^sdgo:SDGCodeCompact
	"01.05.01" ^^sdgo:SDGCode
	"11.5.1" ^^sdgo:SDGCodeCompact
	"11.05.01" ^^sdgo:SDGCode
	"13.1.1" ^^sdgo:SDGCodeCompact
	"13.01.01" ^^sdgo:SDGCode
	"C200303" ^^sdgo:SDGPerm
skos:exactMatch	http://purl.unep.org/sdg/SDGIO_00020006
skos:custodianAgency	"UNDRR"

[14] https://unstats.un.org/sdgs/indicators/database/.

3.5   Linking the SDG Ontology

The SDG ontology has been enriched with additional mappings to existing vocabularies and ontologies in order to facilitate content cataloguing, semantic search, and content linking. Specifically, each goal, target and indicator has been mapped with topics and concepts defined in UNBIS and EuroVoc[15] thesauri. Identifiers have also been mapped to external ontologies like SDGIO and Wikidata[16]. Wikidata is a free and open structured knowledge base that can be read and edited by both humans and machines [4]. Figure 2 depicts association of sdg:1 to wikidata and SDGIO via *skos:exactMatch*, as well as concept mappings to UNBIS and EuroVoc via *dct:subject*.

Mapping the SDG elements to both UNBIS and EuroVoc thesauri enables knowledge discovery as both contain large number of concepts across many domains. The UNBIS Thesaurus contains more than 7000 concepts across 18 domains and 143 micro-thesauri with lexicalizations in the six official languages of the UN, providing one of the most complete multilingual resources in the organization. EuroVoc is European Union's multilingual and multidisciplinary thesaurus that contains more than 7000 terms, organized in 21 domains and 127 sub-domains. Section 5 provides further details on the importance of linking to external vocabulary for extracting relevant SDGs.

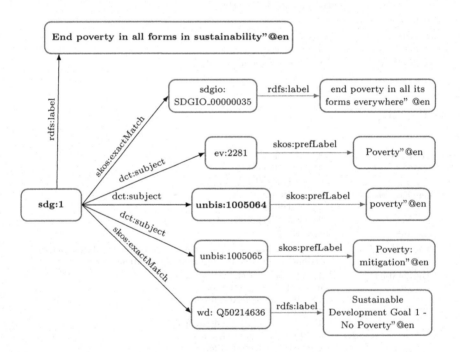

Fig. 2. SDG Goal#1 linked to other vocabularies including UNBIS and EuroVoc.

15 https://op.europa.eu/en/web/eu-vocabularies.
16 https://www.wikidata.org/.

4   Evaluation and Impact of the SDG

In this section we evaluate and assess the impact of the SDG KOS under several dimensions, including usability, logical consistency and support of multilingualism.

4.1   Usability

The resource is mainly modelled as a SKOS concept scheme, for ease of consumption and interpretation of the SDG taxonomy by SKOS-compliant tools. As a complement to that, the ontology vocabulary provides different subclasses of the *skos:Concept* (adopted in the KOS) for clearly distinguishing the nature of Goals, Targets, Indicators and Series, and subproperties of *skos:broader* and *skos:narrower*. OWL axioms constrain the hierarchical relationships among them (for example, Targets can only be under Goals and have Indicators as narrower concepts).

Both the ontology and the SKOS content are served through multilingual descriptors (see Sect. 4.4), thus facilitating interpretation of the content across various idioms and annotation of textual content with respect to these global indicators. *skos:notations* are provided in three different formats (according to various ways in which the global indicators codes have been rendered). For each format, a different datatype has been coined and adopted, so that platforms with advanced rendering mechanisms (e.g. VocBench [9]) can select the proper one and use it as a prefix in the rendering of each global indicator (e.g. ⟨notation⟩ and ⟨description⟩).

4.2   Resource Availability

The SDGs are available on the site of the statistical division of the UN through a web interface[17], allowing for the exploration of their content, and as Excel and PDF files. The Linked Open Data (LOD) version of the dataset is available on the metadata portal of the UN, with separate entries for the ontology[18] and the taxonomy of global indicators[19]. The namespace of SDG ontology and KOS have been introduced in Sect. 3. As a large organization with a solid management of its domain, the LOD version of the dataset does not rely on an external persistent URI service (e.g. PURL, DOI, W3ID) as the metadata.un.org URIs can be considered persistent and reliable. All URIs resolve through content negotiation. The ontology offers a web page for human consumption describing its content, resolving to the ontology file[20] in case of requests for RDF data. The KOS provides an explorable taxonomy on a web interface at the URI of the concept scheme and human-readable descriptions (generated after the RDF data)

---

[17] https://unstats.un.org/sdgs/indicators/database/.

[18] http://metadata.un.org/sdg/ontology.

[19] http://metadata.un.org/sdg/.

[20] e.g. http://metadata.un.org/sdg/static/sdgs-ontology.ttl for Turtle format.

of each single global indicator at their URIs. All of them http-resolve to RDF in several serialization formats (currently Turtle, RDF/XML, NT and JSON-LD).

The project related to the development of the SDG data and the data itself (available as download dumps) are available under a public GitHub repository[21].

Sustainability. SDGs are a long-term vision of the United Nations with an end date of year 2030. As such, the SDG KOS and associated tools and libraries will be actively maintained and updated over the years and are expected to be reachable even in case the SDG mission is considered concluded.

Licensing: The SDG Knowledge Organization System is made available free of charge and may be copied freely, duplicated and further distributed provided that a proper citation is provided. License information is also available on its VoID descriptors.

4.3   VoID/LIME Description

Metadata about the linked open dataset has been reported in a machine-accessible VoID [1] and LIME [5] files at UN Metadata site[22]. The VoID file also contains entries linking the download dumps.

VoID is an RDF vocabulary for describing linked datasets, which has become a W3C Interest Group Note[23]. VoID provides the policies for its publication and linking to the data [6] and also defines a protocol to publish dataset metadata alongside the actual data, making it possible for consumers to discover the dataset description just after encountering a resource in a dataset. Developed within the scope of the OntoLex W3C Community Group[24], LIME is an extension of VoID for linguistic metadata. While being initially developed as the metadata module of the OntoLex-Lemon model[25] [7], LIME intentionally provides descriptors that can be adapted to different scenarios (e.g. ontologies or thesauri being lexicalized, resources being onomasiologically or semasiologically conceived) and models adopted for the lexicalization work (*rdfs:labels*, SKOS or SKOS-XL terminological labels or Ontolex lexical entries).

The VoID description is organized by first providing general information about the dataset through the usual Dublin core [2] properties, such as description, creator, date of publication, etc. Of particular notice is the dct:conformsTo property, pointing in this case to the SKOS namespace and which can be adopted by metadata consumers in order to understand the core modelling vocabularies being adopted representing the dataset. The description is followed by a few *void:classPartitions* providing statistics about the types of resource characterizing the type of dataset (as informed by the aforementioned *dct:conformsTo*).

In the case of SDG, the template for SKOS has therefore been applied, providing statistics for *skos:Concepts*, *skos:Collections* and *skos:ConceptSchemes*,

---

[21] https://github.com/UNStats/LOD4Stats/wiki.

[22] http://metadata.un.org/sdg/void.ttl.

[23] http://www.w3.org/TR/void/.

[24] https://www.w3.org/community/ontolex/.

[25] https://www.w3.org/2016/05/ontolex/.

reporting a total of 812 concepts, 1 concept scheme and 1 collection. The description continues with typical *void* information, such as statistics about the number of distinct subjects (1002), objects (6842), triples (14645), availability of a SPARQL endpoint and downloadable data dump (*void:dataDump*), which we provided for the full dump as well as for some partitioned versions of the dataset (e.g. ontology only, ⟨ Goal, Target, Indicator ⟩ only, etc.). Finally, a list of subsets are then described in detail in the rest of the file. This list is mainly composed of *void:Linksets*, which are datasets consisting of a series of alignment triples between the described dataset and other target datasets, and of *lime:Lexicalizations*, the portions of the described dataset containing all the triples related to the (possibly multiple, as in this case) lexicalizations that are available for it. Each lexicalization is described in terms of its lexicalization model (which in the case of the SDGs is SKOS), of the natural language covered by the lexicalization, expressed in terms of ISO639-1 2-digit code as a literal (through property *lime:language*), and of ISO639-1 2-digit code and ISO639-3 3-digit code in the form of URIs using the vocabulary of languages[26] of the Library of Congress[27]. It also includes information about the lexicalized dataset (*lime:referenceDataset*) and void-like statistical information such as the total number of lexicalized references, the number of lexicalizations, the average number of lexicalizations per reference and the percentage of lexicalized references. More details about the available lexicalizations will be provided in Sect. 4.4 on multilingualism.

4.4 Multilingualism

As the SDGs are a United Nations resource, multilingualism is an important factor and a goal to be achieved. Currently, the resource is available in three languages: English, French and Spanish. As reported in the LIME metadata within the VoID file, English is currently the most represented language (being the one natively used for redacting the SDGs), with 99.9% of resources (813 out of 814) covered by at least a lexicalization (which means it includes the Series linked to the SDGs as well) and an average number of 1,021 lexicalizations per resource, thus allowing for some cases of synonymy. French and Spanish follow almost equally with 422 and 420 lexicalizations respectively covered (roughly 51.4% of the resources). This is approximately equal to the total number of Goals, Targets and Indicators combined, and excludes the Series which still have to be translated to these languages. Other languages are being planned to be added to the list of lexicalizations.

4.5 A Comparison with the SDGIO Ontology

The SDGIO claims to be an Interface Ontology (IO) for SDGs, providing "a semantic bridge between 1) the Sustainable Development Goals, their targets,

---

[26] http://id.loc.gov/vocabulary/.

[27] https://loc.gov/.

and indicators and 2) the large array of entities they refer to" . To achieve this objective, it "imports classes from numerous existing ontologies and maps to vocabularies such as GEMET to promote interoperability" . Among various connections, SDGIO strongly builds on multiple OBO Foundry ontologies "to help link data products to the SDGs" . The SDGIO offers a very specific interpretation, where the various Goals, Targets and Indicators are instances of their respective classes and then Indicators have also a "sustainable development goal indicator value" class (which contains, as subclasses, the various indicators) to contain values for these indicators. The SDGIO does not include any information about the Series. Differently from the objectives of SDGIO, which is focused on its interfacing aspect and is based on a strong commitment to OBO ontologies, our mission was to build the official representation of SDGs and to place it under a largely interoperable, yet neutral, perspective. To this end, we represented SDG elements as ground objects, providing an ontology for describing their nature and mutual relationships, which builds in turn on top of the SKOS vocabulary, for purposes of visualization in SKOS-compliant consumers.

5 Knowledge Discovery and Linking SDGs

The SDG ontology is part of an emerging system of SDG-related ontologies that aim to provide data inter-operability and a flexible interface for querying linkages across independent information systems. Mapping the identifiers described in these ontologies to each other and to external vocabularies allows SDG data to be clearly identified and found by semantic web agents for establishing further links and connections thereby facilitating knowledge discovery.

A pilot application, LinkedSDG[28], has been built to showcase the usefulness of adopting SDG KOS for extracting SDG related metadata from documents and establishing the connections among various SDGs. The application automatically extracts relevant SDG concepts mentioned in a given document using SDG KOS and provides their unified overview. All SDGs related to the identified concepts are displayed in an interactive wheel chart that users can further explore by drilling into associated goals, targets, indicators and series. Figures 3 and 4 depicts different components of application including concept extraction, map, SDG wheel chart and associated data series for one of the Voluntary National Reviews (VNRs)[29]. The application can process documents written in any one of the six UN official languages.

The two key analytical techniques employed in LinkedSDG are taxonomy-based *term extraction* and *knowledge graph traversal*. The term extraction mechanism, implemented using the *spaCy* library[30], scans the submitted document for all literal mentions of the relevant UNBIS and EuroVoc concept labels, based on the initially detected language of the document, and associates them with their

---

[28] http://linkedsdg.apps.officialstatistics.org/, source code for the application available at: https://github.com/UNGlobalPlatform/linkedsdg.

[29] See https://sustainabledevelopment.un.org/ for VNR documents.

[30] https://spacy.io/.

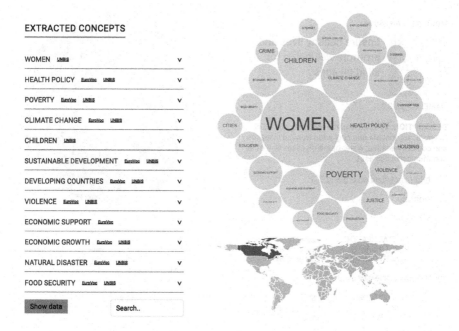

Fig. 3. Application displaying extracted concepts and corresponding tag cloud, and a map highlighted with geographic regions mentioned in a document.

respective concept identifiers. The traversal, performed using SPARQL via the underlying *Apache Jena* RDF store[31], starts from these extracted concept identifiers, following to broader ones, to finally reach those connected directly to the elements of the SDG system via the *dct:subject* and *skos:exactMatch* predicates. Then, the algorithm traces the paths to broader SDG entities in the SDG KOS hierarchy. For instance:

- **text**: "[...] beaches, estuaries, dune systems, mangroves, marshes lagoons, swamps, reefs, etc. are [...]"
- **extracted concept**: WETLANDS (unbis:1007000) via the matched synonym "marshes"
- **traversed path**: WETLANDS - (broader) → SURFACE WATERS (unbis:1006307) - (broader) → WATER (unbis:030500)
- **connected target**: 6.5 By 2030, implement integrated water resources management at all levels, including through transboundary cooperation as appropriate
- **connected goal**: 6. Clean water and sanitation

The computation of the final relevance scores for specific goals, targets and indicators relies on their exact positioning in the SDG hierarchy, which is reflected by the SKOS representation of the system, and on their types, asserted

---

[31] https://jena.apache.org/.

MOST RELEVANT SDGS

 Ensure healthy lives and
promote well-being for
all at all ages

NAME: Target 3.3

DESCRIPTION: By 2030, end the epidemics of AIDS,
tuberculosis, malaria and neglected tropical diseases
and combat hepatitis, water-borne diseases and other
communicable diseases

URI: http://metadata.un.org/sdg/3.3

KEYWORDS:

HEALTH UNBIS

MENTAL HEALTH	EuroVoc UNBIS
PUBLIC HEALTH	EuroVoc UNBIS
HEALTH CONTROL	EuroVoc UNBIS

COMMUNICABLE DISEASES UNBIS

TUBERCULOSIS	UNBIS
AIDS	EuroVoc UNBIS
POLIOMYELITIS	UNBIS

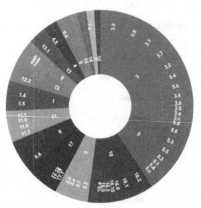

DATA SERIES

Tuberculosis incidence (per 100,000 population)

country	year	value
Canada	2000	6.4
Canada	2001	6.6
Canada	2002	6.1

1 2 3 4 5 ≥ ≫

Fig. 4. Application showing the most relevant SDG keywords corresponding to Target 3.3, an interactive SDG wheel corresponding to a document and related data series for one of the Indicators

in the SDG ontology. Intuitively, the broader the terms (i.e., the higher in the hierarchy) the higher score they receive, as they aggregate the scores in the lower parts of the hierarchy.

The application also provides access to the statistical data of the specific SDG series, which is represented as linked open statistical data using the *RDF Data Cube* vocabulary[32]. The relevant SDG series identifiers are referenced from the extraction results delivered by the application and independently served by the platform's dedicated GraphQL API[33]. Consequently, SDG KOS fueling the LinkedSDG platform supports the user in the entire journey from a text document to the relevant statistics, helping put the originally unstructured, third-party information, in the context of narrowly focused, UN-owned structured data.

6   Conclusion

The integration of multiple sources and types of data and information is fundamental to guide policies aimed to achieve the 2030 Agenda for Sustainable Development. The complexity and scale of the global challenges require solutions that

---

[32] https://www.w3.org/TR/vocab-data-cube/.

[33] http://linkedsdg.apps.officialstatistics.org/graphql/.

take into account trade-offs and synergies across the social and economic dimensions of sustainable development. In order to foster a holistic approach through coordinated policies and actions that bring together different levels of government and actors from all sectors of society, it is crucial to develop tools that facilitate the discovery and analysis of interlinkage across various global SDG indicators, as well as across other sources of data, information and knowledge maintained by different stakeholder groups.

The SDG KOS is an attempt to provide stakeholders a means to publish the data using common terminologies and URIs centred around the SDG concepts, thus helping break information silos, promote synergies among communities, and enhance the semantic interoperability of different SDG-related data and information assets made available by various sectors of society.

Acknowledgements. Much of the work towards developing the SDG KOS and the LinkedSDG pilot application was conducted in the context of a UN DESA project funded through the EU grant entitled "SD2015: Delivering on the promise of the SDGs". The authors would like to acknowledge the invaluable contributions and guidance from Naiara Garcia Da Costa Chaves, Susan Hussein, Flavio Zeni, as well as from many other colleagues from UN DESA, the Dag Hammarskjöld Library, and the Secretariat of the High Level Committee on Management of the UN Chief Executive Board for Coordination.

References

1. Alexander, K., Cyganiak, R., Hausenblas, M., Zhao, J.: Describing linked datasets - on the design and usage of void, the vocabulary of interlinked datasets. In: Linked Data on the Web (LDOW) Workshop, in Conjunction with 18th International World Wide Web Conference (2009)
2. Bird, S., Simons, G.: Extending Dublin Core metadata to support the description and discovery of language resources. Comput. Humanit. **37**(4), 375–388 (2003)
3. Buttigieg, P.L., Jensen, M., Walls, R.L., Mungall, C.J.: Environmental semantics for sustainable development in an interconnected biosphere. In: ICBO/BioCreative (2016)
4. Erxleben, F., Günther, M., Krötzsch, M., Mendez, J., Vrandečić, D.: Introducing Wikidata to the linked data Web. In: Mika, P., et al. (eds.) ISWC 2014. LNCS, vol. 8796, pp. 50–65. Springer, Cham (2014). https://doi.org/10.1007/978-3-319-11964-9_4
5. Fiorelli, M., Stellato, A., McCrae, J.P., Cimiano, P., Pazienza, M.T.: LIME: the metadata module for OntoLex. In: Gandon, F., Sabou, M., Sack, H., d'Amato, C., Cudré-Mauroux, P., Zimmermann, A. (eds.) ESWC 2015. LNCS, vol. 9088, pp. 321–336. Springer, Cham (2015). https://doi.org/10.1007/978-3-319-18818-8_20
6. Gandon, F., Sabou, M., Sack, H., d'Amato, C., Cudré-Mauroux, P., Zimmermann, A.: The semantic web. latest advances and new domains. In: ESWC 2015-European Semantic Web Conference, vol. 9088, p. 830. Springer (2015). https://doi.org/10.1007/978-3-319-18818-8
7. McCrae, J.P., Bosque-Gil, J., Gracia, J., Buitelaar, P., Cimiano, P.: The OntoLex-Lemon model: development and applications. In: Proceedings of eLex 2017 Conference, pp. 19–21 (2017)

8. Miles, A., Matthews, B., Wilson, M., Brickley, D.: SKOS Core: simple knowledge organisation for the Web. In: International Conference on Dublin Core and Metadata Applications, pp. 3–10 (2005)

9. Stellato, A., Fiorelli, M., Turbati, A., Lorenzetti, T., van Gemert, W., Dechandon, D., Laaboudi-Spoiden, C., Gerencsér, A., Waniart, A., Costetchib, E., Keizer, J.: VocBench 3: a collaborative semantic web editor for ontologies, thesauri and lexicons. Semantic Web **11**(5), 855–881 (2020)

10. Dag Hammarskjold Library of United Nations, N.Y.: UNBIS Thesaurus, English Edition http://metadata.un.org/thesaurus/about?lang=en

11. United Nations General Assembly: Transforming our world: the 2030 Agenda for Sustainable Development, A/RES/70/1 (2015). http://undocs.org/A/RES/70/1

12. United Nations General Assembly: Work of the Statistical Commission pertaining to the 2030 Agenda for Sustainable Development, A/RES/71/313 (2017). https://undocs.org/A/RES/71/313

RSP4J: An API for RDF Stream Processing

Riccardo Tommasini[1]([✉]), Pieter Bonte[3], Femke Ongenae[3],
and Emanuele Della Valle[2]

[1] Data System Group, University of Tartu, Tartu, Estonia
`riccardo.tommasini@ut.ee`
[2] DEIB, Politecnico di Milano, Milan, Italy
`emanuele.dellavalle@polimi.it`
[3] Ghent University - imec, Ghent, Belgium
`{Pieter.Bonte,Femke.Ongenae}@ugent.be`

Abstract. The RDF Stream Processing (RSP) community has proposed several models and languages for continuously querying and reasoning over RDF streams over the last decade. They each have their semantics, making them hard to compare. The variety of approaches has fostered both empirical and theoretical research and led to the design of RSPQL, i.e., a unifying model for RSP. However, an RSP API for the development under RSPQL semantics was still missing. RSP community would benefit from an RSP API because it can foster comparable and reproducible research by providing programming abstractions based on RSPQL semantics. Moreover, it can encourage further development and in-use research. Finally, it can stimulate practical activities such as tutorials, lectures, and challenges, e.g., during the Stream Reasoning Workshop.

In this paper, we present RSP4J, a flexible API for the development of RSP engines and applications under RSPQL semantics. RSP4J offers all the necessary abstractions required for fast-prototyping of RSP engines under the proposed RSPQL semantics. Users can configure it to reproduce the variety of RSP engine behaviors in a comparable software environment. To promote systematic and comparative research, RSP4J is open-source, provides canonical citation, permanent web identifiers, and a comprehensive user guide for developers.

1 Introduction

The advent of the Internet of Things and social media has unveiled the streaming nature of information [9]. Data analysis should not only consider huge amounts of data from various complex domains, it should also be executed rapidly, before the data are no longer valuable or representative. Stream Reasoning (SR) is the research area that combines Stream Processing and Semantic Web technologies to make sense, in real-time, of vast, heterogeneous and noisy data streams [13].

Since 2008, the SR community's contributions include data models, query languages, and algorithms, and benchmarks for RDF Stream Processing (RSP). As an extension of the Semantic Web stack, the value of RSP emerges in

© Springer Nature Switzerland AG 2021
R. Verborgh et al. (Eds.): ESWC 2021, LNCS 12731, pp. 565–581, 2021.
https://doi.org/10.1007/978-3-030-77385-4_34

application domains where Data Variety and Data Velocity appear together [10], e.g., Smart Cities, e-Health and news analysis.

RSP approaches extend RDF and SPARQL to represent and process data streams. The community rapidly reached consensus around the use of RDF Streams as the data model. On the other hand, a variety of RSP languages emerged over time, e.g., C-SPARQL, CQELS-QL, SPARQL$_{stream}$, and Strider-QL. Such languages are extensions of SPARQL that support some form of continuous semantics. RSP languages are usually paired with working prototypes that helped proving the feasibility of the approach as well as studying its efficiency. Such variety of languages and systems enriches the state-of-the-art, but it may be hindering adoption and, thus, slow down the technological progress. Indeed, the diversity in the literature often opposes the identification of a clear winner, the establishment of best practices, and calls for comparative research.

Like other communities, e.g., OWL reasoning [20] and Big Data Systems [1], comparative research on and benchmarking of RSP engines is extremely hard. In fact, the semantics of different RSP languages do not completely overlap [12]. Moreover, the development of RSP engines, which are time-based systems, implies a number of design decisions that are often hidden in the code [7]. Such decisions, which fall into the notion of *execution semantics*[1], hamper the performance comparison, making it hard to reproduce the same behavior in two different systems and, thus, generalise the conclusions.

In summary, the lack of standardization and shared design principles are obstructing the growth of the communities. Indeed, as prototyping efforts remain isolated, the costs of development and maintenance of prototypes remain on the shoulder of individual researchers. Nevertheless, the problem did not remain unnoticed. The OWL reasoning community worked on shared APIs to standardise the evaluation of OWL reasoners [16], fostering a number of initiative like the OWL Reasoning Evaluation (ORE) challenges [20]. The Big Data Systems community witnessed the publication of a number of surveys and unification projects. In particular, Apache Beam is an attempt to uniform the APIs for stream and batch Big Data processing [17].

The RSP community is also working actively on solving this issue, focusing on (i) designing best practices [24,27] (ii) disseminating the approaches [15], and (ii) developing benchmarks that take correctness and execution semantics into account [3,18]. A recent important result is RSPQL [14], a reference model that unifies existing RSP dialects and the execution semantics of existing RSP engines. Although RSPQL is a first step towards a community standard, existing prototypes still do not follow shared design principles.

In line with the OWL APIs and Apache Beam initiative, *an API based on RSPQL would reduce the maintenance cost of existing engines, foster adoption of RSP engines, open new research opportunities in Stream Reasoning.*

In this paper, we present RSP4J, a configurable RSPQL API and engine, that builds on the lessons learned by developing the existing prototypes, and bringing RSP research to the next level. We believe RSP4J can foster fast-prototyping,

---

[1] also known as execution semantics.

empirical and comparative research, as well as easing the dissemination of RSP via teaching. To this extent, RSP4J includes (i) all the necessary abstractions to develop RSP engines under the proposed RSPQL semantics and (ii) an implementation, i.e. YASPER, based on Apache Commons RDF[2], with the goal of showcasing the API's potential. Moreover, RSP4J can reproduce the variety of RSP engines in a comparable software environment.

In summary, the goals of RSP4J are (i) fostering the design and development of RSP engines under fixed RSPQL semantics, (ii) unifying the existing prototypes and their results, (iii) providing a framework for fair comparison of results and (iv) presenting a high-level API for easy adoption for RSP developers. RSP4J is open-source and is maintained on Github[3]. It has a canonical citation and permanent URL[4]. Moreover, it comes with an actively maintained documentation and a *Ready2GoPack* for increased availability to new members of the RSP community. RSP4J was already used in a number of tutorials and lectures, i.e. ISWC17, ICWE18, ESWC19, TheWebConf19, RW18/20.

The remainder of the paper is organized as follows: Sect. 2 discusses the potential impact of RSP4J in terms of use-cases, and afterwards presents the requirement analysis. Section 3 presents the background, concepts and definitions used throughout the rest of the paper, while Sect. 4 outlines architecture of RSP4J, its modules, and shows how it satisfies the requirements. In Sect. 5, we presents the related work. Finally, Sect. 6 concludes the paper and summarizes the most important contributions for RSP4J as a resource.

2 Impact: Use Cases and Requirements for an RSPQL API

In this section, we discuss the potential impact of RSP4J as a resource. To this extent, we present different use cases that concern state-of-the-art prototypes for Stream Reasoning and RDF Stream Processing. We highlight the challenges that such use cases unveil, and we elicit a set of requirements for RSP4J in order to address such challenges. Table 1 summarizes the relationship between the challenges (C_i) and requirements (R_j).

2.1 Use Cases

Fast Prototyping. In 2008, the first Stream Reasoner prototype came out [31]. Since then, the SR community has designed a number of working prototypes [5,8,19,23], with the intent of proving the feasibility of the vision. E-health, smart cities, and financial transaction are examples of use cases where such prototypes were successfully used. Nevertheless, the effort of designing and engineering good prototypes is extremely high, and often their maintenance is unsustainable. In fact, prototypes are often designed with a minimal set of requirements and

---

[2] http://commons.apache.org/proper/commons-rdf/.

[3] https://github.com/streamreasoning/rsp4j.

[4] https://w3id.org/rsp4j.

without shared design principles. In such scenarios (C1) adding new operators, (C2) new types of data sources to consume, or (C3) experimenting with new optimisations techniques requires huge manual efforts or is almost impossible.

Comparable Research and Benchmarking. Aside developing proof-of-concepts, the SR/RSP communities have focused a lot on Comparative Research (CR) [24,27] and benchmarking [3,18,22,26,32]. CR studies the differences and similarities across SR/RSP approaches. Stream Reasoners and RSP engines can only be compared when they employ the same semantics. Thus, a fair comparison demands a deep theoretical comprehension of the approaches, a proper formulation of the task to solve, and an adequate experimentation environment [28]. Consequently, it is currently hard to (C4) reproduce the behavior of existing approaches in a comparable way. Moreover, experimentation is limited by (C5) the lack of parametric solutions, i.e. the configurability of the operators allowing to match engine behavior. On the other hand, research on benchmarking aims at pushing the technological progress by guaranteeing a fair assessment. While some of the challenges are shared with CR [27,28], benchmarking is empirical research. To this extent, (C6) monitoring both the execution of continuous queries, as well as (C7) the engine behavior at run-time are of paramount importance. Unfortunately, not all the existing prototypes provide such entry points, and only black-box analysis is possible, e.g. it is impossible to measure the performance of each of the engine's internal operators.

Dissemination. Although SR research is at its infancy, a lot has been done on the teaching side. As prototypes and approaches reach maturity, several tutorials and lectures were delivered at major venues, including ICWE, ESWC, ISWC, RW, and TheWebConf [10,11,15]. These tutorials were often practical and aimed at engaging with their audience using simple yet meaningful applications. Nevertheless, existing prototypes were not designed for teaching purposes. Thus, they lack important features like the possibility to (C8) inspect the engine behaviors and (C9) they are not designed to ease the understanding at various levels of abstraction. Indeed, prototypes often (C10) neglect their full compliance to the underlying theoretical framework for practical reasons. Although this approach often benefits performance, it makes the learning curve more steep.

2.2 Requirements

Now we present the requirements that an RSPQL API should satisfy. We elicit the requirements from the challenges presented above. Although the requirements could be generalized for any RSP engine and Stream Reasoner, we restrict our focus to Window-based RDF Stream Processing Engines, i.e., those covered by the RSPQL specification.

Table 1. Challenges vs Requirements

Req	C1	C2	C3	C4	C5	C6	C7	C8	C9	C10
R_1	✓	✓	✓		✓		✓			
R_2			✓					✓		✓
R_3								✓	✓	✓
R_4		✓	✓	✓						
R_5	✓	✓	✓			✓	✓			

R_1 **Extensible Architecture.** An RSP API should allow the easy addition of data sources (C2) and operators (C1), and the design of optimization techniques (C3). Moreover, An RSP API should allow experimentation by allowing the addition of execution parameters (C5), and should ease the extension of engine capabilities (C7).

R_2 **Declarative Access.** An RSP API should be accessible in a declarative and configurable manner (C4). It should allow querying according to a formal semantics, e.g., RSPQL (C10), and should allow controlling the engine and the query lifecycles (C8).

R_3 **Programming Abstractions.** An RSP API should provide programming abstractions that allow interacting with the engine at various levels of abstractions (C9), abstractions that are based on a theoretical framework (C10), and that provide a blueprint to make sense of the engine behavior (C8).

R_4 **Experimentation.** An RSP API should be suitable for experimentation and, thus, should foster comparative research. To this extent, it should allow experimentation with optimizations techniques (C3), enabling to execute experiments using alternative configurations (C5). Last but not least, the reproducibility of state-of-the-art solutions should be a priority to enable replication studies (C4).

R_5 **Observability.** An RSP API should be observable by design, enabling the collection of metrics at different levels, i.e., stream level, operator level, query level (C6), and engine level (C7). Observability should be independent from architectural changes (C1 and C2), and ease study of optimizations (C3).

3   Background

In this section, we summarize the knowledge necessary to understand the main concepts of RSP4J. RSP4J is based on RSPQL, which in turn relies on the Continuous Query Language (CQL) [4] for its operation structure, SPARQL 1.1 semantics for RDF querying, and the SECRET model [7] for its operational semantics. Notably, we assume some knowledge on RDF and SPARQL semantics[5].

Definition 1. *A data stream S is an infinite sequence of tuples $\langle d_i, t_e, t_p \rangle$ where, d_i is a data item, and t_e/t_p are respectively the event time and the processing time timestamps. An **RDF Stream** is a stream where the data item d_i is an RDF object and t_e/t_p are timestamps indicating event time and processing time, respectively.*

In the literature, there are many definitions of data stream, with a general agreement on considering them as unbounded sequences of time-ordered data. Different notions of time are relevant for different applications. The most important ones are the time at which a data item reaches the data system (*processing time*), and the time at which a data item was produced (*event time*) [2]. In RSP, streams are represented as RDF objects, as stated by Definition 1 [14].

---

[5] For a comprehensive analysis we suggest [21].

Operationally, stream processing requires a special class of queries that run under continuous semantics (vid. Definition 2). In practice, continuous queries consume one or more infinite inputs and produces an infinite output [25]. Arasu et al. [4] proposed a query model for processing relational streams based on three families of operators, as depicted in Fig. 1. RSPQL extends these operators families to work on RDF Streams.

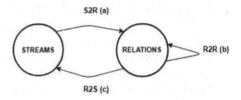

Fig. 1. The CQL query model, i.e., the S2R, R2R, and R2S operators.

Definition 2. *Under continuous semantics, the result of a query is the set of results that would be returned if the query were executed at every instant in time.*

Stream-to-Relation (S2R) (vid. Fig. 1 a), i.e., is a family of operators that bridges the world of streams with the world of relational data processing. These operators chunk the streams into finite portions. A typical operator of this kind is a Time Window operator. In RSPQL, a time-based window operator is defined as in Definition 3.

Definition 3. *The time-based window operator* $\mathbb{W}$ *is a triple* (α, β, t^0) *that defines a series of windows of width* (α) *and that slide of* (β) *starting at* t^0.

Relation-to-Relation (R2R) (Fig. 1 b), i.e., is a family of operators that can be executed over the finite stream portions. In the context of RSPQL, R2R operators are SPARQL 1.1 operators evaluated under continuous semantics.

To clarify this intuition, Dell'Aglio et al. introduce the notion of a Time-Varying Graph and RSPQL dataset [14]. A **Time-Varying Graph** is the result of applying a window operator $\mathbb{W}$ to an RDF Stream $\mathcal{S}$ (vid. Definition 4), while the RSPQL dataset (SDS) is a an extension of the SPARQL dataset for continuous querying (vid. Definition 5).

Definition 4. *A **Time-Varying Graph** is a function that takes a time instant as input and produces as output an RDF Graph, which is called instantaneous.*
Given a window operator $\mathbb{W}$ *and an RDF Stream S, the Time-Varying Graph* $TVG_{\mathbb{W},S}$ *is defined where the* $\mathbb{W}$ *is defined.*

In practice, for any given time instant t, $\mathbb{W}$ identified a subportion of the RDF Stream S containing various RDF Graphs. The Time-Varying Graph function returns the union (*coalescing*) of all the RDF Graphs in the current window[6].

Definition 5. *An **RSPQL dataset** SDS extends the SPARQL dataset[7] as follows: an optional default graph* A_0, n $(n \geq 0)$ *named Time-Varying Graphs, and* m $(m \geq 0)$ *named sliding windows over* k $(k \leq m)$ *data streams.*

---

[6] The current window identified by $\mathbb{W}$ with the oldest closing time instant at t.

[7] https://www.w3.org/TR/rdf-sparql-query/#specifyingDataset.

An RSPQL query is continuously evaluated against an SDS by an RSP engine. The evaluation of a RSPQL query outputs an instantaneous multiset of solution mappings for each evaluation time instant. The RSP engine's operational semantics determines the set ET of evaluation time instants.

Finally, *Relation-to-Stream* (R2S) is a family of operators that returns to the world a set of infinite data from the finite ones, i.e., Fig. 1 (c). RSPQL includes three R2S operators: (i) the **RStream** that emits the current solution mappings; (ii) the **IStream** that emits the difference between the current solution mappings and previous ones, and; (iii) the **DStream** that emits the difference between the previous solution mappings and the current ones.

When developing Stream Processing Engines to evaluate continuous queries there are a number of design decisions that might impact the query correctness. Such decisions, which are usually hidden in the query engine implementation, define the so called *operational semantics* (also known as execution semantics). Botan et al. [7], with their SECRET model, identified a set of four primitives that formalise the operational semantics of window-based stream processing engines. RSPQL incorporates these primitive and applied them on existing RSPQL engines: (i) *Scope* is a function that maps an event-time instant t_e to the temporal interval where the computation occurs. (ii) *Content* is a function that maps a processing-time instant t_p to the subset of stream elements included in the interval identified by the scope function. (iii) *Report* is a dimension that characterizes under which conditions the stream processors emit the window content. SECRET defines four reporting dimensions: (**CC**) *Content Change*: the engine reports when the content of the current window changes. (**WC**) *Window Close*: the engine reports when the current window closes. (**NC**) *Non-empty Content*: the engine reports when the current window is not empty. (**P**) *Periodic* the engine reports periodically. (iv) *Tick* is a dimension that explains what triggers the report evaluations. Possible Ticks are: time-driven, tuple-driven, or batch-driven.

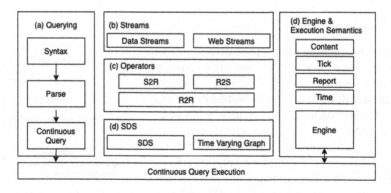

Fig. 2. RSP4J's Modules: (a) Querying (b) Streams, (c) Operators, (d) the SDS, and (e) Engine and Execution Semantics

4   RSP4J

In this section, we present RSP4J's architecture, its components, and we show it satisfies the requirements (cf Sect. 2). Figure 2 shows RSP4J core modules, i.e., (a) Querying, (b) Streams, (c) Operators, (d) the SDS, and (e) the Engine with Execution Semantics. To provide concrete examples of RSP4J, we will use Yet Another Stream Processing Engine for RDF (YASPER). YASPER is a strawman proposal[8] designed for teaching purposes in the context of [15].

4.1   Querying

```
PREFIX : <http://example.org#>
REGISTER RSTREAM <output> AS
SELECT AVG(?v) as ?avgTemp
FROM NAMED WINDOW :w1 ON STREAM :stream1 [RANGE PT5S STEP PT2S]
WHERE {
    WINDOW :w1 { ?sensor :value ?v ; :measurement: ?m }
    FILTER (?m == 'temperature')
}
```

Listing 1.1. An example of RSPQL query.

The query module contains the elements for writing RSPQL programs in a declarative way (R_2). The syntax is based on the proposal by the RSP community. At this stage of development, RSP4J accepts SELECT and CONSTRUCT queries written in RSPQL syntax (e.g. Listing 1.1)[9]. Although RSPQL [14] does not discuss how to handle multi-streams, RSP4J does, allowing its users to fully replicate the behavior of existing systems (cf R_4).

Moreover, RSP4J includes the `ContinuousQuery` interface that aims at making the syntax extensible (cf R_1). Indeed, RSP4J users can bypass the syntax module and programmatically define extensions in the query language.

4.2   Streams

The *Streams* module allows providing your own implementation of a data stream. It consists of two interfaces inspired by VoCaLS [30]: the `Web-Stream` and `WebDataStream`. `WebStream`, represents the stream as a Web resource, while `Web-DataStream`, represents the stream as a data source. Figure 3 provides an overview of the relationships across these classes and interfaces. The `WebStream` does not include any particular logic. It is identified by an HTTP URI so it

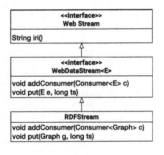

Fig. 3. Streams interface.

---

[8] https://en.wikipedia.org/wiki/Straw_man_proposal.
[9] The RSP W3C Community group has started working towards a common syntax and semantics for RSP (https://github.com/streamreasoning/RSP-QL).

can be de-referenced and then consumed through an available endpoint [30]. Listings 1.11 shows the implementation of the `WebDataStream` interface, which exposes two methods: `put` and `addConsumer`. The former allows injection of timestamped data items of type E by producers; the latter connects the stream to interested consumers, e.g., window operators, or super-streams. The interface is generic, and it allows RSP4J's users to utilize multiple RDF Stream representation, i.e., either RDF Graphs or Triples, or even non-RDF Web Streams. A `WebDataStream` might also include some metadata relevant for the processing, i.e., links to ontologies, SHACL schemas, or alternative endpoints.

```
RDFStream implements WebDataStream<Graph> {
    protected List<Consumer<Graph>> cs = new ArrayList<>();
    @Override
    public void addConsumer(Consumer<Graph> consumer) {
        cs.add(consumer);}
    @Override
    public void put(Graph g,long ts) {
        cs.forEach(c -> c.notify(g, ts)); }
}
```

Listing 1.2. YASPER's WebDataStream implementation.

4.3 Operators

RSP4J core includes separate interfaces for all the RSPQL families of operators: *StreamToRelation, RelationToRelation,* and *RelationToStream.* These abstractions act both as lower level APIs for RSP4J's users (cf R_3) as well as a suitable entrypoint for extensions and optimizations (cf R_1). Moreover, each operator lifecycle could be monitored independently (cf R_5).

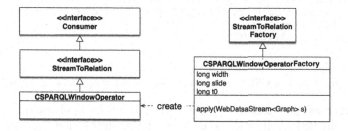

Fig. 4. UML class diagram for the S2R package as used by C-SPARQL.

The **Stream To Relation** operator family bridges the world of RDF Streams to the world of finite RDF Data. RSPQL defines a *Time-Based Sliding Window* operators for processing RDF Streams. When applied to an RDF stream, RSPQL's S2R operator returns a function called Time-Varying Graph, that given a time instant t, materializes an Instantaneous (finite) RDF Graph.

```
public interface StreamToRelationOperator<I,O> extends Consumer<I> {
    String iri();
    Report report();
    Tick tick();
    Content<I, O> materialise(long now);
    List<Content<I, O>> materialise(long now);
    TimeVarying<O> addConsumer(SDS<O> content);
    Content<I, O> compute(long t_e, Window w);
}
```

Listing 1.3. RSP4J S2R operator interface.

```
public interface StreamToRelationOperatorFactory<I,O> {
    String iri();
    TimeVarying<O> apply(WebDataStream<I> stream);
    default boolean named() { return iri() != null;}
}
```

Listing 1.4. RSP4J S2R operator factory interface.

To represent such behavior, RSP4J includes two interfaces, i.e., the **Stream-ToRelationFactory** interface and the **StreamToRelation** (S2R) operator. The former, exemplified in Listing 1.4, is used to instantiate the latter. It exposes the **apply** method that takes a generic **WebDataStream<I>** as input, and returns a Time-Varying object **TimeVarying<O>**, decoupling the Type of the input stream content from the output Time-Varying Object. Listing 1.5 shows part of an implementation of the **StreamToRelationOperatorFactory** that instantiates C-SPARQL's *Time-Based Sliding Window*.

```
public class CSPARQLS2RFactory implements S2R<Graph,Graph> {
    private final long a, b, t0;
    private final ContinuousQueryExecution context;
    @Override
    public TimeVarying<Graph> apply(WebDataStream<Graph> s) {
     CSPARQLS2ROp op = new CSPARQLS2ROp(iri,a,b,scope,tick,report);
     s.addConsumer(op);
     return op.set(context);
    }
}
```

Listing 1.5. The CSPARQL's time-based window operator in YASPER.

The **StreamToRelation** operator is responsible for applying the windowing algorithm. In RSP4J, it is a special kind of **Consumer** that receives the data from the streams, cf Listing 1.3. Listing 1.5 shows that the factory instantiates a **CSPARQLS2ROp**, which is a **StreamToRelationOperator**, and registers it as stream consumer. Then, it obtains a **TimeVarying<Graph>** from the **ContinuousQueryExecution** context. We explain the details about the **TimeVarying<O>** when discussing the RSPQL Dataset *SDS*.

Figure 4 shows the UML class diagram of the S2R package. **CSPARQLWindowOperator** is a **StreamToRelation** operator, which creates a **TimeVarying<Graph>** if applied to a **WebDataStream<Graph>**.

In RSPQL, the **Relation To Relation** operator family corresponds to SPARQL 1.1 algebraic expressions evaluated over a given time instant. The evaluation of the Basic Graph Pattern produces a time-varying sequence of solution mappings, which can be consumed by SPARQL 1.1 operators.

```
public interface RelationToRelationOperator<T> {
    Collection<SolutionMapping<T>> eval(long ts);
}
```

Listing 1.6. RSP4J R2R operator interface.

Listings 1.6 shows the RSP4J interface that covers this functionality. Similarly to the S2R operators, the interface is generic to let the RSP4J's users decide the internal representation of the query solution, e.g., the bindings.

The **RelationToStream** operator family allows going back from the world of Solution Mappings to RDF Streams. According to RSPQL the evaluation of an R2S operator takes as input a sequence of time-varying solution mappings. In RSP4J, we generalized this idea as shown in Listing 1.7, i.e., we allow the user to also provide the solution mapping incrementally as soon as they are produced.

```
public interface RelationToStreamOperator<T> {
  T eval(SolutionMapping<T> sm, long ts);
  default Collection<T>
  eval(Collection<SolutionMapping<T>> s, long t){
    return s.stream().map(sm -> eval(sm, t)).collect(Collectors.toList()
    );
    }
}
```

Listing 1.7. RSP4J R2S operator interface.

4.4 SDS and Time-Varying Graphs

Like in SPARQL, the query specification and the SDS creation are closely related. An RSPQL dataset SDS is an extension of the SPARQL dataset to support the continuous semantics. As indicated in Sect. 3, the SDS is time-dependent as it contains Time-Varying Graphs. RSP4J includes both the abstractions, i.e., the SDS and the TimeVarying Graphs (cf R_3).

Listing 1.8 shows RSP4J's **SDS** interface. The generic parameter is inherited by the generic nature of RSP4J's Time-Varying objects. The `consolidate` method consolidates the SDS content by recursively consolidating every Time-Varying Object it contains.

```
public interface SDS<E> {
    default void consolidate(long t) {
        asTimeVaryingEs().forEach(tvg -> tvg.consolidate(ts));
    } ...
}
```

Listing 1.8. RSP4J's SDS Interface.

Listing 1.9 shows a Time-Varying Graph that is the result of the application of the Window Operator to an RDF Streams. The method `materialize` consolidates the content at a given time instant ts. To this extent, it exploits the `StreamToRelationOperator` interfaces, freezing and polling the active window content. The *coalesce* method ensure only one graph, among those selected during the windowing operation, is returned. According to RSPQL such graph corresponds to the union of the RDF graphs in the window.

```
public class TimeVaryingGraph implements TimeVarying<Graph> {
    private IRI name;
    private StreamToRelationOperator<Graph, Graph> op;
    @Override
    public void materialize(long ts) {
        graph = op.getContent(ts).coalesce(); }...
}
```

Listing 1.9. YASPER's Time Varying Graph Implementation.

As time progresses, the *SDS* is reactively consolidated into a set of (named) Instantaneous Graphs[10] at the time t at which a Time-Varying Graph is updated.

Therefore, RSP4J includes the **SDSManager** and **SDSConfiguration** interfaces. The former controls the creations, detection, and the interactions with the **SDS**; ideally this represents a starting point for federated query answering and/or multi-query optimisation. The latter makes the execution parametric e.g., for enabling different approaches for window management, or alternative output serializations, e.g., JSON-LD or Turtle.

4.5   Engine, Query Execution, and Execution Semantics

This module includes the abstractions to control and monitor the engine and the query lifecycle (cf R_4 and R_5). Moreover, we explain RSP4J's parametric execution semantics (R_4).

The **Engine** interface allows controlling RSP4J's capabilities, e.g., query registration and cancellation. It is based on the VoCaLS service feature idea [30]. Each engine can implement different interfaces, each of which correspond to a particular feature. By querying the implemented interfaces it is possible to list all the features exposed by the engine of choice, e.g., stream registration, RSPQL support, or formatting the results in JSON-LD format.

RSP4J can reproduce the **execution semantics** of common RSP engines by configuring SECRET's primitives: `Tick` is represented as an enumeration, i.e., tuple-based, time-based, and batch. `Scope` is a parameter accessible through the `Time` interface. `Time` controls the time progress w.r.t. the stream consumption. It is initialized with the system initial timestamp at configuration time. It keeps track of the evaluation timestamps ET, and exposes the time-progress to the user

---

[10] Slowly evolving RDF graph are represented as a (named) Time-Varying Graph too.

both for event-time and processing-time[11]. Report is represented as a collection of ReportingStrategies. RSP4J core includes RSPQL's reporting policies, i.e., On-Content-Change, Non-Empty-Content, Periodic, and On-Window-Close. Last but not least, the Content interface represents the data items in the active window. It is generic and exposes the *coalesce* allows alternative implementations of the Time-Varying Graph functions.

```
public interface Time {
    long getScope();
    long getAppTime();
    void setAppTime(long now);
    ET getEvaluationTimeInstants();
    void addEvaluationTimeInstants(TimeInstant i);
    default long getSystemTime() {
        return System.currentTimeMillis();}
}
```

Listing 1.10. RSP4J's Time Interface.

The **ContinuousQueryExecution** interface represents the ever-lasting computation required by continuous queries. It allows monitoring and controlling the query life-cycle. Moreover, in order to make observable (R_5) the SDS and the operators involved in querying, the interface includes getters.

```
public interface ContinuousQueryExecution<I, E1, E2> {
    <O> WebDataStream<O> outstream();
    ContinuousQuery getContinuousQuery();
    SDS<E1> sds();
    StreamToRelationOperator<I, E1>[] getS2R();
    RelationToRelationOperator<E2> getR2R();
    RelationToStreamOperator<E2> getR2S();...
}
```

Listing 1.11. An example of RSP-QL Query.

5   Related Work

In this section, we present the work related to RSP4J. We present the most popular RSP engines, and how they differ in terms of RSPQL semantics, complicating fair comparison.

The C-SPARQL Engine [5] is an RSP engine that adopts a black box approach by pipelining a DSMS system with a SPARQL enige. The DSMS is used to execute the S2R operators and the execution semantics, while the SPARQL engine performs the evaluation of the queries implemented as the R2R operator. C-SPARQL supports the Window Close and Non-empty content reporting policies while employing RStreams as R2S operators.

---

[11] RSPQL determines the evaluation time instant set ET wrt the reporting policy and the input data. Instead, RSP4J serves time as it receives data, i.e., by consuming the streams. Thus, RSP4J's ET is built progressively. While the RSPQL's ET is deterministic, RSP4J ET might not be deterministic in case of distributed computations.

The CQELS Engine [19] takes a white box approach, such that it has access to all the available operators, allowing it to optimize query evaluation. Compared to C-SPARQL, it supports the Content Change reporting strategy. Furthermore, CQELS supports the IStream R2S operator instead of the RStream.

Morph$_{stream}$ [8] focuses on querying virtual RDF streams with SPARQL$_{stream}$. Thus, compared to C-SPARQL and CQELS, it uses Ontology Based Data Access to virtually map raw data to RDF data. Similar to C-SPARQL it supports the Window Close and Non-empty content reporting policies. Morph$_{stream}$ is the only engine that supports all R2S operators.

Strider [23] is a hybrid adaptive distributed RSP engine that optimizes the logical query plan according to the state of the data streams. It is built upon Spark Streaming and borrows most of its operators directly from Spark. Strider translates Strider-SQL queries to Spark Streaming's internal operators. It inherits the Window Close reporting policy from Spark Streaming, and supports the RStream as R2S operator.

In addition to the rigid yet explicit characteristics that each engine has, they also have inherent subtle differences. For example, none of them allows to define the starting timestamp t^0 as part of the time-based sliding window operators definition. This means that the starting time is supplied by the engine itself and in case of processing time engines are bound to produce different results. Differences like the t^0 make impossible to correctly compare the results produced by the various engines. RSP4J allows to customize the inner wiring of the engines, in order to align their semantics and allowing them to produce comparable results.

6   Conclusion, Discussion, and Roadmap

In this paper, we presented RSP4J, a flexible API for RSP development, adhering to the semantics of RSPQL, and YASPER, i.e., a strawman RSP engine implementation designed for teaching purposes in the context of RW [15].

RSP4J aims at solving three use case: fast prototyping, benchmarking comparative research, and dissemination via teaching. Thus, we designed it to fulfill, i.e., a set of requirements: (I) an extensible architecture, (II) declarative access through a uniform query language according to the RSPQL semantics; (III) the necessary programming abstractions; (IV) enable experimentation and fair comparison and (V) observability by design. In Sect. 4, we explained how each RSP4J module solves a subset of requirements. Differently than the state-of-the-art RSP prototypes which only solve requirement R_2 by providing a declarative access, RSP4J fulfills all the set requirements (cf Sect. 4). Moreover, two RSP engines already bind to RSP4J: (i) YASPER[12], which is a strawman implementation based on Apache RDF Commons[2], and C-SPARQL 2.0[13] a new version of the C-SPARQL engine [5].

---

[12] https://github.com/streamreasoning/rsp4j/tree/master/yasper.

[13] https://github.com/streamreasoning/csparql2.

Roadmap. RSP4J's future work includes a number of initiatives. We plan to bind even more engines, i.e., Morph$_{stream}$ and CQELS and run a reproducibility challenge in the context of the upcoming stream reasoning workshop. In the mid term, we would like to abstract RSP4J specification and provide access in other languages, e.g., Python. In the long-term, we would like to include abstraction to control the stream publication lifecycle [29]. Moreover, we would like to investigate how to combine RSP4J with other stream reasoning framework [6].

Acknowledgment. Dr. Tommasini acknowledges support from the European Social Fund via IT Academy program, and from the European Regional Development Funds via the Mobilitas Plus programme (grant MOBTT75). Moreover, the authors would like to acknowledge the support of Robin Keskisärkkä and Daniele Dell'Aglio in earlier versions of this work.

References

1. Affetti, L., Tommasini, R., Margara, A., Cugola, G., Della Valle, E.: Defining the execution semantics of stream processing engines. J. Big Data **4**, 12 (2017)
2. Akidau, T., et al.: The dataflow model: a practical approach to balancing correctness, latency, and cost in massive-scale, unbounded, out-of-order data processing (2015)
3. Ali, M.I., Gao, F., Mileo, A.: CityBench: a configurable benchmark to evaluate RSP engines using smart city datasets. In: Arenas, M., et al. (eds.) ISWC 2015, Part II. LNCS, vol. 9367, pp. 374–389. Springer, Cham (2015). https://doi.org/10.1007/978-3-319-25010-6_25
4. Arasu, A., Babu, S., Widom, J.: The CQL continuous query language: semantic foundations and query execution. VLDB J. **15**(2), 121–142(2006)
5. Barbieri, D.F., Braga, D., Ceri, S., Della Valle, E., Grossniklaus, M.: C-SPARQL: a continuous query language for RDF data streams. Int. J. Semant. Comput. **4**(1), 3–25 (2010)
6. Beck, H., Dao-Tran, M., Eiter, T., Fink, M.: LARS: a logic-based framework for analyzing reasoning over streams. In: Bonet, B., Koenig, S. (eds.) Proceedings of the Twenty-Ninth AAAI Conference on Artificial Intelligence, 25–30 Jan 2015, Austin, Texas, USA, pp. 1431–1438. AAAI Press (2015)
7. Botan, I., Derakhshan, R., Dindar, N., Haas, L.M., Miller, R.J., Tatbul, N.: SECRET: a model for analysis of the execution semantics of stream processing systems. PVLDB **3**(1), 232–243 (2010)
8. Calbimonte, J.P., Jeung, H., Corcho, O., Aberer, K.: Enabling query technologies for the semantic sensor web. Int. J. Semant. Web Inf. Syst. (IJSWIS) **8**(1), 43–63 (2012)
9. Della Valle, E., Ceri, S., van Harmelen, F., Fensel, D.: It's a streaming world! reasoning upon rapidly changing information. IEEE Intell. Syst. **24**(6), 83–89 (2009)
10. Della Valle, E., Dell'Aglio, D., Margara, A.: Taming velocity and variety simultaneously in big data with stream reasoning. In: DEBS, pp. 394–401. ACM (2016)
11. Della Valle, E., Tommasini, R., Balduini, M.: Engineering of web stream processing applications. In: d'Amato, C., Theobald, M. (eds.) Reasoning Web 2018. LNCS, vol. 11078, pp. 223–226. Springer, Cham (2018). https://doi.org/10.1007/978-3-030-00338-8_8

12. Dell'Aglio, D., Calbimonte, J.-P., Balduini, M., Corcho, O., Della Valle, E.: On correctness in RDF stream processor benchmarking. In: Alani, H., et al. (eds.) ISWC 2013, Part II. LNCS, vol. 8219, pp. 326–342. Springer, Heidelberg (2013). https://doi.org/10.1007/978-3-642-41338-4_21

13. Dell'Aglio, D., Della Valle, E., van Harmelen, F., Bernstein, A.: Stream reasoning: a survey and outlook. Data Sci. **1**(1–2), 59–83 (2017)

14. Dell'Aglio, D., Della Valle, E., Calbimonte, J., Corcho, Ó.: RSP-QL semantics: a unifying query model to explain heterogeneity of RDF stream processing systems. Int. J. Semant. Web Inf. Syst. **10**(4), 17–44 (2014)

15. Falzone, E., Tommasini, R., Della Valle, E.: Stream reasoning: from theory to practice. In: Manna, M., Pieris, A. (eds.) Reasoning Web 2020. LNCS, vol. 12258, pp. 85–108. Springer, Cham (2020). https://doi.org/10.1007/978-3-030-60067-9_4

16. Horridge, M., Bechhofer, S.: The OWL API: a Java API for OWL ontologies. Semant. Web **2**(1), 11–21 (2011)

17. Karau, H.: Unifying the open big data world: the possibilities₊ of apache BEAM. In: 2017 IEEE International Conference on Big Data, BigData 2017, Boston, MA, USA, 11–14 Dec 2017, p. 3981. IEEE Computer Society (2017)

18. Kolchin, M., Wetz, P., Kiesling, E., Tjoa, A.M.: YABench: a comprehensive framework for RDF stream processor correctness and performance assessment. In: Bozzon, A., Cudre-Maroux, P., Pautasso, C. (eds.) ICWE 2016. LNCS, vol. 9671, pp. 280–298. Springer, Cham (2016). https://doi.org/10.1007/978-3-319-38791-8_16

19. Le-Phuoc, D., Dao-Tran, M., Xavier Parreira, J., Hauswirth, M.: A native and adaptive approach for unified processing of linked streams and linked data. In: Aroyo, L., et al. (eds.) ISWC 2011, Part I. LNCS, vol. 7031, pp. 370–388. Springer, Heidelberg (2011). https://doi.org/10.1007/978-3-642-25073-6_24

20. Parsia, B., Matentzoglu, N., Gonçalves, R.S., Glimm, B., Steigmiller, A.: The OWL reasoner evaluation (ORE) 2015 competition report. J. Autom. Reasoning **59**(4), 455–482 (2017)

21. Pérez, J., Arenas, M., Gutierrez, C.: Semantics and complexity of SPARQL. ACM Trans. Database Syst. (TODS) **34**(3), 1–45 (2009)

22. Le-Phuoc, D., Dao-Tran, M., Pham, M.-D., Boncz, P., Eiter, T., Fink, M.: Linked stream data processing engines: facts and figures. In: Cudré-Mauroux, P., et al. (eds.) ISWC 2012, Part II. LNCS, vol. 7650, pp. 300–312. Springer, Heidelberg (2012). https://doi.org/10.1007/978-3-642-35173-0_20

23. Ren, X., Curé, O.: Strider: a hybrid adaptive distributed RDF stream processing engine. In: d'Amato, C., et al. (eds.) ISWC 2017, Part I. LNCS, vol. 10587, pp. 559–576. Springer, Cham (2017). https://doi.org/10.1007/978-3-319-68288-4_33

24. Scharrenbach, T., Urbani, J., Margara, A., Della Valle, E., Bernstein, A.: Seven commandments for benchmarking semantic flow processing systems. In: Cimiano, P., Corcho, O., Presutti, V., Hollink, L., Rudolph, S. (eds.) ESWC 2013. LNCS, vol. 7882, pp. 305–319. Springer, Heidelberg (2013). https://doi.org/10.1007/978-3-642-38288-8_21

25. Terry, D.B., Goldberg, D., Nichols, D.A., Oki, B.M.: Continuous queries over append-only databases. In: Proceedings of the 1992 ACM SIGMOD International Conference on Management of Data, San Diego, California, USA, 2–5 June 1992, pp. 321–330. ACM Press (1992)

26. Tommasini, R., Balduini, M., Della Valle, E.: Towards a benchmark for expressive stream reasoning. In: Joint Proceedings of RSP and QuWeDa Workshops co-located with 14th ESWC 2017, vol. 1870, pp. 26–36 (2017)

27. Tommasini, R., Della Valle, E., Balduini, M., Dell'Aglio, D.: Heaven: a framework for systematic comparative research approach for RSP engines. In: Sack, H., Blomqvist, E., d'Aquin, M., Ghidini, C., Ponzetto, S.P., Lange, C. (eds.) ESWC 2016. LNCS, vol. 9678, pp. 250–265. Springer, Cham (2016). https://doi.org/10.1007/978-3-319-34129-3_16

28. Tommasini, R., Della Valle, E., Mauri, A., Brambilla, M.: RSPLab: RDF stream processing benchmarking made easy. In: d'Amato, C., et al. (eds.) ISWC 2017, Part II. LNCS, vol. 10588, pp. 202–209. Springer, Cham (2017). https://doi.org/10.1007/978-3-319-68204-4_21

29. Tommasini, R., Ragab, M., Falcetta, A., Valle, E.D., Sakr, S.: A first step towards a streaming linked data life-cycle. In: Pan, J.Z., Pan, J.Z., et al. (eds.) ISWC 2020, Part II. LNCS, vol. 12507, pp. 634–650. Springer, Cham (2020). https://doi.org/10.1007/978-3-030-62466-8_39

30. Tommasini, R., et al.: VoCaLS: vocabulary and catalog of linked streams. In: Vrandečić, D., et al. (eds.) ISWC 2018, Part II. LNCS, vol. 11137, pp. 256–272. Springer, Cham (2018). https://doi.org/10.1007/978-3-030-00668-6_16

31. Walavalkar, O., Joshi, A., Finin, T., Yesha, Y., et al.: Streaming knowledge bases. In: Proceedings of the Fourth International Workshop on Scalable Semantic Web knowledge Base Systems (2008)

32. Zhang, Y., Duc, P.M., Corcho, O., Calbimonte, J.-P.: SRBench: a streaming RDF/SPARQL benchmark. In: Cudré-Mauroux, P., et al. (eds.) ISWC 2012, Part I. LNCS, vol. 7649, pp. 641–657. Springer, Heidelberg (2012). https://doi.org/10.1007/978-3-642-35176-1_40

WasmTree: Web Assembly for the Semantic Web

Julian Bruyat[1]([⊠]), Pierre-Antoine Champin[1,2], Lionel Médini[1],
and Frédérique Laforest[1]

[1] Université de Lyon, INSALyon, UCBL, LIRIS CNRS UMR 5205, Lyon, France
{julian.bruyat,pierre-antoine.champin,lionel.medini,
frederique.laforest}@liris.cnrs.fr
[2] W3C/ERCIM, Valbonne, France

Abstract. Today, Javascript runtimes intend to process data both at
server and client levels. In this paper, we study how Rust and Web
Assembly can contribute to implement efficient Semantic Web libraries
for the Javascript ecosystem. We propose WasmTree, a new implementation of the RDFJS `Store` and `Dataset` interfaces in which the processing is carefully split between the Web Assembly and Javascript layers. Experiments show that our best setup outperforms state-of-the-art
implementations for fine-grained data access and SPARQL queries.

Keywords: Semantic Web · Web assembly · RDFJS · Indexing

1 Introduction

Nowadays a large number of RDF libraries help application developers take
advantage of Linked Data and the Semantic Web. On the server side, when
high performance is needed, it is usual to use compiled languages, such as C or
Rust. But until recently, in browsers, only libraries written in Javascript (JS)
could be used, such as N3.js [16] or Graphy [13]. With the development of Web
Assembly [14] (WASM), browsers and other JS runtimes are able to run compiled
and highly optimized libraries with near-native performance.

Our aim is to build an efficient RDF library for JS runtimes. We propose
WasmTree[1][2], a fast in-memory implementation of the RDFJS API in which
the processing is carefully split between the WASM and JS layers. Section 2
presents the state of the art of RDF libraries for JS environments. Section 3
presents several attempts to implement efficient Semantic Web libraries using
Rust and WASM, the last being WasmTree. Section 4 evaluates these approaches
in comparison with other libraries. Finally, we conclude with open issues.

---

[1] https://www.npmjs.com/package/@bruju/wasm-tree.

[2] https://github.com/BruJu/WasmTreeDataset/tree/master/wasm-tree-frontend.

R. Verborgh et al. (Eds.): ESWC 2021, LNCS 12731, pp. 582–597, 2021.
https://doi.org/10.1007/978-3-030-77385-4_35

2   State of the Art

RDF Dataset: RDF [9] is the core data model of the Semantic Web. The building block of RDF data is a *triple* composed of a subject (an IRI or a blank node), a predicate (an IRI) and an object (an IRI, blank node, or literal). A set of triples is an *RDF graph*. As graphs are rarely used in isolation, the RDF recommendation defines the notion of *RDF dataset*, composed of one default graph and zero or more named graphs. A dataset can therefore be seen as a set of *quads*, composed of a subject, a predicate, an object, and a graph name (the latter being an IRI, a blank node, or a special marker for the default graph).

Indexing: The most straightforward data structure for representing an RDF graph or dataset is to store triples or quads with their constituting terms directly in the data structure, like in Graphy [13]. Another approach is to store, on one side, a mapping between RDF terms (IRIs, literals, blank nodes) and short identifiers (usually integers), and on the other side, a set of triples or quads where the constituting terms are referred to by their identifiers. This is the approach chosen by HDT [10]. This approach is more memory-efficient and makes it easier to use sorted data structures. On the other hand, it requires an additional step to map identifiers and terms when quads are ingested or retrieved.

RDF in JS Runtime Environments: In order to foster interoperability in Semantic Web developments on JS runtimes (browsers, Node.js, Deno[3]...), the RDFJS W3C Community Group[4] was formed in 2013. It has proposed three specifications [3–5] defining APIs for RDF building blocks, datasets and streams. In the two latter, a `Dataset` interface and a `Store` interface are defined, a store being a dataset usable in an asynchronous fashion. The most prominent implementations of these APIs are Graphy for `Dataset` which uses 1 indexing tree (by Graph then Subject then Predicate then Object, or GSPO) and N3.js for `Store` which stores the data in 3 different indexes (SPO, POS and OSP) for each graph.

Another notable project using the RDFJS interfaces is Comunica [15], a highly modular framework allowing, in particular, to execute SPARQL [11] queries against any `Store` implementation.

Web Assembly: Most JS runtimes nowadays make use of Just In Time (JIT) compilation, which largely increases the performance of JS code. However, since 2015, another approach has been explored, which lead to the standardization of Web Assembly (WASM) in 2019. WASM is a low-level binary language which, alongside JS, is executable in most JS runtimes. WASM files are much smaller than equivalent JS files, and are compiled *ahead of time*, saving time at execution and opening the way to more aggressive optimizations. WASM is executed in a

---

[3] https://deno.land/.

[4] https://www.w3.org/community/rdfjs/.

virtual machine in order to be portable, but at the same time is very close to machine code, in order to achieve near-native performance.

For security and portability reasons, WASM code can only work on a *linear memory*. More precisely, this linear memory is allocated by JS code as an array of bytes, and provided to the WASM code. Communication between JS code and WASM code is only possible through function calls returning integers or floating point numbers and modifications in this array. At the time of writing, a dozen languages can be compiled to WASM[5], Rust being one of them.

Rust: [12] is a programming language created by Graydon Hoare, first released in July 2010 and supported until 2020 by Mozilla. Rust emphasizes performance, reliability and productivity. Performance is ensured by the fact that everything in Rust is explicit; for example, Rust has no exception mechanism nor garbage collector. Reliability is ensured by an original ownership model, guaranteeing memory-safety and thread-safety. Yet, productivity is made possible by powerful abstractions, carefully designed to have minimal or zero cost at runtime.

A few RDF libraries exist in Rust. Sophia [8] provides generic interfaces for graphs and datasets, aiming to play the same role as RDFJS in the JS ecosystem. Oxigraph[6] provides a persistent dataset storage and SPARQL query engine.

Rust was one of the first languages that could be compiled to WASM. What sets Rust apart from other WASM-enabled languages is the wasm-bindgen tool. We have described above how the WASM virtual machine can only work on and communicate through its linear memory, which is seen by JS code as an array of numbers. Communicating other data types to JS code requires an additional layer of JS "glue code" to re-interpret the content of the linear memory into the corresponding abstraction. Such glue code is automatically generated by wasm-bindgen, requiring only that the Rust code be annotated using a set of dedicated keywords. To the best of our knowledge, Rust and C++ (with Emscripten) are the only languages equipped with such tools.

3   Towards an Efficient Implementation of RDFJS

We have developed a fast in-memory implementation of the RDFJS `Dataset` interface usable in any JS runtime. To ensure efficiency, we have developed a new dataset structure in the Rust language. Based on the WASM principles, it is compiled and exported to JS runtimes using the wasm-bindgen tool, so that JS runtime developers can use it from their JS code. We first present two approaches that are more straightforward ways to implement a RDFJS library using WASM, but underperform. Then based on these observations, we present WasmTree.

---

[5] https://webassembly.org/getting-started/developers-guide/.
[6] https://github.com/oxigraph/oxigraph.

3.1   General View of Our Approach

Our **Dataset** structure implementation is separated into two parts:

- A bidirectional *term mapping* to store the correspondence between terms and their integer identifiers.
- A *forest* of B-Trees [2]. Each B-Tree sorts quads of identifiers in a given order e.g. SPOG, GPOS. Details are provided hereafter.

The term mapping is used to convert quads of terms into quads of identifiers and conversely. To provide constant lookup time, this mapping is implemented as a hashmap to map terms to identifiers, and a vector to map identifiers to terms (identifiers are assigned in sequence). Details about how this mapping is implemented and used are provided in the following subsections.

The quads of identifiers are stored in several B-Trees. The reasons are the followings:

- If we classify search patterns according to which positions (Subject, Predicate, Object or Graph name) are fixed (as opposed to a wildcard), there are 15 classes of patterns (the "all-wildcards" pattern is not interesting). For each class of patterns, we need a B-Tree sorted by the fixed positions, so that all matching quads can be efficiently located and iterated over.
- While up to 16 different sort orders are possible (SPOG, OSPG, OPSG ...), 6 sort orders are sufficient to optimally answer any pattern. Indeed, when a pattern is queried, any sort order starting with the fixed positions of the pattern is appropriate; for example if the subject (S) and the object (O) are fixed (which we will refer to as a S?O? in this paper, using ? as a wildcard), any of the following trees could be used: **SO**PG, **SO**GP, **OS**PG and **OS**GP. Note that this is possible because the order of the resulting quads can not be specified using the RDFJS APIs.
- As all classes of patterns will not necessarily be used in practice, we initialize our structure with only one B-Tree. The other five B-Trees are built lazily when a pattern is queried for which the available trees are not suited. This enables to speed up the initial dataset load. For example a tree that starts with SO will only be required when the pattern S?O? is queried.
- B-Trees are preferred over binary trees to benefit from the principle of locality of reference[7]: by using B-Trees, up to 2B-1 quads can be stored in the same node, which is more cache friendly. This choice is also reinforced by the fact that the Rust standard library offers functions to directly extract a range from a B-Tree, which helps code maintainability.

This B-Tree structure is common among all our implementations and implemented in Rust. On the other hand, the management of the term mapping, and more generally the way to retrieve the stored quads from WASM memory to the JS code, comes in three different propositions:

---

[7] https://en.wikipedia.org/wiki/Locality_of_reference.

– The naive TreeDataset approach is a full-Rust implementation of the dataset, which is compiled in WASM and exposes individual quads to JS.
– The all-at-once TreeDataset approach also uses a full-Rust implementation of the dataset compiled in WASM, but reduces the number of exchanges between WASM and JS code by transmitting all quads as one single string serialized using the N-Quads format [7].
– The WasmTree approach implements only the B-Trees in Rust, while the term mapping is managed by JS code.

3.2 Naive TreeDataset Approach

In this first approach, we have implemented both the B-Trees and the term mapping in Rust, in a structure called TreeDataset. More precisely, TreeDataset complies with the Sophia API [8]. The Sophia and the RDFJS APIs are quite similar. In particular, both provide methods to retrieve a subset of quads matching a given pattern. The main difference is the return value of pattern matching methods: Sophia returns a stream of quads that can be lazily evaluated, while the Dataset interface returns a new dataset containing all the match quads.

To hash a term, we use the default Rust hasher implementation. Every part of the term is hashed successively and then the hash code is produced with the SipHash algorithm. For example, if the term is an IRI, the Rust hasher is used on that IRI. If the term is a non language literal, the hasher is used on both the IRI and the datatype.

By writing an adapter annotated with wasm-bindgen, the dataset structure is compiled in WASM. Thanks to the generated JS glue code, this implementation can be used in a JS code like any other RDFJS Dataset implementation.

Figure 1 shows the process to iterate on all quads. An iterator object is first constructed from the list of all quads stored in the output dataset. This iterator is then exported to the JS user. When the user code requests the next quad, the returned quad is produced by Rust code.

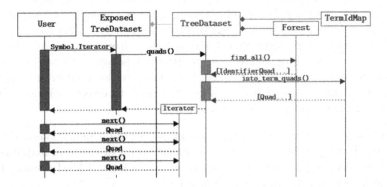

Fig. 1. Process to retrieve quads from a TreeDataset - naive TreeDataset approach. The left blue part is in JS, while the right red part is a WASM built from Rust

As shown later in Sect. 4, naively adapting through WASM a Rust API to a JS API, however similar, leads to bad performance. Indeed, there is a cost for every individual exchange between the JS code and the WASM code, meaning it is better if data is sent in bulk[8].

Another drawback of this approach is related to memory leaks. Unlike JS, WASM does not have a garbage collector. While the WASM memory is implicitly allocated by classes generated by the JS glue code when the constructor is used, the user has to explicitly free it using the `free` method. This means that the whole datastructure representing the dataset in WASM needs to be explicitly deallocated, which is uncommon for JS developers and is not part of the RDFJS specification. Recent versions of JS introduce the FinalizationRegistry, which can be used as a destructor: this is used by recent versions of wasm-bindgen. So when the JS object that owns a part of the WASM memory is destroyed, the memory is freed. In our implementation, we prefer to rely as little as possible on allocated objects to ensure compatibility with older versions of JS runtimes, but also provide a library that conforms to JS developers current idioms.

To solve these performance issues, the next sections present two other approaches aiming at mutualizing exchange costs and reducing the number of WASM allocated objects.

3.3   All-at-Once TreeDataset Approach

We tried a different strategy for iterating over quads: rather than retrieving a single quad from the WASM dataset at each iteration, we export all quads at once, using a textual serialization format.

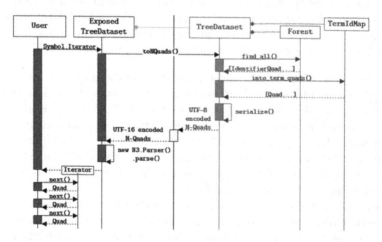

Fig. 2. Process to retrieve quads from a TreeDataset - All-at-once approach. The left blue part is in JS, while the right red part is a WASM built from Rust

---

[8] As a side experiment, we tried to send 1,000,000 integers from WASM to JS: sending in bulk the whole array was 8 times faster than sending the integers one by one.

Figure 2 presents the different steps of this approach: we first serialize all the quads in the N-Quads format [7] into a big string. JS retrieves this string by calling the `toNQuads` function, which first takes care of transcoding it from UTF-16 to UTF-8, then uses the N-Quads parser of N3.js to get a list of quads.

Unfortunately, our experiments described in Sect. 4.2 show that this approach is slower than the previous one. This is mainly due to the high cost of interpreting the N-Quads formatted string received by the JS code, even though N-Quads are a very simple and straightforward format.

3.4   WasmTree: A Hybrid Implementation

Our last implementation, which is the main contribution of this work, consists in splitting wisely the work between WASM code and JS code. Previous approaches fail because of the cost of exchanging and reinterpreting complex data (in our case objects and strings), as they are not trivially copyable[9] from the WASM memory to the JS memory. So we decided to do computation-intensive integer manipulation (i.e. the construction, storage and manipulation of the B-Trees structure) in WASM, and to handle strings (i.e. the mapping between identifiers and terms) in JS. Thus, only integers need to be exchanged across the WASM-JS boundary. More precisely, the JS part implements the RDFJS `Dataset` interface with three main components:

- The term mapping, implemented with an array and a standard JS dictionary; as the array only accepts simple strings as keys, we use the notion of concise term[10] to unambiguously encode RDF terms into strings.
- A handle to the WASM structure that contains the forest of B-Trees.
- An identifier list representing the quads in the dataset. Elements of this list are read four at a time (subject, predicate, object, graph name). The role of this list is to serve as a cache to limit exchanges with the WASM memory.

When a new WasmTree instance is created by the user, it is created with no forest and no identifier list. Iterating over the quads of the dataset is performed using the identifier list, as illustrated in Fig. 3. If the list is absent, it is first recomputed from the forest. If there is no forest, an empty identifier list is used instead. When methods modify the content of the dataset (`add`, `addAll`, `delete`...), the terms received as parameters are converted to identifiers, the changes are applied to the forest, and the identifier list is deleted as its content no longer reflects the content of the forest.

The `match` method takes a quad pattern and builds a new dataset containing only the matching quads. First, the terms in the pattern are converted to identifiers, and the forest is requested for matching quads (it is more efficient than

---

[9] By "trivially copyable", like in C++, we mean that to copy the data, the underlying bytes can be copied from one location to another. An array of 32 bits integers is trivially copyable from WASM to JS with the Int32Array object type. A string is not trivially copyable because of the different encodings.

[10] https://graphy.link/concise.

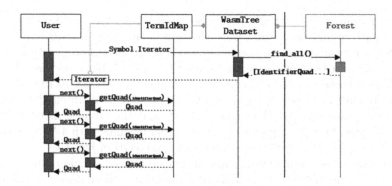

Fig. 3. Process to retrieve quads from a TreeDataset - WasmTree approach. The left blue part is in JS, while the right red part is a WASM built from Rust

browsing the identifier list). This produces a new identifier list, which is used to build a new dataset containing that list, but no forest. The identifier list returned by the forest in WASM is a plain `Uint32Array` Javascript object, meaning that the garbage collector is able to manage it. It is also cheap to produce, as it only requires to copy a segment of the WASM linear memory. The mapping of terms is not duplicated, but shared with the original dataset.

The benefit of this design is that, once an identifier list has been retrieved, and as long as that dataset is not modified, no exchange is required with WASM. Furthermore, while the `match` method is required by the RDFJS API to return a full-fledged dataset, in most cases, this dataset will be iterated over and dismissed, therefore spending time indexing its quads into B-Trees would be useless. However, the indexing (forest reconstruction) will happen lazily if the dataset was to be modified or queried again with `match`.

Our `Dataset` interface also provides a `free` method which is not part of the RDFJS API. It removes the forest and the identifier list, and frees the WASM memory segment allocated to the former. From the the end-user's point-of-view, it has the effect of emptying the dataset.

By using a similar split between WASM and JS code, we also developed an implementation of the RDFJS `Store` interface. The main differences between `Dataset` and `Store` are that `Store` methods are asynchronous and the `match` method in `Store` returns a stream of quads instead of a new dataset. Our implementation is based on an asynchronous call on a function which starts with retrieving the identifier list corresponding to the pattern, and then rebuilds a quad by using the identifier list and the JS dictionary every time a `data` message is emitted.

4   Evaluation

In this section, we evaluate the performance of WasmTree in three different situations: first, we study the amounts of time and memory required to initialize a dataset from an N-Quad file, second we evaluate its performance on a simple task of pattern matching, third we evaluate it in the case of a SPARQL query.

All these evaluations have been performed using the following setup. Compilation tasks have been performed using Rust Compiler 1.43.0, and wasm-bindgen 0.2.63. Benchmarks have been coded and run on the NodeJS 10.19.0 platform. API tests have been performed on a PC equipped with an Intel(R) Core(TM) i5-1035G1 processor, 16 GB of DDR4 RAM, and the Ubuntu 20.04 LTS OS. SPARQL tests have been performed on a virtual machine with 4 VCPUs (based on 2600 MHz Intel Xeon Skylake processors) and 8 GB of RAM.

The two first experiments (dataset initialization and simple pattern matching) were conducted under the following conditions: the datasets we used are extracts of various sizes (up to 1 million quads) from the *Person data* dataset of the 2016-10 dump[11] of DBpedia [1] in N-Triples format, considered as an RDF dataset containing one default graph. All measures were performed 50 times and the average was computed. Both experiments were performed using the RDFJS API and the N3.js parser to read the dataset. A step by step guide to reproduce the experiments can be found at https://github.com/BruJu/wasm_rdf_benchmark/tree/eswc2021.

4.1 Evaluation of Dataset Initialization

We herein evaluate the cost, in time and memory, of initializing a dataset from an N-Quads file containing 1 million quads, in different implementations. By initializing, we mean here all the operations required to make the dataset available to the JS application: reading and parsing the data, and populating data structures. For the TreeDataset approaches and WasmTree, we tested a lazy configuration, where only one of the six B-Trees is constructed (default), and a greedy configuration immediately building all six B-Trees.

Time: Fig. 4b shows initialization speed for several RDFJS `Dataset` implementations. We also compare N3.js using its synchronous `addQuad` function. With only one index, WasmTree is 1.30 times faster than N3.js, and is 1.06 times faster than Graphy, which doesn't resort to a dictionary and directly stores quads in its hashtree. When building greedily its 6 indexes, WasmTree is 1.32 times slower than Graphy, and 1.06 times slower than N3.js.

The table in Fig. 4a shows that the difference between filling one and six indexes is the same (2.1 s) for our two implementations. This is not surprising as they use the same data structures for indexes. This corroborates our hypothesis that the poor performance of TreeDataset are related to storing strings in the term mapping in the WASM memory. The lost time is more impacting in terms of initialization speed for WasmTree as a 2.1 s difference represents a higher ratio of the total time. In real world applications, the lazy indexing strategy will ensure the users benefit from the fastest initialization time, amortizing the cost of creating the missing indexes over the use of the dataset.

---

[11] https://wiki.dbpedia.org/develop/datasets/downloads-2016-10.

	# of indexes	Time (s)	Memory (kB)
TreeDataset	*1*	10.825	**30,982**
TreeDataset	*6*	12.976	**30,994**
WasmTree	*1*	**5.343**	411,093
WasmTree	*6*	7.457	407,511
Graphy	*1*	**5.653**	595,890
N3.js	*3*	6.985	1,286,967

(a) Time and memory used at initialization.

(b) Initialization speed. Higher is better

Fig. 4. Time and memory used to initialize a 1 M quad dataset in various RDFJS implementations.

Memory: The table in Fig. 4a also exhibits an estimation of the memory used to store the different benchmarked RDFJS implementations. These estimations are based on the peak virtual memory usage, as provided in Linux by the `VmPeak` field of the file `/proc/self/status`. This introduces a bias because JS may allocate memory before the garbage collector has freed memory blocks that are not used anymore. Actually, we see that this method is not precise enough to measure the difference between one and six indexes within the same implementation, therefore the most relevant information from these measures is the order of magnitude.

We can see that implementations relying on WASM are more compact than pure JS implementations. TreeDataset, used by the naive approach and the all-at-once approach, entirely based on Rust data structures stored in the WASM memory, is by orders of magnitude the most memory-efficient. However, its initialization time and its poor query performance (as shown in Sect. 4.2) make it non satisfying. The hybrid approach (WasmTree) still consumes less memory than the best pure JS implementation in our study (Graphy).

The difference between pure Rust implementations (TreeDataset), those using fewer JS structure (WasmTree, Graphy) and those using many JS structures (N3.js), demonstrates that Rust structures compiled into WASM are much more compact than comparable JS structures. Additionally, we already remarked that the memory used by WASM B-Trees is negligible compared to the term mapping and the noise induced by the garbage collector. This motivates our choice to store several indexes in WASM memory in order to improve speed.

4.2 Evaluation of Simple Pattern Matching

We now proceed to evaluate the performance of extracting quads matching a given pattern. This corresponds to simple queries such as "find all quads about person X" or "find all resources of type Person".

For each measure, we load a dataset and call the method `match` twice with the given pattern, measuring the time taken by the second call. The first method call ensures that lazily built indexes and caches are computed. The cost of these operations is considered irrelevant here as 1) it will be amortized on multiple calls, and 2) different implementations will trigger them at different times or for different queries, making comparisons less meaningful. We then measure the time it takes to iterate over all the quads of the `Dataset` returned by the second call to `match`.

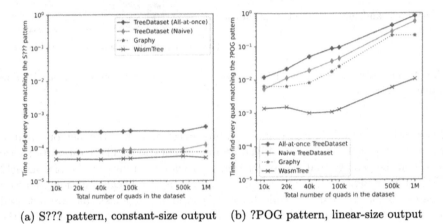

(a) S??? pattern, constant-size output   (b) ?POG pattern, linear-size output

Fig. 5. Time (in seconds) to iterate over quads matching a given pattern.

Performance with Different Patterns: The first set of measures we ran is for querying the dataset for quads having a given subject. We chose that subject in such a way that the number of matching quads was the same (seven) regardless of the dataset size. TreeDataset and WasmTree use their SPOG index to answer this query. The unique index used by Graphy is also optimal in this case (GSPO, with only one graph in the dataset). The results are shown in Fig. 5a.

TreeDataset is slower than Graphy, a pure JS implementation. This can be explained by the fact that the time saved by using WASM is lost in the translation process with JS. The all-at-once approach is the worst, being twice as slow as the naive approach. The reason for these poor performance will be explored later with Fig. 6a. On the other hand, WasmTree reduces the number of exchanges (one array describing all the quads instead of individual quads) and the complexity of the exchanged data (integers rather than strings). This reaches the best trade-off, where the manipulations of numbers are most efficiently handled by WASM code, while string manipulations are left to JS.

We see that the size of the input dataset has only a minimal impact on all implementations. This shows that the choice of B-Trees, that have a $\mathcal{O}(\log n)$

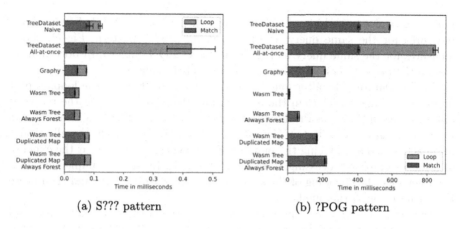

(a) S??? pattern   (b) ?POG pattern

Fig. 6. Workload distribution when matching over a certain pattern.

complexity for searching quads, is a viable alternative to hashmaps with $\mathcal{O}(1)$ complexity (as used by Graphy).

Figure 5b shows the result of a second set of measures, where we are now looking for every resource of type Person in the default graph. For every dataset size, the retrieved quads represent about 13% of the total dataset size. In other words, the output size in this benchmark is linear with the dataset size. For this query pattern (?POG), Graphy's GSPO index is not theoretically optimal, which would make the comparison unfair, as our implementation always uses an optimal index. However, in this particular dataset, all the subjects are of type Person, so they all match the pattern. Graphy is therefore not sanctioned for having to loop on all the subjects.

We can see that the order remains the same: WasmTree is still the most efficient solution, followed by Graphy and then TreeDataset. The gap between different options is bigger, and increases with the size of the output: instead of being 1.5 times faster than Graphy as in Fig. 5a, WasmTree is now 4 to 35 times faster than Graphy, scaling better as the output size grows.

We also benchmarked our implementation of the `Store` interface using Wasm-Tree and compared it to N3.js in similar conditions. We found that WasmTree also outperforms N3.js. For example, when looking for every person in the dataset, WasmTree is on par with N3.js for small datasets, but becomes increasingly faster (up to 13.671 times) when the input dataset grows. Using the `Store` interface of WasmTree makes the iteration over all quads 2.73 to 8.22 times slower than using its `Dataset` interface; it means that in practice, consuming an asynchronous stream of quads is more time consuming than populating an intermediate dataset.

Workload Distribution: In Fig. 6, we focus on the `Dataset` interface, to study how the overall time measured previously is distributed between finding the matching triples (match), and iterating over them (loop)[12]. While Fig. 6a shows measures for the same query as Fig. 5a, using a S??? pattern, Fig. 6b shows measures for the same query as Fig. 5b, using a ?POG pattern. In both figures, we use the biggest version of our test dataset (1M quads).

In TreeDataset, the all-at-once approach is very inefficient: the looping part is up to 11 times slower than the naive approach, especially when the returned dataset is small (Fig. 6a). Profiling the code reveals that 22% of the time spent is used by the garbage collector. Compared to the naive approach, the all-at-once approach aimed at reducing the number of exchanges, but that is at the expense of a more complex processing to retrieve all quads. Indeed the implementation has to change the encoding of the string from UTF-8 to UTF-16, and then parse the string to build the quads.

TreeDataset is always slower to loop on all quads than Graphy. The total time for the latter is even lower than the match time for TreeDataset. The match operation has limited exchange with WASM: it consists in only one function call. We can deduce that the cost of interpretation of the WASM code and our code are not efficient enough to beat Graphy, both for small and big results. It can be explained because Graphy does not build a whole new dataset when the `match` method is called: the returned dataset shares data structures with the source dataset, unlike TreeDataset that copies the quads and creates a new independent dataset.

WasmTree, on the other hand, is faster than all the other approaches, especially during the loop, and when the output dataset is big (Fig. 6b). This confirms that the computation intensive part of the processing is mostly handled by WASM code (in the `match` method), making quick and easy the remaining task of the JS code handling the loop. Thanks to the compactness of the B-Trees stored in the WASM memory, we can afford to store indexes for all possible patterns, while Graphy is bound, with a unique index, to be less efficient for some patterns.

Ablation Study: WasmTree uses two different strategies to be fast. The first one consists in caching the list of identifiers in an array, as described at the end of Sect. 3.4. The second one consists in sharing the term mapping between a dataset and the (sub-)datasets returned by the `match` method. In Figs. 6a and 6b, we studied the impact of these optimizations by removing the first one ("Always Forest"), removing the second one ("Duplicated Map") and removing both.

The sharing of term mappings is what saves most time, dividing by 2 the total time for the S??? benchmark. Producing an independent dataset when the `match` method is called is expensive, as it requires to produce and populate a new term mapping, and this operation has to be done in JS. It results in similar to slightly worse performance as compared to Graphy. When producing a dataset that shares the term mapping, WasmTree is 1.4 to 19 times faster than Graphy, which shares its index and has no mapping.

---

[12] This distinction is not relevant for the `Store` interface, where the iteration is performed in an asynchronous fashion.

The caching of the identifier list has a bigger impact when the output dataset is large (?POG benchmark). Indeed, when there are few elements, the identifier list memory representation in JS and the B-Tree one in WASM are close. In the S??? benchmark, as there are only 7 quads to return, both representations are an array of 28 integers. In the default WasmTree implementation, the identifier list is already in the JS environment, so it does not call a WASM function to retrieve it. The "WasmTree Always Forest" implementation retrieves the identifier list from the WASM environment. When there are less than 2B elements, it consists in simply copying the root element of the B-Tree. This is the only difference between the two, and explains the small measured difference in time, as shown in Fig. 6a.

In every benchmark but memory consumption, WasmTree, the implementation that splits works between WASM and JS is better than TreeDataset: having faster initialization time, faster quad retrieval and being less error prone, as users do not have to care about freeing memory except for the datasets. Moreover, the identifier list permits users to forget about freeing the datasets produced by match, as they do not actually allocate WASM memory.

4.3 Evaluation of SPARQL Queries

To get a broader insight on performance, our third set of experiments evaluates performance on SPARQL [11] queries. SPARQL allows to express complex queries, contrarily to the simple query patterns studied in the previous section.

We used the Berlin SPARQL Benchmark [6] (BSBM), a benchmarking framework for SPARQL. It can generate synthetic datasets about products, vendors and consumers, and realistic queries over these datasets. It provides a driver that can submit a set of queries (a *query mix*) to a SPARQL endpoint and measure its performance. We are interested here in information retrieval: the driver sends a query mix made of 25 queries, generated from 12 query templates from the "Explore" use-case of BSBM. For example, in the first template "Find the name of all products having [two specific features]", the driver randomly chooses the two features for each query.

As described in Sect. 2, Comunica can be used to setup a SPARQL endpoint above any implementation of the RDFJS Store interface. We use Comunica v1.13.1 to expose a SPARQL endpoint above our RDFJS implementation. In this section, we will compare the default configuration (using N3.js) with a Comunica SPARQL endpoint backed by WasmTree.

Oxigraph, which we also described in Sect. 2 is a Rust library implementing a dataset and a SPARQL engine. It can be compiled to WASM, providing its own API which only partially complies with RDFJS, but exposes SPARQL functionalities. It was therefore straightforward to use it to build a Node.js-based SPARQL endpoint, where the whole query processing is done in WASM.

Performance. Table 1 shows that, when it comes to executing SPARQL queries, replacing N3.js with WasmTree as Comunica's store allows to execute almost 7

Table 1. Performance of three SPARQL endpoints, with a dataset of 2000 products (725305 quads). Measured from 100 executions after a warmup of 20 executions.

	Query mixes per hour	Acceleration compared to		
		Oxigraph	Comunica +WasmTree	Comunica +N3.js
Oxigraph	8877.66		×19.90	×135.25
Comunica + WasmTree	446.22	×0.05		×6.80
Comunica + N3.js	65.64	×0.007	×0.15	

times more queries in the same time. WASM increases performance even when used only for a part (finding quads) of a more complex operation (executing a query plan and computing joints). Oxigraph is itself 20 times faster than Comunica with WasmTree. The difference can be explain both by the efficiency of WASM for complex processing paying off compared to the cost of transferring the results, but also the fact that Oxigraph is not limited by the RDFJS API, which enables it to use better query plans.

Memory Limitations. We initially tried to run the BSBM driver with a scale factor of 10,000 (corresponding to a dataset of 4 M quads), but we ran into memory shortage. For Comunica-based approaches, this was solved by increasing the memory allocated to JS. However, for Oxigraph, the limitation was due to WASM itself, which uses 32bit addresses, and is therefore structurally limited to handling 4 GB of linear memory. This limit is easily reached with big RDF datasets. The strict limitation is less impacting on WasmTree, because it only uses WASM memory for BTrees.

5   Conclusion and Perspectives

In this work, we studied how we can use Rust and WASM to build efficient RDF libraries for JS runtimes. Our experiments show that using WASM naively does not improve performance. In an effort to reduce the costs related to exchanging information between WASM and JS, we have proposed WasmTree, a hybrid implementation providing an efficient distribution of tasks between the two languages. On simple pattern matching queries, it outperforms two state-of-the-art JS libraries: Graphy and N3.js.

In the context of SPARQL query evaluation, the fastest approach by far is the one relying entirely on WASM (Oxigraph). However, the WASM intrinsic memory limitations hinder the scalability of this approach. WasmTree, on the other hand, improves the performance of the Comunica framework while being much less affected by this scalability issue.

However, the forest structure, which is the only part implemented in Rust for WasmTree, has no access to the actual terms in the graph. Thus, semantic processing such as inferences, which could benefit from the performance gain of WASM, can not directly be implemented on the WASM side. To tackle this problem, we should refine the hybridization between the two sides of our implementation. Some clues are the following: we could fix once and for all the identifier of semantically loaded IRIs (such as `rdfs:subClassOf`), or enable the term mapping to share some specific identifiers with the index, depending on the inference ruleset. These ideas will be for further work.

Acknowledgment. This work was partly supported by the Fédération Informatique de Lyon within the Repid project, and by the EC within the H2020 Program under grant agreement 825333 (MOSAICrOWN).

References

1. Auer, S., Bizer, C., Kobilarov, G., Lehmann, J., Cyganiak, R., Ives, Z.: DBpedia: a nucleus for a web of open data. In: Aberer, K., et al. (eds.) ASWC/ISWC -2007. LNCS, vol. 4825, pp. 722–735. Springer, Heidelberg (2007). https://doi.org/10.1007/978-3-540-76298-0_52
2. Bayer, R., McCreight, E.: Organization and maintenance of large ordered indices. In: Proceedings of the 1970 ACM SIGFIDET (Now SIGMOD) Workshop on Data Description, Access and Control, pp. 107–141. SIGFIDET 1970. ACM, New York, NY, USA (1970). https://doi.org/10.1145/1734663.1734671
3. Bergwinkl, T.: RDF/JS: Dataset specification. W3C Community Group Final Report, W3C, March 2019. https://rdf.js.org/dataset-spec/. Accessed 15 Dec 2020
4. Bergwinkl, T., Verborgh, R.: RDF/JS: Stream interfaces. W3C Community Group Draft Report, W3C, May 2019. http://rdf.js.org/stream-spec/. Accessed 15 Dec 2020
5. Bergwinkl, T., Verborgh, R.: RDF/JS: Data model specification. W3C Community Group Draft Report, W3C, July 2020. http://rdf.js.org/data-model-spec/. Accessed 15 Dec 2020
6. Bizer, C., Schultz, A.: The Berlin SPARQL benchmark. Int. J. Semant. Web Inf. Syst. (IJSWIS) **5**(2), 1–24 (2009)
7. Carothers, G.: RDF 1.1 n-quads. W3C recommendation, W3C, February 2014. http://www.w3.org/TR/n-quads/
8. Champin, P.A.: Sophia: a linked data and semantic web toolkit for rust. In: The Web Conference 2020: Developers Track, April 2020. https://www2020devtrack.github.io/site/schedule
9. Cyganiak, R., Wood, D., Lanthaler, M.: RDF 1.1 Concepts and Abstract Syntax. W3C Recommendation, W3C, February 2014. https://www.w3.org/TR/rdf11-concepts/
10. Fernández, J.D., Martínez-Prieto, M.A., Gutiérrez, C., Polleres, A., Arias, M.: Binary RDF representation for publication and exchange (HDT). J. Web Semant. **19**, 22–41 (2013)
11. Harris, S., Seaborne, A.: SPARQL 1.1 Query Language. W3C Recommendation, W3C, March 2013. http://www.w3.org/TR/sparql11-query/
12. Matsakis, N.D., Klock, F.S.: The Rust language. ACM SIGAda Ada Lett. **34**(3), 103–104 (2014)
13. Regalia, B.: Graphy.js homepage. https://graphy.link/. Accessed 15 Dec 2020
14. Rossberg, A.: WebAssembly Core Specification. W3C Recommendation, W3C, December 2019. https://www.w3.org/TR/wasm-core-1/
15. Taelman, R., Van Herwegen, J., Vander Sande, M., Verborgh, R.: Comunica: A Modular SPARQL Query Engine for the Web. In: Vrandečić, D., et al. (eds.) ISWC 2018. LNCS, vol. 11137, pp. 239–255. Springer, Cham (2018). https://doi.org/10.1007/978-3-030-00668-6_15
16. Verborgh, R.: N3.js homepage. https://github.com/rdfjs/N3.js/. Accessed 15 Dec 2020

ParaQA: A Question Answering Dataset with Paraphrase Responses for Single-Turn Conversation

Endri Kacupaj[1(✉)] ⓘ, Barshana Banerjee[1], Kuldeep Singh[2] ⓘ,
and Jens Lehmann[1,3] ⓘ

[1] University of Bonn, Bonn, Germany
{kacupaj,jens.lehmann}@cs.uni-bonn.de, s6babane@uni-bonn.de
[2] Zerotha Research and Cerence GmbH, Aachen, Germany
kuldeep.singh1@cerence.com
[3] Fraunhofer IAIS, Dresden, Germany
jens.lehmann@iais.fraunhofer.de

Abstract. This paper presents ParaQA, a question answering (QA) dataset with multiple paraphrased responses for single-turn conversation over knowledge graphs (KG). The dataset was created using a semi-automated framework for generating diverse paraphrasing of the answers using techniques such as back-translation. The existing datasets for conversational question answering over KGs (single-turn/multi-turn) focus on question paraphrasing and provide only up to one answer verbalization. However, ParaQA contains 5000 question-answer pairs with a minimum of two and a maximum of eight unique paraphrased responses for each question. We complement the dataset with baseline models and illustrate the advantage of having multiple paraphrased answers through commonly used metrics such as BLEU and METEOR. The ParaQA dataset is publicly available on a persistent URI for broader usage and adaptation in the research community.

Keywords: Question answering · Paraphrase responses · Single-turn conversation · Knowledge graph · Dataset

Resource Type: Dataset
License: Attribution 4.0 International (CC BY 4.0)
Permanent URL: https://figshare.com/projects/ParaQA/94010.

1 Introduction

In recent years, publicly available knowledge graphs (e.g., DBpedia [21], Wikidata [40]) and Yago [36]) have been widely used as a source of knowledge in several tasks such as entity linking, relation extraction, and question answering [22]. Question answering (QA) over knowledge graphs, in particular, is an essential task that maps a user's utterance to a query over a knowledge graph (KG) to retrieve the correct answer [34]. With the increasing popularity of

© Springer Nature Switzerland AG 2021
R. Verborgh et al. (Eds.): ESWC 2021, LNCS 12731, pp. 598–613, 2021.
https://doi.org/10.1007/978-3-030-77385-4_36

Table 1. Comparison of ParaQA with existing QA datasets over various dimensions. Lack of paraphrased utterances of answers remains a key gap in literature.

Dataset	Large scale (>=5K)	Complex questions	SPARQL	Verbalized answer	Paraphrased answer
ParaQA (This paper)	✓	✓	✓	✓	✓
Free917 [8]	✗	✓	✗	✗	✗
WebQuestions [4]	✓	✗	✗	✗	✗
SimpleQuestions [6]	✓	✗	✓	✗	✗
QALD (1–9)[a]	✗	✓	✓	✗	✗
LC-QuAD 1.0 [38]	✓	✓	✓	✗	✗
LC-QuAD 2.0 [10]	✓	✓	✓	✗	✗
ComplexQuestions [3]	✗	✓	✗	✗	✗
ComQA [1]	✓	✓	✗	✗	✗
GraphQuestions [35]	✓	✓	✓	✗	✗
ComplexWebQuestions [37]	✓	✓	✓	✗	✗
VQuAnDa [20]	✓	✓	✓	✓	✗
CSQA [31]	✓	✓	✗	✗	✗
ConvQuestions [9]	✓	✓	✗	✗	✗

intelligent personal assistants (e.g., Alexa, Siri), the research focus has been shifted to conversational question answering over KGs that involves single-turn/multi-turn dialogues [33]. To support wider research in knowledge graph question answering (KGQA) and conversational question answering over KGs (ConvQA), several publicly available datasets have been released [4,31,38].

Motivation and Contributions. In dialog systems research, we can distinguish between single-turn and multi-turn conversations [7,19]. In single-turn conversations, a user provides all the required information (e.g., slots/values) at once, in one utterance. Conversely, a multi-turn conversation involves anaphora and ellipses to fetch more information from the user as an additional conversation context. The existing ConvQA [9,31] datasets provide multi-turn dialogues for question answering. In a real-world setting, user will not always require multi-turn dialogues. Therefore, single-turn conversation is a common phenomenon in voice assistants[1]. Some public datasets focus on paraphrasing the questions to provide real-world settings, such as LC-QuAD2.0 [10] and ComQA [1]. The existing ConvQA datasets provide only up to one verbalization of the response (c.f. Table 1). In both dataset categories (KGQA or ConvQA), we are not aware of any dataset providing paraphrases of the various answer utterances. For instance, given the question "How many shows does HBO have?", on a KGQA dataset (LC-QuAD [38]), we only find the entity as an answer (e.g. "38"). While on a verbalized KGQA dataset [20], the answer is verbalized as "There are 38 television shows owned by HBO." Given this context, the user can better verify that the system is indeed retrieving the total number of shows owned by HBO. However, the answer can be formulated differently using various paraphrases such as "There are 38 TV shows whose owner is HBO.", "There are 38 television

---

[1] https://docs.microsoft.com/en-us/cortana/skills/mva31-understanding-conversations.

programs owned by that organization" with the same semantic meaning. Hence, paraphrasing the answers can introduce more flexibility and intuitiveness in the conversations. In this paper, we argue that answer paraphrasing improves the machine learning models' performance for single-turn conversations (involving question answering over KG) on standard empirical metrics. Therefore, we introduce ParaQA, a question answering dataset with multiple paraphrase responses for single-turn conversation over KGs.

The ParaQA dataset was built using a semi-automated framework that employs advanced paraphrasing techniques such as back-translation. The dataset contains a minimum of two and a maximum of eight unique paraphrased responses per question. To supplement the dataset, we provide several evaluation settings to measure the effectiveness of having multiple paraphrased answers. The following are key contributions of this work:

- We provide a semi-automated framework for generating multiple paraphrase responses for each question using techniques such as back-translation.
- We present ParaQA - The first single-turn conversational question answering dataset with multiple paraphrased responses. In particular, ParaQA consists of up to eight unique paraphrased responses for each dataset question that can be answered using DBpedia as underlying KG.
- We also provide evaluation baselines that serve to determine our dataset's quality and define a benchmark for future research.

The rest of the paper is structured as follows. In the next section, we describe the related work. We introduce the details of our dataset and the generation workflow in Sect. 3. Section 4 describes the availability of the dataset, followed by the experiments in Sect. 5. The reusability study and potential impact is described in Sect. 6. Finally, Sect. 7 provides conclusions.

2   Related Work

Our work lies at the intersection of KGQA and conversational QA datasets. We describe previous efforts and refer to different dataset construction techniques.

KGQA Datasets. The datasets such as SimpleQuestions [6], WebQuestions [42], and the QALD challenge[2] have been inspirational for the evolution of the field. SimpleQuestions [6] dataset is one of the most commonly used large-scale benchmarks for studying single-relation factoid questions over Freebase [5]. LC-QuAD 1.0 [38] was the first large-scale dataset providing complex questions and their SPARQL queries over DBpedia. The dataset has been created using pre-defined templates and a peer-reviewed process to rectify those templates. Other datasets such as ComQA [1] and LC-QuAD 2.0 [10] are large-scale QA datasets with complex paraphrased questions without verbalized answers. It is important to note that the answers of most KGQA datasets are non-verbalized. VQuAnDa [20] is the only QA dataset with complex questions containing a single verbalized answer for each question.

---

[2] http://qald.aksw.org/.

Conversational QA. There has been extensive research for single-turn and multi-turn conversations for open-domain [7,23,43]. The research community has recently shifted focus to provide multi-turn conversation datasets for question answering over KGs. CSQA [31] is a large-scale dataset consisting of multi-turn conversations over linked QA pairs. The dataset contained 200K dialogues with 1.6M turns and was collected through a manually intensive semi-automated process. The dataset comprises complex questions that require logical, quantitative, and comparative reasoning over a Wikidata KG. ConvQuestions [9] is a crowdsourced benchmark with 11K distinct multi-turn conversations from five different domains ("Books", "Movies", "Soccer", "Music", and "TV Series"). While both datasets cover multi-turn conversations, none of them contains verbalized answers. Hence, there is a clear gap in the literature for the datasets focusing on single-turn conversations involving question answering over KGs. In this paper, our work combines KGQA capabilities with the conversational phenomenon. We focus on single-turn conversations to provide ParaQA with multiple paraphrased answers for more expressive conversations.

Dataset Construction Techniques. While some KGQA datasets are automatically generated [32], most of them are manually created either by (i) using in-house workers [38] or crowd-sourcing [10], (ii) or extract questions from online question answering platforms such as search engines, online forum, etc. [4]. Most (single-turn/multi-turn) conversational QA datasets are generated using semi-automated approaches [9,31]. First, conversations are created through predefined templates. Second, the automatically generated conversations are polished by in-house workers or crowd-sourcing techniques. CSQA [31] dataset contains a series of linked QA pairs forming a coherent conversation. Further, these questions are answerable from a KG using logical, comparative, and quantitative reasoning. For generating the dataset, authors first asked pairs of in-house workers to converse with each other. One annotator in a pair acted as a user whose job was to ask questions, and the other annotator worked as the system whose job was to answer the questions or ask for clarifications if required. The annotators' results were abstracted to templates and used to instantiate more questions involving different relations, subjects, and objects. The same process was repeated for different question types such as co-references and ellipses. ConvQuestions-[9] dataset was created by posing the conversation generation task on Amazon Mechanical Turk (AMT)[3]. Each crowd worker was asked to build a conversation by asking five sequential questions starting from any seed entity of his/her choice. Humans may have an intuitive model when satisfying their real information needs via their search assistants. Crowd workers were also asked to provide paraphrases for each question. Similar to [31], the crowd workers' results were abstracted to templates and used to create more examples. While both conversational QA datasets use a relatively similar construction approach, none of them considers verbalizing the answers and providing paraphrases for them.

---

[3] https://www.mturk.com/.

Table 2. Examples from ParaQA.

Question	What is the television show whose judges is Randy Jackson?
Answer verbalizations	1) American Idol is the television show with judge Randy Jackson
	2) The television show whose judge Randy Jackson is American Idol
	3) The TV show he's a judge on is American Idol
Question	How many shows does HBO have?
Answer verbalizations	1) There are 38 television shows owned by HBO
	2) There are 38 TV shows whose owner is HBO
	3) There are 38 television shows whose owner is that organisation
	4) There are 38 television programs owned by that organization
Question	From which country is Lawrence Okoye's nationality?
Answer verbalizations	1) Great Britain is the nationality of Lawrence Okoye
	2) Great Britain is Lawrence Okoye's citizenship
	3) The nationality of Lawrence Okoye is Great Britain
	4) Lawrence Okoye is a Great British citizen
	5) Lawrence Okoye's nationality is Great Britain
Question	Does Sonny Bill Williams belong in the Canterbury Bankstown Bulldogs club?
Answer verbalizations	1) Yes, Canterbury-Bankstown Bulldogs is the club of Sonny Bill Williams
	2) Yes, the Canterbury-Bankstown Bulldogs is Bill Williams's club
	3) Yes, the Canterbury-Bankstown Bulldogs is his club
	4) Yes, Canterbury-Bankstown Bulldogs is the club of the person
	5) Yes, the club of Sonny Bill Williams is Canterbury-Bankstown Bulldogs
	6) Yes, Bill Williams's club is the Canterbury-Bankstone Bulldogs

Paraphrasing. In the early years, various traditional techniques have been developed to solve the paraphrase generation problem. McKeown [25] makes use of manually defined rules. Quirk et al. [30] train Statistical Machine Translation (SMT) tools on a large number of sentence pairs collected from newspapers. Wubben et al. [41] propose a phrase-based SMT model trained on aligned news headlines. Recent approaches perform neural paraphrase generation, which is often formalized as a sequence-to-sequence (Seq2Seq) learning. Prakash et al. [29] employ a stacked residual LSTM network in the Seq2Seq model to enlarge the model capacity. Hasan et al. [17] incorporate the attention mechanism to generate paraphrases. Work in [12] integrates the transformer model and recurrent neural network to learn long-range dependencies in the input sequence.

3 ParaQA: Question Answering with Paraphrase Responses for Single-Turn Conversation

The inspiration for generating paraphrased answers originates from the need to provide a context of the question to assure that the query was correctly understood. In that way, the user would verify that the received answer correlates with the question. For illustration, in our dataset, the question "What is the commonplace of study for jack McGregor and Philip W. Pillsbury?" is translated to the corresponding SPARQL query, which retrieves the result "Yale University" from the KG. In this case, a full natural language response of the result is "Yale

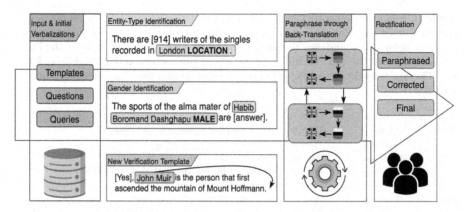

Fig. 1. Overview of dataset generation workflow. Our proposed generation workflow consists of 6 modules in total. The first module is "**Input & Initial Verbalization**", which is responsible for producing the initial verbalized results for each input question. The next three modules ("**Entity-Type Identification though Named Entity Recognition**", "**Gender Identification**", and "**New Verification Template**") are applied simultaneously and provide new verbalized sentences based on the initial ones. Subsequently, the paraphrasing module, named "**Paraphrase through Back-Translation**", applies back translation to generated answers. Finally, in the last step ("**Rectify Verbalization**"), we rectify all the paraphrased results through a peer-review process.

University is the study place of Jack McGregor and Philip W. Pillsbury.". As can be seen, this form of answer provides us the query result and details about the query's intention. At the same time, we also provide alternative paraphrased responses such as, "Yale University is the place where both Jack McGregor and Philip W. Pillsbury studied.", "Yale is where both of them studied.". All those answers clarify to the user that the question answering system completely understood the question context and the answer is correct. They can also verify that the system retrieves a place where "Jack McGregor" and "Philip W. Pillsbury" went for their studies. Table 2 illustrates examples from our dataset.

3.1 Generation Workflow

For generating ParaQA, we decided not to reinvent the wheel to create new questions. Hence, we inherit questions from LC-QuAD [38] and single answer verbalization of these question provided by VQuAnDa [20]. We followed a semi-automated approach to generate the dataset. The overall architecture of the approach is depicted in Fig. 1.

Table 3. Examples generated from each automatic step/module of our proposed generation framework. The presented responses are the outputs from the corresponding modules before they undergo the final peer-review step. The bold text of the initial answer indicates the part of the sentence where the corresponding module is focusing. The underlined text on the generated results reveals the changes made from the module.

Entity-type	Question	Count the key people of the Clinton Foundation?
	Initial	There are 8 key people in the **Clinton Foundation**
	Generated	There are 8 key people in the organisation
Gender	Question	Which planet was first discovered by Johann Gottfried Galle?
	Verbalized answer	The planet **discovered by Johann Gottfried Galle** is Neptune
	Generated	The planet he discovered is Neptune
Verification	Question	Does the River Shannon originate from Dowra?
	Initial	Yes, **Dowra** is the source mountain of **River Shannon**
	Generated	Yes, River Shannon starts from Dowra
Paraphrase	Question	Who first ascended a mountain of Cathedral Peak (California)?
	Initial	**The person that first ascended** Cathedral Peak (California) is John Muir
	Generated (en-de)	The first person to climb Cathedral Peak (California) is John Muir
	Generated (en-ru)	The person who first climbed Mount Katty Peak (California) is John Muir

Input & Initial Verbalization

Our framework requires at least one available verbalized answer per question to build upon it and extend it into multiple diverse paraphrased responses. Therefore, the generation workflow from [20] is adopted as a first step and used to generate the initial responses. This step's inputs are the questions, the SPARQL queries, and the hand-crafted natural language answer templates.

Entity-Type Identification Though Named Entity Recognition

Named Entity Recognition (NER) step recognizes and classifies named entities into predefined categories, for instance, persons, organizations, locations, etc. Our aim here is to identify the entity category (or entity-type) and span and replace it with a predefined value in the response. This stage allows us to accomplish more general verbalization since question entities are swapped with their type categories. The whole process is performed in 2 steps: 1) A pre-trained NER [18] model is employed to locate entities in the initial generated responses. Discovered entities are replaced with their type category such as "ORG, PRODUCT, LOC, PERSON, GPE". 2) A predefined dictionary is used to substitute the type categories with different words such as "the organization, the person, the country". Table 3 presents a generated example from the entity-type identification step.

Gender Identification

In this step, we create new responses by replacing the question entities with their corresponding pronouns, e.g. "he, she, him, her". This is done by identifying the entity's gender. In particular, we query the KG with a predefined SPARQL query that extracts the gender of the given entity. Based on the position of the entity in the answer, we replace it with the appropriate pronoun. Table 3 illustrates a generated example from the gender identification step. In peer-review process, we verify the dataset to avoid any bias in the genders considering we extract gender information from DBpedia and sometime KG data quality is not perfect.

New Verification Template

Considering that, on verification questions, all triple data is given (head, relation, tail). We introduce a verbalization template that interchanges the head and tail triple information and generate more diverse responses. Table 3 provides a generated example from this process.

Paraphrase Through Back-Translation

After having assembled sufficient answers for each question, we employ a paraphrasing strategy through a back-translation approach. In general, back-translation is when a translator (or team of translators) interprets or re-translate a document that was previously translated into another language back to the original language. In our case, the two translators are independent models, and the second model has no knowledge or contact with the original text.

In particular, inspired by [11,14], our initial responses alongside the new proposed answer templates are paraphrased using transformer-based models [39] as translators. The model is evaluated successfully on the WMT'18[4] dataset that includes translations between different languages. In our case, we perform back-translation with two different sets of languages: 1) Two transformer models are used to translate the responses between English and German language (en→de→en). 2) Another two models are used to translate between English and Russian language (en→ru→en). Here it is worth mentioning that we also forwarded output responses from one translation stack into the other (e.g., en→de→en→ru→en). In this way, we generate as many as possible different paraphrased responses. Please note that the selection of languages for back translation was done considering our inherited underlying model's accuracy in machine translation tasks on WMT'18. Table 3 illustrates some examples from our back-translation approach.

Rectify Verbalization

After collecting multiple paraphrased versions of the initial responses, the last step is to rectify and rephrase them to sound more natural and fluent. The rectification step of our framework is done through a peer-review process to ensure the answers' grammatical correctness. Finally, by the end of this step, we will have at least two and at most eight diverse paraphrased responses per question, including the initial answer.

---

[4] http://www.statmt.org/wmt18/translation-task.html.

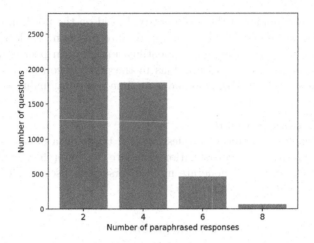

Fig. 2. Total paraphrased responses per question.

3.2 Dataset Statistics

We provide dataset insights regarding its total paraphrased results for each question and the percentage of generated answers from each module on our framework. Figure 2 illustrates the distribution of 5000 questions of ParaQA based on a total number of paraphrased responses per question. As seen from the figure, more than 2500 questions contain at most two paraphrased results. A bit less than 2000 questions include at most four answers, while around 500 have no less than six paraphrased answers. Finally, less than 100 examples contain at most eight paraphrased results. Figure 3 depicts the percentage of generated answers for each step from our generation workflow. The first step (input and initial verbalization) provides approximately 30% of our total results, while the next three steps (entity type identification, gender identification, and new verification templates) produce roughly 20% of responses. Finally, the back-translation module generates no less than 50% of the complete paraphrased answers in ParaQA.

4 Availability and Sustainability

Availability. The dataset is available at a GitHub repository[5] under the Attribution 4.0 International (CC BY 4.0)[6] license. As a permanent URL, we also provide our dataset through figshare at https://figshare.com/projects/ParaQA/94010. The generation framework is also available at a GitHub repository[7] under the MIT License[8]. Please note, the dataset and the experiments reported in the paper are in two different repositories due to the free distributed license agreement.

---

[5] https://github.com/barshana-banerjee/ParaQA.

[6] https://creativecommons.org/licenses/by/4.0/.

[7] https://github.com/barshana-banerjee/ParaQA_Experiments.

[8] https://opensource.org/licenses/MIT.

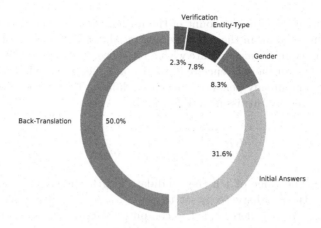

Fig. 3. Percentage of generated results from each step.

Sustainability. The maintenance is ensured through the CLEOPATRA[9] project till 2022. After that, the maintenance of the resource will be handled by the question and answering team of the Smart Data Analytics (SDA)[10] research group at the University of Bonn and at Fraunhofer IAIS[11].

5   Experiments

To assure the quality of the dataset and the advantage of having multiple paraphrased responses, we perform experiments and provide baseline models, which researchers can use as a reference point for future research.

5.1   Experimental Setup

Baseline Models

For the baselines, we employ three sequence to sequence models. Sequence to sequence is a family of machine learning approaches used for language processing, and used often for natural language generation tasks. The first model consists of an RNN [24] based architecture, the second uses a convolutional network [15], while the third employs a transformer network [39].

Evaluation Metrics

BLEU (Bilingual Evaluation Understudy). BLEU score introduced by [28] is so far the most popularly used machine translation metric to evaluate the quality of the model generated text compared to human translation. It aims to count the n-gram overlaps in the reference by taking the maximum count of

---

[9] http://cleopatra-project.eu/.
[10] https://sda.tech/.
[11] https://www.iais.fraunhofer.de/.

each n-gram, and it clips the count of the n-grams in the candidate translation to the maximum count in the reference. Essentially, BLEU is a modified version of precision to compare a candidate with a reference. However, candidates with a shorter length than the reference tend to give a higher score, while the modified n-gram precision already penalizes longer candidates. Brevity penalty (BP) was introduced to rectify this issue and defined as:

$$BP = \begin{cases} 1, & c \geq r \\ exp(1 - \frac{r}{c}), & c < r \end{cases} \qquad (1)$$

Where it gets the value of 1 if the candidate length c is larger or equal to the reference length r. Otherwise, is set to $exp(1 - r/c)$. Finally, a set of positive weights $\{w_1, ..., w_N\}$ is determined to compute the geometric mean of the modified n-gram precision. The BLEU score is calculated by:

$$BLEU = BP \cdot exp(\sum_{n=1}^{N} w_n log(P_n)), \qquad (2)$$

where N is the number of different n-grams. In our experiments, we employ $N = 4$ (which is a default value) and uniform weights $w_n = 1/N$.

METEOR (Metric for Evaluation of Translation with Explicit ORdering). METEOR score, introduced by [2], is a metric for the evaluation of machine-translation output. METEOR is based on the harmonic mean of unigram precision and recall, with recall weighted higher than precision.

BLEU score suffers from the issue that the BP value uses lengths that are averaged over the entire corpus level, leading to having individual sentences a hit. In contrast, METEOR modifies the precision at sentence or segment level, replacing them with a weighted F-score based on mapping uni-grams and a penalty function that solves the existing problem. Similar to BLEU, METEOR score can be in the range of 0.0 and 1.0, with 1.0 being the best score. Formally we define it as:

$$F_{mean} = \frac{P \cdot R}{\alpha \cdot P + (1 - \alpha) \cdot R},$$

$$Pen = \gamma \cdot \left(\frac{ch}{m}\right)^{\beta}, \qquad (3)$$

$$METEOR = (1 - Pen) \cdot F_{mean}$$

where P and R are the uni-gram precision and recall respectively, and are used to compute the parametrized harmonic mean F_{mean}. Pen is the penalty value and is calculated using the counts of chunks ch and the matches m. α, β and γ are free parameters used to calculate the final score. For our experiments we employ the common values of $\alpha = 0.9$, $\beta = 3.0$ and $\gamma = 0.5$.

Table 4. BLEU score experiment results.

Model	Input	One response	Two responses	Multiple paraphrased
RNN [24]	Question	15.43	18.8	22.4
	SPARQL	20.1	21.33	26.3
Transformer [39]	Question	18.3	21.2	23.6
	SPARQL	23.1	24.7	28.0
Convolutional [15]	Question	21.3	25.1	**25.9**
	SPARQL	26.02	28.4	**31.8**

Training and Configurations

The experiments are performed to test how easy it is for a standard sequence to sequence model to generate the verbalized response using as input only the question or the SPARQL query. Inspired by [20], during our experiments, we prefer to hide the query answer from the responses by replacing it with a general answer token. In this way, we simplify the model task to predict only the query answer's position in the final verbalized response.

Furthermore, we perform experiments with three different dataset settings. We intend to illustrate the advantage of having multiple paraphrased responses compared to one or even two. Therefore, we run individual experiments by using one response, two responses, and finally, multiple paraphrased responses per question. To conduct the experiments for the last two settings, we forward the responses associated with their question into our model. We calculate the scores for each generated response by comparing them with all the existing references. For the sake of simplicity, and as done by [16], the final score is the maximum value achieved for each generated response.

For fair comparison across the models, we employ similar hyperparameters for all. We utilize an embeddings dimension of 512, and all models consist of 2 layers. We apply dropout with probability 0.1. We use a batch size of 128, and we train for 50 epochs. Across all experiments, we use Adam optimizer and cross-entropy as a loss function. To facilitate reproducibility and reuse, our baseline implementations and results are publicly available[12].

5.2 Results

Table 4 and Table 5 illustrate the experiment results for BLEU and METEOR scores, respectively. For both metrics, the convolutional model performs the best. It outperforms the RNN and transformer models in different inputs and responses. Here, it is more interesting to notice that all models perform better with multiple paraphrased answers than one or two responses. At the same time, the scores with two answers are better than those with a single response. Hence, we can assume that the more paraphrased responses we have, the better the

---

[12] https://github.com/barshana-banerjee/ParaQA_Experiments.

Table 5. METEOR score experiment results.

Model	Input	One response	Two responses	Multiple paraphrased
RNN [24]	Question	53.1	56.2	58.4
	SPARQL	57.0	59.3	61.8
Transformer [39]	Question	56.8	58.8	59.6
	SPARQL	60.1	63.0	63.7
Convolutional [15]	Question	57.5	58.4	**60.8**
	SPARQL	64.3	65.1	**65.8**

model performance. Concerning the experiment inputs (Question, SPARQL), as indicated by both metrics, we obtain improved results with SPARQL on all models and responses. As expected, this is due to the constant input pattern templates that the SPARQL queries have. While with questions, we end up having a different reworded version for the same template. We expect the research community to use these models as baselines to develop more advanced approaches targeting either single-turn conversations for QA or answer verbalization.

6 Reusability and Impact

ParaQA dataset can fit in different research areas. Undoubtedly, the most suitable one is in the single-turn conversational question answering over KGs for supporting a more expressive QA experience. The dataset offers the opportunity to build end-to-end machine learning frameworks to handle both tasks of query construction and natural language response generation. Simultaneously, the dataset remains useful for any QA sub-task, such as entity/relation recognition, linking, and disambiguation.

Besides the QA research area, the dataset is also suitable for Natural Language Generation (NLG) tasks. As we accomplish in our experiments, using as input the question or the query, the NLG task will generate the best possible response. We also find ParaQA suitable for the NLP area of paraphrasing. Since we provide more than one paraphrased example for each answer, researchers can experiment with the dataset for building paraphrasing systems for short texts. Furthermore, our dataset can also be used for the research involving SPARQL verbalization, which has been a long-studied topic in the Semantic Web community [13, 26, 27].

7 Conclusion and Future Work

We introduce ParaQA – the first single-turn conversational question answering dataset with multiple paraphrased responses. Alongside the dataset, we provide a semi-automated framework for generating various paraphrase responses using back-translation techniques. Finally, we also share a set of evaluation baselines and illustrate the advantage of multiple paraphrased answers through commonly used metrics such as BLEU and METEOR. The dataset offers a worthwhile contribution to the community, providing the foundation for numerous research lines in the single-turn conversational QA domain and others. As part of future work, we look to work on improving and expanding ParaQA. For instance, supporting multi-turn conversations together with paraphrased questions is also in our future work scope.

Acknowledgments. The project leading to this publication has received funding from the European Union's Horizon 2020 research and innovation program under the Marie Skłodowska-Curie grant agreement No. 812997 (Cleopatra).

References

1. Abujabal, A., Roy, R.S., Yahya, M., Weikum, G.: Comqa: a community-sourced dataset for complex factoid question answering with paraphrase clusters. In: NAACL (Long and Short Papers), pp. 307–317 (2019)
2. Banerjee, S., Lavie, A.: METEOR: An automatic metric for MT evaluation with improved correlation with human judgments. In: Proceedings of the ACL Workshop on Intrinsic and Extrinsic Evaluation Measures for Machine Translation and/or Summarization, pp. 65–72. Association for Computational Linguistics (2005)
3. Bao, J., Duan, N., Yan, Z., Zhou, M., Zhao, T.: Constraint-based question answering with knowledge graph. In: COLING, pp. 2503–2514 (2016)
4. Berant, J., Chou, A., Frostig, R., Liang, P.: Semantic parsing on freebase from question-answer pairs. In: EMNLP, pp. 1533–1544 (2013)
5. Bollacker, K., Evans, C., Paritosh, P., Sturge, T., Taylor, J.: Freebase: A collaboratively created graph database for structuring human knowledge. In: SIGMOD, pp. 1247–1250. ACM (2008)
6. Bordes, A., Usunier, N., Chopra, S., Weston, J.: Large-scale simple question answering with memory networks. arXiv preprint arXiv:1506.02075 (2015)
7. Boussaha, B.E.A., Hernandez, N., Jacquin, C., Morin, E.: Deep retrieval-based dialogue systems: A short review. arXiv preprint arXiv:1907.12878 (2019)
8. Cai, Q., Yates, A.: Large-scale semantic parsing via schema matching and lexicon extension. In: ACL (2013)
9. Christmann, P., Saha Roy, R., Abujabal, A., Singh, J., Weikum, G.: Look before you hop: Conversational question answering over knowledge graphs using judicious context expansion. In: CIKM, pp. 729–738 (2019)
10. Dubey, M., Banerjee, D., Abdelkawi, A., Lehmann, J.: LC-QuAD 2.0: a large dataset for complex question answering over Wikidata and DBpedia. In: Ghidini, C., et al. (eds.) ISWC 2019, Part II. LNCS, vol. 11779, pp. 69–78. Springer, Cham (2019). https://doi.org/10.1007/978-3-030-30796-7_5
11. Edunov, S., Ott, M., Auli, M., Grangier, D.: Understanding back-translation at scale. In: ACL (2018)
12. Egonmwan, E., Chali, Y.: Transformer and seq2seq model for paraphrase generation. In: Proceedings of the 3rd Workshop on Neural Generation and Translation, pp. 249–255. ACL, Hong Kong (Nov 2019)
13. Ell, B., Harth, A., Simperl, E.: SPARQL query verbalization for explaining semantic search engine queries. In: Presutti, V., d'Amato, C., Gandon, F., d'Aquin, M., Staab, S., Tordai, A. (eds.) ESWC 2014. LNCS, vol. 8465, pp. 426–441. Springer, Cham (2014). https://doi.org/10.1007/978-3-319-07443-6_29

14. Federmann, C., Elachqar, O., Quirk, C.: Multilingual whispers: generating para-phrases with translation. In: Proceedings of the 5th Workshop on Noisy User-Generated Text (W-NUT 2019), pp. 17–26. ACL (2019)

15. Gehring, J., Auli, M., Grangier, D., Yarats, D., Dauphin, Y.N.: Convolutional Sequence to Sequence Learning. arXiv e-prints arXiv:1705.03122 (May 2017)

16. Gupta, P., Mehri, S., Zhao, T., Pavel, A., Eskenazi, M., Bigham, J.: Investigat-ing evaluation of open-domain dialogue systems with human generated multiple references. In: SIGdial, pp. 379–391. ACL (2019)

17. Hasan, S.A., et al.: Neural clinical paraphrase generation with attention. In: Clin-ical Natural Language Processing Workshop (ClinicalNLP), pp. 42–53 (Dec 2016)

18. Honnibal, M., Montani, I.: spaCy 2: Natural language understanding with Bloom embeddings, convolutional neural networks and incremental parsing (2017)

19. Huang, M., Zhu, X., Gao, J.: Challenges in building intelligent open-domain dialog systems. ACM Trans. Inf. Syst. (TOIS) **38**(3), 1–32 (2020)

20. Kacupaj, E., Zafar, H., Lehmann, J., Maleshkova, M.: VQuAnDa: verbalization question answering dataset. In: Harth, A., et al. (eds.) ESWC 2020. LNCS, vol. 12123, pp. 531–547. Springer, Cham (2020). https://doi.org/10.1007/978-3-030-49461-2_31

21. Lehmann, J., et al.: Dbpedia - a large-scale, multilingual knowledge base extracted from Wikipedia. Semant. Web **6**, 167–195 (2015)

22. Liu, K., Feng, Y.: Deep learning in question answering. In: Deng, L., Liu, Y. (eds.) Deep Learning in Natural Language Processing, pp. 185–217. Springer, Singapore (2018). https://doi.org/10.1007/978-981-10-5209-5_7

23. Lowe, R., Pow, N., Serban, I., Pineau, J.: The Ubuntu dialogue corpus: a large dataset for research in unstructured multi-turn dialogue systems. In: SigDial, pp. 285–294. Association for Computational Linguistics (2015)

24. Luong, M.T., Pham, H., Manning, C.D.: Effective Approaches to Attention-based Neural Machine Translation. arXiv e-prints arXiv:1508.04025 (Aug 2015)

25. McKeown, K.R.: Paraphrasing questions using given and new information. Am. J. Comput. Linguist. **9**(1), 1–10 (1983)

26. Ngonga Ngomo, A.C., Bühmann, L., Unger, C., Lehmann, J., Gerber, D.: Sorry, i don't speak SPARQL: translating SPARQL queries into natural language. In: Proceedings of the 22nd International Conference on World Wide Web, pp. 977–988 (2013)

27. Ngonga Ngomo, A.C., Bühmann, L., Unger, C., Lehmann, J., Gerber, D.: SPARQL2NL: verbalizing SPARQL queries. In: Proceedings of the 22nd Inter-national Conference on World Wide Web, pp. 329–332. ACM (2013)

28. Papineni, K., Roukos, S., Ward, T., Zhu, W.J.: Bleu: a method for automatic evaluation of machine translation. In: Proceedings of the 40th Annual Meeting of the Association for Computational Linguistics (2002)

29. Prakash, A., et al.: Neural paraphrase generation with stacked residual LSTM networks. In: COLING (Dec 2016)

30. Quirk, C., Brockett, C., Dolan, W.: Monolingual machine translation for para-phrase generation. In: Proceedings of the 2004 Conference on Empirical Methods in Natural Language Processing, pp. 142–149. Association for Computational Lin-guistics (Jul 2004)

31. Saha, A., Pahuja, V., Khapra, M.M., Sankaranarayanan, K., Chandar, S.: Complex sequential question answering: Towards learning to converse over linked question answer pairs with a knowledge graph. In: Thirty-Second AAAI Conference (2018)

32. Serban, I.V., et al.: Generating factoid questions with recurrent neural networks: the 30 m factoid question-answer corpus. arXiv preprint arXiv:1603.06807 (2016)

33. Shen, T., et al.: Multi-task learning for conversational question answering over a large-scale knowledge base. In: Proceedings of the 2019 Conference on Empirical Methods in Natural Language Processing and the 9th International Joint Conference on Natural Language Processing (EMNLP-IJCNLP), pp. 2442–2451. Association for Computational Linguistics (2019)

34. Singh, K., et al.: Why reinvent the wheel: let's build question answering systems together. In: Proceedings of the 2018 World Wide Web Conference, pp. 1247–1256 (2018)

35. Su, Y., et al.: On generating characteristic-rich question sets for QA evaluation. In: Proceedings of the 2016 Conference on Empirical Methods in Natural Language Processing (2016)

36. Suchanek, F.M., Kasneci, G., Weikum, G.: Yago: a core of semantic knowledge. In: Proceedings of the 16th International Conference on World Wide Web, pp. 697–706 (2007)

37. Talmor, A., Berant, J.: The web as a knowledge-base for answering complex questions. arXiv preprint arXiv:1803.06643 (2018)

38. Trivedi, P., Maheshwari, G., Dubey, M., Lehmann, J.: LC-QuAD: a corpus for complex question answering over knowledge graphs. In: d'Amato, C., et al. (eds.) ISWC 2017, Part II. LNCS, vol. 10588, pp. 210–218. Springer, Cham (2017). https://doi.org/10.1007/978-3-319-68204-4_22

39. Vaswani, A., et al.: Attention is all you need. In: Advances in Neural Information Processing Systems 30: Annual Conference on Neural Information Processing Systems, pp. 5998–6008 (2017)

40. Vrandečić, D., Krötzsch, M.: Wikidata: a free collaborative knowledgebase. Commun. ACM **57**(10), 78–85 (2014)

41. Wubben, S., van den Bosch, A., Krahmer, E.: Paraphrase generation as monolingual translation: data and evaluation. In: Proceedings of the 6th International Natural Language Generation Conference (2010)

42. Yih, W.T., Richardson, M., Meek, C., Chang, M.W., Suh, J.: The value of semantic parse labeling for knowledge base question answering. In: Proceedings of the 54th Annual Meeting of the Association for Computational Linguistics (2016)

43. Zamanirad, S., Benatallah, B., Rodriguez, C., Yaghoubzadehfard, M., Bouguelia, S., Brabra, H.: State machine based human-bot conversation model and services. In: Dustdar, S., Yu, E., Salinesi, C., Rieu, D., Pant, V. (eds.) CAiSE 2020. LNCS, vol. 12127, pp. 199–214. Springer, Cham (2020). https://doi.org/10.1007/978-3-030-49435-3_13

kgbench: A Collection of Knowledge Graph Datasets for Evaluating Relational and Multimodal Machine Learning

Peter Bloem[✉][iD], Xander Wilcke[iD], Lucas van Berkel[iD], and Victor de Boer[iD]

Informatics Institute, Vrije Universiteit Amsterdam, Amsterdam, The Netherlands
{p.bloem,w.x.wilcke,v.de.boer}@vu.nl, l.12.van.berkel@student.vu.nl

Abstract. Graph neural networks and other machine learning models offer a promising direction for machine learning on relational and multimodal data. Until now, however, progress in this area is difficult to gauge. This is primarily due to a limited number of datasets with (a) a high enough number of labeled nodes in the test set for precise measurement of performance, and (b) a rich enough variety of multimodal information to learn from. We introduce a set of new benchmark tasks for node classification on RDF-encoded knowledge graphs. We focus primarily on node classification, since this setting cannot be solved purely by node embedding models. For each dataset, we provide test and validation sets of at least 1 000 instances, with some over 10 000. Each task can be performed in a purely relational manner, or with multimodal information. All datasets are packaged in a CSV format that is easily consumable in any machine learning environment, together with the original source data in RDF and pre-processing code for full provenance. We provide code for loading the data into numpy and pytorch. We compute performance for several baseline models.

Keywords: Knowledge graphs · Machine learning · Message passing models · Multimodal learning

1 Introduction

The combination of knowledge graphs and machine learning is a promising direction of research. In particular, the class of machine learning models known as *message passing models* offer an interesting set of abilities [1,35]. These models operate by propagating information along the structure of the graph and are trained end-to-end, meaning all information in the graph can potentially be used if it benefits the task. Even the contents of the literals may be used by attaching encoder networks to learn how literals should be read, leading to an end-to-end model for multimodal learning on knowledge graphs. The message

---

P. Bloem, X. Wilcke and L. van Berkel—Contributed equally to this paper.

R. Verborgh et al. (Eds.): ESWC 2021, LNCS 12731, pp. 614–630, 2021.
https://doi.org/10.1007/978-3-030-77385-4_37

passing framework is also a promising direction for interpretable machine learning, as the computation of the model can be directly related to the relational structure of the data [9].

Unfortunately, the progress of message passing models and related machine learning approaches has been difficult to gauge due to the lack of high quality datasets. Machine learning on knowledge graphs is commonly evaluated with two abstract tasks: *link prediction* and *node labeling*. In the latter, the model is given the whole graph during training, together with labels for a subset of its nodes. The task is to label a set of withheld nodes with a target label: a class for node classification or a number for node regression.

While link prediction is probably more popular in recent literature, node labeling is more promising for developing message passing models. In link prediction, it is not clear whether message passing models offer an advantage over embedding models on currently popular benchmarks, without a considerable increase in computational requirements. In node labeling, however, the task cannot be solved from node embeddings alone. In some way, the deeper structure of the graph *needs* to be taken into account, making it a better testing ground for message-passing algorithms such as R-GCNs [28] and R-GATs [6].

In this work, we specifically focus on knowledge graphs that are built on top of the *Resource Description Framework* (RDF). The most common datasets used in node classification on such knowledge graphs are the AIFB, MUTAG, BGS and AM datasets, which were first collected and published for this purpose in [22]. Their details are given in Table 1. These datasets are well suited to message passing methods since they are relatively small, allowing a message passing model to be trained full-batch so that we can gauge the performance of the model independent of the influence of minibatching schemes. However, this small size of the graphs also means a small number of labeled instances, and, in particular, a small *test set*, sometimes with less than 50 instances.

While limited training data is often a cause for concern in machine learning, limited test data is usually the greater evil. With limited training data, we may have a model that fails to perform well, but with limited test data we cannot even tell how well our model is performing. In statistical terms: a performance metric like accuracy is an estimate of a true value, the expected accuracy under the data distribution, based on a sample from that distribution; the test set. The larger that sample, the more accurate our estimate, and the smaller our

Table 1. The currently most commonly used benchmark datasets for node classification.

Dataset	AIFB	MUTAG	BGS*	AM*
Entities	8 285	23 644	87 688	246 728
Relations	45	23	70	122
Edges	29 043	74 227	230 698	875 946
Labeled	176	340	146	1 000
Classes	4	2	2	11

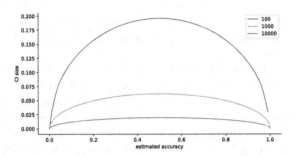

Fig. 1. The size of a 95% confidence interval around an estimate of accuracy for a two-class problem, with test sets of 100, 1 000 and 10 000 instances. Note that 10 000 instances are required before we can tell apart all estimates that differ by 0.01.

uncertainty about that estimate. Figure 1 shows the size of the 95% confidence intervals for different test set sizes on a balanced binary classification problem. We see that only at 10 000 instances do we have sufficient certainty to say that a model with a measured accuracy of 0.94 is most likely better than one with a measured accuracy of 0.93. The test set sizes in Table 1 do not allow for anything but the most rudimentary discrimination.

Additionally, while these datasets provide some multimodal data in the form of literals, these literals are usually not annotated with datatypes, whereas their modalities remain restricted to simple strings containing natural language, or structured information like numerical values and dates. Richer multimodal information like images, audio, or even video would present a more exciting challenge for the possibility of integrating such data in a single end-to-end machine learning model.

To overcome these problems, we introduce `kgbench`: a collection of evaluation datasets for node labeling on knowledge graphs. Each dataset comes with a test set of between 2 000 and 20 000 labeled nodes, allowing for precise estimates of performance.

Each dataset can be used in two different ways. In the **relational** setting, each node is treated as an atomic object, with literals considered equal if their lexical content is equal. This mode can be used to evaluate relational machine learning models, as in [6,23,28]. In the **multimodal** setting, the *content* of literal nodes is taken into account as well, as described in [34,35]. In addition, each dataset can also be used to evaluate link prediction models with by ignoring the node labels (see Sect. 2.3 for details).

The datasets are offered as RDF, with each dataset packaged both in N-Triples and in HDT [10] format. Additionally, since loading RDF into machine learning environments can be non-trivial, we offer pre-processed versions of each dataset, which contain integer indices for all nodes and relations in the graph. These are stored as a set of CSV files, to ensure that they can be directly read by a large number of machine learning libraries. We also provide explicit dataloading code for Numpy and Pytorch, as well as scripts to converts any RDF-encoded knowledge graph to this format.

All data and code is hosted on Github.[1] To ensure long term availability and to provide a permanent identifier, snapshots are also hosted on Zenodo.[2] Each dataset is licensed under the most permissive conditions allowed by the licenses on the source datasets.

1.1 Related Work

Similar efforts to ours include: CoDEx [25], a link prediction benchmark including multilingual literals, and RichPedia [32], a large-scale multimodal knowledge graph with no specific machine learning task attached. Other link prediction research has included new benchmark data [15,30]. Our datasets are, to the best of our knowledge, the first node labelling benchmarks that focus on large test set size and multimodal learning. In [22], node labeling tasks on large knowledge graphs are included, but the number of total instances in the dataset never exceeds 2 000, and canonical snapshots of the knowledge graphs are not provided.

The field of knowledge graph modeling by machine learning methods can be divided into two main camps: pure embedding methods, which learn node embeddings directly, and message passing approaches, which learn from the graph structure more explicitly. For pure embedding methods, [24] serves as a good overview of the state of the art. Message passing methods are popular [1], but in the specific domain of knowledge graphs there has been less progress, with R-GCNs [28] and R-GATs [6] as the main approaches. Other approaches include kernel methods [7] and feature-extraction approaches [23].

2 Method

In this section we detail the main design choices made in constructing the tasks and datasets in kgbench. Our data model in all cases follows RDF. That is, a knowledge graph is defined as a tuple $G = (V, R, E)$, with a finite set of nodes V, a finite set of relations R and a finite set of edges (also known as *triples*) $E \subseteq V \times R \times V$. The nodes in V can be atomic entities,[3] or *literals*, defined by a string which is optionally tagged with a datatype annotation (an IRI expressing the type of data) or a language tag.

2.1 Desiderata

A good machine learning benchmark must satisfy a large number of constraints. We have focused primarily on the following.

Large test sets. A large test set is essential for accurate performance estimates. This is our primary concern.

---

[1] https://github.com/pbloem/kgbench.

[2] Details, including DOIs, under the following references amplus [3], dmgfull and dmg777k [36], dblp [4], mdgenre and mdgender [2].

[3] Entities may be *resources*, identified by an IRI, or *blank nodes*.

Manageable graph size. A small benchmark dataset allows for quick evaluation of hypotheses and quick iteration of model designs, and keeps machine
learning research accessible.

Small training sets. Keeping the number of training instances relatively low
has several benefits: it leaves more instances for the validation and test sets,
and it makes the task more difficult. If the instances are more sparsely labeled,
models are forced to use the graph structure to generalize. It is common practice, once hyperparameter tuning is finished, to combine the training and validation sets into a larger training set for the final run. Normally this conveys
only a very small extra advantage. In our case, adding the validation data
often has a very large effect on how easy the task becomes, and which structure can be used to solve. **For this reason, in our tasks, practitioners
should only ever train on the training data, no matter what set is
being evaluated on.**

Multimodal literals. Where possible we offer literals of multiple modalities.
We annotate existing strings with datatypes and language tags, and add
images and spatial geometries. These are placed into the graph as literals
rather than as hyperlinks, making the dataset self-contained.

2.2 Data Splitting and Layout

Each dataset provides a canonical training/validation/test split. We also split off
a meta-test set if the data allows. This is an additional set of withheld data. It
serves as an additional test set for review studies over multiple already-published
models. This provides the possibility to test for overfitting on the test set if
the dataset becomes popular. **Any practitioner introducing a single new
model or approach, should ignore the meta-test set.**[4]

Each dataset is provided as an RDF graph, with the target labels kept in
separate files. We emphatically choose *not* to include the target labels in the
dataset, as this would then require practitioners to manually remove them prior
to training, which creates a considerable risk of data leakage.

Preprocessing. The most common preprocessing step for relational machine
learning is to map all relations and nodes to integer indices. We have preprocessed all datasets in this manner and provided them as a set of CSV files (in
addition to the original RDF). While a collection of CSV files may not be in
keeping with the spirit of the Semantic Web, this format greatly facilitates reading the data into any data science or machine learning software, without the
need to parse RDF or load the data into a triple store.

This format also allows practitoners to choose between the relational and
multimodal setting in a simple manner. If only the integer indices are read,
then the data is viewed purely from a relational setting. The mappings from the

---

[4] It is common practice to not publish the meta-test set to ensure that it is not used
by practitioners until it is necessary. In our case this makes little sense, since the
meta-test set could easily be derived from the available raw data manually.

```
 1  @prefix :        <http://kgbench.info/dt#> .
 2  @prefix rdfs: <http://www.w3.org/2000/01/rdf-schema#> .
 3  @prefix xsd:  <http://www.w3.org/2001/XMLSchema#> .
 4
 5  :base64Image a rdfs:Datatype ;
 6      rdfs:subClassOf xsd:base64Binary ;
 7      rdfs:label "Base64-encoded image"@en ;
 8      rdfs:comment "An image encoded as a base64 string"@en .
 9
10  :base64Video a rdfs:Datatype ;
11      rdfs:subClassOf xsd:base64Binary ;
12      rdfs:label "Base64-encoded video"@en ;
13      rdfs:comment "A video encoded as a base64 string"@en .
14
15  :base64Audio a rdfs:Datatype ;
16      rdfs:subClassOf xsd:base64Binary ;
17      rdfs:label "Base64-encoded audio"@en ;
18      rdfs:comment "An audio sequence encoded as a base64 string"@en .
```

Listing 1.1. A small ontology (kgbench.info/dt.ttl) for base64-encoded image, audio, and video.

integer indices to the string representations of the nodes provide the multimodal layer on top of the relational setting.

2.3   Link Prediction

Our focus is node labeling, but since link prediction is an unsupervised task, each of our datasets can also be used in link prediction, both for purely relational settings and for multimodal settings. In such cases, we suggest that the following guidelines should be followed:

- The triples should be shuffled before splitting. The validation, test, and meta-test set should each contain 20 000 triples, with the remainder used for training. We include such a split for every dataset.
- In contrast to the node labeling setting, we do not enforce limited training data. The final training may be performed on the combined training and validation sets, and tested on the test set.
- Practitioners should state that the data is being *adapted* for link prediction, and whether the dataset is being used in relational or in multimodal setting.

2.4   Expressing Binary Large Objects

No convention currently exists for encoding images, videos, or audio in literals. A convention in the realm of relational databases is to store complex datatypes as Binary Large OBjects (BLOBs). Here, we chose to adopt this convention by encoding binary data in base64 encoded string literals. The conversion to and from binary data is well supported by many popular programming languages.

To express that a certain string literal encodes a complex type it should be annotated as such using a suitable datatype. The straightforward choice for this datatype would be xsd:base64Binary. However, this does little to convey the

Table 2. Statistics for all datasets. We consider a dataset "GPU friendly" if the R-GCN baseline can be trained on it with under 12 GB of memory and "CPU-friendly" if this can be done with under 64 GB. mdgender is not meant for evaluation (see Sect. 5).

Dataset		amplus	dmgfull	dmg777k	dblp	mdgenre	mdgender*
Triples		2 521 046	1 850 451	777 124	21 985 048	1 252 247	1 203 789
Relations		33	62	60	68	154	154
Nodes		1 153 679	842 550	341 270	4 470 778	349 344	349 347
	Entities	1 026 162	262 494	148 127	4 231 513	191 135	191 138
	Literals	127 517	580 056	192 143	239 265	158 209	158 209
Density		$2 \cdot 10^{-6}$	$3 \cdot 10^{-6}$	$7 \cdot 10^{-6}$	$1 \cdot 10^{-6}$	$1 \cdot 10^{-5}$	$1 \cdot 10^{-5}$
Degree	Avg	4.37	4.47	4.53	9.83	7.17	6.89
	Min	1	1	1	1	1	1
	Max	154 828	121 217	65 576	3 364 084	57 363	57 363
Classes		8	14	5	2	12	9
Labeled	Total	73 423	63 565	8 399	86 535	8 863	57 323
	Train	13 423	23 566	5 394	26 535	3 846	27 308
	Valid	20 000	10 001	1 001	20 000	1 006	10 005
	Test	20 000	20 001	2 001	20 000	3 005	10 003
	Meta	20 000	10 001		20 000	1 006	10 007
Source		[5]	see text		[21, 29, 31]	[12, 31]	[12, 31]
GPU friendly		✓		✓			
CPU friendly		✓	✓	✓		✓	✓
Datatypes[a]							
Numerical		8 418	64 184	8 891		1 387	1 387
Temporal		6 676	463	290		37 442	37 442
Textual		56 202	340 396	117 062	239 265	51 852	51 852
Visual		56 130	58 791	46 061		67 528	67 528
Spatial			116 220	20 837			

[a] Numerical includes all subsets of real numbers, as well as booleans, whereas date, years, and other similar types are listed under temporal information. Textual includes the set of strings (possibly without datatype, its subsets, and raw URIs (e.g. links). Images and geometries are listed under visual and spatial information, respectively

type of information which it encodes, which makes it difficult to build machine learning models that distinguish between these types. To accommodate this distinction, we instead introduce a small collection of datatype classes to annotate binary-encoded strings in accordance with their information type (Listing 1.1).[5]

3   Datasets

Table 2 lists the datasets contained in kgbench and their basic statistics, as well as an overview of the distribution of modalities per dataset. All datasets were created by combining publicly available data sources, with no manual annotation. Enrichment was limited to combining data sources, and annotating literals.

---

[5] The same may be achieved with additional triples. While this would remove the need for new datatypes, it would render the isolated literal meaningless. This contrasts with most other datatypes, which still convey their meaning in isolation.

Table 3. The class mapping for the `amplus` data. The original categories are translated from their original Dutch names.

Original	Class	Frequency
Furniture, Glass, Textile, Ceramics, Sculpture, Arts & crafts	Decorative art	25 782
Prints	Prints	22 048
Coins & tokens, Archaeological artifacts, Measures & weights	Historical artifacts	7 558
Drawings	Drawings	5 455
Non-noble metals art, Noble metal art	Metallic art	4 333
Books, Documents	Books & documents	4 012
Paintings	Paintings	2 672
Photographs	Photographs	1 563

3.1 The Amsterdam Museum Dataset (`amplus`)

The Amsterdam Museum is dedicated to the history of Amsterdam. Its catalog has been translated to linked open data [5]. The AM dataset, as described in Table 1, is already established as a benchmark for node classification: the task is to predict the type of a given collection item.

In the original version, the number of labeled instances is arbitrarily limited to 1000, resulting in small test set sizes. We return to the original data and make the following changes: we collect all collection items as instances, annotate a large number of literals with the correct datatype, and insert images as base64 encoded literals. We also include only a subset of the relations of the original data to make the dataset both small and challenging. Finally, we remap the categories to a smaller set of classes to create a more balanced class distribution. The mapping is given in Table 3.

The `amplus` data is provided under a Creative Commons CC-BY license.

3.2 The Dutch Monument Graph (`dmgfull`, `dmg777k`)

Like `amplus`, the Dutch Monument Graph (DMG) is a dataset from the Digital Humanities. Encompassing knowledge from several organizations, the DMG contains information about 63 566 registered monuments in the Netherlands.

Engineered with the goal of creating a highly multimodal dataset, the DMG contains information in six modalities, five of which are encoded as literals. This includes the often common numerical, temporal, and textual information, but also visual information in the form of images, and, more uniquely, several different kinds of spatial information. Taken all together, these modalities provide the monuments with a diverse multimodal context which includes, amongst other things, a short title, a longer description, a construction date, the city and municipality it lies in, several images from different directions, a set of geo-referenced coordinates, and a polygon describing its footprint.

Five different knowledge graphs from four different organizations,[6] were combined to form the DMG. The information from these organizations was combined using entity resolution based on string comparison, matching municipality and city names, as well as multi-part addresses. Once merged, the information was cleaned and provided with accurate class and datatype declarations where missing.

The 777k-variant is a subset encompassing 8 399 monuments created by sampling monuments from the top-5 monument classes that have no missing values. Both datasets are published under the CC-BY license.

3.3   The Movie Dataset (mdgenre, mdgender)

The Movie datasets are subsets of Wikidata [31] in the movie domain. We select any movies that are recorded as ever having won or been nominated for an award. Every person affiliated with any of these movies is also selected if the relation between the movie and the person is in a whitelist.

This whitelist consists of relations that satisfy the conditions that 1) every relation needs to have a Wikidata prefix, and 2) the relations do not direct to an identifier tag outside of Wikidata. Every triple that contains a movie or individual on their respective lists and a relation on the whitelist is extracted. This creates a graph that is centred around movie-related data with a longest path of 4 hops.

The main objective of this dataset is to predict the genre of the movies. Movies can have multiple genres, which is not practical when creating a single-label classification problem. Therefore, movies are assigned a genre based on a solution to the Set Cover Problem, which was derived using [38]. Each movie is assigned a single genre of which it already was part. This simplifies the multi-label classification objective to a multiclass classification objective. Additionally, the Movie Datasets also contain a gender objective, which we include as a sanity check as the objective is considered easier compared to the genre objective (see Sect. 5 for a discussion). As the classification in the Wikidata knowledge base is already suitable for multiclass classification, no further constraining as with the genres is necessary.

We download thumbnail images from URLs in Wikidata and include these as base64-encoded string literals. We also include thumbnails of images in the Internet Movie Database (IMDb) by matching the IMDb-identifier in Wikidata.

The relational data in these datasets is taken from Wikidata, and provided under the same CC0/Public domain license that applies to Wikidata. For 40 449 out of the 68 247 images in this dataset, we extracted thumbnails from larger images published by IMDb. The copyright of the original images resides with their producers. We assert no rights on this part of the data for redistribution or use outside non-commercial research settings. The remainder of the thumbnails is taken from the Wikimedia repository, and distributed under the individual license of each image.

---

[6] (1) the Dutch Cultural Heritage Agency, www.cultureelerfgoed.nl, (2) the Dutch Cadastre, Land Registry and Mapping Agency, www.kadaster.nl, (3) Statistics Netherlands, www.cbs.nl, and (4) Geonames, www.geonames.org.

3.4   The DBLP Dataset (dblp)

The DBLP repository [29] is a large bibliographic database of publications in the domain of computer science. This was converted to RDF under the name L3S DBLP, of which we used the HDT dump[7]. To provide a classification task on this data we extracted citation counts from the OpenCitations project [21] using the REST API. We checked all DOIs of papers in the DBLP dump, giving us a set of 86 535 DOIs that are present in both databases. These are our instances.

We also extract information from Wikidata about researchers. We use the XML dump of DBLP [29] to extract ORCiDs, which allows us to link 62 774 people to Wikidata. For each person linked, we extract triples from the one-hop neighborhood in Wikidata. We use 24 relations from the DBLP data and 44 relations from Wikidata.

Since we are focusing on classification tasks, we turn the prediction of the citation count into two classes: those papers which received one citation, and those which received more (due to the skewed distribution this the closest to a median-split). We have also preserved the original citation counts in the data, so the task can also be treated as a node regression task. This dataset is provided under a CC0/Public domain license.

4   Code and Baselines

In addition to the datasets in their RDF and CSV formats, we also provide scripts to convert any arbitrary RDF-encoded graph to our CSV format. To import these datasets into a machine learning workflow, we further provide a small Python library that loads any dataset that makes use of our CSV format into a object containing Pytorch [20] or Numpy [19] tensors, together with mappings to the string representations of the nodes. This provides both a utility sufficient for the majority of current machine learning practice, and a reference implementation for any setting where such a dataloader does not suffice.

In addition to the new datasets of Table 2, the repository also includes legacy datasets aifb and the original Amsterdam Museum data, named am1k here. These are useful for debugging purposes.

The dataloader allows the data to be loaded in a single function call. It also provides utility functions for pruning the dataset to a fixed distance around the instance nodes, and for re-ordering the nodes so that the datatypes are ordered together (which may reduce expensive tensor indexing operation in implementing multimodal models). We also provide three baseline models as reference for how to use the data in practice:

Features. This model extracts binary graph features about the set of triples incident to the instance node, which are then used by a logistic regression classifier. Over the whole set of training instances, all of the following binary features are considered: (a) whether a particular predicate p is present or

---

[7] Available at https://www.rdfhdt.org/datasets/.

Table 4. Performance of baselines on the datasets in the collection. The R-GCNs could not be trained on `dblp` in under 64 Gb of memory.

Setting	Baseline	`amplus`	`dmgfull`	`dmg777k`	`dblp`	`mdgenre`
Relational	Features	0.72	0.73	0.42	0.72	0.66
	R-GCN	0.77	0.71	0.70	-	0.63
Multimodal	MR-GCN	0.86	0.76	0.57	-	0.62

not, (b) whether a particular predicate is present in a specific direction, i.e. outgoing or incoming, and (c) whether a particular predicate, in a particular direction, connects the instance node to a specific node n. For all collected features, the information gain is computed for splitting the training instances on that feature. The k features with the highest information gain are kept and used to train a classifier.

R-GCN. The default classification R-GCN model [28]. It contains two R-GCN layers that are fed with a one-hot encoding of the nodes, which is mapped, via a hidden layer, to class probabilities. By default, a hidden size of 16 is used, with a basis decomposition of 40 bases. This baseline is purely relational, and ignores multimodal information.

MR-GCN. We provide a stripped-down version of the MR-GCN model [34]. Unlike the original, this model does not train its feature extractors end-to-end, which means that no backpropagation is needed beyond the R-GCN layer, saving memory. The literal features are extracted by pretrained models: a Mobilenet-v2 [26] for the images and DistilBERT [27] for literals. After feature extraction, the features are scaled down to a uniform input dimension d by principal component analysis.

4.1   Baseline Performance

Table 4 shows the accuracies of the three baseline models on the datasets in `kgbench`. The R-GCN models were trained for 50 epochs with default hyperparameters. That is, a two-layer model, with ReLU activation and a hidden size of 16. Training was done full-batch for 50 epochs with the Adam optimizer with default parameters and a learning rate of 0.01. A $0.5 \cdot 10^{-3}$ L2 penalty was applied to the weights of the first layer. The features baseline was run with $k = 2000$ and a logistic regression classifier with no regularization.

These numbers should be taken as broad baselines for how default models perform on these datasets, and not as the last word of the performance of, for instance, the R-GCN. It may well be possible to achieve better performance with more extensive hyperparameter tuning, a different architecture, or more training epochs. In particular, the MR-GCN used here is likely considerably less performant than the fully end-to-end version.

5 Discussion

While only a small proportion of benchmarks datasets that are published achieve broad community-wide uptake, those that do ultimately have a profound impact on the direction in which technology is developed. A dataset like ImageNet [8] was developed in a time when no models were available that could solve the task, but it is now commonly used to pretrain computer vision models that are widely distributed and used in production systems. Even a dataset like FFHQ [13], which was specifically compiled with diversity and representation in mind has led to pre-trained models that contain bias, which is ultimately exposed in downstream applications [17].

For this reason we consider it wise to discuss both the biases present in the data and the implications of setting certain labels as training targets.

5.1 Bias in Training Data

A common source of discussion in AI Ethics is the bias present in training data, especially where the representation of people is concerned [16]. A case in point are the mdgenre and dblp datasets, which both contain the "Sex or Gender" property of Wikidata.[8] In the former, a disproportionate number of the actors in the data are men. While this may be an accurate reflection of a bias in the world,[9] it means that actions taken based on the predictions of a production model trained on this data, may end up amplifying the data biases.

We have chosen not to de-bias the data for various reasons. First, we can only correct for the biases for which we have attributes (such as sex, gender, race, or religion). Second, even if we resample in this way, the biases may still manifest, for instance in the completeness of the data for men and women. Finally, debiasing the data ourselves, by a fixed strategy removes the possibility of investigating the debiasing method itself.

In short, we take it as a given that the data is biased. Since the data was largely retrieved completely as found in the wild, with only crude filtering based on node neighborhoods and relation whitelists, we may assume that these biases are reflective of the biases in real-world data. This may be used to study data bias in knowledge graphs, but any model trained on these datasets should not be put into production without careful consideration.

5.2 Choice of Target Relations

In all cases, our primary reasons for setting a particular target relation are technical. It is challenging to find a set of classes that are well-balanced, offer a large amount of instances, and provide a challenging task. Moreover, in the multimodal setting, a variety of literals with different modalities must be available, all of which can be shown to contribute to the task.

---

[8] https://www.wikidata.org/wiki/Property:P21.

[9] Even this is not a given. In many cases, the models themselves also amplify the biases present in the data [37].

This narrow range of requirements can lead difficult choices: in our search for suitable targets, we noted that the category "Sex or gender" in Wikidata, satisfied our technical requirements very well. However, training a model to predict this relation is to train (in part) a gender classifier, which is a controversial subject [11]. The following reasons have been posed for why such classifiers would be undesirable:

– Both sex and gender are not well captured by binary categories. Even the range of 36 categories offered by Wikidata (of which 8 are present in the Movie data) is unlikely to capture the spectrum of possibilities.
– People with gender identities outside the male/female categorization are at risk of oppression or discrimination. An oppressive regime may abuse gender and sex classifiers for large scale detention or prosecution. While there are currently no such systems employed to our knowledge, such practices do already exist in the related cases of race and ethnicity classification [18].
– The possibility of gender classification from external features may falsely imply a strong or causal relationship. Here, a comparable case is [14,33], where a classifier was built to predict sexual orientation. Besides the possibilities for abuse noted previously, such classifiers are often misinterpreted as showing strong causal links, for instance between physical features and the target class. In fact, all that can really be inferred is a weak correlation, which may well be based on incidental features, such as lighting, or personal choices such as clothing and make-up.

On the other hand, the inclusion of sex and gender as features in the data is important for the study of algorithmic bias. Simply removing the sex or gender attribute as a *target* class, but not as a feature of the data, also does not circumvent these issues. In a link prediction setting rather than a node labeling setting, every relation in the data becomes both feature and target. In such settings the two cannot be separated, and the problem remains.

Ultimately, we have chosen to include the dataset, with the "Sex or gender" attribute in place. We urge that practitioners use these datasets with care. For the gender-prediction task `mdgender` itself, we recommend strongly that this dataset be used only as a test case in development,[10] and not to report model performance in general settings, unless the task at hand is specifically relevant to the issue of sex or gender bias.

6   Conclusion

In this work, we have introduced a collection of multimodal datasets for the precise evaluation of node classification tasks on RDF-encoded knowledge graphs.

---

[10] The task in its current setup is too easy to serve as a good benchmark (which we have deliberately refrained from fixing). However, it is unique among these datasets in offering a strong guarantee that the images can be used to predict the target label with good accuracy. This property may be useful in debugging models, which can then be evaluated on the other tasks.

All datasets are available on GitHub and Zenodo in N-Triples and HDT format. Also provided are CSVs with an integer-to-label mapping, which can be loaded into Numpy and Pytorch by using the provided dataloader code. To support images, videos, and audio sequences, we also introduced a modest ontology to express these datatypes as binary-encoded string literals. For all datasets, we demonstrated their performance using several baseline models.

6.1 Limitations

To add extra modalities to our data, we have relied primarily on images. Other modalities are available: for instance Wikidata contains a rich collection of audio clips which provide an additional modality. Even small videos might be suitable.

An important consideration in constructing our graphs was to keep the total size of the graph relatively small. This means that the graphs presented here paint a slightly simplified image of real-world knowledge graphs. A model that performs well on these graphs can most likely not be applied directly to knowledge graphs found in the wild, as these will have magnitudes more relations, and relevant information stored more steps away from the instance nodes.

6.2 Outlook

To stimulate adoption of the benchmark, we have aimed to offer a simple and unambiguous way to load the data (including baseline implementations for reference) and to host the data in multiple, redundant places (Zenodo and Github). As the data is used, we will offer a leader board on the Github page to track top performance and collect papers making use of the data.

The ultimate test of a benchmark task is whether it can be solved. In cases like speech-to-text, we can use human performance as an upper bound, but in a relational learning setting this is difficult to measure. Our baseline tests show that simple baselines reach low, but above-chance performance, with plenty of room for growth. It is difficult to establish what the performance ceiling is, but we hope that by providing a good number of datasets, we increase the probability that one of them will turn out to contain that particular trade-off between difficulty and simplicity that typifies the most enduring benchmark tasks.

Our ultimate hope is that these benchmarks stimulate more principled research towards models that learn end-to-end from relational and multimodal data, and that such models help to bridge the gap between statistical and symbolic forms of knowledge representation.

Acknowledgements. We thank Emma Beauxis-Aussalet for illuminating discussions on the broader impact statement. We thank Rein van 't Veer for invaluable assistance with the geometry modalities in the DMG dataset.

References

1. Battaglia, P.W., et al.: Relational inductive biases, deep learning, and graph networks. arXiv preprint arXiv:1806.01261 (2018)
2. van Berkel, L., Bloem, P., Wilcke, X., de Boer, V.: kgbench: mdgenre and mdgender, December 2020. https://doi.org/10.5281/zenodo.4361795
3. Bloem, P., Wilcke, X., van Berkel, L., de Boer, V.: kgbench: amplus, December 2020. https://doi.org/10.5281/zenodo.4361762
4. Bloem, P., Wilcke, X., van Berkel, L., de Boer, V.: kgbench: dblp, December 2020. https://doi.org/10.5281/zenodo.4361787
5. de Boer, V., et al.: Amsterdam museum linked open data. Semantic Web **4**(3), 237–243 (2013)
6. Busbridge, D., Sherburn, D., Cavallo, P., Hammerla, N.Y.: Relational graph attention networks. arXiv preprint arXiv:1904.05811 (2019)
7. De Vries, G.K.D., De Rooij, S., et al.: A fast and simple graph kernel for rdf. DMoLD **1082** (2013)
8. Deng, J., Dong, W., Socher, R., Li, L.J., Li, K., Fei-Fei, L.: Imagenet: a large-scale hierarchical image database. In: 2009 IEEE Conference on Computer Vision and Pattern Recognition, pp. 248–255. IEEE (2009)
9. Feng, Y., Chen, X., Lin, B.Y., Wang, P., Yan, J., Ren, X.: Scalable multi-hop relational reasoning for knowledge-aware question answering. arXiv preprint arXiv:2005.00646 (2020)
10. Fernández, J.D., Martínez-Prieto, M.A., Gutiérrez, C., Polleres, A., Arias, M.: Binary RDF representation for publication and exchange (HDT). J. Web Semantics **19**, 22–41 (2013)
11. Hamidi, F., Scheuerman, M.K., Branham, S.M.: Gender recognition or gender reductionism? the social implications of embedded gender recognition systems. In: Proceedings of the 2018 CHI Conference on Human Factors in Computing Systems, pp. 1–13 (2018)
12. IMDB: The Internet Movie Database, accessed October 2020. http://imdb.com
13. Karras, T., Laine, S., Aila, T.: A style-based generator architecture for generative adversarial networks. In: Proceedings of the IEEE Conference on Computer Vision and Pattern Recognition, pp. 4401–4410 (2019)
14. Levin, S.: New AI can guess whether you're gay or straight from a photograph. The Guardian (2017). https://www.theguardian.com/technology/2017/sep/07/new-artificial-intelligence-can-tell-whether-youre-gay-or-straight-from-a-photograph
15. Liu, Y., Li, H., Garcia-Duran, A., Niepert, M., Onoro-Rubio, D., Rosenblum, D.S.: MMKG: multi-modal knowledge graphs. In: Hitzler, P., et al. (eds.) ESWC 2019. LNCS, vol. 11503, pp. 459–474. Springer, Cham (2019). https://doi.org/10.1007/978-3-030-21348-0_30
16. Mehrabi, N., Morstatter, F., Saxena, N., Lerman, K., Galstyan, A.: A survey on bias and fairness in machine learning. arXiv preprint arXiv:1908.09635 (2019)
17. Menon, S., Damian, A., Hu, S., Ravi, N., Rudin, C.: Pulse: self-supervised photo upsampling via latent space exploration of generative models. In: Proceedings of the IEEE/CVF Conference on Computer Vision and Pattern Recognition, pp. 2437–2445 (2020)
18. Mozur, P.: One month, 500,000 face scans: How china is using a.i. to profile a minority. The New York Times (2019). https://www.nytimes.com/2019/04/14/technology/china-surveillance-artificial-intelligence-racial-profiling.html
19. Oliphant, T.E.: A guide to NumPy, vol. 1. Trelgol Publishing USA (2006)

20. Paszke, A., et al.: Pytorch: An imperative style, high-performance deep learning library. In: Advances in Neural Information Processing Systems, pp. 8026–8037 (2019)
21. Peroni, S., Shotton, D.: Opencitations, an infrastructure organization for open scholarship. Quant. Sci. Stud. **1**(1), 428–444 (2020)
22. Ristoski, P., de Vries, G.K.D., Paulheim, H.: A collection of benchmark datasets for systematic evaluations of machine learning on the semantic web. In: Groth, P., et al. (eds.) ISWC 2016. LNCS, vol. 9982, pp. 186–194. Springer, Cham (2016). https://doi.org/10.1007/978-3-319-46547-0_20
23. Ristoski, P., Paulheim, H.: RDF2Vec: RDF graph embeddings for data mining. In: Groth, P., et al. (eds.) ISWC 2016. LNCS, vol. 9981, pp. 498–514. Springer, Cham (2016). https://doi.org/10.1007/978-3-319-46523-4_30
24. Ruffinelli, D., Broscheit, S., Gemulla, R.: You can teach an old dog new tricks! on training knowledge graph embeddings. In: International Conference on Learning Representations (2019)
25. Safavi, T., Koutra, D.: CoDEx: a comprehensive knowledge graph completion benchmark. In: Proceedings of the 2020 Conference on Empirical Methods in Natural Language Processing (EMNLP). pp. 8328–8350. Association for Computational Linguistics, Online, November 2020. https://doi.org/10.18653/v1/2020.emnlp-main.669. https://www.aclweb.org/anthology/2020.emnlp-main.669
26. Sandler, M., Howard, A., Zhu, M., Zhmoginov, A., Chen, L.C.: Mobilenetv 2: inverted residuals and linear bottlenecks. In: Proceedings of the IEEE Conference on Computer Vision and Pattern Recognition, pp. 4510–4520 (2018)
27. Sanh, V., Debut, L., Chaumond, J., Wolf, T.: Distilbert, a distilled version of bert: smaller, faster, cheaper and lighter. arXiv preprint arXiv:1910.01108 (2019)
28. Schlichtkrull, M., Kipf, T.N., Bloem, P., Berg, R.v.d., Titov, I., Welling, M.: Modeling relational data with graph convolutional networks. arXiv preprint arXiv:1703.06103 (2017)
29. dblp team, T.: dblp computer science bibliography, converted by l3s (2017). http://downloads.linkeddatafragments.org/hdt/dblp-20170124.hdt
30. Tiwari, A.K., Nadimpalli, S.V.: Learning semantic image attributes using image recognition and knowledge graph embeddings. I.J. Image, Graphics and Signal Processing (2020). https://doi.org/10.5815/ijigsp.2020.05.05
31. Vrandečić, D., Krötzsch, M.: Wikidata: a free collaborative knowledgebase. Commun. ACM **57**(10), 78–85 (2014)
32. Wang, M., Wang, H., Qi, G., Zheng, Q.: Richpedia: a large-scale, comprehensive multi-modal knowledge graph. Big Data Research **22**, 100159 (2020). https://doi.org/10.1016/j.bdr.2020.100159. https://www.sciencedirect.com/science/article/pii/S2214579620300277
33. Wang, Y., Kosinski, M.: Deep neural networks are more accurate than humans at detecting sexual orientation from facial images. J. Pers. Soc. Psychol. **114**(2), 246 (2018)
34. Wilcke, W., Bloem, P., de Boer, V., van t Veer, R., van Harmelen, F.: End-to-end entity classification on multimodal knowledge graphs. arXiv p. arXiv-2003 (2020)
35. Wilcke, W., Bloem, P., De Boer, V.: The knowledge graph as the default data model for learning on heterogeneous knowledge. Data Sci. **1**(1–2), 39–57 (2017)
36. Wilcke, X., Bloem, P., van Berkel, L., de Boer, V.: kgbench: dmgfull and dmg777k, December 2020. https://doi.org/10.5281/zenodo.4361779

37. Zhao, J., Wang, T., Yatskar, M., Ordonez, V., Chang, K.W.: Men also like shopping: Reducing gender bias amplification using corpus-level constraints. arXiv preprint arXiv:1707.09457 (2017)
38. Zhu, G.: A new view of classification in astronomy with the archetype technique: an astronomical case of the NP-complete set cover problem. arXiv preprint arXiv:1606.07156 (2016)

The SLOGERT Framework
for Automated Log Knowledge Graph
Construction

Andreas Ekelhart[1]([✉])(iD), Fajar J. Ekaputra[2](iD), and Elmar Kiesling[1](iD)

[1] WU (Vienna University of Economics and Business), Welthandelsplatz 1,
1020 Vienna, Austria
{andreas.ekelhart,elmar.kiesling}@wu.ac.at
[2] TU Wien (Vienna University of Technology), Favoritenstraße 9-11/194,
1040 Vienna, Austria
fajar.ekaputra@tuwien.ac.at

Abstract. Log files are a vital source of information for keeping systems running and healthy. However, analyzing raw log data, i.e., textual records of system events, typically involves tedious searching for and inspecting clues, as well as tracing and correlating them across log sources. Existing log management solutions ease this process with efficient data collection, storage, and normalization mechanisms, but identifying and linking entities across log sources and enriching them with background knowledge is largely an unresolved challenge. To facilitate a knowledge-based approach to log analysis, this paper introduces SLOGERT, a flexible framework and workflow for automated construction of knowledge graphs from arbitrary raw log messages. At its core, it automatically identifies rich RDF graph modelling patterns to represent types of events and extracted parameters that appear in a log stream. We present the workflow, the developed vocabularies for log integration, and our prototypical implementation. To demonstrate the viability of this approach, we conduct a performance analysis and illustrate its application on a large public log dataset in the security domain.

Keywords: Knowledge graphs · Log analysis · Log vocabularies · Graph modelling patterns

1 Introduction

Log analysis is a technique to deepen an understanding of an operational environment, pinpoint root causes, and identify behavioral patterns based on emitted event records. Nearly all software systems (operating systems, applications, network devices, etc.) produce their own time-sequenced log files to capture relevant

This work was sponsored by the Austrian Science Fund (FWF) and netidee SCIENCE under grant P30437-N31 and the Austrian Research Promotion Agency FFG under grant 877389 (OBARIS). The authors thank the funders for their generous support.

© Springer Nature Switzerland AG 2021
R. Verborgh et al. (Eds.): ESWC 2021, LNCS 12731, pp. 631–646, 2021.
https://doi.org/10.1007/978-3-030-77385-4_38

events. These logs can be used, e.g., by system administrators, security analysts, and software developers to identify and diagnose problems and conduct investigations. Typical tasks include security monitoring and forensics [23,38], anomaly detection [11,16,28], compliance auditing [25,39], and error diagnosis [6,44]. Log analysis is also a common issue more generally in other domains such as power systems security [35], predictive maintenance [40], workflow mining [3,4], and business/web intelligence [17,30].

To address these varied applications, numerous log management solutions have been developed that assist in the process of storing, indexing, and searching log data. However, investigations across multiple heterogeneous log sources with unknown content and message structures is a challenging and time-consuming task [22,41]. It typically involves a combination of manual inspection and regular expressions to locate specific messages or patterns [34].

The need for a paradigm shift towards a more structured approach and uniform log representations has been highlighted in the literature for a long time [19,21,34], but although various standardization initiatives for event representation were launched (e.g., [8,9,18,29]), none of them has seen widespread adoption. As a result, log analysis requires the interpretation of many different types of events, expressed with different terminologies, and represented in a multitude of formats [29], particularly in large-scale systems composed of heterogeneous components. As a consequence, the analyst has to manually investigate and connect this information, which is time consuming, error prone and potentially leads to an incomplete picture.

In this paper, we tackle these challenges and propose Semantic LOG ExtRaction Templating (SLOGERT), a framework for automated Knowledge Graph (KG) construction from unstructured, heterogeneous, and (potentially) fragmented log sources, building on and extending initial ideas [12]. The resulting KGs enable analysts to navigate and query an integrated, enriched view of the events and thereby facilitate a novel approach for log analysis. This opens up a wealth of new (log-structured) data sources for KG building.

Our main contributions are: *(i)* a novel paradigm for *semantic log analytics* that leverages knowledge-graphs to link and integrate heterogeneous log data; *(ii)* a *framework to generate RDF from arbitrary unstructured log data* through automatically generated extraction and graph modelling templates; *(iii)* a *set of base mappings, extraction templates, and a high-level general conceptualization* of the log domain derived from an existing standard as well as vocabularies for describing extraction templates; *(iv)* a prototypical *implementation* of the proposed approach, including detailed documentation to facilitate its reuse, and *(v)* an evaluation based on a realistic, multi-day log dataset [27]. All referenced resources, including the developed vocabularies[1], source code[2], data, and examples, are available from the project website[3].

---

[1] https://w3id.org/sepses/ns/log#.

[2] https://github.com/sepses/slogert/.

[3] https://sepses.ifs.tuwien.ac.at/.

The remainder of this paper is organized as follows: we introduce our log KG building approach in Sect. 2 and evaluate it in Sect. 3 by means of example use cases. We then contrast the approach against the state of practice (Sect. 4) and review various strands of related work (Sect. 5); finally, we conclude in Sect. 6 with an outlook on future work.

2   Building Knowledge Graphs from Log Files

In this section, we introduce the SLOGERT (Semantic LOG ExtRaction Templating) log KG generation framework and discuss its architecture, components, and their implementation. The associated workflow, illustrated in Fig. 1, transforms and integrates arbitrary log files provided as input. It consists of two major phases: (1) template extraction, which results in an RDF pattern for each type of log message that appears in the sources; and (2) graph building, which – based on these patterns – transforms raw log data into RDF.[4]

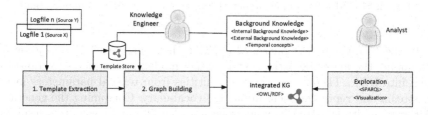

Fig. 1. SLOGERT workflow

In the *Template Extraction* phase, SLOGERT will automatically generate event templates from unstructured log data by identifying the different types of log messages and their variable parts (i.e., parameters) in the raw log messages. For this, we rely on a well-established log parser toolkit [46] that generates *extraction templates*, which at this stage do not provide any clues about the semantics of the log message or the contained parameters. To enrich these extraction templates with semantics, we next annotate the parameters (variable parts) according to their type as well as extract relevant keywords from the log messages, which are used to link each log template with relevant CEE [29] annotations.

We then use this information to associate each log extraction template with a corresponding *RDF graph modelling template* (represented as Reasonable Ontology Templates (OTTRs)). The resulting graph modelling templates can be annotated, adapted, extended and reused, i.e., they only have to be generated (and optionally extended) once from raw log data in which unknown log events appear.

---

[4] A more detailed documentation and pseudocode specification of the process is available at https://github.com/sepses/slogert/.

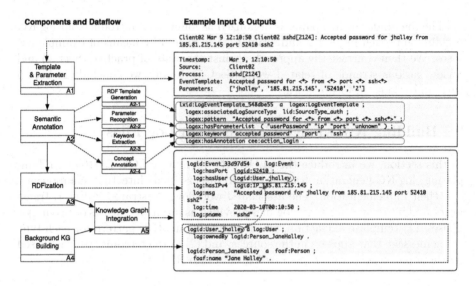

Fig. 2. SLOGERT components and processing of a single example log line

In the *Graph Building* phase, SLOGERT then parses each line in a log file and applies the matching extraction and RDF modelling templates to transform them into RDF. Thereby, we generate entities from textual parameters in the log stream and represent them in our log vocabulary. Combining the generated RDF from multiple, potentially heterogeneous log files and log sources results in a single integrated log KG. This graph can contextualize the log data by linking it to existing background knowledge – such as internal information on assets and users or external information, e.g., on software, services, threats etc.

Finally, analysts can explore, query, analyze, and visualize the resulting log KG seamlessly across log sources.

2.1   SLOGERT Components

Following this high-level outline of the SLOGERT workflow, this section describes each component in more detail. For a dynamic illustration of the overall process by way of an example log line, cf. Fig. 2.

Phase 1: Template Extraction

Template & Parameter Extraction (A1), i.e., the first step in the process from raw log lines to RDF, relies on LogPAI[5] [46], a log parsing toolkit that identifies constant strings and variable values in the free-text message content. This step results in two files, i.e., *(i)* a list of log templates discovered in the log file, each including markings of the position of variable parts (parameters), and *(ii)* the

---
[5] https://github.com/logpai/logparser.

actual instance content of the logs, with each log line linked to one of the log template ids, and the extracted instance parameters as an ordered list.

This process is fully automated and applicable to any log source, but depending on the structure of the log messages, it may not necessarily result in clearly separated parameters. As an example, consider that a user name next to an IP address will be identified as a single string parameter, as they usually change together in each log line. To achieve better results, LogPAI therefore accepts regular expression specifications of patterns that should be extracted as parameters, if detected. We take advantage of this capability by defining general regex patterns for common elements and including them in the configuration. At the end of this stage, we have *extraction templates* and the associated extracted instance data, but their semantic meaning is yet undefined.

Semantic Annotation (A2) takes the log templates and the instance data with the extracted parameters as input and *(i)* generates RDF rewriting templates that conform to an ontology and persists the templates in RDF for later reuse (A2-1), *(ii)* detects (where possible) the semantic types of the extracted parameters (A2-2), *(iii)* enriches the templates with extracted keywords (A2-3), and *(iv)* annotate the templates with CEE terms (A2-4).

For the parameter type detection (A2-1), we first select a set of log lines for each template (default: 3) and then apply rule-based Named Entity Recognition (NER) techniques. Specifically, we use TokensRegex from Stanford CoreNLP [5] to define patterns over text (sequences of tokens), and map them to semantic objects. CoreNLP can detect words in combination with (POS) tags and named entity labels as part of the patterns.

Such token-based extraction works well for finding patterns in natural language texts, but log messages often do not follow the grammatical rules of typical natural language expressions and contain "unusual" entities such as URLs, identifiers, and configurations. For those cases, we additionally apply standard regex patterns on the complete message. For each identified parameter, we also define a type and a property from a log vocabulary to use for the detected entities. In case a parameter does not result in any matches, we mark it as unknown.

In our prototype, we collect all parameter extraction patterns in a YAML configuration file and model a set of generic patterns that cover various applications, including the illustrative use cases in Sect. 3. These patterns are reusable across heterogeneous log sources and can be easily extended, e.g., with existing regex log patterns such as, e.g., Grok[6]. For the semantic representation necessary to allow for a consistent representation over heterogeneous log files, we followed the Ontology 101 methodology [33], extended a prior log vocabulary [26] and mapped it to the Common Event Expression (CEE) [29] taxonomy. Furthermore, we persist our ontology with a W3ID namespace (i.e., https://w3id.org/sepses/ns/log#) and use Widoco [14] for the ontology documentation.

Our vocabulary core represents log events (`log:Event`) with a set of fields (sub-properties of the `log:hasParameter` object property and `log:parameter`

---

[6] https://github.com/elastic/logstash/blob/v1.4.2/patterns/grok-patterns.

datatype properties). Each log event originates from a specific host (log:
hasSourceHost) and exists in a specific log source (log:hasLogSource, e.g.,
an FTP log file). The underlying source type (e.g., ftp) is expressed by log:
SourceType, and the log format is represented as log:Format (e.g., syslog).
Furthermore, a log event template is tagged with its underlying action (e.g.,
login, access), domain (e.g., app, device, host), object (e.g., email, app), service
(e.g., auth, audit), status (e.g., failure, error), and a subject (e.g., user) based
on the CEE specification[7].

Once we have identified extraction templates for events and parameters, we
can generate corresponding RDF generation templates for each of them. This
step expresses the patterns that determine how KGs are built from the log
data as reusable OTTR [1] templates, i.e., in a language for ontology modeling
patterns. As all the generated templates are reusable and should not have to be
regenerated for each individual instance of a log file, we persist them in RDF
with their associated hash (based on the static parts of the log messages) as
identifier. Finally, as a prerequisite to generate the actual KG from these OTTR
templates, we transform all log line instances of the input into the stOTTR
format, a custom file format similar to Turtle, which references the generated
OTTR templates.

Phase 2: Graph Building. In this step, we generate a KG based on the OTTR
templates and stOTTR instance files generated in the extraction component.

RDFization (A3). For the conversion of OTTR templates and instance files, we
rely on Lutra[8], the reference implementation for the OTTR language. Thereby,
we expand the log instance data into an RDF graph that conforms to the log
vocabulary and contains the entities and log events of a single log file.

Background KG Building (A4). Linking log data to background knowledge
through the use of appropriate identifiers is a key step that facilitates enrichment with both local context information and external knowledge. The former
represents information that is created and maintained inside the organization
and not intended for public release. Examples include, e.g., the network architecture, users, organizational structures, devices, servers, installed software, and
documents.

This knowledge can either be maintained manually by knowledge engineers or
automatically by importing, e.g., DHCP leases, user directories with metadata,
or software asset information. The dynamic nature of such information (e.g., a
user switches department, a computer is assigned a new IP address, software is
uninstalled) necessitates a mechanism to capture temporal aspects. To this end,
RDF-Star can be used to historize the contained knowledge.

The second category, external knowledge, links to any publicly available
(RDF) data sources, such as, e.g., IT product and service inventories, vulnerability databases, and threat intelligence information (e.g., collected in [24]).

---

[7] https://cee.mitre.org/language/1.0-beta1/core-profile.html.

[8] https://ottr.xyz/#Lutra.

Knowledge Graph Integration (A5) combines the KGs from the previously isolated log files and sources into a single, linked representation. Key concepts and
identifiers in the computer log domain follow a standardized structure (e.g., IP
and MAC addresses, URLs) and hence can be merged using the same vocabulary. In case external knowledge does not align with the generated graphs (e.g.,
entity identifiers differ), an additional mapping step has to be conducted before
merging. Existing approaches, such as the Linked Data Integration Framework
Silk[9] can be used for this purpose.

3   Use Cases and Performance

We illustrate the presented approach and its applicability to real-world log data
based on a systematically generated, publicly available data set that was collected from testbeds over the course of six days [27]. Furthermore, we report on
the performance of the developed prototype (cf. Sect. 3.3).

3.1   Data Source

The AIT log dataset (V1.1)[10] contains six days of log data that was automatically generated in testbeds following a well-defined approach described in [27]. It
is a rare example of a readily available realistic dataset that contains related log
data from multiple systems in a network. In addition, information on the setup
is provided, which can be used as background knowledge in our approach. As
detailed information on the context of the scenario was not available, we com-
plemented it with synthetic example background knowledge on the environment
that the data was generated in for demonstration purposes.

Each of the web servers runs Debian and a set of installed services such as
Apache2, PHP7, Exim4, Horde, and Suricata. Furthermore, the data includes
logs from 11 Ubuntu hosts on which user behavior was simulated. On each web
server, the collected log sources include Apache access and error logs, syscall logs
from the Linux audit daemon, suricata logs, exim logs, auth logs, daemon logs,
mail logs, syslogs, and user logs. The logs capture mostly normal user behavior;
on the fifth day of the log collection (2020-03-04), however, two attacks were
launched against each of the four web servers. In total, the data set amounts to
51.1 GB of raw log files.

3.2   Use Cases

In this scenario, we assume that activities have raised suspicion and an analyst
wants to conduct a forensic analysis based on the available log data. We will
illustrate how our proposed framework can assist in this process. To this end,
we first processed all raw logs[11] with SLOGERT and stored them together with

---

[9] http://silkframework.org/.

[10] https://zenodo.org/record/4264796.

[11] From the audit logs, we only extracted the time frame relevant for the investigation.

Table 1. Query result for activities of a given user in the network (excerpt)

Template	Timestamp	Host	SourceType	Annotations
108cf6f8	2020-03-04T19:26:00	mail.cup.com	messages	failure,login
...	...	...	...	
108cf6f8	2020-03-04T19:28:59	mail.cup.com	messages	failure,login
108cf6f8	2020-03-04T19:29:00	mail.cup.com	messages	failure,login
c9f3df73	2020-03-04T19:29:07	mail.cup.com	syslog	login,success

the background knowledge in a triple store[12]. Overall, we collected 838.19MB of raw log files, resulting in 84,827,361 triples for this scenario.

```
PREFIX log: <https://w3id.org/sepses/ns/log#>
PREFIX logex: <https://w3id.org/sepses/ns/logex#>
PREFIX rdfs: <http://www.w3.org/2000/01/rdf-schema#>
PREFIX xsd: <http://www.w3.org/2001/XMLSchema#>

SELECT ?template ?timestamp ?host ?sourceType ?annotations
WHERE {
        ?logEvent a log:Event ;
           log:time ?timestamp ;
           log:hasSource ?source ;
           logex:template ?templateId ;
           log:hasSourceHost / log:host ?host .
    ?templateId rdfs:label ?template .
    ?source log:hasSourceType / rdfs:label ?sourceType .
        ?logEvent log:hasUser / log:user.name "daryl" .
    FILTER (xsd:dateTime(?timestamp) > "2020-03-04T18:30:00"^^xsd:dateTime)
    OPTIONAL {
        { select ?templateId (group_concat(?anno;separator=',') as ?annotations) where {
               ?templateId a logex:LogEventTemplate ;
                   logex:hasAnnotation/rdfs:label ?anno
           } group by ?templateId } }
} ORDER BY ?timestamp
```

Listing 1: SPARQL query to show activities of a user

Listing 1 demonstrates how an analyst can query the activities associated with a given username (i.e., daryl). The query illustrates the ability to access integrated log data and the flexibility of SPARQL as a query language for log data analytics.

Table 1 shows an excerpt of the query results, with the template name, timestamp of the event, host, type of log, and automatically extracted CEE [29] annotation labels. The template associated with each log event makes it possible to easily identify events of the same type; human-readable labels can optionally be assigned in the template library.

As a simple illustrative example, the query makes use of only a small subset of the available extracted properties. To explore the context and increase an analyst's understanding of the situation in the course of an investigation, other

---

[12] GraphDB 9.5, https://graphdb.ontotext.com.

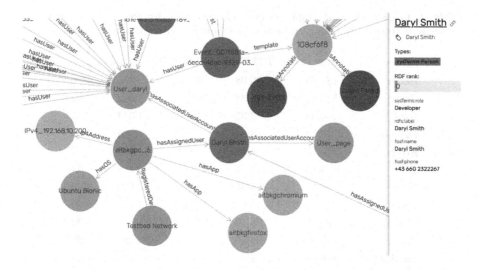

Fig. 3. Graph exploration: context information for `User_daryl`

extracted properties such as IP addresses, processes, commands, files, URLs, and email addresses can be added. These extracted entities establish links among log events and connect them to background knowledge, allowing the analyst to explore the log data from multiple perspectives in order to "connect the dots", e.g., in the context of attacks.

As an example, consider that the sequence of login failures in a short time period evident in Table 1 suggests a possible brute force attack, and the successful login shortly thereafter is alarming. To explore this further, the analyst can construct an enriched view on the available log events by visualizing the data (e.g., using GraphDB) and interactively following links of interest. The graph structure makes it possible to navigate the contextualized log data with interlinked background knowledge that otherwise is typically stored in external documentation or only exists in analysts' heads. In the example in Fig. 3, the analyst started from the username `daryl` and navigated to the Person associated with the account; from there, she can obtain additional information about the person, such as the role in the company, contact information, assigned devices, and additional usernames (e.g., `User_page`). In a similar manner, the analyst could integrate and explore external RDF data sources. We can also see how events are connected to the user in the selected time frame, and how the templates are annotated with detected CEE terms.

3.3   Performance

For each log source in the AIT log dataset – collected from four servers in a testbed environment – we ingest the raw log files[13] and execute all steps in

---

[13] Note that we only used a relevant subset of the high-volume audit logs, but the full time range for all other logs.

Table 2. Log sources and graph output. The run-time for the following phases is measured in seconds: template extraction (P1) and graph building (P2)

Source	Raw (MB)	TTL (MB)	HDT (MB)	P1 (s)	P2 (s)
Access	131.80	526.08	87.57	336	1398
Audit	525.41	2026.38	305.45	6652	6799
Auth	0.48	3.35	0.34	3	5
Daemon	0.58	3.94	0.63	5	6
Error	0.17	0.69	0.15	3	2
Fast	3.15	15.89	2.34	5	34
Mail	58.27	295.36	39.52	146	690
Main	1.96	13.81	3.02	6	20
Messages	28.60	108.10	12.55	34	199
Sys	87.78	408.50	53.05	297	909
Total/Merged	838.19	3402.11	498.36	7486	10062

the workflow according to Fig. 2. As the graph generation is split into multiple processing steps, we measure the execution time for each phase (i.e., template extraction and graph building) on a single machine with a Ryzen 7 3700X processor (64 GB RAM).

Table 2 shows the input log sources with their total file sizes over all four servers. Furthermore, it lists the sizes of the generated (intermediate) KGs in Turtle format (TTL), as well as in compressed format (HDT). At the end of the SLOGERT process, all intermediate graphs are merged into a single KG. In our illustrative scenario, we processed 838.19 MB of raw log data in total and generated a KG from it that is 498.36 MB in HDT format. Note that whereas the resulting TTL graph files were approx. four times the raw input size, the compressed HDT data, which can also easily be queried with SPARQL, is about 40% smaller than the original log file. The size of the generated graphs could further be reduced by *(i)* not including the full original raw input message (currently we keep it as message literal), and/or *(ii)* discarding unknown parameters, and/or *(iii)* extracting only the specific classes and properties necessary for a given set of analytic tasks.

In terms of processing time graph building (P2) is the most time consuming phase (approx. 168 min)[14]. We see that run-time scales linearly with file size; it can easily be reduced by parallelizing the semantic annotation and graph generation phases. Our prototype converts the log events into batches – the number of log lines per batch (200k in our experiments) can be configured. Although we executed the process on a single machine in sequence, each batch file could easily be processed in parallel. Taking the audit log as example, all audit log event lines were split into 200k batches (13 files), taking approx. 17 min each to build the KG.

---

[14] The Lutra team is working on performance according to their release notes.

Table 3. Comparison of SLOGERT with existing LMSs

Aspect	Existing LMSs	SLOGERT
Mode	Online & Offline	(Currently) offline
Storage	Proprietary databases	RDF & HDT compression
Extraction	Regex filters	Template-based
Normalization	Fields	Entity hierarchies and links
Background knowledge	-	RDF linking
Data insights	Dashboards and reports	Graph queries and navigation

4   State of the Practice

Commercially available Log Management Systems (LMSs) – such as Splunk[15], Graylog[16], or Logstash[17] – prioritize aggregation, normalization, and storage over integration, contextualization, linking, enrichment, and rich querying capabilities. They are typically designed to allow scalable retention of large log data and focus on reporting and alerting based on relatively simple rules.

Table 3 compares and contrasts SLOGERT with such existing LMSs. Whereas some tasks, such as *log collection* from raw logs, can rely on available standard mechanisms, the approach differs fundamentally in terms of *event and parameter detection, normalization, background knowledge linking*, and the way that *insights* can be gained.

In particular, SLOGERT *(i)* automatically classifies events and assigns types from a taxonomy based on the static parts of the messages and *(ii)* identifies and annotates variable parts of the messages. Although existing LMSs often also include a predefined and limited set of extractors to identify relevant patterns (e.g., IP address, date/time, protocol), they do not capture entities, their relationships, and the nature of these relationships in a graph structure. Furthermore, they are limited in their representational flexibility by the structure of the underlying, typically relational, storage.

The graph-based approach makes it possible to link assets to concepts and instances defined in background knowledge in order to enrich log events with additional internal or external knowledge. For instance, multiple usernames can be linked to the same person they belong to or software assets can be linked to public sources such as the Cyber-security Knowledge Graph (CSKG) [24] to include information about their vulnerabilities.

Finally, whereas existing LMSs typically provide relatively static dashboards and reports, SLOGERT opens up possibilities for exploration through graph

---

[15] https://splunk.com.
[16] https://www.graylog.org/.
[17] https://logstash.net.

queries and visual navigation, providing a new flexible perspective on events, their context, and their relationships.

Overall, no comparable graph-based semantic systems exist – current state-of-the-art message-centric log management systems focus on aggregation, management, storage, and manual step-by-step textual search and interpretation with implicit background knowledge. SLOGERT makes it possible to automatically contextualize, link and interpret log events. It complements, but does not replace established log management solutions with additional techniques to extract, enrich, and explore log event data. Specifically, our current focus is facilitating deeper inspection of subsets of log data from selected log sources, e.g., in a relevant time frame. To this end, we have developed flexible mechanisms for fully automated ad-hoc extraction and integration.

5 Related Work

Log parsing and extraction Logs, i.e., records of the events occurring within an organization's systems and networks [21], are composed of log entries, each of which provides information related to a specific event that has occurred. These log entries typically consist of a structured part with fields such as a timestamp, severity level etc., and an unstructured message field. Whereas conventions for the structured parts are somewhat standardized (e.g., in [2])), there is little uniformity on the content of the message field, despite numerous standardization attempts (e.g., IDMEF [18], CEE [29], CIM [9] and CADF [8]). Because log messages are produced from statements inserted into the code, they often do not follow typical natural language grammar and expression, but are shaped according to the code that generates them. Specifically, each log message can be divided into two parts: a constant part (i.e., fixed text that remains the same for every event instance) and a variable part that carries the runtime information of interest, such as parameter values (e.g., IP addresses and ports).

Traditional manual methods for analyzing such heterogeneous log data have become exceedingly labor-intensive and error-prone [15]. Furthermore, the heavy reliance on regular expressions in log management results in complex configurations with customized rules that are difficult to maintain as systems evolve [15]. These limitations of regex-based event extraction motivated the development of data-driven approaches for automated log parsing (e.g., [42]) that leverage historical log messages to train statistical models for event extraction. [15] provides a systematic evaluation of the state-of-the-art of such automated event extraction methods. We leverage these methods as the first step in our automated KG construction workflow. Specifically, our template extraction is based on the Log-PAI logparser toolkit [46], which provides implementations of various automated event extraction methods.

Log representation in Knowledge Graphs has attracted recent research interest because graph-based models provide a concise and intuitive abstraction for the log domain that can represent various types of relations flexibly. Therefore, a variety of approaches that apply graph-based models and graph-theoretical analysis techniques to log data have been proposed in the literature, covering applications such as query log analysis [10,45], network traffic and forensic analysis [7,43], and security [36]. Whereas these contributions are focused on graph-theoretical metrics and methods, another stream of knowledge-graph-centric literature has emerged more recently. CyGraph [32], e.g., develops a property graph-based cybersecurity model and a domain-specific query language for expressing graph patterns of interest. It correlates intrusion alerts to vulnerability paths, but compared to our approach, it does not aim for semantic lifting of general log data.

In terms of semantic KGs, existing approaches have focused either on structured log data only [31], or on tasks such as entity [20] and relation [37] extraction in unstructured log data. Whereas some of the extraction methods introduced in this context are similar to our approach, their focus is less on log representation, but on cybersecurity information more general (e.g., textual descriptions of attacks).

Other contributions have focused on a conceptualization of the log domain and the development of appropriate vocabularies for log representation in KGs [13]. Another recent, more narrowly focused approach [26] that does not cover general extraction introduces a vocabulary and architecture to collect, extract, and link heterogeneous low-level file access events from Linux and Windows event logs. Finally, [24] provides a continuously updated resource that links and integrates cybersecurity information, e.g., on vulnerabilities, weaknesses, and attack patterns, providing a useful linking target in the context of this log extraction framework.

6   Conclusions and Future Work

This paper introduced SLOGERT, a flexible framework and workflow for automated KG construction from unstructured log data. The proposed workflow can be applied to arbitrary log data with unstructured messages and consists of a template extraction and a graph building phase. Our prototype demonstrated the viability of the approach, particularly if the messages in the log sources do not require frequent relearning of the extraction templates. Configurability and extensibility were key design goals in the development of SLOGERT. For arbitrary log data with unstructured messages in a given log domain, the framework generates a keyword-annotated RDF representation. The demonstrated configuration covers standard concepts for various log sources relevant in a cybersecurity context, however, they can easily be adapted for different log domains.

An inherent limitation evident from our experiments was a sensitivity to the training data set during template extraction; specifically, entities can not be properly identified if there is too little variation in the variable parts of a given log message. This limitation can be tackled through larger log collections, ideally through a community effort towards creating a shared library of extraction templates for standard log data sources.[18] More broadly, we also envisage a community-based effort to develop mappings, extensions for specific log sources,

---

[18] Note that the template representation in RDF simplifies sharing.

and shared domain knowledge such as vulnerability information and threat intelligence.

Due to the widespread use of unstructured log data in numerous domains and the limitations of existing analytic processes, we expect strong adoption potential for SLOGERT, which in turn could also drive adoption of Semantic Web technologies in log analytics more generally. Furthermore, we also expect impulses for KG research and takeup by KG builders that need to integrate log data into their graphs.

In our own research, we will apply the proposed approach in the context of semantic security analytics[19]. Our immediate future work will focus on the integration into logging infrastructures, e.g., by supporting additional formats and protocols. Furthermore, we will focus on graph management for template evolution and incremental updating of log KGs.

Conceptually, our bottom-up extraction approach provides a foundation for future work on linking it to higher-level conceptualizations of specific log domains (e.g., based on DMTF's CIM [9] or the CADF [8] event model). Potentially, this can also provide a foundation for research into event abstraction, i.e., automatically transforming a sequence of individual log events into higher-level composite events or log-based anomaly detection, e.g., through combinations of rule-based methods and relational learning and KG embedding techniques.

References

1. pOTTR: Reasonable Ontology Templates Primer. https://primer.ottr.xyz/
2. Textual Conv. for Syslog Management. https://tools.ietf.org/html/rfc5427
3. van der Aalst, W.M.P.: Process Mining. Springer, Heidelberg (2011). https://doi.org/10.1007/978-3-642-19345-3
4. Bao, L., Busany, N., Lo, D., Maoz, S.: Statistical log differencing. In: 34th IEEE/ACM International Conference on Automated Software Engineering, pp. 851–862 (2019)
5. Chang, A.X., Manning, C.D.: TokensRegex: defining cascaded regular expressions over tokens. Technical report, CSTR 2014–02, Dep. of CS, Stanford University (2014)
6. Cui, W., et al.: REPT: reverse debugging of failures in deployed software. In: 12th USENIX Conference on OS Design and Implementation, pp. 17–32. USENIX Association (2018)
7. Djidjev, H., Sandine, G., Storlie, C.: Graph based statistical analysis of network traffic. In: 9th Workshop on Mining and Learning with Graphs, p. 8 (2011)
8. DMTF: Cloud Audit. Data Federation. https://www.dmtf.org/standards/cadf
9. DMTF: Common Information Model. https://www.dmtf.org/standards/cim
10. Donato, D.: Graph structures and algorithms for query-log analysis. In: Ferreira, F., Löwe, B., Mayordomo, E., Mendes Gomes, L. (eds.) CiE 2010. LNCS, vol. 6158, pp. 126–131. Springer, Heidelberg (2010). https://doi.org/10.1007/978-3-642-13962-8_14
11. Du, M., Li, F., Zheng, G., Srikumar, V.: DeepLog: anomaly detection and diagnosis from system logs through deep learning. In: 2017 ACM SIGSAC Conference on Computer and Communications Security, pp. 1285–1298. ACM (2017)

---

[19] https://w3id.org/sepses.

12. Ekelhart, A., Ekaputra, F.J., Kiesling, E.: Automated knowledge graph construction from raw log data. In: Proceedings of the ISWC 2020 Demos and Industry Tracks, vol. 2721, p. 5. CEUR (2020). http://ceur-ws.org/Vol-2721/paper552.pdf
13. Ekelhart, A., Kiesling, E., Kurniawan, K.: Taming the logs - vocabularies for semantic security analysis. Procedia Comp. Sci. **137**, 109–119 (2018)
14. Garijo, D.: WIDOCO: a wizard for documenting ontologies. In: d'Amato, C., et al. (eds.) ISWC 2017. LNCS, vol. 10588, pp. 94–102. Springer, Cham (2017). https://doi.org/10.1007/978-3-319-68204-4_9
15. He, P., Zhu, J., He, S., Li, J., Lyu, M.R.: An evaluation study on log parsing and its use in log mining. In: 2016 46th Annual IEEE/IFIP International Conference on Dependable Systems and Networks (DSN), pp. 654–661. IEEE (2016)
16. He, S., Zhu, J., He, P., Lyu, M.R.: Experience report: system log analysis for anomaly detection. In: 2016 IEEE 27th International Symposium on Software Reliability Engineering (ISSRE), pp. 207–218. IEEE (2016)
17. Hussain, T., Asghar, S., Masood, N.: Web usage mining: a survey on preprocessing of web log file. In: 2010 Internationl Conference on Information and Emerging Technologies, pp. 1–6. IEEE (2010)
18. IETF: RFC4765. https://www.ietf.org/rfc/rfc4765.txt
19. Jayathilake, D.: Towards structured log analysis. In: 2012 9th International Conference on Computer Science and Software Engineering (JCSSE), pp. 259–264. IEEE (2012)
20. Jia, Y., Qi, Y., Shang, H., Jiang, R., Li, A.: A practical approach to constructing a knowledge graph for cybersecurity. Engineering **4**(1), 53–60 (2018)
21. Kent, K., Souppaya, M.P.: Guide to comp. security log management. Technical report. NIST SP 800–92, National Institute of Standards and Technology (2006)
22. Kent, K., Souppaya, M.P.: Sp 800–92. guide to computer security log management. Technical report, Gaithersburg, MD, USA (2006)
23. Khan, S., et al.: Cloud log forensics: foundations, state of the art, and future directions. ACM Comput. Surv. **49**(1), 1–42 (2016)
24. Kiesling, E., Ekelhart, A., Kurniawan, K., Ekaputra, F.: The SEPSES knowledge graph: an integrated resource for cybersecurity. In: Ghidini, C., et al. (eds.) ISWC 2019. LNCS, vol. 11779, pp. 198–214. Springer, Cham (2019). https://doi.org/10.1007/978-3-030-30796-7_13
25. Kirrane, S., et al.: A scalable consent, transparency and compliance architecture. In: Gangemi, A., et al. (eds.) ESWC 2018. LNCS, vol. 11155, pp. 131–136. Springer, Cham (2018). https://doi.org/10.1007/978-3-319-98192-5_25
26. Kurniawan, K., Ekelhart, A., Kiesling, E., Froschl, A., Ekaputra, F.: Semantic integration and monitoring of file system activity. In: 2019 SEMANTiCS Conference, p. 5 (2019)
27. Landauer, M., Skopik, F., Wurzenberger, M., Hotwagner, W., Rauber, A.: AIT log data set v1.1 (November 2020). https://doi.org/10.5281/zenodo.4264796
28. Meng, W., et al.: LogAnomaly: unsupervised detection of sequential and quantitative anomalies in unstructured logs. In: 28th International Joint Conference on Artificial Intelligence, pp. 4739–4745 (2019)
29. MITRE: Common Event Expression. https://cee.mitre.org
30. Neelima, G., Rodda, S.: Predicting user behavior through sessions using the web log mining. In: 2016 International Conference on Advances in Human Machine Interaction (HMI), pp. 1–5. IEEE (2016)
31. Nimbalkar, P., Mulwad, V., Puranik, N., Joshi, A., Finin, T.: Semantic interpretation of structured log files. In: 2016 IEEE 17th International Conference on Information Reuse and Integration (IRI), pp. 549–555. IEEE (2016)

32. Noel, S., Harley, E., Tam, K., Limiero, M., Share, M.: CyGraph. In: Handbook of Statistics, vol. 35, pp. 117–167. Elsevier (2016)
33. Noy, N.F., McGuinness, D.L., et al.: Ontology development 101: a guide to creating your first ontology (2001)
34. Oliner, A., Ganapathi, A., Xu, W.: Advances and challenges in log analysis. Commun. ACM **55**(2), 55–61 (2012)
35. Pan, S., Morris, T., Adhikari, U.: Developing a hybrid intrusion detection system using data mining for power systems. IEEE Transa. Smart Grid **6**(6), 3104–3113 (2015)
36. Pei, K., et al.: HERCULE: attack story reconstruction via community discovery on correlated log graph. In: 32nd Annual Conference on Computer Security Applications, ACSAC 2016, pp. 583–595. ACM Press (2016)
37. Pingle, A., Piplai, A., Mittal, S., Joshi, A., Holt, J., Zak, R.: RelExt: relation extraction using deep learning approaches for cybersecurity knowledge graph improvement. arXiv:1905.02497 [cs] (2019)
38. Raftopoulos, E., Egli, M., Dimitropoulos, X.: Shedding light on log correlation in network forensics analysis. In: Flegel, U., Markatos, E., Robertson, W. (eds.) DIMVA 2012. LNCS, vol. 7591, pp. 232–241. Springer, Heidelberg (2013). https://doi.org/10.1007/978-3-642-37300-8_14
39. Reuben, J., Martucci, L.A., Fischer-Hübner, S.: Automated log audits for privacy compliance validation: a literature survey. In: Aspinall, D., Camenisch, J., Hansen, M., Fischer-Hübner, S., Raab, C. (eds.) Privacy and Identity 2015. IAICT, vol. 476, pp. 312–326. Springer, Cham (2016). https://doi.org/10.1007/978-3-319-41763-9_21
40. Sipos, R., Fradkin, D., Moerchen, F., Wang, Z.: Log-based predictive maintenance. In: 20th ACM SIGKDD International Conference on Knowledge Discovery and Data Mining, KDD 2014, pp. 1867–1876. ACM Press (2014)
41. Svacina, J., et al.: On vulnerability and security log analysis: a systematic literature review on recent trends. In: Proceedings of the International Conference on Research in Adaptive and Convergent Systems, RACS 2020, pp. 175–180. ACM, New York (2020)
42. Tang, L., Li, T., Perng, C.S.: LogSig: generating system events from raw textual logs. In: 20th ACM International Conference on Information and Knowledge Management, CIKM 2011, p. 785. ACM Press (2011)
43. Wang, W., Daniels, T.E.: A graph based approach toward network forensics analysis. ACM Trans. Inf. Sys. Sec. **12**(1), 412–433 (2008)
44. Yuan, D., Mai, H., Xiong, W., Tan, L., Zhou, Y., Pasupathy, S.: SherLog: error diagnosis by connecting clues from run-time logs. ACM SIGPLAN Not. **45**(3), 143 (2010)
45. Zhang, J., Jie, L., Rahman, A., Xie, S., Chang, Y., Yu, P.S.: Learning entity types from query logs via graph-based modeling. In: 24th ACM International on Conference on Information and Knowledge Management, CIKM 2015, pp. 603–612. Association for Computing Machinery (2015)
46. Zhu, J., et al.: Tools and benchmarks for automated log parsing. In: 2019 IEEE/ACM 41st International Conference on Software Engineering: Software Engineering in Practice (ICSE-SEIP), pp. 121–130. IEEE (2019)

P2P-O: A Purchase-To-Pay Ontology for Enabling Semantic Invoices

Michael Schulze[1,2,3](✉), Markus Schröder[1,2], Christian Jilek[1,2],
Torsten Albers[3], Heiko Maus[2], and Andreas Dengel[1,2]

[1] Department of Computer Science, Technische Universität Kaiserslautern,
Kaiserslautern, Germany
{michael.schulze,markus.schroder,christian.jilek,andreas.dengel}@dfki.de
[2] Smart Data and Knowledge Services Department, Deutsches Forschungszentrum
für Künstliche Intelligenz GmbH (DFKI), Kaiserslautern, Germany
heiko.maus@dfki.de
[3] Development Department, b4value.net GmbH, Kaiserslautern, Germany
torsten.albers@b4value.net

Abstract. Small and medium-sized enterprises increasingly adopt electronic invoices and digitized purchase-to-pay processes. A purchase-to-pay process begins with making a purchase order and ends with completing the payment process. Even when organizations adopt electronic invoices, knowledge work in such processes is characterized by assimilating information distributed over heterogeneous sources among different stages in the process. By integrating such information and enabling a shared understanding of stakeholders in such processes, ontologies and knowledge graphs can serve as an appropriate infrastructure for enabling knowledge services. However, no suitable ontology is available for current electronic invoices and digitized purchase-to-pay processes. Therefore, this paper presents P2P-O, a dedicated purchase-to-pay ontology developed in cooperation with industry domain experts. P2P-O enables organizations to create semantic invoices, which are invoices following linked data principles. The European Standard EN 16931-1:2017 for electronic invoices was the main non-ontological resource for developing P2P-O. The evaluation approach is threefold: (1) to follow ontology engineering best practices, we applied OOPS! (OntOlogy Pitfall Scanner!) and OntoDebug; (2) to evaluate competency questions, we constructed a purchase-to-pay knowledge graph with RML technologies and executed corresponding SPARQL queries; (3) to illustrate a P2P-O-based knowledge service and use case, we implemented an invoicing dashboard within a corporate memory system and thus enabled an entity-centric view on invoice data. Organizations can immediately start experimenting with P2P-O by generating semantic invoices with provided RML mappings.

Keywords: Semantic invoice · E-procurement · Purchase-to-pay process · Enterprise knowledge graph · Corporate memory · RML

© Springer Nature Switzerland AG 2021
R. Verborgh et al. (Eds.): ESWC 2021, LNCS 12731, pp. 647–663, 2021.
https://doi.org/10.1007/978-3-030-77385-4_39

1   Introduction

Small and medium-sized enterprises (SMEs) increasingly adopt electronic invoices and move towards digitizing their purchase-to-pay processes. A purchase-to-pay or procure-to-pay process begins with making a purchase order and ends with completing the payment process [19]. In such processes, invoice processing is an ubiquitous task [19]. This requires besides information on invoices, also information on other documents, such as delivery notes, credit notes or reports on service provisions. Also frequently needed is background information from various data collections, such as suppliers, product catalogs or purchase-to-pay policies. Therefore, this kind of knowledge work is characterized by searching and assimilating information distributed over heterogeneous sources among different stages in the process. Jain and Woodcock [19] estimate that 21% of tasks in the field of invoice processing will be hard to process automatically. Consequently, even when SMEs adopt electronic invoices, human effort in purchase-to-pay processes will continue to be essential.

To assist knowledge workers in such digitized purchase-to-pay processes, knowledge graphs [9] can serve as an appropriate infrastructure for enabling knowledge services by integrating distributed and heterogeneous information from document-based and other data sources. We envision a personal "information butler" [6], who is able to proactively deliver pertinent information depending on a given work context [21]. In purchase-to-pay processes, this context might be a task involving verification of a corrective invoice based on an initial invoice, a purchase order and reports on service provisions. Having a purchase-to-pay knowledge graph also enables the integration into a knowledge description layer of a corporate memory [1]. This provides an appropriate infrastructure for knowledge services embedded into the office environment of daily work [24].

In line with the definition of a knowledge graph suggested by Ehrlinger and Wöß [9], we see an ontology as an inherent part of a knowledge graph. However, to the best of our knowledge, there is no purchase-to-pay ontology available suiting our requirements and goals. These are as follows: describing and interrelating information on current electronic invoices, relating invoices to a corresponding purchase-to-pay process and adhering to industry standards. Related and established ontologies in the field, such as the Financial Industry Business Ontology (FIBO) [3] or the GoodRelations Ontology [17], have a different focus and thus do not provide sufficient vocabulary to meet these requirements. Therefore, this paper presents P2P-O, a dedicated purchase-to-pay ontology.

P2P-O is developed in cooperation with industry domain experts and aligned with the core invoice model of the European Standard EN 16931-1:2017 (EN16931) [10]. Thus, electronic invoices can be upgraded to semantic invoices, which we define as invoices following linked data principles. Besides enabling knowledge services, semantic invoices also enable new kinds of queries. This is evident in the case of incorporating linked open data[1] in federated queries, thus allowing SMEs, for example, to filter which of their products are sold in cities

---

[1] https://www.lod-cloud.net/.

with more than 50 000 inhabitants. Adoption of e-invoices is also associated with positive social and financial consequences. It is estimated that the adoption saves one million metric tons of $CO2$ emissions a year[2]. Also, it helps with reducing the VAT gap resulted from tax fraud and tax evasion [22]. Financial resources that could be freed up for society. Additionally, it is estimated that in the European Union the adoption can save up to 0.8% of the gross domestic product (GDP) [4,10]. This is in particular due to resulted process efficiency [10]. By providing added value and incentives in form of semantic knowledge services, we also aim to increase adoption rates, especially those from SMEs because their rate is only half the rate of big enterprises (22%) (See Footnote 2).

The rest of the paper is structured as follows. The next section introduces purchase-to-pay processes and the European Standard EN16931 [10] as the main non-ontological reused resource. Section 3 presents the ontology and describes the developing and modeling process. Section 4 elaborates on the evaluation approach and on an example use case, and Sect. 5 covers related resources. We conclude with Sect. 6 and provide an outlook on future work.

2   Foundations

2.1   Purchase-To-Pay Processes and Electronic Invoices

The BPMN[3] diagram in Fig. 1 depicts a simple instance of a purchase-to-pay process that starts with the sending of a purchase order from the buyer to the seller. After delivering the requested goods or providing the services, the seller sends an electronic invoice to the buyer. In the case of the process in Fig. 1, a dispute is depicted and thus, finally, a credit note sent to the buyer. Because P2P-O's focus is on electronic documents in such purchase-to-pay processes, Fig. 1 leaves out the actual payments made by the participants as well as the physical exchange of goods.

In practice, purchase-to-pay processes can take on more diverse and complex forms. For instance, instead of sporadic purchase orders (Fig. 1), processes can be periodic based on a contract. Also, despatch and receiving advice documents or service provision documents can be part of purchase-to-pay processes. For a more detailed overview, we kindly refer the reader to the European Standard EN-16931 [10]. In addition, with respect to the participants in purchase-to-pay processes, buyer, seller, receiver, payee and the respective taxable persons do not necessarily have to be the same [10]. Summarizing, purchase-to-pay processes are characterized by numerous heterogeneous documents, especially in SMEs where ERP Systems are often missing, as well as by diverging processes.

---

[2] https://eur-lex.europa.eu/LexUriServ/LexUriServ.do?uri=COM:2010:0712:FIN:en: PDF.

[3] https://www.omg.org/spec/BPMN/2.0/.

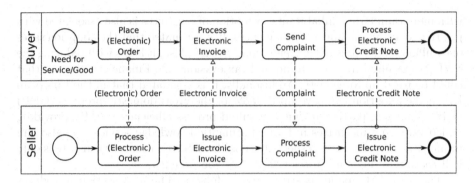

Fig. 1. BPMN diagram of a simplified purchase-to-pay process with a dispute

2.2   The Core Invoice Model in EN 16931-1:2017

In the European Standard EN 16931-1:2017 [10], the CEN-CENELEC Management Centre introduces the *core invoice model*. We reused this standard because of its general approach: the model specifies 161 core information elements for electronic invoices that are sufficient for most transactions. Examples for information elements are the invoice number or the buyer name. In transactions where the core invoice model is not sufficient, it can be extended.

In the *core invoice model* [10], information elements are organized hierarchically at different levels. On the first level (document level), some elements are not further divided (e.g. the invoice number). Higher levels can group further information elements together. For example, information elements with respect to the seller are grouped at the second level (e.g. seller name) and they can be further divided to a third level (e.g. seller postal address). Information elements in EN16931 are depicted in a tabular form with the following columns:

ID: identifier, e.g. BT-1 for the information element "invoice number"
Level: level of the information element, e.g. + for the first level
Cardinality: cardinality of the information element, e.g. 1..n
Business Term: name, e.g. "invoice number"
Description: further details about the information element
Usage Note: notes about the practical usage of the information element
Requirement ID: the particular requirement specified in EN16931 which is addressed by the information element, e.g. R56
Semantic Data Type: data type, e.g. Text, Identifier or Code

This list will be referred when the modeling process in Sect. 3.2 is covered. E-invoices cannot be considered in isolation from the respective purchase-to-pay process as its context. Therefore, EN16931 specifies 12 kinds of purchase-to-pay processes that are supported by the invoice model without any extensions. [10]

Table 1. Excerpt of competency questions for P2P-O.

Identifier	Competency question
C1	What is the reference number of an invoice?
C2	What is the total amount without value added tax of an invoice?
C3	Who is the seller on an invoice?
C4	Who is the buyer on an invoice?
C5	What are items listed on the invoice?
C6	What is the address of the buyer?
C7	To what price and quantity was an item on an invoice purchased?
C8	What are attributes of an item on an invoice?
C9	Which organizations purchased an item?
C10	Which organizations sold an item?
C11	To what sort of purchase-to-pay processes does a document belong to?
C12	What are the documents in a purchase-to-pay process?
C13	Which items on invoices have the colors red and blue?
C14	To which addresses an organization ordered an item?
C15	Which and how many items an organization sold in cities with more than 50 000 inhabitants?

3   P2P-O: The Purchase-To-Pay Ontology

3.1   Methodology of the Developing Process

Because EN16931 [10] was the main non-ontological resource for developing P2P-O, we followed the NeOn methodology [32] since it provides established guidelines for this exact scenario. Additionally, we incorporated advice from Grüninger and Fox [15], Hitzler et al. [18] and McDaniel and Storey [25]. For publishing P2P-O, we followed FAIR principles [33]. The iterative process for developing P2P-O is depicted in Fig. 2. At first, we specified requirements, scope and competency questions together with domain experts from the TRAFFIQX network[4] (examples in Table 1). The set of competency questions has been derived from the requirement specification in EN16931 [10] and has been then enriched. Classes and properties for potential use have subsequently been derived from EN16931 [10] until a conceptual model was achieved. Lessons learned from conversations with experts were, for example, which elements on invoices are frequently used and how P2P-O needs to be designed to allow for common extensions.

To reuse ontologies and to incorporate them into P2P-O, we applied, in addition to guidelines in the NeOn methodology [32], the validation process for ontologies suggested by McDaniel and Storey [25]. Accordingly, we verified the adequacy of ontologies based on our requirements, and we assessed them by means of OOPS! (OntOlogy Pitfall Scanner!) [29] and OntoDebug [31]. These tools have also been employed for P2P-O's evaluation.

---

[4] https://www.traffiqx.net/en/about-us.

3.2   General Modeling Process

This section describes the general modeling process with the *core invoice model* [10] as its basis. More detailed modeling aspects are addressed in the respective ontology modules in Sect. 3.3. Each column of the core invoice model (Sect. 2.2) has been implemented as follows. For the ID of information elements, we introduced the annotation property *seeEN16931-1-2017* so that resources in P2P-O are linked to information elements in EN16931 [10]. This way, it is also possible to query these elements to see how they are modeled in P2P-O. As a result, modeling decisions can be traced from the original invoice model to the ontology and backwards. For the "Business Term" in EN16931 [10], *rdfs:label* is used and for the "Description"-column *rdfs:comment*. Usage Notes, however, are modeled with the annotation property *usage note* from FIBO [3]. Cardinality statements were encoded with OWL class restrictions. For the data type *Text* in EN16931 [10], `xsd:string` was used. This was also used for the type *Code* because it only consists of one text field [10]. However, for the identifier datatype in EN16931 also information regarding the identifier scheme and its version is needed [10]. Therefore, we modeled it as a dedicated class *Identifier* rather than as a property like in Schema.org [16] or DCMI Metadata Terms [5].

3.3   Ontology Description

P2P-O comprises seven modules, 54 classes, 169 properties and 1438 axioms. Table 2 summarizes reused ontologies and vocabularies. An important requirement for reusing ontologies was that a permissive license has been specified. To not clutter P2P-O, only selected statements are reused instead of importing entire ontologies. This was especially problematic in the case of FIBO [3] due to long import chains. Figure 3 illustrates an excerpt of P2P-O's schema which will be referred at appropriate places in the following remarks on the various modules.

Table 2. Reused ontologies and vocabularies in P2P-O.

Prefix	Namespace	Source
vcard	http://www.w3.org/2006/vcard/ns#Address	[42]
fibo-fnd-	https://spec.edmcouncil.org/fibo/ontology/FND/.	[3]
omg	https://www.omg.org/spec/LCC/Countries/CountryRepresentation/	[28]
foaf	http://xmlns.com/foaf/0.1/	[34]
org	http://www.w3.org/ns/org#	[41]
xsd	http://www.w3.org/2001/XMLSchema	[37]
ontodebug	http://ainf.aau.at/ontodebug#	[31]
skos	http://www.w3.org/2004/02/skos/core#	[35]
dcterms	http://purl.org/dc/terms	[5]
owl	http://www.w3.org/2002/07/owl#	[36]
rdf	http://www.w3.org/1999/02/22-rdf-syntax-ns#	[39]
rdfs	http://www.w3.org/2000/01/rdf-schema#	[40]

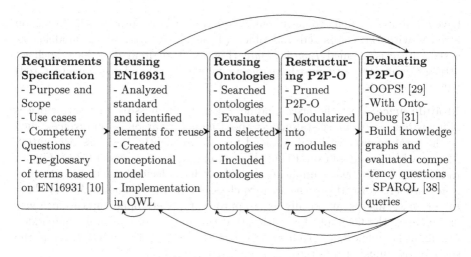

Requirements Specification	Reusing EN16931	Reusing Ontologies	Restructur-ing P2P-O	Evaluating P2P-O
- Purpose and Scope - Use cases - Competeny Questions - Pre-glossary of terms based on EN16931 [10]	- Analyzed standard and identified elements for reuse - Created conceptional model - Implementation in OWL	- Searched ontologies - Evaluated and selected ontologies - Included ontologies	- Pruned P2P-O - Modularized into 7 modules	-OOPS! [29] -With Onto-Debug [31] -Build knowledge graphs and evaluated compe-tency questions - SPARQL [38] queries

Fig. 2. Methodology for developing P2P-O based on the NeOn methodology [32]

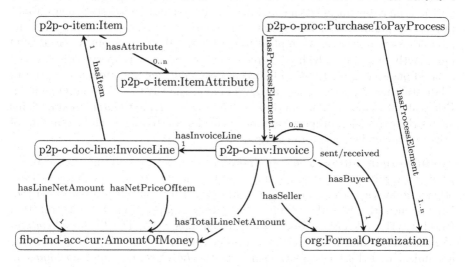

Fig. 3. Excerpt of classes and their relationships in P2P-O. *AmountOfMoney* [3] and *FormalOrganization* [41] are reused.

Module *item*. The *item* module allows the description of specific items or products listed on invoices. The term "item" not only refers to a specific traded product, for example a printer, but to anything that can be listed on invoices, for example a working hour. In the purchase-to-pay domain, the term "item" is according to domain experts and EN16931 [10] the preferable one opposed to the term "product". However, the term "product" is also commonly used interchangeably and therefore included as a synonym for item. According to EN16931 [10], it is only required for an item to have a name, but it can optionally have attributes as well. To easily enable queries such as "retrieve all leitems on invoices with the colors red and blue" (Table 1), an attribute is modeled as a separate class named *ItemAttribute* (Fig. 3). If an item does have such an attribute, this attribute must have one name (e.g. color) and one value (e.g. red) [10].

Module *price*. With the *price* module, it is not only possible to describe prices of items but also to make statements about monetary amounts on invoices, such as the total amount with value added tax. Consequently, the class *AmountOf-Money*, which is reused from FIBO [3], is extensively used across P2P-O (Fig. 3). In contrast to EN16931's implications [10], we have decided not to link the *currency*-property directly to the *Invoice*-class but to the *AmountOfMoney*-class. In our view, this is semantically more appropriate, opens opportunities for reuse and includes the flexibility for stating that the amount of the total value added tax might be in another currency. All other instances of *AmountOfMoney* in the same invoice must still link to the same currency [10].

Module *documentline*. The *documentline* module is responsible for lines or positions on a document. As a core function, it enables to make statements about prices and quantities of items listed on documents. Therefore, it imports the modules *item* and *price*. As implied by EN16931 [10], a document line in P2P-O has exactly one item, which is expressed by the *hasItem*-property (Fig. 3). The assured one-to-one relationship between *DocumentLine* and *Item* is essential to relate statements on document line level unambiguously to a corresponding item. Prices about items are made in this module rather than in the *item* module. This allows the expression of more than one price for an item and the traceability of prices to the context of a transaction.

Module *organization*. The *organization* module is for describing organizations participating in purchase-to-pay processes. It heavily reuses vocabularies from other ontologies because adequate solutions for our purposes already existed. For instance, this module includes *FormalOrganization* from The Organization Ontology [41] and *Address* from the vCard Ontology [42]. The *BusinessRelationship*-class is intended to describe a dyadic business relationship. Organizations are linked to a business relationship via the *hasCustomer*- and *hasSupplier*-property. *BusinessRelationship* is not implied by EN16931 [10] but introduced in P2P-O. It is useful to make statements about typical characteristics of a business relationship, such as customer or supplier numbers. These are indeed specified by EN16931 but on the document level [10].

Module *document*. The *document* module provides classes and properties that are essential for purchase-to-pay documents in general. For more granular vocabulary regarding invoices, which are special kinds of documents, we created a separate module. A document could have been sent or received by an organization. In P2P-O this is expressed by the properties *sent* and *received*. Because information about organizations is needed, the *organization* module is imported. Cross-references between documents can be expressed by using the *references* object property.

Module *invoice*. Because of the focus of P2P-O on invoices, the *invoice* module is the largest sub-module. It imports the modules *document* and *documentline* directly and therefore all other previously introduced modules indirectly as well. It extends the taxonomy of the *document* module and provides more granular vocabulary for kinds of invoices such as *E-FinalInvoice* and *E-PartialInvoice*. To distinguish credit notes from ordinary invoices, *E-CreditNote* and *E-CommercialInvoice* are made disjoint. Therefore, for ordinary invoices, we recommend to use the class *E-CommercialInvoice* instead of the class *E-Invoice*.

Furthermore, this module implements all constraints an invoice must satisfy according to EN16931 [10]. For instance, it must have exactly one seller and one buyer. Particular total amounts are mandatory, like the amounts with and without value added tax. Not mandatory information, such as the allowance amount, are provided as well. An invoice also needs to have at least one instance of the class *InvoiceLine* (Fig. 3), which is modeled as a subclass of *DocumentLine*. In P2P-O this is expressed by the *hasInvoiceLine*-property. Information on invoice line level can be thus related unambiguously to information on invoice level, such as the seller and buyer.

Module *process*. According to process requirements in EN16931 [10], the *process* module provides classes for describing specific kinds of purchase-to-pay processes. These are, for instance, a process in which invoiced items are purchased periodically or the payment amount due is paid in advance. These classes are not modeled as disjoint to each other because an instance of a purchase-to-pay process might fit more than those classes [10]. For example, a process may include both, a paying upfront and a corrective invoicing process. Documents and purchase-to-pay processes are linked via the *hasProcessElement*-property and the inverse property *isProcessElementIn* (Fig. 3). With the properties *followsDocument* and *precedesDocument*, it is further possible to express that a document precedes or follows another document in a process.

3.4 Availability and Maintenance

P2P-O is available at https://purl.org/p2p-o and its accompanying resources at https://purl.org/p2p-o#res. For publishing and documenting the ontology, we used WIDOCO [12] to stick to open standards and best practices. Also, resources for building knowledge graphs with P2P-O are made available (e.g. RML mappings [7]) as well as an invoice generator for test and evaluation purposes. Because P2P-O should be easily reusable and adoptable by organizations, the ontology is published under a business friendly permissive license.

Every module of P2P-O has its own version number. When a module becomes backwards incompatible, which we try to avoid, it will be annotated accordingly. The ontology is maintained by a focus group composed of researchers at DFKI[5] and domain experts from the TRAFFIQX[6] network. In monthly meetings, P2P-O related topics, issues and applications are discussed. Because of this

---

[5] https://comem.ai.

[6] https://www.traffiqx.net/en/about-us.

research-industry cooperation, P2P-O and its accompanying resources aim to contribute to the adoption of semantic web technologies, especially the adoption in SMEs by considering their particular challenges.

3.5 Reusability

Because P2P-O is grounded in the core invoice model of EN16931 [10], it is designed to cover the most common purchase-to-pay processes and invoices, and it is also extendable to more specific information needs. This is essential because information needs in the purchase-to-pay domain can vary depending on the concrete application scenario. For instance, in the manufacturing sector, detailed information on invoiced products is valuable, whereas in the service sector, information in supporting documents of an invoice is more important.

Whereas in the presented use case in Sect. 4.3 only a small subset of purchase-to-pay documents in the TRAFFIQX network have been lifted up to linked data, the transaction volume alone in this network amounts to 40 million per year. Globally, according to Billentis [22], 55 billion e-invoices have been processed in 2019 and the tendency is rising. Noteworthy, P2P-O not only covers e-invoices but also related documents in respective purchase-to-pay processes. For easier reuse, P2P-O is modularized and documented with WIDOCO [12].

4 Evaluation and Use Case

4.1 Evaluation Based on Ontology Evaluation Tools

To ensure that P2P-O is aligned with current ontology engineering standards, it was iteratively tested against best practices formulated by OOPS! (OntOlogy Pitfall Scanner!) [29]. This tool was in particular valuable for identifying issues concerning modeling inverse relationships and providing a license. To ensure that P2P-O is correct and consistent even when users extend it, the OntoDebug [31] plugin in Protégé [26] was used to annotate test cases and to debug P2P-O.

4.2 Evaluation by Constructing and Querying a Purchase-To-Pay Knowledge Graph

On the one hand, we evaluated P2P-O with real-world invoices from the TRAF-FIQX network (see Sect. 4.3), which may not be published. On the other hand, to provide a publicly available data set, we evaluated P2P-O with generated test-invoices from our invoice-generator. With this generator it is possible to produce invoices and credit notes in different syntaxes, such as UBL v2.1[7]. These invoices are inspired by the real ones and are in XML.

---

[7] https://www.iso.org/standard/66370.html.

To construct purchase-to-pay knowledge graphs for evaluating competency questions (Sect. 3.1), we created tailored RML mappings [7] with the use of the CARML extension[8]. It was additionally used because of its ability to deal with namespaces. Thus, we transformed heterogeneous XML-based invoices into semantic invoices. With provided RML mappings, organizations can immediately start experimenting with P2P-O and building purchase-to-pay knowledge graphs. Figure 4 illustrates a part of a constructed knowledge graph in GraphDB[9]. Shown is an excerpt of two invoices (0815-9923-1-a, 08315-93229-1-a) and their relations to each other. Our RML mappings only assert that, for instance, an invoice line has an item; but because of enabled inference, the inverse property *isItemOf* is also available to traverse and query the knowledge graph. To evaluate competency questions (Table 1), we executed respective SPARQL [38] queries. Listing 1.1 illustrates the federated query for retrieving items sold in cities with more than 50 000 inhabitants (competency question C15 in Table 1).

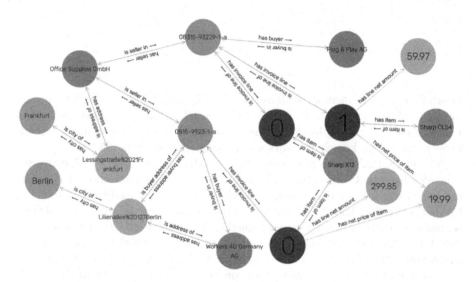

Fig. 4. Screenshot of two synthetic sample invoices in a purchase-to-pay knowledge graph in GraphDB (https://www.ontotext.com/products/graphdb/).

4.3 Use Case: Applying P2P-O in a Corporate Memory System

After applying artificially generated invoices (Sect. 4.2), we employed real-world invoices from the TRAFFIQX network. This network utilizes an internal intermediate format for their invoices which we exploited to convert 2000 of them into semantic invoices. This enabled the use within a knowledge description

---

[8] https://github.com/carml/carml.

[9] https://www.ontotext.com/products/graphdb/.

Listing 1.1. Federated SPARQL [38] query for items sold in cities with more than 50 000 inhabitants by using P2P-O's vocabulary and DBpedia [2].

```
PREFIX p2po-inv: <https://purl.org/p2p-o/invoice#>
PREFIX p2po-line: <https://purl.org/p2p-o/documentline#>
PREFIX p2po-org: <https://purl.org/p2p-o/organization#>
PREFIX rdf: <http://www.w3.org/1999/02/22-rdf-syntax-ns#>
PREFIX rdfs: <http://www.w3.org/2000/01/rdf-schema#>
PREFIX dbo: <http://dbpedia.org/ontology/>
select * where {
<https://comem.ai/org/Office%20Supplies%20GmbH> p2po-inv:isSellerIn
?inv.
?inv p2po-inv:hasBuyerAddress ?buyerAddress ;
     p2po-inv:hasInvoiceLine ?invLine .
?invLine p2po-line:hasItem ?item ;
         p2po-line:lineInvoicedQuantity ?qty ;
         p2po-line:hasLineNetAmount ?lineNetAmount .
?item rdfs:label ?itemLabel .
?lineNetAmount rdfs:label ?amountLabel .
?buyerAddress p2po-org:hasCity ?city .
?city rdfs:label ?cityLabel .
SERVICE <http://dbpedia.org/sparql> {
?dbCity a ?dbO ;
        rdfs:label ?cityLabel .
?dbCity dbo:populationTotal ?population .
FILTER ((?dbO = dbo:City || ?dbO = dbo:PopulatedPlace ) &&
?population > 50000) }}
```

layer of a corporate memory such as the DFKI CoMem[10]. CoMem is a corporate memory infrastructure realizing knowledge-based services using enterprise and personal knowledge graphs. With the Semantic Desktop ecosystem, it embeds these services into knowledge workers' working environments [23,24].

Therefore, P2P-O was published in the CoMem ontology server. A converter was added to the CoMem semantification service which then allowed populating knowledge graphs in CoMem's knowledge base. This enabled the usage of CoMem's existing knowledge services, such as proactive information delivery, semantic search, or ontology-based named entity recognition [20]. Thus, as a use case for a P2P-O-based knowledge service, we implemented a context-specific dashboard within CoMem. With widgets, the user can now grasp context-specific information of an entity, such as items on an invoice (Fig. 5). From those widgets, a user can browse to other resources to see the knowledge space from those resources with other respective context-specific widgets.

---

[10] https://comem.ai.

4181698507 - Invoice Overvi...		4181698507 - Process Context			Invoice Lines			
Reference Number	4181698507	Purchase Order	4171622070	12.03.2018				
Sender	BusinessStore Germany GmbH	Credit Note	5091249651	14.04.2018	Search			
Receiver	HOT + COLD Germany GmbH				Position ↑	Article	Anzahl	Article Price
Invoice Date	22.03.2018				1	Buerofix 5678	2	0,18
Delivery Date	22.03.2018				2	HP Laser Jet HX Toner	8	138,0x
Total Invoice Amount	18768,05				3	Logitec DH 455	23	16,04
Total Article Amount	17428,66				4	Beltz Green Wonder	4	0,80
Currency	EUR				5	Flipchart-Plus	10	9,96

Fig. 5. Excerpt from the context-specific dashboard within CoMem with synthetic sample data.

5   Comparison to Related Resources

Semantic technologies in e-procurement, which includes purchase-to-pay processes, are widely recognized for integrating heterogeneous data [30]. In subdomains of e-procurement such as e-awarding [30], ontologies and knowledge services have been successfully applied. For instance, the LOTED2 ontology [8] for tenders. Nečaský et al. [27] present an ontology-based knowledge service for filling out contracts. In purchase-to-pay processes, however, although knowledge work is essential [19], ontology-based knowledge services are largely neglected.

The work of Escobar-Vega et al. [11] addresses semantic invoices in particular. Their approach is to create an ontology out from Mexican electronic invoices with XSL Transformations. Therefore, this approach is rather document-oriented. Resources for creating semantic invoices and the ontology are not publicly available. FIBO [3] is an established ontology in the field of finance with a broad scope. It provides, for instance, vocabulary for loans and investments but not for invoices or purchase-to-pay processes. Likewise, GoodRelations [17] is an established ontology but in the field of e-commerce. It is well-suited to describe offers, products and prices. However, it also does not cover invoice specific vocabulary such as "item" and "invoice line" or a taxonomy for purchase-to-pay documents because this is not in the scope of GoodRelations. The upcoming e-procurement ontology[11] is an endeavor of the European Union towards a uniform vocabulary in the public e-procurement domain. In the current version 2.0.0, the concept of invoice and alike is also missing. Schema.org [16] provides invoiceto related

---

[11] https://github.com/eprocurementontology/eprocurementontology.

vocabulary. P2P-O may be able to extend it with more detailed vocabulary necessary for invoice processing as well as with vocabulary that allows to relate invoices purchase-to-pay processes. Thus, vocabulary is provided that conceives invoices as part of such processes. The Aggregated Invoice Ontology[12], a dedicated invoice ontology, is not accessible and thus not reusable anymore. However, it was constructed for a pharmaceutical case study and shows the merits and the need of shared invoice vocabulary [13,14].

6   Conclusion and Future Work

Owing to the shortcoming of dedicated purchase-to-pay ontologies, P2P-O was presented, a modularized ontology which reuses the core invoice model of the European Standard EN16931 [10]. To evaluate competency questions, a purchase-to-pay knowledge graph with RML [7] technologies has been constructed and corresponding SPARQL [38] queries executed. In contrast to other contributions, we also provided ready-to-use resources to enable organizations to generate semantic invoices. With a context-specific dashboard, a P2P-O-based knowledge service was illustrated. Its assistance allows an entity-centric view on invoice data by browsing a purchase-to-pay knowledge graph. Future research will focus on enhancing this assistance by applying P2P-O in real-time assistance scenarios and by incorporating other purchase-to-pay data such as business e-mails.

Acknowledgements. This work was funded by the Investitions- und Strukturbank Rheinland-Pfalz (ISB) (project InnoProm) and the BMBF project SensAI (grantno. 01IW20007).

References

1. Abecker, A., Bernardi, A., Hinkelmann, K., Kühn, O., Sintek, M.: Toward a technology for organizational memories. IEEE Intell. Syste. **13**, 40–48 (1998)
2. Auer, S., Bizer, C., Kobilarov, G., Lehmann, J., Cyganiak, R., Ives, Z.: DBpedia: a nucleus for a web of open data. In: Abere, K., et al. (eds.) ASWC/ISWC -2007. LNCS, vol. 4825, pp. 722–735. Springer, Heidelberg (2007). https://doi.org/10.1007/978-3-540-76298-0_52
3. Bennett, M.: The financial industry business ontology: best practice for big data. J. Bank. Regu. **14**(3), 255–268 (2013)
4. Capgemini Consulting: Sepa: potential benefits at stake (2007). https://www.cep.eu/fileadmin/user_upload/cep.eu/Analysen_KOM/KOM_2009_471_SEPA/Capgemini-Report_on_SEPA__engl.__.pdf. Accessed 18 Dec 2020
5. DCMI Usage Board: DCMI Metadata Terms (2006). https://www.dublincore.org/specifications/dublin-core/dcmi-terms/2006-12-18/. Accessed 18 Dec 2020
6. Dengel, A., Maus, H.: Personalisierte wissensdienste: das unternehmen denkt mit. IM+io Fachmagazin **3**, 46–49 (2018)

---

[12] http://ontologydesignpatterns.org/wiki/Ontology:Aggregated_Invoice_Ontology.

7. Dimou, A., Sande, M.V., Colpaert, P., Verborgh, R., Mannens, E., de Walle, R.V.: RML: a generic language for integrated RDF mappings of heterogeneous data. In: Proceedings of the Workshop on Linked Data on the Web Co-located with the 23rd International World Wide Web Conference on CEUR Workshop Proceedings, vol. 1184. CEUR-WS.org (2014)
8. Distinto, I., d'Aquin, M., Motta, E.: Loted2: an ontology of European public procurement notices. Semant. Web **7**(3), 267–293 (2016)
9. Ehrlinger, L., Wöß, W.: Towards a definition of knowledge graphs. In: Proceedings of the Posters and Demos Track of the 12th International Conference on Semantic Systems - SEMANTiCS2016. CEUR Workshop Proceedings, vol. 1695. CEUR-WS.org (2016)
10. EN 16931–1:2017: Electronic invoicing - part 1: Semantic data model of the core elements of an electronic invoice. Standard, European Committee for Standardization (2017)
11. Escobar-Vega, L.M., Zaldivar-Carrillo, V., Villalon-Turrubiates, I.: Semantic invoice processing. J. Intell. Fuzzy Syst. **34**, 2913–2922 (2018)
12. Garijo, D.: WIDOCO: a wizard for documenting ontologies. In: d'Amato, C., et al. (eds.) Widoco: a wizard for documenting ontologies, Part II. LNCS, vol. 10588, pp. 94–102. Springer, Cham (2017). https://doi.org/10.1007/978-3-319-68204-4_9
13. Gómez-Pérez, J.M., Méndez, V.: Towards supporting interoperability in e-invoicing based on semantic web technologies. In: Handbook of Research on E-Business Standards and Protocols: Documents, Data and Advanced Web Technologies, pp. 705–724. IGI Global (2012)
14. Gómez-Pérez, J.M., Méndez, V., Candini, J., Muñoz, J.C.: Electronic invoice management in the pharmaceutical sector: the pharmainnova case. In: Suárez-Figueroa, M.C., Gómez-Pérez, A., Motta, E., Gangemi, A. (eds.) Ontology Engineering in a Networked World, pp. 407–422. Springer, Heidelberg (2012). https://doi.org/10.1007/978-3-642-24794-1_19
15. Grüninger, M., Fox, M.S.: The role of competency questions in enterprise engineering. In: Rolstadås, A. (ed.) Benchmarking — Theory and Practice. IAICT, pp. 22–31. Springer, Boston, MA (1995). https://doi.org/10.1007/978-0-387-34847-6_3
16. Guha, R.V., Brickley, D., Macbeth, S.: Schema.org: evolution of structured data on the web. Commun. ACM **59**(2), 44–51 (2016)
17. Hepp, M.: GoodRelations: an ontology for describing products and services offers on the web. In: Gangemi, A., Euzenat, J. (eds.) EKAW 2008. LNCS (LNAI), vol. 5268, pp. 329–346. Springer, Heidelberg (2008). https://doi.org/10.1007/978-3-540-87696-0_29
18. Hitzler, P., Gangemi, A., Janowicz, K., Krisnadhi, A., Presutti, V. (eds.): Ontology Engineering with Ontology Design Patterns - Foundations and Applications, Studies on the Semantic Web, vol. 25. IOS Press (2016)
19. Jain, K., Woodcock, E.: A road map for digitizing source-to-pay (2017). https://www.mckinsey.com/business-functions/operations/our-insights/a-road-map-for-digitizing-source-to-pay. Accessed 18 Dec 2020
20. Jilek, C., Schröder, M., Novik, R., Schwarz, S., Maus, H., Dengel, A.: Inflection-tolerant ontology-based named entity recognition for real-time applications. In: 2nd Conference on Language, Data and Knowledge (LDK 2019), Leipzig, Germany, 20–23 May 2019. OpenAccess Series in Informatics (OASIcs), vol. 70, pp. 11:1–11:14. Schloss Dagstuhl - Leibniz-Zentrum für Informatik (2019)

21. Jilek, C., Schröder, M., Schwarz, S., Maus, H., Dengel, A.: Context spaces as the cornerstone of a near-transparent and self-reorganizing semantic desktop. In: Gangemi, A., et al. (eds.) ESWC 2018. LNCS, vol. 11155, pp. 89–94. Springer, Cham (2018). https://doi.org/10.1007/978-3-319-98192-5_17
22. Koch, B.: The e-invoicing journey 2019–2025 (2019). https://www.billentis.com/The_einvoicing_journey_2019-2025.pdf. Accessed 18 Dec 2020
23. Maus, H., Jilek, C., Schwarz, S.: Remembering and forgetting for personal preservation. In: Mezaris, V., Niederée, C., Logie, R.H. (eds.) Personal Multimedia Preservation. SSCC, pp. 233–277. Springer, Cham (2018). https://doi.org/10.1007/978-3-319-73465-1_7
24. Maus, H., Schwarz, S., Dengel, A.: Weaving personal knowledge spaces into office applications. In: Fathi, M. (ed.) Integration of Practice-Oriented Knowledge Technology: Trends and Prospectives, pp. 71–82. Springer, Berlin (2013). https://doi.org/10.1007/978-3-642-34471-8_6
25. McDaniel, M., Storey, V.C.: Evaluating domain ontologies: clarification, classification, and challenges. ACM Comput. Surv. **52**(4), 70:1–70:44 (2019)
26. Musen, M.A.: The protégé project: a look back and a look forward. AI Matters **1**(4), 4–12 (2015)
27. Nečaský, M., Klímek, J., Mynarz, J., Knap, T., Svátek, V., Stárka, J.: Linked data support for filing public contracts. Comput. Ind. **65**(5), 862–877 (2014)
28. Object Management Group (OMG): Languages, Countries And Codes Specification Version 1.1 (2020). https://www.omg.org/spec/LCC/About-LCC/. Accessed 18 Dec 2020
29. Poveda-Villalón, M., Gómez-Pérez, A., Suárez-Figueroa, M.C.: Oops! (ontology pitfall scanner!): an on-line tool for ontology evaluation. Int. J. Semant. Web Inf. Syst. (IJSWIS) **10**(2), 7–34 (2014)
30. Rodríguez, J.M.Á., Gayo, J.E.L., de Pablos, P.O.: New trends on e-procurement applying semantic technologies: current status and future challenges. Comput. Ind. **65**(5), 800–820 (2014)
31. Schekotihin, K., Rodler, P., Schmid, W.: OntoDebug: interactive ontology debugging plug-in for protégé. In: Ferrarotti, F., Woltran, S. (eds.) FoIKS 2018. LNCS, vol. 10833, pp. 340–359. Springer, Cham (2018). https://doi.org/10.1007/978-3-319-90050-6_19
32. Suárez-Figueroa, M.C., Gómez-Pérez, A., Fernández-López, M.: The NeOn methodology for ontology engineering. In: Suárez-Figueroa, M.C., Gómez-Pérez, A., Motta, E., Gangemi, A. (eds.) Ontology Engineering in a Networked World, pp. 9–34. Springer, Heidelberg (2012). https://doi.org/10.1007/978-3-642-24794-1_2
33. Wilkinson, M.D., et al.: The fair guiding principles for scientific data management and stewardship. Sci. Data **3**(1), 160018 (2016)
34. World Wide Web Consortium: FOAF Vocabulary Specification 0.99 (2004). http://xmlns.com/foaf/0.1/. Accessed 18 Dec 2020
35. World Wide Web Consortium: SKOS Simple Knowledge Organization System Reference (2009). http://www.w3.org/TR/skos-reference/. Accessed 18 Dec 2020
36. World Wide Web Consortium: OWL 2 Web Ontology Language Primer (Second Edition) (2012). http://www.w3.org/TR/owl2-overview/. Accessed 18 Dec 2020
37. World Wide Web Consortium: W3C XML Schema Definition Language (XSD) 1.1 Part 1: Structures (2012). https://www.w3.org/TR/2012/REC-xmlschema11-1-20120405/. Accessed 18 Dec 2020
38. World Wide Web Consortium: SPARQL 1.1 Query Language (2013). https://www.w3.org/TR/sparql11-query/. Accessed 18 Dec 2020

39. World Wide Web Consortium: RDF 1.1 Primer (2014). http://www.w3.org/TR/2014/NOTE-rdf11-primer-20140624/. Accessed 18 Dec 2020
40. World Wide Web Consortium: RDF Schema 1.1 (2014). http://www.w3.org/TR/2014/REC-rdf-schema-20140225/. Accessed 18 Dec 2020
41. World Wide Web Consortium: The Organization Ontology (2014). http://www.w3.org/TR/vocab-org/. Accessed 18 Dec 2020
42. World Wide Web Consortium: vCard Ontology - for describing People and Organizations (2014). http://www.w3.org/TR/vcard-rdf/. Accessed 18 Dec 2020

KOBE: Cloud-Native Open Benchmarking Engine for Federated Query Processors

Charalampos Kostopoulos, Giannis Mouchakis, Antonis Troumpoukis,
Nefeli Prokopaki-Kostopoulou, Angelos Charalambidis⬤,
and Stasinos Konstantopoulos[(✉)]⬤

Institute and Informatics and Telecommunications, NCSR "Demokritos",
Agia Paraskevi, Greece
{b.kostopoulos,gmouchakis,antru,nefelipk,
acharal,konstant}@iit.demokritos.gr

Abstract. In the SPARQL query processing community, as well as in the wider databases community, benchmark reproducibility is based on releasing datasets and query workloads. However, this paradigm breaks down for federated query processors, as these systems do not manage the data they serve to their clients but provide a data-integration abstraction over the actual query processors that are in direct contact with the data. As a consequence, benchmark results can be greatly affected by the performance and characteristics of the underlying data services. This is further aggravated when one considers benchmarking in more realistic conditions, where internet latency and throughput between the federator and the federated data sources is also a key factor. In this paper we present KOBE, a benchmarking system that leverages modern containerization and Cloud computing technologies in order to reproduce collections of data sources. In KOBE, data sources are formally described in more detail than what is conventionally provided, covering not only the data served but also the specific software that serves it and its configuration as well as the characteristics of the network that connects them. KOBE provides a specification formalism and a command-line interface that completely hides from the user the mechanics of provisioning and orchestrating the benchmarking process on Kubernetes-based infrastructures; and of simulating network latency. Finally, KOBE automates the process of collecting and comprehending logs, and extracting and visualizing evaluation metrics from these logs.

Keywords: Benchmarking · Federated query processing · Cloud-native

1 Introduction

Data federation and distributed querying are key technologies for the efficient and scalable consuming of data in the decentralized and dynamic environment

© Springer Nature Switzerland AG 2021
R. Verborgh et al. (Eds.): ESWC 2021, LNCS 12731, pp. 664–679, 2021.
https://doi.org/10.1007/978-3-030-77385-4_40

of the Semantic Web. Several federation systems have been proposed [2,4,10], each with their own characteristics, strengths, and limitations. Naturally, consistent and reproducible benchmarking is a key enabler of the relevant research, as it allows these characteristics, strengths, and limitations to be studied and understood.

There are several benchmarks that aim to achieve this, but, similarly to the wider databases community, to release a benchmark amounts to releasing datasets, query workloads, and, at most, a benchmark-specific evaluation engine for executing the query load [5,8,9]. Research articles using these benchmarks need to specify what software has been used to implement the SPARQL endpoints, how it has been configured and distributed among hardware nodes, and the characteristics of these nodes and of the network that connects them to the federation system. Reproducing an experiment from such a description is a challenging and tedious task. Based on our own experience with federated query processing research we have been looking for ways to minimize the effort required and the uncertainty involved in replicating experimental setups from the federated querying literature. Our first step in that direction was to complement a benchmark we previously proposed [11] with Docker images of the populated triple store installations and of the federation systems used for that work.

In this paper we present KOBE,[1] an open-source[2] benchmarking engine that reads benchmark definitions and handles the distributed deployment of the data sources and the actual execution of the experiment. This includes instantiating a data source from dataset files, configuring and initializing the federation engine, connecting them into a virtual network with controlled characteristics, executing the experiment, and collecting the evaluation results. The main objective of KOBE is to provide a generic and controlled benchmarking framework where any combination of datasets, query loads, querying scenarios, and federation engines can be tested. To meet this goal, KOBE leverages modern Cloud-native technologies for the containerization and orchestration of different components.

In this paper we will first introduce the core concepts of a federated query processing experiment and the requirements for consistently and reproducibly carrying out such experiments (Sect. 2) and then present KOBE, its system components and how experiments are provisioned and orchestrated (Sect. 3). We then discuss how logs are collected and evaluation metrics visualized (Sect. 4), and how users can extend the library of benchmarks and federation engines to prepare their own experiments (Sect. 5). We close with a comparison to related systems (Sect. 6), conclusions and future work (Sect. 7).

2   Benchmarking Concepts and Requirements

We start by discussing the requirements for a benchmarking experiment of a federated query processor. First, we briefly introduce the main concepts of a federated query processing experiment:

---

[1] Previously demonstrated in ISWC 2020, with extended abstract proceedings [6].
[2] See https://github.com/semagrow/kobe.

Data source: An endpoint that processes queries. A data source is characterized by a dataset label, with data sources characterized by the same dataset serving the exact same data.

Benchmark: A collection of data sources, the latency and throughput of these data sources, and a list of query strings. Benchmarks are defined independently of the federator that is being benchmarked.

Federator: A federated query processor that provides a single endpoint to achieve uniform and integrated access to the data sources.

Experiment run: A specific experiment, where (a) a specific federator has been configured to be able to connect to the data sources foreseen by the benchmark; and (b) the query load foreseen by the benchmark has been applied to the federator.

Experiment: The repetition of multiple runs of the same benchmark. An experiment is stateful, in the sense that the federator and data source instances are not terminated and maintain their caches and, in general, their state between runs.

Having these elements in place allows for the following tests, commonly used to evaluate query processing systems in general and federated query processing systems in particular:

- Comparing the first run for a query against subsequent runs; to understand the effect of caching.
- Observing if performance degrades for large numbers of runs by comparison to smaller numbers of runs; to understand if there are memory leaks and other instabilities.
- Observing if performance degrades for large numbers of experiments executed concurrently; to perform stress-testing.
- Comparing the performance of the same federation engine, on the same datasets, over different data sources; to understand the effect of current load, implicit response size limits, allocated memory, and other specifics of the query processing engines that implement the data sources.
- Comparing the performance of different federation engines on the same experiment; to evaluate federation engines.

Based on the above, we will now proceed to define the requirements for a benchmarking system that supports automating the benchmarking process.

2.1 Data Source Provisioning

In order to reliably reproduce evaluation results, there are several parameters of the data source implementation that need to be controlled as they affect evaluation metrics. These include the software used to implement the SPARQL endpoint and its configuration, the memory, processing power, disk speed of the server where it executes, the quality of the network connection between the data server and the federation engine, etc.

Replicating a specific software stack and its configuration can be captured by virtualization and containerization technologies, so we require that a benchmarking engine use recipes (such as a Dockerfile for Docker containers) that prepare each endpoint's execution environment.

The characteristics of the computing infrastructure where the data service executes and of the network connection between the data service and the federation engine can be naturally aggregated as the latency and throughput at which the federation engine receives data from it. So, one requirement from benchmarking engines is that latency and throughput can be throttled to a maximum, although other conditions might make a data service even less responsive than these maxima: e.g., a data source might be processing an extremely demanding query or might be serving many clients in a stress test scenario.

Based on this observation, we require that benchmarking engines allow the experiment description to include the latency and throughput between the data sources and the federation. And, in fact, that these parameters are specific to each data source. Technically, this requires that the architecture foresees a configurable proxy between the federator and each data source, so that each experiment can set this parameter to simulate the real behaviour of SPARQL query processors.

Naturally, this is in addition to the obvious requirement to control the data served and the way that data is distributed between data services.

2.2   Sequential and Concurrent Application of Query Workload

The benchmarking engine should automate the process of applying a query load to the federation engine. The queries that make up the query load should be applied either sequentially to evaluate performance on different queries or concurrently to stress-test the system.

Technically, a benchmarking system should include an orchestrator that can read such operational parameters from the experiment definition and apply them when serving as a client application for the federation engine.

2.3   Logs Collection and Analysis

One important requirement of a benchmarking system is that the experimenter can have easy access on several statistics and *key performance indicators* of each conducted experiment. An effective presentation of such indicators can offer to the experimenter the ability to compare the performance of different setups of the same benchmark (e.g., different federators or data sources) and to draw conclusions for a specific setup by examining time measurements for each phase of the query processing and several other metrics.

Metrics that are important for the experimenter to analyze the effectiveness of a federator in a specific benchmark, include the following:

– The *number of returned results* can be used to validate the correctness of the query processing by verifying that the federator returns the expected number of results. Naturally, this validation is incomplete as the results might have the correct cardinality and still be different from the correct ones. However, many errors can be very efficiently caught by simply comparing cardinalities before proceeding to the detailed comparison.

- The *total time to receive the complete result set* indicates how the engine performs overall from the perspective of the client. This is the most common key indicator that most benchmarks consider.
- Although different federated query processing architectures have been proposed, there is some convergence on *source selection, query planning*, and *query execution* as beeing the main query processing phases. Regardless of whether these phases execute sequentially or are adaptive and their execution is interwined, the *breakdown of the query processing time into phases* provides the experimenter with insights regarding the efficiency of the federation engine and how it can be improved.
- The *number of sources accessed* during processing a specific query can be used to evaluate the effectiveness of source selection in terms of excluding redundant sources from the execution plan.

The aforementioned key performance indicators can be computed by different pieces of software during an experiment execution. For instance, the first two metrics of the above list should be computed by the evaluator (i.e., the software that poses the queries to the federator), while the last two metrics can be computed only by the federation engine itself. In order for these metrics to be available to the experimenter, the benchmarking system must collect and process the log lines emitted by the federation engine and the other components. This will produce an additional requirement on the compatible format of the log lines of the systems under test.

3   The KOBE System

The *KOBE Benchmarking Engine (KOBE)* is a system that aims to provide an extensible platform to facilitate benchmarking on federated query processing. It was designed with the following objectives in mind:

1. to ease the deployment of complex benchmarking experiments by automating the tedious tasks of initialization and execution;
2. to allow for benchmark and experiment specifications to be reproduced in different environments and be able to produce comparable and reliable results;
3. to provide to the experimenter the reporting that is identified by the requirements in Sect. 2.

In the following sections we will present the architecture and components of KOBE and its key features.

3.1   Deployment Automation

One of the major tasks that KOBE undertakes is the deployment, distribution and resource allocation of the various systems (i.e., the database systems, the federator and others) that participate on a specific experiment. In order to achieve this task, KOBE employs Cloud-native technologies to facilitate the deployment on cloud infrastructures. Each system is deployed in an isolated environment with user-defined computational resources and network bandwidth. In particular, KOBE leverages containerization technologies to support the deployment of systems with different environments and installation requirements. An immediate consequence of employing those technologies is that KOBE is open and can be extended with arbitrary federators and database systems.

KOBE consists of three main subsystems that control three aspects of the benchmarking process:

– The *deployment subsystem* that is responsible for deploying and initializing the components required by an experiment. This subsystem handles the allocation of computational resources for each component.
– The *networking subsystem* that is responsible for connecting the different components of an experiment and imposes the throughput and latency limitations described by the benchmark.
– The *logging subsystem* that manages the logs produced by the several components (i.e., the data sources, federators and evaluators) and produces meaningful diagrams and graphs about the benchmarking process.

KOBE relies on Kubernetes[3] to allocate cluster resources for the benchmark execution. It deploys ephemeral containers with the individual components of a benchmarking experiment. The orchestration of that deployment and the communication with the underlying Kubernetes cluster is performed by the *KOBE operator*. The KOBE operator runs as a daemon and continuously monitors the progress of each running experiment in the cluster. This controller is also responsible for the interpretation of the experiment specifications (see Subsect. 3.2) to complete deployment commands of the components of the experiment.

The network subsystem is controlled by Istio[4], a Cloud-native controller that tightly integrates with Kubernetes to provide a service mesh layer. The KOBE operator utilizes the functionality of Istio to setup the network connections between the data sources and the federating engine. The quality of those network connections can be controlled by the KOBE operator to provide the simulated behavior specified by the specific experiment. It is worth noting that those network links are established in the service mesh layer of the cluster and as a result one can have multiple experiments with different networking topologies running at the same time in the cluster.

The logging subsystem of KOBE is implemented as an EFK stack, a popular solution for a centralized, cluster-level logging environment in a Kubernetes

---

[3] cf. https://kubernetes.io.
[4] cf. https://istio.io.

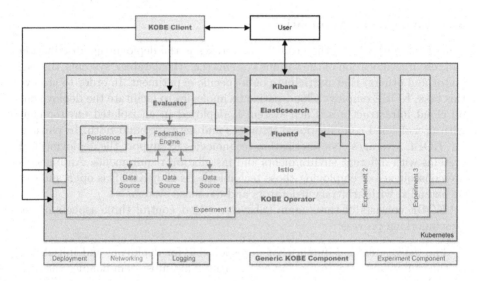

Fig. 1. Information flow through a KOBE deployment: The user edits configuration files and uses kobectl (the KOBE command-line client) to deploy and execute the benchmarking experiments, at a level that abstracts away from Kubernetes specifics. Experimental results are automatically collected and visualized using the EFK stack.

cluster. EFK stack consists of (a) Elasticsearch[5], an object store where all logs are stored in a structured form, used for log searching, (b) Fluentd[6], a data collector which gathers logs from all containers in the cluster and feeds them into Elasticsearch, and (c) Kibana[7], a web UI for Elasticsearch, used for log visualization. Since the metrics of our interest are produced from the federator and the evaluator, and, as we will see in Sect. 4, these logs are of a specific form, Fluentd is configured to parse and to keep only the logs of these containers using a set of regular expression patterns for each type of KOBE-specific logs.

Figure 1 illustrates the relationships between the individual components and the information flow through this architecture. In a typical workflow, the user uses kobectl (the KOBE command-line client) to send commands to the KOBE operator. The operator, itself deployed as a container in the Kubernetes cluster, communicates with the Kubernetes API and with Istio in order to deploy the corresponding containers and establish the network between them. Moreover, a Fluentd logging agent is attached to each related container in order to collect the respective log output. The user also uses kobectl to provide a query load to the evaluator. The query evaluator is also deployed as a containerized application and is responsible for applying the query load to the federator and for measuring the latter's response.

---

[5] cf. https://www.elastic.co/elasticsearch.

[6] cf. https://www.fluentd.org.

[7] cf. https://www.elastic.co/kibana.

During the execution of the experiment, Fluentd collects the log output from the evaluator, and parses it to extract evaluation metrics which are stored in Elasticsearch. If the federation engine is KOBE-aware, then it also produces log lines following the syntax understood by Fluentd so that fine-grained metrics about the different stages of the overall query processing are also computed and stored in Elasticsearch. The user connects to Kibana to see visualizations of these metrics, where we have prepared a variety of panels specifically relevant to benchmarking federated query processors.

3.2   Benchmark and Experiment Specifications

An important aspect of benchmarking is the ability to reproduce the experimental results of a benchmark. KOBE tackles this important issue by defining declarative specifications of the benchmarks and the experiments. Those descriptions can be serialized in a human-readable format (we use YAML as the markup language) and shared and distributed as artifacts.

These specifications are grouped around the various components of an experiment including the benchmark, the evaluator, the data source systems, the data federator and the network topology. Typically, those specifications are partitioned in a series of files; each file includes informations about different elements of the experiment. For example, one specification describes a specific federator and a different specification includes information about the set of datasets and querysets.

The main idea of this organization is that each specification can be provided by a different role. For example, the federator (resp. dataset server) specification should be provided by the *implementor of the federator* (resp. *dataset server*). These specifications include, for example, details about the correct initialization of a federation engine. Moreover, the benchmark specification should be provided by the *benchmark designer* and the more specific details such as the computational resources and the network topology by the *experimenter*. The relevant pages of the online KOBE manual[8] give details about these parameters.

It is worth noting that the specifications are declarative in the sense that they describe the desired outcome rather than the actual steps one needs to follow to reproduce the experiment. The KOBE operator interprets these specifications as the necessary interactions with Kubernetes and Istio to deploy an experiment.

3.3   Experiment Orchestration

The KOBE operator is continuously monitoring for new experiment specifications that are submitted to KOBE by the user via a command-line client application. Upon a new experiment submission, the KOBE operator compiles new deployments for the data sources. The data sources consists of a list of dataset files, that is the serializable content of the dataset, and specifications about the database system that will serve this dataset. The deployment of a data source

---

[8] https://semagrow.github.io/kobe/references/api.

is performed in two phases: in the first phase the data files are downloaded and imported into the database system and in the second phase the system is configured and started for serving.

When all data sources are ready for serving, the federating engine is started. Similarly, the federating engine is deployed in two phases. In the first phase, the federation of the specific instances of data sources is established. This includes the specific initialization process that a federation engine might need. For example, some engines need the generation of a set of metadata that depend on the specific datasets that they federate. The second phase start the actual federation service. After that, the network connections are established and the network quality characteristics are configured.

In that stage the experiment is ready to proceed with querying the federation. This is accomplished by an evaluator component that reads the query set from the benchmark specification and starts sending the queries to the endpoint of the federator. The evaluator is just another container that is deployed in the cluster. During the query evaluation, potential logs that are produced by the federation engine and the evaluator are collected and visualized to the user. The experiment completes when the evaluator finished with all the queries.

4   Collecting and Analysing Evaluation Metrics

In Sect. 2.3 we stipulated that benchmarking engines should include a mechanism that collects and analyzes the logs from multiple containers in order to compute evaluation metrics, and to present them to the experimenter in an intuitive way.

4.1   Collecting the Evaluation Metrics

In KOBE, the following benchmarking metrics are treated: the duration of the query processing phases (source selection, planning, and execution); the number of sources accessed during a query evaluation from the federator; the total time to receive the complete result set of a query; and the number of the returned results of a query. We assume that the federator and the evaluator calculate these metrics and produce a corresponding log message for each metric.

Notice, though, that many executions of several experiments can result in multiple query evaluations. As a result, many log messages that contain the same metric can appear. In order to differentiate between these query evaluations and to collect all logs that refer to the same query that belongs to a specific run of an experiment, each log message should also provide the following information:

Experiment name: This information is used to identify in which experiment the given query evaluation belongs.
Start time of the experiment: Since one experiment can be executed several times, this information is used to link to the given query evaluation with a specific experiment execution.
Query name: Each query has a unique identification name in an experiment. This information is used to refer to the name of the query in the experiment.

Run: Each experiment has several runs, meaning that the evaluation of a query happens multiple times in a specific experiment execution. This information identifies in which run of the experiment the given query evaluation belongs.

An important problem that arises is that this information is only available to the evaluator and cannot be accessed by the federator directly. Any heuristic workarounds that try to connect the evaluator log to the federator log using, for instance, the query strings would not work, as query strings are not unique. Especially in stress-testing scenarios, the exact same query string might be simultaneously executed multiple times, so that a combination of query strings and timestamps would not be guaranteed to work either. To work around this problem, the KOBE evaluator uses SPARQL comments to pass the query *experiment* id to the federator, and the latter includes those in its logs. Then, the federator can retrieve this information by parsing this comment. This approach has the advantage that even if a federation engine has not been modified to produce log lines that provide this information, the query string is still in a valid, standard syntax and the comment is ignored. The fine-grained time to complete each step in the typical federated query processing pipeline cannot be retrieved, but the experiment can proceed with the end-to-end query processing measurements provided by the evaluator.

4.2   Visualizing the Evaluation Metrics

In this subsection, we describe the visualization component of KOBE. In particular, we present the three available dashboards. For every dashboard we provide some screenshots of the graphs produced for some experiment runs.

Details of a Specific Experiment Execution. The dashboard of Fig. 2 focuses on a specific experiment execution. It comprises:

1. Time of each phase of the query processing for each query of the experiment.
2. Total time to receive the complete result set for each query of the experiment.
3. Number of sources accessed for each query of the experiment.
4. Number of returned results for each query of the experiment.

The first and the third visualizations are obtained from the logs of the federator engine, if available. The second and the fourth visualizations are obtained from the logs of the evaluator, so they are available even for federators that do not provide KOBE-specific logs. The values in each visualization can be also exported in a CSV file for further processing.

As an example, we consider an experiment execution for the life-science (ls) query set of the FedBench benchmark for a development version of the Semagrow federation engine. This visualization can help us, for instance, to observe that the query execution phase of the federation engine dominates the overall query processing time in all queries of the benchmark except ls4.

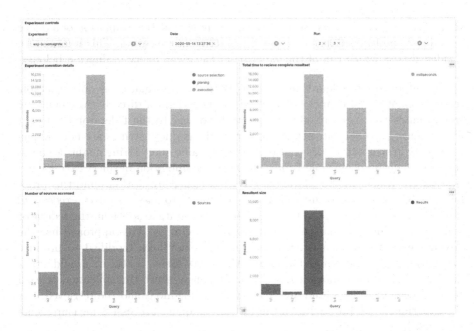

Fig. 2. Details of a specific experiment execution

Comparisons of Experiment Runs. The dashboards depicted in Fig. 3 and Fig. 4 can be used to draw comparisons between several runs in order to directly compare different configurations of a benchmark. The dashboard of Fig. 3 can be used for comparing several experiment executions. It consists of two visualizations:

1. Total time to receive the complete result set for each experiment execution.
2. Number of returned results for each specified experiment execution.

These visualizations are obtained from the logs of the evaluator. Each bar refers to a single query of the experiments presented. The dashboard of Fig. 4 displays the same metrics. The main difference is that it focuses on a specific query and compare all runs of this query for several experiment executions. Contrary to the visualizations of the other two dashboards, each bar refers to a single experiment run, and all runs are grouped according to the experiment execution they belong to.

Continuing the previous example, we consider three experiment executions that refer to for the life-science queryset of FedBench; one for the FedX federator and two for the Semagrow federator. In Fig. 3 we can observe that all executions return the same number of results for each query, and that the processing times are similar, with the exception of the ls6 query for the FedX experiment. Moreover, we can observe that all runs return same number of results, and that the processing times for each run are similar; therefore any caching used by the federators does not play any significant role in speeding up this query.

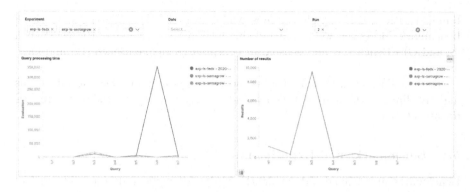

Fig. 3. Comparison of three experiment executions

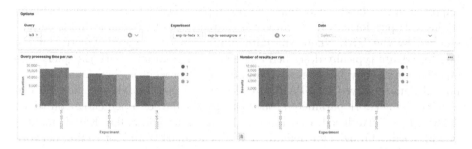

Fig. 4. Comparison of all runs of the ls3 query for three experiment executions

5   KOBE Extensibility

It is apparent that a well-designed and well-executed benchmarking experiment needs contributions from different actors. For example, a benchmark designer may provide a benchmark that is designed to compare a particular aspect of different federators. On the other hand, the specifications of each federator should ideally be provided by their respective implementors.

KOBE provides various extensibility opportunities and by design welcomes contributions from the community. In particular, KOBE can be extended with respect to the database systems, federators, query evaluators and benchmarks that comprise an experiment.

We currently provide specifications for two database systems, namely for Virtuoso[9] and Strabon[10] and for two federators, FedX [10] and Semagrow [2]. These systems have very different requirements in terms of deployment, providing strong evidence that extending the list of supported RDF stores will be straightforwrd.

We also provide a range of benchmark and experiment specifications for existing federated SPARQL benchmarks. Currently, the benchmarks that are already

---

[9] cf. https://virtuoso.openlinksw.com.

[10] cf. http://strabon.di.uoa.gr.

bundled with KOBE include the most widely used LUBM [5] and FedBench [9] benchmark. Moreover, we also include big RDF data benchmarks BigRDFBench [8] and OPFBench [11] and geospatial benchmarks GeoFedBench [12] and Geographica [3].

In the following, we briefly discuss the process of defining these specifications and give links to the more detailed walk-throughs provided in the online KOBE documentation.

5.1   Benchmarks and Experiments

Benchmarks are defined independently of the federator and comprise a set of datasets and a list of queries. Datasets are described in terms of the data and the system that should serve them. Data can be provided as a data dump to be imported in the database systems. For example, RDF data can be redistributed in the N-Triples format. Each dataset is characterized by its name and is parameterized by the URL where the data dump can be accessed. Queries of the benchmark are typically described as strings and annotated with the query language in which they are expressed; supporting heterogeneous benchmarks where not all data is served by SPARQL endpoints. A benchmark specification can also include network parameters, such as a fixed delay, or a percentage on which delay will be introduced as part of fault injection. The online KOBE manual provides walk-throughs for defining a new benchmark[11] and for tuning network parameters.[12]

An experiment that evaluates the performance of a federator over a given benchmark is defined using a strategy for applying the query load to the federator and the number of runs for each query of the experiment. The experimenter specifies an experiment by providing a new unique name for the experiment, the unique name of the benchmark and the federator specification. Moreover, an experiment includes a specific query evaluator, and the number of runs of the experiment. The query evaluator applies the query load to the federator. The one currently bundled with KOBE performs sequential querying, meaning that the queries of the benchmark are evaluated in a sequential manner. The online KOBE manual provides walk-throughs for defining a new experiment[13] and for extending KOBE with a new evaluator.[14] Furthermore, the manual also provides a walk-through for defining and visualizing new metrics.[15]

---

[11] https://semagrow.github.io/kobe/use/create_benchmark.

[12] https://semagrow.github.io/kobe/use/tune_network.

[13] https://semagrow.github.io/kobe/use/create_experiment.

[14] https://semagrow.github.io/kobe/extend/add_evaluator.

[15] https://semagrow.github.io/kobe/extend/add_metrics.

5.2 Dataset Servers and Federators

Dataset servers can be also integrated in KOBE. The dataset server specification contains a set of initialization scripts and a Docker image for the actual dataset server. The initialization scripts are also wrapped on isolated Docker containers and are used for properly initializing the database system. Typically, it includes the import of the data dump and indexing of the database. The dataset server specification may also include other parameters for network connectivity such as the port and the path to the listening SPARQL endpoint. A walk-through for adding a new dataset server is provided in the online KOBE manual.[16]

Federators can also be added to the KOBE system by providing the appropriate specification. That specification resembles the specification of a ordinary dataset server. The main difference is on the initialization phase of a federator. Typically, the initialization of a federator may involve the creation of histograms from the underlying datasets. Thus, in KOBE, the federator initialization is performed in two steps: the first step extracts needed information from each dataset and the second step consolidates that information and properly initializes the federator. As in the dataset server, the initialization processes are provided as containerized Docker images by the implementor of the federator. A walk-through for adding a federator is provided in the online KOBE manual.[17]

Federator implementors should also consider a tighter integration in order to benefit from the detailed log collection features for reporting measurements that can only be extracted by collecting information internal to the federator (Sect. 4). Therefore, a log line from a federator should be enhanced to include the evaluation metrics and the query parameters discussed in Sect. 2.3. More details about how a federator should be extended to provide detailed logs are given in the online KOBE manual.[18] This tighter integration is not a requirement, in the sense that the overall end-to-end time to evaluate the query and the number of returned results are provided without modifying the source code of the federation engine (as we have done in the case of FedX).

6 Comparison to Related Systems

To the best of our knowledge, the only benchmark orchestrator that directly targets federated query processors is the orchestrator distributed with the Fed-Bench suite [9]. As also stated in the introduction, it is in fact the limitations of the FedBench orchestrator that originally motivated the work described here. Specifically, FedBench does not support the user with either container-based deployment or collecting federator logs to compute detailed metrics.

HOBBIT [7], on the other hand, is a Docker-based system aiming at benchmarking the complete lifecycle of Linked Data generation and consumption.

---

[16] https://semagrow.github.io/kobe/extend/add_dataset_server.

[17] https://semagrow.github.io/kobe/extend/add_federator.

[18] Specifically, see the first step of the walk-through for adding a new federator. See also details about collecting logs to compute evaluation metrics https://semagrow.github.io/kobe/extend/support_metrics.

Although HOBBIT tooling can support with collecting logs and visualizing metrics, HOBBIT as a whole is not directly comparable to KOBE. In the HOBBIT architecture, the benchmarked system is perceived as an opaque container that the system tasks and measures. KOBE exploits the premise that the benchmarked system comprises multiple containers one of which (the federator) is tasked and that this one container communicates with the rest (the data sources). By exploiting these premises, KOBE goes further than HOBBIT could have gone to automate the deployment of the modules of an experiment and the control of their connectivity. In other words, KOBE aims at the federated query processing niche and trades off generality of purpose for increased support for its particular purpose.

A similar conclusion is also reached when comparing KOBE with scientific workflow orchestrators. Although (unlike HOBBIT and like KOBE) scientific workflow orchestrators are designed to orchestrate complex systems of containers, they focus on the results of the processing rather on benchmarking the processors. As such, they lack features such as controlling network latency.

Finally, another unique KOBE feature is the mechanism described in Sect. 4.1 for separating the logs of the different runs of an experiment. This especially useful in stress-testing scenarios where the same query is executed multiple times, so that the query string alone would not be sufficient to separate log lines of the different runs.

7 Conclusions

We have presented the architecture and implementation of the KOBE open benchmarking engine for federation systems. KOBE is both open-source software and an open architecture, leveraging containerization to allow the future inclusion of any federation engine. KOBE also uses Elasticsearch as a log server and Kibana as the visualization layer for presenting evaluation metrics extracted from these logs, again emphasizing openness by supporting user-defined ingestion patterns to allow flexibility in how evaluation metrics are to be extracted from each federator's log format. Deployment depends on Kubernetes, which is ubiquitous among the currently prevalent Cloud infrastructures. These features allow experiment publishers the flexibility needed for sharing federated query processing experiments that can be consistently reproduced with minimal effort by the experiment consumers.

Although originally developed for our own experiments, we feel that the federated querying community can extract great value from the abstractions it offers, as it allows releasing a benchmark as a complete, fully configured, automatically deployable testing environment.

As a next step, we are planning to expand the library of federators bundled with the KOBE distribution, and especially with systems that will verify that KOBE operates at the appropriate level of abstraction away from the specifics of particular federators. For instance, adding Triple Pattern Fragments [13] will verify that adaptive source selection and planning can operate within the KOBE framework.

Another interesting future extension would be support for the detailed evaluation of systems that stream results before the complete result set has been obtained. This requires adding support for calculating the relevant metrics, such as the diefficiency metric [1].

Acknowledgments. This project has received funding from the European Union's Horizon 2020 research and innovation programme under grant agreement No 825258. Please see http://earthanalytics.eu for more details.

References

1. Acosta, M., Vidal, M.-E., Sure-Vetter, Y.: Diefficiency metrics: measuring the continuous efficiency of query processing approaches. In: d'Amato, C., et al. (eds.) ISWC 2017, Part II. LNCS, vol. 10588, pp. 3–19. Springer, Cham (2017). https://doi.org/10.1007/978-3-319-68204-4_1
2. Charalambidis, A., Troumpoukis, A., Konstantopoulos, S.: SemaGrow: optimizing federated SPARQL queries. In: Proceedings of the 11th International Conference on Semantic Systems (SEMANTiCS 2015), Vienna, Austria, Sept 2015 (2015)
3. Garbis, G., Kyzirakos, K., Koubarakis, M.: Geographica: a benchmark for geospatial RDF stores (long version). In: Alani, H., et al. (eds.) ISWC 2013, Part II. LNCS, vol. 8219, pp. 343–359. Springer, Heidelberg (2013). https://doi.org/10.1007/978-3-642-41338-4_22
4. Görlitz, O., Staab, S.: SPLENDID: SPARQL endpoint federation exploiting VOID descriptions. In: Proceedings of the 2nd International Workshop on Consuming Linked Data (COLD 2011), vol. 782, Bonn, Germany, Oct 2011. CEUR (2011)
5. Guo, Y., Pan, Z., Heflin, J.: LUBM: a benchmark for OWL knowledge base systems. Web Semant. **3**(2) (2005). https://doi.org/10.1016/j.websem.2005.06.005
6. Kostopoulos, C., Mouchakis, G., Prokopaki-Kostopoulou, N., Troumpoukis, A., Charalambidis, A., Konstantopoulos, S.: KOBE: Cloud-native open benchmarking engine for federated query processors. Posters & Demos Session, ISWC 2020 (2020)
7. Ngonga Ngomo, A.C., Röder, M.: HOBBIT: Holistic benchmarking for big linked data. In: Processings of the ESWC 2016 EU Networking Session (2016)
8. Saleem, M., Hasnain, A., Ngonga Ngomo, A.C.: BigRDFBench: A billion triples benchmark for SPARQL endpoint federation
9. Schmidt, M., Görlitz, O., Haase, P., Ladwig, G., Schwarte, A., Tran, T.: FedBench: a benchmark suite for federated semantic data query processing. In: Aroyo, L., et al. (eds.) ISWC 2011, Part I. LNCS, vol. 7031, pp. 585–600. Springer, Heidelberg (2011). https://doi.org/10.1007/978-3-642-25073-6_37
10. Schwarte, A., Haase, P., Hose, K., Schenkel, R., Schmidt, M.: FedX: a federation layer for distributed query processing on linked open data. In: Antoniou, G., et al. (eds.) ESWC 2011, Part II. LNCS, vol. 6644, pp. 481–486. Springer, Heidelberg (2011). https://doi.org/10.1007/978-3-642-21064-8_39
11. Troumpoukis, A., et al.: Developing a benchmark suite for semantic web data from existing workflows. In: Proceedings of the Benchmarking Linked Data Workshop (BLINK), (ISWC 2016), Kobe, Japan, Oct 2016 (2016)
12. Troumpoukis, A., et al.: GeoFedBench: a benchmark for federated GeoSPARQL query processors. In: Proceedings Posters & Demos Session of ISWC 2020 (2020)
13. Verborgh, R., et al.: Triple pattern fragments: a low-cost knowledge graph interface for the web. J. Web Semant. **37–38**, 184–206 (2016)

CSKG: The CommonSense Knowledge Graph

Filip Ilievski[(✉)], Pedro Szekely, and Bin Zhang

Information Sciences Institute, University of Southern California, Los Angeles, USA
{ilievski,pszekely,binzhang}@isi.edu

Abstract. Sources of commonsense knowledge support applications in natural language understanding, computer vision, and knowledge graphs. Given their complementarity, their integration is desired. Yet, their different foci, modeling approaches, and sparse overlap make integration difficult. In this paper, we consolidate commonsense knowledge by following five principles, which we apply to combine seven key sources into a first integrated CommonSense Knowledge Graph (CSKG). We analyze CSKG and its various text and graph embeddings, showing that CSKG is well-connected and that its embeddings provide a useful entry point to the graph. We demonstrate how CSKG can provide evidence for generalizable downstream reasoning and for pre-training of language models. CSKG and all its embeddings are made publicly available to support further research on commonsense knowledge integration and reasoning.

Keywords: Commonsense knowledge · Knowledge graph · Embeddings

Resource type: Knowledge graph
License: CC BY-SA 4.0
DOI: https://doi.org/10.5281/zenodo.4331372
Repository: https://github.com/usc-isi-i2/cskg

1 Introduction

Recent commonsense reasoning benchmarks [3,27] and neural advancements [16, 17] shed a new light on the longstanding task of capturing, representing, and reasoning over commonsense knowledge. While state-of-the-art language models [8,17] capture linguistic patterns that allow them to perform well on commonsense reasoning tasks after fine-tuning, their robustness and explainability could benefit from integration with structured knowledge, as shown by KagNet [16] and HyKAS [18]. Let us consider an example task question from the SWAG dataset [38],[1] which describes a woman that takes a sit at the piano:

---

[1] The multiple-choice task of choosing an intuitive follow-up scene is customary called question answering [19,38], despite the absence of a formal question.

© Springer Nature Switzerland AG 2021
R. Verborgh et al. (Eds.): ESWC 2021, LNCS 12731, pp. 680–696, 2021.
https://doi.org/10.1007/978-3-030-77385-4_41

```
Q: On stage, a woman takes a seat at the piano. She:
1. sits on a bench as her sister plays with the doll.
2. smiles with someone as the music plays.
3. is in the crowd, watching the dancers.
-> 4. nervously sets her fingers on the keys.
```

Answering this question requires knowledge that humans possess and apply, but machines cannot distill directly in communication. Luckily, graphs of (commonsense) knowledge contain such knowledge. ConceptNet's [29] triples state that pianos have keys and are used to perform music, which supports the correct option and discourages answer 2. WordNet [21] states specifically, though in natural language, that pianos are played by pressing keys. According to an image description in Visual Genome, a person could play piano while sitting and having their hands on the keyboard. In natural language, ATOMIC [26] indicates that before a person plays piano, they need to sit at it, be on stage, and reach for the keys. ATOMIC also lists strong feelings associated with playing piano. FrameNet's [1] frame of a performance contains two separate roles for the performer and the audience, meaning that these two are distinct entities, which can be seen as evidence against answer 3.

While these sources clearly provide complementary knowledge that can help commonsense reasoning, their different foci, representation formats, and sparse overlap makes integration difficult. Taxonomies, like WordNet, organize conceptual knowledge into a hierarchy of classes. An independent ontology, coupled with rich instance-level knowledge, is provided by Wikidata [34], a structured counterpart to Wikipedia. FrameNet, on the other hand, defines an orthogonal structure of frames and roles; each of which can be filled with a WordNet/Wikidata class or instance. Sources like ConceptNet or WebChild [31], provide more 'episodic' commonsense knowledge, whereas ATOMIC captures pre- and post-situations for an event. Image description datasets, like Visual Genome [14], contain visual commonsense knowledge. While links between these sources exist (mostly through WordNet synsets), the majority of their nodes and edges are disjoint.

In this paper, we propose an approach for integrating these (and more sources) into a single Common Sense Knowledge Graph (CSKG). We suvey existing sources of commonsense knowledge to understand their particularities and we summarize the key challenges on the road to their integration (Sect. 2). Next, we devise five principles and a representation model for a consolidated CSKG (Sect. 3). We apply our approach to build the first version of CSKG, by combining seven complementary, yet disjoint, sources. We compute several graph and text embeddings to facilitate reasoning over the graph. In Sect. 4, we analyze the content of the graph and the generated embeddings. We provide insights into the utility of CSKG for downstream reasoning on commonsense Question Answering (QA) tasks in Sect. 5. In Sect. 6 we reflect on the learned lessons and list the next steps for CSKG. We conclude in Sect. 7.

Table 1. Survey of existing sources of commonsense knowledge.

	Describes	Creation	Size	Mappings	Examples
Concept net	Everyday objects, actions, states, relations (multilingual)	Crowd-sourcing	36 relations, 8M nodes, 21M edges	WordNet, DBpedia, OpenCyc, Wiktionary	/c/en/piano /c/en/piano/n /c/en/piano/n/wn /r/relatedTo
Web child	Everyday objects, actions, states, relations	Curated automatic extraction	4 relation groups, 2M nodes, 18M edges	WordNet	hasTaste fasterThan
ATOMIC	Event pre/post-conditions	Crowd-sourcing	9 relations, 300k nodes, 877k edges	ConceptNet, Cyc	wanted-to impressed
Wikidata	Instances, concepts, relations	Crowd-sourcing	1.2k relations, 75M objects, 900M edges	various	wd:Q1234 wdt:P31
WordNet	Words, concepts, relations	Manual	10 relations, 155k words, 176k synsets		dog.n.01 hypernymy
Roget	Words, relations	Manual	2 relations, 72k words, 1.4M edges		truncate antonym
VerbNet	Verbs, relations	Manual	273 top classes 23 roles, 5.3k senses	FrameNet, WordNet	perform-v performance-26.7-1
FrameNet	Frames, roles, relations	Manual	1.9k edges, 1.2k frames, 12k roles, 13k lexical units		Activity Change_of_leadership New_leader
Visual genome	Image objects, relations, attributes	Crowd-sourcing	42k relations, 3.8M nodes, 2.3M edges, 2.8M attributes	WordNet	fire hydrant white dog
ImageNet	Image objects	Crowd-sourcing	14M images, 22k synsets	WordNet	dog.n.01

2 Problem Statement

2.1 Sources of Common Sense Knowledge

Table 1 summarizes the content, creation method, size, external mappings, and example resources for representative public commonsense sources: Concept-Net [29], WebChild [31], ATOMIC [26], Wikidata [34], WordNet [21], Roget [13], VerbNet [28], FrameNet [1], Visual Genome [14], and ImageNet [7]. Primarily, we observe that the commonsense knowledge is spread over a number of sources with different focus: commonsense knowledge graphs (e.g., ConceptNet), general-domain knowledge graphs (e.g., Wikidata), lexical resources (e.g., WordNet, FrameNet), taxonomies (e.g., Wikidata, WordNet), and visual datasets (e.g., Visual Genome) [11]. Therefore, these sources together cover a rich spectrum of knowledge, ranging from everyday knowledge, through event-centric knowledge and taxonomies, to visual knowledge. While the taxonomies have been created manually by experts, most of the commonsense and visual sources have been created by crowdsourcing or curated automatic extraction. Commonsense and common knowledge graphs (KGs) tend to be relatively large, with millions of nodes and edges; whereas the taxonomies and the lexical sources are notably smaller. Despite the diverse nature of these sources, we note that many contain mappings to WordNet, as well as a number of other sources. These mappings might be incomplete, e.g., only a small portion of ATOMIC can be mapped to ConceptNet. Nevertheless, these high-quality mappings provide an opening for consolidation of commonsense knowledge, a goal we pursue in this paper.

2.2   Challenges

Combining these sources in a single KG faces three key challenges:

1. The sources follow **different knowledge modeling approaches**. One such difference concerns the relation set: there are very few relations in ConceptNet and WordNet, but (tens of) thousands of them in Wikidata and Visual Genome. Consolidation requires a global decision on how to model the relations. The granularity of knowledge is another factor of variance. While regular RDF triples fit some sources (e.g., ConceptNet), representing entire frames (e.g., in FrameNet), event conditions (e.g., in ATOMIC), or compositional image data (e.g., Visual Genome) might benefit from a more open format. An ideal representation would support the entire granularity spectrum.

2. As a number of these sources have been created to support natural language applications, they often contain **imprecise descriptions**. Natural language phrases are often the main node types in the provided knowledge sources, which provides the benefit of easier access for natural language algorithms, but it introduces ambiguity which might be undesired from a formal semantics perspective. An ideal representation would harmonize various phrasings of a concept, while retaining easy and efficient linguistic access to these concepts via their labels.

3. Although these sources contain links to existing ones, we observe **sparse overlap**. As these external links are typically to WordNet, and vary in terms of their version (3.0 or 3.1) or target (lemma or synset), the sources are still disjoint and establishing (identity) connections is difficult. Bridging these gaps, through optimally leveraging existing links, or extending them with additional ones automatically, is a modeling and integration challenge.

2.3   Prior Consolidation Efforts

Prior efforts that combine pairs or small sets of (mostly lexical) commonsense sources exist. A unidirectional manual mapping from VerbNet classes to WordNet and FrameNet is provided by the Unified Verb Index [33]. The Predicate Matrix [6] has a full automatic mapping between lexical resources, including FrameNet, WordNet, and VerbNet. PreMOn [5] formalizes these in RDF. In [20], the authors produce partial mappings between WordNet and Wikipedia/DBpedia. Zareian et al. [37] combine edges from Visual Genome, WordNet, and ConceptNet to improve scene graph generation from an image. None of these efforts aspires to build a consolidated KG of commonsense knowledge.

Most similar to our effort, BabelNet [22] integrates many sources, covers a wide range of 284 languages, and primarily focuses on lexical and general-purpose resources, like WordNet, VerbNet, and Wiktionary. While we share the goal of integrating valuable sources for downstream reasoning, and some of these sources (e.g., WordNet) overlap with BabelNet, our ambition is to support commonsense reasoning applications. For this reason, we focus on commonsense knowledge graphs, like ConceptNet and ATOMIC, or even visual sources, like Visual Genome, none of which are found in BabelNet.

3   The Common Sense Knowledge Graph

3.1   Principles

Question answering and natural language inference tasks require knowledge from heterogeneous sources (Sect. 2). To enable their joint usage, the sources need to be harmonized in a way that will allow straightforward access by linguistic tools [16,18], easy splitting into arbitrary subsets, and computation of common operations, like (graph and word) embeddings or KG paths. For this purpose, we devise five principles for consolidatation of sources into a single commonsense KG (CSKG), driven by pragmatic goals of simplicity, modularity, and utility:

P1. Embrace heterogeneity of nodes One should preserve the natural node diversity inherent to the variety of sources considered, which entails blurring the distinction between objects (such as those in Visual Genome or Wikidata), classes (such as those in WordNet or ConceptNet), words (in Roget), actions (in ATOMIC or ConceptNet), frames (in FrameNet), and states (as in ATOMIC). It also allows formal nodes, describing unique objects, to co-exist with fuzzy nodes describing ambiguous lexical expressions.

P2. Reuse edge types across resources To support reasoning algorithms like KagNet [16], the set of edge types should be kept to minimum and reused across resources wherever possible. For instance, the ConceptNet edge type /r/LocatedNear could be reused to express spatial proximity in Visual Genome.

P3. Leverage external links The individual graphs are mostly disjoint according to their formal knowledge. However, high-quality links may exist or may be easily inferred, in order to connect these KGs and enable path finding. For instance, while ConceptNet and Visual Genome do not have direct connections, they can be partially aligned, as both have links to WordNet synsets.

P4. Generate high-quality probabilistic links Inclusion of additional probabilistic links, either with off-the-shelf link prediction algorithms or with specialized algorithms (e.g., see Sect. 3.3), would improve the connectedness of CSKG and help path finding algorithms reason over it. Given the heterogeneity of nodes (cf. P1), a 'one-method-fits-all' node resolution might not be suitable.

P5. Enable access to labels The CSKG format should support easy and efficient natural language access. Labels and aliases associated with KG nodes provide application-friendly and human-readable access to the CSKG, and can help us unify descriptions of the same/similar concept across sources.

3.2   Representation

We model CSKG as a **hyper-relational graph**, describing edges in a tabular
KGTK [10] format. We opted for this representation rather than the traditional
RDF/OWL2 because it allows us to fulfill our goals (of simplicity and utility)
and follow our principles more directly, without compromising on the format. For
instance, natural language access (principle P5) to RDF/OWL2 nodes requires
graph traversal over its `rdfs:label` relations. Including both reliable and probabilistic nodes (P3 and P4) would require a mechanism to easily indicate edge
weights, which in RDF/OWL2 entails inclusion of blank nodes, and a number
of additional edges. Moreover, the simplicity of our tabular format allows us to
use standard off-the-shelf functionalities and mature tooling, like the `pandas`[2]
and `graph-tool`[3] libraries in Python, or graph embedding tools like [15], which
have been conveniently wrapped by the KGTK [10] toolkit.[4]

The edges in CSKG are described by ten columns. Following KGTK, the
primary information about an edge consists of its `id`, `node1`, `relation`, and
`node2`. Next, we include four "lifted" edge columns, using KGTK's abbreviated
way of representing triples about the primary elements, such as `node1;label` or
`relation;label` (label of `node1` and of `relation`). Each edge is completed by two
qualifiers: `source`, which specifies the source(s) of the edge (e.g., "CN" for ConceptNet), and `sentence`, containing the linguistic lexicalization of a triple, if given
by the original source. Auxiliary KGTK files can be added to describe additional
knowledge about some edges, such as their weight, through the corresponding edge
`ids`. We provide further documentation at: https://cskg.readthedocs.io/.

3.3   Consolidation

Currently, CSKG integrates seven sources, selected based on their popularity in existing QA work: a commonsense knowledge graph ConceptNet, a
visual commonsense source Visual Genome, a procedural source ATOMIC, a
general-domain source Wikidata, and three lexical sources, WordNet, Roget,
and FrameNet. Here, we briefly present our design decisions per source, the
mappings that facilitate their integration, and further refinements on CSKG.

3.3.1   Individual Sources

We keep the original edges of **ConceptNet** 5.7 expressed with 47 relations
in total. We also include the entire **ATOMIC** KG, preserving the original
nodes and its nine relations. To enhance lexical matching between ATOMIC
and other sources, we add normalized labels of its nodes, e.g., adding a
second label "accepts invitation" to the original one "personX accepts per-
sonY's invitation". We import four node types from **FrameNet**: frames,
frame elements (FEs), lexical units (LUs), and semantic types (STs), and we

---

[2] https://pandas.pydata.org/.
[3] https://graph-tool.skewed.de/.
[4] CSKG can be transformed to RDF with `kgtk generate-wikidata-triples`.

reuse 5 categories of FrameNet edges: frame-frame (13 edge types), frame-FE (1 edge type), frame-LU (1 edge type), FE-ST (1 edge type), and ST-ST (3 edge types). Following principle P2 on edge type reuse, we map these 19 edge types to 9 relations in ConceptNet, e.g., is_causative_of is converted to /r/Causes. **Roget** We include all synonyms and antonyms between words in Roget, by reusing the ConceptNet relations /r/Synonym and /r/Antonym (P2). We represent **Visual Genome** as a KG, by representing its image objects as WordNet synsets (e.g., wn:shoe.n.01). We express relationships between objects via ConceptNet's /r/LocatedNear edge type. Object attributes are represented by different edge types, conditioned on their part-of-speech: we reuse ConceptNet's /r/CapableOf for verbs, while we introduce a new relation mw:MayHaveProperty for adjective attributes. We include the *Wikidata-CS* subset of **Wikidata**, extracted in [12]. Its 101k statements have been manually mapped to 15 Concept-Net relations. We include four relations from **WordNet** v3.0 by mapping them to three ConceptNet relations: hypernymy (using /r/IsA), part and member holonymy (through /r/PartOf), and substance meronymy (with /r/MadeOf).

3.3.2   Mappings

We perform node resolution by applying existing identity mappings (P3) and generating probabilistic mappings automatically (P4). We introduce a dedicated relation, mw:SameAs, to indicate identity between two nodes.

WordNet-WordNet. The WordNet v3.1 identifiers in ConceptNet and the WordNet v3.0 synsets from Visual Genome are aligned by leveraging ILI: the WordNet InterLingual Index,[5] which generates 117,097 mw:SameAs mappings.

WordNet-Wikidata. We generate links between WordNet synsets and Wiki-data nodes as follows. For each synset, we retrieve 50 candidate nodes from a customized index of Wikidata. Then, we compute sentence embeddings of the descriptions of the synset and each of the Wikidata candidates by using a pre-trained XLNet model [36]. We create a mw:SameAs edge between the synset and the Wikidata candidate with highest cosine similarity of their embeddings. Each mapping is validated by one student. In total, 17 students took part in this validation. Out of the 112k edges produced by the algorithm, the manual validation marked 57,145 as correct. We keep these in CSKG and discard the rest.

FrameNet-ConceptNet. We link FrameNet nodes to ConceptNet in two ways. FrameNet LUs are mapped to ConceptNet nodes through the Predicate Matrix [6] with 3,016 mw:SameAs edges. Then, we use 200k hand-labeled sentences from the FrameNet corpus, each annotated with a target frame, a set of FEs, and their associated words. We treat these words as LUs of the corresponding FE, and ground them to ConceptNet with the rule-based method of [16].

Lexical matching. We establish 74,259 mw:SameAs links between nodes in ATOMIC, ConceptNet, and Roget by exact lexical match of their labels. We restrict this matching to lexical nodes (e.g., /c/en/cat and not /c/en/cat/n/wn/animal).

---

[5] https://github.com/globalwordnet/ili

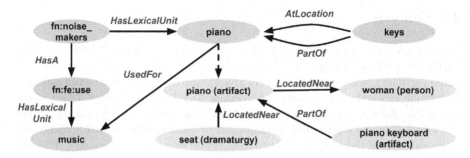

Fig. 1. Snippet of CSKG for the example task of Sect. 1. CSKG combines: 1) lexical nodes (piano, keys, music; in blue), 2) synsets like piano (artifact), seat (dramaturgy) (in green), and 3) frames (`fn:noise_makers`) and frame elements (`fn:fe:use`) (in purple). The link between `piano` and `piano (artifact)` is missing, but trivial to infer. (Color figure online)

3.3.3   Refinement

We consolidate the seven sources and their interlinks as follows. After transforming them to the representation described in the past two sections, we concatenate them in a single graph. We deduplicate this graph and append all mappings, resulting in CSKG*. Finally, we apply the mappings to merge identical nodes (connected with `mw:SameAs`) and perform a final deduplication of the edges, resulting in our consolidated CSKG graph. The entire procedure of importing the individual sources and consolidating them into CSKG is implemented with KGTK operations [10], and can be found on our GitHub.[6]

3.4   Embeddings

Embeddings provide a convenient entry point to KGs and enable reasoning on both intrinsic and downstream tasks. For instance, many reasoning applications (cf. [16,18]) of ConceptNet leverage their NumberBatch embeddings [29]. Motivated by these observations, we aspire to produce high-quality embeddings of the CSKG graph. We experiment with two families of embedding algorithms. On the one hand, we produce variants of popular graph embeddings: TransE [4], DistMult [35], ComplEx [32], and RESCAL [24]. On the other hand, we produce various text (Transformer-based) embeddings based on BERT-large [8]. For BERT, we first create a sentence for each node, based on a template that encompasses its neighborhood, which is then encoded with BERT's sentence transformer model. All embeddings are computed with the KGTK operations `graph-embeddings` and `text-embeddings`. We analyze them in Sect. 4.2.

The CSKG embeddings are publicly available at http://shorturl.at/pAGX8.

---

[6] https://github.com/usc-isi-i2/cskg/blob/master/consolidation/create_cskg.sh.

4 Analysis

Figure 1 shows a snippet of CSKG that corresponds to the task in Sect. 1. Following P1, CSKG combines: 1) lexical nodes (piano, keys, music), 2) synsets like piano (artifact), seat (dramaturgy) (in green), and 3) frames (`fn:noise_makers`) and frame elements (`fn:fe:use`). According to P2, we reuse edge types where applicable: for instance, we use ConceptNet's `LocatedNear` relation to formalize Visual Genome's proximity information between a woman and a piano. We leverage external links to WordNet to consolidate synsets across sources (P3). We generate further links (P4) to connect FrameNet frames and frame elements to ConceptNet nodes, and to consolidate the representation of `piano (artifact)` between Wikidata and WordNet. In the remainder of this section, we perform qualitative analysis of CSKG and its embeddings.

4.1 Statistics

Basic statistics. of CSKG are shown in Table 2. In total, our mappings produce 251,517 `mw:SameAs` links and 45,659 `fn:HasLexicalUnit` links. After refinement, i.e., removal of the duplicates and merging of the identical nodes, CSKG consists of 2.2 million nodes and 6 million edges. In terms of edges, its largest subgraph is ConceptNet (3.4 million), whereas ATOMIC comes second with 733 thousand edges. These two graphs also contribute the largest number of nodes to CSKG. The three most common relations in CSKG are: `/r/RelatedTo` (1.7 million), `/r/Synonym` (1.2 million), and `/r/Antonym` (401 thousand edges).

Connectivity and centrality. The mean degree of CSKG grows by 5.5% (from 5.26 to 5.55) after merging identical nodes. Compared to ConceptNet, its degree is 45% higher, due to its increased number of edges while keeping the number of nodes nearly constant. The best connected subgraphs are Visual Genome and Roget. CSKG's high connectivity is owed largely to these two sources and our mappings, as the other five sources have degrees below that of CSKG. The abnormally large node degrees and variance of Visual Genome are due to its annotation guidelines that dictate all concept-to-concept information to be annotated, and our modeling choice to represent its nodes through their synsets. We report that the in-degree and out-degree distributions of CSKG have Zipfian shapes, a notable difference being that the maximal in degree is nearly double compared to its maximal out degree (11k vs 6.4k). To understand better the central nodes in CSKG, we compute PageRank and HITS metrics. The top-5 results are shown in Table 3. We observe that the node with highest PageRank has label "chromatic", while all dominant HITS hubs and authorities are colors, revealing that knowledge on colors of real-world object is common in CSKG. PageRank also reveals that knowledge on natural and chemical processes is well-represented in CSKG. Finally, we note that the top-centrality nodes are generally described by multiple subgraphs, e.g., `c/en/natural_science/n/wn/cognition` is found in ConceptNet and WordNet, whereas the color nodes (e.g., `/c/en/red`) are shared between Roget and ConceptNet.

Table 2. CSKG statistics. Abbreviations: CN = ConceptNet, VG = Visual Genome, WN = WordNet, RG = Roget, WD = Wikidata, FN = FrameNet, AT = ATOMIC. Relation numbers in brackets are before consolidating to ConceptNet.

	AT	CN	FN	RG	VG	WD	WN	CSKG*	CSKG
#nodes	304,909	1,787,373	15,652	71,804	11,264	91,294	71,243	2,414,813	**2,160,968**
#edges	732,723	3,423,004	29,873	1,403,955	2,587,623	111,276	101,771	6,349,731	**6,001,531**
#relations	9	47	9 (23)	2	3 (42k)	3	15 (45)	59	**58**
Avg. degree	4.81	3.83	3.82	39.1	459.45	2.44	2.86	5.26	**5.55**
Std. degree	0.07	0.02	0.13	0.34	35.81	0.02	0.05	0.02	**0.03**

Table 3. Nodes with highest centrality score according to PageRank and HITS. Node labels indicated in bold.

PageRank	HITS hubs	HITS authorities
/c/en/**chromatic**/a/wn	/c/en/**red**	/c/en/**blue**
/c/en/**organic_compound**	/c/en/**yellow**	/c/en/**red**
/c/en/**chemical_compound**/n	/c/en/**green**	/c/en/**silver**
/c/en/**change**/n/wn/artifact	/c/en/**silver**	/c/en/**green**
/c/en/**natural_science**/n/wn/cognition	/c/en/**blue**	/c/en/**gold**

4.2 Analysis of the CSKG Embeddings

We randomly sample 5,000 nodes from CSKG and visualize their embeddings computed with an algorithm from each family: TransE and BERT. The results are shown in Fig. 2. We observe that graph embeddings group nodes from the same source together. This is because graph embeddings tend to focus on the graph structure, and because most links in CSKG are still within sources. We observe that the sources are more intertwined in the case of the BERT embeddings, because of the emphasis on lexical over structural similarity. Moreover, in both plots Roget is dispersed around the ConceptNet nodes, which is likely due to its broad coverage of concepts, that maps both structurally and lexically to ConceptNet. At the same time, while ATOMIC overlaps with a subset of ConceptNet [26], the two sources mostly cover different areas of the space.

Table 4 shows the top-5 most similar neighbors for /c/en/turtle/n/ wn/animal and /c/en/happy according to TransE and BERT. We note that while graph embeddings favor nodes that are structurally similar (e.g., /c/en/turtle/n/wn/animal and /c/en/chelonian/n/wn/animal are both animals in WordNet), text embeddings give much higher importance to lexical similarity of nodes or their neighbors, even when the nodes are disconnected in CSKG (e.g., /c/en/happy and at:happy_that_they_went_to_the_party). These results are expected considering the approach behind each algorithm.

Table 4. Top-5 most similar nodes for `/c/en/turtle/n/wn/animal` (E1) and `/c/en/happy` (E2) according to TransE and BERT.

	TransE	BERT
E1	/c/en/chelonian/n/wn/animal	/c/en/glyptemys/n
	/c/en/mud_turtle/n/wn/animal	/c/en/pelocomastes/n
	/c/en/cooter/n/wn/animal	/c/en/staurotypus/n
	/c/en/common_snapping_turtle/n/wn/animal	/c/en/parahydraspis/n
	/c/en/sea_turtle/n/wn/animal	/c/en/trachemys/n
E2	/c/en/excited	/c/en/bring_happiness
	/c/en/satisfied	/c/en/new_happiness
	/c/en/smile_mood	at:like_a_party_is_a_good_way_to_...
	/c/en/pleased	/c/en/encouraging_person's_talent
	/c/en/joyful	at:happy_that_they_went_to_the_party

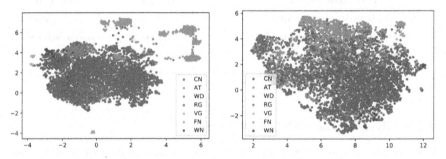

Fig. 2. UMAP visualization of 5,000 randomly sampled nodes from CSKG, represented by TransE (left) and BERT (right) embeddings. Colors signify node sources. (Color figure online)

Word Association with Embeddings. To quantify the utility of different embeddings, we evaluate them on the *USF-FAN* [23] benchmark, which contains crowdsourced common sense associations for 5,019 "stimulus" concepts in English. For instance, the associations provided for day are: night, light, sun, time, week, and break. The associations are ordered descendingly based on their frequency. With each algorithm, we produce a top-K most similar neighbors list based on the embedding of the stimulus concept. Here, K is the number of associations for a concept, which varies across stimuli. If CSKG has multiple nodes for the stimulus label, we average their embeddings. For the graph embeddings, we use logistic loss function, using a dot comparator, a learning rate of 0.1, and dimension 100. The BERT text embeddings have dimension 1024, which is the native dimension of this language model. As the text embedding models often favor surface form similarity (e.g., associations like daily for day), we devise variants of this method that excludes associations with Levenshtein similarity higher than a threshold t.

We evaluate by comparing the embedding-based list to the benchmark one, through customary ranking metrics, like Mean Average Precision (MAP) and Normalized Discounted Cumulative Gain (NDCG). Our investigations show that TransE is the best-performing algorithm overall, with MAP of 0.207 and NDCG of 0.530. The optimal BERT variant uses threshold of $t = 0.9$, scoring with MAP of 0.209 and NDCG of 0.268. The obtained MAP scores indicate that the embeddings capture relevant signals, yet, a principled solution to USF-FAN requires a more sophisticated embedding search method that can capture various forms of both relatedness and similarity. In the future, we aim to investigate embedding techniques that integrate structural and content information like RDF2Vec [25], and evaluate on popular word similarity datasets like WordSim-353 [9].

5 Applications

As the creation of CSKG is largely driven by downstream reasoning needs, we now investigate its relevance for commonsense question answering: 1) we measure its ability to contribute novel evidence to support reasoning, and 2) we measure its role in pre-training language models for zero-shot downstream reasoning.

5.1 Retrieving Evidence from CSKG

We measure the relevance of CSKG for commonsense question answering tasks, by comparing the number of retrieved triples that connect keywords in the question and in the answers. For this purpose, we adapt the lexical grounding in HyKAS [18] to retrieve triples from CSKG instead of its default knowledge source, ConceptNet. We expect that CSKG can provide much more evidence than ConceptNet, both in terms of number of triples and their diversity. We experiment with four commonsense datasets: CommonSense QA (CSQA) [30], Social IQA (SIQA) [27], Physical IQA (PIQA) [3], and abductive NLI (aNLI) [2]. As shown in Table 5, CSKG significantly increases the number of evidence triples that connect terms in questions with terms in answers, in comparison to Concept-Net. We note that the increase is on average 2–3 times, the expected exception being CSQA, which was inferred from ConceptNet.

We inspect a sample of questions to gain insight into whether the additional triples are relevant and could benefit reasoning. For instance, let us consider the CSQA question "Bob the lizard lives in a warm place with lots of water. Where does he probably live?", whose correct answer is "tropical rainforest". In addition to the ConceptNet triple /c/en/lizard /c/en/AtLocation /c/en/tropical_rainforest, CSKG provides two additional triples, stating that tropical is an instance of place and that water may have property tropical. The first additional edge stems from our mappings from FrameNet to ConceptNet, whereas the second comes from Visual Genome. We note that, while CSKG increases the coverage with respect to available commonsense knowledge, it is also incomplete: in the above example, useful information such as warm temperatures being typical for tropical rainforests is still absent.

Table 5. Number of triples retrieved with ConceptNet and CSKG on different datasets.

	Train			Dev		
	#Questions	ConceptNet	CSKG	#Questions	ConceptNet	CSKG
CSQA	9,741	78,729	125,552	1,221	9,758	15,662
SIQA	33,410	126,596	266,937	1,954	7,850	16,149
PIQA	16,113	18,549	59,684	1,838	2,170	6,840
aNLI	169,654	257,163	638,841	1,532	5,603	13,582

Table 6. Zero-shot evaluation results with different combinations of models and knowledge sources, across five commonsense tasks, as reported in [19]. CWWV combines ConceptNet, Wikidata, WordNet, and Visual Genome. CSKG is a union of ATOMIC and CWWV. We report mean accuracy over three runs, with 95% confidence interval.

Model	KG	aNLI	CSQA	PIQA	SIQA	WG
GPT2-L	ATOMIC	59.2($\pm$0.3)	48.0($\pm$0.9)	67.5($\pm$0.7)	53.5($\pm$0.4)	54.7($\pm$0.6)
GPT2-L	CWWV	58.3($\pm$0.4)	46.2($\pm$1.0)	68.6($\pm$0.7)	48.0($\pm$0.7)	52.8($\pm$0.9)
GPT2-L	CSKG	59.0($\pm$0.5)	48.6($\pm$1.0)	68.6($\pm$0.9)	53.3($\pm$0.5)	54.1($\pm$0.5)
RoBERTa-L	ATOMIC	**70.8($\pm$1.2)**	64.2($\pm$0.7)	72.1($\pm$0.5)	63.1($\pm$1.5)	59.6($\pm$0.3)
RoBERTa-L	CWWV	70.0($\pm$0.3)	**67.9($\pm$0.8)**	72.0($\pm$0.7)	54.8($\pm$1.2)	59.4($\pm$0.5)
RoBERTa-L	CSKG	70.5($\pm$0.2)	67.4($\pm$0.8)	**72.4($\pm$0.4)**	**63.2($\pm$0.7)**	**60.9($\pm$0.8)**
Human	–	91.4	88.9	94.9	86.9	94.1

5.2 Pre-training Language Models with CSKG

We have studied the role of various subsets of CSKG for downstream QA reasoning extensively in [19]. Here, CSKG or its subsets were transformed into artificial commonsense question answering tasks. These tasks were then used instead of training data to pre-train language models, like RoBERTa and GPT-2. Such a CSKG-based per-trained language model was then 'frozen' and evaluated in a zero-shot manner across a wide variety of commonsense tasks, ranging from question answering through pronoun resolution and natural language inference.

We select key results from these experiments in Table 6. The results demonstrate that no single knowledge source suffices for all benchmarks and that using CSKG is overall beneficial compared to using its subgraphs, thus directly showing the benefit of commonsense knowledge consolidation. In a follow-up study [11], we further exploit the consolidation in CSKG to pre-train the language models with one dimension (knowledge type) at a time, noting that certain dimensions of knowledge (e.g., temporal knowledge) are much more useful for reasoning than others, like lexical knowledge. In both cases, the kind of knowledge that benefits each task is ultimately conditioned on the alignment between this knowledge and the targeted task, indicating that subsequent work should further investigate how to dynamically align knowledge with the task at hand.

6   Discussion

Our analysis in Sect. 4 revealed that the connectivity in CSKG is higher than merely concatenation of the individual sources, due to our mappings across sources and the merge of identical nodes. Its KGTK format allowed us to seamlessly compute and evaluate a series of embeddings, observing that TransE and BERT with additional filtering are the two best-performing and complementary algorithms. The novel evidence brought by CSKG on downstream QA tasks (Sect. 5) is a signal that can be exploited by reasoning systems to enhance their performance and robustness, as shown in [19]. Yet, the quest to a rich, high-coverage CSKG is far from completed. We briefly discuss two key challenges, while broader discussion can be found in [11].

Node resolution. As large part of CSKG consists of lexical nodes, it suffers from the standard challenges of linguistic ambiguity and variance. For instance, there are 18 nodes in CSKG that have the label 'scene', which includes WordNet or OpenCyc synsets, Wikidata Qnodes, frame elements, and a lexical node. Variance is another challenge, as `/c/en/caffeine`, `/c/en/caffine`, and `/c/en/the_active_ingredient_caffeine` are all separate nodes in ConceptNet (and in CSKG). We are currently investigating techniques for node resolution applicable to the heterogeneity of commonsense knowledge in CSKG.

Semantic enrichment. We have normalized the edge types across sources to a single, ConceptNet-centric, set of 58 relations. In [11], we classify all CSKG's relations into 13 dimensions, enabling us to consolidate the edge types further. At the same time, some of these relations hide fine-grained distinctions, for example, WebChild [31] defines 19 specific property relations, including temperature, shape, and color, all of which correspond to ConceptNet's `/r/HasProperty`. A novel future direction is to produce hierarchy for each of the relations, and refine existing triples by using a more specific relation (e.g., use the predicate 'temperature' instead of 'property' when the object of the triple is 'cold').

7   Conclusions and Future Work

While current commonsense knowledge sources contain complementary knowledge that would be beneficial as a whole for downstream tasks, such usage is prevented by different modeling approaches, foci, and sparsity of available mappings. Optimizing for simplicity, modularity, and utility, we proposed a hyper-relational graph representation that describes many nodes with a few edge types, maximizes the high-quality links across subgraphs, and enables natural language access. We applied this representation approach to consolidate a commonsense knowledge graph (CSKG) from seven very diverse and disjoint sources: a text-based commonsense knowledge graph ConceptNet, a general-purpose taxonomy Wikidata, an image description dataset Visual Genome, a procedural knowledge source ATOMIC, and three lexical sources: WordNet, Roget, and FrameNet. CSKG describes 2.2 million nodes with 6 million statements. Our analysis showed that CSKG is a well-connected graph and more than 'a simple sum of its parts'. Together with CSKG, we also publicly release a series of graph and text embeddings of the CSKG nodes, to facilitate future usage of the graph. Our analysis showed that graph and text embeddings of CSKG have complementary notions of similarity, as the former focus on structural patterns, while the latter on lexical features of the node's label and of its neighborhood. Applying CSKG on downstream commonsense reasoning tasks, like QA, showed an increased recall as well as an advantage when pre-training a language model to reason across datasets in a zero-shot fashion. Key standing challenges for CSKG include semantic consolidation of its nodes and refinement of its property hierarchy. Notebooks for analyzing these resources can be found on our public GitHub page: https://github.com/usc-isi-i2/cskg/tree/master/ESWC2021.

Acknowledgements. This work is sponsored by the DARPA MCS program under Contract No. N660011924033 with the United States Office Of Naval Research, and by the Air Force Research Laboratory under agreement number FA8750-20-2-10002.

References

1. Baker, C.F., Fillmore, C.J., Lowe, J.B.: The berkeley framenet project. In: Proceedings of the 17th international conference on Computational linguistics (1998)
2. Bhagavatula, C., et al.: Abductive commonsense reasoning. arXiv preprint arXiv:1908.05739 (2019)
3. Bisk, Y., Zellers, R., Bras, R.L., Gao, J., Choi, Y.: Piqa: Reasoning about physical commonsense in natural language. arXiv preprint arXiv:1911.11641 (2019)
4. Bordes, A., Usunier, N., Garcia-Duran, A., Weston, J., Yakhnenko, O.: Translating embeddings for modeling multi-relational data. Adv. Neural Inf. Process. Syst. **26**, 2787–2795 (2013)
5. Corcoglioniti, F., Rospocher, M., Aprosio, A.P., Tonelli, S.: Premon: a lemon extension for exposing predicate models as linked data. In: Proceedings of the Tenth International Conference on Language Resources and Evaluation (LREC 2016) (2016)
6. De Lacalle, M.L., Laparra, E., Aldabe, I., Rigau, G.: Predicate matrix: automatically extending the semantic interoperability between predicate resources. Lang. Resour. Eval. **50**(2), 263–289 (2016)
7. Deng, J., Dong, W., Socher, R., Li, L.J., Li, K., Fei-Fei, L.: ImageNet: a large-scale hierarchical image database. In: 2009 IEEE Conference on Computer Vision and Pattern Recognition, pp. 248–255. IEEE (2009)
8. Devlin, J., Chang, M.W., Lee, K., Toutanova, K.: Bert: Pre-training of deep bidirectional transformers for language understanding. arXiv preprint arXiv:1810.04805 (2018)
9. Finkelstein, L., et al.: Placing search in context: The concept revisited. In: Proceedings of the 10th International Conference on World Wide Web, pp. 406–414 (2001)
10. Ilievski, F., et al.: KGTK: a toolkit for large knowledge graph manipulation and analysis. In: Pan, J.Z., et al. (eds.) ISWC 2020, Part II. LNCS, vol. 12507, pp. 278–293. Springer, Cham (2020). https://doi.org/10.1007/978-3-030-62466-8_18

11. Ilievski, F., Oltramari, A., Ma, K., Zhang, B., McGuinness, D.L., Szekely, P.: Dimensions of commonsense knowledge. arXiv preprint arXiv:2101.04640 (2021)

12. Ilievski, F., Szekely, P., Schwabe, D.: Commonsense knowledge in WikiData. In: Proceedings of the WikiData Workshop, ISWC (2020)

13. Kipfer, B.: Roget's 21st century thesaurus in dictionary form (éd. 3) (2005)

14. Krishna, R., et al.: Visual genome: connecting language and vision using crowd-sourced dense image annotations. Int. J. Comput. Vis. **123**(1), 32–73 (2017)

15. Lerer, A., et al.: Pytorch-biggraph: A large-scale graph embedding system. arXiv preprint arXiv:1903.12287 (2019)

16. Lin, B.Y., Chen, X., Chen, J., Ren, X.: KagNet: Knowledge-aware graph networks for commonsense reasoning. arXiv preprint arXiv:1909.02151 (2019)

17. Liu, Y., et al.: Roberta: A robustly optimized BERT pretraining approach. arXiv preprint arXiv:1907.11692 (2019)

18. Ma, K., Francis, J., Lu, Q., Nyberg, E., Oltramari, A.: Towards generalizable neuro-symbolic systems for commonsense question answering. In: EMNLP-COIN (2019)

19. Ma, K., Ilievski, F., Francis, J., Bisk, Y., Nyberg, E., Oltramari, A.: Knowledge-driven data construction for zero-shot evaluation in commonsense question answering. In: 35th AAAI Conference on Artificial Intelligence (2021)

20. McCrae, J.P.: Mapping wordnet instances to Wikipedia. In: Proceedings of the 9th Global WordNet Conference (GWC 2018), pp. 62–69 (2018)

21. Miller, G.A.: Wordnet: a lexical database for English. Commun. ACM **38**(11), 39–41 (1995)

22. Navigli, R., Ponzetto, S.P.: BabelNet: building a very large multilingual semantic network. In: Proceedings of ACL (2010)

23. Nelson, D.L., McEvoy, C.L., Schreiber, T.A.: The university of South Florida free association, rhyme, and word fragment norms. Behav. Res. Methods Instrum. Comput. **36**(3), 402–407 (2004). https://doi.org/10.3758/BF03195588

24. Nickel, M., Tresp, V., Kriegel, H.P.: A three-way model for collective learning on multi-relational data. ICML **11**, 809–816 (2011)

25. Ristoski, P., Paulheim, H.: RDF2Vec: RDF graph embeddings for data mining. In: Groth, P., et al. (eds.) ISWC 2016, Part I. LNCS, vol. 9981, pp. 498–514. Springer, Cham (2016). https://doi.org/10.1007/978-3-319-46523-4_30

26. Sap, M., et al.: Atomic: an atlas of machine commonsense for if-then reasoning. In: Proceedings of the AAAI Conference on Artificial Intelligence (2019)

27. Sap, M., Rashkin, H., Chen, D., LeBras, R., Choi, Y.: Socialiqa: Commonsense reasoning about social interactions. arXiv preprint arXiv:1904.09728 (2019)

28. Schuler, K.K.: VerbNet: A broad-coverage, comprehensive verb lexicon (2005)

29. Speer, R., Chin, J., Havasi, C.: Conceptnet 5.5: an open multilingual graph of general knowledge. In: Thirty-First AAAI Conference on Artificial Intelligence (2017)

30. Talmor, A., Herzig, J., Lourie, N., Berant, J.: Commonsenseqa: A question answering challenge targeting commonsense knowledge. arXiv preprint arXiv:1811.00937 (2018)

31. Tandon, N., De Melo, G., Weikum, G.: Webchild 2.0: fine-grained commonsense knowledge distillation. In: ACL 2017, System Demonstrations (2017)

32. Trouillon, T., Welbl, J., Riedel, S., Gaussier, É., Bouchard, G.: Complex embeddings for simple link prediction. In: ICML (2016)

33. Trumbo, D.: Increasing the usability of research lexica. Ph.D. thesis, University of Colorado at Boulder (2006)

34. Vrandečić, D., Krötzsch, M.: WikiData: a free collaborative knowledgebase. Commun. ACM **57**(10), 78–85 (2014)

35. Yang, B., Yih, W.T., He, X., Gao, J., Deng, L.: Embedding entities and relations for learning and inference in knowledge bases. arXiv preprint arXiv:1412.6575 (2014)
36. Yang, Z., Dai, Z., Yang, Y., Carbonell, J., Salakhutdinov, R.R., Le, Q.V.: XLNet: generalized autoregressive pretraining for language understanding. In: Advances in Neural Information Processing Systems, pp. 5754–5764 (2019)
37. Zareian, A., Karaman, S., Chang, S.F.: Bridging knowledge graphs to generate scene graphs. arXiv preprint arXiv:2001.02314 (2020)
38. Zellers, R., Bisk, Y., Schwartz, R., Choi, Y.: Swag: A large-scale adversarial dataset for grounded commonsense inference. arXiv preprint arXiv:1808.05326 (2018)

In-Use Track

A Knowledge Graph-Based Approach for Situation Comprehension in Driving Scenarios

Lavdim Halilaj[1]([⊠]), Ishan Dindorkar[2], Jürgen Lüttin[1],
and Susanne Rothermel[1]

[1] Bosch Corporate Research, Renningen, Germany
{lavdim.halilaj,juergen.luettin,susanne.rothermel}@de.bosch.com
[2] Robert Bosch Engineering and Business SPL, Bengaluru, India
ishan.dindorkar@in.bosch.com

Abstract. Making an informed and right decision poses huge challenges for drivers in day-to-day traffic situations. This task vastly depends on many subjective and objective factors, including the current driver state, her destination, personal preferences and abilities as well as surrounding environment. In this paper, we present *CoSI* (Context and Situation Intelligence), a Knowledge Graph (KG)-based approach for fusing and organizing heterogeneous types and sources of information. The KG serves as a coherence layer representing information in the form of entities and their inter-relationships augmented with additional semantic axioms. Harnessing the power of axiomatic rules and reasoning capabilities enables inferring additional knowledge from what is already encoded. Thus, dedicated components exploit and consume the semantically enriched information to perform tasks such as *situation classification*, *difficulty assessment*, and *trajectory prediction*. Further, we generated a synthetic dataset to simulate real driving scenarios with a large range of driving styles and vehicle configurations. We use KG embedding techniques based on a Graph Neural Network (GNN) architecture for a classification task of driving situations and achieve over 95% accuracy whereas vector-based approaches achieve only 75% accuracy for the same task. The results suggest that the KG-based information representation combined with GNN are well suited for situation understanding tasks as required in driver assistance and automated driving systems.

Keywords: Situation comprehension · Knowledge graph · Knowledge graph embedding · Graph neural network

1 Introduction

Safe driving requires an understanding of the current driving situation which includes perceiving the current traffic situation, comprehending their meaning and predicting what could happen in the near future. Situation Awareness

© Springer Nature Switzerland AG 2021
R. Verborgh et al. (Eds.): ESWC 2021, LNCS 12731, pp. 699–716, 2021.
https://doi.org/10.1007/978-3-030-77385-4_42

(SA) is a concept that attempts to describe and integrate these cognitive processes [12]. SA is the driver's useful moment-to-moment knowledge and understanding of the driving environment but does not include the decision making. SA by machine could assist the driver and reduce accidents by warning about difficult driving situations. However, the behaviour of the driver in the vast range of situations is not well understood [7].

Vehicles with driver assistance systems (DAS) [4] aim to take some work-load off the driver to improve comfort and efficiency and to enhance driving safety. These systems are aware of the driving situation and benefit from the concept of SA at different task levels of perception, decision making and action [33]. A shared control driver assistance system based on driver intention identification and situation assessment has been proposed in [28]. The application of driver safety warning, particularly collision warning has been described in [25].

Automated Driving Systems (ADS) require the system rather than the driver to maintain high safety performance. A number of metrics to define the driving safety performance of ADS and compare it to that of human driven vehicles have been proposed in [42]. Currently, in many highly automated driving scenarios, the driver is required to take-over the driving task in cases where the system is not capable to handle the situation safely [1]. This requires machine perception to assess the current driving situation followed by scene understanding and decision making. Whereas much progress has been made in machine perception, scene understanding and prediction of the next actions of the traffic participants is still subject to extensive research [10].

In this paper, we propose CoSI, a Knowledge Graph (KG)-based approach for representing numerous information sources relevant for traffic situations. It includes information about driver, vehicle, road infrastructure, driving situation and interacting traffic participants. We built an ontology to encapsulate the core concepts crucial for the driving context. Concepts from external ontologies are reused, enabling an easy extension and interlinking with different data sources as well as facilitating data extraction. We describe how the knowledge in the KG is utilized via an embedding method such as Graph Neural Networks (GNN) to implement typical classification and prediction tasks used in DAS and ADS. Our approach is evaluated on a synthetically generated dataset comprising a large number of traffic situations and driving styles. We also compare the performance of our proposed approach with classic vector-based feature representations.

2   Related Work

Some key tasks in DAS and ADS are the detection and tracking of the relevant traffic participants, prediction of their possible actions, understanding of the traffic situation and planning of the next movement based on the actual context. According to [26] approaches for vehicle motion prediction can be grouped into *Physics-based, Maneuver-based* and *Interaction-based*.

Classical *Rule-based decision-making* systems in automated driving are limited in terms of generalization to unseen situations. Deep reinforcement learning

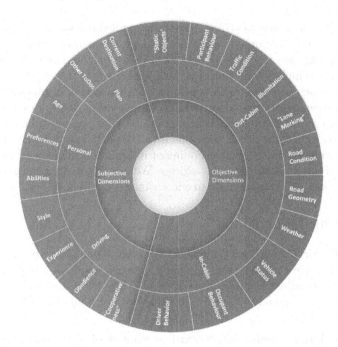

Fig. 1. Driving Dimensions. Categories of driving dimensions: 1) *Objective Dimensions*, further divided in Out-Cabin and In-Cabin; and 2) *Subjective Dimensions*, grouped in Personal, Driving, and Plans.

(DRL) is therefore used to learn decision policies from data and has shown to improve rule-based systems [29]. Different deep neural approaches and feature combinations for trajectory prediction are described in [27] in which surrounding vehicles and their features are extracted from fixed grid cells. Convolutional neural networks (CNN) that use fixed occupancy grids are limited by the grid size and the number of vehicles considered [30]. Recurrent neural networks (RNN) are able to model temporal information and variable input size, but are not well suited to handle a variable number of objects permutation-invariant w.r.t. the input elements [20]. When RNNs are combined with an *Attention* mechanism, they can be used to create a representation which is permutation invariant w.r.t. the input objects [38]. *Deep Sets* provide a more flexible architecture that can process inputs of varying size [43] and are used for DRL in Automated Driving [20]. One limiting factor of these approaches is the implicit and informal representation of entities and relational information between entities.

Ontologies on the other hand encompass the formal definition of entities and their relations. Authors in [6] present an approach that uses ontologies to represent knowledge for driver assistance systems. A traffic intersection description ontology for DAS is described in [21]. It also uses logic inference to check and extend the situation description and to interpret the situation e.g. by reasoning about traffic rules. An ontology-based driving scene modeling, situation assessment, and decision making for ADS is proposed in [19].

Graph Neural Networks (GNN) have been applied to model traffic participant interaction [8, 11]. VectorNet, a hierarchical graph neural network is used for behaviour prediction in traffic situations [15]. A behaviour interaction network that captures vehicle interactions has been described in [13].

Our approach in comparison is overarching, consisting of phases for perception, knowledge ingestion, and situation comprehension. It exploits relationships between the ego and foe vehicles from a graph-based representation. Personal and subjective aspects of the driver and other involved participants are covered as well. Our motivation is that explicit encoding of information might lead to improved modelling of interactions between vehicles. We use multi-relational graph convolution networks [41] that are able to encode multi-modal node features.

3   Driving Dimensions

Assisting the driver with fully-informed decisions about steering, acceleration, breaking, or more complex tasks like lane changing requires a high level of situation understanding. Figure 1 illustrates an overview of dimensions divided in two main groups, namely *Objective Dimensions* and *Subjective Dimensions*.

Objective Dimensions. There exist a number of dimensions that can be explicitly perceived from sensors or derived via specific methods. This group comprises dimensions presented in [16], which are related to dynamics, complexity and uncertainty impacting the drivability of a driving scene irrelevant of the driver personality. The ability to scrutinize them in a right manner directly influences the comprehension of the occurring events. Potential hazardous situations can only be identified by further investigating the interactions and the intent of road participants [36]. This information is rather implicit and has to be inferred by combining observations with additional algorithmic procedures.

Considering the origin of these dimensions, they are divided into two categories: 1) *Out-Cabin*; and 2) *In-Cabin*. The *Out-Cabin* category comprises information happening outside the vehicle boundaries. Such information include the actual traffic, road and weather conditions, static objects, illumination, and others. All kind of information pertaining to what is happening inside the vehicle belongs to the *In-Cabin* category. It consists of information related to driver status, occupant behavior, vehicle status, and others.

An exhaustive list of the objective dimensions including their categorization and further details which impact the drivability of a scene are presented in [16].

Subjective Dimensions. Objective dimensions alone are not sufficient for a personalized situation assessment. It heavily depends on the individuality of the driver itself. Not each explicitly perceived situation occurring in a given driving scenario is considered the same or has the equal level of difficulty. Therefore, a number of subjective dimensions are crucial in determining correct situation classification or difficulty level. The subjective subcategories cover information pertaining to *personal*, *driving*, and *current plans*.

In general, each subcategory belonging to the outer circle can have tens of signals coming from sensors through different transmission channels like Controller Area Network (CAN) bus. These signals include information such as gaze direction, drowsiness, inside- and outside-temperature, fuel consumption, number of occupants. Next, special processing units consume and manage retrieved signals to generate appropriate notifications to the driver or actions to the vehicle.

4   Approach

Achieving a *high level of intelligence* is possible by fusing and enriching collected data from different sources such as connected sensors. This enables autonomous vehicles to react according to the situation within a driving environment [9]. With the aim of covering the entire process, we designed a flow-oriented architecture composed of three main phases, namely: 1) *Contextual Observation*; 2) *Knowledge Ingestion*; and 3) *Situation Comprehension*. Each phase comprises a number of components dedicated to perform specific tasks as shown in Fig. 2.

4.1   Contextual Observation

Intelligent vehicles are equipped with a number of sophisticated sensors that sense the surrounding of the vehicle. Typically, the average number of sensors in a smart vehicle is ranging from 70 up to 100 [18], monitoring various types of events as well as stationary and mobile objects. This includes observing the driver and occupant(s), engine status, and the road network. Spatial and temporal information is obtained for each observed object. A wide range of sensors, e.g. light and rain sensors, internal and external cameras, Radar and Lidar are used for perception tasks. Each sensor may be built via a specific technology and standard, thus generating data in various formats with a different granularity.

4.2   Knowledge Ingestion

Situation comprehension requires integrating and structuring the abundance of information from various sources. Raw signals from sensors are transformed and enriched with additional semantics. Further, contextual information and user characteristics are injected to support a personalized situation assessment.

Knowledge Graph. The KG serves as a coherence component comprising fundamental ontologies to capture information about entities and their relationships. We see a KG as a set of triples $G = H, R, T$, where H is a set of entities, $T \subseteq E \times L$, a set of entities E or literal L values and R, a set of relationships connecting H and T. These triples are represented using Resource Definition Framework (RDF) as a modeling language. Encoding additional formal axioms enables inferring new facts out of given ones via automated reasoning techniques.

Once the transformation process is realized, i.e. converting input data of any format to triples, the output is stored in a knowledge graph. Information in the

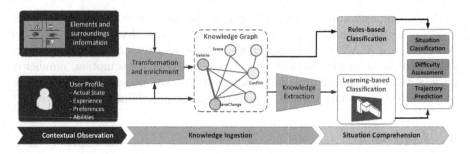

Fig. 2. CoSI Pipeline. The pipeline is comprised of three consecutive phases: 1) *Contextual Observation* - capture information about the surroundings and the user; 2) *Knowledge Ingestion* - transform, enrich and ingest information on the KG; and 3) *Situation Classification* - assess the situation type considering the contextual knowledge.

KG is aggregated and organized in an intuitive and hierarchical way, making it easy to exploit and understand by humans. An excerpt of the CoSI KG (CKG) is given in Fig. 3, showing how *scenery information* is represented via instances (*assertional box*) of ontological concepts (*terminological box*). Apart from sensor data, it captures the information related to the driver such as preferences and abilities modeled according to the CoSI ontology as described in the following.

Ontology. We developed the CoSI ontology based on the dimensions and their respective categories described in Sect. 3. It captures relevant information coming from sensors mounted in a given vehicle. The human description of crucial concepts: Scene, Situation and Scenario given in [37] are used as a basis to create formal definitions using ontological axioms. Additionally, the ontology models different user characteristics such as preferences (e.g., preferred driving style or safety measures), experience and (dis)abilities. In the following, the respective definitions of core concepts of the CoSI ontology are given:

- *Scene*: A scene describes a snapshot of the environment including the scenery and dynamic elements, as well as all actors' and observers' self-representations, and the relationships among those entities [37].
- *Situation*: A situation is the entirety of circumstances considered for the selection of an appropriate behavior pattern at a particular point of time. It entails all relevant conditions, options and determinants for behavior [37].
- *Scenario*: A scenario describes the temporal development between several scenes in a sequence of scenes. Actions, events and goals may be specified to characterize this temporal development in a scenario [37].
- *Observation*: Act of carrying out an (Observation) Procedure to estimate or calculate a value of a property of a FeatureOfInterest [17].
- *Driver*: A driver is a specific type of user. It encapsulates all relevant attributes associated to a driving context where driver is the main subject.
- *Profile*: A user profile is a structured data representation that is used to capture certain characteristics about an individual user[1].

---

[1] https://en.wikipedia.org/wiki/User_profile.

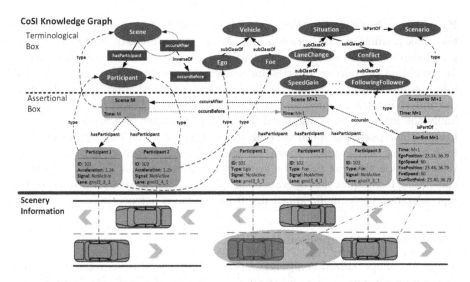

Fig. 3. CoSI Knowledge Graph. An excerpt of the CoSI KG representing respective situations occurring in two consecutive scenes: 1) the bottom layer depicts scenery information among participants; 2) the top layer includes concepts such as classes and relationships representing the domain knowledge; and 3) the middle layer contains concrete instances capturing the scenery information based on the ontological concepts.

- *Preference*: A preference is a technical term in psychology, economics and philosophy usually used in relation to choosing between alternatives. For example, someone prefers A over B if they would rather choose A than B[2].

The CoSI ontology is built on principles for an easy extension and exploration. Concepts from external ontologies such as Schema.org and SOSA ontology[3], are reused to enable interlinking with different data sources. Currently, it contains 51 classes, 57 object datatype properties and 3 annotation properties.

Transformation and Enrichment. This component performs a semi-automatic conversion of sensor data to the RDF representation via both declarative and imperative approaches. Using the declarative approach, a number of mappings of sensor data to the ontological concepts are defined. The imperative approach is realized in cases when it is necessary to perform complex transformations. In these cases, additional queries are executed on-the-fly to enrich sensor data with new relationships. For instance, raw data generated from sensors are augmented with additional semantic information in order to establish new type definitions or missing relationships between scenes, e.g. *occursAfter*.

---

[2] https://en.wikipedia.org/wiki/Preference.
[3] https://schema.org/, https://www.w3.org/TR/vocab-ssn/.

Knowledge Extraction. Performing tasks such as knowledge graph completion, link prediction, classification, or other types of downstream tasks requires knowledge to be consumed based on various perspectives. This component allows for execution of complex queries and traversing the graph to retrieve relevant information. Various views of the information can be created on the fly while the underlying knowledge structure remains unchanged. For instance, while originally the information is organized from the perspective of a Scene, i.e. participants, their position, speed as well as the type of situation happening in it; by traversing the graph through specific queries, another view from the ego vehicle perspective can easily be generated as illustrated in Fig. 4. As a result, embedding techniques that operate on graph level, can efficiently learn the vector representation of symbolic knowledge from the "new perspective".

4.3 Situation Comprehension

A number of specialized components perform dedicated tasks related to situation comprehension, such as *Situation Classification*, *Difficulty Assessment*, and *Trajectory Prediction*. These components can be built on different paradigms, namely 1) Rule-based; and 2) Learning-based classification.

- *Rule-based Classification* Components following this paradigm rely on a number of declarative rules to perform logic-based classification tasks. They harness the expressive power of the knowledge graph structure which in combination with reasoning techniques provide interpretable results.
- *Learning-based Classification* Components employ a number of techniques that learn common patterns from a large number of observations. Therefore, it is possible to make predictions or classifications based on a given sample data used for training without pre-defining explicit rules.

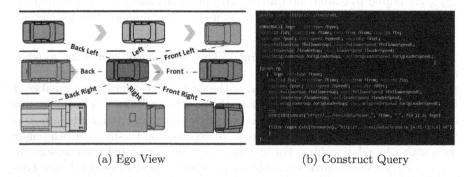

(a) Ego View   (b) Construct Query

Fig. 4. Ego Vehicle Perspective. a) A traffic situation from the ego vehicle (green) perspective in the center and eight foe vehicles in its vicinity. b) A SPARQL query constructing a graph-based view on the fly from ego perspective. (Color figure online)

Table 1. Simulation Parameters. Simulation parameters of the driver and vehicle that were varied to generate a large range of driving situations.

Parameter	Description
lcSpeedGain	Driver's eagerness for speed gain by overtaking
lcCooperative	Driver's cooperativeness in reducing speed for other vehicles
σ (sigma)	Driver's imperfection in realizing desired speed
τ (tau)	Driver's reaction time in seconds
minGap	Driver's target gap between ego and foe vehicle
maxSpeed	Vehicle's maximum speed
maxAccel	Vehicle's maximum acceleration

5 Implementation

Our objective is to evaluate how well our KG-model can represent traffic situations. Particularly, we focus on situations with interacting vehicles, where vehicles base their behaviour on current and predicted behaviour of other nearby vehicles, considered a notoriously challenging task. We thus define driving situation classification as our evaluation task. To validate the benefit of our model with as little influence from other factors, we deliberately define the task on single *scenes*. Models that exploit temporal information are very likely to lead to better results, since some situations such as merging or overtaking are manifested via a gradual change of the lane ID over time. However, here we only validate the underlying static knowledge and exclude effects of temporal information.

5.1 Dataset Generation

Experimental Setup. Experiments on recorded test drives is prohibitive [22] as it would require huge amounts of test data without assurance that enough examples of critical driving situations are included. We therefore use simulated data for our experiments. An advantage of this approach is that it allows to specifically generate critical driving scenes which we are interested in, both in terms of driving behaviour and situation criticality.

We use *Simulations of Urban Mobility* (SUMO)[4], an open source, highly portable, microscopic and continuous multi-modal traffic simulation package to generate driving data. We generated a dataset[5] comprising more than 50'000 driving examples on a 40 km long highway section around the Gothenburg city as shown in Fig. 5a. It is circular in shape with three lanes in each direction.

Scenarios. We varied simulation parameters such as time-to-collision (TTC) (i.e. the time until a collision between two entities would occur if both continue with the present velocities) of drivers and vehicles to simulate different driving styles

---

[4] https://www.eclipse.org/sumo/.
[5] https://github.com/siwer/Retra.

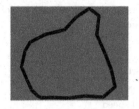      

(a) Gothenburg's Highway   (b) Lane change situation   (c) Collision situation

Fig. 5. Sumo traffic simulations. Examples of traffic simulations using SUMO: a) A snapshot of a highway around the city of Gothenburg; b) A situation where ego vehicle is switching the most left lane; and c) An example with a collision situation happening.

and vehicle types as listed in Table 1. This leads to the generation of various driving scenarios as described in Table 2.

Car Following Model. The standard car following model in SUMO is described in [24]. It is based on the assumption that the speed of the ego vehicle is adapted according to the speed of the preceding vehicle. Further, a desired gap between the ego and the leading vehicle as well as reaction and braking time are taken into account to ensure that no collision will occur. Figure 5c depicts a situation where a collision between the ego and the foe is happening.

Lane Change Model. The lane change model considers different motivations of the driver (route, speed gain, rule-following, cooperativeness and other factors) for lane changes on multi-lane roads and related speed adjustments [14]. Figure 5b shows an example where the ego vehicle is performing a lane change.

5.2 CoSI Knowledge Graph

Data generated from SUMO are provided in XML format which are then transformed and enriched on-the-fly to RDF representation. As a result, the CoSI Knowledge Graph (CKG) is created with over 915 million triples. There are more than 84K *Conflict Scenarios* containing millions of instances of different types of situations, such as *Following Leader, Following Follower, Crossing, Merge* etc. These instances consist of information about the conflict points, speed of ego and foe vehicle, and the direction of movement, respectively. Further, CKG has more than 10K *Lane Change Scenarios*, which also contains millions of instances of different lane change situations, categorized in respective ontological classes, such as *Speed Gain, Keep Right*, or *Sublane*.

5.3 KG-Based Situation Classification

This component is implemented according to the principles of the learning-based paradigm. It uses a *Relational Graph Convolutional Network* [34] (R-GCN), an

Table 2. Driving Scenarios. Different driving scenarios are simulated by varying simulation parameters of vehicle and the driving style.

Driving scenario	Description
1	Successful lane change
2	Abandoned lane change
3	Dangerous lane change (small gap, small TTC values)
4	Dangerous close car following (small gap, small TTC values)
5	Unexpected stopping of leading vehicle
6	Unexpected pedestrians on road
7	Collision between ego and foe vehicle

extension of *Graph Convolutional Network* (GCN) [23], to directly operate on a graph and learn its embeddings. Each layer l of the *R-GCN* calculates:

$$H^{(l+1)} = \sigma(\sum_{r\in\mathbb{R}} \hat{A}^r H^{(l)} W^{(l)}) \tag{1}$$

where $\hat{A}^r$ is the normalized adjacency matrix of the graph G, $W^{(l)}$ is the weight matrix for layer (l) and σ the activation function, such as *ReLU*. $H^{(l)} \in \mathbb{R}^{N \times D}$ is the matrix of activation's in the lth layer and H^0 the $N \times D$ matrix of D-dimensional node embeddings for nodes N in the graph. Similar as in [41], we extend the matrix of node embeddings H with feature embeddings for each node forming a *Multimodal Relational Graph Convolutional Network* (MRGCN):

$$H^{(l+1)} = \sigma(\sum_{r\in\mathbb{R}} \hat{A}^r H_I^{(l)} W_I^{(l)} + \hat{A}^r H_F^{(l)} W_F^{(l)}) \tag{2}$$

where $W_I^{(l)}$ and $W_F^{(l)}$ are the learnable weights for the structural and feature components, respectively.

5.4   Vector-Based Situation Classification

To compare the performance of the KG-based classification with traditional feature based classifiers we implemented three methods described below. The features are extracted from our KG to represent vector-based features. To deal with a varying number of foe vehicles, we formed samples with tuples of the ego vehicle, a foe vehicle and their relational information such as TTC and distance.

- *Support Vector Machine (SVM)* SVMs are a set of supervised learning methods that use a subset of the training samples, the so-called support vectors, in the decision function.
- *Decision-Tree Classifier (DTC)* The fact that we have both, numerical and categorical features representing driving situations, the application of decision tree fits well to our classification task.

– *Multi-Layer Perceptron (MLP)* Finally, we use a multi-layer perceptron neural network and train in with back-propagation for the classification task.

6 Evaluation

We empirically study the accuracy of our knowledge graph-based approach in a situation classification task. In this section, we describe in detail the experiment configuration for both, the KG-based as well as for the vector-based approaches, as well as the achieved results. To evaluate the performance of our KG-model, we compare classification results with vector-based feature representation in combination with different classifiers.

6.1 Experiment Configuration

For our experiments, we used a sub-set of the CKG with 6.4 million triples, representing around 226K Conflict Situations, each described with 28 triples on average. This is further divided in 134K for training, 46K for validation and 46K for testing. To investigate the relative importance of different features, we performed experiments with single features and combined features as shown in Table 3. The 5 most important features were selected based on heuristics. For each vehicle we have about 10 features on average (e.g., position, speed, acceleration, steering angle). The number of other features (e.g., minTTC, velocity difference, etc.) depends on the number of vehicles in the vicinity (50 m radius) around ego. The numeric features are normalized before further processing by the classifiers. MRGCN is implemented using one hidden layer with 40 nodes[6], trained in full batch mode with an ADAM optimizer. MLP uses 2 hidden layers with 40 hidden neurons per layer trained in full batch mode with an ADAM optimizer. SVM is implemented with radial basis function kernels and DTC uses the *Classification And Regression Trees* algorithm.

6.2 Results and Discussion

Results for the different methods and different number of features are shown in Table 3. The overall best results are obtained by the MRGCN method using the 5 most important features. For MRGCN, the performance using all features is slightly lower than for the 5 most important ones. For the vector-based methods SVM and DTC, best results are obtained using all features. When only one feature is used, DTC and MLP achieve the best performance.

The experiments show that our KG-based classifier achieves considerably better results than all vector-based classifiers, in case when 5 most important or all features are used, respectively. This suggests that the graph-based representation provides more discriminating information compared to the classic feature vector-based representation.

---

[6] https://gitlab.com/wxwilcke/mrgcn.

Table 3. Classification accuracy. Accuracy for different features and different algorithms for the task of situation classification.

	MRGCN	SVM	DTC	MLP
Single features				
Vehicle signal	0.468	0.510	**0.511**	**0.511**
Longitudinal lane position	0.501	0.566	0.507	**0.569**
Steering angle	0.607	0.524	**0.641**	0.510
Distance between vehicles	**0.673**	0.529	0.491	0.542
Lane ID	0.883	0.520	**0.890**	0.514
Combined features				
ALL 36 features	**0.938**	0.708	0.750	0.733
5 most important features	**0.953**	0.648	0.746	0.742

Classification experiments with single features show that vector-based methods are superior to KG-based classifier for all features except *Distance between vehicles*. This suggests that KG-based methods have no clear advantage in simple situations but outperform vector-based methods in complex situations where multiple relationships and interactions exist between participants. It indicates that KG-based methods could also perform well in more complex tasks that consider much rich context as well as domain knowledge about the driver.

We did not consider temporal information for our classification experiment. We believe that a superior performance of the KG-based method in learning relational information suggests that the method will also be able to learn temporal relations between nodes. The conducted experiments were the first attempts to prove the advantage of our CoSI approach and further experiments for tasks in automated driving will be the subject of future research.

7 Usage and Lessons Learned

7.1 Usage

Bosch has been pushing research in automated driving for many years and as a result, many technologies are ready for highly automated driving today [5]. For example, Bosch has developed automated valet parking, the first fully automated system (SAE level 4). Therefore, the approach described here is one of the many ongoing activities to address the challenges in automated driving [3]. It represents one component of the overall architecture for an autonomous driving system [2].

The behavior of highly automated driving (HAD) systems especially in critical driving situations is crucial for their validation [39]. However, the validation based on recorded test drives would require millions or billions of test kilometers which makes it unfeasible [22]. Thus, alternate methods of validation including simulation are a common practice [44]. We therefore used simulated data to validate our approach. On the other hand, HAD vehicles will contain sensors and perception units providing information about the driving scene surrounding the ego-vehicle, similar to the information provided by the simulation tool (e.g. position, speed, and driving direction of nearby vehicles). We therefore expect that our approach is generic enough and will also perform well on real-world data.

7.2   Lessons Learned

Maturity of Semantic Technologies. For many years now, semantic technologies are widely used in specific domains e.g. education, life sciences and cultural heritage [31]. Recent advances of vendors such as Stardog, OntoText, and Cambridge Semantics[7] on their respective solutions offer support for many use cases with different requirements and scenarios. Their primary function as triple stores is improved considerably, being now able to manage and query knowledge graphs with trillions of triples without experiencing significant degradation in performance. Other features such as knowledge exploration, visualization, or validation techniques are now inseparable and fully integrated in many triple stores. A wide range of industry related solutions can be implemented and fully operate in production, instead of a prototypical level. Therefore, we also consider their application in the automotive domain to be promising.

Integration with Existing Data Sources. Typically, the sophisticated triple stores provide support for the *Ontology-Based Data Access* (OBDA) principles [32]. OBDA enables accessing heterogeneous data sources via ontologies and a set of mappings, that interlink this data with the ontological concepts.

There are two main forms for realizing a data integration scenario: 1) *virtual data access* - data are kept in the original format but are transformed on-the-fly and accessed as RDF triples; 2) *materialization of triples* - data from relational tables are materialized in RDF triples to special named graphs. We followed a hybrid approach using both forms depending on the requirements and constraints:

- *Virtual data access* is seen as a preferred solution in cases when it is crucial to avoid: 1) synchronization issues with data frequently changing; 2) replicating resources; and 3) issues with migrating legacy systems.
- *Materialization of triples* is applied to prevent from: 1) performance degradation of running systems while executing complex queries; 2) safety and security issues with read/write permissions; and 3) issues with heavyweight reasoning for non-RDF data.

---

[7] https://www.stardog.com,   https://www.ontotext.com,   https://www.cambridge semantics.com.

Applicability of Knowledge Graph Embeddings. Knowledge graphs are powerful in encapsulating and representing prior knowledge, leveraging rich semantics and ontological structures. Additional rules and axioms encoded manually support the reasoning process where new facts are inferred from the existing ones. On the other hand, a number of knowledge graph embedding (KGE) methods are presented for learning latent information in a KG using low dimensional vectors [40]. They perform tasks such as knowledge graph completion, entity recognition and classification as well as *downstream tasks* like recommendation systems, question answering and natural language processing.

Despite the fact that from their intrinsic nature, knowledge graphs are very flexible, we faced a number of challenges while preparing the data to be optimally processed by KGE methods. In particular, we had to define special queries each time when the information is scattered in n-ary relationships more than one hop away from the main node. A number of slightly different views are created on the fly comprising additional information encapsulated in main nodes. As a result, the KGE methods performed better in terms of achieving a higher accuracy.

8   Conclusions

This article presents CoSI, an approach for enabling situation comprehension using knowledge graphs. The CoSI ontology as the skeleton of CKG provides a semantic representation of core concepts in a driving context. Thus, our approach is able to effectively integrate data from heterogeneous sources and structures it into a common knowledge graph. To demonstrate the applicability of our approach, we performed a number of empirical evaluations with different machine learning methods. Results show that our approach achieves higher accuracy in the task of situation classification compared to traditional methods. This indicates that CKG can well represent complex information of the driving domain and when combined with graph-based neural networks leads to superior performance, achieving over 95% accuracy.

As future work, we plan to further expand the CoSI ontology with more fine-grained entities covering additional objective and subjective dimensions. Next, we will complement our approach via implementing the classification based on axiomatic rules described in [35]. Therefore, tasks such as *difficulty assessment* and *trajectory prediction* can be performed following *rule- and learning-based* paradigms, respectively. In order to improve tasks related to situation comprehension, we will further exploit objective dimensions, i.e. related to the context and time. Another goal is to include subjective dimensions in KGE methods for achieving a more personalized situation comprehension.

References

1. Bazilinskyy, P., Petermeijer, S.M., Petrovych, V., Dodou, D., Winter, J.D.: Take-over requests in highly automated driving: a crowdsourcing survey on auditory, vibrotactile, and visual displays. Transp. Res. Part F-Traffic Psychol. Behav. **56**, 82–98 (2018)

2. Becker, J., Helmle, M., Pink, O.: System architecture and safety requirements for automated driving (2017)
3. Becker, J., Kammel, S., Pink, O., Fausten, M.: Bosch's approach toward automated driving. at - Automatisierungstechnik **63**, 180–190 (2015)
4. Bengler, K., Dietmayer, K., Färber, B., Maurer, M., Stiller, C., Winner, H.: Three decades of driver assistance systems: review and future perspectives. IEEE Intell. Transp. Syst. Mag. **6**, 6–22 (2014)
5. Bolle, M., Knoop, S., Niewels, F., Schamm, T.: Early level 4/5 automation by restriction of the use-case. In: Internationales Stuttgarter Symposium (2017)
6. Buechel, M., Hinz, G., Ruehl, F., Schroth, H., Gyoeri, C., Knoll, A.: Ontology-based traffic scene modeling, traffic regulations dependent situational awareness and decision-making for automated vehicles. In: IEEE IV, pp. 1471–1476 (2017)
7. Campbell, K.: The shrp 2 naturalistic driving study: Addressing driver performance and behavior in traffic safety (2012)
8. Chen, C., et al.: Gated residual recurrent graph neural networks for traffic prediction. In: AAAI (2019)
9. Datta, S.K., Costa, R.P.F.D., Härri, J., Bonnet, C.: Integrating connected vehicles in internet of things ecosystems: challenges and solutions. In: 17th International Symposium on WoWMoM, Portugal, pp. 1–6. IEEE Computer Society (2016)
10. Di, S., Zhang, H., Li, C.G., Mei, X., Prokhorov, D., Ling, H.: Cross-domain traffic scene understanding: a dense correspondence-based transfer learning approach. IEEE Trans. Intell. Transp. Syst. **19**, 745–757 (2018)
11. Diehl, F., Brunner, T., Truong-Le, M., Knoll, A.: Graph neural networks for modelling traffic participant interaction. In: IEEE IV, pp. 695–701 (2019)
12. Ding, C., Mao, Y., Wang, W., Baumann, M.: Driving situation awareness in transport operations. In: Computational Intelligence for Traffic and Mobilit (2013). https://doi.org/10.2991/978-94-91216-80-0_3
13. Ding, W., Chen, J., Shen, S.: Predicting vehicle behaviors over an extended horizon using behavior interaction network. In: ICRA, pp. 8634–8640 (2019)
14. Erdmann, J.: Lane-changing model in sumo. In: SUMO2014. Reports of the DLR-Institute of Transportation Systems Proceedings, vol. 24, pp. 77–88. Deutsches Zentrum für Luft- und Raumfahrt e.V., May 2014. https://elib.dlr.de/89233/
15. Gao, J., et al.: VectorNet: encoding HD maps and agent dynamics from vectorized representation. In: IEEE/CVF Conference on Computer Vision and Pattern Recognition (CVPR), pp. 11522–11530 (2020)
16. Guo, J., Kurup, U., Shah, M.: Is it safe to drive? An overview of factors, metrics, and datasets for driveability assessment in autonomous driving. IEEE Trans. Intell. Transp. Syst. **21**(8), 3135–3151 (2020)
17. Haller, A., et al.: The modular SSN ontology: a joint W3C and OGC standard specifying the semantics of sensors, observations, sampling, and actuation. Semant. Web **10**(1), 9–32 (2019)
18. Hamid, S.A., Hassanein, H.S., Takahara, G.: Vehicle as a resource (VAAR). IEEE Netw. **29**(1), 12–17 (2015)
19. Huang, L., Liang, H., Yu, B., Li, B., Zhu, H.: Ontology-based driving scene modeling, situation assessment and decision making for autonomous vehicles. In: 2019 4th Asia-Pacific Conference on Intelligent Robot Systems (ACIRS), pp. 57–62 (2019)
20. Hügle, M., Kalweit, G., Mirchevska, B., Werling, M., Boedecker, J.: Dynamic input for deep reinforcement learning in autonomous driving. In: IEEE/RSJ International Conference on Intelligent Robots and Systems (IROS), pp. 7566–7573 (2019)
21. Hülsen, M., Zöllner, J.M., Weiss, C.: Traffic intersection situation description ontology for advanced driver assistance. In: IEEE IV Symposium, pp. 993–999 (2011)

22. Kalra, N., Paddock, S.: Driving to safety: how many miles of driving would it take to demonstrate autonomous vehicle reliability? Transp. Res. Part A-Policy Pract. **94**, 182–193 (2016)
23. Kipf, T.N., Welling, M.: Semi-supervised classification with graph convolutional networks. In: 5th ICLR (2017). https://openreview.net/forum?id=SJU4ayYgl
24. Krauss, S., Wagner, P., Gawron, C.: Metastable states in a microscopic model of traffic flow. Phys. Rev. E **55**, 5597–5602 (1997)
25. Kusano, K., Gabler, H.C.: Safety benefits of forward collision warning, brake assist, and autonomous braking systems in rear-end collisions. IEEE Trans. Intell. Transp. Syst. **13**, 1546–1555 (2012)
26. Lefèvre, S., Vasquez, D., Laugier, C.: A survey on motion prediction and risk assessment for intelligent vehicles. ROBOMECH J. **1**, 1–14 (2014)
27. Lenz, D., Diehl, F., Truong-Le, M., Knoll, A.C.: Deep neural networks for Markovian interactive scene prediction in highway scenarios. In: IEEE Intelligent Vehicles Symposium, IV 2017, pp. 685–692. IEEE (2017)
28. Li, M., Cao, H., Song, X., Huang, Y., Wang, J., Huang, Z.: Shared control driver assistance system based on driving intention and situation assessment. IEEE Trans. Industr. Inf. **14**, 4982–4994 (2018)
29. Mirchevska, B., Pek, C., Werling, M., Althoff, M., Boedecker, J.: High-level decision making for safe and reasonable autonomous lane changing using reinforcement learning. In: 21st ITSC, pp. 2156–2162 (2018)
30. Mukadam, M., Cosgun, A., Nakhaei, A., Fujimura, K.: Tactical decision making for lane changing with deep reinforcement learning (2017)
31. Petersen, N., Halilaj, L., Grangel-González, I., Lohmann, S., Lange, C., Auer, S.: Realizing an RDF-based information model for a manufacturing company – a case study. In: d'Amato, C., et al. (eds.) ISWC 2017. LNCS, vol. 10588, pp. 350–366. Springer, Cham (2017). https://doi.org/10.1007/978-3-319-68204-4_31
32. Poggi, A., Lembo, D., Calvanese, D., Giacomo, G.D., Lenzerini, M., Rosati, R.: Linking data to ontologies. J. Data Semant. **10**, 133–173 (2008)
33. Röckl, M., Robertson, P., Frank, K., Strang, T.: An architecture for situation-aware driver assistance systems. In: IEEE 65th Vehicular Technology Conference - VTC-Spring, pp. 2555–2559 (2007)
34. Schlichtkrull, M., Kipf, T.N., Bloem, P., van den Berg, R., Titov, I., Welling, M.: Modeling relational data with graph convolutional networks. In: Gangemi, A., et al. (eds.) ESWC 2018. LNCS, vol. 10843, pp. 593–607. Springer, Cham (2018). https://doi.org/10.1007/978-3-319-93417-4_38
35. Schukraft, M., Rothermel, S., Luettin, J., Halilaj, L.: Towards a rule-based approach for estimating the situation difficulty in driving scenarios. In: 7th International Conference on Vehicle Technology and Intelligent Transport System (VEHITS) (2021, to appear)
36. Takahashi, R., Naoya Inoue, Y.K., Kobayashi, S., Inui, K.: Explaining potential risks in traffic scenes by combining logical inference and physical simulation, vol. 6, pp. 248–255 (2016)
37. Ulbrich, S., Menzel, T., Reschka, A., Schuldt, F., Maurer, M.: Defining and substantiating the terms scene, situation, and scenario for automated driving. In: 18th ITSC, Gran Canaria, Spain, pp. 982–988. IEEE (2015)
38. Vinyals, O., Bengio, S., Kudlur, M.: Order matters: sequence to sequence for sets. In: Bengio, Y., LeCun, Y. (eds.) 4th International Conference on Learning Representations, ICLR 2016 (2016)
39. Wang, C., Winner, H.: Overcoming challenges of validation automated driving and identification of critical scenarios. In: IEEE ITSC, pp. 2639–2644 (2019)

40. Wang, Q., Mao, Z., Wang, B., Guo, L.: Knowledge graph embedding: a survey of approaches and applications. IEEE Trans. Knowl. Data Eng. **29**, 2724–2743 (2017)
41. Wilcke, W.X., Bloem, P., de Boer, V., t Veer, R., van Harmelen, F.: End-to-end entity classification on multimodal knowledge graphs abs/2003.12383 (2020)
42. Wishart, J., et al.: Driving safety performance assessment metrics for ads-equipped vehicles (2020)
43. Zaheer, M., Kottur, S., Ravanbakhsh, S., Poczos, B., Salakhutdinov, R.R., Smola, A.J.: Deep sets. In: Advances in Neural Information Processing System, vol. 30 (2017)
44. Zofka, M.R., Klemm, S., Kuhnt, F., Schamm, T., Zöllner, J.M.: Testing and validating high level components for automated driving: simulation framework for traffic scenarios. In: 2016 IEEE Intelligent Vehicles Symposium (IV), pp. 144–150 (2016)

Pay-as-you-go Population of an Automotive Signal Knowledge Graph

Yulia Svetashova[1(✉)], Lars Heling[2(✉)], Stefan Schmid[1], and Maribel Acosta[3]

[1] Bosch Corporate Research, Robert Bosch GmbH, Renningen, Germany
stefan.schmid5@de.bosch.com
[2] Institute AIFB, Karlsruhe Institute of Technology, Karlsruhe, Germany
lars.heling@kit.edu
[3] Center of Computer Science, Ruhr University Bochum, Bochum, Germany
maribel.acosta@rub.de

Abstract. Nowadays, cars are equipped with hundreds of sensors that support a variety of features ranging from basic functionalities to advanced driver assistance systems. The communication protocol of automotive signals is defined in DBC files, yet, signal descriptions are typically ambiguous and vary across manufacturers. In this work, we address the problem of extracting the semantic data from DBC files, which is then managed in an Automotive Signal Knowledge Graph (ASKG). We developed a semi-automatic tool that automatically extracts signals from DBC files and computes candidate links to the ontology. These candidates can then be revised by experts who can also extend the ontology to accommodate new signal types in a pay-as-you-go manner. The knowledge provided by the experts is stored in the ASKG and exploited by the tool thereafter. We conducted an evaluation of the tool based on a targeted experiment with automotive experts and report on the first lessons learned from the usage of the tool in the context of the Bosch automotive data lake. The results show that our solution can correctly populate the ASKG and that the expert effort is reduced over time.

1 Introduction

In automotive engineering, signal processing technologies enable the communication between electronic control units (ECUs) in the car. The ECUs and sensors involved in the communication over the Controller Area Network (CAN) of a car are defined in DBC files[1] A variety of applications rely on logs of the messages transmitted on the CAN bus to analyze and improve the interaction of the ECUs. Therefore, understanding the meaning of the data from DBC files is crucial for

---

[1] Vector Informatik GmbH. DBC Communication Database for CAN, https://www.vector.com/.

Electronic supplementary material The online version of this chapter (https://doi.org/10.1007/978-3-030-77385-4_43) contains supplementary material, which is available to authorized users.

© Springer Nature Switzerland AG 2021
R. Verborgh et al. (Eds.): ESWC 2021, LNCS 12731, pp. 717–735, 2021.
https://doi.org/10.1007/978-3-030-77385-4_43

subsequent analyses over this data. Moreover, a machine-processable representation of the data semantics facilitates data integration and process automation, which are key requirements for Bosch [14].

Nonetheless, the effective processing of DBC files is not straightforward. The first challenge is associated with the type of identifiers used in DBC files. These identifiers are usually composed of short, abbreviated terms that are difficult to disambiguate. An example of such identifiers is *ACC_Status*, which could refer to the status of the *Adaptive Cruise Control* or the *Automatic Climate Control* component. In turn, the process of extracting the semantics from these identifiers is a challenging task. The second challenge is associated with the heterogeneity of the identifiers. Typically, manufacturers use different identifiers to represent the same signals, which makes it difficult to generalize the techniques developed for a specific DBC file.

In this work, we present a novel tool, called CANNOTATOR, which implements a pay-as-you-go approach that combines automatic techniques with human interaction to represent automotive signals defined in DBC files in an Automotive Signal Knowledge Graph (ASKG). At the core of the ASKG is the Vehicle Signal Specification Ontology [8] (VSSo), which is populated and extended with the signals captured in DBC files. CANNOTATOR implements an entity extraction component, that expands the signal identifiers and computes candidate links to the signal classes defined in the ontology. These candidates may be revised by automotive experts before they are added to the ASKG. The goal of ASKG is to establish a Knowledge Base of automotive signals that supports a variety of processes and tools at Bosch in the future. These use cases range from semantic search of datasets in our automotive data lake to entity recognition and linking for NLP in requirements management tools. CANNOTATOR is currently used and evaluated in two pilot projects in different business divisions: Bosch Powertrain and Chassis Systems Control Solutions, prior to a widespread rollout at Bosch.

In this paper, we evaluate CANNOTATOR in the context of the Bosch automotive data lake [14], where we manage in the order of 10^5 automotive sensor signals from many different projects and test scenarios at Bosch. With CANNOTATOR, experts are able to expand their domain ontology in a pay-as-you-go manner as the need for new concepts arises – without the need of consulting one of the scarce ontology experts. The tool automatically learns from the interactions with the experts and captures their domain knowledge. This continuously improves the tool in being able to process more signals automatically and in assisting experts by providing better recommendations. Our results show that CANNOTATOR effectively assists engineers to expand both the ontology model and the instance data (i.e., signals) in the ASKG.

Listing 1.1. Example: Message description for steering sensor from a DBC file.

```
1  BO_ 380 POWERTRAIN_DATA: 8 PCM
2   SG_ PEDAL_GAS : 7|8@0+ (1,0) [0|255] "" EON
3   SG_ ENGINE_RPM : 23|16@0+ (1,0) [0|15000] "rpm" EON
4   SG_ GAS_PRESSED : 39|1@0+ (1,0) [0|1] "" EON
5   SG_ ACC_STATUS : 38|1@0+ (1,0) [0|1] "" EON
6   SG_ BRAKE_SWITCH : 32|1@0+ (1,0) [0|1] "" EON
7   SG_ BRAKE_PRESSED : 53|1@0+ (1,0) [0|1] "" EON
8   SG_ CHECKSUM : 59|4@0+ (1,0) [0|15] "" EON
```

The remainder of the paper is organized as follows. Section 2 introduces the preliminaries. Our approach is presented in Sect. 3 and evaluated in Sect. 4[2]. Section 5 discusses related work and we conclude in Sect. 6 with an outlook to future work.

2   Preliminaries

First, we describe the automotive signal data used as input to construct the ASKG. Then, we present the Vehicle Signal Specification Ontology as the schema of the ASKG.

Automotive Signal Data. The Controller Area Network (CAN) is a vehicle bus system used in the majority of today's cars to enable communication between electronic control units (ECUs) that support a variety of features in the car. For the development of complex CAN networks, car manufacturers and their suppliers commonly use the DBC File Format to describe CAN messages. The central object types in a DBC file are *nodes* (i.e., the ECUs), *message*, and *signals*. Listing 1.1 shows an example CAN bus message definition. A message definition starts with the keyword BO_ and is followed by the message identifier (380), message name (POWERTRAIN_DATA), message size (8 bytes) and the node emitting this message (PCM). In the following lines (Line 2 to Line 8), the signals that constitute the message are defined. The signal definition starts with the keyword SG_ and is followed by details about the signal. For example, on Line 3 the signal name (ENGINE_RPM) is defined which is followed by additional information, including the starting bit (23) in the message, signal size 16, byte order (0), value type (+), value range ([0|15000]), the unit (rpm) and the intended receiver (EON).

The example reveals some of the syntactic and semantic challenges when trying to automatically match the natural language names to a corresponding semantic model. Engineers use different syntax to delimit words, such as underscores (ENGINE_RPM), hyphens (ENGINE-RPM) or camel-casing (EngineRpm, or EngineRPM). Moreover, they apply different abbreviation methods, such as disemvoweling (PWR = power), acronyms (PCM = powertrain control module) or shortenings (Req = request).

---

[2] Developed semantic artifacts, the detailed setup of the evaluation experiment and its results are available at https://github.com/YuliaS/cannotator.

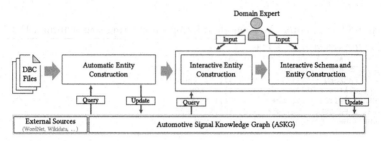

Fig. 1. Overview of the CANNOTATOR architecture

Vehicle Signal Specification Ontology. We use the Vehicle Signal Specification Ontology (VSSo) [8] for modeling the ASKG. This ontology is an extension to the Vehicle Signal Specification (VSS),[3] modelled with constructs from the Web Ontology Language (OWL) [11] to express relationships and restrictions. VSSo relies on the SOSA ontology[4] to represent sensors and observations. In this work, we distinguish three main concepts in the VSSo ontology:

Branch. In this context, a branch corresponds to a car part. Branches may be structured in hierarchies using `rdfs:subClassOf`. Examples of top branches in VSSo are *Body*, *ADAS*, and *Cabin*. Branches are associated with signals. These associations are modelled with `owl:Restriction` on the branch property `vsso:hasSignal`.

Signal. VSSo classifies signals into observable and actuable signals. According to the VSSo specification, the choice of making a signal observable or actuable is based on the existence of the sensor and actuator entries of each VSS signal. In VSSo, signals may be annotated with an abstract definition of the unit using the QUDT[5] ontology, e.g., Length Unit. In addition, VSSo includes human-readable descriptions with the predicates `rdfs:label` and `rdfs:comment`. Also, the URIs defined in the VSSo ontology are created with camel case strings for the term at the end.

Sensor or Actuator. A sensor is a car component that measures a physical variable. An actuator consumes the outcome of sensors to perform actions in the car. In VSSo, the classes sensor and actuator are not necessarily disjoint. Sensors and actuators are associated with signals through restrictions on the signal property `sosa:isObservedBy`.

3   Automotive Signal Knowledge Graph Population

Given the VSSo as initial schema and a set of DBC files, the problem addressed in this work is to extract the semantics from the signal descriptions provided

---

[3] https://github.com/GENIVI/vehicle_signal_specification.

[4] http://www.w3.org/ns/sosa/.

[5] https://qudt.org.

in the DBC files to populate a knowledge graph (i.e., ASKG) of classes and instances of automotive signals. The ASKG population comprises (i) extending the schema by creating new classes and linking them to existing concepts in the KG, and (ii) creating instances for signals from the DBC file descriptions according to the schema.

We propose a novel semi-automatic tool called CANNOTATOR (cf. Fig. 1), which combines automatic techniques with domain expert input to accurately populate an ASKG from the data encoded in DBC files. Our tool processes automotive signal descriptions with the following three main components:

1. **Automatic Entity Construction:** Extracts information from the signal description texts and predicts the signal class of the entity to be added to the ASKG.
2. **Interactive Entity Construction:** Consults experts to create a new signal entity, in the case that a reliable signal class candidate could not be determined automatically.
3. **Interactive Schema Construction:** Extends the ASKG schema with the help of a domain expert, assisted by an adequate Graphical User Interface (GUI).

The central goal of our approach is to minimize the interactions with the domain experts during the ASKG population process. For this, CANNOTATOR operates in a pay-as-you-go fashion such that information provided by the experts is learned by the tool and considered when processing signal descriptions subsequently.

3.1   Automatic Entity Construction

This component aims at automatically populating the ASKG by constructing new signal entities from signal description using the existing schema. For a given signal, the metadata for constructing a new entity is obtained from the descriptions in the DBC File. The component first implements lightweight NLP techniques to the signal name and its unit text to obtain a set of potential expansions, which then map to concepts in the ASKG. Finally, the component uses a complete signal description to identify the corresponding signal class in the KG. During this process, existing information from the KG as well as external data sources are used to aid automatic signal class identification.

Expanding Signal Names. The signal names in the DBC files are often composed of several abbreviations or acronyms, which are concatenated using different separators such as camel casing, underscores, or hyphens. Therefore, our tool first splits a given signal name string s into a set of tokens T_s. For example, $s =$ "ENGINE_RPM" is split into $T_s = \{$ENGINE, RPM$\}$. For each of the resulting tokens, this component expands the original signal names into full words which can then be matched to identifiers in the ASKG. The expansion relies on knowledge acquired from external sources and that is encoded in the ASKG. Formally, an expanded token is defined as follows.

Definition 1 (Expanded Token). *Given a token t, an expanded token e for token t is a 3-tuple* $e := (t, exp, u)$ *with a token string t, an expansion of the token string exp, and the IRI of the source for the expansion u.*

To obtain expanded tokens, CANNOTATOR leverages the KG which contains mappings from abbreviations to expansions that have been created or confirmed by domain experts before. Each mapping in the ASKG is annotated with the IRI of the source. We scraped data on common automotive abbreviations from the Web as the initial abbreviation expansions for the KG. For example, we processed abbreviations provided in Wikipedia[6] and added the expansions to the ASKG. In our example, we obtain the mapping RPM to "revolutions per minute" from Wikipedia and, therefore, we have an expanded token $e_1 = $ (RPM, *revolutions per minute*, <https://en.wikipedia.org/>). Since not all tokens are abbreviations but potentially regular words, e.g. ENGINE, we also leverage the WordNet KG[7] to determine whether a token is a word, i.e., $exp = t$. When querying WordNet, we apply lowercasing, lemmatization, and stemming to the token, to increase the chances of finding a correct match.

Since there might be several expansions in the ASKG for an abbreviation, the tool keeps all options for a given token t in a set of expanded tokens E_t. For example, a second expansion for RPM might be provided by another source as $e_2 = $ (RPM, *rotations per minute*, <http://example.org/car_abbreviations>) and hence, $E_t = \{e_1, e_2\}$. Note that, keeping several possible expansions may increase the chances of finding the corresponding signal class in the KG in the later processing steps. However, if the number of possible expansions is large, it can also become overwhelming and time consuming for domain experts if their input is required. To overcome this, the sources are annotated with trust scores. Formally, we define the trust score as a partial function $\tau : I \mapsto [0, 1]$ that maps an IRI to a trust score value. A higher trust score value indicates higher trustworthiness of the source associated with the IRI and reflects the likelihood of an expansion to be correct. The domain experts can provide feedback on the correctness of these expansions to improve the trustworthiness of the expansions. In this case, the source provenance information is updated to the IRI identifying the domain expert which will have a higher trust score than the Web sources. The experts can also add new expansions to the KG that will be considered when processing future signal names. Lastly, if no expansion could be found, the token itself is considered the expansion and no source is associated with this information, i.e., $E_t = \{(t, t, \text{null})\}$. For example, signal names frequently contain numeric identifiers, which do not need to be expanded. Once this process has been applied to all tokens of a signal name, we construct complete expansions for the entire signal name.

Definition 2 (Expanded Signal Name). *Given a signal name s, an expanded signal name* $S = \{e \mid e \in E_t, \forall t \in T_s\}$ *is a set of token expansions for all tokens of the signal name* T_s. *Further, we denote the set of all possible signal name expansions that can be obtained for a signal as* $\mathscr{S} = \{S_1, \ldots, S_n\}$.

---

[6] From the article: https://en.wikipedia.org/wiki/Automotive_acronyms_and_abbreviations.

[7] http://wordnet-rdf.princeton.edu/.

Algorithm 1: Signal Class Linking

Input: Expanded Signal Names $\mathscr{S}$, Similarity Threshold θ

1   $M = \emptyset$
2   **for** $S \in \mathscr{S}$ **do**
3     $D =$ empty dictionary
4   **for** $(t, exp, u) \in S$ **do**
5       $C = \mathtt{candidatesFromKG}(exp)$
6   **for** $(U, L) \in C$ **do**
7         $\delta_U = \mathtt{similarity}(U, exp)$
8         $\delta_L = \mathtt{similarity}(L, exp)$
9         $\delta = \max\{\delta_U, \delta_L\}$
10   **if** $\delta > \theta$ **then**
11         $D[U] = D[U] \cup \{(exp, \delta)\}$
12   **for** $(key\ U,\ value\ V) \in D$ **do**
13   **if** $|V| > 1$ **then**
14         $\bar{\delta} = \frac{1}{|V|} \sum_{(exp, \delta) \in V} \delta$
15         $M = M \cup \{(S, U, \bar{\delta}, \mathrm{T}(S))\}$
16   **return** M

In other words, an expanded signal name S is a combination of expansions for each token in the signal name. The set of all possible such combinations for a given signal name is given by $\mathscr{S}$. For our previous example the expansions are[8]
$\mathscr{S} = \{$

$S_1 = \{(\texttt{ENGINE}, \text{engine}, \texttt{<wn>}), (\texttt{RPM}, \text{revolutions per minute}, \texttt{<wp>}))\}$,
$S_2 = \{(\texttt{ENGINE}, \text{engine}, \texttt{<wn>}), (\texttt{RPM}, \text{rotations per minute}, \texttt{<ex>}))\}\}$

Furthermore, the trust score of an expanded signal name can be defined as the average trust score values of the sources that contributed to the token expansions.

Definition 3 (Expanded Signal Name Trust Score). *Given an expanded signal name S, the trust score T for S is given as $\mathrm{T}(S) := \frac{1}{|S|} \sum_{(t, exp, u) \in S \wedge u \neq null} \tau(u)$.*

Unit Linking. After processing the name of the signal, the tool aims at matching the unit of the signal description to the corresponding unit instance in the QUDT ontology. This allows for a better candidate selection later when trying to map the signal to an existing signal class in the KG, as the unit information can help to select the corresponding class. Moreover, in the case that no automatic mapping can be found, this additional information is passed to the experts. Since a variety of unit texts can be encountered and the units in the QUDT ontology typically only have one label (e.g., "Kilometer per Hour" for $\mathtt{qudt:KiloM\text{-}PER\text{-}HR}$), the tool resorts to the Wikidata SPARQL endpoint[9] to retrieve more candidate units. This is possible, since Wikidata links most of the unit instances to QUDT with the "QUDT Unit ID" property ($\mathtt{wd:P2968}$) and provides several labels for a single unit (e.g., "km/h","kmh", "kph", "Kilometer per Hour", etc.).

---

[8] $\mathtt{wn}$, $\mathtt{wp}$, $\mathtt{ex}$ stand for the IRIs of WordNet, Wikipedia, and the example source, respectively.
[9] https://query.wikidata.org/.

Signal Class Linking. Given a set of expanded signal names and links to QUDT unit instances, the approach computes matches for the corresponding signal class in the ASKG schema. This process is detailed in Algorithm 1. The input is a set of signal name expansions $\mathscr{S}$ and a similarity threshold θ. The algorithm iterates over all expanded signal names in $\mathscr{S}$ (Lines 2–15); for each expanded token in a given expanded signal name, a set of candidates from the KG is computed (Line 5). This candidate selection uses a SPARQL query to retrieve the URI (U) and the text label (L) of all signal classes where the expanded to token exp is either a sub-string of the URI or text label (`rdfs:label` or `rdfs:comment`) from the KG schema. For example, for the expanded signal name $S_2 = \{$(`ENGINE`, *engine*, `<wn>`), (`RPM`, *rotations per minute*, `<ex>`)$\}$, we would obtain several candidates for the token "engine" such as `vsso:EngineLoad`, `vsso:EngineOilTemperatur`, `vsso:RotationSpeed`, etc. For each candidate, we then determine a normalized string similarity ($\delta \in [0, 1]$) based on the iterative Levenshtein distance between exp and the candidate URI[10] δ_U (Line 7) and the text label δ_L (Line 8). If the maximum of the similarity values (δ) exceeds the predefined similarity threshold (θ), we consider the candidate an option for the token and add it to a dictionary D that maps the candidate URI to the expanded token and the similarity value (Line 11). After all tokens of an expanded signal name have been processed, we determine whether the same candidate URI has been selected for more than one token (Lines 13–15). The idea is as follows: if several tokens of an expanded signal name map to the same signal class and the computed similarity is high, then it is very likely that this is a correct match. The output of the algorithm is a set M of signal class from the ASKG schema that matches one signal name expansion $S \in \mathscr{S}$. Each match consists of the expanded signal name S, the URI of the candidate instance U, the confidence of the match $\bar{\delta}$ and the trust score of the signal name expansion $\mathrm{T}(S)$. In our example, both tokens "engine" and "rotations per minute" map to `vsso:RotationSpeed` due to the match with the `rdfs:comment` "Engine speed measured as rotations per minute". Thus, the signal class `vsso:RotationSpeed` is considered a match and is added to M.

After all possible classes have been determined for a signal, they are ordered by decreasing similarity $\bar{\delta}$. We use the trust score as a tie-breaker if two matches yield the same similarity. If the similarity exceeds a predefined threshold, we automatically add an instance to the signal class in the KG. Otherwise, the information is passed to the Interactive Entity Construction component. In our example, `ENGINE_RPM` is automatically added to the ASKG using the `vsso:RotationSpeed` class as shown in Listing 1.2.

---

[10] For hash-URIs/slash-URIs we consider the text after the hash/last slash.

Listing 1.2. Instance for `vsso:RotationSpeed` and resulting axioms. `vsso-ext` are annotations by the CANNOTATOR to represent the signal in the ASKG

```
1  @prefix askg: <http://www.bosch.com/ns/askg#>.
2  @prefix vsso-ext: <http://www.bosch.com/ns/vsso-ext#> .
3
4  askg:s002  a vsso:RotationSpeed ;
5        rdfs:label "Engine Revolutions Per Minute";
6        qudt:unit unit:RevolutionsPerMinute;
7        vsso-ext:dbcFileName "bmw_i8kk09.dbc";
8        vsso-ext:originalSignalName "ENGINE_RPM";
9        vsso-ext:expandedSignalName "Engine Revolutions Per Minute"@en;
10       vsso-ext:messageName "380Powertrain Data"@en.
```

Fig. 2. CANNOTATOR GUIs: 1) Interactive Entity Construction. 2) Interactive Schema Construction generated from Template User Interface (TUI) ontology descriptions

3.2 Interactive Entity Construction

The domain experts are only involved to process signals for which no corresponding signal class could be identified automatically. In this case, the experts provide structured input that is added to ASKG through a GUI (cf. Fig. 2 (1)). At the top, the original signal name and corresponding message name are displayed as well as the suggested expanded signal name. Below, if there are signal class candidates that match the given expanded signal name (i.e., $|M| > 0$), they are displayed with the corresponding VSSo signal class name and mapping's similarity score. If a correct signal class has not been automatically added due to a similarity score below the threshold θ, the domain expert can directly create the new signal instance by pressing the "Add Signal Instance" button. Further below, there are three expandable sections that can be used by the domain experts to enrich the information about a signal by (i) adding links between tokens of the signal name and other types of classes in the schema (such as branches), (ii) providing expansions for abbreviations, and (iii) providing the correct tokenization of a signal name. With the "Submit" button, the experts can add this additional information to the KG which triggers a re-processing of the current signal description. As a result, new signal class candidates might be generated, so that the signal can be either added automatically to the KG or displayed to the domain expert for further manual processing.

Listing 1.3. Pattern *Observable Signal*

```
1  ?classIRI rdf:type owl:Class;
2    rdfs:label ?label;
3    rdfs:comment ?comment;
4    rdfs:subClassOf vsso:ObservableSignal,
5      [rdf:type owl:Restriction;
6      owl:onProperty qudt:unit;
7      owl:allValuesFrom ?unit],
8      [rdf:type owl:Restriction;
9      owl:onProperty sosa:isObservedBy;
10     owl:allValuesFrom ?sensor].
```

Listing 1.4. Class `vsso:RotationSpeed`

```
1  vsso:RotationSpeed rdf:type owl:Class;
2    rdfs:label "Speed"@en;
3    rdfs:comment "Rotations per minute."@en;
4    rdfs:subClassOf vsso:ObservableSignal,
5      [rdf:type owl:Restriction;
6      owl:onProperty qudt:unit;
7      owl:allValuesFrom qudt:AngularVelocityUnit],
8      [rdf:type owl:Restriction;
9      owl:onProperty sosa:isObservedBy;
10     owl:allValuesFrom vsso:RotationalSpeedSensor].
```

Listing 1.5. OTTR Template for *Observable Signal*

```
1  vsso-template:ObservableSignal [owl:Class ?classIRI,
2  rdf:Literal ?label, rdf:Literal ?comment,
3  owl:Class ?unit, owl:Class ?sensor] :: {
4    ottr:Triple(?classIRI, rdfs:label, ?label),
5    ottr:Triple(?classIRI, rdfs:comment, ?comment),
6    o-owl:SubClassOf(?classIRI, vsso:ObservableSignal),
7    o-owl:SubObjectAllValuesFrom(?classIRI,qudt:unit,?unit),
8    o-owl:SubObjectAllValuesFrom(?classIRI,
9        sosa:isObservedBy, ?sensor) }.
```

Listing 1.6. OTTR Instance

```
1  vsso-template:ObservableSignal (
2    vsso:RotationSpeed,
3    "Rotation Speed"@en,
4    "Rotations per minute."@en,
5    qudt:AngularVelocityUnit,
6    vsso:RotationalSpeedSensor
7  ).
8
9
```

3.3 Interactive Schema Construction

If no candidate classes are found in the schema, domain experts can create a new signal class. The Interactive Schema Construction component allows for extending the VSSo through a Graphical User Interface (GUI) with new classes, which are immediately accessible for annotating new instances. The GUIs are generated automatically with an ontology-driven process: Ontology Patterns → Reasonable Ontology Templates (OTTR) → Template User Interface (TUI) ontology → GUI with Input Validation.

Ontology Patterns. This component is based on ontology design patterns, defined as "modelling solutions to solve a recurrent ontology design problem" [5]. We use an extended notion of patterns to indicate recurring patterns of axioms in an ontology [9].

The VSSo is both, pattern-inspired and densely interlinked by several recurrent axiom patterns. Firstly, it relies on patterns from the SOSA ontology for modeling sensors, actuators, and observations [8]. Secondly, VSSo was auto-generated from the Vehicle Signal Specification through instantiations of the repetitive axiom structures to define certain types of information (signals, branches, sensors). For example, all signals are defined as subclasses of `vsso:ObservableSignal` and value restrictions on properties `sosa:isObservedBy` and `qudt:unit`. Listing 1.3 shows the pattern for observable signals; leading question marks denote variable elements in the patterns. In our example, `vsso:RotationSpeed` can be instantiated by this pattern as shown in Listing 1.4.

Repetitive structures in VSSo can be captured by seven patterns: *Observable Signal, Actuable Signal, Observable and Actuable Signal, Branch, Sensor, Actuator,*

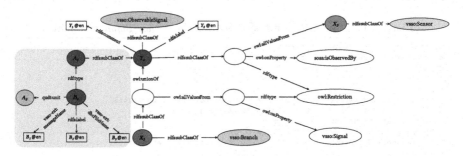

Fig. 3. Template to add new signal classes and instances (indicated in gray) to VSSo

and *Unit*. We derived these patterns by abstracting from how various classes with the same frequent super-classes are defined in VSSo. To guarantee uniformity and consistency of schema construction, new classes should also become the instantiations of patterns. CANNOTATOR enables that by exposing patterns as templates.

OTTR Templates. A template is an abstraction over the underlying pattern. Users of templates create *instances* from templates by providing values to the parameters. These values can be named classes, object and datatype properties, individuals, and plain literals. A template is instantiated by the replacement of its parameters by the provided values. For CANNOTATOR, we used the OTTR [15] OWL vocabulary to record templates and their instances and the instance expansion tool Lutra[12].

Listing 1.5 shows the OTTR template for the *Observable Signal* pattern and the instance of this template for our example class vsso:RotationSpeed. Each argument in the instance corresponds to a parameter in a template (e.g., ?classIRI ← vsso:RotationSpeed). The replacement of parameters in a template by instance arguments will generate the class definition given above in the Listing 1.4.

In total, we constructed eight templates: seven – to create classes in the schema according to the mentioned patterns in VSSo and one template to instantiate DBC signal entities (see Fig. 3). For the latter template, the automated entity linking component provides the values for its parameters. For the interactive schema construction, we actively involve the domain experts. Addressing this, we developed a new module of CANNOTATOR with a graphical user interface that assists the users in completing the templates in a user-friendly and intuitive way based on their domain expertise.

Template User Interface Ontology and GUI Generation. Figure 2 (2) shows the graphical user interface of CANNOTATOR with an example of the form for the *Observable Signal* template. Each form element corresponds to a parameter of an OTTR template. The schema-construction process is straightforward: the expert fills in the form, either providing values into text fields or selecting the values from the drop-down menus.

Listing 1.7. Template UI description for *Observable Signal* template

```
 1 @prefix ui: <http://www.w3.org/ns/ui#>.
 2 @prefix tui: <http://www.bosch.com/ns/tui#> .
 3 @prefix vsso-tui: <http://www.bosch.com/ns/vsso-tui#> .
 4
 5 vsso-tui:ObservableSignalIRI a tui:HiddenParameter ;
 6   tui:processingDirective [vsso-tui:ObservableSignalName, func:mintIRI] .
 7 vsso-tui:ObservableSignalName a tui:FreeParameter ;
 8   tui:validationFunction func:notEmpty ;
 9   tui:parameterGuiFormType ui:TextField ;
10   tui:parameterGuiFormLabel "Provide a name for this observable signal" .
11 vsso-tui:ObservableSignalDescription a tui:FreeParameter .
12 vsso-tui:ObservableSignalUnit a tui:BoundParameter ;
13   tui:validationFunction func:notNull ;
14   tui:parameterGuiFormType tui:SingleDropDown ;
15   tui:parameterGuiFormLabel "Select unit of measurement for this signal" ;
16   tui:parameterFormFillerQuery "SELECT * WHERE {?s rdfs:subClassOf qudt:Unit .}".
17 vsso-tui:ObservableSignalSensor a tui:BoundParameter ;
18   tui:dependsOn vsso-tui:ObservableSignalUnit .
19 vsso-tui:ObservableSignal a tui:Template;
20   tui:parameters ( vsso-tui:ObservableSignalIRI, vsso-tui:ObservableSignalName,
21   vsso-tui:ObservableSignalDescription, vsso-tui:ObservableSignalUnit,
22   vsso-tui:ObservableSignalSensor ) ;
23   tui:ottrTemplate vsso-template:ObservableSignal.
```

CANNOTATOR implements an ontology-driven generation of this graphical user interface. To this extent, we propose the Template UI (TUI) ontology which maps the elements of the GUI to elements of the OTTR templates. We distinguish three main types of parameters depending on how users interact with them. For `FreeParameters`, users can freely provide values. For `BoundParameters`, a user selects values from a list. `HiddenParameters` are not shown to users and their values are derived from other parameter values. In Fig. 3, we denote bound parameters with circles and variables X_i, and free parameters with rectangles and variables Y_j. Listing 1.7 shows a fragment of the *Observable Signal* UI template: Line 5 represents a hidden parameter for a signal URI, whose value is derived from the class label parameter defined in Line 7. Parameter in Line 12 will be used to select a unit of measurement for this signal from a list.

The parameter descriptions are used to render the GUI form for a template. A field can be either a `ui:TextField` for `Free` parameters or a `ui:Classifier`. For the fields of type `ui:Classifier`, TUI defines the specializations `tui:SingleDropDown` and `tui:MultipleDropDown`, which provide a list of options generated dynamically by evaluating SPARQL queries over the ASKG (e.g., see Line 16 in Listing 1.7).

To minimize the effort of domain experts, CANNOTATOR automatically fills in some of the form fields by exploiting the dependencies between parameters specified by the property `tui:dependsOn` (see, e.g., Line 18 in Listing 1.7). Thus, if a unit of measurement was selected, the system re-runs a SPARQL query for sensors and pre-selects a corresponding sensor in a drop-down list based on the query evaluation result.

Lastly, CANNOTATOR can change the type of a parameter defined in the TUI descriptions of templates. It happens, for example, if the automated entity generation component obtains a similarity score that exceeds a threshold for the linked sensor or unit entities. Then the parameter's type is set to `Hidden` and its form field is not rendered.

Expert Input Validation and Triple Generation. CANNOTATOR validates the expert input based on the validation functions specified in the TUI templates. These validations can check for empty mandatory fields (e.g., Line 8, Listing 1.7), formatting (date, number, etc.), and potential inconsistencies generated from the data provided by the experts. If the validation fails, CANNOTATOR communicates the reason to the user and asks for correct input. After validation, the tool checks for duplicate concepts by evaluating SPARQL queries against the ASKG. If there exist classes with identical names, labels, or values of restrictions on properties in their class definitions, the user is asked to either (1) confirm that the existing class can fully suit the purpose of signal description (and discard the new class), or (2) change the name or definition of the new class.

For `tui:HiddenParameters`, CANNOTATOR generates their values by applying processing functions to their source parameters. In our example, it passes the value of the parameter `vsso-tui:ObservableSignalName` to a function `func:mintIRI` (see Line 6 in Listing 1.7), which outputs the IRI.

Finally, CANNOTATOR constructs an OTTR instance and runs Lutra to generate triples that are added to the ASKG. In this step, the tool will also extend the ASKG by adding the corresponding signal entity associated with the newly created signal class. The updated ASKG is immediately available to other users or other components.

Learning from Expert Input. CANNOTATOR is designed to learn from the input provided by experts with the interactive components. The VSSo extension and the addition of signal instances to the ASKG, as well as recorded interactions of domain experts with the tool, lead to a continuous improvement of the Automatic Entity Construction component. After each feedback iteration, we say that CANNOTATOR has been *trained*, as more linguistic cues for finding matching signal instances and class candidates become available. In consequence, the manual steps that require a domain expert's attention are naturally reduced over time. In the following section, we will evaluate the usage of CANNOTATOR and focus specifically on the learning aspect.

4 Evaluation

We evaluate CANNOTATOR in a controlled setting to empirically study its performance. In a user study, we investigated the usability with 12 experts at Bosch: 5 software engineers with a background in Semantic Technologies and 7 domain experts with a background in automotive engineering. We focused on the following core questions:

Q1 How well does the template-based schema construction support experts?
Q2 What percentage of signal names can be handled in a fully automated manner?

Q3 How does the performance of the system improve over time by learning?

Input Data. We randomly selected 200 English signal descriptions out of the 31017 signals from the 82 DBC of different car manufacturers provided by *opendbc*[11]. We excluded object detection data and metadata signals, such as checksums or counters. Two domain experts annotated these 200 signals using our system. Then we selected the 150 signals with the highest inter-rater agreement score as the ground truth. The agreement meant the selection of the same VSSo term for a signal name by both experts or the usage of the same options (superclass, sensor, unit) in the template when the term was missing in VSSo.

Initial vs. Trained System. We prepared two CANNOTATOR instances to evaluate the improvement of a *Trained System* over an *Initial System*. The *Initial System*, contained only default knowledge sources in the automated entity construction component and the initial knowledge graph with the VSSo and the QUDT Unit ontology. The *Trained System* contained the input provided by the domain expert from annotating 100 signals of the ground truth dataset. During the annotation process, the KG was extended with the expansions, token relations, alignments, signal instances, and 132 new classes provided by the experts. The KG statistics for both CANNOTATOR systems are shown below.

System	Triples	Classes	Instances
Initial	20569	304	0
Trained	32155	436	100

For the experiments with the users, we created 24 DBC files with 5 signals in each file. The signals for the 12 files to be annotated with the *Initial System* were randomly sampled from the ground truth set of 150 signals. The signals to be annotated with the *Trained System* were sampled at random from the subset of 50 signals not used for training.

Expert Annotations. Each participant of the experiment was provided with a short introduction to the concept of ontologies, the structure of VSSo, the specifics of the data, and the tool itself. Thereafter, the participants used CANNOTATOR to annotate two DBC files with 5 signal names each. For the first file, they used the *Initial System*, and for the second the *Trained System*. After assessing the candidates provided by the tool, the participants annotate the signals by (1) picking a candidate to *align* the signal, or (2) creating a class to *extend* the ontology using the interactive schema construction component. Note that the input was different for all users because we randomly sampled signals from the subset of the ground truth, which was not used for training the system.

Evaluation Metrics. We measured correctness, calculated as the percentage of successfully completed tasks, as the metric for the effectiveness of our approach.

---

[11] https://github.com/commaai/opendbc, retrieved on Jul 27, 2020.

Absolute correctness for our tasks is not attainable due to the complexity of the automotive domain and the diversity of CAN-bus data. As the metric for efficiency, we used the time users spent on a task. We report the results for the annotation and the extension separately because the time needed to perform these tasks is different. In summary, we report on the following metrics: (1) **TimeAlign**, mean time a user needed to annotate a signal where the decision was to accept the suggested alignment; (2) **TimeExt**, mean time a user needed to annotate a signal where the decision was to create a new signal class; (3) **TimeAnnot**, mean time a user needed to annotate a signal; (4) **CorrAlign**, percentage of correctly aligned signals (w.r.t. the ground truth); (5) **CorrExt**, percentage of correctly chosen options in the schema construction form; (6) **CorrAnnot**, percentage of correctly annotated signals (aligned or constructed). We compute these metrics separately for the annotations obtained by the *Initial System* and the *Trained System*.

4.1   Performance Results

As a result of our evaluation, we obtained 10 annotations from each participant. An annotation could either be an alignment when the user pointed to a VSSo class corresponding to a DBC signal name or a schema extension when the user created a new schema element. The submitted input was compared with the ground truth.

Figure 4 and Table 1 show the performance results for all metrics. As expected, the time for alignment annotations (TimeAlign) is considerably lower than for extensions (TimeExt). For the *Initial System* state, the mean time (in seconds) needed for the alignments was 51 s; extensions took 183.5 s. These averaged into 107 s per annotation. The mean correctness was 97% for the aligned signals. Schema extensions resulted in 92% correct choices; the correctness of decisions on the level of the signal set was also 92%. In the *Trained System*, the majority of the annotations corresponded to alignments; the mean time per alignment was 43 s (TimeAlign) as well as per annotation in general (TimeAnnot). Only in one case, the user decided to extend the schema, which took 75 s (left out from Fig. 4); this is considerably faster than the average reported for the *Initial System* state. Correctness was 100% for aligned signals in the *Trained System*. Note that we could not compute this metric for the extensions as the ground truth since for the single extensions provided by the domain expert was modeled as an alignment in the ground truth. Yet, this decreased the overall correctness for the annotations to 97%.

The time spent on schema extensions and their correctness provide insights into **Q1**: in the case that a signal class was not yet present in our ASKG, the experts provided correct template-based schema extensions in a time-efficient manner.

Moreover, our experiment showed that CANNOTATOR effectively learns with expert input: on average, the *Initial System* found alignment candidates for 68% of the signals (for the rest, the users created schema extensions) and the *Trained System* for 100% of the signals. With respect to **Q2**, 28% of the candidates

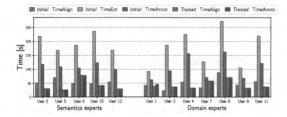

Fig. 4. Time spent by each user in the annotations

Table 1. Summary of results

Metric		System state	
		Initial	Trained
TimeAlign	[s]	50.92	42.75
TimeExt	[s]	183.50	75.00
TimeAnnot	[s]	107.25	43.33
CorrAlign	[%]	97.25	100.00
CorrExt	[%]	91.67	NA
CorrAnnot	[%]	91.67	97.25

generated by the *Initial System* had similarity scores above 90%, which could potentially be handled fully automatically. In comparison, candidates provided by the *Trained System* had higher average similarity scores with 69% above 90% similarity. Yet, human involvement was needed as the tool generated multiple candidates with a high similarity score; in this case, expert input ensures that correct signal instances are added to the ASKG.

Regarding **Q3**, our experiments showed that CANNOTATOR provided more automated alignments in the trained state and, therefore, fewer schema extensions were needed. Overall, the users were two times faster and provided more accurate results using the *Trained System* instead of the *Initial System*.

5   Related Work

Data and Metadata Management Solutions. Various solutions have been proposed for the large-scale data management of the enterprise data, which offer such functionalities as metadata management and mapping-based data integration (Karma [6], Sansa [10], Ontop [1], or Silk [16]). To the best of our knowledge, none of the existing systems implement schema extension by non-experts combined with the automated mapping candidate generation. These aspects were addressed by several standalone tools and frameworks, which CANNOTATOR builds on.

Abbreviation Expansion. The automatic expansion of abbreviations and acronyms has been studied by a variety of works [2,13,19]. Such approaches typically rely on either large corpora to discover abbreviations or leverage the abbreviation's context to determine its expansion. Since the textual data of signal descriptions in DBC files is limited in size and barely provides context, we rely on predefined acronyms and abbreviations which can be extended by the domain experts such that our system improves over time.

Template-Based Ontology Extension Tools and GUIs. Our system adopts ontology templates to involve domain experts in the schema and entity construction process. Frameworks and software tools relevant for our approach were developed in the biomedical domain [3,7,12,18]. We could reuse none of the tools directly due to their high domain specificity and limited interaction capabilities.

Therefore, we rely on a general template framework called Reasonable Ontology Templates (OTTR) [15] and the tool Lutra[12] for axiom generation. We build template-based GUIs, which is similar to recent works on Web form generation for the interaction with knowledge graphs such as [17] or Shex Form[13]. In contrast to these works that focus on instance data, CANNOTATOR allows for consistently extending the schema of the ASKG.

Automotive Ontologies. A variety of ontologies have been developed for the automotive domain. Feld and Müller [4] propose a high-level ontology to describe users, vehicles, and the current driving situation to support Human-Machine Interfaces. Moreover, the W3C Automotive Ontology Community Group[14] proposes vocabularies to improve the interoperability of data in the automotive domain on the Web. However, as these ontologies do not allow for describing ECUs and automotive signals, we use the Vehicle Signal and Attribute Ontology (VSSo) [8] as the schema of the ASKG. The VSSo, which is derived from the Vehicle Signal Specification (VSS)[3], provides a formal model of car signals to improve the interoperability for car development applications.

6   Conclusions

We presented a novel tool that assists automotive experts at Bosch in extracting and managing the semantics of CAN signals in an Automotive Signal Knowledge Graph (ASKG). For this, CANNOTATOR implements an entity construction component that automatically extracts signals from DBC files and computes candidate links to the ontology. Experts can then revise these candidates and if necessary extend the schema of the ASKG on-the-fly to accommodate new signal types in a pay-as-you-go manner.

As we have demonstrated through our experiment, CANNOTATOR is capable of learning from the interactions with the domain experts and using this knowledge to improve its assistance capabilities. The results showed that the tool, after some usage by the domain experts, is able to process more signals fully automatically, and also provides higher quality recommendations to the experts. Both lead to a significant reduction in the time that is required by the human experts.

A key lesson learned while designing the automatic entity construction component was the observation that, at first, few restrictions (low threshold) should be applied to the candidate selection. For example, we started by using SPARQL queries with basic string matching filters to obtain candidates from the VSSo, because we found that too restrictive queries (i.e., queries with more triple patterns and constants) would lead to no matches. As the KG grows, the candidates increased, and therefore, the queries can be more restrictive by taking for instance the unit or the branch of a signal into account.

---

[12] https://gitlab.com/ottr/lutra/lutra.
[13] https://github.com/ericprud/shex-form.
[14] https://www.w3.org/community/gao/.

Another lesson learned is that existing template frameworks based on simple tabular interfaces to create template instances [7,15] are not suitable for interactive schema extension by domain experts. Firstly, they are not capable of providing assistance to the users and involve the experts interactively in the process (e.g. to validate a system recommendation). Secondly, they do not allow to pre-fill the templates with results from the automatic entity construction component or prior input from experts.

Finally, the usage of CANNOTATOR revealed current shortcomings to be addressed in future work: (1) some experts tend to extend the schema instead of spending more time assessing the candidates, and (2) experts sometimes chose inadequate signal classes instead of extending the schema. The key to address these issues is to improve both the ranking of the automatically generated suggestions as well as the usability of the GUIs allowing users to explore the current schema of ASKG during extension.

References

1. Calvanese, D., et al.: Ontop: answering SPARQL queries over relational databases. Semant. Web **8**(3), 471–487 (2017)
2. Chopard, D., Spasić, I.: A Deep Learning Approach to Self-expansion of Abbreviations Based on Morphology and Context Distance. In: Martín-Vide, C., Purver, M., Pollak, S. (eds.) SLSP 2019. LNCS (LNAI), vol. 11816, pp. 71–82. Springer, Cham (2019). https://doi.org/10.1007/978-3-030-31372-2_6
3. Dietze, H., et al.: TermGenie–a web-application for pattern-based ontology class generation. J. Biomed. Semant. **5**(1), 1–13 (2014)
4. Feld, M., Müller, C.A.: The automotive ontology: managing knowledge inside the vehicle and sharing it between cars. In: AutomotiveUI, pp. 79–86. ACM (2011)
5. Gangemi, A., Presutti, V.: Ontology design patterns. In: Handbook on Ontologies (2009)
6. Gupta, S., et al.: Karma: a system for mapping structured sources into the semantic Web. In: ESWC (2012)
7. Jupp, S., et al.: Webulous and the Webulous Google Add-On-a web service and application for ontology building from templates. J. Biomed. Semant. **7**(1), 1–8 (2016)
8. Klotz, B., Troncy, R., Wilms, D., Bonnet, C.: VSSo: the vehicle signal and attribute ontology. In: SSN@ ISWC, pp. 56–63 (2018)
9. Ławrynowicz, A., Potoniec, J., Robaczyk, M., Tudorache, T.: Discovery of emerging design patterns in ontologies using tree mining. Semant. web **9**(4), 517–544 (2018)
10. Mami, M.N., et al.: Semantic data integration for the SMT manufacturing process using SANSA stack. In: ESWC (2020)
11. Motik, B., et al.: Owl 2 web ontology language: structural specification and functional-style syntax. W3C Recommendation **27**(65), 159 (2009)
12. O'Connor, M.J., Halaschek-Wiener, C., Musen, M.A.: M2: a language for mapping spreadsheets to owl. In: OWLED, vol. 614 (2010)
13. Pakhomov, S., Pedersen, T., Chute, C.G.: Abbreviation and acronym disambiguation in clinical discourse. In: AMIA (2005)
14. Schmid, S., Henson, C., Tran, T.: Using knowledge graphs to search an enterprise data lake. In: Hitzler, P., et al. (eds.) ESWC 2019. LNCS, vol. 11762, pp. 262–266. Springer, Cham (2019). https://doi.org/10.1007/978-3-030-32327-1_46

15. Skjæveland, M.G., Lupp, D.P., Karlsen, L.H., Forssell, H.: Practical ontology pattern instantiation, discovery, and maintenance with reasonable ontology templates. In: ISWC 2018
16. Volz, J., et al.: Silk-a link discovery framework for the web of data. In: LDOW, vol. 538 (2009)
17. Wright, J., Rodríguez Méndez, S.J., Haller, A., Taylor, K., Omran, P.G.: *Schímatos*: a SHACL-based web-form generator for knowledge graph editing. In: Pan, J.Z., et al. (eds.) ISWC 2020. LNCS, vol. 12507, pp. 65–80. Springer, Cham (2020). https://doi.org/10.1007/978-3-030-62466-8_5
18. Xiang, Z., et al.: Ontorat: automatic generation of new ontology terms, annotations, and axioms based on ontology design patterns. J. Biomed. Semant. **6**, (2015). https://doi.org/10.1186/2041-1480-6-4
19. Zhang, W., Sim, Y.-C., Su, J., Tan, C.-L.: Entity linking with effective acronym expansion, instance selection and topic modeling. In: IJCAI, Citeseer (2011)

Correction to: A Semantic Framework to Support AI System Accountability and Audit

Iman Naja, Milan Markovic, Peter Edwards, and Caitlin Cottrill

Correction to:
Chapter "A Semantic Framework to Support AI System Accountability and Audit" in: R. Verborgh et al. (Eds.): *The Semantic Web*, LNCS 12731, https://doi.org/10.1007/978-3-030-77385-4_10

In the original version of this chapter, figure 3 was incorrect. This has been updated in the chapter as seen below.

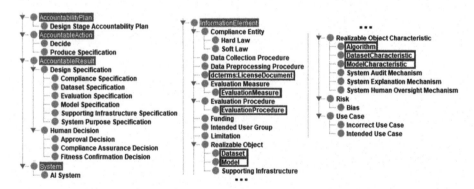

Fig. 3. RAInS classes as subclasses of SAO classes (in blue-filled rectangles). Third party classes reused from ML Schema and Dublin Core vocabulary have green borders. (Color figure online)

The updated version of this chapter can be found at
https://doi.org/10.1007/978-3-030-77385-4_10

Author Index